American Reference Books Annual

1998 VOLUME 29

AMERICAN REFERENCE BOOKS ANNUAL

1998 VOLUME 29

Bohdan S. Wynar EDITOR IN CHIEF
Ed Volz ASSOCIATE EDITOR

ASSISTANT EDITOR
Melissa R. Root
EDITORIAL ASSISTANT
Shannon M. Graff

Comprehensive annual reviewing service for
reference books published in the United States and Canada

1998

LIBRARIES UNLIMITED
ENGLEWOOD, COLORADO

Copyright © 1998 Libraries Unlimited, Inc.
All Rights Reserved
Printed in the United States of America

No part of this publication may be reproduced, stored in a retrieval system, or transmitted, in any form or by any means, electronic, mechanical, photocopying, recording, or otherwise, without the prior written permission of the publisher.

LIBRARIES UNLIMITED, INC.
P.O. Box 6633
Englewood, CO 80155-6633
1-800-237-6124
www.lu.com

Library of Congress Cataloging-in-Publication Data

American reference books annual, 1970-
  Englewood, Colo., Libraries Unlimited.

    v. 19x26 cm.

Indexes:
  1970-74. 1v.
  1975-79. 1v.
  1980-84. 1v.
  1985-89. 1v.
  1990-94. 1v.

    I. Reference books--Bibliography--Periodicals.
I. Wynar, Bohdan S. II. Volz, Ed. III. Root, Melissa R. IV. Graff, Shannon M.
Z1035.1.A55 011'.02
ISBN 1-56308-623-9(1998 edition)
ISSN 0065-9959

Contents

Introduction xiii
Contributors xv
Journals Cited xxix

Part I
GENERAL REFERENCE WORKS

1—General Reference Works

Acronyms and Abbreviations 3
Almanacs 3
Bibliography 5
  Bibliographic Guides 5
  National and Trade Bibliography 7
    International 7
    United States 8
    Canada 9
    South Africa 9
Biography 10
  International 10
  United States 13
  Canada 16
  Ireland 16
  Latin America 17
Dictionaries and Encyclopedias 17
Directories 25
Government Publications 29
Handbooks and Yearbooks 31
Indexes 32
Museums 35
Periodicals and Serials 36
Quotation Books 37

Part II
SOCIAL SCIENCES

2—Social Sciences in General

Social Sciences in General 43

3—Area Studies

General Works 47
United States 48
  General Works 48
  Florida 49
  Louisiana 49
  New York 49
Africa 50
  General Works 50
  Benin 51
  Lesotho 51
  Sub-Saharan Africa 52
Asia 52
  General Works 52
  Afghanistan 53
  China 53
  India 54
  Indonesia 54
  Japan 54
  Kurdistan 55
  Vietnam 55
Australia 56
Canada 56
Developing Countries 56
Europe 57
  General Works 57
  Czech Republic 57
  Finland 58
  Former Soviet Republics 58
  France 61
  Great Britain 61
  Hungary 62
  Ireland 62
  Luxembourg 62
  Scotland 63
  Spain 64
Latin America and the Caribbean 64
  General Works 64
  Brazil 64
  Mexico 65
  Venezuela 65
Middle East 66
  General Works 66
Oceania 66
Pacific Area 67
  Samoan Islands 67
South Atlantic Ocean 67

4—Economics and Business

General Works 69
  Bibliography 69
  Biography 70
  Dictionaries and Encyclopedias 70
  Directories 73
  Handbooks and Yearbooks 74
  Indexes 77
Business Services and Investment Guides . . . 78
  Dictionaries and Encyclopedias 78
  Directories 78
  Handbooks and Yearbooks 79
Consumer Education 81
Finance and Banking 84
Industry and Manufacturing 86
International Business 89
  General Works 89
    Bibliographies 89
    Directories 90
    Handbooks and Yearbooks 91
  Asia 93
  Canada 93
  Latin America and the Caribbean 94
Labor 95
  Bibliography 95
  Dictionaries and Encyclopedias 95
  Directories 97
  Handbooks and Yearbooks 99
Management 106
Marketing and Trade 108
Real Estate 115
Taxation 115

5—Education

General Works 117
  Bibliography 117
  Biography 117
  Dictionaries and Encyclopedias 118
  Directories 118
  Handbooks and Yearbooks 121
  Indexes 122
Alternative Education 122
Computer Resources 123
Elementary and Secondary Education . . . 124
  Bibliography 124
Higher Education 125
  Directories 125
  Handbooks and Yearbooks 129
Nonprint Materials and Resources 135
Vocational and Continuing Education . . . 136

6—Ethnic Studies and Anthropology

Anthropology and Ethnology 139
Ethnic Studies 141
  General Works 141
  Blacks 145
  Hispanic Americans 150
  Indians of North America 151
    Biography 151
    Chronology 151
    Dictionaries and Encyclopedias 152
    Handbooks and Yearbooks 153
  Latin Americans 154

7—Genealogy and Heraldry

Genealogy 157
  Bibliography 157
  Directories 158
  Handbooks and Yearbooks 159
  Indexes 163
Heraldry 163
Personal Names 164

8—Geography and Travel Guides

Geography 167
  General Works 167
    Atlases 167
      United States, 167; *International*, 167
    Bibliography 171
    Dictionaries and Encyclopedias 173
    Handbooks and Yearbooks 174
Place-Names 176
Travel Guides 176
  General Works 176
  Directories 176
  Handbooks and Yearbooks 177
  United States 179
  Africa 184
  Canada 184
  Europe 185
    General Works 185
    Greece 186
  International Travel 187

9—History

Archaeology 189
American History 190
  Archives 190
  Atlases 191
  Bibliography 191

Biography 192
Chronology 193
Dictionaries and Encyclopedias 194
Handbooks and Yearbooks 196
Indexes 199
African History 200
Asian History 203
European History 204
General Works 204
British 205
French 207
German 207
Greek 208
Hungary 209
Icelandic 209
Irish 209
Italian 210
Latvian 210
Lithuanian 211
Polish 211
Soviet 212
Sweden 213
Latin American and Caribbean
History 213
Middle Eastern History 214
World History 215
Atlases 215
Bibliography 217
Chronology 218
Dictionaries and Encyclopedias 219
Handbooks and Yearbooks 220

10—Law

General Works 223
Bibliography 223
Biography 224
Dictionaries and Encyclopedias 225
Directories 228
Handbooks and Yearbooks 230
Indexes 237
Criminology 238
Bibliography 238
Dictionaries and Encyclopedias 239
Handbooks and Yearbooks 240
Environmental Law 242
Human Rights 244
Intellectual Property 245
Victims of Abuse 246

11—Library and Information Science and Publishing and Bookselling

Library and Information Science 247
General Works 247
Dictionaries and Encyclopedias 247
Directories 248
Handbooks and Yearbooks 249
Archives and Manuscripts 250
Cataloging and Classification 251
Information Technology 251
Intellectual Freedom and Censorship . . . 252
Interlibrary Loan 253
School Libraries 253
Special Libraries and Collections 254
Technical Services 255
Publishing and Bookselling 256
General Works 256
Bibliography 256
Biography 257
Catalogs and Collections 257
Directories 258
Handbooks and Yearbooks 261

12—Military Studies

General Works 263
Bibliography 263
Dictionaries and Encyclopedias 265
Directories 267
Handbooks and Yearbooks 268
Air Force 269
Army 270
Navy 271
Uniforms 272
Weapons 273

13—Political Science

General Works 275
Bibliography 275
Biography 277
Directories 277
Quotation Books 277
Politics and Government 278
United States 278
Almanacs 278
Bibliography 279
Biography 281
Dictionaries and Encyclopedias 284
Directories 286
Handbooks and Yearbooks 288
Indexes 294

13—Political Science (continued)

Politics and Government (continued)
- Canadian 294
- European 295
  - General Works 295
  - British 295
  - Russian 296
  - Middle Eastern 297
- **Ideologies** 297
- **International Organizations** 298
- **International Relations** 299
- **Public Policy and Administration** 302

14—Psychology and Parapsychology

- **Psychology** 305
  - Bibliography 305
  - Biography 306
  - Dictionaries and Encyclopedias 307
  - Indexes 307
- **Parapsychology** 308

15—Recreation and Sports

- **General Works** 311
  - Biography 311
  - Dictionaries and Encyclopedias 312
  - Handbooks and Yearbooks 312
  - Indexes 314
- **Baseball** 315
- **Basketball** 318
- **Boxing** 320
- **Card Games** 320
- **Football** 321
- **Golf** 322
- **Hockey** 322
- **Tennis** 323
- **Track-Athletics** 323
- **Wrestling** 323

16—Sociology

- **General Works** 325
- **Abortion** 325
- **Aging** 327
- **Community Life** 329
- **Death** 331
- **Disabled** 332
- **Family, Marriage, and Divorce** 335
- **Gay and Lesbian Studies** 336
- **Philanthropy** 337
  - Bibliography 337
  - Dictionaries and Encyclopedias 337
  - Directories 338
- Handbooks and Yearbooks 340
- **Sex Studies** 342
- **Social Welfare and Social Work** 343
- **Youth and Child Development** 344

17—Statistics, Demography, and Urban Studies

- **Demography** 347
- **Statistics** 349
  - General Works 349
  - International 349
  - United States 352
- **Urban Studies** 353

18—Women's Studies

- **Almanacs** 357
- **Bibliography** 358
- **Biography** 360
- **Chronology** 360
- **Dictionaries and Encyclopedias** 361
- **Handbooks and Yearbooks** 362
- **Indexes** 363

Part III
HUMANITIES

19—Humanities in General

- **Humanities in General** 367

20—Communication and Mass Media

- **General Works** 371
  - Bibliography 371
  - Dictionaries and Encyclopedias 372
  - Directories 374
  - Handbooks and Yearbooks 375
- **Authorship** 376
  - General Works 376
  - Handbooks and Yearbooks 377
  - Style Manuals 380
- **Newspapers and Magazines** 382
- **Radio, Television, Audio, and Video** ... 385

21—Decorative Arts

- **Collecting** 389
  - General Works 389
  - Antiques 393
  - Baseball Cards 394
  - Books 395
  - Coins (and Paper Money) 395
  - Dolls 398

Firearms	399
Memorabilia	400
Pottery	401
Stamps	402
Toys	402
Crafts	403
Fashion and Costume	404
Interior Design	405
Photography	405

22—Fine Arts

General Works	407
Bibliography	407
Biography	409
Catalogs and Collections	410
Dictionaries and Encyclopedias	410
Directories	413
Handbooks and Yearbooks	414
Indexes	417
Architecture	418
Drawing	422
Graphic Arts	422
Painting	423
Sculpture	424

23—Language and Linguistics

General Works	425
Bibliography	425
Dictionaries and Encyclopedias	426
Directories	427
Handbooks and Yearbooks	427
English-Language Dictionaries	429
General Usage	429
Abridged	431
Etymology	432
Foreign Words and Phrases	434
Grammar	434
Idioms, Colloquialisms, Special Usage	435
Juvenile	436
New Words	437
Obsolete Words	437
Other English-Speaking Countries	438
Slang	439
Synonyms and Antonyms	439
Terms and Phrases	440
Unabridged	441
Non-English-Language Dictionaries	442
General Works	442
Chinese	442
French	443
German	445
Hani	447
Hebrew	448
Italian	448
Latin	450
Mayan	450
Portuguese	451
Russian	452
Spanish	454
Swedish	455
Yiddish	456

24—Literature

General Works	457
Bibliography	457
Bio-bibliography	458
Biography	459
Handbooks and Yearbooks	462
Indexes	466
Children's and Young Adult Literature	466
General Works	466
Bibliography	466
Biography	468
Handbooks and Yearbooks	468
Children's Literature	469
Bibliography	469
Biography	471
Handbooks and Yearbooks	471
Young Adult Literature	473
Bibliography	473
Biography	475
Handbooks and Yearbooks	476
Drama	477
Essays	478
Fiction	479
General Works	479
Crime and Mystery	480
Historical Fiction	482
Romances	482
Science Fiction, Fantasy, and Horror	483
Short Stories	484
National Literature	486
American Literature	486
General Works	486
Bio-bibliography, 486; Biography, 487; Dictionaries and Encyclopedias, 488; Handbooks and Yearbooks, 489	
Drama	489

24—Literature (continued)

National Literature (continued)
  American Literature (continued)
    Individual Authors 490
      Stephen Crane, 490; Emily Dickinson, 490; Lorraine Hansberry, 491; Edgar Allan Poe, 491; Eudora Welty, 492; Laura Ingalls Wilder, 492
    Poetry 492
  British Literature 494
    General Works 494
      Bibliography, 494; Biography, 495; Catalogs and Collections, 496; Handbooks and Yearbooks, 496
    Drama 497
    Fiction 498
    Individual Authors 498
      Jane Austen, 498; Robert Browning, 499; George Gordon Byron, 499; Geoffrey Chaucer, 500; Charles Dickens, 500; Arthur Conan Doyle, 501; G. A. Henty, 501; W. Somerset Maugham, 502; William Shakespeare, 502; William Butler Yeats, 505
  African Literature 505
  Argentine Literature 506
  Canadian Literature 506
  East European Literature 507
  French Literature 507
  German Literature 508
  Irish Literature 509
  Italian Literature 510
  Latin American and Caribbean Literature 510
  Russian Literature 511
  Spanish Literature 512
Poetry 512

25—Music

General Works 515
  Bibliography 515
  Biography 520
  Dictionaries and Encyclopedias 523
  Discography 523
  Handbooks and Yearbooks 524
  Indexes 525
Children's 526
Composers 527
Instruments 530
Musical Forms 531
  Classical 531
  Operatic 532
  Orchestral 533
  Popular 534
    General Works 534
    Band 535
    Country 535
    Jazz 537
    Rap 538
    Rock 538
  Sacred 541
  Symphonic 542

26—Mythology, Folklore, and Popular Culture

Folklore 543
Mythology 546
Popular Culture 548

27—Performing Arts

General Works 551
Dance 552
Film, Television, and Video 554
  Bibliography 554
  Bio-bibliography 554
  Biography 555
  Chronology 558
  Dictionaries and Encyclopedias 558
  Directories 560
  Filmography 561
  Handbooks and Yearbooks 566
  Indexes 572
  Videography 573
Theater 574
  Bibliography 574
  Dictionaries and Encyclopedias 575
  Directories 576
  Handbooks and Yearbooks 576

28—Philosophy and Religion

Philosophy 579
  Bibliography 579
  Dictionaries and Encyclopedias 581
  Directories 584
Religion 585
  General Works 585
    Bibliography 585
    Biography 587
    Dictionaries and Encyclopedias 587
    Handbooks and Yearbooks 592
    Quotation Books 595
  Bible Studies 596
    Bibliography 596

Dictionaries and Encyclopedias	597
Handbooks and Yearbooks	599
Christianity	600
Bibliography	600
Dictionaries and Encyclopedias	601
Directories	604
Handbooks and Yearbooks	604
Hinduism	604
Judaism	605
Mormon Church	607

Part IV
SCIENCE AND TECHNOLOGY

29—Science and Technology in General

Bibliography	611
Biography	611
Chronology	613
Dictionaries and Encyclopedias	613
Directories	617
Handbooks and Yearbooks	618
Indexes	620

30—Agricultural Sciences

General Works	621
Food Sciences and Technology	621
Dictionaries and Encyclopedias	621
Handbooks and Yearbooks	623
Quotation Books	625
Forestry	625
Horticulture	626
Dictionaries and Encyclopedias	626
Handbooks and Yearbooks	627

31—Biological Sciences

General Works	631
Biology	632
Botany	633
General Works	633
Flowering Plants	634
Fungi	635
Grasses and Weeds	636
Herbaceous Plants	637
Ivy	637
Trees and Shrubs	638
Natural History	638
Zoology	639
Birds	639
Domestic Animals	640
Fishes	642
Mammals	643

Primates	644
Reptiles and Amphibians	645

32—Engineering

General Works	647
Automotive Engineering	647
Chemical Engineering	648
Civil Engineering	648
Electric Engineering and Electronics	650
Genetic Engineering	652
Materials Science	652
Mechanical Engineering	653
Safety Engineering	654
Soils Engineering	654
Stationary and Custodial Engineering	655
Tools	655

33—Health Sciences

General Works	657
Atlases	657
Bibliography	658
Biography	660
Dictionaries and Encyclopedias	660
Directories	662
Handbooks and Yearbooks	662
Medicine	667
General Works	667
Dictionaries and Encyclopedias	667
Directories	670
Handbooks and Yearbooks	672
Alternative Medicine	675
Ophthalmology	679
Pediatrics	679
Psychiatry	680
Specific Diseases and Conditions	681
General Works	681
AIDS	681
Childbirth	682
Diabetes	683
Poisoning	683
Pharmacy and Pharmaceutical Sciences	684

34—High Technology

General Works	687
Computing	689
Optical Storage Devices	691
Microforms	691
Robotics	692
Telecommunications	692
Directories	692
Handbooks and Yearbooks	697

35—Physical Sciences and Mathematics

Physical Sciences 701
   General Works 701
   Chemistry 702
   Earth and Planetary Sciences 703
     General Works 703
     Astronomy and Space Sciences 704
     Climatology and Meteorology 706
     Geology 707
     Mineralogy 708
     Oceanography 708
     Paleontology 709
   Physics 710
Mathematics 712

36—Resource Sciences

Energy Resources 715
Environmental Science 716
   Bibliography 716
   Biography 717
   Dictionaries and Encyclopedias 717
   Directories 719
   Handbooks and Yearbooks 720

37—Transportation

General Works 723
Air 723
Ground 724
Water 726

   Author/Title Index 727

   Subject Index 757

Introduction

PURPOSE AND SCOPE

American Reference Books Annual, a far-reaching reviewing service for reference books, is now in its 29th volume. The 1,651 books and CD-ROMs reviewed in this volume cover imprints from 1997 and some from 1996 that were received too late to be reviewed in the previous volume. Titles not reviewed in ARBA 97, due to database development work delays, have been reviewed in ARBA 98. In the 29 volumes of ARBA published since 1970, a total of 50,198 titles have been reviewed. Five cumulative indexes for ARBA cover the years 1970-1974, 1975-1979, 1980-1984, 1985-1989, and 1990-1994. These indexes expedite the use of the annual volumes.

ARBA differs significantly from other reviewing media in its basic purpose, which is to provide comprehensive coverage of English-language reference books published in the United States and Canada during a single year. The categories of reference books reviewed in ARBA and the policy regarding them can be summarized as follows: (1) Dictionaries, encyclopedias, indexes, directories, bibliographies, guides, concordances, atlases, gazetteers, and other types of ready-reference tools are routinely reviewed in each volume of ARBA; coverage of this category of reference materials is nearly complete. (2) General encyclopedias that are updated annually, yearbooks, almanacs, indexing and abstracting services, and other annuals or serials are usually reviewed at intervals of three, four, or five years. The first review of such works generally provides an appropriate historical background. Subsequent reviews of these publications attempt to point out changes in scope, editorial policy, and similar matters. (3) New editions of reference books are ordinarily reviewed with appropriate comparisons to the older editions. (4) Traditionally, foreign reference titles have been reviewed only if they had an exclusive distributor in the United States. In 1987 coverage was expanded to include Canadian publications that do not have U.S. distributors. Prices for such titles are in Canadian dollars unless otherwise indicated. Substantial coverage of Canadian reference publications has been achieved and will continue until it is as complete for Canada as it is for the United States. Other foreign-title coverage is restricted to English-language publications from Great Britain, as well as a few select sources from Australia and other countries. (5) Government publications are reviewed on a highly selective basis because other Libraries Unlimited works, *Government Reference Books* and *Government Reference Serials,* provide the library professional with comprehensive coverage of government reference publications. In ARBA 98 only Library of Congress publications and international publications, such as those of the United Nations, are covered. (6) Reprints are reviewed in ARBA on a selective basis as they often are produced in limited quantities. (7) Titles produced for the mass market in the areas of collectibles, travel guides, and genealogy receive selective coverage.

Certain categories of reference books are usually not reviewed in ARBA: those of fewer than 48 pages, those produced by vanity presses or by the author as publisher, and those generated by library staffs for internal use. Highly specialized reference works printed in a limited number of copies and that do not appeal to the general library audience ARBA serves may also be omitted.

Because there has been a significant increase and interest in electronic publishing, ARBA has begun reviewing this medium. More than 90 CD-ROMs receive comprehensive and lengthy evaluations in this edition. Future volumes will continue to include reviews of these state-of-the-art information storage devices in a variety of subject areas.

REVIEWING POLICY

To ensure well-written and erudite reviews, the ARBA staff maintains a roster of more than 400 scholars, practitioners, and library educators in all subject specialties at libraries and universities throughout the United States and Canada. Because ARBA is not a selective reviewing source, such as *Choice* or *Library Journal*, the reviews are generally longer and more critical, to detail the strengths and weaknesses of important reference works. Reviewers are asked to examine books and provide well-documented critical comments, both positive and negative. Coverage usually includes the usefulness of a given work; organization, execution, and pertinence of contents; prose style; format; availability of supplementary materials (e.g., indexes, appendixes); and similarity to other works and previous editions. Reviewers are encouraged to address the intended audience but not necessarily to give specific recommendations for purchase. An adequate description and evaluation of the reference book are sufficient. All reviews in ARBA are signed.

ARRANGEMENT

ARBA 98 consists of 37 chapters, an author/title index, and a subject index. It is divided into four alphabetically arranged parts: "General Reference Works," "Social Sciences," "Humanities," and "Science and Technology." "General Reference Works" is subdivided by form: bibliography, biography, catalogs and collections, dictionaries and encyclopedias, handbooks and yearbooks, indexes, and so on. Within the remaining three parts, chapters are organized by topic. Thus, under "Social Sciences" the reader will find chapters titled "Economics and Business," "Education," "History," "Law," and "Sociology."

Each chapter is subdivided to reflect the arrangement strategy of the entire volume. There is a section on general works followed by a topical breakdown. For example, in the chapter titled "Performing Arts," "General Works" is followed by "Dance" and "Film, Television, and Video." The latter is divided into sections by format, which include "Biography" and "Filmography." Subdivisions are based on the amount of material available on a given topic and vary from year to year.

ACKNOWLEDGMENTS

In closing, we wish to express our gratitude to the many talented contributors without whose support this volume of ARBA could not have been compiled. We would also like to thank the members of our staff who were instrumental in its preparation: Pamela J. Getchell, Stephen Haenel, Kay Minnis, Beth Partin, Judy Gay Matthews, and especially Shannon M. Graff, the recently-appointed ARBA Assistant Editor.

Bohdan S. Wynar, Editor in Chief

Editorial Staff

Bohdan S. Wynar, Editor in Chief
Ed Volz, Associate Editor
Melissa R. Root, Assistant Editor
Shannon M. Graff, Editorial Assistant

Contributors

Gordon J. Aamot, Head, Foster Business Library, Univ. of Washington, Seattle.

Stephen H. Aby, Education Bibliographer, Bierce Library, Univ. of Akron, Ohio.

Anthony J. Adam, Reference Librarian, Prairie View A & M Univ., Coleman Library, Tex.

January Adams, Asst. Director/Head of Adult Services, Franklin Township Public Library, Somerset, N.J.

Sandra Adell, Asst. Professor, Dept. of Afro-American Studies, Univ. of Wisconsin, Madison.

Bev Cummings Agnew, Reference Librarian, Univ. of Colorado Law School Library, Boulder.

Mark A. Allan, Reference Librarian, New Mexico State Univ., Las Cruces, N.Mex.

Walter C. Allen, Assoc. Professor Emeritus, Graduate School of Library and Information Science, Univ. of Illinois, Urbana.

Donald Altschiller, Reference Librarian, Boston Univ.

Elizabeth L. Anderson, Part-Time Instructor, Lansing Community College, Mich.

Frank J. Anderson, Librarian Emeritus, Sandor Teszler Library, Wofford College, Spartanburg, S.C.

Robert T. Anderson, Professor, Religious Studies, Michigan State Univ., East Lansing.

Charles R. Andrews, Dean of Library Services, Hofstra Univ., Hempstead, N.Y.

Hermina G. B. Anghelescu, Fulbright Doctoral Student/Teaching Assistant, Graduate School of Library and Information Science, Univ. of Texas, Austin.

Susan B. Ardis, Head, McKinney Engineering Library, Univ. of Texas, Austin.

Melvin S. Arrington Jr., Assoc. Professor of Modern Languages, Univ. of Mississippi, University.

Susan C. Awe, Arvada Branch Manager, Jefferson County Public Library, Colo.

Mary A. Axford, Reference Librarian, Georgia Institute of Technology, Atlanta.

Susan D. Baird-Joshi, Database Programmer/Analyst, Rho, Redmond, Wash.

Christopher Baker, Professor of English, Armstrong Atlantic State Univ., Savannah, Ga.

Jan Bakker, Resource Center Director, North Central Regional Educational Laboratory, Oak Brook, Ill.

Jack Bales, Reference Librarian, Mary Washington College Library, Fredericksburg, Va.

Robert M. Ballard, Professor, School of Library and Information Science, North Carolina Central Univ., Durham.

Gary D. Barber, Head of Reference, Daniel A. Reed Library, State Univ. of New York, Fredonia.

Helen M. Barber, Reference Librarian, New Mexico State Univ., Las Cruces.

Suzanne I. Barchers, Author/Consultant, Denver, Colo.

Donald A. Barclay, Asst. Director of the Medical Informatics Education Center, Houston Academy of Medicine—Texas Medical Center Library.

David Bardack, Professor, Dept. of Biological Sciences, Univ. of Illinois, Chicago.

Craig W. Beard, Reference Librarian, Mervyn H. Sterne Library, Univ. of Alabama, Birmingham.

Sandra E. Belanger, Reference Librarian, San Jose State Univ. Library, Calif.

Carol Willsey Bell, Head, Local History and Genealogy Dept., Warren-Trumbull County Public Library, Warren, Ohio.

George H. Bell, Assoc. Librarian, Daniel E. Noble Science and Engineering Library, Arizona State Univ., Tempe.

Adrienne Antink Bendel, Medical Group Management Association, Lakewood, Colo.

Kenneth W. Berger, Team Leader, Reference/ILL Home Team, Perkins Library, Duke Univ., Durham, N.C.

Bernice Bergup, Humanities Reference Librarian, Davis Library, Univ. of North Carolina, Chapel Hill.

John B. Beston, Professor of English, Nazareth College of Rochester, N.Y.

Barbara M. Bibel, Reference Librarian, Science/Business/Sociology Dept., Main Library, Oakland Public Library, Calif.

David Bickford, Information Specialist, Univ. of Phoenix, Ariz.

Terry D. Bilhartz, Assoc. Professor of History, Sam Houston State Univ., Huntsville, Tex.

John D. Blackwell, Co-ordinator of Information Services, Arthur A. Wishart Library, Algoma Univ. College, Sault Ste. Marie, Ont.

Ron Blazek, Professor, School of Library Science, Florida State Univ., Tallahassee.

Richard Bleiler, Reference Librarian, Univ. of Connecticut, Storrs.

Laura K. Blessing, Personnel Librarian, Univ. of Texas, Arlington.

Marcia Blevins, Reference Supervisor, McMinnville Public Library, Oreg.

Daniel K. Blewett, Reference Librarian, Cudahy Library, Loyola Univ., Chicago.

Edna M. Boardman, Library Media Specialist, Minot High School, Magic City Campus, N.D.

Mary Pat Boian, Assoc. Editor, *Foster's Botanical & Herb Review*, Beaver, Ark.

Bobray Bordelon, Social Science Reference Center, Firestone Library, Princeton Univ. Libraries, N.J.

Mary L. Bowman, Reference Librarian, Noel Memorial Library, Louisiana State Univ., Shreveport.

James K. Bracken, Head, Second Floor Main Library Information Services, Ohio State Univ., Columbus.

William Bright, Research Associate in Linguistics, Univ. of Colorado, Boulder.

Georgia Briscoe, Assoc. Director and Head of Technical Services, Law Library, Univ. of Colorado, Boulder.

Natalie Brower-Kirton, Staff, Libraries Unlimited, Inc.

Barbara E. Brown, (formerly) Head, General Cataloguing Section, Library of Parliament, Ottawa, Ont.

Sue Brown, Reference Librarian, Louisiana State Univ., Shreveport.

Vik Brown, Assoc. Professor, Music Librarian, Southern Utah Univ. Library, Cedar City.

Patrick J. Brunet, Library Manager, Western Wisconsin Technical College, La Crosse.

Betty Jo Buckingham, (retired) Consultant, Iowa Dept. of Education, Des Moines.

John R. Burch Jr., Technical Services Librarian, Hagan Memorial Library, Cumberland College, Williamsburg, Ky.

Frederic F. Burchsted, Reference Librarian, Widener Library, Harvard Univ., Cambridge, Mass.

Robert H. Burger, Head, Slavic and East European Library, Univ. of Illinois, Urbana-Champaign.

Joanna M. Burkhardt, Head Librarian, College of Continuing Education Library, Univ. of Rhode Island, Providence.

Ingrid Schierling Burnett, Reference Librarian, Univ. of Southern Colorado Library, Pueblo.

Hans E. Bynagle, Library Director and Professor of Philosophy, Whitworth College, Spokane, Wash.

Christopher Byrne, Staff, Libraries Unlimited, Inc.

Diane M. Calabrese, Freelance Writer and Consultant, Silver Spring, Md.

Luiz Alberto Cardoso, D.D.S., Governors Park Dental Group, Denver, Colo.

Joseph L. Carlson, Library Director, Vandenberg Air Force Base, Calif.

Ruth A. Carr, Chief, U.S. History, Local History and Genealogy Div., New York Public Library.

G. A. Cevasco, Assoc. Professor of English, St. John's Univ., Jamaica, N.Y.

Bert Chapman, Government Publications Coordinator, Purdue Univ., West Lafayette, Ind.

Boyd Childress, Reference Librarian, Ralph B. Draughon Library, Auburn Univ., Ala.

Dene L. Clark, Reference Librarian, Auraria Library, Denver, Colo.

Juleigh Muirhead Clark, Independent Librarian, Golden Retriever Research, Williamsburg, Va.

Paul F. Clark, Assoc. Professor, Pennsylvania State Univ., University Park.

Stella T. Clark, Professor, Foreign Languages, California State Univ., San Marcos.

Richard W. Clement, Assoc. Special Collections Librarian, Univ. of Kansas, Lawrence.

Barbara E. Clotfelter, Head, Business Dept., Birmingham Public Library, Ala.

Harriette M. Cluxton, (formerly) Director of Medical Library Services, Illinois Masonic Medical Center, Chicago.

Gary R. Cocozzoli, Director of the Library, Lawrence Technological Univ., Southfield, Mich.

Joshua Cohen, Director for Outreach and Continuing Education, Mid-Hudson Library System, Poughkeepsie, N.Y.

Donald E. Collins, Assoc. Professor, History Dept., East Carolina Univ., Greenville, N.C.

Barbara Conroy, Career Connections, Santa Fe, N.Mex.

Kay O. Cornelius, (formerly) Teacher and Magnet School Lead Teacher, Huntsville City Schools, Ala.

Paul B. Cors, Catalog Librarian, Univ. of Wyoming, Laramie.

Bob Craigmile, Reference Librarian, Pitts Theology Library, Emory Univ., Atlanta, Ga.

Kathleen W. Craver, Head Librarian, National Cathedral School, Washington, D.C.

Mark J. Crawford, Consulting Exploration Geologist/Writer/Editor, Madison, Wis.

Milton H. Crouch, Asst. Director for Reader Services, Bailey/Howe Library, Univ. of Vermont, Burlington.

George M. Cumming Jr., Librarian and Systems Administrator, Center for European Studies, Harvard Univ., Cambridge, Mass.

Gregory Curtis, Director, Northern Maine Technical College, Presque Isle.

Elizabeth D'Antonio-Gan, Instructor/Reference Librarian, Auraria Library, Denver, Colo.

Joseph W. Dauben, Professor of History and History of Science, City Univ. of New York.

Donald G. Davis Jr., Professor, Graduate School of Library and Information Science, Univ. of Texas, Austin.

Dominique-René de Lerma, Professor, Conservatory of Music, Lawrence Univ., Appleton, Wis.

Gail de Vos, Adjunct Assoc. Professor, School of Library and Information Studies, Univ. of Alberta, Edmonton.

Bonnie A. Dede, Head, Special Formats Cataloging, Univ. of Michigan Library, Ann Arbor.

Barbara Delzell, Research and Development Center Manager, Hewlett-Packard, Vancouver, Wash.

Margaret Denman-West, Professor Emeritus, Western Maryland College, Westminster.

Donald C. Dickinson, (retired) Professor, Graduate Library School, Univ. of Arizona, Tucson.

John B. Dillon, European Humanities Bibliographer, Memorial Library, Univ of Wisconsin, Madison.

David Dodd, Branch Manager, Aptos Library, Santa Cruz City-County Library System, Calif.

David A. Doman, PAC Instruction Specialist, Pikes Peak Library District, Colorado Springs, Colo.

Margaret F. Dominy, Head, Mathematics-Physics-Astronomy Library, Univ. of Pennsylvania, Philadelphia.

G. Kim Dority, Assoc. Director/Project Manager, the Library, National Cable Television Center and Museum, Denver, Colo.

Kristin Doty, Freelance Librarian, Brunswick, Maine.

Lamia Doumato, Head of Reader Services, National Gallery of Art, Washington, D.C.

Christine Drew, Coordinator of Library User Services, St. Norbert College, Todd Wehr Library, Green Bay, Wis.

John A. Drobnicki, Asst. Professor/Reference Librarian, City Univ. of New York—York College.

Joe P. Dunn, Charles A. Dana Professor of History and Politics, Converse College, Spartanburg, S.C.

Lee S. Dutton, Librarian, Hart Southeast Asia Collection, Founders Library, Northern Illinois Univ., De Kalb.

Cheryl J. Eckl, Staff, Libraries Unlimited, Inc.

David Eggenberger, Freelance Writer and Editor, Vienna, Va.

Jennifer Comi Ellard, Young Adult Librarian, San Antonio Public Library, Tex.

Marie Ellis, (retired) English and American Literature Bibliographer, Univ. of Georgia Libraries, Athens.

Marcus P. Elmore, Managing Editor of *Physiological Zoology*, Univ. of Colorado, Boulder.

Jean Engler, Reference Librarian, Koelbel Public Library, Englewood, Colo.

Edward Erazo, Reference/Outreach Librarian, New Mexico State Univ., Las Cruces.

Jonathon Erlen, Curator, History of Medicine, Univ. of Pittsburgh, Pa.

Patricia A. Eskoz, (retired) Catalog Librarian, Auraria Library, and Asst. Professor Emeritus, Univ. of Colorado, Denver.

G. Edward Evans, Univ. Librarian, Charles Von der Ahe Library, Loyola Marymount Univ., Los Angeles, Calif.

Elaine Ezell, Library Media Specialist, Bowling Green Jr. High School, Ohio.

Andrew Ezergailis, Professor of History, Ithaca College, N.Y.

Ian Fairclough, Serials Cataloger, Coe Library, Laramie, Wyo.

Kathleen Farago, Reference Librarian, Cleveland Heights-University Heights Public Library, Ohio.

Evan Ira Farber, College Librarian Emeritus, Earlham College, Richmond, Ind.

Lesley S. J. Farmer, Library Media Teacher, Tamalpais UHSD, Corte Madera, Calif.

Megan S. Farrell, Collection Development Librarian and Asst. Professor, Dupre Library, Univ. of Southwestern Louisiana, Lafayette.

Eleanor Ferrall, Librarian Emerita, Arizona State Univ., Tempe.

Ken Feser, Systems Librarian, Cleveland Museum of Art, Ohio.

Judith J. Field, Senior Lecturer, Program for Library and Information Science, Wayne State Univ., Detroit, Mich.

George L. Findlen, Dean, General Education and Educational Services, Western Wisconsin Technical College, La Crosse.

Joan B. Fiscella, Bibliographer for Professional Studies, Library, Univ. of Illinois, Chicago.

Virginia S. Fischer, Reference/Documents Librarian, Univ. of Maine, Presque Isle.

Jerry D. Flack, Assoc. Professor of Education, Univ. of Colorado, Colorado Springs.

Michael Florman, Staff, Libraries Unlimited, Inc.

James H. Flynn Jr., (formerly) Operations Research Analyst, Dept. of Defense.

Michael A. Foley, Honors Director, Marywood College, Scranton, Pa.

Harold O. Forshey, Assoc. Dean, Miami Univ., Oxford, Ohio.

Joanna F. Fountain, Adjunct Faculty, Graduate School of Library and Information Science, Univ. of Texas, Austin.

Lynne M. Fox, Information Services and Outreach Librarian, Denison Library, Univ. of Colorado Health Sciences Center, Denver.

A. David Franklin, Professor of Music, Winthrop Univ., Rock Hill, S.C.

David K. Frasier, Asst. Librarian, Reference Dept., Indiana Univ., Bloomington.

Suzanne G. Frayser, Social Science Research Consultant and Faculty, Univ. College, Univ. of Denver, Colo.

Susan J. Freiband, Assoc. Professor, Graduate School of Librarianship, Univ. of Puerto Rico, San Juan.

David O. Friedrichs, Professor, Univ. of Scranton, Pa.

Ronald H. Fritze, Assoc. Professor, Dept. of History, Lamar Univ., Beaumont, Tex.

Paula Frosch, Assoc. Museum Librarian, Thomas J. Watson Library, Metropolitan Museum of Art, New York.

Thomas K. Fry, Assoc. Director, Public Services, Penrose Library, Univ. of Denver, Colo.

Sandra E. Fuentes, Student, Graduate School of Library and Information Science, Univ. of Texas, Austin.

Monica Fusich, Reference and Instruction Librarian, Henry Madden Library, Fresno, Calif.

Ahmad Gamaluddin, Professor, School of Library Science, Clarion State College, Pa.

Vera Gao, Catalog Librarian, Auraria Library, Univ. of Colorado, Denver.

Zev Garber, Professor and Chair, Jewish Studies, Los Angeles Valley College, Calif.

Joan Garner, Staff, Libraries Unlimited, Inc.

Gregg S. Geary, Music Librarian, Sinclair Library, Univ. of Hawaii, Honolulu.

Pamela J. Getchell, Staff, Libraries Unlimited, Inc.

Gerald L. Gill, Assoc. Professor/Business Reference Librarian, James Madison Univ., Harrisburg, Va.

John T. Gillespie, College Professor and Writer, New York.

Elizabeth A. Ginno, Coordinator of Library Computer Information Resources, Univ. Library, California State Univ., Hayward.

Edwin S. Gleaves, State Librarian and Archivist, Tennessee State Library and Archives, Nashville.

Barbara B. Goldstein, Media Specialist, Magothy River Middle School, Arnold, Md.

Anthony Gottlieb, Psychiatrist, Denver, Colo.

Allie Wise Goudy, Professor, Western Illinois Univ., Macomb.

Shannon M. Graff, Staff, Libraries Unlimited, Inc.

M. Patrick Graham, Director, Pitts Theology Library, Emory Univ., Atlanta, Ga.

Pamela M. Graham, Latin American and Iberian Studies Librarian, Columbia Univ., New York.

Marilynn Green, Librarian, NASA Johnson Space Center, Scientific and Technical Information Center, Houston, Tex.

Rachael Green, Reference Librarian, Noel Memorial Library, Louisiana State Univ., Shreveport.

Stephen W. Green, Coordinator, Reference and Instruction Services, Auraria Library, Denver, Colo.

Richard W. Grefrath, Reference Librarian, Univ. of Nevada, Reno.

Arthur Gribben, Professor, Union Institute, Los Angeles, Calif.

Margarete Gross, Librarian, Chicago Public Library.

Laurel Grotzinger, Professor, Univ. Libraries, Western Michigan Univ., Kalamazoo.

Kwabena Gyimah-Brempong, Professor of Economics, College of Business Administration, Univ. of South Florida, Tampa.

Stephen Haenel, Staff, Libraries Unlimited, Inc.

Susan B. Hagloch, Director, Tuscarawas County Public Library, New Philadelphia, Ohio.

Blaine H. Hall, English Language and Literature Librarian, Harold B. Lee Library, Brigham Young Univ., Provo, Utah.

L. Hallewell, Professor, Essex, England.

Deborah Hammer, Head, History, Travel and Biography Div., Queens Borough Public Library, Jamaica, N.Y.

Gary Handman, Head, Media Resources Center, Univ. of California, Berkeley.

Joseph Hannibal, Curator of Invertebrate Paleontology, Cleveland Museum of Natural History, Ohio.

Roland C. Hansen, Readers' Services Librarian, the School of the Art Institute of Chicago.

Constance Hardesty, Editorial Consultant, Denver, Colo.

Roberto P. Haro, Director and Professor, San Francisco State Univ., Calif.

Chauncy D. Harris, Samuel N. Harper Distinguished Service Professor Emeritus of Geography, Univ. of Chicago.

Marvin K. Harris, Professor of Entomology, Texas A & M Univ., College Station.

Ann Hartness, Asst. Head Librarian, Benson Latin American Collection, Univ. of Texas, Austin.

Ralph Hartsock, Senior Music Catalog Librarian, Univ. of North Texas, Denton.

Karen D. Harvey, Assoc. Dean for Academic Affairs, Univ. College, Univ. of Denver, Colo.

Joy Hastings, Manager, Technical Library, Hunt-Wesson, Inc., Fullerton, Calif.

Deborah S. Hatfield, Head Librarian, Lexmark Information Center, Univ. of Kentucky, Lexington.

Robert J. Havlik, Librarian Emeritus and Exhibit Coordinator, Univ. of Notre Dame, Ind.

Fred J. Hay, Librarian of the W. L. Eury Appalachian Collection and Assoc. Professor, Center for Appalachian Studies, Appalachian State Univ., Boone, N.C.

Lucy Heckman, Reference Librarian (Business-Economics), St. John's Univ. Library, Jamaica, N.Y.

James S. Heller, Director of the Law Library and Assoc. Professor of Law, Marshall-Wythe Law Library, College of William and Mary, Williamsburg, Va.

David Henige, African Studies Bibliographer, Memorial Library, Univ. of Wisconsin, Madison.

Carol D. Henry, Librarian, Lyons Township High School, LaGrange, Ill.

Mark Y. Herring, Dean of Libraries, Oklahoma Baptist Univ., Shawnee, OK.

Susan Davis Herring, Reference Librarian, Univ. of Alabama Library, Huntsville.

Janet Hilbun, Garland ISD-Librarian, Texas Woman's Univ.

Marquita Hill, Cooperating Professor of Chemical Engineering, Univ. of Maine, Orono.

V. W. Hill, Social Sciences Bibliographer, Memorial Library, Univ. of Wisconsin, Madison.

Christopher J. Hoeppner, Reference Instruction Librarian, DePaul Univ., Chicago.

Richard E. Holl, Asst. Professor, History Dept., Lees College, Jackson, Ky.

Susan Tower Hollis, Assoc. Dean and Center Director, Central New York Center of the State Univ. of New York.

Paul L. Holmer, Reference Librarian, Buley Library, Southern Connecticut State Univ., New Haven.

Curtis D. Holmes, Aurora Hinkley High School, Colo.

Shirley L. Hopkinson, Professor, Div. of Library and Information Science, San Jose State Univ., Calif.

Renee B. Horowitz, Professor, Dept. of Technology, College of Engineering, Arizona State Univ., Tempe.

C. D. Hurt, Director, Graduate Library School, Univ. of Arizona, Tucson.

Jonathan F. Husband, Program Chair of the Library/Reader Services Librarian, Henry Whittemore Library, Framingham State College, Mass.

Ludmila N. Ilyina, (retired) Professor, Natural Resources Institute, Winnipeg, Man.

David Isaacson, Asst. Head of Reference and Humanities Librarian, Waldo Library, Western Michigan Univ., Kalamazoo.

Barbara Ittner, Staff, Libraries Unlimited, Inc.

Peter B. Ives, Business Librarian, Parish Memorial Library, Univ. of New Mexico, Albuquerque.

Eugene B. Jackson, Professor Emeritus, Graduate School of Library and Information Sciences, Univ. of Texas, Austin.

Peggy Jobe, Government Publications Librarian for International Documents, Univ. of Colorado, Boulder.

D. Barton Johnson, Professor Emeritus of Russian, Univ. of California, Santa Barbara.

Marjorie H. Jones, Educational Media Specialist, Bryan Senior High School, Omaha, Neb.

Raymond E. Jones, Assoc. Professor of English, Univ. of Alberta, Edmonton.

Kelly M. Jordan, Engineering Reference Librarian, Pennsylvania State Univ., University Park.

Suzanne Julian, Public Services Librarian, Southern Utah Univ. Library, Cedar City.

Jane Jurgens, Reference Librarian, St. Cloud State Univ., Minn.

Elaine F. Jurries, Coordinator of Serials Services, Auraria Library, Denver, Colo.

Sue Kamm, Head, Audio-Visual and Stack Maintenance Divisions, Inglewood Public Library, Calif.

Thomas A. Karel, Assoc. Director for Public Services, Shadek-Fackenthal Library, Franklin and Marshall College, Lancaster, Pa.

Edmund D. Keiser Jr., Professor of Biology, Univ. of Mississippi, University.

John Laurence Kelland, Reference Bibliographer for Life Sciences, Univ. of Rhode Island Library, Kingston.

Dean H. Keller, Assoc. Dean of Libraries, Kent State Univ., Ohio.

Barbara E. Kemp, Asst. Director, Dewey Graduate Library, State Univ. of New York, Albany.

Caroline M. Kent, Head of Research Services, Widener Library, Harvard Univ., Cambridge, Mass.

Jackson Kesler, Professor of Theatre and Dance, Western Kentucky Univ., Bowling Green.

Robert H. Kieft, Coordinator for Reference Services and Collection Development, Magill Library, Haverford College, Pa.

Vicki J. Killion, Asst. Professor of Library Science and Pharmacy, Nursing and Health Sciences Librarian, Purdue Univ., West Lafayette, Ind.

Sung Ok Kim, Senior Asst. Librarian/Social Sciences Cataloging Librarian, Cornell Univ., Ithaca, N.Y.

Norman L. Kincaide, Citation Editor, Shepard's/McGraw-Hill, Inc., Colorado Springs, Colo.

Christine E. King, Reference—Music Library, State Univ. of New York, Stony Brook.

Janet J. Kosky, Circulation/Reference Librarian, Mukwonago Community Library, Wis.

Diane Kovacs, Internet Consultant/ Library School Faculty, Kent State Univ., Ohio.

Lori D. Kranz, Freelance Editor; Assoc. Editor, *The Bloomsbury Review*, Denver, Colo.

Betsy J. Kraus, Librarian/Technical Editor, Environmental Evaluation Group, Albuquerque, N.Mex.

Linda A. Krikos, Head, Women's Studies Library, Ohio State Univ., Columbus.

Marlene M. Kuhl, Library Manager, Baltimore County Public Library, Reisterstown Branch, Md.

Colby H. Kullman, Assoc. Professor and Editor, *Studies in American Drama*, Univ. of Mississippi, University.

Natalie Kupferberg, Health Sciences Library Coordinator, Ferris State Univ., Big Rapids, Mich.

Keith Kyker, Educational Media Specialist, Okaloosa County Schools, Valparaiso, Fla.

Robert V. Labaree, Reference/Public Services Librarian, Von KleinSmid Library, Univ. of Southern California, Los Angeles.

Linda L. Lam-Easton, Assoc. Professor, Dept. of Religious Studies, California State Univ., Northridge.

Lizbeth Langston, Reference Librarian, Univ. of California, Riverside.

Mary Larsgaard, Asst. Head, Map and Imagery Laboratory Library, Univ. of California, Santa Barbara.

Binh P. Le, Reference Librarian, Abington College, Pennsylvania State Univ., University Park.

Charles Leck, Professor of Biological Sciences, Rutgers Univ., New Brunswick, N.J.

Hwa-Wei Lee, Dean of Libraries, Ohio Univ., Athens.

R. S. Lehmann, Rocky Mountain BankCard System, Colorado National Bank, Denver.

Polin P. Lei, Assoc. Librarian, Information Services, Arizona Health Sciences Library, Tucson.

Richard A. Leiter, Director, Law Library, Howard Univ., Washington, D.C.

John A. Lent, Drexel Hill, Pa.

Charlotte Lindgren, Professor Emerita of English, Emerson College, Boston.

Larry Lobel, Virtuoso Keyboard Services, Petaluma, Calif.

Koraljka Lockhart, Publications Editor, San Francisco Opera, Calif.

Elisabeth Logan, Assoc. Professor, School of Library and Information Studies, Florida State Univ., Tallahassee.

Jeffrey E. Long, Interlibrary Loan/Photocopy Services Library Assistant, Lamar Soutter Library/Univ. of Massachusetts Medical Center, Worcester.

Jeffrey R. Luttrell, Leader, Humanities Cataloging Team, Princeton Univ. Library, N.J.

Ron Maas, Staff, Libraries Unlimited, Inc.

Marit S. MacArthur, Reference Librarian, Auraria Libraries, Univ. of Colorado, Denver.

Sara R. Mack, Professor Emerita, Dept. of Library Science, Kutztown Univ., Pa.

Theresa Maggio, Head of Public Services, Southwest Georgia Regional Library, Bainbridge.

Linda Main, Assoc. Professor, San Jose State Univ., Calif.

Kay Mariea, Staff, Libraries Unlimited, Inc.

S. D. Markman, Professor Emeritus, Art Dept., Duke Univ., Durham, N.C.

Judith A. Matthews, Physics-Astronomy/Science Reference Librarian, Main Library, Michigan State Univ., East Lansing.

Judy Gay Matthews, Staff, Libraries Unlimited, Inc.

Debby Mattil, Staff, Libraries Unlimited, Inc.

George Louis Mayer, (formerly) Senior Principal Librarian, New York Public Library and Part-Time Librarian, Adelphi, Manhattan Center and Brooklyn College.

Peter H. McCracken, Reference Librarian, Joyner Library, East Carolina Univ., Greenville, N.C.

James R. McDonald, Professor of Geography, Eastern Michigan Univ., Ypsilanti.

Christopher Michael McDonough, Lecturer, Dept. of Classics, Princeton Univ., N.J.

Dana McDougald, Lead Media Specialist, Learning Resources Center, Cedar Shoals High School, Athens, Ga.

Peter Zachary McKay, Business Librarian, Univ. of Florida Libraries, Gainesville.

Robert B. McKee, Professor, Mechanical Engineering, Univ. of Nevada, Reno.

Marian B. McLeod, Professor of Speech Communication and Theater, Trenton State College, N.J.

Jean C. McManus, Reference Librarian and Adjunct Professor, Hesburgh Library, Univ. of Notre Dame, Ind.

Margo B. Mead, Technology Instruction Librarian, Louis M. Salmon Library, Univ. of Alabama, Huntsville.

Sue Lyon Mertl, President, Lyon Consulting Group, Inc., Marietta, Ga.

Michael G. Messina, Assoc. Professor, Dept. of Forest Science, Texas A & M Univ., College Station.

G. Douglas Meyers, Chair, Dept. of English, Univ. of Texas, El Paso.

George A. Meyers, Chairman, National Labor Commission, Baltimore, Md.

Robert Michaelson, Head Librarian, Seeley G. Mudd Library for Science and Engineering, Northwestern Univ., Evanston, Ill.

Bogdan Mieczkowski, Professor of Economics, Ithaca College, N.Y.

Bill Miller, Director of Libraries, Florida Atlantic Univ., Boca Raton.

Elizabeth B. Miller, Instructor, College of Library and Information Science, Univ. of South Carolina, Columbia.

Richard A. Miller, Professor of Economics, Wesleyan Univ., Middletown, Conn.

Carol L. Mitchell, Southeast Asian Bibliographic Services Librarian, General Library System, Univ. of Wisconsin, Madison.

James Moffet, Head, Reference Dept, Baldwin Public Library, Birmingham, Mich.

Paul A. Mogren, Head of Reference, Marriott Library, Univ. of Utah, Salt Lake City.

Janet Mongan, Research Officer, Cleveland State Univ. Library, Ohio.

Terry Ann Mood, Humanities Bibliographer, Univ. of Colorado, Denver.

Anne C. Moore, Electronic Resources Librarian, New Mexico State Univ., Alamogordo.

Debra L. Moore, Reference Librarian, Loyola Marymount Univ., Los Angeles, Calif.

Gerald D. Moran, Director, McCartney Library, Geneva College, Beaver Falls, Pa.

Betty J. Morris, Staff, Libraries Unlimited, Inc.

Walt Mundkowsky, Freelance Film and Music Critic, Beverly Hills, Calif.

Craig A. Munsart, Teacher, Jefferson County Public Schools, Golden, Colo.

Paul M. Murphy III, Paramedic, Chapel Hill, NC.

James M. Murray, U.S. Courts Library, Spokane, Wash.

Charles Neuringer, Professor of Psychology and Theatre and Film, Univ. of Kansas, Lawrence.

John Newman, Univ. Archivist, Colorado State Univ., Fort Collins.

Danuta A. Nitecki, Assoc. Univ. Librarian, Yale Univ., New Haven, Conn.

Eric R. Nitschke, Reference Librarian, Robert W. Woodruff Library, Emory Univ., Atlanta, Ga.

Christopher W. Nolan, Head, Reference Services, Maddux Library, Trinity Univ., San Antonio, Tex.

Carol L. Noll, Volunteer Librarian, Schimelpfenig Middle School, Plano, Tex.

O. Gene Norman, Head, Reference Dept., Indiana State Univ. Libraries, Terre Haute.

Marilyn Strong Noronha, (retired) Reference Librarian, Harleigh B. Trecker Library, Univ. of Connecticut, West Hartford.

David G. Nowak, Asst. Professor and Reference Librarian, Mississippi State University Libraries, Mississippi State.

Marshall E. Nunn, Professor, Dept. of History, Glendale Community College, Calif.

Barbara J. O'Hara, Adult Services Librarian, Free Library of Philadelphia, Pa.

Herbert W. Ockerman, Professor, Ohio State Univ., Columbus.

Lawrence Olszewski, Manager, OCLC Information Center, Dublin, Ohio.

Ray Olszewski, Computer Systems Specialist, Nueva School, Hillsborough, Calif.

Berniece M. Owen, Coordinator, Library Technical Services, Portland Community College, Oreg.

John Howard Oxley, Halifax, N.S.

Mark Padnos, Humanities Reference Librarian, Mina Rees Library, Graduate School and Univ. Center, City Univ. of New York.

Joseph W. Palmer, Assoc. Professor, School of Information and Library Studies, State Univ. of New York, Buffalo.

Penny Papangelis, Health Sciences Librarian, Western Kentucky Univ., Bowling Green.

J. Carlyle Parker, Librarian and Univ. Archivist Emeritus, Library, California State Univ., Turlock.

Maureen Pastine, Univ. Librarian, Paley Library, Temple Univ., Philadelphia, Pa.

Elizabeth Patterson, Head, Reference and Computer Reference Services, Robert W. Woodruff Library, Emory Univ., Atlanta, Ga.

Gari-Anne Patzwald, Freelance Editor and Indexer, Lexington, Ky.

Harry E. Pence, Professor of Chemistry, State Univ. of New York, Oneonta.

Karin Pendle, Professor of Musicology, Univ. of Cincinnati, Ohio.

Julia Perez, Biological Sciences Librarian, Michigan State Univ. Libraries, East Lansing.

Kevin W. Perizzolo, Staff, Libraries Unlimited, Inc.

Glenn Petersen, Professor of Anthropology and International Affairs, Graduate Center and Baruch College, City Univ. of New York.

C. Michael Phillips, Asst. Reference Librarian, Robert Scott Small Library, College of Charleston, S.C.

Jack E. Pontius, Assoc. Librarian, Pennsylvania State Univ., St. College.

Francis Poole, Assoc. Librarian, Univ. of Delaware Library, Newark.

Phillip P. Powell, Asst. Reference Librarian, Robert Scott Small Library, College of Charleston, S.C.

Carl Pracht, Reference Librarian, Southeast Missouri State Univ., Cape Girardeau.

Ann E. Prentice, Dean, College of Library and Information Services, Univ. of Maryland, College Park.

Pete Prunkl, Freelance Writer, Hickory, N.C.

Randall Rafferty, Reference Librarian, Mississippi State Univ. Library, Mississippi State.

Varadaraja V. Raman, Professor of Physics and Humanities, Rochester Institute of Technology, N.Y.

Lisé Rasmussen, Reference Librarian, Dowling College, Oakdale, N.Y.

Jack Ray, Asst. Director, Loyola/Notre Dame Library, Baltimore, Md.

Nancy P. Reed, Media Specialist, St. Mary Middle/High School, Paducah, Ky.

James Rettig, Asst. Univ. Librarian for Reference and Information Services, Swem Library, College of William and Mary, Williamsburg, Va.

Diane B. Rhodes, Life Sciences and Agriculture Librarian, Arizona State Univ., Tempe.

Jo Anne H. Ricca, Staff, Libraries Unlimited, Inc.

Robert B. Marks Ridinger, Head, Electronic Information Resources Management Dept., Univ. Libraries, Northern Illinois Univ., De Kalb.

Constance Rinaldo, Head, Collection Services, Biomedical Libraries, Dartmouth College, Hanover, N.H.

Anne F. Roberts, Adjunct Professor, School of Education, State Univ. of New York, Albany.

William B. Robison, Asst. Professor, History, Southeastern Louisiana Univ., Hammond.

John M. Robson, Institute Librarian, Rose-Hulman Institute of Technology, Terre Haute, Ind.

JoAnn V. Rogers, Professor, College of Library and Information Science, Univ. of Kentucky, Lexington.

Deborah V. Rollins, Reference Librarian, Univ. of Maine, Orono.

John B. Romeiser, Professor of French and Dept. Head, Univ. of Tennessee, Knoxville.

Melissa Rae Root, Staff, Libraries Unlimited, Inc.

Elizabeth McClure Rosen, Media Specialist, Champaign Unit 4 Schools, Ill.

Marjorie N. Rosenthal, (retired) Librarian, South Huntington Public Library, N.Y.

Samuel Rothstein, Professor Emeritus, School of Librarianship, Univ. of British Columbia, Vancouver.

Michele Russo, Acting Director, Franklin D. Schurz Library, Indiana Univ., South Bend.

Kenneth I. Saichek, President, Saichek/Vail Associates and C.E.O., Kybercom, Wauwatosa, Wis.

Nadine Salmons, Technical Services Librarian, Fort Carson's Grant Library, Colo.

Edmund F. SantaVicca, Librarian, Information Commons, Estrella Mountain Community College Center, Litchfield Park, Ariz.

Frederick A. Schlipf, Executive Director, Urbana Free Library and Adjunct Professor, Graduate School of Library and Information Science, Univ. of Illinois.

Diane Schmidt, Asst. Biology Librarian, Univ. of Illinois, Urbana.

Steven J. Schmidt, Assoc. Librarian, Indiana Univ./Purdue Univ. at Indianapolis Libraries.

Willa Schmidt, Reference Librarian, Univ. of Wisconsin, Madison.

Ralph Lee Scott, Assoc. Professor, East Carolina Univ. Library, Greenville, N.C.

Robert A. Seal, Univ. Librarian, Texas Christian Univ., Fort Worth.

Ravindra Nath Sharma, Library Director, West Virginia State College, Institute.

Earl Shumaker, Government Documents/Map Librarian, Elmer E. Rasmuson Library, Univ. of Alaska, Fairbanks.

Bruce A. Shuman, Adjunct Professor, Univ. of South Florida, Tampa.

Stephanie C. Sigala, Head Librarian, Richardson Memorial Library, St. Louis Art Museum, Mo.

Susan M. Sigman, Staff, Libraries Unlimited, Inc.

Linda Keir Simons, Head of Client Services, Univ. of Dayton Library, Ohio.

Esther R. Sinofsky, Library Media Teacher, Alexander Hamilton High School, Los Angeles, Calif.

Robert M. Slade, Independent Consultant, North Vancouver, B.C.

Jeanette C. Smith, Grants Officer, New Mexico State Univ. Library, Las Cruces.

Nathan M. Smith, Director, School of Library and Information Sciences, Brigham Young Univ., Provo, Utah.

Mary Ellen Snodgrass, Freelance Writer, Charlotte, N.C.

Lynn K. Sorenson, Humanities and Social Sciences Librarian, Michigan State Univ., Okemos.

Steven W. Sowards, Head, Social Sciences/Humanities Reference, Michigan State Univ. Libraries, East Lansing.

Jerri Spoehel, Freelance Writer and Editor, Las Cruces, N.Mex.

Howard Spring, Asst. Professor, Univ. of Guelph, Ont.

Jan S. Squire, Reference and Instructional Services Librarian, Univ. of Northern Colorado, Greeley.

Karen Y. Stabler, Head of Information Services, New Mexico State Univ. Library, Las Cruces.

Victor L. Stater, Assoc. Professor of History, Louisiana State Univ., Baton Rouge.

Allen E. Staver, Assoc. Professor, Dept. of Geography, Northern Illinois Univ., De Kalb.

Kay M. Stebbins, Coordinator Librarian, Louisiana State Univ., Shreveport.

Lillian Jane Steele, Historian, Old Salem, Inc., Winston-Salem, N.C.

Norman D. Stevens, Director Emeritus, Univ. of Connecticut Libraries, Storrs.

John P. Stierman, Reference Librarian, Western Illinois Univ., Macomb.

John W. Storey, Professor of History, Lamar Univ., Beaumont, Tex.

William C. Struning, Professor, Seton Hall Univ., South Orange, N.J.

Bruce Stuart, Professor and Parke-Davis Chair, Univ. of Maryland, Baltimore.

Mila C. Su, Senior Asst. Librarian, Pennsylvania State Univ., Altoona.

Timothy E. Sullivan, Asst. Professor of Economics, Towson State Univ., Md.

Tom Sullivan, Asst. Editor, *Mobile Computing Magazine*, New York.

Richard H. Swain, Reference Librarian, West Chester Univ., Pa.

James H. Sweetland, Assoc. Professor, School of Library and Information Science, Univ. of Wisconsin, Milwaukee.

Nigel Tappin, (formerly) General Librarian, North York Public Library, Ont.

Deborah A. Taylor, Staff, Libraries Unlimited, Inc.

Glynys R. Thomas, Sawyer Library, Suffolk Univ., Boston.

Katherine Margaret Thomas, (formerly) Biologist, Long Point Bird Observatory, Toronto.

Paul H. Thomas, Head, Catalog Dept., Hoover Institution Library, Stanford Univ., Calif.

Sharon Thomerson, Patron Services Librarian, Villa Library, Jefferson County Public Library, Lakewood, Colo.

Mary Ann Thompson, Asst. Professor of Nursing, Saint Joseph College, West Hartford, Conn.

Peter Thorpe, Professor Emeritus, Univ. of Colorado, Denver.

Linda D. Tietjen, Senior Instructor, Instruction and Reference Services, Auraria Library, Denver, Colo.

Bruce H. Tiffney, Assoc. Professor of Geology and Biological Sciences, Univ. of California, Santa Barbara.

Andrew G. Torok, Assoc. Professor, Northern Illinois Univ., De Kalb.

Gregory M. Toth, Reference Librarian, State Univ. of New York, Brockport.

Mary L. Trenerry, Media Specialist, Millard Public Schools, Omaha, Nebr.

Carol Truett, Assoc. Professor, Appalachian State Univ., Boone, N.C.

Dean Tudor, Professor, School of Journalism, Ryerson Polytechnical Institute, Toronto.

Elias H. Tuma, Professor of Economics, Univ. of California, Davis.

Diane J. Turner, Science/Engineering Liaison, Auraria Library, Univ. of Colorado, Denver.

Robert L. Turner Jr., Librarian and Asst. Professor, Radford Univ., Va.

Michele Tyrrell, Media Specialist, Arundel Senior High School, Gambrills, Md.

Arthur R. Upgren, Professor of Astronomy and Director, Van Vleck Observatory, Wesleyan Univ., Middletown, Conn.

Judith A. Valdez, Instructor/Reference Librarian, Auraria Library, Univ. of Colorado, Denver.

Joyce Kasman Valenza, Librarian, Wissahickon High School, Ambler, Pa.

Susanna Van Sant, Librarian, Michigan State Univ., East Lansing.

Debra S. Van Tassel, Reference Librarian, Univ. of Colorado, Boulder.

Vandelia L. VanMeter, Professor and Library Director, Spalding Univ., Louisville, Ky.

Jennie Ver Steeg, Education Liaison/Social Science Librarian, Northern Illinois Univ., De Kalb.

Dario J. Villa, Reference Librarian/Bibliographer, Ronald Williams Library, Northeastern Illinois Univ., Chicago.

Kathleen J. Voigt, Head, Reference Dept., Carlson Library, Univ. of Toledo, Ohio.

Bridget Volz, Freelance Librarian and Weaver, Denver, Colo.

Ed Volz, Staff, Libraries Unlimited, Inc.

David V. Waller, Asst. Professor of Sociology, Dept. of Sociology and Anthropology, Univ. of Texas, Arlington.

Jeff Wanser, Coordinator, Reference and Government Documents, Hiram College Library, Ohio.

Richard S. Watts, Coordinator, Technical Processing Dept., San Bernardino County Library, Calif.

J. E. Weaver, Dept. of Economics, Drake Univ., Des Moines, Iowa.

Bruce H. Webb, Librarian/Asst. Professor, Rena M. Carlson Library, Clarion Univ., Pa.

David S. Webster, Assoc. Professor of Educational Administration and Higher Education, Oklahoma State Univ., Stillwater.

Karen T. Wei, Head, Asian Library, Univ. of Illinois, Urbana.

Michael Weinberg, Reference Librarian, Ronald Williams Library, Northeastern Illinois Library, Chicago.

Lynda Welborn, Director of Libraries, Colorado Academy, Denver.

Andrew B. Wertheimer, Librarian, Woodman Astronomical Library, Univ. of Wisconsin, Madison.

Lee Weston, Reference Services Manager, James A. Michener Library, Univ. of Northern Colorado, Greeley.

Lucille Whalen, Dean of Graduate Programs, Immaculate Heart College Center, Los Angeles, Calif.

Carol Wheeler, Government Documents Reference Librarian, Univ. of Georgia Libraries, Athens.

Cathy Seitz Whitaker, (formerly) Social Work Librarian, Hillman Library, Univ. of Pittsburgh, Pa.

David L. White, Professor, History Dept., Appalachian State Univ., Boone, N.C.

Marilyn Domas White, Assoc. Professor, College of Library and Information Services, Univ. of Maryland, College Park.

Robert L. Wick, Asst. Professor and Fine Arts Bibliographer, Auraria Library, Univ. of Colorado, Denver.

Agnes H. Widder, Humanities Bibliographer, Michigan State Univ., East Lansing.

Albert Wilhelm, Professor of English, Tennessee Technological Univ., Cookeville.

Connie Williams, Information Manager, Merrick & Company, Aurora, Colo.

Lynn F. Williams, Professor, Div. of Writing, Literature, and Publishing, Emerson College, Boston.

Robert V. Williams, Assoc. Professor, College of Library and Information Science, Univ. of South Carolina, Columbia.

Wiley J. Williams, Professor Emeritus, School of Library Science, Kent State Univ., Ohio.

Frank L. Wilson, Professor and Head, Dept. of Political Science, Purdue Univ., West Lafayette, Ind.

Mark A. Wilson, Professor of Geology, College of Wooster, Ohio.

Celia J. Wintz, Faculty, Houston Community College, Tex.

Glenn R. Wittig, Director of Library Services, Criswell College, Dallas, Tex.

Raymund F. Wood, Editor, *The Westerners*, Encino, Calif.

Bohdan S. Wynar, Staff, Libraries Unlimited, Inc.

Eveline L. Yang, Manager, Information Delivery Programs, Auraria Library, Univ. of Colorado, Denver.

Hope Yelich, Reference Librarian, Earl Gregg Swem Library, College of William and Mary, Williamsburg, Va.

Henry E. York, Head, Collection Management, Cleveland State Univ., Ohio.

Arthur P. Young, Director, Northern Illinois Libraries, Northern Illinois Univ., De Kalb.

Louis G. Zelenka, Freelance Librarian, Douglas, Ga.

Magda Želinská-Ferl, Professor/Faculty Advisor, Union Institute, Los Angeles, Calif.

L. Zgusta, Professor of Linguistics and the Classics and Member of the Center for Advance Study, Univ. of Illinois, Urbana.

Anita Zutis, Adjunct Librarian, Queensborough Community College, Bayside, N.Y.

Journals Cited

FORM OF CITATION	JOURNAL TITLE
BL	Booklist
BR	Book Report
Choice	Choice
C&RL	College & Research Libraries
EL	Emergency Librarian
JAL	Journal of Academic Librarianship
LJ	Library Journal
RBB	Reference Books Bulletin
RQ	RQ
SLJ	School Library Journal
SLMQ	School Library Media Quarterly
VOYA	Voice of Youth Advocates

Part I
GENERAL REFERENCE WORKS

1 General Reference Works

ACRONYMS AND ABBREVIATIONS

1. **Buttress's World Guide to Abbreviations of Organizations.** 11th ed. Revised by L. M. Pitman. London, Blackie Academic & Professional/Chapman & Hall; distr., Detroit, Gale, 1997. 1149p. $180.00. ISBN 0-7514-0261-3.

Published regularly in the United Kingdom since 1954, this standard reference book continues to increase its usefulness. The 10th edition concentrated on expanding coverage of the Far East, Australia, and Latin America. The current edition emphasizes additional coverage of organizations from the United States, the United Kingdom, Australia, Central and Eastern Europe, and the former Soviet Union. National and international organizations are included; local organizations are not.

More than 9,000 of the entries are new or revised. The names of the organizations are given only in the language of the acronym, but there are cross-references to acronyms in other languages for the same organization. For example, the reference for the UN reads "UN United Nations = NN.UU, ONU," and both of the other acronyms are found in their appropriate alphabetic place. If appropriate, acronyms for parent organizations are provided.

The guide is not intended to give information about the organizations, other than the acronym and its expansion. A bibliography is provided, however. *Buttress's World Guide to Abbreviations of Organizations* is recommended, particularly for larger libraries and any library dealing with international organizations.

—**Mary A. Axford**

ALMANACS

2. *The New York Times* **1998 Almanac.** John W. Wright, ed., with editors and reporters of *The Times*. Toronto, Penguin Books Canada, 1997. 988p. index. $10.95pa. ISBN 0-14-051405-8.

This reference work makes some fairly strong claims for itself, and most of them are valid. The best way to describe this work is to compare it to its more famous counterpart, *The World Almanac and Book of Facts* (see entry 3). Both almanacs include the same categories of information, such as chronology of the year; major news stories of the year; U.S. history; U.S. presidential biographies; world history; world geography; economic and climate data; major awards in the arts, sciences, and sports; and a wide variety of U.S. demographic information. *The World Almanac* probably has more data, but *The New York Times Almanac* prefers to expand on selected items and provide more in-depth information. For example, both almanacs list all the Nobel prize-winners, but *The New York Times Almanac* explains why they won.

This is a comprehensive reference volume. However, it may be debatable as to whether it is the most comprehensive almanac ever published—one of its claims. It is well organized, the table layout is easy to read, and the typeface does not invite eye strain. In addition, even the paper version is well bound and lies flat when opened. It is affordable and an excellent choice for both home and library use.

—**Deborah S. Hatfield**

3. **The World Almanac and Book of Facts 1997.** Mahwah, N.J., World Almanac Books, 1996. 975p. illus. maps. index. $27.95; $9.95pa. ISBN 0-88687-801-2; 0-88687-800-4pa. ISSN 0084-1382.

Readers of *American Reference Books Annual* have no doubt played the "Ready Reference Desert Island Game," in which colleagues name the minimum number of reference sources with which they could answer the maximum number of questions. No doubt, too, *The World Almanac and Book of Facts* (WA) is one of the titles that washed ashore with almost every such Biblio-Crusoe. Almanacs descend etymologically from medieval Arabic and physically from heavenly charts for astronomers, astrologers, and agriculturists. WA has grown steadily over the years, has used multiple indexing schemes, and has developed a less densely packed layout. The almanac lost its advertising in 1945 and its New York orientation in the late 1960s, when the last vestiges of the much merged *New York World* disappeared; it gained color maps in 1967; color news photographs in 1994; and a larger, easier-on-the-eye format in the 1995 hardcover edition.

Complete still with calendars and the whereabouts of celestial bodies, the presence of Steven J. Gould's article on dinosaurs' cultural appeal, "Offbeat News Stories," Internet addresses, a windchill chart, presidential election returns, "Shortest Navigable Distance Between Ports," notable disasters, cancer prevention advice, a digest of world history, Newbery medalists, and divorce laws, not to mention the text of the Declaration of Independence, the 1948 NCAA hockey champion, the Roman Catholic Church's North American cardinals, and Idaho's 1995 barley harvest make the paperback cover's claim, "#1 FOR FACTS AND FUN," hard to dispute, especially at $9.95. For autodidacts, waiting room browsers, trivia buffs, social historians, and yes, even librarians with entire continents of reference collections, WA may be the most varied reference source available.—**Robert H. Kieft**

4. **The World Almanac for Kids 1998.** Mahwah, N.J., World Almanac Books, 1997. 320p. illus. maps. index. $16.95; $8.95pa. ISBN 0-88687-813-6; 0-88687-812-8pa.

The World Almanac for Kids 1998 is a comprehensive, well-designed reference volume well suited for students in grades 3-5. The information is plentiful and well organized. Photographs, charts, graphs, and illustrations are appropriate and well produced. The almanac is divided into content-related chapters (countries, environment, law, money, and so forth) that are further subdivided into shorter one- or two-page sections. The chapters are arranged alphabetically. A table of contents and an index are included. Like most almanacs, this volume is printed on medium-grade newsprint—a bit thicker than newspaper stock, but with a similar grayish hue. The hardbound edition features a coated cardboard cover and the stitch-and-glue binding found in similar publications. The spine features no special reinforcement. A paperbound volume is also available.

The true usefulness of any age-specific work must be evaluated based on the needs of the audience. In making a list of several elementary-oriented research questions and researching those, this reviewer found that all of the questions were answered at least partially by this volume. Such typical elementary topics as states, U.S. presidents, and health and nutrition are covered adequately. Political maps and flags of the world are featured in 30 color pages. Such topics as currency exchange rates, world religions, and letter writing are explained. Many articles give Website addresses. More than a dozen content-related puzzles are also included; however, duplication permission for the puzzles is not expressly granted.

An index is an important part of any almanac, and this index falls short of expectations. In the search for the answer to one of the research questions—"Which U.S. city gets the most rain?"—the index was useless. "Rain" is not included in the index, and the pages listed under "weather" did not lead to the information. Instead, the information sought was found in the "United States: Facts & Figures" section. How many fourth-graders would be able to find this information? *The World Almanac for Kids 1998* deserves a place in the children's reference section of school and public library shelves. That place should be alongside traditional complete almanacs, which provide better indexing and a more exhaustive representation of pertinent information.—**Keith Kyker**

BIBLIOGRAPHY

Bibliographic Guides

5. **ARBA Guide to Subject Encyclopedias and Dictionaries.** 2d ed. By Susan C. Awe. Englewood, Colo., Libraries Unlimited, 1997. 482p. index. $65.00. ISBN 1-56308-467-8.

Initially, one may think that another guide to reference books is superfluous and tedious, yet a serious perusal of the *ARBA Guide to Subject Encyclopedias and Dictionaries* will convince even the most skeptical librarian of its inherent usefulness. This volume will prove invaluable to general reference librarians who must work in many fields, for it covers the areas of the social sciences, the humanities, and science and technology. The 36 separate chapters document the individual subject areas and provide full bibliographic citations and reviews from 10 years (1986-1996) of *American Reference Books Annual*. The reviews themselves, as well as the citations, have in many cases been expanded or revised to include new information, especially updated prices.

The author has carefully selected the encyclopedias and dictionaries in this volume with an eye on the most useful sources; she based her selections on organization of the book, its contents, its intended audience, and its special features. Excluded from this collection are general dictionaries and encyclopedias, those that deal with specific languages, and reprints of any kind. To assist the collection development librarian, there are two indexes to the volume: an author/title index and a subject index, both of which are comprehensive, listing all terms used throughout the text. A quick glance through the pages will reaffirm the fact that most everyone is unfamiliar with such sources as *The Dictionary of Stylistics* contained in the chapter on communication and mass media or with the *Encyclopedia of Wood Joints* found in the section devoted to the decorative arts.—**Lamia Doumato**

6. **Bibliographic Index 1996: A Cumulative Bibliography of Bibliographies.** Laurel Cooley, ed. Bronx, N.Y., H. W. Wilson, 1996, 1997. 1155p. $250.00. ISSN 0006-1255.

The Bibliographic Index series began with coverage for 1937-1942 and has been published continuously ever since. Each volume is an alphabetic subject list of bibliographies published separately or appearing as parts of books, pamphlets, and periodicals. Library of Congress subject headings are used for subject terms. Generally speaking, bibliographies with less than 50 citations are excluded, unless they are bibliographies of works by or about individuals. There are approximately 2,800 periodicals from which these bibliographies are culled, and for the most part these are indexed by H. W. Wilson. The scope is also narrowed by including those bibliographies that appear in the Roman alphabet and that were published in the previous five years.

This index resembles the others in format; in typeface; and most importantly, in comprehensive, well-defined coverage. Several sample citations with explanations are given to aid the user. Lists of abbreviations of journals cited and of abbreviations used in the citations are also provided. These annual volumes are extremely useful sources for both the student and the advanced researcher.

—**Robert H. Burger**

7. **The Eighteenth Century: A Current Bibliography n.s.15—for 1989.** Jim Springer Borck, ed. New York, AMS Press, 1996. 489p. index. $112.50. ISBN 0-404-62220-8.

This volume is another installment (v. 15) of the important title, *The Eighteenth Century: A Current Bibliography*. This bibliography is a collaborative project under the general editorship of Borck, with many other scholars and graduate assistants. Most of the listed items are books and articles that were published in 1989, with some earlier publications included. The volume is divided into 6 principal parts: printing and bibliographic studies; historical, social, and economic studies; philosophy, science, and religion; fine arts; literary studies; and individual authors. Many entries are extensively annotated, either from original reviews or by the editor and his staff. Book reviews are cited frequently, and Borck often furnishes an indication of whether the book was favorably or negatively reviewed. The comprehensive index provides access by authors, editors, and reviews. A table of contents and keyword access in the index would have improved this compilation, but it must nevertheless be judged indispensable to scholars and students of this period.—**Arthur P. Young**

8. **The Reader's Catalog: An Annotated Selection of More Than 40,000 of the Best Books in Print in Over 300 Categories.** 2d ed. Geoffrey O'Brien, ed. New York, Reader's Catalog, 1997. 1968p. illus. index. $34.95pa. ISBN 0-924322-01-2.

This is the 2d edition of a work first published in 1989 (see ARBA 91, entry 4). As with the 1st edition, this volume is a browser's guide to 40,000 books in print, but because some of the titles in the 1st edition are now out of print, and editorial judgment varies, many of the titles in the 2d edition are different from those in the 1st. Other differences from the original include 320 instead of 208 categories of books; 36 timelines, maps, and "picture galleries"; 750 line drawings by the caricaturist David Levine; a new section on business and reference books; and an increase in the number of pages devoted to most of the categories.

This reviewer essentially agrees with the assessment of the 1st edition in *American Reference Books Annual*: This book can be useful to a book lover but is of dubious reference value. The preface never defines what the editor means by a "best book." Although the selection of books is often interesting to a book lover, the annotations that accompany many of the entries are unpredictable, ranging from briefly descriptive to rather lengthy and sometimes marvelously opinionated. Because the general editor, O'Brien, is a poet, and other contributing editors work for the *New York Review of Books* (the 1st edition was the brainchild of Jason Epstein, cofounder of that learned, liberal journal), many annotations reflect a depth of scholarship that seems a bit at odds with the supposed mass appeal of this list. Any browser is likely to be both pleased and displeased with this book: This reviewer was happy, for instance, with the introductory few sentences on the novelist Iris Murdoch and the annotations for her works, but less than satisfied with the sparse entries on Thomas Mann.

The book does have both a nicely detailed specific subject as well as a general table of contents (although the tab color-coding system does not work very well, because the volume does not really have protruding tabs); the separate subject, title, and author indexes are also useful. Although there were a few drawings and photographs in the 1st edition, the 750 drawings by Levine in this edition are a distinct advantage: these are often more insightful than pages of critical commentary. Librarians looking for more comprehensive guidance to best books in print should stick with an old stand-by such as *The Reader's Adviser* (see ARBA 97, entry 11, for a review of the CD-ROM version). Potential users of *The Reader's Catalog* may want to wait until the World Wide Web site is up (www.nybooks.com), which promises to be frequently updated and to include Levine's drawings. The Website, it is only fair to point out, will compete with Amazon (www.amazon.com), the popular online "bookstore."—**David Isaacson**

9. **Recommended Reference Books for Small and Medium-sized Libraries and Media Centers 1997.** Bohdan S. Wynar, ed. Englewood, Colo., Libraries Unlimited, 1997. 321p. index. $45.00. ISBN 1-56308-555-0.

This is the 17th appearance of this annual, intended to provide guidance to smaller libraries in choosing reference material. Continuing the past pattern, reviews are selected and reprinted in their entirety from the full *American Reference Books Annual* (ARBA), with the addition of a code indicating suitability for college, school, and public libraries. This year's offering includes 555 reviews from the 1,449 in ARBA 97.

Arrangement follows the ARBA pattern—general tools, then 36 subject categories, subdivided as needed. Each entry includes full bibliographic description and price, a signed evaluative review, and citations to other reviews in a number of standard library review sources. Access is provided by author/title and subject indexes. It should be noted that in addition to print titles, this series is beginning to include more machine-readable sources, with at least 9 CD-ROMs covered this year in addition to reference to machine-readable versions of printed sources.

Aside from the fact that the price is about half that of the full ARBA for only one-third of the entries, the only criticism that can be made is the lack of clear selection criteria. Lacking such a statement, one can only wonder at the inclusion of titles clearly not recommended; others specifically recommended only for "research libraries," "larger collections," and the like; and titles with such comments as "optional," "best used as a supplementary source," or "limited appeal." The full ARBA is as much a year's record of reference publishing as a selection and review source; because this subject is specifically those items "recommended" for small and medium-sized organizations, more clarity in the criteria and more care in the selection would be helpful.—**James H. Sweetland**

10. **The Sabin Collection Catalog.** [CD-ROM]. Woodbridge, Conn., Primary Source Media, 1997. Minimum system requirements: IBM or compatible 386. Double-speed CD-ROM drive. MS-DOS 5.0. Windows 3.1. 4MB RAM. 5MB hard disk space. VGA color monitor. Mouse. Printer (optional). $1,995.00. ISBN 1-57803-054-4.

In the 1860s, an English expatriate, Joseph Sabin, began the task of producing a bibliography of all extant books on U.S. history, culture, and life. The first volume of his *Bibliotheca Americana: A Dictionary of Books Relating to America from Its Discovery to the Present* was printed in 1867, and his task was finished in 1936 by Wilberforce Eames for the Bibliographical Society of America. The final product was a set of 39 volumes containing more than 100,000 entries. Although it is not the only Americana bibliography produced in the nineteenth century (some would argue it was far from the best), it was certainly the largest. Also, according to Michael Zinman's "critical mess" theory, the sheer amassing of so many titles easily makes it one of the most important. The original work was one of those monumental tasks that, to the eyes of the modern bibliographer (assisted by computers, records available across the network, downloading, and personal bibliographic managers) seems almost unbelievable. The original print bibliography, for all of its problems, remains a useful part of any Americana research collection.

Primary Source Media has selected from the original 100,000-plus entries in excess of 14,000 of the "most significant" of the included titles, located the printed works, and reproduced them in microform under the title *The Sabin Collection*. The reviewed title is the CD-ROM catalog to this collection. The actual software (CD Answer by Dataware Technologies) used to organize this catalog is somewhat gruesome in its use. It has the look of a modern graphical user interface, but navigation is not intuitive, and its explanations are terribly jargon-laden. One can appreciate Primary Source Media's need to use a generic piece of software, but one hopes that in the future, a better solution will be found. In fairness, the disc is functional, if awkward and unnecessarily abstruse.

That being said, this catalog has many useful qualities. The bibliographic content of the records is substantive (much more so than the nineteenth-century entries of the original *Bibliotheca Americana*). Although the catalog is clearly intended to be used directly with the purchased microform collection, any library that generates regular use of the original Sabin bibliography would find it useful. Clearly, a huge number of the titles Sabin included in the original work would not be found here, but for those that are, the added access points would make their location significantly easier than using the original author-only access. It should be considered for purchase by any library owning the microform collection, *The Sabin Collection*, as well as any university or specialized research collection with a strong Americana component.

—**Caroline M. Kent**

National and Trade Bibliography

International

11. **Cumulative Book Index 1995: A World List of Books in the English Language.** Nancy C. Wong and others, eds. Bronx, N.Y., H. W. Wilson, 1995, 1996. 2v. priced on a service basis rate. ISSN 0011-300X.

Even in these infocratic days, *Cumulative Book Index* (CBI) is one of those publications that, like the proverbial famous speaker, "truly needs no introduction," so familiar is its self-effacing brown buckram to generations of library school students. Published since the early 1930s with coverage beginning in 1928, this classic succeeds an earlier *Cumulative Book Index* and the *United States Catalog*, over the years becoming a sidekick to the *National Union Catalog* (NUC) and, more recently, a subordinate of both the cumulations of NUC and the shared cataloging utilities OCLC and RLIN.

CBI compiles entries for English-language publications throughout the world from review copies supplied by publishers and from Library of Congress (LC) and British MARC tapes; it arranges entries in one alphabetic sequence by author, title, and subject. The preface enumerates publications included and excluded, pledges adherence to LC subject headings and filing rules, describes a full complement of cross-references, and notes inclusion of items published pre-1995 or early in 1996 if H. W. Wilson received news of them in calendar 1995. A directory of publishers and distributors concludes the set.

Most librarians today probably reach first for OCLC or RLIN rather than CBI, even in its several electronic forms, for answers to bibliographic questions. However, for libraries or their patrons without access to the national utilities, for those who prefer turning the pages of multiple volumes, and for students learning the traditions of the librarian's trade, CBI does the job.—**Robert H. Kieft**

12. **International Books in Print 1997: English-Language Titles Published in Africa, Asia, Australia, Canada, Continental Europe, Latin America, New Zealand, Oceania, and the Republic of Ireland. Part I: Authors-Title List.** Barbara Hopkinson and Irene Izod, eds. New Providence, N.J., K. G. Saur, 1997. 2v. index. $795.00/set. ISBN 3-598-22285-8. ISSN 0170-9348.

13. **International Books in Print 1997: English-Language Titles Published in Africa, Asia, Australia, Canada, Continental Europe, Latin America, New Zealand, Oceania, and the Republic of Ireland. Part II: Subject Guide.** Barbara Hopkinson and Irene Izod, eds. New Providence, N.J., K. G. Saur, 1997. 2v. index. $795.00/set. ISBN 3-598-22286-6. ISSN 0170-9348.

International Books in Print has a subtitle: *English Language Titles Published in Africa, Asia, Australia, Canada, Continental Europe, Latin America, New Zealand, Oceania, and the Republic of Ireland.* This subtitle describes the scope of this standard directory that lists approximately 17,000 new titles available from 7,074 publishers in 138 countries. The *Subject Guide* is based on a modified version of the 20th edition of the Dewey Decimal Classification. The 1st edition of this directory, published in 1979, contained 80,000 titles and was reviewed in ARBA on several occasions. It is an important directory for international publishing in the English language and should be found on the shelves of most large university and public libraries.—**Bohdan S. Wynar**

14. **Whitaker's Books in Print 1997: The Reference Catalogue of Current Literature.** London, J. Whitaker & Sons; distr., New Providence, N.J., R. R. Bowker/Reed Reference Publishing, 1997. 5v. index. $640.00/set. ISBN 0-85021-263-4. ISSN 0953-0398.

Whitaker's Books in Print has been reviewed in ARBA on several occasions (see ARBA 94, entry 6). This is a standard British bibliography providing the most comprehensive listing of British books in print. In addition to British publications, *Whitaker's* lists English-language titles published in continental Europe, plus titles available to the trade through a sole stockholding agent based in the United Kingdom.

Whitaker's was first published in 1874 as *The Reference Catalogue of Current Literature.* It contained the catalogs of 135 publishers, with 35,000 titles listed in a separate index. The catalogs were dropped after the 1932 edition, and in 1971 *Whitaker's* adopted its practice of listing in a single sequence the books both about and by a person. The book continues to be updated weekly, from listings in *The Bookseller.* The present edition contains details of some 770,000 titles from 31,000 publishers and has more than 13,400 pages. More than one million amendments (additions, corrections, deletions, and price changes) have been made from the 1996 edition. This remains an essential source for libraries interested in British publications.—**Bohdan S. Wynar**

United States

15. **Books in Print 1997-98.** 50th ed. New Providence, N.J., R. R. Bowker/Reed Reference Publishing, 1997. 9v. index. $525.00/set. ISBN 0-8352-3935-7. ISSN 0068-0214.

16. **Subject Guide to Books in Print 1997-98.** 41st ed. New Providence, N.J., R. R. Bowker/Reed Reference Publishing, 1997. 5v. $369.95/set. ISBN 0-8352-3957-8. ISSN 0000-0159.

R. R. Bowker's familiar *Books in Print* (BIP) publications are well known to librarians and publishers, primarily in their print iterations but more recently as CD-ROMs. (For a review of previous volumes see ARBA 96, entries 15 and 16, and for CD-ROM, see entry 17.) The 50th edition of *Books in Print* contains over 1,350,000 active titles and over 1,433,700 active ISBNs published by 57,600 U.S. publishers. Bound in nine volumes, the set includes four volumes arranged by author and four by title. The 9th volume is devoted to publisher information and includes names, addresses, and ordering information of all publishers mentioned in the author and title volumes.

The 41st annual edition of *Subject Guide to Books in Print* follows the headings assigned by the Library of Congress and also includes two unique features. In volume 5 there is a subject thesaurus that lists all subject headings used in *Books in Print, Paperbound Books in Print, Children's Books in Print, Forthcoming Books,* the *Software Encyclopedia, Ulrich's International Periodicals Directory,* and *American Men and Women of Science.* Second, *Subject Guide* now includes annotated entries, using information provided by participating publishers. This feature improves upon an already invaluable source.

Both sets remain an important reference tool, providing access to the U.S. annual publishing output that is available in no other print source.—**Bohdan S. Wynar**

17. Rinderknecht, Carol, and Scott Bruntjen, comps. **A Checklist of American Imprints for 1845: Items 45-1–45-7137.** Lanham, Md., Scarecrow, 1996. 539p. $67.50. ISBN 0-8108-3109-0. ISSN 0361-7920.

This is another volume in the continuing Checklist series. Items are presented in alphabetic order by the author's full name. Rather than use "dash-on entries" for representing the same author in the second or subsequent items in the same volume, the full author's name is used each time. This repetition is particularly helpful for an author such as "New York," which has dozens of entries. The user does not have to keep turning back to the first entry to determine the author.

Location symbols follow each entry. The checklist uses the National Union Catalog (NUC) symbol for the library. The entry numbers have a prefix of two numbers representing the year. Thus, when the indexes are compiled for the decade of the 1840s the user will not have to examine the entry numbers on the spine of the individual Checklists to find the correct volume.—**Rachael Green**

Canada

18. **Canadian Books in Print 1997: Author and Title Index.** Marian Butler, ed. Buffalo, N.Y., University of Toronto Press, 1997. 1283p. $155.00. ISBN 0-8020-4999-0. ISSN 0068-8398.

The *Canadian Books in Print: Author and Title Index* is issued quarterly—the hardcover edition is followed by complete microfiche editions in April, July, and October of each year. As in previous editions *Canadian Books in Print 1997* is compiled from listings obtained from Canadian publishers. All replies received before August 31, 1996, have been included in the present volume that contains 42,000 entries, including 4,000 entries with a 1996 imprint. As is well known, *Canadian Books in Print* is the most comprehensive source for Canadian imprints complementing and supplementing Bowker's *Books in Print* (see entry 15) and *Whitaker's Books in Print* (see entry 14). For a more complete listing of all books written by Canadian authors or books dealing with Canadian subjects, *Canadiana* should be consulted, published by the National Library of Canada.—**Bohdan S. Wynar**

South Africa

19. Musiker, Reuben, and Naomi Musiker. **Guide to South African Reference Books.** 6th ed. Herndon, Va., Mansell/Cassell, 1997. 240p. index. $89.50. ISBN 0-7201-2224-4.

The 6th edition of this long-running reference work (first published in 1955) includes 1,139 mostly annotated citations to works primarily in English that deal with all aspects of South Africa and are either traditional reference works or works that do an adequate job covering a topic when a reference source is lacking. The number of entries is double that of the previous edition published by Clio Press in 1979 under the title *South Africa* as volume 7 of the World Bibliographical Series (updated in 1994 by Geoffrey Davis; see ARBA 96, entry 122). Most bibliographies are excluded, however, except for a few basic cardinal subject bibliographies. Instead, readers are referred to Reuben Musiker's *South African Bibliography* (3d ed.; see ARBA 97, entry 551). Given that users seldom read introductions and that there are bibliographies listed in the guide at hand, this may cause some users to miss important works.

This edition is updated to include the most recently published reference works, some of which are listed under new topics, such as "Value Added Tax," and some of the older works represented in earlier editions have been dropped. It would have been nice if, in updating the contents, the authors had included materials available through computerized media, such as CD-ROMs and the Internet. The entries are arranged by the Dewey Decimal Classification system and indexed by author, title, and subject. This arrangement has its oddities. "People's Studies" (i.e., ethnographies) is found between meteorology and flora and includes such subdivisions as "Chinese people." Books on the "Cape Malays," however, are found both under "People's Studies" and under "Genealogy," with one particular title being listed in each section but having different pagination each time. The subject index term "Apartheid, Struggle Against," lists only eight items, some of which seem only indirectly associated with the topic, whereas other titles listed in this work that deal more directly with the topic were not indexed. Also, although the extremely important *South African Survey* (formerly entitled *Race Relations Survey*) is published by the well-known South African Institute of Race Relations, there is no reference to that body in the index. These quibbles aside, this is a useful revision of an important bibliography that libraries collecting Africana will want to have.

—**Paul H. Thomas**

BIOGRAPHY

International

20. **Biography Index: A Cumulative Index to Biographical Material in Books and Magazines. September 1995-August 1996.** Charles R. Cornell and Rene J. Montalvo, eds. Bronx, N.Y., H. W. Wilson, 1995, 1996. 681p. index. $190.00. ISSN 0006-3053.

In a previous review of this title (see ARBA 93, entry 33), the reviewer says it all: "Writing a review of *Biography Index* is really an exercise in describing the obvious." He notes generations of reference librarians since 1946 have gone to it as the preferred initial source for dependable biographies. The different emphasis intended for the present review is to look at the quality of the indexing headings actually used and the distribution of entries in the "Index to Professions and Occupations" that occupies pages 489-681 and to observe how reference questions in this area are handled at the local Association of Research Libraries member library.

The prefatory note indicates "The *Index* is comprehensive in scope and is intended to serve general and scholarly reference needs." Where do the listees come from? Mainly from the 1,105 (source of 21,560 entries) relevant titles of the 2,700 to 3,000 titles the H. W. Wilson staff regularly scans in preparing the other company tools. Finally, there were 116 component books.

The initial scanning of the entries in the "Index to Professions and Occupations" was to look for subjects having 100 or more entries. The most populated subjects were "Authors, American" (1,530 entries); "College Professors and Instructors" (1,080); "Actors and Actresses" (950); "Historians" (360); "Illustrators" (360); "Lawyers" (350); "Authors, English" (330); "Football Players" (325); "Singers" (315); and "Children of Prominent Parents" (300). The examination of the headings for difficulty and consistency showed that they were user friendly. Boy George is under "B," for example, as is "Brandy, (Singer)." Anyone who can handle telephone "yellow pages" would be fine.

When the local undergraduate library's head instructor/librarian was contacted, she did not have a paperback copy of *Biography Index* but instead had some experimental databases with biographical content she used heavily when doing demonstrations for classes. The reference staff on duty at the main library's reference desk does a quick search on the experimental databases while a patron waits. They also had a complete set of bound volumes at an index table of *Biography Index*. The staff is aware that the experimental databases do not distinguish between such entries as for the two Brandy's (Brandy the singer and Brandy the liqueur). *Biography Index* is recommended generally and broadly.—**Eugene B. Jackson**

21. **Biography Today: Profiles of People of Interest to Young Readers. 1996 Annual Cumulation.** Laurie Lanzen Harris and Cherie D. Abbey, eds. Detroit, Omnigraphics, 1997. 398p. illus. index. $52.00. ISBN 0-7808-0070-2.

Biography Today offers a profile of 40 people that young readers, 9 years old and up, are interested in learning about. Ranging from football coach Don Shula and the stars of *Beverly Hills 90210*, to guitar guru Jerry Garcia, a whole spectrum of celebrities is covered in this volume. Although some of the celebrities, such as the stars of *Beverly Hills 90210* may not seem worthy of study, this is a book for children and is made better by including them.

Throughout the year, three softcover issues are published, for which subscriptions can be purchased. In January they are alphabetized and compiled into one hardbound edition, which provides a cumulative index. Additionally, new information for selected individuals who have appeared in past volumes is added to an appendix in the annual cumulation. Each biographical entry ranges from five to six pages in length and contains information on birth, youth, early memories, education, first jobs, marriage and family, hobbies, career highlights, honors, and awards. A photograph of the profiled individual is included, and the entry ends with a list of suggestions for further reading. The annual cumulation also contains cumulative name, general, places of birth, and birthday indexes. The general index includes occupations, organizations, and ethnic and minority origins.

Biography Today is designed for young readers and, therefore, written on a basic level that is easy for children to understand. Quotes from the profiled people help children get to know them and to see how they feel about issues, life, childhood, or the value of working toward a dream. Although it is aimed at young readers, this book is not censored so as to shelter them from important facets of celebrities' lives, such as racism, drug use, or childhood poverty.

The real value of this book is the choices it makes when selecting whom to profile. From people children see on television nearly every day like Dave Thomas, to entries about a spelling bee winner and a geography bee winner, nearly all those profiled were in the news that year. And most of the entries are celebrities children can look up to for inspiration.—**Tom Sullivan**

22. **Current Biography Yearbook 1996.** Judith Graham and others, eds. Bronx, N.Y., H. W. Wilson, 1996. 710p. illus. index. $72.00. ISBN 0-8242-0908-7. ISSN 0084-9499.

H. W. Wilson's venerable *Current Biography Yearbook* (CBY) continues to maintain its place as a reference standard that should be owned by most libraries, judging by its latest installment in the series. Each yearbook is a compilation of the year's monthly issues of *Current Biography* (CB); separate subscriptions are required. *Current Biography 1940-Present*, a cumulative edition, is also available on the World Wide Web and on CD-ROM (see entry 22). The 1996 issue of the yearbook has a crop of 180 "living leaders," including Michael Bloomberg, Christiane Amanpour, Don Imus, Astrid Lindgren, Dennis Rodman, Faith Ringgold, Will Shortz, and P. L. Travers (who died in 1996). Ten biographies are updates from those in previous yearbooks.

Biographees complete questionnaires that form the primary material for each profile in CB; suggestions and corrections are solicited for publication in the CBY. Editors find supplementary information in magazines and other cited sources. The biographies, which are fascinating to read, owe much of their appeal to extensive use of direct quotations by and about the subject. Editors give a well-rounded picture of each individual by combining a detailed overview of his or her career with background information, such as childhood events, anecdotes, and memorable experiences. Black-and-white photographs accompany each article; their quality varies widely. Many are too dark or grainy, and although sources are credited, none are dated. In a separate section, brief obituaries (140 this year) summarize life accomplishments for those persons who have been featured in CB. Lists of the titles of biographical reference sources and periodicals consulted; an index to subjects by profession (e.g., film, journalism, social sciences); and a 1991-1996 cumulative index complete the yearbook.—**Deborah V. Rollins**

23. **DISCovering Biography.** [CD-ROM]. Detroit, Gale, 1997. Minimum system requirements: IBM or compatible 386 (486DX/33MHz or higher highly recommended). CD-ROM drive (double-speed or faster recommended) with MS-DOS CD-ROM Extensions 2.2. DOS 5.0. Windows 3.1. 8MB RAM. 5MB hard disk space. SVGA monitor (256-color display) and graphics card. Windows-compatible mouse. Printer (optional). $300.00/stand-alone version; $400.00/2-8 users. ISBN 0-7876-0919-6.

This disc can be used as a general biographical reference work but is designed as a well-conceived high school or junior college teaching tool for instructing students how to do research using CD-ROMs. The authors have selected approximately 2,000 names as being of particular interest to a youthful audience. Although the canonical names are there (Moses, Aristotle, Leonardo da Vinci, John Locke), much attention is directed toward the contemporary and multicultural. The "Biography Units" outlined in the accompanying Teacher's Guide list the study categories "Fine & Performing Artists" (e.g., Little Richard, Tito Puente, and Beverly Sills); "Winning Sports Personalities"; "Women in Politics and Government"; "Multicultural Authors"; and "On the Shoulders of Giants," the more traditional figures of biographical and historical study. The Guide also describes various collaborative and cross-curricular student projects. Each entry contains an extensive biography (with photograph), a bibliography by and about the subject, and a "Life & Times" outline of people and events important during the subject's life span. The biographies are generally well written—even those of such controversial figures as Louis Farrakhan.

An accompanying User's Manual contains instructions on Windows and navigating and searching the disc program. A Help Card summarizes the different search modes, for example, name, subject, place, timeline, full text, and "custom," as well as browsing, saving, and printing texts. The "custom search" capability enables the user to select any combination of categories to identify and group names. Thus, by selecting "Native American" from the "Ethnicity" category, "Poet" from "Occupation," and "Female" from "Gender," the user will be guided to Native American women poets Paula Gunn Allen and Leslie Marmon Silko. *DISCovering Biography* is an attractive and useful package for classroom or individual use.

—**D. Barton Johnson**

24. **Larousse Dictionary of Women.** Melanie Parry, ed. New York, Larousse Kingfisher Chambers, 1996. 741p. illus. $40.00. ISBN 0-7523-0015-6.

With nearly 3,000 entries including biblical, legendary, historical, and modern figures, the *Larousse Dictionary of Women* provides a concise starting point for information on women. Each entry includes the woman's full name as she is best known, with indications of other names (actors are listed under their stage name, with a note on their birth name); birth and death dates, when known; a one-line summary of her activities; and a brief description of her accomplishments. Many entries are illustrated. This work also includes a chronology of women's achievements, beginning with Eve and concluding with the 1997 standouts. Brief quotations by women on women and men on women round out the work. The international scope of the work includes many women who may not be known outside their own countries. Although the work is comprehensive, entries are of necessity short.

There are improvements that could be made in future editions. Geographic and occupational indexes would assist a student seeking information on women in a particular field. Although the editor notes the source of much information in the Larousse database, brief bibliographic citations would help researchers as well.

Even with the omissions noted, *Larousse Dictionary of Women* will be useful in academic, public, and secondary school libraries.—**Sue Kamm**

25. **Newsmakers 1997: The People Behind Today's Headlines.** Frank V. Castronova and Sean R. Pollock, eds. Detroit, Gale, 1997. 4v (subscription includes 3 quarterly paperback issues and 1 cumulative hardback). illus. index. $125.00/yr. ISBN 0-7876-0103-9. ISSN 0899-0417.

For young students who see names and faces in the news but who may not know anything about these people, *Newsmakers 97* can be a helpful tool. Three paperback volumes and one cumulative volume come per year, covering the people of greatest interest to youngsters. The range of people highlighted in this edition is excellent, from movie stars almost every teenager will know, such as Gwyneth Paltrow and Matthew McConaughey, to writers they may not have studied yet in school, such as Edward Albee and Kenzaburo Oe. In fact, the strength of these books is coverage of the newsmakers with which students are less likely to be familiar. It is these people that often have the most to teach students.

Each description of a newsmaker begins with typical biographical information: birth date and place, as well as who the parents are and their occupations. The next step, naturally, is a description of their childhood that looks toward the future and what made them famous. The final aspect to each description is a brief synopsis of exactly why that person is in the news. For authors, a list of works is included; for filmmakers and actors, a list of films; and for musicians, a list of recordings. Each section includes quotations from the highlighted individual. Although these are taken from outside sources rather than from the individuals directly, they are still valuable to show young students the real side of stars. Additionally, it is here that students can draw inspiration. A list of sources from which information was gathered on the celebrities closes out each section.

The $125 subscription includes all the volumes. What makes this series worth the money, however, is the timeliness of the three paperback versions.—**Tom Sullivan**

26. **Nobel Prize Winners 1992-1996 Supplement: An H. W. Wilson Biographical Dictionary.** Clifford Thompson, Edward Moran, and Selma Yampolsky, eds. Bronx, N.Y., H. W. Wilson, 1997. 165p. illus. $35.00. ISBN 0-8242-0906-0.

This supplement to *Nobel Prize Winners*, published in 1987 by H. W. Wilson (see ARBA 88, entry 32), continues the original edition's format, which is the hallmark of the Wilson biographical dictionaries. Each biography in the strictly alphabetic arrangement runs from two to three pages in length, with an accompanying photograph and bibliographies of works by and about the subject.

The first list in the book contains the names of the 55 Nobel prize-winners included in the volume. Following that list is a list of all Nobel prize-winners from 1901 to 1996 grouped by prize category and year for all prize categories. Next, the names of prize-winners appear by country of residence, which, according to a notation on the page, has been rearranged "to reflect all geopolitical changes" (p. 17). This particular list makes for fascinating browsing. Bosnia and Costa Rica, for example, have only 1 winner each, and the United Kingdom has 86. Equally interesting is the place of birth of winners who are not native-born. For example, Rudyard Kipling is listed as having been born in Germany, as is Henry Kissinger. The final list is of the names of the prize-winners who have died since 1991, such as Menachem Begin and Isaac Bashevis Singer.

The Nobel laureates were invited to contribute essays that explained their work and why they had pursued this course. In some instances, the unsigned articles come from the Wilson biographical publication, *Current Biography* (see entry 22); others are based on the subjects' autobiographies appearing in the Nobel Foundation's *Les Prix Nobel*. Wilson has done its usual skillful job of producing a usable and valuable biographical dictionary deserving of a place in every reference collection.—**Nancy P. Reed**

27. **100 Greatest.** Danbury, Conn., Grolier, 1997. 12v. illus. maps. index. $249.00/set. ISBN 0-7172-7691-0.

Although this attractive 12-volume set holds a great deal of appeal in terms of subject matter and presentation, it lacks substance. Each book focuses on 100 outstanding examples of a given topic or field (e.g., women, tyrants, disasters, inventions). Students will surely be attracted to such volumes as "100 Greatest Disasters" and "100 Amazing Animals," but the information offered is spare. Each entry is given a page of coverage, with approximately one or two paragraphs of description. These are supplemented by large color photographs and sidebars of interesting facts. In addition, each book has an index and several games or activities based on some of the information. Cataloging cards are provided with the set.

Some of the books are organized in topical sections. For example, in "100 Greatest Men," there are sections on humanitarians, scientists, musicians and composers, and so forth. Within these sections, entries are arranged chronologically. Other volumes are simply arranged chronologically. Criteria for selection are not stated, and therefore it is difficult to assess the choices. However, this type of reference is bound to raise questions about the inclusion (or exclusion) of specific people or events (e.g., Mikhail Gorbachev as one of the 100 greatest men of all time). Because the entries are brief, it is also unfortunate that they do not direct students to sources for further information.

The publicity information for this set states that it is aimed at readers in grades 5 or higher, but the typeface size, layout, and content (or lack thereof) seem geared to a younger audience. More important, most of the information contained in this collection can easily be found in a general encyclopedia, so librarians with limited budgets should give careful consideration to the purchase.—**Barbara Ittner**

United States

28. **The Complete Marquis Who's Who on CD-ROM.** [CD-ROM] (2 discs). New Providence, N.J., Marquis Who's Who/Reed Reference Publishing, 1996. Minimum system requirements (Windows version): IBM or compatible 386. CD-ROM drive. Windows 3.1. 4MB RAM. Hard disk. Minimum system requirements (Macintosh version): 68020 processor. CD-ROM drive. 6MB RAM. Hard disk. $995.00.

Marquis Who's Who biographical works are essential for academic libraries and businesses in which data on people are important. Therefore, when this reference standard appears in a new form (i.e., on CD-ROM) for the first time, it is an occasion to be noticed. Unfortunately, this premier edition does not live up to the print volumes' distinguished history.

The Complete Marquis Who's Who on CD-ROM consists of two discs, one for current volumes and a second for previous entries, each of which must be searched separately. In many ways, this electronic version is a tremendous improvement over the book-bound data in print format. Simple name and address searching is easier than ever before, although the latter occasionally suffers from an inconsistency in the use of abbreviations. Approximately 750,000 biographical sketches published during the past 10 years in the 18 regional and specialized titles issued by Marquis Who's Who are now searchable via only 2 CD-ROMs. Entries are updated every six months with the inclusion of new biographees as well as selected updates of previous entries. The CD-ROMs include every entry from *Who's Who in America* and *Who Was Who in America*, as well as volumes covering the East, West, Midwest, South and Southwest, the world, education, U.S. nursing, entertainment, finance and industry, religion, advertising, U.S. law, women, human services professionals, science and engineering, and emerging leaders in the United States. The price of the electronic version was recently cut in half, thereby reducing it to within the budgets of many libraries that may not have been able to purchase it otherwise.

Marquis Who's Who has obviously put much work, thought, and effort into producing this electronic version. Searchers may retrieve the desired biographies by using any number of search methods: keyword(s), Boolean, wildcard, and field searching, among others. The basic search is simple. Through the use of a series of fill-in-the-blank templates, data may be retrieved according to a biographee's name, birthplace, birth year, death date, address, zip code, educational background, place of employment, professional and other organizations, occupation, family name of wife, and so on. Searchers may highlight records, add notes to individual entries, and compile edited versions of specific records via shadow files. Installation is easy, but access to records suffers severe limitations.

Several significant additional problems were found in using this work. Many of the problems are a result of the way in which records were compiled. Rather than going for uniformity, Marquis used two types of biographical record formats: 90 percent are in category form, and 10 percent are in sketch format. With some exceptions, each of these categories must be searched separately in order to ensure that a biographee is, or is not, included. In most instances, searches do not permit the inclusion of both city and state. Because of this, users attempting to find persons born in Miami, Oklahoma are subjected to a long list of hits that includes every individual born in Miami, Florida, and Miami, Ohio. Inconsistency in the use of abbreviations is fairly widespread.

In addition to difficulties in retrieval because of lack of consistency within records and other causes, this tool is disappointing for other reasons. The expertise necessary to effectively search the database almost necessitates the thorough study of the 112-page printed guide that accompanies the two discs; unfortunately, this guide has no index. The brief lifespan of this CD-ROM, which is timed to cease functioning after 248 days, requires the lease of expensive updates every 8 months. The necessity to continually lease updates, combined with the fact that the discs are limited to a 10-year time span, almost requires that university libraries, which are accustomed to maintaining older volumes for historical purposes, must also purchase the hardcover print volumes. The cumulative effect of these criticisms is that, despite the inclusion of so much data, much will be missed through searches that have too many unnecessary impediments to them.

Despite its faults, libraries in which biographical searches form a major part of their reference work should consider inclusion of this title. Marquis Who's Who states that changes are planned that will alleviate some of the above problems, and other modifications are being discussed.—**Donald E. Collins**

29. **Concise Dictionary of American Biography.** 5th ed. New York, Scribner's/Simon & Schuster Macmillan, 1997. 2v. index. $235.00/set. ISBN 0-684-80549-9.

This 5th edition of *The Concise Dictionary of American Biography* is a 2-volume reference set that includes all of the entries found in the parent set as well as all its supplements. The coverage of the work includes all outstanding Americans who died prior to January 1, 1981. Of the more than 19,000 Americans profiled, over 1,000 are new to this edition. All of the original articles have been condensed, but the integrity of important biological facts is maintained.

The main body of the dictionary is alphabetized by surname, and two special indexes are included. They are indexed according to occupations and according to birthplace. This is a must-purchase item for academic and public libraries.—**Mary L. Bowman**

30. Wetterau, Bruce. **The Presidential Medal of Freedom: Winners and Their Achievements.** Washington, D.C., Congressional Quarterly, 1996. 546p. illus. index. $67.00. ISBN 1-56802-128-3.

The Presidential Medal of Freedom is the U.S.A.'s highest civilian honor. Established in 1963, it had been given to 331 people by September 29, 1995. Wetterau's book first describes the historical background of the award, the methods of selection, and the conduct of the ceremonies. It then gives, for each recipient (in chronological order), the official citation, a photograph, and a one- to two-page biographical account. The book also includes a brief bibliography and a name and occupations index. Primarily, this is a biographical reference book. Its value is to be gauged by the importance of its subject matter, the degree to which it offers new information, and by how well it has been written. Unfortunately, it falls short on all three counts.

The medal winners apparently have been selected by the presidents themselves (no doubt with the aid of advisers) and for reasons unspecified; there are no review boards or official criteria. As a result, the choice of recipients seems to have been determined more by political or personal considerations than by pure merit. How else to account for the dozens of people whose names are scarcely recognizable or, worse still, are well known but hardly impress readers as being distinguished (e.g., Martha Raye, Louis L'Amour, and Richard Petty)? Ironically, the capriciousness of the selection process means that the reference value of this publication is higher than it may have been otherwise. Wetterau claims, unjustly, that "a significant part of this material cannot be found in any other available source," but many of the people he writes about are indeed sufficiently obscure to make his accounts useful.

Unfortunately, however, Wetterau's biographical sketches are often so laudatory and deferential that they lack credibility. Is Joe DiMaggio "revered around the world"? One doubts it. Has James Cagney "left his mark on the hearts of all Americans"? Ditto. Funeral-style eulogies do not command confidence as information sources. The physical appearance is sumptuous; as a piece of bookmaking, the book is inexpensive at the published price. However, the price is too high for the limited value that the book will have for most libraries. [R: Choice, April 97, p. 1318]—**Samuel Rothstein**

31. **Who's Who in the East 1997-1998.** 26th ed. New Providence, N.J., Marquis Who's Who/Reed Reference Publishing, 1996. 1044p. index. $279.00. ISBN 0-8379-0628-8. ISSN 0083-9760.

The 26th edition of *Who's Who in the East* provides biographical information on select individuals from the eastern section of North America. Biographees represent Connecticut, Delaware, Maine, Maryland, Massachusetts, New Hampshire, New Jersey, New York, Pennsylvania, Rhode Island, Vermont, portions of Virginia, and Washington, D.C. The Canadian provinces of New Brunswick, Newfoundland, Nova Scotia, Prince Edward Island, Quebec, and the eastern section of Ontario are also included.

Inclusion in the volume is based on reference value and achievement in one of the fields represented, such as art, business, education, government, law, media, medicine, religion, and so forth. More than 23,000 entries are listed from biographees who furnished their own data or approved of data compiled by Marquis Who's Who staff members. Data include name, occupation, vital statistics, education, professional certification, address, and the like. A valuable feature of this volume is the "Professional Index," where biographees are listed by occupation; under each occupation names are listed alphabetically by country, state, and city. This volume is recommended for public and academic libraries in the region represented and for other libraries whose budgets permit.—**Mary L. Bowman**

32. **Who's Who in the West 1998-1999.** 26th ed. New Providence, N.J., Marquis Who's Who/Reed Reference Publishing, 1997. 897p. index. $272.95. ISBN 0-8379-0928-7. ISSN 0083-9817.

Like its predecessors, the 26th edition of *Who's Who in the West* is an essential reference for libraries in the western United States and western Canada. The volume contains about 19,500 names of individuals who live in western North America or live elsewhere but have made a significant contribution to the West. Criteria for inclusion are based on position or individual achievement as well as the likelihood the person will be the subject of a reference inquiry in a library. As with all of these publications, a name does not automatically remain in the volume with each new edition, so libraries need the complete set on hand as biographical reference.

Individuals included must be living, and generally, the listing includes facts relating to vital statistics, family, and professional activities. Addresses are provided for those who release them. Most of the entries are generated by the individual included, but not before they are screened by the staff. A profession index further divided geographically is also included.

Marquis publications are well-respected classics, which librarians generally refer to. They are widely indexed in paper and online sources and are a must for libraries with a reference section. This type of resource is not currently duplicated on the World Wide Web, although Marquis does sell it on CD-ROM.

One wonders, however, why Marquis, a division of Reed, has to charge $272.95 for the one-volume work. This alone may limit its placement in some libraries that ought to have it.—**Paul A. Mogren**

Canada

33. **Canadian Newsmakers 1997.** Toronto, Gale Canada, 1997. 170p. illus. index. $150.00/yr. ISBN 1-896413-41-2. ISSN 1206-8764.

Fifty "newsmakers" comprise this volume of a new series on notable Canadians. Coverage is broad, with personalities in politics, the arts, the media, sports, film, and science. Organized alphabetically by name, each person's entry is three to five pages in length and includes a black-and-white photograph, a telegraphic-style biography and career summary, a profile, a list of works (if applicable), and a brief bibliography. The profiles—drawn from such Canadian sources as *The Globe and Mail* and *Maclean's* magazine—are both interesting and informative. This premier issue includes Prime Minister Jean Chrétien; Canada's first female police chief, Christine Silverberg; media moguls Conrad Black and Israel Asper; and actor Michael J. Fox, singer Alanis Morissette, author Carol Shields, and figure skater Elvis Stojko.

The annual subscription fee includes three quarterly issues and one cumulative hardcover volume. An occupation index and a subject index in each issue refer only to issue number, not page number. *Canadian Newsmakers* is a convenient resource, but with its rather steep price, not all libraries will be able to afford it.—**Lori D. Kranz**

Ireland

34. Ó Céirín, Kit, and Cyril Ó Céirín. **Women of Ireland: A Biographic Dictionary.** Minneapolis, Minn., Irish Books & Media, 1996. 248p. illus. index. $19.95pa. ISBN 0-937702-16-1.

This is the first biographical dictionary on significant deceased women of Ireland to be published. The authors are a nurse with experience in health care, social work, and journalism and a secondary school teacher, lecturer, journalist, published poet, painter, editor, and translator. The publisher is a small press whose previous titles are maps and guides to regions of Ireland and a book on medieval Galway. The work at hand is a paperback with a sewn binding and a nice presentation. The authors' goal is to make women more visible in Irish history. No specific criteria for inclusion are provided, aside from the exclusion of living persons. The authors admit to subjectivity and personal choice in an effort to show Irish women's achievements, especially how they have risen above challenges and limitations.

The text is nicely illustrated in black-and-white; the alphabetically arranged entries provide life dates, occupation or significance, family background, historical context, and "flavour of each subject's life," trying to appeal to and educate readers with a limited knowledge of Irish history. No further references are provided at the conclusion of the entries, which is regrettable, although there is a basic bibliography at the end of the work. The illustrations do not provide provenance, which a quality work should do. An appendix that classifies according to occupation, pursuits, concerns, interests, and so forth provides access to public figures, revolutionaries, educators, social welfare activists, evangelists, missionaries, and visual artists, thus promoting work on women in various modes of life. The general index covers all names included in the text and organizations and some historical events.

Obviously, notable Irish women are included in some biographical sources on British women, but this is a fine first effort and breaks new ground. *Women of Ireland* is recommended for all reasonably sized academic libraries, especially those with active women's studies clienteles, and public libraries with Irish interests. [R: LJ, 15 Mar 97, pp. 57-8]—**Agnes H. Widder**

Latin America

35. **Who's Who in Latin America: Government, Politics, Banking, & Industry.** 4th ed. Bettina Corke, ed. New York, Norman Ross, 1997. 2v. index. $99.00/volume; $149.00/set. ISBN 0-88354-226-9 (v.1); 0-88354-227-7 (v.2); 0-88354-225-0 (set). ISSN 1068-7896.

Who's Who in Latin America provides brief biographical information on significant persons in government, politics, banking, and industry in Latin America and the Caribbean in the twentieth century. Updated editions are published about every four years. The 1st edition (1984) included 1,000 biographies covering 28 countries. This new 4th edition has expanded to 2,000 biographies covering an additional 8 Caribbean countries. In spot-checking and comparing the 3d and 4th editions, many entries are the same. However, in the latest version, some entries have additional information, and very few have been deleted.

Another country-specific reference source is Roderic Ai Camp's *Who's Who in Mexico Today* (see ARBA 89, entry 135). Examples of additional general biographies are *Biographical Dictionary of Latin American and Caribbean Political Leaders* (see ARBA 89, entry 618), which contains 450 biographies of nineteenth- and twentieth-century figures, and Ronald Hilton's *Who's Who in Latin America* (3d ed.; see ARBA 72, entry 226). The latter book is more inclusive than this new edition. Information for the work under review was compiled from questionnaires sent to individuals and information from newspaper articles and other publications. Because current biographical information on Latin American leaders is difficult to find, this book is useful. It is recommended for public and academic libraries with an interest in Latin America.—**Karen Y. Stabler**

DICTIONARIES AND ENCYCLOPEDIAS

36. **Academic American Encyclopedia.** Danbury, Conn., Grolier, 1997. 21v. illus. maps. index. $795.00/set. ISBN 0-7172-2064-8.

Grolier's standard-bearer is one of the multivolume encyclopedia sets regularly reviewed in these pages (see ARBA 95, entry 41, and ARBA 93, entry 57, for the most recent analyses). The set has been consistently praised for the currency of its information, the quality of its illustrations, and the clarity of its text and organization. The compliments are justified on all counts. The 1997 set contains summary information for the 1996 baseball season and the 1996 elections. Illustrations are relevant, reproduced well, and number more than 16,000. The text of the 32,000 entries manages to be cogent but still comprehensible to a wide-ranging audience (students and at-home users from middle school through college). Approximately a third of the entries are biographical. Cross-references, bibliographies, and a separate index volume serve to intensify the set's value and assist its use.

Librarians are familiar with the handful of multivolume encyclopedias currently being produced. Only novices wholeheartedly recommend purchase of one set over another, for each emphasizes and excels in different aspects of information delivery. Grolier's product has shorter entries than comparable encyclopedias and is at the low end on total page count and number of illustrations. The differences among all these products, however, are based in priority, not quality. This reviewer turns to the *Academic American Encyclopedia* for its lucid, concise text. This set's strength is in its syntax.—**Ed Volz**

37. **The Cambridge Encyclopedia.** 3d ed. David Crystal, ed. New York, Cambridge University Press, 1997. 1303p. illus. maps. $54.95. ISBN 0-521-58459-0.

This one-volume encyclopedia serves as a transition between two worlds, offering both the quick information fix of the handheld desk dictionary and the diversity of the multivolume encyclopedia. In Crystal's third *Cambridge Encyclopedia*, the format is larger, the atlas is expanded, the ready-reference section is no longer yellow, and the color news photographic plates are dropped, which leaves the atlas and updated world flags the only color in the volume. The preface briefly and thoroughly describes *Cambridge*'s scope and explains the encyclopedia's editorial conventions as well as the process of selecting contributors and revisions by an almost exclusively British roster of academics. That process, which accounted for expanded subject coverage in the 2d edition, continues here with further expansion of political and sports entries, revisions for recent government reorganization in Britain, and other changes. The volume claims 26,000 entries for persons, places, events, and concepts, with another 10,000 bits of data in the Ready Reference tables of measurements, terrestrial features, languages, sports records, national leaders, abbreviations, and so on. Entries are boldfaced and cross-referenced. The illustrations and maps are clear black-and-white drawings, although some tables have the gray look of a photocopier background. The writing is accessible to high school students, and even middle school students may find it useful for short reports.

The 5th (1993) edition of *Cambridge*'s chief competitor, the long-running *Columbia Encyclopedia* (see ARBA 95, entry 49), claims 50,000 entries (many with bibliographies), lacks *Cambridge*'s almanac features, and, with longer entries, is bulkier and heavier. For example, *Cambridge* gives "United States" one column on a two-column page, whereas *Columbia* gives it a two-page map and seven, three-column text pages. *Columbia*'s small print and three-column layout is daunting and not as easy on the eye as *Cambridge*'s design. *Cambridge* will nicely serve those who want something reasonably portable for their home, office, or ready-reference desk; those who want more information and have keen eyes may prefer *Columbia* on a dictionary stand.—**Robert H. Kieft**

38. **The Cambridge Factfinder.** 2d ed. David Crystal, ed. New York, Cambridge University Press, 1997. 891p. illus. maps. index. $16.95pa. ISBN 0-521-56597-9.

The Cambridge Factfinder is a thoughtfully organized almanac of facts with a European/world perspective. Cambridge University Press has taken great pains to choose facts that readers are most likely to need by studying the results of a data search project that tracked the questions most people asked when using their *Cambridge Encyclopedia* (see ARBA 96, entry 44). Two hundred fifty experts then organized the facts into areas of knowledge and added an exhaustive index at the end. Sources are listed for statistical information, and facts that are open to interpretation are noted.

Useful as a companion to U.S. almanacs, the *Factfinder* contributes unique coverage of the world, history, and social issues. The history section is indicative of the useful information one will find. This section lists the dynasties of China and ancient Egypt, rulers of the Roman Empire, a map of the chief Roman roads, diagrams of the British royal family tree and the European royal families descended from Queen Victoria, the family tree of the Hapsburgs, major wars, the Crusades, great explorers, and world political leaders and rulers. The environment section describes multilateral treaties concerning the environment, world forest depletion with maps, charts on greenhouse gases, a chart of acid rain damage worldwide, and more. Priced modestly, this title is recommended for all school and public libraries.

—**Carol D. Henry**

39. **Children's Encyclopedia.** [CD-ROM]. New York, DK Multimedia, 1997. Minimum system requirements: IBM or compatible Pentium 75MHz. Quad-speed CD-ROM drive. Windows 95. 16MB RAM. 25MB hard disk space. 800 x 600 pixels, 16-bit color monitor. Mouse. 8-bit sound card. Loudspeakers or headphones. $39.95. ISBN 0-7894-2233-6. (Also available in Macintosh version: ISBN 0-7894-2236-0.)

The Dorling Kindersley (DK) Eyewitness book series has been a staple of school media centers and children's library collections for several years. Now, DK Multimedia offers the Eyewitness *Children's Encyclopedia* CD-ROM as a continuance of its high-concept publishing efforts.

Program installation is simple and quick. Although only newer machines will easily meet the system requirements, older school and library computers may fall short. When accessing the program, the user is given an option to access the DK Internet Website, DK Online. (An Internet connection is required to access this feature.) After a brief registration process, the user is given a list of linked Websites. Exiting the browser software takes the user back to the encyclopedia's start-up screen.

Each user must log on to the CD-ROM encyclopedia before accessing information. This process may prove tiresome to busy library personnel who typically load several different CD-ROM encyclopedias into the computer throughout the day. The user is then presented with the Navigator, a graphic interface to the information available through the encyclopedia. The easiest way to access the information is to use the "Search" function and type the desired topic. Users can access all media—articles, video, animations, and others—or restrict the search to a single presentation style.

The typical entry consists of about 100 words and at least one illustration of the topic. "Fact Files" and "Amazing Facts" sections are frequently offered. A helpful *see also* section is provided, which includes many topics. Almost any article can begin an exciting, eclectic knowledge quest. Such quests can also begin by investigating the 20 "virtual worlds." In these virtual reality presentations, users can click "world" elements to access certain sections of the encyclopedia. For example, by clicking the movie theater in the "City" world, the user can learn about motion pictures. Additionally, a slot machine-style button on the Navigator can send the user to a randomly selected article.

But what about the information? After spending a few hours on the program, one nine-year-old said, "It's fun, but I couldn't use it for a report." Although the Eyewitness *Children's Encyclopedia* is intuitive, fun, and beautifully made, its value as a research tool is limited. Several topics of interest to children (dogs, cats, horses) have minimal representation. Articles about countries contain only the information available in a print children's almanac, and states fare worse under the regional approach. Also missing are audio files. Although filled with sound effects, the sounds of animals, musical instruments, and vocal performers are missing.

Clearly designed for the casual elementary-age explorer, the Eyewitness *Children's Encyclopedia* is an inexpensive and professionally produced CD-ROM. However, a student requiring more than cursory information on most topics would quickly discover the program's inadequacies.—**Keith Kyker**

40. **Collier's Encyclopedia.** New York, Collier Newfield, 1997. 24v. illus. maps. index. $1,499.00/set. ISBN 1-57161-093-6.

First published in 1950, *Collier's Encyclopedia* has established a reputation as a reliable and comprehensive information source for young adult and adult readers. This new edition continues that tradition with 24 volumes containing some 23,000 articles. Using a relatively broad subject base, *Collier's* publishes lengthy, detailed, and often fascinating articles in those areas deemed pertinent to the curricula of colleges and secondary schools, as well as some elementary schools. The organization and writing style reflect this audience, and it could be contended that *Collier's* is geared to more literate and sophisticated reference book users than other encyclopedias.

Each entry clearly defines its subject and proceeds with a general explanation that presents readers with relevant facts. If deemed necessary, references to other articles or sources of further information about the topic are listed. Written primarily by academics and scholars, the articles are somewhat uneven in style, but most are clear and engaging. A list of approximately 5,000 contributors with their affiliations precedes the text and includes such luminaries as Kip Thorne, Margaret Mead, Louis Shore, and Isaac Asimov. Unlike some other encyclopedias (e.g., *World Book*), *Collier's* does not avoid controversial material (e.g., mathematician Alan Turing's homosexuality). In fact, these authors sometimes veer from factual data into critique or opinion, which makes for spirited, although not totally objective, reading. An example of this is the rather lengthy article on art, in which the author suggests that a specific painting by René-François-Ghislain Magritte "perhaps more than any other illuminates the nature of art."

Keeping material current and achieving well-balanced coverage are always the major challenges of encyclopedias. On this score, *Collier's* is certainly adequate. According to the publisher, this edition contains 57 new entries, 148 new capsule biographies, 78 completely rewritten articles, and 1,189 updated or revised articles. Examples of new articles are those on Maya Angelou, the Dalai Lama, suicide, and vertigo; heavily revised articles include those on black holes, Nicaragua, and rock music. Other updates have also been made, such as in the article on alcoholism, where it is noted that the term has been abandoned by scientists in favor of the more specific terms "alcohol dependence," "alcohol abuse," and "problem drinking." New maps and illustrations have also been added. However, with revisions, there is always room for improvement. This reviewer observed that although the changes in the former Soviet Union are documented with new entries of adequate length for individual nations (such as the 9-page article on Ukraine, ably written by Alexander Motyl), the entry for the Union of Soviet Socialist Republics, which no longer exists, lingers on in a 63-page spread. In the same vein, illustrations for the article on U.S. painting includes works only up through 1947, and the text discusses art movements only through the 1970s.

Regarding balance of coverage, a pervasive bias toward Western history and learning was found. This bias is readily apparent in the article on art, where only 1 of the 60 excellent illustrations represents Asian art. Other problems with balance of coverage were also noted, for although there is an exemplary 26-page discussion of black Americans, there are no entries for Asian Americans or Hispanic Americans.

The format and typography of this work are appealing and clear, and there are now a number of color illustrations. Although placed appropriately, illustrations are not graphically integrated, being treated more as footnotes or additional information rather than the focus of the text. Color and registration also create minor problems in color illustrations as well as the transparency overlays. On the other hand, the black-and-white illustrations (such as those that appear in the article on anatomy) are excellent. It is unfortunate that more are not used in place of the substandard color reproductions.

As noted in previous reviews (see ARBA 92, entry 39, for example), the main weakness of the set is its accessibility. Because of the broad subject base, readers are compelled to use the analytic index, which is still rather difficult to use. The typeface is small, and the index does not differentiate primary entries from other coverage, so it may take readers several tries to find the information they seek. Finally, although some articles list sources for further information, most are cited in the bibliography, which appears in volume 24 with the index. However, notes on using the bibliography and the index should help adults master accessibility, and with practice younger users should also be able to overcome search problems.

All in all, the publisher has produced a solid and dependable reference work. Although it is more expensive than its main competitors (*New Encyclopaedia Britannica* is $995 for 32 volumes and *Encyclopedia Americana* is $995 for 30 volumes), its broad, narrative approach will appeal more to some users. Despite its problems, the set will continue to serve its audience well, and it is therefore recommended for high school, community college, and some public and home libraries.—**Barbara Ittner**

41. **Collier's Encyclopedia 1998.** [CD-ROM]. New York, Collier Newfield, 1997. 3 discs. Minimum system requirements: IBM or compatible 486/66MHz. CD-ROM drive. 16MB RAM. 50MB hard disk space. SVGA, 256-color monitor. $99.95. ISBN 0-87177-513-1.

Collier's Encyclopedia on CD-ROM is formatted for Windows 95 and for use with Internet Navigator. It is embodied on three discs and is designed to run from one CD-ROM drive. This means changing discs for some searches, but the process is fairly easy, if a little inconvenient. Considering the amount of information contained on the discs, it is understandable.

Collier Newfield's policy is constant revision and updating of article entries, which is apparent in this latest version. The 1998 edition contains 57 new entries that are mostly biographical but with some topical areas covered as well. There are 148 new capsule biographies that include a wide range of people from the fields of music and sports. There are 78 completely rewritten articles and 1,189 updated or revised articles, which include such topics as libraries; books; music genres (jazz, blues, ragtime, opera, rock); international literature areas (Chinese, Japanese, Arabic, Germanic); areas of education; astronomy and astrophysics; and country and geographic areas (Africa, Latin America, and the former Soviet Union). There are 98 new contributors out of the total of 4,600 educators, scientists, and business leaders who supply articles. The 1998 edition has 470 new illustrations, most in color, and 62 revised or replaced maps.

The layout of the opening screen of the encyclopedia is fairly easy to read and use. Several icons are located along the left side of the screen. The first choice is the Encyclopedia A-Z, then a World Atlas of maps from De Agostini Rand-McNally. The American Heritage Dictionary follows and then a choice to perform Simulations. A Timeline, Internet access, and Help conclude the choices. Located horizontally along the top of the screen are Netscape icons and navigational icons for the database. Immediate searching of the encyclopedia is available on the first screen. There are also choices to enter the encyclopedia by the volume desired, to open the multimedia index, to use the Topic Finder, and to open random articles.

Upon opening the encyclopedia, an alphabetic list of volumes appears. Once a selection is made, an alphabetic list of articles within the volume appears. At the top of the list, two-letter guides appear as a shortcut for entering the list of articles. Once an article is selected, the screen divides into three parts. The article is displayed in a window along the right. On the left side of the screen are two smaller windows. The top window allows for a display of the article's outline, and the bottom window allows for the pulling in of multimedia items, such as videos, sound, and pictures related to the article being displayed. An article title will display if the words searched match the article title. If there is no matching title, then the articles that contain the relevant words or articles are displayed. The articles are assigned a relevancy code. One can use Boolean logic or type in a natural language question. Articles can be searched using the Topic Finder, which displays broad general areas first and then more specific areas, or by clicking on Random Article. By selecting the Multimedia Gallery, one is able to display maps, pictures, movies, sounds, or World Wide Web links to the Internet.

Under each selection is an alphabetic list of titles. The dictionary allows searching for words of which one is not sure of the spelling by using a truncation symbol. The simulations and activities section provides lessons designed so that one can walk through an experiment or activity using the interactivity of the encyclopedia. The timeline allows one to search for major events and view the timeline by decade. Interactivity is provided so that links clicked on bring up the corresponding encyclopedia article. One useful feature of the encyclopedia is the interactivity with the Internet. It appears to be a seamless function that allows great ease in searching the encyclopedia or other components and then connecting to the Internet directly or through links provided in the article entries to see related Websites. This interactivity promotes access to the most current information and latest updates

Collier's strengths are its in-depth articles and ongoing revisions and updates. The encyclopedia is geared toward those with at least a high school reading level. This CD-ROM package is highly recommended for its currency and breadth and depth of coverage.—**Jan S. Squire**

42. **The Columbia Encyclopedia.** [CD-ROM]. New York, Columbia University Press, 1997. Minimum system requirements (Windows version): IBM or compatible 486. CD-ROM drive with MS CD-ROM Extensions 2.0. MS-DOS 6.2. Windows 3.1. 8MB RAM. Minimum system requirements (Macintosh version): 68030. CD-ROM drive. 8MB RAM. $195.00. ISBN 0-231-10520-7.

The Columbia Encyclopedia has established a reputation as an almost indispensable ready-reference tool in libraries of all types and sizes. The most current print edition (see ARBA 95, entry 49) has been further revised and expanded and made available in CD-ROM format. There are 900 new articles and 3,000 revised ones, with an additional 13,000 cross-references (or, as they function here, hyperlinks).

There are two search options: browsing and keyword searching. The default browsing list is all 51,053 alphabetically arranged entries (including blind entries), but the user can select 1 of 11 categories (such as "Science and Technology," "Philosophy and Religion," and "Sports and Everyday Life") and 1 or more subcategories. Whereas in browse mode one is simply electronically thumbing through the entry headings, search mode allows keyword access to the entire text of the encyclopedia. The user can also limit searches to subsets of the whole work by choosing 1 or more of the 11 subject categories. A search can consist of up to four words or phrases combined with Boolean operators. Browsing uses implicit right-hand truncation; keyword searching offers four truncation options: right-hand, left-hand, simultaneous right- and left-hand, and internal (which is not documented in the online help).

The articles themselves include pronunciation where it is deemed necessary, and a pronunciation key can be opened from the menu bar. Hyperlinked cross-references in the text are in bold typeface, as are links to tables ("Sites of the Modern Olympics," "Chronology of Popes," and the like). The user can also view a list of related articles, some of which do not appear as hyperlinks. True to its heritage, this work emphasizes text. However, unlike its print counterpart (which has a few maps and line drawings), it contains no illustrations at all (not to mention no video or sound clips).

Although the content of *The Columbia Encyclopedia* on CD-ROM is accurate, readable, and reasonably up-to-date, the presentation leaves something to be desired. The interface, although simple and uncluttered, is unattractive and not easy on the eyes. There is no option for changing the yellow text on black background or the blue letters on olive buttons to something more appealing or easy to read. The window, which on this reviewer's PC occupied only about 33 percent of the screen, cannot be resized, and even on a Pentium 166 MHz, searching and displaying was often ponderously slow. The text of the articles can be printed but not copied-and-pasted or saved to a file.

The publishers have not exploited computer, CD-ROM, or multimedia technology to create an encyclopedia that can easily compete with such products as *The World Book Multimedia Encyclopedia* (see ARBA 96, entry 51), *Microsoft Encarta* (see ARBA 95, entry 60), and *The New Grolier Multimedia Encyclopedia* (see ARBA 95, entry 42), with which they compare it. There may be libraries that need exactly what the Columbia disc has to offer. However, if choosing between it and the others just mentioned, they may want to pass it up until the disc undergoes a substantial makeover.—**Craig W. Beard**

43. **Grolier Multimedia Encyclopedia, 1998.** deluxe ed. [CD-ROM]. Danbury, Conn., Grolier Electronic Publishing, 1997. 2 discs. Minimum system requirements: IBM or compatible 486DX/33MHz. Double-speed CD-ROM drive with Microsoft CD-ROM Extensions 2.2 (Extensions only necessary for Windows 3.1). MS-DOS 5.0. Windows 3.1. 8MB RAM. 10MB hard disk space. SVGA 256-color monitor. Microsoft or compatible mouse. Wave-table sound card. Speakers or headphones. Printer (optional). Optional online requirements: Modem. Access to the World Wide Web using an Internet service provider. $59.99. ISBN 0-7172-3400-2.

This CD-ROM is a most impressive multimedia encyclopedia that will enhance and improve research for elementary through adult students. The deluxe edition of the *Grolier Multimedia Encyclopedia* is relatively easy to use and simply fun to browse. It features the "Online Knowledge Explorer," which contains access to two other Grolier encyclopedias and links to specially selected World Wide Web addresses. *The New Book of Knowledge* (see entry 46) is one alternative reference link, as is the well-known *Encyclopedia Americana* (see ARBA 90, entry 50). The *Grolier Internet Index* provides access to Websites that complement and enhance the information contained in the articles. Users must provide their own Web access.

Images, videos, sounds, maps, timelines, tours, an atlas, a yearbook, and *The American Heritage College Dictionary* add to the variety of multimedia available. Especially impressive are the maps that allow the user to zero in on smaller and smaller areas, even down to street corners with names. The tours are beneficial for those who need to research a topic and do not know where to begin, because the user is guided through related sights, sounds, and articles.

Technical support is helpful and accessible. If users desire a more than minimum response time, pay special heed to the minimum system requirements and exceed them. *Grolier Multimedia Encyclopedia* is definitely a worthwhile investment and a beneficial addition to the collection.—**Mary L. Trenerry**

44. **International Year Book, 1997: Covering the Year 1996.** New York, Collier Newfield, 1997. 576p. illus. maps. index. $199.95.

This yearbook is intended to update the coverage of previous printed editions of *Collier's Encyclopedia* (see ARBA 95, entry 48), bringing earlier sets up-to-date and delaying the need for buying a new edition. Despite the name, however, this is not a 1997 yearbook. Like 1997's almanacs, it covers 1996's significant events. As for the arrangement, first comes a lavishly illustrated, 12-page summary of 1996's signal events worldwide. Next come several lengthy, signed feature articles, similarly enhanced by full color. Among topics are Guglielmo Marconi (100 years after his invention of radio), the Smithsonian Institution, tattoos and tattooing, new and notable bridges of the world, Copenhagen, and a roundup of the 1996 Olympic Games with all results and names. The following section is an alphabetically arranged series of *Collier's*-format articles (with mostly black-and-white illustrations) dealing with significant events in the nations of the world, as well as articles dealing with current trends for computers, crime, and education. A final section provides nine newly written or extensively revised articles from the 1997 edition of *Collier's*, covering such topics as the Dalai Lama, football, and jazz.

Even though almanacs are fine sources of brief factual information, the yearbook format allows much more in-depth coverage of a year's transition, entertainment, sports, and politics, nation by nation throughout the world, and the use of eye-catching color photography is extremely commendable. A note of caution: Although the encyclopedia articles follow the usual standards and protocols of straightforward, unbiased reporting, feature articles (particularly the ones on the U.S.'s 1996 elections and tattooing) reflect the distinct points of view of their writers, occasionally causing objectivity to be compromised. The overall work, however, succeeds as one of the best treatments going of an entire year's events, and all articles are literate, readable, and interesting. In fact, even without its excellent reference value, this book can easily be browsed just for its interesting feature stories. Libraries already owning *Collier's* should definitely consider a standing order of the yearbook. Others may wish to consider this book as a stand-alone volume for its extensive and excellent coverage of a tumultuous year. For a roundup of the signal events of the previous calendar year, it is hard to find a better treatment.—**Bruce A. Shuman**

45. Kabdebo, Thomas, and Neil Armstrong, with Etaín Ó Síocháin. **Dictionary of Dictionaries and Eminent Encyclopedias: Comprising Dictionaries, Encyclopedias, and Other Selected Wordbooks in English.** 2d ed. New Providence, N.J., Bowker-Saur/Reed Reference Publishing, 1997. 418p. index. $130.00. ISBN 1-85739-103-9.

This 2d edition of *Dictionary of Dictionaries and Eminent Encyclopedias* is conveniently arranged and easy to use. There are 1,400 subject headings, which is 400 more than the 1st edition, and 8,000 dictionary titles.

Actual dictionaries were used for most of the quoted sources. This reference work does not claim to list all of the dictionaries in print or out of print; however, it is, for the most part, comprehensive in listing the types of dictionaries available. The subject headings are helpful with easy-to-understand terms, topics, and subjects. The categories are alphabetic, with the dictionaries listed by title beneath each listing. Each entry begins with a heading in bold print, followed by a title and a description of the work. Quoted sources are italicized. Within most entries, other dictionaries are listed with explanations of the various types available, their features, or the technical or social novelties of the dictionary world. "Alternate accessibility" is the stated purpose of the index. Titles, personal names, and headings are referred to in the three indexes.

This reference work certainly presents relevant information in a convenient structure. However, the cost is prohibitive to all but the most dedicated "dictionarians."—**Sue Brown**

46. **The New Book of Knowledge.** Danbury, Conn., Grolier, 1997. 21v. illus. maps. index. $725.00/set. ISBN 0-7172-0528-2.

It is not an easy task to provide a thought-provoking review of an item whose previous annual editions have been so well covered (see ARBA 95, entry 61, for a review of the 1994 edition). All interested parties are referred to the excellent and thorough evaluation of the set in general (including comparisons) in *Kister's Best Encyclopedias* (2d ed.; see ARBA 95, entry 57).

An encyclopedia primarily intended for children in the intermediate and middle school grades (3-9), *The New Book of Knowledge* is "uniquely related to the needs of modern young people . . . who need an encyclopedia that will help them understand the constantly changing realities of the world around them" (preface). To ensure utmost accuracy, every article, map, drawing, photograph, diagram, chart, and fact box is checked by skilled researchers so that the information provided is correct and current. Where authorities disagree or information is unknown, the reader is so informed. Editorial policy is to present fact, not opinion.

As with all earlier editions, the 1997 edition of *The New Book of Knowledge* is designed for educational use at home as well as for classroom and library use. Its content was selected by educators who analyzed curriculum requirements of school systems across the nation, by librarians familiar with the research needs of the intended audience (children and young adults), and by cultural specialists who considered the interests and needs of users beyond the classroom and library settings. In addition to the abundance of accurate, up-to-date information, the text is enhanced by many informative projects, experiments, illustrations, games, and activities. The articles are written or reviewed by experts in their respective fields, and almost all are signed. The few unsigned articles are written by staff editors who are familiar with the needs and ability levels of young readers and are subject-matter specialists. The set contains more than 13,000 color illustrations that were carefully checked for accuracy. Most of the artwork was commissioned especially for this publication. The more than 1,000 maps were prepared by skilled cartographers in collaboration with geographers and subject editors. The maps are clear, accurate, informative, attractive, and easy to understand.

The "pyramid" approach of the set, wherein articles begin simply and become more complex as the text progresses, is an effective writing technique that allows the youngest readers to benefit from each article. It should be noted that even though *The New Book of Knowledge* may include slightly fewer entries than other similar encyclopedias, the set offers longer articles with more in-depth coverage. Technical terms are printed in bold typeface and are defined in context. When the number of terms makes it relevant, some articles include a glossary. The encyclopedia is organized alphabetically in unit letter volumes. Each of the 20 volumes contains an index that is cross-referenced to the entire contents of the set. The often-criticized "Dictionary Entries" are printed in front of each index. Grolier intends to phase out the separate "Dictionary Entries," incorporating the sometimes ephemeral entries into the main body of the encyclopedia.

The 1997 set includes 20 new articles, 84 completely rewritten articles, and 227 revised articles. Highlights of this edition include the addition of articles on international cities; articles in the life sciences, mathematics, physical sciences, and weather have been updated; the excellent coverage of the humanities is enhanced by the ongoing revision of mythology, legends, and folklore; profiles of 40 children's authors have been added in the excellent section on children's literature; several half-page biographies have been added throughout the set as part of the ongoing revision process; 4 presidential biographies were updated as part of the major revision of presidential biographies; and the article on the Olympics was updated to reflect the 1996 Summer Games in Atlanta. A complete list of authors, reviewers, and consultants appears in Volume 20.

The set is accompanied by the newly revised paperback text, "Home and School Reading and Study Guides." A new "Activities Section" has been added to replace the instructional paperback "Teaching Basic Reference Skills With . . . The New Book of Knowledge." This instructional guide is intended to assist teachers, librarians, and parents in making optimal use of *The New Book of Knowledge*. The guide's stated intent is to teach children the lifelong habit of turning to reference sources for information. A section of the "Home and School Reading and Study Guides" contains activity sheets that are designed to help students learn how to find, organize, and use the information in the set and build good research skills in the process.

In conclusion, *The New Book of Knowledge* continues to provide "excellent coverage of both curriculum-related and out-of-school subjects of interest and concern to young people. The bottom line: an outstanding encyclopedia for young people" (*Kister's*, p. 200). This encyclopedia is highly recommended for library, classroom, and home use.—**Sharon Thomerson**

47. **Oxford Family Encyclopedia.** Steve Luck, ed. New York, Oxford University Press, 1997. 744p. illus. maps. $45.00. ISBN 0-19-521367-X.

Choice of subjects to cover is always a major problem in designing a reference work. The decision here seems to be to cover as many topics as possible by shortening individual articles. The vast majority of entries are no more than a paragraph, and many are a single sentence. Common terms are not included and entries tend to be modern. Contemporary U.S. singer Madonna gets an entry, a large in-column picture, and a large caption. However, the turn-of-the-century physician-poet, John McCrae, is not included. There is also a subtle, but quite definite, U.S. bias both as to choice of topics covered and the writing itself, which is odd given that copyright is held by a British firm. This reviewer found the ordering of entries, which is crowded, difficult to get used to. The book alphabetizes letter-by-letter, which can be confusing. "Easter" comes before "Easter Island," which comes before "Eastern Cape," all natural enough, but "Eastern Cape" and "Eastern Orthodox Church" come before "Easter Rising," which itself comes before "East India Company."

The book is heavily illustrated, with scientific graphics predominating. In many cases, however, the "cutaway" or otherwise explanatory drawings are difficult to follow, even when the captions are studied closely. Individual articles in the encyclopedia are concise, and bits and pieces of the topic or story have to be gathered across the whole collection of articles. In trying to research the Boer War, entries for Afrikaans, Afrikaner, Bantu, Boer, Boer Wars (see South African Wars), Cape Province, Dutch, Dutch East India Company (see East India Company), Eastern Cape, East India Company, Free State, Great Trek, Huguenots, Kimberley, Netherlands, Orange Free State, South Africa (see country feature), South African Wars, Transvaal, Xhosa, Zulu, and Zulu War have to be found. This work is definitely a candidate for a CD-ROM product with a cross-reference feature. However, some work will have to be done on the cross-references first: Terms mentioned in the articles having their own entries in the encyclopedia are sometimes printed in uppercase letters (indicating that a reference exists) and sometimes are not. In any case, tracing down the cross-references, and even related topics that are not referenced, is necessary in order to attempt to gain a complete picture. The handling of technology is disappointing. The definition of a computer virus is flatly wrong, referring to "[p]art of a computer program" and disruptive or corrupting software, while saying nothing about reproduction and spread. The entry for computer network is correct for the most part, but the illustration, which tries to explain the carrier sense multiple access with collision detection (CSMA/CD) scheme, talks about colliding data packets producing an "electronic shock wave." The explanation of multiplexing of telephone voice conversations over digital lines is completely misleading in its implication that the technology relies on short sampling times.

For a quick lookup or casual browsing, a single-volume encyclopedia probably makes more sense than a multivolume monster. There is a wealth of information available in this work for the satisfaction of idle curiosity. The number of errors found in such a short acquaintance, however, seems to indicate that this is not a book that can be relied upon without checking other sources as well.—**Robert M. Slade**

48. **Pockets: Encyclopedia.** By John Farndon. New York, DK Publishing, 1997. 512p. illus. maps. index. (DK Pockets). $14.95 flexibinding. ISBN 0-7894-1498-8.

Want an encyclopedia that is both handy and unconventional? This well-illustrated, pocket-size encyclopedia is one of a series of fact-packed miniguides in a wide range of fields covering such diverse topics as aircraft, castles, clogs, gemstones, and many more (for example, see entries 1467 and 1645). Unlike the others in the series, this is a general encyclopedia covering physical and biological sciences, technology, transportation, countries of the world, and history. Smaller topics are covered in two adjoining pages with outstanding color illustrations, captions, fact boxes, and timelines. For example, the section on galaxies has an informational beginning definition of the concept, four color illustrations including pictures of the different galaxy types, the Milky Way galaxy and the Andromeda galaxy, and two galaxy facts. A timeline of world history and a reference section with units of measurement, conversions, wars and battles, and good indexes end the book. This encyclopedia would be an excellent way to introduce students to concepts and a useful source for illustrations. Its unconventional size has drawbacks, but it will be attractive to students.—**Carol D. Henry**

DIRECTORIES

49. **Awards, Honors, & Prizes 1997: An International Directory of Awards....** 13th ed. Donna Batten, ed. Detroit, Gale, 1997. 2v. index. $420.00/set. ISBN 0-7876-0877-7. (Volumes also available separately.)

This 2-volume set is comprehensive in its coverage of awards, honors, and prizes and their sponsors in virtually every aspect related to human endeavor worldwide. Volume 1 covers 5,000 organizations in the United States and Canada and the 17,000 awards they sponsor, 300 of which are new to this volume. Volume 2 covers 3,500 international and foreign organizations in more than 100 countries and the 9,000 awards they sponsor, 150 of which are new listings. The preface and introduction of each volume list a representative selection of notable awards and a selected list of awards new to the volume. Each volume contains an alphabetic and numerical list, sponsors and their contact information, and names and descriptions of each award sponsored. A line separates each sponsor's section. Within the information provided for each award are the award's purpose, eligibility requirements, application due date, type of award given, date established, and current status. Because of the size and volume of the work and the fact that information was obtained through surveys and follow-up telephone calls, there is bound to be some out-of-date information. For example, the Pritzker Architecture Prize lists the address as unknown as of 1995. By searching the Internet, one is able to obtain the address and other information. Also listed as "address unknown" was the Professional Basketball Writers Association of America, but it was quickly found in the *Encyclopedia of Associations*.

There are three indexes in each volume; a subject index of awards, an organization name index, and an award name index. There are approximately 400 broad subject categories and cross-references based on the awards' principal target areas. The entries are listed alphabetically by name, and awards named for persons are listed by the person's last name. There are some problems for such a comprehensive index. Subject assignments are based on the awards' principal areas of interest according to the descriptions, but in looking at random descriptions for some awards, it is difficult to readily identify the subject category in which it was placed. For example, Canadian Phytopathological Society's Glenn Anderson International Lectureship on World Food Security mentions plant science, world food security, food supplies, and lectureships. The entry was under botany, not under any of the aforementioned words. At the least, a cross-reference from plant to botany would have been helpful. The organization and award name indexes are the same for both volumes and they cross-reference each other. Entries are arranged alphabetically with volume and entry number cited.

Although there are some minor faults with this work, it is a comprehensive, useful, and singular reference work. This edition incorporates some previous recommendations from an earlier review (see ARBA 93, entry 66), but there still needs to be consideration of including running titles in both volumes. In volume 1 the sponsors' name and in volume 2 the country and the sponsor's name would be very useful. In volume 2, the alphabetic country divisions are hard to recognize; it would help to have the country name in either a larger typeface or some clearer form of delineation. This work is still somewhat expensive, so consideration should be given as to whether it is necessary to buy every edition. There is a companion work—*World of Winners* (see ARBA 93, entry 1314)—that identifies the recipients of the awards. Diskette and magnetic tape versions are available, as are customized mailing labels.—**Jan S. Squire**

50. **Directories in Print: A Descriptive Guide to Print and Non-Print Directories....** 15th ed. Dawn Conzett DesJardins, ed. Detroit, Gale, 1997. 2v. index. $345.00/set. ISBN 0-7876-0185-3. ISSN 0899-353X.

This reference standard, now in its 15th edition, provides astounding access to more than 15,000 directories, buyer's guides, rosters and other address lists published in the United States and worldwide. Volume 1 of this 2-volume set consists of descriptive listings arranged by 26 broad subject areas covering business, education, science and technology, hobbies and leisure activities, medicine, and community services and social concerns, to name a few. Volume 2 contains subject, title, and keyword indexes and an alternate formats index indicating those items that are available on magnetic tape, diskette, CD-ROM, microfiche, 3 by 5" cards, mailing labels, computer printouts, and other formats.

Each entry contains up to 28 pieces of information, including directory title, mailing and e-mail addresses, telephone and fax numbers, price, availability online, circulation, language of the directory, and much more. All entries from the previous edition have been updated, and 775 additional entries from the supplement to the 14th edition have been added. New to this edition are directories of U.S., state, city, and local government scope. This work is highly recommended for academic and public libraries and for special libraries with a focus on business.—**Elaine F. Jurries**

51. **Fulltext Sources Online, July 1997: For Periodicals, Newspapers, Newsletters, Newswires, & TV/Radio Transcripts.** Ruth M. Orenstein, ed. Needham Heights, Mass., BiblioData, 1997. 558p. index. $118.00; $195.00/yr. spiralbound. ISBN 1-879258-19-6. ISSN 1040-8258.

Fulltext Sources Online (FSO) has been an important source of periodical information in all types of libraries since its 1988 launch. It provides an alphabetic listing (by title) of periodicals, newspapers, newsletters, and newswires that are available in full text through various online services as well as on the Internet. To her credit, the editor painstakingly defines the various meanings of *full text* in the directory. First, *full text* when referring to a periodical means that "complete articles are found online. It does not mean that a periodical is found cover-to-cover in the database." Second, in regard to the articles themselves, "in general, the term means that the entire *text* of an article is available online." That means that charts, graphs, illustrations, or photographs will not usually be included.

Updated twice a year, FSO includes approximately 7,000 records. Entries note title; regional or geographic orientation; name(s) of search services carrying the publication online in full text; name or number of database, section, or file containing the publication; dates of coverage; frequency of updating; lag time for updating; amount of full-text coverage; whether database contains current material only; what length of time is considered "current"; and the Internet uniform resource locator (URL), if one exists. Happily, FSO continues to improve. The inclusion of URLs is new to this edition, as is the addition of 500 new titles plus coverage of H. W. Wilson's *Readers' Guide to Periodical Literature*, *Humanities*, *General Science*, and *Business Abstracts Fulltext* databases (see entry 70). Internet information includes listings for about 1,000 URLs, all with free access, plus a table of 442 URLs for journals that post free back issues. (Access to these URLs is provided free to FSO subscribers through its "Private Zone" Website.) In an era in which "access" is quickly superseding "ownership" in every information center or library, FSO remains a reliable and useful navigational tool.—**G. Kim Dority**

52. **Government Phone Book USA 1997: A Comprehensive Guide to Federal, State, County, and Local Government Offices in the United States.** 5th ed. Detroit, Omnigraphics, 1997. 1656p. index. $185.00. ISBN 0-7808-0071-0. ISSN 1062-1466.

This volume has expanded greatly since its original volume, titled *The Government Directory of Addresses and Telephone Numbers* (see ARBA 96, entry 732, and ARBA 93, entry 740). The quick reference listings now include state and agency abbreviations. A new feature is the URL addresses for most of the executive, federal, regional, and state offices. Also provided are e-mail addresses for various departments, offices, and contact persons. Specific fax numbers of these offices and additional offices are also given. Unfortunately, the preface states that the information for Congress contains outdated information (from November 1994). The URL addresses should have been checked because the majority of the Senate addresses were changed by eliminating the "gov//" with the second slash becoming a "~." In most instances, having the domains for the Senate and House of Representatives can give one access to an individual. There is now a separate section on United States Courts as well as a listing in the Federal Regional section. Along with state, county, municipal, and local government office information, maps of the counties of each state are another new feature. Most of the data were provided by Carroll Publishing, who also produces the multivolume *Carroll Directories* (see ARBA 96, entries 721-729).

With these new revisions, the *Government Phone Book* serves well as a one-volume resource when compared to similar resources, with the understanding that the information is more dated than information available with a subscription to the four volumes (federal, congress, state, and municipal) of Leadership Directories's *Yellow Book*.—**Mila C. Su**

53. **The Instant National Locator Guide.** 3d ed. San Francisco, Calif., Creighton-Morgan, 1997. 1v. (various paging). maps. $29.95pa. ISBN 0-9620096-3-6.

The 3d edition of this work provides the ZIP codes and telephone area codes for over 20,000 towns and cities in the United States. The main section is an alphabetic listing of towns and cities, with each entry including the area code, the name of the county seat, the 1990 population, and the ZIP code. The subsequent section includes state maps indicating the first three ZIP code digits (area not precisely defined), city, county and town names, and selective road mileage distances. The next section lists the counties by state with the name of the county seat. The fourth and fifth sections contain a reverse ZIP code directory and an area code directory to identify states.

Although this guide provides a lot of information, it does have several limitations. If a city has more than one ZIP code, the range of numbers is listed but not the specific code. In order to find the right code the *National 5-Digit Zip Code and Post Office Directory* (see ARBA 97, entry 52) will need to be consulted. Similarly, because the area codes within some cities are different, dialing telephone directory assistance service may prove to be more useful. Finally, the North American Numbering Plan (NANP) is currently renumbering the area codes of many cities and states; the most updated information is now available on the Internet. [R: LJ, 15 May 97, p. 72]—**Donald Altschiller**

54. **PhoneDisc Powerfinder.** [CD-ROM]. Carter Lake, Iowa, PhoneDisc, 1996. 6 discs. Minimum system requirements (Windows version): IBM or compatible 386XT. CD-ROM drive. DOS 3.1. Windows 3.1. 4MB RAM. 500K hard disk space. Minimum system requirements (Macintosh version): Macintosh Plus/Classic. CD-ROM drive. System 6.04. $99.95.

Having access to 114 million residential and business listings for $100 is a good deal, provided that users can find what they are looking for most of the time. That is what *PhoneDisc Powerfinder* supplies. This CD-ROM telephone directory is easy to install and easy to search when searching the basics. Users can export in a variety of formats, and the user manual gives clear instructions for using advanced features, such as deduplicating or selecting noncontiguous listings.

Less pleasing are the facts that one cannot choose multiple Standard Industrial Classifications for a business search and that deduplicating is not available for exporting. Limiting within a name is slow. Accuracy of entries is a problem as well. These lists did not seem to have been updated within the past year. Listings for businesses and residences that had been gone or had moved up to three years ago were found.

If a library anticipates heavy business usage, it probably ought to go with one of the telephone directories specifically created for the business market. For home use, public libraries, or the small business that has to stretch its dollars, this program would be a good buy.—**Deborah S. Hatfield**

55. **Toll-Free Phone Book USA 1997: A Directory of Toll-Free Telephone Numbers for Businesses and Organizations Nationwide.** Detroit, Omnigraphics, 1997. 1118p. index. $75.00pa. ISBN 0-7808-0173-3. ISSN 1092-0285.

This 1st edition of *Toll-Free Phone Book USA* joins a long list of directories located both on the Internet and in print. This volume is a spin-off of *The National Directory of Addresses and Telephone Numbers* by the same publisher (see ARBA 96, entry 56, for a review of the 1995 edition). In addition to toll-free telephone numbers, the book offers other contact data, including full name of company, complete mailing address, regular telephone number, fax number, e-mail and World Wide Web addresses if available, and a classification code indicating business activity or type of organization.

The main emphasis of listings is on business; however, entries are also provided for such organizations as associations, colleges and universities, the media, political groups, travel providers, and U.S. government agencies. The text is arranged alphabetically by name of organization and geographically by state, and a classified section is arranged by type of business.

Other features of the directory include an area code guide with recent and upcoming changes, a list of area codes in numerical order, a list of area codes in state order, and a table of abbreviations used in the directory. This book is a useful ready-reference item, even though it is not as comprehensive as *The National Directory*.—**Mary L. Bowman**

56. **U.S. Homes.** [CD-ROM]. Carter Lake, Iowa, PhoneDisc, 1996. 2 discs. Minimum system requirements (Windows version): IBM or compatible 386XT. CD-ROM drive. DOS 3.1. Windows 3.1x. 4MB RAM. 1MB hard disk space. Minimum system requirements (Macintosh version): Macintosh Plus/Classic. CD-ROM drive. System 6.04. 1MB RAM. $39.95.

U.S. Homes CD-ROM from PhoneDisc has both advantages and disadvantages. On the plus side, the User Manual is organized and well written. On the negative side, the manual is written for all the various PhoneDisc products and mentions that a feature is available in versions with business listings. It is unnecessarily confusing.

The software is reasonably intuitive. The main feature is a "search by name" function. Precision can be increased using the "limit" button, which brings up a screen of possible limits, including city, state, street, zip code, area code, and more. Results can be printed in various formats, including labels, and exported to mail merge programs. Another advantage is that the CD-ROM contains the software so that the information can be used on MS-DOS, Windows NT or 95, and MacOS. The primary drawback is typical of this type of product—currency of listings. The box claims the product is the "new 1997 updated version." A check of known listings shows that if the person has moved in the last two years the listing is likely to be out of date. It seems unlikely this problem will be solved satisfactorily until someone arranges a Web interface to the needed databases that is updated in real time or, say, once a day or even weekly. PhoneDisc does have a Web page (http://www.phonedisc.com/index.html). It is not particularly useful but does have contact information. Overall, PhoneDisc is a good attempt but has problems yet to be resolved.—**Mary A. Axford**

57. **U.S. Homes and Business.** [CD-ROM]. Carter Lake, Iowa, PhoneDisc, 1996. 3 discs. Minimum system requirements (Windows version): IBM or compatible 386XT. CD-ROM drive. DOS 3.1. Windows 3.1. 4MB RAM. 1MB hard disk space. Minimum system requirements (Macintosh version): Macintosh Plus/Classic. CD-ROM drive. System 6.04. 1MB RAM. $49.95.

U.S. Homes and Business is simple to use. The manual may be needed for installation and to read about all the features of this program; however, the manual is not needed to run the program and to search for telephone numbers. There are 3 discs, 1 for business and 2 for homes (East and West) with maps to determine which disc is needed when searching for a number in a specific state. In addition to telephone numbers, the disc provides addresses for businesses as well as individuals. Users may search by name, by business type, or by specific zip code areas and Standard Industrial Classification codes. Printing formats include labels with zip+4 and postal bar codes. Names and addresses may be exported one at a time, and the labels will begin to print when there is a full page of addresses. There was no mention of update frequency for these discs. However, *U.S. Homes and Business* is recommended for anyone who needs this service. These three discs certainly are an improvement over paperback telephone books, and the printing formats make this a useful item.—**Sue Brown**

58. **Washington '97: A Comprehensive Directory of the Key Institutions and Leaders of the National Capital Area.** 14th ed. Washington, D.C., Columbia Books, 1997. 1250p. index. $85.00pa. ISBN 1-880873-25-7. ISSN 0083-7393.

Annually published in the spring, the 14th edition of Columbia Books' reference directory for metropolitan Washington, D.C., continues the tradition of a concise albeit selective guide to both public and private institutions and individuals in leadership positions for this area. As in previous editions, the contents are divided into 17 organizational chapters, each with an introductory background essay prefacing main entries, including name, address, telephone and fax numbers, membership, succinct description, officers' names, and other detailed information as appropriate.

The 2d section of the volume, which comprises half of its 1,250 pages, is a combined alphabetic index of organizations (distinguished by boldfaced capital letters) and individuals (upper and lower case). Individuals are indexed to position and organizational affiliation, but organizational entries are followed by the page number corresponding to an entry in the initial chapters. In response to reader suggestions, this latest edition features enhanced headings at the top of the page and an expanded business section.

Highly recommended as a primary ready-reference tool for the Washington, D.C., area, the directory's ease-of-use format brings together a diverse group of organizations and associations. Although not comprehensive in scope, it serves well as a first-stop information source in determining what directory may provide further information on any particular organization or individual.—**Virginia S. Fischer**

59. **Zip Code Finder.** Skokie, Ill., Rand McNally, 1997. 432p. maps. $7.95pa. ISBN 0-528-81516-4.

This is an up-to-date, portable, inexpensive, but hardly complete zip code finder for approximately 120,000 places in the United States. Most information is gleaned from other Rand McNally products, such as the *Commercial Atlas & Marketing Guide, 1997.* This reference tool is ideal for the small business owner, the person on the road, and the mail patron living a distance from the nearest post office or library. Unfortunately, because of its size, there are no specific street zip codes.

In addition to zip codes, the guide includes standard address abbreviations, useful toll-free reservation numbers, telephone area codes and time zone tables and maps, current national postal rates and regulations, private carrier rates, and U.S. Postal Service business centers. An indication of postal section, census-designated place, and use of italics for county designation are added to this newest edition. Many specific government agency zip codes are included.

The volume has a clean layout for the amount of information included. The typeface is clear, with bold typeface for headers in the introductory section. Liberal use of abbreviations helps clarity in the five-column page layout. The only fault in layout are the maps; these could use improvement. The overlay of zone lines over small typefaced city names makes text sometimes hard to read.—**Nadine Salmons**

GOVERNMENT PUBLICATIONS

60. Hardy, Gayle J., and Judith Schiek Robinson. **Subject Guide to U.S. Government Reference Sources.** 2d ed. Englewood, Colo., Libraries Unlimited, 1996. 358p. index. $45.00. ISBN 1-56308-189-X.

This updated edition to the 1985 bibliography *Subject Guide to U.S. Government Reference Sources* contains more than 800 new entries (see ARBA 86, entry 66). The scope of the work is selective rather than comprehensive, focusing on original works that should be available in depository library collections. Entries are arranged under four broad subject divisions—general reference sources, social sciences, science, and technology and humanities—with further subdivisions added as needed. Emphasis is placed on documents of at least 80 pages in length. Valuable new items were identified from federal government Internet and World Wide Web sites. Annotations were created upon direct examination of the actual item and are designed not to repeat information readily apparent in the bibliographic record. The title/subject index has been augmented to include entries for variant titles of an item, and there is even a subject index to bibliographies of Government Printing Office (GPO) publications.

The items chosen for this guide take fully into account the migration of government documents from print to electronic format. Therefore, the selection philosophy emphasizes access over format. In fact, entries span a wide range of formats, including reference books, CD-ROMs, and Internet and Websites.

Moreover, the editors are careful to indicate when a particular item is available in multiple formats. It should be noted, however, that government information accessible through the Web is in constant flux and needs monitoring almost on a daily basis. Librarians working in nondepository libraries will find this *Subject Guide* a useful starting point for selecting government resources in a variety of formats for their core collection.—**David G. Nowak**

61. **Information Sources in Official Publications.** Valerie J. Nurcombe, ed. New Providence, N.J., Bowker-Saur/Reed Reference Publishing, 1997. 564p. index. (Guides to Information Sources). $95.00. ISBN 1-85739-151-9.

This new work provides bibliographic essays on official publications of countries and the United Nations as well as coverage of other intergovernmental organizations. The chapters, which cover the regions of the world (with an additional chapter covering the United Nations), outline the organization of governments of individual countries in the region and mention publications of legislative, executive, judicial, and sometimes statistical bodies. Previously published guides, bibliographic control, and availability of publications are also discussed. Some chapters provide an overview of the region. When available, information about electronic sources is provided. Other features of this guide include a contents, list of abbreviations, and index.

In spite of the valuable information contributed by regional or country experts, this work has significant shortcomings. As the introduction explains, some countries were inadvertently omitted, others were included in the wrong region, and others receive only a brief mention. Finding where a country is covered in this guide can be a challenge. The contents lists the regional chapters and specifies only a few countries. The index provides access by country name but often provides numerous page listings. The index does provide other access points; however, they reflect the wide coverage received by different countries. Also, page headers are inconsistent; sometimes both region and country appear at the top of the page and sometimes only the region. There are numerous other problems, including inaccurate, incomplete, or inconsistent bibliographic information provided for sources; run-on sentences, especially in the introduction; and text missing from the bottom third of page 476 of the review copy.

This new work makes frequent reference to other sources for additional information, especially the 1990 edition of *Guide to Official Publications of Foreign Countries* (see ARBA 92, entry 49), which arranges information by country and uses standard subject categories to make finding specific information much easier. (The 1997 edition of *Guide to Official Publications of Foreign Countries* was not available for comparison at the time this review was being written.) It is a shame that Nurcombe's guide is so inconsistent, because the information it provides for official publications of some countries is much more extensive and current than anything previously published.—**Carol Wheeler**

62. **NTIS OrderNOW: Your Government Research Companion.** [CD-ROM]. Baltimore, Md., National Information Services Corporation, 1991, 1996. Minimum system requirements: IBM or compatible 386. CD-ROM drive. DOS 3.3. 2MB hard disk space. 250K conventional memory. 1MB extended memory. Color or monochrome monitor. $124.00/yr.

The National Technical Information Service (NTIS) distributes technical reports and other information produced under contract to agencies of the U.S. government, state and foreign governments, and such intergovernmental organizations as the World Bank. NTIS publications include worldwide scientific, technical, and business related information, and other materials in a wide variety of formats—paper, microfiche, CD-ROMs, audiovisual media, and tape and diskette products. Although NTIS is an agency of the Department of Commerce's Technology Administration, it is a self-sustaining agency relying on sales of its products rather than appropriations for day-to-day operating expenses. Through 1996, NTIS provided access to its publications in *Government Reports Announcements and Index* (GRAI), issued since 1946 under varying titles. In 1996, NTIS ceased publication of GRAI and began publishing its catalog on CD-ROM as *NTIS OrderNOW*, whose title emphasizes the sales mission of the agency.

NTIS OrderNOW includes bibliographic entries for materials distributed by NTIS from January 1995 to the present. Coverage reflects date of inclusion in the database rather than date of publication. The annual subscription price includes quarterly updates, which are supplemented by the NTIS OrderNOW Online Service at http://www.ntis.gov/ordernow. OrderNOW Online furnishes complete bibliographic entries for materials added to the database in the last 90 days. In both the CD-ROM and online service, each bibliographic entry gives an accession number, title, personal authors, performing organization, document type, language, source of item, publication date, price, abstract, keywords, subject categories, country of publication, and report number. Menus contain context-sensitive commands and help screens.

The *NTIS OrderNOW* CD-ROM supports novice, advanced, and expert searches. The novice search includes search for author, title, abstract, and keyword terms that may be used with Boolean connectors and truncation. The advanced mode features fielded searching of any of the elements of the bibliographic record. The expert mode comprises Boolean set combinations, fielded searching, and search save options. The novice and advanced searches supply a browse feature for the index terms that have been included in each field. Citations can be downloaded to disk, printed, transferred to an NTIS order form that can be printed and mailed, or e-mailed to NTIS.

NTIS publications are rich sources of information for many disciplines. The word "technical" does not adequately describe the contents or scope of NTIS publications, which may cover business and management studies, international marketing reports, materials and chemical science data, technology innovations, engineering studies, environmental studies, and other information. For many reports, NTIS is the sole supplier of bibliographic access and acquisition. Because of the rich and diverse content of the collections, online and CD-ROM versions of the historic NTIS bibliographic citations are also available from vendors such as DIALOG, SilverPlatter, and others. Dates of coverage for online and CD-ROM products vary by vendor. Libraries that subscribed to the print product should consider subscription to *NTIS OrderNOW* for continued coverage of technical literature. Libraries that have not subscribed to GRAI may want to consider the CD-ROM because of the enhanced search capabilities included in the product. The disc is recommended for all libraries with an interest in science, communications, technology, engineering, biotechnology, agriculture, engineering, business, and the environment.—**Peggy Jobe**

HANDBOOKS AND YEARBOOKS

63. **Verify Those Credentials: Do You Know Who You're Dealing With?** Michael Sankey and Carl R. Ernst, eds. Tempe, Ariz., Facts on Demand Press/BRB, 1997. 472p. maps. $19.95pa. ISBN 1-889150-00-2.

How would people know if a potential employee misrepresented his or her educational background or other credentials on a résumé? Does a child day care center meet state licensing/registration requirements? Is a certain beautician certified by his or her state's licensing board? The answers to these and many more questions regarding credentials of individuals and organizations can be found in this one-stop resource.

Verify Those Credentials begins with a brief explanation of the verification process, including specific hints and strategies. The next section consists of 51 state chapters (all 50 states plus the District of Columbia). Each chapter starts with a state overview, followed by an alphabetic listing of degree-granting educational institutions within the state. Information listed for each institution includes address, telephone and fax numbers, and business hours of the office where records are kept; enrollment; degrees granted; and an indication of how many years back the records are maintained. In the next part, addresses and telephone numbers of trade and vocational schools are listed. The final part of each state chapter gives state licensing and business registration information, listed under 12 broad subject categories, such as construction and manufacturing, education, health and beauty, and social services. Occupational titles and services are found under these 12 categories and are followed by a "key number" that leads to the agency listing to call to verify information on credentials in this area.

The book ends with appendixes of sample release forms, telephone area code changes for 1996-1997, and a final appendix that gives helpful information on privacy issues. This resource would be a welcome and easily affordable addition to any library's collection.—**Laura K. Blessing**

64. **The World Book Year Book, 1997: The Annual Supplement to** *The World Book Encyclopedia.* **A Review of the Events of 1996.** Chicago, World Book, 1997. 525p. illus. maps. index. $29.40. ISBN 0-7166-0497-3.

There has been a long-standing professional discussion among librarians about the value of adding encyclopedia yearbooks to collections. One side points out that it is wise to buy entire new sets of encyclopedias as new editions become available; the other side points to the value of frequent updates through yearbooks.

This discussion has been extended with the advent of online or World Wide Web-based encyclopedias now so readily available to libraries, even the smallest ones, at a relatively inexpensive cost and with frequent updates. Further, many patrons, especially children, prefer the online access to encyclopedias with the ease of searching and flashy graphics.

With this in mind, the 1997 yearbook of *The World Book Encyclopedia* has been published and distributed to customers. What are the advantages of a yearbook, and what are the advantages of this one in particular? Many patrons, especially students, wish to see a list of the past year's events in one place. The monthly breakdown here is excellent, with good descriptions and pictures of the singular events of each month. In addition, the events of the year are further described in more than 250 topical articles arranged alphabetically. Usually, the topical articles are a half-page to one page in length, with clear color pictures. Also, there are 10 "special reports" on specific topics, such as mad cow disease, Ella Fitzgerald, and whether the British monarchy will survive. These articles are 4 to 10 pages in length and are well written with pictures included. As a snapshot of the year 1996, this volume is an excellent portrayal. As with all World Book products, the authors of the articles are identified, and a short biography is included.

What, then, are the disadvantages of acquiring this yearbook? Numerous online services are now available that focus on the past year's events, rendering this type of published work somewhat superfluous as a recent summary of the year's events. Many libraries have storage concerns as well. Just how far back should a library keep yearbooks? Are the data presented incorporated in subsequent editions of the encyclopedia? When should a library start to acquire yearbooks, and what happens if there is a scattered run of them in one's collection? These questions are important; each library must answer them before spending funds to obtain this yearbook.

Last, the discussion on the pros and cons of yearbooks speaks to a larger issue about the archival nature of information. In 25 years when students wish to see what happened in a particular year in the past, will the data be available concisely and permanently? Could that famous assignment where students are asked to find information about the year and day of their birth be handled by libraries of the future? With the uncertainty of the answers to these questions, it is recommended that libraries with collections of any encyclopedia yearbooks continue to select them. World Book does an excellent job.

—**Paul A. Mogren**

INDEXES

65. **Book Review Digest: March 1996 to February 1997 Inclusive.** Martha T. Mooney and others, eds. Bronx, N.Y., H. W. Wilson, 1996, 1997. 2688p. priced on a service basis rate. ISSN 0006-7326.

As more standard references go online than many traditional librarians would like, it is comforting to see this 1996 annual cumulation of *Book Review Digest* as a solid, well-bound volume, presenting this useful and accurate information in the tradition begun in 1905. One hopes that in spite of the popularity of the electronic version, the paper copy will still remain available.

The prefatory and explanatory notes are brief and clear, conveying quickly to the reader how books are selected and the organization of the volume. The sample entry, on a single page, is a model of simple and competent layout. The 1996 cumulation includes reviews from March 1996 through February 1997. Books listed must have had two or more reviews in the extensive list of periodicals surveyed. Arrangement is by main entry, usually by author, with a subject and title index. Of the five entries thoroughly checked for this review, all of the bibliographic information is accurate and the summaries of reviews, including long ones, are all pertinent and fair.

The paper is thin, the typeface is small, and the volume is bulky, but this is an excellent example of the compiler's art. Most libraries of any size probably already subscribe.—**John Newman**

66. **PCI: Periodicals Contents Index.** [CD-ROM]. Alexandria, Va., Chadwyck-Healey, 1993-1997. Minimum system requirements: IBM or compatible 386/33MHz. CD-ROM drive, tower, or stack with controller card. Microsoft CD-ROM Extensions 2.1. MS-DOS 2.1. Windows 3.1. 8MB RAM. 4MB hard disk space. VGA color monitor. ISBN 0-89887-116-6. (Inquire with publisher for prices.)

Electronic indexes, though popular, usually cover only relatively recent years. PCI is an effort to extend the range of indexing retroactively. You can buy its whole range, or segments; it will eventually cover 3,500 periodicals in the humanities and social sciences from the date of their initial publication. Coverage is international and multilingual, and includes western European languages. Web, CD-ROM DOS, and CD-ROM Windows versions are available as well as a magnetic tape of USMARC data to use with your local software. The CD-ROM version under review used MS-DOS software but ran adequately under Windows 95 in DOS emulation mode. A user manual is included.

PCI is similar in concept to that used by the UnCover database/document delivery service. It contains the tables of contents of each journal issue and a bibliographic record for the journal. You can look up what was published in a particular issue of a particular journal, or you can search the words in the table of contents by a keyword search. This approach expedites coverage of a large number of journals, but does not provide the good access of an index using controlled vocabulary descriptors.

In general, the software is easy to use. There are two main search modes, the Main search screen and the Journal search screen. The Main screen has nine fields; one or several can be used for any particular search. You can use the Boolean *and*, *or*, or *not*, as well as adjacency or proximity searching and wild cards. A list of available terms can also be viewed. The fields are keyword, article title, author, heading, journal, journal keyword, language, subject, year, and segment (in case multiple segments were purchased). The "heading" categories appear to be page headings and are seldom useful; the 33 "subject" categories are extremely general, such as history (the Americas). Typing in a search and hitting Enter will bring up a screen showing the search terms and the number of hits found. Previous search strategies and results are also shown; at this point the results of several searches can be combined using Boolean logic. Particular citations can be added to the Selected Citations screen. If the Local Holdings module is chosen (included), the software will indicate if the library holds that article.

Periodicals Contents Index fills a major gap in retrospective electronic indexing of a large number of humanities and social science journals. It will not replace more specific indexes with retrospective coverage, however, because of its lack of controlled vocabulary descriptors and abstracts. In a day when library patrons increasingly expect full-text access, it will have to compete with more limited but full-text sources such as DUSTER. Nonetheless, it will be a useful addition to large academic libraries, especially those with substantial retrospective journal holdings in the humanities and social sciences.

—**Marit S. MacArthur**

67. **Personal Name Index to** *The New York Times Index*. **1975-1993 Supplement, Volume 5.** By Byron A. Falk Jr. and Valerie R. Falk. Sparks, Nev., Roxbury Data Interface, 1996. 567p. $86.75. ISBN 0-89902-139-5.

68. **Personal Name Index to** *The New York Times Index*. **1975-1993 Supplement, Volume 6.** By Byron A. Falk Jr. and Valerie R. Falk. Sparks, Nev., Roxbury Data Interface, 1996. 572p. $86.75. ISBN 0-89902-140-9.

Volumes 5 and 6 of the *Personal Names Index* are the last in a set that indexes the personal names found in the *New York Times Index* (NYTI) from 1975 to 1993. These indexes are a listing of personal names that have variant spellings or are misspelled in the NYTI. This "index to an index" seeks to provide users with a cohesive and cross-referenced alphabetic list of names. The authors state in the introduction that they do not seek to distinguish persons who have identical names and that all citations for a person may not be listed together. Therefore, there may be an inclusion within a name entry of variant spellings, misspellings of a name, or several name entries that reflect those variations. Within each entry the date of the NYTI and page the name is listed on is included and arranged in a chronological manner. Under the name Christopher Reeve there are several notations as well as a listing for Christopher Reeves where there is one notation. This date and page notation is also reflected under Reeve. Nancy Reagan is listed with a cross-reference to Mrs. Ronald Reagan, so there is a listing for that name variation, but there is also a listing for Mrs. Ronald Wilson Reagan.

These indexes are comprehensive and straightforward and provide an excellent way to quickly identify names and their variant spellings and place those names within a date context. The indexes provide a useful resource in searching for biographical information in the NYTI. These volumes are highly recommended for academic and research libraries. [R: C&RL, Mar 97, pp. 184-85]—**Jan S. Squire**

69. **Readers' Guide Abstracts Full Text Mega Edition.** [CD-ROM]. Norwood, Mass., SilverPlatter, 1997. 2 discs. Minimum system requirements: IBM or compatible 386SX. ISO 9660-compatible CD-ROM drive and controller with MS-DOS CD-ROM Extensions 2.1. MS-DOS or PC-DOS 3.1. Windows 3.1. 4MB RAM. 8MB hard disk space. VGA monochrome monitor (color monitor recommended). Windows-compatible mouse. Windows-compatible printer. $2,795.00/single user.

Readers' Guide Abstracts Full Text Mega Edition is produced by H. W. Wilson, and the WinSPIRS Version 2.0 search and retrieve software that allows searching of the bibliographic and full-text databases together is produced by SilverPlatter. This CD-ROM database indexes more than 240 of the most popular general interest periodicals published in the United States and Canada. More than 120 of these journals are in full text. This product covers news; current events; and all subject areas, including business, fashion, politics, crafts, food, education, sports, history, and science. Extra features include graphic support; translated versions in Spanish, French, and German are available from SilverPlatter. Presently, full text is only available in the subset of 1994 to the present.

The speed of searching on a disc with 640,000-plus bibliographies is impressive. The simultaneous display of the search results on the same window is also sleek. The display functions are transparent: Users can turn on the brief record or the full record display at the click of a button. The Limit button refers to publication year, physical description, language, document type, full-text indicator, and text size using such operators as equal, less than, greater than, greater than or equal to, and less than or equal to. Other limits, such as "Freud in au" or "Freud in ti," are not transparent, and the Boolean operators, such as *and*, *in*, *near*, *not*, *with*, and *or*; the truncation symbol "*"; or the combination of sets are left for the experienced searchers to enjoy. End users may need an instructional session before they can benefit fully from what this database can offer. The Download and Print buttons are prominently displayed. The index button leads to an alphabetic listing of terms with number of records and occurrences. The Contents and Thesaurus buttons are available for full-text display only. Within the citations, there are searched terms linking to other references. Citations can be marked Search, Print, or Sort using a variety of fields.

In sum, this version of the *Readers' Guide* is an improvement over other SilverPlatter CD-ROM products this reviewer has used. The speed of retrieval is excellent, and the visual display is pleasing. As is usual with many CD-ROM products, there is a need to have a simplified reference card to lead users to the obscure functions of the software. Until the 1983-1993 subset includes full text, it is confusing for this set of data to be named *Full Text Mega Edition*. The World Wide Web version of this product is similar but contains e-mail capability, which is quite useful for online users.—**Polin P. Lei**

70. **Readers' Guide to Periodical Literature 1995: An Author and Subject Index.** Jean M. Marra and others, eds. Bronx, N.Y., H. W. Wilson, 1995, 1996. 2652p. $220.00. ISSN 0034-0464.

An old favorite, this author/subject index to about 240 general interest, English-language periodicals has not changed much in format since its last ARBA review (see ARBA 92, entry 60) but has increased the number of journals covered by about 28 percent. It remains an index; the abstracts to selections of *Readers' Guide* appear in a related Wilson product, *Readers' Guide Abstracts*, available online and in CD-ROM format. Like many indexes, the introduction fails to report some relevant information, such as average time lag between an indexed article's publication and indexing, number of subject terms assigned per entry, indication of whether all or only major articles are covered, and a list of subject headings. This information would facilitate use and perhaps raise the user's confidence level in editorial decisions. However, the publisher still lists all journals indexed and solicits librarians' opinions about journal coverage. This is apparent with the use of *see* and *see also* references connecting related subjects and entry terms, the combined author/subject index that collocates articles both by and about specific authors, and the separate listing of book reviews. For libraries that do not provide online or CD-ROM access to *Readers' Guide Abstracts* or comparable databases such as *Magazine Index*, the hardcopy of *Readers' Guide to Periodical Literature* is still a very useful index to the general periodicals held by most libraries.—**Marilyn Domas White**

71. **Yearbook of International Organizations 1997/98.** 34th ed. Union of International Associations, ed. New Providence, N.J., K. G. Saur, 1997. 4v. index. $1,170.00/set. ISBN 3-598-23357-4. ISSN 0084-3814.

The *Yearbook of International Organizations* has been reviewed in ARBA on several occasions (see ARBA 93, entry 75; ARBA 88, entry 71; and ARBA 87, entry 70). In comparison to the 1991/92 3-volume edition, the present 34th edition consists of 4 volumes: Organization Description, Country Directory of Secretariats and Membership, Subject Directory and Index, and International Organization Bibliography and Resources. This indispensable reference tool for college, research, and large public libraries is supplemented by quarterly publications of *The International Congress Calendar* and *CD-ROM Yearbook*, an enriched, multilingual version of all volumes of the *Yearbook of International Organization* and *Who's Who in International Organizations* (see ARBA 93, entry 784).—**Bohdan S. Wynar**

MUSEUMS

72. **Museum Premieres, Exhibitions, & Special Events: The Nationwide Guidebook of Museum Exhibitions and Special Events for Travelers and Research Professionals.** Paul D. Groenier and Sally E. Miller, eds. St. Louis, Mo., Museum Information Services, 1997. 818p. illus. index. $29.95pa. ISBN 1-888187-97-4.

This annual publication professes to be "the only nationwide museum guidebook specializing in exhibitions and special events." More than 10,000 museum exhibitions and events are included in this easy-to-use directory. In the current edition, an introductory section covers museum premieres for 1997; explanatory text and selected illustrations from museums across the country describe unique major exhibitions. Examples include "Walkabout! An Exciting Australian Adventure" at the Florida Museum of Natural History and "Faberge in America," a traveling exhibit organized by the Fine Arts Museum of San Francisco.

Next comes "Scheduled Museum Exhibitions and Events Listed by State." Within the state entries, cities are arranged alphabetically, and their respective museums are detailed. Inclusive dates and subject matter are listed for all exhibits to be held in a given museum during the current year. Permanent exhibitions are described: open hours, prices, addresses, and telephone numbers—in short, all the necessary information for each museum. In checking the state of Oregon, this reviewer found the entries for each city's museum to be as hoped and to have little extras, such as a mention of one of the Portland zoo's favorite elephant's birthday celebration event.

The final keyword section is labeled "Reference Indexes of Museums, Major Exhibitions and Keywords." Here is the breakdown: museums alphabetically by name, museums with free admission (very useful!), major exhibitions for 1997, keywords—general museum information, keywords—temporary exhibitions, keywords—traveling exhibitions, keywords—special events programs, and keywords—travel tours. Because it is easy to get lost in all these keyword indexes, there is a handy black box device every few pages that lists the various indexes and the appropriate pages. This reference tool will fit right into a mid-sized public library's reference collection, and most college and university libraries will find it a valuable annual purchase as well. [R: Choice, Jan 97, p. 772]—**Marcia Blevins**

73. **Museums of the World.** 6th ed. New Providence, N.J., R. R. Bowker/Reed Reference Publishing, 1997. 673p. index. $425.00. ISBN 3-598-20605-4.

There are a number of specialized directories of museums, such as *University and College Museums, Galleries, and Related Facilities: A Descriptive Directory* (see ARBA 97, entry 62), that list over 1,100 museums and galleries in the United States. The 4th edition of this universal directory was reviewed in ARBA 94 (see entry 60), and previously in ARBA 92 (see entry 64). This is a standard work, familiar to many art librarians as the most current and comprehensive source of foreign art museum addresses and contact information. The scope of this resource tool has been enlarged, and the number of museums listed was increased from 24,624 in the 5th edition to 27,380 in the latest volume. This is an expensive and essential directory that reflects Bowker's usual high standards of accuracy and comprehensiveness.

—**Bohdan S. Wynar**

74. **150 Years of America's Smithsonian: Discovering, Imagining, Remembering.** [CD-ROM]. New York, Macmillan Digital, 1996. Minimum system requirements (Windows version): IBM or compatible 486/33MHz. Double-speed CD-ROM drive. Windows 3.1. 8MB RAM. VGA 256-color monitor with 640 x 480 resolution. Minimum system requirements (Macintosh version): LCIII/Performa 475. Double-speed CD-ROM drive. System 7.01. 8MB RAM. 256-color monitor. $39.95. ISBN 1-57595-012-X.

After 150 years the Smithsonian has collected more than 140 million objects. During 1997 a traveling exhibit was created to visit sites across the country. This CD-ROM is designed to allow a user to experience the show. The program installed on my PC with Windows 95 without any problem. The menu offers choices of a guided tour, a timeline, or a find. Broken into three categories—discovering, imagining, and remembering—a user can choose how to experience the exhibit. Each piece includes a photograph and information describing it. Video and audio clips are included with some of the entries. Although this is an interesting document regarding the exhibit, as a reference tool it will have limited value. There is no clear information about why certain objects are included in the exhibit or their relation to each other except as samples of each category. Although billed as a multimedia product, it uses little of the interactive potential of CD-ROM; there are no hypertext links connecting like objects. Navigating through the exhibit is easy, but attempting to retrace steps is not. The Find feature will allow a method of choosing only video clips, but there could be an easier method of doing this. Each entry is clearly illustrated with assistance to zoom or further information, but the best method of viewing the exhibit is sequentially. This product is a nice review of the exhibit, but of little reference value. [R: LJ, Aug 97, p. 147]—**Joshua Cohen**

PERIODICALS AND SERIALS

75. **CPI.Q: Canadian Periodical Index.** [CD-ROM]. Toronto, Gale Canada, 1997. Minimum system requirements: IBM or compatible. ISO 9660-compatible CD-ROM drive with interface card and connecting cable. DOS 3.1. Windows 3.0. 8MB RAM. 12MB hard disk space. Windows-supported monitor. Windows-supported mouse. Windows-supported printer. $1,999.00. ISBN 1-896513-37-4.

More than 400 general interest and academic periodicals, mostly Canadian, are indexed in *CPI.Q*. Coverage is from 1988 to the present, with full-text articles (rekeyed and lacking graphics) from 150 of these periodicals since January 1995 provided. Currently, the database contains more than 30,000 full-text articles, including ones from the Canadian newspaper *The Globe and Mail*.

Databases that feature full-text articles are always welcome, and this product is well done and easy to use. Although the subscription includes a quick reference guide, it may not be necessary to use it. The icons on the tool bar make sense, as do the search field icons. The system allows both simple queries and sophisticated searches. Using Boolean operators if desired, it is possible to search all available fields by keyword or specifically by article title, author, date, periodical, or subject. The researcher can also specify only full-text articles or only those in a particular language. A click of the mouse allows someone to toggle between a French- and an English-language interface.

Gale Canada has augmented the list of citations and articles with information from its own reference databases. A query on acid rain, for example, included a scientific essay on that subject, whereas one on Jean Chrétien offered a short biography on the Canadian prime minister. This enhancement is useful, particularly for students and others needing encyclopedic information in order to put the articles in perspective. Another nice feature is the serials holdings module that allows libraries to indicate on the results screen which periodicals they own. Monthly updates of the disc are available, and the cost is reasonable. Because it serves both general and academic needs, this product would be useful in public, school, and academic libraries in Canada and in libraries elsewhere that offer Canadian studies.

—**Hope Yelich**

76. **Hudson's Subscription Newsletter Directory.** 13th ed. Joan W. Artz, ed. Rhinebeck, N.Y., Hudson's, 1996. 499p. index. $159.00pa. ISBN 0-9617642-6-0. ISSN 1046-8110.

A selective worldwide listing of newsletters, this directory has some 4,800 entries. Excluded are newsletters that are not published regularly; have controlled circulation; depend on advertising or newsstand distribution; or are publications of reporting services, associations, leagues, clubs, or foundations.

An entry may include the publishing company name; the street address; telephone and fax numbers; the editor's name; an e-mail address; the price; the frequency; the year founded; key numbers to pertinent footnotes (e.g., what PR the newsletter is interested in receiving); and a brief description of contents. Verification letters were sent to the publisher of each newsletter to ensure accuracy and up-to-date information. Missing information was either not given or not verified.

Entries are arranged by subject category and alphabetically within the subject. Titles are printed in large, bold typeface, and all data (except for the newsletter descriptions) are in a fairly large typeface, making the information easy to read. Various indexes allow access to the entries by publisher and geographic location as well as list publications and editorial and publishing personnel alphabetically. A curious (and short) list of suppliers to the industry (many have advertised in the directory) is also included. Potential purchasers of the directory need to be aware that the copyright date is 1996; thus, the information was as correct as the editor could attain at that time.—**Jo Anne H. Ricca**

77. **Readers' Guide for Young People.** [CD-ROM]. Bronx, N.Y., H. W. Wilson, 1997. Minimum system requirements (DOS version): IBM or compatible. CD-ROM drive. DOS 3.1. 640K RAM. 3MB hard disk space. Hayes or compatible modem (optional). Minimum system requirements (Macintosh version): 68020, 68040, or PowerPC. System 7.0. 2MB RAM. 10MB hard disk space. $395.00/3 times per year; $695.00/6 times per year; $1,295.00/monthly. ISSN 1091-7586.

Readers' Guide for Young People contains a great deal of useful, current information. Although designed for students in upper elementary through middle school, the disc is difficult to use. The content, readability, and format seem to be geared to an older audience than intended. Reading the screen is challenging because of a small font and unappealing color combinations. Both subject and keyword searching are available for 21 magazines, with indexing and abstracts for 64 titles. A subject search for "snowboarding" yielded 14 hits, about half in full text. In a keyword search, there were 38 hits for the Persian Gulf War, with a similar number in full text.

In comparison, *EBSCO's PrimarySearch* (EBSCO Publishing) has an easier layout for young readers, clear directions at the bottom of each screen, and a greater scope with 33 full-text magazines and indexing and abstracts for 115 titles. *PrimaryTOM on CD-ROM* (Information Access Company) has also been on the market for a significant length of time and includes 30 full-text magazines. Although the cost combined with the coverage, difficulty in use, and unattractive screens make the Wilson product a questionable purchase at this time, newer versions may correct some of these flaws.—**Lynda Welborn**

QUOTATION BOOKS

78. **Contemporary Quotations in Black.** Anita King, comp. and ed. Westport, Conn., Greenwood Press, 1997. 298p. illus. index. $39.95. ISBN 0-313-29122-5.

A companion volume to King's earlier *Quotations in Black* (see ARBA 82, entry 444) that recalled the voices of slavery and its descendants, this work records the voices of 236 contemporary African Americans and black Africans speaking out about their lives, their work, their frustrations, their inspirations, and their hopes and progress in their continuing quest for the end of racism, for equality, and for human dignity. The more than 1,000 quotations taken from books, speeches, magazines, and newspaper articles published from the late 1980s to 1996 were selected for their clarity of thought and their emphasis on faith and the uplifting of African Americans and humanity in general. Those quoted include journalists, musicians, athletes, political figures, physicians, scientists, playwrights and novelists, artists, social activists, dancers, and actors and directors, with nearly half the quotations coming from women.

Arranged alphabetically by speaker, from Hank Aaron to Bruce McMarion Wright, judge, author, and poet, the entries can also be accessed through a thorough subject and keyword index. Enhancing the collection are 40 full-page portraits of some of the quotees. Each entry briefly identifies the person, and each saying is followed by its source. Most of these quotations have not been anthologized before, so this will be a valuable addition to the quotation collections of all libraries. *Contemporary Quotations in Black* is highly recommended for all users regardless of race or color, for everyone shares the common humanity reflected in these voices. [R: RBB, 15 Oct 97, pp. 426-27]—**Blaine H. Hall**

79. **Criminal Quotes: The 1,001 Most Bizarre Things Ever Said by History's Outlaws, Gangsters, Despots, and Other Evil-Doers.** Andrew Chesler and H. Amanda Robb, eds. Detroit, Visible Ink Press/Gale, 1997. 175p. index. $12.95pa. ISBN 0-7876-0937-4.

The subtitle is truly descriptive of this source. The "bad guys" range from Nero, Idi Amin, Adolf Hitler, and other Nazis; to Charles "Lucky" Luciano, Al Capone, and other gangsters; to Mark David Chapman (killed John Lennon), Timothy McVeigh, and the Unabomber. "Bad girls" are not forgotten. They include Mary Elizabeth Wilson (poisoned three husbands), Eva Braun, Queen Christina, Amy Fisher, and Lynette "Squeaky" Fromme. The quotations are arranged alphabetically by subject, such as admiration, boredom, confessions, final words, lies, and wishes, and then alphabetically by person cited.

The table of contents cross-references related topics (e.g., spouses and marriage). A selective bibliography is provided. The index includes one- to two-sentence descriptions of each person's criminal activity. Instead of the usual straightforward, uninteresting layout, the quotations on each page are indented at different spacings. At least one quotation per two-page spread is in a larger typeface.

Librarians should put this book in the reference section if quotation books are constantly researched. The volume is so much fun to browse, it would be a shame not to offer it to patrons as a circulating book.—**Esther R. Sinofsky**

80. **Famous Lines: A Columbia Dictionary of Familiar Quotations.** By Robert Andrews. New York, Columbia University Press, 1997. 625p. index. $29.95. ISBN 0-231-10218-6.

Tracking down quotations from partially recalled line fragments has always been a challenge for reference librarians; the fresh approach taken in *Famous Lines* makes that job easier and much more fun. *Famous Lines* updates the traditional quotation books by including such current subject headings as abuse, AIDS, the Gulf War, robots, and sexual harassment in addition to the old standards life, love, and death. Not only are the subject headings current, but the sources are today's personalities as well as classical writers and philosophers. Here one finds Monty Python, Woody Allen, and Maya Angelou sharing pages with William Shakespeare, Charles Dickens, and Thomas Jefferson.

Andrews, editor of *The Columbia Dictionary of Quotations* (see ARBA 95, entry 88), has selected more than 6,000 quotations to include in *Famous Lines*. The book is arranged alphabetically by subject, from abandonment to zoos. The subjects are helpfully printed in large bold typeface, which is a definite asset for finding the subject with a flip-through-the-book approach. For the more methodical, there are two useful indexes in the back of the book—an index to sources and an index to keywords. In both of these indexes, the pages are arranged for easy viewing; that is, the typeface is clear, and the entries are given good, open spacing. Some of the sources, such as Shakespeare, have many entries following the main heading, but the format makes it easy to find a specific subject and page. Valuable commentary accompanies many of the entries, offering background for the quotation or the name of the source movie, book, or poem. For instance, the explanation for a quotation "Beep! Beep!" under the general subject of communication informs the user that this was the only dialogue between the Road Runner and Wile E. Coyote. Additional information about the cartoon is included. The explanations are a significant feature of the book because they give the quotation more validity, prevent misuse of the quotation, and, in some cases, encourage further research.

Although not intended to be used as a sole or primary source quotation book, *Famous Lines* will add depth and currency to any library's reference collection. It is valuable for catching phrases from pop culture and issue-oriented works.—**Marcia Blevins**

81. Fitton, Robert A., comp. **Leadership: Quotations from the World's Greatest Motivators.** Boulder, Colo., Westview Press, 1997. 338p. index. $19.00pa. ISBN 0-8133-3288-5.

Leadership is yet another book of quotations, this one consisting of statements by "the world's greatest motivators" on the topic of leadership. The compiler holds military degrees and positions and has let his background influence his choice of authors and respective quotations. On a page chosen at random (page 130), dealing with the subject of human nature, there are three quotations by Brigadier General S. L. A. Marshall, one by Somerset Maugham, one by Field Marshal Bernard Montgomery, and one from *The New York Times* of 1919 on the subject of seclusion at the Military Academy. This page is typical of the ratio of military to civilian quotations. Occasionally appearing are sayings from the Bible,

Ralph Waldo Emerson, or even Confucius. The subjects covered include experience, courage, obedience, luck, fate, morale, humor, and rank and file. The sources are referenced poorly, sometimes with only the author's name, other times with at least the name of the book but without page or chapter numbers.

This book should be titled *The Military on Leadership*. Those who would benefit from this focus will probably find something of worth in this noncomprehensive survey. The rest of quotation seekers should stick with *Bartlett's Familiar Quotations* (Time-Life Books, 1995).—**Kenneth I. Saichek**

82. Gaither, Carl C., and Alma E. Cavazos-Gaither. **Statistically Speaking: A Dictionary of Quotations.** Philadelphia, Institute of Physics Publishing, 1996. 420p. illus. index. $39.00pa. ISBN 0-7503-0401-4.

This may well be, as the authors claim in their preface, the first book of quotations related exclusively to probability and statistics. Designed as a resource for "the individual who loves to quote—and to quote correctly," this accessible volume contains nearly 300 pages of verified quotations, carefully grouped under 60 statistical motifs ranging from actuary, bayesian, and correlation, to chance, gambling, and randomness. The entries are both amusing and enlightening. The authors range from ancient to contemporary, renowned to unknown. The text is interspersed with black-and-white cartoons to illustrate the use, or misuse, of statistics in quotations. Two indexes allow users to find quotations on a specific subject, locate citations by others on the same subject, and identify what an individual has said on a variety of statistical points. A 20-page bibliography and 9 pages of copyright permissions lend credence to the assertion that every method was employed to provide the fullest possible attribution for each quotation.

Of particular interest to those engaged in statistical research, this compilation is recommended for most libraries and any individual who recognizes that "a knowledge of statistics is like a knowledge of foreign languages or of algebra; it may prove of use at any time under any circumstances" (Arthur L. Bowley, p. 237). [R: Choice, June 97, p. 1639]—**Debra S. Van Tassel**

83. **The Oxford Dictionary of Quotations.** 4th ed. Angela Partington, ed. New York, Oxford University Press, 1996. 1075p. index. $39.95. ISBN 0-19-860058-5.

During the 4 years following the publication of the 4th edition (see ARBA 93, entry 92), the editors at the Oxford dictionary factory have compiled, computerized, and consulted to produce this fine, current reference tool. The revision of the 4th edition includes a brief section on "Sayings of the 90s," which is interesting and may be the basis of yet another publication, as are the added sections of "Popular Misquotations" and "Slogans," not extensive but also promising for the future. The work is totally user friendly with an alphabetic author format, including pseudonyms (e.g., Saki) and most familiar forms (e.g., George Eliot). The instructions on how to use the dictionary are clear and concise. The index is easy to use: Quotations are indexed by a number of keywords that make searching uncomplicated and the references simple to decipher.

In comparison with many of the current reference books of quotations, this would appear to be the most complete and certainly the most reader-accessible. From the Bible to George Bush, William Shakespeare to Susan Sontag, this volume reflects the statements of politicians and poets, critics and clergy, along with all those other phrases worth treasuring. Well produced, with a clean typeface and a spine that allows the book to stay open easily, this is an excellent choice for any library, and at this price, it is certainly a great bargain. [R: SLJ, May 97, pp. 160-62]—**Paula Frosch**

84. **Simpson's Contemporary Quotations: The Most Notable Quotes from 1950 to the Present.** rev. ed. James B. Simpson, ed. New York, HarperCollins, 1997. 657p. index. $35.00. ISBN 0-06-270137-1.

"There are things that get whispered about that writers are there to overhear," says Ann Beattie, anthologist. Simpson may not have eavesdropped to gather his quotations, but he achieves similar results. Quoting entertainers, journalists, poets, novelists, essayists, reporters, politicians, sports figures, humorists, and artists, among many others—people prominent and obscure—Simpson documents the era with more than 11,300 quotations taken from 4,000-plus written and oral sources of the past half-century. However, this edition emphasizes the years 1988-1995, making earlier editions (see ARBA 89, entry 76) valuable for fuller coverage of the period.

The work is organized into three broad categories: the world, humankind, and communication and the arts. These categories are divided into 25 subject categories, including government, business, education, religion, fashion, literature, food and drink, music and dance, science, radio and television, family life, and sports. The subject categories are further subdivided into 55 sections, under which the sayings are arranged alphabetically by the person quoted. To ease finding the correct quotation, the book also provides source, subject, and key line indexes. Each statement is documented, provided with a context when needed, and dated.

If what the critic Elizabeth Janeway says about anthologies ("as long as mixed grills and combination salads are popular, anthologies will undoubtedly continue in favor") is true, then this revised and expanded collection of bon mots, witticisms, epigrams, profundities, and other well-turned phrases and expressions will surely find favor with anyone looking for a useful, entertaining read. The volume is recommended for libraries needing an excellent, extensive compendium of contemporary quotations.—**Blaine H. Hall**

85. Thomsett, Michael C., and Jean Freestone Thomsett. **War and Conflict Quotations: A Worldwide Dictionary of Pronouncements from Military Leaders, Politicians, Philosophers, Writers, and Others.** Jefferson, N.C., McFarland, 1997. 296p. index. $45.00. ISBN 0-7864-0314-4.

The Thomsetts, authors of two similar works devoted to political quotations (1994) and sex and love quotations (see ARBA 96, entry 889), point out in their introduction that "it may be said that history is primarily a chronicle of the conflicts of the human race, and politicians and philosophers have had much to say on these topics." This work is a topical guide to a vast range of those comments.

The book's 2,700 quotations are arranged by 87 subjects; these range from action, aggression, alliances, and appeasement to victory, Vietnam, war and peace, and weapons. The authors have forsworn the usual organizational approaches of quotation books (i.e., alphabetic by individual's name or chronological). Instead, within subject categories, the quotations are arranged so that complementary or similar statements are together, with contradictory statements in close proximity. Each quotation is followed by its author, the work in which it appeared, and the date. Two indexes—one by person cited and the other by keyword-in-context—provide alternative access to the quotations.

War and Conflict Quotations is similar to other such works in that within its covers one finds both desolation and inspiration. Thucydides tells readers that "Peace is an armistice in a war that is continuously going on," whereas Anwar as-Sadat teaches that "Peace is much more precious than a piece of land." Ralph Waldo Emerson notes that "Life is a search after power," while a pensive Steven Vincent Benét muses that "We thought, because we had power, we had wisdom." However, perhaps the most interesting statement comes from billionaire Warren Buffet: "If past history was all there was to the game, the richest people would be librarians."—**G. Kim Dority**

Part II
SOCIAL SCIENCES

2 Social Sciences in General

SOCIAL SCIENCES IN GENERAL

86. **Encyclopedia PLUS of World Problems and Human Potential.** 4th ed. [CD-ROM]. Edited by the Union of International Associations. New Providence, N.J., K. G. Saur/Reed Reference Publishing, 1996. Minimum system requirements (Windows version): IBM or compatible 486. DIN/ISO 9660 CD-ROM drive. MS-DOS 3.3. Windows 3.1. 4MB RAM. 7MB hard disk space. EGA or VGA monitor. Minimum system requirements (Macintosh version): 68020 processor. DIN/ISO 9660 CD-ROM drive. System 7. 6MB RAM. 7MB hard disk space. $595.00/yr. ISBN 3-598-40294-5.

The *Encyclopedia PLUS of World Problems and Human Potential* provides four article databases, a list of international organizations, and a bibliography. The text databases include World Problems, Human Development, Strategies—Actions—Solutions, and Human Values. In addition, the CD-ROM provides a demonstration program and a list of international meetings on the subject of world problems. Each of the searchable databases is an alphabetic list of terms, with articles on the subject and subject links to other terms.

Each text database must be searched separately. They are searchable by a sequential exploration of the records by scrolling up and down, by an inspection of records selected by a search, by following the hypertext links provided at the end of each article, by a special "backtrack" icon that returns the user to the starting point, by switching between databases when one or more is open, and by "jump links" that can be customized before the search begins. While a search is underway, it is possible to tag records for later display or printing. In addition, a special program called a shadow file is provided, which allows the user to personalize a database by overlaying to a UIA CD-ROM database. All searching can be done through the use of this shadow file, which will also allow the user to place notes in the text, create bookmarks, highlight material, modify the layout, and edit the text. By saving the shadow file, all of the changes may be stored for later use or additional searching. Searching may also be done using Boolean terms, wildcards, word combinations, and shortcut keys.

The disc is configured for both Windows and Macintosh operating systems, and it is easy to install and use. An installer program is included that places all of the programs in the proper place. The program does take almost 7MB of hard disk space, which may be a problem if a number of other CD-ROMs are mounted on the same computer.

The text provided in the information databases tends to be brief and simply written. Often it is presented in outline form. Users can follow the subject links to find additional information in an almost endless loop. Each entry provides a brief bibliography, but it is not made clear if this is where the information in the article has been obtained or if the bibliography is a list of additional reading. There is no specific documentation of the information in the articles. Although there is much information contained in these databases, one has the feeling that most of it is rather elementary and lacks depth. Because of this fact, the disc is more suitable for undergraduate research or for use by high school students preparing term papers. Also, the databases make for interesting browsing through the use of the hyperlinks, allowing the discovery of related information one may not have ordinarily considered.—**Robert L. Wick**

87. Gallup, George, Jr. **The Gallup Poll: Public Opinion 1995.** Wilmington, Del., Scholarly Resources, 1996. 301p. index. $65.00. ISBN 0-8420-2595-2. ISSN 0195-962X.

The format of this annual publication remains unchanged since the 1993 edition (see ARBA 95, entry 92). Sampling methods, poll accuracy, and regions are the same. What has changed, of course, are the topics surveyed during 1995. These include, but are not limited to the Whitewater affair, the bombing in Oklahoma

City, the trial of O. J. Simpson, the Pope's visit to the United States, the Million Man March on Washington, and the shutdown of the federal government because of failure to agree on a budget. As in past editions, question results are classified by various factors, such as age, gender, and race. In addition, surveys of the honesty and ethical standards of people in various professions as well as the most admired man and most admired woman appear as they have in previous years. Many of these findings are followed by longer explanatory notes. Reference librarians will find the chronology of events that appears in the front of each volume useful for school projects. An exhaustive index makes this fascinating glimpse of our world in 1995 easy to use.—**January Adams**

88. Malone, John. **Predicting the Future: From Jules Verne to Bill Gates.** New York, M. Evans, 1997. 194p. index. $19.95. ISBN 0-87131-830-X.

Humans have been trying to predict the future for ages, whether motivated by reasons of religion, science, imagination, entertainment, or commerce. Furthermore, some of the predictions to date have been spectacularly correct (e.g., the atomic bomb) and incorrect (e.g., space travel). These facts, along with our endless fascination with such predictions, are the motivation behind this book. It is a collection of more than 100 predictions, many scientific in nature, arranged chronologically by year from 1858 through 1996. For each prediction there is a date in which it was made, the name of the predictor, and a one- to two-page summary of the reasons for the prediction and its success or failure. Many notable fiction writers are included (e.g., H. G. Wells and Jules Verne), as are diplomats and politicians (e.g., Benjamin Disraeli and Grover Cleveland), corporate moguls (e.g., Henry Ford), and scientists and inventors (e.g., Thomas Edison and Albert Einstein). The predictions themselves relate primarily to the areas of science, medicine, and technology, although there are a few that deal with politics and social life. Indexes to predictions and predictors are included as well as a bibliography of consulted and relevant works.

Given the nature of the topic and the level of the writing, the book's target audience appears to be secondary school students. But there is little scientific or educational purpose to these stories. They are isolated vignettes, with no discussion of underlying processes involved in creative writing, scientific research, or invention. Most certainly the book does not address "where we've been, how we got to where we are, and where we may go yet," as the dust jacket suggests. Students fascinated with science may find this an additional boost to their interests, particularly if they consult some of the works cited in the bibliography. Other than that, the book is what it appears to be at first glance, a quirky and readable overview of scientific facts. School and public libraries may find it of interest.—**Stephen H. Aby**

89. **PAIS Select. Volume 1, Number 2, February, 1997.** [CD-ROM]. New York, Public Affairs Information Service, 1997. Minimum system requirements: IBM or compatible 486. Double-speed CD-ROM drive. DOS 4.x. Windows 3.1x. 8MB RAM. 4MB hard disk space. VGA color monitor. Printer (Laser or InkJet for printing images). $950.00/yr.

The name *PAIS* is generally enough to get the attention of scholars and librarians. PAIS, or the Public Affairs Information Service, has long been associated with the excellent indexing it provides to materials in the political sciences and related areas. Indeed, PAIS has had a lock on that discipline for many years.

PAIS Select (PS) is, thankfully, no exception. For libraries wanting full-text access to almost 2,500 articles, without the angst of World Wide Web access and browsers, PS offers the perfect modus vivendi. Updated twice a year, PS provides full-text access to select pamphlets and articles in the PAIS International database. More than 300 magazines are covered, including such titles as *Background Notes*, *Black Scholar*, *Dissent*, *Foreign Policy*, *Judicature*, *Russia Review*, *World and I*, and literally hundreds more.

The search engine is nothing to sneeze at, either. Featuring the usual author, title, and subject access points, PS also provides keyword, truncation (*,?), and browse lists. Boolean operators (AND, OR, NOT) and proximity operators (ADJ, NEAR) are also available. Full text here means tables and graphs, and the print commands provide crisp, clear results, at least on a laser printer.

The bright yellow command buttons and the green and blue toolbar look of the search screen are a pleasing eye-grabber. Once the search is executed, the yellow command buttons can take the user from full text to bibliographic source and back again. DOS is also available. Terms used are highlighted in the document in red. Articles appear in descending chronological order. Navigation is as easy as reading the monitor. Even with a high speed machine with more than adequate memory, however, searches with a large number of hits (in this case 50 or more) took about 60 seconds to load. One wonders if students will be patient for repeatedly long searches. PS is the perfect solution for the library wanting to offer sophisticated access to scholarly materials, but on a restricted financial diet. [R: RBB, 15 Feb 97, p. 1039]—**Mark Y. Herring**

90. Parker, Philip M. **National Cultures of the World: A Statistical Reference.** Westport, Conn., Greenwood Press, 1997. 249p. index. (Cross-Cultural Statistical Encyclopedia of the World, v.4). $79.50. ISBN 0-313-29770-3.

This statistical compendium provides data across all countries and territories for social, economic, cultural, and resource factors from approximately 1994. The other volumes in this series available thus far are *Religious Cultures of the World*, *Linguistic Cultures of the World*, and *Ethnic Cultures of the World* (see entries 331, 990, and 1368). The author of the volume under review teaches multivariate statistics, research methodology, and international marketing at the European Institute of Business Administration (INSEAD).

Chapter 1 provides background and methodological information. Chapter 2 contains a theoretical essay on the influences of resource and climatic factors on variation between societies drawing on the work of Adam Smith and Baron de Montesquieu. Chapters 3 through 9 have statistical tables. They are organized with an initial summary table of average values, followed by a table of the same variables arranged by country. An impressive array of measures are covered, from the economic, demographic, and social through the religious, ethnic, and linguistic to the mineral, land, marine, and climatic. Chapter 10 is a selected bibliography. Access points include the table of contents and indexes by subject and by country or territory. The latter seems unnecessary as the references are mostly to tables that are arranged by country.

Inevitably there are minor points of contention. Although variables are generally well labeled, for a few measures (e.g., GNP, savings, inflation, and birth and death rates) units are not specified. There are also some typographic errors. Statistical sources cited include a few older editions of annual works (e.g., *The Statesman's Year-Book, 1989-1990*).

A highly useful statistical source with significant methodological and theoretical insights, this book should be acquired by social science research collections with client interests in econometrics and in comparative studies in the social sciences. Larger general collections should also consider it where funds permit.—**Nigel Tappin**

91. Schlachter, Gail Ann, and R. David Weber. **Money for Graduate Students in the Social Sciences 1996-1998.** San Carlos, Calif., Reference Service Press, 1996. 328p. index. $40.00. ISBN 0-918276-33-0.

For the first time, information on financial aid for graduate students in all branches of the social sciences has been gathered together in one reference volume. The scope is broad. Social science is interpreted as encompassing the usual fields identified by the term, plus other areas not always included under social science in curriculum organization. Thus, business, education, library and information science, and psychology are covered.

Entries are listed alphabetically by title under two categories. "Study and Teaching" lists 727 fellowships, loans, and traineeships that support structured and unstructured study or training on the graduate level. "Research and Creative Activities" describes 246 grants, awards, and other aid programs that support those projects. Each entry concisely states the source of funding, the address, the purpose of the award, eligibility requirements, financial data, the amount and distribution of awards, the duration, limitations, special features, the number awarded per year, and deadlines.

Supplements include a directory of state sources of information on educational benefits and guaranteed student loan programs and a bibliography of directories and other books on financial aid in education. The entries are thoroughly indexed by program title, by sponsoring organization, by residency and tenability restrictions, and by subject. A calendar index lists specific deadline dates by month. One of the authors is a specialist in library and information science, the other in social science. This excellent guide will be of value to students who are contemplating graduate studies and to counselors and librarians. Two companion reference works cover the sciences and the humanities (see entries 848 and 1411).—**Shirley L. Hopkinson**

92. **Social Sciences Abstracts Full Text.** [CD-ROM]. Bronx, N.Y., H. W. Wilson, 1997. Minimum system requirements (Windows version): IBM or compatible 386SX. CD-ROM drive. DOS 3.1. Windows 3.1. 4MB RAM (8MB recommended). 14MB hard disk space. Printer (optional). Hayes or compatible modem (for online capabilities). Minimum system requirements (Macintosh version): 68020 or Power PC. CD-ROM drive. System 7.0. 2MB RAM. 10MB hard disk space. $2,995.00/yr.

The format of this product will be immediately recognized by users familiar with the CD-ROM version of *Readers' Guide to Periodical Literature* (see entry 70) as the standard H. W. Wilson interface. Search options are by subject, independent keyword, and free-text browsing. Notable is the inclusion of such series publications as the *Annual Review of Sociology*, some of which are also partially accessible in full text via sites on the World Wide Web. The chief value of this tool is the provision of full-text copy from many professional social science periodicals that library collections in high schools, rural libraries, and smaller public library systems are unlikely to hold locally or to be able to access. Individual collection information can be added via the journal holdings manager feature of the software. This disc is most suitable for adoption by academic libraries supporting undergraduate and graduate programs in the social sciences that have not acquired more specialized resources, such as Sociofile, PsycLit or Ageline.—**Robert B. Marks Ridinger**

93. **Social Sciences Index. April 1995 to March 1996.** Cheryl Ehrens and others, eds. Bronx, N.Y., H. W. Wilson, 1995, 1996. 2504p. priced on a service basis rate. ISSN 0094-4920.

This latest volume of the *Social Sciences Index* offers an occasion to praise the continued availability of "hard copy" research tools. In an era when scholars and general readers have growing numbers of electronic data banks, it is still valuable for many to be able to pore over such indexes as these for exploring categories and subjects that may not have occurred to people sitting at their computers. This index is the standard for the social sciences. It covers 415 major serial publications in the social sciences. Although the index is an old one, it has remained up-to-date in the journals that it covers by regular "subscriber votes." As a result, *Social Sciences Index* continues to cover traditional titles but has also reached out to include serials in newer areas, such as women's studies, minority studies, environmentalism, and so on. The index allows for searches by author and by subject. The subject classifications are extensive and include frequent cross-references to link subject headings. Subject classifications are kept up-to-date with new terms based on changing scholarly interests or new avenues of research introduced on a regular basis. *Social Sciences Index* remains essential for all college and university libraries and larger community libraries.—**Frank L. Wilson**

94. **Sociofile: 1974-December 1996.** [CD-ROM]. Baltimore, Md., National Information Services Corporation, 1997. Minimum system requirements: IBM or compatible 386. CD-ROM drive. 3MB RAM. 480K conventional memory. 2.5MB hard disk space. Color or monochrome monitor. $2,095.00/yr.

This thorough and multifaceted tool is replete with bells and whistles to excite even those most technically challenged. Unfortunately, *Sociofile* is not self-explanatory or user-friendly. If the intent is to challenge users to find what information is not provided, the disc is a success. It is hard to point out something that is missing, unless it is one little word: simplicity.

However, installation is easy, although the requirement for the install code could keep some reference librarians digging through the trash every update (they are listed on each update cover letter and are case sensitive). Function keys activate help screens, searches, the display of records, clear screens, and exit commands, all of which are useful functions. Adding to the user's confusion are the autodex (automatic index) key for displaying words that match what is entered, a rotated index for displaying the word entered and all phrases associated with it, a thesaurus, scroll keys, a commands menu (of which there are more than a dozen and a half), clear and copy keys, a save key, advanced and expert search modes, and an options menu (of which there are 14). The User's Guide is 80 pages long, and the "quick reference" card contains more than 100 items with explanations.

Boolean operators obtain records, as do proximity (nearX or adjX, where "X" equals a number) operators. Truncation is also available, as is "P.I.C.," or plurals, international variants, and compound words. Search terms are highlighted in retrieved records. *Sociofile* allows searching in English and Spanish. Although the searching mechanism may be loaded to a LAN, the database information remains on CD-ROM and must be replaced with each update and remain accessible to the LAN.

There can be no doubt that this disc will provide libraries with information at their fingertips. The information is from standbys that have served information needs well for years: ERIC, Sociological Abstracts, Child Abuse and Neglect, Family Studies Database, and more. There is also no question that librarians will need to be in close proximity wherever such discs are in use.—**Mark Y. Herring**

3 Area Studies

GENERAL WORKS

95. **Lands and Peoples.** Danbury, Conn., Grolier, 1997. 6v. illus. maps. index. $259.00/set. ISBN 0-7172-8020-9.

96. **Lands and Peoples Special Edition: The Changing Face of Europe.** Danbury, Conn., Grolier, 1996. 130p. illus. maps. index. free with set. ISBN 0-7172-8019-5.

Public and school libraries need no introduction to this social studies reference tool. It is the resource of choice for any librarian helping a child locate country information. The set has become a standard over the years because of its content and the ongoing revision policy of the editors. The 1997 edition sports a new cover design even though the basic arrangement of the information remains the same. The six main volumes are arranged by continent, and the countries of that continent are arranged geographically. Quick access to a specific country is provided by the table of contents, which lists countries alphabetically.

There is an overview article for each continent accompanied by a facts and figures box that serves as a quick reference to historical, topographic, economic, and demographic facts as well as pertinent political information. Main articles explore the geography, people, culture, economy, and history of each country. Country articles also have fact boxes. Country entries are enhanced by the use of sidebars to discuss specific issues and topics related to the country. The "Facts and Figures" section of the index volume contains 27 useful tables and 8 maps. Many of the tables are comparative and will be useful to students and librarians searching for such things as the longest river in Africa.

Volume 6, *Central and South America*, was selected for major revision in 1997. Every article has either been replaced or has undergone major revision (50 to 99 percent of the content has been revised). All maps have been replaced or updated to reflect the latest borders and place-names. New to the volume are two introductory articles that give an overview of the region. Of the 345 articles in the set as a whole, 2 are new and 235 have been revised. Twenty of these reflect major revisions. Among the 300 maps, there are 17 new maps and 23 revised maps. There are also 276 new 4-color photographs. The index volume, including the "Facts and Figures" statistical appendixes, has been expanded and redesigned.

The impact of the disintegration of communism in Europe is the focus of the 1997 special edition. Part 1 is a discussion of the roots and characteristics of communism and its effect on the people who lived under its rule. Part 2 is a timetable of events tracing developments in the communist world from 1944 onward. Post-1992 events are presented in two spreads, one for Central Europe and the Balkans and the other for republics of the former Soviet Union. Names and terms in bold typeface refer to main entries appearing in the next section, which is an alphabetic list of 121 short articles covering all former communist countries, new successor states, geographic regions, personalities, terms, and organizations. The historical, cultural, and political complexity of the former communist world can only be highlighted in 125 pages, but the major players and issues are identified in a way that makes the information accessible to young people and provides a starting point for further research. The supplemental volume is designed to be used with the main volumes of *Lands and Peoples*. The consistent quality of this resource and its ease of use continue to make it indispensable to libraries serving upper elementary and middle school students.
—**Marlene M. Kuhl**

97. **The World Guide 1997/98: A View from the South.** 10th ed. Oxford, England, New Internationalist Publications; distr., Atlantic Highlands, N.J., Humanities Press, 1997. 628p. maps. index. $80.00; $39.95pa. ISBN 1-869847-42-3; 1-869847-43-1pa.

Published in Spanish since 1979 and English since 1984 under variant titles, this work is intended to provide an alternative to what the editors feel is an overload of information from the perspective of the industrialized nations. There are 2 main sections: The 1st provides approximately 1 page of text and another of graphs and tables for 22 "Global Problems." The larger section, by country, typically consists of two or three pages text, plus two small outline maps (one regional, one of the country); a box of standard statistics; and some icons repeating significant statistics in graphic form. There is one full-color political map; other graphics involve a couple of shades of green and gray but are generally legible. Access points include a table of contents and an index, mostly for proper names with some subjects. A brief, unannotated bibliography is attached.

Because the work's major point—the implicit bias of most reference tools of its kind—is valid, it is most unfortunate that the guide remains flawed. The little documentation, when provided at all, tends to a brief author/title/date citation, even when the item cited is a lengthy series published over several years. The index is curious; even though each paragraph in each article is numbered, index entries list only a page number. Selection of entries is also strange: For example, although Catholicism (presumably of the Roman variety), Buddhism, and Islam receive coverage, there is no index term for Jews (except one reference for Ashkenazim). Many technical terms used in the text are not indexed, such as the "Boxers" of the Boxer Rebellion. Others, such as the Monroe Doctrine, certainly a sore point for South Americans, get only a brief reference. Numerous minor errors are not only aggravating but make one wonder about the overall care taken with facts—for example, English is not the official language of the United States.

As an alternative view of the world, and thus a supplement to other standard works in the typical U.S. library, this guide has some value. Unfortunately, its quality as a general reference book has not improved. A CD-ROM version of this source is also available (1997) but was not seen by this reviewer.

—**James H. Sweetland**

UNITED STATES

General Works

98. **Encyclopedia of Rural America: The Land and People.** Gary A. Goreham, ed. Santa Barbara, Calif., ABC-CLIO, 1997. 2v. illus. index. $175.00/set. ISBN 0-87436-842-1.

The *Encyclopedia of Rural America* is a comprehensive reference book of American rural life with more than 230 entries that cover a broad range of disciplines, including agriculture, the arts, business and economics, the environment, health and medicine, history, humanities, policy issues, and social sciences.

Organized for easy use, each alphabetic entry begins with a concise definition of the term and is followed by subentries relating to the topic. Written by experts in their fields, each entry also includes cross-references and references for further reading. A selected bibliography and a comprehensive index complete the reference.

Distinguishing itself from general works, this encyclopedia not only presents information, but also demonstrates the effects of urbanization on rural America. Due to the numerous interconnections that exist between rural and urban America, this resource is intended for several audiences—people who work with rural residences or in rural areas, including county commissioners, newspaper editors, clergy, legal staff, government officials, librarians, teachers, counselors, and industry leaders as well as academic faculty, researchers, and students.—**Deborah A. Taylor**

Florida

99. **Florida Almanac 1997-1998.** 11th ed. By Del Marth and Martha J. Marth. Bernie McGovern, ed. Gretna, La., Pelican Publishing, 1997. 452p. illus. maps. index. $14.95pa. ISBN 1-56554-258-4. ISSN 0361-9796.

Now in its 11th edition, the *Florida Almanac* continues to be one of the best state almanacs in the United States. The almanac was originally created in response to a newspaper editor's request for a comprehensive source on the state in one volume. It fulfills that request well. In addition, the current edition contains a table of contents with listings of the topics covered in each section. The lack of a table of contents was a major criticism of earlier reviews of this serial (see ARBA 82, entry 369 and ARBA 73, entry 420). There continues to be a detailed index at the end of the volume. Sections include climate and weather, geography (with a fine explanation of sinkholes and their formation), history (with a valuable chronology dating from 10,000 B.C.E. to the present), archaeology, historical landmarks, waterways and boating, wildlife, tourism, agriculture and industry, the military, space exploration, and sports. The almanac will appeal to both residents and anyone considering relocating to Florida. It contains more than the necessary demographics, county maps, educational institutions, government and election information, and crime and vital statistics. For example, the section on flowers, which is important for the state known as the "land of flowers," includes lists of native, imported, and endangered flowers as well as a monthly planting schedule. For the tourist there are sections on major attractions; state parks; lodging; major festivals; and regulations for boating, fishing, and hunting.

The *Florida Almanac* is an outstanding purchase for any library in the region as well as libraries in colder climates with resident "snowbirds" who will travel there. It is a fine example of a comprehensive state handbook and a great reference tool.—**Ingrid Schierling Burnett**

Louisiana

100. **Louisiana Almanac.** 1997-98 ed. Milburn Calhoun and Jeanne Frois, eds. Gretna, La., Pelican Publishing, 1997. 695p. illus. maps. index. $26.00; $16.95pa. ISBN 1-56554-243-6; 1-56554-248-7pa. ISSN 0896-6206.

This 15th edition of the *Louisiana Almanac* (see ARBA 93, entry 110, for a review of an earlier edition) continues its reputation as a compendium of information about all aspects of the state. In the foreword, the editors acknowledge that much of the material is compiled from a variety of sources and in some cases photocopied, accounting for the variety of fonts and styles. The source of the information is noted in most instances. Popular topics such as sports and tourism are included as well as the standard entries about history, population, government, and politics. Natural resources, education, employment, and health are also presented. The almanac is illustrated with black-and-white drawings and maps. The table of contents and the index guide the user to specific topics. Some of the charts are difficult to read because of the small typeface, but these limitations are offset by the amount of information packed into the book. Because of the four-year interval between editions, libraries will want to purchase the hardback. Anyone with an interest in Louisiana will appreciate this title.—**Margo B. Mead**

New York

101. Wertsman, Vladimir F. **New York, the City in More Than 500 Memorable Quotations: From More Than 500 Authors....** Lanham, Md., Scarecrow, 1997. 190p. index. $35.00. ISBN 0-8108-3088-4.

This quotation book is a comprehensive and well-documented international list of more than 500 memorable quotations on New York City from the sixteenth century to the present. Arranged alphabetically by author, the volume includes brief biographical information with references and indexes that are supplied by writers, statespeople, educators, scientists, actors, and others. Another important aspect is the thoroughness of the basic indexes, listed by subject, in the back of the book. However, the subject "Transportation" lists the entry number rather than the page number. The final index is chronological.

The book is well coordinated by the author. Much information can be gleaned, whether the sayings come from the general public, statespeople, or entertainment celebrities. One example comes from comedian and former rabbi Jackie Mason (1930-): "The best [in NYC] is that it's the most exciting, vital, vibrant city around. But no matter where you go to enjoy it, you're bound to get mugged" (1993). The volume is highly recommended for academic, public, and special (fine arts or entertainment) libraries and for other institutions.—**Lisé Rasmussen**

AFRICA

General Works

102. **Africa in Figures 1996.** By the United Nations Economic Commission for Africa. New York, United Nations, 1996. 83p. $12.00pa. ISBN 92-1-025117-2. S/N E/F.96.II.K.8.

This volume is the 3d edition of an annual series intended to present in monograph form information drawn from the Regional Statistical Data Base maintained by the Economic Commission for Africa (ECA). The 1st section compares the status of Africa with the world in terms of surface area and population, education, national accounts, agriculture, energy, and external trade. The 53 nations of the continent are then presented through detailed, single-page tables covering demographic and social indicators, environment-related factors, the gross national product, the status of transport and communications networks, finance and prices (including exchange rates and consumer price indexes), and the information on principal imports and exports. Libraries that hold *Africa South of the Sahara* (see entry 108) or possess a major international documents collection containing the ECA's *African Statistical Yearbook* will find this new series best used for quick reference.—**Robert B. Marks Ridinger**

103. Bever, Edward. **Africa.** Phoenix, Ariz., Oryx Press, 1996. 302p. illus. maps. index. (International Government & Politics Series). $34.95pa. ISBN 0-89774-954-5.

At first glance, this book looks like another country handbook. In reality, it is a useful introduction to the political history of Africa and its individual countries. The volume's core, a country-by-country review, focuses entirely on the political background and governments of each country, accompanied by a short statistical profile. Sections on each country cover events up to the mid-1990s. In addition, the work includes a 50-page history of the continent, covering ancient Africa, European colonialism, and independence. Also included are two chapters addressing international relations and "common challenges," such as population growth and ethnic tensions. Clear black-and-white maps show Africa's geographic features and political boundaries. A short bibliography, a glossary, and a detailed index conclude the book.

The brief statistical section on each country, covering such basics as population and foreign debt, is taken from secondary sources and is somewhat out-of-date. This is excusable given the difficulty of finding statistics on African nations and the strong historical focus of the book. The sweeping but concise review of African history makes this book a basic text as well as a quick reference book. Students are likely to want to borrow it for use outside the library. At such a reasonable price, some libraries may want a copy for reference and a second copy to circulate. [R: Choice, May 97, pp. 1471-72]—**Cathy Seitz Whitaker**

104. Hall, David E. **African Acronyms and Abbreviations: A Handbook.** New York, Mansell/Cassell, 1996. 364p. $120.00. ISBN 0-7201-2275-9.

National and international government, business, social, cultural, and educational organizations use acronyms and abbreviations to shorten communications. The life of any of these institutions is not the story of this book; instead, Hall presents a progress report of his findings on the correct identifications of their tricky labels that have been common in this century. Getting the title right is the problem attacked here. This thorough book is a trustworthy authority for Africanists facing the mistakes, misunderstandings, multiple organizations with the same initials, varying interpretations of the same office's name, or elusive meanings of the letters.—**Elizabeth L. Anderson**

105. Zell, Hans M., and Cecile Lomer. **The African Studies Companion: A Resource Guide & Directory.** 2d ed. New Providence, N.J., Hans Zell/Reed Reference Publishing, 1997. 276p. index. $75.00. ISBN 1-873836-41-4.

This is a welcome revision of a useful guide to African studies. Intended as a desktop companion and working tool for scholars, students, teachers, and librarians, its aim is to provide an introduction to general and current sources (primarily in English) on African studies. As with the 1st edition (see ARBA 91, entry 93), more specialized materials (e.g., country-level bibliographies) are generally not included.

This 2d edition, however, is considerably larger: 935 annotated items versus 667 in the 1st edition; although 40 titles listed in the original were dropped from the initial 2 chapters on major reference sources and bibliographies, 114 titles were added this time around. Also, this edition has added e-mail addresses and Websites where available and complete international calling codes for all telephone and fax numbers. Similarly, details of Internet access to library online public access catalogs are also incorporated where applicable. Older materials felt to be outdated have been dropped, as have materials for children and young adults that the authors felt were better covered elsewhere.

Once again, chapters cover periodical publications, major libraries, Africana publishers and dealers, major regional and international organizations that deal with Africa, major donor agencies and foundations active in Africa, African studies associations and societies, academic and literary awards, and a final section on Africana abbreviations and acronyms. This guide is recommended for any library with any interest in Africa.—**Paul H. Thomas**

Benin

106. Eades, J. S., and Chris Allen, comps. **Benin.** Santa Barbara, Calif., Clio Press/ABC-CLIO, 1996. 261p. index. (World Bibliographical Series, v.192). $82.50. ISBN 1-85109-145-9.

Researchers working on sub-Saharan African countries generally do not have ready-references to works done on the region. The World Bibliographical Series is generally changing that situation. *Benin*, a recent addition to the series compiled by Eades and Allen, is an important bibliographic source of reference material on Benin. Covering works from both anglophone and francophone sources and materials from precolonial times to the present, this 278-page bibliography neatly complements the *Historical Dictionary of Benin* compiled by Samuel Decalo (2d ed.; see ARBA 89, entry 91). The book is organized according to subject matter and covers all aspects of research on Benin, including the country and its peoples, geography, environment and resources, history, economy, politics, international relations, religion, libraries, and statistical data. Each entry is accompanied by a short summary in English as well as references to related materials that are not entries in the bibliography itself. This feature makes the bibliography far more extensive than the 759 entries it contains and also makes it enjoyable to read. The entries in the bibliography are not arranged in alphabetic order.

The two indexes—an author index and a subject index—are useful. The compilers provide an extensive and excellent introduction to the bibliography that skillfully ties all the materials together. The introduction also solves the potential confusion that could otherwise have arisen because of the commonality of the country's name with the city of Benin in Nigeria and the University of Benin in Togo. Despite the paucity of material in recent times, especially during the Mathieu Kerekou socialist period, the compilers have done an excellent job in presenting a comprehensive bibliography of Benin. This is an informative book that belongs in every reference library and must be on the shelf of everyone interested in research work on Benin in particular and West Africa generally.—**Kwabena Gyimah-Brempong**

Lesotho

107. Johnston, Deborah, comp. **Lesotho.** rev. ed. Santa Barbara, Calif., ABC-CLIO, 1996. 197p. index. (World Bibliographical Series, v.3). $74.00. ISBN 1-85109-247-1.

Lesotho is a small, landlocked nation entirely surrounded by South Africa (with all that implies for its political and economic development), and perhaps for this reason it has attracted a fair amount of attention. Indeed, the author of this revision is a South African economist who at one time was employed by Lesotho's Ministry of Finance. This bibliography is typical of the books in this series. It is designed for English speakers and is a good first place to begin for people who are unfamiliar with Lesotho. Its 563 selections (books, government reports, and journal articles in English through 1995) are arranged by topic (geology, history, trade, and so forth) and are carefully annotated, with author, title, and subject indexes and a map appended. A short but useful introduction precedes the bibliography. Libraries having the earlier edition (see ARBA 82, entry 331) will want to retain it, because even though this revised edition contains many updated entries, the earlier edition was close to being comprehensive, having 2,562 entries, and it included works in languages other than English.—**Paul H. Thomas**

Sub-Saharan Africa

108. **Africa South of the Sahara 1997.** 26th ed. London, Europa; distr., Detroit, Gale, 1996. 1111p. $350.00. ISBN 1-85743-029-8. ISSN 0065-3896.

This by-now venerable reference tool appears in its latest edition with the format unchanged. There are 8 introductory essays, a few of intrinsic value, and a bibliography of current awareness journals, all of which total about 60 pages. A further 60 pages are devoted to discussing the various international and regional organizations as they relate to Africa, and then the 50 countries of sub-Saharan continental and insular Africa are treated alphabetically. Each treatment is broken down into physical and social geography, recent (postindependence) history, economics, a statistical survey, a directory, and a bibliography. Readers are told that "all statistical and directory material . . . have been extensively updated, revised and expanded" (p. v), and it is probably true that these two categories have been and will continue to be the most heavily used in this source. Some 50 scholars have contributed to this work, most of them British, and most country sections are the result of several hands. The latest information—included in a stop-press section—seems to date from October 1996. The statistical data are of necessity selective, and anyone attempting a broad survey would need to supplement them. The directory is extensive, although probably not comprehensive. Telephone and fax numbers are usually included, but the value of this material would benefit from having e-mail addresses as well where appropriate.

Although hardly inexpensive, *Africa South of the Sahara* is probably the best value for libraries not wishing to be comprehensive in their attention to Africa. For instance, it costs less than twice as much as a single *Country Report/Country Profile* from the Economist Intelligencer Unit, which may in its turn cover two or three countries. Appearing quarterly, the *Country Report* is more current but not necessarily more accurate. After all, users of all the African statistical compendia must reconcile themselves, not to being right, but only to being able to cite a source.—**David Henige**

ASIA

General Works

109. **Bibliographic Guide to East Asian Studies 1995.** New York, G. K. Hall/Simon & Schuster Macmillan, 1996. 668p. $210.00. ISBN 0-7838-1320-1. ISSN 1046-8765.

G. K. Hall's bibliographic series surveys, comprehensively and often annually, publishing activity in more than 20 geographic or subject disciplines. Entries are compiled from the cataloging records of the New York Public Library, the Library of Congress, and occasionally other major research libraries. Formats include monographs, serials, CD-ROMs, other audiovisual materials, and online resources. Full Library of Congress cataloging is given for each title. Access is alphabetic by integrated main entry. Coverage in the current series is for materials with imprint dates later than 1989. Titles range from one to three volumes in format.

The East Asian volume (see ARBA 94, entry 107, for an earlier review) contains the cataloging records of materials published in or about any East Asian country: China, Hong Kong, Japan, North and South Korea, and Taiwan. Titles (approximately 3,500) in all languages are included. Source collections are the Library of Congress and the New York Public Library's Oriental Division. Imprints 1990 and newer are listed and were cataloged by the two libraries between September 1, 1994, and December 31, 1995.

This volume and others in its series are prosaic by the standards of even the subject bibliography genre. Nonetheless, acquisitions librarians and others performing collection development work will be drawn to this reliable, comprehensive source. Few tools are as useful and trustworthy for the maintenance of current awareness in a field of study. A migration to the CD-ROM format would perhaps reduce the purchase price of this information and would certainly save library shelf space. Libraries of sufficient size and degree of research activity will find most of the G. K. Hall bibliographies indispensable.—**Ed Volz**

Afghanistan

110. Adamec, Ludwig W. **Historical Dictionary of Afghanistan.** 2d ed. Lanham, Md., Scarecrow, 1997. 499p. (Asian/Oceanian Historical Dictionaries, no.5). $58.00. ISBN 0-8108-3312-3.

This 1-volume concise historical dictionary of Afghanistan is the 2d edition of a 1991 publication (see ARBA 93, entry 121), with updated information on recent changes in a country wracked by continuing struggles and turmoil. As a dictionary, its numerous entries provide brief descriptions of major historical events and periods; important places; significant aspects of culture, religion, economy, and politics; as well as notable personalities of the past and present. Written by a well-qualified specialist on Middle Eastern studies who just published a related reference work, *Dictionary of Afghan Wars, Revolutions, and Insurgencies* (see ARBA 97, entry 106), this latest work includes, aside from the main dictionary, an extensive chronology from ca.2000-1000 B.C.E. to March 20, 1997, and a useful bibliography of selected books and articles, mostly in English, arranged by broad subjects. Although the contents of this historical dictionary overlap other works by the same author, it is more comprehensive in historical coverage than the others.—**Hwa-Wei Lee**

China

111. Hayford, Charles W., comp. **China.** new ed. Santa Barbara, Calif., Clio Press/ABC-CLIO, 1997. 601p. index. (World Bibliographical Series, v.35). $150.00. ISBN 1-85109-235-8.

Although a new edition of an earlier (1983) book of the same title by Peter Cheng, this volume by Hayford appears to be a totally new bibliography on China. The 1,502 annotated entries consist largely of more recent (1980-1995) publications on China by Western sources, mostly in English, but also including reprints or translations of standard works and classics. The subject coverage, under 44 topics, is broad indeed—from "Agriculture and Rural Political Economy" to "Tourism and Travel Guides." The volume is intended for general readers seeking to learn more about China and needing a single but extensive guide to a wide range of English-language materials readily accessible in libraries. Companion volumes in the same series provide more detailed coverage of related areas, such as *Hong Kong* (1990); *Macau* (1989); *Taiwan* (1990); and *Tibet* (see ARBA 93, entry 130). Separate author, title, and subject indexes conclude the volume. Because of the price, this title is recommended for major reference or bibliographic collections.—**Hwa-Wei Lee**

112. Wang, Richard T. **Area Bibliography of China.** Lanham, Md., Scarecrow, 1997. 334p. index. (Scarecrow Area Bibliographies, no.13). $59.00. ISBN 0-8108-3350-6.

There are still too few good survey bibliographies for Chinese studies, the most notable recent contribution being Charles W. Hayford's new edition of *China* (see entry 111). Wang's contribution also covers English-language monographic literature, and although his are predominantly from the 1990s, there are more than twice as many citations than in *China* (at less than half the price). However, Wang's entries are not annotated and the layout is different. The volume is alphabetically arranged by subject headings and subheadings, sometimes specific (e.g., "Bicycle Industry," "Longevity Techniques," and "Music Bells"). Some geographic and political entities (Hong Kong, Taiwan, Macao, and others) are given separate headings. An author index is provided, but given the lack of cross-references and the idiosyncratic assignment of citations under headings, the lack of a subject index is particularly frustrating. For example, there are no cross-references between *Literature* (and its subheadings) and *Short Stories, Fiction,* or *Poetry*. With online bibliographic access (through OCLC and RLIN) more than matching this coverage, the limited time span of publications, and the lack of annotations, this resource will be attractive only as a supplement to *China* and to comprehensive subject collections.—**Kenneth W. Berger**

India

113. Johnson, Gordon. **Cultural Atlas of India.** New York, Facts on File, 1996. 240p. illus. maps. index. $50.00. ISBN 0-8160-3013-8.

This excellent cultural atlas deals with the Indian subcontinent, which is the home of 20 percent of the world's population. Four major religions of the world—Hinduism, Buddhism, Sikhism, and Jainism— had their birth on this ancient land. People of other religions of the world, including Christians, Muslims, and Jews, have also lived on the subcontinent for centuries, which is solid proof of successful diversity. The book introduces readers to the rich cultural history, different religions, arts and architecture, social and political organizations, literature, science, and other aspects of a remarkable people and unique land.

The book is divided into three parts, and the first two parts are devoted to India. Part 1 deals with the physical and cultural background of India, encompassing land, climate, agriculture, people, religion, architecture, and the society. Part 2 covers the prehistory and early history of India, the medieval period dominated by Muslim rule, the history of the state of Bengal, rising Maratha power, and the impact of Europeans' rule in India. There is a special chapter on the making of modern India that discusses the rise of nationalism; the role of Mahatma Gandhi in gaining independence for India from British rule; the introduction of railways; Indian dress; music, dance, drama, and cinema; the partition of India in 1947; and economic development.

Part 3 of this atlas has short chapters on the other countries of the Indian subcontinent, including Bangladesh, Bhutan, Nepal, Pakistan, and Sri Lanka. There are a few chapters on regions of India also, such as the Northwest, the Northeast, and Central India. It includes a glossary of Indian names and words; a bibliography on different subjects; a gazetteer; a list of contributors; an index; and a chronological table of the cultural, economic, and political history of India. There are more than 250 beautiful illustrations and 36 color maps to support the text. It is difficult to write a book about the Indian subcontinent in 240 pages, but Johnson has done a remarkable job of introducing India and other South Asian countries in brief to readers. *Cultural Atlas of India* is an excellent addition to the literature and is recommended for all types of libraries.—**Ravindra Nath Sharma**

Indonesia

114. Rony, A. Kohar, comp. **Unveiling Indonesia: Indonesian Holdings in the Library of Congress: A Bibliography.** Washington, D.C., Library of Congress, 1996. 2v. illus. maps. index. $77.00pa./set. ISBN 0-8444-0877-8.

The Library of Congress holds approximately 17,000 items in its Indonesian collection. Those titles are listed as brief, numbered entries in this two-volume paperback bibliography, providing a valuable resource for those investigating the world's fourth most populous nation. Entries are arranged by broad subject categories, such as reference and general works, creative expression, the economy, and science. The bibliographic citations are presented in main entry order and are not annotated.

Published so that the resources of the Library of Congress may be shared, this work is both well intended and utilitarian. Unembellished bibliographies excite only the most serious of researchers; this title's depth and scope will please that audience. [R: LJ, 15 Sept 97, p. 96]—**Ed Volz**

Japan

115. **Japanese Studies in Canada: The 1990s.** Tokyo, Japan Foundation and Ann Arbor, Mich., Association for Asian Studies, 1996. 1v. (various paging). index. (Japanese Studies Series, no.25). $12.00pa. ISBN 0-924304-35-9.

Although sponsored by an interested party, this book is thoroughly professional and is informative beyond the standard range of reference sources. The volume concentrates on the period of 1988 to 1995, picking up after two earlier similar studies, and it draws recommendations for the future. Ably edited by Suzanne Culter of McGill University, the book contains two interesting essays on the state of Japanese studies and two main reference parts, the first a directory of Japanese studies in Canada, listing the specialists, the institutions and their programs, and other resources. The 2d reference part contains 10 indexes of names, disciplines, occupations, and the like.

The book gives guidance to those intending to include Japanese studies in their education and to those who look to use their interests in Japan for gainful employment. It provides profiles of experts on Japan, location of resources, and by implication the strengths of the programs. The guide reveals incidentally some curious demographic characteristics of the specialists on Japan and several characteristics of the markets for Japanese skills, such as the primacy of the main academic discipline over the area of specialized study. Nonacademic resources are included, as is a separate list of fellowships and grant recipients listed according to the granting institution. This reviewer found the book fun to examine. [R: Choice, Mar 97, p. 1135]—**Bogdan Mieczkowski**

Kurdistan

116. Meho, Lokman I., comp. **The Kurds and Kurdistan: A Selective and Annotated Bibliography.** Westport, Conn., Greenwood Press, 1997. 356p. index. (Bibliographies and Indexes in World History, no.46). $79.50. ISBN 0-313-30397-5.

A 24-page introduction to this bibliography presents general information on the Kurds and their nonexistent state of Kurdistan. This introductory essay describes the geography, language, religion, and tribal culture of the 30 million Kurds who are scattered among Turkey, Iran, Iraq, Syria, and Azerbaijan (with the largest number in Turkey). This information is followed by a brief history of the Kurds since 1918 in each of the five neighboring nations.

The bibliography begins with the usual general works and then proceeds with expected subdivisions ranging from "Description and Travel" to "Culture and Arts." Almost all of the 814 entries carry an annotation varying from 50 to 250 words in length. The material is in English except for an infrequent French entry where there is no English equivalent. The focus is on recent titles. A comprehensive system of cross-references and helpful indexes of authors, titles, and subjects are available.

This volume is number 46 in the World History series of Greenwood Press, which includes such titles as *Contemporary Italy* (1996); *Wartime Poland, 1939-1945* (see entry 480); and *The Russian Revolution 1905-1921* (see ARBA 96, entry 548). The audience for the review volume is media, the academic community, and Middle East researchers. The compiler of this bibliography is an adjunct lecturer at North Carolina Central University with on-the-ground experience in the Middle East.—**David Eggenberger**

Vietnam

117. Singleton, Carl. **Vietnam Studies: An Annotated Bibliography.** Pasadena, Calif., Salem Press and Lanham, Md., Scarecrow, 1997. 303p. index. (Magill Bibliographies). $44.00. ISBN 0-8108-3317-4.

A number of reference bibliographies on Vietnam, the Vietnamese, and related topics are now available to readers. Singleton's annotated guide aids access to selected English-language books on the people, culture, and history of Vietnam, the war (sometimes called the "Second Vietnam War"), Vietnamese Americans, and related topics. Annotated entries for books on diverse aspects of Vietnam studies are arranged by subject. Bibliographic coverage is rather limited, however: French- or Vietnamese-language works are not cited, and few of the many available Vietnam-related journal articles are cited. The volume includes references to some English-language books recently published in Vietnam. Author and subject indexing of entries is provided, but the absence in the citations of information on book pagination is problematic.

David G. Marr's excellent annotated bibliography, *Vietnam* (see ARBA 94, entry 122), covers the history and culture of Vietnam in detail. It includes references to selected English-, French-, and some Vietnamese-language books and also to many journal articles. Marr's coverage of the Vietnam War is somewhat abbreviated, and publications on Vietnamese Americans are not included. Some substantial bibliographies on the 1955-1975 war (or aspects of the war) are available, for example, Christopher L. Sugnet and John T. Hickey's *Vietnam War Bibliography* (see ARBA 84, entry 1522). Entries in the latter work are arranged by author, and the annotations are brief.—**Lee S. Dutton**

AUSTRALIA

118. Kepars, I., comp. **Tasmania.** Santa Barbara, Calif., Clio Press/ABC-CLIO, 1997. 164p. index. (World Bibliographical Series, v.194). $56.50. ISBN 1-85109-273-0.

As another in ABC-CLIO's extended series of bibliographic guides to almost 200 countries, this is a skillful and generally useful guide to books and journals about Tasmania. Some 537 items are listed under approximately 30 miscellaneous categories that seem to be arranged at random, such as geography, discovery and exploration, history, convicts, and aborigines. Full bibliographic information is given for each entry, and each is accompanied by a brief descriptive annotation. There are separate indexes by author, title, and subject to simplify access to the contents. The selection of material is adequate, and there is little doubt that this is the best available printed guide to literature dealing with Tasmania.

Although most large academic libraries will undoubtedly continue to purchase this volume and other titles in the series, such printed guides are no longer the best approach to obtaining information concerning relatively obscure parts of the world. Comparison of the contents of this volume against the online catalog of a large academic library indicates that less than 10 percent of the items listed are available in that library. For most users of such a library, especially students, a bibliographic guide to material not readily available in that library is of limited value. Unfortunately, this guide, like the others in the series, fails to describe the ample information on Tasmania, or virtually any other country, that is now immediately accessible on the World Wide Web. A quick search of that resource, for example, turned up some 30 sources including an excellent comprehensive index to all Tasmanian information on the Internet. Those resources may not provide the same depth as a printed guide, but because all of the information is immediately available, they are a far more useful starting point. Series such as the World Bibliographical Series need to begin to list Internet resources. Libraries need to review the continued desirability of purchasing bibliographic guides that primarily feature material they do not own in favor of reliance on Internet resources.—**Norman D. Stevens**

CANADA

119. **Junior Worldmark Encyclopedia of the Canadian Provinces.** Timothy L. Gall and Susan Bevan Gall, eds. Detroit, U*X*L/Gale, 1997. 225p. illus. maps. index. $34.95. ISBN 0-7876-1490-4.

Designed for students in the middle grades, this 1-volume resource devotes a generous section to each of the 10 Canadian provinces and 2 territories and to Canada as a whole. Elements such as fishing, domesticated animals, forestry, labor, taxation, and housing are identically numbered in each chapter and set apart with boldfaced headings. This provides for quick location and ready comparisons. Each chapter has a black-and-white political map and a chart of frequently sought facts. Features of each chapter are lists of premiers, population profiles, black-and-white pictures, charts, graphs, and bibliographies of books that teachers and schools may consult or add to their collections. Also provided are a glossary, a list of abbreviations, and an index.

The book has several egregious omissions: It has no physical maps at all, no color prints of flags and provincial coats of arms, and no portraits of political leaders. A comparison with a recent edition of *World Book Encyclopedia* (see ARBA 97, entry 48) shows that each provincial profile will have facts the other does not. However, *World Book* will provide most of the information contained in this book, often in a more attractive format and with color pictures, physical maps, and color prints of flags and coats of arms.—**Edna M. Boardman**

DEVELOPING COUNTRIES

120. Arnold, Guy. **The Resources of the Third World.** Chicago, Fitzroy Dearborn, 1997. 381p. maps. $75.00. ISBN 1-57958-014-9.

The annual *World Development Report* issued by the World Bank classifies countries according to several criteria, among which the income level of their economies is a determinant factor. Other factors include the resources available to a country, agricultural capacity, minerals, the ability to add value to raw materials, and the state of education and training of the population. Based on this classification, there are three categories of countries: low-, middle-, and high-income economies. The first two categories are known as the Third World or South, whereas the last category represents the rich or developed countries, or the North.

The Resources of the Third World focuses on the countries of the South that have a per capita income below $3,000. Part 1, an overview, analyzes the factors that determine the level of wealth or poverty of a country and the relationship between the advanced economies of the North and the developing economies of the South within the context of globalization. Special attention is paid to the resources of population; agriculture; the mineral resource base; oil and its impact; communications; mechanisms of control (e.g., aid, the International Monetary Fund, and debt); the international drug trade; and the global market.

Part 2, the country surveys' examines 5 groups of states: "the three giants" (Brazil, China, and India); "the crossover states" (Argentina, Indonesia, Iran, Israel, Kazakhstan, South Korea, Malaysia, Mexico, Singapore, South Africa, Taiwan, Thailand, Turkey, and Venezuela); "the oil states" (Algeria, Bahrain, Brunei, Gabon, Iraq, Kuwait, Libya, Nigeria, Oman, Qatar, Saudi Arabia, and the United Arab Emirates); 80 "low- and middle-income economies"; and 35 "mini-states." Each section is preceded by an introduction. Every country survey comprises general information (area, population, capital and major cities, language(s), religion(s), date of independence, gross national product, land, and climate) and an introduction, followed by data on economy, agriculture, mining and manufacturing, infrastructure, and political considerations and assessments. For a series of well argued reasons, the work does not consider the European part of the former Soviet Union and the Eastern European states as belonging to the Third World, and therefore these countries are not included in the study. An appendix provides brief information on the dependent territories. Ten black-and-white maps illustrate and support the text. The volume represents a valuable reference source for economists, businesspeople, and students.—**Hermina G. B. Anghelescu**

EUROPE

General Works

121. **Europe on File.** New York, Facts on File, 1997. 2v. maps. index. $185.00/set looseleaf w/binder. ISBN 0-8160-3508-3.

Information for 200 European countries and microstates is included in this 2-volume, tabbed binder set. Each country's entry contains several maps, including general maps, topographical maps, maps showing major transportation routes, and maps representing the location of natural resources. There is also a section of regional maps of Europe, which displays such information as acid rain levels and deforestation. A fact sheet outlines the ethnic makeup of the country, its governmental organization, major and minor religions, and population. Another fact sheet gives cultural facts such as holidays, recreational activities, and foods. A timeline tracing the country's history runs parallel to a timeline of world history. Economic and demographic statistics are presented by several pages of chart, graphs, and tables. An index and a bibliography add to the convenience of this set. The looseleaf format makes photocopying easy, and the concise, one-stop collection of information will be beneficial to students. Nonetheless, it should be viewed as a supplement to more comprehensive sources, such as *Lands and Peoples* (see entries 95 and 96) or *Statesman's Yearbook* (see ARBA 96, entry 102).—**Marlene M. Kuhl**

Czech Republic

122. Lunt, Susie, comp. **Prague.** Santa Barbara, Calif., Clio Press/ABC-CLIO, 1997. 182p. index. (World Bibliographical Series, v.195). $85.00. ISBN 1-85109-252-8.

Volume 68 of the World Bibliographical Series, published in 1986, was dedicated to Czechoslovakia and was compiled by David Short (see ARBA 87, entry 127). Eleven years later, the same series dedicates an entire volume to Prague, the capital of Czechoslovakia—now the capital of the Czech Republic after the former Czechoslovakia split into two independent countries in 1993: the Czech Republic and Slovakia. This is an excellent reference work covering a wide spectrum of information on the city, including issues focusing on people, geography, history and archaeology, politics and government, health and welfare, education, religion, science and technology, the environment, literature, the arts, architecture, archives and libraries, museums, food and drink, and the media. The introduction presents a nutshell overview of most of the above subjects.

By careful selection of entries, the work reflects both the recent changes in the political, economic, and social aspects of everyday life, and it does not omit materials published during the communist regime—a gloomy period in the country's history, terminated by the 1989 "Velvet Revolution." The 533 entries are annotated and are primarily in English or in major Western European languages. The materials are mostly books, but periodical and journal articles have been selected to illustrate aspects that have not been covered by monographs. The three indexes—by authors (personal and corporate), titles, and subjects—ensure quick access to the volume.—**Hermina G. B. Anghelescu**

Finland

123. Screen, J. E. O., comp. **Finland.** rev. ed. Santa Barbara, Calif., Clio Press/ABC-CLIO, 1997. 246p. index. (World Bibliographical Series, v.31). $68.00. ISBN 1-85109-265-X.

In the 15 years since the publication of the 1st edition of this bibliography (see ARBA 83, entry 322), enormous changes have taken place in Finland. The hold of the former Soviet Union has been broken, and the country's ever-growing relationships with Western Europe and the rest of the world have had a tremendous impact on the Finnish people. Nearly all of the works cited in this volume are in the English language. Many reflect upon and assess the changes. Others report current developments in science and technology, politics and government, the economy and trade, and even the arts and literature. Guides to libraries, archives, museums, and art galleries; the mass media; and the press are also included.

Citations are gathered under broad subject headings, then arranged under more specific subdivisions. The method of arrangement varies. For history and travel, the arrangement is chronological. Under other subjects, the most highly recommended or the most recent are listed first. The annotations are succinct. Some are descriptive, others interpretive or analytic. Some evaluate the importance of the work or its origins. An index combines author, title, and subject entries in one alphabet.

This compilation shows the same level of scholarship and thoroughness of research common to the nearly 200 other bibliographies in the World Bibliographical Series. The editorial standards for the series generally require compilers to limit the number of citations carried over from previous editions and to limit inclusions to works still in print. For this reason, libraries holding the 1st edition should retain it when the 2d is acquired. The two volumes will complement each other. This work will be of great use to scholars and researchers in Finnish and area studies and will be a necessary purchase in libraries holding the series.—**Shirley L. Hopkinson**

Former Soviet Republics

124. **The Baltics Information Sources Directory 1996.** Published for Luxembourg, EUSIDIC, by New York, TFPL, 1996. 178p. index. $50.00pa. ISBN 1-870889-62-2.

This directory is the commercial release summarizing the results of the Baltics Information Landscape research project, commissioned from EUSIDIC (the European Association of Information Services) in December 1994. The directory was compiled by a project team coordinated by TFPL Ltd.—one of the leading international providers of professional services to all sectors of the information market.

The directory is a list of information resources and services available within and about Estonia, Lithuania, and Latvia. The goal of the work is to support industrial and business development and to provide a "framework of information services that could be made available across the improved data network" (p. iv), which is being developed with support from the European Commission. The project team identified 777 individual sources covering the Baltic states, of which 568 are native to the area. The sources cover business information, marketing, science and technology, regulatory documents, finance and finance raising, training and education, news and current affairs, and official statistics. All of these statistics are illustrated with tables and charts.

The organization of the entries provides a consistent treatment of the material throughout the directory, an aspect that ensures easy retrieval. The main entry is in English and is followed by its name in the vernacular language, for example, Latvia University Library—Latvijas Universitates Biblioteka. Following this information is the name of the contact person; type of expertise (individuals or collection); sector heading (services, commerce or technical, marketing); sector descriptor (library, environmental services, health/medical/welfare, sales/marketing/distribution); subject heading (training/education/information, scientific/technical/information services); subject descriptors (legal, scientific information services, training and education information, official statistics); type of source; type of information; format of information; authors; publisher; year of publication; frequency of publication; geographic coverage; languages; and country of origin. When the entry refers to a public institution, other relevant descriptors are assigned, such as number of volumes (books, periodicals, manuscripts, microforms, CD-ROMs); hours available, and patron accessibility. Supplementary information is provided under notes.

The three indexes—country of origin index, subject index, and organization index—give quick access to the 777 entries of the book. This directory is an excellent resource for locating information on Estonia, Lithuania, and Latvia. The work should serve as an example for similar projects aiming at sharing information sources on other excommunist countries in Central and Eastern Europe that have not constituted the subject of this type of research. All libraries should have a copy of this valuable work.
—**Hermina G. B. Anghelescu**

125. Batalden, Stephen K., and Sandra L. Batalden. **The Newly Independent States of Eurasia: Handbook of Former Soviet Republics.** 2d ed. Phoenix, Ariz., Oryx Press, 1997. 233p. maps. index. $34.95pa. ISBN 0-89774-940-5.

As the former Soviet Union disintegrated along the fault lines of its ethnic republics, a new group of independent countries with difficult and unfamiliar names and still more mysterious culture and history began to be heard on the evening news. Some of the world's most important politics and most difficult challenges are located in these new countries: the lingering and still unsolved puzzle of Chernobyl's environmental disaster, nuclear proliferation, the drying up of the Aral Sea, among others.

This 2d edition is an update of the 1993 handbook, providing current statistical profiles, demography, government, education, economics, geography, and communications. The book is divided into four sections, each covering a region. Unfortunately, the authors have omitted the Baltic states with less than convincing logic. The historical and contemporary influences of Russia and the Soviet Union are too important, even if in a negative sense, to omit them from the handbook. For this reason, this book cannot be considered a comprehensive resource. For each country, information is divided into a "History and Description" and "Contemporary Issues" sections. The subcategories vary by country. The information is necessarily brief for a book of this size.

A map of each republic and general maps of regions are included, as well as an afterword; a glossary, which should have been more detailed a bibliography for each region and an index. A statistical index or summary of all the countries and regions together would have added to the book's usefulness.

The book is intended as a general reference to provide current information to students, librarians, teachers, scholars, and the general public. In this it succeeds, but with the flaws and missed opportunities cited above. The importance of these new states and the scarcity of good, easily accessible general information about them argue the need for the book as well.—**Curtis D. Holmes**

126. **Bibliographic Guide to Slavic, Baltic, and Eurasian Studies 1996.** New York, G. K. Hall/Simon & Schuster Macmillan, 1997. 3v. $690.00/set. ISBN 0-7838-1755-4. ISSN 0162-5322.

The source material for this three-volume set is MARC copy from the New York Public Library and the Library of Congress. The more than 21,000 records describe titles that are published in the Commonwealth of Independent States in the Russian language or published in 1 of 7 former Soviet Republics or published in either the non-Romance- or Germanic-speaking countries of Eastern and Central Europe. Materials written in a Baltic, Slavic, or non-Western European language are also included, as are titles concerning Eastern Europe or the former Soviet Union.

This component of the G. K. Hall bibliographic series (see entry 109 for a thorough review of the series) began in 1978 and totals 91 volumes. Introductory material lists guidelines for the remote access of the New York Public Library's collection and includes the Slavic and Baltic Division's World Wide Web address (http://www.nypl.org/research/chss/slv/slav.balt.html).—Ed Volz

127. **Eastern Europe and the Commonwealth of Independent States 1997.** 3d ed. London, Europa; distr., Detroit, Gale, 1996. 926p. $425.00. ISBN 1-85743-025-5. ISSN 0962-1040.

No changes in structure have been introduced in this reference book since its last edition in 1994. The publisher has maintained its successful combination of lengthy signed introductory essays, country profiles, and a final section with short biographies of important political figures. New articles on the environment and Chechnya have been added to the topics retained from earlier editions, which include international relations, business and economic conditions, religion, social policy, and the conflicts in Yugoslavia. Reappearing texts have been revised, in some cases substantially, with bibliographies updated.

Each of the 27 country sections begins with a short description of the country's geography and a chronology. Two short, signed articles on history and the economy are followed by a section of statistical tables and a directory of agencies in government, politics, trade and industry, and the media. The introductory paragraphs that precede many sections in the directory are especially useful, giving a summary of the history and organization of the agency. A brief bibliography closes each country chapter. Finally, the "Political Profiles" section, including 250 short biographies of political figures (50 more than in the last edition) completes the volume. Hewing to the tradition established in earlier editions, the publisher does not provide an index. This would be helpful; this reviewer, for example, had to search a bit to find a paragraph on organized crime in the Russian Federation.

There have been many changes in the region since the 1994 edition of *Eastern Europe*. This new edition, with its substantial updates, is welcome.—**V. W. Hill**

128. **Russia & Eurasia Facts & Figures Annual, Volume 21.** Theodore W. Karasik, ed. Gulf Breeze, Fla., Academic International Press, 1996. 379p. maps. $96.50. ISBN 0-87569-177-3.

129. **Russia & Eurasia Facts & Figures Annual, Volume 22.** Lawrence R. Robertson, ed. Gulf Breeze, Fla., Academic International Press, 1997. 468p. $96.50. ISBN 0-87569-185-4.

USSR Facts & Figures Annual has been renamed *Russia & Eurasia Facts & Figures Annual* for volumes 21 and 22, with identical geographic coverage. The volumes are organized into three major sections: "CIS Affairs," "Russian Affairs," and "Coverage of the Former USSR Republics," including Armenia, Azerbaijan, Belarus, Estonia, Georgia, Kazakhstan, Kyrgyzstan, Latvia, Lithuania, Moldova, Tajikistan, Turkmenistan, Ukraine, and Uzbekistan. It should be noted, however, that the first section covers all former republics, with the exception of the three Baltic countries, and information contained in these volumes is based on official sources. Larger libraries will appreciate the information contained here, especially the chronology; information on government, security, and crime; political parties; the economy; and so forth. Russia is covered in more detail, and information on the former Soviet Republics is adequate. There are other publications on this topic, such as a much more comprehensive and critical volume, *Russia and the Commonwealth of Independent States*, edited by Zbigniew Brzezinski and Paige Sullivan (M. E. Sharpe, 1997).—**Bohdan S. Wynar**

130. **USSR Population Census, 1989.** [CD-ROM]. Minneapolis, Minn., East View Publications, 1996. Minimum system requirements: IBM or compatible 486. CD-ROM drive. Windows 3.1. 8MB RAM. Graphic adapter capable of displaying at least 256 colors. $785.00.

There are abundant data here, not only about the 1989 census of the USSR but, at least in terms of aggregate data at the country level, from nine other censuses dating back to 1897. This CD-ROM product is the most comprehensive source of information currently available on the population of the USSR during that entire period. It contains 12 volumes of data that cover size and distribution of the population, age and marital status, number and composition of families, number of children born in the USSR, housing conditions, education level, nationality composition, means of livelihood, social composition, distribution of employed population by economic status, occupations, and duration of stay in permanent residence. It is possible to view all of that information and to search it by subject, nationality, and geographic unit.

Unfortunately, even on a sophisticated computer the searches run slowly. There are also some peculiar formulations, including one that appears to allow a search by any subject, but when a nonstandard subject is entered, the program indicates that it is not a valid field and then only provides a list of the searchable subjects. That is typical of the search capabilities of this product. It is in almost every respect extremely difficult to access. This CD-ROM is not meant for the casual user, or even the student, looking for basic information; it is obviously meant for, and suitable for, only the advanced researcher. It takes a good deal of time and effort, especially because no good guide comes with it and the on-screen instructions offer minimal assistance, to gain full access to the data. Even advanced users will require the assistance of someone versed in the use of CD-ROM products to find what they are looking for. Other printed sources of information, even though they are less complete, should be far more satisfactory for most people seeking information about the population of the USSR.—**Norman D. Stevens**

France

131. Hudson, Grace L., comp. **Corsica.** Santa Barbara, Calif., Clio Press/ABC-CLIO, 1997. 198p. maps. index. (World Bibliographical Series, v.202). $67.00. ISBN 1-85109-263-3.

Corsica, with its checkered history and its attraction as a tourist spot, has engendered much attention and a large volume of published literature in a number of languages. Because it is the policy of the World Bibliographical Series editors to focus primarily on English-language materials, most of the citations are for works in English, originally or in translation. In certain subject areas where there are insufficient publications in English, works in other languages, primarily French, have been included. Where the writings are plentiful, the bibliography is highly selective. In subject areas where duplications are scarce, an attempt has been made to include all useful items. For subjects such as politics, works have been chosen to represent varying points of view.

Books, periodical articles, conference reports, theses, and special issues of periodicals are listed. All works cited have been read or personally examined by the highly qualified compiler. More than 400 citations are listed under 39 chapter or subject headings. Annotations vary somewhat in length, but all give a succinct and clear description of the contents. Some include an evaluation of the author's qualifications or of sources used. An introduction gives an overview of Corsica's history and geography and describes the culture of the Corsicans. Supplementary materials include a chronology of events from ca.6500 B.C.E. to 1997; three small black-and-white maps; an index of authors, titles, subjects, and place-names in one alphabetic sequence; and addresses of tourist offices and a bookseller. This bibliography will be of use to students, researchers, information specialists, and the general reader with an interest in Corsica.—**Shirley L. Hopkinson**

Great Britain

132. Shaw, Gareth, and Allison Tipper. **British Directories: A Bibliography and Guide to Directories Published in England and Wales (1850-1950) and Scotland (1773-1950).** 2d ed. Herndon, Va., Mansell/Cassell, 1997. 459p. illus. maps. index. $150.00. ISBN 0-7201-2329-1.

City and town directories are useful current sources for locating people, whereas older directories continue to provide historians and genealogists with much useful information. In this 2d edition, Shaw and Tripper update their valuable 1989 publication (see ARBA 90, entry 133). The new edition again lists 2,222 British directories published before 1950 and continues the clear arrangement and intensive indexing of its predecessor. Unfortunately, the daunting price may discourage many libraries from acquiring this excellent guide.—**Ronald H. Fritze**

Hungary

133. Sarkozi, Matyas, comp. **Budapest.** Santa Barbara, Calif., Clio Press/ABC-CLIO, 1997. 109p. index. (World Bibliographical Series, v.198). $54.00. ISBN 1-85109-261-7.

This bibliography containing 341 items is an excellent guide to books and lengthy articles on Budapest. Most of them are written in English, but there are several German-language articles and Hungarian-language books that are richly illustrated albums where the text is of secondary importance. The book is divided into 21 sections, the largest of which contains memoirs and travelers' accounts (58 citations) and history (58 citations). Taken together, the contents of the various sections cover every conceivable aspect of one of the oldest settlements in Europe. Each entry is accompanied by a brief informative annotation that sometimes provides citations to other relevant literature of Budapest.

Access to the contents is provided by three separate indexes: author, title, and subject. The compiler has also provided an unkeyed map that shows the districts of the city. The bibliography should be useful for anyone interested in Budapest.—**Robert H. Burger**

Ireland

134. **Irish Almanac and Yearbook of Facts 1997.** Pat McArt and Dónal Campbell, eds. Derry, Northern Ireland, Artcam Publishing; distr., Chester Springs, Pa., Dufour, 1997. 318p. $9.95pa. ISBN 0-9529596-1-5.

The publication of the *Irish Almanac and Yearbook of Facts* is a welcome assist to the individual with a need to know about modern Ireland and things Irish. Launched jointly by Bernie Ahearn, leader of Fianna Fáil, Ireland's largest political party, and John Hume, leader of Northern Ireland's Social Democratic Labor Party (SDLP), at the European Finance Convention in Dublin in November 1996, the *Irish Almanac* represents two years of planning and research by McArt and Campbell culminating in a truly definitive reference source on Ireland for the 1990s and beyond. The editors have made available a wide range of information that is not readily accessible but that is important for an intelligent understanding of modern Ireland. The volume is full of details on the key personalities and important events that have shaped the political, social, and economic landscape of modern Ireland. Especially interesting are the sections on Ireland's increasingly significant role as a member state in the European Union, the focus on towns and cities other than (although not exclusive of) Dublin, the segments on historical movements and organizations (with distinctions drawn between the Official and Provisional Irish Republican Army), description of the government systems north and south of the border, a catalog of local and national newspapers and periodicals, and much more.

In compiling the *Irish Almanac*, the editors have done a distinctive service for anyone interested in Ireland and its people. Future plans involve an increase from 320 to 520 pages, with substantial new sections on Irish-American associations and prominent business and political figures of Irish descent, as well as a CD-ROM and a Website. The one item that may puzzle some readers is the seemingly insensitive inclusion of a chainsaw-wielding butcher boy—going to work on a very imposing bovine carcass in an abattoir—amid serious and somber pictures of "troubles," funerals, and important political functions.

—**Arthur Gribben**

Luxembourg

135. Christophory, Jul, and Emile Thoma, comps. **Luxembourg.** rev. ed. Santa Barbara, Calif., Clio Press/ABC-CLIO, 1997. 327p. index. (World Bibliographical Series, v.23). $90.00. ISBN 1-85109-249-8.

Given the growing importance of Luxembourg as a center of European Union activities, this updated edition of a bibliography first published in 1981 (see ARBA 82, entry 344) is timely. Christophory, a collaborator on the earlier work, is a former director of the country's National Library, and Thoma has been editor of the annual *Bibliographie luxembourgeoise* since 1976. Both bring considerable professional and personal understanding to this work.

With 1,058 entries, the new edition more than doubles the original book's 427 entries. There are 37 subject categories covered, including history, population, and education, which have been preserved, and the newer categories of tourism and travel and cuisine. Arrangement within the categories continues to be a mystery, but separate author, title, and subject indexes facilitate use. French- and German-language entries predominate over English ones, making the annotations especially helpful. Other useful features are a 12-page introduction that provides an overview of the tiny country's history, present status, and idiosyncratic language and a list of around 100 addresses of important publishers, editors, and printing presses. Updating and significant expansion of this useful introductory work make its purchase worthwhile.

—**Willa Schmidt**

Scotland

136. **Dictionary of Scottish Quotations.** Angela Cran and James Robertson, eds. Edinburgh, Mainstream Publishing; distr., North Pomfret, Vt., Trafalgar Square, 1996. 431p. index. $39.95. ISBN 1-85158-812-4.

More than 4,000 quotations by Scots and about Scotland are assembled in this work. Arranged alphabetically by speaker or writer (or in cases of multiple authorship under the name of the document and in the case of unknown authorship under "anonymous"), the quotations relate to subject areas ranging from education, food, and religion to science, literature, and sports. Those quoted include such notables as Protestant reformer John Knox and poet and songwriter Robert Burns, as well as many lesser-known individuals. Under each name, the editors state the person's career (e.g., philosopher, comedian, poet) and provide birth and death dates if available. A brief introduction instructs readers on how to use the book.

Although some may question the usefulness of the book's organization, the detailed subject index that precedes the annotations gives users the opportunity to locate quotations on specific topics. There is also a keyword index that furthers accessibility. Offering general readers insight into Scottish culture and society, this work will be of special interest to students of Scottish life and history. [R: LJ, 15 Sept 97, p. 95]

—**Barbara Ittner**

137. Mullay, Sandy. **The Edinburgh Encyclopedia.** Edinburgh, Mainstream Publishing; distr., North Pomfret, Vt., Trafalgar Square, 1996. 384p. illus. index. $39.95. ISBN 1-85158-762-4.

Edinburgh, the once and (perhaps) future capital of Scotland, is one of Europe's most historic and attractive cities. With its impressive castle dominating the scene; its bustling, compact shopping district; and its world-famed summer arts festival, the town attracts tourists by the thousands and is considered one of Great Britain's most favorable residential and commercial locations.

In this work, Mullay, a native of the city whose great affection for it is clearly in evidence, presents a comprehensive—almost exhaustive—collection of assorted information about the place. The entries are arranged alphabetically, from "Abbeys" to "Zoos," and are usefully cross-referenced. Charts, tables, and numerous intriguing photographs illuminate the entries; there is an index and a modest bibliography; and Mullay's writing style is light and accessible. No detail seems too trivial for the author, reflecting his long research interests, and this thoroughness certainly makes the book the unquestioned authority on the city. However, such items as a list of every cinema ever known to have existed (with opening and closing dates) represent a level of specialization that borders on the arcane.

Whether encyclopedic format is the best way of presenting what is essentially a comprehensive history of the city seems doubtful, as there is inevitably a choppy quality about it. Nonetheless, this is an intriguing compendium reflecting the multifaceted character of one of the world's more fascinating cities. *The Edinburgh Encyclopedia* should be of considerable interest to anyone who has ever lived or spent appreciable time in Edinburgh. [R: Choice, July/Aug 97, p. 1782]—**James R. McDonald**

Spain

138. Shields, Graham, comp. **Madrid.** Santa Barbara, Calif., CLIO Press/ABC-CLIO, 1996. 250p. index. (World Bibliographical Series, v.193). $84.00. ISBN 1-85109-250-1.

Madrid, renowned for its vitality and fabulous monuments and museums, is the capital and largest city of Spain. It is also the center of Spain's air, road, and rail networks. Considering the popularity of Madrid as a travel destination, this book is a timely and useful addition to the nearly 200 other volumes in the series. A 10-page introduction orients readers to the early history of the area, cultural aspects, and the unique character of this fascinating city with its vibrant streets and noisy cafés. Thematic chapters include a chronology; useful addresses (no e-mail addresses are included); geography, atlases, and maps; tourism, guidebooks, and travelers' accounts; archaeology and history; population, language, religion, and society; economy; education; literature and the arts; sports and recreation; mass media; and much more. The annotations offer both analytic and critical descriptions of the 538 main entries and over 600 subentries.

Main entries with foreign-language titles are followed by English translations. The English-language publications listed are up-to-date and easily available; all annotations are in the English language. Coverage in the various sections is generous. As is typical of the series, the history section is the largest, followed by the arts (27 pages), guidebooks (17 pages), and the environment (16 pages). Customs and folklore seems underrepresented with only 11 entries on 4 pages. Cross-references are numerous and lead directly to items of primary importance. For example, *The Prado* listing on page 27 leads to item 380 in the main body of the text, where an annotation of approximately 190 words describes this world-class museum. Useful appendixes include maps of the Madrid metro system and the city center. Adequate margins and white space have produced a volume that is easy to read. The binding is sturdy and will stand up to heavy use. This bibliography deserves a place in most public libraries, especially in those collections that include other titles in the series.—**Judy Gay Matthews**

LATIN AMERICA AND THE CARIBBEAN

General Works

139. **Bibliographic Guide to Latin American Studies 1996.** New York, G. K. Hall/Simon & Schuster Macmillan, 1997. 2v. $595.00/set. ISBN 0-7838-1764-9. ISSN 0162-5314.

MARC copy from the New York Public Library and the Library of Congress provides the source material for most of the titles in G. K. Hall's respected bibliographic series (see entry 109 for a complete review of the series). This two-volume entry (last reviewed in ARBA 94 [see entry 141]), however, is based upon publications cataloged by the Nettie Lee Benson Latin American Collection at the University of Texas at Austin. Some titles from the Library of Congress have been included to ensure comprehensiveness. Titles are in all formats and languages, including Latin American Indian dialects. Serials were not selected for inclusion from the University of Texas OCLC tapes that were used. Any discipline is represented if written about by a Latin American author. The book's introductory section is presented in both Spanish and English.—**Ed Volz**

Brazil

140. Dickenson, John, comp. **Brazil.** rev. ed. Santa Barbara, Calif., Clio Press/ABC-CLIO, 1997. 244p. index. (World Bibliographical Series, v.57). $85.00. ISBN 1-85109-259-5.

Brazil has a long history of subtle influence in the Anglo-American world, but the popular, and even academic, influence of Brazilian culture tends to end with the samba and carnival. Few Americans even know that Brazilians speak Portuguese, not Spanish, or that Brazil is considered one of the emerging powers in the post-Cold War era, with an economy, culture, and political system that extensively shapes other regions. Having access to information about emerging countries, such as Brazil, is critical to understanding their place in the world. It is also important to those having research or personal interests in these countries or cultures. The World Bibliographical series, which this book is a part of, tackles the task of compiling a variety of printed information about specific countries.

This revised edition of *Brazil* attempts to update both bibliographic resources and to better reflect current conditions. An introduction provides critical background information and the subject categories seem logical and easy to use. Bibliographic entries include short, useful descriptions that vary from a sentence to several paragraphs. The compiler wisely manages to eliminate older or repetitive works, while keeping classic ones that are critical to understanding Brazil. Although most works are in English, there are also a variety of Portuguese-language works where translations are not available, as well as journal and article citations. The three indexes—author, title, and subject—provide flexible access to the material. There are a few errors, for example Nancy Scheper-Hughes classic work *Death Without Weeping* is called *Death by Weeping*, but overall the material is clear and accurate.

Although no bibliography can be comprehensive, *Brazil* appears well thought out and should provide English speakers with an excellent resource. At $85 it is affordable and recommended for all libraries, except perhaps secondary schools or small libraries that would have few of the bibliographic citations available. It is a must for university and research libraries, and the revised edition is well worth the cost of updating the older 1984 version. That work should be retained, however, for works from the 1970s and 1980s that have been eliminated from the new edition.—**Luiz Alberto Cardoso**

Mexico

141. **Encyclopedia of Mexico: History, Society & Culture.** Michael S. Werner, ed. Chicago, Fitzroy Dearborn, 1997. 1749p. illus. maps. index. $250.00/set. ISBN 1-884964-31-1.

More than 300 scholars in 7 countries collaborated to produce this 1,700-page, 2-volume encyclopedia on Mexico. It covers the people, events, institutions, processes, society, and culture from Mexican history that are critical to the understanding of modern-day Mexico. All the article-length entries are signed and include select bibliographies.

The alphabetic list of entries is accompanied by thematic outlines, which have four divisions: culture, economy, geography and demography, and politics. These in turn are subdivided into topical entries, such as education, language, literature, popular culture, philosophy and social thought, and religion. Larger topics, such as motion pictures, radio, education, architecture, and visual arts, appear as several entries divided by periods. Entries on current topics of interest that distinguish this reference on Mexico from similar works include the Zapatista Rebellion in Chiapas, gender, feminism, cuisine, and the earthquake of 1985. In fact, the entry on Cuauhtemoc Cárdenas, the popular leader and presidential hopeful, is particularly current because it mentions his recent election as mayor of Mexico City. The index has extensive cross-references, which are useful for finding acronyms of Mexican political parties and government agencies. There are ample maps, graphs, and tables as well as photographs, drawings, and other illustrations—all black-and-white—that add considerably to the work.

This fine encyclopedia has some of the most scholarly, in-depth, complete, and current coverage of historical and cultural topics on Mexico available in English. It is destined to become the reference of choice for questions in the humanities and social sciences.—**Edward Erazo**

Venezuela

142. Rudolph, Donna Keyse, and G. A. Rudolph. **Historical Dictionary of Venezuela.** 2d ed. Lanham, Md., Scarecrow, 1996. 954p. (Latin American Historical Dictionaries, no.3). $110.00. ISBN 0-8108-3029-9.

The authors of the new edition of *Historical Dictionary of Venezuela* have expanded and made numerous improvements in both the quality and quantity of material included. The entries vary from a short paragraph to multiple pages in length, as in the treatment of petroleum. The dictionary is much improved in its scholarly erudition; for example, the entries are more comprehensive. An extensive bibliography (1,891 items) of English and Spanish materials is included. The bibliography is organized into numerous broad topical areas, such as "Agriculture" and "Agrarian Reform—Society and Social Conditions." Also provided for many entries are *see* references. This dictionary will be well used in any academic library and in large public libraries.—**Dario J. Villa**

MIDDLE EAST

General Works

143. **Bibliographic Guide to Middle Eastern Studies 1996.** New York, G. K. Hall/Simon & Schuster Macmillan, 1997. 694p. $215.00. ISBN 0-7838-1771-1. ISSN 1058-644X.

This entry in G. K. Hall's comprehensive subject bibliography series (see entry 109 for a complete review of the series) is a one-volume work compiled from the cataloging records of the Library of Congress and the Middle East section of the New York Public Library's Jewish Division. Last reviewed in ARBA 93 (see entry 159), the latest volume has materials with copyrights of 1990 or newer that were cataloged in 1996 and are listed with full bibliographic data. An integrated main entry format is used, and the New York Public Library holdings are identified. Works in the modern Arabic, Persian, and Turkish languages are included. Serials are listed as well as book and nonbook items. The scope is interdisciplinary, covering a variety of topics such as anthropology, finance, literature, and politics. Librarians and academics expect G. K. Hall's bibliographies to be reliable and thorough. This title will not disappoint and should be added to respectable multicultural collections.—**Ed Volz**

OCEANIA

144. Thawley, John. **Australasia and South Pacific Islands Bibliography.** Lanham, Md., Scarecrow, 1997. 587p. index. (Scarecrow Area Bibliographies, no.12). $74.00. ISBN 0-8108-3240-2.

This book cites sources on Australia, Melanesia (excepting the Indonesian part of New Guinea), Micronesia, and Polynesia (excluding Hawaii). New Zealand comes under Polynesia. The bibliography includes materials from the past 50 years, because earlier periods are already covered. Items cited are primarily in English, although with strong French involvement in the area, some are in that language. The volume will be welcomed by researchers of these vast regions of the Southern Hemisphere.

The bibliography itself is arranged in five main sections, for the regions given above and the South Pacific in general. Subdivision is then by country or territory, with each of these further divided by subject. The Australian section amounts to almost 40 percent of the whole; Micronesia, 6 percent; Melanesia, 20 percent (60 percent of that on Papua); Polynesia, 25 percent (about 60 percent of that on New Zealand); and the South Pacific in general, 10 percent. Subject divisions largely follow Library of Congress practice. The bibliography is described as selective, but it is not annotated.

Additional features include a detailed table of contents, an overview map of the region (which is a bit small), a brief introduction by the bibliographer, an author index, and selective lists of journals and databases dealing with the region. The physical production is of high quality with good binding and paper meeting the permanence of paper standards of the American National Standard for Information Sciences. The author is an Australian academic and special librarian and bibliographer who moved to the United States in late 1995.

This thorough work should be acquired by research collections covering the South Pacific. It will also be useful for large general collections where funds and client interests warrant.—**Nigel Tappin**

PACIFIC AREA

Samoan Islands

145. Hughes, H. G. A. **Samoa (American Samoa, Western Samoa, Samoans Abroad).** Santa Barbara, Calif., Clio Press/ABC-CLIO, 1997. 342p. index. (World Bibliographical Series, v.196). $70.00. ISBN 1-85109-253-6.

This evaluative bibliography is another fine addition to ABC-CLIO's World Bibliographical Series. It covers all aspects of the literature on this Polynesian group. The British-based, academic author clearly has a deep understanding of his subject. Materials from the past two decades are emphasized, but earlier works of enduring value are included. References are made to other relevant bibliographies, and most of the material is in English, with some featured in German, French, and Samoan.

The volume starts with an essay outlining the main facts of Samoan affairs. A helpful feature is the long chronology, which provides historical information about this much mythologized archipelago. There is also a glossary of Samoan words.

The bibliography is divided into 42 sections with further subdivisions. The topics range from anthropology and language to travelers' accounts, flora and fauna, politics, Robert Louis Stevenson, and audiovisual media. Annotations are evaluative and usually the length of a paragraph. In addition to a detailed table of contents, access is provided through author, title, and subject indexes.

There are references to three World Wide Web addresses at the end of the introduction. At the time of this review only one was working, and it led to a brief promotional site for the government of Western Samoa.

This fine work in a quality series should be acquired by research collections specializing in the Pacific islands, Polynesia, and Samoa. For less focused libraries, John Thawley's *Australasia and South Pacific Islands Bibliography* (Scarecrow, 1997) might be more appropriate.—**Nigel Tappin**

SOUTH ATLANTIC OCEAN

146. Day, Alan, comp. **St. Helena, Ascension, and Tristan da Cunha.** Santa Barbara, Calif., ABC-CLIO, 1997. 260p. index. (World Bibliographical Series, v.197). $70.00. ISBN 1-85109-272-2.

The World Bibliographical Series is made up of separate volumes on nearly every country in the world plus some cities and regions. This volume provides a bibliography of three small British dependencies off the coast of Africa in the South Atlantic. The annotated entries are organized by subject categories, such as history, geography, flora and fauna, politics, education, and so on. Among these sections is one on Napoleon Bonaparte and St. Helena, perhaps the dependencies' most notable historical association. Most citations are to English-language materials. They include works from as far back as the seventeenth century to the mid-1990s.

Not many people are interested in doing work on St. Helena, Ascension, and Tristan da Cunha. With a total population of less than 9,000 and noted only for a U.S. satellite tracking station on Ascension, these British colonies attract little attention. Those who are interested will find this a comprehensive and useful introduction to the most important literature on these three dependencies.—**Frank L. Wilson**

4 Economics and Business

GENERAL WORKS

Bibliography

147. **Bibliographic Guide to Business and Economics 1995.** New York, G. K. Hall/Simon & Schuster Macmillan, 1996. 3v. $650.00/set. ISBN 0-7838-1309-0. ISSN 0360-2702.

This three-volume set was last reviewed in ARBA 92 (see entry 121). MARC copy from the New York Public Library and the Library of Congress provides the source material for this entry in G. K. Hall's respected series (see entry 109 for a complete review of the series). Titles are in all languages and formats, including conference papers. The disciplines represented include the various business, economic, and financial fields one would expect, as well as agriculture, communications, population, statistics, and transportation. Records are printed three columns to the page in an integrated main entry order.—**Ed Volz**

148. Crainer, Stuart. **The Ultimate Business Library: 50 Books That Shaped Management Thinking.** New York, AMACOM, 1997. 323p. index. $24.95. ISBN 0-8144-0395-6.

Stuart Crainer's *The Ultimate Business Library: 50 Books That Shaped Management Thinking* provides a summary of the 50 greatest books on management. The selection is based on opinions from experts in both the United States and the United Kingdom. Selections span the centuries and range from *The Art of War* by Sun Tzu (500 B.C.) to Gary Hamel and C. K. Prahalad's *Competing for the Future* (1994). Other authors represented include Abraham Maslow, Peter F. Drucker, Rosabeth Moss Kanter, Dale Carnegie, Niccolo Machiavelli, Henry Ford, Adam Smith, and Max Weber. Each entry provides biographical information about the author, a description of the work, and a discussion of its contribution to management. Additionally, Gary Hamel, a noted author in management, wrote the foreword and a brief commentary on each book. Hamel groups the books within specific issues in management, including leadership, customers, competition, efficiency, and strategy, which enables readers to focus in on their specific areas of interest. The appendix contains a list and brief description of 50 additional titles that had been considered for the list of greatest books. A bibliography for further reading is also provided.

This important work is primarily recommended to academic library collections. Business librarians or collection development librarians will want to use this book to build or enhance management holdings. Business faculty should consider this book in preparing assignments.—**Lucy Heckman**

149. **International Bibliography of Business History.** Francis Goodall, Terry Gourvish, and Steven Tolliday, eds. New York, Routledge, 1997. 668p. index. $125.00. ISBN 0-415-08641-8.

This is an excellent reference in terms of coverage, diversity of scholarly viewpoints in the selection, relevance, and quality of annotation. Although only three people are listed as editors, a large number of people from around the world participated in selecting the 4,421 entries, which cover general sources, primary and extractive industries, traditional and heavy industries, light manufacturing industries, trade and distribution, banking and finance, utilities, transport and other services, strategy and structure (approaches to business history), and entrepreneurship and management. The entries are listed alphabetically by author in each category. These categories are treated differentially in terms of space allocation and the number of entries from different parts of the world. For example, general sources fill 22 pages, whereas utilities and transport occupy 100 pages. Light manufacturing sources are classified as from the United Kingdom, the United States, and the rest of the world. In contrast, banking and finance entries are classified as from 15 countries and several regions. This differentiation may be only, in part, a function of the limited number of studies of business in the various countries and regions. The index of authors and industries is fairly comprehensive.

Another attractive feature of this volume is that it complements existing business references by filling gaps evident in those references. This reference should be of great use to business students and historians. It would have been of even greater use had it included theories of business or history of thought in business as a separate category. Although references to theory and thought are partially covered under entrepreneurship and management, a separate section would have been a major contribution, especially to academicians and graduate students of business, economics, and history.—**Elias H. Tuma**

Biography

150. **Who's Who in Asian Banking & Finance 1998-1999 International Edition.** John L. Pellam, ed. Laguna Beach, Calif., Barons Who's Who, 1997. 304p. illus. $210.00. ISBN 1-882292-12-X. ISSN 1059-5392.

This volume is a current compilation of personal and professional biographical information on 1,851 individuals of influence throughout Hong Kong, Indonesia, Japan, Malaysia, the People's Republic of China, the Philippines, the Republic of Korea (South Korea), Singapore, Taiwan (Republic of China), Thailand, and Vietnam. Selection of entries was made from the fields of banking, finance, economics, venture capital, and investment: a few of the regions' investors and prominent business leaders are also included. Individuals managing banking and investment firms and financial executives have been chosen primarily on their value as business contacts. Special attention has been paid to executives of firms with stock exchange prominence and those involved in economics and governmental economic policy.

The book is set up with a biography section and a company profile section. The main biography section provides information about the person's professional endeavors: past and present job functions; employer; education; professional memberships; honors and awards; and contact address, telephone number, and fax number. The company profiles list 1,552 banks and financial institutions within the Pacific Rim region. Each listing gives contact data, addresses, telephone and fax numbers, and key employees. Both the biographical and company sections are in alphabetic order. This book is recommended for large public and university libraries with business collections. Special business libraries for banks and financial institutions and businesses who have trade and banking interests in the Pacific Rim countries would find this volume an essential directory for current information on their business contacts.
—**Kay M. Stebbins**

Dictionaries and Encyclopedias

151. Black, John. **A Dictionary of Economics.** New York, Oxford University Press, 1997. 507p. (Oxford Paperback Reference). $12.95pa. ISBN 0-19-280018-3.

A Dictionary of Economics is a compilation of technical terms used in economics, along with terms from the related disciplines of statistics, finance, and general business. Written for British readers, its intended audiences are good students of economics in undergraduate courses and lay readers of such journals as *The Economist*. The high quality of the book makes it a useful reference for U.S. readers, although the pervasive Britishness of the writing imposes some limits on its usefulness outside the United Kingdom.

The core material—definitions of the technical terms used in economic writing—is first class throughout. The range of terms defined is broad, and the definitions are models of good writing: clear, accurate, and concise. Aside from the minor need to adjust to British English spellings (e.g., labour), the U.S. reader will have no trouble here. The treatment of statistical and econometric terminology is equally effective.

The less central material in the book is more severely limited by its British focus. Readers familiar with usage differences will not be slowed down by references to "flats" and "holidays," but some students may find these differences distracting. More serious is an apparent bias toward British usages in business jargon. For example, the term "white knight" is listed, but not "greenmail" or "poison pill." The dictionary lists "pay controls" and "death duties," but not "wage controls" or "estate taxes." "Golden handshake" is defined, but not "golden parachute."

Coverage of U.S. government activities is hit or miss. The generic discussion of social security benefits uses only U.K. examples, and there is no entry for FICA. The Bureau of Economic Analysis gets an entry, but not the Bureau of Labor Statistics. Also the U.S. business censuses, such as the Census of Manufactures and the Census of Retailing, are not listed.

Although somewhat selective, the dictionary does an adequate job of covering tertiary material. It touches on major environmental issues, for example. Even with its real limitations for U.S. audiences, the dictionary provides a useful supplement for U.S. students of economics and business, due mainly to its excellent treatment of the technical language of economics and econometrics.—**Ray Olszewski**

152. **An Encyclopedia of Keynesian Economics.** Thomas Cate, Geoff Harcourt, and David C. Colander, eds. Northhampton, Mass., Edward Elgar, 1997. 638p. $235.00. ISBN 1-85898-145-X.

John Maynard Keynes merits a voluminous treatment, and so do the many writers who contributed to Keynesian economics. Some 110 of them are included in this encyclopedia, with approximately 140 contributors who each give a synoptic account of the creators of Keynesianism or of its key concepts, such as the liquidity trap, incomes policies, the relative income hypothesis, or the IS/LM model; of institutions, such as the Keynes proposal for an International Clearing Union; and schools of thought, such as the Lausanne School, which provided some antecedents of Keynesianism. Each entry contains references to related subjects or persons, and each has a useful—and sometimes, as in the case of William Baumol, extensive—bibliography. Important contributors, at the present time rarely mentioned (as in the case of Ragnar Frisch), are preserved here for interested scholars. Some of the items in this reference source summarize the overall influence of Keynes, as on national income accounting, or on the question of "what remains of Keynes?" Other items provide a view of alternative schools of economic thought, such as the classical, the monetarist, and the new classical, thus deepening the intellectual content of this encyclopedia. This reviewer found using this source exhilarating and endowed with additional interest in view of the 1997 discussion on the inclusion or noninclusion of Keynesian economics in introductory economics textbooks. The editors should be applauded for helping to preserve a part of intellectual heritage.

—**Bogdan Mieczkowski**

153. Folsom, W. Davis. **Understanding American Business Jargon: A Dictionary.** Westport, Conn., Greenwood Press, 1997. 235p. $65.00. ISBN 0-313-29991-9.

Folsom's dictionary is designed to be a practical reference tool for students, managers, and international businesspeople trying to understand the patois of U.S. business. The entries are arranged alphabetically, in an unconventional letter-by-letter scheme, in order to accommodate the large number of multiword phrases that occur in business jargon. An added, welcome feature is the frequent inclusion of quotations from business periodicals and newspapers, where the term is used in context. The author has also supplied a list of acronyms often used in the business environment.

Folsom's work is useful for the intended audience, especially foreigners. Unfortunately, he does not explain the criteria for including terms in his dictionary. A bibliography of similar dictionaries is provided, and the user will infer that this, as well as the sources used for quotations of the words used in context, constitute the base from which his terms were culled. In spite of this lexicographical lapse, and some minor typographical errors in some terms (e.g., "bib leagues" for *big leagues* and "xeriod" for *xeroid*), students of U.S. business should value this dictionary highly.—**Robert H. Burger**

154. **Knowledge Exchange Business Encyclopedia.** Lorraine Spurge, ed. Santa Monica, Calif., Knowledge Exchange, 1997. 747p. illus. index. $45.00. ISBN 1-888232-05-6.

As business becomes increasingly complex, new concepts and techniques evolve to enable further expansion of knowledge and to promote communication. Consequently, the already large number of business terms constantly increases, making it difficult to keep abreast. *Knowledge Exchange Business*

Encyclopedia provides an accessible, concise, and comprehensive source of current business knowledge. It serves the business student just learning business terminology and technology, as well as the seasoned manager who wants to keep informed. Although designed as a reference volume, colorful illustrations, sidebars highlighting important points, numerous examples, and a precise yet relaxed style of presentation invite casual reading as well.

Profiles of business leaders, key industries, and selected growth companies furnish useful and interesting insights into U.S. business. An index of entries by discipline, a general index, and the use of cross-references enable readers to easily locate terms of specific interest. Data tables summarizing the U.S. economy add to the broad spectrum of useful knowledge condensed into this single volume. The book is attractive as well as authoritative and offers excellent value. In future editions, the editor may wish to consider including one or two suggestions for further reading with respect to complex topics for which it would be impractical to include extensive details.—**William C. Struning**

155.   Krouglov, Alexander, Katya Kurylko, and Dmytro Kostenko. **English-Ukrainian Dictionary of Business.** Jefferson, N.C., McFarland, 1997. 119p. $28.50. ISBN 0-7864-0301-2.

This Ukrainian dictionary contains current English terminology used in business sectors. Approximately 1,700 entries consist of the required form of a word, various translations, interpretations, and useful phrases. The dictionary is compiled alphabetically; English word combinations are provided in alphabetic order under the corresponding keyword, regardless of whether or not the keyword appears first in the phrase. Within each entry, the word combinations are listed alphabetically according to the English word beginning the phrase.

There are 2 so-called sections in the dictionary: The English section includes about 15 percent of the dictionary's mass, and the Ukrainian section contains 85 percent. The words in the English section have their grammatical categories indicated. If a word is used only in the singular or plural, this too is indicated in parentheses. Where English terms yield more than one equivalent in Ukrainian, the Ukrainian words are listed according to the following convention: synonyms are separated by commas, whereas words of similar meaning are separated by a semicolon. Different meanings of the same term are enumerated. All nouns in the Ukrainian section, other than those appearing in oblique cases, have their definitions followed by their gender, and if the noun is used in the plural, a plural marker is used. Words having more than one syllable have their stress indicated. There is also a list of abbreviations at the end of the dictionary. The user is advised that English does not have a single norm for fixing the forms of abbreviations or acronyms.

Although designed for Ukrainian businesspeople, the dictionary's value extends mostly to professional interpreters and trade consultants who do not know updated Ukrainian well enough to read this book. In today's Ukraine, readers prefer to use English words, such as *display* and *printer*, *standard* and *progress*, *dispute* and *discussion*.—**Ludmila N. Ilyina**

156.   **Routledge German Dictionary of Business, Commerce and Finance: German-English/English-German. Wörterbuch für Wirtschaft, Handel, und Finanzen Englisch.** New York, Routledge, 1997. 961p. $125.00. ISBN 0-415-09391-0.

This impressive dictionary is truly a team product that economically comprises maximum information on its double-column pages. Sections on features, the use of the source, and abbreviations allow the user to make the most of this compendium, while the appendix includes business correspondence (including a handy job application for the translator who uses this dictionary); job titles; a list of stock exchanges in North America, the United Kingdom, and France; financial and economic indexes; basic translation information on countries; and a table on cardinal and ordinal numbers. The latter is a source of a minor criticism because periods and commas that have opposite meanings on the continent and in the United States are not shown, and so 1,000 could be translated as meaning 1.000.

The two main parts of the dictionary are compendious and well done, including examples of the use of words. They show some difficulties in translation as well. For instance, *venture capital* has no strict equivalent in German, and is rendered by several descriptive translations, whereas *Fertigkeit* is translated as *person skill* instead of *personal skill(s)*. Among the useful and interesting features this reviewer found was the distinction between English and American terms (there are also distinctions between Swiss and Austrian German), and information about the obsoleteness of some terms. Thus, this dictionary allows the user to keep up with changing language norms. Cross-references expand the choices available to translators. Translations are conveniently divided into the areas to which they pertain, such as accounting, banking, finance, or law. Grammar is stressed, while grammatical codes allow the translator to avoid some potential pitfalls, as do indications of formal, informal, and jargon uses. The value of this extensive dictionary increases with the inevitable expansion of commercial relations within the European Union and between Germany and the English-speaking world.—**Bogdan Mieczkowski**

157. **Wiley's English-Spanish, Spanish-English Business Dictionary.** By Steven M. Kaplan. New York, John Wiley, 1996. 580p. $19.95pa. ISBN 0-471-12665-9.

Obtaining accurate terminology in the rapidly changing field of international business has always presented librarians with a challenge, beginning with the appearance of I. de Veitelle's *Mercantile Dictionary* in 1864. Since the late 1980s, both British and American publishers have produced reference works addressing the needs of companies and individuals dealing with the expanding markets of the Hispanic world. The present original volume is based on American English and offers extensive coverage of more than 40,000 words and phrases from the fields of accounting, advertising, commerce, economics, finance, trade, taxation, securities, banking, real estate, management, and insurance. Acronyms and abbreviations are not included. A particularly useful feature for speakers of either language is the arrangement of entries by phrasal groups based on a common first term. The author has compiled three other similar bilingual dictionaries in business, psychology and psychiatry, and law (for example, see entries 157 and 519). An inexpensive price makes this an essential addition to all reference collections, although public libraries and university collections supporting degree programs in all business fields will find it most useful.—**Robert B. Marks Ridinger**

Directories

158. **Business: Name & Business Type Index.** [CD-ROM]. Carter Lake, Iowa, PhoneDisc, 1996. Minimum system requirements (Windows version): IBM or compatible 386XT. CD-ROM drive. DOS 3.1. Windows 3.1x. 4MB RAM. 1MB hard disk space. Minimum system requirements (Macintosh version): Macintosh Plus/Classic. CD-ROM drive. System 6.04. 1MB RAM. $39.95.

Included in one CD-ROM are the names, addresses, telephone numbers, Web addresses, Metropolitan Statistical Areas (MSA), and Standard Industrial Classification (SIC) codes for U.S. businesses. The documentation did not say how many businesses the product included, but a quick search showed that more than 983,000 businesses started with "A." Indexes by name and SIC provide quick access, and a count button tells how many records were in the list. Two clicks of the mouse lead to 54,082 travel agencies.

Advanced search features allow the user to locate information using alternative spellings of last names; alternate first names, such as "Bob" for "Robert"; and first initial matches. The search can be done for anywhere in the city, state, or country. A user can further refine a search by specifying criteria for address, telephone, MSA, part of a name, and the radius from a geographic center. The user can store a geographic center location in the program by its 5-digit zip code, its latitude and longitude using a reference point from the NAD-1927 datum, or a reference point from a global positioning system (GPS) receiver. According to the documentation, a GPS receiver plugged into the computer will show and update the user's current location in real time on the screen. Travelers with laptops and CD-ROM drives can use this feature to direct themselves to their appointments. The help system also discusses several GPS manufacturers and describes GPS status messages.

There are several features that make this product valuable. Installation on the hard drive is optional, and the program runs fast from a CD-ROM drive. There are customization options for screen presentation and several options for directly dialing the phone number from the computer. Finally, printing address labels, including postal barcodes, is simple.

The major problem of the program is that the content is static. The only option for updating records is to buy an upgrade or export the information into another application and update it manually. The information's benefit is problematic, especially if the user lives in an area like Seattle, Washington, where one area code has recently split into three.—**Susan D. Baird-Joshi**

159. **Hoover's Billion Dollar Directory: The Complete Guide to U.S. Companies.** Austin, Tex., Hoover's, 1997. 1200p. index. $149.95. ISBN 1-57311-019-1.

Hoover's is known for producing attractive, easy-to-use business directories featuring concise company profiles. *Hoover's Billion Dollar Directory* focuses on publicly traded U.S. companies. Each entry includes address, telephone, and fax number; CEO; CFO; fiscal year-end; ticker symbol; and Website address, if available. Five years of financial data are given, followed by a summary describing the company's business. Three indexes provide access to the companies by industry, headquarters location, and ticker symbol. A company rankings section lists the top 500 companies by sales, market value, and 3-year sales growth. Although this directory is fairly straightforward, there are a few caveats. *Hoover's Billion Dollar Directory* excludes companies traded on the U.S. stock exchanges but headquartered in other countries, such as Glaxo Wellcome or British Airways. Also, the directory assumes the parent company name is known, and no subsidiaries are listed. A separate index of companies with *see* references would be helpful to aid in locating entries in the directory. Libraries owning Standard & Poor's *Stock Reports* will not find this to be a necessary purchase. However, students and job-seekers researching companies will like finding directory information, company background history, and financial data all in one volume.—**Barbara E. Clotfelter**

160. **Peterson's Guide to MBA Programs 1998: A Comprehensive Directory....** 3d ed. Princeton, N.J., Peterson's Guides, 1997. 1193p. illus. index. $24.95pa. ISBN 1-56079-862-9. ISSN 1080-2533.

Published annually, this comprehensive directory of MBA programs in the United States, Canada, and international business schools provides information on some 900 institutions with full-time, part-time, joint-degree, distance learning, and executive MBA and master's-level business programs. In addition to introductory information about choosing, getting admitted, and paying for the MBA, this annual directory offers well-written profiles for individual institutions, providing necessary details about graduate business programs, admission requirements, faculty, finances, international students, and placement. In a separate section called "Highlights," the student will find brief information about enrollment (full-time, part-time, average age, average class size, and so forth). All in all, this is probably the best directory of MBA programs available.—**Bohdan S. Wynar**

161. Schraepler, Hans-Albrecht. **Directory of International Economic Organizations.** Washington, D.C., Georgetown University Press, 1997. 460p. index. $65.00. ISBN 0-87840-633-6.

This comprehensive directory covers some 90 main organizations or their groupings, some with additional affiliated organizations. The information includes addresses; the legal basis; objectives; membership; structure; and activities, including publications. The main parts cover the United Nations system, according to its functional divisions; the British Commonwealth regional organizations by areas (with an omission of the Andean Pact); and the banks and funds covered by geographic areas of operation. Separate sections provide more than 300 abbreviations of names of the various international organizations and institutions; historical dates; tables of the membership of major international groupings (demonstrating, among others, the virtual isolation of North Korea); and an index.

The directory is an excellent source of data, although it fails to list bibliographic sources for researchers interested in particular organizations. It is up-to-date, listing as it does various post-Soviet organizations and memberships, and it perceptively indicates the increasing role played by international organizations within the framework of growing global interdependence. The resource is highly recommended for reference libraries, including those of multinational enterprises.—**Bogdan Mieczkowski**

Handbooks and Yearbooks

162. **Extractives, Manufacturing, and Services: A Historiographical and Bibliographical Guide.** David O. Whitten and Bessie E. Whitten, eds. Westport, Conn., Greenwood Press, 1997. 523p. index. (Handbook of American Business History, v.2). $115.00. ISBN 0-313-25199-1.

It has been 7 years since the publication of volume 1 of the Handbook of American Business History series (see ARBA 92, entry 206). The original volume focused on 23 manufacturing industries, as defined by the Enterprise Standard Industrial Classification (ESIC). This 2d volume adds 16 industries, including printing and publishing, and 4 chapters on transportation. Each contributor was given tremendous latitude by the editors; the result is a lack of coherence in style, scope, and coverage. The introduction serves as a guide to each chapter and updates the general business history bibliography from the original volume. It mentions the prevalence of computers and telecommunications in today's business environment but fails to provide an update to the industries that were covered in the first volume. Each chapter provides a concise history of the industry with an emphasis on bibliographies. The index is excellent.

Using the industries defined by the largely unknown ESIC is a surprising choice. The use of a more widely used classification system, such as the upcoming North American Industrial Classification System or the International Standard Industrial Classification, would have made the work more compatible with business research. Because of the amount of time passed between volumes, the original entries are now only useful for historical research. If this pace continues, it will take decades for the entire system to be covered. The bibliographies and histories are valuable as a starting point for the junior business historian; however, the series needs much work.—**Bobray Bordelon**

163. Harris, Wayne. **CyberTools for Business.** Austin, Tex., Hoover's, 1997. 185p. illus. index. $19.95pa. ISBN 1-57311-025-6.

Hoover's, well-known for its directories, has created a basic guide to browsing the World Wide Web. Useful for experienced and novice searchers, the 100 sites described here are well-chosen, stable ones offering both user support and clarity of purpose. Organized in six categories, search engines are explained, and users are directed to news, advice, corporate, and investment data sources. Focused on features and benefits, each clearly written report provides basic information (e.g., URL, value) and an analysis of a site's pros and cons. All required costs are identified along with the benefits to be gained. There is a topical index and a directory of 4,000 corporate Websites, which should increase access to individual, company, and site names. The potential difficulties inherent in most guides to World Wide Web resources have been avoided by limiting content to the more stable sites and emphasizing Web use to save time and money. This volume will prove attractive to libraries at all levels as well as for individual purchase.
—**Sandra E. Belanger**

164. **Hoover's Handbook of Private Companies 1997.** Austin, Tex., Hoover's, 1997. 663p. index. $99.95. ISBN 1-57311-017-5. ISSN 1073-6433.

This handbook covers 600 major nonpublic business enterprises. Entries for 405 of these are brief capsules containing contact information (including World Wide Web site address), a paragraph-length company description, and the names of key officers and competitors. The remaining 195 organizations are covered in greater depth, each receiving a two-page entry that includes a history of the company and an overview of its current operations, along with expanded directory data and limited financial information—typically, sales and net income figures—for the most recent 10 years. The front of the volume offers lists ranking the companies by sales and number of employees and reprinting *Inc.* magazine's most recent list of the 500 fastest-growing private companies in the United States. The companies are indexed by industry and headquarters location, and a third index has entries for people, brands, and companies named in the profiles.

Hoover's handbooks and other publications have been well regarded for providing a great deal of information in affordable packages. Gathering information about privately held businesses is a challenge to the researcher and reference librarian, and since its introduction three years ago (see ARBA 95, entry 192), this handbook has quickly become a highly valued source. Especially useful is its inclusion of charitable and not-for-profit organizations and government-owned enterprises, all of which get minimal coverage in other sources of this kind. Since the earlier edition the editors have increased the number of organizations treated and, of course, updated the content. This is a title that continues to merit a place in any business collection.—**Christopher J. Hoeppner**

165. **Medieval and Early Modern Data Bank.** [CD-ROM]. Baltimore, Md., National Information Services Corporation, 1996. Minimum system requirements: IBM or compatible 386. CD-ROM drive. 3MB RAM. 480K conventional memory. 2.5MB hard disk space. Color or monochrome monitor. $395.00.

The purpose of *Medieval and Early Modern Data Bank* (MEMDB) is to provide research scholars with the opportunity to access, display, and generate reports of numerical data pertaining to European economic history from 800 to 1815 C.E. MEMDB contains four data banks with more than 210,000 electronic records produced by scanning pages from primary text materials. The databases include all currency exchange quotations compiled by Peter Spufford from his *Handbook of Medieval Exchange* (1986), prices drawn directly from *Inquiry into the History of Prices in Holland* (1946) by N. W. Posthumus, grain prices supplied by Rainer Metz and collected for the print edition of *Getreideumsatz Getreide-und Brotpreise in Koln 1368-1797* (1976-1977) by Dietrich Eberling and Franz Irsigler, and finally monetary data from *Geld, Wahrung und Preisent Wicklung: Der Neiderrheinraum im Europaischen Vergleich: 1350-1800* by Rainer Metz.

The ROMWright bibliographic search and retrieval software, developed by the National Information Services Corporation, provides novice, advanced, and expert search modes with full Boolean, proximity, and truncation capabilities for maximum flexibility in composing a keyword search. For the nonspecialist searcher unfamiliar with the technical language or the subject scope of each data bank, the AUTODEX (AUTOmatic inDEX), available in all search modes, is an indispensable search aid. As words are typed into a search field, the AUTODEX appears automatically with the closest word to the original input highlighted in the index. Each index term in the AUTODEX records the count of records in which the term occurs at least once, which simplifies browsing by revealing the depth to which a topic is covered in the database. The variant search feature expands retrieval by accommodating for plurals, compounds, and British or American spelling alternatives. Systems librarians can customize the software to LAN specifications and modify features of a particular search mode to fit the degree of patron experience with database searching. A variety of output functions allow patrons to tag records in a specified citation display and to choose among several full-record formats for downloading.

Originating as a project at Rutgers University sponsored by Research Libraries Group, MEMDB exists admittedly as an electronic version of previously published print resources. However, the advantage of the electronic version is that it allows the researcher to search all four data banks individually, concurrently, or in any combination, thereby liberating the scholar from the time-consuming tedium of consulting indexes to multiple print titles with multiple volumes often with confusing or clumsy cross-references. Moreover, the original documentation from the print resources is accessible when relevant in the notes field of records displaying numeric data. Consequently, the benefits of the print resources are not lost in the migration to an electronic format. The CD-ROM is recommended for purchase by university libraries with graduate programs in economics or history.—**David G. Nowak**

166. **Small Business Sourcebook: The Entrepreneur's Resource.** 10th ed. Amy Lynn Park and Eva M. Felts, eds. Detroit, Gale, 1997. 2v. index. $290.00/set. ISBN 0-8103-5798-4.

In the past year and a half, it has become more and more obvious that many businesses are communicating and trading via the Internet. It is not uncommon to see a company's World Wide Web address imprinted across the side of a city bus in a splashy advertisement. Recent survey statistics support this trend, and forecasts have been made that Internet-related commerce will increase from $15 billion in 1996 to $200 billion in the year 2000. Although small businesses have been slower to jump on the bandwagon, they can no longer ignore the Internet. The 10th edition of *Small Business Sourcebook* is significantly updated to respond to this trend. Included are company or personal e-mail addresses, Websites, and Internet databases for related resources. In addition, several small business profiles are combined, others are eliminated due to lack of interest, and a new emphasis is placed on rapidly growing new businesses such as those in the information industry.

The contents of this 2-volume guide are arranged in 4 major sections. The 1st, "Specific Small Business Profiles," lists sources of information to establish and run 312 types of small businesses as varied as nanny services, computerized billing services, convenience stores, and Internet/online service providers. Each small business profile includes annotated sources for start-up information, associations and organizations, reference works, consultants, libraries and research centers, computerized and Internet databases, sources of supply, trade shows and conventions, videos, trade periodicals, franchising opportunities, and educational programs. New to this section is licensing information. Section 2 covers general small business topics in 79 chapters on current issues, such as office automation, substance abuse in the workplace, customer service, and more. Each chapter organizes information sources under the same categories as listed in section 1. The 3d section, "State Listing," offers sources of assistance for each state, territory, and Canadian province. A new category in this section is the chambers of commerce. Other categories include small business development centers, better business bureaus, minority business assistance programs, financing and loan programs, incubators/research technology parks, educational programs, legislative assistance, and publications. The 4th section, "Federal Government Assistance," lists specific offices in 49 federal government agencies that address small business issues, programs, assistance, and policy. Of additional value to users are the glossary of small business terms, Standard Industrial Classification codes for profiled small businesses, a master list of small business profiles, and a master index.

This comprehensive and well-organized reference work should be among the first library resources a fledgling entrepreneur will want to look at as well as a resource for a seasoned entrepreneur who is considering business expansion. The resource is easy to use, and it is updated yearly. Librarians may also want to use it as a collection development tool.—**Elizabeth D'Antonio-Gan**

Indexes

167. **Business Periodicals Index. Volume 38: August 1995-July 1996.** Hiyol Yang and others, eds. Bronx, N.Y., H. W. Wilson, 1995, 1996. 2v. priced on a service basis rate. ISSN 0007-6961.

When was the last time you used a Wilson index? Chances are it was not recently. Today's libraries seem to have relegated print indexes of periodicals to use on only two occasions: when the computers are down, or for coverage of the years preceding available electronic indexes. In taking a closer look at the *Business Periodicals Index*, what one sees is a venerable index—solid and reliable, covering more than 400 periodicals. If people are accustomed to computerized indexes, they may be a little surprised to realize the citations are listed in alphabetic order by article title rather than by date, and they may find it restrictive to be limited to only one year's worth of entries.

Loaded with *see* and *see also* references, the index offers an alphabetic arrangement of subject headings followed by a section at the end giving book review citations. The subject headings can be quirky. The information is not difficult to find; it is just not where users think it will be. For example, there is no listing for "dress code," although "dress" leads to "clothing and dress," which has a *see also* reference to "Employees—clothing and dress." Most patrons want keyword searching, the ability to print full-text articles, and the immediacy of computerized indexes. Although this index offers none of these features, it remains a quality product. *Business Periodicals Index* is recommended for larger collections.
—**Barbara E. Clotfelter**

168. **Hoover's Handbooks Index 1997.** Austin, Tex., Hoover's, 1997. 245p. $34.95. ISBN 1-57311-022-1.

Since its introduction several years ago, the Hoover's Handbook series has been well regarded as a reasonably priced source of company information. This volume consists of three indexes. The first two list companies by industry and by headquarters location. The third integrates the main index from each of the four handbooks (*American Business* [see ARBA 96, entry 191], *Emerging Companies, Private Companies* [see entries 164 and 173], and *World Business* [see ARBA 96, entry 201]). The third index includes not only companies but also brands and people named in the handbook entries. In all, the series profiles about 1,400 companies.

The indexes are extensive and well prepared. However, because they appear simply to integrate what appears in the respective handbooks, the volume's chief value is in reducing the number of lookups required to locate desired material. Selectors are likely to arrive at differing conclusions as to whether this convenience is worth the price of a separate index volume. This is particularly true because many users are apt to know which volume is the appropriate place to begin a particular search, depending on whether the target company is public, private, or based outside the United States.—**Christopher J. Hoeppner**

169. **Index of Economic Freedom, 1997.** Kim R. Holmes, Bryan T. Johnson, and Melanie Kirkpatrick, eds. New York, Wall Street Journal and Washington, D.C., Heritage Foundation, 1997. 486p. maps. $24.95pa. ISBN 0-89195-240-3.

The *Index of Economic Freedom, 1997* measures the degree of economic freedom in 150 countries. The authors contend that the most important reason for world poverty is the repressive economic policies of governments and the existence of unequivocal relationships between the degree of economic freedom in a country and its prosperity. Furthermore, they condemn U.S. foreign aid as detrimental to the recipient countries. For each country the economic policy and activity are rated in ten areas: trade policy, taxation policy, government intervention in the economy, monetary policy, capital flows and foreign investment, banking policy, wage and price controls, property rights, regulation, and the black market. Chapter 4 provides a detailed explanation of the method used to construct the index. The findings of the study are illustrated with color-coded maps, statistically correlated curves, and tables that rank each country on each economic factor with cumulative index scores. The five countries ranked as having the greatest economic freedom are Hong Kong, Singapore, Bahrain, and New Zealand, with Switzerland and the United States tied for fifth place. The bottom five countries are Vietnam, Iraq, Cuba, Laos, and North Korea. Chapter 5 contains brief portraits of each country with a discussion of the 10 factors used to rank it.

This is the 3d edition of the *Index of Economic Freedom*, previously published by the libertarian Cato Institute. The index is constructed by the conservative Heritage Foundation and co-published with *The Wall Street Journal*.—**Peter Zachary McKay**

BUSINESS SERVICES AND INVESTMENT GUIDES

Dictionaries and Encyclopedias

170. Scott, David L. **Wall Street Words: An Essential A to Z Guide for Today's Investor.** rev. ed. New York, Houghton Mifflin, 1997. 433p. $12.00pa. ISBN 0-395-85392-3.

Since Scott's original dictionary (see ARBA 89, entry 193) was published a decade ago, the Dow Jones has risen 400 percent and many new instruments have appeared. In particular, the derivatives field has exploded. Three hundred new entries have been added to the 3,600 terms in the original edition. Even though some of the newer areas of interest such as inflation-indexed securities and PCS options are absent, this work seems to be the most comprehensive and timely investments dictionary available. By scanning standard professional and popular business serials for terms, Scott clearly defines in simple language most words that an investor would encounter. Although the focus is on investment terminology, the basics of accounting and economics are also treated. Acronyms are cross-referenced to their full terms. In the last few years, a number of similar titles by different authors have appeared. A major competitor is Richard Maturie's *Wall Street Words: From Annuities to Zero Coupon Bonds* (Probus, 1995). Maturi's guide includes more detailed definitions and textbook examples; the drawback is that his work defines about one-sixth the number of terms that Scott's does.

Practical investment tips from industry insiders are sprinkled throughout the guide. In addition, more than 60 case studies help to give the reader real-life examples of the terminology. The book concludes with nearly five pages of technical analysis chart patterns.

The sheer number of clearly defined terms coupled with its low cost make Scott's dictionary a must for all business reference collections.—**Bobray Bordelon**

Directories

171. Robertson, Malcolm J. **The Directory of Listed Derivative Contracts 1996/97.** New York, John Wiley, 1996. 366p. $150.00. ISBN 0-471-96368-2.

Financial researchers often need to know the markets in which an option or future is traded. Although other directories provide exchange listings and products, this work goes a step further by providing not only details about the exchange and its contracts but by including an index of contracts. An international view of the markets for a product is easily obtainable. This biennial directory covers more than 850 contracts traded on 90 exchanges in 40 countries. Individual options on equities are not listed. Because of the exponential growth in the number of contracts, this is a snapshot. Each exchange listing includes standard directory data, trading methods, key exchange methods, key exchange personnel, and an alphabetic list of contracts traded. The contract specifications detail contract size, delivery format, trading months and hours, quotation method, value, daily price limit, position limit, last trading day, and delivery day. For options, type and strike price interval are also given. The directory's easy-to-use format, detailed content, and unique indexing make it an essential tool for any reference collection serving investors or financial researchers.—**Bobray Bordelon**

172. **Walker's Manual of Unlisted Stocks.** San Mateo, Calif., Walker's Western Research, 1996. 513p. index. $75.00. ISBN 0-9652088-9-3.

What is the difference between publicly held companies, whose securities are listed and traded on stock exchanges or markets such as the New York Stock Exchange or the National Association of Securities Dealers Automated Quotation System, and those traded through market makers? Although obvious differences are size and number of shareholders, another difference lies in criteria for listing, which include asset base, number of shares publicly traded, and total market value of traded shares. Some companies choose not to list their shares because of high listing fees, annual and quarterly filing requirements by the Securities and Exchange Commission, public exposure on management decisions, and interference by outside investors.

The companies listed in this title are those either sold on regional exchanges (Boston Exchange, Chicago Exchange, Pacific Stock Exchange [now the Pacific Exchange]) or over-the-counter (either through the online bulletin board or the printed Pink Sheets). The profiles include a company description (name, address, telephone number, and a brief note on the company's business); per-share information (stock price for a given year or period, earnings per share, price/earnings ratio, book value per share, price/book value percentage, and dividends per share); annual financial data; compound growth percentages; comments; officers and ownership information; and other information, including the transfer agent, auditor, market maker, broker dealer, location where the stock is listed, and so on. Historical vignettes on eight companies, including the Kohler Co. and Rand McNally, provide additional information on those firms.

There are several indexes: by company name, by geographic locale, by U.S. state, by Standard Industrial Classification code, by total revenues, by market capitalization, and so forth. The introduction, in addition to explaining the tables, discusses considerations for investors, such as performance, financial strengths, products and markets, and ownership. Public libraries, particularly those serving an investment-minded clientele, and business school libraries will find the work useful. Although there is no indication of how often the book will be updated, a compilation on at least an annual basis would be helpful.
—**Sue Kamm**

Handbooks and Yearbooks

173. **Hoover's Handbook of Emerging Companies 1997.** Austin, Tex., Hoover's, 1997. 327p. index. $39.95. ISBN 1-57311-010-8. ISSN 1069-7519.

This work is now in its 4th annual edition and appears as one of a four-title series being made available by Hoover's as an indexed set (see entry 168). Others are *Hoover's Handbook of American Business* (see ARBA 96, entry 191), *Hoover's Handbook of World Business* (see ARBA 96, entry 201), and *Hoover's Handbook of Private Companies* (see entry 164). The aim is to provide vendors with accurate and authoritative information, and the method of inclusion is explained. The 250 companies profiled here have been identified as the hottest of the emerging companies from the standpoint of growth potential and future gains. These companies have been traded in the United States, possess revenues between $20 million and $1 billion, and have experienced sales growth of at least 25 percent over the past 5 years. In addition, they have had positive net income for the past year. Fully 135 companies have repeat status from the 3d edition; others have fallen off the pace, been merged or acquired, or have grown mature and are no longer considered "emerging."

The handbook begins with a list of abbreviations, a table of contents, and an alphabetic list of companies profiled. A useful inclusion is a "list of lists," which provides 11 listings from Hoover's of top companies in different aspects, such as sales, quotas, stock appreciation, and the like. Eleven additional listings are given from other publications (e.g., *Forbes, Business Week, Fortune*). How to use the handbook is explained, and the sections of each profile are clarified. The overview provides a thumbnail description of the company (history, strategy, reputation); "Who" furnishes the names of officers and legal representatives along with their ages and salaries; "Where" identifies headquarters, addresses, key sites, and sales/profit information by unit; "What" enumerates products, services, and brand names; "Key Competitors" names rival companies; and "How Much" presents data on financial performance in six-year tables (earnings, sales, stock prices, and so forth). This section also furnishes year-end statistics on debt ratios, return on equity, and long-term debt. Excellent indexes are provided for locating profiles by industry; by headquarters location; and by brands, company name, and people.—**Ron Blazek**

174. **"How Much Can I Make?" Actual Sales and Profit Potential for Your Small Business.** 2d ed. Genevieve Graves and Minjia Qiu, eds. Oakland, Calif., Source Book Publications, 1997. 446p. index. $29.95pa. ISBN 1-887137-10-6.

This is the 2d edition of a book previously published under the title *Franchising: The Bottom Line*. The body of the work comprises earnings claim statements from 167 franchisers. These statements are financial information presented to prospective investors by franchisers based on the results of franchisees currently in operation. A detailed company profile accompanies each statement. The introductory section offers the authors' commentary on how to critically evaluate an earnings claim statement and worksheets for use in this evaluation, plus an overview essay and annotated bibliography about the franchising industry. Indexes, both alphabetic and by industry, complete the volume.

The author has written extensively about the franchising industry for many years and this work can be thought of as a complement to his *Bond's Franchise Guide* (see ARBA 97, entry 180). The *Guide* offers less extensive information on more than 2,300 franchise opportunities, whereas *"How Much Can I Make?"* provides much greater detail on only a fraction of that number. Thus, it is less a directory than a detailed presentation of the type of information an investor needs to consider before making an intelligent decision about pursuing a business opportunity. Even for investors who are not interested in a specific franchiser represented here, it would still be wise to examine others in the same industry for comparative purposes. Also, entrepreneurs who are interested in independently starting a small business that will compete with franchises in a particular industry will be well-advised to consult this book for insights into the economics of their chosen field. This book is recommended for collections serving entrepreneurs and small business owners.—**Christopher J. Hoeppner**

175. Shilling, Henry. **The International Guide to Securities Market Indices.** Chicago, Fitzroy Dearborn, 1996. 1030p. $125.00. ISBN 1-884964-48-6.

This interesting and worthwhile directory profiles more than 400 international securities indexes. Each profile contains a performance graph and record for the past 10 years, minimum and maximum values, average annual price return and total return, standard deviation, number of issues, market value, selection criteria, base date, computation methodology, deviation instruments, subindexes and related indexes, background, publisher/producer name, and short editorial comments. The introductory material includes common computational formulas, and examples of the math formulas are found in the 187 pages of appendixes. Any variation from the standard formulas is detailed within the particular profile. Other appendixes cover derivative instruments, a glossary, lists by asset size and country, and brief data on an additional 200-plus supplemental securities market indexes (mainly smaller secondary indexes or benchmarks of special interest).

The principal value of the guide is the coverage of how the indexes are computed. Reasonably priced for this type and size of directory, the work is clearly presented and easy to use. *The Handbook of Financial Market Indexes, Averages, and Indicators* (see ARBA 91, entry 171) also reviews major stock indexes but covers fewer and is dated. A WorldCat search found no other recent title covering the topic. The Fitzroy Dearborn guide is highly recommended for academic and larger public library business collections.
—**Patrick J. Brunet**

176. **The Topline Encyclopedia of Historical Charts.** March 1997 ed. Boulder, Colo., Topline Investment Graphics, 1997. 30v. index. $249.00/set looseleaf w/binders.

The Topline Encyclopedia is a 3-binder work comprising 30 sets of charts. The sets may be ordered in any combination at a lower price. Each set consists of 12 charts focusing on a particular variable or data series of interest to investors. These range from economic measures, such as interest rates and consumer prices in various countries, to foreign currency exchange rates, stock indexes, bonds, commodities, precious metals, and more. Each of the 30 sets begins with a detailed explanation of what the chart represents and how the underlying data were obtained and computed. The charts are printed on heavy paper and sold in looseleaf binders for easy copying. The publisher permits unlimited copying of all charts.

For investors and analysts looking for graphic presentations of investment data, this publication is a bonanza the likes of which will not be found elsewhere. Two things would make the encyclopedia even more valuable: presentation of the charts in machine-readable format and inclusion of the underlying data. The publisher maintains that the paper format allows much greater precision than machine-readable formats, and presumably licensing issues may preclude publication of the data. These considerations aside, *The Topline Encyclopedia* will be of real value to investors who want to go beyond tips and newsletters to take a careful, historical look at markets and the variables that impact them.

The publisher has long provided custom charts drawn to order. This publication makes the most commonly requested charts available at a reasonable price. The set is recommended for libraries serving investors, with one caveat—some of the included charts are, arguably, rather esoteric (e.g., Coppock Curves and the McClellan Oscillator), even for relatively sophisticated investors. Some purchasers may want to select a subset of the charts at a lower price.—**Christopher J. Hoeppner**

177. Troy, Leo. **Almanac of Business and Industrial Financial Ratios 1996.** 27th ed. Englewood Cliffs, N.J., Prentice Hall, 1996. 740p. index. $89.95pa. ISBN 0-13-520503-4.

Business students and investors frequently request industry-wide financial data. These data, often represented in the form of established financial ratios, allow the researcher to benchmark a company's financial performance relative to the performance of its competitors. Of the handful of competing publications offering industry ratios, Troy's *Almanac of Business and Industrial Financial Ratios* stands out as particularly easy to use and attractive in its layout.

Ratios are derived from corporate tax return information from the Internal Revenue Service and are organized according to four-digit SIC codes. For each SIC code, data are presented for 37 key measurements of financial health. For each of the 37 items, data are presented globally for all companies in the SIC code. In addition, the same 37 measurements are listed for categories of company size as determined by assets. This feature is particularly helpful for making meaningful comparisons because a company's size will often influence its financial ratios. An additional feature that proves to be particularly useful is a 10-year historical table showing trends for 13 key measurements. These tables provide a long-term perspective that is sometimes difficult to find in financial reference materials.

This book represents a good value for its price and is recommended for medium and large public libraries and academic libraries.—**David Bickford**

CONSUMER EDUCATION

178. Achar, Rajani, and others. **Shopping with a Conscience: The Informed Shopper's Guide to Retailers, Suppliers, and Service Providers in Canada.** Etobicoke, Ont., John Wiley & Sons Canada, 1996. 434p. index. $18.95pa. ISBN 0-471-64172-3.

Aimed at conscientious shoppers in Canada, this volume, produced by EthicScan, Canada's oldest and largest corporate social responsibility research firm, advances concentrated information about 10 major ethical concerns that can affect purchasing policies of individuals and organizations for 16 major service sectors. These concerns include gender and family issues, community responsibilities, progressive staff policies, labor relations, environmental performance, environmental management, management practices and consumer relations, sourcing and trading policies, candor, and Canadian content (the degree to which company decisions are made in Canada).

The text, directed at both potential customers and students of consumer studies, is well organized and highly accessible. The introductory information discusses the criteria used to formulate the ratings and the businesses included in the study and offers table summaries of the social, labor, and environmental performance of the individual companies analyzed. The assessment of these individual businesses, organized alphabetically within the service sectors, are then discussed in greater detail. Each entry includes background information on the company and its history in Canada, a brief summary of the findings for each of these issues, and the raw scores they obtained in the study. These scores are compared in rating tables within each sector. The service sectors are introduced with a brief discussion of the particular ethical challenges that they face. The policy of the authors is not to tell their readers what to think, but "just to offer the information." This tactic is carried out well, notwithstanding that some of the material is already dated; one of the major companies discussed, Consumers Distributing, is no longer in business.

—Gail de Vos

179. **The Essential Business Buyer's Guide.** By the Staff of *Business Consumer Guide*. Naperville, Ill., Sourcebooks, 1997. 436p. index. $18.95pa. ISBN 1-57071-130-5.

The staff of the *Business Consumer Guide* has created a handy volume filled with helpful and friendly advice regarding more than 110 business products and services. Although designed as an aid for the buying process, it also gives purchasers one less thing to worry about by identifying potential blunders. For instance: Some cordless telephones will not work during a power outage; if buying a paper shredder, one must be sure the power switch is easily accessible because neckties can become entangled; the U.S. Postal Service is the only business that can deliver to military addresses or post office boxes; and if a company uses a music-on-hold system, it should not play a radio station unless it has checked to be sure a competitor does not advertise on the same station.

The table of contents lists the topics alphabetically. Topics covered include 401(k) plans, beverage services, chairs, ground shipping, international callback services, off-site storage, recycling, safes, telephone systems, trade show displays, and video conferencing services. Each profile for the business product or service begins with a brief introduction, followed by a chart listing the major vendors. Buying points, pricing, and special tips are discussed and, depending on the topic, words or phrases unique to the topic are defined. An exhaustive index is provided, as well as a list of topics by category.

The staff of the *Business Consumer Guide* has also developed BuyersZone, a World Wide Web site. The icon for BuyersZone is included at the end of many of the profiles to indicate that additional purchasing information, vendor links, and user forums can be found on the Web. This title is practical, well planned, and affordable. It is recommended to all libraries.—**Barbara E. Clotfelter**

180. Kent, Cassandra. **Household Hints & Tips.** New York, DK Publishing, 1996. 192p. illus. index. $19.95pa. ISBN 0-7894-0432-X.

Divided into 9 sections, this little handbook dispenses wisdom with "more than 2,000 ingenious solutions to everyday problems in and around the home." It covers the basics of house cleaning, stain removal, clothes and laundry, care and repair, home improvements, home maintenance, food and drink, housekeeping, and health and safety. The neophyte is sure to appreciate this collection, and the more experienced will enjoy the convenience of having new and old tips collected together.

Copious illustrations and photographs are used throughout, whether necessary for clarity or not. For instance, lists of stain removal cleaners and solvents would probably fit the bill just as well as titled pictures of plain bottles and accessories. The pictures do make the book less text intensive and, therefore, probably more enjoyable for most readers. In other words, this book is arranged in typical DK format.

Special features include a quick reference box that denotes chapter contents at the beginning of each section and boxes with traditional tips, warnings, and safety information scattered throughout the text. In addition, there are five icons that pop up from time to time, presenting traditional wisdom, moneysaving and timesaving tips, bright ideas, and green alternatives that make chores go quicker, easier, or more efficiently. One of the most important features is the "Getting Organized" section at the beginning of the book, which points out the necessity for a home log book—one of the best tips for the busy household of today.

There are a few tips that the author might want to reconsider before another printing of this book. Of primary importance is the addition of a warning concerning the cold mixture recommended on page 179. Doctors warn that honey should not be given to children under the age of one due to the risk of botulism spores that their little bodies are unable to metabolize. Another item suggests a method for reviving dried mascara, which opthamologists recommend throwing out.

Although this book does not answer all house questions, it is a good overview of solutions to common problems. It is great for someone going "out on their own" for the first time or for anyone who would just like to have answers to a lot of life's little household problems in one book.—**Jo Anne H. Ricca**

181. **The National Directory of Catalogs 1997.** New York, Oxbridge Communications, 1997. 1159p. index. $495.00pa. ISBN 0-917460-85-5. ISSN 0163-7010.

This 7th edition of *The National Directory of Catalogs* contains close to 9,000 entries for business-to-business and consumer mail-order catalogs. The 1990 premier edition (see ARBA 91, entry 194) held slightly more than half that number of entries (approximately 5,000) and cost a mere $145.

The directory is arranged in 200-plus subject categories. Each entry lists catalog company name followed by catalog name, address, telephone and fax numbers, description of product carried, target audience, sales volume, catalog circulation, list rental information, payment information, frequency of catalog issue, number of pages and size of catalog, use of color, type of binding, paper stock, key staff names (including buyers), and name and address of management company if catalog is handled by an outside firm. A company name index; a catalog title index; and an index to companies by state, including Canadian provinces and Mexican states, are included. This directory is essential for businesses engaged in mail order, businesses wanting to start mail order, and businesses wanting to place products in the most appropriate catalogs. Special libraries in this arena will want to purchase this new edition if they do not have a recent edition. The *National Directory of Catalogs* is substantially more comprehensive than either the *Catalog of Catalogs* (see ARBA 95, entry 226) or the *Directory of Mail Order Catalogs* (9th ed.; see ARBA 96, entry 219).—**Thomas K. Fry**

182. **Orion Blue Book: Computer 1997.** fall ed. Scottsdale, Ariz., Orion Research, 1997. 744p. $375.00/yr. ISBN 0-932089-78-x. ISSN 0883-4881.

For 25 years Orion Research has been providing blue book values on equipment ranging from guns and cameras to power tools and car stereos. Their fall 1997 edition is a valuable asset in obtaining retail values for company's computer systems. Roger Rohrs, the publisher, has been thorough and accurate in his research for this volume. Acronyms and abbreviations used throughout the book are clearly displayed in the front matter, providing ease of use and classification. Several tips are available for retailers that are solid guidelines for the growing used computer industry. Orion provides two Internet sites and an e-mail address where demonstration products are available. Products purchased over the Internet are available with a discount. There is a directory of manufactures that details all of the vendors represented in the book and displays the contact information. With about 960 manufacturers, even small businesses are represented in the book. "Mom and pop" computer retailers are listed, and their contact information was verifiable. The book's detail is noticeable while browsing the volume; general specifications for all computer systems and items such as dot pitch for monitors and dots per inch for printers are included. Overall, organization is excellent, and the book is available on 3.5-inch floppy disk for DOS or Windows. This is one of the most comprehensive computer guides available on the market.—**Christopher Byrne**

183. Palder, Edward L. **The Catalog of Catalogs V: The Complete Mail-Order Directory.** Bethesda, Md., Woodbine House, 1997. 520p. index. $24.95pa. ISBN 0-933149-88-3.

The ease and convenience of mail-order shopping has led to the publication of this ever-expanding directory, now in its 10th year. Approximately 14,000 companies, grouped into nearly 850 subject areas, offer a diverse line of products, from tattooing and egg crafting supplies to toys and games. The catalog can create new business prospects and sales leads or supply craft buffs or gardeners, and it is intended for a wide range of shoppers.

Entries, arranged by subject sections and subsections, contain the name of company, the address, the telephone number, the cost of the catalog, and a brief description of the merchandise offered. An introduction alerts readers to possible problems encountered by mail-order customers, and a corporate index and subject index, with cross-references, help locate appropriate catalogs.

Although this catalog attempts to include the widest possible range of products, principal ones may be overlooked. The category "Suspenders" is included, whereas swimwear is not. At least one major mail-order company, Lands' End, does not appear in this directory. To the author's credit, it is his plan to periodically update, revise, and expand the information given, and he gives an invitation to submit suggestions for future editions, which should result in an even more complete catalog. [R: LJ, 15 Feb 97, p. 128]—**Anita Zutis**

FINANCE AND BANKING

184. Moles, Peter, and Nicholas Terry. **The Handbook of International Financial Terms.** New York, Oxford University Press, 1997. 605p. $95.00. ISBN 0-19-828885-9.

Authors Moles and Terry, members of the finance faculty at Edinburgh University Management School, have produced a first-rate reference volume covering 14,000 definitions of terms, concepts, laws, and institutions relating to financial markets around the world. Definitions are clear and usually concise. Common terms (e.g., callable, Paris Bourse, risk premium, expected value, index fund, Beta) are augmented by less common terms (e.g., binomial option pricing model, vertical bull spread, masharaka, facultative reinsurance), colloquial terms (e.g., beamer, repos, G-hedge, Baba, box, strips), and financial institutions (e.g., ICC, SVT, CVM). Several entries go well beyond definitions. These are particularly good and of greater length: risk, options pricing, options strategies, stock index, and Federal Reserve (of the United States). About 1,600 abbreviations and acronyms are listed and identified in a separate section; most are defined in the main text. Over 200 international currencies are listed by country separately—lek, pula, and dirham for Albania, Botswana, and Morocco. An excellent 24-page essay titled "Getting Going with the A to Z of Entries" introduces some operations of international financial markets.

Entries on the tools of statistics are understandably short, and thus the reader may require additional references. The *McGraw-Hill Pocket Guide to Business Finance* (see ARBA 93, entry 241) provides the coverage of the quantitative tools that this handbook lacks. A less complete and less expensive dictionary is Barron's 4th edition of *Dictionary of Finance and Investment Terms* (see ARBA 96, entry 220), which lacks the international scope of this book.—**Richard A. Miller**

185. **Plunkett's Financial Services Industry Almanac.** Jack W. Plunkett, Karen Barbier, and Robin Mina, eds. Galveston, Tex., Plunkett Research, 1996. 690p. index. $129.99pa. ISBN 0-9638268-4-0.

Plunkett's Financial Services Industry Almanac provides a timely and comprehensive guide to the financial services industry of the United States. The guide features profiles of 500 of the leading U.S. financial firms, including not only banks but companies offering services relative to investments, insurance, stocks, trusts, credit cards, tax preparation, financial data (software and processing), and online banking, as well as firms providing financial services via the Internet. In effect, the editors reach beyond traditional institutions to capture the broad panorama of firms that use recent technological, legal, economic, and cultural changes in the way U.S. companies and individuals manage their money. In this way, the book distinguishes itself from most others in the field, which are restricted to a particular area, such as banking.

Pertinent details of each entry include products and services offered; areas of specialization; names of key officers; addresses; contact numbers (telephone, fax, e-mail, World Wide Web); financial data (sales, profits, number of employees, amount spent on research); brands; areas of the United States covered; competitive advantages; opportunities for women and minorities; top-line salaries and benefits; growth plans; and special features. Care has been taken to make the guide user friendly by adding features such as a glossary; an overview (including excellent historical tables on U.S. and global economics and finances); a separate list of financial services contacts (addresses, telephone numbers, and Websites); reviews of key industries (e.g., banking, insurance); and lists of firms by industry and location. Useful information is offered on careers in various areas of the financial services industry.

Indexing of firms by alphabet, subsidiary, brands, selected affiliations, and apparent climate for women and minorities provides quick access for particular interests. A diskette is enclosed that contains essential data and reduces the effort required in creating, for example, mailing lists. Well researched and presented, this almanac is an excellent value in terms of information versus cost. It will appeal to a broad spectrum of library users. One hopes the publisher has plans to update this useful volume.—**William C. Struning**

186. Salda, Anne C. M. **Historical Dictionary of the World Bank.** Lanham, Md., Scarecrow, 1997. 281p. (International Organizations Series, no.11). $68.00. ISBN 0-8108-3215-1.

The International Bank for Reconstruction and Development (World Bank) plays an influential and often high-profile role in the economic development of many contemporary developing countries. Not only does it lend money, provide technical assistance, and influence economic and financial policies to these countries, but the adoption of its programs is seen as a stamp of approval that opens access to private international capital for a country. Despite this high-profile and often controversial role played by the bank, there are few sources that provide adequate information about the history, structure, and operation of the bank and its affiliate institutions. *Historical Dictionary of the World Bank* fills this gap. The 281-page book provides copious information about the World Bank that has hitherto not been available in any single volume.

The majoring of the book, covering pages 26 to 207, is devoted to the dictionary itself. This section provides entries on the World Bank's activities from such subjects as acquired immunodeficiency syndrome (AIDS) to world tables. Each entry gives sufficient detail and is put in a historical context that makes it understandable and enjoyable to read. Part 3 of the book is a statistical appendix that furnishes information on membership, capital subscription, and lending activities of the bank. Part 4 is a comprehensive list of the bank's publications. Perhaps the most interesting and informative part of the book is the introductory chapter covering the first 25 pages. In this short section, the author brilliantly describes the historical context within which the bank was created; the major personalities behind its creation; objectives of the bank, its growth, and changes in objectives; the structure of the bank; and how some of its affiliates came to be created. The historical chronology of events that precede the introduction makes the book user friendly. The book is also well written.

By putting the activities of the World Bank in a historical context, this book will do more to educate the public about the bank than any effort the bank itself may produce. The dictionary is recommended for all who are interested in the activities of the World Bank.—**Kwabena Gyimah-Brempong**

187. **Walker's Manual of Community Bank Stocks.** Lafayette, Calif., Walker's Manual, 1997. 1v. (various paging). index. $100.00. ISBN 0-9652088-7-7.

Community banks are often the lifelines of small towns. They provide a source of investment for local inhabitants and loans for area businesses and citizens and, according to *Walker's Manual of Community Bank Stocks*, can be good investments that supply consistent returns. The manual covers 502 community banks that are traded over-the-counter. As a handbook, the manual serves two possible functions: as an investment analysis guide and as a local banking directory.

The manual does not try to give investment advice. Instead, it provides ownership and officer information, loan mix, per share information, annual financial data (1993-1996), and financial comments. This information can be used to measure performance and financial strength. Indexes by financial measures and ratios also give useful financial information. For some of the banks, the data can be easily obtained from Securities and Exchange Commission (SEC) information. However, many of the banks do not have to file with the SEC, and the data are more difficult to obtain. The profiled companies are not ones that services such as Value Line normally cover. As with any handbook, one would have to supplement the information furnished with other sources.

The majority of the banks are listed in major comprehensive banking directories. Standard directory information is given. A brief profile is supplied with the founding date. In addition to the financial indexes, there are indexes by geographic area and additional company name cross-references. An appendix lists World Wide Web addresses for approximately 10 percent of the companies. *Walker's Manual of Community Bank Stocks* is more appropriate for libraries providing investment advisory services than research libraries.—**Bobray Bordelon**

188. **World Economic Outlook, May 1997: A Survey by the Staff of the International Monetary Fund.** Washington, D.C., International Monetary Fund, 1997. 207p. (World Economic and Financial Surveys). $35.00pa. ISBN 1-55775-648-1. ISSN 0256-6877.

World Economic Outlook is published as part of the International Monetary Fund's (IMF) study of economic developments and policies in its member countries and in the global economic system. The IMF published this series annually from 1980 through 1983, and has published it biennially since 1984.

The focus of the May 1997 volume is "Globalization: Opportunities and Challenges." Presented are historical statistics and projections in the forms of charts and tables, with accompanying analysis in essay format by IMF staff. Statistics are given for both advanced economies and developing countries. The volume is composed of the following sections: global economic prospects and policies; world economic situation and short-term prospects; meeting the challenges of globalization in the advanced economies; globalization and opportunities for developing countries; integration of transition countries into the global economy; and globalization in historical perspective. The statistical appendix consists of tables plus a list of country classifications and compositions of groups for advanced economies and developing countries.

The tables provide both historical data and projections for categories of output, inflation, financial policies, foreign trade, current account transactions, balance of payments and external financing, external debt and debt service, flow of funds, and medium-term baseline scenario. For most of the tables, historical data are presented for 1989-1996, with projections for 1997 and 1998. This volume and its series provide needed data for the study of the international economy and country comparisons. It is highly recommended to academic and research library collections.—**Lucy Heckman**

INDUSTRY AND MANUFACTURING

189. **Business & Industry.** [CD-ROM]. Beachwood, Ohio, Responsive Database Services, 1997. Minimum system requirements: IBM or compatible 386. CD-ROM drive. DOS 3.0. Windows. 8MB RAM. 7MB hard disk space. $2,397.00/yr./single user. (Other pricing options available).

Business & Industry is an extensive and practical electronic database of some 350,000 records outlining business information that has been compiled from more than 700 business trade magazines, regional newspapers, newsletters, international trade journals, and business dailies from more than 30 countries. Approximately 60 percent of these records contain the full text of articles, and the remaining records are abstracts. Despite covering a diverse array of business publications, entries within this database seem to consistently gather together the various facts, figures, and events contained within these published articles. Data, tables, and rankings are provided in a concise and factual manner for a great many companies, products, markets, and industries. As a CD-ROM, this is a handy reference device because users can readily search this large database by word, business subject, company, industry, brand names, and slogans as well as by publication date, journal name, and geographic areas.

A variety of users may benefit from and use this database in alternative ways. Academic users will most likely be interested in developing and comparing case studies and research papers. The relevant and timely material will be useful and necessary for consultants. Practitioners, investors, and prospective job candidates can review and evaluate companies, markets, and industries. Searches can be modified to detect specific information, as well as providing the ability to survey large amounts of data quickly and efficiently. The database's search engine also sorts the results by the frequency of selected search terms. Another useful and practical feature of this database is its ability to display a search history, which is invaluable to any user conducting multiple searches. [R: LJ, 15 June 97, p. 107]—**Timothy E. Sullivan**

190. **The Directory of Business to Business Catalogs, 1997: A Comprehensive Source of Suppliers to Meet Most Day-to-Day Business Needs.** Lakeville, Conn., Grey House Publishing, 1997. 598p. index. $135.00pa. ISBN 0-939300-81-8.

This directory points people to companies that publish product catalogs to meet the operational needs of all kinds of businesses. Using this tool, a purchasing officer could locate catalogs that sell things to keep a company functioning, such as sanitation equipment, restaurant supplies, uniforms, or office equipment. Some of the more interesting types of products are optical equipment, including microscopes and fiber optic components; mailing list companies; business seminars; plastics; dental; gifts; and law enforcement and prison management. Companies represented cover a broad spectrum of industries. They include easily recognizable companies, such as Girl Scouts of the U.S.A., Breck's Dutch Bulbs, and the National Wildlife Federation. There are also specialty companies, such as National Parachute Industries and Antique Electronic Supply, which sells vacuum tubes and electronic parts.

A complete listing could include the following: contact information; e-mail, World Wide Web home page, and toll-free telephone number; a one-line description of the products in the catalog; officers' names; number of employees; sales volume; years in business; international distribution information; and the kinds of credit cards accepted. It also includes whether the company sells the catalog's mailing list and who manages the list. Some companies will also trade names. Finally, regarding the catalog itself, a listing could include the frequency of circulation, the name and address of the printer, and a one-word description of the stock, binding, printing method, color, and cost of the publication. In addition to a table of contents organized by subject, two indexes for company name and geographic location provide additional access points. Grey House Publishing also sells the directory listing on diskette as an ASCII text file, making it possible for users to upload the information into a database.

Any large service or manufacturing company, library, or school system would benefit from having this in its purchasing department. Any manufacturer or publisher that wants to sell products through a catalog could also use this to locate probable matches.—**Susan D. Baird-Joshi**

191. **Energy & Environmental Industry Survey 1997.** Ruth M. Bennett, comp. and ed. Lilburn, Ga., Fairmont Press, 1997. 109p. $95.00. ISBN 0-88173-281-8.

The 8,200 members of the Association of Energy Engineers were polled on their opinions of the energy and environmental marketplace and asked to provide salary data. The return rate was 8.6 percent, and this work is based on the returned surveys. They were asked to evaluate products and detail purchasing trends for energy management systems, lighting, motors, and drives. Other questions involved cogeneration and independent power production, energy services, and demand-side management.

A reproduction of the original questionnaire serves the purpose of an index, and the overall work acts as both a codebook and source of data. This highly specialized study is written for industry insiders and makes no attempt to explain terminology or acronyms. Researchers investigating the energy and environmental industry who need technical information and human resource executives seeking specialized compensation data may also find this survey useful. Results are only given for the current year; a time series would make the data more useful for comparative purposes. It is not mentioned when this annual survey was first conducted or if the data are available in machine-readable form. This work is recommended for special libraries in the energy and environmental industry and research libraries that have a strong interest in this field.—**Bobray Bordelon**

192. **Hoover's Company Capsules on CD-ROM.** [CD-ROM]. Austin, Tex., Hoover's, 1997. Minimum system requirements (Windows version): IBM or compatible. CD-ROM drive. Windows 3.1. 4MB RAM. 20MB hard disk space. Minimum system requirements (Macintosh version): System 7.0. CD-ROM drive. 4MB RAM. 20MB hard disk space. $449.95.

Containing key contact and business industry information on more than 10,000 U.S. companies, this powerful database would fill the needs of every marketing professional, corporate librarian, or business researcher. Developed in Claris's FileMaker Pro, the interface is intuitive, the search capabilities are strong, and the installation is easy. Each listing contains up to 65 bits of information about a company, including several fields the user can customize. The primary information given is company contact information; metropolitan area; the names of the CEO, CFO, and human resources executive; a brief description of the company; fiscal year ending; amount of sales for the previous year; how much the sales changed from the previous year; number of employees; stock exchange; ticker symbol; and primary industry. For a more in-depth analysis of select companies and their histories, one should refer to *Hoover's Company Profiles on CD-ROM* (see entry 193).

Full database capabilities exist. A user can edit, duplicate, and export existing records and import new or revised records. The operator can select which fields to export and choose from a variety of formats. Unfortunately, the headers do not export, and the program truncates the description. The import mechanism allows users to map their information to specific fields in the database before importing the records. All fields can be searched using free-text and wildcard characters; industry description and metropolitan area have drop-down lists. The operator can also sort by one of 10 fields and create address labels or letters for all records, the found record set, or one record.

The most useful and timely feature of the CD-ROM is the hypertext links in the database to a company's homepage on the World Wide Web and to a Website for stock trading information. For example, if a user's Internet connection is active, he or she can click on http://www.hoovers.com, and the Web browser will open to Hoover's Website. Clicking on the stock symbol for Weyerhaeuser Company will take users to DBC Online (http://www.dbc.com) and show the fundamental stock data for that company.—**Susan D. Baird-Joshi**

193. **Hoover's Company Profiles on CD-ROM.** [CD-ROM]. Austin, Tex., Hoover's, 1997. Minimum system requirements: IBM or compatible. CD-ROM drive. DOS 6.0. Windows 3.1. 4MB RAM (8MB for Windows 95). 4MB hard disk space. $449.95/single user; $549.95/2-8 users.

The computer-based version of Hoover's Handbooks (see entries 164, 168, and 173, for example), this product has interesting, lively profiles of about 2,700 public, private, and government-operated companies in the United States and abroad. Four key criteria influenced the selection of the companies: size, growth, visibility, and coverage of each industry. These factors lead to some obvious inclusions, such as Digital Equipment Corporation, UPS, the Big Six accounting firms, Chevron Corporation, and Harvard University. There are some surprising inclusions (the AFL-CIO, The John D. and Catherine T. MacArthur Foundation, Heineken N.V.) and omissions (Adobe and REI).

Like any good reporter, each profile answers the essential questions: who (chief officers and key competitors), what (products or services), when (history), where (location and primary geographic areas of business), why (mission and motivation), and how much (financials for up to 10 years and year-end statistics). Hypertext links point to competitors' profiles, but the links are difficult to activate. Unfortunately, Hoover's buried the subsidiaries, collaborators, and other important business partners in the text instead of putting them in a separate section.

The interface is user-friendly. Fifteen minutes of exploration will get the user up and running quickly. In addition to a sophisticated Find feature, five indexes (company name; headquarters location; industry; keyword; and "sounds like," or Soundex) provide additional entry points into the information. The writing is excellent—funny, irreverent, and full of puns, when appropriate. Microsoft, Inc., is "the 800-pound gorilla of computerdom." The Walt Disney Corporation's "Dumbo-sized acquisition" of ABC, Inc., "left its competitors looking goofy." Aladdin Knowledge Systems Ltd., a Tel Aviv-based company that manufactures hardware to prevent software theft, "sails the cyber seas" to prevent software piracy and keep "the software genie in the lamp." An excellent companion to *Hoover's Company Capsules on CD-ROM* (see entry 192), this product would be a good addition to any marketing group or academic business library's collection.—**Susan D. Baird-Joshi**

194. **International Yearbook of Industrial Statistics 1997.** By the United Nations Industrial Development Organization. Lyme, N.H., Edward Elgar, 1997. 680p. $175.00. ISBN 1-85898-632-X.

This yearbook is a thorough compilation of manufacturing and industrial statistics in the countries of the world. The book is handy for those in need of such information and is easy to use. This version is an update of the 1st edition (see ARBA 97, entry 196) and covers data for the years 1985 through 1994.

The initial 113 pages contain some general information: the manufacturing sector, the manufacturing branches (containing lists by major products), share of females in total employment by branch, and selected characteristics of branches. Part 2 (country tables) takes up pages 117 to 680. The countries, arranged alphabetically, begin with an introductory page and then three to five pages of statistics, arranged by category under ISIC number. The first table presents employment: number of establishments, number of employees, and wages and salaries paid to employees. The following table presents output in producers' prices, value added, and gross fixed capital formation. A final table lists index numbers of industrial production.

The products are arranged by category under ISIC number. These cover, for example, food products, printing and publishing, petroleum products, iron and steel, fabricated metal products, and professional and scientific equipment. These categories are then further broken down. By studying part 1, which lists products by country, and part 2, which lists countries with their products, one could learn the relative output of each.—**Barbara E. Brown**

195. **Manufacturers Phone Book USA 1997.** Detroit, Omnigraphics, 1997. 925p. $125.00. ISBN 0-7808-0299-3. ISSN 1092-1338.

The title of this specialized reference work aptly describes its contents. The book contains useful listings for approximately 41,300 U.S. manufacturing companies. The listings are categorized alphabetically by company name, geographically by state, and by product type. Each listing includes the company's address; telephone and fax numbers; and, where available, toll-free numbers, e-mail, and World Wide Web addresses. This book's primary audience is the business community, including manufacturers themselves, as well as marketing and sales departments, dealers, and others. It also could prove useful in an academic setting as a resource for researchers and for job-hunters.—**Paul F. Clark**

196. **Thomas Register of American Manufacturers, 1997.** 87th ed. New York, Thomas Publishing, 1997. 33v. illus. index. $210.00/set.

197. **Thomas Register on CD-ROM, 1997.** [CD-ROM]. New York, Thomas Publishing, 1997. Minimum system requirements: IBM or compatible 486. Windows-supported CD-ROM drive (double-speed or faster recommended). DOS 3.3. Windows 3.1. 16MB RAM. 5MB hard disk space. VGA monitor. Windows-supported mouse. Windows-supported printer. $210.00.

The *Thomas Register* is an extensive and comprehensive inventory of the many and diverse products and services available from U.S. manufacturers. Volumes 1 through 22 contain more than 56,000 alphabetically listed product and service headings. Within each of these headings is a list of manufacturers and suppliers arranged alphabetically by states as well as by cities within individual states. Scattered throughout these listings are advertisements that provide comparative details about various manufacturers and suppliers. Volumes 23 and 24 provide company profiles on some 152,000 alphabetically arranged U.S. firms. In a typical entry, the company's name is followed by a concise list of the firm's products, along with contact information, asset ratings, data on subsidiaries, and even if the company provides export services. Volumes 25 through 33 contain alphabetically arranged catalog descriptions, pictures, technical sketches, and diagrams of product lines for some 2,400 companies. Entries throughout this ample and impressive register are cross-referenced and indexed, which makes it a practical albeit weighty directory of the distribution, location, and activity of U.S. manufacturers and suppliers.

This directory is also available on CD-ROM. In its electronic format, the directory permits users to more easily search and compare information because items are indexed and cross-referenced. The CD-ROM contains an interactive tutorial to guide users through the practical features of the register. Users can not only search by types of products and services available, by company name, and by brand names, but also attach and edit notes to a specific record or company.—**Timothy E. Sullivan**

198. **WEFA Industrial Monitor 1997.** Priscilla Trumbull, ed. New York, John Wiley, 1997. 1v. (various paging). index. $59.95. ISBN 0-471-19946-X. ISSN 1093-6580.

As a tool for economic analysis of various industries, this annual work reviews more than 130 major U.S. industries. WEFA, a firm that provides economic forecasts, reports here on agriculture, mining, and construction; manufacturing; transportation, communications, and utilities; wholesale and retail trade; and various service industries. Each report examines the significant areas for that industry. For example, the chapter on retail trade begins with an analysis of supply and demand conditions as well as price trends for each industry. In addition, each section includes tables showing trends and forecasts. A valuable contribution in the industry structure section is a discussion of possible threats. Under "Food Stores," for instance, mention is made of potential competition with grocery chains by such retailers as Wal-Mart and Kmart because their new supercenters also sell food.

For some industries, however, the contributors to this volume appear to overlook an important trend—the influence of the Internet. Its effect on many industries, ranging from online real estate listings to online bookstores (such as Amazon.com), needs to be addressed. Despite the above omission, this industry monitor is a valuable reference tool for anyone who requires information on economic trends in specific industry sectors. Depending on user needs, the CD-ROM version (which is sold separately) also would be an important resource.—**Renee B. Horowitz**

INTERNATIONAL BUSINESS

General Works

Bibliographies

199. Schreiber, Mae N. **International Trade Sources: A Research Guide.** New York, Garland, 1997. 327p. index. (Research and Information Guides in Business, Industry, and Economic Institutions, v.12; Garland Reference Library of Social Science, v.1068). $55.00. ISBN 0-8153-2109-0.

Adding a title dealing with international trade should enhance the scope of Garland's Research and Information Guides in Business, Industry, and Economic Institutions series. Unfortunately, this title has only a slightly broader scope than Ruth Pagell's *International Business Information* (see ARBA 95, entry 255), but is not as comprehensive, accurate, or as detailed as this award-winning title. The one strength that the title at hand has over the Pagell title is the number of Websites that have been included.

The subtitle states that the volume is a research guide, but it is not a good resource for a researcher. Many of the titles listed do not indicate that they are 2d or 3d editions, others do not indicate that they have ceased publication, and some of the annotations are not very descriptive or at best incomplete. References to the Standard Industrial Classification (SIC) code have been included, although no mention is made that it has been superseded by the North American Industry Classification System (NAICS). This change has long been known, but Websites to NAICS have only recently been mounted. Some of the Websites that the author has included here have changed, but this is to be expected as the migration toward electronic resources continues.

Libraries that own the 1st edition of the Pagell title should wait for the new edition that is in preparation rather than acquiring this title. If there is a need for electronic addresses for government sites, there are books published by the National Journal or Congressional Quarterly that are published more regularly. Interest in international business is increasing, and resource publications in this area are multiplying. Unfortunately, this book does not serve its intended clientele well.—**Judith J. Field**

Directories

200. **International Directory of Consumer Brands and Their Owners.** London, Euromonitor; distr., Detroit, Gale, 1996. 553p. index. $450.00. ISBN 0-86338-694-6.

Business researchers and students will quickly and easily find comprehensive information about consumer brands and their owners worldwide, except for Europe, in this new directory. With its sister publication, *European Directory of Consumer Brands and Their Owners* (see ARBA 93, entry 288), this complete reference source provides comprehensive information on brands, their owners, countries where they are marketed, and competing brands in their specific product sectors. Both directories are included on the CD-ROM titled *World Database of Consumer Brands and Their Owners* (Gale, 1997). More than 16,000 brands and about 3,000 companies in approximately 60 countries are covered in the international directory.

This directory is divided into two sections with section 1 focusing on brands and their owners by product sector and subsector. The brands are classified alphabetically, including the owner's name and country, main product sector, product type, and a further product categorization such as the specific variety. Section 2 profiles the brand-owning companies, listed alphabetically by country, with a complete index of brand names and companies at the end of the volume.

Each company's entry includes contact data along with the names of key personnel, number of employees for recent years, details of sales geography, and manufacturing capacity. The table of contents and introduction also provide useful information to users. This information is a wonderful product but very expensive.—**Susan C. Awe**

201. **World Investment Directory 1996: Foreign Direct Investment, Legal Framework, and Corporate Data. Volume V: Africa.** By the United Nations Conference on Trade and Development. New York, United Nations, 1997. 462p. $75.00pa. ISBN 92-1-104475-8. S/N E.97.II.A.1.

Published as part of a United Nations effort to systematically gauge the world's $2.7 trillion foreign investment, this directory covers 53 African economies with 4 to 11 pages of pages of data each. Each country begins with definitions and sources of data and includes a brief summary of governmental policy toward foreign investment and its international investment position. Tables give investment flows, geographic distribution of investment (both inward and outward), largest foreign affiliates, index of the significance of foreign investment in the host economy, and a list of names for the largest foreign companies in the host economies (which is of particular value). Last, a list of national and international laws and treaties is provided, as well as a short bibliography of official and secondary sources used to compile the work. As with virtually all UN publications, there are extensive technical notes.

This title is part of a seven-volume series that covers each of the Second and Third World areas (see entry 207 for a review of the West Asia volume). The summary of governmental economic policy provided here is less useful than that of the World of Information's *Economic and Business Report: Africa Review*, which, in its textual review, complements this volume's tabular data. The closest title to compare is the International Monetary Fund's *Balance of Payments Statistics Yearbook*, which is as current and more detailed on type of investment but covers fewer years and is weaker on investment direction. Because *Balance of Payments Statistics Yearbook* is published annually and is slightly less expensive, libraries that need only one volume may want to chose that publication as a better value. The two works are, however, highly complementary, and libraries with serious foreign investment demand will want both.

The volume under review is done well and is reasonably priced for this type of reference. It is highly recommended for graduate business collections and large public libraries. Libraries that have country or regional collection strengths will find volumes in this set for their areas a worthwhile purchase.

—**Patrick J. Brunet**

Handbooks and Yearbooks

202. **Hoover's Global 250: The Stories Behind the Most Powerful Companies on the Planet.** Austin, Tex., Hoover's, 1997. 612p. index. $29.95pa. ISBN 1-57311-008-6.

This fine Hoover product gives two pages of useful data for 250 of the most influential, global business giants outside of the United States, with one giant flaw. The volume follows Hoover's standard format. One page is text, containing an overview of the company and the company's history. The second page gives officers (sometimes with compensation); location, telephone, and fax numbers; 1995 sales; key competitors; major products or services; a chart of 12 financials for 1986-95; a stock price history chart; and nine financials for the company's last fiscal year (either FY95 or FY96). The data is prefaced by 60 pages of lists, such as top 100 European stock companies or non-U.S. company stocks available through U.S. markets.

This title, like so many of the Hoover publications fills a need for low cost, reliable business data. Normally it can be stated that there is nothing comparable in quality and price and Hoover publications are a great value. However, Hoover has published the exact same material in hardback form under the title *Hoover's Handbook of World Business, 1996-1997* (Hoover's, 1996). The text and data are exactly the same except for the title, introduction, and the price ($44.95). This reviewer could not find any statement that tells the user that the material is a duplicate of the other title in either work, the Hoover Website, or in the publisher catalogs. Obviously the paperback is a better value. For content and utility, the Global 250 is highly recommended for academic and public libraries.—**Patrick J. Brunet**

203. **National Accounts Statistics: Main Aggregates and Detailed Tables, 1993.** By the Department for Economic and Social Information and Policy Analysis, Statistics Division. New York, United Nations, 1996. 2v. $135.00/set. ISBN 92-1-161381-7.

This is the 37th issue of this work (see ARBA 95, entry 254, and ARBA 91, entry 900, for reviews of earlier versions). It consists of statistical tables for 182 countries in 2 parts or volumes. Part 1 has tables covering Afghanistan to Jordan, and part 2 covers Kazakhstan to Zimbabwe. A four-page introduction describes the nature and organization of the work as a whole. A 14-page essay describes the System of National Accounts (SNA), which is used to describe data from "transaction flows in an economy." An 11-page essay describes the System of Material Product Balances (MPS), which is used to standardize data from centrally planned economies. Raw data are provided to the United Nations by each country, but the UN Statistical Division must then spend an immense amount of time formulating and applying the SNA and MPS in order to make the data as comparable as possible. Indeed, this work embodies a valiant effort to make the national accounts statistics as comparable as can be.

The table for each country contains (where available) statistics from 1980-1982 through 1992. A table can contain up to 51 categories of statistics, and the header for each country describes the peculiarities of the statistics for each country within the context of the SNA and MPS. The data presented are the best available, but for technical and political reasons the data are not identical for each country. The most obvious problem is that there is only a bare minimum of data for some countries, but there is a large amount of data given for other countries. Only gross domestic product and gross national product are given for the Russian Federation, but there are 40 pages of statistics for Sweden. As one would expect, the freer and more developed the economy, the more data are presented.—**Richard H. Swain**

204. **The Thunderbird Guide to International Business Resources on the World Wide Web.** By Candace Deans and Shaun Dakin. New York, John Wiley, 1997. 142p. maps. $21.95pa. ISBN 0-471-16016-4.

Although print publications of World Wide Web-accessible materials are often quickly out of date, this book provides organized and annotated information about many international business resources on the World Wide Web that are stable as well as valuable. It is organized by major geographical region, making it easy to find resources that are specific to a region or country. The table format for each entry is particularly clear and readable. This guide is recommended for use at a reference desk because the format will make it simple to make single copies or to add URLs to a local WWW electronic library collection. The coverage is restricted to WWW sites and does not include discussion lists, newsgroups, or other Internet-accessible resources. This outstanding book is strongly recommended for anyone using the Web for business research. [R: Choice, Jan 97, p. 766]—**Diane Kovacs**

205. **World Country Analyst.** [CD-ROM]. Detroit, Gale, 1997. Minimum system requirements: IBM or compatible 386 (486 or higher recommended). CD-ROM drive. DOS 5.0. Windows 3.1. 8MB RAM. SVGA 256-color monitor. Mouse. $425.00/stand-alone; $475.00/2-8 users. ISBN 0-7876-1638-9.

The *World Country Analyst* states that it provides businesspeople with economic and business information on foreign countries—drawing heavily from government sources—which is true. What is not stated is that this information is almost all available, and more, in *Department of Commerce's National Trade Data Bank* (NTDB), available on CD-ROM and in an online version through STAT-USA.

The *World Country Analyst* software proved difficult to install under Windows 95 until everything from the Windows startup menu was removed. There is a brief, yet reasonable, manual provided. Online help is meager, but the software is fairly easy to use and intuitive. The software is probably easier to use than that of the NTDB but is less sophisticated. A search can be done by country, topic, clickable map, full text, and custom search, including phrase and word searches using the functions AND and NOT. A full-text search on Mexico resulted in a screen showing a colored flag, a list of 429 topics, and the beginning of the text of the first topic. If Mexico is searched under country, however, only 132 hits are made. Clicking on one of the list of topics will display a single map in the right window. Unfortunately, the screen appears to use frames, so the text cannot be expanded to fill the whole screen. It is possible to print or download all or part of the document text, map, or flag, but not the list of topics. There is information on particular industries and the country in general, including topics such as human rights practices. Almost all of this information can be found on the NTDB, and although no credit or date is given for the individual source, it is obviously from the Department of Commerce's Market Research Reports and Country Commercial Guides, as well as from other departments such as State and Labor. Formatting of documents is sloppy at times, with stray lines at the beginning or end. This is most likely the result of poor division of longer documents. A few tables appear in a scrambled display. Aside from ethical problems of sources not being credited or dated, it is difficult for the user to know how current the information is, except for dates in the text itself. Most of the information appears to be relatively recent, although not as current as the NTDB. However, the labor trends document contains 1990-1991 data, whereby most libraries government publications depository collections have 1995-1996 foreign labor trends. Also, the original source's references to other sources for the user to consult are omitted.

Aside from the above issues, this is a source of considerable useful information for businesspeople, providing easy-to-use software. Anyone considering its purchase, however, should consider the other alternatives—the National Trade Data Bank on CD-ROM or a subscription to STAT-USA. Both contain significant information not present in the *World Country Analyst*, including references to other electronic sources. The NTDB CD-ROM may cost less for a single copy, and both NTDB and STAT-USA will provide more current information.—**Marit S. MacArthur**

206. Zuckerman, Amy. **International Standards Desk Reference: Your Passport to World Markets....** New York, AMACOM, 1997. 324p. index. $35.00. ISBN 0-8144-0316-6.

This is an excellent book on an important but often little noticed or understood subject of international standards. Standards can lead to better goods and services, help suppliers enter markets, and increase customer satisfaction. They can also be a major barrier to international trade, with their use in this regard growing as tariff levels are reduced. The primary audience for this well-written book is the people who run the companies affected by the standards.

Standards can cover many areas, such as product, quality assurance, health and safety, and environmental concerns. They can vary by industry and by country. The book explains how the standards are set and how businesses can comply with them. In the United States, compliance is largely through nongovernmental organizations, but in the countries of the European Union, governments are usually actively involved in their establishment and enforcement. The major players in international standards are groups in the United States and the European Union, but the book includes what is happening in Asia, South America, and many developing countries. Advice is given on what businesses need to know and how they should act to meet the standards for their industries. Numerous addresses are given to aid that effort. Even though the author makes an arcane subject filled with acronyms clearer, it will be necessary to supplement this text with more recent information, as this is a continuously changing field. [R: LJ, 1 Mar 97, p. 70]
—J. E. Weaver

Asia

207. **World Investment Directory 1996: Foreign Direct Investment, Legal Framework, and Corporate Data. Volume VI: West Asia.** By the United Nations Conference on Trade and Development. New York, United Nations, 1997. 138p. $35.00pa. ISBN 92-1-104476-6. S/N E.97.II.A.2.

This West Asia volume of the *World Investment Directory 1996* is one of a set of seven, six of which are geographic and the last an overview called *Global Trends*. Like the other regional volumes, its contents are arranged in three sections: introduction, technical introduction, and tables. Underlying the banality of these headings is a unique agglomeration of statistics and rankings drawn from published and unpublished sources. The introduction is a brief survey of the legal framework and foreign direct investment trends handled in eight pages of text and twice as many pages of tables. Appropriately referenced, there are two pages of endnotes. The technical introduction explicates foreign direct investment data by source, noting variations of definition in national and international legal and accounting practices. A necessary glossary explains the terms and categories employed throughout the work.

In the largest section, country tables (called "Tables" in the table of contents), nations from Bahrain to Yemen exhibit statistics and rankings, such as "Foreign Direct Investment Flows" and "Largest Foreign Affiliates in Host Country." A handy matrix chart in the technical introduction shows which countries have which of the 19 categories of data. This chart is quite helpful. For instance, one can see at a glance that five entire categories of data are lacking for the West Asian countries. Six other categories have only one to four nations reporting. Despite this weakness, key themes are covered for West Asia: foreign direct investment flow and its geographic and sectoral distribution, the geographic distribution of foreign direct investment stock, and rankings of the largest foreign and domestic corporations in and from the specified nation. The last country table is a useful compilation of the national laws and international treaties that would affect transnational corporations for each country.

The West Asia volume is recommended for collections used by patrons interested in research on trade with the Middle East, excluding Africa. (The Africa [see entry 201] and West Asia volume was split for 1996.) Six-volume sets were issued in 1992 and 1994, so the title appears to be biennial.—**Peter B. Ives**

Canada

208. **Canadian Company Histories, Volume 1.** Tina Grant, ed. Toronto, Gale Canada, 1996. 293p. index. $170.00; $125.00 (U.S.). ISBN 1-896413-06-4.

Gale Canada is a division of the same company (ITP Thomson) that owns *The Globe and Mail* in Toronto. This book details in 4 double-column pages the basic history of 80 Canadian companies that did $1 billion (Canadian) in annual revenues in their most recent reporting year. For some reason, ITP Thomson is not among these companies, even though competing media giants such as Southam and Rogers Communications are.

Arrangement is alphabetic by corporate name, and corporate logos are included in most cases. After basic directory data (names, addresses, Standard Industrial Classifications, incorporation date, stock exchanges traded on), there is a narrative profile written mostly on a freelance basis by one of 24 authors (usually from the United States). This profile is based on annual reports, newspapers, business news sources, magazines, and material from the companies themselves. Each profile concludes with a brief bibliography of recent books and articles and an author's name. At the back of the volume, there are indexes to companies, people, and industries. Overall, the book is fair, with balance in the profiles. However, the title is grossly overpriced for the announced audience (librarians, researchers, and students). Also, there is no indication of when volume 2 will appear.—**Dean Tudor**

Latin America and the Caribbean

209. **Consumer Latin America 1997.** 4th ed. London, Euromonitor; distr., Detroit, Gale, 1997. 359p. maps. $830.00pa. ISBN 0-86338-624-5.

Euromonitor's standard series format offers regional commentary with statistics derived from national, international, and Euromonitor sources. With the 4th edition, 2 countries previously included (Bolivia and Paraguay) have been excluded. Three of the eleven organizational sections present the relative strengths and weaknesses of the region, concentrating on important regional developments and economic factors; for example, inflation rates ranging from 3.4 percent (Argentina) to 84.4 percent (Brazil).

The remainder of the volume contains detailed background and consumer market data for each country; however, for effective analysis, other resources should be consulted, because the problem noted previously with the lack of analysis of business trends continues. Rather than a topical index, content and location can be pinpointed with the detailed table of contents and the list of tables. A comparison with the newly available CD-ROM version may eliminate both the analytic and access difficulties noted; the promotional literature describes the manipulation and comparison of data through calculations and charts that can be customized.

The Euromonitor series, although expensive, remains an excellent analysis of the trading environment and a useful statistical source for businesses, investors, and students of international business.
—**Sandra E. Belanger**

210. **Economic Survey of Latin America and the Caribbean 1995-1996.** By the Economic Commission for Latin America and the Caribbean. New York, United Nations, 1996. 335p. $75.00pa. ISBN 92-1-121215-4. ISSN 0257-2184. S/N E.96.II.G.12.

This volume is the latest issue of the annual *Economic Survey of Latin America and the Caribbean*, prepared by the United Nations since 1983. The 1st part contains sections devoted to such topics as economic policy, structural reform, finance, inflation, investment and saving, and employment and wages. In the 2d part, 8 to 10 pages are devoted to each country, covering general trends, economic policy, and the main variables, with statistics going back several years. The 3d part deals with Caribbean economics.

A list of tables and charts included in each part is given in the table of contents. A statistical annex is contained on two enclosed diskettes. The layout of the text is clear and easy to read. The text appears in double columns, but the charts and tables run across the page. On the whole, this is a useful cumulation of economic details for Latin America and the Caribbean. It is also issued in Spanish as *Estudio Económico de America Latina y el Caribe*.—**Barbara E. Brown**

211. **Hoover's Masterlist of Major Latin American Companies 1996-1997.** Austin, Tex., Reference Press, 1996. 149p. index. $79.95. ISBN 1-878753-69-X.

In a sense, this book may be looked upon as an inexpensive version or abridgment of D. Shave's monumental and expensive *Major Companies of Latin America 1996* (see ARBA 97, entry 247). The entries here are concise, with the barest minimum of information regarding the companies listed, a sort of "yellow-pages" telephone book. Nevertheless, for the price, *Hoover's Masterlist* is well worth the money if all one requires are addresses, telephone numbers, type of industry or commercial enterprise, and names of managers or officers.—**S. D. Markman**

LABOR

Bibliography

212. Switzer, Teri R. **Telecommuters, The Workforce of the Twenty-First Century: An Annotated Bibliography.** Lanham, Md., Scarecrow, 1997. 176p. index. $34.00. ISBN 0-8108-3210-0.

This book is an annotated bibliography on telecommuting, with its primary focus on telecommuting as an alternative to working in the traditional office. Some citations are to articles about home business. There are 649 entries organized into 7 chapters from a variety of sources, mostly magazines. The first 3 chapters on monographs, general issues, and management and human resource issues have 337 entries. Then come chapters on environmental, legal, and tax concerns; telecommuting programs (articles that discuss different real-life applications of working away from the traditional office); and hardware and software issues. The last chapter, on telecommuting resources, is broken down into sections on magazines, tapes, videos, and newsletters; directories; Internet resources; selected World Wide Web engines; selected Websites; reports, policies, and procedures; consultants; associations; and companies with telecommuters. The entries are largely dated in the late 1980s and early 1990s; the most recent were published in 1995. This book is likely to become dated quickly because the subject matter is rapidly changing, with relevant articles being published frequently. Libraries that allow patrons to use indexes and Internet access may not find this bibliography especially valuable.—**J. E. Weaver**

Dictionaries and Encyclopedias

213. **Career Discovery Encyclopedia.** Holli Cosgrove, ed. Chicago, J. G. Ferguson Publishing, 1997. 6v. illus. index. $129.95/set. ISBN 0-89434-184-7.

More than 500 occupations are described in this 6-volume set for upper elementary and middle school children. Each entry is two pages in length and includes a description of the work, training needed, salaries, demand, addresses to write for more information, and a picture of a person engaged in the occupation. Suggestions (such as potential auditors volunteering to be treasurer for a school club) are given for curious children who wish to further understand the skills and qualities needed for an occupation. Cross-references are displayed in a circle at the beginning of each article and invite the child to browse the volumes. Of use to librarians and teachers are the indexes—especially the general index and the index to skills groupings, which list occupations under such headings as "people skills" or "organizational skills."

The information is usually clearly and uniformly presented. Exceptions to this appear in the category "Outlook," which tells the reader, in a phrase, about the future. "Average," "About as Fast as the Average," and "Faster Than the Average" are rankings not explained, neither in the preface nor in specific articles. The authors also vary in describing salaries—some state the year(s) in which the salary is based; some do not. Although librarians will know to check the publishing date for a clue, most children will not. It is refreshing not to find this set a regurgitation of the *Occupational Outlook Handbook* (see ARBA 94, entry 281, and ARBA 91, entry 249), yet one wonders what the sources of the information are: government, industry, or personal experience? In general, this is a worthy set, with an engaging format and interesting descriptions; however, these aspects should be considered in the next edition.—**Juleigh Muirhead Clark**

214. **Encyclopedia of Careers and Vocational Guidance.** 2d ed. [CD-ROM]. Chicago, J. G. Ferguson Publishing, 1997. Minimum system requirements (Windows version): IBM or compatible 386. Double-speed ISO 9660-compatible CD-ROM drive. Windows 3.1. 8MB RAM. 10MB hard disk space. SVGA monitor and graphics card. Microsoft-compatible mouse. Minimum system requirements (Macintosh version): MacOS 7.0. Double-speed ISO 9660 CD-ROM drive. Foreign File Access extension. 8MB RAM. 10MB hard disk space. 640 x 480 pixels color monitor. Macintosh mouse or pointing device. $199.95 (single user); $299.95 (2-8 users); $399.95 (9+ users). ISBN 0-89434-171-5 (single user); 0-89434-172-3 (2-8 users); 0-89434-173-1 (9+ users).

215. **Encyclopedia of Careers and Vocational Guidance.** 10th ed. Chicago, J. G. Ferguson Publishing, 1997. 4v. illus. index. $149.95/set. ISBN 0-89434-170-7.

Encyclopedia of Careers and Vocational Guidance (ECVG) continues to be one of the standard tools for libraries in the area of career development. This 10th edition continues the topical arrangement first tried in the previous edition (see ARBA 94, entry 386). In this format, volume 1 surveys 67 major industries, such as accounting, automotives, energy, hospitality, public relations, and toys and games. The remaining 3 volumes comprise alphabetic listings of individual jobs within industries; for example, the information services industry profile links to job descriptions for archivists, database administrators, indexers, librarians, library media specialists, and library technicians. In addition to the industry profiles, volume 1 includes 2 appendixes, 1 on career resources and associations for individuals with disabilities, the other focusing on internships, apprenticeships, and training programs.

The industry profiles lead off with an industry overview, including history and development, followed by a description of the industry's structure, the various careers within the industry, employment opportunities, and the industry outlook. A list of sources of additional information and links to related articles complete each industry section. The job profiles found in volumes 2 through 4 lead off with a paragraph-length description of each job, then provide a history of the job; describe the nature of the work; its requirements; opportunities for experience and exploration; methods of entering the profession; paths for advancement; employment outlook; entry-level, average, and high earnings; and conditions of work. As with the industry overviews, the job entries conclude with a list of sources of additional information and links to related articles. For example, the "librarians" entry lists (with their respective Website addresses) the American Library Association, the Special Libraries Association, the American Association of Law Libraries, and the Music Library Association as information sources.

For those libraries that can afford its higher cost, the 2d edition of the CD-ROM version of the ECVG offers additional text as well as enhanced searching capability. A database of 152 military careers put together by the U.S. Department of Defense describes each job's background, what activities are involved, work environment, and other useful information. Search capabilities include searching by interest and ability; training or education requirements; school subject (e.g., biology, mathematics); and numerous other fields. The CD-ROM version not only supports full printing options but also offers a letter-writing function that allows users to create and print a personalized letter of inquiry to any association or agency listed in the ECVG.

The information in the encyclopedia is thorough, reliable, and current. Whether in print or electronic format, it remains an important resource for school, academic, and public libraries.—**G. Kim Dority**

216. **JIST's Electronic Enhanced Dictionary of Occupational Titles.** 2d ed. [CD-ROM]. Indianapolis, Ind., JIST Works, 1997. Minimum system requirements: IBM or compatible 386SX with Intel or Pentium processor (486DX recommended). CD-ROM drive. Windows 3.0. 4MB RAM. VGA monitor (SVGA preferred). Mouse. Windows-compatible printer. $295.00.

JIST's Electronic Enhanced Dictionary of Occupational Titles combines the information of four familiar occupational resources—*Dictionary of Occupational Titles* (DOT; see ARBA 79, entry 855), *Guide for Occupational Exploration* (GOE; JIST Works, 1996), *Occupational Outlook Handbook* (OOH; see entry 238), and the *Worker Traits Data Book* (WTDB; JIST Works, 1994)—on one CD-ROM. The DOT covers 12,741 jobs, whereas the OOH information encompasses 250 occupations from the 1996-1997 edition and includes a color photograph of a worker performing a task from that job. Military jobs are divided by branch of service and are listed with the civilian equivalent. Clicking on one of the jobs takes the user to the DOT information with links to the OOH and the WTDB. The user may look up information in this resource through five choices: DOT numbering system, GOE interest groups, OOH clusters, military occupations, and the general search function. The search function allows for multiple criteria and the use of operators to narrow the search; it also provides a list of available words and allows searches to be saved.

Cross-references are extensive. With any occupation, the researcher may click at the top of the entry for related information within the other resources. Related jobs listed at the end of the article may also be clicked for a direct link to information on that job. With the Back, Home, Print, and Exit buttons, it is easy to flip back and forth between the entries. The print function gives the user the ability to print any of the occupational reports. Program information from the main menu provides sources used, ways to use the program, and information about the program plus additional content from the DOT, the OOH, and the WTDB. This electronic resource will be useful for students researching occupations or the job market, as well as for counselors and employment professionals.—**Elaine Ezell**

217. **VGM's Careers Encyclopedia: A Concise, Up-to-Date Reference for Students, Parents, & Guidance Counselors.** 4th ed. By the Editors of VGM Career Horizons. Lincolnwood, Ill., VGM Career Horizons/National Textbook, 1997. 456p. index. $39.95. ISBN 0-8442-4525-9.

This career encyclopedia provides detailed information on approximately 200 of the most popular jobs in the United States today. The jobs, ranging from blue collar to professional, appear in alphabetic order. The table of contents is an alphabetic list as well. The index consists of a keyword list, and it includes association names as well as numerous cross-references and *see also* references. Each occupational entry follows a uniform pattern, describing "The Job"; "Places of Employment and Working Conditions"; "Qualifications, Education, and Training"; "Potential and Advancement"; "Income"; and "Additional Sources of Information." The entries for many occupations list related jobs. The editors use such phrases as "strong demand," "average growth," or "little growth" to describe the job outlook for each occupation through the year 2005.

Public and academic libraries of all sizes require current information about occupations and the educational requirements for those occupations. Guidance counselors in secondary and academic institutions likewise need such basic material. *VGM's Careers Encyclopedia* is a basic, one-volume source eminently suitable for high school and junior college students seeking career advice. Libraries and schools with limited budgets will find this title to be current and authoritative. Academic libraries and public libraries serving a medium-sized or larger clientele should consider the four-volume *Encyclopedia of Careers and Vocational Guidance* (see entries 214 and 215), a much more comprehensive source. Libraries that can afford to duplicate holdings should also consider the *Occupational Outlook Handbook* (see entry 238).—**Dene L. Clark**

Directories

218. Betrus, Michael. **The Guide to Executive Recruiters.** new ed. New York, McGraw-Hill, 1997. 874p. index. $25.95pa. ISBN 0-07-006280-3.

More than 6,000 recruiting firms in the United States are listed in this geographically arranged work. Each entry gives contact information, minimum salary placed, and recruiting specialty. Useful indexes follow the main body of the work: by industry (64 classifications) and by company name. Short chapters at the beginning of the book outline the process of working with recruiters and suggest that the job-hunter will have more success using a contingency firm (rather than a retained firm); however, in the entries that follow, there is no indication of the firm's status. Furthermore, no information as to how and when this information was gathered is described.

This book may be compared to *The Directory of Executive Recruiters* (25th ed., Kennedy Publications, 1996), which gives information on 4,400 firms. These entries include more information and are listed alphabetically by company under two main headings: retainer firms and contingency firms. Five indexes assist users to further narrow their search: industry, functions, geography, key principal, and company name.

For an executive job-hunter, the directory is preferable, but with a few improvements, the guide could be just as helpful. An exhaustive collection will want both titles.—**Juleigh Muirhead Clark**

219. **Directory of U.S. Labor Organizations.** 1997 ed. C. D. Gifford, ed. Washington, D.C., BNA Books, 1997. 138p. index. $55.00pa. ISBN 1-57018-081-4. ISSN 0734-6786.

The 1997 edition of the *Directory of U.S. Labor Organizations* brings up to the beginning of 1997 the rapidly shifting structure of the U.S. labor movement. In order to keep up with the changes in composition and leadership, the directory is now being published annually instead of biennially. Most of the changes have been a result of the marked increase in mergers, but many are a result of a decline in membership that began in the 1970s. According to the U.S. Bureau of Labor Statistics, there have been 133 union mergers between 1955 and 1995. Most of these mergers were a result of smaller organizations being absorbed by larger unions. Almost half were accounted for by four major unions, the Service Employees Industrial Union, the Machinists, the United Food and Commercial Workers, and the Communication Workers, all affiliated with the AFL-CIO.

This edition of the directory carries a breakdown of mergers that have taken place between 1985 and March 1997. The 1997 edition also provides new data, including general e-mail and Website addresses. As in previous editions, the directory supplies a wide range of information concerning the structure, leadership, and membership of the AFL-CIO, including several charts. The directory also furnishes brief biographies of AFL-CIO President John J. Sweeney, Secretary-Treasurer Richard L. Trumpka, and Executive Vice President Linda Chavez-Thompson, the new leadership elected at the 1995 AFL-CIO Convention.—**George A. Meyers**

220. **The JobBank Guide to Employment Services 1998-1999.** Steven Graber and others, eds. Holbrook, Mass., Adams Publishing, 1997. 429p. index. $200.00. ISBN 1-55850-826-0.

This employment guide is published every other year by Adams Publishing, known for its annual "companion directory" to this guide, *The National JobBank* (see entry 237), and dozens of geographic-specific JobBank series titles, as well as other job-related titles. This is the 6th edition of *The JobBank Guide to Employment Services*, and it provides information on more than 5,000 employment service firms. The employment services are listed alphabetically by state and then by agency type within each state in the 1st section and listed by more than 70 specializations in the 2d section. The work distinguishes agencies that offer services under one or more categories of these five types of employment services: temporary employment agencies, permanent employment agencies, executive search firms, contract services firms, and career/outplacement counseling firms.

Each listing contains some or all of the following information: name of employment service; mailing address; telephone, toll-free telephone, and fax numbers; recorded job line; contact person and title or department; e-mail address; World Wide Web address; employment service profile; area of specialization; positions commonly filled; benefits available; corporate headquarters location; other area, national, and international locations; average salary range of placement; and number of placements per year. The index is arranged by specialization and by state within the specialization for optimal use. Adams Media's CareerCity Website, an electronic career center at www.careercity.com, now houses the missing résumé and cover letter advice section found in the previous edition of this guide.

Given today's increased employee mobility and the changing job market, this reference makes a welcome source for job-seekers thinking of moving or getting employment assistance in a job search just about anywhere in the country. The tool is highly recommended.—**Edward Erazo**

221. Oldman, Mark, and Samer Hamadeh. **America's Top Internships.** 1998 ed. New York, Princeton Review/Random House, 1997. 408p. $21.00pa. ISBN 0-679-78394-6.

Engagingly written by two recent college graduates who, together, have completed a total of eight internships as each acquired a bachelor and master's degree from Stanford University, this directory profiles 107 of the firms offering the best internships in the United States. To illustrate the diversity of the internships profiled, the entities range from giants in the computer field to organizations in arts management. In fact, every conceivable facet of corporate society, both for profit and nonprofit, is included. The entries range from the environmental field to fashion model management, and from public policy think tanks to television production.

The companies offering internships appear in alphabetic order by firm name. Each entry consists of three to four concisely edited pages, all in a common format. A table on the first page of each entry denotes selectivity, compensation, quality of life, location(s), fields (of endeavor), duration, prerequisites, and deadlines. A "busyword meter" for each entry appears on the same page as the table. The authors have done their homework. In most cases, a history of each firm is provided as well as a history of the firm's internship program. Past interns who have completed the programs are extensively quoted and frankly describe pluses and minuses of their experiences. A number of useful tables in the appendix categorize the 107 firms. Categories included range from "highest compensation" to "most selective," and from "internships open to graduate students" to "free housing." Other tables in the appendix list "internships of interest" and "internships by location." This work is highly recommend for all academic libraries, most secondary school libraries, and all mid-size and large public libraries.—**Dene L. Clark**

Handbooks and Yearbooks

222. Bolles, Richard Nelson. **Job-Hunting on the Internet.** Berkeley, Calif., Ten Speed Press, 1997. 110p. illus. (The Parachute Library). $4.95pa. ISBN 0-89815-909-1.

Excerpted and expanded from the author's well-known publication, *What Color Is Your Parachute?*, this book has added Internet job-hunting to its repertoire. First, nine large, gateway locations, comprising university-sponsored, commercial, and favorite sites, are identified. This list is followed by a discussion of the benefits and limitations in using the Internet for job listings, résumés, career counseling, contacts, and research. Obviously based on extensive research, the World Wide Web sites, evaluated and annotated, offers discussion of guidelines, exercises, techniques, opportunities, specialized resources, and other forms of assistance. A symbol, the parachute, connotes the best within each category. Advice for the unsuccessful job search and basic search instruction complete the volume.

This handy reference guide, also available on the Internet (http://www.washingtonpost.com/parachute) offers a realistic approach to job hunting. Even though the Internet is shown as both a superlative and a limited tool, patrons will appreciate the oft-neglected security considerations covered here. The lack of a master site list and index presupposes a readership, for the printed version, limited to those moving through the entire process.—**Sandra E. Belanger**

223. **Career Perspectives Software Series.** [CD-ROM]. Moravia, N.Y., Chronicle Guidance, 1997. Minimum system requirements: IBM or compatible Pentium-grade 486. CD-ROM drive. Windows 3.1. 8MB RAM. 33MB hard disk space. VGA monitor. $250.95.

When examining electronic devices such as CD-ROMs, one notices there often is an embarras de richesses of information. Unfortunately, the emphasis is too often on the embarras, rather than the richesses. Chronicle Guidance Publications has produced a CD-ROM that brings this to mind. Clearly there is a considerable amount of material here. Often getting there, however, can be difficult. Installation is fairly easy, however, some configuration is required. Available to the user are four databases: CGP Career Perspectives Occupations Briefs for two-year, four-year, high school, and "all subjects" careers. Access to each requires a CAN code that accompanies the CD-ROM. All occupation codes come from several sources: Holland Code, Dictionary of Occupations Titles, Guide for Occupational Exploration, and SIC codes for industry careers. Thus, while viewing a brief or summary of a chosen career, users may click on related codes for information about those areas. Special counselor features provide two useful hallmarks for helping students. Counselors may print by brief number as well as results from optional criteria searches. The optional criteria search allows for exact matching by name, data, people, reasoning skills needed, language, and specific vocational prep time. Users are reminded that choosing too many may result in a null set. Each entry provides the familiar outline of careers listed in printed sources, such as the *Dictionary of Occupational Titles*. A brief introduction about the career is followed by a description of work performed, working conditions, training required, qualifications (both personal and educational), entry methods, advancements, and more. In all, over 640 briefs covering more than 2,500 occupations are included. CGP updates the material on a four-year cycle. In the hands of a qualified user, this CD-ROM will reap its richest harvest. Even in the hands of patrons with limited knowledge of the printed tools, CGP will prove helpful. Although the information, clickable options, and search options are overwhelming at times, this CD-ROM will be put to good use almost anywhere it finds a home.—**Mark Y. Herring**

224. Cook, Mary F. **The Human Resources Yearbook 1996/1997.** Englewood Cliffs, N.J., Prentice Hall Career & Personal Development, 1996. 1v. (various paging). index. $79.95. ISBN 0-13-244583-2. ISSN 0887-5316.

Designed to help human resource professionals keep up-to-date in the rapidly changing business environment, this annual covers current issues, trends, legislative developments, and court cases. This year's foreword identifies as major issues the flattening of business organizations and outsourcing selected functions for the sake of flexibility, the resulting employee confusion, and the role of human resource managers in providing leadership and addressing ethical and technological issues. The yearbook is a compilation of articles reprinted from magazines and journals, government publications, and other reports.

Chapters are organized around broad areas, including perennial topics such as compensation, employee training, and employee performance. Other chapters address current topics, such as managing workplace violence, a diverse workforce, a contingent workforce, family issues, and information systems. A chapter on services and resources lists consultants or other companies by function (e.g., arbitration, benefits, dependent care, safety); associations; magazines and looseleaf services; and books for the previous three years. Each chapter begins with a brief listing of contents and an introduction and update to the topic that sets the context and highlights specific issues. Occasionally the chapter introduction will refer to a discussion in an earlier volume to indicate developments or trends. The yearbook's extensive glossary defines terms specific to human resource concerns and includes a list of abbreviations and acronyms. A combined subject, personal name, and legal case index completes the work.

The yearbook is useful for those in the human resources field or for those needing an easily accessible overview of the issues. Although some of the material included is otherwise not easily available, much has been published in professional journals. Therefore, it is recommended for libraries without access to professional human resources literature.—**Joan B. Fiscella**

225. Exter, Thomas G. **The Official Guide to American Incomes.** 2d ed. Ithaca, N.Y., New Strategist, 1996. 364p. index. $89.95. ISBN 1-885070-00-4.

This 2d edition, a useful, reasonably priced statistical compendium, contains current and historical statistics from U.S. government and private sources. The 300 clear, concise tables represent unpublished (50 percent), census Website (27 percent), and author-calculated (5 percent) 1994 data, with some tables reflecting trends since the late 1960s or mid-1970s. The introductory material focuses on major demographic trends and data importance but fails, like the 1st edition (see ARBA 94, entry 283), to explain how the data have been analyzed. Following the structure adopted previously, each chapter offers a brief introduction, highlights several results, and presents tables in nine topical areas (e.g., consumer spending, poverty results) for the United States, with some regional data. A detailed list of tables, a brief glossary, and a topical index complete the volume.

Some of the problems noted with the 1st edition have been addressed; for example, some tables now include Asians/Pacific Islanders. Although patrons will be delighted with access to hard-to-find numbers, the presentation relies too heavily on demographic jargon and poor indexing. The list of tables more clearly defines the content than the index, which fails to incorporate more general terminology and to refer users from those terms to demographic jargon that has not been defined in the glossary. [R: Choice, Mar 97, p. 1146]—**Sandra E. Belanger**

226. Farr, J. Michael, LaVerne L. Ludden, and Paul Mangin, comps. **The Enhanced Occupational Outlook Handbook.** Indianapolis, Ind., JIST Works, 1997. 761p. $34.95pa. ISBN 1-56370-312-2.

JIST Works offers a compilation of the *Occupational Outlook Handbook* (OOH; see entry 238) and the *Dictionary of Occupational Titles* (DOT; 4th ed.; see ARBA 93, entry 301) in this rendering. The table of contents resembles that of the OOH, listing the same topical arrangement of careers and the same job titles. The entries give the text from the OOH and continue with related occupations taken from the DOT. In the OOH, only the DOT reference numbers are given; *The Enhanced Occupational Outlook Handbook* (EOOH) expands this information by reprinting most of each individual DOT entry. For example, for information about horseshoers, the nearest OOH topic is "Animal Caretakers, Except Farm"; following the text are five DOT entries (which would not all appear together in the DOT), one of which describes the work of a horseshoer and lists the DOT codes (GOE, GED, SVP). The EOOH leaves out two bits of information from the DOT entry: The date the definition was formulated and the strength rating; that is, how much strength does an individual need to do this work?

The introduction describes fully how to use the fat (200-plus pages longer than the OOH), paperbound volume. However, there is no index to help the user go straight to "horseshoers." One must use the topical approach laid out in the table of contents. Also missing from the EOOH are the general job search articles appearing in the beginning of the OOH. Users browsing for career possibilities will prefer this combined format to the more intimidating DOT, and the volume should be a welcome addition to a popular career collection. Career professionals will want to keep the originals for the additional information and more specific access method.—**Juleigh Muirhead Clark**

227. Farr, J. Michael. **America's Top Jobs for People Without College Degrees.** 3d ed. Indianapolis, Ind., JIST Works, 1997. 361p. (Top Jobs). $14.95pa. ISBN 1-56370-282-7.

Part of JIST Work's Top Job series and a new edition of *America's Top Technical and Trade Jobs*, this reasonably priced, paperbound volume contains four parts: job descriptions, labor market trends, job-hunting advice, and articles of interest. Section 1 (the majority of the contents) reprints 100 job descriptions (50 more than the 2d edition) from the *Occupational Outlook Handbook 1996-97* (OOH; see entry 238). Section 2 also depends heavily on the OOH for charts and facts but is rearranged and expanded to improve readability. In section 3, Farr guides career-seekers with helpful charts and questionnaires to match their skills to careers. He outlines job search skills in a friendly, organized way and includes brief assistance with résumés, communication, and coping—both emotionally and financially. Suggestions for further reading lead one to many other JIST Works publications. The articles in section 4 are reprinted from various Department of Labor publications. Sections 2 and 3 are identical in the Top Job books examined, but the articles in section 4 vary. The book is well formatted—the typeface is clear, with varying fonts, boldface, and italics for emphasis. The format and the emphasis on 100 "top jobs" for people without college degrees will appeal to people who do not want to tackle the OOH or the alarming array of career advice books available.—**Juleigh Muirhead Clark**

228. Farr, J. Michael. **America's Top Office, Management, Sales, & Professional Jobs.** 3d ed. Indianapolis, Ind., JIST Works, 1997. 377p. (Top Jobs). $14.95pa. ISBN 1-56370-291-6.

This paperbound volume contains four parts: job descriptions, labor market trends, job-hunting advice, and "Good Articles." Section 1 (the majority of the contents) reprints 100 job descriptions (40 more than the 2d edition) from the *Occupational Outlook Handbook 1996-97* (OOH; see entry 238), the majority in business. Disturbingly, librarians will note that careers for library assistants are described, but not careers in librarianship (or even information science). Section 2 also depends heavily on the OOH for charts and facts but is rearranged and expanded. In section 3, Farr aids the undecided with helpful charts and questionnaires to match skills to careers. He outlines job search skills in a friendly, organized way and offers cursory assistance with résumés, communication, and coping. Suggestions for further reading lead one primarily to other JIST Works publications. The "Good Articles" and appendixes are reprinted from various Department of Labor publications. Sections 2 and 3 are identical in the Top Job books examined, but the articles in section 4 vary. The book is well formatted in a clear typeface with varying fonts, boldface, and italics for emphasis.

Complementary books on the job-seeking process for business to consider are *Business and Finance Career Directory* and *Marketing and Sales Career Directory* (both Visible Ink Press, 1992), which include informative job descriptions written in a conversational style by people in the field but focus more attention on likely companies to approach. Also of interest is *Peterson's Job Opportunities in Business* (see ARBA 96, entry 280), which lists companies and notes what type of people (accountants, market researchers) they hire.—**Juleigh Muirhead Clark**

229. Fisher, Helen S. **American Salaries and Wages Survey: Statistical Data Derived from More Than 300 Government, Business, & News Sources.** 4th ed. Detroit, Gale, 1997. 805p. $110.00pa. ISBN 0-7876-0059-8. ISSN 1055-7628.

The 4th edition of this directory is a compilation of 4,402 occupations with their respective salaries and wages garnered from more than 300 sources, including federal, state, regional, and local government sources and many trade associations and industry journals. This edition has expanded its coverage from the 3d edition (see ARBA 96, entry 266) in every section, and the user will now find more than 38,000 salaries on more than 4,400 occupational classifications in this volume. The data collected cover the period from January 1993 through February 1997. The 3d edition included material from January 1990 through December 1995, so there is overlap. Human resources departments can consult this book for generic job classification guidelines on general salary ranges applicable for a particular geographic region. These salary ranges do not reflect other benefits, such as a uniform allowance or any other supplemental compensation packages. One of the appendixes includes employment projections by occupation from 1994 and 2005. If this book is judiciously used as a starting point for an analysis of salary classifications, it can be of value.—**Judith J. Field**

230. **Handbook of U.S. Labor Statistics: Employment, Earnings, Prices, Productivity, and Other Labor Data.** Eva E. Jacobs, ed. Lanham, Md., Bernan Press, 1997. 316p. index. $59.00pa. ISBN 0-89059-062-1.

This 1st edition contains valuable statistical labor information compiled by the U.S. Bureau of Labor Statistics (BLS). Published by Bernan Press, the work continues and updates the *Handbook of Labor Statistics*, published by the BLS until 1989. The *Handbook of U.S. Labor Statistics* includes tables on labor market conditions, prices, and productivity grouped into chapters according to subject matter. A detailed table of contents, as well as an index, provides access to the data. The primary focus of the tables is national in scope, but the work does include state and city data. The BLS studies labor conditions in selected foreign countries, and one chapter consists of tables comparing U.S. data with data from nine other countries. Notes prefacing each chapter describe the data therein and offer additional sources of information.

The tables run the gamut from size of labor force and employment status to hours and earnings, and from projections of employment by occupation and industry to prices and living conditions. Tables display historical timelines, on occasion providing data as early as the 1930s. Selected tables on producer price indexes and consumer price indexes provide data as early as 1913. The BLS's statistical correlation breakdowns on concepts relating to sex, race, Hispanic origin, age, marital status, educational attainment, and employment/presence and age of children are of much more recent vintage, resulting in shorter timeline tables. All of the data are available in BLS publications, but not in a single publication and not in a historical timeline series. The handbook is a mandatory purchase for medium and large public libraries and academic libraries with business programs.—**Dene L. Clark**

231. **JIST's Electronic Occupational Outlook Handbook.** 2d ed. [CD-ROM]. Indianapolis, Ind., JIST Works, 1996. Minimum system requirements: IBM or compatible 386SX with an Intel or Pentium processor (486DX recommended). CD-ROM drive. Windows 3.0. 4MB RAM. 3.7MB hard disk space. VGA monitor (SVGA monitor preferred). Mouse. Windows-compatible printer. $129.00.

JIST's Electronic Occupational Outlook Handbook uses the entire text of the 1996-1997 edition of the familiar *Occupational Outlook Handbook* (OOH; see entry 238) published by the U.S. Department of Labor every two years. The 250 occupations described in the OOH are cross-referenced with the *Guide for Occupational Exploration* (GOE; JIST Works, 1996); interest groups and the 7,700 specific job descriptions from the *Dictionary of Occupational Titles* (DOT; see ARBA 79, entry 855). The user may choose to search by 1 of 4 methods: the 12 OOH clusters, jobs by names, interest areas, or DOT codes and titles. The OOH descriptions give the most extensive information. Each entry is arranged in the same format: nature of work, working conditions, employment, training, job outlook, earnings, related occupations, and sources of additional information. The entry concludes with a list of specific job titles from the DOT that when clicked give the DOT description for that job. Color photographs of a worker from each occupation are included.

The main screen has four options: the OOH, the GOE, the DOT, and general information. General information includes an extensive employment outlook by the Bureau of Labor Statistics, recommendations on locating a job and evaluating job offers, résumé and interview tips, and sources of additional career information. Throughout the program the user has the option to return to the home screen, print, exit the program, or go back a screen. The ability to change preferences, as well as page and printer setups, is a useful feature. The program is user friendly and can be used easily by students seeking career information or adults in the fields of counseling and employment.—**Elaine Ezell**

232. **JIST's Multimedia Occupational Outlook Handbook.** 2d ed. [CD-ROM]. Indianapolis, Ind., JIST Works, 1997. Minimum system requirements: IBM or compatible 386. CD-ROM drive. Windows 3.1. 8MB RAM. SVGA 640 x 480 pixels, 256-color monitor. Mouse. Printer (for printing). $295.00.

Based on the *Occupational Outlook Handbook* (see entry 238) published every two years by the U.S. Department of Labor, this CD-ROM program is a user-friendly alternative for students who like to use computers rather than books to find information. The Main Menu presents three options: Search by Occupational Cluster, Search Alphabetically, and Search by Custom Criteria. When one chooses Search by Occupational Cluster, a screen then presents a number of clusters, such as "Administrative Support, Including Clerical," "Construction Trades," or "Service Occupations." If one clicks on "Professional Specialty Occupations," the next screen offers "Teachers, Librarians, Counselors, etc." After selecting that, the next screen offers "Adult Education Teachers," "Archivists and Curators," "College and University Faculty," "Counselors," "Librarians," and "Special Education Teachers." Thus, each broad cluster has been subdivided into individual professions.

Information offered for each profession chosen includes nature of the work, working conditions, employment, education/training, job outlook, earnings, related occupations, and more information sources. There are buttons for Back, Print, Help, and To Menu at each step. When Print is selected, all of the above information is printed rather than only the most recent, a sad lesson learned after getting 35 pages of print-out.

When the user selects Search Alphabetically, a screen appears that has a large button for every letter in the alphabet. If one is interested in finding information about veterinarians, one can click on the V button and the list of all occupations beginning with the letter "V" appears. Clicking on the desired profession will then lead to the information described in the above paragraph. When one selects Search by Custom Criteria, there are three lists from which choices must be made: "Minimum Earning Requirements," "Job Growth Outlook," and "Education/Training Requirements." Based upon the choices made, a list of professions meeting all three combined criteria appears. From there, one may click on any one of those to go to the primary information for that profession. If no profession meets all three criteria, such a message is given and one must adjust choices.

Other content of the program includes "Tomorrow's Jobs," which presents highlights of the Bureau of Labor Statistics projections of industry and occupational employment and the labor force; "Sources of Career Information," which identifies selected sources of information about occupations and career planning, counseling, training and education, and financial aid; "Finding a Job and Evaluating a Job Offer," which includes a list of where to learn about job openings; "Occupational Information Included in the Handbook," which is an overview of how the occupational descriptions are organized; "Data for Occupations," which presents summary data on 79 additional occupations for which employment projections are prepared, but for which detailed occupational information is not developed; and "Assumptions and Methods," which describes the steps by which the Bureau arrives at employment projections. Although this version claims to be multimedia, it is modest in such features as color and a voice speaking information when a new screen is first encountered. This lack of graphics is somewhat disappointing, as the earlier edition showed video clips of workers engaged in various occupations.

Although the same basic information can be obtained in the print version, it is important to provide students with electronic research tools. Because the information is authoritative and thorough, is presented in an easy-to-use format, and covers a subject widely studied across the curriculum, this disc is a good reference program that belongs in any library serving youth or job-seeking adults.—**Dana McDougald**

233. **Job Hunter's Sourcebook: Where to Find Employment Leads and Other Job Search Resources.** 3d ed. Kathleen E. Maki, ed. Detroit, Gale, 1996. 898p. index. (A Gale Career Information Guide). $70.00. ISBN 0-8103-9075-2. ISSN 1053-1874.

In today's competitive job market, up-to-date references of this type are essential for assisting job-seekers in finding career information. This 3d edition of the *Job Hunter's Sourcebook* (JHS) provides just such information, and its coverage of occupations is impressive. This edition varies from the 2 previous editions (see ARBA 94, entry 279, and ARBA 92, entry 222) not in the number of entries of sources, 10,403 (many of which are duplicate entries listed under several occupations), but in the number of categories for specific professions and vocational occupations: 179, up from 155 in the 1st edition and 165 in the 2d. New also to this edition are e-mail addresses and Website information (URLs) for some of the entries. Additionally, the reference sources section has 26 essential topics of job-hunting information, including electronic databases, periodicals, and software; tips for finding jobs, such as interview skills; and opportunities for special populations (e.g., military, minority, and young and old workers). A thorough index assists job-seekers in finding occupations and sections of interest easily. The three-column format maximizes the amount of information on a page yet is easy to read.

This work is similar in size and scope to another Gale reference, *Professional Careers Sourcebook* (Gale, 1996), which lists 121 occupations. JHS differs in its much wider audience and leads on all kinds of jobs, not just those that require a degree. This reference will get ample use. It is reasonably priced and highly recommended for public and academic libraries.—**Edward Erazo**

234. Lauber, Daniel. **Government Job Finder 1997-2000.** 3d ed. River Forest, Ill., Planning/Communications, 1997. 325p. illus. index. $32.95; $16.95pa. ISBN 1-884587-08-9; 1-884587-05-4pa.

Lauber has done an excellent job of providing people who are seeking positions in the government sector with a wide array of sources that can be used to identify available jobs at local, state, regional, and federal levels. In this edition, he has included Internet addresses and Websites plus online databases, recommended professional and trade periodicals, and a comprehensive list of government agencies directories. Approximately 98 percent of the contents have been revised when compared to the 2d edition published in 1994 (see ARBA 95, entry 315), reflecting the volatile nature of this material. In addition to sources, the author has included information to help guide the job-seeker through applying for a job and interviewing, plus some salary guidelines. This book can be updated by visiting the Job Finders' Internet homepage. Libraries with extensive career collections will want to acquire multiple copies of this title. Small libraries and job placement centers will consider this title an absolute must for their collections because it is so comprehensive and inexpensive.—**Judith J. Field**

235. Lauber, Daniel. **Non-Profits and Education Job Finder 1997-2000.** River Forest, Ill., Planning/Communications, 1997. 340p. illus. index. $32.95; $16.95pa. ISBN 1-884587-09-7; 1-884587-06-2pa.

The edition of this title that covers the years 1997 to 2000 contains 2,222 sources of job leads and job-search resources in the nonprofit and education fields. This edition is divided into 30 chapters. The core material for individual disciplines, such as the arts, housing, museums, social services, and the like, is found in chapters 4 through 29, with each chapter devoted to a different specialty, all in alphabetic order. Chapter 30 is a geographic listing of resources by state for users who wish to target a specific geographic locale. The typical user may proceed immediately to these core chapters, but the author wisely cautions the reader, again and again, to read chapters 1-3 before proceeding. Chapter 1 is an excellent overview of job-hunting tools. Chapter 2 is a detailed discussion of the online job search and includes countless sources on e-mail, the World Wide Web, Gopher servers, newsgroups, mailing lists, and bulletin board services as well as a discussion of books that will simplify online job searches. Chapter 3 reports on offline job-hunting tools that are common to all in the nonprofit sector and in education.

Until the recent past, jobs and internships in the nonprofit sector were often filled by word of mouth. Today, nonprofits use advertising in specialty and trade periodicals, job hotlines, and the Internet as well as networking. *Non-Profits and Education Job Finder* is worth its weight in gold as the only reference tool to explore all these venues. It is highly recommended for most academic libraries as well as all mid-sized and large public libraries.—**Dene L. Clark**

236. **Mandated Benefits: 1997 Compliance Guide.** By McGladrey & Pullen, LLP. New York, Panel/Aspen, 1997. 1v. (various paging). index. price not reported. ISBN 1-56706-403-5.

Mandated Benefits is a comprehensive publication designed to provide accurate and authoritative information in regard to relations between employers and employees. The publisher, Panel, is a division of Aspen. The guide is written by specialists to assist business professionals in the area of human resources, as well as for owners of small and medium-sized businesses and their legal and financial advisers. It seeks to provide practical, solution-based, how-to information.

The publication details federal and state laws and regulations in addition to many useful exhibits demonstrating, for example, how to fill out forms for such subjects as mandated pay penalties, work required materials, medical and health care benefits, training, layoffs and termination, and discretionary benefits. Other topics, such as the Americans with Disabilities Act, the Federal Family and Medical Leave Act of 1993, sexual harassment, and privacy in the workplace are also discussed. The 1997 edition contains revised and updated information and four new chapters: "Assessing Your Company's Liability Risks," "Affirmative Action/Equal Employment Opportunity," "Requirements of COBRA," and "Recordkeeping Requirements." Each chapter begins with brief comments regarding the subject covered. *Mandated Benefits* can save much time in research, not only for new employers, but for employers in general.
—**George A. Meyers**

237. **The National JobBank 1998.** 14th ed. Michelle Roy and others, eds. Holbrook, Mass., Adams Publishing, 1997. 1099p. index. $320.00. ISBN 1-55850-825-2.

This is the 14th edition of a compendium containing more than 20,000 profiles of potential employers. The entries provide key employment information on typical job positions, principal education background required, and contact information to inquire about employment. The text is arranged alphabetically first by state and then by employer. An effort has been made to include e-mail addresses and World Wide Web site information when known. There is a modest index by major industry grouping and a list of companies arranged by states. At the back of the book is a brief, 18-page guide on how to do a job search, which should prove useful when others books on résumés and cover letters are missing from the collection. This title has proven to be useful to libraries that maintain a career guidance collection, and this new edition should be acquired because of the volatility of this type of information.—**Judith J. Field**

238. **Occupational Outlook Handbook.** 1996-97 ed. Lanham, Md., Bernan Associates, 1996. 507p. illus. index. $32.00pa. ISBN 0-89059-060-5.

Occupational Outlook Handbook (OOH) was first published in 1946 at the request of the Veterans Administration to assist World War II veterans in locating information about careers. OOH was first available to the public in its 1949 edition. It was updated periodically until 1966. Since 1966, it has been published biennially. The 1996-97 volume is the 22d edition.

This handbook is a standard reference tool. It offers descriptions of approximately 259 occupations listed in clusters of related jobs. The descriptions account for 87 percent of the jobs available in the current economy (110 million jobs). Descriptions are approximately two pages in length. They cover the nature of the work, working conditions, training and education needed, average earnings, and job prospects in that field for the near future. A photograph of someone performing each job is included. In addition, a list of 79 other occupations (5 percent of all jobs) is appended, with brief, one-paragraph descriptions of the job and job prospects. The remaining 8 percent of jobs in the current economy are not described; they are considered to be peripheral categories from which no meaningful information could be extracted.

Projections of industry and occupational employment and the labor force are given for the years 1994 to 2005. These projections are illustrated with charts and graphs. The assumptions and methods used in preparing employment projections are described. The volume also includes selected sources of information about careers, career planning, counseling, training and education, and financial aid. A state-by-state list of contacts at Departments of Labor and other employment offices is given as well. There is a brief section offering advice for finding a job and evaluating a job offer.

An index matches job titles with the *Dictionary of Occupational Titles* (4th ed.; see ARBA 93, entry 301) numbers. Titles and numbers for reprints of individual categories of jobs are listed. A final index lists references and *see* references for subjects throughout the volume. Job-seekers and career planners will find this volume both timely and useful.—**Joanna M. Burkhardt**

239. Stuart, Ralph B., III. **Safety & Health on the Internet.** Rockville, Md., Government Institutes, 1997. 198p. illus. index. $39.00pa. ISBN 0-86587-523-5.

This text is typical of the simplistic yet surprisingly popular niche of Internet subject guides that have sprung up like mushrooms in the past two or three years. Aimed at occupational safety and health professionals, it weaves a minimal overview of Internet terminology, tools, and protocols with coverage of relevant safety information resources and research advice. Special emphasis is given to SAFETY, an electronic discussion list launched by the author, even so far as to include the SAFETY mailing list "welcome" file as an appendix. Initial chapters provide an extremely brief introduction to the Internet and scant explanations of a handful of basic concepts and terms (client and server, World Wide Web and e-mail addresses, newsgroups). Another chapter suggests search strategies for locating occupational and environmental safety information online. Tips on professional networking and how to participate in electronic discussion lists are also supplied. An annotated directory of selected government, academic, commercial, and professional health-related Websites and a directory of discussion lists follow. (As is the case with all Internet guides that include resource directories, some of this information is destined to become obsolete as Web links and discussion list locations change.) Some simple graphics are sprinkled throughout the text. A short glossary and index are included. Despite weak overall coverage of Internet technology and concepts, this may be a useful primer for the researcher who is an Internet novice and wants a crash course in accessing health and safety information resources online.—**Judith A. Matthews**

240. **U.S. Employment Opportunities.** Denver, Colo., Washington Research Associates, 1997. 1v. (various paging). $184.00.yr. looseleaf w/binder. ISBN 0-937801-11-9. ISSN 1076-4798.

This looseleaf service attempts to provide career information for white-collar job-seekers. The information is categorized into 14 major U.S. industry groupings. The publisher supplies a year of supplements as part of the subscription price. Each industry section gives a summary of what is happening in the industry, including background information on the industry and what the employment outlook is. Most of these sections are approximately eight pages in length, except for the sections dealing with employment in the federal government and teaching, which are longer. In many of the sections, quotations from publications such as *Fortune* are furnished, but not the citation. There is nothing unique about the material provided. Part 2 of each section lists companies with a brief general description of their business and the address of their human resources office. A list of relevant periodicals and other job information services are also found here. Some of the sections are fairly comprehensive, and others are not. The reader will also note that these sections are not in alphabetic order, nor do they include World Wide Web addresses.

The introductory material includes a two-page article entitled "On-line Jobmarket Research—A Primer." Considering that the issue this reviewer evaluated was published in February 1997, this was a scanty article dealing with online employment opportunities. Since then, more sites have been developed, and many can be located by consulting the homepages of various libraries with large career centers. In contrast, librarians will find the article in the June 1997 issue of *Searcher* entitled "Job Search Sites on the Web" by Aggi Raeder very comprehensive.

Public libraries, placement services, and career counselors are always seeking new creditable career information resources; unfortunately, this is not a such a resource. Only the largest career information centers should consider this item for purchase.—**Judith J. Field**

MANAGEMENT

241. Avery, Christine, and Diane Zabel. **The Quality Management Sourcebook: An International Guide to Materials and Resources.** New York, Routledge, 1997. 327p. index. $125.00. ISBN 0-415-10831-4.

The purpose of this work is to provide a resource for information about quality management. It begins with an overview of the total quality management (TQM) movement, including basic TQM concepts. An annotated bibliography of some of the most important works on quality improvement follows.

The next section of this sourcebook examines applications of TQM. Writings summarized here are organized according to the U.S. government's system for classifying economic activities. Thus, the authors look at books and articles about quality in the construction industry, publishing, pharmaceuticals, hospitals, educational institutions, and other manufacturing and service areas. Most of these works are case studies that analyze TQM implementation in particular companies or institutions. Other subdivisions of this book focus on various essential aspects of quality management, such as teams, customers, analytic and statistical tools, corporate culture, leadership, training, and communication. Another section includes quality in the future and the role of ISO 9000. Also of help to researchers are the glossary of terms associated with TQM and name, title, and subject indexes.

Although new books on quality improvement will continue to appear, the authors have made their sourcebook independent of time constraints by defining strategies for ongoing research. They list presses that publish books about quality improvement, databases, training materials, executive development programs, quality management consultants, and TQM associations. Perhaps most useful is the list of periodicals and newsletters relating to quality. Such information, added to the authors' recommendation of Internet sources, ensures that Avery and Zabel's work remains an outstanding resource for up-to-date material on total quality management. [R: Choice, June 97, p. 1635]—**Renee B. Horowitz**

242. Keen, Peter G. W. **Business Multimedia Explained: A Manager's Guide to Key Terms & Concepts.** Boston, Harvard Business School Press; distr., New York, McGraw-Hill, 1997. 379p. index. $39.95; $24.95pa. ISBN 0-87584-718-8; 0-87584-772-2pa.

Depending upon one's perspective, business multimedia tends to be seen as either "presentation" software (about as welcome as a vacation slide show) or an oxymoron. Keen, in the preface and introduction, does suggest some potentially useful applications in training and specialized forms of modeling. He makes a reasonable argument for further investigation of the topic, although nowhere near a compelling case for investment in the technology. His examples are isolated, and the results, although suggestive, are not backed up by any kind of analysis, let alone conclusive evidence.

The majority of the book is a glossary. A variety of terms, phrases, and concepts prompt miniessays, generally a page or two in length. Entries are numerous but by no means exhaustive. For example, compact disc technology is represented by listings for "CD-Audio," "CD-I," "CD Plus," "CD-R," "CD-ROM," "CD Technology," and "CD- XA," but not "CD-RW" (rewritable). In the introduction, Keen insists that the book is not about the Internet—but a great many of the terms are. The essays cannot really be called definitions, because many times they overlook important aspects of the technologies in question or get them wrong. For example, the entry for "CD-XA" states that it is a file format that is unique in storing both video and sound together, but the book's own coverage of the Motion Picture Expert Group standard contradicts this statement. The listing for Virtual Reality Modeling Language (VRML) makes no mention of the need for a compatible browser and states that VRML is not interactive. The book does provide a sort of "once over lightly," with a few nods to such controversial topics as censorship and pornography.
—**Robert M. Slade**

243. Kemper, Robert E. **Quality, TQC, TQM: A Meta Literature Study.** Lanham, Md., Scarecrow, 1997. 559p. index. $59.50. ISBN 0-8108-3346-8.

This interesting study compiles the most influential writings of the last half-century on "quality." Using citation indexing as a meta-analysis methodology, the author attempts to identify the present state of quality knowledge. To define "quality," the author, a professor of management at Northern Arizona University, uses both a dictionary definition and a definition from an authoritative business text. For the purposes of the study, "quality" was also seen as interchangeable with the following terms found in the literature: property, attribute, character, and trait. The process of quality also includes at least six other variables: effectiveness, efficiency, leadership, management, assertiveness, and cooperation. The intended audience consists of readers with a general interest in quality—managers, supervisors, and others who practice, or (as the author says) should practice, quality routinely; researchers investigating quality; and students seeking an imaginative area for interesting study and research.

This work is arranged in 2 related parts. The 1st section is a 40-page bibliographic essay that discusses key theoretical approaches and authors. It also lists the most-cited quality literature identified in the study. These lists include key sources of quality literature; most-cited authors (cited at least five times); most-cited professional associations; most-cited publishers; most-cited periodical sources; and works about or based on the philosophy of W. Edwards Deming. The 2d section, which comprises the majority of the work, is an alphabetically arranged list of 5,839 citations covering some aspect of quality. Items from the "key sources" list are identified by bold typeface, and a number noting multiple citings is also included if appropriate. The work also includes subject and contributor indexes.

This work is significant in several ways. First, it identifies the most influential works—as determined by citation analysis—from many different areas of quality research. Second, its scope is such that it has allowed the author to assemble a broad range of quality literature. The result is a work that not only pulls together much of the literature on quality, but also identifies the elite literature for researchers and other interested persons. Flipping back and forth between the lists and citations may be tiresome for researchers and librarians, but both will find this work useful. It is highly recommended for academic and public libraries serving users with interests in quality.—**Gordon J. Aamot**

244. Landskroner, Ronald A. **The Nonprofit Manager's Resource Directory.** New York, John Wiley, 1996. 522p. $65.00pa. ISBN 0-471-14839-3.

This directory is a compendium of more than 2,000 information sources that any not-for-profit organization needs. It brings together both reference and bibliographic citation information in an annotated guide format. The chapters cover subjects in a wide spectrum of topics, such as financial management, human resources, governance and boards, legal issues, marketing, planning, volunteerism, and 10 other areas. Within each chapter, resources are grouped into these subsections: providers of products and services (generally commercial companies); support organizations; subject-interest periodicals; publications/ software/tapes; and, where relevant, Internet resources, e-mail addresses, and Websites.

With few exceptions, entries have a descriptive annotation, and many are quite extensive. Entries relevant to another chapter are repeated with cross-references to the main annotation. An unusual feature is the directory of colleges and universities offering classwork on managing nonprofit organizations, which includes a description of the programs of study. The appendix surveys general reference books serving nonprofit interests (e.g., *Encyclopedia of Associations* [Gale, 1997]) that would be found in most libraries.

Many items covered here could be found in other reference books, but not without a laborious search process. The annotations add much value, and the bibliographic sections will be highly effective as a collection development tool. The logical arrangement and up-to-date content will provide an excellent introduction for any user. It is unfortunate that there is no index, but the expanded table of contents and cross-references will provide adequate access for most users. [R: Choice, Mar 97, p. 1138]—**Gary R. Cocozzoli**

245. **Management Consulting: Exploring the Field, Finding the Right Job, and Landing It!** [CD-ROM]. Boston, Harvard Business School Press, 1996. Minimum system requirements (Windows version): IBM or compatible 486. Double-speed CD-ROM drive. Windows 3.1. 8MB RAM. SVGA 256-color monitor. Soundblaster-compatible sound card. Minimum system requirements (Macintosh version): 68040. Double-speed CD-ROM drive. 8MB RAM. 8 bit color monitor (16 bit recommended). $39.95. ISBN 0-87584-752-8.

This well-designed, easy-to-install, smooth-running hypermedia CD-ROM teaches prospective consultants about the work, client expectations, major firms, and strategies for successfully obtaining work. Text introductions, a glossary, self-tests of management concepts, QuickTime movie clips, and listings for 50 top firms are all integrated into a lively and colorful approach to educating the viewer. Viewers are given a rare and relatively candid peek into the world of consulting. Industry representatives with varying years of experience share their views on a variety of topics. Case interviews, standard practices, and general impressions are shared by emissaries from all segments of the business, representing a variety of ethnic and racial groups. Unfortunately, although most female informants are asked about balancing work and home responsibilities, few of the male informants give opinions on that topic. In addition to this slight evidence of sexism in the interviews, a more glaring flaw is the lack of an index or table of contents, which would allow the viewer to track completion of sections or to pick up easily where they had left off. Despite these annoyances, the disc offers libraries a rich resource of information about the work of management consulting and major firms in the area in an appealing, engaging format.—**Lynne M. Fox**

MARKETING AND TRADE

246. **The American Marketplace: Demographics and Spending Patterns.** 3d ed. Janet Heslop, ed. Ithaca, N.Y., New Strategist, 1997. 417p. index. $89.95. ISBN 1-885070-07-1.

The American Marketplace is a reference tool for librarians and researchers who need demographic, spending, and lifestyle statistics. Each of the tables is based on information from government databases: the Census Bureau, the National Center for Education Statistics, the National Center for Health Statistics, and the Bureau of Labor Statistics. The New Strategist authors analyzed the numbers and compiled each of the tables so that researchers can see the trends quickly without having to calculate the statistics themselves. The statistics are accompanied by an analysis of the numbers.

The tables of statistical information are divided into eight topic areas with headings listed in alphabetic order: education, health, income, labor force, living arrangements, population, spending, and wealth. The statistics are current through 1995. Each statistical table is documented with a source note if the researcher wants to check the original sources of information. An appendix provides World Wide Web addresses or telephone numbers, as well as a glossary. A researcher or librarian can access statistics of

U.S. consumers and their spending habits in one handy volume instead of surfing the Internet for hours or sifting through piles of printed reports. *The American Marketplace* will be helpful in reference departments of public and academic libraries.—**Kay M. Stebbins**

247. **American Women: Who They Are & How They Live.** By the Editors of New Strategist Publications. Ithaca, N.Y., New Strategist, 1997. 400p. index. $89.95. ISBN 1-885070-08-X.

New Strategist is a company that publishes statistical books aimed at the business community, particularly those in marketing who want to know as much as possible about potential consumers. Many of their books deal with a particular segment of the population (e.g., teenagers, ethnic groups, Generation Xers). This edition looks at women born in the United States since World War II and how the changes in women's lives and attitudes have altered buying habits.

The nine chapters in *American Women* suggest the broad focus of this study: There is a chapter each on attitudes, education, health, income, the labor force, living arrangements, population, spending, and wealth. The text consists of tables preceded by a few paragraphs that explain the significance of the particular table. Perhaps because this is designed for the business community, short and sweet is the rule—readers are alerted to particularly significant information by a bullet or text in bold typeface. Much of the information, which is admirably up-to-date, comes from government sources, although private and trade publications are also represented. The source of the data is clearly printed under each table. The book is easy to use and, although it lends itself to browsing, also has an index and a short glossary.

No subject is treated in depth, but the compilers have chosen a fascinating mixture of facts to illustrate women's lives today. Books of statistics are always in demand, and this one will be a good acquisition for collections in academic and public libraries.—**Hope Yelich**

248. **Business Sales Leads.** 1997 ed. [CD-ROM]. Carter Lake, Iowa, PhoneDisc, 1997. 2 discs. Minimum system requirements (Windows version): IBM or compatible 386. CD-ROM drive. Windows 3.1. 4MB RAM. Minimum system requirements (Macintosh version): Macintosh Plus/Classic. CD-ROM drive. System 6.04. $79.95.

In the past few years, many companies have developed CD-ROMs full of telephone directory information. Naturally, they have improved as technology has improved and the data have been "matched" to an electronic format. The *Business Sales Leads* product is terrific. The CD-ROM no longer has to be installed on a PC's hard drive; the software needed to run the disc is on the disc! This feature alone makes it perfect for library circulating collections.

Businesses can be searched on disc 1 by name, type, or Standard Industrial Classification, and then limited by city, state, street, zip code, county, Metropolitan Statistical Area, area code, or "within a mile circle." Disc 2 can be searched by business name, address, and telephone, with the same "limit" choices. Both discs can be limited to businesses or residences or both listings as well. Help screens are easy to locate and useful. Printing is quick and easy, and an export feature allows fast, flexible, predefined or customized formats. If a PC has a modem, an "auto dial" feature saves even more time.

Businesses can find new customers, conduct direct mail campaigns, enlarge telemarketing efforts, designate research markets, assign sales territories, and locate suppliers. Individuals will use it to find lost friends and plan trips. Reasonably priced, this or one of PhoneDisc's other business discs may be perfect for individuals or a library or business.—**Susan C. Awe**

249. **Consumer Sales Leads.** 1997 ed. [CD-ROM]. Carter Lake, Iowa, PhoneDisc, 1997. 5 discs. Minimum system requirements (Windows version): IBM or compatible 386. CD-ROM drive. Windows 3.1. 4MB RAM. Minimum system requirements (Macintosh version): Macintosh Plus/Classic. CD-ROM drive. System 6.04. $79.95.

Identifying qualified sales leads for direct mail and telemarketing can often be difficult and expensive. One database of nationwide "white pages" that is both economical and easy to use is PhoneDisc's *Consumer Sales Leads*. The database is structured the same as another PhoneDisc product, *PowerFinder*. The search can be made by name, address, and phone number or limited by any geographic field, from zip code to metropolitan statistical area and area codes. Searching across discs is easy. By simply switching to a new disc and pressing the disc icon, the search is automatically repeated.

Consumer Sales Leads exports into formats suitable for spreadsheets, organizers, word processors, and mailing label programs and contains printing options for a wide variety of labels. It also includes some census information, including median household income and mean housing value. Unfortunately, these data are not searchable or complete in all records.

Because searching is limited to geographic fields and does not include any kind of demographic data, *Consumer Sales Leads* is a misleading name. However, for the price, it is a good start, and for libraries it is an excellent alternative to published telephone books.—**Deborah S. Hatfield**

250. **The Directory of Business Information Resources, 1997.** 5th ed. Leslie Mackenzie and Amy Lignor, eds. Lakeville, Conn., Grey House Publishing, 1997. 1308p. index. $150.00pa. ISBN 0-939300-79-6.

Although the title of this directory indicates coverage of all types of business information sources, it is in fact focused on the needs of marketers, market researchers, advertisers, and public relations personnel wanting to reach a target market or audience. Organized in 93 industry-specific chapters, the directory's more than 10,000 resources include associations, newsletters, magazines, trade shows, directories, and databases. The industries covered range from very high tech (e.g., computers and data processing, telecommunications) to industrial (e.g., building and construction, electrical and electronics manufacturers) to services (exhibits and meeting planners, marketing services). Within chapters, resources are listed alphabetically under the categories of associations, newsletters, and so forth. Every entry includes basic directory information as well as at least one line of descriptive text. Beyond that, entries may also offer tax numbers, date of establishment or founding, membership counts (for associations), circulation and subscription price (for newsletters and magazines), and dates and attendance numbers (for conferences and trade shows). Surprisingly, e-mail and URL addresses are still not included.

There seems to be little consistency in providing the supplementary information; one assumes it would have been available universally if the publisher had made the effort to track it down. Another question arises over selection criteria: Because there is no statement setting out what is included and why, and selection is necessarily selective rather than comprehensive, a reader would assume that the most important items are included in each category. However, this is often not the case. An example is the inclusion of the *Wisconsin Library Association Bulletin* among the six newsletters listed for the "Libraries" section. Although the *WLA Bulletin* is no doubt an exemplary publication, its inclusion here seems somewhat odd at best. Additionally, there is no entry under "Associations" for American Society of Information Scientists (ASIS), one of the most important and influential organizations in the library and information science profession.

The strength of this directory is that it does an adequate job of assembling in one place six key components of marketing and public relations resources for a broad range of industries. However, a check of several industries indicates the coverage is selective rather than comprehensive, and the information is so minimal that it provides only a starting place for tracking down answers rather the than answers themselves. It would be helpful for a preliminary marketing overview, but for more thorough marketing plans one would still need *Encyclopedia of Associations* (Gale, 1997) and similar directories. However, despite these drawbacks, *The Directory of Business Information Resources* could function as a one-stop source for small public libraries in a pinch.—**G. Kim Dority**

251. **Handbook of World Mineral Trade Statistics 1990-1995.** By the United Nations Conference on Trade and Development. New York, United Nations, 1997. 291p. $46.00pa. ISBN 92-1-112407-7. S/N E.97.II.D.3.

Responding to the need for global trade data on minerals, the United Nations (UN) has issued the first comprehensive source providing both import and export quantities and values for selected nonfuel minerals and metals for 197 countries and territories. These areas are further divided into regions and subregions with their own aggregate figures.

Following a summary table on the value of world exports and imports of minerals, the handbook presents data on over 60 metals and minerals. The commodities covered represent 93 percent of the 1995 world trade in minerals. Each mineral comes with its Standard International Trade Classification (SITC) and Harmonized Commodity Description and Coding System (HS) class numbers. The export and import data for six years by country and region, given in quantity (weight) and value (U.S. dollars) is also included. The final section has production statistics from 1990.

The organization is in standard UN tabular format. The numbers are small but legible, with no charts or graphs to break up the presentation. The sources of data are reputable including the U.S. Bureau of the Mines, the British Geological Survey, and the World Bureau of Metal Statistics. The United Nations intends to continue and expand this publication in the future to eventually include "all mineral and metals playing a role in world trade; with special attention to minerals and metals of specific interest to developing countries."

This source contributes significantly to the knowledge of global minerals trade and is a welcome addition in this important area. However, it is a specialized publication and would not be suitable for all collections. Libraries serving users in the minerals industry or ancillary industries would find this a useful reference.—**Gerald L. Gill**

252. **International Trade Statistics Yearbook, 1995. Annuaire Statistique du Commerce International.** By the Department for Economic and Social Information and Policy Analysis, Statistics Division. New York, United Nations, 1996. 2v. $135.00/set. ISBN 92-1-061169-1. S/N E/F.97.XVII.2.

The International Trade Statistics Yearbook contains data regarding individual countries' external trade performances in terms of overall trends in current value and in volume and price, importance of trading partners, and significance of individual commodities imported and exported. The two-volume work is made up of charts containing statistics through 1995. Data are presented in English and in French.

The first volume consists of detailed import and export trade data by individual country. Data are presented in national currency, but some countries give the information in U.S. dollars. Data analysis for imports is based on the *Classification by Broad Economic Categories* and for exports on the *Classification of Commodities by Industrial Origin*. Economic categories and specific industries are arranged according to the *International Standard Industrial Classification of All Economic Activities* (SITC). The second volume contains commodity tables detailing the total trade of commodities analyzed by regions and countries.

The statistics presented here are compiled from national published sources; the data are from governments and the United Nations publications, including *Monthly Bulletin of Statistics* and *Statistical Yearbook*. This comprehensive work is highly recommended for academic and research collections.

—**Lucy Heckman**

253. Koschnick, Wolfgang J. **Dictionary of Social and Market Research.** New York, John Wiley, 1996. 416p. $59.95. ISBN 0-470-23733-3.

A serious difficulty that plagues practitioners and students of social and marketing research is the vast number of terms, concepts, and techniques that are required to enable meaningful communication. Koschnick's *Dictionary of Social and Market Research* provides concise and authoritative definitions and explanations of more than 2,500 technical terms that are most likely to be encountered in the practice or study of behavioral research. More than simply a dictionary, this reference volume can be used as an overview of current research practices. Entries have been carefully cross-referenced, so that definitions used in explaining a given term are themselves defined. Most of the explanations can be understood by readers with little technical background, although some of the more quantitative entries can best be appreciated by those who have studied or practiced social or market research or who are familiar with mathematical or statistical terminology. Even students of statistics may benefit from the insightful definitions. The book is remarkable for the broad range and depth of information, understandable to a reader with only modest technical training, and compressed into a single volume.—**William C. Struning**

254. **Market Share and Business Rankings Worldwide.** [CD-ROM]. Detroit, Gale, 1997. Minimum system requirements: IBM or compatible 386 (486DX recommended). ISO 9660 CD-ROM drive with Microsoft CD-ROM Extensions 2.2 (double-speed or faster recommended). DOS 5.0. 4MB RAM (8MB or more recommended). 5MB hard disk space. VGA monitor and graphics card. Windows-compatible mouse. Windows-compatible printer. $1,495.00. ISBN 0-7876-0282-5.

The *Market Share and Business Rankings Worldwide* CD-ROM product includes the print contents of current and past editions of Gale products, such as the *Market Share Reporter*, *World Market Share Reporter*, *Business Rankings Annual*, and *European Business Rankings*. The information contained within this database includes corporate, industrial, and organizational rankings by a variety of criteria, such as market share, revenue, numbers of stores or outlets, research and development, opinion polls, and almost any other category imaginable. Access to these data is provided by means of several menu options.

Individuals can search by company or institution (the latter including some political entities and nonprofit organizations), by type of industry, by brand, and by geographic location. Full-text (including Boolean) searching is also available, as well as Extended Searching, which allows one to limit a search to some commonly searched fields. Finally, Expert Searching, although more complicated, is useful in performing searches for specific criteria in a variety of different fields.

Although the inclusion of these data in a searchable format is useful, the database suffers from a lack of a controlled vocabulary. For example, a search for AFSCME or the Church of Jesus Christ of Latter-day Saints will result in no hits, as compared with a search for the American Federation of State, County, and Municipal Employees or the Mormon Church. Furthermore, field-specific searching may retrieve seemingly incongruous results. An extended search for Pink Floyd requires that one must enter the name of the band in the "Person" field rather than the "Company," "Institution," or "Brand" fields in order to retrieve data, bringing to mind the eternal question of which band member is named Pink. The information contained within this product is also necessarily uneven, as it depends upon primary data collection and analysis that is not done consistently across all industrial classifications or businesses.

At approximately $1,500, many libraries may choose to buy one or more of the individual print titles that this database compiles. However, the product is recommended for libraries with a high demand for market share and business ranking data, for libraries with patrons requiring the advantages of a searchable database, or for libraries choosing to make use of networked information sources. It is also recommended for libraries with comprehensive business collections as well as pertinent special libraries.

—**Mark A. Allan**

255. Metz, Allan, comp. **A NAFTA Bibliography.** Westport, Conn., Greenwood Press, 1996. 491p. index. (Bibliographies and Indexes in Economics and Economic History, no.18). $89.50. ISBN 0-313-29463-1.

As stated in the introduction, this volume is the first book-length bibliography covering the development, passage, and status of the North American Free Trade Agreement (NAFTA). The bibliography covers English-language books, journal articles, and other materials from 1988 through 1995, excluding review literature, television transcripts, and letters to the editor. Works in which NAFTA is not the primary focus are also excluded unless the item is unique or covers a particular subject matter.

The book is divided into 3 format-based parts. The 1st part covers serial publications. Items indexed are arranged under broad subject headings, such as "business," and are defined as either multiple entries or single entries. Multiple entries list articles from the same magazine that have appeared over time. Most of these entries are not annotated. Single entries are annotated, for the most part, and are derived from scholarly journals. The multiple entry lists are especially useful because they identify those magazines that contain comprehensive coverage of NAFTA. The 2d part covers books, government documents, selected dissertations, and pamphlets. Entries are categorized by format and then chronologically by publication date. Of particular use in this section are references to special reports from research institutes. The final part covers nonbook materials. This section is rather lean but does introduce the reader to a variety of useful sources, although only six Internet sites are listed, and they are not accompanied by any commentary about their specific content or usefulness. Author and subject indexes complete the volume.

The book's strengths are notable. It is generally well organized, the content has been informed by a broad range of indexing services, and the inclusion of both magazines and scholarly serials adds a significant dimension to the understanding of NAFTA's development. However, aside from the choice of typeface that makes the pages difficult to read, the lack of clearly delineated criteria used for selecting or not selecting materials beyond references to language and period leaves the reader without any framework for understanding what additional resources have been excluded from the bibliography. [R: Choice, May 97, pp. 1476-78]—**Robert V. Labaree**

256. Mitchell, Susan. **Generation X: The Young Adult Market.** Ithaca, N.Y., New Strategist, 1997. 261p. index. $69.95. ISBN 1-885070-09-8.

Generation X may be smaller in numbers than the Baby Boomers, but people should not deny their buying clout in specific markets. From beer to baby food, the buying habits of the 18- to 34-year-old segment of the U.S. population are analyzed in Mitchell's work.

The nine chapters of this book cover nine categories from "Attitude" to "Wealth." Within the 9 chapters are 95 tables of data. Explanation and analysis, including future trends, precede each table. The data have been thoroughly compiled from reliable sources, such as the Census Bureau, the Bureau of Labor Statistics, and the General Social Survey of the University of Chicago's National Opinion Research Center. The source of the data is included with each table. The tables are well designed and easy to read. The book contains an index and a glossary of terms used in the tables. Readers will learn, for example, that Generation X is officially defined as people in the United States born between 1965 and 1976.

Mitchell has painted a demographic picture of the wants and needs of the Generation X market. This book is a concise reference to what those markets are or could be and will give market researchers additional insight into what products and services to sell to this market segment. It is a useful marketing tool for many different industries and should be included in the collection of business schools as well.

—**Deborah S. Hatfield**

257. Mogelonsky, Marcia. **Who's Buying Food & Drink: Who Spends How Much on Food and Alcohol, At and Away from Home.** Ithaca, N.Y., New Strategist, 1996. 283p. index. $69.95. ISBN 1-885070-04-7.

258. Wellner, Alison Stein. **Who's Buying for the Home: Who Spends How Much on Products and Services for the Home.** Ithaca, N.Y., New Strategist, 1996. 496p. index. $89.95. ISBN 1-885070-05-5.

These two new publications by New Strategist provide researchers, consumers, students, marketing managers, and others with interesting details on what consumers are spending money on in their homes and for food and drink at and away from home. Both books use data from the Bureau of Labor Statistics Consumer Expenditure Survey, which since the mid-1800s has collected 35,000 spending records from 25,000 U.S. households each year. As the twentieth century draws to a close, people in the United States are more interested in food than ever before, and are outfitting and operating their "castles" in new, expensive ways.

Who's Buying for the Home tracks spending on many products and services by the demographics that influence how people spend (e.g., age, income, household type, region of the country, race, education, number of earners in the household, and occupation). Section 1 covers shelter, and 2, household operations. Aside from covering the obvious—rent and furniture—computers and software, power tools, postage and stationery, bedroom linens, plumbing supplies, and telephone services are also surveyed. Average spending tables showing the big spenders, per capita tables showing individuals, indexed tables revealing households spending above and below the average, and total spending tables on the overall size of the market and market share tables show how much of the market is controlled by household agents. Both books include projections by age of total spending and market shares to the year 2000. [R: Choice, May 97, p. 1482]—**Susan C. Awe**

259. **Plunkett's Retail Industry Almanac.** Jack W. Plunkett, ed. Galveston, Tex., Plunkett Research, 1997. 682p. index. $129.99pa. ISBN 0-9638268-5-9.

In this retail trade guide, Plunkett covers the retail industry in detail. The introductory chapter contains an overview of the retail industry with trends and statistics. Chapters 2 through 5 discuss useful retail industry contact sources with World Wide Web addresses; online retailing and nonstore retailers; retail sites on the Web by broad subject with Web addresses; malls, superstores, and shopping centers; and employment, careers, earnings, and job outlook in the retail trade.

Chapter 6, the main section of the book, provides profiles with data on 491 companies that Plunkett calls "The Retail 500." Each business profile includes store data; types of business; brands, divisions, and affiliates; chief officers to contact, telephone and fax numbers; address and Internet address; financial information; salaries and benefits information; competitive advantage; locations; and growth plans and special features. Appendix 1 contains monthly sales and inventory statistics, explanatory material on terms, information on reliability of data, factors for adjusting seasonal variations, and Standard Industrial Classifications. In the back of the book, a helpful combined index lists companies by store name, subsidiaries, brand names, and selected affiliations to provide a variety of access.

The detailed and varied information found here on retail trade is difficult to easily access elsewhere in one volume. The almanac should be a welcome addition to business and large public and academic libraries that deal with the retail trade side of business.—**O. Gene Norman**

260. **Review of Maritime Transport 1997.** By the UNCTAD Secretariat. New York, United Nations, 1997. 133p. $50.00pa. ISBN 92-1-112412-3. ISSN 0566-7682. S/N GV.E.97.II.D.9.

Published by the United Nations Conference on Trade and Development, this annual compendium provides trends, developments, and statistics in world maritime transport. In addition, the work discusses the economic aspects of seaborne trade, the expansion of the world merchant fleet, the productivity of the world fleet, the variable freight markets, the increased port traffic, and the additional globalization of activities of service providers. Fifty-one tables list such current data as world output, exports and imports by major region, and the most important maritime countries or areas. A list of six boxes indicates such information as vessel and registry groupings used in the *Review*. Twelve graphs illustrate such concepts as a forecast of future world seaborne trade for the next eight years. Supplementary material in the back of the volume, referred to as annex 1 through annex 5, contains more data, including a classification of countries, a group of statistical tables, and a list of shipping Internet sites. The addition of an index would improve access to specific information in the *Review*.

This handy publication provides much detailed information that would be difficult to locate in another single volume. Business, public, and academic libraries requiring information on international trade and shipping should find this volume useful.—**O. Gene Norman**

261. Russell, Cheryl. **The Mid-Youth Market: Baby Boomers in Their Peak Earning and Spending Years.** Ithaca, N.Y., New Strategist, 1996. 271p. index. $69.95. ISBN 1-885070-06-3.

Russell, a nationally known demographer and authority on the Baby Boomers, has analyzed trends in Boomers' families and households and produced tables based on census data. The eight chapters cover population, households and living arrangements, labor force, income and assets, spending, health, education, and attitudes and behavior. The chapter on attitudes and behavior also uses data from the 1994 General Social Survey of the University of Chicago's National Opinion Research Center.

Baby Boomers are now in their peak earning, spending, and saving years. In industry after industry—automotive, home furnishings, apparel—Boomers have boosted the bottom lines. Marketers, researchers, students, and business owners/managers will see how the 35 to 54 age group is expanding. In addition, as Boomers guide their children and help their parents, this "mid-youth" market will be the most dominant consumer force the United States has ever known.

In addition to a detailed table of contents to assist users in locating data, a lengthy index and a glossary of terms used in the tables and texts are provided. For further information, the original source for the data in the tables is listed at the bottom of each table. The millions of self-indulgent, demanding, fun-loving Boomers are showing businesses and society in general that the "youth market" is just a state of mind.—**Susan C. Awe**

262. **Services—The Export of the 21st Century: A Guidebook of US Service Exporters.** [rev. ed.] Joe Reif and others, comps. and eds. San Rafael, Calif., the Northern California Export Council and World Trade Press, 1997. 180p. $19.95pa. ISBN 1-885073-41-0.

This how-to manual and sourcebook runs the gamut of service export know-how and opportunities. The guide is aimed at service firms who are interested in expanding internationally and seeks to provide them with the basic strategies and tools to accomplish that objective. Although less than 200 pages, its 8 1/2-by-11-inch size allows for significant amounts of information to be presented. The first six chapters after the overview cover export basics, such as the export decision, marketing and market research, trade barriers, U.S. government regulations, and finance. These chapters include case studies, highlighted additional information emphasizing practical considerations, and occasionally lists of additional information. The case studies consist of one-page examples describing how one company has dealt with the challenges of exporting its particular service. These studies are tied into the chapter they accompany.

The 2d part, comprising all of chapter 8, is devoted to examining and analyzing 20 industries. The industries encompass banking, computer services, entertainment, franchising, insurance, retailing, and telecommunications, among others. Each industry report reviews the domestic and international markets, market barriers, market channels, opportunities in various regions, best bets for export opportunities, sources of assistance, and helpful publications. Internet sites are given where applicable. Further information is provided by the appendixes, which include data on associations, U.S. government contacts, trade statistics, and a bibliography.

On the whole, this is a well-written and -researched reference. One error, however, did surface. The authors cite the *U.S. Industrial Outlook* (see ARBA 94, entry 218) and *Worldcasts* (Information Access Company) as active sources, when both ceased publication in 1994. Despite this mistake, this excellent reference manual on marketing services overseas is appropriate for public and academic libraries.—**Gerald L. Gill**

REAL ESTATE

263. Shim, Jae K., Joel G. Siegel, and Stephen W. Hartman. **Dictionary of Real Estate.** New York, John Wiley, 1996. 307p. illus. (Business Dictionary Series). $19.95pa. ISBN 0-471-01335-8.

Providing succinct and precise definitions of a full spectrum of terms relating to real estate, this volume is accessible to the layperson who may be involved with a first real estate transaction and needs to define a term quickly. At the same time, the dictionary provides enough information about a term or concept to serve as an accurate introduction for the student or professional in the field. The coverage is admirably broad, including such areas as appraisal, escrow, law, agency and ethics, and even architecture and construction. Another strength is the inclusion of examples, applications, diagrams, and the like. With 3,000 terms defined in 300 pages, entries are short. Those people involved in real estate practice will obviously need to go beyond a basic definition, but for both a general and a professional audience, this volume provides an excellent place to start to understand an unfamiliar term.—**JoAnn V. Rogers**

TAXATION

264. Collins, James T., and Robert M. Kozub. **State and Local Taxation Answer Book.** Gaithersville, Md., Aspen, 1997. 1v. (various paging). index. (The Panel Answer Book Series). $118.00. ISBN 1-56706-374-8.

This book is an attempt to provide tax practitioners with information on a wide range of state and local tax issues in a question-and-answer format. Questions are grouped in 20 chapters under broad headings, such as real property taxes, personal property taxes, corporate franchise and income taxes, and sales and use taxes. A brief table of contents and a complete list of questions begin the volume. The back of the book features a highly detailed subject index, separate indexes by court decision and Internal Revenue Code section, a glossary of tax terms, and a directory of state tax departments. The publisher indicates that the book will be updated periodically.

This is definitely a source for the professional and not the layperson. With this caveat, the book fulfills its purpose well. For tax professionals, the question-and-answer format and variety of finding aids make this an ideal quick reference or starting point for in-depth research. Answers are concise, with examples frequently provided, as well as ample references to primary sources of law. Although the book may not enable a business manager without a tax background to deal with a complex question single-handedly, it could certainly assist the manager in understanding the issues and in discussing them intelligently with a professional. The work is recommended for libraries serving tax practitioners and business managers.—**Christopher J. Hoeppner**

5 Education

GENERAL WORKS

Bibliography

265. **Bibliographic Guide to Education 1996.** New York, G. K. Hall/Simon & Schuster Macmillan, 1997. 886p. $385.00. ISBN 0-7838-1756-8. ISSN 0147-6505.

The cataloging records from Columbia University's Teachers College and the New York Public Library comprise the entries listed in this G. K. Hall bibliographic title (see entry 109 for a thorough review of the series). Typical of the series, the scope here is international and multilingual, with nonbook materials (except serials) included. Administrative reports from departments of education (both domestic and foreign) are covered as well. More than 200 separate educational systems are represented, categorized into standard disciplines within the broad field of education. One unexpected topic was nursing education. The activity level of research in education will make this volume a necessary purchase for many libraries, if they can absorb the book's relatively high cost (see ARBA 94, entry 303, for an earlier review).—**Ed Volz**

Biography

266. Ohles, Frederik, Shirley M. Ohles, and John G. Ramsay. **Biographical Dictionary of Modern American Educators.** Westport, Conn., Greenwood Press, 1997. 432p. index. $79.50. ISBN 0-313-29133-0.

This book is a major revision of the *Biographical Dictionary of American Educators* (see ARBA 79, entry 695), originally published in 1978. The 410 bibliographic entries were selected from a list of nearly 1,500 names submitted by education agencies from the 50 states, and include many women and educators of color that may have been overlooked in the original work. Although those mentioned are not necessarily people of historical prominence, each educator included has "made a distinctive contribution to a facet of education in this country." Of the included educators 173 were born before 1900. Among the selection criteria are a birth date before January 1, 1935, or the candidate being deceased; such criteria allow the significance of an individual's long-term contribution to education to be assessed effectively.

Each bibliographic entry includes family background, educational and career accomplishments, publications and honor, and a reference list. In addition to the alphabetic listing of comprehensive bibliographic entries, the book includes appendixes of birthplaces, states of major service, field of work, chronology of birth years, a chronological listing of important dates in American education, and a comprehensive index.

At a time when American education is confronting increasing criticism from many fronts and attempting solutions such as the implementation of national and local standards, this book provides a strong historical perspective for what has gone on before. Such concepts as implementation of driver's education classes (Amos Neyhart, 1933), a field trip consisting of an all-night bus tour through New York City as part of a social studies class (Roma Gans, 1940s), or adapting the study of physics to elementary school students (Robert Karplus, 1960s), demonstrates that much of what is good in education today has strong historical foundations.—**Craig A. Munsart**

Dictionaries and Encyclopedias

267. **Dictionary of Multicultural Education.** Carl A. Grant and Gloria Ladson-Billings, eds. Phoenix, Ariz., Oryx Press, 1997. 308p. index. $49.95. ISBN 0-89774-798-4.

Approximately 100 scholars have contributed highly informative, richly context-laden, and consistently well-written entries to this exemplary resource for multicultural educators. Noting that the term "multicultural education" and the vocabulary associated with it have suffered from a lack of clarity, the editors offer this dictionary as an explication of more than 150 critical terms that are used in multicultural education. Terms are arranged alphabetically and fall into three main categories: broad terms examined in relation to multicultural education (e.g., "culture" and "race"); methodological/theoretical/conceptual terms (e.g., "ethnography" and "neo-Marxism"); and key court cases (e.g., *Brown v. Topeka Board of Education* and *Plessy v. Ferguson*). Always attributed, entries often include extensive bibliographies, and when possible they are cross-referenced to other entries.

This dictionary is not simply a traditional kind of definitional work, however. As scholar-activists who see multicultural education contributing to equity and social justice, the editors have also included a "Multicultural Education Resources" appendix of organizations, Websites, and Department of Education–funded assistance centers. The last term in this book is *xenophobia*; this important reference work, which belongs in all libraries, may help make that word obsolete.—**G. Douglas Meyers**

268. **International Encyclopedia of the Sociology of Education.** Lawrence J. Saha, ed. New York, Pergamon Press/Elsevier Science, 1997. 961p. index. (Resources in Education). $432.00. ISBN 0-08-042990-4.

This volume is another of the several spin-offs from the highly respected 1994 12-volume publication *The International Encyclopedia of Education* (2d ed.; see ARBA 95, entry 337). The approximately 150 articles in this compilation are organized into 10 sections, each dealing with a division of the main discipline, educational sociology. Examples are social theories, research traditions, the family and schooling, and teachers in society. Each article supplies an overview of the topic, gives background historical information, outlines issues and problems, and reports on significant recent research findings. A sampling showed that each of these articles and their accompanying bibliographies were verbatim reprints from the parent set, in which coverage ends around 1990. Updating of articles such as those that deal with educational technology would have been welcome.

Like the parent set, the tone of the articles is scholarly and theoretical; emphasis is on English-speaking countries, particularly the United Kingdom and the United States; and coverage excludes higher education. The choice of articles for inclusion has been judicious, and the organization logical and thorough. New to this volume are a preface outlining in detail the plan of the volume and introductory overviews of each section, all written by the book's editor, who is from the Australia National University in Canberra. Supplementary material includes a list of contributors, a name index listing all people whose works are cited, and an extensive subject index. This is an impressive, well-written, erudite volume that is recommended for professional and academic collections that do not own the parent set.—**John T. Gillespie**

Directories

269. **Big Book of Opportunities for Women: The Directory of Women's Organizations.** Elizabeth A. Olson, ed. Chicago, J. G. Ferguson Publishing, 1997. 455p. index. $39.95. ISBN 0-89434-183-9.

As a guide for women needing assistance for funding in order to attend colleges and universities, women who are searching for programs offering special assistance to women with disabilities, displaced homemakers, or women who are searching for assistance with almost any aspect of their educational or career interests, this volume is a real find. Its ease of use is a definite asset. The book is organized into five major sections, including programs for majors in specific fields, programs for majors in more than one field, organizations helping specific groups, sources of educational and career assistance, and publications of special interest to women. Other information directories of special interest to women are included in a bibliography at the end of the volume, along with an in-depth index to this volume.

The first section covers many subject majors, from agriculture to art, music, and drama; business; education; engineering; health; humanities; journalism and mass communications; law; library and museums studies; religion and theology; science; and social science. Each entry is numbered for simple access from the index and includes the name of the institution, organization, or association listed, along with address, telephone number, and a very brief abstract of assistance available. For future revisions of this volume it would be useful to include the Websites available for much of this information.

There is much information on scholarships, fellowships, loans, grants, counseling services, women's research centers, job counseling services, and prizes or honors available for women—more than 4,000 programs of assistance. For example, in the humanities section, organizations such as the American Council of Learned Societies, the American Historical Association, *Glamour*, the National Endowment for the Humanities, Pen American Center, and United Daughters of the Confederacy are listed, along with many colleges and universities offering degrees in the noted subject fields. The same is true of the minority women's organizations listed, from the Association of Black Women in Higher Education to the Gamma Phi Delta Sorority. More than 80 women's 2- and 4-year colleges are featured, and it is noted if they have become co-ed.

Although there are, undoubtedly, some missing higher education programs that would be of assistance to women, some omitted organizations of assistance to women, and other additional programs specifically of interest to women, the number and variety of sources listed in this volume should stimulate those searching for additional resources into thinking of other potential sources to approach for help within their locale, state, or region.—**Maureen Pastine**

270. **Certification and Accreditation Programs Directory: A Descriptive Guide....** Michael A. Paré, ed. Detroit, Gale, 1996. 620p. index. $89.50pa. ISBN 0-7876-0463-1. ISSN 1084-2128.

The purpose of this premier edition of the *Certification and Accreditation Programs Directory* is to bring together "detailed information on requirements and procedures for approximately 1600 voluntary certification programs for individuals and over 200 accrediting organizations for educational programs, institutions, businesses, and service providers in one easy-to-use volume." The term *voluntary* separates this volume from the *Professional and Occupational Licensing Directory* (see ARBA 94, entry 800), which lists certifications that are required in order for professionals to work or practice their profession.

This directory is conveniently divided into two main sections. "Certification Programs," the first section, is further subdivided into occupations that are listed in the contents in the front of the volume as well as in a master index in the back. Each certification entry lists the specific title awarded, number of individuals certified, contact information on the organization, requirements for certification, examination information, recertification information, and fees and endorsements or accreditation of certification programs. The second section, "Accreditation Programs," provides contact information for the accrediting organization, number of institutions accredited, application procedures, accreditation procedures, renewal information, fees, and endorsements or accreditation of accreditation programs.

There is a comprehensive master index listing all certification titles, names of certification granting and accrediting organizations, subject headings, and job titles. An alphabetic list of certification acronyms is provided in an appendix. This is a handy reference tool for those needing information on voluntary certification and accreditation programs.—**Sue Brown**

271. **Directory of Education Grants: A Reference Directory Identifying Educational Grants Available to Nonprofit Organizations.** Loxahatchee, Fla., Research Grant Guides, 1996. 152p. index. $59.50pa. ISBN 0-945078-15-3.

This reference directory identifies 650 qualified foundations awarding educational grants to all types of nonprofit organizations. The subjects cover the following categories: adult education, cultural education, elementary/secondary education, health education, higher education, libraries, literacy, medical education, minorities, religious education, scholarships/financial aid, science and mathematics, and special education/disabled.

The state-by-state arrangement helps in a research effort to target only those sources awarding grants in a particular geographic area. Several feature articles will help in proposal strategies, among them "A Fund-raiser's Guide to Education Grants," "A Grant Seeker's Guide to the Internet," and "Ten Tips for More Competitive Grant Proposals." An alphabetic index and a subject index conclude the volume.

Research Grant Guides has been publishing directories on fund-raising guidance for 19 years. This title helps applicants match their proposals to a funder's educational interests. It is an essential research tool for nonprofit organizations.—**Kathleen J. Voigt**

272. Hammer, Patricia Cahape, and Heather Beasley, comps. **Native Education Directory 1997: Organizations and Resources for Educators of Native Americans.** Charleston, W.Va., ERIC Clearinghouse on Rural Education and Small Schools, 1996. 102p. index. $12.00pa. ISBN 1-880785-17-X.

In any reference material of this kind there are several requirements: the information must be carefully selected, logically organized, and complete and descriptive enough that it is user friendly and presents what people actually need. This reference meets those criteria. Reflecting the age of technology, each entry in the directory lists the mailing address, contact person, telephone number, fax number, e-mail address, and a brief description. There are five major sections with rational subsections, making the directory exceptionally useful. In addition, sprinkled throughout the directory are sidebars or additions of important information that are particularly convenient or that may not be readily available, such as "Federal Hotlines and Information Services" or "Other Useful Directories and Guides Related to American Indian and Alaska Native Education." Sections include international, national, and multistate nongovernmental organizations; federal programs; media, periodicals, publishers, and producers; state and territorial governmental and nongovernmental organizations; and colleges and universities offering Native studies, Native language instruction, supportive services, or scholarships for Native students.

Although the directory has been compiled for educators of Native Americans, it would be of great value for those who work with Native American people in any capacity, who are interested in American Indian history and cultures, or who teach non-Natives about Native Americans. Many of the resources, such as periodicals, publishers, e-mail addresses, or Websites, could be used in nearly every school. Recognizing that the Internet is always changing, it is still a true service to have an extensive listing of Native American Websites. Frankly, the directory is also interesting reading and a strong affirmation of the continuity of Native American cultures.

Finally, the information reflects what people have told the compilers, and consequently there are no endorsements for the programs or organizations. However, with so much information available, including the convenient e-mail, fax number, and Website information, the reader cannot only readily search for a particular resource but compare multiple resources to meet a particular need. This inexpensive resource should be in every high school and certainly in all schools that serve Native American students. [R: Choice, July/Aug 97, p. 1782]—**Karen D. Harvey**

273. Washburn, David E., and Neil L. Brown. **The Multicultural Education Directory.** Bloomsburg, Pa., Inquiry International, 1996. 265p. $39.95. ISBN 0-9635521-3-9.

Washburn has a lengthy background in ethnic studies and wrote *Ethnic Studies, Bilingual/Bicultural Education and Multicultural Teacher Education in the United States* (see ARBA 81, entry 465). Although many titles promote multiculturalism and suggest methods for teaching in a multicultural classroom, Washburn and Brown attempt to provide teachers, administrators, and curriculum designers with a practical means to locate the particulars of multicultural programs in each of the larger school districts in the United States.

Each of the approximately 300 programs covered by this directory is described using one of the categories in Christine E. Sleeter and Carl A. Grant's *Making Choices for Multicultural Education: Five Approaches to Race, Class, and Gender* (Prentice Hall, 1993). Most of the information for the directory was obtained through a questionnaire that determined what elements were studied in a particular curriculum (e.g., art, beliefs); groups studied; disciplines participating in the curriculum; social goals; school goals; and curricular and instructional aims that each district was hoping to achieve through a multicultural education program. Some entries have full descriptions of programs, others only a contact name, and each entry notes whether any handouts or other elements of the curriculum are available for purchase or use. There is no index, but adequate cross-referencing is achieved with the table of contents and the chapter organization. This reference will be useful for educators, curriculum designers, and administrators responsible for curriculum decisions, to see who is doing what, where. The directory is for comprehensive or graduate-level education collections.—**Glynys R. Thomas**

Handbooks and Yearbooks

274. **Guide to Federal Funding for Education, 1997.** 23d ed. Elizabeth A. Bernhard, Jody Feder, and Alvin C. Lin, eds. Washington, D.C., Education Funding Research Council, 1997. 2v. index. $388.95/yr. looseleaf with binder. ISBN 0-933538-63-4. ISSN 0275-8393.

With all of the fiscal uncertainties facing institutions of higher education, particularly public universities, more emphasis is being put forth by both faculty and administrators to fund research projects. This guide, designated for research purposes as the "#1 information resource for federal aid to education," emphasizes the financial increases in the field with the current presidential and congressional focus on public schools. This hefty two-volume reference work is in looseleaf format with topical divisions; subscribers also receive the twice-monthly *Federal Grant Deadline Calendar* updating deadlines and new available monies.

The guide lists new services, what online grant information is available from the government, a grantmakers directory listing key program officials, reproducible copies of application forms, an expanded section that describes and updates the funding status of programs listed, and an index telling how competitive a program is. According to the guide, some $50 billion is available in federal aid for education programs in 1997. The audience for this work is primarily educators in universities, community colleges, and schools of all types, as well as for state and local agencies, day care, health care, and other providers of services for children.

This is a comprehensive federal guide for funding in education and would be welcomed by all the institutions and professionals for which it was written. It covers many subjects, from bilingual education and arts and humanities to technology for education and adult education and literacy. Special groups are also highlighted: Native Americans, veterans, the disabled, the disadvantaged, and teachers for teacher training.

—**Anne F. Roberts**

275. **The Guide to the Evaluation of Educational Experiences in the Armed Services, 1996. Volume 1: Army.** Washington, D.C., American Council on Education; distr., Phoenix, Ariz., Oryx Press, 1996. 1v. (various paging). index. $35.00pa. ISBN 1-57356-055-3.

276. **The Guide to the Evaluation of Educational Experiences in the Armed Services, 1996. Volume 2: Navy.** Washington, D.C., American Council on Education; distr., Phoenix, Ariz., Oryx Press, 1996. 1v. (various paging). index. $35.00pa. ISBN 1-57356-056-1.

277. **The Guide to the Evaluation of Educational Experiences in the Armed Services, 1996. Volume 3: Air Force, Coast Guard, Department of Defense, Marine Corps.** Washington, D.C., American Council on Education; distr., Phoenix, Ariz., Oryx Press, 1996. 1v. (various paging). index. $35.00pa. ISBN 1-57356-057-X.

Those people who need this guide will probably already know about its 50-year track record. They will also be familiar with the dense, daunting content, turgid style, and relentless organization. Basically, these volumes are a guide for postsecondary institutions to evaluate the college credit potential of various military training experiences. The three volumes, one each for the Army and Navy and another for the other services, are clearly and consistently organized and fully and accurately indexed. The introductory material, sample entries, and appendixes are as clear as possible for such heavy material. The descriptions of military courses and occupational specialties and the credit recommendations for them are the heart of the volumes. Academic libraries and such places as college admissions offices will find this guide invaluable but not fun.—**John Newman**

278. Kopka, Deborah L. **School Violence: A Reference Handbook.** Santa Barbara, Calif., ABC-CLIO, 1997. 184p. index. (Contemporary World Issues). $39.50. ISBN 0-87436-861-8.

Goal 7 of the Educate America Act of 1994 envisions schools free of violence and related youth pathologies by the year 2000. This volume in the Contemporary World Issues series rightly identifies a need for information that defines the term according to the current (not necessarily conventional) wisdom. It gives a bit of history, provides a chronology of prevention efforts beginning in 1968, collects basic statistics, outlines legislation, and briefly reviews prevention strategies and the biographies of key players. The book helps the reader contact organizations by giving addresses, telephone and fax numbers, and e-mail addresses where available. It lists detailed information sources—periodicals; books; and many nonprint sources, including online services, films, and videotapes. Notes and bibliographies serve researchers at a variety of levels.

This source will be helpful to program planners, writers and journalists, school officials, law enforcement units, and other groups and agencies that deal with violence among youth. The author is not an authority on the topic but is a thorough researcher and an experienced "specialist in the design, development, and delivery of educational media for youth." Not an in-depth treatment, this book is nonetheless a starting place for persons seeking sources of data and information and would best serve as a U.S., not a world, source.—**Edna M. Boardman**

Indexes

279. **Education Index: A Cumulative Author Subject Index to a Selected List of Educational Periodicals, Yearbooks, and Monographs. July 1995 to June 1996.** Barbara Berry and Mildred A. Donahue, eds. Bronx, N.Y., H. W. Wilson, 1995, 1996. 1871p. priced on a service basis rate. ISSN 0013-1385.

Education Index has an important niche in the educational research marketplace. As an index primarily to the educational journal literature, it includes roughly half of the journals covered by the Educational Resources Information Center (ERIC) indexes and databases. However, the volume does index some journals not covered by ERIC, and it also indexes educational yearbooks and a significant number of monographs. In short, if a researcher is really digging for appropriate material on an educational topic, *Education Index* is an essential research tool.

Bibliographic references in the index are arranged by author and subject in one alphabetic sequence; they are then listed alphabetically by title. The citations include the author, article title, journal name, volume, pages, month/season, and year. Issue numbers are excluded. Journal names are often abbreviated, although they are fully spelled out in a list of journal abbreviations at the front of the volume. *Education Index* also includes citations to reviews of other media; these are found under the headings "Videotape Reviews/Single Works," "Motion Picture Reviews/Single Works," and "Computer Programs/Evaluation." Book reviews are found in a separate section in the back of the volume and are arranged alphabetically by the book's author. Law cases are cited under the subheading "Suits and Claims" within various subject categories.

The print version of *Education Index* does not include abstracts, which can help in determining the value of an article. Also, unlike the *Readers' Guide to Periodical Literature* (see entry 70), it continues to abbreviate journal titles, which can be a minor inconvenience. However, the index's ease of use and its inclusion of citations for monographs and reviews earn it a fundamental place among educational research sources. The work is highly recommended both for college and university libraries supporting teacher education programs and for larger public libraries.—**Stephen H. Aby**

ALTERNATIVE EDUCATION

280. Burgess, William E. **The Oryx Guide to Distance Learning: A Comprehensive Listing of Electronic and Other Media-Assisted Courses.** 2d ed. Phoenix, Ariz., Oryx Press, 1997. 497p. index. $98.50pa. ISBN 1-57356-073-1.

The 2d edition of this guide provides detailed, objective information on over 4,000 courses offered for credit through 434 accredited institutions. The number of courses listed is more than double the number in the 1st edition published in 1994 (see ARBA 95, entry 342), and the courses represent a wider variety of delivery options, but the guide's purpose, audience, and organization remain the same.

The bulk of the volume is comprised of information arranged by state, then alphabetically by institution. Information such as institutional profile, credit and grading policies, tuition, and course descriptions are provided. E-mail addresses are included in program contact information, but surprisingly few URLs for institutional Websites are listed. Three indexes—subject, institution, and delivery system—are organized geographically and alphabetically, as is the main entry section. Public and academic librarians will find this work a fine resource for potential distance learner patrons, although the guide is similar enough to the much less expensive and more visually attractive *Peterson's Distance Learning 1997* (see ARBA 97, entry 291) that it may not be the first choice for small- and medium-sized collections.

—**Jennie Ver Steeg**

COMPUTER RESOURCES

281. Cooper, Gail, and Garry Cooper. **Virtual Field Trips.** Englewood, Colo., Libraries Unlimited, 1997. 168p. index. $24.00pa. ISBN 1-56308-557-7.

This little book grows better the more closely the user examines it. The authors state in their introduction that they have designed *Virtual Field Trips* to assist teachers to plan class trips "without worrying about weather and lost and wandering children . . . completely unconstrained by the boundaries of place and time." They have achieved their goal with flying colors, producing a teachers' handbook that should be made available to anyone who works with young people.

Virtual Field Trips is divided into 13 chapters organized by subject. The first chapter, "Historic Time Travel," contains listings for 19 sites, which range from the Paleolithic Painted Cave to the Gulf War. Each site citation is followed by a brief annotation describing the site and its attraction for young people. Subjects are cross-referenced, with many *see* and *see also* entries in each chapter. Chapter 13 presents sites specifically suitable for primary-age children, such as Mr. Rogers' Neighborhood and Pooh's Page. A comprehensive index makes this book even more user-friendly.

A random sampling of 10 of the sites found 8 active, 2 which needed some truncating of the address (a process clearly explained by the authors in the introduction), and 1 which is no longer active. This is a good average, considering the ephemeral nature of some Websites. The authors have included their e-mail addresses, so the readers can contact them about changes of site addresses as well as new interesting sites they have discovered.

This book is highly recommended for the school professional library, especially because of its reasonable cost. Teachers will find a great deal of lesson-planning assistance in *Virtual Field Trips*.

—**Nancy P. Reed**

282. Sorrow, Barbara Head, and Betty S. Lumpkin. **CD-ROM for Librarians and Educators: A Guide to Over 800 Instructional Resources.** 2d ed. Jefferson, N.C., McFarland, 1996. 405p. index. $45.00pa. ISBN 0-7864-0176-1.

This update to the original 1993 edition of this work (see ARBA 94, entry 1920) has several notable differences from the original. Aside from a slight subtitle change, it has more than doubled in size, increasing from 150 pages to more than 400 pages, while adding 500 titles to its listings. There is also a new section on early education. Arrangement is still by broad subjects, which include aerospace/aviation, AIDS, art, audiovisual, business, careers, computers, current events, dictionaries, education, encyclopedias, geography, government, health, history, indexes, language, literature, mathematics, music, reference, religion, science, and stories. The choice of these topics makes the work especially useful for schools, colleges, and libraries of all types, as well as the general public.

Another noteworthy change is the sizable price increase, which may make the work too expensive for individuals and organizations with small budgets. The easy-to-use format of the work remains the same, with an index arranged by CD-ROM title. Annotations, although not evaluative, do provide selection guidance by indicating the nature of each database, and most indicate age level of the intended audience. It is interesting that after three years the revised work still does not include *The World Book New Illustrated Information Finder* (see ARBA 95, entry 67)—the CD-ROM version of this standard K-12 school encyclopedia.

Because this work is selective in nature, with each work having been carefully reviewed or evaluated against a basic set of criteria, omission of a title could be construed as indicating that a CD-ROM product is without educational value. This is disturbing given the fact that the above title is missing. Nonetheless, the work is recommended for school, public, and other general libraries as well as individuals who can afford it, although it probably should be supplemented with more current titles.—**Carol Truett**

ELEMENTARY AND SECONDARY EDUCATION

Bibliography

283. **El-Hi Textbooks and Serials in Print 1997: Including Related Teaching Materials K-12.** 125th ed. New Providence, N.J., R. R. Bowker/Reed Reference Publishing, 1997. 2056p. index. $149.00/set. ISBN 0-8352-3915-2. ISSN 0000-0825.

This edition lists 90,120 elementary, junior, and senior high school textbooks and pedagogical books. It includes six indexes. The main index is topically arranged by 21 broad subject areas and 321 more specific subdivisions with appropriate cross-references. The author and title indexes guide the user to the page of the complete listing in the subject index. The series index is arranged by 22 main subject categories and includes full information for each series. As in most R. R. Bowker publications, there is detailed instruction on how to use this volume. *El-Hi Textbooks and Serials in Print* has been reviewed in *American Reference Books Annual* many times and is the standard source of information on textbooks and serials. It remains an essential purchase.—**Bohdan S. Wynar**

284. Harms, Jeanne McLain, and Lucille J. Lettow. **Picture Books to Enhance the Curriculum.** Bronx, N.Y., H. W. Wilson, 1996. 521p. index. $38.00. ISBN 0-8242-0867-6.

Picture Books to Enhance the Curriculum consists of a list of picture books arranged thematically to provide elementary school teachers and educators an avenue to a multidimensional, literature-based curriculum. The inclusion of stories and colorful illustrations and the presentation of various themes in the planned curriculum augments the teaching process with the use of visual aids and classroom discussion initiators. The authors state in the introduction that this book is not intended to be an exhaustive list of titles under each subject but rather a collection of titles most often found in children's literature collections and in professional collection development sources. For instance, *Children's Catalog* (see entry 586) is readily available.

The book under review has an accessible arrangement that can be used easily in curriculum development. The text is divided into three different indexes. The "Themes Index," the first, offers an author-title list under each subject. The second, the "Picture Book Index," includes an alphabetic arrangement by author of each title listed in the first section. Every title gives complete bibliographic information, a brief annotation, and a list of other subjects that can be used when discussing the book. The last index, the "Title Index," includes an alphabetic list of the titles, followed by the authors' names. There is a key to the themes that is listed at the beginning of the book and includes *see* and *see also* references for simplified access.

Harms and Lettow's book is an easy-to-use and well-arranged presentation of picture books by subject. The authors state that the book is designed to enhance teaching in elementary schools, but this book could also be used in a public library setting when developing programs for children. Including the number of titles and the range of publication dates that were used in the book would have added to the information already given, but these omissions do not detract from the overall usefulness of the material. The annotations and additional subject listings for each title make this a worthwhile addition to the titles presented in *A to Zoo* (see ARBA 94, entry 1176).—**Bridget Volz**

HIGHER EDUCATION

Directories

285. **The A's and B's of Academic Scholarships 1997/98.** 19th ed. Ann Schimke, ed. Alexandria, Va., Octameron; distr., Chicago, Dearborn Trade, 1996. 177p. $9.00pa. ISBN 1-57509-010-4.

Scholarships are a mysterious part of the college world. We know they exist, we know people who have them, but we wonder how many schools offer them and to whom, how to qualify, how much money is given, and how long a particular scholarship lasts. These questions are answered in Schmike's *The A's and B's of Academic Scholarships*. This guide gives the college-bound student a simple rundown of the scholarships available at U.S. universities and colleges. The book is divided up by state and then alphabetically by college or university. A simple table format is used, which lists the names of the scholarship programs, number of awards, money, qualifications, restrictions, renewability, and application dates. The result is an easy-to-scan resource, to fully understand each entry, one must read Schmike's notes in the beginning of the book.

The only drawback to this work is that the editor fails to include a list of addresses and telephone numbers for each of the schools. It would add some pages to the book, but would save the user much time by having to find the information elsewhere. In spite of this major shortcoming, it is a useful resource and a worthwhile purchase.—**Kelly M. Jordan**

286. **The Complete Book of Colleges.** 1998 ed. New York, Princeton Review/Random House, 1997. 1468p. index. $26.95pa. ISBN 0-679-77889-6.

The Complete Book of Colleges has more than 1,400 listings of American colleges and universities arranged alphabetically. Despite the odd alphabetic arrangement, no *see* references are provided, even in the alphabetic index. Entries starting with "University of" do not fall under the letter "U," but the state or city they are located in. University of Minnesota, for instance, comes after Minneapolis College of Art and Design. Each entry is devoted one full page, but many have only one column of text. Most entries include contact information as well as the following standard format: e-mail address, CEEB and ACT codes, statistics on students and faculty, a listing of academic programs, services, facilities, admissions, costs, and financial aid. Some of the information in this book is inaccurate, out of date, and confusing. The University of Minnesota at Crookston, for example, has only the address, telephone number, and e-mail address listed; the rest of the page is blank. After a quick look on the World Wide Web, this reviewer found that the University of Minnesota at Crookston has a detailed Website. This book could be much improved. With access to so much information about colleges and universities available online, there are no excuses for such poor editing. For free online directories of American colleges, Mike Conlon has a meta-listing of links at http://www.clas.ufl.edu/CLAS/american-universities.html and Petersons.com offers yet another listing at http://www.petersons.com/. Petersons.com does not provide the level of detail that they do in their famous print *Peterson's Guide to Four-Year Colleges* (Peterson's Guides, 1996), however, their Website does allow a variety of search options.

A free offer for a CD-ROM comes with this book, but one must send in an enclosed postcard to obtain the CD-ROM. It was not received within one month, so the CD-ROM was not reviewed. The book mentions a companion Internet address: http://www.weapply.com/. At this Website, geared toward high school students, you can download application forms and search for colleges.

Seven indexes are provided in the blue pages in the back of the book: alphabetic, by state, size (only large, medium, or small), environment (urban or rural), cost, selectivity, and "apply." The selectivity index provides only three levels: mega-selective, selective, not-selective. The "apply" index corresponds with the CD-ROM. It lists all colleges that have electronic duplicates of their college admissions forms on the CD-ROM. The alphabetic index is not necessary, because the book is already arranged this way, and it does not give any much needed cross-references. *The Complete Book of Colleges* does not supply an index by majors, which would add value to its use. This guide is not recommended. For the same price *Peterson's Guide to Four-Year Colleges*, even though not perfect, has far better indexing, more schools listed (more than 2,000 total), and more accurate information.—**Christine Drew**

287. **The Complete Scholarship Book.** By Student Services, Inc. Naperville, Ill., Sourcebooks, 1996. 612p. index. $22.95pa. ISBN 1-57071-127-5.

This title details information on more than 5,000 sources of college financial aid provided by nongovernmental organizations. The introduction includes an informative section, which any student would find helpful, with 52 excellent tips for optimizing money for college. The main section of the book lists the funding sources in alphabetic order. Information consists of name, amount of aid available, deadline, field of intended study, address, and other pertinent data. An icon representing special criteria (specific majors, athletics, disability, ethnicity, and so forth) is printed beside each entry to allow for easy visual identification. Indexes for major/career objectives, special criteria, and schools complete the volume.

More than half of the entries are for college-specific scholarships; however, it should be noted that not all universities are represented. Additionally, the list of scholarships from specific universities is far from complete. For example, it lists only two scholarships available from Indiana University. Nothing in the introduction explains how the information is obtained. The promotional materials for *The Complete Scholarship Book* inform readers that Student Services, Inc., also furnishes a free scholarship search database available on the World Wide Web (http://www.fastweb.com). This database contains 180,000-plus awards and is updated daily. A puzzling query is why nothing about this Website appears anywhere in the book itself.

Although one may question the completeness of *The Complete Scholarship Book*, it is generally useful. In any case, the volume is an affordable addition to any reference collection.—**Michele Russo**

288. Custard, Ed, and Dan Saraceno. **The Complete Book of Catholic Colleges.** 1998 ed. New York, Princeton Review/Random House, 1997. 268p. index. $21.00pa. ISBN 0-679-77889-6.

Princeton Review guides are standard reference tools for all high school and public libraries, and this one, devoted solely to 193 Catholic colleges and universities in the United States and Puerto Rico, is no exception. It is highly recommended as a purchase for all Catholic high school libraries. Replete with useful statistics concerning enrollment, environment, cost, admissions, selectivity, level of athletic competition, and majors offered, this guide is accessible and informative.

One-page entries for each college or university are arranged alphabetically. An initial paragraph describes the college's setting; year founded; dominant academic majors; and any distinguished campus art galleries, arenas, museums, or sports programs. The second part of the entry, "Admissions," provides the details concerning high school required courses, test and interview requirements, and availability of financial assistance.

"Financial Aid," the third component, supplies users with school and state financial aid deadlines, available loan programs, and filing requirements. The last part of the entry contains a chart with statistical data about the ethnic and gender diversity of the student body, most popular majors, a freshman profile, and the selectivity of admissions.

The remaining pages provide a listing of colleges and the presence or absence of each profile element such as financial aid or interview necessary, Newman Centers and other Catholic ministries, and useful patron saints. Indexes include alphabetized lists of all the colleges and universities cited; a selectivity ranking ranging from the most to the least selective; colleges by state; and colleges by enrollment size and by urban, suburban; and rural determinations.—**Kathleen W. Craver**

289. Edwards, Alan F., Jr. **Interdisciplinary Undergraduate Programs: A Directory.** 2d ed. Oxford, Ohio, Association for Integrative Studies and Acton, Mass., Copley Publishing Group, 1996. 435p. index. $24.95pa. ISBN 0-87411-881-6.

Like many other directories, this one is based on data gathered through a survey, but it is clearly intended more as a vehicle for presenting the findings of that survey to interested scholars, administrators, and planners than as a comprehensive guide for prospective students or guidance professionals. The author acknowledges that this edition, like the 1st (see ARBA 87, entry 356), represents only a sample of interdisciplinary programs: those that both responded to the survey and met the specific Association for Integrative Studies criteria spelled out in the introduction to this volume.

Nonetheless, this new edition of the directory clearly reflects the persistence of the interdisciplinary movement in U.S. higher education and the increasing number and diversity of interdisciplinary programs, describing 410 in existence in the 1995-1996 academic year, as compared with 235 in 1986 when the 1st edition appeared. Program descriptions are arranged by institution name and include details on the size and type of each program, constituent courses, administrative structure, historical development, and contact information. Appendixes analyze the program list by state and by program type (including broad disciplinary areas) and provide index access to the program descriptions. *Interdisciplinary Undergraduate Programs* continues to be a unique reference work that will be of greatest interest to researchers and practitioners in interdisciplinary higher education. [R: Choice, May 97, p. 1474]—**Gregory M. Toth**

290. Kravets, Marybeth, and Imy Wax. **K & W Guide to Colleges for the Learning Disabled.** 1998 ed. New York, Princeton Review/Random House, 1997. 697p. index. $25.00pa. ISBN 0-375-75043-6.

First published in 1991, this 4th edition of *K & W Guide to Colleges for the Learning Disabled* is a resource guide for students with learning differences. It would also be a valuable source for parents and professionals in helping students identify colleges that will fill all of their needs—educationally, culturally, and socially. The title was conceived independently by the authors more than 20 years ago, but it took until 1987 for their paths to cross, and until 1991 for its first publication to appear.

The 2-page profiles of 310 colleges provide comprehensive information about their services or programs: admissions requirements (general and for students with learning differences), graduation requirements, policies, housing, cost, and student body demographics. In addition, a quick contact reference list covering 1,000 schools supplies school names, addresses, names of individuals who direct the schools' programs or services for students with learning differences, program titles, and telephone numbers. Also included is a section on "getting ready"; a guide to admission, application, and search processes; and a section of helpful advice and encouraging thoughts from a broad spectrum of individuals. When using this guide, users can differentiate between three categories: structured programs that offer the most comprehensive services for students with learning differences, coordinated services that are not as comprehensive, and services that are the least comprehensive but comply with the federal mandate requiring reasonable accommodations to all students.

The authors are nationally respected experts in their field, and with each edition of this title they have expanded their information and included more tips and strategies and more colleges and universities. The *K & W Guide* is a one-of-a-kind resource for all public libraries and university libraries as well.

—**Kathleen J. Voigt**

291. **National Guide to Funding for Higher Education.** 4th ed. Elizabeth H. Rich, ed. New York, Foundation Center, 1996. 1275p. index. $145.00pa. ISBN 0-87954-661-1.

National Guide to Funding for Higher Education is the essential guide to grant-making foundations for academia. There are 4,314 grant-making foundations identified, plus 163 direct corporate giving programs and 102 public charities, for a total of 4,579 grant-making entities interested in supporting higher education. This is almost twice the number identified in the 1989 edition (see ARBA 91, entry 317). Two billion dollars of support is identified from 825 foundations.

This edition has improved indexing using the Grants Classification System (GCS), which provides a more comprehensive and precise terminology. The introduction has a significant section that clearly defines what a foundation is, how to seek grants from a foundation, grant-seeking from a corporation, the sources of the information in each entry, and where to receive other helpful information.

Each entry provides the legal name of the foundation; mailing address; history; telephone number; contact person, donors, or principal contributors; foundation type; fiscal year, date, and deadlines for applications; assets; gifts received; expenditures; qualifying distributions; grants paid; application information; publications; officers, principal administrators, trustees, or directors; and recent grants in higher education. The indexes are comprehensive.

An excellent grant-seeking and fund-raising glossary is also included as well as a bibliography of funding in higher education and a publications and services list of the Foundation Center. The directory has a list of "cooperating collections" in each of the states. The entries are arranged by state and then in alphabetic order. This is an essential purchase for every library in academia.—**Gerald D. Moran**

292. **Peterson's Competitive Colleges 1997-1998.** 16th ed. Princeton, N.J., Peterson's Guides, 1997. 458p. index. $16.95pa. ISBN 1-56079-764-9. ISSN 0887-0152.

Unlike the street-level *Princeton Review Student Access Guide to the Best 309 Colleges* (see ARBA 96, entry 358), which gives the best party schools and drinking spots from a student's perspective, this Peterson guide, in its 16th edition (beginning in 1981), provides up-to-date information for 375 colleges and universities in the United States in concise, 1-page "briefs." Each page gives a paragraph of a type of "mission statement" for the college, followed by highlights on academics, computers on campus, campus life, and the applying process. Also provided in boxes at the bottom are statistics on how many students who applied actually were admitted, a composite of the student body, how many returned after the freshman year, what the careers of the graduates were, and what the costs of tuition and room and board are.

In addition to the majority of the book, there is a majors index and a geographic index. Also supplied are some practical and well-written introductory essays by knowledgeable people from a variety of the institutions surveyed on the following topics: choosing the right college, understanding the college admissions process, applying to professional colleges for art and music, and paying for college. This up-to-date compendium will be useful for parents and students as well as academic, public, and school libraries. Guidance counselors may also want to have a copy handy for referral.—**Anne F. Roberts**

293. **Peterson's Guide to Two-Year Colleges 1998.** 28th ed. Princeton, N.J., Peterson's Guides, 1997. 825p. illus. maps. index. $21.95pa. ISBN 1-56079-784-3. ISSN 0894-9328.

Peterson's Guides certainly has experience in providing concise, useful information in a manner that is sensible to the person who needs a specific type of information; this guide reflects that expertise. There are essentially 5 major components to this reference to 2-year or community colleges: (1) what one needs to know; (2) quick-reference college search indexes; (3) more than 1,500 college profiles; (4) in-depth descriptions of a small number of colleges; and (5) a comprehensive index. Two-year colleges are often the first step to higher education for those who are uncertain about their career goals; who are restricted financially; who need to develop their academic skills; who are adult, working students with family and work responsibilities; or who have special career needs. The information in the beginning of the book, "What You Need to Know About Two-Year Colleges," is especially helpful. There is a section, "Returning to School: A Guide for Adult Students," that realistically and empathetically addresses the concerns and problems faced by older students who are balancing uncertainty and adult constraints with their hopes and dreams.

The guide is organized to be user friendly; it is possible to search for colleges with particular majors, to review colleges within each state (and U.S. territories), and to easily find comprehensive information that is important to the individual. In-depth descriptions of a smaller number of colleges make it possible to explore the diversity that exists within the 1,500, 2-year colleges that are profiled. Certainly a valuable tool for the high school or career counselor, this guide should also be readily accessible to the general population, which generally continues to be engaged in the pursuit of lifelong learning opportunities.
—**Karen D. Harvey**

294. **Peterson's Scholarships for Study in the USA & Canada 1998.** Princeton, N.J., Peterson's Guides, 1997. 421p. index. $21.95pa. ISBN 1-56079-948-X.

A blurb on the cover of this directory reads "Non-institutional Money for International Students." The work describes some 900 programs for graduate students and more than 200,000 undergraduate scholarships. In addition to general information, this directory offers basic information about Fulbright fellowships, information about loans in financing an American education, and a chapter on "Scholarship Frauds: Advice for International Students." A glossary of special terminology and several indexes conclude this helpful annual.—**Bohdan S. Wynar**

Handbooks and Yearbooks

295. **Asian Higher Education: An International Handbook and Reference Guide.** Gerard A. Postiglione and Grace C. L. Mak, eds. Westport, Conn., Greenwood Press, 1997. 403p. index. $95.00. ISBN 0-313-28901-8.

"Asia, home to a majority of the world's population as well as most of the fastest growing academic systems, is centrally important in higher education" (preface). The first sentence of this unique and valuable reference book sets forth its basic rationale. Its purposes are to help readers gain an understanding of Asian higher education in 20 key representative countries and regions and to place its subject in global, cultural, political, and socioeconomic contexts.

The handbook accomplishes this (after particularly perceptive remarks in a preface and an introduction) by means of 20 alphabetically arranged chapters; 19 of these chapters are on individual countries and 1 is on a country plus a region (Papua and New Guinea and the Pacific Islands). Coverage is selective: Iran is here (is it a Middle Eastern or Southwest Asian country?), but other important Asian countries and regions are missing, such as Australia, New Zealand, Hawaii, Okinawa, and Easter Island. Discussion of Guam, Fiji, Samoa, French Polynesia, and other Pacific territories is in general rather than specific terms.

Each chapter contains profiles of the country or area's higher education system, history, changing functions and patterns, response to internal demand, and future trends and developments. Statistical tables and data accompany the texts, and each chapter has its own bibliography. The contributors write with considerable authority; almost all of them are indigenous to the country or society they describe. Approximately half of them are women. The editors are prominent experts at the University of Hong Kong and the Chinese University of Hong Kong, respectively. There is a selected general bibliography. The entries are unannotated, and some of them duplicate entries in the bibliographies at the end of each chapter. The index and "Notes About the Editors and Contributors" enhance the book's value.

Please note that this book is not a directory; see *World List of Universities and Other Institutions of Higher Education* (20th ed.; see ARBA 96, entry 361) for this information. Nor does it contain in-depth descriptions of individual colleges, universities, and institutes; see *The World of Learning* (Gale, 1996) for these profiles. Nevertheless, *Asian Higher Education* does admirably achieve its stated objectives in a highly professional manner.—**Marshall E. Nunn**

296. **College Handbook for Transfer Students 1997.** 7th ed. New York, College Entrance Examination Board, 1996. 551p. index. $17.95pa. ISBN 0-87447-546-5.

More than 2,600 accredited 2 and 4 year colleges that accept transfer students are described in this guide. For each school the book includes transfer-out data; 1995 transfer student profile; credit transfer; admission requirements with deadlines and selection criteria; special services for transfers; annual expenses and financial aid; and availability of early morning, evening, and Saturday classes. All information was verified with the schools in 1996; thus, readers should confirm all information of any school that attracts their interest before making any final decisions. This handbook is the only one available that is written specifically on the issue of student transfer.—**Jo Anne H. Ricca**

297. **CollegeSource: College Catalogs on CD-ROM.** [CD-ROM]. San Diego, Calif., Career Guidance, 1996. Minimum system requirements: IBM or compatible 486SX/16MHz. CD-ROM drive. DOS 3.3. Windows 3.1. 8MB RAM. 17MB hard disk space. VGA monitor. Mouse. $798.00 (national); $348.00 (regional).

The *CollegeSource* CD-ROM provides access to college catalogs both in the United States and overseas. Several versions are available, including the full version of 6 discs that costs almost $800 per year, and the product may be purchased by regions, including Eastern, Northcentral, Southern, and Western for about $350 per year. The international collection provided in the full version includes the more than 600 colleges and universities throughout the world that are the most prominent (e.g., Cambridge University, the University de Paris, the University of Port Elizabeth, the American University of Cairo, Lund University, the Universitet Oslo, Leiden University). Also, the full version includes all accredited U.S. colleges and universities, some 3,400 in all.

Searching is relatively simple, but some of the advanced search functions will require training. Users can search by individual colleges, by majors, by state or region, by size of enrollment, by types of degrees, and even by levels of tuition. Another useful feature is the possibility of searching by colleges affiliation, such as religious affiliation or other affiliations with social or political groups. The cost search produces a list of colleges and universities based on the cost of tuition and room and board, along with other costs that may be searched by priority order. More advanced searching is possible if several elements are put together to obtain priority lists. On a basic level, one can simply call up the catalog of the college or university of interest.

Although most of the features of *CollegeSource* work quite well, there are some problems. Some of the more advanced searches take quite a bit of time to be completed. (This is, of course, related to the clock speed and other capabilities of the computer being used.) Also, some of the catalogs have evidently been scanned into the database, as the typeface has not come out clearly and portions are extremely hard to read. In some cases when a particular subject is clicked, nothing appears on the screen except the same subject terms. If no information is present on that subject in that catalog, it would be nice to have a dialog box informing users of that fact.

Because of the cost, *CollegeSource* is not for all library collections but should be considered for larger academic and public libraries where students are searching for graduate programs. The product is of prime importance for college and high school advising centers.—**Robert L. Wick**

298. **The Financial Aid Book: The Insider's Guide to Private Scholarships, Grants, and Fellowships.** 2d ed. Compiled by Student Financial Services. Seattle, Wash., Perpetual Press; distr., Chicago, Independent Publishers Group, 1996. 537p. index. $19.95pa. ISBN 1-881199-30-4.

This eye-catching book is a directory for introducing students to private scholarships, grants, and fellowships. Because of the increasing cost of higher education in the United States, any amount of financial aid would be helpful for most students, yet many of them do not know that private scholarships other than state and federal grants and loans are available. This reliable guide provides 3,500 sources of funds: 2,700 sources for scholarships and grants; 200 sources for student loans; and 600 sources for fellowships, internships, and research opportunities. It also provides the most accurate and up-to-date information available, owing to the Student Financial Services research team that investigated scholarship offerings and interviewed financial aid experts.

Each entry gives exact names, addresses, telephone and fax numbers, college majors or interests, amount of scholarship, number of scholarships, application deadline, and eligibility criteria. Good features of the directory include a comprehensive indexing system in six different groups of categories; special tips from financial aid experts that increase the chances to apply; and four steps of the application process, including sample letters of request and sample essays for applicants. This scholarship directory makes the application complete, without help from any other references. It is recommended to all levels of libraries, including school, college, research, and public.—**Sung Ok Kim**

299. **The Government Financial Aid Book: The Insider's Guide to State & Federal Government Grants and Loans.** 2d ed. Compiled by Student Financial Services. Seattle, Wash., Perpetual Press; distr., Chicago, Independent Publishers Group, 1996. 162p. $9.95pa. ISBN 1-881199-31-2.

The glut of financial aid guides often overwhelms many students, but reference librarians may recommend *The Government Financial Aid Book* as an accessible, accurate, and specialized resource that is easy to use. Although the book is not designed to be comprehensive, the "Introduction to Financial Aid" and "Common Questions" sections will cover the questions of many financial aid applicants. Furthermore, there is enough information on programs for physically challenged and minority students to be of use as a starting point for financial aid research.

The book contains features designed to make users more comfortable. There are a number of worksheets and sample forms. Sufficient white space, balanced fonts, and limited tables help to avoid the cramped, gray look of other financial aid books. A glossary precedes each chapter, and the entry format is consistent. One added feature is a list of typical starting salaries for college graduates, which helps the reader put repayment expenses into perspective.

Academic librarians can use this book to assist college students who have questions concerning Stafford loans, Perkins loans, and Pell grants. Users will find directions for filling out forms, information on fund disbursement, and important phone numbers. The book will direct students to check with their financial aid office for information that varies according to the college's own procedures. School and public librarians can show younger students to the "High School Programs" section, where they will find a list of scholarships and a college prep guide. The prep guide is a planning calendar that begins the freshman year of high school and stresses preparation tasks, such as visiting the guidance counselor by the sophomore year. Although the early start for the schedule of tasks may be overly optimistic, it stresses that the earlier one thinks about funding college, the better one's chances of receiving financial aid.

By making government financial aid procedures understandable, this inexpensive paperback will be an excellent addition to ready-reference or college and career collections. *The Government Financial Aid Book* is recommended for secondary school, academic, and public libraries.—**Sandra E. Fuentes**

300. **The Grants Register 1998.** 16th ed. New York, St. Martin's Press, 1997. 730p. index. $115.00. ISBN 0-312-17585-X. ISSN 0072-5471.

The new edition of this 20-year-old standard title lists graduate and postgraduate study, research, and professional development opportunities worldwide. A random selection of entries yields as many opportunities outside the United States as within. However, U.S. citizens must carefully screen out those opportunities that apply only to citizens of other countries. The book lists over 3,000 awards, 10 percent more than in the last edition. Past users will like the index of discontinued awards. For those seeking information on a specific funding opportunity, the book contains an index of awards and another index of awarding organizations. All areas of study and research seem to be represented.

The key to accessing this book's value is in the subject and eligibility guide, which uses the list endorsed by the International Association of Universities at UNESCO. Unfortunately, some of the entries in that list, printed at the head of the subject and eligibility guide, are in the guide itself. Further, once in the guide, one must plow through about 16 boldfaced subdivisions by major industrialized countries or regions of the world within each of about 25 subdivisions of an area of interest. That makes this resource difficult to use as a reference book; it may be easier to use when issued on CD-ROM in January 1998.

Entries are revised and enlarged for this edition, listing mailing address, fax, and, if available, e-mail and the Website address, with contact office or name. Entry sections include eligibility, level of study, type, number of awards given in a year, value of award (given in the currency of the country of issue), length of tenure, country of study, application procedure, closing date each year, and additional information. All seem to be available to all applicants in an eligibility area. However, I did find one entry that was available only to those enrolled in a certain university, something that should not be included in a reference work of this scope. Library reference collections will want this current edition but may want to wait for the CD-ROM available in 1998 to see if it is easier to use.—**George L. Findlen**

301. Guernsey, Lisa. **College.edu: On-Line Resources for the Cyber-Savvy.** Alexandria, Va., Octameron; distr., Chicago, Dearborn Trade, 1997. 99p. $9.00pa. ISBN 1-57509-030-9.

Subject-specific guides to Internet resources have become ubiquitous and often out of date before they hit the market. Many are hastily compiled and written by unqualified authors who seem less interested in contributing accurate and selective tools than in cashing in on the Internet publishing frenzy of the last few years.

This particular guide, however, is an exception for many reasons. Aimed at the college-bound student dizzied by the vast amount of information available online, this is a handy guide to college-shopping (including virtual campus tours), standardized tests, the application process, and seeking financial aid. Also included are a listing of fun sites, an FAQ (frequently asked questions) section for Internet newcomers, and two Internet Website address indexes (subject and alphabetic). The initial chapter includes a 10-step guide to college hunting that will walk even the most baffled user through the process.

Setting the guide apart from its competition is the author's appropriate treatment of the audience and the organization and currency of the information included. The tone is casual and relaxed. The text includes substantive resource annotations, and covers new topics such as distance learning and electronic college applications. The author advises critical perusal of college Web information, and includes Internet site warnings and recommendations throughout. General sound advice and tips for both students and parents are also included.

One cannot expect a sophisticated treatment of Internet technology and terms with this level of guide, and some explanations could be expanded. On the whole, however, the author has provided a good starting point for those seeking a future alma mater online. Anyone bound for higher education—not just high school seniors—could benefit from this guide.—**Judith A. Matthews**

302. Mitchell, Robert. **The Multicultural Student's Guide to Colleges: What Every African-American, Asian-American, Hispanic, and Native American Applicant Needs to Know About America's Top Schools**. rev. ed. New York, Noonday Press/Farrar, Straus & Giroux, 1996. 745p. $25.00pa. ISBN 0-374-52476-9.

The Multicultural Student's Guide to Colleges does not give rankings but provides an overview of the multicultural experience at each profiled college or university. Using a combination of mailed questionnaires, telephone interviews, and campus visits, the author describes academics and student life at 203 colleges and universities. These schools represent 47 states and the District of Columbia. Entries for Alaska, Hawaii, and Nevada are not included.

The strength of this work is its use of student perspective. There is an objective fact box for each entry, but the longer narrative portion draws heavily from student interviews. This provides a frank discussion of campus race relations that is not always available from an admissions office. Sometimes the reported problems are disturbing, but applicants and prospective students benefit from a realistic report. The college students quoted in this guide are supportive of higher education and quick to give advice on how to "survive and thrive" at their schools.

For each school, the guide attempts to list statistics on nonwhite student enrollment, retention student-faculty ratios, and median ACT and SAT scores. However, these statistics come from the colleges and universities themselves, via responses to mailed questionnaires. Most schools sent back the majority of requested data, but occasionally portions are unavailable. The most frequently omitted item is a racial breakdown of tenured and nontenured faculty. Out of the 203 colleges and universities profiled, 11 failed to return any statistical data.

Most entries also include lists of the top majors, scholarships for nonwhite students, recent nonwhite campus speakers, remediation programs, and academic support services. In the narrative portion of several entries, multicultural students describe an individual dean, staff person, or faculty member as an important resource for support. Prospective students may want to check with the admissions office to learn whether or not an important support individual is still employed with the college or university.

Because this guide was published in 1996, information may be two to three years old, depending on the academic year reported. A phone call by this reviewer to Farrar, Straus, & Giroux received no indication of a date for another revision. Despite this problem the book fills a niche. Multicultural students need to know if a college will respect their concerns. *The Guide* answers like a trusted relative who is an alumnus. This reference guide is recommended for high school libraries and multicultural resource centers. Academic and public libraries may also consider purchasing a copy. [R: VOYA, June 97, pp. 141-42]
—**Sandra E. Fuentes**

303. **Peterson's College Money Handbook 1998**. 15th ed. Princeton, N.J., Peterson's Guides, 1997. 713p. index. $26.95pa. ISBN 1-56079-932-7.

With higher education costs escalating and the kinds of financial aid proliferating, an up-to-date reference work to guide applicants through the maze of financial information and procedures is a necessity. This reference book accomplishes the task at hand. Information was gathered by sending questionnaires to more than 2,000 accredited institutions of higher education in the United States and U.S. territories that offer four- or five-year baccalaureate degrees through full-time, on-campus programs of study.

Section 1 provides an introduction with advice on how to use this book. The 2d section explains the basics of financial aid while pinpointing the trouble areas and questions that most concern parents and students. Worksheets are included for calculating costs, matching financial aid and financial need, and comparing financial aid and family contributions. Section 3 contains the 15 most-often-asked questions and answers of financial aid administrators.

Section 4 explains the federal grant programs, the Work-Study program, and low-interest loans. Section 5 describes state-sponsored college savings programs, and section 6 lists specific grants and loans available from state sources. The 7th section examines freshman-year costs and how to reduce sticker shock. A table in this section provides some quick answers charting what the average student receiving financial aid really pays at particular institutions.

Section 8 contains 1,767 individual college financial aid profiles arranged alphabetically by school name. These profiles contain data supplied by each college and university for full-time students enrolled for the fall of 1996. Each provides specific information on expenses, basic facts about the school, a summary of the schools' undergraduate financial aid resources, detailed data on need-based and nonneed awards for freshmen and how to apply for each, a list of money-saving options, and contacts for further information.

The final section provides six indexes providing valuable information for prospective students in matching specific programs with their specific needs. This reference book is accompanied by an IBM compatible disk, *Peterson's Financial Aid Planner*.—**Vik Brown**

304. **Peterson's Scholarship Almanac: Key Facts You Need to Know About Scholarships.** Princeton, N.J., Peterson's Guides, 1997. 506p. index. $9.95pa. ISBN 1-56079-94908.

Peterson's Guides is the country's largest education/communication company, providing the academic community with print directories, software, and online services in support of education access and career choice. The present volume provides a general overview of several alternatives on how to pay for college, listing in part 2 some 500 of the largest scholarships that can assist students. The price for 4 years at state-supported colleges can be more than $40,000, and private colleges and universities can cost more than $100,000. This almanac is a sensible general-orientation source.—**Bohdan S. Wynar**

305. **The Princeton Review Student Advantage Guide to Visiting College Campuses.** 1997 ed. By Janet Spencer and Sandra Maleson. New York, Princeton Review/Random House, 1996. 367p. maps. index. $20.00pa. ISBN 0-679-77852-7.

This guide is intended as an aid to prospective students and their parents planning to visit colleges and universities of interest. Approximately 250 schools in 50 states, mostly private institutions with some state universities, are included. For some states, not a single school is listed, and no criteria are given for the selection of the institutions discussed. This is strictly a guidebook for reaching the school and for short stays in the area. No information on curricula, notable faculty, or strengths or weaknesses of the educational programs is given.

Entries are arranged under state and are accompanied by a small state road map. Each entry provides the address, telephone number, and location and hours of the admissions office, as well as a vacation schedule of the school. A sidebar contains specifics on campus tours, interviews, class visits, and overnight dormitory stays. Supplementary paragraphs briefly describe transportation to the institution, directions, a few hotels or motels nearby, and local attractions. Once again, no criteria for inclusion are given. Two appendixes provide regional mileage matrices and college calendars. A short introduction suggests points to consider during observations and questions to ask officials and students.

This compilation should be useful to the audience for whom it is intended—private preparatory schools and large public high school collections. High school counselors may also find it helpful.
—**Shirley L. Hopkinson**

306. Re, Joseph M. **Financial Aid FinAncer: Expert Answers to College Financing Questions.** Alexandria, Va., Octameron, 1997. 63p. illus. $6.00pa. ISBN 1-57509-027-9.

This slender paperback is one of a series of 16 titles from Octameron dealing with various aspects of applying to, financing, and succeeding in college. This volume is targeted for prospective college students and their parents, and its focus is on the financial aid process, especially as it is affected by various family circumstances. Application procedures, determination of family contribution, and the various forms of financial aid are all covered, as well as alternative financing strategies and special considerations for graduate students. Information is presented in a question-and-answer format and accessed solely through a brief table of contents. There is no index or list of references. Thus, although useful material is presented in a convenient and nonthreatening package, this is not a quick reference work a brief treatise to read through continuously, if selectively. Also, its size and binding render it less than ideal as an addition to conventional print reference collections. Nonetheless, this and other titles in the series would be useful to high school guidance counselors and college admissions and financial aid offices wishing to make this information available to their clientele. Academic and public libraries may want to purchase it to supplement the introductory material found in other reference works on the subject.—**Gregory M. Toth**

307. Schlachter, Gail Ann, and R. David Weber. **High School Senior's Guide to Merit and Other No-Need Funding 1996-1998.** San Carlos, Calif., Reference Service Press, 1996. 338p. index. $25.95. ISBN 0-918276-29-2.

High school seniors and their families are faced with the reality of ever-increasing college costs. This reality is particularly apparent in middle-income households in which the income appears to exceed need. The ultimate reality is these students still require outside funding. *High School Senior's Guide* fills an interesting niche. This directory includes 1,034 merit and no-need funding opportunities from a wide range of sources. The introduction discusses the selection criteria regarding the inclusion or exclusion of a potential funding source. The reader is given information about the directory's arrangement and use of the directory. One page is devoted solely to a sample entry and a definition of each section within an entry.

The portion of the directory listing financial aid possibilities is divided into four sections by general subject, including "Any" for the large number of entries not fitting a specific category. Entry format is clear and easily understood, containing such information as address and telephone numbers, purpose of the fund, eligibility requirements, financial data, and application deadlines. The indexing is varied, providing for a number of potential points of access. These include subject, program title, residency requirements, and tenability requirements (geographic requirements for use). Helpful, too, is an explanation at the head of each index and directions on how to use that particular index.

This is a useful directory that may assist motivated high school seniors to locate additional funding for their higher education. Just in reviewing the book, this reviewer found a potential funding source for his high school senior.—**Phillip P. Powell**

308. Spille, Henry A., David W. Stewart, and Eugene Sullivan. **External Degrees in the Information Age: Legitimate Choices.** Phoenix, Ariz., American Council on Education and Oryx Press, 1997. 239p. index. (American Council on Education/Oryx Press Series on Higher Education). $34.95pa. ISBN 0-89774-997-9.

This work is a combination and expansion of two earlier works: *The Adult Learner's Guide to Alternative and External Degree Programs* (see ARBA 94, entry 393) and *Diploma Mills: Degrees of Fraud* (Oryx, 1989). A major difference in this work from *The Adult Learner's Guide* is the exclusion of campus-based degree programs for those that are "campus-free." This work is half the size of the original, which contained 272 entries. Although it is stated that the focus is on programs that are "campus-free," many of the entries list a required minimal time on campus. The guide is intended for those adults who have work and family demands and require flexibility and freedom from "'weekend colleges' and evening courses," while seeking a degree from an accredited institution.

The tie-in to *Diploma Mills* is done in several chapters in part 1. Discussions focus on comparing and contrasting nonaccredited institutions, which target nontraditional students by promoting fast and easy degrees using computer and telecommunications technologies, with legitimate degree programs. There are helpful discussions on accreditation, what diploma mills are and their characteristics, and selecting an external degree program. A useful summary chart of state statutes that govern degree granting institutions is provided.

Part 2 contains the results of 140 returned surveys from 1996 that were sent to institutions offering accredited external degree programs. Entries are alphabetic by state and then institution name. Entries include; address, telephone and fax numbers; e-mail address; degrees offered; program mission statement; accreditation held; admission requirements; credit hour requirements; minimum campus time; tuition and fees; credit awards for examinations or prior learning; and a description of how the program is offered and the technology utilized. There are two indexes; one for each part. The index for part 1 is arranged by field of study, and the second is alphabetic by institution name.

This book is useful to those who are interested in applying to legitimate, accredited institutions that offer external degrees, and for those looking for a general referral and information directory on such programs. Because it has fewer entries, it should be noted that it is not a comprehensive work of all external degree programs offered. [R: RBB, 15 Oct 97, p. 428]—**Jan S. Squire**

309. Sumner, David E. **Graduate Programs in Journalism and Mass Communications.** Ames, Iowa, Iowa State University Press, 1996. 183p. index. $19.95pa. ISBN 0-8138-2187-8.

As time nears the close of the twentieth century, among the fastest-growing areas of study are the fields of journalism and mass communications. This growth means that more people are needing quick access to information about graduate programs in those fields. Sumner's guidebook is one of the first resources to offer descriptions of both master's and doctoral programs in these fields, with a special focus on advertising, public relations, news and editorial journalism, broadcasting, mass communications, and film studies.

Basically, the volume is made up of three indexes. One covers master's programs, another focuses on doctoral programs, and a third deals with majors and areas of concentration. The majority of the work consists of program descriptions, offered alphabetically by state. Each entry offers a complete list of graduate courses offered; admission and degree requirements; tuition; financial aid; enrollment figures; and the name, address, and telephone number of the contact person at each school.

Many students become disgruntled because universities frequently do not clearly identify their programs as professional or research. This fact makes it hard for students to select the school with the right program track for them. *Graduate Programs in Journalism and Mass Communication* is intended as a tool to simplify this search for people looking to pursue graduate study and for academic advisers who need to keep abreast of the current trends in graduate programs. [R: Choice, Mar 97, pp. 1143-44]
—**Steven J. Schmidt**

NONPRINT MATERIALS AND RESOURCES

310. **Film & Video Finder.** 5th ed. Medford, N.J., published for the National Information Center for Educational Media (NICEM), Plexus Publishing, 1996. 3v. index. $295.00/set. ISBN 0-937548-29-4.

Produced by the National Information Center for Educational Media (NICEM), *Film & Video Finder* may be the single most important print source for providing directory information on educational films and videos. It provides subject, title, and series access to more than 123,000 films and videos for schools, vocational education, and business, as well as directory information on 14,000 producers and distributors. Primary access to the film and video descriptions is provided by both subject and title indexes. The subject index comprises volume 1 and is arranged alphabetically by more than 2 dozen major subject headings (e.g., history—world and business and economics). These, in turn, can include dozens of subheadings, also arranged alphabetically. Within subheadings, films or videos are arranged alphabetically by title.

For a complete description of the film or video, the user must look up the title alphabetically in the accompanying title volumes (volume 2, A-K; volume 3, L-Z). Here, one finds descriptive information on the item that includes the title; media type (e.g., 16mm, VHS); running time; series title; grade/audience level; price; order number; Library of Congress number; descriptive paragraph; distributor; producer; and date. Series titles are also listed alphabetically, with each title in the series itemized. The producer/distributor directory in volume 1 lists addresses and telephone numbers, where available, and cross-references producers/distributors by full name and by abbreviation. Volume 1 also provides a subject heading outline and a comprehensive subject heading index.

This source is also available in CD-ROM format (*A-V Online* from SilverPlatter) and online through the Knight-Ridder (DIALOG) database service, among others. However, the print version is suitably descriptive and easy to use and should be an acceptable alternative to the electronic formats. Overall, this source is essential for both public and academic libraries.—**Stephen H. Aby**

311. **IDEA: International Directory of Educational Audiovisuals.** [CD-ROM]. Caterham, England, Oxmill Publishing and Albuquerque, N.Mex., National Information Center for Education Media, 1996. Minimum system requirements: IBM or compatible 386. CD-ROM drive with MS CD-ROM Extensions. Windows 3.1. 4MB RAM. 5MB hard disk space. Windows-compatible printer. $320.00/yr./institutions; $640.00/yr./individuals and networks. ISSN 1358-8648.

The National Information Center for Education Media (NICEM) provides bibliographic, acquisitions, and descriptive information on all varieties of educational and instructional media. Its database adds approximately 20,000 records a year and now totals more than 400,000 items. *IDEA* is a selective, CD-ROM version of the NICEM database, including some 300,000 items that were added to the database after 1984.

For each item in the database, there are categories of information for the distributor, series, abstract, subject(s), audience, language, publication year, media, length, special feature(s) (such as color), and price. The HEADFAST/Hunter software is fairly straightforward for searching, marking records, printing, and downloading. The "Audio Visual Titles Search Form" screen allows the user to do Boolean searching for global text, title words, subject words, series words, audience, media, and publication year. Other fields of information can be added to this list and searched as well. Screen displays can be changed from three- or four-column displays to detailed or full formats; the full format includes addresses, telephone numbers, and fax numbers for the distributor. Overall, the software creates a nice balance between ease of use and searching and output options.

Identifying relevant media materials by a range of variables is important for teachers and media librarians, among others. Yet this kind of searching is tedious in print indexes to media. However, *IDEA* offers powerful search capabilities, broad subject and audience coverage, and ease of use, making it an excellent resource for those engaged in detailed searching of instructional media. A clearly written "User Notes" booklet accompanies the disc, which quickly explains the software and walks the user through some practice searches. Public and academic libraries, particularly those serving teacher education programs, should like this at its institutional single-user ($320) and network ($640) prices.—**Stephen H. Aby**

312. **Index to AV Producers & Distributors 1997.** 10th ed. Medford, N.J., for NICEM (the National Information Center for Educational Media), Plexus Publishing, 1996. 626p. $89.00pa. ISBN 0-937548-30-8.

Index to AV Producers & Distributors 1997 contains more than 23,600 archival and current listings of production/distribution companies and institutions for 425,000 nonprint media titles. Information has been supplied by the producers, distributors, and the Library of Congress. Each entry includes, when available, name; address; telephone and fax numbers; e-mail; Website; media type; subject headings under which media are indexed; and codes for each producer, distributor, and production group. Physical arrangement of the information is by subject heading outline, producer/distributor by subject, alphabetic name list, and alphabetic code (standard acronym) list.

The audience for this reference tool encompasses media staff; library personnel; teachers; trainers; researchers in large academic, public, and school libraries; and information specialists in corporate settings. The resources cover all levels of instruction and education from preschool to postgraduate.

The index is published for the National Information Center for Educational Media (NICEM), a division of Access Innovations, Inc. (a database management company headquartered in Albuquerque, New Mexico). Print indexes are published by Plexus Publishing; online access is available through DIALOG and on CD-ROM from SilverPlatter.—**Bonnie A. Dede**

VOCATIONAL AND CONTINUING EDUCATION

313. Barnhart, Phillip A. **The Guide to National Professional Certification Programs.** 2d ed. Amherst, Mass., HRD Press and Boca Raton, Fla., CRC Press, 1997. 302p. $99.95. ISBN 0-8493-9960-2.

The expansion of voluntary professional certification by professional associations and trade organizations is revealed by this revision of the 1994 edition (see ARBA 96, entry 267). One of the major career fields exploding now is that of information systems specialists. Certifications are created, sponsored, or affiliated with professional associations and trade organizations and are often based on portfolio, competence, or curriculum. They are usually used to set objective standards of performance in specific occupational areas and to ascertain job-related expertise.

The arrangement is by occupational clusters, enabling the user to check a field or specialty comprehensively. Easy access to specific job titles is provided through an index. A second index provides access alphabetically through the association's or organization's acronym.

For each certification, the sponsoring organization is identified and described, complete with URLs and e-mail addresses. The number of certified individuals and costs of certification is given, and the education and experience requirements for eligibility are described. The nature of required examinations addresses the scope, content, and type of questions. Prescribed curricula and portfolio essentials are clearly given, as are recertification requirements.

This is a valuable reference work used by human resource managers for employment qualifications as well as for personnel development and by individuals directing their own career development with advanced credentialing.—**Barbara Conroy**

314. **A Guide to College Programs in Hospitality and Tourism: A Directory of CHRIE Member Colleges and Universities.** 5th ed. New York, John Wiley, 1997. 470p. illus. index. $29.95pa. ISBN 0-471-23923-2.

The tourism industry is the fastest-growing sector of the U.S. job market. Therefore, there should be a lot of interest in careers in hospitality and tourism services. These fields are much more diverse, however, than most people envision, including food services of all kinds, lodging, recreation, travel, and convention and meeting services. This directory is produced by the Council on Hotel, Restaurant, and Institutional Education (CHRIE), which is the main association for individuals and organizations involved in this area of higher education. It provides information about employment prospects and postsecondary programs that prepare students for careers in hospitality and tourism.

The first section of the directory focuses on careers, the purpose and structure of hospitality and tourism education, and tips for selecting programs. The remainder of the guide consists of program listings, organized by the type of degree awarded; associate degrees, certificates, and diplomas; baccalaureate degrees; and graduate degrees. The arrangement within each section is alphabetic and includes many foreign schools. Each listing includes student enrollment, institution and program features, accreditation, admission and graduation requirements, and financial aid. Access is provided through geographic, specialization, and alphabetic indexes.

This directory provides a useful starting point for students considering a career in this field and belongs in all career collections.—**Christine E. King**

315. **The National Guide to Educational Credit for Training Programs.** 1997 ed. E. Nelson Swinerton and Jo Ann Robinson, eds. Phoenix, Ariz., American Council on Education and Oryx Press, 1997. 1557p. index. $85.00pa. ISBN 1-57356-035-9. ISSN 0275-4142.

Skills training opportunities outside colleges and universities are increasingly being used to qualify individuals for employment and career advancement. This volume lists and describes more than 7,000 training opportunities offered through business, industry, labor unions, professional associations, institutes, and government agencies. Entries for each of the 260-plus organizational sponsors give general information about the organization, its training and educational activities, and the information contact person.

Each course entry gives title and course number, location, duration, and dates. In addition, it describes the content, competencies, methodology, objectives, and semester hour equivalency. This information is used by counselors and academic advisers to determine course equivalencies for prerequisite or transfer requirements of potential students. With this resource, individuals can locate high-quality alternative sources of credit for specific areas of training or find potential employers with training opportunities.

To qualify for a listing, organizations must submit course documentation for rigorous review and evaluation. The American Council on Education has published this title since 1975.—**Barbara Conroy**

316. Phifer, Paul. **College Majors and Careers: A Resource Guide for Effective Life Planning.** 3d ed. Chicago, J. G. Ferguson Publishing, 1997. 188p. index. $14.95. ISBN 0-89434-179-0.

This work functions as a basic introduction and guide to choosing academic fields of study and future careers. Accordingly, the major portion of text is given over to profiling 61 college majors or fields of study. Each profile opens with a 100-word scope statement of the discipline, followed by a list of related occupations (with an indication of educational level needed for that occupation). Discussions of related avocational and leisure-time activities, related skills, values and personal attributes often associated with this area, sources for further exploration, and a list of related organizations complete the profile. Following this is another large section that provides explanations and exercises for self-discovery, to assist in choosing a suitable field for study and career.

These two major sections are prefaced by an introduction, a guide to using the text, and an explanation of who might profit most from the information contained therein. Appendixes include descriptions of selected occupations, skill statements, definitions of values and personal attributes, publishers, a list of college majors and related high school courses, and a table indicating the number of degrees awarded by fields. Comprehensive indexes, by major and by occupation, complete the volume.

This guide is highly recommended for high school libraries and counselors and in similar academic settings where students need access to such information. The book is intelligible and well organized.

—**Edmund F. SantaVicca**

6 Ethnic Studies and Anthropology

ANTHROPOLOGY AND ETHNOLOGY

317. **Anthropological Literature on Disc.** [CD-ROM]. New York, G. K. Hall/Simon & Schuster Macmillan, 1996. Minimum system requirements: IBM or compatible. CD-ROM drive with Microsoft CD-ROM Extensions 2.0. 512K RAM. $995.00.

Anthropological Literature on Disc is an annually published CD-ROM product that offers excellent bibliographic coverage for its narrowly defined range of topics. This product emphasizes anthropology, archaeology, and linguistics, with more limited coverage of sociology, history, demography, geography, and human genetics. A number of foreign-language publications are indexed, which is appropriate for the disciplines of anthropology and archaeology. Although obituaries are usually indexed, book, film, and video reviews are excluded. This index of journals and edited works spans the years from 1971 to 1996. Such standard search features as truncation, wildcards, and nested logic are available. Browsable phrase indexes include authors, titles, subjects, and several others. Although the subject indexing is thorough, there are no cross-references in the subject listings, and a number of items were found indexed by title under the initial article "The." Included in the search software are such features as field searching as well as several display and sort options. This CD-ROM product is undoubtedly the most comprehensive and authoritative source for anthropological literature and related disciplines available in an online format. It is simple to navigate and relatively easy to use. This product is highly recommended for all academic libraries.
—**Stephen W. Green**

318. **Atlas of Threatened Cultures.** Paul Mason, ed. Austin, Tex., Raintree/Steck-Vaughn, 1997. 96p. illus. maps. index. $32.83. ISBN 0-8172-4755-6.

Raintree/Steck-Vaughn's atlas of world cultures threatened by encroaching civilization, industrialization, and depletion of natural resources is an indispensable work for school and public libraries. Although the subject matter is sobering, 29 uplifting entries stress life, vigor, and group solidarity. The table of contents precedes a pictorial explanation of the work's organization; a two-page introduction to use demonstrates the interrelation of text, maps, photographs, and sidebars. A preface explains the concept of threatened cultures.

Bright and appealing in style and layout, the work features crayon-bright maps keyed to particular threats, such as loss of language; environmental degradation; aftereffects of communism and Christian missionaries; and suicide, despair, and alcoholism. Crisp photographs enhance the text by showing families and tribes working, dancing, healing, eating, herding, dressing in ritual costume, and carrying out traditions and ceremonies. A spectacular choice of illustrations appears on page 36, featuring a Huichol agricultural celebration, a hand-made mythic story cloth, and natives enjoying the scenery of the Sierra Madre Occidental. Cutlines clearly identify photographs. Sidebars append important data—nearby cultures under threat; description of language groups; direct citations from native people; and such details as the importance of camels to the Bedouin economy, an aboriginal child taming a kangaroo, the definition of *caravan*, and Rigoberta Menchú's receipt of the 1992 Nobel peace prize.

The text is made more appealing than the usual atlas format with a balance of simple explanation and corroborative dates and statistics. Foreign words such as *shtetl, murran, potlatch, billabong, terra nullius, kwoth,* and *klezmer* appear in italics. Back matter offers additional reference sources for young and adult readers; a list of Websites; and three indexes on lifestyles, threats, and peoples. The editor has kept to a minimum difficult, abstract terms. A few unavoidable technical terms—"assimilation of majority culture" and "sedentarization of nomads"—challenge an inexperienced or disadvantaged reader. Diction is at times weak, for example, "and do fortune-telling" and "are in danger of ceasing to exist." Also, the dependence on passive verbs frequently avoids the subject of blame, as with "This treaty of Waitangi was not honored" and "they are considered to be among the Mexican peoples whose cultures has been least affected by Western culture." The fair allotment of native activities to male and female, old and young, sets this reference book far above others still locked into patriarchy. Overall, the work treats a serious subject with respect for cultural differences and lauds achievements and lifestyles of indigenous peoples. Well done! [R: RBB, 15 May 97, pp. 1610-11]—**Mary Ellen Snodgrass**

319. **Bibliographic Guide to Anthropology and Archaeology 1995.** New York, G. K. Hall/Simon & Schuster Macmillan, 1996. 707p. $245.00. ISBN 0-7838-1304-X.

The latest volume in the notable series begun in 1987, this work aims to provide comprehensive access to recent material in the indicated subject areas. The contents represent all publications cataloged between September 1, 1994, and December 31, 1995, at the Tozzer Library of Harvard University, one of the premier collections of anthropological literature in the United States and formerly a part of the Peabody Museum of Archaeology and Ethnology. Types of materials included here are books, serials, microforms, maps, manuscripts, and video recordings, in languages ranging from the familiar English, French, Spanish, Dutch, German, and Italian through Chinese, Russian, Swedish, Latvian, and Croatian. Entries provide full Library of Congress cataloging information for each item (making this volume useful for both reference and technical processing personnel) and are arranged alphabetically by subject headings. The guide would be most useful for large public libraries engaged in continuing acquisition of substantial anthropology holdings and university or museum libraries supporting master's and doctoral programs in anthropology or archaeology.—**Robert B. Marks Ridinger**

320. **History of Physical Anthropology: An Encyclopedia.** Frank Spencer, ed. New York, Garland, 1997. 2v. illus. maps. index. (Garland Reference Library of Social Science, v.677). $175.00/set. ISBN 0-8153-0490-0.

In 1986, Greenwood Press published Frank Spencer's *Ecce Homo: An Annotated Bibliographic History of Physical Anthropology* (see ARBA 88, entry 404). Spencer has also authored a monograph about the history of physical anthropology (Academic Press, 1982), as well as several other books on human evolution. His latest effort is a highly welcome addition to the pool of anthropology reference works. Physical anthropology does not receive a great deal of space in most general anthropology reference works, and these two volumes will fill a gap. More than 160 scholars from around the world contributed 1 or more entries. Entries arranged in alphabetic order fall into three broad categories: subjects in a specific field of inquiry (e.g., australopithecines) or theory (e.g., catastrophism), intellectual and institutional development of the field in countries (e.g., Germany), and biographical sketches (e.g., Charles Darwin). All entries identify the contributor(s) of the material; many of the subject entries have multiple contributors.

To fully exploit the richness of the set, one needs to use either the name or the subject index. Even biographical entries have *see also* references. For prolific writers, the bibliography at the end of the article supplies a variety of information. As an example, Pierre Teilhard de Chardin's entry includes selected works and archival, primary, and secondary resources. Spencer and his contributors took a broad approach when it came to naming people involved in the field; the name index is 31 pages in length, with a typical page listing more than 120 people. The coverage is from classical times (Plato and Pliny) up to the present. Certainly not all the people listed in the index have a biographical entry, and at times it is difficult to determine how the biographees were selected. For example, there is an entry for Louis Leakey but none for his wife Mary or their son Richard, both of whom had/have active careers in the field. Content of entries is solid, if at times brief. In the essay on the history of the field in Germany, there is a short section on the National Socialist Period (1933-1945) that does state the field contributed the "scientific" basis for the "ethnic cleansing" that took place, but also suggests the contribution was "indirect." The section does provide a citation to an article that deals with the field and National Socialism in depth. The preceding is a matter of emphasis and interpretation, and this reviewer encountered no factual errors. The encyclopedia would be a valuable addition to any anthropological or general academic reference collection.—**G. Edward Evans**

321. **Nations of Africa.** By the Diagram Group. New York, Facts on File, 1997. 112p. illus. maps. index. (Peoples of Africa). $19.95; $95.00/set. ISBN 0-8160-3488-5; 0-8160-3482-6/set.

322. **Peoples of Central Africa.** By the Diagram Group. New York, Facts on File, 1997. 112p. illus. maps. index. (Peoples of Africa). $19.95; $95.00/set. ISBN 0-8160-3486-9; 0-8160-3482-6/set.

323. **Peoples of East Africa.** By the Diagram Group. New York, Facts on File, 1997. 112p. illus. maps. index. (Peoples of Africa). $19.95; $95.00/set. ISBN 0-8160-3484-2; 0-8160-3482-6/set.

324. **Peoples of North Africa.** By the Diagram Group. New York, Facts on File, 1997. 112p. illus. maps. index. (Peoples of Africa). $19.95; $95.00/set. ISBN 0-8160-3483-4; 0-8160-3482-6/set.

325. **Peoples of Southern Africa.** By the Diagram Group. New York, Facts on File, 1997. 112p. illus. maps. index. (Peoples of Africa). $19.95; $95.00/set. ISBN 0-8160-3487-7; 0-8160-3482-6/set.

326. **Peoples of West Africa.** By the Diagram Group. New York, Facts on File, 1997. 112p. illus. maps. index. (Peoples of Africa). $19.95; $95.00/set. ISBN 0-8160-3485-0; 0-8160-3482-6/set.

This set was created specifically for middle and high school students. Peoples of Africa presents the different cultures and traditions of the major ethnic groups. Each volume presents information on history (including timelines), language, way of life, social structure, culture, and religion, putting it in the context of the particular group's environment—land, climate, vegetation, and wildlife. Special features on cultural and political topics are included, as are a chronology and pictorial history of the region, a glossary, and a language tree.

Facts on File is usually consistent in its published books. However, this set falls flat. Even though the information is current and the topics included are important, the lack of photographs and color illustrations is noticeable. The color (or lack of) is in black, rust, and gray tones, somewhat reminiscent of the early rotogravures. For example, when the wildlife and vegetation of each area are shown, only the names are given. There is no way for the reader to know the colors. If research by students includes the reproduction of specific animals and vegetation, another book will need to be used. The *Nations of Africa* volume shows flags, but once again without color. The color key is at the bottom of the picture. Also, indigenous words (e.g., Mahdi, shari'a) are used without pronunciation guides, which would cause difficulty for students giving an oral report.

When doing serious research, students today like to use books that are pleasing to the eye. These books certainly would provide all the information needed for any report about Africa. However, students would not gravitate toward these readily due to the blandness of the illustrations. The price of $95 for a 6-volume set is not too much money considering the information found in these books, but a better choice may be the Enchantment of the World series (Children's Press, 1982-), with useful information as well as illustrations and photographs, so that students can get a feel for the continent of Africa.—**Barbara B. Goldstein**

ETHNIC STUDIES

General Works

327. **Guide to Multicultural Resources 1997/1998.** Alex Boyd, Curt Idrogo, Lotsee Patterson, and Kenneth Yamashita, eds. Fort Atkinson, Wis., Highsmith Press, 1997. 580p. index. $49.00pa. ISBN 0-917846-83-4. ISSN 1050-4249.

As with prior editions, there are five major sections in this volume—African, Asian, Hispanic, and Native American, and multicultural resources. Boyd prepared the African American and multicultural American section, Yamashita handled the Asian and Pacific American material, Idrogo was responsible for Hispanic American data, and Patterson compiled the Native American resources chapter. This edition is 100 pages longer than the 1993 version (see ARBA 94, entry 400). Most of the added space is for new entries of groups involved in some manner of multicultural activities.

Entry format is the same as in the past, with the addition of e-mail addresses. The introductory essays for each cultural section are similar to those in the previous edition, with the added feature of some statistical tables. The statistics cover such topics as population, economic conditions, education attainment, and health issues. There are a few specialized tables for each group (for example, a table of the major Asian and Pacific Islanders groups in the United States). One useful feature of each section is the video listings. Entries provide the basic information needed to acquire a title, a brief annotation, and the intended audience by grade level.

Certainly there are other sources that provide more listings or more statistics for each of the groups. However, the advantage of this publication is the depth it provides for each group in a single volume. Another excellent feature is the indexing: There are organizational, geographic, subject, publication, and video indexes, as well as one for executive directors of the organizations. This guide is a publication well worth the price.—**G. Edward Evans**

328. Herbst, Philip H. **The Color of Words: An Encyclopaedic Dictionary of Ethnic Bias in the United States.** Yarmouth, Maine, Intercultural Press, 1997. 259p. $24.95. ISBN 1-877864-42-0.

The Color of Words should be included in any U.S. reference collection where the origin of words and phrases and the language of racism and bigotry are of concern. This dictionary defines and explains the origin of hundreds of epithets, stereotypes, and other words that betray bias or are used in the sociological study of racism. Although a large portion of the dictionary is, naturally, devoted to racism against Native Americans, Asians, African Americans, Hispanics, and Jews, some entries also address European immigrant groups and poor or marginalized Caucasian groups. The book itself is a lesson on how thoughtlessly people use such hurtful phrases as "Indian Giver," "Poor White Trash," or "Montezuma's Revenge." This thorough and enlightening volume is an essential purchase for every reference collection. [R: LJ, 1 May 97, p. 96; RBB, 15 Oct 97, p. 426]—**Lynne M. Fox**

329. Lilley, William, III, Laurence J. DeFranco, and William M. Diefenderfer III. **The State Atlas of Political and Cultural Diversity.** Washington, D.C., Congressional Quarterly, 1997. 298p. maps. $200.00; $250.00 (with disk). ISBN 1-56802-177-1; 1-56802-274-3 (with disk).

Congressional Quarterly is a well-known publisher of many standard reference sources dealing with U.S. government. *The State Atlas of Political and Cultural Diversity* is one such reference source. It provides an analysis of U.S. census data to show how 15 of the nation's largest and most important racial, ethnic, and ancestral groups are distributed among 6,744 state legislative districts. For example, there are many state and senate districts in which 50 percent or more of the represented population are African-Americans. Maps and tables show the average household income of the districts, the percentage of people with a college education, and the percentage receiving social security. This work will be of interest to larger library collections.—**Bohdan S. Wynar**

330. **Minority Organizations: A National Directory.** 5th ed. Elizabeth H. Oakes, ed. Chicago, J. G. Ferguson Publishing, 1997. 636p. index. $49.95pa. ISBN 0-89434-176-6. ISSN 0162-9034.

The new publisher of this title provides information on 5,891 organizations, which is fewer than the number included in previous editions of this title by Garrett Park Press. The 3d edition of this title (see ARBA 88, entry 407) provided information for over 7,700 organizations, and the 4th edition included approximately 9,700 organizations. The entries are alphabetically arranged and can be accessed by using either the state index or the general index. The entries have been expanded to include e-mail addresses, Websites, and TDD (telecommunications device for the deaf) numbers. Unfortunately, the editor uses an extremely broad definition of what constitutes a minority organization to include organizations that have a peripheral program or unit for minorities but whose focus is in other areas. For example, there is an entry for the National Federation of Community Broadcasters because some minority groups use one of its publications. These questionable additions make for a thick directory with a large number of entries, but also limit its usefulness.—**John R. Burch Jr.**

331. Parker, Philip M. **Ethnic Cultures of the World: A Statistical Reference.** Westport, Conn., Greenwood Press, 1997. 408p. index. (Cross-Cultural Statistical Encyclopedia of the World, v.3). $95.00. ISBN 0-313-29767-3.

With all due respect to the author and publishers, this is one of the most unserviceable books this reviewer has ever been asked to review: It is part of a series meant to provide comparative statistical data to development agencies and marketing operations; the four volumes in the series deal respectively with religious, linguistic, national, and ethnic "cultures" (see entries 90, 990, and 1348), although what actually appear are populations categorized almost at random.

Aside from the glaring lack of a competent editor, the book's most fundamental flaw is its attempt to map categories that have been deliberately chosen because they ignore national boundaries (i.e., "ethnic" groups) onto bounded national territories ("nation-states"). At its core, then, the book is oxymoronic. To cite but two typically egregious examples, it posits an ethnic group it calls "Mestizo" (which is simply Spanish for "mixed") that is distributed in 19 nation-states in Africa; the Caribbean; the South Pacific; and North, Central, and South America. This is followed three lines later by the ethnic group "Mixed," distributed among 14 countries in Africa, the Caribbean, the South Pacific, and the Indian Ocean. If readers turn to the tabulations, they find that Mestizos have a 0.6 risk of earthquakes (p. 281) and a typhoon risk of 0 (p. 373); the "Mixed" have 0 risk of both earthquakes (p. 282) and typhoons (p. 374). Prima facie differences in the threats typhoons pose to points in mainland Africa and Caribbean islands, for example, are of overwhelming magnitude; obviously, these figures are meaningless. Tabulated distributions of mineral resources, literacy levels, and the majority of the volume's other listings are similarly absurd.—**Glenn Petersen**

332. Schaefer, Christina K. **Guide to Naturalization Records of the United States.** Baltimore, Md., Genealogical Publishing, 1997. 394p. illus. $25.00. ISBN 0-8063-1532-6.

Similar to census forms, U.S. naturalization records provide a variety of information, including place and date of birth, places of residence, occupation, port and date of entry into the United States, and other valuable data. This information, culled by librarians, demographers, and genealogists, supplies primary source material on U.S. immigrants. Because these naturalization records are scattered in a wide variety of local, municipal, and state agencies throughout the United States, this guide is an important, indeed unique, source.

The majority of the book is arranged alphabetically by state. Each chapter includes state and county resources in addition to addresses of other pertinent organizations and a suggested reading list. An introductory chapter briefly overviews the naturalization process and gives a chronological survey of the history of naturalization in the United States. Furthermore, the volume includes a chapter on records in U.S. territories and possessions, the records of Native Americans (who were not considered U.S. citizens until 1924), and a glossary of naturalization terms. The author must be commended for the diligent and time-consuming work performed to assemble this source. It is an outstanding reference work.

—**Donald Altschiller**

333. **U*X*L Multicultural CD: A Comprehensive Resource on African Americans, Hispanic Americans, and Native North Americans.** [CD-ROM]. Detroit, U*X*L/Gale, 1997. Minimum system requirements: IBM or compatible 286 (386 or higher recommended). ISO 9660-compatible CD-ROM drive with MS-DOS CD-ROM Extensions 2.1 (double-speed or faster recommended). DOS 3.3. 640K RAM. 10MB hard disk space. VGA monitor and graphics card. Mouse (optional). Printer (optional). $325.00/stand-alone version. ISBN 0-7876-1285-5. (Also available in Macintosh version.)

In the past, current history and social studies textbooks have focused on the lives of the controlling figures and events in North American history. Often these are one-sided presentations because the history of the North American continent is not one story but actually a collection of stories of the different peoples inhabiting the area. The *U*X*L Multicultural CD* was developed to overcome this limitation by giving students and teachers a more complete picture of North American history and culture in presenting the stories of African Americans, Hispanic Americans, and Native North Americans. Although primarily targeting the younger student in grades 5 and up, this CD-ROM resource is an excellent addition to any multicultural collection, including those at the undergraduate level. It offers fast, easy access to a wide variety of information on North America's largest and most often studied ethnic groups.

The disc explores diverse subject areas. Its 3,400 entries cover historical and current events, prominent figures, and cultural aspects of the daily life of the three ethnic groups. The work offers biographies on more than 500 prominent individuals, both living and deceased, who have made significant contributions. The CD-ROM also includes more than 900 photographs, illustrations, and maps, as well as a glossary. A special feature of the disc is an option to create a timeline. The timeline examines the social, cultural, political, economic, and educational impact of the groups, spanning from prehistory to modern times. The teacher's guide that is provided is designed to suggest creative, interactive activities for further support of the in-depth use of the CD-ROM.

With help from the user's manual, the software is easy to install. The disc is available in both DOS and Macintosh formats. There are search options for both simple and complex assignments. Students can select a subject, period, person, or issue to quickly retrieve information that can be printed or saved to a disk for use outside the library. The user's manual also provides an index or list of subject terms divided by ethnic group as a word list. Detailed on-screen help is available from most screens simply by selecting the Help button with the mouse. The Help screen that appears gives help for the operation that is currently in use. There are two additional features of the Help button that are extremely useful. Selection of the Tutorial button at the bottom of any Help screen brings up a tutorial that shows a few sample searches. Selection of the Navigation button, which is also at the bottom of any Help screen, brings up a summary of the navigation options available in the program.

U*X*L Multicultural CD furnishes a diverse and dynamic approach to multiculturalism not afforded in standard history or social studies texts. It is recommended for any multicultural collection. [R: RBB, 15 May 97, p. 1610]—**Judith A. Valdez**

334. **World Directory of Minorities.** Edited by the Minority Rights Group. London, Minority Rights Group International; distr., Concord, Mass., Paul & Company Publishers, 1997. 840p. maps. index. $145.00. ISBN 1-873194-36-6.

The objective of the latest edition of the *World Directory of Minorities*, edited by the Minority Rights Group, is "to provide an authoritative and concise reference book on the contemporary situation of minorities worldwide." The *World Directory* meets this objective effectively. The new edition is nearly doubled in length and provides geopolitical, historical, and religious information on minorities in more than 200 nations and dependent territories. This directory is an excellent starting point for a variety of research endeavors related to minority groups.

This edition provides new features and a more consistent structure than its predecessor. The book's 11 chapters correspond to geopolitical world regions. A written overview, a map, and names of section contributors begin each chapter. Within the chapters, users will find the minority group entries organized by country or political territory. Students can quickly locate statistics that include land area, population, real per capita gross domestic product, and the main languages and religions of each country. Because all region and country sections contain "further reading" lists, a researcher can easily compile bibliographies.

This directory also includes contact information—sometimes with e-mail addresses—for "minority-based and advocacy organizations." Patrick Thornberry, the *World Directory* legal consultant, includes his own essay on legal standards for minority rights. The appendix contains 23 documents, either in full text or a substantive excerpt, related to the rights of minorities and indigenous peoples. The index to minority names describes how to use cross-references to find group names. Short biographical notes on the contributors enhance the authority of the work.

With so much new material, librarians may not notice the omission of some detailed maps that were present in the previous edition, which showed the location of settlement areas, provincial borders, transportation routes, or disputed territories. Librarians will need to direct users to other resources for this information.

The *World Directory of Minorities* is highly recommended for academic, government, law, and news agency libraries. The price may deter small organizations, but private and nonprofit groups involved with immigration law, amnesty, and race issues should consider investing in this excellent resource. This title is also strongly suggested for large public libraries.—**Sandra E. Fuentes**

Blacks

335. The African American Almanac. 7th ed. L. Mpho Mabunda, ed. Detroit, Gale, 1997. 1270p. illus. maps. index. $165.00. ISBN 0-8103-7867-1.

This newly updated and revised 7th edition of this respected work is, as Chuck Stone writes, "the ultimate one-stop, interdisciplinary authority on Americans in the African Diaspora" (p. xiii). It includes 27 chapters including such typical almanac features as chronology, firsts, and important documents. Also featured is considerable history as well as law, politics, economics, demography, family life, education, religion, fine arts, popular culture, science, sports, and the military. The almanac provides directories of organizations and institutions; many brief biographies; an extensive, classified bibliography; lists of African American award-winners and historic sites; a detailed index; and much more.

It is unfortunate that an outstanding reference work on this topic contains so many errors. The index is computer-generated and displays the problems of machine indexing (e.g., Muddy Waters is indexed only under Waters, Muddy). Included are questionable and incomplete statistics (only 10 percent of Haitians practice voodoo); outdated terminology ("Bush Negro"); omission of important historical figures (Henri Christophe) and of important details (books by Cornel West, Rosa Parks's training at the Highlander School); exclusion of awards (Toni Morrison's Nobel prize for literature); and mislabeled pictures (Phippa Schuyler's photographs are reversed). Furthermore, a number of the chapter authors are not included in either the list of contributors or the list of advisory board members.

It is wonderful to see two chapters devoted to African American music. Unfortunately, other than the jazz section, which is quite accurate and balanced, the music sections (especially for the blues) contain many errors. The treatment of gospel is egregiously brief for such an important and influential genre.—**Fred J. Hay**

336. The African American Encyclopedia Supplement. Kibibi Voloria Mack, ed. North Bellmore, N.Y., Marshall Cavendish, 1997. 2v. illus. index. $149.95/set. ISBN 0-7614-0563-1.

These 2 volumes are an alphabetically arranged supplement to the 1993, 6-volume set of the same title (see ARBA 94, entry 402). Reviews of the original set, although generally lacking critical analysis, welcomed the new reference tool. The supplement with its 505 additional entries (71 are updates) will also be welcomed. Its format follows that of the original: mostly short, unsigned articles with a scattering of longer pieces (usually signed and sometimes with a bibliography) and many black-and-white photographs. Following the articles are an African American timeline from 1619 to 1996; an annotated, classified bibliography; an annotated filmography of feature films and documentaries; a list of the "100 Most Profitable Black-Owned Businesses, 1995"; lists of black achievements in various sports; a list of African Americans by profession; and a detailed, comprehensive index to the whole 8 volumes.

Generally accurate in detail, there are only a few errors (e.g., sociologist Guy B. Johnson was white, not black). The greater danger lies in its avoidance of controversy and complexity (e.g., *Ebony* is praised, but the entry does not mention the charges of its elitism) and in what the encyclopedia omits (e.g., in spite of its emphasis on popular culture, it gives insignificant coverage to two of African America's most significant contributions to world culture, blues and gospel).

This encyclopedia lacks the grandeur and scholarly depth of the recent *Encyclopedia of African-American Culture and History* (see ARBA 97, entry 331). Also its contributors, unlike the editor of the aforementioned title, are not the academic stars of African American studies. This supplement is easy reading, is attractively laid out, and has good-quality reproductions. The encyclopedia is designed for use by students from middle school through lower-level undergraduates.—**Fred J. Hay**

337. African-American Orators: A Bio-Critical Sourcebook. Richard W. Leeman, ed. Westport, Conn., Greenwood Press, 1996. 452p. index. (Bio-Critical Sourcebooks on American Orators). $95.00. ISBN 0-313-29014-8.

Public speaking has long played a central role in the African American heritage; the voices of influential orators such as Martin Luther King Jr., Sojourner Truth, and Frederick Douglass have echoed throughout U.S. history down to the present day. Leeman, a professor of communication studies, has assembled this collection of critical bio-bibliographies of notable African American speakers in order to convey to readers the vibrancy of this form of communication, to engender appreciation for the ideas and ideals expressed therein, and to act as a catalyst for further research in this area. The volume is intended for broad interdisciplinary use by students, teachers, activists, and general readers in college, university, institutional, and public libraries.

An informative introduction emphasizes themes common to the orators treated: the quest for freedom and equality of treatment, the upholding of U.S. ideals, and black pride. The body of the work includes entries on 43 representative orators from the mid-nineteenth century to the present, contributed by speech communication faculty members from a variety of U.S. universities. Each alphabetic entry consists of a biographical essay, a critical analysis of the orator's speeches, a list of information sources, and a chronology of major speeches. Information sources include research collections and collected speeches, selected critical studies, and selected biographies. The chronology of speeches lists the title, date, and source of the text for the speech. The number of orators covered was restricted in order to enable the essays to be as comprehensive as possible. The book is indexed by personal name and by subject.

Well written, this book is successful on many levels: in providing information on a specific aspect of American history, in providing insightful analyses of African American rhetoric, and in being an unusually interesting and inspiring reference work. Part of the Greenwood Press series Bio-Critical Sourcebooks on American Orators, it differs from other volumes in the series in that it is not a summary of conclusions of the discipline but is intended as a prologue to research yet to come in an area previously neglected. The sourcebook is recommended for a general audience as well as specialists.

—**Jeanette C. Smith**

338. Altman, Susan. **The Encyclopedia of African-American Heritage.** New York, Facts on File, 1997. 308p. illus. maps. index. $37.95. ISBN 0-8160-3289-0.

People, places, and events that played an important role in African American history and culture are included in this encyclopedia. Some coverage of Africa and the African Diaspora is also provided. Entries vary in length from a paragraph to several pages. Black-and-white photographs are furnished in many entries; "Recommended Readings" are listed in a few. A bibliography of sources consulted is supplied, as is an unfortunately rudimentary index, which provides access to main entries and little else.

In a work as comprehensive as this one, errors (e.g., Pygmies are not nomadic, and the influential Blind Lemon Jefferson—whose inclusion should be applauded—certainly did not pick his guitar with a knife) and omissions (e.g., Alex Haley's plagiarism settlements involving his celebrated book *Roots*, place of birth in some biographical entries, radical poet Nikki Giovanni now writes children's books) are unavoidable. There is also a curious neglect of the contemporary African American intellectual; for example, there are no entries for Henry Louis Gates, bell hooks, Cornel West, or Manning Marable. While sympathetic to Afrocentrist interpretations, the book includes entries for neither Afrocentrism nor its more prominent advocates, such as Molefi Asante or Leonard Jeffries. However, in a work of this scope, these errors are relatively minor.

It is unusual for a reference book designed for public and school libraries to be executed with such care for accuracy and balance, especially in such a growth market as African American reference book publishing. Juvenile literature author Altman has produced a useful, dependable, and attractive encyclopedia. [R: RBB, 15 Mar 97, p. 1256]—**Fred J. Hay**

339. **Bibliographic Guide to Black Studies 1995.** New York, G. K. Hall/Simon & Schuster Macmillan, 1996. 342p. $190.00. ISBN 0-7838-1308-2. ISSN 0360-2710.

The source material for this one-volume entry in G. K. Hall's series (see entry 109 for a complete review) is cataloging copy from the New York Public Library's Schomburg Center for Research in Black Culture. This annual, last reviewed in ARBA 96 (see entry 398), acts as a supplement to the *Dictionary Catalog of the Schomburg Collection of Negro Literature and History, The New York Public Library* (G. K. Hall, 1962; *First Supplement*, 1967; *Second Supplement*, 1972). Together, they comprise a subject holdings list for the New York Public Library. Books for all age levels are included, if written by or about people of African descent. Some nonbook materials are listed (e.g., microform and videos), but serials are excluded. Topics that are emphasized include the arts, biography, geography, history, religion, and sports. This volume is an essential source for African American studies departments and larger general collections.—**Ed Volz**

340. Clark, Edward. **Dictionary Catalog of the Collection of African American Literature in the Mildred F. Sawyer Library of Suffolk University.** Boston, Suffolk University, 1996. 220p. illus. $20.00pa. ISBN 0-9650710-0-6.

This book lists the 4,500 items found in the collection of African American literature at Suffolk University. The collection comprises a partnership between Suffolk University, the Museum of Afro-American History, and the National Park Service. The objective of the collection is to gather the works of all African American writers from the eighteenth century to the present, with special emphasis on writers from New England. Many of the books and periodicals listed can be found in large libraries. The cooperative agreement used by the various participating agencies is included in the preface.

There are four sections in the book: periodicals; books, manuscripts, and microfilm; catalogs and guides to other collections; and books in the library of the Museum of Afro-American History. Brief bibliographic data are included for each entry, but no annotations are provided. No subject index is found. Various black-and-white photographs are provided to make the book more interesting. This catalog is recommended only to libraries wanting a bibliography of this special collection, or to libraries working to expand their African American literature collections and seeking a list of possible purchases.—**Carl Pracht**

341. **A Comprehensive Name Index for** *The American Slave*. Howard E. Potts, comp. Westport, Conn., Greenwood Press, 1997. 390p. $95.00. ISBN 0-313-29204-3.

This index—10 years in the making—is an outstanding contribution to scholarship in U.S. history, folklore, anthropology, genealogy, and African American studies. Potts indexes the more than 40 volumes, in 3 series, of slave oral histories collected by the Works Progress Administration (WPA) and Fisk University in the 1920s and 1930s and published under the editorship of George P. Rawick as *The American Slave: A Composite Autobiography* by Greenwood Press beginning in 1972.

Separate indexes for slave location (county and state), narrator, master, interviewer, and narrator birth year are included. Each index includes all of these categories of information as well as narrator's age at time of interview, volume and page number, and the number of pages. Individual former slaves were given multiple entries if they had been slaves in more than one county or owned by more than one master. These multiple listings make possible the study of slave movements and changing ownership patterns.

Systematic sampling would undoubtedly turn up errors, but for an index of this magnitude it appears to be amazingly error-free. Historian Charles Joyner's foreword describes the various slave narrative collection projects, the history of their publication, and their use by historians and other scholars. Unfortunately, this excellent index does not include the 159 WPA Virginia slave narratives discovered and published by Charles Perdue et al. as *Weevils in the Wheat* (Virginia, 1976). The title under review supersedes, in most respects, Donald Jacobs's *Index to the American Slave* (Greenwood Press, 1981), which is still useful for its crude subject indexing.—**Fred J. Hay**

342. Cramer, Clayton E. **Black Demographic Data, 1790-1860: A Sourcebook.** Westport, Conn., Greenwood Press, 1997. 165p. index. $59.95. ISBN 0-313-30243-X.

The majority of this book is composed of tables and graphs, more than 140 of each. The first third of the book includes six chapters discussing the use of census data for the study of antebellum African American demographics and the effects of emancipation, manumission, slave-dumping, and internal migration. Changes in census categories and procedures through time are explained, and the controversies surrounding the 1840 census are discussed. Also included are a bibliography of cited sources and a much too brief and selective index.

The tables and graphs are presented in two sections; the first presents data in percentages and the second section in raw numbers. The same categories and arrangement are used in both sections. The data for free black, slave, and total black population from the censuses of 1790-1860 are presented in both tabular and graphic form for each state and also by geographic region. The second section also includes graphs comparing percentages of free blacks to slaves in total black population for each state and region. Also included are the same data for "ahistoric regions": Union slave states, all slave states, Union states, Confederate states, and Union free states.

Cramer, a graduate student and author of previous books, has done a satisfactory job in discussing African American demographics and the census. The graphs and tables make for a useful ready-reference compilation. The book would have been more useful and easy to use if the publisher had enlarged the graphs and tables (there is considerable blank space even on these 9-by-6-inch pages) and improved their presentation.—**Fred J. Hay**

343. **Facts on File Encyclopedia of Black Women in America.** Darlene Clark Hine and Kathleen Thompson, eds. New York, Facts on File, 1997. 11v. illus. index. $29.95/volume; $329.00/set. ISBN 0-8160-3425-7 (v.1); 0-8160-3430-3 (v.2); 0-8160-3644-6 (v.3); 0-8160-3427-3 (v.4); 0-8160-3431-1 (v.5); 0-8160-3426-5 (v.6); 0-8160-3434-6 (v.7); 0-8160-3429-X (v.8); 0-8160-3436-2 (v.9); 0-8160-3435-4 (v.10); 0-8160-3428-1 (v.11); 0-8160-3424-9/set.

The 11 volumes of this set, covering the areas of pre-1900 history; literature; dance, sports, and the visual arts; business and the professions; music; education; religion and community; law and government; theater and entertainment; social activism; and sciences and health constitute a reworking and updating of Hine's impressive earlier 2-volume compilation, *Black Women in America* (see ARBA 94, entry 965). This set, however, targets a more general, less scholarly audience. Each volume contains a lengthy introduction, alphabetically arranged entries for individuals and groups pertaining to the area in question, a chronology, a brief bibliography, and an index. Each volume also repeats two lists that provide access to all other volumes, one giving entries by volume, the other an alphabetic list of entries in the whole set. The final volume also includes a master index to the entire set. Access to the readable, nicely illustrated biographies is thus provided for well.

Given considerable duplication with the earlier title—many entries are repeated verbatim, and the same photographs are featured—it is disturbing that little mention is made of a connection. Only footnotes found after the introductory essays mention that most of the latter are adapted from topical articles in BWA. For example, BWA entries on slavery and the civil rights movement were used in slightly altered form for the introduction to volume 1 describing pre-twentieth-century history. Public and high school libraries that do not own BWA will find this set a worthwhile purchase, and libraries serving specialized audiences may consider purchasing individual volumes. Those libraries already owning the earlier encyclopedia may want to rely on other sources for the updated portion of this expensive set and better use their dollars elsewhere.—**Willa Schmidt**

344. Foner, Eric. **Freedom's Lawmakers: A Directory of Black Officeholders During Reconstruction.** rev. ed. Baton Rouge, La., Louisiana State University Press, 1996. 298p. illus. index. $19.95pa. ISBN 0-8071-2082-0.

Before the American Civil War, the Supreme Court decreed that no black person could be a citizen of the United States. In 1860, only five Northern states allowed blacks to vote on an equal basis with whites. Virtually unheard of was officeholding by blacks. However, after the war, large numbers of black Americans were elected to office only a few years after the destruction of slavery. *Freedom's Lawmakers*, a product of painstaking research, is a monument to the formerly forgotten black officials of the Reconstruction period and to their struggle for equality before the law of all citizens of the United States.

The introduction to this biographical directory provides an interesting and meaningful historical perspective and includes several tables noting the public offices held by blacks after Reconstruction, occupations, literacy status, and many other details. A list of general sources is followed by a section of several group portraits. The directory consists of 1,510 short biographical entries in alphabetic order, many accompanied by portraits. Complete entries (many entries are incomplete because of lack of documented information) contain dates of birth and death, state, free or slave status at birth, black or mulatto status, literacy status, occupation(s), a biographical sketch, service as an elected official, and a list of sources. Several new entries were added to this revised edition. The book concludes with several indexes: by state; by occupation; by office; by birth status (free or slave); and by topic, such as "Abolitionist Movement" or "Freedman's Savings Bank."

Freedom's Lawmakers is a substantial contribution to Reconstruction history. Its compilation of facts is useful in dispelling stereotypes critical of the qualifications of black officeholders, such as illiteracy (in fact, 83 percent were able to read and write). In addition, the volume brings to life the memory of many black officials whose lives were formerly shrouded in obscurity. The reference is recommended for historical research in public and university libraries. [R: RBB, 15 Feb 97, p. 1041]—**Penny Papangelis**

345. **Index to Black Periodicals 1995.** New York, G. K. Hall/Simon & Schuster Macmillan, 1996. 381p. $99.00. ISBN 0-7838-2110-7. ISSN 0899-6253.

Previously published under the titles *Index to Periodical Articles by and About Blacks*, *Index to Periodical Articles by and About Negroes*, and *Index to Selected Periodicals* (see ARBA 94, entry 403, and ARBA 91, entry 389), this annual index covers journals of general and academic interest, ranging from *Jet* to *Black Issues in Higher Education*. Authors, subjects, and cross-references are filed in a single alphabetic arrangement. Book, film, and theater reviews are also included. The citations include author, title, publication, volume, date, and pagination.

Unfortunately, some problems previously noted about earlier volumes still persist. The number of journal titles covered has continued to decline from 39 in 1988 to 34 in 1991, and now down to 29 in 1995. In addition, the use of Library of Congress subject headings is not consistent; more cross-references would also aid the reader. Nevertheless, this reference source provides access to serials not indexed elsewhere and, thus, still serves as a useful index to black magazines and journals.—**Donald Altschiller**

346. Ross, Leon T., and Kenneth A. Mimms. **African American Almanac: Day-by-Day Black History.** Jefferson, N.C., McFarland, 1997. 177p. index. $29.95. ISBN 0-89950-675-5.

This book was published without adequate editing; it is rife with error. Many types of error are evident: error in factual content (e.g., Zora Neale Hurston's *Tell My Horse* is not about African Americans in the South; W. E. B. Du Bois received his Ph.D. from Harvard, not Berlin); location (George Wallace was not governor of Georgia; Alabama authorities did not chase James Brown into South Carolina; and throughout there is confusion about the Dominican Republic, Santo Domingo, and Haiti); proofreading (Erroll not Earl Garner, UNIA not UIA, Arthur Ashe was once "topseeded"); chronology (Louis Armstrong was not the first African American to play riverboats, and W. C. Handy could not both be born and publish the "Memphis Blues" in 1912); and of omission (mention of Toni Morrison's Pulitzer but not Nobel prize; inclusion of Ernestine Anderson but not the more influential Ma Rainey, Billie Holiday, or Mahalia Jackson; discussion of Jermaine Jackson but not his more famous siblings).

The almanac includes a preface with quotations but no citations; a chapter on significant events not associated with a single day (many of them inexplicably so—was there not a specific day on which Oscar De Priest was elected to Congress?); chapters for each month; an appendix of inventors and their patents; and a woefully inadequate bibliography and index. Month chapters are arranged by day of the month, and under each date events are listed in order of the year in which they occurred. This book is so egregiously flawed that it should be added only to comprehensive collections in African American studies. [R: LJ, 1 April 97, p. 84]—**Fred J. Hay**

347. Stuhr-Rommereim, Rebecca. **Autobiographies by Americans of Color 1980-1994: An Annotated Bibliography.** Troy, N.Y., Whitston Publishing, 1997. 262p. index. $29.50. ISBN 0-87875-466-0.

Autobiographies by Americans of Color fills a need as a readers' advisory tool. Autobiographies present a tapestry of human experiences and views of culture. This work closes a gap left by older bibliographies on specific ethnic and racial groups that are out-of-date. Nearly 500 works are cited and described. A wide variety of subjects are addressed in the autobiographies, including sports, politics, religion, and social issues. Entries include references to earlier autobiographical efforts and provide alternative publishing information when there have been several editions of an autobiography. Annotations provide descriptions and give a flavor of the autobiography for the prospective reader. Some annotations furnish quotations from the original work. A thorough and well-organized index assists the reader in locating autobiographies that address certain events or themes or that were written by specific ethnic or racial groups.

Most public and academic libraries will find this a welcome addition to their collection. The volume may also serve as a collection development tool for libraries with an interest in collecting a broad range of autobiographical books.—**Lynne M. Fox**

Hispanic Americans

348. Kanellos, Nicolás. **Hispanic Firsts: 500 Years of Extraordinary Achievement.** Detroit, Gale, 1997. 372p. illus. index. $44.95. ISBN 0-7876-0517-4.

This reference tool presents a yearly chronology of the contributions and achievements of Hispanics to the development of U.S. culture and civilization. It documents the firsts, the significant accomplishments of Hispanics in the United States in 14 subject areas: art and design, business and commerce, education, film, government, labor, literature, media, military, performing arts, religion, science and technology, sports, and theater. The period ranges from the sixteenth century through 1996.

Most entries are brief, one or two paragraphs in length. The focus is on Mexican Americans and Puerto Ricans, although the ethnic affiliation is not included consistently in each entry. Events of particular importance are highlighted in the text. They are often accompanied by black-and-white illustrations or photographs. These add greatly to the book's interest. The entries include a brief citation (author, title, and pages) to the source of the information. Cross-references are provided. The book's design makes it easy to read. The color photograph of César Chávez on the cover is eye-catching.

A brief introduction explains the book's conceptual basis. As part of the preliminary materials there is also a monthly "Calendar of Firsts" and a long foldout timeline of important Hispanic events from 1509 to 1997. The bibliography contains references to books and articles for further information about the history of Hispanic peoples in the United States. There is an index by year, as well as a general index. The author is a well-known, respected scholar and professor of Hispanic literature at the University of Houston. He is the founder of Arte Publico Press and has written award-winning reference books on Hispanic cultures in the United States and on Hispanic Americans.

The book is a noteworthy contribution to broadening the scope of U.S. history. It is a useful, interesting addition to reference collections, particularly in high school, community college, and public libraries serving Hispanic communities.—**Susan J. Freiband**

349. Meier, Matt S., with Conchita Franco Serri and Richard A. Garcia. **Notable Latino Americans: A Biographical Dictionary.** Westport, Conn., Greenwood Press, 1997. 431p. illus. index. $65.00. ISBN 0-313-29105-5.

Over the last several years, a number of reference works have been published focusing on the Hispanic American community in the United States. Meier, an author of several books on Chicano ethnic studies and history, has compiled a biographical dictionary of 127 Latinos from all walks of life who have made a significant contribution in their respective fields. Sports figures (Jose Conseco), politicians (Lincoln Diaz-Balart), entertainers (Gloria Estefan), performing artists (Jose Limon), and other luminaries are given three-page entries on their personal and professional lives. The emphasis always includes the struggles or prejudices these people faced in becoming ultimately positive role models for contemporary Latino youth.

The writing style is more simplistic than that of entries appearing in *Notable Hispanic American Women* (see ARBA 94, entry 962), but is usually more detailed than biographical entries published in *The Latino Encyclopedia* (see ARBA 97, entry 337). There is approximately an 80 percent overlap in coverage with these two reference works alone. An appendix, which is arranged by professionals in the field, is a good ready reference source for determining which Latinos were dancers, artists, lawyers, etc. This work is a reasonably good choice for school, public, and community college libraries. [R: LJ, 15 April 97, p. 70]—**Judith A. Valdez**

Indians of North America

Biography

350. Johansen, Bruce E., and Donald A. Grinde Jr. **The Encyclopedia of Native American Biography: Six Hundred Life Stories of Important People....** New York, Henry Holt, 1997. 463p. illus. index. (A Henry Holt Reference Book). $50.00. ISBN 0-8050-3270-3.

Do not think of this encyclopedia as a dry, sterile tome resting on a shelf waiting for someone who needs to write a quick report or verify a questionable fact or date. It is tempting to simply state that the volume belongs in every school library or on the desk of every teacher who teaches American history. Although those are certainly commendable goals, this encyclopedia is a readable, enjoyable, and essential book for anyone who has a personal or professional interest in the lives and accomplishments of Native American people; it is not just a "library" book.

The lives of 600 historical and contemporary people are examined from a Native American perspective. The well known and the lesser known are included—writers, artists, politicians, athletes, warriors and soldiers, politicians, and religious leaders. For many entries, there are quotations that the authors have included in order "to transport the reader into the mind of another human being." These quotations do indeed accomplish that objective.

The authors bring their scholarship in Native American studies and their commitment to the people to give life to the stories and contributions of Native Americans and important non-Native Americans who have been a part of history. Enormous difficulties were encountered in creating this biographical reference; the issue of names alone is staggering. The introduction states, "A Native person, particularly a man, might have as many as a half-dozen names during a lifetime.... Confusion may also arise in the matter of the names we have listed for tribal affiliations, because Native tribal and national names are a mixture of those given by European immigrants." However, these problems themselves are instructive as a part of Native American life and history, and the explanation of them assists the reader in understanding the lives and times of the people.

"Practical" and "useful" are the words that keep coming to mind. There are quotations, additional books or resources listed for further information in many entries, photographs, and an index that is exceptionally helpful. The index lists names, tribes, treaties, and concepts and cross-lists them when appropriate. For some readers, it would have been beneficial or convenient to have included an additional separate list of the contemporary Native American people who were described in the book; it is still too easy to focus on the historical instead of the enduring importance of Native American people.

Having intended to scan a reference book, this reviewer found that the book was engaging reading and extraordinarily difficult to set aside. Again, the encyclopedia is an indispensable reference for schools and public and personal libraries.—**Karen D. Harvey**

Chronology

351. Hazen-Hammond, Susan. **Timelines of Native American History: Through the Centuries with Mother Earth and Father Sky.** New York, Perigee Books/Putnam, 1997. 332p. index. $16.00pa. ISBN 0-399-52307-3.

Timelines of Native American History is much more than a chronological listing of 1,500 years in the saga of native peoples of North America. Its author has drawn on a variety of sources for an abundance of information about the history and culture of many of the extant 500-plus tribes, as well as others long vanished.

The first listing in the chronologically arranged material is "Before 20,000 B.C." The last entry, "2000 and Beyond," records this Sioux prophecy: "Whites will all die, and Native people will reclaim their ancestral lands." Many pages also contain sidebars with biographies, individual tribal histories and customs, excerpts from treaties and speeches, and folktales. The author uses pictographs to key entries by the following 10 geographic divisions: Alaska, Northwest Coast, California, Plateau, Great Basin, Southwest, Great Plains, Northeast, Southeast, and all regions. A bibliography and index are included in the end material.

Written in the present tense in unpretentious language, this volume is filled with interesting and little-known information: The costliest Indian war was between 1835 and 1837, against Osceola and his Seminoles, and "A well-trained Apache archer could shoot so fast that he would be drawing the bow for his ninth arrow before the first hit its mark." Not surprisingly, the material tends to be biased toward Native Americans. The information is inclined to be scattered, so that one must read nearly a dozen separate entries to find all the references to Tecumseh, and the Nez Perce, treated in several entries, fail to appear in the index. Despite these shortcomings, *Timelines of Native American History* remains a valuable addition to a too-long-neglected body of information. [R: LJ, 1 June 97, p. 90]—**Kay O. Cornelius**

Dictionaries and Encyclopedias

352. **The American Indian: A Multimedia Encyclopedia.** [CD-ROM]. New York, Facts on File, 1996. Minimum system requirements (Windows version): IBM or compatible 386/16MHz. Double-speed CD-ROM drive. MS-DOS 5.0. Windows 3.1. 8MB RAM. 2MB hard disk space. Color monitor. Mouse. Windows-compatible sound card. Printer. Minimum system requirements (Macintosh version): 68030. Double-speed CD-ROM drive. System 7.1. 4MB RAM. 1.3MB hard disk space. 13-inch, 256-color monitor. Printer. $149.95.

One of the disappointments faced by users of general Native American reference works is the lack of scope given to the tribes. This deficiency often occurs because reference materials oversimplify the subject matter in order to present it in a few pages. Sadly, somewhere in those pages the real character and experience of the Native American is often missed or ignored. Facts on File's latest version (2.0) of *The American Indian: A Multimedia Encyclopedia* on CD-ROM is working to break this trend. Thanks to CD-ROM technology's ability to use pictures, video, sound, and large bodies of text, the user is given an almost overwhelming amount of information on the Native American experience, both past and present.

Version 2.0 features much of the same material found on the first CD-ROM (see ARBA 94, entry 414): descriptions of the tribes and their histories; biographies of key players in history; text from treaties and military orders; and maps and timelines. The update also continues where the first left off by adding an overview of Native American folklore, a directory of cultural institutions and organizations, and a glossary of terms associated with the tribes. The end product is an adequate overview of Native Americans, enhanced by wonderful pictures, video, and sound. Even though the CD-ROM has agreeable graphics, there are two negatives that tarnish this otherwise fine work: the inequity in the coverage of the tribes and the light attention paid to Native Americans of the present day. These are areas that need improvement in future versions.—**Kelly M. Jordan**

353. **Encyclopedia of North American Indians.** Frederick E. Hoxie, ed. New York, Houghton Mifflin, 1996. 756p. illus. maps. index. $45.00. ISBN 0-395-66921-9.

No book of this scope can promise to be comprehensive, but *Encyclopedia of North American Indians* goes a long way to convey the lives and issues of Native North Americans. Its contributors number more than 260, and many are tribal members as well as scholars. All were encouraged to provide subjective as well as objective comments on the topics, resulting in a wide range of voices from around the continent and some fascinating reading. The political correctness also extends to the subjects chosen—especially those dealing with stereotypes and controversial matters, such as "Indian Alcoholism," "Mascots and Other Public Appropriations of Indians and Indian Culture by Whites," "Savages," and "Repatriation."

The alphabetized entries number 447: 100 tribes, including major languages and language groups; 100 biographies; 100 short essays on important issues, eras, and traditions; and definitions of events and terms, including major battles and treaties. No entry is longer than 1,500 words, but *see also* references, along with recommended reading, expand the reader's options. Although biographical entries do not cover living persons, entries on Native art, literature, organizations, and relatively recent events discuss the movers and shakers in Native American life today.

By and large, the essays are well written and interesting. One wishes there were more illustrations, however, which would certainly increase the cost. A list of contributors (with bylines), a contributors index, and a general index round out this encyclopedia, which is recommended for all public and college libraries.—**Lori D. Kranz**

354. **The Encyclopedia of North American Indians.** Tarrytown, N.Y., Marshall Cavendish, 1997. 11v. illus. maps. index. $459.95/set. ISBN 0-7614-0227-6.

Unique in its presentation and organization, *The Encyclopedia of North American Indians* explores the history, culture, individuals, nations, and tribes of North American Indians throughout the Americas, including every state and province of the United States, Canada, Mexico, Greenland, the Caribbean, Central America, and parts of South America. This 11-volume set is rich in its inclusion, scope, scholarship, and content with more than 1,700 entries and 1,400 illustrations, many of them in color. Rather than the typical organization by nation and tribe, this set is alphabetic by topic. Included are historical events as well as current issues. There is strong coverage of contemporary people in the arts, politics, education, and sports with articles on Sherman Alexie, Maria Tallchief, Wilma Mankiller, Russell Means, and many others.

Articles range in length from a few paragraphs to several pages for subjects of broader significance. All entries are readable and contain extensive *see also* references and suggestions for further reading. One of the strengths of this work is its assertion that Native Americans are not an extinct culture. The set looks at the multitude of ways that Native people participate in an ethnically diverse culture while upholding tradition. Volume 11 serves as both a general and topical index; in addition, appendixes of specific nations and tribes, suggestions for further reading, a pronunciation guide, population, and Native centers and museums are found here. The contributors are recognized authorities in the field of Native American studies. Of the 60 writers and consultants, 2/3 of them are members of Native communities, and they have contributed 80 percent of the content.

The targeted audience of this encyclopedia is the student in middle or high school, but its coverage and visual appeal make it useful for both school and public libraries with readers of all ages. Although other single-volume works with a focus on nations and tribes are available, *The Encyclopedia of North American Indians* provides the most complete information on the topic. It will be heavily used and is a highly recommended purchase.—**Lynda Welborn**

355. **Scholastic Encyclopedia of the North American Indian.** By James Ciment, with Ronald LaFrance. New York, Scholastic, 1996. 224p. illus. maps. index. $17.95. ISBN 0-590-22790-4.

Scholastic Encyclopedia of the North American Indian includes information concerning 143 groups of American Indians in alphabetical order, but it is not an ordinary encyclopedia. In his introduction, Ronald LaFrance, a Ph.D. and an Iroquois, states that there is no single Indian culture and that Indian tribes are as different from one another as the Spanish are from the French or the English from the Dutch. Indian tribes are portrayed in three time frames: past, present, and future. This work seeks to avoid creating new stereotypes or reinforcing old ones.

Information about each of the listed tribes includes its language family, lifeways, location, and its own name for the tribe. Sidebars on each page contain further information about specific members of the tribe, past or present, and aspects of the tribe's life. Many photographs and drawings are used throughout the book. Helpful end material includes a timeline; list of museums and resources; and maps showing regions and peoples, language families, forced migrations, and the loss of land. Topics printed in red in the subject index show the best place to look for specific information.

This volume lends itself more to browsing than to finding facts quickly. No subject heading is provided for "Delaware," and a student must go to four entries to get complete information about "Shawnee." Users should be aware that bias toward the Indian occasionally distorts historical fact, and some of the terms and language seem beyond upper elementary level. However, despite its shortcomings, *Scholastic Encyclopedia of the North American Indian* offers a lot of information at a reasonable price.—**Kay O. Cornelius**

Handbooks and Yearbooks

356. **Handbook of North American Indians. Volume 17: Languages.** Ives Goddard, ed. Washington, D.C., Smithsonian Institution; distr., Government Printing Office, 1996. 957p. illus. maps. index. $74.00. ISBN 0-16-048774-9.

This volume, although it was some 25 years in the making, has been worth the wait: It summarizes and epitomizes research in Native American linguistics during the twentieth century and instantly becomes the most comprehensive and authoritative reference volume available for the topic. Of the 27 chapters, the first 13 deal with general aspects of the research area, such as the history of the field, implications for culture history, contact between languages, native writing systems, onomastics, "ethnography of speaking" (ethnolinguistic and sociolinguistic approaches), "discourse" (especially traditional narratives), and "nonspeech communication systems" (including sign language and pictographs).

Following these 13 chapters is a chapter by the editor on the classification of the native languages of North America, which is certain to be highly influential; this is a major contribution to the current and fiercely raging controversy regarding historical relationships among Native American languages, provoked by Joseph H. Greenberg's book *Language in the Americas* (Stanford University Press, 1987). Taking a conservative position diametrically opposed to that of Greenberg, Goddard recognizes a large number of distinct language families. He insists that mergers of these into a smaller number of larger families, of greater time depth, must be regarded as unsubstantiated hypotheses.

The next 12 chapters constitute grammatical sketches of languages, ranging from Yupik (Eskimoan) of Alaska to Shoshone (Uto-Aztecan) of the Great Basin. Each sketch includes a short vocabulary. A final chapter called "Sources," by H. J. Landar, is a useful list of names designating languages and ethnic groups, with references to the large bibliography that follows. A pocket in the back of the book contains a colored map, 19 by 22 inches, displaying the language families recognized in the editor's classification. This will be attached promptly to the office walls of many scholars in the field. Even more than Goddard's chapter, which it illustrates, the map will shape our views of Native American language relationships well into the twenty-first century.—**William Bright**

357. Heard, J. Norman. **Handbook of the American Frontier: Four Centuries of Indian-White Relationships. Volume 4: The Far West.** Lanham, Md., Scarecrow, 1997. 369p. (Native American Resources Series, no.1). $59.50. ISBN 0-8108-3283-6.

Fourth in a series of geographically oriented volumes published during the past 10 years, this latest volume focuses on the Southwest, Pacific coast, and Rocky Mountain regions. Alphabetically organized, it consists of hundreds of entries ranging from one paragraph to two pages in length, describing the interaction between Native Americans and whites up to the end of the nineteenth century. Entries are clearly written, with bibliographic citations accompanying each. Extensive coverage is given to military encounters, the fur trade, and missionization, with little ethnographic material. For example, the entry on the Navajo largely describes their military and reservation history, but no mention is made of economy, social organization, or religion. The Spanish period north of Mexico is well covered, but entries stop at the Canadian border.

A comparison with the *Encyclopedia of the Far West* (see ARBA 92, entry 84) and the more extensive *Encyclopedia of the American West* (see ARBA 97, entry 415) reveals that Heard's volume has some unique entries, including biographical material. There is no index; the fifth volume in the series is intended for that purpose. This handbook is a useful supplement to the above-mentioned works, to be used in conjunction with sources that more fully describe Native American life. It is recommended for all libraries. [R: LJ, Aug 97, p. 78]—**Jeff Wanser**

Latin Americans

358. Schon, Isabel. **The Best of the Latino Heritage: A Guide to the Best Juvenile Books About Latino People and Cultures.** Lanham, Md., Scarecrow, 1997. 285p. index. $37.50. ISBN 0-8108-3221-6.

This annotated bibliography includes selected fiction and nonfiction books for children and teens, from kindergarten to high school, published in English in the United States. It is a cumulation of the best titles from the author's previous books, as well as titles recently published. The book is aimed at librarians and teachers interested in "exposing students to the cultures of Latino people through noteworthy books for children and adolescents."

The guide is arranged in 20 chapters by country: Argentina, Bolivia, Chile, Colombia, Costa Rica, Cuba, the Dominican Republic, Ecuador, El Salvador, Guatemala, Honduras, Mexico, Nicaragua, Panama, Paraguay, Peru, Puerto Rico, Spain, Uruguay, and Venezuela. In addition, it includes chapters on people of Latino heritage in the United States, Central America in general, and Latin America in general. Within each chapter, the books are arranged alphabetically by author. In addition to author and title, each bibliographic citation includes translator, place of publication, publisher, date of publication, pages, format, ISBN, price, and grade level. The annotations, mostly short paragraphs, are both descriptive and evaluative, expressing the author's opinion of the strengths and weaknesses of each title.

In the brief preface, Schon mentions the criteria used to select the books: presentation of material, quality of art and writing, entertainment and appeal to intended audience, recent information, and interest level and involvement of the reader. The guide also includes three indexes by author, title, and subject. Schon is a recognized expert and authority in the field of Spanish-language books for children and young adults. She has written 13 other books published by Scarecrow, including the well-known series, Books in Spanish for Children and Young Adults and A Hispanic Heritage. She is a member of the faculty and founding director of the Center for the Study of Books in Spanish for Children and Adolescents at California State University, San Marcos. This latest title is another useful, convenient resource for school and children's librarians in building or evaluating their collections of books for children and teenagers about Latino people and cultures.—**Susan J. Freiband**

7 Genealogy and Heraldry

GENEALOGY

Bibliography

359. **Genealogical & Local History Books in Print: General Reference & World Resources Volume.** 5th ed. Marian Hoffman, comp. and ed. Baltimore, Md., Genealogical Publishing, 1997. 353p. illus. index. $25.00pa. ISBN 0-8063-1538-5.

With the countless genealogy books on the market today, it is difficult and time consuming to sort through all the titles. There is a need for a comprehensive source to organize this information and *Genealogical and Local History Books in Print: General Reference and World Resources* fills this void.

The purpose of this work is two-fold: it organizes the genealogy books by type and provides the researcher with information about each book and where to purchase it. This reference covers a variety of subjects—church records, military records, dictionaries, land records, archives, religious and ethnic groups, newspapers, and other. Books on a variety of countries, from Australia and Russia to Ireland and Japan are featured here. For each book listed in this guide information is given on the author, title, date of publication, pagination, indexing and illustration (if present), format (paper or hard-cover), and a vendor identification number. The vender identification number leads to an index in the front of the book, which provides a list of the book vendors names, addresses, phone numbers, and shipping information. This is not a detailed book; it simply provides the researcher with a list of books by subject and vendor information. It does not review the books, nor does it list their contents. Although it would be helpful to have a review or a list of the contents, *Genealogical and Local History Books in Print* does provide a much needed service by categorizing the books by subject, thereby making it a worthwhile genealogy reference source.—**Kelly M. Jordan**

360. **Genealogical & Local History Books in Print: U.S. Sources & Resources Volume.** 5th ed. Marian Hoffman, comp. and ed. Baltimore, Md., Genealogical Publishing, 1997. 2v. index. $50.00pa./set. ISBN 0-8063-1535-0.

The purpose of this work is to provide the user with a source to consult for information on currently available books for sale. In the field of genealogy and local history, it is frequently difficult to find ordering information. One is happy to see this work updated, the 4th edition having been published in 1992.

The easy-to-use format contains major regions of the United States (New England, Mid-Atlantic, South, Midwest, and West) and then each state alphabetically. Within each state, items are listed by counties or sometimes by regions. Each entry lists the title, author, and number of pages, as well as the code number for the vendor who sells the book. A separate list of vendors, in each volume, gives the address and shipping charges for that vendor. In addition, the work is enhanced by the inclusion of an author index, a title index, and an index to advertisers.

This publication needs some careful editing to improve its usefulness. There is no Pennsylvania County in Pennsylvania, nor a Burlingham County in New Jersey. It would be helpful if some vendors used more detail in describing the items listed. For example, a book listed under New Lisbon, Ohio, is never listed under the county, Columbiana. Nevertheless, the set is highly recommended for serious researchers and all genealogical libraries.—**Carol Willsey Bell**

361. Kemp, Thomas J. **The Genealogy Annual, 1995: A Bibliography of Published Sources.** Wilmington, Del., Scholarly Resources, 1996. 397p. $95.00. ISBN 0-8420-2661-4. ISSN 1090-7440.

This is a comprehensive bibliography of genealogies, handbooks, and other source material published in 1995. The work is divided into three sections: "Family Histories," "Guides and Handbooks," and "Genealogical Sources by State." The "Family Histories" section comprises most of the volume. It consists of references to U.S. and international single and multifamily genealogies. Most seem to be self-published. Many seem to be owned only by the Library of Congress, so getting access to many of the family histories may be difficult. Each genealogy is listed alphabetically by the major surnames in each book. The "Guides and Handbooks" section is divided into two parts, the United States and international. The United States section is arranged alphabetically by subject, but the international section is arranged by areas or countries of the world. The "Genealogical Sources by State" section is arranged alphabetically by state and then by city or county. It includes information on cemetery, census, military, and other useful records. This work appears to be the first volume of, one hopes, an annual publication. *The Genealogy Annual* will be useful in any library that has patrons asking for genealogical information. [R: RBB, 1 Mar 97, p. 1195]—**Robert L. Turner Jr.**

362. Zubatsky, David S., and Irwin M. Berent. **Sourcebook for Jewish Genealogies and Family Histories.** Teaneck, N.J., Avotaynu, 1996. 456p. $69.50. ISBN 1-886223-03-3.

The *Sourcebook for Jewish Genealogies and Family Histories* is a comprehensive bibliography of published and nonpublished Jewish genealogies, family histories, and individual family names compiled from books, newspapers and journal articles, Jewish encyclopedia entries, family papers, and family trees. The authors have attempted to include not only collections from U.S. archives and libraries, but also from Austria, the Netherlands, England, Germany, and Israel. This work enables genealogists and historians to determine primary sources on Jewish families in a variety of times, places, and backgrounds.

This book begins with an introduction defining the purpose of the book. It is important to note that no information from private collections is included. If a particular family's history or genealogy does not span three generations it is not included. If one family had many surnames, the family is only listed under the main name. This books if the first of its type since Herman Meyer's 1942 *Bibliographia Genealogica Judaica*. Annotations are also included.

A listing of the major sources that were used in compiling this book are included, which will allow the reader further sources to research. The reader will find the section on "How to Use This Bibliography" contains important information and should be consulted before using this bibliographic reference. There is also a section on the most frequently cited journal and monograph abbreviations. General works, abbreviations, and most cited Jewish genealogic journals are also listed.

This books fulfills a special need. For the researcher trying to obtain information about Jewish families, this book will be a valuable resource. A Jewish library, Hebrew school, or Jewish day school would all benefit from this book. [R: RBB, Jan 97, p. 900]—**Barbara B. Goldstein**

Directories

363. Thode, Ernest. **Address Book for Germanic Genealogy.** 6th ed. Baltimore, Md., Genealogical Publishing, 1997. 196p. $24.95pa. ISBN 0-8063-1526-1.

The *Address Book* continues to be an excellent, comprehensive handbook for genealogists, researchers, and family historians seeking the location of specific resources related to Germany both in the United States and in Germany. The 6th edition is a welcome resource updating many addresses and adding others.

This edition includes the name and address of societies outside of Europe, a list of archives in the United States, religious organizations, booksellers and importers in the United States and Europe, foreign offices in North America, the location of map resources, ship and riverboat records, a list of German national archives and organizations, European national or provincial archives, municipal and county archives in Germany, religious archives (both Catholic and Protestant), historical and genealogical societies, libraries, museums, and the names of genealogists working with German records.

Examples of form letters, both in English and German, are provided, which can be used when corresponding with organizations in Germany. An added feature of this new edition includes World Wide Web links to various organizations in the United States and Germany.

The *Address Book for Germanic Genealogy* is a welcome addition to any academic or public library with even a small collection of genealogical materials.—**Jane Jurgens**

Handbooks and Yearbooks

364. Bremer, Ronald A. **Compendium of Historical Sources: The How and Where of American Genealogy.** rev. ed. Bountiful, Utah, AGLL, 1997. 914p. maps. index. $69.95pa. ISBN 1-877677-15-9.

If ever there was a one-stop guide for genealogists, this is it. After perusing these pages one can become truly amazed about who knows what about whom on this planet. The contents are grouped into three subject areas: the nuts and bolts of genealogical research, records, and special topics. Using the nuts and bolts section, which provides basic how-to information, and the records, a beginning genealogist could find an abundance of information about ancestors. Topics include general principles of genealogical research; an explanation of proxy research, with sample letters written in several languages requesting proxy research; how to request genealogy books through interlibrary loan; note-keeping tools with charts, graphs, and a research organizer; surname registries; birth date and formula patterns; the repository at Salt Lake City, Utah; the Loyalist Microfilm Collection; and useful sources in the public library.

Chapters on records exhaustively list places to go for information on file: national, state, court, land, county, WPA ("Historical Records Survey Program" for selective counties), vital, census, immigration, naturalization and passenger lists, church, military, insurance, colleges and universities before 1900, fraternal societies and alliances, and the railroad. Special topics cover supplementary sources and information pertinent to genealogical research: a list of 24 major genealogical periodicals, Canadian sources, museums, the Library of Congress, the Daughters of the American Revolution Library, nontraditional record sources and repositories, a list of U.S. place-names during the 1870s, U.S. townships, and 31 special items not covered elsewhere. A glossary explains any term a person may come across during their research, particularly legal terms and abbreviations. To locate a source, one should first go to the well-organized table of contents before looking at the brief index; the latter is a supplement to the table of contents and is not exhaustive.

The only complaint about this book is that it does not include any Internet sources. Nonetheless, serious genealogists, public libraries, and institutions with related genealogical records should add this book to their collections.—**Susan D. Baird-Joshi**

365. Hone, E. Wade. **Land & Property Research in the United States.** Salt Lake City, Utah, Ancestry, 1997. 517p. maps. index. $44.95. ISBN 0-916489-68-X.

Genealogy, like real estate, has a saying: "Location, location, location." Land and property records are vital to genealogical research because land records go back further in time than virtually any other type of record and, in the United States, land records apply to more people than any other type of written record. Eighty-five percent of all U.S. citizens owned or leased land prior to the Civil War; hence, the importance of land and property records.

This work is divided into five sections. The first is "Pre-U.S. Possessions," which includes chapters on Spanish, British, French, and Mexican possessions. Each chapter has information on historical background, records, repositories, and references. The second section is on "State-Land States," treating lands that were initially controlled and dispersed by the state governments. The chapters in this section deal with organization, records, and strategies for using these types of records. The third section is about lands that were initially controlled and dispersed by the U.S. government. The chapters in this section also deal with organization, records, and strategies for use. The fourth section concerns lands in all land transactions following the initial sale by the federal or state government. These are called individual or private lands. The fifth section features Native American land records.

Two appendixes that occupy more than half of the book follow. The first is a "Tract Book and Township Plat Map Guide to Federal Land States," and the second is "Land Office Boundary Maps for All Federal Land States." This is the largest section of the work and allows one to easily find out which office held the land records that are of interest. This volume will be a standard work for those interested in land records.—**Robert L. Turner Jr.**

366. Kemp, Thomas Jay. **Virtual Roots: A Guide to Genealogy and Local History on the World Wide Web.** Wilmington, Del., Scholarly Resources, 1997. 279p. $65.00; $24.95pa. ISBN 0-8420-2718-1; 0-8420-2720-3pa.

The World Wide Web has become a popular medium for information dissemination, and genealogy offices and researchers have embraced this technology to the fullest. There are thousands of genealogy Websites devoted to a whole host of topics—from county records to those focusing on surnames. With the boom in Websites, a need arises for someone to organize these resources for easier navigation and reference. *Virtual Roots: A Guide to Genealogy and Local History on the World Wide Web* answers this call.

Kemp's directory organizes genealogy Websites into four sections: general subjects, which covers a wide range of topics, such as cemetery records, religious groups, heraldry, and obituaries; United States, which focuses on state resources, such as archives, libraries, and historic societies; international, which focuses on the genealogy offices and ancestral information of other nations; and family associations, which is devoted to family names and clans.

The contents of the directory are rather simple. The book is divided into four sections, with the entries in alphabetic order, for easy skimming. Each listed Website includes who created the site and how to get in touch with the author or organization by mail, e-mail, or telephone. To alert readers to the Websites the author found useful, the labels "extraordinary" and "outstanding" are used. There are 130 in the directory that bear this mark. For novice Web surfers who do not know basic Internet terminology, Kemp has also included a short glossary of terms describing such frequently encountered words as e-mail, TELNET, and URL.

It is important to note that *Virtual Roots* does not attempt to provide total coverage of genealogy Websites. Instead, Kemp's focus is on the 1,000 best sources that are good starting points in genealogical research. With its concise and easy-to-read format, this work is a welcome addition to any genealogical collection.—**Kelly M. Jordan**

367. Mix, Ann Bennett. **Touchstones: A Guide to Records, Rights, and Resources for Families of American World War II Casualties.** Bountiful, Utah, AGLL, 1996. 133p. index. $34.95; $19.95pa. ISBN 1-877677-72-8; 1-877677-73-6pa.

Academic researchers often dismiss the work of amateur enthusiasts, particularly when the outcome of that enthusiasm is a reference book. Mix reveals typical amateur characteristics in *Touchstones*. The style is personal and emotional, the syntax is chilling, the index is inadequate, and the review copy is badly printed. That said, this is a competent, complete, and interesting assembly of useful information. Everything needed to gain access to the records of U.S. World War II casualties is here, including both governmental and unofficial sources. The objective data are accurate and up-to-date, many with fax numbers and e-mail addresses. Many, perhaps most, of the annotations begin with "This," and they are not always easy to read, but they do contain pertinent information about the entries they support. Sections cover military service records, burials, medals and awards, repositories, organizations, and much more. A great deal of ancillary information is included, which a professional researcher may have left out, but which may, in fact, be helpful to persons who do not have access to large reference collections. At $19.95 for the paperback version, this would be a reasonable purchase for individuals, and the guide is worth serious consideration for library collections that emphasize family history.—**John Newman**

368. Ryskamp, George R. **Finding Your Hispanic Roots.** Baltimore, Md., Genealogical Publishing, 1997. 290p. illus. index. $19.95pa. ISBN 0-8063-1517-2.

For those people tracing ancestors from Mexico, Central or South America, Spain, or the Caribbean, this new resource from the author of *Tracing Your Hispanic Heritage* (Hispanic Family History Research, 1984) will bring them up-to-date. The handbook is an excellent introduction to research basics as well as a major guide to unique aspects of Hispanic genealogy, such as birth and baptismal names and titles, language and handwriting, and notarial records. The author has added some key features, including information on computer searching and family history centers. The book also contains a useful selective bibliography of reference works organized by country and a helpful list of Hispanic genealogical societies in the United States. Ryskamp is an accredited genealogist with expertise in Spanish-language research and an assistant professor of history at Brigham Young University. His new book is more concise and less expensive than its predecessor and merits a place in libraries' genealogy sections.—**Jean Engler**

369. Schleifer, Jay. **A Student's Guide to Jewish American Genealogy.** Phoenix, Ariz., Oryx Press, 1996. 168p. illus. maps. index. (Oryx American Family Tree Series). $24.95. ISBN 0-89774-977-4.

Although designed for students, this attractive and carefully crafted volume—the 13th in the Oryx Press series on ethnic genealogy—also offers much of value to the mature family historian. Schleifer begins by concisely tracing the story of the Hebrew people from their origins 4,000 years ago, through the Jewish Diaspora, their global migrations, the horrors of the Holocaust, the creation of Israel in 1948, and the accomplishments of prominent Jews in the contemporary United States. He notes that "wherever they have wandered, Jews have always carried with them strong faith, an independent spirit, and a high regard for work and education" (p. 36). Their peripatetic, often tragic, history has made the family of paramount importance to the Jewish people.

The second half of the book provides detailed, practical guidance for undertaking family history research. Numerous illustrations enhance Schleifer's text, creating a greater sense of immediacy for the reader. Each chapter has a substantial annotated bibliography. The book also gives addresses for obtaining information as well as advice on using state-of-the-art software, Internet resources, and Mormon Family History Centers and concludes with a brief glossary of terms and a comprehensive index. Throughout, the author emphasizes the importance of starting with one's immediate family, and he frankly admits that there may be many obstacles in research. Even though the search may never be finished, he urges finding an appropriate way to preserve one's findings and share them with other family members. Above all, Schleifer succeeds in instilling a sense of pride in one's roots and the importance of celebrating "heritage and the bond of family" (p. 158). This guide is essential for all genealogical, school, and public collections.
—**John D. Blackwell**

370. **The Source: A Guidebook of American Genealogy.** rev. ed. Loretto Dennis Szucs and Sandra Hargreaves Luebking, eds. Salt Lake City, Utah, Ancestry, 1997. 834p. maps. index. $49.95. ISBN 0-916489-67-1.

This newly revised edition of *The Source* is arranged by major topics, such as census, court, church, land, and military records. These topics are treated in more detail than the 1st edition, by state or by area, in a readable manner.

Updating and revising the 1984 edition (see ARBA 85, entry 379) was a monumental task, using 17 contributors from various areas of expertise. Constantly changing prices or addresses are always a problem with this type of work, and the reader needs to be aware of some problems that were noted: (1) prices of Ohio vital records are incorrect; (2) Ohio's three volumes on Revolutionary soldiers are not listed; (3) citations to published works do not always list the most current edition; (4) some addresses have not been revised—one known to this reviewer changed in 1982!; (5) Ohio was omitted from the Special Census Schedules list, 1850-1880; and (6) census of industry is not explained.

The genealogist has much to learn from *The Source*, despite some shortcomings. Discussions about record types are well written and informative, although sometimes too brief. A detailed index greatly enhances the work, as do seven appendixes. This guide is highly recommended for genealogical libraries and individuals who are seriously pursuing the study of genealogy.—**Carol Willsey Bell**

371. **Ultimate Family Tree Deluxe.** [CD-ROM]. (3 discs). Larkspur, Calif., Palladium Interactive, 1997. Minimum system requirements (Windows version): IBM or compatible 486DX/33MHz. Double-speed CD-ROM drive. Windows 3.1. 8MB RAM (16MB recommended). 50MB hard disk space. SVGA, 256-color monitor. 14.4K bps modem (optional). Scanner (optional). Minimum system requirements (Macintosh version): 68040/33MHz or PowerMac. Double-speed CD-ROM drive. System 7.1. 8MB RAM. 45 MB hard disk space. SVGA, 256-color monitor. Word processor to preview and print reports (Microsoft Word recommended). 14.4K bps modem (optional). $59.99.

From installation to data entry, this program is user friendly, with prompts to assist throughout the process. The deluxe version includes components to create a family journal, a picture album, and Webpages to participate in Internet online discussions. The CD-ROM includes copies of an Internet browser as well as AT&T World Net Service software for users without an Internet provider. The opening screen is clean and well designed with options for going into eight components. "Family Tutor" launches the selected browser and provides links to five major sections, including a glossary. This is a self-directed workshop on genealogical records, techniques for gathering data, tools for research, and templates for letters to request information from outside sources. An audiovisual selection is available for each of the following: marriage and divorce; civil court; estate; religions; census (federal and state); military records; birth and death; land, property, and tax; cemetery and mortuary; immigrations and naturalization; and newspapers. "World Photo Studio" contains photographs that create a "family album." Directions for importing personal photographs and illustrations are included. The "Records Requester" includes a database of state, national, and county offices. By completing the on-screen request form, a letter can be prepared to send to the appropriate agency. "Social Security Death Index" (included on two additional CD-ROMs) is searchable by name. The gazetteer dates are 1833 and 1853, helping researchers locate towns that may not be on current maps.

The primary function of the program is to provide a database of genealogical records. It begins with tips for using the program, which is an excellent way to learn the software. There are two editing modes, normal and advanced, as well as a Wizard. New data are entered in the blanks with help available to explain terms, options, and the process. To test the software further, 1,788 records were imported from another genealogical record program. It converted the records in just over six minutes. A couple of errors occurred in the conversion, such as recording that this reviewer was deceased. Editing provided an opportunity to learn more about the program and to prepare the information for publication on a Website.

The 353-page manual is easy to use with many screen illustrations, step-by-step instructions, and importing instructions from previous versions and other standard genealogical formats. A glossary and a section on frequently asked questions are also provided in the manual. Librarians will find the tutorial an excellent resource for beginning genealogy researchers. The additions included in the deluxe edition will also be valuable in a library, especially if a printer is available for form letters. When it comes to actually using the "Family Tree Maker" component, patrons will probably prefer to own the program, as the personal data files will not fit on a floppy disk. The limited version is also sold separately.—**Donald E. Collins**

372. Willard, Jim, and Terry Willard, with Jane Wilson. **Ancestors: A Beginner's Guide to Family History & Genealogy.** New York, Houghton Mifflin, 1997. 212p. illus. $16.00pa. ISBN 0-395-85410-5.

There is always need for a good how-to book for beginners in family history and genealogical research that includes up-to-date information. Chapter nine of this work, "High-tech Help Computers and Genealogy," contains a good summary of genealogy on the Internet, CD-ROMs, computer software, and large databases.

The book's subtitle, *A Companion to the PBS Television Series Ancestors: A Ten-Part Series Celebrating the Significance of Family History*, summarizes the majority of the contents of the book. Fortunately, many chapters include more narrative and how-to instructions than were presented on television. This is a well-written, even inspirational work. However, despite this and its information, it is not recommended as a good introductory book to family genealogy. It will be too advanced for most beginners because much of the "how-to" gets lost in the narrative. The lack of an index also diminishes its value. Illustrations include 43 unidentified photographs, many unrelated to the subjects presented; seven pages of half-tone photos, with paragraphs overlaid; and only 20 identified photographs.

Because of media hype, this work may be in many libraries, but two other better beginning guides for family history and genealogical research should be in their collections: Desmond Walls Allen and Carolyn Earle Billingsley's *Beginner's Guide to Family History Research*, 3d ed. (Conway, Ark.: Research Associates, 1997) and Emily Anne Croom's *Unpuzzling Your Past: A Basic Guide to Genealogy*, 3d ed. (Cincinnati, Ohio: Betterway Publications, 1995). [R: LJ, 15 Mar 97, p. 58]—**J. Carlyle Parker**

Indexes

373. **Periodical Source Index CD-ROM.** [CD-ROM]. Orem, Utah, Allen County Public Library and Ancestry, 1997. Minimum system requirements: IBM or compatible 486/33MHz (486/66MHz or better recommended). Double-speed CD-ROM drive. Windows 3.1. 8MB RAM (16MB recommended). 15MB hard disk space. $99.95.

With the appearance of the electronic version, this index assumes new significance as a major source for genealogy and history in the United States, Canada, and the world. Although many are familiar with this index, it has been largely ignored because it was limited to only the largest institutions, and the complex arrangement of the 27 print volumes made searches cumbersome and tedious. Produced by the staff of the Allen County Public Library in Fort Wayne, Indiana, the product's stated purpose is to index every genealogical and local history periodical published in the United States and Canada since 1800. The word "local" is misleading, however, because the CD-ROM's comprehensive indexing covers virtually every local, state, and national genealogical and historical periodical in these countries. Few titles are omitted, and the comprehensive inclusion of even the most obscure periodicals will be a pleasant surprise to many. Perhaps the major significance of this undertaking is that many hundreds, if not a thousand or more, periodicals that have failed to be indexed elsewhere are covered, thereby greatly increasing the availability of sources for historians and genealogists. Of further importance, the index provides the names and addresses of libraries that hold each title, making retrieval easier, and provides subscription information for interested persons. More than a million titles are included, and subject searches cover nearly every area of history.

The *Periodical Source Index CD-ROM* (PERSI) is easy to install and is user friendly. It is this reviewer's opinion that every possible point of access to its massive contents has been made available. Hypertext links allow researchers to move easily through the index. A main menu offers users eight approaches to locating data: keyword(s); surname (full-name searches are extremely limited); search of titles only; geographic location and type of record; how-to articles; identification of specialized periodicals, with the ability to scan the complete table of contents of each; and searches for Canadian, United States, and foreign periodicals by keyword and location. Other useful features include SOUNDEX searching for variant spellings, lists of library holdings of each title, and subscription information, including prices, for each title. The manual is short, clear, and good, as is the online help feature.

Criticisms are minor, given the magnitude of the work. PERSI does not index every name in an article as many first-time users often assume. Instead, only the single main person, surname, or subject is indexed, although this is sometimes extended to two or three key subjects or names. There is also no author index, and article titles are rewritten or revised when the subject is not clearly stated. Despite minor shortcomings, however, this reviewer, as both a historian and librarian, is greatly impressed. PERSI is highly recommended to individuals for home purchase, and should be seriously considered by every library and institution with an interest in history or genealogy.—**Donald E. Collins**

HERALDRY

374. **Ultimate Pocket: Flags of the World.** New York, DK Publishing, 1997. 240p. illus. maps. index. $12.95. ISBN 0-7894-2085-6.

This book, which was produced in association with the Flag Institute of Chester, United Kingdom, contains individual profiles of more than 300 flags. This attractively designed, compact book is arranged by continent. The countries are not listed in alphabetic order, which necessitates the use of the table of contents or the index. International flags and signal flags are also included in the back of the book, and a collection of the key flags in world history appears in the front matter. Nearly every country is allocated one page, which includes a color illustration of its flag; brief notes concerning the history and origin of the flag; a colored illustration of the emblem, seal, or arms of the nation and the standard or arms of the sovereign; and a locator map showing the country's location in relation to the countries around it. Provincial, regional, and subnational flags, as well as flags of overseas territories, republics, states, and cantons are included following the page with the national flag. These flags usually are grouped together, several to a page, with brief histories of origin. This up-to-date flag book is a recommended for all library collections.—**J. Carlyle Parker**

PERSONAL NAMES

375. Beider, Alexander. **Dictionary of Jewish Surnames from the Kingdom of Poland.** Teaneck, N.J., Avotaynu, 1996. 570p. illus. $69.50. ISBN 0-9626373-9-4.

In this companion volume to *A Dictionary of Jewish Surnames from the Russian Empire*, Beider covers the area known as "Congress Poland," which existed from 1815 through 1917. After a general discussion of Eastern European Jewish onomastics and a history of Jewish surnames in Poland, including geographic distribution, the main section comprises approximately 32,000 surnames. Each alphabetically arranged entry includes the location where the name occurred (based on civil records), etymology, and related surnames. An appendix explains the Daitch-Mokotoff soundex system, and all the surnames included in the dictionary are rearranged in soundex order. Users unfamiliar with alternate spellings, particularly as a result of Polish rules and transliterations from Yiddish and Russian, will have to use the soundex to locate their name. For example, Ringelblum is not included in the dictionary but the soundex would direct the user to "Ryngielblum." Because the author covered only Russian Poland, his subsequent volume will likely be on Austrian Poland, because Galicia (including Krakow and Lvov) also had a substantial Jewish population.

Although *Jewish Family Names and Their Origins: An Etymological Dictionary* (see ARBA 94, entry 441) by Heinrich W. and Eva H. Guggenheimer includes twice as many surnames, including Ashkenazic, Sephardic, Oriental, and modern Israeli names, this current volume is more comprehensive for a smaller area. This dictionary, published by Avotaynu (publisher of the authoritative Jewish genealogical journal of the same name), should become the standard source in this area.—**John A. Drobnicki**

376. Grehan, Ida. **The Dictionary of Irish Family Names.** Boulder, Colo., Roberts Rinehart, 1997. 332p. $24.95. ISBN 1-57098-137-X.

Grehan continues her work in the study of Irish names with the publication of *The Dictionary of Irish Family Names*. Covering more than 550 examples, this work is arranged in alphabetic order, except for names beginning with "O'," which appear under the first consonant.

Under the most common form of a name, the reader will find an ancient version—for example, O Murchu for Murphy. Variants for Murphy are Maccamore, MacMurrough, O Morchoe, and O Murchadha. The writer states that Murphy is "the most numerous of all Irish names in Ireland, and is even more common in the USA." The entry continues with information concerning the history of the name and lists the parts of Ireland in which the name was prevalent. Rounding out the sketch are data about famous personages bearing the name.

This work is a readable and welcome addition to the ever-growing collection of books on the study of names. It is highly recommended.—**Carol Willsey Bell**

377. Ingraham, Holly. **People's Names: A Cross-Cultural Reference Guide....** Jefferson, N.C., McFarland, 1997. 613p. index. $65.00. ISBN 0-7864-0187-7.

This volume is intended for writers, whether preparing fiction for print or scripts for screen or television or merely hoping to enter the field. Essentially it enables a fiction writer to invent personal names with imagination and accuracy. There are more than 100 languages here, divided into groups, such as Western Europe, North America, the Pacific, and so forth. Under each group are a dozen or so specific languages—English, Frisian, Italian, and so on—with lists of male and female names and family names in some cases. Alternate forms are often shown (e.g., Howard, Howie, Ward) and occasional comments are made, such as "sometimes also for boys." In the case of such languages as Arabic, the meaning is given: Majd-al-Din means "Exaltation of Islam." Pronunciation is given for difficult non-English names, using a column headed "sounds like" for each letter or syllable of that language.

The quantity of names is considerable; there are approximately 70 Tahitian female names and even more male names. North American names are grouped into Arapaho, Algonquian, and so forth, and many native names are translated—Kiowan Non-son-gee, for example, means "New Fire." There is also a long section on historical names and ancient languages. A chapter on fictitious ("Shadow") languages, for "out-of-this-world" fiction; a bibliography; and an index conclude the work.

The introduction contains much valuable advice about selecting names and traps to be avoided, as well as the danger of being sued. The paragraphs on "feeling" the period of history being written about and not including a modern name, such as Ashley, in a Regency story, are extremely helpful. The work is strongly recommended for public libraries and for colleges where journalism or any sort of creative writing is part of the curriculum.—**Raymund F. Wood**

378. Sierra, Judy. **Celtic Baby Names: Traditional Names from Ireland, Scotland, Wales, Brittany, Cornwall & the Isle of Man.** Eugene, Oreg., Folkprint, 1997. 121p. index. $14.95pa. ISBN 0-9636089-5-9.

This interesting compilation guides the user to over 1,200 personal names and nicknames from the six Celtic languages: Irish, Gaelic, Welsh, Breton, Cornish, and Manx. The author suggests that there is currently a lot of interest in Celtic names, not only for infants, but for adults looking for meaningful names and authors seeking names for literary characters.

Arranged first by area of origin and then alphabetically by name, each entry contains the pronunciation, etymology (when known), and sex to which attributed. Some colorful examples are Auron (Welsh), meaning "golden goddess"; Gwencalon (Breton), meaning "shining heart"; and Riordan (Irish) meaning "royal poet." The currently popular name Liam is the Irish form of William, short for Uilliam, which is derived from the Anglo-Norman Guillaume.

A pronunciation guide is included as well as information about Celtic realms, a calendar of Celtic saints, and a complete index. This guide is highly recommended as a helpful addition and complement to the material available on Great Britain. [R: Choice, Oct 97, p. 268]—**Carol Willsey Bell**

8 Geography and Travel Guides

GEOGRAPHY

General Works

Atlases

United States

379. **Indiana: Atlas of Historical County Boundaries.** John H. Long, ed. Peggy Tuck Sinko, comp. New York, Scribner's/Simon & Schuster Macmillan, 1996. 394p. maps. index. $125.00. ISBN 0-13-309550-9.

One of the major research questions for many genealogists is, in which county will one find the public records of their ancestors? The answer may be difficult because of county boundary changes. This book will help solve this problem for most genealogists researching in Indiana, as well as other problems for geographers, historians, political scientists, and historical statisticians. The preface and introduction include the history of the development of the atlas. Also provided are the sources for the legislative acts for each county's creation, with authorization and effective dates, and a consolidated chronology of the state and county boundaries.

The majority of the atlas consists of 101 individual county chronologies, historical boundary outlines, and changes superimposed over outline maps. The county chronology explains the county or counties from which a county was created and the county or counties created from it. The outline map pages contain the names of present-day communities and geographic features (however, they lack points to mark locations of communities); map scales; number of square miles; and a county locator map showing the county's location in its part of an outline map of the state. Also included in this book are a useful group of 15 census outline maps for Indiana from 1800 (territory) to 1990 and 13 maps of the territories and states of the Old Northwest, plus related chronologies. The atlas supplies a comprehensive bibliography and an index of places and their counties.

Indiana is volume 9 in a projected series covering all states except Alaska, which has no counties. This series will supersede Long's five-volume *Historical Atlas and Chronology of County Boundaries, 1788-1980* (G. K. Hall, 1984). This long-needed, excellent book is recommended as an absolutely necessary acquisition for all Indiana libraries and for libraries throughout the nation that serve patrons doing Indiana genealogical and local geographic and historical research.—**J. Carlyle Parker**

International

380. **Answer Atlas.** Skokie, Ill., Rand McNally, 1996. 176p. illus. maps. index. $12.95pa. ISBN 0-528-83872-5.

The *Answer Atlas* is a unique volume combining an answer section with an up-to-date map section. The 50-page answer section includes 2 main parts. The 1st part contains more than 130 intriguing questions, such as "Where in South America could you find places in which no rainfall has ever been recorded?" and "Is Venice, Italy really sinking?" Answers accompany the questions. The 2d part is entitled

"World Superlatives, Facts and Rankings" and includes 30 pages that readers will find useful when trying to locate statistics and interesting information on such topics as the universe and solar system; the Earth; continents and islands; mountains, volcanoes, and earthquakes; oceans and lakes; rivers; climate and weather; population; the world's most populous cities; and countries and flags.

The remaining two-thirds of the *Answer Atlas* features maps from *Goode's World Atlas* (19th ed., Rand McNally, 1995). General maps are organized by continents and further break down into countries or groups of countries on one- and two-page spreads. Others include physical, political, population, precipitation, and demographic maps. Special pages are inserted with information on current topics, such as urbanization in North America and the destruction of the rain forest.

A short glossary and an index of approximately 5,000 entries are appended to the main text. This medium-sized atlas (8½ x 11 inches) with softbound cover is a fine introductory atlas for home or school use.
—**Vik Brown**

381. **Children's Illustrated Atlas.** 1997 ed. Chicago, World Book, 1997. 288p. illus. maps. index. $29.95. ISBN 0-7166-4033-3.

Children's Illustrated Atlas is a clearly and simply written atlas intended for use by young, elementary-age children. The moderately oversized (9 by 14 inches) volume presents an overview of the Earth, with brief text that is enhanced by more than 400 color illustrations and 250 color photographs. Cartoon characters are introduced in the first section, "You and Your World," and serve as tour guides to enliven the explanatory material introducing students to basic map skills and terminology. More than 100 basic maps are interspersed throughout the book.

The majority of this volume is divided into 15 sections, each introducing a major region of the world. Each section begins with a welcome page and then presents colorful two-page spreads acquainting the students with the countries in the region, the land, plants and animals, growing and making (farming and manufacturing), people and how they live, the cities, and occasionally special sections such as "Through Europe by Truck."

Young students will enjoy this introductory atlas. A simple index and a pronouncing gazetteer are included. This atlas is fine for home or elementary school use.—**Vik Brown**

382. **Collins Concise Atlas of the World.** rev. ed. New York, HarperCollins, 1996. 160p. maps. index. $16.00pa. ISBN 0-00-448368-5.

HarperCollins has reworked the *Collins Atlas of the World* to produce this latest volume. The *Collins Concise Atlas of the World* consists of three sections. The 1st section is a 23-page geographic encyclopedia that features essays and maps on such topics as population, oceans, and earthquakes. The 2d section is a collection of 96 updated maps. Finally, the world data section is presented, containing five pages of informative statistical data followed by an exhaustive index of place-names. The atlas is square-bound with thick paper covers. The geographic encyclopedia and maps sections feature vivid colors printed on high-quality semireflective paper.

Although the maps themselves are well prepared, their presentation in this volume often undermines their ability to communicate geographic information. In the foreword, the editor states that although the size of the volume is smaller (8½ by 11 inches), the scale of the maps has not been reduced. This decision to put large maps in a small volume results in presenting most of the maps as two-page spreads. The square-bound atlas lies flat only after the user forcefully presses down on the binding. Important information is often lost in between the two pages. For example, on the map entitled "Central America and the Caribbean," the nations Guatemala, El Salvador, and Belize are lost in the binding until the user flattens the atlas. Furthermore, with few exceptions, the atlas features only physical maps. Although the index of place-names is complete, the user is offered only page number and geographic coordinates (latitude and longitude) instead of the letter/number system (for example, G-2) featured in other popular atlases.

Libraries may wish to purchase a copy of the *Collins Concise Atlas of the World* for the reference desk to answer ready-reference queries needing only very general information. However, the presentation prohibits this volume from taking a place among the standard, full-sized forms.—**Keith Kyker**

383. **Concise Atlas of the World.** 3d ed. New York, Oxford University Press, 1996. 176p. illus. maps. index. $39.95. ISBN 0-19-521265-7.

Concise Atlas of the World is an up-to-date, attractive, introductory atlas suited for home and school use. Its moderately oversized format (9¼ by 12½ inches), beautiful graphics, and clear writing style indicate a desire to keep the student in mind. The excellent map quality is the same as seen in the larger *Oxford Atlas of the World* (4th ed.; see ARBA 97, entry 376).

Individual sections are arranged by color-coded edges. The first eight-page section includes statistics about countries and physical dimensions of the world, followed by a useful description of map projections and a user guide. A special 48-page U.S. map section comes next, offering an abundance of multicolored political, topographic, and climate maps, as well as a number of close-ups of urban areas. An index completes this section. A colorful 32-page introduction to world geography explores engaging and timely topics, including tourist spending, notable earthquakes since 1900, a list of oil spills, a description of the Beaufort wind scale, and predominant world languages and religions. The section contains many colorful graphs and pictures and a subject index. A longer "World Maps" section has 177 pages of clear and legible colored maps, many of them 2-page spreads.

A general index of more than 40,000 place-names and features follows. An interesting "Regions in the News" page concludes the atlas, which shows small maps featuring current world "hot spots," such as Bosnia, the West Bank and Gaza Strip, and Taiwan. Flags of the world are displayed on the end papers.
—**Vik Brown**

384. **Concise World Atlas.** New York, DK Publishing, 1997. 250p. maps. index. $19.95. ISBN 0-7894-1062-1.

Like many DK Publishing titles, this work is long on gorgeous graphics and short on text. But here it works just fine, providing readers maps that, in the words of the publisher, "combine the latest cartographic information with state-of-the-art computerized terrain modeling."

The atlas leads off with 12 thematic maps (for example, "political world," "population," "world climate," "global conflict"), then breaks into coverage by continent. The United States is represented by maps of the Northeast, the Southeast, the Central States, the West, and the Southwest. As would be expected in an atlas that measures about 6 by 8 inches, detail is somewhat minimal. Nevertheless, maps show political and state borders, population and administrative centers, and airports. Supplementing the volume's 74 maps are a listing of overseas territories and dependencies; a glossary of geographic terms; and an index/gazetteer that lists, defines, and locates each of the 20,000 places and countries identified in the atlas. Although obviously no substitute for the standard atlases libraries normally have on hand, this work could be a handy backup for ready-reference questions or for home or student use.
—**G. Kim Dority**

385. **Hammond Explorer Atlas of the World.** Maplewood, N.J., Hammond, 1996. 120p. illus. maps. index. $15.95. ISBN 0-8437-1194-9.

Over 100 computer-generated maps comprise this world atlas, with each of the 6 continental sections being introduced by a political map of that continent (Antarctica is combined with Africa). Various colors are used to differentiate the individual countries. Features, including major highways, airports, native reservations, and railroads, are highlighted by the use of different colors and textures. Maps of major, well-known cities are included.

The book opens with information on interpreting maps, map projections, and suggestions on how to use the atlas, including symbols, abbreviations, and scales. A section on geographic comparisons includes six pages of flags of all the nations of the world followed by important geographic data: area, population, page location, capital, largest city, highest point, and monetary unit. Tables of information on world statistics are given in rank order on dimensions of the earth's principal geographic features plus the solar system.

An extensive index containing more than 6,000 entries extends the usefulness of this general world atlas. Cities are identified by state and country location. Other geographic names are noted by their type, such as, rivers, islands, and capitals. This is a general world atlas for home or school use.—**Elaine Ezell**

386. **Macmillan Centennial Atlas of the World.** New York, Macmillan Library Reference/Simon & Schuster Macmillan, 1997. 463p. illus. maps. index. $175.00. ISBN 0-02-861264-7.

New techniques and innovations in cartography have made possible the state-of-the-art maps and satellite photographs in this new atlas created by the Bertelsmann Cartographic Institute. Computer cartography—the map designs were digitally scanned—as well as more realistic use of color representing the world as seen from space and the use of the same unified and detailed scale of 1:4 million for depiction of all of the world's land surfaces are just a few of the outstanding features that make this atlas so superior.

The large-format atlas (45 by 30 centimeters) opens with 32 pages of satellite photographs of such landmarks as the Grand Canyon, the Amazon River, star dunes in eastern Algeria, and the Namib Desert. (Satellite photographs also introduce each map section.) Following the table of contents are keys to the maps; map samples with explanations of scale, color, shading, legends, and the like; and detailed explanations of map symbols. A section in a scale of 1:35,500,000 provides an introduction to the world and its major structures, its division into oceans and land masses, and the continents and their relative geographic positions. In the main section of the atlas, countries' maps are arranged by continent at the 1:4 million scale; regions of the United States and southern Canada at the 1:2 million scale follow the main section. Next is a section of political maps and quick reference facts, and a final section presents a series of maps of major cities of the world. The index contains more than 150,000 entries, each with country abbreviation, page numbers, and grid locations.

Additional outstanding features of this atlas are its details of continental road networks, route numbers and classifications, an indication of distances between points, locations of airports and important natural and cultural sites, an easy-to-read typeface, and a locator map in the top right of each two-page spread. A supplemental CD-ROM entitled *Planet Earth* allows the computer user to explore thematic maps, natural landscapes, and world wonders.—**Dana McDougald**

387. **Maps of the World.** Danbury, Conn., Grolier, 1997. 10v. illus. maps. index. $319.00/set. ISBN 0-7172-7662-7.

The commendable premise of this set of books is to introduce young students to the world of maps. Despite the publisher's claims that this is a comprehensive resource of world maps, the set will have limited value outside the United States because the information about other countries is too general to be of significant use. The 1st volume provides a clear, concise, and helpful overview of types of maps, definitions of terms found on maps, and intriguing "geofacts" about geographic features. This volume also includes a valuable 15-page resource unit on map skills that is reproduced in its entirety in volumes 3, 4, 8, 9, and 10. Volumes 2, 3, and 4 concentrate on political, physical, and cultural maps of the United States. Although these volumes include an abundance of data, they are not as useful as they could be because the data are inconsistent. A map showing the crime rate, for example, is based on 1993 figures, and a corresponding map on police officers is compiled from 1982 statistics.

Volumes 5, 6, and 7 provide political maps and accompanying descriptions of geographic, economic, and historical information for the rest of the world. Each of these 3 volumes includes the same comprehensive place index. Volume 5, which encompasses Africa and Asia, files the countries of the Middle East alphabetically with those of Asia. France, Germany, Russia, and the United Kingdom are the only countries that warrant a double-page spread in volume 6 (Australia and Europe), but 18 pages are dedicated to Canada in volume 7 (North and South America). The data for volumes 8, 9, and 10 are primarily based on 1996 estimates, but again contain inconsistencies. For example, both maps of world television and radio receivers are compiled from 1993 statistics, the world map of telephone ownership from 1994 estimates, and the map on newspapers from 1992 estimates. Volume 10, *U.S. and World History Atlas*, although illustrating key moments in world history accompanied by text summaries and arranged by date or theme, devotes the majority of its pages to the history of the United States. Perhaps this emphasis would not be a liability if the title of the set was not *Maps of the World*.—**Gail de Vos**

388. **The New Comparative World Atlas.** Maplewood, N.J., Hammond, 1997. 96p. illus. maps. index. $14.95; $9.95pa. ISBN 0-8437-7101-1; 0-8437-7100-3pa.

This medium-format, thin atlas is more useful for orientation than for detailed reference. The worldwide thematic maps of global physical and human elements and relationships are simplified enough to be easily comprehensible. The continental physical, political, and comparative maps present essential facts with clarity. However, the computer-generated physical maps of subcontinental regions are hard to read because the colors are too dark and the names often are not well placed to avoid interfering lines. A table of populations of major world cities, world statistics, and a brief index complete the volume. Reference collections in libraries generally will need a larger, more detailed atlas.—**Chauncy D. Harris**

389. **Oxford Desk Reference Atlas.** New York, Oxford University Press, 1996. 160p. illus. maps. index. $18.95. ISBN 0-19-521263-0.

This atlas is published in the United States by the Oxford University Press; however, it was prepared and published in Great Britain by the prestigious atlas and map publisher, George Philip & Son. It is 6-by-9-inches in size, with 47 double-paged maps, approximately 7-by-9-inches in size. Regardless of the small size of the maps, nearly all the printed data is readable without a magnifying glass. Unfortunately, the inside margins between facing pages are too wide for easy reading. Map scales range from 1:5,000,000 to 1:100,000,000. Five of the maps are political maps, including the world and some of the continents. The rest of the maps are physical. The index, like most atlases, does not represent every community appearing in the atlas; however, it is 63 pages and contains approximately 18,750 entries. Two convenient features of this atlas are that the tables of world statistics for counties and physical characteristics provide measurements both in metric (kilometers) and imperial (miles). The world statistics also include the populations of cities with over 600,000 inhabitants. These statistic tables are one of the preliminary sections of the atlas. Another section is a collection of 13 essays on various subjects often included in atlases and three pages of the flags of 165 countries.

This atlas is perfect for any reference desk to explain atlas arrangement, content, use, and for answering simple reference questions requiring the use of an atlas. For atlases with additional maps and more detail, patrons could be referred with ease to two larger atlases that are arranged similarly—the *Concise Atlas of the World* (see entry 383) and *Atlas of the World* (2d ed.; see ARBA 94, entry 446).

—**J. Carlyle Parker**

390. **Planet Earth: Macmillan World Atlas.** New York, Macmillan Library Reference/Simon & Schuster Macmillan, 1997. 415p. illus. maps. index. $34.95. ISBN 0-02-861266-3.

Thanks to computer, satellite, and communications technology, cartography has come a long way since maps were drawn by hand and the margins were labeled "terra incognita." *Planet Earth* is a fine example of this progress. Herein are maps of the world's regions with up-to-date information, naturalistic colors to represent ecological zones and topographic features, detailed transportation networks (including airports and railroads), time zones, climate, and cultural sites.

What sets this atlas apart from others is the use of the same scale (1:5,000,000) for all the maps (except Antarctica and some small islands), thereby providing a far more accurate view of the world. Each chapter opens with a color satellite image of the continent covered and, in the margin, locator maps with page numbers for the areas included in that chapter. These locator maps are repeated in the margin of each map to help orient the viewer. A separate section highlighting the United States and southern Canada in more detail (1:2,500,000) will be especially useful to the domestic traveler. The index to 105,000 place-names at the back is coded with icons symbolizing geographic features.

Planet Earth is an authoritative, attractive, and user-friendly atlas. Its reasonable price makes it affordable for most libraries.—**Lori D. Kranz**

Bibliography

391. **Bibliographic Guide to Maps and Atlases 1996.** New York, G. K. Hall/Simon & Schuster Macmillan, 1997. 812p. $360.00. ISBN 0-7838-1770-3. ISSN 0360-5889.

Most of the titles in G. K. Hall's subject bibliography series (see entry 109 for a thorough review) are compiled from the collections of the Library of Congress and the New York Public Library. That is the case with the volume at hand. Previously reviewed in ARBA 92 (see entry 413), the scope of this volume is standard as well: materials that have imprints of 1990 or newer and that were cataloged in 1996. All languages and all formats (book, nonbook, serials) are included. The typical integrated main entry sort is used, with complete MARC bibliographic copy presented in a three-column format that features a clear, if small, typeface. Access points are names of geographic entities; persons, places, and regions; corporate and conference names; titles; and topics. Maps, atlases, and globes, as well as all aspects of cartography, are covered in depth, making this an automatic purchase for map and cartographic collections.—**Ed Volz**

392. McIlwaine, John. **Maps and Mapping of Africa: A Resource Guide.** New Providence, N.J., Hans Zell/Reed Reference Publishing, 1997. 391p. index. $100.00. ISBN 1-873836-76-7.

The goal of this book is to open up to researchers interested in Africa some of the works that exist for both maps as sources and mapping as an art and a science. The author, an Africana bibliographer, has long had an interest in cartography and has now combined both his vocation and his avocation to create this superb reference book.

This work lists 3,131 citations culled from monographs, journal articles, conference proceedings, doctoral dissertations, and some masters' theses and indexed both by subject and name (but not title). Lest there be any doubt, what this book is not is a list of individual maps on Africa. To be sure, some individual maps, those published in monographs or articles, are listed; but McIlwaine's guide is primarily a reference source that provides citations to those sources (bibliographies, catalogs, and the like) that do list individual maps on Africa. The guide covers cartographic activity dealing with Africa from ancient times up to the present (1995 in general, although a few "significant" items from 1996 have been included) and is divided into 3 general parts. Although all 3 parts are further subdivided into sections, some of which are unique to each part, they all contain, where available, the following types of materials: a guide to bibliographies and catalogs of maps; a list of all significant individual works of cartographic reference (e.g., atlases, school atlases, gazetteers, and related topographic reference works); and a bibliography of writings on maps, surveying, place-names, map collections, and other cartographic topics.

The 1st part deals with the continent as a whole. In particular, it includes sections on map collections and bibliographies of travel and exploration up to the twentieth century, followed by maps divided up by periods. The 2d part of the guide lists materials created and published by colonial and overseas agencies, and the 3d part treats Africa by region and country (including North Africa, Egypt, the islands of the Atlantic [St. Helena, Ascension, Tristan da Cunha, and Cape Verde], and the islands of the Indian Ocean [Madagascar, Comoro Islands, Mauritius, Réunion, and the Seychelles]). This 3d part also includes some pilots (sailing guides and directions) and the annual reports and serial publications produced by the relevant mapping agencies and local cartographic and survey journals in their respective countries.

This guide appears to be comprehensive in scope and should prove essential to both researchers and librarians. It belongs in all collections of any significance that deal with Africa or with maps. Although the author points out some areas where further work or expansion could be done, it is difficult to believe this work will soon be surpassed (unless McIlwaine himself comes out with a new edition).—**Paul H. Thomas**

393. Sukhwal, B. L., and Lilawati Sukhwal. **Political Geography: A Comprehensive Systematic Bibliography.** New York, AMS Press, 1996. 715p. index. (AMS International Studies, no.1). $159.50. ISBN 0-404-63151-7.

This bibliography, listing at most 17,382 unique entries, is touted as a comprehensive bibliography of political geography monographs, government documents, pamphlets, and journal articles in English and a selective bibliography of similar materials in European and other languages. The "other languages" are not specified. Excluded are book reviews, newspaper articles, and conference papers not published as journal articles or in books. Assessing the bibliography's comprehensiveness is difficult because the authors do not clearly specify their selection procedures and principles. For example, dates of coverage are not named explicitly; the earliest date found through browsing the entries is 1902 , and the latest is 1994.

B. L. Sukhwal is a university professor and author of several books on the political geography of India; Lilawati Sukhwal is classified as a researcher and graduate student adviser in the introduction, although the bibliography lists no published works by her. The authors scanned more than 270 journals and bibliographies of political geography books; solicited publication lists from all political geographers, many of whom responded; and looked individually at each item in the bibliography. The only sources identified are *Current Geographical Publications*; the *American Geographical Research Catalog*; *Professional Geographer*; and University Microfilm, Ann Arbor, Michigan. No annotations are included. The book contains an author index but no title index.

The bibliography is arranged in 17 subject-oriented chapters, each of whose scope is clearly delineated in the introduction. The text covers, for example, international political geographic patterns, military geography and geostrategy, colonies and resurgent nationalism, and electoral geography. The table of contents and the introduction constitute the only access to the subject content; there is no subject index. Each chapter is divided into several subsections, usually "General and Theory" first, then others appropriate to the chapter. Within each subsection, the items are divided into books and journal articles and then alphabetically by author. The sections devoted to books include all nonjournal materials. Entries are duplicated if they cover more than one subject, which makes it impossible to ascertain the actual number of unique items in the bibliography. A standard, consistent bibliographic format is used for each item, with entry under the personal or institutional author. Issue numbers are occasionally omitted for journal articles, a minor flaw. Some foreign titles are translated into English.

Aside from the political geography listings in the standard geographic indexes and bibliographies, the only sources covering comparable literature are André-Louis Sanguin's *Géographie Politique: Bibliographie International* (Montreal, les Presses de l'Université du Québec, 1976), and Martin Ira Glassner's *Bibliography on Land-Locked States* (4th ed., Kluwer Academic, 1995). Neither has annotations. Sanguin covers fewer journals and is not as current as the Sukhwal and Sukhwal bibliography. Glassner focuses more narrowly on access to and from the sea and sea resources for landlocked states, but covers international law and economics as well as political geography. He duplicates Sukhwal and Sukhwal for some journals and countries and in some languages and is a good match in currentness, but the bibliography under review covers all countries, emphasizing only political geography. Glassner also has a title index.

The literature of political geography is widely dispersed across many materials and disciplines, so any source that collocates the materials in one bibliography is useful. The source would be more helpful, however, if it included annotations and a title index and if the introduction had more specifically delineated critical scope characteristics, such as date and language coverage, the sources the authors searched for items, and their criteria for inclusion. [R: Choice, April 97, pp. 1316-17]—**Marilyn Domas White**

Dictionaries and Encyclopedias

394. Bendall, Sarah. **Dictionary of Land Surveyors and Local Map-Makers of Great Britain and Ireland, 1530-1850.** 2d ed. Buffalo, N.Y., University of Toronto Press, 1997. 2v. illus. maps. index. $150.00/set. ISBN 0-7123-4509-4.

Planned since 1947, the 1st edition of this dictionary was published in 1975 and 1976. Two supplements were added by 1979, and the resource was published then as a single volume. The 2d edition, a two-volume set, is broader both in scope (the start date of coverage was moved back 20 years to 1530) and comprehensiveness (this edition has 13,744 entries). The 1st volume contains a general introduction, a lengthy guide discussing how to use the book, and a variety of indexes, to the surveyors and the places where they practiced and lived, to the types of maps they produced (e.g., railway, township), and others. A general index lists personal, corporate, and place names as well as subjects. The 2d volume is the dictionary itself, with the entries arranged from A to Z on 578 pages. Each surveyor's entry contains name, dates, geographic area of practice, types of maps done, name of sponsor or patron if applicable, partnerships, education, and other data. The length of the entries vary from a single line to 20 or more.

This revised and expanded edition of a unique resource will be a necessary purchase for large geography and cartography collections.—**Ed Volz**

395. **The Houghton Mifflin Dictionary of Geography: Places and Peoples of the World.** New York, Houghton Mifflin, 1997. 458p. maps. $22.00. ISBN 0-395-86448-8.

Billed in the preface as being "a concise and authoritative guide to the places and peoples of the world," this dictionary lives up to its claims. The limits as to what is covered are spelled out in the preface. There are over 10,000 entries arranged in a single alphabet on two-column pages. Headings are printed in bold typeface, and entry information is set in a legible Roman typeface. Syllables and pronunciations are indicated and there are numerous cross-references. Entries range in length from about 15 words to a couple of hundred words. Scaled sketch maps accompany many of the country entries. Seven full-page, colored maps of continents and the world, with scales and projections indicated, are in the center of the volume. These were created especially for this book. Both physical and political geography are considered.

Emphasis is on places where people live, languages, populations, and forms of government. Up-to-date information about recent changes in European, African, and Asian countries, such as Algeria, Laos, Serbia, USSR, and Yugoslavia are included, with brief histories and current status. Principal physical features of our world (e.g., deserts, mountains, and rivers) are noted. Terms relating to geography and geology are listed and defined. Back matter includes a list of abbreviations and geographic features. A five-page currency table, listed alphabetically by country, indicates basic unit (dinar, dollar, peso, etc.) and subunit (centimes, cents, centavos, etc.) The reasonable price will make it affordable for students and home libraries.—**Frank J. Anderson**

396. **Merriam-Webster's Geographical Dictionary.** 3d ed. Springfield, Mass., Merriam-Webster, 1997. 1361p. maps. $29.95. ISBN 0-87779-546-0.

The 3d edition of this well-known, geographic dictionary will be a welcome addition to reference collections. It contains more than 48,000 entries—an increase of about 1,000 over the 1972 edition. There are also 252 detailed maps in black and white, as compared to 218 in the earlier edition. The visual quality of the maps is greatly improved.

This work identifies and locates both land features, such as mountains, deserts, and lakes, and human geography, such as cities, states, countries, and even well-known neighborhoods (Chelsea—in London). Major constructions, such as dams, the Great Wall of China, Chesapeake Bay Bridge Tunnel, and ruins (Machu Picchu, Tikal), are also included.

Information about the United States and Canada at the state level is given more detail than it is for other countries. It is unfortunate that Mexico was not included in this enhanced coverage, given its major significance as a tourist destination for other residents of North America, its increasing economic importance as a trading partner, and the high profile of its states that border the United States in recent years.

Entries provide pronunciation, variant spellings, alternate and former names, location, population, area, and landform descriptions, as well as political divisions, major economic activities, important educational and cultural institutions, and historical notes through the mid-1990s, when appropriate.

This revision reflects the ever-evolving interest in different places dictated by current events. The entry for Bosnia and Herzegovina is an example. Not only has it been expanded and updated, but a map that did not appear in the 1972 edition is included. Bahrain is accorded similar treatment in contrast to the earlier edition, which had a brief entry for that Persian Gulf country, as is Uzbekistan, and other former republics of the Soviet Union. Geopolitical changes within countries are also incorporated into this new edition. Brazil, where five areas achieved statehood between 1979 and 1990, is a good example. A glossary, with brief definitions of geographic terms used in the dictionary is a new feature of this edition. This fine, basic reference tool is recommended for all libraries with a need for geographic information.
—**Ann Hartness**

Handbooks and Yearbooks

397. **Companion Encyclopedia of Geography: The Environment and Humankind.** Ian Douglas, Richard Huggett, and Mike Robinson, eds. New York, Routledge, 1996. 1021p. illus. maps. index. $160.00. ISBN 0-415-07417-7.

Geography is a crossroad of many fields: history, economics, biology, astronomy, and even politics. The fabulously rich vein of information in this book weaves its way through a global view of the interrelationships between humans and our habitat in a style that is both easy to understand and endlessly fascinating. Eminent scholars of both the physical and human environments focus on the larger theme of the evolution of the earth as a habitat. In 45 chapters, essays are grouped in 6 parts. Part 1 provides an outline of the origin and evolution of the Earth and explores the ever-changing climate, biosphere, human evolution, and the emergence of Homo sapiens. A chapter on the geography of language includes changes in languages, place-names, and linguistic and political boundaries. Religion and modifications of the Earth by humans in pre-industrial times is also covered. Part 2 addresses European settlement and expansion, origins of the world economy and agriculture, changes in global demography, origins of modern environmentalism, and political aspects of urbanization. Part 3 addresses issues concerned with global political geography, Third World urbanization, the international debt crisis, the impact of science and technology since World War II, and anticipated changes in the environment in the future. Part 4 concentrates on contemporary problems: climatic variations and global changes, water and other natural resources use and management, environmental hazards, the nature of Third World cities, and the quality of life (human welfare and social justice). Part 5 covers geography in higher education, achievements of spatial science, geography and humanism in the late twentieth century, and other theoretical developments. Part 6 looks to the future of the discipline. Each essay is authoritative and includes an up-to-date list of references. An essential index concludes the volume. Deservedly, this book has been selected as a *Choice* Outstanding Academic Book of 1997.

Despite the price, this searching investigation of geography in all its aspects—past and future—is a fine selection for any library that wishes to strengthen its reference collection.—**Judy Gay Matthews**

398. **Outline Maps on File.** New York, Facts on File, 1997. 1v. (various paging). maps. index. $165.00 looseleaf w/binder. ISBN 0-8160-3476-1.

Like its relatives from the same publisher—*State Maps on File*, *Historical Maps on File*, and *Maps on File* (respectively 1984, 1984, and 1989)—the object of this volume is to provide quick answers to that perennial reference-desk query, "Where can I find a map of [geographic area], 8½ by 11 inches, that will photocopy well?" The major difference is that these maps are indeed outline maps, that is, they have no place-names on them; only major physical features (e.g., rivers, mountains) and capital cities are indicated, and only with symbols. The maps are arranged by continent, with the continents other than North America first; then come the Americas and regional maps (e.g., East Africa) of continents last. Maps are for individual countries—wisely, both current and past (for example, both Yugoslavia and Bosnia-Herzegovina)—except for the United States and Canada, for each of which are maps of individual states or provinces. The maps are for nonprofit, education, or private use photocopying only.

Because there is a sentence on each map at the bottom stating, "All electronic storage, reproduction or transmittal is copyright protected by the publisher," one wonders if this volume's contents will at some point be issued on CD-ROM, so that users can customize digital maps as they can these hardcopy maps. Be warned: This is a looseleaf volume, for ease of removing maps to be photocopied, which means that on the open shelves, many of these maps may well be removed and never reappear.—**Mary Larsgaard**

399. Penn, James R. **Encyclopedia of Geographical Features in World History: Europe and the Americas.** Santa Barbara, Calif., ABC-CLIO, 1997. 317p. illus. maps. index. $55.00. ISBN 0-87436-760-3.

The author of this encyclopedia, an assistant professor of geography and anthropology at Southern Louisiana University, must have some misconception about the function of an encyclopedia. According to the preface, "this work is not a gazetteer or geographical dictionary, but rather a compendium of selected geographical features that have rich historical associations." The articles are usually one, two, or three pages in length and cover such topics as "Continental Divide" or "Colorado Plateau." Indeed, the illustrations are fine, and the text is readable. There are two or three references for further reading. This volume is a trade coffee-table book, certainly not an information sourcebook, encyclopedia, or compendium. The integral relationship between people and their natural environment is the topic of many scholarly books, including reference books. It is a topic of tremendous interest to many people. This "encyclopedia" is not going to assist readers in their quest to understand a delicate relationship between people and nature.—**Bohdan S. Wynar**

400. **World Facts & Maps.** Skokie, Ill., Rand McNally, 1997. 216p. maps. $10.95pa. ISBN 0-528-83695-1. ISSN 1057-9834.

Like all Rand McNally products, this one is full of crucial information and locator maps for various countries around the world. The 1st section starts with "hot spots" and provides an overview of 41 centers of conflict, including such information as chronological perspectives, issues and events, and background data. The next section gives profiles, important facts, and locator maps on every country in the world and is subdivided into people, languages, politics, economy, land, history, and politics.

As the world races headlong toward a more global market, this volume is absolutely essential for every citizen and particularly every student and should be required reading in at least some of the courses taught at both the high school and university levels. The maps are all in gray tones but are detailed enough to locate the country, its neighbors, and important landmarks. The paper, printing, and binding are acceptable for a paperback; for the price, the volume is quite a bargain.—**Herbert W. Ockerman**

PLACE-NAMES

401. Room, Adrian. **Placenames of the World: Origins and Meanings of the Names for over 5000 Natural Features....** Jefferson, N.C., McFarland, 1997. 441p. $65.00. ISBN 0-7864-0172-9.

The literature on geographic names is extensive, covering the etymology of the place-names for individual countries, cities, provinces, or even towns. Most of these works are monographs, specializing in specific geographic areas ranging from Afghanistan to Zululand (now called KwaZulu). Surprisingly, few works survey the entire world's place-names. *Names and Their Histories* by Isaac Taylor (London, 1898) was a useful dictionary on geographic nomenclature, but it is now significantly outdated.

Room, a prolific author of reference works on toponyms and onomastics, has compiled this new work covering the origins of the place-names for more than 5,000 natural features, countries, municipalities, territories, and historic sites. (The author uses "placename" as one word even though most dictionaries hyphenate the term.) Each entry contains a short description and the geographic location plus a brief etymology and significant historical references. Cross-references provide former names and alternate spellings of current names. An introductory chapter offers an interesting and useful survey on the classification and origin of place-names. The appendixes provide a variety of helpful information: indigenous country names, bilingual place-names, and words derived from place-names. One problem is that the "select bibliography" needs annotations, which would greatly assist readers pursuing further research. *Placenames of the World* is an excellent ready-reference work.—**Donald Altschiller**

TRAVEL GUIDES

General Works

Directories

402. Barish, Eileen. **Vacationing with Your Pet: Over 23,000 Listings of Hotels, Motels, Inns, Ranches and B&Bs That Welcome Guests with Pets.** 3d ed. Gardena, Calif., SCB Distributors, 1997. 720p. illus. $19.95pa. ISBN 1-884465-07-2.

The 3d edition of *Vacationing with Your Pet* is an essential guide to traveling with pets. The first half of the guide helps the reader prepare to travel with animals with sections on training pets, tips for getting ready to travel by plane or car, what to pack, ways to have a better vacation with pets, tips for travel safety, and emergency and medical advice. The book also has helpful sections on grooming, calming pets with massage, and fitness for Fido. The section on moving with a pet is beneficial and offers many tips that are not often thought of during the hustle and bustle of moving. In addition, there is an enjoyable section on pet poems, recipes for dog biscuits, and a list of other pet-friendly titles.

The second half of the guide consists of a comprehensive directory of pet-friendly lodging in the United States and Canada. Approximately 3,000 new entries have been added to this edition, bringing the list of accommodations to more than 23,000. Entries ranging from rustic ranches to fancy bed-and-breakfasts provide information for a variety of price ranges. Divided by state and by city, each entry includes the address and telephone of each hotel/motel along with rate information. Boldfaced subject headings and fun illustrations make this book easy to use. After using this guide to make some travel arrangements, this reviewer found that it is valuable, accurate, and full of sound advice. It is a real time-saver for people traveling with their four-legged friends.—**Natalie Brower-Kirton**

403. **Hostelling North America, 1997: The Official Guide to Hostels in Canada and the United States of America.** Washington, D.C., Hostelling International, 1996. 415p. illus. maps. index. $6.95pa.

Many people may not realize that hostels can be a fun, clean, and inexpensive place for budget-minded individuals and families to stay when traveling. No longer catering only to youth travelers with spartan, dorm-style accommodations, hostels come in all forms, from cabins and hotels to homes, lodges, and mansions. This slender volume packs all the information one needs to locate any of the 222 hostels in the United States and Canada. The introduction, in no less than five languages (English, French, German, Spanish, and Japanese), explains the hosteling concept, membership/nonmembership use, hostel customs, and more. Listings appear to provide all the necessary data. Detailed are location, telephone number, hours of operation, facilities, eating arrangements, credit card acceptability, family/group availability, reservation requirements, and so forth. A photograph of the hostel, directions, and a map, plus a brief discussion of the area, accompany each description. All this appears on one page, so the typeface is small but not difficult to read. Preceding each hostel description is an overview of the area, lists of useful/helpful organizations, discount programs and activities, and other local activities and restaurants. A geographic index provides access. Informative and easy to use, this pocket-sized resource should find lodging in any collection.—**Joy Hastings**

404. **Travel and Vacation Phone Book USA: A Pocket Guide to 100 Major Travel Destinations in the United States.** Detroit, Omnigraphics, 1997. 605p. maps. $50.00pa. ISBN 0-7808-0295-0.

This guide provides condensed travel information for 100 cities in the United States. No criteria for choosing these cities are given, but the locations represent a selection of popular business and vacation travel destinations. Thus, in addition to the largest cities, a town such as Hot Springs, Arkansas, is included, but no cities from Wyoming or North Dakota appear. A useful list of the telephone numbers and addresses of national credit card, airline, and rental car companies; visitor bureaus; and similar services begins the work, followed by several-page entries on each of the featured cities.

Entries list a variety of travel and lodging services, as well as area colleges, attractions, and events. The choices are obviously quite selective; for example, San Antonio includes a list of about 2 dozen hotels and 20 restaurants. These choices consist of mostly moderate to upscale establishments, including both local independents and national chains. A few major shopping centers and local banks are noted. A nice feature is the inclusion of Internet addresses for colleges, universities, and mass media entities. Other categories include museums, zoos, and parks; sports teams and venues; information sources such as libraries and chambers of commerce; demographics; and climate.

As a basic outline of services and lodging in major cities, this book presents substantial data clearly. Entries are commendably accurate and current. However, the volume is much more appropriate for business travel than it is for vacation use. No descriptive or evaluative information is offered for any of the establishments or attractions, hotel rates are not listed, and most of the coverage focuses on the central city's core. Much of the same data, with the addition of credible evaluations and prices, can be found in *Mobil Travel Guide: Major Cities* (Fodor's Travel Publications, 1997) for less than half the price of this work.

—**Christopher W. Nolan**

Handbooks and Yearbooks

405. **Fodor's Healthy Escapes.** 5th ed. By Bernard Burt. New York, Fodor's Travel Publications/Random House, 1997. 387p. maps. $17.00pa. ISBN 0-679-03229-0.

Health spas are one of the fastest growing vacation destinations. This travel guide lists more than 240 fitness-focused resorts in the United States (including Hawaii), Canada, Mexico, and the Caribbean. The facilities are listed in the table of contents by geographic region and in directories alphabetically by name and by type of program. Each spa is categorized by holistic health, children's fitness, life enhancement, nutrition and diet, preventive medicine, spiritual awareness, sports conditioning, stress control, taking the waters, vibrant maturity, weight management, nonprogram resorts, and luxury pampering.

The hotel entries give a description of the sleeping room accommodations, rates, meal plans, directions, a detailed enumeration of the exercise equipment on-site, swimming facilities, golf and tennis availability, and any other services offered. These services may include massage, aromatherapy, herbal wraps, skin and beauty care, and the like. The author provides a glossary defining the treatments available from algotherapy to Zen shiatsu. Also helpful is a list of the local sights that can be visited when one is not exercising. Facility adaptations for the physically impaired are noted. The reader is also informed if the destination caters only to women or to a specific age group. Regardless of the size of one's budget or current level of fitness, a reader can use this guide to find a compatible spot for a healthy vacation.

—Adrienne Antink Bendel

406. **The Milepost: Trip Planner for Alaska & Western Canada.** 49th ed. Bellevue, Wash., Vernon, 1997. 770p. illus. maps. index. $21.95pa. ISBN 1-878425-29-3.

This standard travel guide has been published annually since 1949 (see ARBA 80, entry 584, and ARBA 75, entry 634). The work is conveniently divided into sections covering highways, major attractions, railroads, marine routes, and general information. Users can quickly get their bearings by looking at the table of contents and the introduction, which includes how to read a highway log. Travelers will find the removable foldout map of the region especially handy in determining how far to go each day (a mileage chart of 30 principal points is on the map's verso). More detailed sectional maps are bound in where appropriate.

The narrative portion of the guide follows the mileposts for each route, with detailed descriptions of nearby attractions; practical information on accommodations, road conditions, gas stations, hospitals, and restaurants; plus statistical data on population and elevations. Cautionary notes on possible road hazards, such as ore trucks or deer, are also included. Advertisements are interspersed throughout the text, highlighting points of interest and times of special events.

This guide will prove invaluable to anyone planning a trip to Alaska, the Yukon, the Northwest Territories, or western British Columbia. Whether driving or going by air or water, travelers will need to study the guide well beforehand because its encyclopedic size makes it cumbersome to tote around. It is important to note that the coverage of Canadian sites is limited to points immediately east of Alaska, omitting Banff and Jasper parks. *The Milepost* is recommended for circulating collections in most public libraries.

—Gary D. Barber

407. **Thomas Cook International Air Travel Handbook 1997: A Guide to the World's Major Airports, Their Facilities, and Transport Connections.** Lincolnwood, Ill., Passport Books/National Textbook, 1997. 256p. maps. index. $24.95pa. ISBN 0-8442-9188-9.

The *Thomas Cook International Air Travel Handbook* is a must-have book for air travelers. It details all of the major airports and provides valuable travel information about the countries where the airports are located around the world. Section 1, "Air Travel Facts," provides travel data for every country where an airport is located. The arrangement of countries is in alphabetic order, and the entries supply the language spoken; time zone; address of the airport; e-mail address; locale information about nearest city; health advice about food, water, and vaccines; currency; postage; business and banking hours; public holidays; and the types of driver's license required. The pertinent visa and passport information and regulations for the listed countries are current, but the book urges travelers to check with the authorities to make sure that they have all of the correct documents before traveling.

The "A to Z of Air Travel" section is authored by David Wickers, travel correspondent for the Sunday *London Times*. It defines frequent fliers, j-class, traveling with kids, queues, open jaws, and lost luggage, for example. The section even diagrams and labels a printed ticket. The Airport Directory describes 100-plus getaway airports around the world. Each airport is listed alphabetically and gives information about telephone area codes; currency and banking; time zones; postal addresses and e-mail addresses; distance from the nearest large city; emergency numbers; airport facilities, such as duty-free shops and malls and restaurants; smoking policies; luggage and ground transportation services with local telephone numbers; and regional air connections. The terminal information accompanied by diagrams of the terminal and an area map with major street and highways helps travelers locate where they are in relation to other parts of the city and other locales. The "traveller's notes" are very helpful. For example, the note for Abu Dhabi informs travelers that "gold is duty free and the best value for the duty-free items for sale, and always ask permission to photograph local people, especially women." A blank evaluation form is provided at the end of the book for readers to submit feedback on their travel experiences to the publisher.

The "Destinational Index" is an alphabetic list of destinations listed by the Public Transport and Regional Air Connections tables of all the gateway airports. It advises the traveler of the nearest gateway and the air and land connections available to travel from the gateway airport. This book is recommended for public, academic, and especially business and special libraries.—**Kay M. Stebbins**

United States

408. **America's Best Bed & Breakfasts: Over 2,000 Delightful Places to Stay in All 50 States.** 2d ed. New York, Fodor's Travel Publications/Random House, 1997. 639p. illus. maps. $18.00pa. ISBN 0-679-03302-5.

For this 2d edition, Fodor's has completely updated its list of bed-and-breakfasts by sending reviewers to more than 2,000 locations. The reviewers evaluate the accommodations, setting, and amenities to give the reader some feel for what to expect. Regional maps at the front of the book pinpoint the locations of the bed-and-breakfasts. Entries for individual sites are arranged alphabetically by state. Most states are then divided into geographic regions. Within those regions featured, the bed-and-breakfasts are listed alphabetically, followed by a short list of basic information about other bed-and-breakfasts in the area.

Listings cover a wide range of accommodations, from small houses with one or two rooms to much larger inns. All entries include name, address, and telephone and fax numbers. Descriptions of the featured bed-and-breakfasts detail setting, history, architecture and layout of the house, innkeepers, special amenities, entertainment and activities nearby, meals served, and if there is a restaurant (a dining facility serving at least two meals that is open to the public). Number of rooms; with or without private bath; and other features such as telephone, TV/VCR, air conditioning, whirlpool, fireplaces, and so on are described. Common areas are listed, as are price range, meals available, credit cards accepted, and any restrictions the landlords may impose (smoking, pets, children). A list of "other choices" follows the featured bed-and-breakfasts. These descriptions are short but supply basic information. Reservations services are also listed where available.

Fodor's gives little information as to what criteria were used by their reviewers or how a featured bed-and-breakfast differs from the "other choices" listed. This guide is not exhaustive. There is no explanation as to what was included and what was excluded. What it does, this guide does well. Finding a bed-and-breakfast to suit particular needs is easy with this guide.—**Joanna M. Burkhardt**

409. **America's Best Hotels and Restaurants: The 4-Star and 5-Star Winners of 1997.** New York, Fodor's Travel Publications/Random House, 1997. 248p. (Mobil Travel Guide). $11.00pa. ISBN 0-679-03323-8. ISSN 1086-1726.

Few honors in the hospitality industry are more coveted than the four and five stars awarded by the Mobil Travel Guide. This guide rates establishments using information gathered by a team of culinary and hospitality experts. Quality of food, service, decor, comfort, amenities, or a combination of the above must meet specific criteria to receive the award. This small volume features more than 460 of these premier establishments in the United States and Canada. Each entry provides location, telephone and fax numbers, and a brief description of the establishment emphasizing what is special about the property. Following this information is further detail on amenities and facilities, shops, rates, programs and services, and the like. For restaurants, signature dishes, decor, costs, wine selection, hours, reservation policies, and more are noted. This resource is the one to consult for unique dining and lodging experiences. It is a useful reference at an affordable price.—**Joy Hastings**

410. Barnes, Rik. **Complete Guide to American Bed and Breakfast.** 5th ed. Gretna, La., Pelican Publishing, 1997. 956p. illus. maps. $19.95pa. ISBN 1-56554-268-1. ISSN 1059-6917.

Published since 1986, this directory is now in its 5th edition and lists over 2,000 accommodations. Inexpensive bed and breakfast inns are convenient for a tourist who has limited financial resources and is willing to stay in guest houses offering a variety of lodging. As in previous volumes, the listings are arranged alphabetically by state, city, and inn. The typical information includes name, address, and telephone number; name of innkeeper; number of rooms; rates; credit cards; and restrictions, if any.

—**Bohdan S. Wynar**

411. Bourie, Steve. **American Casino Guide.** 1997 ed. Dania, Fla., Casino Vacations; distr., Chicago, Login Publishers Consortium, 1997. 244p. maps. index. $12.95pa. ISBN 1-883768-06-3. ISSN 1086-9018.

Look no more, because here is one of the best choices among up-to-date gaming guides. *American Casino Guide* provides the lucky purchaser or reader with terrific information on casino games and more than 500 gaming locations throughout the United States. Buyers should not overlook the 42 potentially money-saving coupons for food, cruise rides, and room rates in Atlantic City, Las Vegas, and other gaming locations. The guide is a useful primer on basic casino games, such as roulette, blackjack, and craps, and also gives tips on slot machine playing.

The directory portion of the book is arranged by state and then by city. Native American gaming establishments are listed separately within each state. Casino listings include cruise liner and riverboat gaming opportunities. Even the cruise departure times are given. Each directory entry provides full address and telephone number, a map location, a toll-free number, restaurant information, hours of operation, size of gaming area, and any special or unusual features. Only the lowest and highest room rates are given for the hotels. The AAA Tour Book series is much better for giving room prices and ratings for some of these rooms. An overview of gaming history, rules and regulations, and gambling or bet limitation information is summarized for each of the 30 states offering some form of legalized gaming. The guide is a superb selection and is reasonably priced for public libraries or those people considering combining some gaming action with their travel plans.—**Stephen W. Green**

412. Breining, Greg. **Minnesota.** New York, Compass American Guides/Fodor's Travel Publications/Random House, 1997. 345p. illus. maps. index. $18.95pa. ISBN 1-878867-48-2.

Compass American Guides is an imprint of Fodor's Travel Publications. *Minnesota* is the latest in a series that offers history, commentary, and lavish color photography on the state as opposed to the usual lists of hotels, restaurants, shops, and places of interest found in other travel guides. The reader will learn about the Dakota War, the early history of St. Paul, and the pleasure of boating on the Mississippi River. However, although names and addresses of sites are given throughout the narrative, operating hours and travel directions are not. The 25-page traveler's information section lists a bare minimum of lodgings (and none under $70) and a similarly sparse number of restaurants (only 2 for Duluth). There are two pages on "Minneapolis Music," but no mention of shops except for the Mall of America. Although entertaining to read and delightful to look at, these coffee-table guides are only for the traveler with a suitcase large enough for another guidebook with more specific and practical information.—**Deborah Hammer**

413. **California.** New York, DK Publishing, 1997. 630p. illus. maps. index. (Eyewitness Travel Guides). $29.95 flexibinding. ISBN 0-7894-1451-1.

California is a remarkably compact travel guide. In 630 pages, the writers have packed as many maps, site descriptions, street guides, floor plans, color photographs, and hotel and dining advice as one can imagine ever needing. This is especially noteworthy because the subject is the most populous U.S. state and the third largest state in area. Indeed, this single state offers many more tourist attractions than many nations. The guide is divided into 12 color-coded sections that include its 2 most populous cities, Los Angeles and San Francisco and the Bay Area, and 10 larger geographic regions, including the Mojave Desert, the High Sierras, and wine country. Within each section, readers find historical and background information, maps, colorful photographs, and star visitor attractions such as museums and state and national parks.

The guide opens with lively and informed writing about the history, geography, and geology of California. California's earthquakes are explained, as are the varying climate conditions tourists may expect to find throughout the state. Overviews of the arts in California and its literary history are also shared. Maps are everywhere in the guide. Street-by-street maps of unique neighborhoods are both attractively presented and highly useful. The traveler should be able to easily follow these helpful maps to the "star sights" or main attractions found in the vicinity guide. Special walking tours of unique neighborhoods are highlighted throughout the guide. Sidebar information about people, history, and events enriches the travel reading experience. For example, in addition to the inviting four-page description of the marvels to be found at Disneyland, a boxed profile of its creator, Walt Disney, is provided.

In addition to the 12 chapters devoted to specific cities and regions, a separate "Travelers' Needs" section highlights places to stay and dine, unique shopping opportunities, and specialized vacations (e.g., rock climbing or bird-watching treks). Just in case something is missing or readers desire more detailed information about particular regions, the addresses and telephone numbers of all major tourist sites and attractions are provided. Personal health and security information is even furnished. The travel guide sports a comprehensive index, and its cardstock cover and flexibinding insure that the travel guide can tolerate heavy use and endure plenty of punishment by travelers. The one drawback is the small typeface size.

The Golden State remains one of the great tourist Meccas of the world. This amazingly comprehensive guide provides a superb introduction to all its wonders.—**Jerry D. Flack**

414. Carlson, Barbara. **Food Festivals: Eating Your Way from Coast to Coast.** Detroit, Visible Ink Press/Gale, 1997. 428p. illus. index. $14.95pa. ISBN 1-57859-003-5.

The book at hand is a traveling "foodies" guide to more than 400 food festivals across the United States, grouped by state. The festivals were selected for their ability to reflect the abundance and diversity of the U.S. harvest as well as foods native to a particular region. The individual entries, listed chronologically by exact or approximate date, give a bit of local history along with a description of the festival's major events and notable dishes. Travel directions and a contact person/organization are listed. Carlson, a newspaper reporter, also includes some photographs and recipes from the festivals. A food-type index, a general index, a date index, and a cook-offs and recipe contests index make the book easy to use. *Food Festivals* is an entertaining, fun to browse volume for the circulating collection of all sizes of libraries.
—**Deborah Hammer**

415. Doerper, John. **Pacific Northwest.** New York, Compass American Guides/Fodor's Travel Publications/Random House, 1997. 373p. illus. maps. index. $19.95pa. ISBN 1-878-86785-7.

The first thing one notices about this travel guide is Greg Vaughn's sublime color photography of such sites as Seattle by moonlight, Vancouver Island at sunset, and a tidal pool along the Oregon coast filled with starfish and anemones. Vaughn so expertly captures the exceptional beauty of the Pacific Northwest with his color-soaked images that readers will surely be convinced that this is a region of North America that they must see for themselves. All that is left for Doerper to do is fill in the blanks, which he does expertly. Doerper, a noted food and wine writer, provides text that is both appealing and informative. He supplies all the information one expects from a travel guide, providing a capsule history of the two-nation region along with enticing descriptions of the scenic highlights and major commercial and cultural attractions. Doerper adds more, however. Drawing upon his food and wine background, he encourages readers to seek out particularly excellent venues for Northwest cuisine—oysters, salmon, apples, hazelnuts, and cheese—as well as fine domestic wines. He reviews restaurants and provides maps and details for regional food and wine tours.

Twenty-seven large and reader-friendly maps provide orientation to the fifteen regions highlighted in *Pacific Northwest*, which begin with lower British Columbia (Vancouver, Victoria, and the Fraser River Valley) and end with southern Oregon. To enrich the history and local color of the region, Doerper includes occasional essays and literary extracts, such as a historical account of Robert Gray's discovery of the Columbia River in 1792 and a 1922 first-person account of Kwakiutl chief Dan Cranmer's "potlatch" off the coast of Vancouver Island. Archival photographs expand these historical perspectives and provide a background context that contributes to the reader's greater appreciation of the history, culture, and sense of place. In addition to the expert descriptions of these 15 regions, Doerper provides comprehensive information at the end of the guide about transportation, accommodations, camping, skiing, and crossing the border between the United States and Canada. The book is well indexed. For example, the reader need only look up the word "oyster" to find eight pages devoted to directing the traveler to the best possible sources for that delicacy.

The breathtaking combination of snow-capped mountains and ocean found in the Pacific Northwest makes it one of the most beautiful regions in all of North America. Add to that allure tantalizing regional foods and wines, and the sum is an irresistible vacation destination. Combining their very considerable talents for words and photographic images, Doerper and Vaughn have produced a travel guide that beckons travelers to a first-person sampling of a special place.—**Jerry D. Flack**

416. **Florida.** New York, DK Publishing, 1997. 384p. illus. maps. index. (Eyewitness Travel Guides). $24.95 flexibinding. ISBN 0-7894-1946-7.

This beautiful, colorful guide is designed to help visitors get the most out of a Florida vacation. The pages are filled with colorful illustrations, expert recommendations, and detailed practical information for the person who wants to explore the land, the people, and the history of Florida to the fullest.

The guide is divided into 5 sections. The 1st section, "Introducing Florida," provides maps of the whole state and puts Florida in its cultural and historical context. The 2d and 3d sections, "Miami Area by Area" and "Florida Area by Area," describe the most important sights for the visitor to see using maps, photographs, and illustrations. The six regions mentioned are each given a chapter, including the Gold and Treasure Coasts, Orlando and the Space Coast, the Northeast, the Panhandle, the Gulf Coast, and the Everglades and the Keys. Topics covered in these sections include architecture, food, and sports. Each region shows a map with the sights at a glance for quick reference. The sights in each area are described individually, with addresses, open hours, and other practical information. Graphic 3-D drawings of the interiors of historic buildings are provided; theme parks are shown in a bird's-eye view, with top attractions noted. The 4th section, "Traveler's Needs," recommends hotels and restaurants. The "Where to Stay" category provides prices for hotels and describes which credit cards are accepted, children's facilities, swimming pool facilities, and restaurant and kitchen facilities. The "Where to Eat" section provides price categories that include a three-course meal, a glass of house wine, and unavoidable extras for restaurants. It also describes the credit cards accepted, children's facilities, early bird specials, good regional cuisine (Florida specialties or dishes with Hispanic or Caribbean influence), and bar facilities. Other points of interest in this section include what to eat, shopping, entertainment, sports, and outdoor activities. The 5th section, "Survival Guide," includes practical tips on dress, travel information, currency and banking, personal security and health, and communications.

Color coding and a general index makes the guide easy to use. This travel guide is excellent because of its beautiful color illustrations and the abundance of information provided. It is highly recommended as a Florida travel guide.—**Betty J. Morris**

417. Schimke, Ann. **Great Escapes: The Spring Breaker's Guide to Beaches and Beyond.** Alexandria, Va., Octameron; distr., Chicago, Dearborn Trade, 1997. 134p. index. $9.00pa. ISBN 1-57509-031-7.

This is a handy guide for college students designed to help them plan their "most important week of the academic year, Spring Break." The author covers all of the bases, from "Beach Breaks" and "Slopeside Breaks," to "Alternative Spring Breaks."

The "Beach Spring Break" chapter offers a guide to the most popular American beaches—Panama Beach, Daytona Beach, Key West, South Padre Island, and Lake Havasu City—and international beach destinations, such as Cancun, Montego Bay, Negril, Nassau, and Paradise Island. The guide includes the following topics: how to get there, description of the beach, nightlife (with names of the hotspots and their addresses), the demographics of the beach population, alcohol policy, and transportation. At the end of each section, Schimke provides Internet Web resources. The chapter titled "Slopeside Spring Break" discusses tour operators and U.S. ski resorts from Vermont to California as well as Canadian resorts. Each site description includes toll-free telephone numbers and the Internet Web addresses.

If the beach and slope sites are not of interest to readers, information about "trail breaks" is outlined for the hiker and camper. U.S. national parks, the Grand Canyon, Yosemite National Park, and the Everglades, as well as the state parks, Slide Rock State Park in Arizona and Bahia Honda in Florida, are discussed in this section. Long-distance hiking trails, such as the Appalachian National Scenic Trail and Pacific Crest National Scenic Trail, are described, and each trail's telephone number and Web address are included.

Alternative spring break ideas are presented for students who want to spend their time as volunteers for community service projects. They include building houses for low-income families, serving meals to the homeless, helping AIDS patients in clinics, tutoring Head Start children, working on Indian reservations, and other service projects. A list of alternative spring break programs is given, with telephone numbers and Web addresses included.

The last chapter suggests additional travel guides for backpacking across Europe and attending music festivals and provides destinations to travel for students who want to "head out" across the United States, Canada, or Europe. An appendix of the Websites mentioned throughout the book is provided at the end of the book.

This book is the only book dedicated to the subject of spring breaks and is recommended for all academic and large public libraries with collegiate communities. It is written in a friendly and informative style. The publisher encourages students to write or e-mail their spring break adventures or misadventures for inclusion in future editions of this book.—**Kay M. Stebbins**

418. **The Traveler's Sourcebook 1997: A Practical Guide to Information on Recreational and Business Travel in the United States.** Darren L. Smith and Nancy V. Kniskern, eds. Detroit, Omnigraphics, 1997. 306p. index. $48.00. ISBN 0-7808-0174-1.

This new reference book for travelers is designed to help the businessperson and the outdoor enthusiast in planning trips in the United States. The 83 chapters, arranged alphabetically by subject, are essentially lists of organizations to contact for information on transportation, lodging, business conventions, and recreational opportunities. Each chapter begins with cross-references to related chapters, as well as helpful tips on various aspects of travel and tourism. The sources listed, some of which are also accessible online, will provide free or low-cost information to the interested traveler. Such topics as traveling with children and pets, travel clubs for almost any interest, health, insurance, and travel magazines are a nice touch. Recreational travelers will appreciate the chapters devoted to particular activities (even dogsledding and whale watching). The master index at the back includes both activities and organizations for simple access. The two-column format throughout the book leaves enough white space to be easy on the eye.

The editors of *The Traveler's Sourcebook* invite readers' comments and suggestions for the next edition of what will apparently be an annual publication. The information found here can also be obtained from numerous other references, but combining it between two covers gives it one-stop shopping appeal. It may not contain every source a traveler would read, but it is a good start and is recommended for purchase by public libraries.—**Lori D. Kranz**

419. **Where to Play in the USA: The Gaming Guide.** Michael Sankey and Timothy O. Russell, eds. Tempe, Ariz., Facts on Demand Press/BRB, 1997. 338p. maps. $19.95. ISBN 1-889150-03-7.

This book is a recreational guide for the gambler and traveler who is looking for some legal gaming action along the way. Here is a fairly comprehensive list of virtually every casino, riverboat, and cruise ship gambling junket; harness, thoroughbred horse, and greyhound racing track; and even jai alai courts existing in the United States. The status of state lottery ticket sales is included as well. The main body of the text is arranged by state and subdivided by gaming activity. A general spotting map of legal gaming locations within each state's borders is accompanied by directory listings of gaming site, address, general gaming information, room rates, scope of gaming activities, and any feature attraction. A highly selective list of campgrounds located near some of the gaming attractions is also provided. Tribal casinos, a growing segment of the gaming industry, are given a separate heading under each state. The extent and size of each gambling site listing can vary considerably from entry to entry.

Four appendixes include cruise ship gambling; card rooms in California, Montana, North Dakota, and Washington State; a few Internet gaming sites; and several relevant state regulatory agencies, such as tourism, gaming commission, and so on. As up-to-date and more comprehensive in overall gaming site enumeration than the *American Casino Guide* (see entry 411), *Where to Play* offers the reader less basic information or tips on more popular casino games. This traveler's guide also lacks the money-saving coupons found in the *American Casino Guide*. The title under review is an especially good choice, however, for the budget-conscious traveler whose main or secondary purpose is some form of gaming. It would be a good selection for public libraries of all sizes.—**Stephen W. Green**

Africa

420. Taussig, Louis. **Resource Guide to Travel in Sub-Saharan Africa, Volume 2: Central and Southern Africa.** New Providence, N.J., Bowker-Saur/Reed Reference Publishing, 1997. 468p. maps. index. (Resource Guides to Travel). $125.00. ISBN 1-873836-50-3.

Volume 1 of this guide, covering Eastern and West Africa, was published in 1994. This 2d volume is designed for librarians engaged in collection development or reference work in this field and for those planning to live in or travel to Africa, be it by tour package, self-drive, or backpacking.

This work is prefaced by a good overview of travel literature, which is where the user should start when consulting it. It is then divided into 2 parts. The 1st part consists of lists of published materials, books, guides, magazines, and other literature, as well as maps, videos, and films. Over 1,400 entries are provided in this section. Although not extensive, reference is made to Internet resources as well. The 2d part lists about 350 organizations that help facilitate travel—travel bookstores; government tourist agencies; and publishers, conservation, and outdoor pursuit clubs and societies. Entries in both parts are eloquently annotated. Whenever available, entries for organizations list telephone numbers, hours of operation, fax numbers, addresses, and other useful information.

The cutoff date for published items was December 1996, although the author has updated it. For example, Congo (Democratic Republic) is listed in place of Zaire. There are two indexes: one for journal titles, organizations, clubs, and societies, and the second for places, subjects, and activities. Unfortunately, there is no general author/title index. Four maps are included.

As with volume 1, Taussig has defined travel in a very broad sense. Everything from bungee jumping to language courses and ecotourism is included. The wealth of information found in this volume is incredible. Once again Taussig has outdone himself and produced a rich, wonderful sourcebook that has no competitor and that has instantly become the standard reference tool on the topic. This is a must-have for any reference collection remotely concerned with travel in Africa.—**Paul H. Thomas**

Canada

421. **Fodor's Exploring Canada.** New York, Fodor's Travel Publications/Random House, 1997. 288p. illus. maps. index. $22.00pa. ISBN 0-679-03203-7.

Fodor's Exploring series represents a new generation of travel guide designed to serve as a pictorial introduction to a region. *Exploring Canada* employs lavish color photographs and illustrations on every page, along with evaluative descriptions of features to assist in planning trips and to entertain the armchair tourist.

An overview section introduces Canada's arts, culture, cuisine, social issues, and people and presents the country's history and key events in a nutshell. Each geographic section also has an overview, accompanied by facts, quotations, maps, or tips on every page of the text. The arrangement is by province or region, moving eastward from British Columbia to Newfoundland, with attractions highlighted at cities or geographic areas. A rating system (from "Do Not Miss" to "Non-essential") will help tourists who may be overwhelmed in deciding what to see when planning a vacation. The numerous informative sidebar sections cover a variety of topics germane to Canada (e.g., "Great Explorers," "Mounties," "Salmon"). The final section offers some general travel tips and has a small list of recommended hotels.

Although many travel guides tend to be poorly or underindexed, this book's index is above average and uses boldfaced numbers to indicate major versus minor mention. The numerous photographs are not indexed, a flaw common with other reference works, but a disadvantage for a book that so heavily depends on pictorial representation for its appeal. Another limitation is the high selectivity of sites and cities chosen for inclusion; these tend to be only the traditional tourist stops rather than an in-depth look at available features of more cities and areas. Reading the book is a chore because of the tight construction: The page format and the 5.5-by-11-inch size do not allow for a large enough inner margin, and it is difficult to keep the book open.

With copious information and strong pictorial orientation, this guide is worth consideration by many libraries, even those that normally do not buy travel books. *Exploring Canada* is suitable for reference at those libraries that get frequent travel and geographic questions, especially public libraries, although no aspect is presented in great depth. The primary use for this guide is for trip planning rather than as a take-along guidebook. As such, it complements rather than duplicates traditional guidebooks from AAA, Mobil, Frommer's, or Fodor's.—**Gary R. Cocozzoli**

Europe

General Works

422. **Portugal with Madeira & the Azores.** New York, DK Publishing, 1997. 480p. illus. maps. index. (Eyewitness Travel Guides). $24.95/flexibinding. ISBN 0-7894-1948-3.

In true fashion of DK Publishing's series of Eyewitness Travel Guides, this expansive guide to Portugal, Madeira, and the Azores is colorful, entertaining, and informative. Designed to help users get the most out of their trip to Portugal, this book provides expert recommendations on everything from festivals and beaches to restaurants and lodging. Colorful photographs, three-dimensional maps, and informative timelines are scattered throughout the book, adding to its value.

This guide begins with an introduction to the country of Portugal, including an overview of the culture, most popular months for tourists, and a brief history lesson. It goes on to cover in detail the northern, southern, and central parts of the country, as well as Lisbon and the surrounding islands. Each section includes famous sightseeing attractions of the area, with convenient maps, local restaurants, and customs. Whether the interest is art and architecture or hiking and bird-watching, this guide will contain helpful tidbits on where to go, what to see, and how to get there. The last two sections of the book, "Travelers' Needs" and "Survival Guide," are essential to any traveler new to Portugal. "Travelers' Needs" charts nearly 100 of the most convenient hotels and restaurants and highlights criteria that may influence a traveler's choice, such as price, location, and suitability for families. The "Survival Guide" discusses the details of traveling that are easily overlooked yet essential—transportation within the country, an explanation of local currency, and what to do in the event of an emergency. A two-page list of common phrases completes the guide.

This book contains all the basic elements a traveler would want yet remains convenient because of its small size and flexible binding. This guide would be a welcome addition to the travel collection of any library.
—**Shannon M. Graff**

423. **Warsaw.** New York, DK Publishing, 1997. 288p. illus. maps. index. (Eyewitness Travel Guides). $22.95 flexibinding. ISBN 0-7894-1614-X.

It can be argued that no European country has had a more disastrous history than Poland. Invaded, partitioned, and caught between great powers to east and west, the nation has consistently struggled to maintain its geographic integrity. At the same time, the Polish people have demonstrated a remarkable ability to both conserve and expand their cultural, linguistic, and economic identities, while making the most of any opportunities presented to them.

At the heart of this perseverance has been the capital, Warsaw, and, to the south, the ancient city of Krakow, the embodiment of the Polish nation. Entirely demolished during the desperate fighting of 1944, Warsaw was lovingly restored to its eighteenth-century grandeur. Citizens from across the country volunteered weekends to come to the capital and help with cleanup and reconstruction. Following the collapse of the Soviet empire, Poland moved aggressively into a market-driven economy emulating that of western Europe. The resulting success of this strategy has created more wealth, which is again reflected in the urban landscape of Warsaw.

The Eyewitness Travel Guides have undeniably broken new ground in travel writing and are now the standard against which other guidebooks are measured. These well-organized and lavishly illustrated guides are filled with useful maps, diagrams, practical information, and intelligent text. This latest title will surely prove indispensable to anyone planning a visit to Warsaw, one of the world's most cosmopolitan and enduring cities.—**James R. McDonald**

Greece

424. **Fodor's Exploring the Greek Islands.** New York, Fodor's Travel Publications/Random House, 1997. 288p. illus. maps. index. $22.00pa. ISBN 0-679-03208-8.

Attractively presented and downright fun to read, this travel guide combines practical "how-to" information with an eclectic mix of historical and cultural background material. The introductory section offers concise, charmingly written tidbits on all manner of subjects, ranging from politics, religion, and climate to how to obtain a good meal at an inexpensive restaurant. Also interspersed among the pages of the main section are illuminating sidebars on such topics as the islands' economy, the role of mythology in Greek life, the effects of tourism on island ecology, and so on. Each island is treated individually, with brief descriptions of the main towns and the chief sites. To aid in planning one's itinerary, these towns and sites are rated on the scale from "Not Essential Viewing" to "Do Not Miss." At the end of the book is a much-too-brief section on hotels and restaurants divided into three price categories—unfortunately with no listing of the range of prices included in each category. In the area of the Greek language, the book is on very shaky ground: The pronunciation guide is completely unreliable, and the spelling of island names in Greek is riddled with errors. Although brief, this distinctive guide is useful and well researched.
—**Jeffrey R. Luttrell**

425. **Greece: Athens & the Mainland.** New York, DK Publishing, 1997. 352p. illus. maps. index. (Eyewitness Travel Guides). $24.95 flexibinding. ISBN 0-7894-1452-X.

426. **The Greek Islands.** New York, DK Publishing, 1997. 400p. illus. maps. index. (Eyewitness Travel Guides). $24.95 flexibinding. ISBN 0-7894-1453-8.

Since its inception, the Eyewitness series of travel guides, which now runs to some 20-plus volumes, has been a solid success in an overcrowded market. The reasons for this are evident in these two companion volumes on Greece and its numerous adjacent islands. The formula includes an accessible plan of organization—various regions are color-coded for quick access—and lavish use of maps, diagrams, and photographs (all in color) to highlight major focal points of tourist interest. Introductory sections summarize the geography, history, and culture of the region, and there are detailed chapters on "travelers' needs" and a "survival guide," as well as an overall index. Hotel and restaurant suggestions are diverse but generally upscale, in keeping with the overall series focus, although camping, for example, is lightly passed over.

One of the secrets of Eyewitness's commercial success has been its focus on major areas of high-volume tourism interest (roughly half the publications deal with specific cities) and on regions of maximum tourism expenditure (Europe and the United States). In the present case, this is demonstrated by the separate volume devoted solely to the Greek Islands, which in themselves have become one of Europe's most popular cruising and vacation destinations. This is in contrast to more eclectic offerings, such as those from Fodor's Travel Publications, Frommer's, or Lonely Planet, that are more wide-ranging. An Eyewitness guide to Afghanistan or Cambodia will truly mark the arrival of this series as the world standard. At present, in any case, these are probably the most useful baggage for any visitor to the "cradle of Western civilization."—**James R. McDonald**

International Travel

427. Sakach, Deborah Edwards, and Tiffany Crosswy. **Bed & Breakfast Encyclopedia.** Dana Point, Calif., American Historic Inns, 1997. 948p. illus. maps. $16.95pa. ISBN 1-888050-00-4.

This guide was prepared for travelers wanting to experience local flavor by lodging with residents in homey or romantic surroundings. The bulk of the work provides detailed information on over 2,000 bed and breakfasts (B&Bs), country inns, or homestays in the United States and Canada, some of which are listed in the *National Register of Historic Places*. Besides the expected information, publicity sources and guest comments are given when available, as are special discounts offered by the inn. Establishments in this section are recommended on the basis of visits by the publisher's staff and reports from other unnamed sources; however, specific standards for selection are not given.

Following the detailed entries is a listing of over 13,000 B&Bs that have not been rated or endorsed, providing telephone numbers only. Several additional shorter sections contain a bibliography of international B&B sources, and telephone numbers of reservation services, state inn associations, and tourist offices. The publishers have rated and listed the top 50 B&Bs; the most romantic; the best waterfront inns; those with the best food and best holiday atmosphere; or those distinguished as dude ranches or living history inns. A smattering of B&B recipes dots the work, and a brief article outlines how to start a B&B business.

Perhaps the most interesting and valuable section is an index of the recommended inns listed because of unique features, such as associations with noted personalities or various eras; inns that were plantations, jailhouses, lighthouses, or stagecoach stops; or those related to African American history (to the exclusion of other ethnic groups). There is also an index to the oldest inns in chronological order.

Though touted as the most comprehensive B&B guide on the market, the ambitiousness of covering the entire nation and Canada has to result in only a partial review of lodgings available. For families planning their annual vacation, a more specific region or state guide such as Frommer's or Fodor's may offer more rated choices. However, the broad scope of this work may make it useful to travel agents or those people who have access to the entire country and prefer to stay at bed and breakfast inns. [R: RBB, 15 Sept 97, p. 262]—**Janet J. Kosky**

9 History

ARCHAEOLOGY

428. **The Oxford Companion to Archaeology.** Brian M. Fagan and others, eds. New York, Oxford University Press, 1996. 844p. maps. index. $65.00. ISBN 0-19-507618-4.

This work is organized around several broad themes that explore the tasks, methods, and conclusions of archaeologists, historically and geographically. Fagan is uniquely qualified by knowledge and experience to edit and comment on this comprehensive labor. Topics are arranged alphabetically, but many of the topics are so broad (e.g., "Asia," "History of Archaeology Before 1900," "Byzantine Culture") that specific topics and particular sites or people may be difficult to locate. The volume accommodates this problem with a thorough index and two forms of cross-referencing: asterisks before words that appear as entries and a list of related articles at the conclusion of an entry.

Some browsing is recommended because unique topics do appear, such as "Marxist Theory," "Pseudo-Archaeology," "Structuralism," and articles on other philosophical and ethical issues. No photographs or drawings are found in the main text, but several maps and charts appear in the back of the book. There is a somewhat pronounced focus on British involvement in archaeology. Considering the broad public interest in Syro-Palestinian or "Biblical Archaeology," Palestinian sites (e.g., Megiddo, Lachish) and biblical archaeologists (other than W. F. Albright) are not very visible as contributors or subjects. The style is expository rather than literary, but well informed. [R: LJ, 15 Feb 97, p. 129]

—**Robert T. Anderson**

429. **The Oxford Encyclopedia of Archaeology in the Near East.** Eric M. Meyers, ed. New York, Oxford University Press, 1997. 5v. illus. maps. index. $575.00/set. ISBN 0-19-506512-3.

This work follows not far behind two other recent multivolume sets focusing on the ancient Near East: *The New Encyclopedia of Archaeological Excavations in the Holy Land* (see ARBA 94, entry 489) and *Civilizations of the Ancient Near East* (see ARBA 96, entry 159). Each has its own value; thus they are complementary rather than competitive. The latter deals with the peoples of the area and their culture in thematically arranged articles. The former presents alphabetically arranged entries on important sites in—as the title indicates—the Holy Land. *The Oxford Encyclopedia of Archaeology* is a standard encyclopedia with specific, alphabetically arranged articles on "archaeological techniques, theory, methods, and practice" (p. ix), as well as on sites, archaeologists, structures, materials, and languages.

The editorial team decided on a broad definition of the ancient Near East. Geographically, the boundaries are Anatolia and Armenia to the north, Ethiopia and the Arabian Peninsula to the south, North Africa as far as Morocco to the west, and Iran to the east. Due to the continuing expansion of archaeological work in this area, the chronological starting point was pushed back into prehistory and extended through the Crusades (and, in some cases, beyond). The geographic and chronological boundaries are illustrated in Appendix 2, "Chronologies," and Appendix 3, "Maps," in volume 5.

Most of the more than 1,100 articles (contributed by an international team of 560 scholars) include bibliographies, many of which are annotated. Only sites of major importance are treated in separate entries, but with the assistance of the index, users will be able to find other sites mentioned in articles on regions, countries, and so forth. In addition to the general index, there is a synoptic outline that groups the entries under conceptual categories and subcategories. These points of access are supplemented by a thorough system of cross-references. Although it is outdone by the illustrations in *The New Encyclopedia*, the *Oxford Encyclopedia* is well illustrated with black-and-white photographs, line drawings, and maps throughout.

This is a well-written work, and it is generally clear. However, general readers will find some articles that they will have to read with dictionary in hand because of the use of technical jargon. Thus, the set is highly recommended for collections that serve students and scholars in archaeological studies and recommended with slight reservations for general reference collections. [R: RBB, 15 Mar 97, p. 1260]

—Craig W. Beard

AMERICAN HISTORY

Archives

430. **ArchivesUSA.** [CD-ROM]. Alexandria, Va., Chadwyck-Healey, 1997. Minimum system requirements: IBM or compatible 486/33MHz. High-speed CD-ROM drive with Microsoft CD-ROM Extensions 2.10. MS-DOS 3.3. Windows 3.1 running in enhanced mode. 8MB RAM. 10MB hard disk space. High-density floppy disk drive. VGA color monitor. Microsoft-compatible mouse. various pricing options available. ISBN 0-89887-156-5.

In the past, those searching for archival or manuscript collections had to depend on printed sources. The primary printed source was the *National Union Catalog of Manuscript Collections* (NUCMC) from the Library of Congress and containing 75,000-plus records (1959-1993 in print, 1993-1995 on magnetic tape). In 1982, Chadwyck-Healey began the publication of the *National Inventory of Documentary Sources in the United States* (NIDS) on microfiche, which has the names and detailed subject indexing of more than 42,000 collections from some 300 repositories. With the advent of computerized catalogs, bibliographic records began appearing in OCLC's Union Catalog, RLIN, and in individual library catalogs. Now this electronic product from Chadwyck-Healey makes things much easier for researchers and librarians alike. Both of the two bibliographic sources are combined here, along with the *Directory of Archives and Manuscript Repositories in the U.S.* (1988). The introduction in the user's manual states that the records "from NIDS and NUCMC have been cross-collated and new records created, pooling information from both sources where available." In addition, some 3,000 repositories not listed in either NIDS or NUCMC have information included in this product. For those doing comprehensive research in primary sources, *ArchivesUSA* does not remove the need to search individual printed and electronic catalogs, but this is now the first place to look for citations to collections in the United States.

Installation of the Caravan software is easy using the two installation diskettes sent along. The searching features seem logical and easy to operate. One can search by all keywords, collection name, and collection keyword; collection year or all dates (from, to, only, between); the repository name, repository city, and repository state; and all records, NIDS records only, and NUCMC records only. This reviewer typed in "Loyola University Chicago" for a repository name. A browse list of names came up, the desired institution was highlighted, and the OK button was clicked on. Under the "Summary of Matches," Loyola had 87 collections listed. One can highlight the desired collection, then click on the Full Record Details button. These details include the collection name, dates, repository name, NUCMC number, type and extent of the material, and a text description of the collection. At the bottom of the record is a button to click on to see the NUCMC indexing terms. There is also a button for Repository Details, which include the address, telephone and fax numbers, days and hours of service, materials solicited, total number of volumes, inclusive dates of materials, and a text description of the highlights of the collections. All of this information is contributed by the individual repositories. The software has buttons to copy, cut, and paste text and to print or download text. The accompanying manual is easy to read and includes an index, a list of stopwords, and an explanation of the search fields.

The World Wide Web version (http://archives.chadwyck.com:8085/), is similar to the CD-ROM version. Here there are hot links to an online submission form to submit repository or collection information, repository home pages, and online finding aids. The main difference is that the Web version is updated quarterly, whereas the CD-ROM will be updated once a year. In both versions, the Collection Search is probably the main way to search the database. The database will be updated with NUCMC data from the Library of Congress. Approximately 2,500 new finding aids are added to the NIDS microfiche collection 5 times a year. All indexes will be included in the annual update of *ArchivesUSA*. Subscribers will get Web access to the database as well as the compact disc and will get to keep the CD-ROM if they terminate their subscription.

The subscription price is determined by the type of library and by the book budget: Prices range from $1,995 for a site license for a large library with more than $1,000,000 in its book budget to a $495 single-user license for a special library spending less than $50,000 on its book budget. The standard restrictions apply: The licensee may only use the data for personal or internal organizational purposes and cannot use it to create products that might compete with Chadwyck-Healey. Research and large public libraries should definitely consider this product.—**Daniel K. Blewett**

Atlases

431. **Florida: Atlas of Historical County Boundaries.** Peggy Tuck Sinko and Kathryn Ford Thorne, comps. John H. Long, ed. New York, Scribner's/Simon & Schuster Macmillan, 1997. 323p. maps. index. $125.00. ISBN 0-13-366329-9.

During the First Seminole War (1817-1818) Andrew Jackson and his troops chased the Seminole Indians into Spanish Florida. While there, Jackson deposed local Spanish governments, adding to the mythic status he earned in the Battle of New Orleans. In 1819, the Spanish left for good, ceding both East and West Florida to the United States. Two years later Jackson was named the first provisional governor of the Florida territories. He gave up the post the next year, and in one of his few official acts he divided the complete territory into two counties, using the Suwannee River as a boundary. He named the eastern county St. Johns, and the western county Escambia. During the next 105 years, Florida governments would further divide Florida into its current 67 counties. Although people tend to think of the city as the basic unit of geography, it is the county that issues marriage, birth, and death certificates; records property ownership; maintains tax rolls; and probates wills. *Florida: Atlas of Historical County Boundaries* is a wonderful documentation of the unit of government so critical to Florida's growth and development.

This hardbound volume features several sections useful to the historian, genealogist, teacher, and student. The major part of the work is dedicated to county chronological maps that depict the geographic development of each county. For example, Alachua County has undergone 13 boundary changes. Each change is expertly rendered on political maps that include current county boundaries and names of cities in the area. Dates of these changes and the resulting area (in square miles) are also included. Other sections of the book include a consolidated chronology of state and county boundaries, census outline maps, an index of Florida place-names, and an extensive bibliography.

Although targeted for the serious researcher, *Florida* has something to offer for everyone interested in the Sunshine State. Younger students will marvel at the 1830 Federal Census map, with "Indian Territory" printed where a visitor would now find Disney World. Older students can observe how counties originated around seaports, with later counties added as agricultural importance was realized. Genealogists will find this book a blessing. All libraries with a need for Florida historical information should find a place for this thorough, academic, yet surprisingly accessible volume.—**Keith Kyker**

Bibliography

432. **Civil War Books: A Critical Bibliography.** Allan Nevins, James I. Robertson Jr., and Bell I. Wiley, eds. Baton Rouge, La., for the U.S. Civil War Centennial Commission, Louisiana State University Press, 1967-1969; repr., Wilmington, N.C., Broadfoot Publishing, 1996. 326p. index. $75.00. ISBN 1-56837-321-X.

A facsimile reprint of the original 2-volume work (see ARBA 70, v.1, p.61, for a review of v.2) reprinted by Broadfoot Publishing in 1996, this bibliography consists of 15 subject sections, each arranged alphabetically by main entry. Coverage is for the war years only, excluding causes, background, consequences, and so on. The list includes books and pamphlets and excludes theses, dissertations, journal articles (unless in a monographic collection), manuscript materials, and fiction and other "literary" material. Approximately 6,000 items were selected by the 15 subject experts to represent, apparently, the titles most likely to be consulted by researchers and hobbyists. In addition to copies of the main entry and title page paragraph from Library of Congress cataloging, each entry consists of a one-sentence evaluative annotation by the section compiler.

The major attraction of this work was, and continues to be, the excellent, succinct comments. Surprisingly, a large percentage are at least partially negative; because this is a selective bibliography, one wonders what the compilers thought of the items not listed. The major objection to the work remains its access system. The index is reminiscent of nineteenth-century practice—fairly complete for proper names (persons, battlefields, organizations, and the like) and sparse for other subjects. When combined with the lack of cross-references in the body of the work or even subject tracings from the catalog entries, there is hardly any access to anything except the large topics used as sections.

Quite simply, if a library already owns an earlier version, it does not need this. If it does not have the earlier version, and there is considerable interest in pre-1960s Civil War books, it may want to consider getting the new version for the annotations. It is a shame that the publisher did not feel it worthwhile to reindex this work, because it is well bound, well printed, and not outlandishly priced.

—**James H. Sweetland**

433. Eicher, David J. **The Civil War in Books: An Analytical Bibliography.** Champaign, Ill., University of Illinois Press, 1997. 407p. index. $39.95. ISBN 0-252-02273-4.

This volume represents a remarkable achievement in the field of Civil War literature/bibliography. Eicher, with the cooperation of a board of specialists, presents 1,100 major works in a broad range of Civil War studies. The critical and descriptive annotations are superbly written and closely approximate in both form and style those found in scholarly historical journals. The appeal, nevertheless, is both popular and scholarly. Selections were chosen to appeal to a wide range of interests. Readers will find works dealing with such related but different areas as individual battles and campaigns, diplomacy, the homefront, politics, prisons, medicine, equipment, the press, biography, maps, music, and illustrations. Fiction is not excluded, and reference libraries will appreciate the excellent selection of reference titles.

This volume is well organized for ease of use. Particular works may be located through author and title indexes, and the contents are arranged in logical groupings in which users may easily identify a useful book via a detailed six-page table of contents or by scanning the book itself. Battle literature is listed chronologically, with separate subsections devoted to naval warfare and the war in the West. Biographical works on 350-plus people are organized alphabetically and divided by Union or Confederate allegiance and subdivided into Army, Navy, politics, and other groupings. The remaining titles are categorized according to subsections dealing variously with individual states, regiments, strategy and tactics, women, African Americans, the common soldiers, equipment, fiction, medicine, the press, and other topics of interest. It is also significant that selections for this volume are not limited by date or format of publication. Included are such titles as the *Confederate Veteran*, a periodical devoted to the recollections of southern veterans and others published between 1893 and 1932, and the monumental *War of the Rebellion: A Compendium of the Official Records of the Union and Confederate Armies* (Government Printing Office, 1891-1895). Two appendixes, "Prolific Civil War Publishers" and "A Short List of Civil War Bibliographies," lead readers to additional works on the subject.

This is an excellent book. The price is modest and less than the typical student textbook. As such, it is highly recommended for all libraries with collections on the Civil War and for anyone or any institution having an interest in the area.—**Donald E. Collins**

Biography

434. Barthelmas, Della Gray. **The Signers of the Declaration of Independence: A Biographical and Genealogical Reference.** Jefferson, N.C., McFarland, 1997. 334p. illus. index. $55.00. ISBN 0-7864-0318-7.

The premise of this book is simple—to provide concise biographical and genealogical information on the lives of the signers of the Declaration of Independence. Each of the 56 signers, plus Charles Thomson, the Secretary of the Continental Congress, receives several pages. Well-known signers, such as Thomas Jefferson and Benjamin Franklin, receive the most coverage. For each signer, information is divided into three parts. The first section is a brief look at his life, with particular emphasis on his participation in events of the Revolution; the second gives supplementary information, such as physical appearance, anecdotes, and present-day markers or memorials that commemorate his life; and the third section traces the signer's lineage back several generations. Genealogical information concerns the paternal line of the signer. Each biography is preceded by a portrait.

Although the collection of information about these individuals, who are bound together in history by their participation in a momentous happening, is attractive, informative, and well written, it is difficult to know where this book would fit in library collection policies. The genealogical information is rather difficult reading, as such information always is for those not practiced in following the tangled paths of family descent. Most of the biographical information is available in standard sources, such as the stalwart *Dictionary of American Biography* (see ARBA 96, entry 36), although of course not so conveniently packaged. Libraries with a specialized interest in either American history or in genealogy will be interested in its purchase.—**Terry Ann Mood**

Chronology

435. **Chronicle of America.** rev. ed. New York, DK Publishing, 1997. 1016p. illus. maps. index. $59.95. ISBN 0-7894-2091-0.

Following nine pages of information on world events that led up to the pivotal 1492 voyage, the *Chronicle of America* chronologically traces the history of this country. Representing the early years, a 2-page spread may cover 5 to 10 years, but by 1764, a spread covers the events of 1 year. Each spread includes a number of colorful illustrations or photographs and a sidebar that pinpoints major events of the time. The work concludes with the events of 1997, which are followed by an illustrated list of facts about the presidents, information on each of the 50 states, a chart on the format of the U.S. government, and an amazingly thorough index.

The index makes clear the value of this attractive work to both student and browser. Among the many entries that identify information on historic persons, places, and events are others that indicate coverage on cultural topics over the years, such as abolition, abortion, actors and actresses, advertising, alcoholic beverages, art, automobile, and aviation. There are four columns of "books, fiction," which are listed in the order of coverage, that enhance access to fiction on a given period.

This sturdy book is appropriate for secondary and public libraries. In academic libraries, undergraduates seeking report topics or an overview of an event or time would find this reasonably priced work of value. A worthwhile companion volume is the 1997 edition of *The Encyclopedia of World Facts and Dates*, by Gorton Carruth.—**Vandelia L. VanMeter**

436. Rubel, David. **The United States in the 19th Century.** New York, Scholastic, 1996. 192p. illus. maps. index. (Scholastic Timelines). $18.95. ISBN 0-590-72564-5.

Events, photographs, drawings, and maps are brought together here and organized as a timeline to provide an understanding of the history of the United States during the nineteenth century. The book is arranged into chapters, each representing a different era of the 1800s: "Federalism (1800-1814)," "Era of Good Feelings (1815-1828)," "Jacksonian Democracy (1828-1837)," "Industrialization (1837-1845)," "Manifest Destiny (1845-1854)," "A House Divided (1854-1861)," "The Civil War (1861-1865)," "Reconstruction (1865-1877)," "The Gilded Age (1877-1889)," and "The Gay Nineties (1890-1899)." An introduction before each chapter introduces the era and provides some background information. Each chapter is further divided into four categories—science and technology; arts and entertainment; daily life, social movements, fads, and fashions; and politics—that enable the user to better understand the relationships among events that occurred during the same period. Every right-hand page includes an area that features a person (such as Mathew Brady or Horace Mann), an event (such as the Trail of Tears or the Irish Potato Famine), or a trend (such as transcendentalism or urbanization) that further describes the people and conditions that helped shaped the era.

More than 300 photographs and illustrations, a glossary, and a comprehensive index all increase the enjoyment and usefulness of this attractive and easy-to-use reference.—**Dana McDougald**

Dictionaries and Encyclopedias

437. **The ABC-CLIO Companion to the 1960s Counterculture in America.** By Neil A. Hamilton. Santa Barbara, Calif., ABC-CLIO, 1997. 386p. illus. index. (ABC-CLIO Companions to Key Issues in American History and Life). $60.00. ISBN 0-87436-858-8.

With more than 400 alphabetically arranged topical entries, this work explicates a period of U.S. history whose activities and celebrities have steadfastly eluded dispassionate analysis. Beginning with "Acid" and ending with "Young, Neil," entries are included for events, people, places, organizations, broad topics (e.g., "Rock Music"), individual books, motion pictures, record albums, and catch phrases (e.g., "Far Out"). Although approximately 50 black-and-white illustrations are interspersed throughout the text, the inclusion of more would have strongly enhanced the book's value to students. Following the main text is a five-page chronology, spanning January 1970 through March 1973. Again, more material of this sort would only serve to improve the companion's usefulness. The 16-page bibliography is a strength, although the mere 19 Websites that are listed feel like an afterthought. A combined index ends the book.

It can be difficult to spot biases that parallel one's own, but an empathetic attitude was noticed in many of the entries regarding antiwar groups and activities. Readers with different views could take mild offense.

Both factual and editing errors were noted—Creedence Clearwater Revival is referred to as "Credence Clearwater Revival," the Cream *Wheels of Fire* album is called "Wheels," the rock group Procol Harum's entry varies between the correct spelling and "Procul Harum," and the entry for the Jackson State killings of May 14, 1970, says the event occurred ". . . just five days after . . ." the Kent State killings of May 4, 1970. These are trivial matters, but the book is, after all, intended to be a research tool. The currency of information is commendable. For instance, Allen Ginsberg's April 1997 death date is noted.

This topical dictionary gathers together data that are otherwise scattered throughout disparate sources that are unlikely to be in school or smaller public libraries. Hamilton's survey will be valuable to that market. A better edited, revised edition, illustrated and with a more substantial chronology, could become a seminal reference title.—**Ed Volz**

438. **Dictionary of Afro-American Slavery.** updated ed. Randall M. Miller and John David Smith, eds. Westport, Conn., Praeger/Greenwood Press, 1997. 892p. index. $99.50; $35.00pa. ISBN 0-313-23814-6; 0-275-95799-3pa.

Like the original 1988 edition (see ARBA 90, entry 493), the goal of this updated edition is to provide a synthesis of the best scholarship on the many and diverse features of the slavery experience in North America from the first English settlement to Reconstruction after the Civil War. Although the basics of slavery studies have remained the same since the 1st edition, the update contains new aspects of academic study, including assessment of the social and cultural aspects of slaves on their own terms, not just as victims of bondage; an effort to track slavery, African American culture, and plantation society back to their origins; and renewed interest in slaveholders, including women slaveholders.

The 300 substantial articles on both broad and specific subjects, including regional differences, were written by contributors selected for their scholarly expertise. Each entry ends with a brief list of references recommended for further study. This edition includes a new introduction, a bibliography arranged by topic, and a slavery chronology. It is available in an inexpensive paperback edition, making it available to a wider audience.

The editors see this book not only as a reference tool but also as an expression of the state of the art of the field. Both a valuable and readable resource, it is appropriate for lay readers as well as scholars. Recommended for public and academic libraries.—**Jeanette C. Smith**

439. **Encyclopedia USA: The Encyclopedia of the United States of America Past & Present. Supplement Volume I: Abbe, Robert-Alexander, Robert Evans.** Donald W. Whisenhunt, ed. Gulf Breeze, Fla., Academic International Press, 1997. 248p. $38.50. ISBN 0-87569-076-9.

440. **Encyclopedia USA: The Encyclopedia of the United States of America Past & Present. Volume 24: Dulles, Allen Welsh-Earthquakes in America.** Donald W. Whisenhunt, ed. Gulf Breeze, Fla., Academic International Press, 1997. 250p. $38.50. ISBN 0-87569-076-9.

Here is an encyclopedia that strives to be both exhaustive and substantive. Quite literally, its objective is not only to include every event, place, subject, and person of significance from the precolonial United States to the present, but also to allow the individual authors to be fairly expansive. The result has been a plodding process with no immediate end in sight. Begun in 1983, the work to date spans 6,400 pages, contains 3,078 entries, and features 420 specialists. The 24th volume barely reaches the 5th letter of the alphabet, and the 1st supplement manages to get only about halfway through "A." Even if the publisher's expectation, which frankly seem unwarranted, of completing the task in another 26 volumes or so proves correct, the end is still a decade or more away. With completion so remote, one must also question the wisdom of commencing supplements so soon. One hopes the current editor, a historian of proven ability, will be able to speed the venture along.

It is easy to fault the mechanical aspects of *Encyclopedia USA* but not the quality of its content. Most entries, all of which have a bibliography, are at least a page or two in length, and many are quite lengthy. Accounts of the "Dutch in America" and the "Earp Family," for instance, run to about nine pages, as do the treatments of the "Abortion Issue" and "AIDS." Attention is also given to subjects such as *Dynasty*, the popular television series of the 1980s, comedian Jimmy Durante, historian Will Durant, and the phrase "*E Pluribus Unum*." This is no ordinary encyclopedia. The individual volumes are approximately 250 pages in length, and ultimately the entire set will be indexed. Until then, a list of contents at the back of the two current volumes will guide readers through the material. Although the cost will be steep, university and college libraries should consider adding the complete set to their reference collections. Students interested in the American experience will be the beneficiaries. This is a treasure trove.—**John W. Storey**

441. Hatch, Thom. **Custer and the Battle of Little Bighorn: An Encyclopedia of the People, Places, Events....** Jefferson, N.C., McFarland, 1997. 229p. illus. maps. index. $45.00. ISBN 0-7864-0154-0.

Will interest in George Armstrong Custer and the Battle of Little Bighorn never wane? A query on "George Armstrong Custer" in FirstSearch retrieves just more than 1,200 items; and still the hero versus villain controversy rages, despite voluminous analyses of the battle site, personal letters and narratives from the 1870s from U.S. military men and civilians, as well as drawings and oral history gathered from various Plains Indian tribes. As early as 1953, Colonel W. A. Graham, in *The Custer Myth: A Sourcebook of Custeriana* (Stackpole), included a 600-plus-item bibliography compiled between 1939 and 1952 by Fred Dustin for his own book, *The Custer Tragedy* (Edwards Brothers).

Hatch's 1997 contribution to the Custer literature, *Custer and the Battle of Little Bighorn* is subtitled *An Encyclopedia of the People, Places, Events, Indian Culture and Customs, Information Sources, Art, and Films*. This reference is a 229-page "encyclopedia" that may be described as part annotated bibliography and part historical dictionary. Instead of the more usual chronological, geographic, archaeological, or biographical arrangement, this book is arranged alphabetically. Entries range from paragraph-size (for minor military personnel and popular songs of the day) to multipage (for Custer himself and the Battle of Little Bighorn) and are supplemented by maps, illustrations, and "sources for further study." The entry "Motion Pictures and Videos Relating to Custer and Little Bighorn" lists 40-plus movie and video titles.

The encyclopedia is strengthened by an appendix, "Custer Civil War Chronology and Battle Summary," and a comprehensive back-of-the-book index. The work is prefaced by a list of maps, all drawn by the author, and a list of photographs and illustrations. The author's purpose, "to assist the interested reader in gathering relevant information—fact, theory, speculation—into a manageable perspective," has been met. The encyclopedia is likely to be found in academic and large public libraries and sometimes, despite its title, in the circulating collection (only one of six libraries checked shelves it in reference). Civil War and U.S. history buffs may also want a copy for their collections.

Hatch's encyclopedia summarizes previous scholarly research as well as popular movies, fiction, and art. It may even be part of a trend in specialized reference books that serve almost as "metareference" works: reference works about reference works. [R: LJ, 15 Feb 97, pp. 127-28]—**Linda D. Tietjen**

442. **Reader's Guide to American History.** Peter J. Parish, ed. Chicago, Fitzroy Dearborn, 1997. 880p. index. $125.00. ISBN 1-884964-22-2.

What are the most important books that have been published about the U.S. past? A cast of some 225 distinguished historians provides answers to that question in this ambitious and impressive work. The 880-page, 8½-by-11 inch volume contains some 600 alphabetically arranged historiographic essays about selected topics in U.S. political, social, and economic history. The volume does not attempt to cover topics in art history, literary history, or the history of science and medicine. Minor emphasis is placed on topics relating to the history of technology or popular culture.

Each entry includes a list of approximately 10 major works published on the subject; a 1,500-word essay that attempts to summarize the major arguments of these books; the contributor's name; and where appropriate, a reference to related topics in the volume. In all, more than 5,000 published works are reviewed in this user-friendly guide to secondary literature.

Although some may quibble with the editor's selection of topics, *Reader's Guide to American History* is an important reference tool that will be greatly appreciated by undergraduate, graduate, and professional historians alike. It is strongly recommended for all libraries with collections in American history.
—**Terry D. Bilhartz**

443. **Scholastic Encyclopedia of the Presidents and Their Times.** updated ed. By David Rubel. New York, Scholastic, 1997. 232p. illus. maps. index. $17.95. ISBN 0-590-49366-3.

A revision of the 1994 edition (see ARBA 96, entry 521), this version of the *Scholastic Encyclopedia of the Presidents and Their Times* covers Bill Clinton's reelection; the assassination of Yitzhak Rabin; and the problems, physical and political, of Russia's president Boris Yeltsin. Updated maps and charts are also included.

Attractively arranged and well illustrated, each entry follows the same format. The president's name, term, and picture begin the entry. A mini-fact box containing those items dear to young researchers (e.g., the wife's name and the names of the children) and a personal tidbit—George Bush is cited for his opposition to broccoli and Theodore Roosevelt was the first president to fly in an airplane—follow. Highlights of the administration are given on the outside column of each page, with columns in the interior sections giving cultural events of the period. For example, Gibson Girls, yellow journalism, and breakfast cereals are given as part of the daily life during Grover Cleveland's term. Dates being covered are in blue numbers at the top of each page, making chronology easy to establish.

Added features of this reference book are a history of the White House and a list of presidential election results. A comprehensive index concludes the work. Throughout the essays are words highlighted in red, indicating that the subject is discussed in greater detail elsewhere. The only drawback to this system is that the topic, when found, is not in bold typeface or otherwise noted—one must read the entire page to find the information. This may be discouraging to younger students. A glossary might have been a better approach.

As an overview of the presidents, this is a valuable addition to a reference collection. The format is not overwhelming, concentrated attempts have been made to make the information engaging, and the overall effect of the book is professional and interesting. [R: SLJ, May 97, p. 162]—**Michele Tyrrell**

Handbooks and Yearbooks

444. **American Eras: Civil War and Reconstruction, 1850-1877.** Thomas J. Brown, ed. Detroit, Gale, 1997. 433p. illus. index. $85.00. ISBN 0-7876-1484-X.

This reference tool is the 2d volume in a projected 8-volume series. Each volume will cover a period in 12 chapter headings: world events; the arts; business and the economy; the Civil War; communications; education; government and politics; law and justice; lifestyles, social trends, and fashion; religion; science and medicine; and sports and recreation. With the exception of world events, each chapter begins with an overview, which is followed by a brief chronological list of selected events unique to each subject. The text contains black-and-white photographs. The volume is convenient to use for beginning researchers. It gathers important information on the period in a single source. *Civil War and Reconstruction* is recommended for undergraduate libraries. [R: RBB, 15 Oct 97, p. 425]—**Jane Jurgens**

445. **American Eras: Development of the Industrial United States, 1878-1899.** Vincent Tompkins, ed. Detroit, Gale, 1997. 455p. illus. index. $85.00. ISBN 0-7876-1485-8.

American Eras: Development of the Industrial United States, 1878-1899 vividly brings to life, through text, charts, and visuals, the period of U.S. history and culture during the last two decades of the nineteenth century. The volume is conveniently divided into chapters that encompass all major activities: world events; the arts; business and economy; communications; education; government and politics; law and justice; life-styles, social trends, and fashions; religion; science and medicine; and sports and recreation. Within each chapter appears a basic chronology of important events during the period, a general overview, and a list of several dozen topics within the area that are considered the most important, followed by three or four biographical treatments of "headline makers" and a list of relevant publications. The text is uniformly well written, with a nice balance between factual reconstruction and interpretive summary. Pictures are interspersed throughout the text, and they greatly enhance the volume's value and appeal. The chapter bibliographies are generally excellent, and a list of general references in the rear of the volume will alert readers to sources for further study. The index is exceptionally detailed and easy to use.

The volume is not without imperfection, however. For example, in the section on dime novels, Horatio Alger, the best-selling author of the period acknowledged today as a pioneer in child advocacy, is marginalized in favor of mentioning other dime novel authors. Also, Albert Johannsen's *The House of Beadle and Adams* (1950, 1962), a magisterial work on dime novels, is curiously omitted from the bibliographic listings. Overall, this volume is a perceptive overview of the industrial epoch in the United States, and it is recommended for all types of libraries. [R: RBB, 15 Oct 97, p. 425]—**Arthur P. Young**

446. **DISCovering U.S. History.** [CD-ROM]. Detroit, Gale, 1997. Minimum system requirements: IBM or compatible 386 (486DX/33MHz or higher highly recommended). CD-ROM drive (double speed or faster recommended) with MS-DOS CD-ROM Extensions 2.2. DOS 5.0. Windows 3.1. 8MB RAM. 5MB hard disk space. SVGA monitor (256-color display) and graphics card. Windows-compatible mouse. Printer (optional). $500.00/stand-alone version; $700.00/2-8 users. ISBN 0-7876-0923-4.

This CD-ROM is a comprehensive, interdisciplinary, and cross-linked electronic guide to the significant events, social movements, and notable and diverse persons of American history from the prehistoric era through 1996. This interesting and useful reference work contains more than 2,000 essays covering such topics as government and politics, film and the performing arts, business and industry, science and technology, and various social movements. These entries are supplemented by and hypertext linked to more than 1,500 biographies that provide relevant and personal significance to a variety of historical events. Entries throughout this lively work are concise and factual and should supply users with an awareness of the context under which these events occurred.

The principal strength of this electronic reference work is the ease by which users can search, access, and cross-reference materials. Information is sensibly indexed and organized into five general categories: timelines; names; subjects; places (states, cities, or regions); and primary documents. The timelines furnish a convenient and effective overview of historical eras and supply descriptive chronologies to an assorted array of nearly 10,000 political, social, and economic events. The inclusion of 163 primary documents, including such things as speeches, letters, journal entries, and other personal narratives; contemporaneous newspaper articles; and book excerpts add an invaluable insight that will be of great and practical benefit to users. Among the other effective and accessible features of this reference work are its linked picture gallery and dictionary. As a broad-based reference work, the disc effectively introduces a variety of significant events and persons and will help students to organize and broaden their understanding of U.S. society.—**Timothy E. Sullivan**

447. **Everything Civil War: The Ultimate Guide to Civil War Products, Services....** Spencer Kope, ed. Silverdale, Wash., Willow Creek Press, 1996. 304p. illus. maps. index. (Everything Books). $19.95pa. ISBN 0-9657183-1-6.

According to Kope, *Everything Civil War* is the first of a series of Everything Books that will aim to provide information about products, services, organizations, accommodations, places of interest, and archives associated with certain topics. From more than 1,000 requests for information sent to relevant sources, 550 responded. The result is a unique compendium of information about Civil War references previously unavailable in any one volume.

Of these entries, a foreword lists several entries as "Editor's Choices" that every Civil War enthusiast should know about. These include the United States Civil War Center Internet site; Civil War Round Table Associations; Civil War Trust and the Association for the Preservation of Civil War Sites; music; Civil War news; Civil War site guides; and the U.S. Army Military History Institute. The material is listed alphabetically within categories of products and services, organizations, accommodations, places of interest, and archives. The book also contains more than 200 illustrations and a master index of all entries. Each listing includes the name, mail and electronic addresses, and telephone number, along with a brief annotation. In these pages, the Civil War reenactor can find sources of authentic and reproduction clothing, musical instruments, books, and other accoutrements; the history buff can plan a vacation around Civil War sites; and the scholarly researcher may find some previously unknown sources of information.

Although some of its entries may rapidly become outdated, *Everything Civil War* should be welcomed by the many reenactors. Others interested in this period of U.S. history will welcome it as well. [R: LJ, 15 May 97, p. 70]—**Kay O. Cornelius**

448. Gelbert, Doug. **Civil War Sites, Memorials, Museums, and Library Collections: A State-by-State Guidebook to Places Open to the Public.** Jefferson, N.C., McFarland, 1997. 201p. index. $39.95. ISBN 0-7864-0319-5.

This guidebook takes the user on a state-by-state tour of 1,538 sites, memorials, and library collections connected to the Civil War. The consecutively numbered entries cover 43 states and the District of Columbia; are arranged alphabetically by state and then alphabetically by city within each state section; and are identified as to site, memorial, or collection. Each state section opens with a brief profile of its role in the Civil War and includes Civil War status, 1860 population, number of troops provided, number of known scenes of action, and a Civil War timeline.

The information given in each entry includes location, telephone number, policies, hours, whether or not a fee is charged, and a summary of its Civil War role. The information varies in length from a single paragraph of approximately 50 words to summaries of several hundred words. Although the information is concise, it furnishes the reader with a basic overview of the location's role or connection to the war. When possible, regular reenactments at sites are noted.

An alphabetic appendix of gravesites of significant Civil War individuals gives the name of the individual followed by city and state. A general index consisting primarily of names of individuals and a few vessels follows the appendix. The guidebook will be useful not only to persons planning visits to Civil War sites but also to individuals researching a state's role and participation in the war.

—**Elaine Ezell**

449. **The Longman Companion to America in the Era of the Two World Wars, 1910-1945.** By Patrick Renshaw. White Plains, N.Y., Longman Publishing, 1996. 249p. maps. index. $17.16pa. ISBN 0-582-09115-2.

This book, one in a series of Longman Companions to History, is a handbook of information about the United States from near the end of the Progressive Era to the end of World War II. It consists of seven sections. Section 1, a chronology, lists important domestic events during the years 1910 to 1945, with events concerning U.S. foreign policy included for the years 1941 to 1945. The information is provided in diary style, year by year and month by month, with entries starting with a date or dates, followed by one to several sentences describing important events that happened on those dates.

Section 2, "Foreign Policy," lists the major events in U.S. foreign policy from 1910 to 1940. Section 3, "Constitution and Civil Liberties," includes materials on "The First World War and the Red Scare," "The Republican Ascendancy, 1920-32," and "The Supreme Court in Crisis, 1933-45." Section 4, "Economics and Social History," is the last section that uses the diary format. It contains subsections on agriculture, conservation, commerce and the tariff, banking and finance, industry, industrial production, demography, and industrial workers and labor unions. Section 5 lists, for the years 1910 to 1945, all members of the U.S. president's cabinet, all justices of the U.S. Supreme Court, and selected leaders of the U.S. Congress. Section 6 contains biographies, averaging some 200 words in length, of more than 100 important U.S. personages, most of them political leaders. Section 7 contains a dozen maps.

The book concentrates on the political, economic, and social history of the United States and on U.S. foreign policy. Other than in its brief biographies, which include some distinguished writers, it contains little, if any, information about culture, entertainment, and sports. Renshaw, according to his acknowledgments, relied heavily, for all sections of the book, on other reference books.—**David S. Webster**

450. **The Sixties.** [CD-ROM]. New Rochelle, N.Y., MultiEducator, 1997. Minimum system requirements (Windows version): IBM or compatible 386DX (486 recommended). Double-speed CD-ROM drive. 8MB RAM. SVGA monitor. Sound card. Minimum system requirements (Macintosh version): LC III (040 recommended). Double-speed CD-ROM drive. 8MB RAM. 13-inch monitor. $79.95.

Called a multimedia history on CD-ROM, *The Sixties* is an ambitious attempt to provide a comprehensive overview of a tumultuous decade. Unfortunately, the project does not deliver.

For the most part, the CD-ROM resembles "filmstrips on video," with little interactivity. Black-and-white photographs with voice-overs scroll past at varying rates, but the two do not always relate. Much information, especially the statistics section, is given in the form of bar graphs, with no accompanying text. The "Arts and Culture" section, which students were immediately drawn to because of the music and television connections, is a series of lists—10 top songs, television lineups—with no hypertext links.

The section on the Vietnam War is also problematic. Maps are noninteractive and appear elementary and oftentimes, place-names are obscured by the navigational buttons. The brown background of the opening screen is not only dull, but makes seeing the brown buttons difficult. Again, bar graphs are used to provide information about casualty rates and other data.

The "America of the 60's" section is primarily text. Divided into four sections—African Americans, Native Americans, ethnic groups, and women—it does not deal with individuals. Information on particular individuals must be found in the biography section, which is an alphabetic listing, not a list divided by category or subject.

Lastly, the index is somewhat mixed, at times functioning as a glossary, with full definitions of a topic, whereas at other times only the topic is given. "First" is used as an index term, as in "the first sit-in," "the first bombing," and so on.

The program loads easily on both Windows 3.1 and Windows 95. Print functions also work well. However, navigating through the program is confusing, primarily due to the dark buttons—the forward and back buttons are difficult to distinguish. *The Sixties* would be a marginal purchase for most collections. [R: LJ, July 97, p. 136]—**Michele Tyrrell**

Indexes

451. **Roster of Confederate Soldiers 1861-1865.** Janet B. Hewett, ed. Wilmington, N.C., Broadfoot Publishing, 1995, 1996. 16v. $1,000.00/set. ISBN 1-56837-306-6.

Southerners and descendants of Confederate veterans in search of information on their Civil War ancestors should find the answer to their needs in this monumental new work. This, with its companion set, the 33-volume *Roster of Union Soldiers 1861-1865*, provides the best single source for locating information on individual soldiers in both armies in the war between the states. Even more important than their value as cumulative rosters to the Union and Confederate armies, these works provide, for the first time, comprehensive indexes to the Compiled Military Service Records of the United States National Archives, which contain the unit rosters for every organization in the Confederate and Union armies.

The straight alphabetic arrangement makes this work easy to use, although users should note that in names beginning with initials, the letters are treated as though they are words and are alphabetized that way. This system conforms to the way in which unit service records are arranged, which makes for an easy transition when moving from the roster to searching regimental and other unit service records. Users also need to consider all variant spellings in order to find the sought-after individual. Soldiers named Hammett, for example, might be located under Hamet, Hammit, or similar variations. Unfortunately, *see also* references to variant spellings are omitted. The basic information provided for each soldier is state, rank, military organization, and company. Because most soldiers were privates, this rank is omitted in order to save space. Many men are listed two or more times if they served in more than one unit. Therefore, this greatly lessens the total number of individuals cited in the publisher's advertising literature. A valuable introductory essay discusses additional sources for identifying and finding information on Confederate soldiers, whether they are included in these volumes or not.

Hewett deserves praise for performing the monumental task of transcribing often difficult to read names from 535 reels of microfilm containing the rosters of every regiment in the Confederate army and organizing them into a single alphabetic index of every known soldier listed in those reels. Although the primary purpose is genealogical, they are also useful for scholarly research. By comparing rosters of certain North Carolina Union army regiments with names in the *Roster of Confederate Soldiers*, this reviewer was able to identify and determine the number of rebel soldiers from those units who deserted the Confederate army and entered the Union service.

This work is highly recommended for every library with an interest in genealogy or the Civil War. It would be a great service if Broadfoot or another publisher would create a similar index for Confederate sailors, who are much more difficult to identify and research than are Confederate soldiers. [R: LJ, 1 June 97, pp. 92-94]—**Donald E. Collins**

452. **The Roster of Union Soldiers 1861-1865: United States Colored Troops.** Janet B. Hewett, ed. Wilmington, N.C., Broadfoot Publishing, 1997. 2v. $200.00/set. ISBN 1-56837-344-9.

From "Aanderson, Henry US 55th Col'd. Inf. Co.C" to "Zumwalt, Levi US 68th Col'd. Inf. Co.l," this is an alphabetic roster of nearly 200,000 African Americans who served as volunteer Union soldiers in the U.S. Civil War. The 2-volume hard copy set was transcribed from the 98 reels of National Archives Microfilm Group M589. Only the names of volunteers in a few state-designated units from Massachusetts, Connecticut, and Louisiana have not been included. Also listed are 7,100 (predominantly white) officers in "colored" units, such as "Shaw, Robert G. MA 54th Inf. (Col'd."). Col." Editorial intervention, with the exception of a few minor alphabetic readjustments, has been minimal. A short introduction describes how the roster was derived and what it contains.

From William Wells Brown's *The Negro in the American Rebellion* (1867) to the movie *Glory* (1990) and beyond, people have been supplied with works depicting the military role of African Americans in the Civil War, but to this reviewer's knowledge, this is the first publication between hard covers that gives a near complete listing of the names of the men who took part. No serious African American, genealogical, or Civil War library collection not already owning the National Archives Microfilm Group M589 should be without this set.—**Jonathan F. Husband**

AFRICAN HISTORY

453. Decalo, Samuel. **Historical Dictionary of Chad.** 3d ed. Lanham, Md., Scarecrow, 1997. 601p. (African Historical Dictionaries, no.13). $95.00. ISBN 0-8108-3253-4.

This work is essential in the understanding and improvement of the impoverished and disintegrating country of Chad. Decalo's brilliant research and outspoken descriptions of this century's politics are invaluable. Academic and practical coverage on geography, weather, pollution, investment, and communal relations as civil and military power has gone awry is available here. Most entries discuss political people, parties, and events. Even though most of its 143-page bibliography consists of French-language books, it can fill out information on health, religion, Neolithic and "tribal" art, and other anthropological and human interests. The introduction, acronym list, and chronology provide adequate orientation. Chad's plight may spark interest in this book. Independence—after interference from Sudan, Turkey, Libya, France, and the United States (the latter in an effort to stop aggression by Libyan leader Mu'ammar Gadhafi—may stir concern. Yet newly found oil will make information on Chad irresistible to readers.—**Elizabeth L. Anderson**

454. Decalo, Samuel. **Historical Dictionary of Niger.** 3d ed. Lanham, Md., Scarecrow, 1997. 486p. (African Historical Dictionaries, no.72). $49.00. ISBN 0-8108-3136-8.

Like most of the African Historical Dictionaries, this volume was not actually compiled by a historian but, in this case, by a political scientist. The result is the normal but less useful emphasis on postindependence Niger. At least 60 percent of the entries, and a larger proportion of the available space, is devoted to events and personalities of the past 40 years. As a result, too little attention is given to coverage of the several centuries of history preceding independence. The format is the by-now familiar one: a recent political chronology, a list of acronyms and abbreviations, a few statistical tables, and two maps. The last are entirely inadequate, schematic, lacking detail, and without even scale and orientation. As a result, users will be able to locate few of the place-names and geographic features mentioned in the dictionary entries.

The style of the entries, particularly the genuinely historical ones, is often illusory, leaving readers with the impression, for instance, that Borno and Carthage were contemporaneous states. The emphasis on recent times means that numerous entries for earlier periods are far too brief to have any value at all, consisting merely of a sentence or two. The bibliography is substantial, running to 150 pages, and is certainly not without value, but there is no keying of entries in it to entries in the dictionary proper.

This last comment underscores that, despite more than 20 years of producing the African Historical Dictionaries, Scarecrow, the series editor, and the authors of individual volumes have shown no signs of responding to the substantive criticism that has greeted most of these volumes at one time or another. In these days of continually declining purchasing power, no library should purchase these volumes without good reasons.—**David Henige**

455. Eggers, Ellen K. **Historical Dictionary of Burundi.** Lanham, Md., Scarecrow, 1997. 199p. (African Historical Dictionaries, no.73). $38.00. ISBN 0-8108-3261-5.

The 1st edition of this work appeared in 1976 (see ARBA 77, entry 312), and perhaps Burundi's tragic prominence in the news of late has prompted this new edition. The author is an English instructor who spent a year in Burundi, and this lack of perspective is evident throughout. *Zina* (praise names) is granted more attention than Zaire; infant naming practices more than agriculture; two days in the lives of two U.S. ambassadors more than the economy; and so forth. The writing is oddly awkward as well: describing Ntare I as "the first Burundi monarch whose dynastic name was Ntare I" (p. 106) will make readers wonder how many others were also named Ntare I (none, of course); speaking of "the rotation of kings every four generations" (p. 106) is unintelligible; and referring to "four dynastic lines" (p. 3) is incorrect. Noting that Pierre Buyoya "left office as the result of losing the votes of his constituents" (p. 4) is a most peculiar way to say that he lost the election, and so on throughout. The dates in the lists of kings and heads of state do not always agree with those in the text. Perplexing errors such as these can only undermine credibility in a work intended for casual reference use.

There are a list of acronyms and abbreviations; a 56-page bibliography; and a 46-page chronology, largely devoted to post-1960 events. This work is no better or worse than most other volumes in this series. Its major defects—inaccuracies and no sense of balance—are those that typify the African Historical Dictionaries series. Either flaw would serve to render using this volume risky.—**David Henige**

456. Lobban, Richard Andrew, Jr., and Peter Karibe Mendy. **Historical Dictionary of the Republic of Guinea-Bissau.** 3d ed. Lanham, Md., Scarecrow, 1997. 412p. (African Historical Dictionaries, no.22). $79.00. ISBN 0-8108-3226-7.

This volume is another in the parade of 3d editions of the African Historical Dictionaries series. Potential users may expect that by this time the many defects of this series would have been surmounted, but, even though this edition is better than its previous incarnations (published in 1979 [see ARBA 81, entry 337] and 1988 [see ARBA 89, entry 98]), this can only be faint praise. In fact, this work remains far short of what it could and should be.

Like other entries in the series, the dictionary proper is preceded by a historical chronology, a list of acronyms and abbreviations, and a general introduction, and in this case is followed by several appendixes, including a list of Portuguese governors, some economic data, and a modicum of cultural information. Twelve maps of varying quality are scattered throughout. The list of governors (pp. 396-99) is woefully and inexplicably incomplete and is riddled with errors. The economic data are adventitious and trivial. The bibliography is substantial but, paradoxically, overmatches the likely usership of the work—many citations are to works in French and Portuguese, much of which are in turn virtually unobtainable.

A good dictionary relies on being accurate and correct in its fundamentals. Here there are countless misspellings (pharoah for pharaoh, and so forth), and there are peculiarities of alphabetization as well. Although minor in the singular, these proliferate to an alarming degree and suggest a certain indifference on the part of the authors and their editors. There are also numerous and sometimes lengthy entries that are entirely irrelevant to present-day Guinea-Bissau (Phoenicians, Mungo Park, Mali), whereas other entries, particularly that on Portugal, are strangely short and uninformative. The proportion of entries on postindependence matters is rather less than in most other volumes of this series, but that fact can hardly rescue it from being as unhelpful in practical terms as its predecessors.—**David Henige**

457. Ofcansky, Thomas P., and Rodger Yeager. **Historical Dictionary of Tanzania.** 2d ed. Lanham, Md., Scarecrow, 1997. 291p. (African Historical Dictionaries, no.72). $69.00. ISBN 0-8108-3244-5.

On its chosen topics, the extensive bibliography in this dictionary will be useful to researchers. The fine chronology will suggest what entry in the text has desired data, as will leafing through the dictionary proper and following the dependable *quod vides* and suggested topics at the ends of entries. The past 200 years of European intruders into Tanzanian political, economic, and religious sectors and the African survivors make an embarrassing and alarming story. The recent panicky Burundi and Rwanda migrations added to the cataclysm. The victims, 120 animist and Muslim indigenous cultures, are rarely brought up, except as populations murdered, dispossessed, and subjected to arbitrary schemes or doubling. Biographies of particular European leaders and powerful African losers and short-term winners are a high point of this volume. Their organizations are also described. German and English people are given credit for ending Arab-sponsored slave trading, but not finally until 1922. Independence since 1961 has seen leaders who are authoritarian and foolish, albeit idealistic.

A book for missionaries, do-gooders, and scholars, the dictionary pronounces postcolonial, postsocialist Tanzania as irretrievably in debt to the World Bank and deforested, yet so fragmented by its ethnic groups as to be without threat of civil war. Known as the site of extraordinary Lake Victoria, Mt. Kilimanjaro, and big-game reserves and the venue of *Homo habilis*, David Livingstone and Henry Stanley, Mary and Louis Leakey and Jane Goodall, one could watch Tanzania's future to see what happens after the end of the world.—**Elizabeth L. Anderson**

458. Park, Thomas K. **Historical Dictionary of Morocco.** new ed. Lanham, Md., Scarecrow, 1996. 540p. maps. (African Historical Dictionaries, no.71). $69.50. ISBN 0-8108-3168-6.

William Spencer of Florida State University compiled the 1st, much shorter edition of this reference tool in 1980 (see ARBA 81, entry 339). This new work contains much more information and, like Spencer's work, is more than just a "dictionary." The author's introduction sketches the history of this North African country and explains why most of the sultans are not described in this book. The dictionary portion runs 198 pages, and the entries are longer than in the 1st edition, although there were more entries in the 1980 book. Cross-references are indicated by italics. The lengthy bibliography goes on for 268 pages and has references to many works not in English. This reviewer felt that the bibliography did not come up to standard: Book and journal titles were not underlined, and article titles were not in quotation marks, so it is harder to differentiate the various parts of the bibliographic citation.

Four statistical charts are printed here; these kinds of reference books would benefit from the addition of even more statistical charts. There is no index, but there is a list of acronyms and abbreviations, a glossary, a chronology (1000 B.C.E. to April 1996 C.E.), and a note about transliteration. The first appendix is composed of a chronology of native and foreign rulers during the Islamic era, and the second appendix features a useful description of the holdings of important Moroccan and foreign libraries and archives (but no directory information). Also included is a section consisting of 30 line maps that illustrate the various political divisions, trade and invasion routes, natural resources, and other topics. (The previous edition had only one map of the country.)

Park is a professor of anthropology at the University of Arizona. Jon Woronoff is the series editor. There are relatively few reference books on Morocco available; this book is most welcome. The sturdily bound item under consideration required much work and is recommended for the reference collections of all academic and large public libraries, along with appropriate specialized collections.

—**Daniel K. Blewett**

459. Perkins, Kenneth J. **Historical Dictionary of Tunisia.** 2d ed. Lanham, Md., Scarecrow, 1997. 311p. (African Historical Dictionaries, no.45). $64.50. ISBN 0-8108-3286-0.

This thoroughly updated version of the 1989 edition by the same scholar combines a detailed historical dictionary with a lengthy bibliography. The period after the Arab conquest is emphasized.

The dictionary, about 60 percent of the text, is a series of articles ranging in length from a short paragraph to several pages; typical length is a paragraph or two. The writing is designed to be accessible to a wide audience. Overall the entries provide a readable, fascinating history of this Maghreb country. The publisher states that all entries have been revised where appropriate, taking into account developments since the earlier edition. For example, there is a lengthy article on the 1990-1991 Persian Gulf War.

The bibliography is selective but not annotated. Works in French and English languages dominate, with a selected few from other European languages. It is arranged chronologically and thematically. After brief sections on general historical and reference works about pre-Islamic Tunisia, it features lengthier parts on subsequent eras. Postindependence material is thematically divided and is responsible for almost half of the book. The 114-page bibliography is a major feature enhancing the work's attractiveness. There are other value-added aspects, including a detailed chronology; a list of the rulers of Tunisia; a schematic map; and an introduction to Tunisia's geography, population, economy, and history.

The author is professor of Middle Eastern and North African history at the University of South Carolina and has published extensively in the field. This work should be purchased by all reference libraries with collections in North African studies. General collections should seriously consider it, funds permitting.—**Nigel Tappin**

ASIAN HISTORY

460. Baxter, Craig, and Syedur Rahman. **Historical Dictionary of Bangladesh.** 2d ed. Lanham, Md., Scarecrow, 1996. 285p. (Asian Historical Dictionaries, no.2). $54.00. ISBN 0-8108-3187-2.

Bangladesh may be one of the least-known countries of the world, but the *Historical Dictionary of Bangladesh* will assist anyone who wishes to know more about this country on the Indian subcontinent. After a chronology of important events and an introduction containing interesting demographic information and a short narrative history, the main body of the book begins with entries covering important individuals from all walks of life: such groups as the Abyssinians and Association for Social Advancement or the Dutch East India Company, intellectual movements, geographic regions and features, historical events and terms, political parties, and towns and cities. Entries range from a sentence or two to several paragraphs in length depending upon the significance of the topic and include useful expositions on such subjects as education, elections, health delivery, industry, language, and media in independent Bangladesh.

Five appendixes list principal political personages from the rulers of pre-Muslim dynasties in Bengal to the principal officers of the governments of Bangladesh from 1971 to 1995. The book concludes with an extensive bibliography divided into 12 categories with further subdivisions. This volume updates and expands on the 1989 edition (see ARBA 90, entry 117). A readable and easily accessible work, this historical dictionary should be in any research library and in public libraries serving a population of South Asians in the United States.—**David L. White**

461. Cybriwsky, Roman. **Historical Dictionary of Tokyo.** Lanham, Md., Scarecrow, 1997. 212p. illus. (Historical Dictionaries of Cities of the World, no.1). $49.00. ISBN 0-8108-3234-8.

A new series, Historical Dictionaries of Cities of the World, has been born, and its first volume is *Historical Dictionary of Tokyo*. Tokyo is not only a political and administrative center but also a commercial and educational center of Japan. It is one of the largest, richest, and most important cities in the world. As the editor of the series, Jon Woronoff, stated in the foreword, there are not many books or articles about the city that are available for English readers. A subject search of "Tokyo (Japan)" in Cornell University's research library's database gives 236 clusters, but only 48 entries are English-language materials.

This new dictionary is designed to provide more materials and help English readers learn about the city and seek further study. The dictionary section is the major part of the volume and provides 260 entries in alphabetic order. Main entries are in all capital letters and with bigger fonts than the explanation. The bibliography part of the work gives 341 books and articles that are divided into 13 categories. The work includes essential figures, facts, dates, and significant individuals who had an impact on the city. The volume also contains such useful information as a chronology dating from 628 to 1995, a 16-page introductory note, 3 maps, 4 leaves of pictures, and 3 appendixes.

Although the work is creditable, a few things should be pointed out for improvement in forthcoming editions. Many items in the dictionary section are Japanese-language entries. If the entries were divided by subject or categories and given in an index, readers could have more access when they do not know the specific names. Also, the 13 categories of the bibliography are not in order. If they were listed alphabetically, it would be quicker for readers to search for the desired books or articles.—**Sung Ok Kim**

EUROPEAN HISTORY

General Works

462. **Chronology of European History: 15,000 B.C. to 1997.** rev. ed. John Powell and others. Pasadena, Calif., Salem Press, 1997. 3v. illus. maps. index. $225.00/set. ISBN 0-89356-418-4.

This chronological presentation combines a number of revised entries from 3 older publications with 266 new ones in order to provide a broad overview of European history and culture from 15,000 B.C.E. to 1997. Of the 614 entries, 413 are revisions or replacements of articles from the following titles edited by Frank Magill and published by Salem Press: *Great Events from History: Ancient and Medieval Series* (1972); *Great Events from History: Modern European History* (1973); and *Great Events from History: Worldwide Twentieth Century Series* (1980). The new entries provide coverage from 1973 to 1997 and include coverage of Eastern Europe, the Balkan Peninsula, and the portions of Central Asia that are in the Russian sphere of influence. The addition of approximately 350 photographs and maps addresses a significant void in the original titles.

The entries begin with ready-reference information such as date, locale, category, and key figures. This capsulated information is followed by a signed entry and an annotated bibliography entitled "Additional Reading." Both the original author and the author of the update signed the articles drawn from the previously published titles. The volume features a number of excellent indexes: "Key Word Index," "Category List," "Time Line," "Geographical List," "Personages Index," and "Subject Index." The span of time covered is somewhat misleading. The first entry is about the paintings in the Lascaux Cave, which is given a date of 15,000 B.C.E. The next entry concerns the construction of Stonehenge and is given the date of 3100-1550 B.C.E. A gap of approximately 12,000 years is significant in a publication that purports to cover nearly 17,000 years of European history. This set is appropriate for public and undergraduate libraries.—**John R. Burch Jr.**

463. **European History on File.** By the Diagram Group. New York, Facts on File, 1997. 1v. (various paging). illus. maps. index. $165.00 looseleaf w/binder. ISBN 0-8160-3480-X.

As the introduction to this fact-filled, looseleaf volume points out, Europe's contributions to the world's culture have been monumental despite its small geographic area. This is amply demonstrated by the scope of *European History on File*, which traces the development of western Europe from 2 million B.C.E. to 1995. Ambitious as the concept is, the book does an excellent job of covering the primary aspects of social and intellectual history in Facts on File's familiar graphic and eminently reproducible format. Maps, charts, timelines, and pictorial representations of daily life are organized within major periods of cultural growth, such as classical empires and the twentieth century. Layouts for pages are varied so the narrative retains a fresh interest, although this sourcebook is more likely to be used to answer individual questions and place events in perspective. The beauty of this volume lies in its diversity: One page illustrates how a Paleolithic flint knife was made, and another describes the daily life of a monk. Although the sheer scale of time covered does not allow for in-depth examination of any single topic—World War I has four pages—the amount of factual information is impressive. The index could be more detailed, but this is a minor complaint in a work arranged chronologically and with pages headed as to the content.

European History on File fulfills its intention to be a visually interesting, intensely factual, and easily photocopied source for students and librarians. The price is quite reasonable given the years of use this tool will receive.—**James Moffet**

British

464. **A Bibliography of British History 1914-1989.** Keith Robbins, comp. and ed. New York, Clarendon Press/Oxford University Press, 1996. 918p. index. $160.00. ISBN 0-19-822496-6.

This latest volume in the Bibliography of British History series (see ARBA 77, entry 410 and ARBA 78, entry 368) contains 27,264 entries focusing on the political, economic, and social history of Great Britain between 1914 and 1989. It is designed to meet the needs of students and scholars of history and other disciplines.

The bibliography is divided into 12 major subject areas, such as constitutional and political history, economy and industry, British society, and external relations, with each section subdivided into narrower subsections. The two world wars are treated briefly and only discuss the aspects in which Britain was involved. Each major subject area begins with a brief essay describing what that section covers and suggesting where in the work to locate other relevant material. The book contains an alphabetic author index listing titles and entry numbers.

This fine work should be useful to researchers. However, it is not without a few problems. Although full citations are provided for articles, they are not included for books. The entries under each subject are not arranged in any kind of order; alphabetically by author or chronologically by date of publication would have been useful. Also, a detailed name index would have been helpful for finding biographical materials. Still, this is an important addition to an established series. [R: Choice, Mar 97, p. 1143]—**Kathleen Farago**

465. **Columbia Companion to British History.** Juliet Gardiner and Neil Wenborn, eds. New York, Columbia University Press, 1997. 840p. $40.00. ISBN 0-231-10792-7.

Gardiner and Wenborn's superb reference contains more than 4,500 entries on all aspects of the history of England, Ireland, Scotland, and Wales from the Roman invasion of Britain in 55 B.C.E. to 1979 (some items extend to 1990). Six distinguished historians—David Bates (55 B.C.E.-1068 C.E.), John Gillingham (1068-1485), Diarmaid MacCulloch (1485-1660), Joanna Innes (1660-1801), David Englander (1801-1914), and John Stevenson (1914-1979)—have written most entries for their respective periods; additional specialists have also contributed.

The work provides excellent coverage of traditional topics, including political, constitutional, military, social, economic, and religious history; however, it also devotes considerable space to cultural history, the family, women, and related subjects that have caught historians' attention more recently. The book addresses both domestic history and that of the British Empire and Commonwealth. The work also takes account of the *longue durée* with entries that extend across more than one period, and it includes important historical controversies such as those concerning the Tudor revolution in government and the rise of the gentry. The entries are necessarily rather brief, but they are packed with as much information as a book of this length could possibly hold. There are also useful chronologies, lists of monarchs and prime ministers, and maps.

The book lacks an index, which would have been a useful addition, but the list of entries is so comprehensive and the use of cross-references so extensive that this is not a serious handicap. This reference should be in every library, from the local public branch to the major research institution; every serious student of British history will also want to own a copy of this attractive, compact, and reasonably priced volume.—**William B. Robison**

466. **Historical Dictionary of the British Empire.** James S. Olson, Robert Shadle, and others, eds. Westport, Conn., Greenwood Press, 1996. 2v. index. $195.00/set. ISBN 0-313-27917-9.

Historical Dictionary of the British Empire is a useful reference for students and scholars of Great Britain's empire, with entries ranging from the fifteenth-century explorations of John Cabot to the late twentieth-century Commonwealth. Readers interested in brief summaries of persons and events associated with British imperial history will find these two volumes indispensable. Although many of the entries will not provide the depth of detail specialists may require—the essay on the slave trade, for example, only covers about one page—many of the entries provide bibliographic information for further reading, and there is an appendix listing a variety of recent works on imperial themes. As with any work of this type, some entries are more informative than others, but most do a creditable job of conveying the maximum information in the minimum space. There are some omissions—no entry on the Darien Company, for example (even though the South Sea Company receives deft treatment by Elizabeth Lane Furdell). Also missing is an entry for Daniel Parke, the infamous eighteenth-century governor of Antigua, who was murdered by his subjects in 1710. However, these are relatively minor points; overall, the editors have done a sufficient job of identifying subjects worthy of inclusion. If including every subject worthy of notice had been their goal, two volumes would hardly have been space enough.

In their preface, the editors assert a traditional view of the empire; on balance, they suggest, the empire, for all of its flaws, was not inherently evil. They do not cover up or excuse the mistakes, follies, and crimes of imperialism—Roger Long's description of the Amritsar Massacre and the entry on Bloody Sunday are useful examples of their determination not to allow nostalgia to overwhelm historical reality. Yet they view the British imperial experience in the light of the failed empires of the late twentieth century and the instability and chaos that have been the consequence of those events. Browsing through these volumes conjures up vivid images from Great Britain's past, and one cannot help but think that the editors may well have the best of the argument.—**Victor L. Stater**

467. Panton, Kenneth J., and Keith A. Cowlard. **Historical Dictionary of the United Kingdom. Volume I: England and the United Kingdom.** Lanham, Md., Scarecrow, 1997. 700p. (European Historical Dictionaries, no.17). $79.00. ISBN 0-8108-3150-3.

Part of Scarecrow's ongoing European Historical Dictionaries series, *Historical Dictionary of the United Kingdom* covers the entire sweep of the United Kingdom's history, from prehistoric Britain to the present day. Volume 1 concentrates on the history of England and the U.K. in general; the forthcoming volume 2 will cover Scotland, Wales, and Northern Ireland. This volume's scope is comprehensive, both in time and in material covered, including people, events, institutions, places, and terms. People discussed are not only monarchs and members of the nobility but industrialists, scientists, and statespeople as well. Events run the gamut from the Interregnum to D-Day; institutions and terms are as various as the Crown Courts and the Royal Prerogative. Entries are brief for the most part, with the three pages devoted to Winston Churchill being about the limit. The brevity is necessary when covering an enormous period and a nation that has been influential in almost every field of endeavor but it is somewhat mitigated by the length (more than 150 pages) of the bibliography. This bibliography is subdivided both by period and, within each period, by subject, and offers the person seeking more information ample choices.

The introduction to the dictionary gives an abbreviated historical overview; a look at economic history; a brief discussion of social change in modern times, beginning with the Industrial Revolution; and a quick look at recent changes, both domestically—the loosening of the class structure—and in connection with the world—the Common Market, the privatization of various industries, and the breakup of Empire. Supplementary material includes a chronology of British history that lists events of major significance; a chronology of monarchs; a chronology of governments, political parties, and prime ministers; and various outline maps. One curious and admittedly minor note concerns the chronology of monarchs. This begins with William the Conqueror in 1066. An expanded list including the earlier kings of Wessex, Mercia, and Northumbria (e.g., such personages as Aethelred II, Alfred, Aethelbald, Edgar, and Edmund) would have been helpful.

Libraries that own others in this series know its value. Most libraries with an interest in British history or world history will find this addition useful.—**Terry Ann Mood**

468. **Victorian Database on CD-ROM, 1970-1995.** [CD-ROM]. Edmonton, Alberta, University of Alberta Press, 1996. Minimum system requirements: IBM or compatible 386. CD-ROM drive. MS-DOS 4.1. Windows 3.1. 2MB RAM. $995.00 (U.S.). ISBN 0-919237-33-9.

Researchers in Victorian studies will be excited about this reference CD-ROM. The coverage is massive: indexing for more than 60,000 books and articles from 500-plus journals published from 1970 to 1995. Much more than a literature bibliography, this tool covers every topic related to the Victorian era, from the arts to business, law, sociology, history, medicine, science, and technology. Annual updates are projected and will be cumulative. The search engine and software are powerful, simple to use, and fast. Boolean searching; truncation (including wildcard interior truncation); and searching by keyword, title, and author are supported. Searching can be limited by the year of date of entry, and searches are case insensitive. This is a menu-driven system, although some applications can be done with a mouse.

The citations include descriptors but no abstracts and no full text. Citations retrieved in a search are displayed chronologically with the oldest first. Therefore, when a large set of entries is retrieved, access to the most recent scholarship can be time-consuming. Some surprising typographic errors were found—"Lodnon" for London, "Garlad" for Garland, and "Bradden" for the author Mary Elizabeth Braddon in a descriptor field. Also, descriptors include subject area codes from the *Annual Bibliography of Victorian Studies* but are not described in any online help or accompanying literature. In fact, the code for fiction (GAY) is searchable and can lead to many false hits. The compilers are aware of the problem and intend to address this in future updates.

The high price of the first issue will be a concern for many libraries. Renewal subscriptions are $245 in the United States and $335 in Canada. A 25 percent introductory discount is available for a limited time. If price is not a concern, this reference CD-ROM is highly recommended for libraries with collections and programs in Victorian studies. [R: Choice, April 97, p. 1321]—**Ingrid Schierling Burnett**

French

469. Whaley, Leigh Ann. **The Impact of Napoleon, 1800-1815: An Annotated Bibliography.** Pasadena, Calif., Salem Press and Lanham, Md., Scarecrow, 1997. 209p. index. (Magill Bibliographies). $36.00. ISBN 0-8108-3316-6.

Few people have had such an impact on history—both contemporary and long-term—as Napoleon Bonaparte. From Corsican origins, to revolutionary heroism, to imperial grandeur and command of the most feared European army since Roman times, to the snows of Moscow, exile, and the dramatic "hundred days" ending finally at Waterloo, his life was the stuff of which legends (not to mention novels and films) are made. Even before his demise in 1821, a substantial literature about him had appeared, and by now, as Whaley points out, there are more than 250,000 studies dealing with Napoleon, more than the number of days since his death.

In this work, the latest in the impressive Magill Bibliographies series, Whaley arranges a selected number of the most informative and critical works on the subject into a logical and useful format. Following a particularly insightful essay on the shifting course of Napoleonic historiography, subsequent chapters provide crisply annotated entries on basic source materials, biographies, internal affairs, the Napoleonic legend, military history, women and society under Napoleon, colonial and imperial studies, religion, diplomacy, and culture. Author and subject indexes conclude the work.

Everyone who has even casually delved into French and Napoleonic history has his or her own favorite list of works, not all of which (for obvious reasons) are included here, and it is possible to lament the inclusion of only French- and English-language sources. The stated time frame (1800 to 1815) is also somewhat misleading, because Napoleon was a powerful figure before 1800 and certainly an enduring legend after 1815. Nonetheless, this book is an extremely useful guide to the enormous influence of one of history's most charismatic figures.—**James R. McDonald**

German

470. **Encyclopedia of German Resistance to the Nazi Movement.** Wolfgang Benz and Walter H. Pehle, eds. New York, Continuum Publishing, 1997. 354p. $39.50. ISBN 0-8264-0945-8.

Fortunately, most persons interested in the details of the German resistance to the Nazis will probably have access to sources in the original German, because this translation is not a success. Much of the problem stems from the hybrid nature of the original book. The 10 historical essays on such subjects as "Communist Resistance" and "Youth Opposition" compose part 1. The "Encyclopedia" in part 2 contains 63 shorter entries on specific subjects, including such well-known groups as White Rose and Red Orchestra. Part 3 consists of brief biographical sketches of some 500 persons. Finally, there is a "Cross Reference System" in lieu of an index that seems, even after some study, to make no sense.

Two examples of the treatment of the best-known resistance event, perhaps the only one generally known, illustrate the book's problems. The substantive introductory essay on "Military Resistance" does not discuss Claus Schenk von Stauffenberg's assassination attempt on Adolf Hitler. Instead, the reader is referred to a 2-page entry in part 2. Worse, the biographical entry for von Stauffenberg mentions his military assignments, his wounds, and his execution, but not the plot to kill Hitler that led to his execution. Any reader who did not already know a great deal about these matters would be badly served and misled. The translation does not help; it is technically correct, but does little to render the length and structure of German sentences into comfortable, academic English. Librarians who really need this encyclopedia will buy it, but others should not.—**John Newman**

471. Vincent, C. Paul. **A Historical Dictionary of Germany's Weimar Republic, 1918-1933.** Westport, Conn., Greenwood Press, 1997. 635p. index. $115.00. ISBN 0-313-27376-6.

Vincent has produced a concise, readable resource for undergraduates, teachers, researchers, and interested general readers. As a librarian who has taught German history at Keene State College and written a doctoral dissertation about the Weimar period, he combines an impressive grasp of factual detail with intelligent judgments about events in Germany between the end of World War I and Hitler's ascent to power.

There are nearly 550 entries around a page in length and arranged in alphabetic order. Frequent cross-references and a 40-page index lead readers to related articles and help in locating subjects that could appear under either German or English headings. Thus, users can look under either *Center Party* or *Zentrum*. Most entries identify individuals, mainly from politics but also from journalism, the arts, and economics. Other articles discuss political parties, labor unions, newspapers, and cultural milestones. All entries cite sources for further reading; the bibliography lists 900 books and articles in English and German, some published as recently as 1995. A short glossary translates German political terms and the abbreviations for political parties, such as DNVP, DDP, and DVP. No equivalent work is available on this subject. Comparable volumes like *The Encyclopedia of the Third Reich* (see ARBA 92, entry 493) devote scant attention to the Weimar period, and *Political Leaders in Weimar Germany: A Biographical Study* (see ARBA 94, entry 774) is shorter and limited to politics.

This work has a few inconsistencies and flaws. Headings for some groups (such as parties) are in English, others in German, and there are no maps, illustrations, or tables. The index has a few errors: Some page numbers are incorrect (see Berliner Tageblatt). Nevertheless, academic libraries supporting work in modern German history will find this a welcome addition.—**Steven W. Sowards**

Greek

472. Baker, Rosalie F., and Charles F. Baker III. **Ancient Greeks: Creating the Classical Tradition.** New York, Oxford University Press, 1997. 254p. illus. maps. index. (Oxford Profiles). $35.00. ISBN 0-19-509940-0.

Although the publishers intend *Ancient Greeks* for a young audience, this collection also serves adults as a basic introduction to 37 of ancient Greece's most influential individuals. Three to eight pages of text and illustration are devoted to each person. The authors, both former teachers, provide a biographical narrative accompanied by black-and-white reproductions from art and literature. A sidebar on each person provides birth and death dates, profession, and a brief summary of accomplishments. "Further reading" is a guide to other biographical sources, although most of these are not specifically for young adults.

The book's sensible organization places the biographies in roughly chronological order; these are grouped in five sections by period, each of which is prefaced by a brief historical introduction. Simple maps on two-page spreads show the world of the ancient Greeks as well as the city of Athens, Alexander the Great's conquests, and Persian War battle sites. A chapter on lesser-known individuals ends each section. End matter consists of a timeline, "A Guide to Spelling and Pronunciation" of personal and place-names (with Roman and Greek spellings), a glossary, a bibliography, an index by profession, and a general index.

Ancient Greeks brings to life philosophers, statespeople, dramatists, poets, and scientists whose impact on Western civilization is still evident. The work is recommended for middle school, high school, and public libraries.—**Lori D. Kranz**

Hungary

473. Várdy, Steven Béla. **Historical Dictionary of Hungary.** Lanham, Md., Scarecrow, 1997. 813p. (European Historical Dictionaries, no.18). $75.00. ISBN 0-8108-3254-2.

After beginning this work with a chronology and overview of Hungarian history, Várdy provides over 1,000 entries relating to historical Hungary, which covers a much larger geographic area than present-day Hungary. Entries are alphabetically arranged and provide information on individuals, events, organizations, political parties, and historical topics. There are many cross-references throughout the work, and articles range in length from two sentences to several pages, for example, "Education in Hungary." A few subjects, such as "Holocaust in Hungary," deserved longer entries. Although this is a detailed overall bibliography, it would have been useful if individual articles had suggestions for further reading. Filling a gap in the literature, this volume is recommended for all academic and large public library reference collections.—**John A. Drobnicki**

Icelandic

474. Hálfdanarson, Guðmundur. **Historical Dictionary of Iceland.** Lanham, Md., Scarecrow, 1997. 213p. (European Historical Dictionaries, no.24). $40.00. ISBN 0-8108-3352-2.

Iceland's history has been strongly conditioned by its physical geography (the "fire and ice" of its volcanic origins and glaciation); by its Nordic cultural traditions; by nearly six centuries of often bitterly contested control by Denmark; and by its strategic position as a halfway point between Europe and North America. As a result, Icelanders (today's population is about 300,000) have developed a strong sense of national identity based on language—Icelandic is considered the most pure form of the Scandinavian tongues—and on more than a half-century of independence and economic growth.

This work, the 24th volume in an impressive series of European historical dictionaries, considers all aspects of Icelandic history, from the first arrivals from Norway (about 870) to 1996. The author is one of the most knowledgeable Icelandic historians of modern times, and his brief introduction is a valuable contribution to an understanding of the nation. Entries in the dictionary are alphabetically arranged, extremely detailed, and usefully cross-referenced. A solid bibliography includes primarily book-length works in English. A chronology and notes on the Icelandic language are provided as well. One basic political map of the island is included, although some additional cartography and a few photographs would have considerably enhanced the text.

This is an excellent introduction to one of the world's most unique nations. It is an obvious starting point for anyone interested in exploring Iceland's history and culture.—**James R. McDonald**

Irish

475. Thomas, Colin, and Avril Thomas. **Historical Dictionary of Ireland.** Lanham, Md., Scarecrow, 1997. 263p. (European Historical Dictionaries, no.20). $49.50. ISBN 0-8108-3300-X.

This volume is number 20 in the European Historical Dictionaries series, and it continues the tradition of excellence. The dictionary is a scholarly, clearly written work, packed full of useful information. The main section consists of an A to Z annotated dictionary with entries covering the main events, people, and places in Irish history, from the Book of Kells to Gerry Adams. The 15-page introduction provides a concise overview of Irish history from the Neolithic period until 1922. Eight appendixes list the lords lieutenants and chief secretaries of Ireland, the presidents of Ireland (until 1997), the prime ministers of the Irish Republic (until 1997) and of Northern Ireland (until 1972), the secretaries of state for Northern Ireland (until 1997), and the Church of Ireland and Roman Catholic archbishops. Unfortunately, the moderators of the Presbyterian Church are not included. (Presbyterians are one of the largest religious groups in Ireland.) The work concludes with an extensive bibliography.

The main criticism that can be made about this dictionary is that the criteria for inclusion are not clearly defined. Some Northern Irish people and events are included, but it is impossible to tell on what basis. For example, there are entries for Adams and Ian Paisley, but none for internment, the Troubles, or the Special Powers Act. It would have been even more useful if the historical overview had included a section on recent Irish history. The accompanying chronology goes up to 1996, but the overview stops at 1922. Despite the above criticisms, this dictionary is a useful book that any institution or individual with an interest in Irish studies should acquire.—**Linda Main**

Italian

476. Ingamells, John, comp. **A Dictionary of British and Irish Travellers in Italy, 1701-1800.** New Haven, Conn., for the Paul Mellon Centre for Studies in British Art, Yale University Press, 1997. 1070p. maps. $75.00. ISBN 0-300-07165-5.

Thirty years ago, Brinsley Ford, noted patron, collector, and historian of English art, became fascinated with the Italian influence on British and Irish artists. In the ensuing years, he built up a huge archival collection of letters, memoirs, and reports from eighteenth-century British and Irish travelers to Italy. In 1988, he donated it, along with his unpublished drafts on the subject, to the Paul Mellon Centre. It is from this collection that Ingamells has compiled his dictionary. He has also incorporated additional entries prepared by 22 scholars as well as material from Italian archives. More than 6,000 entries of varying length describe the travels of young persons making the Grand Tour, students of art and architecture, diplomats, merchants, art collectors, Jacobite and Stuart exiles, and Britons residing in Italy.

Although most entries give brief biographical information, the compiler's stated purpose is primarily to answer questions regarding the travelers' presence in Italy, where they were, and when they were there. The narratives are frequently interrelated, and much cross-referencing is necessary. Supplements include 2 black-and-white maps of Italy; a political chronology; a list of rulers of the Italian states or principalities; a section of supplementary biographical notes on selected foreign artists, antiquarians, and diplomats in Italy during the century; a list of 229 painters, 60 architects, 28 sculptors, and 13 engravers in Italy from 1701 to 1800; a chronological list of artists' visits by decade; a list of abbreviations; and a list of abbreviated titles. This truly monumental compilation will be appreciated by scholars and students of the arts; literature; history; and British, Irish, and European culture and civilization.—**Shirley L. Hopkinson**

Latvian

477. Plakans, Andrejs. **Historical Dictionary of Latvia.** Lanham, Md., Scarecrow, 1997. 193p. (European Historical Dictionaries, no.19). $34.50. ISBN 0-8108-3292-5.

Brief historical dictionaries for countries of the world, if done as well as this volume, are useful. This dictionary consists of two parts: naming and defining the movers and the shakers and listing the agencies of history makers, and listing the historical events themselves. It must be noted, however, that the second layer of entries may or may not have a direct relationship with the first.

For a dictionary of this type, its credibility depends on the name the author brings to the endeavor. Plakans was the right scholar to do the job, and he accomplished it with distinction. In less than 200 pages, the author provides a credible set of entries to make sense of Latvia's history, especially its twentieth-century peregrinations. Plakans tends to lean heavily on cultural developments to explain historical events. There are more entries on literary figures than on politicians.

One lapse that should be mentioned is that, for being a historical dictionary, the historians and historical institutions receive short shrift. The only historian who makes it in the dictionary is Arveds Švabe. Although the Latvian Soviet Writer's Union makes it in the dictionary, the Historical Institute of Latvia, which has a much longer standing, does not, nor does its publication, the *Journal of the Historical Institute of Latvia*.—**Andrew Ezergailis**

Lithuanian

478. Sužiedėlis, Saulius. **Historical Dictionary of Lithuania.** Lanham, Md., Scarecrow, 1997. 382p. (European Historical Dictionaries, no.21). $47.50. ISBN 0-8108-3335-2.

This historical dictionary on Lithuania is in effect a brief history of that country. It attempts to introduce the nonspecialist to the most important mileposts of Lithuania's past. Unlike the companion volume on Latvia (see entry 477), which has a cultural emphasis, Sužiedėlis's work concentrates on political events and personalities. The history of Lithuania is long and glorious, and at one time that state contended for leadership as a unifier of Eastern Europe.

Although the work contains information starting from the time of Mindaugas in the thirteenth century, the volume most fully centers on twentieth-century Lithuania, beginning with the Revolution of 1905 and moving on with the declaration of the First Lithuanian republic in 1918, the occupation by the Soviets and the Nazis in the early 1940s, and the Lithuanian resistance against both occupiers from 1940 to 1991. The latest developments in Lithuania, including the regaining of independence, are well represented by entries on the Sajūdis movement and the foremost personalities Kazimiera Prunskiene, Vytautas Landsbergis, and Algirdas Brazauskas.

Appendixes provide pronunciation guides, lists of rulers from 1251 to 1795, and lists of political leaders since 1918. Four maps and a detailed chronology provide further background information. This dictionary is recommended for all college and public libraries.—**Andrew Ezergailis**

Polish

479. Gozdecka-Sanford, Adriana. **Historical Dictionary of Warsaw.** Lanham, Md., Scarecrow, 1997. 319p. (Historical Dictionaries of Cities of the World, no.3). $49.50. ISBN 0-8108-3299-2.

The author, a former Polish journalist now living in the United Kingdom, published five earlier books, two of them in Great Britain. Her present book is a work of love and dedication, which is apparent in the introduction and in individual entries. In the former she traced the history of Warsaw, Poland from the early settlements dating back to fourth century B.C.E., through the settlements of the tenth and eleventh centuries C.E. She goes on to discuss the formal founding of the town around 1300, and presents a detailed sketch to the present conurbation of 2.6 million inhabitants, with 37 institutions of higher learning, the seat of the government, an effervescent cultural life, and most recently, the seat of a stock exchange. The period of the heroic anti-Nazi resistance, unparalleled in the rest of occupied Europe, is properly highlighted, as is the role of the city in the opposition to and in the undermining of the communist rule. The main part of the work occupies 280 pages and includes historical, institutional, and cultural backgrounds as well as biographies of many outstanding citizens, fortunately omitting the recent communist leaders and officials. The current entries include AIDS, homosexuality, John Paul II, and current tourist attractions. The *Historical Dictionary of Warsaw* includes prefatory material on Polish spelling, a chronology of events, a list of the mayors of the city, a list of abbreviations and acronyms, and two maps. It ends with a good bibliography, divided by topics.

This is a useful source for urban and ethnic historians, students of regional culture, readers on local topics, and any person whose stay in Warsaw left them with the unforgettable memory of a vibrant, indomitable center of culture, business, and politics.—**Bogdan Mieczkowski**

480. Okonski, Walter. **Wartime Poland, 1939-1945: A Select Annotated Bibliography of Books in English.** Westport, Conn., Greenwood Press, 1997. 111p. index. (Bibliographies and Indexes in World History, no.45). $65.00. ISBN 0-313-30004-6.

This slim volume (the bibliography itself is 90 pages) presents 408 entries from more than 350 monographs, book chapters, and government documents published between 1940 and 1996. Although it is limited to materials in English, several Polish titles are included if they contain English summaries. Entries give descriptive annotations and are arranged by broad subject and subdivided by topic, with separate author, title, and subject indexes referring to sequential numbers. Based on the book's title, many of the items in the first two chapters ("Poland in the Twentieth Century" and "Pre-War Period, 1919-1939") could have been excluded.

The author attempted to be highly selective, targeting the needs of students, teachers, journalists, and scholars; hence, some of the items listed are owned by only a handful of U.S. institutions (particularly the New York Public Library). Nevertheless, there are several omissions: The section on German concentration camps discusses five books on Auschwitz, but not any on Belzec, Sobibor, or Treblinka, and Emanuel Ringelblum's *Notes from the Warsaw Ghetto* (McGraw-Hill, 1958) and *Polish-Jewish Relations During the Second World War* (Fertig, 1974), both considered classics, are not included. Although this source is more up-to-date and comprehensive for its selected time period, the average student should be able to use the materials covered in *Poland* (rev. ed.; see ARBA 94, entry 134) or *Poland: An Annotated Bibliography of Books in English* (see ARBA 89, entry 121). Because of its high price and lack of journal and dissertation coverage, the book under review is only recommended for comprehensive Eastern European and World War II collections.—**John A. Drobnicki**

Soviet

481. **Critical Companion to the Russian Revolution 1914-1921.** Edward Acton, Vladimir Iu. Cherniaev, and William G. Rosenberg, eds. Bloomington, Ind., Indiana University Press, 1997. 782p. maps. index. $59.95. ISBN 0-253-33333-4.

Eighty years on the other side of the Russian Revolution of 1917 and seven years past the dissolution of the Soviet Union, the editors of this volume, one Russian, one British, and one American, have brought together essays of 46 historians of the Russian Revolution. The work was simultaneously published on both sides of the Atlantic. It consists of freestanding essays organized in seven sections: "The Revolution as Event"; "Actors and the Question of Agency"; "Parties, Movements, Ideologies"; "Institutions and Institutional Cultures"; "Social Groups, Identities, Cultures and the Question of Consciousness"; "Economic Issues and Problems of Everyday Life"; and "Nationality and Regional Questions." Although the volume, in the main, still concentrates on the Bolsheviks and on events in St. Petersburg and the Russian part of the empire, it also signals a melting of hard-core Cold War positions. The contributions by recently liberated Russian scholars are especially welcome. This companion is the major publication on the Russian Revolution to come out in this decade and a milestone in the Western study of the revolution. There is a good index of names and subjects, and each essay contains a brief biography. The work is recommended for all college libraries.—**Andrew Ezergailis**

482. **The Gorbachev Bibliography, 1985-1991: A Listing of Books and Articles in English on Perestroika in the USSR.** Joseph L. Wieczynski, comp. and ed. New York, Norman Ross, 1996. 275p. index. $65.00. ISBN 0-88354-275-7.

This volume, as the title indicates, is a bibliography of the Mikhail Gorbachev era that lasted from 1985 to the demise of the USSR in 1991. The bibliography is limited to writings in the English language and contains at least 7,000 entries. In terms of the volume of writing that the Gorbachev reign produced, it would have few competitors in history. The bibliography is arranged in 36 subsections, starting with a list of textbooks and containing topical subunits, such as agriculture, the coup of 1991, environmental matters, literature, and women's issues. The volume also contains a 41-page index of 4,770 authors whose writings are listed in the volume. This bibliography is a useful research aid for scholars working with contemporary history and is recommended for all research and college libraries.—**Andrew Ezergailis**

Sweden

483. Gould, Dennis E. **Historical Dictionary of Stockholm.** Lanham, Md., Scarecrow, 1997. 257p. illus. maps. (Historical Dictionaries of Cities of the World, no.2). $64.00. ISBN 0-8108-3238-0.

Almost anything the serious reader may want to know about the city of Stockholm and its place in the history of Sweden will be found in this remarkable compendium. Entries cover persons, organizations, places, and events from the popular music group ABBA to the artist Anders Zorn. Some general topics, such as contemporary architecture, the theater, and the labor movement, are also included. The main body of the work is the dictionary, with its entries arranged in one alphabetic sequence. Supplemental sections provide a tremendous amount of additional information and can be used to access statistical, graphic, and rapid reference sources. An introduction presents an overview of the city's geography, history, and government. A 13-page chronology lists important events from 1252 to 1996. Seven maps show districts, the subway system, the county, and the city's relative placement in northern Europe. Eight pages of photographs on four plates show views, the king and queen, and other prominent persons. Appendixes list the mayors of Stockholm, buildings, museums, sporting events, authors connected with Stockholm, and art galleries and museums and include tables of statistics. A 37-page selected bibliography lists publications on every aspect of life in Stockholm and its environs; its people; and their culture, history, economy, and industry; as well as directories and guides to institutions, libraries, newspapers, and periodicals.

This volume is the second work in a new series that aims to provide quick reference to the backgrounds of major cities of the world. It is not a guidebook but will be of interest to serious travelers. The dictionary should be of much value to students and teachers of Swedish history and culture and of area studies.—**Shirley L. Hopkinson**

LATIN AMERICAN AND CARIBBEAN HISTORY

484. Anthony, Michael. **Historical Dictionary of Trinidad and Tobago.** Lanham, Md., Scarecrow, 1997. 670p. (Latin American Historical Dictionaries, no.26). $84.00. ISBN 0-8108-3173-2.

This newest addition to the Latin American Historical Dictionaries series offers a rich and detailed guide to Trinidad and Tobago's past, expanding upon the mere 32 pages devoted to these islands in William Lux's *Historical Dictionary of the British Caribbean*, published in 1975 (see ARBA 76, entry 282). Anthony's intention to include important historical events and facts, "but also to cite people whose activities have in some way made a difference to this country, for better or worse," is largely realized through the comprehensive entries covering diverse topics. The book is divided into 3 main sections: a chronology (1498-1995); the dictionary (1,497 entries and cross-references); and a bibliography (275 items). The bibliography is organized by format, subject, and period where relevant. The author covers political, geographic, economic, sociological, and cultural terms and provides lists of major leaders.

The inclusion of the chronology (with marked terms that guide the reader to relevant individual entries) makes this work a useful tool for new students of the islands' histories, and the number and length of the entries provide much information for the specialist. However, at times the writing could be more concise within entries, and the thorough cross-referencing system reduces the need to repeat facts across entries. The typeface is of noticeably lower quality than that used in other recent volumes in the series (for example, the 2d edition of *The Historical Dictionary of Venezuela* [see entry 142]), making it more difficult for the eye to distinguish between subject headings, entry text, and cross-references. More attention to layout and typeface would have made the bibliography easier to navigate as well. Such aesthetic factors aside, Anthony's work is a welcome addition to the series, and one hopes that individual treatment of other Caribbean nations will appear in the future.—**Pamela M. Graham**

485. Vázquez-Gómez, Juana. **Dictionary of Mexican Rulers, 1325-1997.** Westport, Conn., Greenwood Press, 1997. 191p. index. $65.00. ISBN 0-313-30049-6.

Throughout its history Mexico has experienced a unique variety of social structures and governments that range from the indigenous to the foreign, from revolutionary governments to the present democracy. This political mélange extends to the nation's 185 "rulers," as Vázquez-Gómez labels the leaders who have been in power from 1325 until the present. These have included Aztec emperors; Spanish viceroy; a Hapsburg; high-profile figures such as Juárez Zapata, Pancho Villa, and Carranza; and the current president, Ernesto Zedillo. The author divides the book into four periods—the Aztecs, the Conquest and Colonial period, Independence to the Porfiriato, and the twentieth century. Each chapter consists of a succinct introduction and a short biography of each leader of that period, in chronological order. Biographies include the places of birth and death, time in power, major accomplishments, and noted failures. There are also a glossary and several appendixes that contain definitions of Colonial policies and institutions; descriptions of Mexican plans, treaties, conspiracies, and constitutions; names of political parties; acronyms; and chronological and alphabetic lists of rulers. This succinct, thorough, and user-friendly reference work is recommended to any reader interested in Mexican history, politics, or social structures.—**Stella T. Clark**

MIDDLE EASTERN HISTORY

486. **Ancient Egypt.** David P. Silverman, ed. New York, Oxford University Press, 1997. 256p. illus. maps. index. $35.00. ISBN 0-19-521270-3.

This volume provides a most welcome addition to the many recent books on ancient Egypt. Its editor and contributors rank among the most notable of today's Egyptologists, and each of them describes clearly and succinctly the area about which he or she is writing, including the most recent information on the topic under discussion.

Lavishly illustrated with maps, pictures, and drawings, the book consists of short essays addressing virtually every aspect of the life and times of ancient Egypt under three main topics: the Egyptian world, including a discussion of the dynasties and historical periods, the land, the surrounding world, knowledge in Egypt, and women; belief and ritual, composed of discussions about royalty, mortuary practices, beliefs regarding creation, and ritual actions and beliefs; and finally art, architecture, and language. Under this last heading, the reader learns about pyramids; temples and tombs; Egyptian art; and the signs, symbols, and language of the ancient Egyptians. Each short article includes sidebars or boxes offering brief, detailed discussions of relevant topics, such as the female pharaoh Hatshepsut, the worker's village at Deir el-Medina, and the Egyptian calendar.

A notable and welcome feature is the many in-text page references to the current topic's appearance elsewhere in the volume, permitting the reader to quickly locate other discussions on the subject. The volume's extensive bibliography, arranged by topic, provides another excellent and helpful feature. This book makes a fine addition to any public or school library, and with its bibliography, the library of any undergraduate institution.—**Susan Tower Hollis**

487. Haywood, John. **The Encyclopedia of Ancient Civilizations of the Near East and Mediterranean.** Armonk, N.Y., Sharpe Reference/M. E. Sharpe, 1997. 304p. illus. maps. index. $95.00. ISBN 1-56324-799-2.

This book on Ancient Civilizations is split into three parts: the ancient Near East and Egypt, the Greek world, and the Roman world. It includes chronological tables, an index, a glossary of terms, lists of rulers of each era, and information on further reading. The book contains over 125 color maps and numerous color photographs with illustrations on practically every page. They are not only beautiful but informative and aid in making the book easier to use. This book is perfect for younger students and adults alike because the artwork, photographs, and illustrations capture the reader's interest. In addition, inserts throughout the book highlight certain important historical sites. For example, the insert on Pompeii includes historical facts and a brief description of its importance. Pictures of artifacts found at the site, a photograph of the site today, a map, and an example of the artwork of the time complete the entry. Inserts also convey relevant features such as art, sports, and the technology of each period. For example, the section on ancient Egypt includes inserts on the origins of writing, the pyramids, warfare in ancient Egypt, and Egyptian religion. Other resources, such as the *World Book Encyclopedia* (see ARBA 97, entry 48), provide similar information; however, for more detailed information and illustrations this book is a great resource.—**Natalie Brower-Kirton**

488. Nazzal, Nafez Y., and Laila A. Nazzal. **Historical Dictionary of Palestine.** Lanham, Md., Scarecrow, 1997. 304p. (Asian/Oceanian Historical Dictionaries, no.23). $55.00. ISBN 0-8108-3239-9.

The authors have provided a useful guide to the recently established Palestinian state. They have concentrated "on individuals, events, factions, and institutions that have a historical, political, and social significance in the shaping of the nascent Palestinian State" (p. xi). Thus, the reader will find, in addition to expected entries on figures such as Yāsir Arafāt, short entries on Benjamin Netanyahu, Shimon Peres, and Yitzhak Rabin. Palestinians living in Israel have generally not been included.

An extensive chronology beginning with Omar Ibn al-Khattab's expedition to Jerusalem in 638 and concluding with King Hussein's meeting with Arafāt in Jericho on October 15, 1996, precedes a brief introductory chapter. Some topics covered in the introduction overlap separate treatments in the individual listings. A 75-page bibliography arranged by categories (general, cultural, societal, economic, historical, and political) with subsections should prove to be one of most useful aspects of the book. Because general readers are not likely to be familiar with many of the names included in this dictionary, it will be most useful to those who already have substantial knowledge of the history and culture of the region.

—**Harold O. Forshey**

489. Peck, Malcolm C. **Historical Dictionary of the Gulf Arab States.** Lanham, Md., Scarecrow, 1997. 324p. (Asian Historical Dictionaries, no.21). $45.00. ISBN 0-8108-3203-8.

This small dictionary is intended for academic and other researchers as well as diplomats, businesspeople, and general readers. In addition to providing separate, brief histories of each of these small states, the author offers information on their political, economic, social, cultural, and religious dimensions. As a consequence of the prominence brought to the region by the Persian Gulf War of 1990-1991, the author has chosen to emphasize to some extent current and recent developments.

Entries are wide-ranging although somewhat uneven. They include, in addition to the more obvious subjects, such topics as Australia, a source of alumina for aluminum processing in Bahrain and Dubai, and Zanzibar, which was at one time under the control of Oman. Curiously, a heading, "China," is cross-referenced to a nonexistent entry, "The People's Republic of China." The bibliography of more than 80 pages emphasizing more recent works is helpfully divided into 12 categories. This bibliography is one of the strengths of Peck's work. Also useful are appendixes listing the principal government officials of the Gulf Arab States as well as the United Nations Security Council Resolutions on Iraq, August-November 1990. General readers, especially, will find the dictionary useful.—**Harold O. Forshey**

490. **The Penguin Historical Atlas of Ancient Egypt.** By Bill Manley. New York, Penguin Books, 1996. 144p. illus. maps. index. $16.95pa. ISBN 0-14-51331-0.

This atlas is an impressive array of historical, social, political, and economic information that will assist most high school and college students and adults who are interested in what appears to be all aspects of ancient Egyptian history. Manley has done a first-rate job of composing a work of historical art and compiling it between 150 interesting and colorful pages. The photographs are clear and beautiful.

The book also features a fine list of Egyptian kings and rulers, a creditable index, and a timelime that covers the years 5000 B.C.E. to 305 B.C.E. The only suggestion for improvement would be to print the timeline information in a larger typeface for older adult learners and parents or grandparents who assist their children with homework.—**Lillian Jane Steele**

WORLD HISTORY

Atlases

491. **The Complete Atlas of World History.** Armonk, N.Y., Sharpe Reference/M. E. Sharpe, 1997. 3v. $145.00/set. ISBN 1-56324-854-9.

The history of the world is a big subject to cover in a single book, or in this case, a 3-volume set with a total page count of 400. This atlas is therefore a general reference work and is best suited to public libraries. Volume 1 is entitled "Prehistory and the Ancient World, 4,000,000 Years Ago-AD 600"; volume 2,

"The Medieval and Early Modern World, AD 600-1783"; and volume 3, "The Modern World, 1783-Present." Each volume begins with instructions for using the atlas, a brief introduction, and a series of numbered world maps showing the world at particular dates during the period covered.

The majority of the book consists of regional maps organized chronologically by historical period. All maps appear on two-page spreads with an essay about the region's history during that period, a geographic or thematic timeline, a key, and cross-references to other map spreads. On each regional map are numbered points representing important places and events explained in captions and colored lines for routes of migration, trade, and campaigns. Each volume has its own index, which is limited to regions, people, and kingdoms. Volume 3 also contains an index to the entire series.

Overall production quality of this atlas is adequate, with one caveat: In a few cases, similar colors or values of colors are used on a map, which may make it difficult for some readers to distinguish between areas. Use of brighter colors would have eliminated this problem.—**Lori D. Kranz**

492. **Historical Atlas of the Holocaust.** By the United States Holocaust Memorial Museum. New York, Macmillan Library Reference/Simon & Schuster Macmillan, 1996. 252p. maps. index. $39.95. ISBN 0-02-897451-4.

493. **Historical Atlas of the Holocaust.** [CD-ROM]. New York, Macmillan Library Reference/Simon & Schuster Macmillan, [1996]. Minimum system requirements: IBM or compatible 386. Double-speed CD-ROM drive. Windows 3.1. 4MB RAM (8MB recommended). Sound Blaster-compatible sound board. Speakers or headphones (for audio). $79.95.

The staff of the United States Holocaust Memorial Museum's Wexner Learning Center, led by cartographer Dewey Hicks and historian William Meinecke, have produced this print collection of more than 220 color maps using aerial photographs, German and Allied period maps, and such textual sources as captured documents and survivor testimonies. Maps are of varying scales and arranged by subject (e.g., "Nazi Extermination Camps," "Death Marches and Liberation"), showing political units or locations along with basic physical features (rivers) and human-made objects (railway lines). Maps of individual camps and ghettos are particularly detailed, in the latter instance showing several street names, and the textual material enhances the graphics. Although map colors are appealing, many of the place-names are written in white or other light colors that do not provide enough contrast and that do not photocopy well on noncolor machines. The atlas contains a gazetteer of place-names found on the maps (with alternate spellings and *see* references), but no index of names or subjects. There are a detailed table of contents and an adequate bibliography, as well as a glossary of 60 words and phrases.

The user-driven CD-ROM version of the *Historical Atlas of the Holocaust* offers the same maps as the print version. Unlike some CD-ROMs, hot links on maps are unfortunately displayed in the same typeface as the other place-names—only by using the Tab key or by dragging the mouse can one see the available links. While a map is displayed, there is a *see also* option from the menu bar that offers related maps, as well as options to display related black-and-white photographs and textual material or to attach a bookmark. Text may be printed, but the program does not support printing of maps or images, a major drawback. A glossary provides printed definitions and correct pronunciations of 135 words used in the atlas. Several words, however, are not included, such as *Oswiecim* and *Judenraete*. An index allows the user to click on a place-name and display the relevant map.

Although the print atlas is in color, it does not replace Martin Gilbert's *Atlas of the Holocaust* (see ARBA 95, entry 569), which contains photographs and more maps (in black-and-white, however), including many thematic ones. Most libraries will want both volumes. Libraries expecting the CD-ROM version to be a complete history of the Holocaust will be disappointed, but it succeeds in its limited purpose.

—**John A. Drobnicki**

Bibliography

494. **The Dardanelles Campaign, 1915: Historiography and Annotated Bibliography.** Fred R. van Hartesveldt, comp. Westport, Conn., Greenwood Press, 1997. 163p. index. (Bibliographies of Battles and Leaders, v.21). $69.50. ISBN 0-313-29387-2.

The Bibliographies of Battles and Leaders series from Greenwood Press is a distinguished collection of volumes, but some, such as this one and the compiler's prior contribution on the Battles of the Somme, are a bit esoteric. After 31 pages of narrative historiographic text on such topics as the tactical overview of the campaign, archival sources and other research materials, politics and strategy, the Australian-New Zealand Army Corps who participated in the Gallipoli campaign, and a discussion of who was responsible for failure, the book includes 765 annotated citations.

The scope is comprehensive, and the annotations are informative. This is a good addition to the literature. However, like many others in the series, its audience will be limited. It is recommended for large research libraries.—**Joe P. Dunn**

495. Kavanagh, Gaynor. **A Bibliography for History, History Curatorship, and Museums.** Brookfield, Vt., Scolar Press/Ashgate Publishing, 1996. 221p. index. $54.95. ISBN 1-85928-203-2.

The result of 15 years of experience at the Department of Museum Studies at the University of Leicester, this work with an admitted Anglocentric bias is an outgrowth of a previous local publication. As revealed in the preface, it was "developed to provide a bibliographic source of reference for those engaged in training and research within this field, as well as museum workers and historians," thus indicating its timely (or trendy) attempt to unite historical scholarship and museums.

The work, consisting of nearly 2,000 unannotated entries, divides into 8 sections or chapters: 1 on reference sources, then "History Theory," "History Making" (the largest), "History and the Public," "Forming the Archive," "Managing the Archive," "Histories of History Museums," and "Museum Management and Planning." One needs to understand, in view of the purpose of the work, that in this new interdisciplinary configuration, "museum studies" translates broadly and variously into history making, public and popular history, oral history, history and folklife-ethnographic museums, and sociopolitical exhibitions.

By way of description, a great majority of the entries come from the last two decades, although there are several from the 1950s. Most of the references to U.S. journals appear in the chapter on theory. The 25 publications of the (British) Museum Documentation Association listed on pages 169 to 172 include some entries with identical titles, although different years, and others with identical bibliographical data, although with different titles. An author index concludes the work. This rather specialized work will be helpful for those interested or curious in the new movement to unite libraries, archives, and museums into a common institution.—**Donald G. Davis Jr.**

496. McCarthy, Ronald M., and Gene Sharp. **Nonviolent Action: A Research Guide.** New York, Garland, 1997. 720p. index. (Garland reference library of social sciences, v.940). $99.00. ISBN 0-8153-1577-5.

This volume contains 2,747 entries with adequate but not always consistent bibliographic citations and brief annotations. Listings cover many countries and several continents, but only the English-language publications. This reviewer examined entries under Russia (nos. 1995-2105) with rather mixed results. Half of the entries have little in common with nonviolence and simply describe historical events during the Russian Revolution, Soviet prison camps, and political dissent from 1960 to the 1980s. In addition to Russia, there were 14 other Soviet Republics, such as Ukraine, second in population and now an independent country. There was not a single entry for Ukraine in the subject index. Nevertheless, the guide is a comprehensive source with a subject index, but it should be used with caution by interested students of nonviolence.—**Bohdan S. Wynar**

Chronology

497. Great Events from History: North American Series. rev. ed. Frank N. Magill and John L. Loos, eds. Pasadena, Calif., Salem Press, 1997. 4v. illus. maps. index. $300.00/set. ISBN 0-89356-429-X.

Although in many libraries the name of Magill has become synonymous with questionable study aids such as *Masterplots* (see entry 1085), the editor in recent years has brought out some reference sources that are highly regarded by both users and reference librarians alike. This new 4-volume set is one of them. It combines revised and updated entries from Magill's *Great Events from History: American Series* (1975) with revised ones from *Great Events from History: Worldwide Twentieth Century Series* (1980) and 325 new entries. The coverage is expanded from U.S. history through 1975 to North American history through 1996. Volume 1 begins with the Bering Strait migrations of 15,000 B.C.E. and includes succinct essays on such topics as the Norse expeditions, the Salem witchcraft trials, the Declaration of Independence, and the War of 1812. Concluding essays in Volume 4 cover Bill Clinton, the North American Free Trade Agreement, and the rise of the Internet. Photographs and well-executed maps are scattered throughout each volume.

The format is neat, clean, and easy to follow. Each entry includes the title and year of the event, its locality, subject categories in which the event falls, a list of principal figures involved, and a critical summary of 1,000 to 1,200 words written or updated by an academician. Reference librarians will find particularly useful the annotated bibliography of additional readings following each entry, as well as cross-references to related articles. Librarians and users will also appreciate the indexes. Each volume has a keyword index and a category list (the latter notes the 31 categories and the entries that fall in each). Volume 4 includes a personages index that lists all key figures and a subject index of the events, people, and concepts that receive significant treatment in the essays.

The introduction is a model of clarity and conciseness. This set is sure to be used in every academic and public library and probably many school libraries as well.—**Jack Bales**

498. Junior Chronicle of the 20th Century. New York, DK Publishing, 1997. 336p. illus. maps. index. $39.95. ISBN 0-7894-2033-3.

Each two-page spread in this colorfully illustrated chronology features events of one year of the century on topics as varied as politics, natural disasters, cultural happenings, war, sports, science, and invention. Each concise account is clearly written for the understanding of the intended audience—intermediate and middle school students. At the bottom of each page is a month-by-month highlight of world events. "Special Feature" spreads cover such topics as the Russian Revolution, the Great Depression, the rock 'n' roll years, and the space race. The work concludes with chronological spreads on Hollywood superstars, scientists and inventors, sports stars, world leaders, music makers, and lawbreakers. A thorough index provides access to people, places, and events.

Complementary works suitable for this age group include David Rubel's *Scholastic Timelines: The United States in the 20th Century* (Scholastic, 1995); *Junior Time Lines on File* by Valerie Tomaselli-Moschovitis (see entry 499), which covers the range of world history; and the Day by Day series (e.g., *Day by Day: The Eighties* [see ARBA 96, entry 503]) from Facts on File, which thoroughly treats each decade since the 1940s. From the browsing history buff, who will read all the way through, to the student seeking ideas for a report topic, young readers will find this sturdily bound and attractive book a welcome addition to any library.—**Vandelia L. VanMeter**

499. Tomaselli-Moschovitis, Valerie. **Junior Timelines on File.** New York, Facts on File, 1997. 1v. (various paging). illus. maps. index. $165.00 looseleaf w/binder. ISBN 0-8160-3444-3.

In a looseleaf format, *Junior Timelines on File* offers a comprehensive collection of historical timelines for reference and classroom use. Each page is illustrated with an original drawing or map based on appropriate artifacts, buildings, portraits, or events. These timelines are intended to support the middle school and junior high world history curriculum in three ways: country by country summaries, major trends in world history, and everyday life and human achievement. Thus, the student may research the history of a country or region but may also trace highlights in the production of food; changes in the social status of women; and important dates in the history of architecture, art, literature, religion, and transportation. Emphasis is on North America and Europe. The sturdy stock on which the timelines are printed will hold up to heavy use; permission for reproduction is granted for nonprofit, educational, or private purposes.

Any attempt to provide a chronology of world events in one volume is subject to nit-picking, but overall, this title will prove valuable to its intended audience. The work concludes with a bibliography of suitable recently published books, a helpful glossary, and a thorough index. A worthwhile companion volume is *The Encyclopedia of World Facts and Dates* by Gordon Carruth (see ARBA 95, entry 46).—**Vandelia L. VanMeter**

Dictionaries and Encyclopedias

500. Cook, Chris, and Diccon Bewes. **What Happened Where: A Guide to Places and Events in Twentieth-Century History.** New York, St. Martin's Press, 1997. 310p. maps. $30.00. ISBN 0-312-17278-8.

Organizing a reference work by where events happened is an interesting concept. The entries here are clear and concise, and maps are interspersed with the entries. Entries are arranged alphabetically, with two appendixes at the end listing the changing nations of the world and the major wars of the twentieth century. The organization of the work may have been better served by grouping the entries by region to give the work greater continuity and to demonstrate regional relationships. There is also a major omission in the list of major wars: the Spanish and Chinese Civil Wars are listed, but the Russian Civil War is left out. Cook and Bewes need to do more with this work if it is to rise above the level of an average reference work. There are some cultural references interspersed with historical event places. This work is adequate for high school and public library reference collections.—**Norman L. Kincaide**

501. **History of the Ancient & Medieval World.** Tarrytown, N.Y., Marshall Cavendish, 1996. 12v. illus. maps. index. $459.95/set. ISBN 0-7614-0351-5.

This is a beautifully illustrated 12-volume historical encyclopedia, arranged chronologically, beginning with "Origins of Humanity" and continuing through "Asia, Africa, and the Americas." In between are "Egypt and Mesopotamia," "Ancient Cultures," "The Ancient Greeks," "Greece and Rome," "The Roman Empire," "Religions of the World," "Christianity and Islam," "The Middle Ages," and "Medieval Politics and Life." Each volume contains its own index, timeline, glossary, and bibliography of further reading suggestions.

Colorful illustrations make this a rich historical resource; helpful maps, charts, and abundant photographs of locations and artifacts for each period provide fascinating information, greatly enhancing the easy-to-follow text. This reviewer's mid-size public library will put to immediate use the history covered in these volumes; each year, the local middle schools review Egypt and the Middle Ages. This set will be just what is needed for those annual assignments on Egyptian gods; religious and political beliefs; and medieval traditions, wars, and culture.

The index volume provides five valuable sections. "The Chronicles" is a listing of the ancient kingdoms, rulers, and dynasties in order, something frequently asked for in the library. "The Time Line" is an inclusive listing of the periods from all 11 volumes. "A Glossary" covers the entire set. The "Thematic Indexes" are on broad topics, such as arts and culture, religion, wars and battles, and government and politics. Finally, an "Index" to the entire set completes the volume.

History of the Ancient & Medieval World is a versatile, well-organized reference tool. It would be an asset in middle school, high school, and public library reference collections. [R: RBB, 15 Oct 97, p. 428]

—**Marcia Blevins**

502. **The Holocaust: A Grolier Student Library.** Geoffrey Wigoder, ed. Danbury, Conn., Grolier, 1997. 4v. illus. maps. index. $169.00/set. ISBN 0-7172-7637-6.

In 4 volumes (511 pages), alphabetically arranged entries cover the causes, events, and results of the Holocaust. The roles of significant persons and groups, related events in many nations, and similar topics are also discussed. The volumes are vastly illustrated and include maps, timelines, sidebars, and other study aids; cross-references connect entries. Non-English-language terms are used sparingly and are fully defined. Each volume is indexed; a cumulative index appears in volume 4. Most helpful is the subject index, which will help the reader locate all of the articles that touch on a particular topic, ranging from anti-Semitism to Zionist activities. The bibliographic essay that describes related titles and indicates the grade level is a helpful collection development tool.

Suitable for students grades 7 and up, this set provides excellent support for junior high school units on World War II, genocide, racism, and related topics. Macmillan Library Reference's 1989 *Encyclopedia of the Holocaust* provides more extensive coverage in a multivolume work suitable for high school and adult readers. [R: RBB, 15 Feb 97, p. 1042]—**Vandelia L. VanMeter**

503. The Illustrated Encyclopedia of World History. K. Donker van Heel, ed. Armonk, N.Y., Sharpe Reference/M. E. Sharpe, 1997. 414p. illus. maps. $125.00. ISBN 1-56324-805-0.

In an easy-to-use alphabetic arrangement, this one-volume history of the world offers a broad view of important people, events, wars, treaties, places (but not nations), and cultural trends. Full-color thematic pages that illustrate great historical happenings (e.g., monks and monasteries in the Middle Ages, the Ottoman Turks, Napoleon); illustrations; portraits; and occasional maps provide strong support to the clear, concise text. In the 3-column format, a reader finds 6 lines devoted to Genghis Khan, 30 lines to Adolf Hitler, and 9 lines to Paul Gauguin.

There are *see* references on some thematic pages, as well as occasional *see* references within the text, but there is no indication by bold or italic typeface or other technique that any term within an entry has an entry of its own. This hinders the user in tracing related persons or topics. A scan of the illustrations gives the sense that there is an effort at evenhandedness, but a closer examination leaves many questions—there is a thematic page on China's early dynasties, and another on communist China, but there is no entry or *see* reference for China or any other nation or continent.

This attractive and colorful work is suitable for quick-reference use in school libraries, at the desk, or in the home. Even though the alphabetic arrangement provides access, the necessary sense of context is better provided for students by the timeline/extensive indexing approach used in *The Dorling Kindersley History of the World* (see ARBA 95, entry 587). Libraries serving secondary students and adults who need deeper coverage may prefer to use general encyclopedias, multivolume works, or such one-volume works as *The Hutchinson Dictionary of World History* (see ARBA 95, entry 581), which includes chronologies, lists of leaders, organizations, wars, battles, and disasters.—**Vandelia L. VanMeter**

504. Palmowski, Jan. **A Dictionary of Twentieth-Century World History.** New York, Oxford University Press, 1997. 693p. maps. (Oxford Paperback Reference). $15.95pa. ISBN 0-19-280016-7.

Accurate and up-to-date entries in this alphabetically arranged dictionary provide facts and analyses of more than 2,500 historical figures, movements, and events in the political, diplomatic, and military arenas of the twentieth century. The cutoff date for inclusion in the dictionary is October 10, 1996. World leaders (e.g., Bill Clinton, Benjamin Netanyahu, Kim Yong Sam, Joseph Stalin, Margaret Thatcher, and Boris Yeltsin) have adequate (albeit brief) biographies. Economic, cultural, and religious dimensions of seminal events and movements are given adequate consideration. Attention is paid to major treaties and political agreements, such as the Dayton Accords. Key battles are analyzed, and world events such as the Chernobyl disaster are not ignored. The relative importance of the individuals and events included may not be indicated by their entry length. The ongoing investigation of Hillary and Bill Clinton and the Whitewater controversy receives the same space as Fiorello La Guardia ($2\frac{1}{2}$ inches).

Two central criteria favored selection of entries: Individuals and events had to be genuinely global, and the entries had to be as comprehensive as possible allowing for space restrictions. A few maps and tables are included, but they are of negligible value. No sidebars or illustrations are present to break up the dense, two-column presentation. Cross-references are used judiciously. Birth and death dates are noted, as are inclusive dates to encompass periods in which ideas central to world developments took place. British English is used throughout, but this is not a major distraction. The use of accent marks is restricted to the most common English usage for Spanish, German, French, and Portuguese. There is no pronunciation guide.

Although quite readable, this book has limited reference value, and the information will become quickly dated. Few could quarrel with the selection or quality of the entries, but this is only a springboard to broader research in more comprehensive sources. Students, teachers, and librarians could use this book for a desk reference, but only those willing to browse extensively will appreciate its diverse appeal.—**Judy Gay Matthews**

Handbooks and Yearbooks

505. DISCovering World History. [CD-ROM]. Detroit, Gale, 1997. Minimum system requirements: IBM or compatible 386 (486DX/33MHz or higher highly recommended). CD-ROM drive (double-speed or faster recommended) with MS-DOS CD-ROM Extensions 2.2. DOS 5.0. Windows 3.1. 8MB RAM. 5MB hard disk space. SVGA monitor (256-color display) and graphics card. Windows-compatible mouse. Printer (optional). $500.00/stand-alone version; $700.00/2-8 users. ISBN 0-7876-0925-0.

DISCovering World History, a new addition to the Gale DISCovering Program of CD-ROMs, is a reference and research tool for teachers and students of world history. Patterned after the well-known world history encyclopedias in print (e.g., *An Encyclopedia of World History: Ancient, Medieval, and Modern, Chronologically Arranged*, edited by William L. Langer [5th ed.; see ARBA 73, entry 309]), the database contains overviews of 60 historical eras; a chronological timeline; and detailed essays on political, cultural, and historical events.

The 100 primary documents are not always full text; are not facsimiles; and tend to be legal or governmental documents with only a few personal accounts, diaries, or letters. There are 300 captioned pictures, photographs, and maps linked to the entries. The essays are authoritative, with reliable bibliographies. The language is scholarly, with vocabulary, such as "principal personages," "collusion," "juridical," and "indisputable prerequisites," that will challenge high school students and transcend the reading level of most primary and middle school students.

The coverage of historical overviews extends from the beginning of civilization through the twentieth century, with a view to the future. Individual essays range from the "Upright-Walking Australopithecine" of 30,000,000 B.C.E. to the August 6, 1996, entry "Evidence of Possible Life on Mars." The scope is truly global, with topics ranging from "African Kingdoms and Empires" and the "Aztec, Maya and Inca" to "Japan: Establishment and Development" and "Southeast Asia in the Nineteenth Century." Biographical entries include notables from Aaron and Zoser to Chinua Achebe and Zhou En-lai.

Unlike its print equivalents, however, the hypertext format of *DISCovering World History* allows users to select a point of entry and follow their own path of learning—a process that allows for exploration and reinforces critical analysis. Users may begin with keyword searching (both Boolean logic and bound phrase searching are supported), or, by clicking on one of seven icons, they can search from a timeline; narrow their search by name, subject, or place; search only primary documents; or do custom searching in multiple categories, such as occupation, gender, place, primary documents, and country essays. While the search mechanisms are sophisticated and engaging, the search results may be confusing. Any search may bring up a list of entries that are displayed in a small window at the bottom left of the screen. The majority of the screen is filled with the text of the first entry in the list. This entry may or may not be what the user is seeking, and it is not always apparent how it relates to the search. For example, a Place search on Vietnam brings up a list of 17 entries. The entry for Ho Chi Minh is displayed on the screen. The user must scroll through the entire list of 17 entries to find the country overview of Vietnam, the last entry in the list. Once found, many essays are accompanied by full-color, captioned pictures, photographs, and maps.

Excellent documentation includes a comprehensive, easy-to-use, adequately indexed User's Manual; a concise HelpCard for use at a workstation; and a Teacher's Guide, which provides a number of learning activities designed to achieve specific teaching strategies and learning outcomes. Content learning, such as historical comprehension, comparative analysis, and interdisciplinary causation, is linked with such activities as role playing, research methods, and group collaboration. Installation on a single workstation is straightforward if the system requirements are met and memory is sufficient. The installer may enable or disable printing and saving, limit the number of pages that may be printed, and require a password if desired. Network installation is more involved than with some CD-ROM software, but users of other discs in the DISCovering Program report excellent technical support from Gale. School librarians, teachers, and history students considering purchase of this disc can view a free demonstration from Gale's Internet site (http://www.gale.com).—**Debra S. Van Tassel**

506. **Facts on File World News CD-ROM 1997.** [CD-ROM]. New York, Facts on File, 1997. Minimum system requirements: IBM or compatible 486. Double-speed CD-ROM drive. Windows 3.1. 8MB RAM. 7MB hard disk space. Color monitor. Mouse. Printer (recommended). $995.00.

Most reference librarians consider *Facts on File* to be a core title. It is a source of summaries of the news stories from around the world, and unlike indexes to newspapers, it is not limited to one newspaper or groups of newspapers. *Facts on File* is now available in three formats: traditional print ($725), CD-ROM ($995), and a database from various vendors. The question that librarians have to answer in this electronic age of competing products is whether Facts on File is still core, and if so, which format is best?

Many libraries provide users with access to either the full text of newspapers through a service like Lexis-Nexis or electronic or CD-ROM access to a newspaper indexes like *Newspaper Abstracts* or *Newspaper Index*. Most full-text or index and abstract services will be more up-to-date than the print of CD-ROM *Facts on File*. Although less objective than *Facts on File*, many newspaper indexes now provide geographically diverse coverage, particularly for the United States, because of the newspapers they cover.

The CD-ROM version of *Facts on File* is updated quarterly, whereas the print version is updated weekly. The database is updated monthly or weekly depending on the vendor. Both the CD-ROM and database include coverage since 1980, providing more than 70,000 news articles. The print version's index is updated every two weeks with annual and five-year indexes. The major benefit of the CD-ROM is that it includes keyword searching of both the index and the entries. It also includes features that do not appear in the print version—country profiles and more than 400 primary source documents. Although maps and photographs appear in the print version, the CD-ROM has many more.

The CD-ROM version also has an easy-to-use browser that will look comfortably like Netscape to undergraduates. There are 35 overviews of key topics frequently sought after for term papers on subjects like abortion, capital punishment, and drugs. Different sections are hyperlinked together, allowing the user to move easily from one area to another. News digests are a click away from an overview of a topic like "censorship," and overviews are a click away from related news summaries.

There is still a need in most research libraries for a source like *Facts on File*. The CD-ROM enhancements will attract a new audience and be popular with high school students and college undergraduates interested in one-stop research on hot topics.—**Jack E. Pontius**

507. **History of Humanity. Volume 3: From the Seventh Century BC to the Seventh Century AD.** Joachim Herrmann, Erik Zurcher, and others, eds. Paris, United Nations Educational, Scientific, and Cultural Organization and New York, Routledge, 1996. 626p. illus. maps. index. $149.95. ISBN 0-415-09307-4.

Providing a welcome 3d volume to their multicultural history, UNESCO and Routledge have published a fine reference work to be included with the first 2 volumes of the series (see ARBA 97, entry 479, and ARBA 96, entry 568). This international history breaks with the traditions of the western world and its implied ethnocentrism, which of course it must do to be a truly multicultural history.

Themes are emphasized throughout (where possible), rather than a specific event or events; for example, "Cultural Contacts Between the Greeks and the Orient" and "The Formation of the Classical Andean World." The text is supplemented with many fine figures, maps, and plates. Each section has an excellent bibliography, although several citations may be considered dated. There is also a helpful, detailed index.

History of Humanity is a reference work of value to the collections of college, university, or public libraries. The set could be useful in answering general reference questions or as a guide to the beginning researcher looking for information and details.—**Bruce H. Webb**

508. Schwartz, Richard Alan. **The Cold War Reference Guide: A General History and Annotated Chronology, with Selected Biographies.** Jefferson, N.C., McFarland, 1997. 321p. index. $55.00. ISBN 0-7864-0173-7.

The Cold War Reference Guide is a short narrative-format guide to the events, chronology, and important people of the Cold War. Divided into four sections, this informative volume provides a general history of the Cold War, identifies the highlights of the conflict, details the chronology of events, and provides biographies of important Cold War individuals. The small volume gives a concise and clearly written narrative of the issues that fueled the Cold War and that brought about its end. A part of this conflict was the importance of the perceptions that the respective sides of the conflict had of one another. Schwartz also probes the historical debate over some of the issues, such as the Yalta Conference and the conservative and liberal struggle over the course of U.S. foreign policy.

This volume is not intended to be an encyclopedic treatment of the Cold War, but it is more than just a quick reference guide. A selected bibliography is broken up by subject and adds to an already interesting and effective treatment of the Cold War. The guide is recommended for public, college, university, and private reference collections.—**Norman L. Kincaide**

10 Law

GENERAL WORKS

Bibliography

509. **Bibliographic Guide to Law 1996.** New York, G. K. Hall/Simon & Schuster Macmillan, 1997. 2v. $395.00/set. ISBN 0-7838-1767-3. ISSN 0360-2745.

MARC copy from the New York Public Library and the Library of Congress provides the source material for this title in G. K. Hall's respected bibliographic series (see entry 109 for a complete review). The two-volume set, last reviewed in ARBA 92 (see entry 517), contains items that have an imprint date of 1990 or newer and that were cataloged during the 1996 calendar year. All languages and formats (book, nonbook, serials) are included. The disciplines of law that one expects to see are represented with thoroughness, as are political science fields (diplomacy and international relations) and financial topics (banking and taxation). The straightforward presentation and comprehensiveness of this guide should make it useful to both librarians and law students.—**Ed Volz**

510. DeCoste, F. C., and Lillian MacPherson. **Law, Religion, Theology: A Selective Annotated Bibliography.** West Cornwall, Conn., Locust Hill Press, 1997. 360p. index. $48.00. ISBN 0-933951-75-2.

The purpose of this bibliography is to show the large amount of study done on the historical, cultural, and theoretical intersections between law, religion, and theology as well as to show where such scholarship has been pursued, produced, and published. The authors wanted to be as inclusive as possible, so they focused on literature of a broad, nonspecialized nature to keep the number of entries manageable. Included are journal articles published in English between 1980 and 1996, which are indexed in *Catholic Periodical Index*, *Religion and Theological Abstracts*, *Religion Index*, *Sociofile*, DIALOG, *Wilsondisc*, and *Legal Trac*. However, only *Legal Trac* was checked through 1996; the other indexes were checked only through 1993.

The scholarship of three seminal authors in this area—Harold Berman, Robert Cover, and Thomas Shaffer—is completely included in the bibliography. Works by other authors are not included if they are case commentaries, doctrinal analyses, book reviews, or debates on the Establishment and Free Exercise Clauses of the U.S. Constitution. The brief annotations contain two to six sentences. Subject arrangement by chapter is as follows: "Church and State," "First Nations and Race," International and Comparative Law," "Legal History," "Legal Profession," "Legal Theory," and "Women." The last three chapters cover bibliographies, symposia, and Websites. Indexes by author, topic, and journal complete the work.

—**Georgia Briscoe**

511. McKnight, Jean Sinclair. **Law for the Layperson: An Annotated Bibliography of Self-Help Law Books.** 2d ed. Littleton, Colo., Fred B. Rothman, 1997. 228p. $47.50pa. ISBN 0-8377-0869-9.

It seems rare that anyone can get through modern life without the assistance of a lawyer at some point. Many people want to avoid them at all cost, often by going to their local library for information. This updated edition of *Law for the Layman* by Frank Houdek (see ARBA 92, entry 522) has a new author, a new format, and a gender-sensitive new title. Yet the subtitle, which remains the same, tells it all: *An Annotated Bibliography of Self-Help Law Books.*

McKnight's paperback edition updates the formerly looseleaf bibliography to include publications from 1990 to March 1, 1996. It will assist librarians and patrons who want to know what is available for persons wanting to represent themselves in this legalistic society. The main section of the book is a two-part subject arrangement of the annotated list of self-help law books. Part 1 covers general/comprehensive works, and part 2 is arranged by specific subject. The specific subjects have been expanded from 76 to 96 entries, although many are cross-references. Appearing at the end of each subject area is a jurisdictional list, usually by state. Annotations clearly describe subject content and identify special features, such as sample forms, checklists of things to do, and step-by-step procedures.

As law librarian Houdek said in the original edition, "The plethora of self-help law books presents a problem for the conscientious acquisitions librarian with a limited budget." This book will help one select the most useful books in given areas, and the indexes will be especially helpful. Four indexes—by author, title, jurisdiction, and publishers—will expedite acquisitions. The list of publishers has 55 new entries, totaling 160, an indication of the expanding demand. Many of the publishers are small and difficult to locate. Telephone numbers are thankfully provided.

This annotated list of law books written expressly for the nonlawyer fills a definite need in librarianship. The author also hopes to help people find information that will bring everyone closer to the "elusive goal of justice for all."—**Georgia Briscoe**

512. Raistrick, Donald. **Lawyers' Law Books: A Practical Index to Legal Literature.** 3d ed. New Providence, N.J., Bowker-Saur/Reed Reference Publishing, 1997. 723p. index. $125.00. ISBN 1-85739-087-3.

This title is a monumental achievement in legal bibliography. It endeavors to be a comprehensive bibliography of the legal literature of the United Kingdom. Of course, comprehensiveness as a primary feature of any bibliography is an ideal state that can never be effectively tested. However, with more than 13,000 entries, it is clear that this work comes as close as possible to listing every modern title of value to the student of the law of the United Kingdom.

The only drawback to a work of this magnitude is its size. The bibliography alone is nearly 600 pages of small typeface, and not a single entry is annotated, nor does any entry contain more than the barest essentials of bibliographic information. As a result, the book presents the user with a staggering number of titles that offer no editorial context for the material that is listed other than the location under a particular subject heading. The effect is overwhelming.

Yet this is not to say that the book is not useful. One useful feature is the arrangement of the main bibliography. All entries are arranged according to a thorough and well-thought-out system of subject headings. Plenty of cross-references are available to make use of this bibliography extremely profitable. One interested in obtaining a virtually complete list of materials available in any particular area of the law of the United Kingdom can feel confident that this book will provide it. One challenge presented to the bibliographer by this book is that because the United Kingdom is such an old common law jurisdiction, many works that are considered standard works are themselves very old, and consequently, out of print. It is not uncommon when leafing through the book to find titles with copyright dates from the nineteenth century. This makes using the book for collection development somewhat problematic. Two useful features of the book are appendixes that list the regnal years of British sovereigns and the law reports of the United Kingdom and Ireland. The book is finished with a comprehensive index of authors and titles.

Overall, this index is an overwhelmingly useful compilation of the sources of law for the United Kingdom and related jurisdictions. Its only fault—the size—is the result of its topic, which is itself massive.
—**Richard A. Leiter**

Biography

513. Berry, Dawn Bradley. **The 50 Most Influential Women in American Law.** Los Angeles, Calif., Lowell House; distr., Chicago, Contemporary Books, 1996. 354p. illus. index. $30.00. ISBN 1-56565-469-2.

Nearly 50 percent of law school graduates today are women. Berry has provided an exciting array of stories about women who have overcome tremendous obstacles to influence the practice of law in the United States. These personal stories reveal the intelligence and confidence needed to overcome local and regional customs, and the pressure these women used to pave the way for far-reading reforms in the

American Bar Association, civil rights, personal liberty, and equal rights. These 50 stories provide readers with models and metaphors that will empower everyone to overcome obstacles in personal and professional development, regardless of gender. This book will inspire women who already possess self-assurance or who need to develop it to use the ambition and competitiveness necessary to succeed.

Of course, one wants to ask why these particular women were selected—many were not lawyers, and some were without higher education. The first woman profiled is Margaret Brent, who lived from 1601 to 1671, the first woman to own land in the colonies. Even though the earlier women treated practiced some law in a county bar, they were not recognized by a state bar for more than 200 years, until Arabella Babb Mansfield was admitted to a state bar in 1869 in Iowa. There are some well-known women who were not only admitted to the bar but were also highly influential. Not all of the biographees are women of the legal profession; some are women who influenced the law (e.g., biologist Rachel Carson and civil rights activist Rosa Parks). Other contemporary women include Barbara Jordan, Geraldine Ferraro, Sandra Day O'Connor, Ruth Bader Ginsburg, and Marcia Clark.

Although Berry states that her selections are subjective, she apparently gave too much thought to what would make her book sell, therefore including some contemporary people who have recently been in the headlines. Whether or not their influence is as important as her book title would indicate, only time will tell. The greatest flaw in the book is the gap in coverage between the work of Brent in 1671 and that of Elizabeth Ware Packard in 1816. Influential women of this period should have been listed, but instead Berry has loaded the book with influential women from the second half of the twentieth century. This book is a good read, not an influential reference.—**Gerald D. Moran**

514. **Who's Who in American Law 1996-1997.** 9th ed. New Providence, N.J., Marquis Who's Who/Reed Reference Publishing, 1996. 977p. index. $269.95. ISBN 0-8379-3511-3. ISSN 0162-7880.

The 9th edition of *Who's Who in American Law* contains approximately 22,000 biographical sketches of prominent members of the legal community, including attorneys, judges, legal educators, and other professionals. (See ARBA 95, entry 602 for the content of the sketches and indexing.) The set of individuals profiled in this volume were compared with a group of three articles found in *Forbes* (November 6, 1995) and one in the National Law Journal (April 28, 1997). The former listed 62 of the highest paid or noteworthy attorneys, and the latter included 100 of the most powerful lawyers in the nation. Only about a quarter of the individuals found in the *Forbes* articles were profiled in the title at hand, and fewer than one-half of the *National Law Journal* attorneys were included. Particularly glaring absences include John O'Quinn, a principle attorney in breast implant litigation; Laurence Tribe, a renowned constitutional scholar and Harvard professor; and Barry Scheck, popularly associated with the O. J. Simpson and Louise Woodward trials. Before purchasing this work, libraries may want to consider as alternatives the free West Legal Directory on the World Wide Web or the rather expensive *Martindale-Hubbell Law Directory* (see ARBA 91, entry 581), although neither focus exclusively upon distinguished legal professionals and the scope of entries in these resources may be limited.—**Mark A. Allan**

Dictionaries and Encyclopedias

515. Anglim, Christopher Thomas. **Labor, Employment, and the Law: A Dictionary.** Santa Barbara, Calif., ABC-CLIO, 1997. 549p. index. (Contemporary Legal Issues). $39.50. ISBN 0-87436-825-1.

The majority of this work by a government documents and special collections librarian (at South Texas College of Law) consists of more than 400 entries covering everything from AIDS and affirmative action, to drug use, to the glass ceiling, to religious discrimination in the workplace, sexual harassment, and the zipper clause. Preceding the entries is an overview of the development of U.S. labor and employment law. Entries, ranging in length from a few lines to a few pages, define terms or phrases, summarize the significance of laws and court opinions, provide brief histories of organizations (e.g., the AFL-CIO and government agencies), and usually conclude with *see also* references. *See* references are also liberally used.

This volume is clearly intended for a 1990s audience: witness the inclusion under "Affirmative Action" of the *Texas v. Hopwood* case (1996) and litigation involving California's Proposition 209 (1996). Certain legislation of the 1990s, such as the Americans with Disabilities Act and the Family Medical Leave Act, are entered. There are, however, such retrospective statutes as the Civil Rights acts of 1866 and 1871, and there are court cases from the pre-Civil War period (e.g., *Commonwealth v. Pullis* [1806] and *Commonwealth v.*

Hunt [1842]). Following the main dictionary portion of this treatise are a bibliography of books; a table of cases (case name, legal citation, date); a table of statutes (citation, date); and a subject index with *see* references, personal names cited in the text, and other topics, not all of which are represented by separate entries.

Labor, Employment, and the Law is complementary to *Roberts' Dictionary of Industrial Relations* (4th ed.; see ARBA 96, entry 257), the classic work by reason of the breadth and number of entries (more than 4,400); *The Blackwell Encyclopedic Dictionary of Human Resources Management* (1997); and other standard sources, such as *The Facts on File Dictionary of Personnel Management and Labor Relations* (2d ed.; see ARBA 87, entry 275) and *The Human Resources Glossary* (see ARBA 93, entry 302). The title at hand is suitable for public and academic libraries.—**Wiley J. Williams**

516. **Bieber's Dictionary of Legal Citations: Reference Guide for Attorneys, Legal Secretaries, Paralegals, and Law Students.** Prince's 5th ed. By Mary Miles Prince. Buffalo, N.Y., William S. Hein, 1997. 1v. (various paging). index. $39.50. ISBN 1-57588-285-X.

This standard guide to legal citations is an indispensable reference for all legal practitioners and law students. Because the dictionary has traditionally complemented *The Bluebook: A Uniform System of Citation*, it makes sense to now have the entire 1996 edition of this style guide included in the dictionary's appendix. All citations and abbreviations in the *Dictionary of Legal Citations* are based on *Bluebook* rules or derived from its guidelines. The dictionary entries give the official abbreviation of each journal or law set cited, along with citation examples. An entry on how to cite Internet sources is included, covering such things as bulletin board services (BBSs), listservs, Gopher sites, and online journals. Cross-references to the *Bluebook* and other resources are used throughout. The *Bluebook* portion provides detailed practitioners' notes, general rules of citation and style, rules for foreign and international law materials, and citation examples for law reporters from all U.S. court jurisdictions. This work is a must for all law collections and is highly recommended for most academic and large public libraries. (See ARBA 94, entry 544; ARBA 90, entry 543; and ARBA 88, entry 568, for earlier reviews of the title.)—**Gary D. Barber**

517. **Elsevier's Dictionary of European Community Company/Business/Financial Law in English, Danish, and German.** Hanne Bock, Gisela Frey, and Ian Bock, comps. New York, Elsevier Science, 1997. 539p. index. $203.25. ISBN 0-444-81783-2.

This dictionary contains 6,875 terms in English, many with multiple Danish and German equivalents. The user needs to select the pertinent translation, for example, from the English "payment by installment" to the German *Ratenzahlung* or *Amortisation* or *Abtragszahlung*, which are not synonymous, as many Danish words are not. In the second part of the volume, the Danish and German indexes are specially constructed to allow easier correlation between terms in those two languages. This enables the user not only to find the English equivalents of Danish or German terms, but also to find translations of those terms from German to Danish and vice versa.

The volume includes a reference list of 50 major documents consulted in the preparation of the dictionary. The one-page list of abbreviations does not seem to include all of those used in the basic table, but such abbreviations should be easily understood, such as "dat" for the dative case. In the increasingly cross-country web of Europe, the dictionary will be of help to those who participate in the expanding economic relations between the members of the European Union. The choice of languages indicates the spatial markets of commercial relations this dictionary addresses.—**Bogdan Mieczkowski**

518. **Encyclopedia of the American Constitution.** [CD-ROM]. New York, Macmillan Library Reference/ Simon & Schuster Macmillan, 1996. Minimum system requirements (Windows version): IBM or compatible 386. CD-ROM drive. Windows 3.1. 4MB RAM. 2MB hard disk space. Minimum system requirements (Macintosh version): System 6.0. CD-ROM drive. 4MB RAM. 2MB hard disk space. Color monitor. $275.00.

Librarians familiar with the print version of *Encyclopedia of the American Constitution* (see ARBA 87, entry 711) will recognize the information and format of the CD-ROM version. The content is taken from the 1986 four-volume set and 1992 supplement; the opening screen shows the arrangement of the information into four volumes with the supplement cross-referenced. What is boldfaced as a cross-reference in the print version appears as a hypertext link on the CD-ROM. Appendixes and the glossary are identical, with the addition of hypertext links facilitating the cross-references. Each paragraph of the CD-ROM text is prefaced by a note indicating where the paragraph can be found in the print edition.

Installation of the program using both Windows 3.1 and Windows 95 was quick and effective. The program can also run on Macintosh and DOS platforms. The disc is also networkable; the network version is $125 more. Other than the hypertext links, there are no "bells and whistles"—no graphics, no sound, no video. The CD-ROM includes a wide variety of search techniques, including Boolean searching; truncation; proximity; operators (wildcard, stem, thesaurus); and exact phrases. Although this variety is a strength, the intricacies may be confusing to novice researchers, and it is easy to become lost within the search functions and results. When a search is performed, a list of hits is generated and displayed. One can search each hit for the reference or move within the list of hits by using the toolbelt, a 12-button feature that accesses special functions.

Encyclopedia of the American Constitution, both in print and electronic forms, presumes a high level of comprehension. Many high school students will struggle with the vocabulary and sentence structure, but the resource is an invaluable one nonetheless. Librarians will have to choose whether they feel their clients can be best served by one format or the other; if they have the capacity to network the CD-ROM, the resource would be more widely available. A call to customer service in July revealed that Macmillan has no plans to update the information in either version at this time; this may also be a consideration.

—**Michele Tyrrell**

519. Kaplan, Steven M. **Wiley's English-Spanish, Spanish-English Legal Dictionary. Diccionario Juridico Ingles-Espanol, Espanol-Ingles Wiley.** 2d ed. New York, John Wiley, 1997. 646p. $65.00. ISBN 0-471-16111-X.

The North American Free Trade Agreement and the increasing proportion of Spanish-speaking residents of the United States are two good reasons libraries need bilingual legal dictionaries. This new edition of Kaplan's dictionary is substantially expanded to over 60,000 terms (see ARBA 95, entry 606 for a review of the 1st edition). Another recently revised competitor is *Dahl's Law Dictionary: An Annotated Legal Dictionary, Spanish to English, English to Spanish* (see ARBA 97, entry 486). Both authors are bilingual. Dahl is an attorney; Kaplan is not but was assisted by an eminent Spanish attorney. Both dictionaries omit parts of speech and pronunciation, and contain many brief definitions consisting of a single word or phrase. Dahl also contains many longer, substantive definitions, including the actual text of legal codes from Spain, Latin America, and the United States. However, Kaplan's uniformly brief entries contain more multiple word terms useful for quick access to specific legal meanings, such as *hurto calificado*, meaning "aggravated larceny." A third alternative is *Butterworths Spanish/English Legal Dictionary*, by Guillermo Cabanellas de las Cuevas and Eleanor C. Hoague (Butterworths, 1991), which does contain parts of speech and some longer, multiple definitions for a single term and also offers the convenience of putting the Spanish/English and English/Spanish sections in separate volumes. Perhaps Kaplan's greatest strengths are the sheer number of specific terms and the simplicity of the definitions. Of course, any bilingual legal dictionary is no substitute for a bilingual attorney. This work is recommended for any library with Spanish-speaking and legal constituencies.—**Marit S. MacArthur**

520. Rapalje, Stewart, and Robert L. Lawrence. **A Dictionary of American and English Law, with Definitions of the Technical Terms of the Canon and Civil Laws.** Littleton, Colo., Fred B. Rothman, 1997. 2v. $245.00/set. ISBN 0-8377-2582-8.

This dictionary is the current reprint of a work now more than 100 years of age. In its day, Rapalje and Lawrence's work was a classic case, a standard work for American and English law, as formidable a standard as Black's *Law Dictionary* (West, date not set). All the text is intact here, including the 1883 preface, the typeface, and the at-times hard-to-read print so typical of turn-of-the-century publications. Yet the effort is rewarded a hundredfold with numerous citations, scores of Latin maxims defined, and cases cited. Of course the dictionary's value is not in its contemporaneity (although it will still prove a useful guide) but because it is an expansive snapshot of law as it was once honorably practiced. Moreover, the dictionary's generous sampling of Latinisms makes it valuable as a quick translator. If for no other reason, the two volumes stand as a testament to the utter skill and power of mind that could produce such a prodigious work when personal typewriters were still to come and computers had not seen the light of cognitive day.—**Mark Y. Herring**

Directories

521. BNA's Directory of State and Federal Courts, Judges, and Clerks: A State-by-State and Federal Listing. 1997 ed. Judith A. Miller, with the BNA Library Staff, comps. Washington, D.C., BNA Books, 1996. 548p. illus. index. $115.00pa. ISBN 1-57018-043-1. ISSN 1078-5582.

This standard guide to the national court system begins with an overview of federal and state courts arranged by levels and types. Also included here are the District of Columbia, American Samoa, Guam, the Northern Mariana Islands, Puerto Rico, and the U.S. Virgin Islands. Entries consist of official names of the courts, clerks of the courts, and judges. Geographic jurisdictions are indicated at the third court level, with counties or cities listed alphabetically. Clerks and judges' titles, addresses, telephone and fax numbers, and e-mail and Internet addresses are also given when available.

Each state's court structure is shown in flowchart form. Although there are four levels of courts (courts of last resort, intermediate appellate courts, general-jurisdiction trial courts, and limited-jurisdiction trial courts), the directory excludes limited-jurisdiction courts. Introductory material includes an explanatory sample entry and a map of the United States showing jurisdictional boundaries of courts of appeal and U.S. district courts. The first 3 editions of this guide were limited to state courts (see ARBA 89, entry 511, and ARBA 87, entry 552 for reviews of the 1st 2 editions). Federal courts were added to the 4th edition (see ARBA 93, entry 582). The directory is now published annually in order to keep up with frequent staff and other changes. BNA's World Wide Web address and the compiler's e-mail address are also provided.

Among the added features in the current edition are a directory of electronic public access services to automated information in U.S. federal courts (which includes Internet sites for federal and state courts), a geographic jurisdiction index, and a personal name index. The only negative feature for this reference book is the semiperforated pages, which will only encourage vandalism. A less expensive alternative (for federal courts only) is *The Sourcebook of Federal Courts: U.S. District and Bankruptcy* (see ARBA 97, entry 500). The directory under review, however, is the only comprehensive one, making it an essential purchase for all law libraries and many general collections as well.—**Gary D. Barber**

522. Judicial Staff Directory, 1997. 11th ed. Alexandria, Va., CQ Staff Directories, 1997. 1040p. maps. index. $89.00pa. ISBN 0-87289-123-2. ISSN 1091-3742.

Judicial Staff Directory joins CQ Staff Directories' family of respected directories, which include *Federal Staff Directory* and *Congressional Staff Directory* (see entry 652). Now in its 11th edition, the directory has become a standard reference tool for legal professionals. The softcover volume provides accurate and timely information concerning the federal justice system of the U.S. government, complete with 2,200 biographies.

A color-coded edge-index on the second page takes users quickly and efficiently to the court of their choice. The complete index of individual names in the back of the volume gives telephone numbers for further efficiency. The details and organization of information are complete and user-friendly. Examples include maps illustrating state and county boundaries with circuit and district jurisdictions; listings of telephone numbers for voice and electronic access to case information on circuit-by-circuit and district-by-district bases; and listings of presidential appointments of federal judges alphabetically by name, chronologically by year of appointment, and by appointing president.

Other titles provide some of the same information as *Judicial Staff Directory*, such as *BNA's Directory of State and Federal Courts, Judges, and Clerks* (see entry 521), and *Want's Federal-State Court Directory* (see ARBA 94, entry 564, and ARBA 91, entry 582). Neither is as thorough or easy to use as the CQ title. The reference tool under review is valuable and an excellent value.—**Georgia Briscoe**

523. Law and Legal Information Directory: A Guide to More Than 34,000 National and International Organizations.... 9th ed. Steven Wasserman, Jacqueline Wasserman Monroe, and Bonnie Shaw Pfaff, eds. Detroit, Gale, 1997. 1875p. $370.00. ISBN 0-8103-4896-9. ISSN 0740-090X.

This huge directory is divided into 41 sections; a listing of them in small typeface on the title page consumes 11 lines. Approximately half of the sections are state-by-state listings of various courts, agencies, and offices that deal with specific areas, such as environmental protection, banking, securities, public health, real estate, and boating. Ten of the sections (e.g., law schools, federal regulatory agencies, awards and prizes) have their own alphabetic/keyword/acronym indexes, although the primary arrangement of these sections is alphabetic. New to this edition is a listing of bar examination review courses available in each state (a number of them, such as West Bar Review, are from national companies that are listed for many or all states). Occasionally, the editors may be accused of stretching a point: A section on book and media publishers that "issue a significant portion of their products in the legal field" contains numerous trade and university presses whose coverage of legal topics is fairly incidental compared with their offerings on other subjects. Even though entries in this directory almost always include addresses and telephone numbers (and sometimes a fax number), there are no (as far as this reviewer could see) e-mail addresses or World Wide Web URLs. Massive printed directories of this kind may become increasingly less useful unless they take into account the vast revolution in electronic communication that has been occurring in the past decade.—**Jack Ray**

524. **The Sourcebook of County Court Records: A National Guide to Civil, Criminal, and Probate Records....** 3d ed. Michael L. Sankey and Carl R. Ernst, eds. Tempe, Ariz., BRB, 1997. 639p. (The Public Record Research Library). $35.00pa. ISBN 1-879792-33-8.

This specialized sourcebook could be a godsend to libraries with frequent questions on locating county court records. More than 6,700 court entries are organized alphabetically by state and by county. These courts handle felonies, civil actions of more than $2,500, probate, misdemeanors, evictions, and small claims. Each state section begins with three charts that condense the court structure for courts of original jurisdiction. The charts provide a most useful and quick way to compare state court systems, which vary greatly. However, the charts can oversimplify the situation and possibly misguide users who do not dig deeper into the court profiles.

Introductory pages on searching for court records give practical advice and basic information to the lay reader. Types of litigation, state court structure, and computerization of courts are discussed. The court profile is the meat of this reference tool. Included are the basics: address, telephone number, time zone, and fax number. Valuable information details whether the court accepts searches by telephone, whether the office's records are accessible by modem, the payee for checks, certification fees, the status of online system availability, and so on. The sourcebook appears to be thorough; the 31,000 entries cover every official U.S. Postal Service place-name in the city/county cross-reference section.

Potential purchasers who are wondering if the information in this book is available on the Internet can probably trust the editors' statement that only 15 percent of public records can be found online. No other reference materials satisfy this unique niche.—**Georgia Briscoe**

525. **The Sourcebook of Local Court and County Record Retrievers: The Definitive Guide to Searching for Public Record Information at the State Level.** 3d ed. Michael L. Sankey and Carl R. Ernst, eds. Tempe, Ariz., BRB, 1997. 540p. (The Public Record Research Library). $45.00pa. ISBN 1-879792-37-0.

If researchers are seeking information that has roots in a public record, this may be a book for them. *The Sourcebook of Local Court and County Record Retrievers* is a comprehensive reference of more than 2,400 businesses that retrieve documents from local courts and probates, U.S. District Courts, U.S. Bankruptcy Courts, property liens and recordings, marriage records, divorce records, birth and death records, voter registration records, and federal records centers.

The directory is extremely easy to use, with clear and concise directions in the introduction. Section 1, the county index, is alphabetically organized by state. All the counties are listed alphabetically with the names and telephone numbers of record retrievers who do business in that area. A simple code is used that explains the type of court and county records available, and the key is handily repeated before each state's list. Section 2, the retriever profiles, lists all of the record retrievers mentioned in section 1. Included in the profiles are an address, telephone and fax numbers, retrieval areas, normal turnaround time, and any special services provided. Specific search fees are not mentioned.

This is an ideal directory for legal professionals, investigators, credit and collection personnel, and reference librarians. It is a must-have for genealogical researchers.—**Mary L. Trenerry**

Handbooks and Yearbooks

526. Biskupic, Joan, and Elder Witt. **Guide to the U.S. Supreme Court.** 3d ed. Washington, D.C., Congressional Quarterly, 1997. 2v. illus. index. $299.00/set. ISBN 1-56802-130-5.

This comprehensive reference work examines the history and development of the Supreme Court, along with its people and their decisions. The book is composed of 6 parts divided into numbered chapters for quick and easy reference. Part 1 traces the growth of the Court from an idea to a powerful institution; part 2 examines the Court's influence on the U.S. system of government, the rulings affecting the powers of Congress, the president, the lower federal courts, and the states; part 3 surveys the impact of the Court's rulings on the rights and freedoms of the individual; part 4 examines the influence of public opinion and the press on the Court; part 5 reviews the history of the Court's operations and functions; and part 6 provides biographical sketches and pictures of each of the 108 justices who have served on the Court. A large "Reference Materials" section contains documents and texts that trace the Court's history as well as the full text of 5 landmark rulings and summaries of more than 400 major decisions.

Now in 2 volumes, Congressional Quarterly's *Guide to the U.S. Supreme Court* is completely updated and enlarged to cover recent judicial appointments and legal issues that have developed since the 2d edition was published in 1990. It includes 150 new cases and more than 270 photographs, editorial cartoons, drawings, and maps. Extensive notes and a selected bibliography listing scholarly and general sources of additional information is included for readers who want to pursue their own research on a particular decision or legal issue. Both volumes contain detailed case and subject indexes. The case index includes every decision mentioned in the book, along with a complete legal citation for each case. This 3d edition continues its commitment to providing accurate, thoughtful, and readable information and is highly recommended for all large libraries.—**Deborah A. Taylor**

527. Boire, Richard Glen. **Marijuana Law.** 2d ed. Berkeley, Calif., Ronin Publishing, 1996. 271p. index. $14.95pa. ISBN 0-914171-86-0.

Boire is a California criminal defense attorney who believes that individuals should have just as much freedom to choose to use marijuana as to read what they like. Accordingly, he has written a guide on using the Bill of Rights and other legal protections to resist what he considers to be oppressive governmental interference with using or growing marijuana. He examines in detail how courts have ruled on the legality of various law enforcement stratagems to detect marijuana cultivation, possession, or use. Full legal citations are given for court cases and U.S. Code sections; an appendix lists which states are in which U.S. circuit courts, so that readers can find the legal precedents that apply in their jurisdiction. Another appendix lists legal penalties for marijuana crimes by state. Other topics covered include guides to how law enforcement agencies gather information, searches, drug testing, medical use of marijuana, and what to do if arrested.

Although the book is clearly intended to help readers avoid legal penalties for marijuana use, it also makes clear the legal rights of law enforcement agencies. The book offers a great deal of information on law related to drugs, although someone in legal jeopardy would also need to consult a lawyer. What Boire does not offer is any real discussion of the philosophical, moral, medical, and political issues and arguments related to government regulation of drugs. Libraries interested in those issues may want to consider Erich Goode's *Between Politics and Reason: The Drug Legalization Debate* (St. Martin's Press, 1997).
—**Marit S. MacArthur**

528. **Civil Trial Practice Deskbook.** 1997 ed. Robert A. Robbins, Jane E. Hadro, and Joan C. Rogers, eds. Washington, D.C., BNA Books, 1997. 1007p. index. $250.00pa. ISBN 1-57018-006-7.

This title was compiled with the express purpose of being a complete resource on the art and practice of civil litigation in the United States. It lives up to its ambitious goal with extraordinary clarity and completeness. Understanding the rules of civil procedure and the art of prosecuting or defending a lawsuit within their parameters is something that is at the root of the lawyer's craft. Yet this is not an easy thing to do. As a result, handbooks and guidebooks that help the lawyer comprehend the ins and outs of suing have been a cottage industry throughout legal history. There have been countless attempts to make the complex procedures of civil litigation both understandable and manageable. Essentially, this book is one of the latest in a long tradition in the legal publishing industry; however, it is more than merely another attempt at accomplishing the near impossible. This book succeeds in ways in which others have not been able.

The format of the book is roughly sequential. Each chapter discusses a potential step in the prosecution of a civil case according to the most likely sequence in which it is likely to arise. The topics covered are nearly exhaustive, treating everything from client interview to judgment, including gathering of evidence, selecting expert witnesses and jurors, and tips on opening and closing statements. The boldest feature of the book is its ability to handle with clarity a topic that necessarily contains variations from state to state and from state to federal jurisdictions. In each chapter, differences among the states and federal jurisdictions are clearly spelled out. Each chapter also includes a useful bibliography that directs the user to other important sources of information.

Overall, the book is a well-executed handbook on civil litigation that will be useful to practitioners and *pro se* litigants. It is an appropriate tool for basic reference collections that serve lay patrons who are in need of expert guidance in handling their own lawsuits as well as for libraries serving experienced lawyers. However, as the title of the book implies, its primary audience is members of the bar, and it is intended as a practical reference tool for day-to-day litigation practitioners.—**Richard A. Leiter**

529. **Congressional Quarterly's Guide to the U.S. Supreme Court.** 3d ed. By Joan Biskupic and Elder Witt. Washington, D.C., Congressional Quarterly, 1997. 2v. illus. index. $289.00/set. ISBN 1-56802-130-5.

Lamentably, rational and moral thought in the United States has fallen on hard times. With the passing of the 1960s, ethical decision-making has nose-dive in an abyss from which it may never recover. Much of that decline can be traced to court decisions during the past 20 years. Therefore, this 3d edition of *Congressional Quarterly's Guide to the Supreme Court* is most welcome. What makes the guide so useful is its comprehensive approach to the subject matter. Beginning with the origins of the court, readers are taken on a guided tour from the Constitution to the federal courts, Franklin Delano Roosevelt's threat of packing of the court, and today's various litmus tests. Throughout these hefty volumes, readers will find abundant information on every ruling (more than 150 new cases are examined); the Court's own internal inconsistencies; sidebars of curious but useful information; and graphs, charts, and tables of every turn the Court has made. Indexes of cases, a comprehensive subject index, appendixes of documents (e.g., Declaration of Independence, Articles of Confederation, *Marbury v. Madison*) and tables, and a bibliography of hundreds of sources round out these fine volumes. All of this information is graced by superb writing and provocative thought.

Nothing is left undone in this set. Every difficult case is recalled. Those using the volumes cannot fail to come away with a clear understanding of what the most powerful court in the land has wrought for this country and its citizens. Almost no library, regardless of size, can afford to be without this important guide.
—**Mark Y. Herring**

530. **Employment Discrimination Law.** 3d ed. By Barbara Lindemann and Paul Grossman. Paul W. Cane Jr. and others, eds. Washington, D.C., BNA Books, 1996. 2v. index. $445.00/set. ISBN 0-87179-791-7.

Lindemann and Grossman's treatise is one of the most important works available on the law of employment discrimination. The new edition includes reference to and commentary on Supreme Court cases through the end of the 1995-1996 term and important lower court decisions rendered through late 1995. The continually developing field of employment discrimination law is arguably more volatile today than it was when the 1st edition was published in 1976. Fortunately, as with prior editions, BNA Books plans to publish annual updates.

Employment Discrimination Law is designed for both practitioners and legal scholars. It is heavily footnoted (BNA Books claims the editors supply citations to nearly 7,000 cases), and the table of cases alone takes up more than 200 pages. Dozens of experts had their hand in preparing the 43 chapters. It is to the editors' credit that the text flows as smoothly as it does, although one can identify different styles from chapter to chapter.

Produced by the American Bar Association's Section on Labor and Employment Law, *Employment Discrimination Law* is not a title for most public or even university libraries. It does, however, belong on the shelves of all law libraries, as well as in the offices of those who practice in this area.
—**James S. Heller**

531. Fosbrook, Deborah, and Adrian C. Laing. **A-Z of Contract Clauses.** London, Sweet & Maxwell; distr., Scarborough, Ont., Carswell, 1997. 519p. index. $95.00. ISBN 0-421-50720-9.

This book is unique among law books. In a simple, straightforward format, the authors present the practitioner with a tremendously useful and usable tool for crafting contracts. The book lays out in clear, concise language hundreds, if not thousands, of contract clauses that may be used as models for actual wording of legally binding contracts. As the title implies, the material in the book is arranged in alphabetic order by topic. The topics covered in the book are extremely broad, from ordinary contracts of sale to complex employment agreements and from issues involving jurisdictional agreements to restraint of trade. The material is also organized with a convenient alphanumeric system that allows for easy reference and access to specific clauses. This arrangement will also make for easy updating of the material in the future. The book comes with two computer disks that contain all of the material in the book in a format that will allow for easy "cutting and pasting" in the creation of new contracts.

Despite the book's uniqueness and its practical organization and execution, it suffers from a single flaw from the perspective of libraries in the United States: Contract clauses apply to the law of the United Kingdom and not the law of the United States. This fact is unfortunate because the book should have wide appeal to all libraries that serve patrons with occasional need for materials to help them draft legal contracts. However, for libraries in the United Kingdom, this book will be a necessary addition to the legal reference shelf.—**Richard A. Leiter**

532. **Great World Trials.** Edward W. Knappman, ed. Detroit, Gale, 1997. 536p. illus. index. $50.00. ISBN 0-7876-0805-X.

Gale has followed up its 1994 reference book *Great American Trials* (see ARBA 95, entry 613) with this wonderful overview of great world trials. In his preface, Knappman explains how cases covering 25 centuries of trials from more than 30 countries were selected for inclusion in the present work. The three criteria for selection were political significance, historical significance, and public attention. For example, trials of political significance include cases where governments perceived defendants as threats to the established political order. In several of these cases, the religious and secular worlds combined to exert political power, which accounts for the inclusion of such trials as those of Socrates, Jesus, Thomas More, and Galileo. Trials of historical significance were selected based on their overall impact on history. Here readers will find trials surrounding the French Revolution, various ideological battles, and war crimes, among others. Trials of public attention were selected based on their impact from the rise of mass media. These trials were based on high-profile cases of brutality, notoriety of the victim or the defendant, or a widely perceived case of injustice.

These criteria were used singly and collectively to reduce to 100 cases what can be called "great trials." There is no claim that these are necessarily the greatest trials, but there is no question but that they have impacted parts of the world significantly in one way or another. The book is a model of clarity in organization. There are four tables of contents; each entry includes suggestions for further reading; photographs and drawings enhance the presentations; and a comprehensive index references key figures, subjects, and areas of law. Reference collections of all types would be enhanced by the addition of this collection. It is highly recommended.—**Michael A. Foley**

533. **Information Sources in Law.** 2d ed. Jules Winterton and Elizabeth M. Moys, eds. New Providence, N.J., Bowker-Saur/Reed Reference Publishing, 1997. 673p. index. (Guides to Information Sources). $95.00. ISBN 1-85739-041-5.

In this 2d edition of *Information Sources in Law* in the Guides to Information Sources series, the editors cover new ground by addressing non-English-speaking jurisdictions, whereas the 1st edition dealt mainly with English-speaking jurisdictions. The foreword outlines the countries and jurisdiction units covered, followed by a list of the subjects addressed in each chapter.

The first chapter of this work, "General Sources," elaborates on each type of legal resource covered. It provides a general description of the legal system of each country or organizational unit as well as resource types, including legislation, codes and commentaries, treatises, periodicals, and other serial publications. Each chapter ends with a list of useful addresses, both print and electronic, and a comprehensive "List of Works Cited in the Chapter." A number of electronic sources are included.

Subsequent chapters deal with a country or group of countries and follow the format outlined in the first chapter as closely as possible. Because many of the materials cited are not in English, subject specialists fluent in the various languages comprise the group of 34 contributors to this volume. A very selective country index follows the body of this more than 650-page work.

This detailed and well-edited reference work is a must for any academic, large public, or specialized legal and international collection. The $95.00 price tag is appropriate for the amount of specialized, multilingual research required for its compilation.—**Linda D. Tietjen**

534. **Legal Research: How to Find and Understand the Law.** 5th ed. By Stephen Elias and Susan Levinkind. Janet Portman, ed. Berkeley, Calif., Nolo Press, 1997. 1v. (various paging). illus. index. $19.95pa. ISBN 0-87337-401-0.

The purpose of this guide continues to be the practice of legal research in law libraries. It presents a successful, systematic method for finding answers, learning the legal system, and evaluating decisions. Using a format established with previous editions, an overview of legal research and the law is followed by instructions on identifying problems, locating materials, and understanding such documents as statutes. This guidance is enhanced with hypothetical and self-teaching problems, examples, review questions, unique features, and a topical index. With this edition, chapter discussions have been updated with current terminology (e.g., *cyberlaw*), alternate Internet resources (e.g., Findlaw, Practice Manual Equivalents on the Web), and Internet search strategies. Consideration of the two primary online systems (Lexis and Westlaw) remains somewhat simplistic for the uninitiated, with none of the bibliographic references found elsewhere, and no mention of the access restrictions and printing charges imposed by many libraries.

Even though librarians will continue to rely on the index and lists, a bibliography would ensure that all important legal resources have been acquired. This work continues to improve and is recommended for law libraries and other libraries with extensive legal collections.—**Sandra E. Belanger**

535. MacLeod, Don. **The Internet Guide for the Legal Researcher.** 2d ed. Teaneck, N.J., Infosources, 1997. 1v. (various paging). illus. index. $55.00pa. ISBN 0-939486-46-6.

Everything about the 2d edition of *The Internet Guide for the Legal Researcher* speaks of a work in progress, one which will be continuously updated over time. In fact it appears to be a work that can be almost as easily updated as its primary, ever-changing information source, the Internet. From its chapter/page numbering scheme instead of continuous book numbering and the unjustified text margins, to its 8½-by-11-inch softcover format, this work is more like a looseleaf system than a traditional book. Two 1998 updates are offered as the first means of keeping the information in the book timely.

MacLeod is in charge of Web publications at a law firm in New York City and is the editor in chief of the monthly newsletter *Internet Law Researcher*. The stated purpose of the 2d edition of *The Internet Guide for the Legal Researcher* is to write a book useful for integrating the Internet into day-to-day legal projects in the most jargon-free way. MacLeod has succeeded in writing a book that not only recommends how to get set up for Internet research—everything from choosing an ISP to using e-mail, newsgroups, and various search engine protocols—but manages to do so in an organized and jargon-free manner. Unlike other resources, such as *The Legal List Internet Desk Reference: Law-Related Resources on the Internet and Elsewhere* (Lawyers Cooperative, 1995), this is not a mere checklist of typed URLs but a source that displays the graphics of actual Web pages.

After a thorough introduction to Internet usage, MacLeod explores Web content. Several large chapters, "Federal and International Resources," "State and Local Resources," and "Reference Resources," comprise most of the work.

Following introductory remarks, each page in these chapters follows a similar format: name of the site, URL, a shaded "highlights" box with explanatory text, and a graphic of the site's homepage. The "Federal/International" chapter contains information on numerous government agencies, as well as sites for each federal circuit court district, Thomas, Government Printing Office access, and a one-page overview of international resources. The "State and Local Resources" chapter provides Internet legal resources for each state of the Union.

The last chapter of the book fills in gaps with URLs not fitting neatly into the jurisdiction model. Examples include Websites for the American Bar Association, online newspaper sites, court TV, listservs, and dictionaries, to name a few. Following this chapter are a glossary of terms and an index.

This book was written with inevitable updates required by the Internet in mind. It is a valuable resource, highly recommended for college and university libraries, public libraries, and specialized law or government publications collections. It is a pioneering reference work dealing with the ever-changing, yet imminently unavoidable, resource known as the Internet.—**Linda D. Tietjen**

536. **The MVR Book Motor Services Guide: The National Reference Detailing, in Practical Terms, the Privacy Restrictions....** 1997 ed. Michael Sankey, ed. Tempe, Ariz., BRB, 1997. 270p. (The Public Record Research Library). $19.00pa. ISBN 1-879792-35-4.

537. **The MVR Decoder Digest: The Companion to the MVR Book....** 1997 ed. Michael Sankey, ed. Tempe, Ariz., BRB, 1997. 311p. (The Public Record Research Library). $19.00pa. ISBN 1-879792-36-2.

The *Guide* has, in addition to the subtitle above, information on access procedures, regulations, and systems of all state-held driver and vehicle records. Specifically, the listing for Illinois includes "General Help Numbers and Agencies"; "Driver Licensing Facts" (terms, age, classes, and the like); "Safety and Enforcement" (insurance, alcohol, accident reports); "Obtaining Drive-Related Records" (access, how to obtain); "Vehicle Plates and Facts" (classes, number codes, and so forth); and "Obtaining Vehicle-Related Records" (access, liens, and so on). Entries for other states cover similar topics and information, in greater or lesser detail, depending on the laws of that state.

The *Digest* lists and translates the codes and abbreviations of violations and licensing groups appearing on motor vehicle records for every state. Here, entries provide names of principal officers of the state departments; license classes, restrictions, and endorsements; and violation codes, points, and descriptions, which in the case of Illinois include action codes and the Illinois Vehicle Code. Because state codes vary so widely, there are enormous differences; for example, Indiana's code is summarized in two pages, and some states have no point system.

There is little or nothing here that is not readily available within the individual state. The value of these volumes to larger libraries is the access to information for all the states in one source.—**Walter C. Allen**

538. Paddock, Lisa. **Facts About the Supreme Court of the United States.** Bronx, N.Y., H. W. Wilson, 1996. 569p. illus. index. $55.00. ISBN 0-8242-0896-X.

It would be difficult to find a better one-volume historical survey of the Supreme Court than this one for the general reader. As Paddock writes in the preface, this volume "is a straightforward, chronologically organized reference compilation of essential historical information about one of the nation's oldest and most important institutions." The substantive part of the book opens with a brief but clear and coherent introduction to the nature, purpose, and scope of Supreme Court judicial decision-making, followed by a historical overview of the Supreme Court. For individuals looking for a general introduction to and understanding of the Supreme Court, these opening pages will be extremely helpful.

Thereafter, each chapter provides an overview of the Supreme Court in terms of each of the chief justices. Each of these chapters contains brief biographical information about the people who served on the Court during a particular chief justice's term, some historical information that gives a framework within which to understand some of the issues the Court faced during those years, and a brief explanation of the leading cases decided by the Court in question. In addition, the reader will find the political composition of the Supreme Court for that term, any voting patterns that may have emerged, and any special features of the Court during the term under review.

The appendixes include the Constitution; Title 28; Judiciary and Judicial Procedure of the United States Code Annotated, 1995; and a copy of the rules of the Supreme Court. The book concludes with a helpful glossary, a list of sources for further study, an index of cases, and a general index. If one seeks some quick "facts" about the Supreme Court, this is certainly the work to which to turn.—**Michael A. Foley**

539. Perlman, Seth, and Betsy Hills Bush. **Fund-Raising Regulation: A State-by-State Handbook of Registration Forms, Requirements, and Procedures.** New York, John Wiley, 1996. 2v. (Non-Profit Law, Finance, and Management Series). $295.00/set looseleaf w/binders. ISBN 0-471-14253-0.

As the authors of this collection note in their introduction to the myriad forms and reporting mechanisms mandated by state regulatory agencies, one of the constants in the fund-raising business is the increasing amount of paperwork necessary to meet state reporting requirements. The purpose of this two-volume reference work is to provide a state-by-state guide to the rules and regulations for charities and fund-raising.

Basically, information and representative forms from each state are furnished (with the exception of states such as Delaware, Montana, Nevada, and Wyoming, which had no relevant statutes at the time these volumes were prepared), along with the address of the state registration agency. As the attention of the public becomes more focused on charities and fund-raising activities, nonprofit organizations will need up-to-date information regarding state accountability. This reference work should prove helpful. The 1st volume begins with a brief history of fund-raising regulations, complete with a brief discussion of regulatory trends (including reference to 3 Supreme Court decisions that place some limits on state regulation); required disclosures; commercial coventurers; and sanctions. In addition, the authors offer a guide on how to use these volumes. Before moving to a state-by-state description, the authors provide eight tables that include information on such things as nonprofit organization registration requirements, charitable solicitation disclosures, and professional solicitor disclosures, among others.

Any nonprofit organization that depends on substantive fund-raising activities should have a copy of the guides presented in these volumes. Public libraries should have this set available for use by smaller nonprofit organizations and agencies in their community.—**Michael A. Foley**

540. Renstrom, Peter G. **Constitutional Law and Young Adults.** 2d ed. Santa Barbara, Calif., ABC-CLIO, 1996. 497p. index. $45.00. ISBN 0-87436-850-2.

An update of the 1992 edition, this revision includes cases decided as recently as 1996. The purpose of the book is to introduce young people (secondary and junior college) to the U.S. Constitution, and specifically to the individual rights of the Bill of Rights and the Fourteenth Amendment. The primary component of constitutionalism examined in the book is, according to the author, the institutional restraints on political and governmental power, or what keeps government from violating citizens' rights.

The organization and writing style make this a useful reference tool. Introductory chapters explain the history of the Constitution, the court system, and the juvenile justice system. Remaining chapters examine the evolution of constitutional concepts of interest to young adults. These include such diverse topics as hate speech, capital punishment, abortion clinics, drug testing, homosexual rights, and automobile and school locker searches. The U.S. Constitution, amendments, and names of U.S. Supreme Court justices are appended. The numbering system for cases and other valuable pointers are explained in "A Note on How to Use This Book."

Recent and complete coverage of decisions is always difficult in this format. However, the author could have indicated when he stopped examining U.S. Supreme Court decisions for this revision. This information would have been helpful to those seeking to update the book. Curiously, appendix A does not contain the Twenty-seventh Amendment to the Constitution, although it was ratified in 1992. [R: RQ, Summer 97, pp. 613-14]—**Bev Cummings Agnew**

541. Sitarz, Daniel. **The Complete Book of Personal Legal Forms.** 2d ed. Carbondale, Ill., Nova Publishing, 1997. 253p. index. (The Legal Self-Help Series). $29.95pa (with disk). ISBN 0-935755-28-4.

With the cost of legal assistance in civil matters increasing, many people have turned to self-help law books. The title under review claims to include "all of the legal forms and documents necessary to allow individuals and families to handle their own day-to-day legal problems without the need for an attorney." The 19 chapters include contracts, signatures and notary acknowledgments, powers of attorney, wills and trusts (including living wills), premarital and marital settlement agreements, releases, receipts, leases and sales of real and personal property, documents dealing with personal loans and promissory notes, and miscellaneous documents.

In most cases the documents are similar to the boilerplate forms an attorney uses to complete them. Each chapter is introduced by an overview of the topic covered and a description of the document forms provided. The forms are designed to be photocopied and used as a framework for preparing the finished document, with blanks left for the user to insert information. Questionnaires for completing wills for and preparing for premarital and marital settlement agreements are included. There is a brief glossary of legal terms and an index. Sitarz is careful to point out he need for professional legal help in using these documents, particularly if the individual's situation is complicated.

The software consists of the printed forms in ASCII format and can be used with common word processing programs. Instructions for loading and using the software are clear and easy to understand.

Because the book is available without the accompanying software, librarians may wish to purchase that edition at the reasonable price of $19.95. With or without the software, this title is recommended for public libraries, and may also be useful in educational institutions supporting paralegal or legal secretarial curricula.—**Sue Kamm**

542. Sitarz, Daniel. **The Complete Book of Small Business Legal Forms.** 2d ed. Carbondale, Ill., Nova Publishing, 1997. 253p. index. (The Small Business Library Series). $29.95pa (with disk). ISBN 0-935755-27-6.

Like other titles in the publisher's series of legal self-help books, *The Complete Book of Small Business Legal Forms* is designed to provide a boilerplate for documents the user may need in the course of business. Business operation agreements, including sole proprietorships, partnerships, corporations, and other agreements; contracts; signature and notary acknowledgments; powers of attorney; releases; receipts; real estate and personal property leases and sales; employment documents; credit documents; and purchasing and sale of goods documents are among the topics covered. Each chapter includes an overview of the subject as well as the forms necessary for the transaction described. When used without the accompanying software, the book is designed to be photocopied for the document draft, which can then be typed in a final form. The software includes all the forms in ASCII format, and are compatible with personal computer software. (Macintosh users may obtain a disk for use with their systems from the publisher.) Terms are briefly defined within the text.

The title under review will be useful in public libraries as well as academic and secondary school libraries offering paralegal or legal secretarial courses. Librarians may wish to obtain two copies—one with the software for circulation and the book alone for reference use.—**Sue Kamm**

543. Smith, Robert Ellis. **Compilation of State and Federal Privacy Laws.** 1997 ed. Providence, R.I., Privacy Journal, 1997. 119p. $29.00pa. ISBN 0-930072-11-1.

This book is a compilation of state and federal privacy laws including citations and descriptions of all of the laws affecting privacy. It also provides a brief update on statutory law and court cases dealing with these issues. A convenient addition is the chart that shows what states have laws in regard to many privacy issues. The publication consists of an alphabetic list by state of privacy laws, such as arrest records, bank records, cable television, computer crime, credit, criminal justice, electronic surveillance, employment, government information, insurance, library records, mailing lists, medical, polygraphing, privacy statutes, privileges, school records, social security number, tax records, telephone services, and testing in employment. The appendix lists several federal laws affecting privacy as well as New Jersey's Genetic Privacy Act and Canadian laws of a similar nature. The appendix is easy to use with its alphabetic listing by state within each topic.

This edition contains new laws relating to genetic testing and comparison. The first section of the publication includes laws that permit the expunction or correction of individual arrest records. The next section describes laws setting disclosure and accuracy policies for criminal justice information systems. The section on employment records has especially changed since earlier editions, whereby several states have enacted laws permitting public and private employees to inspect (and in a few cases, correct) their own personnel files. This book should be an excellent addition to the consumer law section of public libraries for attorneys, citizens, legislators, public interest groups, lobbyists, and researchers. The publisher also publishes supplements through the *Privacy Journal* of state and federal laws affecting the confidentiality of personal information.—**Theresa Maggio**

544. **Women's Legal Guide.** Barbara R. Hauser, with Julie A. Tigges, eds. Golden, Colo., Fulcrum, 1996. 526p. index. $39.95; $22.95pa. ISBN 1-55591-913-8; 1-55591-303-2pa.

Women's Legal Guide is a comprehensive guide to legal issues affecting every woman. Hauser is a practicing attorney with a J.D. from the University of Pennsylvania. She is a member of the American Bar Association, the Union Internationale des Avocats, and the International Bar Association (London).

The guide is published with a caveat on the verso page: "This book is not intended to give specific legal advice on any issue. To obtain legal advice, you need to retain an attorney." The preface, written by Hauser, sets out the purpose of the book; the benefit for the reader; why this book is special; authority, organization, and scope of the book; and intended audience.

Written by 29 women lawyers, *Women's Legal Guide* provides up-to-date information and navigates readers through complex legal processes with sample forms, lists, and letters. From a parent who would like to hire a nanny to a businesswoman who needs to be aware of laws governing the workplace, women in all stages of life will find this guide an indispensable resource.

The chapters are arranged in broad topics beginning with personal/body issues, such as health care, patient rights, reproductive rights, and sexual assault. The next group of chapters deals with family law, children's rights, marriage and divorce, adopting a child, and placing a child for adoption. The third section deals with rights, generally in school and the workplace; sexual harassment or discrimination; women in sports; rights of lesbian women; and disabled women. The fourth section treats business law; for example, starting a business, intellectual property rights, real estate, bankruptcy, and consumer rights. The fifth section details issues that will affect women as they move toward the end of their careers and lives and as they care for aging parents. The final chapter and afterword move to a broader arena and spotlight issues of refugee women and the impact the law can have on improving the equality of women on a global basis.

Each of the 25 chapters are organized in the same way, allowing consistency and ease of use. There is a chapter outline that shows each topic to be covered. As one looks through the chapter, the topics, in bold typeface, are listed not only in the text but also in the margin so that the reader can find the specific section quickly. At the end of each chapter there are a bibliography, a list of general resources, and a biographical sketch of the author of the chapter. Topics discussed in the book can be found in the comprehensive index. There are also a glossary and a list of general resources, which includes bibliographic references as well as information on legal organizations in various states.

In today's complex world, women need to be aware of their legal rights. *Women's Legal Guide* is a groundbreaking reference book that pulls together in one volume the information women need to know about how their lives intersect with the law. This comprehensive guide is for every woman.

—**Barbara B. Goldstein**

Indexes

545. **Patent Law Index.** 1997 ed. By Christopher M. Pickett. Washington, D.C., BNA Books, 1997. 503p. $75.00pa. ISBN 1-57018-033-4. ISSN 1092-6828.

Pickett's index is designed to help patent lawyers and others who research patent law to locate quickly any potentially relevant information from federal statutes and regulations, from the *Manual of Patent Examining Procedure* (MPEP), and from three leading treatises on patent law. In Pickett's own words, "My intent was to make the book compact enough to reside on the practitioner's desk where it may be regularly used to guide him or her to the most relevant points of interest. *Patent Law Index* is intended to give the user some definite starting points for research . . . [but] may also alert researchers to issues that they might otherwise have overlooked" (introduction). (Civil War buffs may want to call this "Pickett's Charge.")

The author created 135 topic headings—which in turn are broken down into nearly 3,000 subtopics—to provide citations to specific sections of the primary and secondary sources. He cross-indexes statutes and regulations almost exclusively from Title 35 of the *United States Code* and Title 37 of the *Code of Federal Regulations*; from the MPEP; and from Donald Chisum's *Patent Law Fundamentals*, Peter Rosenberg's *Patent Law Fundamentals*, and Robert Harmon's *Patents and the Federal Circuit*. (Those readers not familiar with these titles of the *U.S. Code* and CFR or with these authors probably do not need this book.) Pickett also includes three indexes by USC, CFR, and MPEP sections, as well as the table of contents from the six referenced sources.

At a modest cost (for law books), *Patent Law Index* probably will be a useful supplemental research aid for some researchers. How helpful will depend on one's own experience.—**James S. Heller**

CRIMINOLOGY

Bibliography

546. Harrison, Ben. **True Crime Narratives: An Annotated Bibliography.** Lanham, Md., Scarecrow, 1997. 748p. index. $65.00. ISBN 0-8108-3260-7.

Harrison has taken on the daunting task of compiling a bibliography of the "true crime" genre—fact-based narratives about crime. Although his study covers only monographs produced in the mid-nineteenth century through 1993, his introductory essay traces the historical origins of the genre from its roots in fifteenth- and sixteenth-century English ballads up through the modern era. Even excluding works of sociology, criminology, and fiction, what remains is more than 3,000 unique bibliographic entries arranged under such broad subject headings as "Classic British Cases" and "Law Enforcement Personnel." Each entry contains a brief, largely nonevaluative, descriptive annotation. Access is provided by an author/title and a subject index. A case name glossary is also included.

In attempting to cover the totality of the so-called true crime genre, Harrison has overextended himself. This compilation lacks focus and comprehensiveness. Had he limited himself solely to murder cases (rather than nonfatal crimes and the like), the study would have proved more useful. Even here, however, there are notable omissions. He lists two titles on Texas-based serial killer Dean Corll but omits David Hanna's paperback account *Harvest of Horror* (1975). Likewise, he notes the book about killer cop Robert Erler but fails to cite the book written by him, *The Catch-Me Killer* (1980). Annotations are often too uneven. In several anthologies of murder cases, Harrison provides names of killers in the style of the popular *The New Murderers' Who's Who* (1989), but in others (e.g., *Practitioners of Murder*) he does not, even though the book covers a manageable number.

Embarrassing misspellings and faulty indexing abound. Florida serial killer Aileen "Lee" Wuornos is cited as "Wuornes" in the index and in one of the two entries on her. Teenaged killer Sean Sellers is cited as "Sellars" in the subject index, whereas the corresponding entry number points to a title on 15-year-old killer Wayne Dresbach. The 1989 book on Sellers, *Devil Child*, has a different entry number. Nor does Harrison cite the book *by* Sellers, *Web of Darkness* (1990). Although useful as a collection aid for large public and academic libraries, aficionados of the genre will be disappointed.—**David K. Frasier**

547. Moses, Norton H., comp. **Lynching and Vigilantism in the United States: An Annotated Bibliography.** Westport, Conn., Greenwood Press, 1997. 441p. index. (Bibliographies and Indexes in American History, no.34). $85.00. ISBN 0-313-30177-8.

A history professor at Montana State University in Billings has compiled this descriptively annotated bibliography of more than 4,200 entries from books, parts of books, articles, government documents, and unpublished theses and dissertations covering the 1760s to the present. After a chapter on general works, a portion of this volume is arranged chronologically from the 1760s to 1996, followed by topical chapters on such subjects as the frontier West; antilynching; fiction, poetry, ballads, and films; and artworks. Each chapter is arranged alphabetically by author or title if the author is unidentified.

An author index of both persons and organizations (e.g., American Civil Liberties Union, National Association for the Advancement of Colored People, U.S. Commission on Civil Rights) is followed by a subject index, which includes numerous geographic locales; names of individuals (William Faulkner, Abraham Lincoln, Franklin and Theodore Roosevelt, and Emmett Till, for example) and organizations; and other topics as varied as blacks as lynchers, the Ku Klux Klan, laws against lynching, and women and lynching. The volume concludes with an additional 21 entries that are not indexed. For serious students of U.S. lynching and vigilantism, this title should prove valuable as a starting point for further research.—**Wiley J. Williams**

548. Nordquist, Joan, comp. **Race, Crime, and the Criminal Justice System: A Bibliography.** Santa Cruz, Calif., Reference and Research Services, 1997. 72p. (Contemporary Social Issues: A Bibliographic Series, no.45). $15.00pa. ISBN 0-937855-88-X.

As the century comes to an end, it is in some respects an unfortunate commentary that interest in the intersection of race, crime, and the criminal justice system has intensified. This interest is a reflection of the persistence of racism as a significant element within the realm of crime and criminal justice and the enduring correlations between race, allegations of criminal conduct, and crime victimization. The present bibliography identifies a wide range of contemporary sources pertinent to the broad topic of race, crime, and the criminal justice system. Although reliance upon online databases obviously increases almost daily, this bibliography is part of a series premised on the notion (a credible one, it seems) that inexpensive print bibliographies can include many marginal sources not necessarily picked up by online searches.

The first half of *Race, Crime, and the Criminal Justice System* is devoted to books and articles on race, ethnicity, and the criminal justice system. In particular, 11 subheadings focus on such topics as the courts, the death penalty, imprisonment, police in the minority community, and minority women and the criminal justice system. The second half of the bibliography focuses on race, ethnicity, inequality, and crime. It attends to the literature on specific groups (e.g., African Americans, Latinos, Native Americans, minority youth, ethnic gangs, and so forth) and crime. A final brief section identifies sources of statistics, bibliographies, and Websites pertinent to the general topic of the bibliography.

Altogether, the modest cost of this bibliography should enhance its appeal to libraries as well as individuals. The bibliography is certainly current, with some 1997 publications. There are no annotations for the more than 800 entries, but researchers on virtually any level should find the bibliography provides a useful point of departure for their exploration of any aspect of race, crime, and criminal justice.

—**David O. Friedrichs**

549. O'Shea, Kathleen A., and Beverly R. Fletcher, comps. **Female Offenders: An Annotated Bibliography.** Westport, Conn., Greenwood Press, 1997. 264p. index. (Research and Bibliographical Guides in Criminal Justice, no.5). $79.50. ISBN 0-313-29228-0.

With an increasing number of women being arrested and convicted of crimes, a bibliography of the extensive but often elusive literature about female offenders is timely. *Female Offenders* includes more than 3,000 numbered entries arranged in such categories as crimes; arrest, prosecution, and sentencing; corrections; and probation and parole.

The bibliography is selective, with an emphasis on materials published in books and in scholarly and professional journals. All materials listed are published in English, and, consequently, international coverage is limited. The compilers excluded materials from the popular media and restricted the numbers of entries for dissertations, reports, and conference papers. As a result, users seeking the unusual or esoteric are unlikely to find it here.

The annotations are of little use. Only one sentence in length, many are little more than paraphrases of titles. In entries for studies, the compilers have deliberately excluded results from the annotations, further limiting their usefulness. Entries include all bibliographic information necessary to locate materials. However, the book's typeface is exceptionally small, making it difficult to browse entries and, perhaps, making it difficult for some people to use the guide. A list of bibliographies, an author index, and an adequate subject index are included.

In spite of its shortcomings, but because of its subject matter, this will be a useful resource for researchers and for law enforcement and criminal justice professionals. The work is recommended for law libraries, criminal justice and women's collections, and larger academic libraries.—**Gari-Anne Patzwald**

Dictionaries and Encyclopedias

550. **Crime and the Justice System in America: An Encyclopedia.** Frank Schmalleger, ed. Westport, Conn., Greenwood Press, 1997. 299p. index. $65.00. ISBN 0-313-29409-7.

The growth of reference works written for nonspecialists in the field of criminology has diversified since the 1983 publication of the *Encyclopedia of Crime and Justice* (see ARBA 84, entry 498). The focus has shifted to such areas as juvenile justice, special interest groups, and philosophic issues. This work, edited by the compiler of *Criminal Justice Ethics: Annotated Bibliography and Guide to Sources* (Greenwood, 1991), is multidisciplinary, taking as its principal subject the years 1960 to 1996. Categories of information include significant terminology, precedent-setting cases, key contemporary and historical figures (ranging from Wyatt Earp to O. J. Simpson and Sandra Day O'Connor), policy initiatives, key research studies and their results, major agencies involved in U.S. criminal justice processes, and social programs. All entries provide a listing of recommended readings for further research. A table of cited cases, both those included and others ranging from 1871 to 1993, allows easy cross-references for practicing lawyers. A valuable bibliographic essay offers librarians and researchers a survey of extant histories, encyclopedias (both on general criminal justice and subfields such as police science and corrections), anthologies, and works on contemporary controversies such as court-ordered drug testing. The book is most useful for large public libraries and university collections supporting criminal justice degree programs.—**Robert B. Marks Ridinger**

551. **Encyclopedia of World Terrorism.** Armonk, N.Y., Sharpe Reference/M. E. Sharpe, 1997. 3v. illus. maps. index. $299.00/set. ISBN 1-56324-806-9.

Often a great gap separates introductory material from the detailed and exhaustive tome. A short article in a magazine or general encyclopedia can be nearly as frustrating as the scholar's prying scrutiny of a subject. Everyone has need from time to time for information that falls between the two extremes. For instance, one can be aware of the Basque separatist movement and the turmoil it raises in Spain, but what if one wants more than a few sound bites from network news or three paragraphs from a national news magazine?

That reality is why *Encyclopedia of World Terrorism* is so useful. Three volumes cover every imaginable aspect of this grim subject, from terrorist fund-raising to terror in ancient Rome. Each section is readable and communicates a great deal of information, like a military intelligence briefing. There are photographs, maps, and diagrams as well as a chronology, a bibliography, and three different types of indexes. There is even an A to Z directory of terrorist groups and individuals.

This encyclopedia is the sort of reference work that librarians dream about. Interested in the psychology of hostages or perhaps Carlos the Jackal? This reviewer started with the Basque separatists and the Tamil Tigers and found a concise, clear guide to these movements. The encyclopedia does not prepare readers to formulate foreign policy, but they will certainly understand the issues and events involved after reading those sections of *Encyclopedia of World Terrorism*. This work is highly recommended for any size library, public or academic. It fills a need for current and reasonably comprehensive information on this important subject.—**George M. Cumming Jr.**

Handbooks and Yearbooks

552. **City Crime Rankings: Crime in Metropolitan America.** 3d ed. Kathleen O'Leary Morgan, Scott Morgan, and Neal Quitno, eds. Lawrence, Kans., Morgan Quitno Press, 1997. 392p. index. $37.95; $72.95 (with disk). ISBN 1-56692-315-8. ISSN 1081-6453.

For those individuals and librarians who experience difficulty in deciphering the statistical data presented in the FBI's annual publication, *Crime in the United States*, Morgan Quitno Press has reformatted the information into the work at hand. Covering the reporting year 1995, 90 simplified tables show the crime numbers, rates, and trends for some 266 U.S. metropolitan areas and more than 300 cities with populations of 75,000-plus. Reacting to criticism that the statistical information in an earlier edition was not adequately analyzed (see ARBA 96, entry 602), the editors have included a "Crime Overview" that briefly comments on the numbers presented. Preceding the government-collected data are the results of the "America's Safest Cities" competition and a joint crime study by the publisher and *Money Magazine* that examines safety levels for 266 metro areas and 202 cities with a population of more than 100,000. Based on their own methodology, the tandem ranked Amherst, New York, as the safest city and Newark, New Jersey, was placed last.

As stated, the FBI-collected statistical data for metropolitan areas and cities are presented in a user-friendly fashion. Twin tables, alphabetized by city and in numerically ranked order, are offered for a variety of categories: murder, rape, aggravated assault, robbery, and various types of property crimes. These tables require no statistical expertise to read and are useful in demonstrating crime trends and rates. *City Crime Rankings* is recommended for public libraries and those individuals who need quick, easy-to-understand statistics concerning crime in several larger U.S. cities and metropolitan areas.—**David K. Frasier**

553. **Guide to Federal Funding for Anti-Crime Programs.** 2d ed. Alvin C. Lin, ed. Arlington, Va., Government Information Services, 1997. 1v. (various paging). $287.45 looseleaf w/binder. ISBN 0-933544-94-4.

Guide to Federal Funding for Anti-Crime Programs is a well-organized and informative resource. Presented in a three-ring binder, the guide provides data on a variety of anticrime programs as well as information on grant-writing in general. The arrangement of the guide is somewhat different from other sources but proves to be effective. A table of contents and a general introduction begin the work, followed by an explanation of its arrangement. Comprehensive indexes follow other introductory material and are extremely useful for locating specific grant programs by name or by type.

The following categories of grants are covered: law enforcement, corrections, courts and legal assistance, substance abuse, crime prevention and public safety, juvenile and youth programs, child and family welfare, victim's services, and education and training for offenders. Each section follows the same format, outlining the purpose of the program, the application procedure, and the selection criteria. The "Program Profile," an information box containing helpful information (including fax numbers, Websites, and e-mail addresses), is especially useful.—**Michele Tyrrell**

554. Hearn, Daniel Allen. **Legal Executions in New York State: A Comprehensive Reference, 1639-1963.** Jefferson, N.C., McFarland, 1997. 365p. index. $65.00. ISBN 0-7864-0386-1.

This work is primarily a collection of entries detailing the crimes that led to execution in New York state, covering from 1639 until the state repealed the death penalty in 1965. The entries are arranged by the date the criminals were executed and include the age and race of the executed, a description of the crime leading to the execution (in some cases, graphic), as well as the date and method of execution. A subsequent section of primary sources, principally composed of local newspaper articles, is arranged chronologically and occasionally provides additional miscellaneous facts for the entries. A bibliography and comprehensive index follow, referencing entries by the criminal's and victim's name, the type and method of crime, and the county of execution. The text provides basic information on all the capital crimes that have led to an execution in the state of New York. When taken as a whole, the entries are useful in showing the application of capital punishment for various offenses for more than 300 years.

The book is entertaining, providing true crime aficionados the essential gory details along with citations for follow-up. Unfortunately, the preface is extremely short (approximately one page), and a more extensive discussion of the legal and social history of capital punishment in New York would have been useful. However, this reference is a mandatory purchase for academic and public libraries in the state of New York and all academic and large public libraries in the northeastern United States. It is an optional title for academic and larger libraries elsewhere.—**Mark A. Allan**

555. **Jane's Police and Security Equipment 1996-97.** 9th ed. Charles Heyman, ed. Alexandria, Va., Jane's Information Group, 1996. 563p. illus. index. $290.00. ISBN 0-7106-1359-8.

In this work, Jane's Information Group, the publishers of defense, aerospace, and transportation information, present the latest in police and security equipment technology. The volume uses the same standard format as other Jane's materials—a highly organized system that makes most other reference books seem messy.

How organized is *Jane's Police and Security Equipment*? First, each piece of equipment is categorized by type, further organized by manufacturing country, and finally, alphabetized. In this case, six sections are devoted to firearms, operational equipment, riot control, communications, access control, and personal protection. Second, each entry is given a complete description, including dimensions, the name of the supplier/manufacturer, production status, and where the equipment is being used. Notations are found with each entry on the status of the information—if the entry is new, or if old, whether or not it has been updated since the last volume. Third and last, clear black-and-white photographs are provided for most of the equipment, as well as colorful advertisements from some of the featured manufacturers.

Jane's standard format and thoroughness make this an ideal reference tool. In addition to the well-laid-out entries, index after index of manufacturers and equipment make the task of searching through the book an easy one. Not surprisingly, this work is a must for those who have a need for information on public safety and security equipment.—**Kelly M. Jordan**

556. Mickolus, Edward F., with Susan L. Simmons. **Terrorism, 1992-1995: A Chronology of Events and a Selectively Annotated Bibliography.** Westport, Conn., Greenwood Press, 1997. 958p. (Bibliographies and Indexes in Military Studies, no.9). $145.00. ISBN 0-313-30468-8.

This detailed chronology, the 5th in a series on international terrorist incidents by the principal author covering the period 1968 to 1995, is compiled from publicly available sources. Domestic incidents are included where relevant to international ones. It is derived from a database maintained by Mickolus's company, Vineyard, which specializes in databases on political violence and contains a partially annotated bibliography.

The introduction explains the rationale for editorial decisions and provides a table on terrorist attacks by month and year for 1992 to 1995. A 102-page chapter provides new information on terrorist incidents from 1950 to 1991. The 803-page chronology is arranged by date of first public knowledge of the incident. Entries range from paragraph-length to several pages. They are assigned 8-digit codes, the first 6 digits denoting date, and the last 2 represent an incident number within it. Acts considered domestic are skipped in this numbering. What makes an event international is not made explicit. The 50-page bibliography is only partly annotated, although it is a useful feature.

The absence of an index is an obstacle to the use of the volume for locating specific terrorists events and organizations. Mickolus explains this by stating that most users wanting nonchronological access will use electronic formats, both textual and numeric, which are available from his company. Although plausible as far as research scholars are concerned, the omission diminishes the volume's value to the broader academic community, including students and nonspecialists.

This thorough chronology on international terrorism from 1992 through 1995 should be strongly considered for research collections. However, the absence of indexes and the availability of electronic forms should be taken into account.—**Nigel Tappin**

557. **Terrorism in the United States.** Frank McGuckin, ed. Bronx, N.Y., H. W. Wilson, 1997. 131p. index. (The Reference Shelf, v.69, no.1). $20.00. ISBN 0-8242-0914-1.

Since its 1st issue in 1922, H. W. Wilson's series The Reference Shelf, this work has provided useful and well-organized sourcebooks for reprints of articles and book excerpts on current topics and social trends in the United States and the world. In addition to this volume, which focuses on the timely topic of "homegrown terrorism," other 1997 titles in the series feature discussions on the issues of multiculturalism, right to privacy, substance abuse, and wildlife conservation. Targeted at the undergraduate student preparing a term paper or speech, material is often taken from popular sources. In the volume under consideration, 18 articles are reprinted from sources such as *National Review*, *The New York Times*, *Time*, and *Good Housekeeping*. Brief editorial comments introduce each of the volume's 4 sections on some aspect of terrorism (politics, adherents, effects, prevention), and a select bibliography cites nearly 100 additional articles, books, and pamphlets on the topic. Particularly useful are appendixes listing organizations involved with terrorism analysis and World Wide Web sites for an additional six information sources (Clinton Administration Counter Terrorism Initiative, and so on). An index is included. Recommended for college and university libraries with undergraduate studies.—**David K. Frasier**

ENVIRONMENTAL LAW

558. Abate, Randall S. **A Directory of Environmental Law Education Opportunities at American Law Schools.** West Hartford, Conn., Graduate Group, 1997. 115p. $27.50 spiralbound.

Intended for use by university faculty, students, and career offices, this directory has the potential to become a useful addition to legal and educational reference collections. Environmental law covers pollution control (e.g., air, water, and hazardous waste) and related fields (e.g., natural resources, energy, and land use), which are special areas of interest to business and industry. Unfortunately, the volume, limited to American Bar Association-approved law schools in the United States, has several major weaknesses. Organized in two parts with considerable wasted space, the volume consists of alphabetic lists of colleges within four topical categories—curricular programs, clinical programs, reviews and journals, and competitions—in the first section, and by state in the second. In addition, no attempt has been made to explain data collection methods, describe program and course content, or highlight the significance for prospective students of clinical or competitive opportunities. An opportunity to create a valuable reference tool was lost with the absence of explanations, indexing, and other relevant data and ensures that users and librarians will have to rely on college catalogs, directories, and Web-based resources for complete answers. This directory is not recommended at this time.—**Sandra E. Belanger**

559. **Environmental Law Handbook.** 14th ed. Thomas F. P. Sullivan, ed. Rockville, Md., Government Institutes, 1997. 587p. index. $79.00. ISBN 0-86587-560-X. ISSN 0147-7714.

This classic primer now in its 14th edition comes out just 2 years after the 13th edition of 1995. The goal of the *Environmental Law Handbook* remains the same: to give reliable, accurate, and practical compliance information from some of the most respected people in the field, all in a clear and concise manner. Comparing the 13th with the 14th edition, one finds the same chapters by the same authors but in a different arrangement. Each major environmental law is covered by a chapter, from the Clean Air Act to the Toxic Substances Control Act. Minor changes reflecting recent legislation and trends have been added since the 13th edition. Only the chapter on enforcement and liability in the 14th edition has a new author and is substantially revised to show the new reorganization of the Environmental Protection Agency's enforcement office.

This book serves primarily as an introduction to those who know little about environmental law. For most such users, the earlier edition would serve almost as well as the most recent edition. This title has some of the shortcomings of handbooks: In being too concise, important details and secondary references are sometimes omitted. Charts that one may expect to find in an environmental handbook, such as lists of hazardous pollutants and lists of nonattainment geographic areas, are not present; neither is a table of cases, nor a glossary. The table of contents is thoroughly detailed, and an index is present, in addition to copious footnotes.

This book does live up to its goal of being readable, clear, and concise. It will provide basic information for general libraries or for legal professionals not practicing in specific areas of environmental law. Whether the 14th edition is worth purchasing if the 13th edition is already owned requires a close judgment call.—**Georgia Briscoe**

560. **Law, Values, and the Environment: A Reader and Selective Bibliography.** Robert N. Wells Jr., ed. Lanham, Md., Scarecrow Press, 1996. 675p. index. $60.00. ISBN 0-8108-3134-1.

The goal of this anthology is to familiarize readers with environmental concerns around the world and potential ways of solving them. Further, the author hopes that the book will direct the international community in organizing protection programs and reductions of hazardous substances. These goals may be too lofty for the complex subjects of the 26 articles that make up the volume.

The anthology's articles are divided into 11 subject areas. The subjects cover the common range of international environmental issues, including population, land, water, space, forests, biodiversity, and so forth. Each subject area is preceded by a brief synopsis on the subject, written by the editor. The synopsis deals mainly with the environmental issues rather than the legal aspects. Approximately one-half of the articles are from law reviews, and the other half are from technology, environmental, or political science journals. Articles from *Popular Science* and *The Futurist* round out the collection.

The editor is a professor of government at St. Lawrence University in Canton, New York. It is presumed that the intended audience is an undergraduate college class. An anthology on the same subject but suitable for law students as well as undergraduates is available for half the price and twice the size. *International Environmental Law Anthology* (Anderson Publishing, 1996) offers much deeper and more complete coverage and includes substantial excerpts from the leading treaties and conventions on environmental law. The Wells book offers only a brief chronological listing of the treaties by subject.

The selective bibliography in this volume is topically organized, with each topic subdivided into documents, books, and articles. Three pages of notes on contributors and a rudimentary glossary are followed by an index, which completes the volume. [R: RQ, Summer 97, p. 616]—**Georgia Briscoe**

561. **TSCA Handbook.** 3d ed. By McKenna & Cuneo, L.L.P. Rockville, Md., Government Institutes, 1997. 402p. index. $95.00pa. ISBN 0-86587-566-9.

The *TSCA Handbook*, now in its 3d edition, is a valuable resource for a specialized audience of businesses and other organizations who deal with hazardous wastes and toxic substances. The handbook is prepared by the environmental law firm of McKenna & Cuneo as a service to clients and others. The book reprints the complete Toxic Substances Control Act (TSCA), describes divisions within the Environmental Protection Agency (EPA) and EPA organizational charts, and provides EPA contact persons and telephone numbers in those divisions. The majority of the volume supplies readable interpretations and guidelines of TSCA, arranged by section and subsection of the Act. A brief, useful index leads users from subjects and substances to the pertinent sections of the Act. The handbook is required reading for anyone responsible for the purchase, inventory, or disposal of the substances controlled by this law, because mistakes that result in violations of the law can have costly legal and financial consequences.—**Lynne M. Fox**

HUMAN RIGHTS

562. **Encyclopedia of American Indian Civil Rights.** James S. Olson, Mark Baxter, Jason M. Tetzloff, and Darren Pierson, eds. Westport, Conn., Greenwood Press, 1997. 417p. illus. index. $65.00. ISBN 0-313-29338-4.

The American Indian, as has been the case with other racial minorities in America, has suffered a multitude of indignities. The *Encyclopedia of American Indian Civil Rights* fill a gap in the literature for student interested in defining the subject and in locating additional readings. The excellent introduction will help users define the main issues. A chronology of "Major Landmarks in the History of American Indian Civil Rights" will also assist in placing this extensive and complicated history into better perspective. Numerous photographs and an extensive bibliography add to the usefulness of this work. This encyclopedia is recommended for undergraduate collections and for high school libraries. [R: RBB, 15 Oct 97, p. 427]—**Dario J. Villa**

563. Frost-Knappman, Elizabeth, and Kathryn Cullen-DuPont. **Women's Rights on Trial: 101 Historic Trials....** Detroit, Gale, 1997. 478p. illus. index. $49.95. ISBN 0-7876-0384-8.

From the cases of Anne Hutchinson to Shannon Faulkner, the 101 trials examined in this fascinating collection cover 400 years of women's legal history in the United States. All of the trials set legal precedents and are representative of a historical period. Each of the six topic sections—crimes of conscience and nonconformity; crime and punishment; rights and responsibilities of citizenship; reproductive rights; marriage, parenting, and divorce; and women at work—begins with an overview of the trials covered in the specific section. Essays 1,000 to 2,000 words in length discuss the trial and court proceedings. For cases that were appealed to a higher court, both lower and higher court proceedings are discussed. Arguments for the plaintiffs and defendants and judicial ruling and rationale are given. Any legislative action resulting from the trial is reported and its impact analyzed.

Fact boxes give pertinent and quick reference information. The boxes include the major points of the case; names of the plaintiffs, defendants, attorneys, and judges; the trial's date and location; the verdict; the sentence; and its historical significance. A bibliography follows each case. There are also photographs and illustrations and a glossary of legal terms. Two tables of contents (chronological and alphabetic), an appendix of legal citations and sources, and an alphabetic index provide quick access by case name, subject, or time period.

This collection of landmark trials is an outstanding resource that provides insight into the continuing challenges to the legal rights of women and identifies key legislative changes within the context of a historical perspective. The guide is highly recommended for high school and public libraries.

—**Marlene M. Kuhl**

564. Gorman, Robert F., and Edward S. Mihalkanin. **Historical Dictionary of Human Rights and Humanitarian Organizations.** Lanham, Md., Scarecrow, 1997. 296p. (Historical Dictionaries of International Organizations, no.12). $44.00. ISBN 0-8108-3263-1.

Historical Dictionary of Human Rights and Humanitarian Organizations presents a compendium of terminology and definitions that establishes a foundation of understanding for the student and scholar alike. The idea of human rights, as so well pointed out by the authors in their excellent introductory essay, "has ancient roots . . . its history can be traced back into the classical Hebrew, Greek and Roman worlds and to the earliest days of Christianity." This excellent source of information discusses many men and women, such as Mohandas Gandhi, who participated in movements for the recognition of human dignity. The majority of the entries give ample coverage, and each provides a selected list of sources used. This is an added benefit for students who plan to conduct further research into the topic. Included is a comprehensive list of acronyms and abbreviations and three appendixes: "Universal Declaration of Rights"; "Covenant on Economic, Social, and Cultural Rights"; and "International Covenant on Civil and Political Rights." This excellent dictionary and sourcebook is highly recommended for all libraries.
—**Dario J. Villa**

565. Luker, Ralph E. **Historical Dictionary of the Civil Rights Movement.** Lanham, Md., Scarecrow, 1997. 331p. (Historical Dictionaries of Religions, Philosophies, and Movements, no.11). $68.00. ISBN 0-8108-3163-5.

Luker has a well-informed background to bring to the compilation of this dictionary. He was himself active in the civil rights movement at Duke University, is an adjunct professor of history at Morehouse College, and has won major awards for other historical writing about the African American struggle for civil rights. In compiling the dictionary, Luker has reflected on what the key events were or are and what students will most likely look up in the course of their studies. Especially useful features at the front of the book are a chronology that runs from 1941 to 1995 and a list of acronyms.

The entries are relatively brief, one-half page to two pages in length, depending on the importance and complexity of the topic. They include biographical sketches of major players and many court cases, both in the U.S. Supreme Court and at lower levels. However, information on teachers, students, journalists, and writers is often difficult to locate. Luker refers to *Plessy v. Ferguson* in the context of *Brown v. Board of Education of Topeka*, when it should probably have its own entry. The bibliography alone, which includes a separate list of primary sources, may be the most useful part of the book for researchers. A "Bibliographical Note" makes readers aware of the relative importance of sources. This dictionary is highly recommended. [R: RBB, 15 Feb 97, p. 1042]—**Edna M. Boardman**

INTELLECTUAL PROPERTY

566. **Copyright Laws and Treaties of the World 1991-1995 Supplement.** Washington, D.C., BNA Books, 1997. 1v. (various paging). $365.00 looseleaf. ISBN 1-57018-010-5.

This book-length cumulation of looseleaf inserts represents the 1991-1995 update for *Copyright Laws and Treaties of the World*, the single source in which those in need may find official English translations of every key worldwide copyright law and agreement. The present supplement includes such important national and multinational documents as the North American Free Trade Agreement, directives from the European Union, the Cartagena Agreement, and the Treaty on the International Registration of Audiovisual Works. The data are authoritative, having been compiled by the United Nations Educational, Scientific, and Cultural Organization (UNESCO) in cooperation with the governmental copyright agencies of the United States and the United Kingdom.

The documents are grouped into two categories: countries, which are arranged alphabetically, and multilateral conventions. The latter are subdivided into international treaties, regional treaties, and other regional instruments. Access to the contents is solely by tables of contents accompanying each document, as there is no index to the overall series.

This work should be a first stop for persons with legal questions concerning such areas as computer programs; literary, musical, and choreographic works; sound recordings; graphic and sculptural works; motion pictures and audiovisual works; and other works of authorship. It is an essential work for libraries and organizations in which questions concerning the ownership of intellectual property is significant, and it should be purchased by those institutions and agencies.—**Georgia Briscoe**

567. **International Treaties on Intellectual Property.** 2d ed. Marshall A. Leaffer, ed. Washington, D.C., BNA Books, 1997. 1036p. index. $125.00pa. ISBN 1-57018-056-3.

Intellectual property rights is a fast growing segment of domestic and international law. This 2d edition reproduces the text of 47 agreements and is nearly twice the size of the 1st edition. The last several years have been an active period for regional and global intellectual property treaties, including portions of NAFTA, the Trade Related Aspects on Intellectual Property (TRIPS) portions of the Uruguay Round of GATT, and European Union conventions. Although older treaties, such as the Berne Convention for the Protection of Literary and Artistic Works, already appear in print in such books as *International Copyright and Neighboring Rights* (London: Butterworths, 1989), some newer texts of international treaties are found readily on the Internet at such Websites as the World Intellectual Property Organization (WIPO) (HTTP://WWW.WIPO.ORG).

International Treaties on Intellectual Property brings together a wide range of the most important international agreements drawn up over the years. This is an excellent core bibliography and contains several useful appendixes, which round out this work's central value to all law, trademark, copyright, and academic libraries.—**Stephen W. Green**

VICTIMS OF ABUSE

568. **Child Abuse: Betraying a Trust.** 1997 ed. Suzanne B. Squyres, Alison Landes, and Jacquelyn Quiram, eds. Wylie, Tex., Information Plus, 1997. 152p. index. $12.95pa. ISBN 1-57302-036-2.

For the numerous students who select child abuse as their research topic and for those who merely want to be better informed on the subject, *Child Abuse* is a useful resource. The information presented is clear and concise. A detailed table of contents is extremely helpful in locating specific data. The book is divided into eight chapters, and each chapter is liberally documented with a variety of charts, graphs, and tables, all of which contain source and date information. The first three chapters are devoted to the history, the definition, and the reporting of child abuse. Subsequent chapters cover reporting abuses, causes and effects, child sexual abuse, and abuse and the law. The last chapter includes information on the controversial False Memory Syndrome. Other sections are furnished that contain important names and addresses for those seeking help or further information, resources, and a small index. Information Plus has provided an excellent source for the student and for those wanting more information about child abuse.

—**Mary L. Trenerry**

11 Library and Information Science and Publishing and Bookselling

LIBRARY AND INFORMATION SCIENCE

General Works

Dictionaries and Encyclopedias

569. **Encyclopedia of Library and Information Science. Volume 57, Supplement 20.** Allen Kent, ed. New York, Marcel Dekker, 1996. 357p. illus. $99.75. ISBN 0-8247-2057-1.

570. **Encyclopedia of Library and Information Science. Volume 59, Supplement 22.** Allen Kent, ed. New York, Marcel Dekker, 1997. 347p. illus. $99.75. ISBN 0-8247-2059-8.

Encyclopedia of Library and Information Science has been reviewed in *American Reference Books Annual* on several occasions, starting with volume 1, published in 1968 and edited by the late Harold Lancour and current editor Kent. One may wish for a new edition of the encyclopedia, but apparently the publisher has decided to continue with supplements. It should be noted that Kent is now professor emeritus at the School of Library and Information Science at the University of Pittsburgh. William Nasri, who also is associated with Pittsburgh, is no longer listed on the title page and has been replaced by Carolyn M. Hall as administrative editor.

Volume 59, Supplement 22, was published in 1997. It contains 14 articles. There is an article on "Archival Science" by Luciana Duranti (School of Library Science at British Columbia) that substantially updates an article on "Archives" published in the 1968 volume, which was written by Robert H. Bahmer, then the archivist at the U.S. National Archives and Records Services. Bahmer's article was brief, and the editorial staff made a correct decision to update and substantially enlarge the article on this important topic. There is, of course, a different emphasis in the article on archival science, which discusses not only the development of archival science but also the rapid changing of structures, organizations, methods of communication, and information technologies. This well-written article contains a comprehensive bibliography. However, the text does contain a few typographic errors (e.g., *Verwaltunslehre* should be capitalized but is not in the text, although it is in the bibliography).

Several articles in this volume cover (and update) such traditionally known topics as "User Needs" and "Strategic Planning Models in Academic Libraries," but in general this supplement covers topics of contemporary interest, such as "Electronic Libraries of the Future," "Object-Oriented Programming Languages: A Natural Framework for Distributed Artificial Intelligence," and "The Interaction-Based Information Retrieval Paradigm." Other volumes have a similar structure, with some articles updating previously written material and others dealing with topics of a more recent nature.

The price per volume today is $99.75 versus $65.00 10 years ago. The encyclopedia will be of interest to large library collections, especially to library schools and other programs that offer library science courses.
—**Bohdan S. Wynar**

571. **International Encyclopedia of Information and Library Science.** John Feather and Paul Sturges, eds. New York, Routledge, 1997. 492p. index. $130.00. ISBN 0-415-09860-2.

This one-volume, British encyclopedia will join a number of other works on this topic, including a multivolume *Encyclopedia of Library and Information Science* (published by Marcel Dekker) or such works as *Harrod's Librarian's Glossary* (Gover, 1995), *Dictionary of Information Science and Technology* (Academic Press, 1992), and *World Encyclopedia of Library and Information Services*, (32d ed.; American Library Association, 1993). The reader will find evaluations of encyclopedias and dictionaries in library and information science in Susan C. Awe's *ARBA Guide to Subject Encyclopedias and Dictionaries* (2d ed.; Libraries Unlimited, 1997). The present volume will nicely supplement and compliment the existing reference sources on this subject. Beverly Lynch is listed as an American consultant, but most contributors are from Great Britain and appended bibliographies in complex articles are, for the most part, British imprints. Some articles are rather brief, such as the one on health science libraries. This work may be classified as a dictionary rather than an encyclopedia.—**Bohdan S. Wynar**

Directories

572. **American Library Directory 1996-97.** 49th ed. New Providence, N.J., R. R. Bowker/Reed Reference Publishing, 1996. 2v. index. $249.95/set. ISBN 0-8352-3755-9. ISSN 0065-910X.

American Library Directory, published annually, is the standard source for information about United States, Canadian, and Mexican libraries. The major portion in this directory consists of lists of public, academic, government, and special libraries in the United States and Canada, followed by a separate and somewhat shorter list of Mexican libraries. Arrangement is geographic; countries are alphabetized by state, region, or province, then by city, and finally by institution or library name. Entries include the name and address of the library, the names of key personnel, and information on the library's holdings. Entries for larger institutions contain additional information (e.g., income, expenditures, subject profile, automation, and publications). Information is based on questionnaires and public records. There are several additional sections: library and award recipients, networks, library schools, library systems, libraries serving blind and physically disabled patrons, state and provincial library agencies, the national interlibrary loan code, and military overseas libraries. The organization index and personnel index conclude the second volume.

As one can expect in a work of this size, some information is dated, and there are some typographic errors. Nevertheless, this directory is the most comprehensive source on North American libraries and will be frequently consulted in reference rooms in many larger library institutions. It should be noted that for the first time, library services and suppliers are accessible at the Reed Reference Publishing Website.
—**Bohdan S. Wynar**

573. **Directory of Federal Libraries.** 3d ed. William R. Evinger, ed. Phoenix, Ariz., Oryx Press, 1997. 379p. index. $97.50. ISBN 1-57356-048-0.

Federal agency libraries represent significant sources of information about governmental activity unknown to most citizens of the United States. These facilities, ranging from national libraries such as the Library of Congress and National Agricultural Library to smaller facilities in communities across the nation, feature unique and diverse collections chronicling various areas of government research and policy development.

Directory of Federal Libraries profiles these libraries. Entries are arranged by governmental branch, independent agencies, and boards, with executive branch agency libraries receiving the most extensive coverage. Individual library entries feature common directory information, such as name, address, telephone and fax numbers, and World Wide Web URL if available. Additional information lists names and numbers of librarians and support personnel, staff and collection size, collection strengths, interlibrary loan services, and available reference and circulation services. It should be noted that many of these libraries are restricted to federal personnel and are not open to the public. Profiled libraries are located in the Washington, D.C., area; throughout the United States; and in foreign countries. Libraries profiled include the Air Force Historical Research Agency Library at Alabama's Maxwell Air Force Base; the U.S. Supreme Court Library; the U.S. Senate Library; Fire Island National Seashore Library; Leavenworth

U.S. Penitentiary Library in Leavenworth, Kansas; Gerald R. Ford Library in Ann Arbor, Michigan; the USIS American Library in Athens; and the Environmental Protection Agency's Atmospheric Sciences Modeling Division Library in Research Triangle Park, North Carolina.

This work is a valuable introduction to the holdings of federal agency libraries. Its exhaustive detail makes it particularly valuable for librarians and library users. Because it is now in its 3d edition, it seems likely that this work will remain an essential reference source for libraries with significant federal documents collections and users requiring information from federal agencies that may not be accessible through the Federal Depository Library Program.—**Bert Chapman**

574. **International Biographical Directory of National Archivists, Documentalists, and Librarians.** Frances Laverne Carroll, ed. Susan Houck, comp. Lanham, Md., Scarecrow Press, 1997. 225p. index. $45.00. ISBN 0-8108-3223-2.

This directory brings together data gathered directly from surveys sent to executive officers of national archives, documentation centers, and libraries as well as information from several specialized biographical sources. Information for 192 countries is included. The completeness of data provided is inconsistent because of differences in organization and staffing of facilities in the countries treated. Most entries give substantial biographical information on executive officers as well as addresses and telephone and fax numbers for the facilities. E-mail addresses are available for a few. Separate indexes for places, institutions, and persons make the book easy to use. The directory will have a limited audience, but those with a need to contact international archivists, documentalists, and librarians will appreciate the scope and accuracy of this carefully compiled volume. [R: LJ, 15 April 97, p. 126]—**Ahmad Gamaluddin**

Handbooks and Yearbooks

575. Berkman, Bob I. **Find It Fast: How to Uncover Expert Information on Any Subject.** 4th ed. New York, HarperPerennial/HarperCollins, 1997. 323p. index. $14.00pa. ISBN 0-06-273473-3.

This guide shows readers how to find information on almost any subject in any format and is intended for the use of non-information specialists, such as students, businesspeople, activists, or freelance writers. The emphasis is on sources that are easy to obtain and use, and the author includes general library resources, supersources (broad-based resources covering many subjects), government publications, business resources, the Internet, and locating experts.

Most of the library-related resources are familiar and predictable (e.g., the H. W. Wilson indexes, various major directories), and the discussions of government and business resources are equally thorough. The greatly expanded Internet chapter describes major news sources, search engines, and newsgroups, and the author quite appropriately includes warnings about the drawbacks of Internet research. The several chapters on finding and interviewing experts may be among the most useful in the guide, as most of the other resources are more easily found. The author's frequent warnings about the need to evaluate the source of information, whether from an "expert," the Internet, or a magazine, if followed, would increase the value of many articles and term papers. *Find It Fast* is a good choice for library purchase, although perhaps it would be more valuable to patrons for home study than as a reference tool for librarians.—**Diane Schmidt**

576. **The Bowker Annual Library and Book Trade Almanac 1997.** 42d ed. Dave Bogart, ed. New Providence, N.J., R. R. Bowker/Reed Reference Publishing, 1997. 839p. index. $175.00. ISBN 0-8352-3906-3. ISSN 0068-0540.

This annual, reviewed in *American Reference Books Annual* many times (see ARBA 96, entry 623), is an essential ready-reference source used by both librarians and patrons. Coverage and structure is similar to that of previous volumes and includes six parts: "Reports from the Field"; "Legislation, Funding, and Grants"; "Library Information Science, Education, Placement, and Salaries"; "Research and Statistics"; "Reference Information"; and "Directory of Organization." There are a number of special reports in the first part, such as evolution of the copyright during 1996, the year's developments in library networking and cooperation, and an article by Paula Montgomery about changes in school library media programs in the 1990s. All in all, this volume is indispensable for all libraries that can afford the rather high price tag.—**Bohdan S. Wynar**

Archives and Manuscripts

577. DeWitt, Donald L., comp. **Articles Describing Archives and Manuscript Collections in the United States: An Annotated Bibliography.** Westport, Conn., Greenwood Press, 1997. 458p. index. (Bibliographies and Indexes in Library and Information Science, no.11). $89.50. ISBN 0-313-29598-0.

This companion volume to DeWitt's earlier *Guides to Archives and Manuscript Collections in the United States* (see ARBA 95, entry 523) delivers a complete source for articles describing archive and manuscript collections held in the United States as well as U.S. holdings found in foreign repositories. The articles cited in the bibliography date from circa 1890 to 1996 and contain detailed descriptions of a specific record series, institution's holdings, and general information to help find similar subject matter in various repositories. DeWitt's annotations concisely provide a general description of an article's content but are detailed enough to enable researchers to easily assess usefulness of a specific topic.

The work is divided into the 13 general sections DeWitt used in his previous guide. Each general section encompasses several subheadings, further dividing the materials into manageable groups, which enables users to easily identify an area of interest. A few new subheadings have been added to allow for information on materials not found in the previous guide. Section headings in this work include general collections, business collections, ethnic minorities and women, U.S. federal archives, fine arts collections, literary collections, political collections, professional groups and organizations, U.S. regional collections, religious groups, and others. All citations are numbered sequentially throughout the volume for easy reference from the index, which includes subjects, personal and corporate names, geographic locations, and specific archival repositories.

A brief introduction to the work provides a glimpse of the other bibliographies and indexes that were used in compiling this work. Unfortunately, the introduction is too brief and does not give users a definitive list of what resources have been covered so that they may safely ignore those in searching for additional relevant articles on a specific topic. Despite these problems, this compilation serves researchers well by bringing copious information on a broad range of subjects together in one work. When used with the author's earlier book, researchers have the opportunity to locate collections, published finding aids, and articles that describe a collection's content and usefulness. No historically oriented collection should be without both volumes.—**Robert V. Williams**

578. Rosenthal, Bernard M. **The Rosenthal Collection of Printed Books with Manuscript Annotations: A Catalog of 242 Editions....** New Haven, Conn., Beinecke Rare Book and Manuscript Library, Yale University; distr., Binghamton, N.Y., Medieval & Renaissance Texts & Studies, State University of New York, 1997. 389p. index. $50.00. ISBN 0-8457-3131-9.

This catalog is a description of both printed books and manuscripts acquired by Yale University in 1995 from the Bernard M. Rosenthal Collection of Printed Books with Manuscript Annotations. The volume is published as a record of this distinct collection, which includes 242 editions and is a complement to the other guides to medieval and renaissance resources at the Beinecke Library.

This beautifully produced book with manuscript annotations differs from most similar works because of the inclusion of an item in the collection that focuses on the presence of manuscript notes, not the printed text. Consequently, a variety of unknown writers receive attention: students, professors, physicians, lawyers, priests, scientists, and classical scholars who have owned and annotated the books in this collection. The annotations are responses to what is printed and thus exist as a part of an organic whole. Most are not meaningful if read in isolation. Rosenthal's unique type of description intends to illuminate this fundamental unity.

Manuscript commentaries contain painstakingly counted numbers of words and detailed information regarding the script. Rosenthal gives random examples by transcribing passages that he considers to be characteristic as well as consistently indicating the presence of vernacular words or sentences. He supplies data with features meriting further study. The bibliographic and historical information, as well as the sample transcriptions of annotations, provides a sound basis for an appreciation of the books. In Rosenthal's preface he discusses how the collection came into being and how it grew. This book is for specialists and scholars interested in the why, how, and what that give insight into the perspective of contemporary readers of included books.—**Magda Želinská-Ferl**

Cataloging and Classification

579. **Abridged Dewey Decimal Classification and Relative Index.** 13th ed. Joan S. Mitchell, Julianne Beall, Winton E. Matthews Jr., and Gregory R. New, eds. Dublin, Ohio, OCLC Forest Press, 1997. 1023p. $90.00. ISBN 0-910608-59-8.

The 13th edition of this venerable classic has been significantly expanded (166 more pages) and updated from the 1990 edition (see ARBA 91, entry 617). More than 40 pages of index terms have been added, and there are new classification schedules for animals, education, life sciences, plants, and public administration. This single volume is a condensed version of the 4-volume *Dewey Decimal Classification*, 21st edition (see ARBA 97, entry 535). It is intended for use by libraries with holdings of up to 20,000 volumes, where little original cataloging is done.

OCLC Forest Press is now publishing a companion workbook for the *Abridged 13*. This spiral-bound volume is designed for either classroom use or self-instruction. Its clear directions on number-building, accompanied by numerous exercises, can help novice catalogers develop confidence as well as competence.

Small and one-person libraries should purchase this update to keep their cataloging practices current.—**Ed Volz**

580. **Sears List of Subject Headings.** 16th ed. Joseph Miller, ed. Bronx, N.Y., H. W. Wilson, 1997. 786p. $54.00. ISBN 0-8242-0920-6.

Minnie Earl Sears developed the first abbreviated list of subject headings in 1923, generating it from the catalogs of nine representative small libraries (as the original subtitle stated). The inclusion of Dewey Decimal Classification numbers has been hit and miss through the years. They were not included until the 4th edition, remained through the 8th edition, and were dropped again until the 11th edition, but have now become a regular feature since 1977. The Dewey numbers included in this volume are from the 13th abridged edition.

This most recent *Sears List of Subject Headings* has broadened its religion headings to better include non-Christian concepts and activities. Some of the other topics that have expanded headings to contemporize the list are body image, computer simulation, forest conservation, hypertext, militia movements, multimedia systems, and the World Wide Web. Sears continues its practice of using the direct form of an entry, varying from the inverted form commonly used by the Library of Congress. This is done because the editor assumes library users think of headings in the linear, not inverted, form. Capitalization practice and the forms of corporate and personal names follow *Anglo-American Cataloguing Rules* (2d ed.; American Library Association, 1988). Filing is in accordance with *ALA Filing Rules* (1980).

This continues to be an essential purchase for smaller libraries; it is the primary resource needed for rudimentary cataloging.—**Ed Volz**

Information Technology

581. **Elsevier's Dictionary of Information Technology in English, German, and French.** By J. P. Hoepelman, R. Mayer, and J. Wagner. New York, Elsevier Science, 1997. 406p. $172.00. ISBN 0-444-88410-6.

The coauthors of this timely multilingual dictionary are professional information scientists whose home base is Stuttgart, Germany. They direct the dictionary to technical translators, to computer scientists, and to students who need to understand international information technology literature. The English section of the dictionary includes full entries for the selected terms: definitions, synonyms, translations with gender indicators, references to related terms, and additional information. Users can go to the German and French sections via convenient thumb indexes. Terms in these sections do not include definitions but refer back to the English entries. The authors define more than 4,500 English terms or phrases, but they have made no attempt to be comprehensive. They do not define commonly used technical terms that appear in most modern dictionaries, but include only the translations. Nor do they include terms whose meanings are apparent from common, nontechnical English definitions.

A clear, easy-to-use product, this is a highly specialized dictionary whose intended audience will be equally specialized. One supposes the audience will simply have to meet the high cost. There are not many other current choices.—**Berniece M. Owen**

582. Liu, Lewis-Guodo. **The Internet and Library and Information Services: Issues, Trends, and Annotated Bibliography, 1994-1995.** Westport, Conn., Greenwood Press, 1996. 300p. index. (Bibliographies and Indexes in Library and Information Science, no.10). $69.50. ISBN 0-313-30019-4.

The explosive growth of the Internet has impacted all areas of society, and none more than libraries. As gateways to the universe of information, libraries have devoted personnel and resources to the Internet while continuing to provide access to print-based materials. Libraries have had to rapidly embrace new technologies, train librarians and public users, develop policies on public access, select resources, provide intellectual access to networked publications, and struggle with issues of preservation and copyright. The volume of published literature about the Internet has also grown rapidly. Liu has examined the published record and selected materials published in 1994 and 1995 from books, conference proceedings, magazine and periodical articles, and other sources that address the policy issues associated with rapid technological change.

The resulting resource opens with a lengthy introductory essay about the impact of the Internet on library and information providers and society in general. The essay is followed by an annotated bibliography of 1,161 entries grouped into 4 themes: Internet development, Internet and libraries, Internet resources and services, and Internet and society. *The Internet and Library and Information Services* includes two indexes: an author index to the annotated works and a general index by subject and keywords. The volume is recommended for libraries with an interest in social policy or library and information sciences.

—**Peggy Jobe**

583. **National Guide to Funding for Information Technology.** Elizabeth H. Rich, ed. New York, Foundation Center, 1997. 199p. index. $115.00pa. ISBN 0-87954-709-X.

In recent years the Foundation Center has produced a number of topical guides as spin-offs of their comprehensive databases; the present guide is of particular interest to readers of *Library and Information Science Annual* (Libraries Unlimited, 1989). The work is arranged alphabetically by state and within states by foundation name. Entries include the sort of information familiar from the *Foundation Directory* (see entry 787), providing the foundation's name, address, telephone number, URL address, contact person, foundation officers, staff size, financial data, and Employer Identification Number. Information on types, purposes, and amounts of grants awarded is provided, as well as information on how to apply and deadlines. Entries in this guide also give information on recent grants for information technology. There are indexes for foundation officers and donors, for types of support, and by subject of the recent grants listed.

As pointed out in the introduction, because many foundations support a wide variety of programs within a specific region, the foundations listed here do not represent all possible sources of foundation funding related to information technology. This is, however, a useful place to start. Because the subject indexing is only for recent grants, it is not comprehensive. For example, George Soros's Central European University Foundation is indexed under Czech Republic and under Hungary because those are sites of its recent grants in information technology, but one cannot find it in the index under *Europe*, *Central Europe*, or *Eastern Europe*. Despite these shortcomings, this is a useful source of possible foundation funding in information technology.—**Robert Michaelson**

Intellectual Freedom and Censorship

584. Foerstel, Herbert N. **Free Expression and Censorship in America: An Encyclopedia.** Westport, Conn., Greenwood Press, 1997. 260p. index. $65.00. ISBN 0-313-29231-0.

Since the end of the Cold War, the United States has become a nation without a common enemy, no longer fearing the outsider from whom the shores must be kept safe, and to the consternation of politician and thriller writer alike, the search for a contemporary threat has proven elusive. However, it would seem that at last, "we have met the enemy and it is us" (to quote Pogo), and those most private parts of people's lives have become the target. Freedom of thought and expression has never been under greater threat than in this current era of deception and disclosure. This remarkable work details the struggle against censorship in all contemporary arenas: Abortion, television violence, pornography on the Internet, homosexuality, and funding for the arts are but a few. In addition, the essays deal with important figures in the conflicts, philosophical attitudes, and specific legal cases.

Alphabetically arranged, the work has citations at the conclusion of each article, as well as recommended references. There is a short, general, selected bibliography; a table of the legal cases cited; and a thorough index. This volume is a masterful work, different from most encyclopedias in that it is the work of only one author who has clearly done intensive research, writes clearly and concisely, and feels very keenly the need to protect the rights and freedoms of all citizens of the United States as guaranteed by the First Amendment. The encyclopedia is highly recommended for all libraries.—**Paula Frosch**

Interlibrary Loan

585. **WLN Interlibrary Loan Policies Directory.** 5th ed. Lacey, Wash., WLN, 1997. 1v. (unpaged). index. $60.00 looseleaf w/binder. ISSN 1093-0027.

This new edition of the *WLN Interlibrary Loan Policies Directory* (see ARBA 94, entry 643) updates the interlibrary loan (ILL) policies of more than 435 North American libraries, the majority of which are in Alaska, Arizona, Idaho, Montana, and Washington. Libraries, all with holdings in the WLN online ILL policy file, are listed alphabetically, but the looseleaf format, which accommodates each library in one page, facilitates rearranging the symbols by NUC symbol. The hard copy version corresponds to the file available from WLN's online system; therefore its purchase by WLN member libraries is less vital because they have access to the information in the WLN files. When appropriate the listings also include holding symbols for competing services, like DOCLINE, SERHOLD, ONTYME, RLIN, and OCLC. Other relevant information includes fax numbers and e-mail, Internet and Ariel addresses. The real benefit, however, especially for non-WLN users, is the information contained in the indexes. One index lists libraries that lend unbound periodicals, another audiovisual materials, and yet another lists libraries that charge fees and prints the price. In this age of greater reliance on resource sharing, such elusive information often needs to be easily at every ILL librarian's fingertips. Depending upon volume, such information could well result in a tradeoff worth more than the $60 price tag.—**Lawrence Olszewski**

School Libraries

586. **Children's Catalog.** 17th ed. Anne Price and Juliette Yaakov, eds. Bronx, N.Y., H. W. Wilson, 1996. 1373p. index. (Standard Catalog Series). $105.00. ISBN 0-8242-0893-5.

The *Children's Catalog* remains the selection tool it has always been for both public libraries and school media centers. It consists of an extensive list of books and magazines of interest to preschool through sixth-grade children. The structure of the 17th edition is identical to earlier editions except for the addition of a separate section listing CD-ROM reference works. The catalog includes nearly 7,000 titles and more than 6,500 analytical entries. The main section, arranged according to the abridged Dewey Decimal Classification, contains full bibliographic data, Sears subject headings, a descriptive annotation, and quoted evaluations from selected book reviews. The 2d section is a comprehensive analytic index of authors, titles, and subjects in addition to such collective works as story collections and anthologies. The 3d section is the above-mentioned list of recommended CD-ROM titles, chiefly interactive multimedia resources. The 4th section is a directory of publishers and distributors.

Because so many schools and public libraries are sharing resources and because Library of Congress subject headings are used most frequently for MARC records, *Children's Catalog* would be more useful for many practitioners if Library of Congress subject headings were listed along with Sears. Nonfiction titles with 1970s and early 1980s copyright dates need to be eliminated from the list, except for those that have historical value. More titles need to be added to the bibliography of most nonfiction subject areas to allow for growth of the core collection in libraries. In order to better serve the needs of students and faculty in schools, bibliographies of the professional collection need more in-depth coverage. A more comprehensive bibliography of CD-ROM reference materials is warranted. Fifteen titles in this edition only scratch the surface. Other audiovisual materials need to be added to represent the media concept in most libraries today. Because of this omission, the practicing children's librarian or media specialist would have to consult *The Elementary School Library Collection* (see ARBA 97, entries 544 and 545) for these materials. The author, title, subject, and analytic indexes could be a separate volume in the future for those libraries that still use it.—**Betty J. Morris**

587. **Senior High School Library Catalog.** 15th ed. Juliette Yaakov, ed. Bronx, N.Y., H. W. Wilson, 1997. 1312p. index. (Standard Catalog Series). $130.00. ISBN 0-8242-0921-4.

Senior High School Library Catalog continues to serve as a comprehensive selection tool for senior high school media centers and public libraries. Books for young people in grades 9 through 12 are included within the scope of the book. Although 5,432 titles and 10,344 analytic entries are furnished in the 15th edition, the number of titles and analytic entries are less than in the 14th edition.

The catalog is organized into 4 sections. The 1st section, "The Classified Catalog," is arranged according to *Dewey Decimal Classification*, 12th abridged edition. It contains Sears subject headings, full bibliographic data, a descriptive annotation, and quoted evaluations from selected book reviews. The 2d section contains an author, title, subject, and analytic index for collective works, such as anthologies and story collections. The 3d section, added to this edition, is a select list of recommended CD-ROM reference works, chiefly interactive multimedia resources for which there is no print equivalent. The 4th section is a directory of publishers and distributors.

Because many libraries are sharing resources and because Library of Congress subject headings are used most frequently for MARC records, *Senior High School Library Catalog* would be more useful for many practitioners had Library of Congress subject headings been listed along with Search subject headings. The addition of more titles to the bibliography in the nonfiction sections is warranted to allow for expanding the core collections of libraries. The inclusion of CD-ROM reference works in the 15th edition is a step in the right direction, although other audiovisual materials need to be included in future volumes to represent the media concept in most libraries. Because of the omission of audiovisual materials from the catalog, the media specialist or practicing young adult librarian must consult other sources for these materials. A separate volume is recommended in the future for the author, title, subject, and analytic index to allow more space in the catalog for audiovisual materials and for expanding bibliographies in the nonfiction sections.—**Betty J. Morris**

Special Libraries and Collections

588. **A Directory of Rare Book and Special Collections in the United Kingdom and the Republic of Ireland.** 2d ed. B. C. Bloomfield, with Karen Potts, eds. London, with the Rare Books Group of the Library Association, Library Association Publishing; distr., Lanham, Md., Bernan Associates, 1997. 740p. index. $195.00. ISBN 1-85604-063-1.

This substantially revised and slightly expanded 2d edition (see ARBA 86, entry 592) provides information on over 1,200 libraries in the United Kingdom and Ireland. "Rare" is defined as printed books before 1850, however, manuscripts and post-1850 material have been included when deemed relevant. All major national and university collections are covered, as are those of public libraries, schools, selected National Trust properties, ecclesiastical bodies, learned societies, and other institutions. Unlike the first edition, only publicly accessible private libraries are mentioned.

Libraries are arranged alphabetically by geographic region. This arrangement renders the index absolutely indispensable, not only for topical access, of course, but more importantly for locating geographic and institutional names, because many American users may be unfamiliar with the British county and town breakdown. The information for each entry includes the address, telephone and fax numbers, hours of operation, conditions of admission, and information services and research facilities available. Descriptions of special collections and listings of published catalogs are often appended. Whereas most entries are typical directory length, some are more elaborate; that for the British Library runs 40 pages and the Bodleian 27.—**Lawrence Olszewski**

589. **Directory of Special Libraries and Information Centers, Volume 1.** 21st ed. Marc Faerber and Sara Rowe, eds. Detroit, Gale, 1997. 2v. index. $535.00/set. ISBN 0-7876-0167-5.

590. **Directory of Special Libraries and Information Centers. Volume 2: Geographic and Personnel Indexes.** 21st ed. Marc Faerber and Sara Rowe, eds. Detroit, Gale, 1997. 1244p. $445.00. ISBN 0-7876-0168-3.

This work is a guide to special libraries, including resource centers, research libraries, archives, information centers, special collections, and documentation centers throughout the United States and Canada. It provides detailed entries on 22,800 facilities, with an expanded focus on international coverage. Entries are arranged alphabetically by the names of organizations and contain the address, staff information, holdings, services, automated operations, computerized information services, and publications. Seven appendixes and a subject index allow the user to retrieve library information by subject fields.

The companion volume 2 provides additional access points through a geographic index and a personnel index. The personnel index is brief, yet it does refer the user to volume 1 for more details. Volume 2 is functional and allows the user to identify libraries located within a particular geographic region, find the number of libraries located in a specific city, or locate the place of employment of a particular librarian.

Smaller libraries may not be able to afford this directory; therefore, it should be noted that the information contained in this directory can also be found in other formats. For example, R. R. Bowker's *American Library Directory* (see entry 572) contains similar information, but for more detailed listings of special libraries, Gale's edition is more comprehensive. This 21st edition continues to be a reference tool of significant value.—**Natalie Brower-Kirton**

Technical Services

591. Stewart, Barbara. **Directory of Library Technical Services Home Pages.** New York, Neal-Schuman, 1997. 249p. illus. index. (Neal-Schuman NetGuide Series). $55.00. ISBN 1-55570-286-4.

This unique and useful directory's primary target audience is the "working technical services librarian," but it includes Websites that library personnel from other areas will also find useful. The directory focuses on three broad areas: Websites that will be useful, timesaving, or of interest to librarians in acquisitions, cataloging, and technical services in general. It is in an easy-to-read format. Each section has a brief overview or introduction, and the entries are arranged in an easily identifiable alphabetic list by Website name. Entries include the Website address and a brief description of the Website's contents. Illustrations of selected Websites are included among the entries.

The acquisition's section of the book includes three subsections. Listed first are library acquisitions' departmental Websites, bindery and preservation Websites, gift and exchange program Websites, and general acquisitions Websites. Next, are Websites of vendors and publishers, which include book and serial jobbers; general and specialty publishers and bookstores; Websites that focus on subject and format specialty; online digital publishers; and out-of-print, rare book, and back issue vendors. Concluding the section are Websites that list e-journals, newsletters, and listservs and those that save time and money by including postal information and currency rates.

The cataloging section of the book includes six subsections of Websites. General cataloging Websites are listed first. Sections that discuss authority control, classification and indexing, bibliographic record formats, and cataloging special formats and subjects follow. There is a section that focuses on concerns of catalogers in three areas: cataloging workstations, library automation vendors, and cataloging outsourcing. The last section includes useful Internet Websites on cataloging organizations, e-journals, newsletters, and discussion lists. The last section of the book is on Websites of special interest for technical services librarians that include technical services departments' Websites, associations, discussion lists, e-journals, and newsletters. Following the last section is an index of keywords.

The index contains broad subject categories with some listings for libraries and companies. A complete name index would have been useful for quickly identifying what publishers and libraries are included. Also, there was a minor page numbering error in the index; the AcqWeb listing says page 156, but it is actually 155.

This is a work that library technical services staff with Internet access should consider having as a shortcut guide to Websites that provide useful and helpful information.—**Jan S. Squire**

PUBLISHING AND BOOKSELLING

General Works

Bibliography

592. Boice, Daniel. **The Mitchell Kennerley Imprint: A Descriptive Bibliography.** Pittsburgh, Pa., University of Pittsburgh Press; distr., Ithaca, N.Y., CUP Services, 1996. 222p. illus. index. (Pittsburgh Series in Bibliography). $75.00. ISBN 0-8229-3948-7.

This bibliography serves as a comprehensive chronicle of the publishing efforts of Mitchell Kennerley, a man responsible for introducing an array of new authors to U.S. readers during the early decades of this century by publishing periodicals and monographs. Titles are arranged in chronological order, with reprintings, separate issues, states, or editions being included under the title. Although there is no attempt to provide full bibliographic description, the author includes a transcription of the title page; pagination; location of copies examined; and additional notes pertaining to copyright, cancel title pages, date of publication, binding, printer, device, earlier editions, later editions, series, price, advertisements, and citation of titles in other bibliographies.

A brief introduction provides an overview of Kennerley and the body of the bibliography. Separate appendixes detail the publishing output of Kennerley's sons, Morley and Mitchell Jr.; titles that Kennerley imported and sold; keepsakes; journals published by Kennerley; titles that Kennerley advertised but that were presumed never published; unpublished works; and catalogs and series. The volume concludes with a valuable list of secondary sources and a comprehensive name and title index.

Those interested in the history of publishing and letters, as well as bibliographers, will find this volume immensely valuable. It will be a solid addition to American and British bibliography.

—Edmund F. SantaVicca

593. Turner, John R. **The Walter Scott Publishing Company: A Bibliography.** Pittsburgh, Pa., University of Pittsburgh Press; distr., Ithaca, N.Y., CUP Services, 1997. 626p. illus. index. (Pittsburgh Series in Bibliography). $100.00. ISBN 0-8229-3965-7.

The 14-page introduction to this volume gives a general overview on Walter Scott, a builder and contractor in Newcastle upon Tyne and the owner of a successful complex of businesses specializing in construction and civil engineering, with emphasis on railway and dock construction. In 1882 Scott decided to acquire the Tyne Publishing Company, a printing and publishing firm, which was on the point of bankruptcy. The history of the Walter Scott Publishing Co., Limited, is traced highlighting the series (Bijou Books, Books of Fairy Tales, Brotherhood Library, Cambridge Library, Camelot Classics, Canterbury Poets, Children's Graphic Picture Books, Children's Hour, Contemporary Science, Emerald Library, Every-Day Help, Great Writers, Half-Roan Library, Hawthorne Library, Hero, Indian Railway Library, Kenilworth Library, Library of Humour, Library of Poetry, Makers of British Art, Million Library, Music Story, New England Library, Oxford Library, Reward, Union Library, Useful Red, Windsor Series of Poetical Anthologies, World's Great Novels, Young Folk's Library, and many others) that made it famous.

The company specialized in reprints, which ensured its financial success throughout its entire existence. Printing major works of English prose and poetry along with translations into English of important foreign-language works was a rewarding publishing strategy. A table, covering the period 1882 to 1927, contains information regarding changes in the title page imprints (title of the firm, address, place of publication) as well as changes in the printer's colophon during the history of the company.

The volume has 1,070 entries, but it provides bibliographic descriptions of a larger number of items because many entries list several editions of the same title under the same entry number, indicated by extensions of *a*, *b*, *c*, and so forth. The description includes references to author, title, year, and place of publication. Each entry includes a quasi-facsimile transcription of the title page, information on advertisements printed on leaves as part of the text, and the transcription of the printer's colophon. Because many titles were included in several series of books, the name(s) of the series are provided, along with the number the book was assigned in those series.

The physical features of each series are described in appendix B, "Books in Series," which is richly illustrated with black-and-white pictures of book covers, spines, or title pages. The location field gives information on the library/libraries that have the title in their collections, with special mention if the author examined the book. If he did not, "NS" standing for "not seen," indicates this aspect. The remaining 5 appendixes contain information structured under the following headings: "Periodicals," "Remainders," "Agency Work," "Titles Published but Not Seen," and "Titles Announced but Not Published." The three indexes allow quick access to the works included in the bibliography that can be retrieved by author, title, or editors; translators; and contributors.—**Hermina G. B. Anghelescu**

Biography

594. **The British Literary Book Trade, 1475-1700.** James K. Bracken and Joel Silver, eds. Detroit, Gale, 1996. 412p. illus. index. (Dictionary of Literary Biography, v.170). $140.00. ISBN 0-8103-9933-4.

In 1475, the printing press was introduced into England. Gale uses this date as a starting point for its survey of the *British Literary Book Trade 1475-1700*, volume 170 of their series Dictionary of Literary Biography. It joins others in the series on the same subject, volumes 106 (1991) and 112 (see ARBA 93, entry 689), which cover 1820-1880 and 1881-1965, respectively, and volume 154, covering 1700-1820 (see ARBA 97, entry 553). Similar volumes exist for the U.S. booktrade.

The British Literary Book Trade consists of 45 chapters, written by experts in the field, that cover various presses and individual printers. Illustrations accompany each chapter, showing pages from various works produced at the particular press or by the particular printer. Title pages, initial letters, illustrations, or sample pages are included as illustrations. Each chapter ends with a list of further references, and an additional, more extensive bibliography follows the entire volume. Many printers associated with the early editions of William Shakespeare are included here—William and Isaac Jaggard, the printers of the First Folio; Thomas Creede; and John Danter. In addition, printers of other authors of this golden age of literature are examined: John Wolfe William Ponsonby, printer and publisher of Edmund Spenser's *Faerie Queen*; John Windet, who printed Francis Bacon's *Essays*; and printers of John Dryden, John Milton, and Ben Jonson.

The volume has a wider scope than only literary publishers, including as well people associated with publishing of scientific works, music, or newspapers and news bulletins. An extensive article recounts the history and significance of the Stationers' Company of London. One confusion is that while the introduction to the volume indicates that Cambridge University Press, the Stationers' Company of London, and Oxford University Press are all included, only the first two actually are. There is no article for Oxford University Press. Although a puzzling discrepancy, this omission does not negate the value of the work; the material that is included far outweighs that which is missing. Libraries that purchase the series will of course receive this volume automatically. Libraries without the set, but with an interest in the book arts and the history of publishing, will find this volume, along with its companions on the same subject, of value.—**Terry Ann Mood**

Catalogs and Collections

595. **Books from Chapel Hill 1922-1997: A Complete Catalog of Publications from the University of North Carolina Press.** Chapel Hill, N.C., University of North Carolina Press, 1997. 463p. $40.00; $19.95pa. ISBN 0-8078-2383-X; 0-8078-4690-2pa.

The University of North Carolina Press has the distinction of being one of the three oldest presses sponsored by a public university in the United States. It was begun in 1922 under the editorship of the prominent librarian Louis R. Wilson, and has continued to develop a unique southern regional voice in the U.S. publishing scene. To celebrate the publisher's 75th anniversary it has released this commemorative bibliography of the 3,000 editions bearing its imprint. The catalog, which was 10 years in the making, is completely revised and expanded from the 2 earlier editions honoring quarter-century anniversaries. This edition includes the previous editors' prefaces from the older volumes, which give a brief glimpse at the history of the press. The preface, by current Press Director Kate Douglas Torrey, is the most capable of succinctly capturing the historical context. One hopes that this aspect can be even further developed

for the next celebration. Each title listed in the catalog includes a complete bibliographic reference and a brief summary statement. A list of award-winning titles (after 1969) is also included. *Books from Chapel Hill 1922-1997* is a fitting tribute to the press and will be of interest to bibliographers and collectors.
—**Andrew B. Wertheimer**

Directories

596. **American Book Trade Directory 1997-98.** 43d ed. New Providence, N.J., R. R. Bowker/Reed Reference Publishing, 1997. 1808p. index. $249.95. ISBN 0-8352-3826-1. ISSN 0065-759X.

This annual guide to U.S. and Canadian booksellers lists more than 31,000 retailers and wholesalers, 879 of which are new to this edition. Divided into 6 sections, the book's 1st section lists 29,920 retail outlets and is arranged geographically by state or province and city. Under each city, bookstores are listed alphabetically by name, and include mailing address, standard address number (SAN), telephone number, store size, number of volumes stocked, and type of books carried. Section 2 contains 1,323 wholesalers, jobbers, and distributors of trade books and magazines. The 3d section provides a list of appraisers of library collections by state, state export representatives, and national and regional associations. Dealers of foreign-language books are listed in section 4, and section 5 is a subject listing. The final section is a complete alphabetic listing to all retail and wholesale outlets included in this directory. This book will be useful for public libraries, publishers, and retail bookstores.—**Debby Mattil**

597. **Antiquarian, Specialty, and Used Book Sellers 1997-98: A Subject Guide and Directory.** 2d ed. James M. Ethridge and Karen Ethridge, eds. Detroit, Omnigraphics, 1997. 861p. index. $85.00pa. ISBN 0-7808-0024-9.

As with its predecessor (see ARBA 94, entry 662), *Antiquarian, Specialty, and Used Book Sellers 1997-98* is useful to librarians, bookdealers, or others who have professional or personal interests in out-of-print book vending or collecting. The majority of the 5,261 dealers within its pages appear here for the first time. For instance, many additional merchandisers are listed whose stock emphasizes children's books or books on the Arctic. Also, many dealers whose operations began prior to the 1990s but were absent from the 1st edition have been added, such as the Haunted Book Shop (1985) and Antonio Raimo Five Books (1980).

Making its debut with this edition is information that identifies dealers' e-mail and World Wide Web addresses, dealer-to-dealer discounts, and such database resources as Interloc and the Automated Bookman. Also for the first time, dealers were asked to classify their stock as "general," "general, with specialties," or "limited to specialties." A higher percentage of booksellers in this revision reflects electronic catalog-based merchandising. The work's subject index has been improved with its inclusion of such new headings as "Chinese literature," "depth psychology," and "artificial intelligence." Furthermore, a sufficient number of subtopic entries have been introduced on behalf of this edition, such as "autographs" and "biography," under "business and industry."

However, there continues to be an insufficiency of cross-references. For example, users are not provided a *see also* notation under "biography" for the entry "diaries and journals." Nor is there a cross-reference under "children's books" to the heading "Little Golden Books." In some cases, helpful cross-referencing terminology in the 1993 edition has been deleted from the new edition. Regrettably, listings of hundreds of solvent booksellers have been dropped from the 2d edition, often because of the prominence of paperbacks or comic books among their stock. Also excised from this edition are data on such dealer sideline wares as audiocassettes, literary posters, and bookends. Of some concern to researchers will be this edition's reduction of typeface, as well as its main entries' clutter of information pertaining to bookseller name, address, telephone number, and year of establishment. These laments aside, this guide is clearly superior to both its previous incarnation and to its rival publication, *Buy Books Where—Sell Books Where* (9th ed., Robinson Books, 1994), which encompasses only about half as many booksellers as the work under review and is generally spotty in its book stock subject descriptors.—**Jeffrey E. Long**

598. **The Association of American University Presses Directory 1996-1997.** New York, Association of American University Presses; distr., Chicago, University of Chicago Press, 1996. 235p. index. $15.95pa. ISBN 0-945103-10-7. ISSN 0739-3024.

The directory of members of the Association of American University Presses (AAUP) provides detailed information on each of its 113 scholarly press members. The directory has several sections. A general information section for authors includes a short bibliography of writing and style manuals and a list of the presses that publish journal titles. A useful "Subject Area Grid" cross-references 135 subject areas with the press names so that one can determine at a glance the subject areas in which a press publishes. The last part of the book gives information on the AAUP, including its board, committees, staff, by-laws, and guidelines for its members.

The main part of the directory contains individual listings of the member presses. The arrangement of the individual press entries is alphabetic based on the state or university name (e.g., the University Press of Colorado is under "C"). Each entry supplies the following information: street, mailing, or warehouse addresses; telephone and fax numbers; e-mail address; homepage address; foreign representatives; staff members and departments; AAUP membership information, including date the press was established, date admitted to the AAUP, the number of book titles in print, and title output by year since 1994; editorial program notes (the presses' publication subject areas, journal titles, series titles, and information on distribution); and joint and copublishing ventures. The index consists of an alphabetic list of the presses' personnel.

This unique directory will be useful and interesting for anyone interested in scholarly presses and their publications. The volume is geared specifically to authors, librarians, booksellers, and those presses looking for membership in the AAUP. The entries furnish a useful starting point for those interested in submitting books or journal articles to respected and recognized presses. The subject grid, although a useful and timesaving feature for identifying subject areas and presses in those areas, is somewhat small in typeface size; however, the small size does allow for all of the subject areas of a press to be viewed on two pages. The directory is recommended for all university and college libraries.—**Jan S. Squire**

599. **Directory of Poetry Publishers, 1997-98.** 13th ed. Len Fulton, ed. Paradise, Calif., Dustbooks, 1997. 342p. index. $21.95pa. ISBN 0-916685-63-2.

Now in its 13th edition, this compendium of poetry publishing is an important contribution to the "Small Press Information Library," of which it has long been a part. As the world of poetry and its publication has expanded, so has the need for a directory to which the interested reader, writer, researcher, or scholar can turn for a full description of the available programs.

The work has listings for magazines/periodicals and presses/book publishers. Each magazine entry includes names; addresses and telephone numbers; editors; founding date; policies; circulation and frequency; and information about special interests, submission quantity, and recent contributors. The list for presses includes similar information plus number of poetry titles published during the past year and a projection for forthcoming years and such items as royalty arrangements and rights purchased. With more than 2,200 citations, this is the single source for information of this type.

The subject index covers a wide range of topics—as broad as humor and haiku and as specific as hunger and libraries. The regional index, which could be quite helpful, has no apparent order beyond the state or country level. However, the publisher informed this reviewer by e-mail that the ordering system is the zip code, lowest to highest: a most peculiar access point and therefore one of which the reader should be made aware at the beginning of the index. Nonetheless, this is a small lack in what is otherwise a most useful work.—**Paula Frosch**

600. **Directory of Publishing 1997: United Kingdom, Commonwealth, and Overseas.** 22d ed. Herndon, Va., Mansell/Cassell, 1996. 507p. index. $95.00pa. ISBN 0-304-33823-0.

Mainstream English-language (non-U.S.) publishing information is provided in this annual directory, which was last reviewed when it was a two-volume work (see ARBA 94, entry 665). Its 650-plus entries are arranged in 5 major groupings: publishers, packagers, authors' agents, trade and allied associations, and services.

Typical entries include an organization's full name, address, telephone and fax numbers, and some e-mail and World Wide Web addresses of editorial offices and ordering locations; names of directors, managers, editors, and other key personnel; number of employees; fields of activity; number of new titles; ISBNs; imprints and series; and association memberships. Some entries give the name of the parent company, associated companies and subsidiaries, partners, distributorships, overseas representation, and annual turnover (revenue). Authors' agents' entries provide rights representation information, but trade and allied services entries are limited to contact information and description of services. The trade listing includes a new section on electronic publishing services, and enhancements related to new media have been made throughout the directory.

Appendixes include fields of activity and ownership of United Kingdom publishers; overseas representatives; firms represented in the U.K.; and indexes to ISBN prefixes, personal names, companies and their imprints, and U.K. publishers' postal codes. Because trade and allied services are not indexed, this directory's greatest value is to book dealers and acquisitions librarians in academic and research settings.—**Joanna F. Fountain**

601. **Directory of Small Press/Magazine Editors & Publishers 1997-1998.** 28th ed. Len Fulton, ed. Paradise, Calif., Dustbooks, 1997. 329p. $23.95pa. ISBN 0-916685-62-4.

As the cover of this biennial states, there are more than 6,000 small press and magazine editors and publishers listed alphabetically by name. Addresses and telephone numbers are included as well. As a companion to the publisher's *International Directory of Little Magazines and Small Presses* (see ARBA 95, entry 669), the book is intended to serve searchers who remember an editor's or publisher's name, but not the press or publication. Unlike the *International Directory*, however, it offers no description of the press or publication. "Legitimate" self-publishers who are not found in the *International Directory* are provided here. This directory is recommended for those who use the latter publication—writers, librarians, and especially those in the publishing industry.—**Lori D. Kranz**

602. **International Book Trade Directory 1997: Europe, Australia, Oceania, Latin America, Africa, and Asia.** 3d ed. Munich, New Providence, N.J., K. G. Saur/R. R. Bowker/Reed Reference Publishing, 1996. 495p. index. (Handbook of International Documentation and Information, v.15). $360.00. ISBN 3-598-22236-X.

The 3d edition of this standard title contains information on approximately 46,300 booksellers in 150 countries. Booksellers are arranged by country and city and then alphabetically by name. Entries provide the firm name, address, telephone and fax numbers, special subject areas if known, and association memberships. A subject index with 23 subsections contains references on various types of booksellers and most popular specialist areas. The coverage is adequate for countries represented in this directory, and it is only unfortunate that several former Soviet republics are not covered, such as Ukraine, Belarus, Georgia, and Armenia. Russia has 19 entries, most of them too brief to be of substantial assistance. The coverage for Western Europe is good, and for most African or Asian countries, it is adequate. Recommended for major corporations interested in book trade and some larger libraries.—**Bohdan S. Wynar**

603. **Publishers Directory, 1998: A Guide to New and Established....** 18th ed. Louise Gagné, ed. Detroit, Gale, 1997. 1936p. index. $330.00pa. ISBN 0-7876-0174-8. ISSN 0742-0501.

This valuable resource has been expanded this year to cover more than 20,000 publishers and distributors in the United States and Canada, with approximately 800 new entries. This directory compares favorably to its traditional competitor, *Literary Market Place* (see ARBA 95, entry 672), which advertises less than 14,000 publisher listings in its latest edition (R. R. Bowker declined to submit a copy for review). *Publishers Directory* provides simplified access to publisher information by grouping all major publishers together with small press, museum, religious, association, corporate, government, electronic, and database publishers in one alphabetic listing. Distributors are listed separately, and both lists are supported by a series of subject, geographic, and traditional alphabetic indexes.

The directory also provides a variety of useful data not easily found in other resources. Publisher entries are updated or added annually as a result of broadcast fax or telephone interviews, and a wide variety of data are requested that do not appear in other directories. Competitive information including discounts, annual sales, percentage of sales by markets, and returns policies are included if the publisher agreed to supply such data. Information on consolidations and amalgamations is a useful feature (although only as accurate as the response to the questionnaire). Publisher imprints are identified as such and are referenced to the parent publisher. E-mail addresses and Websites are included where known, and participation in CIP (Cataloging-in-Publication) is indicated.

As with most publishing directories compiled through invited response, there are occasional occurrences of outdated and incorrect information, usually in staff contacts or other areas where high turnover is a factor. However, the directory's broad coverage and the unique data provided make this a useful resource for any library needing comprehensive access to publisher and distributor information. *Publishers Directory* is also available electronically on diskette or magnetic tape; on CD-ROM through *Gale's Ready Reference Shelf* (see ARBA 97, entry 50); or online via GaleNet.—**Ron Maas**

604. **Publishers' International ISBN Directory 1997/98.** 24th ed. New Providence, N.J., R. R. Bowker/Reed Reference Publishing, 1997. 3v. index. $410.00. ISBN 3-598-21606-8. ISSN 0939-1959.

The 24th edition of *Publishers' International ISBN Directory* contains a considerably greater number of entries than the earlier editions. It comprises 391,837 publishers from 209 countries, an increase of 117 percent since the last printed edition. The geographic section lists 262,620 active publishers with adequate address information. The numerical section contains 402,872 ISBNs, including 29,217 entries marked as ceased publishing. The alphabetic index provides access to all 331,837 publisher entries. It should be noted that at present 140 countries worldwide officially use ISBNs, representing 95 percent of book production. The publisher hopes to publish a CD-ROM version of this directory and then, a year later, a new printed volume. Thus, this new semiannual publication cycle will provide a more up-to-date user service to subscribers of this standard work.—**Bohdan S. Wynar**

Handbooks and Yearbooks

605. Crawford, Tad. **Business and Legal Forms for Authors and Self-Publishers.** 2d ed. New York, Allworth Press, 1996. 191p. index. $19.95pa. ISBN 1-880559-50-1.

The need to help authors maintain their rights in new electronic publishing media (CD-ROM, the Internet, etc.) has brought forth a revision of this useful book, first published in 1990. Written by an attorney specializing in creative copyright and tax laws, this work is divided into three sections. The first section provides a brief overview of contracts and negotiation, the second and largest section explains the need for and use of each of the 20 tear-out legal forms that comprise the third section. A negotiation checklist is included to insure that key points in the contracts are understood, or for use with contract forms provided by someone other than the author. The final section is followed by an index.

Because this edition has been issued mainly to update electronic rights, it seems reasonable to assume it will be available in computer as well as print format for convenience of use, especially by multiple users. This is a must for libraries and anyone with serious literary aspirations.—**Larry Lobel**

12 Military Studies

GENERAL WORKS

Bibliography

606. Chambers, Steven D. **Political Leaders and Military Figures of the Second World War: A Bibliography.** Brookfield, Vt., Dartmouth Publishing/Ashgate Publishing, 1996. 440p. index. $84.95. ISBN 1-85521-646-9.

Chambers has provided an interesting bibliography of important names in the political and military era of World War II. This work is a classed bibliography with five main classes: Allied political leaders, Axis political leaders, Allied military leaders, Axis military leaders, and other notable figures and miscellaneous entries. The military leaders are further divided by country, and political leaders are listed by name and appear to cover only the major players: Winston Churchill, Joseph Stalin, Franklin Roosevelt, Adolf Hitler, and others.

Each leader is covered by a brief one- or two-page biographical introduction and bibliography. The bibliographies are proceeded by a paragraph of annotations of suggested readings, with the annotations referring only to the more well-known biographies. It is a puzzle to the reader what criteria were used for selection. Only books are cited, leaving readers to locate the many periodical articles on their own. In general the volume seems to have been compiled by searching several large computer library catalogs. This results in a bibliography that is neither complete nor annotated. In addition, choices of titles are sometimes odd; for example, detailed Ph.D. dissertations on the speech patterns of World War II political leaders and a correspondence collection between FDR and Pope Pius XII.

The biographical sketches, although balanced, are rather simplistic. For example, the Roosevelt entry reads, "during his terms as president, Roosevelt had his admirers and his detractors." Hitler is similarly described as "the catalyst for change in Europe in the 1930s." Charles de Gaulle's entry covers a scant two paragraphs and lacks the concise phrasing accorded the other leaders as cited above. There are numerous minor inaccuracies in the Stalin thumbnail sketch. Military leaders are arranged alphabetically within the country of their command. Maurice-Gustave Gamelin is given a mere five sentences. There is a miscellaneous grouping at the end that lists collected biographies by class. An author index is provided for each cited biography. There is no general index other than the table of contents. For example, when looking for Klaus Barbie, one can only search through the book. Only when the subject of the biography is a cited author will the person be found in the index, for example Churchill, Dwight Eisenhower, and so on.

Although this is an interesting point of view on World War II, it is better covered by other bibliographers, which the author cites. Most of the information can also be obtained by searching a major library catalog or encyclopedia. In addition, the price seems rather steep for the value.—**Ralph Lee Scott**

607. Croddy, Eric. **Chemical and Biological Warfare: An Annotated Bibliography.** Lanham, Md., Scarecrow, 1997. 429p. index. $45.00. ISBN 0-8108-3271-2.

Although the international community has attempted several times to outlaw chemical and biological weapons, the dangers and the possibility of their use increase daily. This threat is one of the grave concerns of modern warfare. Nevertheless, the subject is little understood beyond a narrow group of specialists. Croddy has done a large service by compiling an exhaustive research source on chemical and biological warfare.

The introduction provides a quick narrative introduction to the topic with definitions and a historical survey. Following are more than 2,100 annotated bibliographic citations divided into 23 topical chapters. Examples include chemical and biological warfare in past and modern history; specific chapters on World War I, World War II, and later conflicts; chemical and biological warfare and civil defense; legal and moral aspects of chemical and biological warfare; and regional studies in the Middle East, Latin America, Asia, the former Soviet Union, and so on. The final chapter consists of a list of 57 Internet sources for further information. The appendixes provide other sources of information, including journals that occasionally deal with chemical and biological warfare issues and signatory nations to the 1993 Chemical Weapons Convention.

The annotations are useful. This timely reference source is a good addition for libraries of all types.—**Joe P. Dunn**

608. Fredriksen, John C., comp. **War of 1812 Eyewitness Accounts: An Annotated Bibliography.** Westport, Conn., Greenwood Press, 1997. 311p. index. (Bibliographies and Indexes in Military Studies, no.8). $79.50. ISBN 0-313-30291-X.

Of course there is nothing inherently wrong with a bibliography of eyewitness accounts of the War of 1812, or any war for that matter. (And one gets the uneasy suspicion that there are more such books about to be born!) Indeed, this one is well done—the annotations fulsome, explicit, and usefully detailed. Its three sections, eyewitness accounts from the military, the Navy, and the civilian population, seem naturally divided, even down to the subdivisions, such as United States and British, American and Canadian armies. Fredriksen is to be commended for not having forgotten his indexes, both by editor and by subject.

What troubles, however, is whether such a tool is worth the price. That is, are there enough military libraries and scholars who will find this tool winsome enough to buy it for what appears to be a quite substantial sum? It would not seem so. Moreover, given the omission in reference to certain important tools in other strategic areas, is this particular subject matter one of such importance that it should supersede all others? Suffice it to say, this tool is for special collections only. [R: C&RL, Sept 97, p. 480]
—**Mark Y. Herring**

609. Jandora, John Walter. **Militarism in Arab Society: An Historiographical and Bibliographical Sourcebook.** Westport, Conn., Greenwood Press, 1997. 142p. illus. maps. index. $65.00. ISBN 0-313-29370-8.

Jandora spent five years as an adviser to the Saudi Arabian National Guard and was activated in the Persian Gulf War and served in the Pentagon and in Riyadh. His earlier study, *The March from Medina: A Revisionist Study of the Arab Conquests* (Kingston Press, 1990), provided background for this useful reference volume.

The eight essays briefly treat warfare in Arab history, or at least in the eastern portion of the Arab world to which the author limits the book. Concise, informative, and well written, the essays are valuable introductory sources for laypeople but will have lesser import for those with greater expertise in the field. Each essay is followed by a selected bibliography. Unfortunately, the book is not quite what the subtitle advertises. The essays are not really historiographical, and the bibliographies, which only cite English-language sources, are not as extensive as desired. Admittedly, this reflects a relative paucity of attention to this subject in the Arab world. At minimum, the author should have annotated the items in the bibliographies. Finally, many of the items are badly out-of-date, and their usefulness is questionable. This is another reason why individual assessments of sources is necessary. The book includes a useful glossary and an alphabetically organized listing of Arab dynasties of the "Arab East."

Because the book is best suited for the relative novice, it is most valuable for college or university undergraduate libraries supporting courses on the Arab world. Some general public libraries may also find it valuable.—**Joe P. Dunn**

610. Noffsinger, James Philip. **World War I Aviation: A Bibliography of Books in English, French, German, and Italian.** rev. ed. Lanham, Md., Scarecrow, 1997. 609p. index. $98.00. ISBN 0-8108-3085-X.

This is an updated and revised edition of the 1987 work (see ARBA 88, entry 681), which includes titles published since then and correction of errors in the previous bibliography. This bibliography is well organized and annotated. Noffsinger provides readers in English, German, French, and Italian with copious lists of published material. The infancy of air war and the brave men who took to the air to defend their respective countries have found a source to refer interested readers and scholars to volumes published during the war up to those published recently. Halftones of vintage photographs and of vintage volumes on the air war during the Great War enhance the value of this extensive bibliography. There is also a priced checklist of books from 1990 to 1996. The list contains books that are valued according to U.S. dollars using 1995 rates. One hopes with the publication of this new edition there may be some interest in reprinting some of the fine works listed in the bibliography. This is an excellent work recommended for public, college, university, and rare book collector reference collections.—**Norman L. Kincaide**

611. Rasor, Eugene L. **The Solomon Islands Campaign, Guadalcanal to Rabaul: Historiography and Annotated Bibliography.** Westport, Conn., Greenwood Press, 1997. 146p. index. (Bibliographies of Battles and Leaders, no.20). $65.00. ISBN 0-313-30059-3.

This is the third of the author's five planned volumes on the Asian/Pacific theater of World War II. He is also working on annotated bibliographies of British statesmen Earl Louis Mountbatten and Lord Arthur James Balfour. This exceptionally good compilation is divided into two parts. The historiographical narrative treats archives, libraries, manuscripts, bibliographies, and the like and provides essays on topics such as strategy and tactics; organization; operations; personalities; diplomacy; logistics; race and barbarity; and the campaign as depicted in fiction, film, and art. Part 2 alphabetically lists 544 annotated citations.

The two parts together provide a comprehensive and exhaustive overview of the subject. Rasor also discusses areas that require further research. Examples include the contributions of Allies, including the Australians, the New Zealanders, the British, the Free French, and natives such as the Fiji Islanders. He also calls for a replacement for Samuel Eliot Morison's classic but dated and insufficient history of the naval battles of the campaign. The book also contains a useful chronology and comprehensive author and subject indexes. Although the book's narrow focus makes it too particular for smaller libraries, large libraries will find this and all its companion volumes exceptional research resources.—**Joe P. Dunn**

Dictionaries and Encyclopedias

612. **Encyclopedia of the War of 1812.** David S. Heidler and Jeanne T. Heidler, eds. Santa Barbara, Calif., ABC-CLIO, 1997. 636p. illus. maps. index. $95.00. ISBN 0-87436-968-1.

In the summer of 1812, the clash of the great European powers was entering its final act. Napoleon led a half-million men into Russia even as French armies continued their four-year fight with the British on the Iberian Peninsula. The crisis between the United States and Great Britain that erupted in the War of 1812 stemmed from the European wars of the French Revolution and their successors, the Napoleonic Wars. This volume contains some 500 alphabetically arranged entries written by 70 contributors examining the military, political, and social history of the War of 1812. The volume also contains the text of important documents, such as the Embargo Act, the Rambouillet Decree, President James Madison's War Message of 1812, and the like. This volume concludes with a brief glossary and a bibliography limited to sources in the English language. David S. Heidler is on the faculty at the University of Southern Colorado, and Jeanne T. Heidler is an associate professor at the U.S. Air Force Academy in Colorado Springs.—**Bohdan S. Wynar**

613. Forty, George. **The Encyclopedia of 20th Century Conflict: Land Warfare.** London, Arms and Armour Press/Cassell Group; distr., New York, Sterling Publishing, 1997. 320p. illus. maps. $34.95. ISBN 1-85409-222-7.

This encyclopedia is part of a trilogy; the other two volumes, by different authors, cover air and naval combat. It is divided into 4 sections: a chronological survey of events; an alphabetic encyclopedia of equipment, concepts, places, battles, wars, and weapons (with detailed topical side bars that do not appear in any particular order); overviews of "the world's foremost military powers"; and brief biographical sketches of important military figures. This work is heavily illustrated with black-and-white photographs, maps, and diagrams. There is a cursory bibliography, but unfortunately no index, which would have been useful considering the amount of information that does not appear in the alphabetically arranged sections. Many of the entries are poorly or subjectively phrased and full of unexplained abbreviations, with much that is misleading, superficial, or simply incorrect. It is unfortunate that such a reasonably priced book, so attractively illustrated, and with so much information is so seriously flawed. This may appeal to some military buffs, but inconsistent quality and ineffective access to information make this unsatisfactory as a reference tool. [R: RBB, 15 Oct 97, pp. 427-28]—**Kenneth W. Berger**

614. **The Grolier Library of World War I.** Danbury, Conn., Grolier, 1997. 8v. illus. maps. index. $249.00/set. ISBN 0-7172-9065-4.

Written for students in grades 7 and higher, *The Grolier Library of World War I* has as its purpose the explication of the conflict that "affected the modern geopolitical landscape of our planet" more than any other. The set is divided into 8 chronologically arranged, 128-page volumes: "The Causes of Conflict, 1914"; "The Race for the Sea, 1915"; "The Lines Are Drawn, 1916"; "The Year of Attrition, 1917"; "The U.S. Enters the War, 1915-17"; "The Eastern Front, 1918"; "A Flawed Victory"; and "1919-39, the Aftermath of War." Each volume contains indexes (subject and biographical) to the entire set, the same 32-word glossary, and the bibliography for the encyclopedia. The format of each volume is identical. Each begins with a comprehensive table of contents listing the subjects covered in the book as well as additional features, such as biographies. This is followed by an introduction explaining the arrangement of the book and a map that focuses on the location of the action in the individual volume. This similarity in format allows each volume to stand alone and makes the information highly accessible.

The editors of *The Grolier Library of World War I* have provided the student researcher with an engaging and information-rich resource. While providing good coverage of the military and political aspects of the war, they have also contributed insights into social history, literature, and medical and technological advances. The use of numerous sidebars giving short biographies of political leaders and military commanders, quotations from letters and diaries, and cross-references to related topics give insights into homefronts as well as battlefronts. The many maps and black-and-white photographs contribute to visual interest.

With its exploration of the causes of the war, ranging back to 1879, and its discussion of the effects of the war, projecting to 1939, this encyclopedia becomes a valuable research tool for issues beyond those indicated in its title. This publication, because of its readability and accessibility, will be a valuable addition to any library or media center.—**Michele Tyrrell**

615. **Modern Campaigns.** Danbury, Conn., Grolier, 1997. 15v. illus. maps. index. $319.00/set. ISBN 0-7172-7678-3.

Modern Campaigns is a series of 15 volumes, each covering an important military conflict of modern times. The conflicts treated cover Civil War campaigns (First Battle of Bull Run, 1861; Antietam, 1862; Chickamauga, 1863; and Vicksburg, 1863); World War I campaigns (Gallipoli, 1915, and Kaiserschlact, 1918); World War II campaigns (France, 1940; Midway, 1942; Guadalcanal, 1942; Kursk, 1943; Normandy, 1944; Operation Bagration, 1944; Arnhem, 1944; and Ardennes, 1944); and a Vietnam campaign (Tet offensive, 1968). Designed for junior high and high school students, each volume describes the events that precipitated the specific conflict; the events of the campaign; and details on the participants, armaments, geographic influences, and other factors that helped determine the outcome of the engagement.

Each volume has 112 pages with numerous captioned photographs (both color and black-and-white), maps, drawings, and timelines, making the set appealing to young adults as well as adults. A table of contents and a master series index in each volume simplifies their use for both researchers and browsers. Also contained in each volume are a chronology of the important dates and events, a guide to further reading, and recommendations for "wargaming" the specific campaign. This series will be a welcome addition to school and public libraries and is within the price range of most libraries.—**Vik Brown**

616. **The Reader's Companion to Military History.** Robert Cowley and Geoffrey Parker, eds. New York, Houghton Mifflin, 1996. 573p. illus. maps. index. $45.00. ISBN 0-395-66969-3.

This companion covers military history from the origin of war to the Persian Gulf War of 1990-1991. It is not meant to be comprehensive but does include 570 entries written by 152 subject specialists. There are 41 maps and 89 black-and-white pictures that enhance the text. The entries are alphabetically arranged and are cross-referenced. The entries are signed, but few contain suggestions for further study. The book concludes with both an index of contributors and a general index.

There are entries from every continent, but the coverage is uneven because of the way the editors selected entries. The editors used two working principles in order to decide what entries should be included and what their length should be. They decided to favor entries that employed Western styles of warfare because that is the dominant style of war today and also to emphasize twentieth-century conflicts. The end result is that coverage from continents such as Asia and Africa is sketchy at best, whereas there is a long entry for World War II, as well as entries for both every major battle and commander in the conflict. The entry for the Persian Gulf War is more than a page long, but there is no entry for the French and Indian War. (It is mentioned in the entry for the Seven Years' War as an afterthought.) This bias severely undermines the usefulness of this title, especially because there is no shortage of information in the reference literature for Western conflicts in the twentieth century.

Scattered throughout the text are little boxes of trivia that list such topics as "The Ten Most Underrated Commanders" and "The Ten Most Important Sea Battles." The information is strictly subjective and is apparently the opinion of the editors, because no source is cited. Aetius is the first commander listed as underrated, which is interesting because the editors did not warrant him a biographical entry. He is mentioned briefly in the entry for Attila.

One hopes more entries will be included in future editions that focus on the non-Western world. That is the only way to truly provide a global perspective on military history. [R: Choice, May 97, p. 1480]

—**John R. Burch Jr.**

Directories

617. Arkin, William M. **The U.S. Military Online: A Directory for Internet Access to the Department of Defense.** Herndon, Va., Brassey's (U.S.), 1997. 240p. illus. index. $29.95pa. ISBN 1-57488-143-4.

In one convenient volume, this work systematically takes the reader through the Internet resources of the entire defense establishment. For example, the Department of Defense starts with DefenseLINK, the master Website with links to all related and subordinate organizations. This book goes even deeper, listing Websites for each service—army, navy, and air force—and those for military installations and facilities in every state and in foreign countries. Research institutes, libraries, and history collections are included, as are sites for policy, weaponry, research and development, and performing business with defense agencies. There are often addresses, telephone numbers, and e-mail addresses given along with URLs. Readers will find the layout of the book clean and attractive, and although the organization of the book is simple and readily apparent, there is an index of organizations at the end.

Why, with all the search engines available on the World Wide Web, would one need a book such as this? For no other reason than that this work will save time. No waiting for search engines to load worthless graphics, or sifting through tens or hundreds of results to find the one needed. By using either the table of contents or the index, one can find the relevant Website instantly. The fact that URLs change and that Websites drop off the Web is a fact of life; however, spot-checking one chapter showed that only 7 of 42 sites listed could not be reached. This is an excellent work that will reward users needing access to the military on the Internet.—**Eric R. Nitschke**

618. **Jane's Military Communications 1997-98.** 18th ed. John Williamson, ed. Alexandria, Va., Jane's Information Group, 1997. 845p. illus. index. $290.00. ISBN 0-7106-1530-2.

This work catalogs current military communications hardware in use or under development by armed forces around the world. Included is equipment for tactical, ground, naval, air force, and satellite system communications. Among other types listed are microwave and tropo scatter systems, encryption and security devices, signal analysis, direction finding, and jamming equipment.

The format is similar to all of Jane's publications. After a foreword that reviews the major trends and events of the past year and discusses implications of developments in progress, the work is organized into chapters by equipment type. Each type is then discussed according to country of manufacture. Clear photographs are provided for almost every piece of equipment listed. The purpose and use of each item is described, the status of those items under development is recorded, and technical specifications noted. There is an index by manufacturer and product name and military designation, as well as a glossary of terms, acronyms, and code names.

This is certainly one of the more specialized of Jane's publications and will be of great value to those who can use and understand it. However, it is not a title that will appeal to general readers or military buffs as does *Jane's All the World's Aircraft* (see ARBA 97, entry 1440) or *Jane's Fighting Ships* (see ARBA 97, entry 573). Because of Jane's reputation and preeminence in the field of military technical information, this work is recommend to those libraries that have readers or support programs in this specialized field.—**Eric R. Nitschke**

Handbooks and Yearbooks

619. **Jane's Electro-Optic Systems 1996-97.** 2d ed. A. P. O'Leary, ed. Alexandria, Va., Jane's Information Group, 1996. 535p. illus. index. $290.00. ISBN 0-7106-1360-1.

This is the 2d edition of the successor to *Jane's Battlefield Surveillance Systems* (published 1988-1995). Included are infrared, thermal imaging, image-intensifying, and laser technology systems designed for combat surveillance, targeting, damage assessment, or countermeasures against other systems. (Radar and acoustic-based technologies are not included.)

The foreword provides a brief overview of types of systems, highlighting the leading products, producers, and developments. The nearly 1,300 entries appear within the broad categories of naval, land (the largest area of application), and airborne systems, with multiple-use systems listed under their predominant application. Typical entries include the name of the system; its generic type; development and description notes; technical specifications; operational status (in production, available, and the like); and contractor. The volume is heavily illustrated with black-and-white photographs and drawings (there are nearly 600 new additions). Supplemental sections include alphabetic indexes of product names and contractors (unfortunately there is no product type index); a directory of contractors; and lists of entries added and deleted in this edition (in addition to extensive updating, there are more than 200 new listings).

The volume is informative, authoritative (within the limits of public information), and reasonably priced. The highly specialized subject matter, however, will likely limit its appeal to comprehensive military technology and contemporary military affairs collections. Potential purchasers should note that *Jane's Electro-Optic Systems* is one of two dozen weapons systems titles included in the *Jane's Defense Equipment Library* on CD-ROM or as a separate CD-ROM priced at $795.—**Kenneth W. Berger**

620. Joes, Anthony James. **Guerrilla Warfare: A Historical, Biographical, and Bibliographical Sourcebook.** Westport, Conn., Greenwood Press, 1996. 312p. index. $89.50. ISBN 0-313-29252-3.

Joes, a political scientist, has written two previous books on guerrilla warfare and a more general analytic history of the Vietnam War. This new volume consists of three parts. Most of the compilation is devoted to brief essays on guerrilla warfare from the American and French Revolutions through present insurgencies in Latin America and Africa. A small sample of the topics include the U.S. Civil War, the Boer War, the activities of Lawrence of Arabia, insurgency against Adolf Hitler and Joseph Stalin, the Greek Civil War, the Huks, Afghanistan, and postcolonial conflict in Africa and Asia. The rather lengthy treatment of the Vietnam conflict under the French and the Americans is out of proportion to the rest of the subjects.

Part 2 consists of brief biographical profiles of individuals who played leading roles in guerrilla conflicts. However, several of the items, examples such as Harry Truman, Ronald Reagan, and Bao Dai, are strange choices. If the criterion is anyone who led a nation that fought guerrillas, a much larger number of world leaders could be included. This is a curious and disappointing part of the book. Part 3, a series of bibliographic essays on some of the topics in part 1, is also less than it could have been. It tends merely to list books in categories rather than provide much analysis or evaluation.

The real question is what audience this compilation will serve. The book is far too superficial for scholars and a bit esoteric for novice students. It seems to be an expensive volume with limited utility.
—**Joe P. Dunn**

621. **The Political Role of the Military: An International Handbook.** Constantine P. Danopoulos and Cynthia Watson, eds. Westport, Conn., Greenwood Press, 1996. 517p. index. $115.00. ISBN 0-313-28837-2.

This handbook illustrates the varying political roles of a range of militaries from around the world. Twenty-seven chapters, each covering a different country, trace the historical background of the military, analyze the political influence of the armed services, evaluate the success of the political role, and project future developments in each country. Economic factors are also discussed; however, each contributor has chosen the relevant variables for each individual nation. There are a complete index and a short biography of each contributor as well as references for each chapter. Intended to create a body of literature that shows how complicated military-civilian relationships are around the world, this handbook is not fully comprehensive in its attempt to represent every country but does provide informative comparisons between the larger, more representative states.—**Natalie Brower-Kirton**

622. **World War II in Europe, Africa, and the Americas, with General Sources: A Handbook of Literature and Research.** Loyd E. Lee, ed. Westport, Conn., Greenwood Press, 1997. 525p. index. $95.00. ISBN 0-313-29325-2.

The writing of history continues to evolve, and different historical subjects have individual historiographies. World War II is no different. The largest war in history has developed, probably, the largest volume of published material in the history of history. To be of any use to scholars and students, this burgeoning scholarship must be critiqued, organized, and cataloged. This handbook of literature and research is an excellent guide to the conflict in Europe, Africa, and the Americas. Each section is preceded by a historiographic narrative and followed by a bibliography. There are author and subject indexes. Contributors are scholars from the fields of military, European, American, and European colonial history.

Scholars and students looking for an updated bibliographic and historiographic treatment of the published and archival material on World War II will be delighted with this work. From first hand accounts to the evolving scholarly treatment of the great conflict that has shaped history, this book is highly recommended for public, college, and university reference collections.—**Norman L. Kincaide**

AIR FORCE

623. **Jane's Military Aircraft Image Library.** [CD-ROM]. Alexandria, Va., Jane's Information Group, 1997. Minimum system requirements: IBM or compatible with a Pentium processor. Double-speed CD-ROM drive. Windows 3.1. 16MB RAM. 2MB hard disk space. Monitor capable of displaying millions of colors. $600.00. ISBN 0-7106-1759-3.

Without question, Jane's is the leader in publishing comprehensive, up-to-date information on the world's military forces, and the *Military Aircraft Image Library* is one of three new CD-ROM products Jane's began marketing in 1997. The CD-ROM is a combination of three print sources—*All the World's Aircraft*, *Aircraft Upgrades*, and *World Air Forces*. This product is priced at $600, whereas the three print sources carry a combined cost of over $1,000 a year. The CD-ROM is sold on a subscription basis and will be updated annually.

Installation is simple (for the purpose of this review, Windows 3.1 was used), yet installation alone does not allow complete access to the full-image library. A subscription tutorial provides the user with instructions on how to activate full images through the use of a 32-digit code, which requires a similar authorization code. It is necessary to contact Jane's in order to obtain this authorization code.

The initial screen provides options for a tutorial, a table of contents, brief product information, subscription information (which includes the subscription tutorial), and the search option. There are six search options—word, company, country, section, title, and caption. The first three are obvious; section searching is by type of aircraft (e.g., fixed wing, rotary wing), title searching is by name of the aircraft, and caption searching looks for words in captions that accompany images. Word searching is easiest, and search options can be combined using Boolean operators. Once a term is selected, results can be displayed in thumbnail form—a smaller image with caption. All 2,430 of the images can then be enlarged with the caption and specific aircraft name, company, country, section, and Jane's reference. Images can be enlarged further to a full screen, or specific sectors of the image can be enlarged to focus on a wing, fuselage, cockpit, and so on. Images can be sorted by company, country, section, and title. Printing and downloading are options. Searching and on-screen navigation are relatively easy, with icons or drop-down menus. Even the novice searcher should be able to use the product effectively. Help screens are available and are well written, concise, and generally useful. Jane's provides a toll-free telephone number and e-mail address for questions. Six calls to Jane's provided good responses. Jane's sources are accurate and reliable; unfortunately, the image library is of limited use to academic and public libraries. Corporate and military libraries are more likely customers and will find the CD-ROM a valuable resource.—**Boyd Childress**

ARMY

624. Emerson, William K. **Encyclopedia of United States Army Insignia and Uniforms.** Norman, Okla., University of Oklahoma Press, 1996. 674p. illus. index. $125.00. ISBN 0-8061-2622-1.

This magnificent work details the history of U.S. Army uniforms and insignia over a span of 200 years. Organized roughly into three major sections, the work begins with a brief discussion of uniforms and their development before dealing at length with the insignia worn by the different branches of the Army (Infantry and Signal Corps, for example) and then, again exhaustively, with uniform apparel. Each of the latter two sections are treated chronologically from the early Republic to the 1980s. Both men's and women's uniforms are included, but strictly combat clothing is not.

It is the detail in which the encyclopedia relates the development and characteristics of the army uniform and the changes distinguishing the various models that make it so valuable a source. The entire volume is fully illustrated with black-and-white photographs conveniently located in or alongside the text in which a particular item is discussed. Contemporary photographs are used almost exclusively to depict specific uniforms. Other photographs provide detailed close-ups of insignia and uniform particulars. The captions accompanying most illustrations are important sources of information in themselves. There is a fine index and the notes, picture credits, and excellent bibliography provide valuable references for the researcher.

This noteworthy study should be included in any academic or public library serving researchers interested in U.S. military history. Even more, however, because of its detail and fine illustrations, it will be of immense value to archivists and genealogists who need to date old photographs. [R: RBB, 1 Mar 97, p. 1186]—**Eric R. Nitschke**

625. Stein, Barry Jason. **U.S. Army Patches: An Illustrated Encyclopedia of Cloth Unit Insignia.** Columbia, S.C., University of South Carolina Press, 1997. 222p. illus. index. $39.95. ISBN 1-57003-179-7.

Every active-duty army soldier or veteran will be able to find his or her special unit cloth insignia in this colorful book. There are more than 1,800 of these patches reproduced in full color on 77 plates. (The color work here is excellent.) From World War I to the present, the patches represent active and inactive units as well as those approved for local wear and many not officially authorized. Each illustrated army unit receives a brief profile reporting its origin, current status, decorations, battle campaigns, and the historical and heraldic significance of its patch. There is a glossary of terms, a brief bibliography, and a useful index citing plate number and text page.

Stein is a businessman supplying military insignia to the U.S. armed forces. He has visited every major U.S. military base in the world. His earlier book, *U.S. Army Heraldic Crests* (see ARBA 94, entry 696), is a standard reference work.—**David Eggenberger**

NAVY

626. Greger, Rene. **Battleships of the World.** Annapolis, Md., Naval Institute Press, 1997. 259p. illus. index. $59.95. ISBN 1-55750-069-X.

This translated ready-reference volume (originally written in 1993 and not updated since) purports to offer more accurate data on battleships and battle cruisers than existing standard works. Because this is a popular naval topic, this volume adds to a crowded field, leaving the much more interesting pre-Dreadnought era relatively neglected. An introduction provides a short illustrated history of the battleship from the rise of the ironclad to 1905, supplemented by a number of useful statistical tables. The main text is organized by country and class and subdivided chronologically (separating reconstructed ships from their original configuration); unfortunately, the arrangement of nations follows no logical order. Data other than tonnage and United States/United Kingdom gun calibers are uniformly metric and include such details as gun performance and weight of armor (which do not agree with other published references, although definition issues make assessing accuracy difficult). An index provides entries for ship names only.

Each class is illustrated with one or more photographs, plus a profile/deck plan line drawing (the scale of these drawings is not stated, but appears to be 1:1300). Most of the photographs are fresh and clear, but unfortunately some are severely guttered. Although the line drawings provide details of underwater form, they are marred by a number of minor or major errors, the most serious of which is the inaccurate representation of the after lower hull forms of the *North Carolina* and *South Dakota* classes.

The book's claim to definitive status is weakened by a number of factual errors, of which the worst is crediting the *Pennsylvania* class with the wrong main armament (10-by-14 inch rather than 12-by-14 inch) on pages 207 and 216. Additionally, the text has a number of translation errors (e.g., "parliament" is used when "legislature" is intended), and some of the individual class descriptions are split between the national introduction and the class page itself, resulting in a confusing presentation. A persistent typesetting error that eliminates spaces between italicized words and regular typeface makes the text more difficult to read. Even though it is sturdily bound and crisply printed on good-quality paper, this title, which itself is based on secondary sources, fails to realize its high aspirations.—**John Howard Oxley**

627. **Jane's Warships Image Library.** [CD-ROM]. Alexandria, Va., Jane's Information Group, 1997. Minimum system requirements: IBM or compatible with Pentium processor. Double-speed CD-ROM drive. Windows 3.1. 16MB RAM. 2MB hard disk space. Monitor capable of displaying millions of colors. $600.00. ISBN 0-7106-1760-7.

Jane's Information Group has made a career of, in the Duke of Wellington's fine phrase, "all the business of war," and the United States and every other country in the world is safer for it. Jane's books on military armament—aircraft, warships, guns, tanks, and the like—have been staple diets for anyone wanting to find out about matters military. Such tools have also been premier reference sources for libraries. Now comes the first of, one hopes, numerous image library CD-ROMs. *Jane's Warships Image Library* is a treasure trove of all things nautical.

Loading is a snap. The disc runs smoothly and fast, if a bit noisily. Yet the attractions are, of course, the ships themselves. *Albania's Whiskey V Class* (SS) is here, along with Austria's River Patrol Craft. The United States proliferates with its Strategic Missile Submarines, cruisers, destroyers (the Arleigh Burke Class Guided Missile Destroyer is especially nice), frigates, and more. Access is by search terms via a word list or by the table of contents. The table of contents is alphabetic by country, followed by warship type and class. Contained herein are line drawings, photographs, and suitable-for-framing color prints. Each one may be zoomed in upon for closer inspection. Some types have multiple photographs showing a sequence of the ship and its warheads, for example. Although the faint of heart may blanch at this CD-ROM, its information is nonetheless useful.—**Mark Y. Herring**

628. **The Naval Institute Guide to the Ships and Aircraft of the U.S. Fleet.** 16th ed. By Norman Polmar. Annapolis, Md., Naval Institute Press, 1997. 580p. illus. index. $79.95. ISBN 1-55750-686-8.

Identical in format to the previous edition (see ARBA 94, entry 705), this volume provides an authoritative, critical look at the state of the U.S. fleet by a foremost expert on the topic. Broad coverage includes organizational and personnel details, as well as equipment (including U.S. Marine Corps amphibious vehicles); addenda are supplied for late-breaking events. The historical background leading to current naval conditions is explored, the current situation is explained, and future programs are projected. From mighty supercarriers to humble radiation test barges, an abundance of facts is presented, some surprising (e.g., only 5 percent of U.S. Navy officers are married). The succinct text is supported by large, high-quality monochrome photographs (of 100 randomly selected pictures, at least 69 percent are new, with credit dates of 1993 or later) with informative captions.

Compared to the major naval annuals, slight discrepancies in some data emerge, with this title probably being the most authoritative unclassified source available. In comparison to the naval/aviation annuals, as well as to titles like the *Naval Institute Guide to World Naval Weapons Systems* (see entry 634), there is slightly less detail on major weapons and electronics. However, this title offers unrivaled treatment of the vast range of auxiliary and support ships forming the vital sinews of globe-girdling naval strength. A few typographic errors were noted—for example, the first Marine forces landed in Saudi Arabia in 1990, not 1991—but these are minor.

Overall, this book is clearly printed on high-quality paper in a sturdy binding. Comprehensively indexed, it is a peerless ready-reference guide to its subject, of definite interest to any library serving a clientele with naval interests.—**John Howard Oxley**

629. **Warships of the USSR and Russia, 1945-1995.** By A. S. Pavlov. Norman Friedman, ed. Annapolis, Md., Naval Institute Press, 1997. 321p. illus. index. $59.95. ISBN 1-55750-671-X.

The contents of this specialized reference book are divided into three sections: ships of pre-World War II design, ships of postwar design, and transports and cargo vessels. War prizes, Lend-Lease ships, civilian ships, unrealized projects, and ships not launched are excluded. There are more than 120 entries for ship classes, which the Russians call "projects." The entries include the ship names, project numbers, North Atlantic Treaty Organization designations, dates of construction, launching, completion, and when stricken from the navy's list, along with technical data as to its displacement, dimensions, armament, armor, machinery, complement, and electronics. All data were gathered from public sources. Of use would be more text analyzing the design, capabilities, and operations of these ships; what is provided is relatively brief. In addition to large surface warships, submarines, patrol boats, and hovercraft are also included.

Most of the ship classes are accompanied by photographs and line drawings (most done by the author). The most interesting pictures are those of the flying boats with eight jet engines mounted above and behind the cockpit, with large missile tubes on the top of the fuselage—these truly look like something out of science fiction. Many of the designs look sleek and appear to have more weapons than comparable Western ships. When examining the superstructures of these ships, many of them are reminiscent of the Imperial cruisers from the Star Wars series. One wonders how these impressive-looking ships would have done in a war against a modern opponent.

This volume is an expanded edition of a smaller-in-scope handbook published in Yakutsk in 1991. The author is a naval architect, and the editor is an international naval expert. Naval enthusiasts will want to read the helpful explanation of Soviet design practice and overall shipbuilding policy provided in the editor's introduction. This sturdily bound item is suitable for the reference and circulating collections of academic and public libraries, and complements the more expensive Jane's Fighting Ships series.—**Daniel K. Blewett**

UNIFORMS

630. Ball, Robert W. D. **British Army Campaign Medals.** Dubuque, Iowa, Antique Trader Publications, 1996. 152p. illus. $29.95. ISBN 0-930625-64-1.

This is a guide to medals awarded for participation in a particular event, battle, or campaign. Medals for valor, good conduct, or length of service are not included; nor are regimental, commemorative, or personal medals. Further, the guide discusses only medals awarded to members of the British Army, not those created by Great Britain to be awarded to members of native armies. Each of the 80 medals is depicted slightly larger (approximately 1.5 times) than actual size in at least 1 color photograph. Most are shown in two photographs, one for the obverse and one for the reverse. Because the British affix metal bars (also called clasps) bearing the names of particular actions or locales to the ribbon, some medals have multiple photographs illustrating these. The photographs are especially clear, and because the book is printed on coated paper, the details come out extremely well. It is interesting to compare these photographs of actual medals with the chromolithographs in John Horsley Mayo's *Medals and Decorations of the British Army and Navy* (2 vols., Westminster, England, Constable, 1897).

The work under review offers more than just photographs, however. The text gives the history of the medal, including the number of soldiers eligible for it; a physical description of the pendant, ribbon, and accompanying bars; and a brief history of the campaign for which it was created. Coverage is from the General Service Medal honoring those who served during the Napoleonic Wars, 1793-1814 (but not issued until 1848), through to the Persian Gulf War medal of 1991. The book concludes with a guide to the value of various medals and a brief bibliography. The guide is recommended for libraries with an interest in the subject.—**Eric R. Nitschke**

WEAPONS

631. Gelbart, Marsh. **Tanks: Main Battle Tanks and Light Tanks.** Herndon, Va., Brassey's (U.S.), 1996. 160p. illus. (Brassey's Modern Military Equipment). $28.95. ISBN 1-85753-168-X.

Unlike most military equipment, tanks exert a deep fascination on the general reader, but enthusiasts may be disappointed in this volume. The main concentration is on modern main battle (heavy) tanks with more than 60 models from 22 different nations. Some 17 light tanks are also mentioned. In both categories technical data are emphasized: weight, armor, dimensions, and armament, with little attention paid to geographic constraints, design philosophy, or tactical doctrine. Thus, the work assumes much prior knowledge from the reader. Even so, this technical material is so limited that the truly well informed will probably find it insufficient to sustain their attention. Perhaps less space should have been devoted to such antique vehicles as the Sherman and T34; instead, space could be given to new tanks, such as France's Leclerc. Insights gained from the Gulf War are a surprising omission, especially because the author is described as having lived in the Middle East.

This book will be useful for those needing a quick reference to current heavy armor. However, its bare format will do little to hold the attention of nonmilitary readers, and military experts will have access to more complete sources of information.—**Paul L. Holmer**

632. **Jane's Air-Launched Weapons Image Library.** [CD-ROM]. Alexandria, Va., Jane's Information Group, 1997. Minimum system requirements: IBM or compatible Pentium 100. Double-speed CD-ROM drive. Windows 3.1. 16MB RAM. 2MB hard disk space. Monitor capable of displaying millions of colors. $995.00. ISBN 0-7106-1654-6.

Herein is another wonderful contribution to the "flinty and steel couch of war." *Jane's Air-Launched Weapons Image Library* is a picture library of fantastic proportions. Not only are color photographs and line drawings here by the hundreds, but so are numerous video clips that will enthrall library patrons for hours. The only difficulty encountered was turning it off in order to write this review.

Loading is easy and quick. Access is identical to *Jane's Warships Image Library* (see entry 627). The tutorial is not only informative but highly entertaining. Here are France's Mistral ATAM (air-to-air) and its Apache Air-to-Surface. Israel's Python Air-to-Air Missile and its AGM-142 Popeye Air-to-Surface Missile are detailed and explained. The video clips show various launchings, explosions, or deployments and can be advanced frame by frame, reversed, and replayed. All photographs and line drawings allow zooming in for closer inspection of various parts, cutaways, and diagrams of missiles. Launching mechanisms are also included when important to the missile viewed.

All libraries will want to consider the set, but it would be especially valuable in school libraries. Libraries displaying both the *Warships* and *Air-Launched Weapons* discs should consider devoting one terminal or station to them. Once out, they are sure to occupy hawks and doves in hours of endless debate over the sinews of war and its associated pageantry.—**Mark Y. Herring**

633. **Jane's Ammunition Handbook 1996-97.** 5th ed. Terry J. Gander and Ian V. Hogg, eds. Alexandria, Va., Jane's Information Group, 1996. 592p. illus. index. $290.00. ISBN 0-7106-1378-4.

Jane's Information Group is a respected, authoritative, and prolific publisher of serious reference books on military subjects, and this 5th edition of an established text meets expected standards. Coverage includes ammunition for small arms, armor, artillery, and rockets. Specialized projectiles for antitank and air defense weapons are also described, as are projected grenades. For each type of ammunition, the entry typically provides information on the weapon that fires it, a brief history of its development, a description accessible to someone with a general knowledge of military weapons, technical data, and a photograph or drawing. Notes indicate whether each entry has been editorially verified or updated.

Sections on important new weapons, such as the Multiple Launch Rocket System (MLRS) that first came to general public attention in the Persian Gulf War, are extensive and accurate. There is an excellent essay on the future of artillery ammunition, including enhanced range and reconnaissance projectiles, and a useful guide to headstamps and color codes of small arms ammunition. Nothing is perfect; although the new .357 SIG handgun cartridge is included, the even newer 400 CORBON is not. Even so, this edition, which has several accurate indexes, is a satisfactory reference book. The handbook will probably be purchased by more military professionals than libraries, but it is the best choice—really the only choice—for those who need this information.—**John Newman**

634. **The Naval Institute Guide to World Naval Weapons Systems 1997-1998.** By Norman Friedman. Annapolis, Md., Naval Institute Press, 1997. 808p. illus. index. $175.00. ISBN 1-55750-268-4.

This version of a major ready-reference source supplements its predecessors (the 1991/1992 edition [see ARBA 91, entry 696] and its 1994 update [see ARBA 95, entry 701]). The scope and range of naval technology available in late 1996 are presented in lavish detail. Adroitly handling a mass of complex technical issues, the foremost commentator on contemporary naval affairs offers a panoramic perspective that has no single-volume counterpart. Weapons in the traditional sense—guns, bombs, torpedoes, and so forth—only occupy 25 percent of the book; its major focus is on naval electronics, so many of the illustrations depict equipment consoles or system block diagrams.

The previous edition has been entirely reworked and updated, shedding some 50 pages in the process. More emphasis is given to surveillance and control systems, and the coverage of tactical data systems has nearly doubled. The reduction in the number of strategic systems and the retirement of many older strike/surface warfare and antisubmarine warfare systems (particularly sonars/underwater fire control systems) correspondingly reduces their prominence. Treatment of electronic warfare systems has been revamped by placing all these items in a separate category, whereas the space devoted to antiaircraft warfare and mines/mine countermeasures remains about the same. Within each of these major categories, entries for specific weapons and components reflect extensive, careful revision.

The monochrome photographs and drawings are crisp and clear. Compared to the 1991/1992 edition, of 100 randomly selected photographs, 23 percent were old, 44 percent were new, and 33 percent had been deleted from one edition to the next. Aside from 31 pages of addenda, the book is comprehensively indexed, but a random selection of 15 index items yielded a 13 percent error rate, with 2 bad pointers (to "Link 14" and "SCALP" respectively; both entries were off by 1 page). The text appears error-free, and only a few minor photograph caption faults were detected.

Crisply printed on acid-free paper, this is a heavy book that strains its binding, although it does lie flat. Prospective purchasers should be aware that this is a highly specialized reference tool with interest limited to military/scientific professionals. Those libraries serving such a clientele should give this volume careful consideration.—**John Howard Oxley**

13 Political Science

GENERAL WORKS

Bibliography

635. Brunk, Gregory G., comp. **Theories of Political Processes: A Bibliographic Guide to the Journal Literature, 1965-1995.** Westport, Conn., Greenwood Press, 1997. 251p. index. (Bibliographies and Indexes in Law and Political Science, no.27). $79.50. ISBN 0-313-30259-6.

    This compilation of more than 10,000 unannotated articles—selected from the compiler's scanning of 250,000-plus articles—is intended to be a general guide to the theoretical journal literature on politics and policy. It covers a 30-year period (1965 to 1995), a time of tremendous explosion in the number of political science and other the social science journals and, indeed, journals in many other disciplines as well. This growth can be seen in the list of 28 journal specializations in the front matter. Most of these areas are clearly in political science or social sciences, but others (e.g., methodology and applied mathematics, religious studies, resources, science and technology, and strategic studies) lie in other disciplines. Articles from these disciplines reinforce Brunk's contention that the increase in scholarly journal literature makes it ever more difficult to keep abreast of the writings in, at best, only a few specialized fields. Brunk further notes that researchers in widely scattered fields have repeatedly stumbled upon the same theoretical problems without realizing what they viewed as new had already been discussed in a separate scholarly literature. The front matter also includes the abbreviations used for the more than 450 journals represented.

    The body of this book is arranged into 22 large topics, from "Attitudes and Beliefs" to "Legislatures and Executives," to "Technology and Resources," and a final "Miscellaneous" category. Each topic is subdivided, alphabetically, by several subtopics. Entry information uniformly includes entry number, author(s), date, title, periodical abbreviation, and citation. Two indexes conclude this volume: by author, which is especially useful for locating all the contributions of prolific writers, and by subject, for locating all entries on a given topic. Brunk, identified in this book as having graduate degrees in political science, economics, and history and having published more than 60 articles and 6 books in the social sciences and the humanities, has provided scholars and researchers with a wide-ranging, quick-identification, unannotated guide to the scholarly periodical literature for the field of political science.—**Wiley J. Williams**

636. Nordquist, Joan, comp. **Hannah Arendt (II): A Bibliography.** Santa Cruz, Calif., Reference and Research Services, 1997. 68p. index. (Social Theory: A Bibliographic Series, no.46). $15.00pa. ISBN 0-937855-91-X.

    This handy bibliography will be welcomed by students and instructors in the many fields to which Arendt's work is relevant. It is part of a series furnishing ready access to the works of major thinkers and the literature on them. It achieves its end admirably. Other subjects in the series read like a who's who of twentieth-century social thinkers with a center-left emphasis. They will also be of interest to academic and public reference libraries. This one is meant to complement the other Arendt bibliography in the series but is complete in itself.

The work has 4 parts. The 1st lists books in English translation by Arendt. Each title is followed by citations of reviews and essays on it from both scholarly and general literature. This will be useful for instructors and students. It then cites books in German by Arendt with the titles of English translations. A 2d section gives 172 essays by Arendt, including multiple publications where applicable. For this part there are two indexes. A title keyword index provides references to the essay entries. A book title index gives access to all essays contained in the 11 anthologies cited. The 3d section begins by listing books about Arendt, then cites dissertations and theses, and ends by noting 4 bibliographies. This section has obvious utility for the serious Arendt scholar. The last part lists 201 essays about Arendt in periodicals and collections. It has a title keyword index providing subject access.

The bibliographic sources indicate that a search was made of about 40 major bibliographic tools in the social sciences, including various books in print and major indexes and abstracts. There are admirably concise and thorough prefatory materials and notes to the indexes.

This work and the series to which it belongs will prove useful for its target audience. Reference libraries should purchase it where ever possible.—**Nigel Tappin**

637. Nordquist, Joan, comp. **Rosa Luxemburg and Emma Goldman: A Bibliography.** Santa Cruz, Calif., Reference and Research Services, 1996. 64p. index. (Social Theory: A Bibliographic Series, no.43). $15.00pa. ISBN 0-937855-85-5.

This addition to a pamphlet series, which has included bibliographies on such social theorists as Antonio Gramsci, Herbert Marcuse, Martin Heidegger, Michel Foucault, and Simone de Beauvoir, contains entries for more than 600 English-language works by and about the socialist revolutionaries Emma Goldman and Rosa Luxemburg. Compiled from mainstream print titles (*National Union Catalog*, *Books in Print*, *Social Science Index*); online databases (First Search, Historical Abstracts); and such specialized sources as *Alternative Press Index* (National Information Services Corporation, 1996) and *The Left Index* (see ARBA 97, entry 61), the bibliography lists books, periodical articles, essays and chapters within books, dissertations, theses, and conference papers.

The bibliography is organized usefully. Sections 1 and 2 include books and essays by Goldman and Luxemburg. Those that have appeared under more than one title or can be found in more than one source are so noted. For example, Goldman's essay "Marriage and Love" receives six citations ranging in publication date from 1911 to 1995. Additionally, in the case of Luxemburg, the original foreign source of her essays is indicated with the translation. Grouped with each work are reviews or critical responses. Sections 3 and 4 list books, dissertations, theses, and articles about Goldman and Luxemburg. Keyword indexes provide access to such topics as war, revisionism, anarchism, and jealousy.

Lacking are annotations, and perhaps more important considering the international prestige and influence of both women, foreign-language critical works. A scholar will have to go beyond what is found here, but this bibliography and, indeed, the entire series, would well serve the undergraduate or curious adult library user.—**Ruth A. Carr**

638. van Wyk, J. J., and Mary C. Custy. **Contemporary Democracy: A Bibliography of Periodical Literature, 1974-1994.** Washington, D.C., Congressional Quarterly, 1997. 449p. index. $120.00. ISBN 1-56802-244-1.

During the past two decades, democratization has emerged as a central issue in political science and other social sciences. The collapse of authoritarianism and the emergence of new democracies have attracted scholarly attention to a variety of dimensions of democratization, such as what historical, social, political, and economic factors produce it; what its consequences are; and how durable the new democracies are. Custy and van Wyk provide an exhaustive list of periodical literature in several disciplines that treat the nature of this new wave of democratization. Contained in the bibliography are almost 8,000 entries drawn from more than 1,400 journals. The listings are not annotated. They are presented alphabetically by author, but an index assists in finding appropriate articles by topic.

The issue of democracy is a broad one, and the literature is vast. The criteria for including an article in this bibliography are not clearly stated. Taking an issue of the *American Political Science Review* at random to see which articles are listed in the van Wyk and Custy bibliography and which are excluded, this reviewer did not understand why an article by Leslie Paul Thiele on Martin Heidegger's notions of freedom was included and another by Arthur Miller, et al., on mass support for change in the former USSR was not. Nevertheless, this is a useful resource for scholars interested in the study of democratization.—**Frank L. Wilson**

Biography

639. **Who's Who in Democracy.** Seymour Martin Lipset, ed. Washington, D.C., Congressional Quarterly, 1997. 247p. illus. index. $85.00. ISBN 1-56802-121-6.

This slim volume contains a preface, an introduction, 156 short biographical sketches, and an index. Men and women from all over the globe appear in alphabetic order, from John Adams, John Locke, and Nelson Mandela through Roh Tae Woo, Elizabeth Cady Stanton, and Boris Yeltsin. Some of these people were (or are) political leaders, others revolutionaries, academics, or reformers. Each contributed in a meaningful way to the spread of democracy or to the common understanding of it. Mandela, to cite just one example, fought for decades against apartheid in South Africa and ultimately became the first president of that country to be elected by a vote of blacks and whites alike. The various composite portraits, taken together, illustrate the richness and complexity of democratic theory and reality.

Who's Who in Democracy succeeds at the most fundamental level. The reader comes away with a better grasp of democracy in all its varieties. The focus on the part that the individual has played in the democratic past is particularly helpful, counteracting the recent preoccupation with structural factors. Lipset shows knowledge that a true understanding of democracy must take into account not only broad, underlying forces such as economics and culture but also the decisions of outstanding leaders. Yet if this conceptual approach is sound, then why is the book not more comprehensive? For example, why include Frederick Douglass but not Harriet Tubman or William Lloyd Garrison? One may properly question the short length of such an important project as well as the selection of certain individuals over others. Still, the virtues of *Who's Who in Democracy* outweigh the faults. The reference is recommended for high school, college, university, and all public libraries.—**Richard E. Holl**

Directories

640. **The Guide to Background Investigations: A Comprehensive Source Directory for Employee Screening and Background Investigations.** 7th ed. Tulsa, Okla., TISI, 1997. 1952p. $129.50pa. ISBN 0-9642388-1-0.

This directory has more than doubled in length over the last several editions. Over 1,200 pages are devoted to state-by-state and county-by-county listings of where to obtain felony, misdemeanor, civil, and other types of records. Complete information is provided as to fees, methods of delivery, turnaround times, and the like. City listings cross-reference counties, and maps are included for each state, as are zip codes. Other sections are given over to federal and educational records, again providing detailed information on how to go about obtaining them. Many new types of records have been added in recent editions, including medical licensing boards, teaching certifications, military records, child and home care licensing, vehicle ownership, tax liens, among others. A useful introduction provides tips on doing background checks and obtaining public records. This is a helpful guide not only for its expressed purpose, but for various legal, educational, and genealogical applications.—**Lee Weston**

Quotation Books

641. **The Oxford Dictionary of Political Quotations.** Antony Jay, ed. New York, Oxford University Press, 1996. 515p. index. $35.00. ISBN 0-19-863158-8.

This dictionary is not the only political quotation book available, but it is one that provides some uncommon gems. The 4000-plus quotations are arranged alphabetically be the name of the author or speaker, supplemented with a keyword-in-context index. With each name, a brief two- to five-word description of the person is provided. In keeping with Oxford University Press's other quotation books, the arrangement is easy to use with its two-column format—one listing the sayings, the other listing the details of the attribution or source.

However, the Oxford resource is not nearly as comprehensive as *The Macmillan Dictionary of Political Quotations* (see ARBA 94, entry 724) with its 11,000 entries. Both the Macmillan title and Gale's *Political Quotations* (see ARBA 91, entry 724) tend to have heavy U.S. coverage. The Oxford dictionary is noteworthy for its unique British coverage. The most heavily quoted include William Shakespeare, Edmund Burke, Winston Churchill, Walter Bagehot, and Benjamin Disraeli. The dictionary is well documented, but not so much as *Respectfully Quoted* (see ARBA 90, entry 82).

The selection does lack statements by women. Although Margaret Thatcher is allowed almost three pages of quotations, neither Elizabeth Cady Stanton, Sandra Day O'Connor, nor Gloria Steinem are quoted. *The Oxford Dictionary of Political Quotations* is a worthwhile, but not essential, purchase for those libraries interested in improving their quotation shelf.—**Christine Drew**

POLITICS AND GOVERNMENT

United States

Almanacs

642. **The Almanac of the Executive Branch 1997/98.** Peggie Rayhawk, Gary P. Osifchin, and Jennifer Margiotta, eds. Washington, D.C., Almanac Publishing, 1997. 815p. illus. index. $149.00pa. ISBN 1-886222-06-1.

This new edition of *The Almanac of the Executive Branch* provides a comprehensive guide to the personnel in the Clinton administration. It includes the names, addresses, brief biographies, and photos of 835 political appointees and other senior staff in the Clinton administration. Included are officials in the White House, cabinet departments, independent agencies and government corporations, and selected multilateral organizations, such as the International Monetary Fund. The information is current with personnel changes made for Clinton's second term through September 1997. Where there are vacancies in the administration, the pending nominees or interim appointments (130 of them) are included. Although the main goal is to discuss the policy-makers, there are useful organizational charts with background information and brief histories of the cabinet departments and major executive agencies. There is a useful listing of Website addresses in one of the appendixes. The indexes are arranged by name and by office and position. This is a valuable resource for those interested in national politics and policy-making in the United States. The one disadvantage is the paperback format. The volume is likely to be used often, and the binding is not strong enough for such use. This work is highly recommended for major public and university libraries.—**Frank L. Wilson**

643. **The World Almanac of U.S. Politics.** 1997-99 ed. Robert J. Wagman and Angela E. Lauria, eds. Mahwah, N.J., World Almanac Books, 1997. 400p. maps. index. $18.95pa. ISBN 0-88687-810-1. ISSN 1043-1535.

Opening this book, one is almost tempted to say, "World Almanac Books has done it again." Just as the current edition of the *World Almanac and Book of Facts* (see entry 3) is a primary resource in any ready-reference collection, *The World Almanac of U.S. Politics* promises to be an equally valuable resource. The publisher issues "the citizen's guide to American government" every two years, after each major election.

This volume is a storehouse of useful information. It contains a history of the political parties, a brief overview of campaign financing, biographies of the president and vice president, e-mail addresses, and congressional Website addresses. The book also lists addresses, electronic and traditional, for frequently requested governmental agencies. After thoroughly covering the national political scene, the editors then turn their attention to state politics, listing elected officials with brief biographical information, voting districts, and a paragraph or two describing the current local political situation. The addition of so much electronic information makes the book particularly valuable because more and more library patrons are wanting the response to their questions to include Internet data.

All this information is available elsewhere, but in scattered locations. *The World Almanac of U.S. Politics* pulls all these valuable data together in one location at a reasonable price. Now instead of having to consult several different sources for information, the reference librarian will be able to use this book as a first stop for answers to political questions.—**Nancy P. Reed**

Bibliography

644. Hollings, Robert L. **Reinventing Government: An Analysis and Annotated Bibliography.** Commack, N.Y., Nova Science Publishers, 1996. 113p. index. $59.00. ISBN 1-56072-264-9.

This sourcebook is limited to the recent proposals for improving the functioning of U.S. government on its three levels, and it features a business management perspective, supplemented by financial and performance auditing. An informative but inadequately edited review essay introduces the subject and its scope. The bibliography covers books; videos; book reviews; and national, state, and local attempts at implementing reforms; it even includes some advertising matter. There is in-depth coverage of the Clinton-Gore initiatives and articles that appeared in *The Washington Post* (especially by Stephen Barr), and the coverage is limited to the 1990s. Appendixes provide lists of associations, publications, and recent conferences concerned with reinventing government. Author and subject indexes close the volume.

The scope of this reference source is chronologically, thematically, and spatially narrow and could be profitably extended by consulting Robert Miewald's *The Bureaucratic State: An Annotated Bibliography* (see ARBA 85, entry 620) and Bogdan Mieczkowski and Oleg Zinam with their comparative setting of *Bureaucracy, Ideology, Technology* (1984) that contains a 26-page bibliography. *The Tides of Reform: Making the Government Work, 1945-95* by Paul Light focuses on the federal branch of the government, has good footnotes, and conveniently divides reform philosophies into scientific management, war on waste, "watchful eye," and liberation management.—**Bogdan Mieczkowski**

645. **James A. Garfield: A Bibliography.** Robert O. Rupp, comp. Westport, Conn., Greenwood Press, 1997. 185p. index. (Bibliographies of the Presidents of the United States). $65.00. ISBN 0-313-28178-5.

This annotated bibliography covers the life of President James Garfield, from his childhood to his assassination and the public mourning that followed. The citations are divided into chapters on Garfield's education, his years as a professor and college president, his entry into Ohio politics, his service in the Civil War as a brigadier general, his time in the House of Representatives, his legal career, his campaign for presidential office, and his 200 days in the White House.

Materials cited are drawn from personal papers, diaries, letters, newspaper accounts, books, pamphlets, and more. Sources are indexed by author and by subject. References are also provided for his key associates, political rivals, colleagues, fellow generals, and relatives. Topics range from the serious to the lighter side. For example, the chapter on the election of 1880 includes a collection of campaign songs. This work is treasure trove for students of Garfield and the Gilded Age.—**Adrienne Antink Bendel**

646. Martin, Fenton S., and Robert U. Goehlert. **American Government and Politics: A Guide to Books for Teachers, Librarians, and Students.** Washington, D.C., Congressional Quarterly, 1997. 204p. index. $27.95. ISBN 1-56802-221-2.

Although primarily intended for the use of high school students, this bibliography can also be useful for beginning college students or academic librarians who are unfamiliar with basic titles in the area of U.S. government. Most of the books included in this guide are also appropriate for academic library collections.

The guide is a selective listing of general books, arranged into 20 broad subject areas. The most substantial areas are "Elections, Campaigns, and Voting," "The President," "Congress," and "Foreign Policy," but other topics like public policy issues, interest groups, and the mass media are also covered. Each item is accompanied by a brief annotation, although there is no indication of the book's current availability. The coverage is limited to books that tend to have a broad appeal; no reference works, statistical compilations, documents, or classic texts are included. Within these limitations, Martin and

Goehlert, who have published many other political bibliographies, have gathered an interesting assortment of titles. Particularly unique and enjoyable is a section of major fictional books on U.S. politics, which, unfortunately, is not annotated.

Academic librarians who need a more comprehensive approach to the literature of U.S. government may need to consult other standard works, such as the section on U.S. sources in Henry York's *Political Science: A Guide to Reference and Information Sources* (see ARBA 91, entry 717) or a more specialized bibliography like *The United States Congress* by Goehlert and Martin (see ARBA 96, entry 715).

—Thomas A. Karel

647. Mulder, John M., Ernest M. White, and Ethel S. White, comps. **Woodrow Wilson: A Bibliography.** Westport, Conn., Greenwood Press, 1997. 438p. illus. index. (Bibliographies of the Presidents of the United States). $95.00. ISBN 0-313-28185-8.

In the 1950s, historians began using social science methodologies to explain historical events, shifting their focus from politics and personalities to psychology, sociology, and statistics. This comprehensive annotated bibliography on Woodrow Wilson reflects a shift back to more traditional historiography. Aimed at both generalists and specialists, the book includes publications up to and including 1994 copyrights. The annotations summarize the arguments presented in each work cited but avoid passing judgment on their quality or validity. The secondary literature listed is meant to complement the 69-volume set of *The Papers of Woodrow Wilson* (Princeton University Press, 1966-1994). A chronology traces events in Wilson's life from his birth (December 28, 1856) to his burial (February 6, 1924).

The 24 chapters (4,216 entries) include, among other things, articles from scholarly journals, doctoral theses, manuscript and archival sources, contemporary newspapers and magazines, writings by Wilson, general biographies, and writings on the elections of 1912 through 1920. The 185 pages devoted to Wilson's presidency are organized by such subtopics as "Wilson, Progressivism, and Domestic Affairs"; "Wilson and Foreign Affairs"; and "Wilson and World War I." Each of these sections is further subdivided. Separate author and subject indexes complete the volume.

This definitive bibliography will serve students and scholars for years to come. Although plans for updating are not mentioned, decennial supplements would be welcomed. All libraries with a set of the *Papers* will need to add this to their collections, but most academic and large public libraries should consider it as well.—**Gary D. Barber**

648. Sayler, James, comp. **Presidents of the United States—Their Written Measure: A Bibliography.** Washington, D.C., Library of Congress, 1996. 216p. illus. index. $19.00pa. ISBN 0-8444-0902-2.

An almost immeasurable amount of scholarship has been devoted to examining the life, actions, and behavior of U.S. presidents and the institution that they occupy. Much of this literature would not be possible without the availability of the president's written word. This book is an unannotated compendium of selected books by and about the presidency and the 42 men who have served as the chief executive of the United States. Each section is devoted to a single president, arranged chronologically from George Washington to William Clinton.

The first set of items listed in each section consists of selected books about the president. This list is followed by a list of general, published papers that encompasses the "formal, multi-volume corpus of a president's papers" and compilations of papers covering the president's term in office. The last heading, "Selected Writings," includes works that are the result of text derived from the presidential papers, either published or unpublished. The criteria used to include a particular item were the authority of the author; the accuracy, comprehensiveness, currency, and uniqueness of the work; and the book's accessibility. Reviews and advice from experts were also cited by the author as helpful in determining inclusion.

Microfilm editions of presidential papers have been excluded. Each book entry includes the Library of Congress call number and footnotes to pertinent information when appropriate. The reader is introduced to each section by an attractive black-and-white portrait of the president. Although most, if not all, of the works cited in this book are included in other bibliographies, this work provides a concise and clearly presented bibliography of works by and about the presidents. [R: Choice, Jan 97, p. 774]

—**Robert V. Labaree**

Biography

649. **The Almanac of the Unelected: Staff of the U.S. Congress 1997.** Steve Piacente and Todd E. Keeler, eds. Washington, D.C., Almanac Publishing, 1997. 823p. illus. index. $275.00. ISBN 1-886222-04-5.

Now in its 10th edition, this directory contains full-page profiles of more than 700 congressional committee and leadership staffers (see ARBA 95, entry 713, for a review of the 1994 edition). One hundred and eighty of the profiles are new to this edition, which gives a vivid indication of the turnover rate among congressional staff. Each profile includes a concise résumé: the position title; an office address and telephone number, the staffer's birth date and place of birth, educational background, professional career, and areas of expertise. A photograph is provided for most of the staffers. The résumé fills one column of text; the other column consists of a narrative description of the staffer's job, with examples of recent legislative efforts and brief quotations. The book is divided into House and Senate sections and arranged within each by leadership positions and committee assignments. The only index is an index of personal names. Most of the people profiled are unknown to the general public, although an occasional familiar name can be spotted. For example, Virginia Thomas (wife of Associate Supreme Court Justice Clarence Thomas) is profiled in her role as Committee Liaison for House Majority Leader Richard Armey.

This is a useful reference work that nicely supplements the standard directories for members of Congress. However, it continues to receive stiff competition from Congressional Quarterly's *Congressional Staff Directory* (see entry 652). The CQ publication may be preferred by most libraries, because it is significantly less expensive as well as substantially longer and is updated twice a year. Either title is highly recommended for political research collections of most libraries.—**Thomas A. Karel**

650. **American Legislative Leaders in the West, 1911-1994.** Nancy Weatherly Sharp, James Roger Sharp, Gina Petonito, and Kevin G. Atwater, eds. Westport, Conn., Greenwood Press, 1997. 396p. index. $99.50. ISBN 0-313-30212-X.

This book, one of a 4-volume series, provides biographical information on 1,466 speakers who have led the state legislatures of Illinois, Indiana, Iowa, Kansas, Michigan, Minnesota, Missouri, Nebraska, North Dakota, Ohio, South Dakota, and Wisconsin. Each entry is written by a historian, political scientist, state librarian, or archivist—totaling over 40 contributors. A 48-page introduction provides useful data on party affiliations, years of service, reasons for leaving the legislature, and other useful information. These are presented in comparison format within the Midwest over time, by state, and between the Midwest and other regions of the country. From the data presented, the editors are able to make important commentaries on shifts in state politics and political party alignments over much of the twentieth century. A series of appendixes provide information on the profession, religion, home counties, and activities of legislators after leaving the speakership. There is also a brief, but useful, bibliography on state politics in the Midwest. Many of the individual biographical notes also include bibliographic information.

This volume will be a useful tool for researchers and scholars interested in state politics. They are likely to find the compilations in the introduction and appendixes more interesting than the bulk of the text dedicated to the biographical entries.—**Frank L. Wilson**

651. **Biographical Directory of the American Congress, 1774-1996.** Alexandria, Va., CQ Staff Directories, 1997. 2108p. illus. $295.00. ISBN 0-87289-124-0. ISSN 1091-0859.

The 16th edition of the *Biographical Directory of the American Congress*, like its predecessors, will continue to be an indispensable reference tool for students and scholars of U.S. history and politics. It is the most comprehensive biographical source on congressional members. The directory provides brief biographical and career information on the 11,400 men and women who served in the U.S. and Continental Congresses between 1774 and 1996.

The directory is divided into sections. The first section, under separate headings, contains the executive officers, which include vice presidents and cabinet members of each administration from 1789 to 1996; the delegates to the Continental Congress; and the members of each Congress, which include congressional leaders and officers from the 1st to the 104th Congress. Neither biographical information nor party affiliation on these individuals is provided. Also included in this section is the "Representatives Under Each Apportionment" table showing the number of congressional seats allotted to each state of the past 21 censuses. The second section, the main text, contains biographical information on members of Congress. Each entry contains date and place of birth, education, employment (prior to and after governmental service), record of governmental service, party affiliation, and date and place of death; entries for living members contain present occupation and place of residency. The information provided for each entry is rather brief; however, it is accurate. At the end of many entries, biographical references are provided for notable congressional figures. Additional biographical references should have been included for certain entries, however. For example, no biographical references are provided for such major figures as Richard Gephardt, Newt Gingrich, and Albert Gore.

The printing, binding, cover, and organization are excellent. Overall, this is an outstanding reference tool. College, public, and school libraries should acquire this work.—**Binh P. Le**

652. **Congressional Staff Directory, Fall 1997.** Alexandria, Va., CQ Staff Directories, 1997. 1280p. illus. maps. index. $227.00pa./yr. ISBN 0-87289-131-3. ISSN 0589-3178.

This venerable directory, now in its 38th year and published in 3 versions annually, provides exhaustive information on the Congress of the United States and the staff that serves it. Biographical entries arranged by state delegations are provided for the House and Senate members, along with lists of cities, counties, and zip codes included in each congressional district. Results of several elections have been added to recent editions, as have state maps outlining the districts. In separate sections for each body, pictures of the members are supplied accompanied by a list of their committee assignments and staffers. The staff of committees and subcommittees are given another section. Biographical entries appear for a selected 3,200 top staffers. All counties and those cities with a population of more than 15,000 are listed by state with an indication of population, congressional district, member, and political party. Concluding the work are two indexes—by keyword and by personal name, the latter including telephone numbers.

This volume is a well-established directory, familiar in format and with a trusted reputation. Moreover, it seems to improve with each passing year, adding new data (fax numbers, e-mail and Website addresses, and so forth) to increase usefulness. The directory remains a solid choice for those needing more detail than the Government Printing Office's *Congressional Directory* offers concerning the key people who make Congress tick.—**Lee Weston**

653. Diller, Daniel C., and Stephen L. Robertson. **The Presidents, First Ladies, and Vice Presidents: White House Biographies, 1789-1997.** Washington, D.C., Congressional Quarterly, 1997. 180p. illus. index. $24.95pa. ISBN 1-56802-311-1.

At first glance, Congressional Quarterly's new volume of presidential biographies seems just another one of the large group of reference books that present presidential information in readily accessible form. Yet closer examination shows that this highly respected publisher of governmental information has again gathered into one handy reference book information that is available elsewhere only in scattered locations. The first chapter makes fascinating reading. "The Daily Life of the President" covers briefly the work habits of the various presidents, the changing roles of the first ladies, and the role of the Secret Service in protecting the first family. This chapter contains two gems of information: a copy of President Clinton's typical daily work schedule and a one-column explanation of the role of the Chief Usher of the White House, taken from J. B. West's book, *Upstairs at the White House*.

The White House biographies start with illustrated biographies of every president running approximately two pages in length. Under the picture of each man is a facsimile of his signature, which is an interesting touch. The wives of the presidents receive one-page coverage with a picture. An interesting insertion in this section is a two-page spread covering "White House Hostesses: Surrogate First Ladies" (pp. 118-19). Biographies, even brief ones, of the 11 women covered here—sisters, daughters, and nieces of the chief executives—are difficult to find. The last group of biographies covers all the vice presidents except those who were later elected president. This volume is an excellent source to use for information about those interesting individuals who have inhabited the president's home throughout the years. It will prove a useful reference in any collection. [R: BR, Sept/Oct 97, pp. 60-61]—**Nancy P. Reed**

654. **The New Members of Congress Almanac: 105th U.S. Congress.** By Hans Johnson and Peggie Rayhawk. Jeffrey B. Trammell and Gary P. Osifchin, eds. Washington, D.C., Almanac Publishing, 1996. 107p. illus. index. $39.95pa. ISBN 1-886222-03-7.

This small booklet introduces readers to the new members of the 105th Congress. The members are organized by state, first for the Senate, and then for the House of Representatives. Each full-page profile includes a photograph, date and place of birth, education, career, primary results, and general election results. The narrative portion of the profile gives personal background on the member, a brief report on his or her campaign, and speculation about congressional goals and issues.

Similar information was provided in a special issue of *Congressional Quarterly Weekly Report*, which was published right after the 1996 election, although the CQ profiles of the new House members are much shorter than what is provided in the book at hand. For libraries that do not subscribe to CQ, this publication will suffice until the next edition of *The Almanac of American Politics* or other congressional directories can be purchased.—**Thomas A. Karel**

655. **Notable U.S. Ambassadors Since 1775: A Biographical Dictionary.** Cathal J. Nolan, ed. Westport, Conn., Greenwood Press, 1997. 430p. index. $95.00. ISBN 0-313-29195-0.

Implementation of U.S. foreign policy depends on many factors, including the personalities of its executors. U.S. ambassadors to countries around the world have often proven to be crucial architects of U.S. foreign policy interests in these countries. *Notable U.S. Ambassadors Since 1775* provides biographical portraits of a select, but diverse, group of individuals who, in the editor's viewpoint, have represented U.S. diplomatic interests with noteworthiness.

Following an introduction, this work presents six- to eight-page biographical vignettes of diplomatic personnel that the editor sees as being significant in the transaction of U.S. foreign policy. Individuals covered include current U.S. Secretary of State, Madeleine Albright; nineteenth-century historian, George Bancroft; twentieth-century economist, John Kenneth Galbraith, a U.S. Ambassador to India; Thomas Jefferson; George Kennan; former U.S. Ambassador to the United Nations, Jeane Kirkpatrick; Reagan Administration Assistant Secretary of State for Near Eastern and African Affairs, Richard Murphy; and Soviet Union specialist, Llewellyn Thompson Jr. Biographical entries also feature listings of works by and about these ambassadors. A select bibliography of primary and secondary sources concludes this volume.

This is a valuable introduction to some of the individuals influencing U.S. diplomatic history. Scholars in this field may quibble about the inclusion or omission of individuals they consider important. Nevertheless, *Notable U.S. Ambassadors Since 1775* will prove useful to students and scholars desiring to learn more about some of the personalities who have shaped U.S. foreign policy.—**Bert Chapman**

656. **Who's Who in Congress 1997: 105th Congress.** Washington, D.C., Congressional Quarterly, 1997. 344p. index. $17.95pa. ISBN 1-56802-076-7. ISSN 1054-9234.

This edition of *Who's Who in Congress* is a concise but thorough look at the men and women who make up the 105th Congress. Each alphabetically arranged, half-page entry gives date of birth, education, occupation, religion, and family status, along with the congressperson's photograph, office and e-mail addresses, and fax numbers. The Congressional Quarterly staff has added staff and committee information along with 1996 voting studies on presidential support, party, and voting participation. Finally, there are 1995 and 1996 interest group rankings from the Americans for Democratic Action, the American Conservative Union, the AFL-CIO, and the Chamber of Commerce of the United States. Supplementary sections list state delegations, committee assignments, each member's vote on 14 major 1996 congressional issues, and a glossary. Although no book of this sort can ever be completely up-to-date, the Congressional Quarterly staff has done an admirable job of compiling frequently requested, current information in a compact, low-cost volume that belongs in every library. Congressional Quarterly also notes that all these facts and statistics are included and expanded upon in the larger, more expensive *Politics in America*.—**Deborah Hammer**

Dictionaries and Encyclopedias

657. Clucas, Richard A. **Encyclopedia of American Political Reform.** Santa Barbara, Calif., ABC-CLIO, 1996. 346p. index. $60.00. ISBN 0-87436-855-3.

Reforming U.S. politics and government has been a constant theme since the beginning of the country. The federal and state governments are emphasized in this encyclopedia, with less discussion of local trends and issues. The scope of years covered is from the mid-1960s to the present. The 10-page introduction provides an overview and discusses the broad themes and high points of this tumultuous period, which was in many respects a political revolution. Happily, the Tax Equity and Fiscal Responsibility Act of 1982, which is not usually in other political dictionaries, is discussed here. Important personages of the time are allocated their own entries, with their pet causes and objectives outlined. Phrases, events, movements, and procedures are explained, and key terms are defined. There are many cross-references within the encyclopedia, and there is a *see also* section at the end of each individual entry. The chronology at the back stretches from 1962 to 1996, but it does not provide a day and month for the events, a serious omission; one should not have to check another source to find out this information. The 17-page bibliography includes books and journal articles but not many official government publications.

Clucas, a political science professor at Portland State University, recently published *The Speaker's Electoral Connection: Willie Brown and the California Assembly* (University of California, Institute of Governmental Studies Press, 1995). The price of the volume at hand seems a little high, and the publisher might sell more copies if it were issued as a trade paperback with a thick cover. This sturdily constructed book is recommended for the reference collections of public and academic libraries, as it has much information not found in the standard political dictionaries.—**Daniel K. Blewett**

658. **The Complete History of Our Presidents.** Vero Beach, Fla., Rourke Enterprises, 1997. 13v. illus. maps. index. $239.95/set. ISBN 0-86593-405-3.

The Complete History of Our Presidents is an excellent encyclopedic history of the U.S. presidency for juveniles. Numerous illustrations, maps, and photographs highlight the easy-to-read text. Each volume contains a glossary with clear, simple explanations of pertinent terms used in the text. In addition, each book has its own index and bibliography, a general chronology and timeline, and a list of all the presidents.

Each volume covers the terms of several chief executives, and students will readily see the larger historical picture. In addition to the general historical information about the presidents, a brief article appears about each first lady and vice president, accompanied by illustrations or photographs. Throughout the series there are selected topics that are covered in one or two pages; for example: "Immigration in the 1850s" (v. 4, p. 29); "African Americans After Reconstruction" (v. 6, p. 47); and "The Space Race" (v. 10, pp. 52-53).

The final volume consists of a 64-page alphabetic index of the entire set. Again, large typeface and generous illustrations make it easy to read. The series is highly recommended for collections that provide service for students in middle school through junior high and the lower high school grades.

—**Bruce H. Webb**

659. **The Encyclopedia of the Republican Party and the Encyclopedia of the Democratic Party.** George Thomas Kurian and Jeffrey D. Schultz, eds. Armonk, N.Y., Sharpe Reference/M. E. Sharpe, 1997. 4v. illus. index. $399.00/set. ISBN 1-56324-729-1.

This encyclopedia treats various aspects of each of today's major U.S. political parties in four volumes, the first two covering the Republican Party and the second two the Democratic Party. Coverage ranges from extended signed essays (with bibliographies) tracing the parties' histories to entries (also with bibliographies) outlining historical stands on major issues (abortion, health care, gun control, trade, minorities, states' rights, and so forth), and provides brief biographies of major figures. Also included are a historical roster of the members of U.S. Congresses, brief descriptions of party conventions and presidential elections dating from the inception of the parties, and texts of all of their platforms. The signed entries are contributed largely by historians and political scientists from academe. Appendixes including additional organizational and electoral information conclude the work. The indexing is split among general, biographical, geographic, and minorities and women topics.

Although this encyclopedia pulls together much information in a relatively convenient format, there are some problems inherent in its organization. In devoting two volumes to each of the parties, the editors have invited duplication of some material. The contributing scholars, for instance, were called upon to provide essays on the same issue or ideology for both of the parties; consequently, there is a fair amount of repetition between these companion pieces. Another editing approach may have reduced the size (and the cost) of this work. Moreover, nearly 800 pages are devoted to platform texts, documents that, in most library settings, can be found in other sources. The biographies are artisanal and informative and are of standard length; hence, George Bush receives as much space as Abraham Lincoln and Franklin Pierce as much as Franklin Delano Roosevelt. The issue and ideology articles reflect a present-day cast (e.g., one will find little in them on such issues as the free coinage of silver). The encyclopedia contains many black-and-white illustrations and photographs; unfortunately, some are of poor quality. Despite these criticisms, the work will fill a need in the public, high school, and undergraduate libraries that can afford it.

—Lee Weston

660. **Encyclopedia of U.S. Foreign Relations.** Bruce W. Jentleson and Thomas G. Paterson, eds. New York, Oxford University Press, 1997. 4v. maps. $450.00/set. ISBN 0-19-511055-2.

With the ending of the Cold War, the complex nature of foreign policy has been recognized. This four-volume set attempts to provide historical perspectives on foreign policy issues. As the editors reflect in their excellent introductory article, Lyndon Johnson relied on the history of the 1930s to base his policies, but other lessons drawn from history might suggest alternative actions. An instructive examination of U.S. foreign relations could be a valuable tool for future policy analysis. With this end in mind, the 373 contributors have written 1,024 articles on U.S. foreign relations since 1776.

The work is organized alphabetically. Entries include names (e.g., all presidents and secretaries of state); countries; events (e.g., the American Revolution); U. S. departments and concepts (e.g., balance of power). The list of contributors is impressive, including Arthur Schlesinger, Walter LaFeber, and Richard Rosecrance. Entries are cross-referenced, and each includes a list of resources for further study. Appendixes supply a detailed chronology of U.S. foreign relations, national data on 185 United Nations members, and an extensive bibliography arranged by subject.

Overall, the encyclopedia is an excellent resource. The entries are clearly written and readable, covering the topic both historically and thematically. Considering the complexity of the subjects, the editors have maintained a remarkable consistency across entries. For instance, such a controversial event as the assassination of Dien Bien Phu is discussed in the article on the Vietnam War and then again in an article, written by a different scholar, on John F. Kennedy. Although there are differences in nuance, there is internal consistency. The only flaw is in a contradiction between the objectives of the work and the arrangement. If, as the editors suggest, the goal of the work is to examine historical precedents, the work may have been arranged within periods rather than alphabetically, but the alphabetic arrangement makes the set easy to use and extremely helpful as a reference tool for student and scholars.

This encyclopedia is a highly worthwhile addition to the field of U.S. foreign policy for its breadth and coverage, especially of theoretical aspects of world politics. The set is recommended for larger public and academic libraries. [R: LJ, 1 April 97, p. 82]—**Joshua Cohen**

661. **The Presidents.** Fred L. Israel, ed. Danbury, Conn., Grolier, 1997. 8v. illus. maps. index. $259.00/set. ISBN 0-7172-7642-2.

The Presidents is an eight-volume set that details the presidencies from George Washington through the 1996 election of Bill Clinton. Coverage includes a chronology; an extensive biography; excerpts from inaugural addresses and other noteworthy speeches or documents; information about family, cabinet, and vice president; and key places associated with various presidents. The set is lavishly illustrated with both color and black-and-white photographs and drawings. A stunning full-page color portrait begins the section on each president. Entries are 20-plus pages, giving a complete overview of each administration. Although the set is easily accessible for middle school students, it will appeal to high school students and adults as well. Volume 8 includes returns for each election with color-coded maps and state-by-state voting statistics, allowing the reader to visually see the country grow. An adequate index is also provided.

The information here is more extensive than the one-volume *Facts About the Presidents* (6th ed.; see ARBA 94, entry 499) or *The Presidents, First Ladies, and Vice Presidents* (see entry 653). The set under review is more readable than *The Presidents: A Reference History* (2d ed.; see ARBA 97, entry 589), which does not include the 1996 election. Because of its currency, its visual appeal, and its content, this set is a must-buy for all schools and public libraries.—**Lynda Welborn**

Directories

662. **Counties USA 1997: A Directory of United States Counties.** Detroit, Omnigraphics, 1997. 573p. maps. index. $85.00. ISBN 0-7808-0094-X.

Arranged alphabetically by state, *Counties USA 1997* provides brief, basic information on each U.S. county. Every entry lists the county seat with address and telephone and fax numbers as well as e-mail and World Wide Web addresses, population statistics, both numbers and densities, land and water areas, elevation, name origin, and a general description of where the county is located. This description and the name origin section sometimes include a bit of local history. The state government pages give e-mail and Web addresses and fax and telephone numbers for the governor and other officials, plus the state library, the highest court, and chamber of commerce; if the state has a Webpage, it is listed as well. Similar listings are given for all U.S. senators and representatives.

The index lists all counties alphabetically, giving the telephone number and citing the appropriate page in the text. Although much of the basic county information will not change, lists of senators and representatives can quickly become outdated, as can Internet/e-mail addresses. Because much of the same information can be found in Omnigraphics's *American Places Dictionary* (see ARBA 95, entry 500), depending upon what is already owned, this is a marginal purchase for libraries.—**Deborah Hammer**

663. **Election Results Directory 1997.** Denver, Colo., National Conference of State Legislatures, 1997. 320p. index. $50.00pa. ISBN 1-55516-778-0.

This annual directory published by the National Conference of State Legislatures, the most important nonpartisan association of state legislators, provides the names, party affiliations, district numbers, home office addresses, and telephone numbers of the members of all state legislative bodies. In addition, there is an information page for each state giving key addresses and telephone numbers, including where to call for information on each house and for copies of bills and other documents. In addition, the state information page supplies brief facts on the state's government, such as party balance, legislative calendar, and term length and limits. A name index at the end of the directory permits users to find information on legislators without knowing their state. The information is useful, easily accessible, and up-to-date. The one shortcoming is the lack of e-mail addresses. However, the editors offer this information along with additional information on gender, leadership positions, and even legislative committee memberships through online services available at an additional cost.—**Frank L. Wilson**

664. **Federal Regulatory Directory.** 8th ed. Washington, D.C., Congressional Quarterly, 1997. 760p. illus. index. $149.95. ISBN 1-56802-095-3.

Although mostly hidden from the public eye, a significant activity of many federal agencies is regulating laws passed by Congress. Regulation encompasses a number of human endeavors and institutions, including, among others, business transactions, the economy, trade, the workplace, natural resources, and commerce. The most comprehensive and penetrating introduction to the federal regulatory system is the latest edition of the *Federal Regulatory Directory*. The directory begins with an essay that outlines the history of federal regulations, the development of social regulation, recent policies promulgated by the Executive Office, common regulatory procedures and processes, and accountability and oversight of agency activities. This essay, as well as the text of more than 100 agency profiles, frames the activities of the regulatory system within the context of the recent Republican Congress and Democratic White House political climate.

The directory is divided into five parts. The 1st part consists of profiles of the 12 major regulatory agencies. Information given includes descriptions of regulatory responsibilities, specific powers and authority, organizational framework and subagency responsibilities, key personnel, and legislation that affects each agency's mission. Major regulatory agency entries conclude with a list of information sources, including publications, libraries, and nongovernmental organizations that monitor their activities. The next 2 sections profile lesser independent regulatory agencies and departmental agencies granted regulatory power. The descriptive analysis of these agencies is less comprehensive, but the informational data given are still useful. The next section includes short profiles of Executive Branch offices and other agencies with minor regulatory responsibilities. The directory concludes with a list of government Internet sites, the text of major regulatory administrative acts and Executive Orders, and instructions for ordering government publications and how to use the *Federal Register* and the *Code of Federal Regulations*.

New to this edition is a more detailed table of contents, content descriptions of agency and nongovernmental Websites, complete coverage of fax and fax-on-demand numbers, an additional number of government hotlines, and complete details about how to order titles from the publications office of each agency. This directory is as essential to a library's reference collection as the *Government Manual*.
—**Robert V. Labaree**

665. **Find Public Records Fast: The Complete State, County, and Courthouse Locator.** Michael Sankey and Carl R. Ernst, eds. Tempe, Ariz., Facts on Demand Press/BRB, 1997. 522p. maps. $19.95pa. ISBN 1-889150-01-0.

At the outset, this useful resource makes clear its intended audience, namely, anyone interested in finding a missing person, locating asset or financial information, checking the background of an individual, or checking the background of a business. The reference is about the paper trails people leave and how others can use them advantageously. The guide explains what public records are; the benefits of public record searching; the location of public records; various categories of public records; how to search; associated costs of searches; online resources; court searches; and searching for real estate, Uniform Commercial Code filings, and sundry county records.

Following this overall introduction comes the profile of each state, containing such information as state agencies (general help telephone numbers), important state Internet sites, public records for state agencies, some details of county courts and recording offices, addresses and telephone numbers for county courts and recording offices, and federal courts. The information for county courts includes not only address and telephone numbers but also hours of operation and, where possible, fax numbers. The work concludes with important information on any state agency public record restrictions, an appeals and federal records center locator, and the U.S. Appeals Courts and Federal Records Centers addresses and telephone numbers.

An additional value of this book is its cost. Those who find they need regular information on public records can afford to purchase a copy. Public libraries should find this a useful reference for their patrons. The material is clearly and coherently presented. The contents may not live up to the title's suggestion that one can find public records fast, but the book will most certainly enable anyone to find those records faster. It is highly recommended.—**Michael A. Foley**

666. **The Librarian's Guide to Public Records: The Complete State, County, and Courthouse Locator.** rev. ed. Michael L. Sankey and Carl R. Ernst, eds. Tempe, Ariz., BRB, 1997. 554p. index. (The Public Record Research Library). $39.00pa. ISBN 1-879792-38-9.

With a new cover, price, ISBN, and format, this revised edition does three things: It outlines techniques for creating trails to public records and information, it gives state-by-state sources for this information, and it provides a valuable new 32-page professional reference section. In their 28-page introduction, the editors distinguish among public records, public information, and personal information; define a public record; and list 23 categories of public records, such as bankruptcy, credit, criminal, legislation and regulations, and litigation and civil judgments. They offer suggestions for effective searching within records at the federal, state, and county levels.

In state-by-state alphabetic order, the profiles capture directory facts and search information for all 50 states. Listed are Internet sites, offices that maintain specific records ranging from criminal records to vital records, and information on recording offices and on county courts by topics handled. Federal court locations and coverage are stated. The final reference section discusses and defines the privacy issue and notes recent legislation pertaining to it. It cites trends and changes in courts and provides directory information and a state location chart for U.S. Appeals Courts and Federal Records Centers. Finally, users are introduced to the types of vendors performing public records and personal information searches, their distinguishing features, and advice for using them.

Both the introduction and the reference section lift this book out of the category of just another directory. A more descriptive title would use the word "citizen" rather than "librarian," because the book's contents will serve a much broader audience than its current title implies. A few grammatical errors and inappropriate word sequences indicate the need for stricter editing of proof pages. This tool will aid those searching for missing persons or checking backgrounds of both businesses and individuals, and students or citizens seeking clarification of division of responsibilities among various courts and government entities.

—**Eleanor Ferrall**

667. **State Staff Directory, Summer 1997.** Alexandria, Va., CQ Staff Directories, 1997. 1919p. illus. index. $175.00pa./yr. ISBN 0-87289-129-1. ISSN 1090-7203.

CQ Staff Directories has expanded its offerings with the 1997 *State Staff Directory*. This new effort is presented with the assumption that such a guide will be increasingly useful as power continues to be shifted from the federal government to the states. This is a comprehensive guide to the 50 states of the United States with contact information and brief biographical sketches on more than 39,000 key players in state government.

Coverage for each state includes the offices of the governor, the lieutenant governor, and policy- and decision-makers in all departments, agencies, boards, and commissions. For smaller units only a few names are listed, but major agencies may have 15 or 20 listings. Each listing consists of name, title, address, and telephone number. Fax numbers and zip codes are provided for the agencies as a whole. State entries also have a legislative section where each legislator is listed, complete with contact and brief biographical information and a list of committee assignments. Each state section begins with a state information page that includes historical, demographic, and budget facts.

At the end of the volume are three substantial sections. The 1st contains more than 800, 1-paragraph biographies of key executive and legislative branch officials. The 2d section is a functional index: a listing of all state agencies under keywords. The 3d section is an index of individuals appearing throughout the volume.

This new title joins at least two similar publications: *State Legislative Leadership, Committees, & Staff* (see ARBA 92, entry 698) and *Carroll's State Directory* (see ARBA 96, entry 726). The titles vary in the level of detail provided for the many categories of information. With so much detail that is subject to constant change, it is questionable if a paper product is now the best format for another state government directory.—**Henry E. York**

Handbooks and Yearbooks

668. **The American Presidency.** [CD-ROM]. Danbury, Conn., Grolier, 1996. Minimum system requirements: IBM or compatible 486DX/33MHz. Double-speed CD-ROM drive. MS-DOS 5.0. Windows 3.1. SVGA 256-color monitor. Microsoft or compatible mouse. Wave table sound card. Speakers or headphones. Printer (optional). Optional online requirements: Modem. Access to the World Wide Web using an Internet service provider. $19.99. ISBN 0-7172-3367-7.

A wag once said that the opposite of progress is Congress. That may well be, but citizens of the United States have long hallowed their presidency. Even after scores of scandals like the XYZ Affair, Teapot Dome, and more have rocked the Oval Office, people of the United States still rally around the office of the president, even after they have abandoned those who sit in the honored seat. The current CD-ROM is a testament to the deification of that office. Grolier has culled from its three basic encyclopedias—*New Book of Knowledge*, *Academic American Encyclopedia*, and the *Encyclopedia Americana* (see entries 36 and 46)—all materials relating to the U.S. presidency and loaded them on disc. The result is a fascinating piece of work that is as informative as it is fun to use.

When users first load *The American Presidency*, they will get QuickTime, AT&T's World Net Service, and Netscape Navigator Software. The World Net Service is AT&T's own browser that relies on Netscape for safe launching. Installation is easy and quick, but users should be advised, for space allocations alone, that the install feature automatically loads these programs. The "Presidential Assistant" takes users on a tour of the disc, but one is hardly needed. Depending on the depth of the information sought, clicking on the appropriate encyclopedia will guide users there. The screens are beautifully arranged and easy to read. Hardly ever is there an occasion for misunderstanding what one needs to click on next. Clicking is just what users will do. More than 800 biographies, general interest articles, facts, figures, and more are here. The "Quick Facts Browser" provides patrons with a brief résumé of any one of the 42 presidents. General articles discuss topics as wide-ranging as suffrage, the ballot box, and the electoral college to documents, speeches, the Constitution, and more. The presidential summaries range in length according to the historical importance of the president. Thus, Chester Arthur's sketch is brief compared to Abraham Lincoln's lengthy article.

The CD-ROM does not miss much chance for fun, either. By clicking on the first line of the opening screen, users will hear "Hail to the Chief" vigorously played. The multimedia section of minidocumentaries contains movie clips of everyone from Franklin Delano Roosevelt to Bill Clinton. Teachers will be particularly delighted to see quizzes for students from grade 3 through adult. The disc is not, however, without it faults. Even as information-rich as this resource is, much of it is of sound-bite quality. The section on scandals is selective, and bias is evident throughout. For example, Ronald Reagan "jammed" through his tax bill relief, "claimed" to have forced Mikhail Gorbachev and the Soviet Union to its knees, while combining "inspiration over management" with "simplistic" leadership. Compare this to the hagiography that passes for biography under Lyndon Johnson, John F. Kennedy, and even the current White House occupant.

The CD-ROM mimics some parts of *Vital Statistics on the Presidency* (Congressional Quarterly, 1996), but the book has fewer articles and more statistics. The disc is also somewhat like National Geographic Society's CD-ROM, *The Presidents: A Picture History of Our Nation* (Educational Media Division, 1996). Yet the current disc has fewer picture and clips, but three times as many articles and biographies. Not all academic librarians will find this CD-ROM useful unless they serve large undergraduate constituencies. Special, public, and school libraries, not to mention many homes, will see this multimedia disc as the godsend it is. [R: RBB, 15 Feb 97, p. 1040]—**Mark Y. Herring**

669. **The Complete Bill of Rights: The Drafts, Debates, Sources, & Origins.** Neil H. Cogan, ed. New York, Oxford University Press, 1997. 705p. $95.00. ISBN 0-19-51-322-X.

This ambitious work focuses on the initial 10 amendments to the U.S. constitution, offering researchers at all levels a documentary record that reveals the processes by which the Bill of Rights emerged. The book is arranged into 10 chapters, 1 for each amendment. The editor, a law school dean, has examined the original manuscripts and newspapers held by the Library of Congress, the National Archives, and the Library Company of Philadelphia. A detailed table of contents serves as an index, listing "Texts" (preliminary drafts, proposals from state conventions, and colonial charters and laws) and "Discussion of Drafts and Proposals" (debates; commentary from contemporary newspapers and pamphlets; and letters and diaries of James Madison, Thomas Jefferson, and many others).

This title is without competition for the most part, but more extensive sources include Philip B. Kurland and Ralph Lerners's 5-volume *Founder's Constitution* (see ARBA 88, entry 575) and John R. Vile's *Encyclopedia of Constitutional Amendments, Proposed Amendments, and Amending Issues* (see ARBA 97, entry 596). This title is highly recommended for school and academic libraries, and all but the smallest public libraries should consider adding it to their collections.—**Gary D. Barber**

670. **Congressional Quarterly Almanac. Volume LII: 104th Congress, 2nd Session...1996.** Washington, D.C., Congressional Quarterly, 1997. 1v. (various paging). index. $345.00. ISBN 1-56802-267-0. ISSN 0095-6007.

The U.S. Congress produces a staggering amount of work on a multitude of public policy issues. The 1996 edition of *Congressional Quarterly Almanac* covers legislation and other issues addressed by Congress during the 1996 election year.

This work begins with an overview of 1996 congressional developments, focusing on the conflict between a Democratic White House and the Republican controlled Congress and significant legislation that was or was not enacted. The heart of *Congressional Quarterly Almanac* provides detailed coverage of legislative developments in areas as diverse as economics, commerce, environment, law, human services, veterans affairs, defense, foreign policy, appropriations, and major political developments including national party conventions and results and analysis of presidential and congressional elections. Detailed topics addressed by Congress during 1996 covered in this almanac include sexual offenders, Medicare reform, Federal Aviation Administration restructuring, "dolphin-safe" tuna legislation, defense depot privatization, and trade sanctions against Iran and Libya.

Appendixes feature a glossary of congressional terms; rosters of congressional members and their committee assignments; voting records of individual representatives and senators on key issues; the test of important documents, such as the State of the Union address and party platforms; and summaries of public laws enacted during 1996.

This work is the finest single-volume reference source available for coverage of 1996 federal legislative developments in print format. Its objective coverage and analysis of congressional events make it an essential source for congressional students and scholars and a staple in academic library reference departments. Although much similar information can be found on the Internet through GPO Access, Thomas, and Congressional Compass, the presence of this printed source in libraries will continue to produce heavy use by library users regardless of their political and electronic sophistication.—**Bert Chapman**

671. **Congressional Roll Call 1996: A Chronology and Analysis of Votes in the House and Senate, 104th Congress, Second Session.** Washington, D.C., Congressional Quarterly, 1997. 1v. (various paging). index. $36.95pa. ISBN 0-87187-902-6. ISSN 0191-1473.

Although not clearly indicated, the text under review is a reprint of the second half of the *Congressional Quarterly Almanac* (see entry 670). Thus, it is worthwhile to point out right away that libraries that already own the almanac have no need to purchase this newer publication.

The work is divided into two sections. The 1st section, "Vote Studies," contains brief analyses of issues, such as presidential support, party unity, and conservative coalitions patterns, as well as the year's key House and Senate votes. These studies should prove valuable for those who study congressional voting behavior and party discipline, which have been the major contentious debates among scholars in recent decades. However, the most informative item in this section, especially for those who want to get a brief survey of the year's major pieces of legislation (e.g., line-item veto, welfare overhaul, immigration, abortion, minimum wage, and so forth), is the House and Senate's key votes. Under each of the above mentioned areas, the reader is provided with a brief but concise discussion of the history of the bill.

The 2d section contains a complete set of roll call vote charts for the House and Senate during the 1996 congressional session. In addition, it also includes indexes of roll call votes and bills on which roll call votes were taken. All in all, this compilation should prove useful as a research tool for interest groups, political science students, and political scientists. Libraries without the *Congressional Quarterly Almanac* should purchase this work.—**Binh P. Le**

672. **The Congressional Yearbook 1996, 104th Congress, 2nd Session.** By Jon Healey and the Staff of Congressional Quarterly. Washington, D.C., Congressional Quarterly, 1997. 310p. index. $23.95pa. ISBN 1-56802-315-4. ISSN 1079-8129.

This 4th volume in the Congressional Quarterly's series reviews the activity of the second session of the 104th Congress. The work is intended to be a text or reader on the formulation of public policy, including details that are only occasionally reported in a self-contained work requiring no further research to understand what occurred on Capitol Hill in 1996. The work succeeds in accomplishing these objectives. The volume begins with an overview that sets the scene for the legislative battles that will ensue. Chapters are divided by subject and then further subdivided by issue. Every bill is referenced to the issue and can be found in the index. The real strength of the work centers on the writing. The authors have transformed the workings of Congress into an interesting narrative. Using subheads like "Filibuster and Fluster" and "A Bumpy Path," they offer thematic insights that illuminate the day-to-day work of the Congress. With imagery such as referring to a piece of legislation as a "tree moving from forest to sawmill to lathe," the reader is drawn into the nature of congressional work. The session itself offered several precursors for the 1997 year. For instance, in a prophetic comment, Senator Fred Thompson is quoted as saying about campaign finance reform, "We'll have to wait until the next real good scandal to get anything done." This book is highly recommended and is especially useful for smaller collections that need a concise summary of the year's congressional events.—**Joshua Cohen**

673. Cook, Rhodes, and Alice V. McGillivray. **U.S. Primary Elections 1995-96.** Washington, D.C., Congressional Quarterly, 1997. 409p. maps. $189.00. ISBN 0-87187-900-X.

This work is the result of Congressional Quarterly's compilation of the primary results from those states that held presidential, senatorial, and gubernatorial primaries in the 1995-1996 election year. U.S. primary elections are offered in one volume. The previously published information can be found separately in Congressional Quarterly's *Presidential Primaries and Caucuses* and *Congressional and Gubernatorial Primaries*. It can also be used with the biennial *America Votes*. The primary results are arranged alphabetically by county for each state; a map of both counties and congressional districts is available. Introductory material includes a brief discussion of the Clinton-Dole contest, along with summaries of primary results for the 1984, 1988, and 1992 elections. Only the most thorough researcher will need this amount of statistical information. Consequently, this excellent reference work is recommended only for large, inclusive collections.—**Deborah Hammer**

674. **Guide to the Presidency.** 2d ed. Michael Nelson, ed. Washington, D.C., Congressional Quarterly, 1996. 2v. illus. index. $299.00/set. ISBN 1-56802-018-X.

Nelson's *Guide to the Presidency* represents one of the most useful reference works recently published on the presidency. Unlike Leonard Levy and Louis Fisher's *Encyclopedia of the American Presidency* (S&S Trade, 1993), which offers an extensive biographical approach to examining the White House, this work focuses on the Executive Office as a administrative branch within the U.S. political system. The 2d edition of the guide is published in 2 volumes, each with a complete index, and containing a total of 37 chapters grouped into 7 parts. Each part, such as "Powers of the Presidency," analyzes a specific element of the Executive Office within the conceptual boundaries of what makes it unique.

This edition includes coverage from 1791 through Bill Clinton's first term in office. The content is also enhanced by the incorporation of recent research on the 1994 Republican election victories, the development of a new post-Soviet world order, and "emerging political trends." In addition, the text of the new edition has been rearranged and rendered more readable. The 2d volume concludes with a number of supplementary materials, such as the text of key historical documents; a collection of tabular and graphical data; and lists of party nominees, cabinet appointments, and other officials. The data are current through the 104th Congress. The essays are all written by experts in their fields, providing an easy-to-understand but comprehensive overview of a particular topic. A selected bibliography concludes each essay. Photographs and other illustrations are included when appropriate, and many chapters are enhanced with side boxes that highlight a specific concept or offer a case study of an event for further clarification.

As with the 1st edition, this is an outstanding reference tool. The 2d edition updates the previous edition with new research on the presidency in an enhanced format.—**Robert V. Labaree**

675. Makinson, Larry, and Joshua Goldstein. **Open Secrets: The Encyclopedia of Congressional Money & Politics.** 4th ed. Washington, D.C., Congressional Quarterly, 1996. 1348p. index. $200.00. ISBN 1-56802-229-8. ISSN 1089-9642.

The new 4th edition of *Open Secrets* is a welcome addition to reference works that supply information on what groups and individuals provide financial support for people elected to Congress. This edition focuses on the 1994 elections only but does offer some retrospective data for comparative purposes. Although many people may think that the defense lobby contributes more money than other groups to senators and representatives, they in fact provided only $9 million to elected officials in the Congress during the 1993-1994 period. The financial sector was far and away the biggest source of campaign contributions in the 1994 elections, giving $68 million. Labor unions were close with $42.5 million.

This reference book is a useful and valuable compendium and a reliable source of data and information on what groups and political action committees (PACs) provided money to Congress members during the 1994 election. For anyone doing research on what a particular member of Congress has spent in the last three elections, the total contributions she or he has received, and the source of such funding, this reference book represents a gold mine of data. The authors of this encyclopedia attempt to be scrupulously correct and exact in the information provided, allowing the serious researcher and informed layperson to rely on one convenient source of authoritative information.

Although it is a rather hefty tome, *Open Secrets* will be well used by library clients looking for statistics, data, and graphics on money that goes to support elected officials in the Congress. As such, it deserves space on the shelves of all public and academic libraries across the United States. One wishes, however, that such data were updated every year or two and were available on CD-ROM or on a database that would allow a library to download pertinent segments easily. *Open Secrets* is highly recommended for all libraries.—**Roberto P. Haro**

676. Ornstein, Norman J., Thomas E. Mann, and Michael J. Malbin, with Amy Schenkenberg. **Vital Statistics on Congress 1995-1996.** Washington, D.C., Congressional Quarterly, 1996. 291p. index. $46.95; $32.95pa. ISBN 0-87187-845-3; 0-87187-846-1pa.

For 16 years, *Vital Statistics on Congress* has provided annual information on the U.S. Congress. The information ranges from campaign financing and elections to staff size, Congressional workloads, actions on the floor, voting records, and so on. What makes these volumes especially useful is that the data are presented in historical context so that trends and anomalies can be observed. For example, the table on the size of Congressional staff includes information on two-year intervals since 1979. The current Congress is seen alongside figures for previous Congresses.

The data are presented clearly in figures and tables that are easily read and understood. The authors, among the best-known observers of Congress, provide some interpretation of the figures in brief introductions to each chapter. These short essays are useful in identifying trends. Because this volume includes data only through the end of the 103d Congress (1993-1994), it catches only the beginning of the Republican return to control of Congress. Information on the 1994 retirements, elections, regional shifts in partisan strength, and campaign finances show the basis of the Republican triumph. The next volume of *Vital Statistics* will catch the impact of Republicans on Congress itself.—**Frank L. Wilson**

677. **Protocol: A Handbook for Legislative Staff.** Denver, Colo., with National Legislative Services and Security Association, National Conference of State Legislatures, 1997. 65p. illus. $20.00pa. ISBN 1-55516-786-1.

The Protocol Manual Committee of the National Legislative Services and Security Association (NLSSA) has prepared this handbook. Their goals were to gather information about the ceremonial practices in use in the U.S. state legislatures, the proper method of addressing dignitaries, the proper manner of mourning the death of state officials, the protocol in hosting international guests, and correct flag etiquette. The handbook examines these topics with varying degrees of completeness. The section on legislative ceremonies deals with opening new sessions, dress codes, and precedence. For each matter there is a table outlining the practices in the 50 states. A remarkable lack of consensus marks these matters. The chapter on mourning state officials has similar tables detailing such matters as who is entitled to a state funeral and policies on attendance and ceremonies. The chapter on hosting international visitors is divided by nations with a short paragraph for each. These paragraphs provide extremely brief advice on greetings, titles, customs, gifts, and conversations. Many useful Websites are listed in the chapter on traveling outside the United States. The chapter on flags summarizes in a clear way standard etiquette regarding the U.S. and state flags.

Most of the material in the handbook would probably be of more use in a legislative reference or other governmental library rather than a public or academic library collection. Certainly, staff involved in dealing with the topics covered will find its systematic coverage useful. The section on dealing with international guests seems more problematic. The information is brief and sometimes seems obvious—do not talk to Arabs about Israel—or amusing—do not chew gum while talking to Poles. There are many handbooks on government etiquette; this one is especially useful for those concentrating on the issues at the state level.—**Henry E. York**

678. Sharp, J. Michael. **Directory of Congressional Voting Scores and Interest Group Ratings.** 2d ed. Washington, D.C., Congressional Quarterly, 1997. 2v. $269.00/set. ISBN 1-56802-182-8.

To ferret out the mysteries of life in Washington, D.C., Congressional Quarterly (CQ) comes to the rescue once more. A treasure trove of all things political, CQ has spent a lifetime making sense of madness, and the tome here is no exception. *Directory of Congressional Voting Scores and Interest Group Ratings* provides statistical profiles of every member of Congress since 1947 and every group to stake out an interest claim. Thus, for any member of Congress during the last 50 years, the directory provides a thumbnail ideological sketch of voting patterns. Additionally provided are members' biographical data.

The scores include concinnity with the Conservative Coalition, Party Unity, Presidential Support, and Voting Participation—all generated by CQ. Other groups treated are Americans for Democratic Action, the American Conservative Union, the American Civil Liberties Union, and the National Taxpayers Union. In all, there are, including CQ's 4, 14 groups with accompanying ratings.

Those interested in voting records will find this guide invaluable. Citizens wanting information on their Congressional contingency will find it in excess. Reference librarians of every description will turn to this new CQ offering as their political vade mecum.—**Mark Y. Herring**

679. Utter, Glenn H., and Ruth Ann Strickland. **Campaign and Election Reform: A Reference Handbook.** Santa Barbara, Calif., ABC-CLIO, 1997. 351p. index. (Contemporary World Issues Series). $39.50. ISBN 0-87436-862-6.

Another in the ABC-CLIO Contemporary World Issues Series, this volume examines the United States' experience with campaign and election reform from the colonial period to the present. The contents are arranged in the same fashion as previous volumes in this series. The introductory essay outlines the history of reform efforts and discusses key issues concerning, among other topics, electoral mechanics, voter fraud, and campaign finance reform. The essay is informative, clearly written, and supported by a strong list of reference. It is followed by a descriptive chronology of events associated with campaign and election reform and biographical sketches of 28 currently active or historically significant individuals who have influenced reform efforts in some way. The 4th chapter summarizes public opinion data and the content of "major" Supreme Court cases. The selected quotes of public officials, special interest group leaders, and scholars successfully reflect contemporary attitudes about reform. The remainder of the book follows more traditional reference tools: a directory of nonprofit, for-profit, governmental, and intergovernmental organizations and agencies concerned with various aspects of reform; an annotated list of books and periodicals divided into six topical sections; and an annotated list of nonprint resources, including a substantial collection of Internet sites. All the sites appeared to be up-to-date at the time of this writing. The book concludes with a glossary and a title/subject/name index.

This book is another fine addition to the Contemporary World Issues Series. *Campaign and Election Reform* succeeds in delivering an accurate overview of the complex issues associated with campaign and election reform and provides a comprehensive selection of reference tools for both the scholar and nonspecialist.—**Robert V. Labaree**

680. Westin, Richard A., comp. **U.S.-Mexican Treaties.** Buffalo, N.Y., William S. Hein, 1996. 11v. $1,250.00/set. ISBN 0-89941-985-2.

Given the explosive growth in trade between the United Mexican States and the United States of America, Westin felt it was imperative that there be a competent collection of multilateral and bilateral treaties between these two nations. The purpose of this particular work is to provide the reader with a useful compilation of these treaties. Westin has included only treaties in force between the two countries.

Beginning with the Treaty of Guadalupe Hidalgo, this set covers those treaties signed during the period from February 1848 through December 1994. In a set of 11 volumes, the compiler provides the full text of these treaties. Although Westin attempted to make this work comprehensive, he admits that because of time and budget constraints, there have been some omissions. However, his intention is to include these omissions by supplementation at some time in the future.

Within the 11 volumes, treaties are arranged chronologically by signing date. A convenient feature is that the compiler has included a chronological and subject index at the front of each volume. These indexes give the signing date, the short title, and the treaty number for each agreement, as well as its location in the set. Westin has also included a list of treaties with multiple signing dates, which directs the reader to the original signing date and its location in the set, to eliminate unnecessary confusion. The individual treaties are coded with at least one traditional reference, for example, Treaties and Other International Acts Series (TIAS) or U.S. Treaties and Other International Agreements (USI). If applicable, a citation to the Statutes at Large is given.

Preceding the full text of the treaty, the compiler supplies a brief, unauthorized description of the contents of each one. Westin states that the summaries are in no way official interpretations but are provided solely for convenience and do not follow a rigid format. This work is recommended for any international law collection. The set is a useful resource for lawyers, government personnel, or businesspeople in both the United States and Mexico.—**Judith A. Valdez**

681. Zimmerman, Doris P. **Robert's Rules in Plain English.** New York, HarperPerennial/HarperCollins, 1997. 128p. index. $4.95pa. ISBN 0-06-273476-8.

Rules are not only needed in groups but required. The only trouble is, *Robert's Rules* are often as unwieldy as most groups—but there is help. Here are rules disambiguated for the most modern-minded people. This book is laid back, but this is not meant disparagingly. No other book comes to mind that so clearly states what officers are to do and how they are to do it. For example, short, succinct rules are provided throughout: Be organized; be temperate; be impartial. Other rules are more procedural: one question at a time and one speaker at a time. Others are explanatory: Once a question is decided, it is not in order to bring up the same motion or one essentially like it at the same meeting. Following each instruction, the actual rules are given and in the context in which they should be employed.

This book should be everywhere: in reference libraries, in churches, in small groups and large, in the hands of every teacher who must oversee young people who must officiate meetings. Its common sense and straightforward advice will make any meeting run smoothly and in order. Aside from all this, it is written so that everyone can understand it.—**Mark Y. Herring**

Indexes

682. **Historic Documents Index, 1972-1995.** Washington, D.C., Congressional Quarterly, 1997. 278p. $93.00. ISBN 1-56802-214-X.

This 25-year cumulative index covers the entire Historic Documents series from its inception in 1972 through 1995. It consolidates the individual five-year indexes found in each volume of Historic Documents and supersedes the previous cumulative index for 1972-1989 (see ARBA 92, entry 702). The appearance of this cumulative index greatly simplifies the task of students and researchers using the series; libraries may want to purchase it even though it duplicates the existing individual volume indexes.
—**Ronald H. Fritze**

Canadian

683. **Canadian Parliamentary: Guide Parlementaire Canadien.** Kathryn O'Handley and Caroline Sutherland, eds. Toronto, Gale Canada, 1997. 1198p. index. $70.00. ISBN 1-896413-43-9. ISSN 0315-6168.

This bilingual (English and French) standard, first published in this format in 1909, is updated in this edition with important, new material. There was a federal election in 1997, which is reflected with the new biographies of the recently elected representatives. The tabulated results of the election are featured as well. New election results are from material concerning the previous elections, which date back to 1867.

The 1st section deals with the federal government and includes 600 pages on the Governor General, the Privy Council, the Senate, the House of Commons, and the Courts. The Library of Parliament and the Parliamentary Press Gallery are also represented here. Most of the information is biographical. There are thumbnail sketches of the legislators and the top bureaucrats, highlighted by personal data, information on each politicians political career and private career, and their addresses and telephone numbers. The 2d part does the same for the 10 provinces and 2 territories—condensed to fit within 500 pages.

It would be helpful if line sketch maps were provided so that users could see where the electoral districts are geographically located. As well, Websites and e-mail addresses would be useful in this age of the Internet. However, this annual continues to be an up-to-date and reliable source about Canada. In addition to material about the Canadian government, there is general information about each province and territory, such as statistics on geography and demography.—**Dean Tudor**

European

General Works

684. Lane, Jan-Erik, David McKay, and Kenneth Newton. **Political Data Handbook: OECD Countries.** 2d ed. New York, Oxford University Press, 1997. 357p. $95.00. ISBN 0-19-828053-X.

The Organization for Economic Cooperation and Development (OECD) is one of the most important collectors of statistical information on the world's major economies. Its membership includes 24 countries: 19 in Western Europe plus the United States, Japan, Canada, Australia, and New Zealand. The vast extent of the data generated by the OECD sometimes makes them difficult to find and use. This volume is a convenient compilation of OECD data of interest to political and social scientists, individuals, and businesses with economic and political interests in other countries. There is an abundance of statistics on these 24 countries produced by these individual countries and by various international organizations. What makes this compilation especially useful is that it presents the data in a uniform manner with common definitions. This assists bringing meaning to the statistics through comparisons among the 24 major countries. The data are also presented historically in five-year intervals, in many cases from 1950 to 1995. The tables are well presented and easily interpreted.

The volume supplies comparative data for the 24 OECD countries on population, social structure, employment, economy, public finance, government structures, political parties and elections, and political communications. It also includes a section on the European Union that discusses member countries' resources, the EU's budget, and EU institutions and decision-making rules. This volume is highly recommended for all libraries.—**Frank L. Wilson**

685. **Who's Who in European Politics.** 3d ed. New Providence, N.J., Bowker-Saur/Reed Reference Publishing, 1997. 873p. index. $299.95. ISBN 1-85739-163-2.

This source, now in its 3d edition, provides, in a standard who's who format, biographical information on 8,000 political figures presently holding elective or appointive political positions in nearly 50 European countries. Approximately 1,500 of the entries are altogether new, and all of them have been submitted to the entrants for their approval and amendment. Although emphasizing professional and political accomplishments, some of the entries provide information on recreational interests as well. The biographical sketches cover nearly 700 pages; the remainder of the volume provides a political directory and biography index for each of the countries represented, which range from the long-standing Western European democracies to the Central and Eastern European nations formerly of the Soviet bloc. The Russian Federation is included, as are the states that emerged out of the breakup of Yugoslavia. Although the directory section is not as detailed as that information found in such a source as *The Europa World Year Book* (Gale, 1997), it nevertheless proves useful, especially as it conveniently refers the reader to the biographical entries. This volume is an excellent source for information regarding personalities across the broad spectrum of European political life, and it is highly recommended to academic and large public libraries.
—**Lee Weston**

British

686. Davies, Philip H. J. **The British Secret Services.** New Brunswick, N.J., Transaction Publishers, 1996. 147p. index. (International Organizations Series, v.12). $59.95. ISBN 1-56000-231-X.

British intelligence organizations remain important players in the international political arena even after the collapse of the British Empire and the end of the Cold War. This particular volume in Transaction Publishers International Organizations Series provides citations to works on British intelligence activities from the sixteenth century, with particular emphasis on works covering the twentieth century.

The British Secret Services opens with an introduction describing the growth and evolution of British intelligence activity, a glossary, and an organizational chart of the British intelligence community showing to which government ministers individual agencies report. The principal contents of this work provide annotated bibliographic citations to journal articles, books, and government documents examining the development of British intelligence. Chapters cover such topics as World War II deception operations, security intelligence from the end of World War II to 1995, the Special Operations Executive, and the Government Code and Cipher school. Entry annotations are from one to two paragraphs in length and cover events in British intelligence history, such as Winston Churchill's attitudes on intelligence, Oleg Penkovsky, Kim Philby, the Falkland Islands War, British intelligence operations in Northern Ireland, and the Matrix-Churchill in the early 1990s concerning British arms sales to Iraq.

The British Secret Services is a solid introduction to literature on the British intelligence community. Bibliographic annotations provide sufficient descriptions and evaluations of the works, and the inclusion of government reports is particularly beneficial. The only criticism of this work is its price, which will probably restrict its market to academic libraries. The book will be particularly useful to libraries desirous of enhancing the quality of their intelligence and modern British history collections. [R: Choice, Mar 97, p. 1134]—**Bert Chapman**

687. Kulisheck, P. J. **The Duke of Newcastle, 1693-1768, and Henry Pelham, 1694-1754: A Bibliography.** Westport, Conn., Greenwood Press, 1997. 139p. index. (Bibliographies of British Statesmen, no.8). $69.50. ISBN 0-313-29501-8.

Thomas Pelham, Duke of Newcastle (1693-1768), and Henry Pelham (1694-1754) served prominently in the British government from the early 1720s until their respective deaths. During their years of prominence, the brothers guided domestic and foreign policy, served under George I and George II, and worked alongside such greats as Robert Walpole and William Pitt. This bibliographic guide provides an excellent foundation for research on these two statesmen.

More than 600 entries with descriptive and evaluative annotations are organized into 14 chapters. Seven chapters deal with primary sources—Pelham papers in archives, published papers of the Pelhams, related papers and memoirs of contemporaries, Parliamentary speeches, pamphlet literature, newspapers, and journals and periodicals. Two larger chapters cover the secondary literature concerning the Pelhams' lives and careers and related special topics. Portraits, satires, and poems as well as places associated with the Pelhams are listed in two chapters. The final three chapters discuss historiography, bibliographies, and reference works on eighteenth-century Great Britain and recent surveys of the eighteenth century. There is also a chronology of the Pelhams and two indexes: to authors and to correspondents and subjects. Forming the latest addition to a useful series, this volume thoroughly covers two important but relatively neglected people.—**Ronald H. Fritze**

Russian Federation

688. **Maximov's Companion to Who Governs Moscow.** Andrei Maximov, ed. New Providence, N.J., Maximov Publications, 1997. 589p. maps. index. $95.00. ISSN 1358-8230.

Maximov's Companion to Who Governs Moscow bills itself as a reference book and telephone directory. In a country like Russia and an important metropolis like Moscow, both of which are undergoing such profound changes, this kind of information can be critical to someone doing business or research in Moscow. However, because of those same changes, the information is unfortunately out-of-date very quickly.

This volume follows 4 successful editions of *Maximov's Companion to Who Governs the Russian Federation*, and it is published once a year. The edition is bilingual and has several indexes including names, licenses, and a glossary of Moscow's territorial administration. There are also maps of administrative areas and charts showing administrative hierarchy. A user would probably have to flip through the volume for a while to find the specific information needed. The level of detail is incredible; for example, if one needs to know the subprefect of the Yasenevo district, it lists the name with telephone number. Of course, the number of people who need to know this information is limited.

The volume is an interesting work, but its limitations and narrow usefulness are obvious. Librarians may want to know of its existence for particular clientele in cities with crucial ties to Moscow, but otherwise it does not seem to be a particularly appropriate investment for most libraries and institutions. For those who are interested, it may be useful to contact the publisher to receive subscription information, so that information can be continually updated.—**Curtis D. Holmes**

Middle Eastern

689. Clements, Frank A., comp. **The Israeli Secret Services.** New Brunswick, N.J., Transaction Publishers, 1996. 80p. index. (International Organizations Series, v.13). $69.95. ISBN 1-56000-228-X.

Within the state of Israel, the Mossad, or the Israeli Secret Service, is allowed out at any moment; indeed, it *is* out every moment. No other agency of its kind enjoys the love and respect of its people more than the Mossad. Its very existence was not generally acknowledged until the 1970s. This slender volume is at once a tribute and a testimony to this service. Clements provides an excellent, thoroughgoing, and informative introduction to the subject matter. Not only are readers introduced to the Mossad, but Clements sets the stage for its creation, growth, and endurance in the face of monumental odds.

Following the introduction are 10 sections, ranging from general works on secret service and intelligence agencies to the more specific ones of Mossad functions: anti-Nazi operations, foreign incursions, rescue operations, and more. Bibliographic entries are most informative, from as brief as 50, to as engrossing as 500, words in length. Author, title, and subject indexes complete this fine volume.

Admittedly, such a tool falls into the category of the most narrowly drawn and intently focused. Yet the care and expertise presented in this volume makes it stand out as a worthy selection for nearly any academic library and most large public ones. [R: Choice, Mar 97, p. 1134]—**Mark Y. Herring**

IDEOLOGIES

690. Garner, Roberta, and John Tenuto. **Social Movement Theory and Research: An Annotated Bibliographical Guide.** Pasadena, Calif., Salem Press and Lanham, Md., Scarecrow, 1997. 274p. index. (Magill Bibliographies). $39.50. ISBN 0-8108-3197-X.

Dynamic and fluid, social movements tend to have a tremendous impact on societies far beyond the periods in which they occur. For example, the various social movements of the 1960s in the United States brought about many changes that continue to play a major role in human relationships today. *Social Movement Theory and Research* is an excellent resource covering the literature from the end of World War II through the mid-1990s. Although the primary focus of this bibliography is on the United States, many of the prominent European thinkers, such as Theodor Adorno, are well represented. According to the authors, three major periods are covered: (1) "The Irrational," the era of McCarthyism in the United States; (2) "The Rational," as exemplified in the civil rights movement under the leadership of Martin Luther King Jr.; and (3) "The Deconstructive Movement," represented by the backlash of de facto segregation and an enduring racism that could not be removed via legislation.

This is an excellent guide and a must-addition to all academic libraries. The introductory essay (40-plus pages) consists of a thorough analysis of the main currents of social movement theory. The book is divided into three sections: books and book chapters, periodical articles, and "Also of Interest." The name and subject index help the student and researcher alike to pinpoint literature or a social thinker of particular interest. This guide is an invaluable reference source for both the student and researcher. It belongs in all academic libraries and large metropolitan libraries.—**Dario J. Villa**

691. Miner, Brad. **The Concise Conservative Encyclopedia: 200 of the Most Important Ideas, Individuals, Incitements, and Institutions that Have Shaped the Movement.** New York, Free Press/Simon & Schuster Macmillan, 1996. 318p. index. $15.00pa. ISBN 0-684-80043-8.

Miner, former literary editor of *National Review*, has produced a vade mecum of sorts for those who wish a thumbnail sketch of what is going on in conservative politics. Brief entries with generous cross-references fill out this slender work. Subjects include people (Harry Jaffa, Thomas Jefferson, Rush Limbaugh, Ronald Reagan); places (Olin Foundation, Intercollegiate Studies Institute, Heritage Foundation); and things (abortion, feminism, liberty, ultramontanism). Intermixed throughout the text are five essays on the origins of conservative thought. Carnes Lord, Jacob Neusner, James V. Schall, Peter J. Stanlis, and Charles R. Kesler bring their lights to bear on the Greco-Roman influences, Jewish contributions,

Christianity, the Reformation, and modernity. For conservatives, the bibliography alone will be worth the price of the book. For liberals, reading the arguments will help them understand the issues from another viewpoint. Each entry also includes quotations from prominent conservatives on the topic defined.

One wishes the selections were not so eclectic, but then almost any such book would be. The text could have been less cluttered-looking, a distracting fault of the publisher. By and large, this is an excellent starting point for anyone wishing to know something about the conservative movement.
—**Mark Y. Herring**

692. **Protest, Power, and Change: An Encyclopedia of Nonviolent Action from ACT-UP to Women's Suffrage.** Roger S. Powers, William B. Vogele, Christopher Kruegler, and Ronald M. McCarthy, eds. New York, Garland, 1997. 610p. illus. index. $75.00. ISBN 0-8153-0913-9.

Nonviolent protest for the liberation of humankind has been a common activity throughout history. No society, including those claiming to adhere to democratic principles, can be free from the struggles to achieve human dignity for all its citizens. There are many individuals who have placed their lives in extreme danger and ultimately paid a high price for their convictions, such as Martin Luther King Jr. in the United States and Mohandas Gandhi in India.

The new *Protest, Power, and Change* provides both the student and scholar with an excellent introduction to the many facets of nonviolent action. Each entry (in alphabetic order) furnishes a comprehensive essay, which may range from several paragraphs to several pages in length. Each entry also includes a bibliography of selected sources for further reading, an added attraction for students interested in pursuing the subject. There are many black-and-white photographs that add another dimension to the text. This reference source is highly recommended for all academic and public libraries—it will be a standard source of information on this fascinating subject.—**Dario J. Villa**

INTERNATIONAL ORGANIZATIONS

693. **International Information: Documents, Publications, and Electronic Information of International Governmental Organizations.** 2d ed. Peter I. Hajnal, ed. Englewood, Colo., Libraries Unlimited, 1997. 528p. index. $105.00. ISBN 1-56308-147-4.

The 1st edition of this title was published in 1988 and featured "Electronic Information" in the title, which is now replaced by "Information Systems." The discussion of electronic information availability is integrated with details regarding traditional printed documents. Eighteen individuals contributed chapters to this title. The European Union, the G-7, the League of Nations, the Organization for Economic Co-operation and Development, and the International Development Center have separate chapters that review the history and structure of the organization, publication characteristics and information contents, distribution channels, bibliographic control, and links to other entities. Deservedly, the United Nations (UN) receives the most coverage, with separate chapters on its electronic information resources, the UN Library, and the UN Scholar's Workstation that has been developed at Yale University. The chapter on the role of the private sector and other non-IGO organizations has sections on Chadwyck-Healey, Congressional Information Service, the Oxford University Press, the Public Affairs Information Service, and Readex. For a variety of reasons, the distribution of information from international governmental organizations is cumbersome and slow, and the aforementioned private publishers are performing a valuable and underrecognized service in providing this information to the public. The last 2 chapters cover collection development and reference work. A 50-page bibliography is provided that includes appropriate Internet Website addresses and a list of abbreviations and acronyms. The book is illustrated with many helpful charts, graphs, tables, and printouts of Internet Web pages. Reference notes are found at the end of the chapters.

The editor, who is the international documents specialist at the University of Toronto library, has written a long list of publications in this field. This reviewer would like to recommend that catalogers add still another subject heading to this title's bibliographic record: International agencies—Handbooks, manuals, etc. A 2d volume is planned to augment and update the information in this volume. This book can be used to help answer reference questions, for collection development purposes, and for those working on research projects requiring international information. This work is recommended for all academic, large pubic, and special libraries.—**Daniel K. Blewett**

694. Spaulding, Seth, and Lin Lin. **Historical Dictionary of the United Nations Educational, Scientific, and Cultural Organization (UNESCO).** Lanham, Md., Scarecrow, 1997. 500p. (International Organizations Series, no.13). $69.00. ISBN 0-8108-3288-7.

UNESCO deals with education, science, culture, and communication issues worldwide, and each area has its own clientele and politics. This requires several different organizations combined into one and makes understanding of its structure and working relationships difficult. Therefore, this book should be helpful for outsiders and also those working in the organization trying to understand the complexities involved.

The 1st section covers abbreviations and acronyms, of which there are many. The 2d section looks chronologically at UNESCO, followed by an introduction covering such areas as the creation of UNESCO and overall development trends, UNESCO's mandate and structure, the UNESCO general conferences, the secretary, publications, and services. The major body of the book is a dictionary covering general and miscellaneous information, education, science, social and human science, culture, communications, documents, libraries, archives, and serial documentation. Intensive appendixes that look at the definition of a region with a view to the execution by the organization of regional activities; the director-general of UNESCO; sessions of the general conference; international days, weeks, years, and decades; UNESCO prizes; declarations, conventions, agreements, and recommendations adopted under the aspect of UNESCO; UNESCO member states and their estimated assessments; the charter of national commissions of UNESCO; the constitution of UNESCO; rules and procedures concerning recommendations to member states and the international convention covered by the terms of Article IV, paragraph 4 of the constitution; directives concerning UNESCO's relation with foundations of similar institutions; directions concerning UNESCO's relation with international nongovernmental organizations; and a UNESCO organizational chart complete the book.

Understanding UNESCO is a monumental task, and this book will be a great help in wading through the bureaucracy. The book is well written, easy to understand, and well referenced. It should be in all major libraries for the general public, and undergraduate through professional people will also be interested.

—**Herbert W. Ockerman**

INTERNATIONAL RELATIONS

695. Atkins, G. Pope. **Encyclopedia of the Inter-American System.** Westport, Conn., Greenwood Press, 1997. 561p. maps. index. $115.00. ISBN 0-313-28600-0.

This encyclopedia describes the complex workings of the Inter-American System (IAS), which the author defines as a "formal, multipurpose, hemisphere-wide regional organization among the American states" (p. 1). The major components of the IAS are the Organization of American States, the Inter-American Development Bank, and the Inter-American Treaty of Reciprocal Assistance Regime. Now in its second century of existence, the IAS has promoted regional accommodation, collective security, economic development, and cultural awareness among its 35 sovereign states. As a regional intergovernmental organization, the IAS also interacts frequently with other international organizations. The IAS has established a cooperative relationship with the United Nations, but retained considerable autonomy. Relations between the IAS and the European Union have sometimes been harmonious and at other points discordant.

The scope and comprehensiveness of this book are impressive. Approximately 250 entries appear, arranged in alphabetic order, covering various organizations, institutions, treaties, conferences, and leaders. The writing is generally clear if somewhat dry. Cross-indexing helps the reader find information easily. Some important people and developments, however, have been left out or get short shrift. These omissions occur most frequently for the early part of the twentieth century. William Howard Taft and his "Dollar Diplomacy," for example, are not mentioned at all. Theodore Roosevelt appears just twice, with no separate biographical sketch. Still, there is considerable substance here—especially regarding pan-American conferences, committees, and associations. Specialists and nonspecialists alike will benefit from this book.—**Richard E. Holl**

696. Bercovitch, Jacob, and Richard Jackson. **International Conflict: A Chronological Encyclopedia of Conflicts and Their Management 1945-1995.** Washington, D.C., Congressional Quarterly, 1997. 372p. maps. index. $85.00. ISBN 1-56802-195-X.

Following a strict set of criteria, the authors have selected 292 conflicts of significance that occurred between 1945 and 1995 for this encyclopedia. They begin the work with two well-written and instructive chapters: "Understanding International Conflict" and "Managing International Conflict." The conflicts then follow in historical order. A brief factual history and any negotiation attempts are given for each. Following the textual content, which ranges from a few paragraphs to a full page, are reference numbers to an extensive reference list of further reading at the back of the book. Different graphs accompany the first two chapters, and some of the conflict entries contain maps. For ease of use and a quick reference, this work should receive a warm reception.—**Jo Anne H. Ricca**

697. Britton, John A. **The United States and Latin America: A Select Bibliography.** Pasadena, Calif., Salem Press and Lanham, Md., Scarecrow, 1997. 277p. index. (Magill Bibliographies). $38.00. ISBN 0-8108-3248-8.

Relations between the United States and Latin America are important because of the proximity of the two areas. The author, a Latin Americanist, has compiled an excellent annotated bibliography covering major topics since the Monroe Doctrine promulgated in 1823 to works written in 1996. Although there are a few articles, most works included are books. The major focus of this bibliography concerns twentieth-century topics.

The author has taken two approaches: traditional diplomatic history and the new international history. He contrasts these two approaches with two well-known twentieth-century Cubans: Fidel Castro and the popular singer and songwriter Gloria Estefan. Using the diplomatic history approach, the author selects important works country by country. Reflecting U.S. policy emphasizing protecting the Panama Canal and its own borders, the preponderance of works included covers Mexico, Central America, and the Caribbean countries. Using the international history approach, the author covers the broader topics of communism, revolution, armed forces in Latin America, immigration, drugs, the North American Free Trade Agreement, and others.

This book is particularly useful for the beginning student who needs to identify themes and read important works. It is highly recommended for academic and public libraries.—**Karen Y. Stabler**

698. **Careers in International Affairs.** 6th ed. Maria Pinto Carland and Michael Trucano, eds. Washington, D.C., Georgetown University Press, 1997. 282p. index. $17.95pa. ISBN 0-87840-630-1.

Intended to introduce job applicants to international job opportunities, this book consists of 16 chapters written by faculty and alumni of Georgetown University's School of Foreign Service and others affiliated with the agencies covered in each chapter. The editors, Carland and Trucano, are the associate director of the Master of Science in Foreign Service program at Georgetown and an alumnus/consultant, respectively. The chapters are comprehensive for U.S. government agencies and international organizations but selective for business, banking, education, and other areas, where the chapters emphasize a representative sample, not all organizations.

After a brief introduction to the nature and focus of the agencies in the chapter, most chapters consist of a list of agencies that provide opportunities for working abroad. Individual agency entries profile the agency briefly in terms of its scope and activities; describe, if possible, the desired skills and experience for positions within the agency; then list the hiring department within the agency, its mailing address, World Wide Web site addresses, and telephone numbers. Not included, sometimes at the agency's specific request, are names of human resource directors, fax numbers, occasionally telephone numbers, and e-mail addresses. These entries are supplemented by more general chapters on the international affairs job market, federal government employment, and job searching via the Internet. The book has a reliable bibliography of related works and an index to agency names.

Entries for the 300-plus organizations listed in the directory have been updated in this edition through independent research and inquiries to the agencies themselves. Most notable are the revisions to business, banking, consulting, and nonprofit agencies with the addition of about 100 new listings, some the result of structural changes in these areas. The book contains current, highly useful content for job-seekers in the international market. The authors are authoritative and write clearly about their relevant areas of interest and expertise. The Foreign Policy Association's (FPA) *Guide to Careers in World Affairs* (3d ed., Impact Publications, 1993) covers similar areas and provides more complete information for the individual agencies, including, for example, the numbers and position titles of professional staff, training programs, and application procedures. *Almanac of International Jobs and Careers* (2d ed.; see ARBA 95, entry 314) is not as thorough as the FPA publication. Containing slightly more recent information, the book would be useful in academic and public libraries not already owning the FPA publication.—**Marilyn Domas White**

699. DeLancey, Mark W., William Cyrus Reed, Rebecca Spyke, and Peter Steen. **African International Relations: An Annotated Bibliography.** 2d ed. Boulder, Colo., Westview Press, 1997. 677p. index. $85.00. ISBN 0-8133-8653-5.

DeLancey, an Africanist who has written many works on the Cameroon and Africa, has updated this new edition (see ARBA 82, entry 533, for a review of the 1st edition) to cover international relations of Africa from 1978 to 1993, with a few entries from 1994 and 1995. Of the 4,365 entries, approximately 60 percent are new and update the 1st edition that covered the years from 1960 to 1978. DeLancey includes primarily articles, but also lists books, pamphlets, and a few documents and dissertations. Most of the entries are from U.S. sources, but there are several foreign entries that may be difficult to locate. Some entries include a brief annotation.

The book is divided into 11 broad topics, with the largest section covering "Economic Factors in African International Relations" and the smallest 2 sections treating the topics of "General Works" and "UN and International Law." Unfortunately, there is no map of Africa. The author and subject indexes greatly improve access to specific topics. This is an excellent comprehensive bibliography that is a must for research libraries with an extensive collection in African studies.—**Karen Y. Stabler**

700. Franklin, Laurel F., comp. **George F. Kennan: An Annotated Bibliography.** Westport, Conn., Greenwood Press, 1997. 141p. index. (Bibliographies of American Notables, no.3). $69.50. ISBN 0-313-28306-0.

George F. Kennan continues to be known as one of the most influential thinkers and writers about United States Cold War diplomacy and especially the relationship with Russia—then the Soviet Union. Franklin has compiled an excellent annotated bibliography that includes extensive sources for materials by and about Kennan. This new resource book includes information on oral histories and a listing of three important archival collections that house pertinent materials by and about Kennan. With respect to the archival collections, Franklin does not include unpublished works in these collections. The list of dissertations that deal with Kennan and U.S. diplomacy is lengthy and impressive. Most of the sources cited in this bibliography are in English. The compiler's intent was to provide the serious student and the layperson with a convenient new tool to identify important sources of information on Kennan. As a result, many of the annotations are descriptive rather than analytic or critical.

Overall, this is an important new tool to access written and oral sources by and about a significant expert on U.S. diplomacy and international relations during a highly turbulent period. Kennan was almost prescient in 1956 when he was interviewed by Joseph Alsop of the *Saturday Evening Post* (November 24, 1956) and stated that Moscow was slowly losing control of its satellite states, and the disintegration of the Soviet system was only a matter of time. The bibliography is highly recommended for large academic libraries and for institutions with a concentration on international relations during the Cold War. Larger public libraries may also want to have this new annotated work.—**Roberto P. Haro**

701. Nash, Jay Robert. **Spies: A Narrative Encyclopedia of Dirty Deeds and Double Dealing from Biblical Times to Today.** New York, M. Evans, 1997. 624p. illus. index. $24.95pa. ISBN 0-87131-790-7.

The world's history of espionage can be traced in this encyclopedia, which can serve as a narrative to read for those fascinated with spying or as a reference tool for those interested in particular facts. In his introduction, the author states that his purpose in writing this book was to "present an historical panorama of espionage through the profiles of agents over the ages." In several hundred basic entries, *Spies* covers spies and espionage agencies from classical and biblical times to the present. The entries range in length from several paragraphs to several pages. These historical sketches include cross-references to other entries in the encyclopedia, useful one-line headers identifying each entry, and often photographs or other graphics. They do not include footnotes or bibliographies of sources. There are a number of supplements to the main text: glossaries of acronyms and of terms; a filmography that identifies spies and spy organizations on which films were based; and a 38-page bibliography that includes government reports, periodical articles, and books.

Nash is a well-known written of popular books on crime and criminals. His latest work will probably be appreciated by the general reader. He does point out that "spies are not to be confused with the common or uncommon criminal." As a reference or history book, the lack of documentation of sources and his popular style will be noted. There have been a number of reference books on espionage published in the 1990s that may well suffice for most reference collections: *Spyclopedia: The Complete Handbook of Espionage* (see ARBA 90, entry 724); *Spies and Provocateurs: A Worldwide Encyclopedia* (see ARBA 94, entry 796); *Spies: The Secret Agents Who Changed the Course of History* (see ARBA 95, entry 765); and *The Guinness Book of Espionage* (see ARBA 95, entry 761).—**Henry E. York**

PUBLIC POLICY AND ADMINISTRATION

702. Baldwin, Carl R. **Immigration Questions & Answers.** rev. ed. New York, Allworth Press, 1997. 172p. index. $14.95pa. ISBN 1-880559-84-6.

Baldwin has revised his 1995 edition of this text to include changes in the immigration law enacted in 1996 and changes brought about by welfare reform, which will have substantive impact on legal immigrants. As Baldwin makes clear, immigration has become quite complex and difficult. Although his book is designed to help people understand and move through the immigration process, Baldwin emphasizes the need to obtain competent legal counsel whenever possible. Toward this end, Baldwin provides an appendix that includes information on how to obtain competent legal counsel as well as information on keeping up with changes in immigration law through a Website and obtaining INS forms. The book is written for the lay reader, and it succeeds admirably. The 20 chapters are brief and concise; topics covered range from "Is Immigration Good for the U.S.?" and "'Green Card' Defined" to issues such as political asylum, how employers can help in the process, and how to become a U.S. citizen. The chapters are formatted as FAQs (frequently asked questions), which enables readers to focus on their specific needs without requiring that the entire book be read. For example, in chapter 10, "If You Are Battered," one of the FAQs is "How do I qualify to file a petition for myself as a battered spouse?"

The focus throughout the text is on the practical and informative aspects of immigration. This reference work is highly recommended not only for libraries in communities with large immigrant populations but also for all libraries that want to offer interested patrons some brief but substantive information on immigration in general.—**Michael A. Foley**

703. Berko, Robert L., Deborah Roberto, and Barbara Lowenstein. **Using Public Records to Find and Investigate Anyone.** Maplewood, N.J., Consumer Education Research Center, 1997. 192p. illus. $25.95pa. ISBN 0-934873-21-6.

This reference work from the Consumer Education Research Center and its executive director Robert Berko provides a clear and substantive guide to locating or investigating individuals through the various paper trails most people leave. As Berko notes, many searches can be as easy as using an Internet database of telephone records or consulting public records, such as marriage, death, divorce, and motor registration, among other sources.

Each chapter offers ample information regarding searches. For example, the chapter on information from media sources includes not only information on newspapers and magazines but also directories, medical boards, bankruptcy records, bankruptcy courts, bar associations, and cemeteries. Another chapter offers a state-by-state guide on where to write for vital records. There is a chapter on the Freedom of Information Act (FOIA) as well as a chapter on how to write an FOIA request letter. A chapter on how to obtain documents from foreign countries, where possible, and a chapter devoted solely to forms for vital records are provided as well. Chapters include information on tracking a family genealogy to using criminal files to find someone. Berko does not underplay how difficult a search may be. Although some information can be accessed quickly and easily, other information can take several years. Still, his message is that perseverance, in the long run, will probably bring rewards. Any reference collection will benefit from the availability of this useful guide.—**Michael A. Foley**

704. Hollings, Robert L. and Christal Pike-Nase, comps. **Professional and Occupational Licensure in the United States: An Annotated Bibliography and Professional Resource.** Westport, Conn., Greenwood Press, 1997. 146p. index. $65.00. ISBN 0-313-30440-8.

This exceptionally well organized bibliography and resource guide focuses on an important area of modern life: licensing occupational and professional activities. Hollings is a researcher in public administration, and Pike-Nase is an analyst with the Pennsylvania General Assembly. The compilers begin with a 13-page, footnoted introduction that serves as a primer on regulation, followed by 10 bibliographic chapters covering 149 sources. This may sound like a small number for a bibliography, but these sources are, for the most part, annotated at length and represent a selection of the best in the literature. The annotations serve more as digests to summarize, outline, and restate important points. Some are short, but others are up to two pages long.

The 1st chapter introduces the history of licensure. The 2d chapter covers general matters and begins with a useful concept index to the issues discussed. Chapters 3 through 9 examine the issues in more detail. They include current trends, disciplinary issues, the role of other agencies, restrictions, impact on consumers, and public board membership. Two directories of licensing regulations are in the 10th chapter, and the last chapter closes with a look at the future. The volume concludes with a list of occupations and professions licensed in every state, most states, and finally, those licensed in only one state. A list of regulators, state agencies, and interest groups and an author and subject index round out this source.

This bibliography and resource guide is well written, focused, and generously annotated. It is recommended for libraries with collections in business and public administration.—**Gerald L. Gill**

705. Nordquist, Joan, comp. **NAFTA and GATT: Environmental and Economic Issues: A Bibliography.** Santa Cruz, Calif., Reference and Research Services, 1996. 72p. (Contemporary Social Issues: A Bibliographic Series, no.43). $15.00pa. ISBN 0-937855-84-7.

This modestly sized bibliography on the environmental and economic issues surrounding both the North American Free Trade Agreement (NAFTA) and General Agreement on Tariffs and Trade (GATT) includes books, pamphlets, some government publications, book chapters, and periodical articles published during the years 1990 to 1996. Entries are concise and unannotated with approximately two-thirds of them devoted to NAFTA and one-third to GATT. There are eight sections, each arranged alphabetically by author. There is no index or alternative means of access to the works included.

This bibliography is produced by the same publisher who does *The Left Index* (see ARBA 97, entry 61), which has been indexing leftist and socialist perspectives on contemporary social issues since 1982. Therefore, it is not surprising that this NAFTA and GATT bibliography makes a special effort to draw from the world of alternative and small press publishers for many of its entries. Many mainstream book publishers and periodicals are included as well. Although Allan Metz has compiled a more comprehensive and often-annotated work in his *NAFTA Bibliography* (see entry 255), Nordquist's work lists many entries, perhaps 50 percent, that are not in Metz. The bibliography in *Greening the GATT* (Institute for International Economics, 1994) by Daniel C. Esty has little overlap with Nordquist's work, perhaps no more than 5 to 10 percent.

Overall, the bibliography at hand is a fairly inexpensive addition for larger public libraries or academic institutions with a clientele interested in either of these major public policy debates. Smaller public libraries will be much less likely to own many of the items included in this specialized subject bibliography.—**Stephen W. Green**

706. **Public Records Online: The National Guide to Private and Government Online Sources of Public Records.** 1997 ed. Carl R. Ernst and Michael Sankey, eds. Tempe, Ariz., Facts on Demand Press/BRB, 1997. 393p. maps. $19.95pa. ISBN 1-889150-02-9.

There are countless sources of public and private information that are available to citizens today. In the past, all government information was available only either by going to the agency that was the custodian of the records or by sending an agent to obtain the information from the records. During the past several years of the "computer revolution," the sources of information have increasingly been found in computerized formats of one kind or another. Although convenient when one knows the exact protocols for obtaining this information, as the revolution has begun to pick up speed, the problem of learning a variety of protocols has all but disappeared. The new difficulty is keeping track of the addresses and protocols of the sources themselves, as well as keeping track of which sources are available in what format.

Online access to public records has become a standard method of retrieving such information. Yet the numbers of sources have become a nearly outrageous figure. Navigating the sources of online information has become a specialty of legal research, and from this book's title, one would expect help in this endeavor. Unfortunately, the guide fails to deliver on this count. Even though it does provide information about a number of materials that are available online, contrary to what the title leads one to believe, this is not its emphasis. This discrepancy is either because the online sources are actually not yet available or because the editors have failed to do their homework. Examination of the book reveals that it is a combination of these two factors.

Primarily, the book serves as a useful source of information about how to obtain various bits of public information the old-fashioned way: by calling the local agencies that store the information or by calling retrieval services. This is helpful information indeed. The book is well laid out, providing a useful list of various businesses and agencies that provide access to various public documents. Material is organized by state and subdivided by types of public information. Two notable services that are not adequately covered in the state sections are Lexis and Westlaw, sources of public records and public legal information. Although the companies are awkwardly described in the company profiles section at the back of the book, they are not listed in the state sections. These two services are the best online sources for this type of information and should feature prominently in any list of online services. In addition, there is little information given on online sources of information about state legislation and administrative agency rulings. This lack renders the usefulness of the compilation somewhat limited.

Overall, the book is useful as a tool to help the researcher find much of the available public information. However, it should not be considered a tool for finding online information because there is little reference to available online sources.—**Richard A. Leiter**

14 Psychology and Parapsychology

PSYCHOLOGY

Bibliography

707. **Bibliographic Guide to Psychology 1996.** New York, G. K. Hall/Simon & Schuster Macmillan, 1997. 165p. $215.00. ISBN 0-7838-1774-6. ISSN 0360-277X.

Compiled from the 1996 cataloging activity of the Library of Congress (LC) and the New York Public Library, this volume in G. K. Hall's respected series (see entry 109 for a thorough review) surveys the behavioral sciences. The materials included have imprints from 1990 to the present, are listed with complete LC cataloging information, and are presented in an integrated main entry format. Titles on the occult and parapsychology are listed, as well as those within the various subfields of psychology. Libraries considering purchase will notice that this resource's cost exceeds one dollar per page.—**Ed Volz**

708. **Medical and Psychological Effects of Concentration Camps on Holocaust Survivors. Volume 4: Genocide: A Critical Bibliographic Review.** Robert Krell and Marc I. Sherman, eds. New Brunswick, N.J., Transaction Publishers, 1997. 365p. index. $49.95. ISBN 1-56000-290-5.

Authored by a Canadian professor of psychiatry and an Israeli Holocaust researcher, this book is a hybrid, consisting of two essays by Krell, 46 annotated bibliographic entries of books, and 2,461 references to journal articles and books.

The annotations, which vary in length from a couple of sentences to a page or more, are descriptive and sometimes also analytical and evaluative. The essays are lively and provocative. In "Psychiatry and the Holocaust," Krell states when speaking of psychiatry and the Holocaust, it "is the story of tremendous moral failures in medicine generally and psychiatry particularly, failures which have been too little examined." He indicts psychiatry for its participation in the pre-war Nazi "Euthanasia Program," in which German psychiatrists put thousands of adult and child mental patients to death; for making unfounded and slanderous statements about the behavior of concentration camp inmates; for its dismal failure at listening to Holocaust survivors' accounts of their horrifying experiences in the camps; and for the unwillingness of most psychiatrists to consider the possibility that its pet theories might be inappropriate to the task of understanding and helping Holocaust survivors.

His second essay, "Survivors and Their Families: Psychiatric Consequences of the Holocaust," elaborates on these points, as over and over we hear about survivors being blamed for any psychological symptoms they came out of the camps with. Psychiatrists were almost total slaves to the prevalent theory that there could be no neurosis without prior personality vulnerability, and Freud's doubt that a terrifying experience by itself could produce a neurosis in adult life was taken as the received word.

These essays are important reading for modern psychiatrists. They raise the question: Are we really less driven by specific theories today, or are we just driven by different theories? The bibliographic parts of the book should be quite helpful to researchers, undergraduates, graduate students, and mental health practitioners with a keen interest in these subjects.—**Anthony Gottlieb**

709. Wilson, C. Dwayne, and Bernard Lubin. **Research on Professional Consultation and Consultation for Organizational Change: A Selectively Annotated Bibliography.** Westport, Conn., in cooperation with NTL Institute for Applied Behavioral Science, Greenwood Press, 1997. 135p. index. (Bibliographies and Indexes in Psychology, no.10). $59.95. ISBN 0-313-28034-7.

As corporate and organizational worlds are revolutionized, the literature on organizational leadership, organizational change, and organizational behavior is expanding. There are now several graduate programs specifically focused on organizational change. A volume identifying the literature on consultation and organizational change is welcome; this bibliography studies two decades of research on consultative practice and its influence on individuals and groups in organizations and how their participation creates organizational change. Leaders who are in business and industrial settings, educational settings at all levels, legal and criminal justice settings, hospital care and health care settings, mental health and psychiatric settings, and leaders in any organizational consultation environment will have a ready source to find the information they need. The bibliography will be a helpful place to seek out what consultation services bring to an organization in the midst of change and challenges from internal and external forces. This is a bibliography of research reports, and it is an efficient volume for a manager or an organizational leader. The volume aids access for those users who require information on consultation for decision-making in organizational and practice-related issues, and it provides resources to researchers who want to uncover new facts regarding consultation practice.

This comprehensive yet succinct, well-organized volume provides administrators with systematic, relevant, and valuable knowledge that will enable them to promote individual, group, and organizational change. It is a valuable volume for professionals in the consultation field and in the field of guiding organizational change, because it provides and sets the stage for direction for further study. Major bibliographic indexes were manually reviewed; therefore, most of the items listed are available through various library services. The major indexing services—ERIC, PsycLit, PAIS, Dissertation Abstracts, Sociofile, and Social Science Index—were also consulted for sources of data. This is a fine work of carefully selected materials in the area of organizational change via consultants. The volume is a must for every advanced student of organizational behavior and especially in the area specialty of consultation for change.—**Gerald D. Moran**

Biography

710. **Biographical Dictionary of Psychology.** Noel Sheehy, Antony J. Chapman, and Wendy A. Conroy, eds. New York, Routledge, 1997. 675p. index. $130.00. ISBN 0-415-09997-8.

Biographical Dictionary of Psychology serves as a current update and expansion of information previously published in Greenwood Press's *Biographical Dictionary of Psychology* (see ARBA 85, entry 666); *A Guide to Psychologists and Their Concepts* (see ARBA 76, entry 1504); and *Women in Psychology: A Bio-bibliographic Sourcebook* (see ARBA 91, entry 918). This resource incorporates biographical information on 500-plus psychologists and individuals who have contributed to the field of psychology. The scope is international and runs from the late 1700s through the late 1900s. The methodology used by the editors in choosing entries included surveying several reference sources in the psychology literature. From that review, additional lists were created and ranked; then experts in the field were consulted and the list was reduced to its current number. It is noted that some individuals chose not to respond, so the editors were not able to produce a substantial entry, and therefore the individual was not included.

Each entry includes name; date and place of birth, and date and place of death if appropriate; nationality; main area of interest according to the American Psychological Association standards; education; principal appointments, honors, and awards; principal publications; and suggested references for further reading. The most confounding part of the entries is the lack of entries on the women who are part of the number of husband-wife teams of psychologists who have similar research interests, complement, and in most cases, enhance their husbands' research. There is not a separate or even supplemental statement about their contributions. In many cases, in the husband's entry, these contributions are not even acknowledged. Aside from this observation, the entries are clearly written using three-quarters to a full page. The only other piece of information missing is current institutional affiliation. [R: RBB, 15 Oct 97, pp. 425-26]—**Mila C. Su**

Dictionaries and Encyclopedias

711. Bäuml, Betty J., and Franz H. Bäuml. **Dictionary of Worldwide Gestures.** 2d ed. Lanham, Md., Scarecrow Press, 1997. 510p. illus. index. $79.50. ISBN 0-8108-3189-9.

Significantly expanding on the 1975 work, this new edition is an exhaustive multicultural directory of gesture and body language that should prove of great interdisciplinary appeal. Arranged alphabetically by individual or grouped gesture ("finger" or "finger, hand"), each entry is subarranged further by meaning ("anger," "approval"). These subcategories describe both the gesture itself and often include a description of its origins and interpretation among different cultures. References to source materials listed in the Bäumls' extensive bibliography are provided for each subcategory. In addition an index of significances—meanings conveyed by gestures among different cultural groups—is provided, enabling users to easily locate different gestures used to display such emotions as astonishment or disbelief. Lastly, an index of countries and peoples is included, enabling the identification of popular gestures used by a specific region or people.

Much more exhaustive than recent works such as Desmond Morris's *Bodytalk: A World Guide to Gestures* (London: Jonathan Cape, 1994), this work will prove useful for students of anthropology, education, psychology, sociology, and many other fields. The thoroughness of this work would have been considerably enhanced by the inclusion of more illustrations or graphics to capture the essence of the descriptions. Entries such as "finger, nose" may be easier to visualize than "hand, knee, lip," but all would be enhanced by the inclusion of a simple line drawing. This is a minor oversight in what is otherwise an extensive guide to the most elemental forms of meaningful human communication throughout the world.
—**Elizabeth Patterson**

Indexes

712. **ClinPSYC: 1980-December 1996.** [CD-ROM]. Baltimore, Md., National Information Services Corporation, 1996. Minimum system requirements: IBM or compatible 386. CD-ROM drive. 3MB RAM. 480K conventional memory. 2.5MB hard disk space. Color or monochrome monitor. call for rates (410-243-0797).

ClinPSYC is a subset of the PsycLIT database produced and owned by the American Psychological Association. As its name implies, *ClinPSYC* covers the psychological literature pertaining to mental disorders, treatment, and mental health. Clinical references and abstracts are of vital interest to psychologists in private practice and academia. The database is leased, at present, to four vendors—Aries Systems, Ovid, SilverPlatter, and the National Information Services Corporation (NISC)—the last the subject of this review. Vendors receive the identical database and add features to make a search easier and more complete. NISC, at present, is the only one of the four not in a full Windows 95 format; users must navigate in DOS using function keys and up and down arrows. By the end of 1997, NISC plans to have Windows 95 and DOS on the same CD-ROM and, if current price differences hold, at $400 per year less than its competition. Libraries can save an additional $300 per year by also subscribing to the paper version of *ClinPSYC*. An annual subscription of NISC's *ClinPSYC* in disc and paper formats is $2,295 for a stand-alone user.

NISC offers three search levels—novice, advanced, and expert. Using the relatively new clinical term *dissociative identity disorder* (previously multiple personality), a novice search yielded 44 abstracts, with 1 by Sander Breiner. Advanced searching showed 13 articles for Breiner, 44 on the topic, and 1 match of author and topic. Expert searching allows the user to string together a wide variety of related searches, such as dissociative identity disorder, schizophrenia, and female (2 entries out of 300,000). The NISC disc automatically searches for plurals (schizophrenias) and misspellings (schizprenia) but not for "schizophrenic."

The 88-page user's manual is generic to all NISC databases. It and training time (15 to 30 minutes) should be shortened considerably in Windows 95. Other NISC search options include automatic indexing where a search goes on as the user types the topic or keywords, truncation where "?"s, as in "schizophrenic?", act as a wildcard to find schizophrenia and schizophrenic, and proximity where the number of words between keywords can be specified. Options can be toggled off if they prove annoying. Libraries considering a new clinical psychology database subscription may want to wait and compare the NISC version of *ClinPSYC* in Windows 95 with its competitors.—**Pete Prunkl**

PARAPSYCHOLOGY

713. **Daily Planetary Guide 1997.** Saint Paul, Minn., Llewellyn, 1996. 195p. illus. maps. $9.95 spiralbound. ISBN 1-56718-926-1.

If a library anticipates, as the millennium approaches, a flood of people wanting to know what the stars hold for them beyond what the horoscope of the local paper can provide, it can make Llewellyn's *Daily Planetary Guide 1997* part of its collection. It is, as the back cover proclaims, "the most consistent, accurate, and complete astrological datebook and desk calendar on the market." Without quibbling over the exact meanings of these adjectives in this context, the book admittedly is jam-packed with pseudoscientific material. A short introduction to "Calendar Astrology" (as opposed to "birth chart horoscopes") is followed by detailed guides to the Zodiacal signs, moon influences, planets and retrogrades, asteroids, aspects and transits, and so on. The guides are helpfully accompanied by descriptions of the amusing little hieroglyphs that dot the pages of the datebook. The introductory section also contains a 27-page collection of weekly forecasts in narrative form by a certain "Don Lewis," whose name may be meaningful to those versed in this subject. The 365 heavily annotated daily entries come next and fill out the main text. All in all, the guide makes for a fascinating artifact of the New Age movement.—**Christopher Michael McDonough**

714. Karcher, Stephen. **The Illustrated Encyclopedia of Divination: A Practical Guide to the Systems That Can Reveal Your Destiny.** Rockport, Mass., Element Books, 1997. 256p. illus. maps. index. $21.95pa. ISBN 1-85230-903-2.

Karcher's book is one of the best examples of the coffee-table book genre. The volume is lovely with many intriguing illustrations, the text is easy to read, and each topic is dealt with concisely. The chapters include "Learning to Listen: Omens, Symbols, and Signs"; "Shamans, Seers, Mediums, and Guides"; "Opening the Book of Fate"; "Revealing the Magic of the Stars"; and "Opening the Gates of the Dreamworld," giving the book a topical organization rather than an alphabetic one. There is not, however, an adequate index, unusual for this type of book. Appropriately for an encyclopedia, Karcher covers virtually all periods and cultures; as he says, "Divining is one of the oldest and most persistent human acts. There is virtually no culture that has not used divination." Thus, the book covers well-known topics, such as astrology, tarot, dreams, the I Ching, and numerology, but also such unusual topics as scapulomancy (a bone-oracle divination), Ifa (Yoruban geomancy), and so on. Inclusion of such topics as fang-shih that have become recently popular in the West indicate the timeliness of the book. Considering the unusual topics, the glossary at the back of the book is useful and nicely done.

The book cannot be called scholarly in that sources of information are not cited. The information seems accurate. The "Further Reading" list serves almost as a bibliography and seems adequate, although not terribly current. In astrology, for example, Karcher lists writers from earlier in this century, such as Dane Rhudyar, Alan Leo, and Margaret Hone, as well as some of the current popular writers, such as Derek and Julia Parker, but not current influential people, such as Liz Greene and Robert Hand. The works for the most part do not appear to be particularly scholarly, which is unsurprising in that the topic is one in which scholars have had little interest. This work is recommended for popular collections in divination, the occult, and the paranormal.—**Mary A. Axford**

715. Kear, Lynn. **Reincarnation: A Selected Annotated Bibliography.** Westport, Conn., Greenwood Press, 1996. 327p. index. (Bibliographies and Indexes in Religious Studies, no.38). $75.00. ISBN 0-313-29597-2.

Kear's excellent new bibliography on reincarnation covers an admirable range of works, from the Buddhist pamphlets of the Venerable Shravasti Dhammika to Shirley MacLaine's famous *Out on a Limb* to the rambling autobiography of perennial *National Enquirer* favorite, Jeanne Dixon. As Kear notes in the introduction, "pro-reincarnation as well as anti-reincarnation books are included." The entries, listed in alphabetic order, give not only the standard items, such as the author's name, the book's title, and the publication information, but generous citations from the authors' works themselves, so readers can form an instant sense of the books' contents and intended uses. These citations provide some rather entertaining reading. In *The World Before* (item 349), for instance, Ruth Montgomery notes that "Gerald Ford was a pacifier in ancient Egypt as well as in Atlantis." Again, in *Heirs to Eternity* (item 514), Clarice Toyne reveals, "I learned that Voltaire was George Bernard Shaw in his next incarnation." Kear's extensive index allows quick access to the various books and subjects within. Indeed, in flipping through the index to unmask more of these unsuspected soul mates (Rudolph Valentino was William the Conqueror, according to item 037! Who knew?), one must wonder whether or not the book could be subtitled, *A Guide to Who Was Who*. Easy to use and wide in scope, *Reincarnation: A Selected Annotated Bibliography* will be a welcome addition to many school and public libraries.—**Christopher Michael McDonough**

716. Ogden, Tom. **Wizards and Sorcerers: From Abracadabra to Zoroaster.** New York, Facts on File, 1997. 246p. illus. index. $40.00. ISBN 0-8160-3151-7.

This one-volume reference provides a historical overview of enchantment, magic, and the occult based on both fact and fiction. The author has been a professional magician who has toured around the world during the past 20 years and who has been interested in the occult all of his life. In the foreword, Ogden states that terms such as *wizard, shaman, witch doctor, warlock,* and *necromancer* are often used interchangeably because people do not make the distinction between practitioners of beneficent magic and their malicious counterparts—a distinction necessary to respectively divide practitioners of so-called white versus black magic. Ogden is also quick to add that these names do not always offer a gender choice (*wizard*, for example). The inclusion of popular supernatural characters with magical powers from films—the Blue Fairy from *Pinocchio*, for example—and of the thumbnail sketches of nearly 200 films makes this reference especially innovative.

The entries range in length from less than a quarter-page to several pages in a generous two-column layout. Topics include magicians and events from world history. Black-and-white illustrations and drawings enhance the work. Most of the dozen or so black-and-white photographs were taken by the author on his travels around the world; in fact, the one criticism of this work is the lack of any color plates or photographs that greatly enhance other encyclopedias of magic. The work includes an index and an extensive bibliography of more than 150 books, as well as 41 articles, 35 sound recordings, and 14 videos. This reference is a real value and is recommended for all libraries.—**Edward Erazo**

717. Snodgrass, Mary Ellen. **Signs of the Zodiac: A Reference Guide to Historical, Mythological, and Cultural Associations.** Westport, Conn., Greenwood Press, 1997. 243p. illus. index. $39.95. ISBN 0-313-30276-6.

This scholarly reference on the 12 signs of the zodiac provides a thorough and authoritative guide on the history, mythology, and culture of people's enduring fascination with the constellations. Snodgrass begins by discussing the superstitions and religious beliefs associated with the zodiac from ancient times and various cultures, in particular the Babylonian, Egyptian, Arabian, Oriental, Grecian, and Roman traditions. The work then proceeds with a chapter on the historical foundation of astrology and the formation of horoscopes before the time of Jesus Christ. Another chapter gives a historical and literary survey by covering centuries 1 through 20. This extensive background information culminates with a final chapter that discusses the zodiac in the arts and sciences, with subheadings as varied as heraldry, cinema, star lore, advertising, and psychology and healing. The work is completed with chapter-length entries on each of the signs and their historical, cultural, and religious contexts.

There are several appendixes: a timeline; a comparative chart of the elements of the constellations; the sun signs linked with geographic areas; and charts of the planets with their corresponding jewels, metals, herbs, colors, shapes, and smells. An extensive bibliography assists researchers in locating additional sources on related topics of the zodiac signs.

This work is packed with information on the signs of the zodiac, with references from ancient to modern times. The author's research, in-depth knowledge, and cultural connections are impressive. Snodgrass is the award-winning author of several other fine reference works. These factors make the work a solid research tool in contrast to the many popular zodiac guides. Librarians, researchers, teachers, and students alike will all welcome this reference.—**Edward Erazo**

15 Recreation and Sports

GENERAL WORKS

Biography

718. Pare, Michael A. **Sports Stars, Series 3.** Detroit, Gale, 1997. 342p. illus. index. $34.00. ISBN 0-7876-1749-0.

This readily accessible reference provides profiles and photographs of 30 amateur and professional athletes. Featured athletes must meet one or more criteria for inclusion: currently active in amateur or professional sports, considered top performers in their field, and role models who have overcome physical or societal obstacles to reach the top of their professions. Both sexes, various cultures, and a wide variety of sports—including auto racing, baseball, basketball, bicycle racing, boxing, figure skating, football, golf, gymnastics, hockey, horse racing, skiing, soccer, speed skating, swimming, tennis, track and field, and yachting—are represented.

Each profile opens with a thumbnail sketch. Following is a section entitled "Growing Up," which is further subdivided into important aspects of the athlete's life, and a section entitled "Superstar," which is subdivided into highlights of the athlete's sports career. Each profile includes at least one black-and-white photograph, and many include additional photographs of the athlete in action. Sidebars provide interesting details or anecdotes, and each profile concludes with a list of sources and an address to write to for further information.

Arranged alphabetically, there are two tables of contents: one in order of appearance of the entries and the other listed by type of sport. A comprehensive index is included. Generous margins, an easy-to-read typeface size, and an eye-catching cover add to the appeal of this resource.—**Dana McDougald**

719. Siegman, Joseph. **Jewish Sports Legends: The International Jewish Sports Hall of Fame.** 2d ed. Herndon, Va., Brassey's (U.S.), 1997. 222p. illus. $29.95. ISBN 1-57488-128-0.

Jewish people have been an integral part of the American and world sports scene for decades. Well-known Jewish athletes like baseball's Sandy Koufax, basketball's Dolph Schayes, and Olympic swimmer Mark Spitz are recognized by sports fan of any era. In a concise, highly illustrated, and rather expensive volume, Siegman (who founded the International Jewish Sports Hall of Fame in Jerusalem) writes brief biographies of these and 250 other less recognized Jewish sports stars. The sketches are arranged alphabetically by sport—baseball, football, and others—and include athletes of several nationalities from the modern era as well as names dating back to the eighteenth century (bowling's John Brunswick, for example). Virtually every entry includes a photograph or illustration.

The book includes few statistical records of athletes—we do not know how many total games Koufax won, for example—and there is little information that cannot be located in some standard source. The price is high, and useful information is at a premium. Libraries with a strong emphasis on sports collections may want to add this title to their collection, but most will find it easy to pass on as a purchase.—**Boyd Childress**

Dictionaries and Encyclopedias

720. **Encyclopedia of Sports Science.** John Zumerchik, ed. New York, Macmillan Library Reference/Simon & Schuster Macmillan, 1997. 2v. illus. index. $200.00/set. ISBN 0-02-897506-5.

This book combines sports and science in a way that the reader or librarian can expect to find satisfactory answers to questions on sports and the human body. Part 1 considers the physics of sports, including questions of "hang time"; ball dynamics; and the basic concepts of force, energy, gravity, and so on. The 29 entries discuss each specific sport or game, such as baseball and boxing, or actions that are common to many games. Part 2 focuses on the human body in relation to sports. Recent information (1996) on performance, injuries, rehabilitation, physiology, biomechanics, and all other concepts that concern athletes is discussed.

The educated reader who has the mildest interest in sports should find this authoritative, well-written book fascinating. Zumerchik has assembled a staff of about 30 knowledgeable contributors. Some are, as expected, from the world of academe—physics, engineering, and psychology—and others are in medical and therapy disciplines. The science, which is written in terms that an educated layperson can understand, can be trusted. Zumerchik has included diagrams and illustrations on nearly every page to aid in reader understanding. Anecdotal notes deftly bring in the names of such famous sports figures as Michael Jordan, Jack Nicklaus, and John Kruk.

An item of particular interest is the use of *see also* references that lead the reader to basic discussions of certain physical phenomena. A list of references following each chapter includes books and articles. This book will appeal to coaches, athletes, students, and the general public. Good use is made of diagrams and drawings to illustrate points made in the text.—**Randall Rafferty**

721. **Encyclopedia of World Sport: From Ancient Times to the Present.** David Levinson and Karen Christensen, eds. Santa Barbara, Calif., ABC-CLIO, 1996. 3v. illus. index. $225.00/set. ISBN 0-87436-819-7.

This three-volume compilation of articles about sports and topics related to them would enrich any collection, but it is essential to none. One of the editors is an anthropologist, and the other is a professional reference book editor. A coherent, literate introduction explains the concept, origins, and process of the book, especially its broad-spectrum approach and reliance on scholarly works about sport. Also useful are a list in each volume of the contents of all volumes and an excellent index. The black-and-white photographs do not add much to the text.

The entries range in length from a little more than one page to several pages and include specific sports (e.g., curling, fencing, and so forth), as well as such general topics as art, ethics, and movies. The editors would have been wiser to leave the latter out because so much subjectivity clearly informed their selection. Also, there is some duplication. Karate, for instance, is covered briefly under "Martial Arts" and more fully on its own. The entries for the sports themselves are generally well written and authoritative, although not always up-to-date. In "Shooting, Pistol," for example, there is no mention of either metallic silhouette or practical pistol competition, both of which are popular in the United States. The editors are to be commended for including valuable material on African, Native American, and Asian topics and such lesser-known sports as arm wrestling, iaido, and trapball.

Smaller libraries and those whose patrons are not particularly interested in sports may be served well enough by the entries for specific sports in general encyclopedias. Larger, more comprehensive collections, especially those that emphasize sports or physical education, may want this publication.—**John Newman**

Handbooks and Yearbooks

722. Gaschnitz, K. Michael. **Professional Sports Statistics: A North American Team-by-Team, and Major Non-Team Events....** Jefferson, N.C., McFarland, 1997. 1338p. $85.00. ISBN 0-7864-0299-7.

At first glance, this book lacks the appeal of certain essential reference volumes. It includes no illustrations, flashy use of color, or slick packaging. This is, however, another comprehensive McFarland reference work, combining over 100 years (1876-1996) of results for 5 major professional sports—baseball, basketball, football, hockey, and soccer. The arrangement is year-by-year, with final team records and standings, playoff results, and individual statistical leaders and award winners listed. All-Star game results, coaching (or managers in the case of baseball) changes, franchise changes, and halls of fame inductees for the individual year are also featured. A brief note on winners of other major sporting events concludes each yearly entry. Where appropriate, recognized professional league records are included, such as the old American Basketball Association, World Hockey Association, American Football League, and Canadian Football League. The result is an extremely useful one-volume reference work, which, although fairly expensive, incorporates information often found in three or four separate sports books. One minor criticism is the lack of a running page headers to indicate the year. Most academic and public libraries, however, will find this a useful reference source.—**Boyd Childress**

723. Killpatrick, Frances, and James Killpatrick. **The Winning Edge: The Student-Athlete's Guide to College Sports.** 5th ed. Alexandria, Va., Octameron; distr., Chicago, Dearborn Trade, 1997. 138p. $9.00pa. ISBN 1-57509-028-7.

The 5th edition of *The Winning Edge* adds an appendix that includes samples of sports résumés and letters as well as a college checklist. This guide really serves students' needs. The 10 chapters in the 1st section continue to provide worthwhile information, insights, and tips to college-bound athletes for working with their parents, counselors, coaches, and recruiters and for understanding their responsibilities on the road to college athletics. The 2d section covers the championship results, sport by sport, of all 3 National Collegiate Athletic Association (NCAA) divisions and the National Association of Intercollegiate Athletes (NAIA) for the top college sports and a few others. At the end of each sport listed, guidance and comments from a top coach in the field are included. Unfortunately, women's ice hockey, played at all division levels at a growing number of universities, is not included. The 3d section provides the graduation rates of NCAA Division 1 and the contact telephone number and address for Division II, III, and the NAIA institutions.

For athletic scholarship books that focus on scholarship grant information, users should refer to *Free Money for Athletic Scholarships* (see ARBA 94, entry 326); *Athletic Scholarships: Thousands of Grants* (see ARBA 95, entry 795); *Peterson's Sports Scholarships and College Athletic Programs* (see ARBA 95, entry 797); and *The Directory of Athletic Scholarship* (see ARBA 88, entry 356). One of the more detailed and useful titles is *Athletic Scholarships: A Complete Guide* (see ARBA 96, entry 799). *The Winning Edge* is a user-friendly resource that best meets the needs of high school and public libraries. High school student athletes may also consider a personal copy a worthwhile purchase.—**Mila C. Su**

724. Mirkovich, Thomas R., and Allison A. Cowgill. **Casino Gaming in the United States: A Research Guide.** Lanham, Md., Scarecrow, 1997. 401p. index. $48.00. ISBN 0-8108-3230-5.

Mirkovich and Cowgill have bundled together an excellent bibliography and reference guide on casino gaming. The audience for this book is scholars, government officials, industry insiders, students, and all others interested in researching the public policy, social, economic, and legal aspects of the U.S. casino gaming business. More than one-half of the book is dedicated to bibliographic citations drawn from monographic and periodical literature, newspaper articles, government publications, and other sources. These citations are subdivided into seven sections, including Native American gaming, riverboats, economic development, and crime. Each citation is complete and includes a well-written, descriptive annotation of variable length. The book's value in terms of timeliness would have been enhanced by including citations beyond the stated 1994 cutoff date. Criteria for inclusion, such as scholarship and importance, accuracy, and uniqueness, are cogent and adhered to throughout.

A directory section lists relevant federal and state agencies, Native American gaming sites, and a selective list of associations and experts in gaming or industry analysts. A detailed subject index and an author index are provided. A minor production error has the header "Subject Index" over all of the author index with the exception of the first page. Mirkovich and Cowgill, both having written on the gaming industry before, are highly qualified to compile this reference work and have provided a terrific service in bringing together much of the quality literature on casino gaming to the serious student, researcher, or investigator. Recreational and serious gambling enthusiasts would be well advised to turn to such books as *American Casino Guide* (see entry 411) to enhance their gaming pleasure.—**Stephen W. Green**

725. **National Sports Policies: An International Handbook.** Laurence Chalip, Arthur Johnson, and Lisa Stachura, eds. Westport, Conn., Greenwood Press, 1996. 442p. index. $99.50. ISBN 0-313-28481-4.

Televised international sporting events prompt many questions about the organization and support of amateur and professional athletes and athletic programs in many countries. *National Sports Policies: An International Handbook* attempts to address those questions for the developed countries of Australia, Brazil, Canada, France, Germany, Hungary, India, Israel, Italy, Japan, Norway, Spain, the United Kingdom, and the United States. The remaining communist nations of China and Cuba receive attention in individual chapters. There is a chapter discussing the use of sport as a tool for rebuilding the national identity in former Soviet bloc European countries. Most chapters include general information about the country's government structure and the relationship between sports and politics. Chapters also address sport participation and financial support for both professional and amateur sports. Charts and graphs are used appropriately to elaborate or illustrate arguments made by the authors. Generous reference lists enhance the chapters and a thorough index completes the volume. One weakness of the volume is the lack of attention to developing and non-Western nation's sports policies. However, this work is an excellent resource for understanding the structure of sports in the countries that currently hold leadership in international sport competition.—**Lynne M. Fox**

726. Wellner, Alison S. **Americans at Play: Demographics of Outdoor Recreation & Travel.** Ithaca, N.Y., New Strategist, 1997. 367p. index. $89.95. ISBN 1-885071-1-X.

This title provides demographic information about Americans' participation in about 60 outdoor recreational activities ranging from walking to football to kayaking. The participation statistics are taken from the USDA Forest Service's 1994-1995 edition of *National Survey on Recreation and the Environment*. These national statistics are broken down by age, income, sex, race, education, and household type and size. No historical data is provided because the survey questions and methodology have changed over time. There is a brief introduction to each activity that discusses current trends and the future of the sport or activity.

One chapter provides data on spending for recreational activities; this data is drawn from the *1995 Consumer Expenditure Survey* done by the Bureau of Labor Statistics. For each category the data are presented as average annual expenditure as well as in index and market share figures. The chapter on recreational travel also draws spending figures from this same survey. All these statistics were presented in the 2d edition of Margaret Ambry's *The Official Guide to Household Spending* (see ARBA 94, entry 927).

Two chapters on recreational participation by high school and college students are included as well as contact information for various organizations (mostly World Wide Web addresses), a brief glossary, and a general index.

The information in presented clearly and all sources are noted. Although it would be of greater use if the information were more detailed, this title should prove useful in most collections.—**Debra L. Moore**

Indexes

727. Meserole, Mike. **The Ultimate Book of Sports Lists 1998.** New York, DK Publishing, 1997. 224p. illus. index. $17.95pa. ISBN 0-7894-2134-8.

Meserole, creator and editor of the *Information Please Sports Almanac* (see ARBA 94, entry 818, and ARBA 91, entry 800), has compiled more than 1,000 lists in the sports of baseball, football, basketball, hockey, golf, tennis, track and field, swimming, soccer, Olympics, horse racing, auto racing, and a miscellaneous category that includes movies. The majority of the lists are documented, so the reader understands the time span or context of the list. For example, in the section on college basketball, under the category of streaks, there is a list of longest winning streaks for the full season with an explanation that this includes post-season and tournaments. The lists mainly highlight single game and single tournament results.

The material is arranged in an easy-to-use format with a good index; however, this resource is far from being the ultimate authority in either sport or list coverage. The author does not address why he chose the information he did other than as entertainment value. This title may be of more interest for personal collections than a library's collection. *Guinness Sports Record Book* (see ARBA 94 entry 825, and ARBA 91, entry 811) covers many more sports even though the focus is on world records. Aside from trivia and statistical use, this volume does not satisfy the reader's curiosity. Andrew Postman's *The Ultimate Book of Sports Lists* (see entry 727) has more entertaining lists than this volume.—**Mila C. Su**

BASEBALL

728. Dittmar, Joseph J. **Baseball Records Registry: The Best and Worst Single-Day Performances....** Jefferson, N.C., McFarland, 1997. 674p. illus. index. $55.00. ISBN 0-7864-0293-8.

Dittmar has assembled a volume that will delight all dedicated baseball fans. The focus is on benchmark games dating from 1901 through 1996. Entertaining, well-written narratives as well as complete box scores for each game are provided, along with accompanying photographs and illustrations. The articles, chronologically arranged and ranging from 2 to 3 pages in length, describe 226 games that produced record-setting events of a single game or doubleheader. The reader will find Roger Clemens's 20 strikeout performance and Willie Mays's 4-home-run game, but not Cal Ripken's, Roger Maris's, or Hank Aaron's lifetime or season record-breaking games. An exception is the Mets' 120th loss of the 1962 season. Despite the absence of these major record-setting events, the volume offers other unique information by describing such unlikely and long-forgotten achievements as that of Cesar "Cocoa" Gutierrez, who in 1970 became the first modern major leaguer to get seven consecutive hits in one game. Appendixes include a master list of all the games included, a breakdown of records by category for each game included, and a listing of record book errors discovered while researching the volume. A short bibliography and index of player and team names conclude the work. The volume is recommended to all libraries with an interest in sports. [R: RBB, 15 Oct 97, p. 425]—**Lee Weston**

729. **The Encyclopedia of Minor League Baseball: The Official Record of Minor League Baseball.** 2d ed. Lloyd Johnson, Miles Wolff, and Steve McDonald, eds. Durham, N.C., Baseball America, 1997. 666p. $48.95; $39.95pa. ISBN 0-9637189-8-3; 0-9637189-7-5pa.

It would be difficult to praise this book too highly: It is packed with information, yet is an exquisite pleasure to peruse. The encyclopedia is perfectly conceived and executed down to the last detail. The largest part is given over to a year-by-year chronicle that lists each league, the teams and their final standings, names of managers and attendance totals for each team, postseason results, and league leaders in various batting and pitching categories. Other features for each year include a list of no-hitters and a chronology of intriguing facts called "This Date in Minor League History." For example, on June 1, 1937, Winston-Salem in the Piedmont League won its 2d game of the season, having gone 1-31 to that point. This large expanse, covering the years 1883 to 1996, is subdivided into 11 sections, with a 1-page overview of minor league ball during each era.

Even this much information would have been a remarkable achievement, but there is a great deal more: an alphabetic list of each league, with a record of each city that was ever in it and the years of participation; a list by city, showing leagues they have been in over the years; a state-by-state organization of the cities and their leagues; league records held by individual players; and all-time minor league individual records. This book must have required an enormous amount of painstaking research, because primary records of the minor leagues are often inconsistent, incorrect, or missing. The result is not merely a stellar sports reference source but an entertaining glimpse of an important aspect of American local history.—**Jack Ray**

730. Faber, Charles F. **Baseball Pioneers: Ratings of Nineteenth Century Players.** Jefferson, N.C., McFarland, 1997. 148p. index. $24.95pa. ISBN 0-7864-0295-4.

The rating system that Faber devised and applied to modern major league baseball players in *Baseball Ratings* (2d ed.; see ARBA 96, entry 804) is here extended to major league players of the nineteenth century. Once again Faber uses criteria that he believes are of the greatest importance in evaluating hitting, fielding, and pitching performances (unlike the earlier book, there is no rating of relief pitchers, because their role before 1900 was marginal) and assigns point totals to players for each year as well as for their careers. Separate ratings for each of the two major leagues (the National League and the American Association) are presented for each year, although many of the lists (e.g., "Ten Best Hitting Pioneer First Basemen") do not distinguish players by their league.

This volume is a notable and intriguing compilation, but it will probably have less general appeal than its twentieth-century counterpart. Other than the top players, such as Willie Keeler and Cy Young, most of these names will be unfamiliar to modern fans. However, in libraries where baseball research interests are strong, this book is a worthwhile addition.—**Jack Ray**

731. **Fodor's Ballpark Vacations: Great Family Trips to Minor League and Classic Major League Baseball Parks Across America.** By Bruce Adams and Margaret Engel. New York, Fodor's Travel Publications/Random House, 1997. 291p. maps. $16.50pa. ISBN 0-679-03152-9.

Fodor's Ballpark Vacations is not the typical baseball travel book. Adams and Engel had their 5- and 8-year-olds along as equal participants, hence the subtitle. Each chapter includes general team information (including a Website), location of the park and how to get there, ticket information and price range, game time, tips on seating (including disability-accessible seating), stadium food, smoking policy, parking, the visiting team hotel, tourism information, and a map of the area. Chapters describe at least three locations, often many miles apart, so the map is regional rather than local. The emphasis is, of course, on keeping young children entertained without breaking the budget. Motels and restaurants described are usually inexpensive but convenient and clean. Fast food is ignored for the kid-appealing but nutritious. Other attractions are meant for short attention spans and to burn off energy before and between games.

Engel and Adams are baseball purists—grass is better than turf; minors are preferable to majors (less than half-a-dozen major league parks are included); fun wins over all—see the chapter on the St. Paul Saints, an independent team owned by Mike Veeck, son of legendary owner Bill Veeck. Also important is the chance for kids to visit with players and other personnel. In Elmira, New York, they met retired judge Dan Donahoe, who has seen everyone from Babe Ruth to a then-batboy named Cal Ripkin Jr. Different, with all the charm of the small parks Engel and Adams so clearly love, this book is highly recommended.
—**R. S. Lehmann**

732. Freese, Mel R. **Charmed Circle: Twenty-Game-Winning Pitchers in Baseball's 20th Century.** Jefferson, N.C., McFarland, 1997. 347p. index. $35.00pa. ISBN 0-7864-0297-0.

How many people know that, of all the pitchers who have pitched in the major leagues since 1901, about 1 in 15 have won 20 games in a season? That information is the most important fact imparted in this book that is not readily found in *The Baseball Encyclopedia* (see ARBA 94, entry 830, for a review of the 9th edition and ARBA 96, entry 803, for a review of the 1995 update). This book does include summations of the careers of all pitchers who ever won 20 games in a season and reflections on many who never won 20. Many interesting conclusions are drawn by the author. However, not all of these conclusions are completely buttressed with statistical analysis. *Charmed Circle* also supplies an appendix listing pitchers by how many times they won 20 or more games in a season.

Charmed Circle is an interesting book, but it does not really belong in a general library reference collection. Libraries with major baseball collections will want to include the volume, and some serious fans will buy it.—**David A. Doman**

733. Light, Jonathan Fraser. **The Cultural Encyclopedia of Baseball.** Jefferson, N.C., McFarland, 1997. 888p. illus. index. $75.00. ISBN 0-7864-0311-X.

This volume, written and compiled as a labor of love by a California employment attorney, fills a huge gap in the reference literature concerning the sport of baseball. The author seeks to shed light on the history and folklore of the game, rather than to add to the ubiquitous and voluminous statistical treatments already available. Some rare errors and omissions notwithstanding (Mile High Stadium was never called Coors Field; Yaz's entry omits his Hall of Fame induction year), he succeeds brilliantly. Undoubtedly, this is one of the most comprehensive, enjoyable, and useful narrative reference works on the game ever published.

Alphabetically arranged from "Hank Aaron" to "Youth Baseball," the encyclopedia is filled with interesting facts, anecdotes, records, quotations, photos, and references to further reading. Besides biographical sketches of all Hall of Fame players, managers, umpires, and executives, countless other subjects are covered in well-written entries. Entries include such topics as commissioners, league presidents, teams, selected parks, rules, broadcasters and broadcasting, salary trends, length of games, types of pitches, gambling, Negro leagues, integration, trades and sales, and baseball in foreign countries, among others. The coverage is truly exhaustive and the writing is highly informative. Indexing and cross-references are excellent as well. If one is planning on purchasing only one nonstatistical reference book about baseball this year, it should be this one.—**Lee Weston**

734. Madden, W. C. **The Women of the All-American Girls Professional Baseball League: A Biographical Dictionary.** Jefferson, N.C., McFarland, 1997. 288p. illus. index. $35.00. ISBN 0-7864-0304-7.

This volume is another of McFarland's interesting baseball reference books. Prepared with the cooperation of the All-American Girls Professional Baseball League Players Association, the dictionary contains entries for more than 600 players who signed contracts with the League (some of whom never played). Content of entries varies depending on the information available. The most complete entries include names (both family and married), date and place of birth, height, weight, field position, team(s), year(s) played, and date of death, where applicable. Brief biographies include information on the players lives before, during, and after their baseball careers. Some of the information was obtained through interviews with the players. Career batting and fielding statistics are summarized. Statistics for some players are incomplete or absent because the League kept statistics only for players who played in 10 or more games in a season. The volume is illustrated with black-and-white photographs and drawings. There is an excellent brief history of the League and an index that lists players by both family and married names (helpful for those looking for Helen Callaghan, the mother of recent major-leaguer Casey Candaele).

This dictionary is an excellent resource and an enjoyable book to read. It is one of those rare books that can be recommended for both circulating and reference collections in public and academic libraries as well as women's studies and sports collections.—**Gari-Anne Patzwald**

735. **Official Baseball Rules, 1997.** St. Louis, Mo., Sporting News Publishing, 1997. 103p. index. $5.95pa. ISBN 0-89204-572-8.

"Baseball is a game between two teams of nine players each. . . ." So begins Rule 1.01 in the 1st of this rulebook's 10 divisions, "Objectives of the Game." Among the other divisions are those concerning the batter, the runner, the pitcher, and the umpire. At the appropriate places, there are detailed diagrams of the field of play, the home plate area, the pitcher's mound, a fielder's glove, and the strike zone (this last diagram, as most fans know, has been redrawn in practice by home plate umpires). Inserted into the rules are italicized notes, examples, and comments of the Official Playing Rules Committee, which interprets or elaborates on the rules. These designations of the committee are accorded the same level of authority as the rules themselves.

The book contains an index of a page and a half in length, but it may not be a simple matter to easily find the rule that applies to a particular matter, because there is no detailed table of contents to scan. Also, some confusion may result from the fact that many of the rules of scoring pertain to batters, runners, pitchers, and so on. Whatever its difficulties, however, this book is an important primary source for professional baseball and belongs in any reference collection covering that sport.—**Jack Ray**

736. **Official Major League Baseball Fact Book, 1997.** Ron Smith, ed. St. Louis, Mo., Sporting News Publishing, 1997. 479p. illus. $19.95pa. ISBN 0-89204-570-1.

This 1st volume in a planned series is a statistical record of the 1996 baseball season, a preview of the 1997 season, and a miniature baseball encyclopedia. It includes team highlights, team and individual statistics, award winners for the 1996 season, and all 1996 player transactions (e.g., trades). Among the more interesting facts are team records in day versus night games, in doubleheaders, and on grass versus artificial turf, as well as a day-by-day account of each team's season. The preview of the 1997 season includes schedules of games, front office and ticket information, and spring rosters.

A "who's who" section includes statistics for Hall of Famers, award winners, current managers and general managers, and selected players. A history section provides standings and highlights of 1876 to 1995 major league seasons as well as statistics and chronologies for current franchises. A section on records features individual lifetime, single season, single game, and post-season records. Information is logically arranged; however, the book would benefit from a more detailed initial table of contents that would make it friendlier to the nonbaseball aficionado. Designed for the individual fan rather than for a reference library, this book will not replace *The Baseball Encyclopedia Update* (see ARBA 96, entry 803) or a subscription to a good source of current baseball news. However, it is an inexpensive and useful annual resource that answers many common and uncommon baseball questions. With the many changes in player-team affiliations, the spring rosters are particularly helpful and they will become more important in the future as the number of major league teams increases. This work is recommended for public and academic library reference collections.—**Gari-Anne Patzwald**

737. **Total Baseball: The Official Encyclopedia of Major League Baseball.** 5th ed. John Thorn, Pete Palmer, Michael Gershman, and David Pietrusza, eds. New York, Viking/Penguin Books, 1997. 2458p. $64.95. ISBN 0-670-87511-2.

Major League Baseball in 1995 endorsed *Total Baseball* as the game's official encyclopedia. The 5th edition continues the dual coverage of its predecessors—statistical summaries in obsessive detail, combined with cogent essays on the sport's peripheral topics. Updated to include information through the close of the 1996 season, this edition has grown 164 pages from the 1st edition in 1989 (see ARBA 92, entry 786).

The volume's biggest sections are the position player and pitcher registers, comprising nearly half of the book. Brief biographical data and career statistics are given for all players past and present. A roster lists managers, coaches, umpires, team owners, and team officials; playoff games are recounted; and statistical leaders identified. The features one looks for in a statistical almanac are all here, clearly arranged and reflecting the accuracy of *Total Baseball*'s dedicated editors.

The thematic essays are what set this title apart from other sports handbooks. Various guest authors contribute discourses on baseball in other countries, collectibles, fantasy baseball, movies about the game, baseball and the law, Jewish players, and other topics. The articles give this book an encyclopedic depth beyond the inert breadth of statistical compilations. There is much to appreciate here. The coverage is laudably inclusive, the price is reasonable, and the binding is obligingly sturdy. *Total Baseball* is recommended to any library needing a current encyclopedia of the game.—**Ed Volz**

738. Wright, Marshall D. **The American Association: Year-by-Year Statistics for the Baseball Minor League, 1902-1952.** Jefferson, N.C., McFarland, 1997. 408p. index. $45.00pa. ISBN 0-7864-0316-0.

Formed in 8 midwestern cities (Columbus, Indianapolis, Kansas City, Louisville, Milwaukee, Minneapolis, St. Paul, and Toledo) that had been deserted by the Western League (which moved to larger cities and became the American League in 1901), the American Association enjoyed unparalleled stability during the 51 seasons covered by this book: Not a single franchise moved. Wright employs the same format he used successfully in *Nineteenth Century Baseball* (see ARBA 97, entry 651): a one-page overview of each season, followed by team-by-team batting and pitching statistics gleaned from baseball guides of the day. An endearing feature of the latter is the presentation of a "typical" lineup composed of the players who appeared in the most games at each position in a given year. Before the mid-1920s, first names of players are rarely given. The season overviews often highlight a player for a particular achievement (e.g., Paul Carter for his all-time low 1.65 earned run average in 1916). In reviewing the records of players who were stars for a number of years, Wright reminds readers that before the 1930s, the minors were not merely a network of "farm teams" but independent (although lesser) leagues in which players sometimes had long and satisfying careers. Overall, this is an excellent trove of baseball history that will be especially appreciated in American Association cities.—**Jack Ray**

BASKETBALL

739. *Inside Sports Magazine* **College Basketball.** 2d ed. By Mike Douchant, with Jim Nantz. Detroit, Visible Ink Press/Gale, 1997. 747p. illus. index. $19.95pa. ISBN 0-7876-1033-X.

If one likes college basketball by the numbers, in excess of 700 pages, this is a commendable reference source. The book is full of statistics on teams, players, and coaches and includes a season-by-season summary of National Collegiate Athletic Association (NCAA) Division I basketball in the initial seven chapters. The focus is on the national championship tournament, but leading teams, team and individual statistical leaders, all-American players, and coaches of the year are included. The NCAA tournament brackets with sites and scores are chapter highlights from championship games beginning in 1939.

Included, but with considerably less coverage, are National Invitational Tournament, junior college, NCAA Divisions II and III, and National Association of Intercollegiate Athletes results and highlights, as well as brief coverage of women's basketball and U.S. participation in the Olympics. A player register, a coaches directory, and a detailed conference directory are useful features, and there is an interesting section on well-known men who played college basketball but made their marks in other walks of life—football and baseball, politics, acting, and business.

If not for the index, this would be close to the perfect reference book. In a word, the index is inexcusable. For example, there are 51 page references to Auburn University, and only 10 are accurate. Yet there are several other mentions of Auburn not in the index. This inaccuracy is a trend, not an exception. There are other minor errors—Alabama's Antonio McDyess averaged 11.4 points per game (not 1.4) in 1994 and Jim McDaniels of Western Kentucky was from Scottsville (not Scottsdale), Kentucky. In all, the troubling index and lesser mistakes detract from an otherwise entertaining and useful basketball volume.—**Boyd Childress**

740. **NCAA Basketball: The Official 1997 Women's College Basketball Records Book.** Overland Park, Kans., National Collegiate Athletic Association and Chicago, Triumph Books, 1996. 318p. illus. $14.95pa. ISBN 1-57243-138-5. ISSN 1089-5299.

The popularity of women's basketball continues to grow. Witness, for example, the public's response to the new WNBA—women's professional basketball. Cincinnati's Riverfront Coliseum was sold out for the 1997 National Collegiate Athletic Association championship game, with nearly 17,000 fans in attendance. Record books have long been a part of men's basketball, and the women's game is now getting equal time. In an indispensable reference volume, women's basketball is summarized by the numbers—Divisions I, II, and III. Individual, team, and conference records are included, as are a handful of pre-NCAA records, as well as a chronology of rule changes for the women's game. Approximately one-half of the book lists teams' 1995-1996 results and 1996-1997 schedules. In conclusion, the NCAA and Triumph Books have produced a useful reference volume that compares favorably with previous men's basketball volumes (see ARBA 97, entry 652, for example) and is a must for comprehensive reference collections.—**Boyd Childress**

741. *The Sporting News* **Official NBA Guide.** 1997-98 ed. Mark Broussard and Craig Carter, eds. St. Louis, Mo., Sporting News Publishing, 1997. 688p. illus. index. $15.95pa. ISBN 0-89204-585-X.

How popular is the NBA? Simply put, as popular as any sport at any time. In November 1997, the NBA signed a four-year television contract with NBC and Turner Sports for $2.64 billion. No professional sport enjoys such a lucrative package at this time. As professional basketball—with superstars like Michael Jordan, Shaquille O'Neal, Charles Barkley, and Karl Malone—grows, so does the demand for information like that found in the *Sporting News* guide. Previous reviews of this guide (ARBA 95, entry 809 and ARBA 89, entry 728) outline the season-by-season team and individual records, and the 1997-1998 edition provides even more coverage. In addition to the in-depth records of each NBA season is a review of the 1997 playoff finals; All-Star game; league draft; and an extensive directory of each team's office personnel, coaching staff, roster, schedule, and media outlets. Also included in the volume are 30 pages of official rules, a network television schedule, and numerous illustrations. This book is a must for public and academic library reference collections.—**Boyd Childress**

742. *The Sporting News* **Official NBA Register 1997-98.** Mark Bonavita, Mark Broussard, and Sean Stewart, eds. St. Louis, Mo., Sporting News Publishing, 1997. 455p. illus. $15.95pa. ISBN 0-89204-587-6.

Basketball used to be a game that was played or watched rather than discussed. Now, with the immense popularity of such National Basketball Association (NBA) stars as Michael Jordan, professional basketball players warrant the same kind of detailed statistical presentation that baseball players have long enjoyed. Thus, *The Sporting News Official NBA Register* appears. The *Official* (that is, published with the approval and collaboration of the NBA itself) *NBA Register* presents the statistical record of all players now active in the league, plus many players of the past ("all-time greats") and the future ("promising newcomers"). Coverage also extends to all current head coaches and notable coaches of the past.

The information offered is almost entirely statistical (no descriptive or "color" material here), but there are some useful additional features. Each player's or coach's entry includes a list of distinguished achievements and honors (e.g., membership on a championship team); pronunciation of the name, where unusual; "transactions" (i.e., trades); and records in college, the European leagues, and the NBA All-Star games. Most important, a clear, albeit small, photograph is given for each person.

It is important to realize that the register covers only individuals, not teams, so the basketball buff will have to look elsewhere for many kinds of information. Still, for statistical accuracy (vouched for by the NBA itself) and comprehensiveness within its designated scope, the *NBA Register* is unrivaled. Add in the welcome low price and the sturdy, attractive format, and the title rates an unqualified recommendation.—**Samuel Rothstein**

BOXING

743. Roberts, James B., and Alexander G. Skutt. **The Boxing Register: International Boxing Hall of Fame Official Record Book.** Ithaca, N.Y., McBooks Press; distr., Chicago, Login Publishers Consortium, 1997. 447p. illus. $19.95pa. ISBN 1-312-432-7600.

A pair of boxing enthusiasts joined together to write this informative book, a definitive record book as well as interesting, good reading. No current record book exists, an annual having stopped in 1987. The annual contained fight records but little personal information about the boxers. *The Boxing Register*, although limited to Hall of Fame members, covers both the records and life stories of boxers and "noncombatants." Although the authors do not intend to update it yearly, they may do a supplement with the 1997 inductees and update the text every other year.

One hundred and eighty boxers are covered with concise biographical information, including their "supporting casts," presented in four sections: pioneers, old-timers, fighters of the modern era, and noncombatants. Boxing's governing bodies, as well as fixes and fallen heroes (the seamy side of boxing) can be found in this title. Skutt did a nationwide search for rare boxing photographs and spent many hours in *The Ring* magazine archives. The illustrations add a pictorial record to this reference book.

An international, equal-opportunity sport, boxing is both an art and a science, and it is very much about personal achievement. Canastota, New York, where the Boxing Hall of Fame is located, welcomes boxing fans and newcomers to the sport. Boxers can study and enjoy this book long after their visit to the Hall of Fame. Well researched and easy to read, *The Boxing Register* is a must for public libraries.—**Kathleen J. Voigt**

CARD GAMES

744. Truscott, Alan. **The Bidding Dictionary.** Oakland, Calif., Lawrence and Leong Publishing, 1996. 272p. $29.95. ISBN 1-877908-06-1.

Bridge is a 4-person, 52-card game, ostensibly with 1 mentally attuned harmonious pair pitted against the other similarly equipped couple. Each player is dealt 13 cards and in a sequence of bidding or passing loosely communicates the strength and suit distribution of this hand to the others. Partnerships use this limited information to arrive at a final contract. Uncontested Standard American auctions beginning "1 club" through "3 no trump" and subsequent sequences that derive from partners' responses are addressed in the first half of this book. Competitive auctions where opponents open the bidding are addressed in the remainder, with 4,788 bidding sequences shown and many footnoted. Reviewing partnership bidding disasters to determine where deviations occurred compared to the dictionary sequence, self-study, recapping and refining, and improving understandings of opponents' bidding are all major uses of this work.

Bridge is inherently imprecise in practice, and a precision approach may delude acolytes pursuing perfection beyond 75 percent or so in their game. Serious players using the Standard American bidding system will benefit most, while others (i.e., Big Club, Weak No-Trump, and the like) will require footnotes to the footnotes to interpret these recipes. Telegraphic style is achieved in the work with abbreviations and notational cross-referencing. Bridge expert Truscott has provided a ready-reference whose regular use by a partnership following play will catalyze bidding improvement by exposing correctable weaknesses and errors.—**Marvin K. Harris**

FOOTBALL

745. Chestochowski, Ben. **Gridiron Greats: A Century of Polish Americans in College Football.** New York, Hippocrene Books, 1997. 300p. illus. index. $24.95. ISBN 0-7818-0449-3.

Both college football and books on the sport are consistently popular among people of the United States. As one of these books, *Gridiron Greats* presents a unique and unusual look at some 250 players and coaches of Polish descent who have played (or coached) college football since 1893. Chestochowski profiles these Polish Americans in sketches averaging one-half to two-thirds of a page in length. The biographical sketches feature college and professional statistics, records, and awards. The arrangement includes All Stars, an all-academic team, an all-Polish future team, and distinguished coaches. To qualify, an individual must have either a father or mother who is Polish. Included are such All-American players as Johnny Lujack and Leon Hart of Notre Dame, Jack Ham and Ted Kwalick of Penn State, Vic Janowicz of Ohio State, and Dan Marino of Pittsburgh. Lujack, Hart, and Janowicz were Heisman Trophy winners. Coaches include Hank Stram; Forest Evashevski; and Joe Restic, recently retired Harvard coach. An index and a brief bibliography conclude the book. The unusual ethnic nature of the book makes it a one-of-a-kind reference volume but also severely limits the potential audience. This is a selection for libraries with exhaustive sports collections only.—**Boyd Childress**

746. Neft, David S, Richard M. Cohen, and Rick Korch. **The Sports Encyclopedia: Pro Football. The Modern Era 1972-1996.** 15th ed. New York, St. Martin's Press, 1997. 623p. $19.99pa. ISBN 1-312-15662-6.

The 15th edition of *The Sports Encyclopedia: Pro Football* is packed with statistical data spanning 14 years. The reader can determine what teams were leaders in any given year from 1972 to 1996. Scores from every game, complete team statistics, and season summaries can be found in this volume. Players' individual statistics are listed by season and career. Breaks in their career are listed and explained. Play-off scores and statistics are displayed for teams that advanced, including box scores. This is the first book where notable defensive statistics are listed as well as all-time leaders for offense and defense. Year-by-year news that is important to team history is given for all National Football League teams, such as moves to new cities and instrumental players added to their rosters.

Overall, the book is comprehensive and complete; however, not all pages are numbered, making navigation difficult. The research for this book is well done. While browsing the compendium, this reviewer was not able to locate any errors in the data or misspellings seen in other statistical registers for professional sports. This volume only spans a period of 14 years, but it does give reference to the other encyclopedias that contain information for other eras. [R: RBB, 1 Sept 97, p. 160]—**Christopher Byrne**

747. **Total Football: The Official Encyclopedia of the National Football League.** By Bob Carroll and others. New York, HarperCollins, 1997. 1652p. $55.00. ISBN 0-06-270170-3.

In this 1st-edition guide to the game of professional football, the reader will find the information necessary to answer almost any question about the game. This volume is the only comprehensive guide to every player in the National Football League (NFL) since its inception in 1920. All results for the annual college draft are listed, as well as the greatest 300 players of all time and the 25 most memorable games played. Because many statistical categories have been constant throughout the league's history (e.g., yards per game), the reader can compare players of today with those of the past. The general history of the sport is also presented, as is information about the NFL's founders, but the book has no photographs. An alphabetic arrangement by player name comprises most of the book, but defunct teams are also given, along with the results of the Super Bowl games. One of the only statistical items not presented is a list of all-time record holders.

Statistical registers should be perfect, but in browsing the volume this reviewer was disappointed to find typographic errors; for example, Al Del Greco (p. 1560) is listed as starting his career in 1964 instead of 1984. The authors provide an address to which corrections may be sent for later editions. Despite its imperfections, *Total Football* is the single most comprehensive guide to the NFL.—**Christopher Byrne**

GOLF

748. *Inside Sports Magazine* **Golf.** By Roger Matuz. Detroit, Visible Ink Press/Gale, 1997. 640p. illus. index. $19.95pa. ISBN 1-57859-007-8.

The back cover of this book proclaims it to be "the world's best book" on golf. It is not quite that good, but it is certainly most useful, and at a cost of $19.95 for 640 pages, the title represents excellent value for the money.

Inside Sports Magazine Golf is a hybrid, combining reference material with sports magazine feature articles. The reference material profiles the leading current players on the three major tours; gives statistical accounts of the major championships during the years; and "previews" the tournaments to be held in the next year (1997). The feature articles offer a miscellany: "magic moments" in tournament play; celebrities talking about golf; golf in movies, song, and literature; and even a golf lesson. In addition, there are useful appendixes giving summaries of the major championships, a glossary of golf terms, and a chronology of golf happenings. The index and the approximately 200 photographs are also most welcome.

The book evinces its sports magazine heredity by its overly jaunty and gushy style and by its more than a few errors. This said, *Inside Sports Magazine Golf* hits the mark for its intended audience of golf fans: just about all the material they are likely to want for reference and plenty of readable information as well. Libraries also will find the book desirable, although whether it should go on the reference shelf is a good question.—**Samuel Rothstein**

HOCKEY

749. *Inside Sports Magazine* **Hockey.** 1997 ed. Zander Hollander, ed. Detroit, Visible Ink Press/Gale, 1997. 725p. illus. index. $19.95pa. ISBN 0-7876-0876-9.

Is greater interest in professional ice hockey a result of the National Hockey League's expansion, or has the continent-wide interest spurred the expansion from 6 teams in 1965 to the current 28? The answer is not clear, but what is certain is that there are now hockey "data books" aplenty. Thus, alongside the well-established *Sporting News Guide* and *Register* (see ARBA 97, entries 657 and 658, respectively), here is the *Inside Sports Magazine Hockey Guide*, covering much the same ground and as big as its two rivals put together.

So what is the difference between them, and why consider the *Inside Sports* title for library purchase? There is indeed much overlap, but the *Sporting News* publications are almost entirely statistical (player and team records in great detail), whereas the *Inside Sports* version emphasizes "reader interest." Approximately three-quarters of the text is given over to the history of the NHL (season by season), sketches of the Hall of Fame players, NHL records, accounts of other professional leagues and college hockey, and so forth. The remainder is devoted to a register of players, official rules, and a well-made index. The large, clear typeface makes for easy reading, and the black-and-white photographs are full page, numerous, and eye-catching.

The *Inside Sports* guide is actually the 5th edition of what was formerly called the *Complete Encyclopedia of Hockey* (see ARBA 94, entry 852), which gives confidence in the reliability and accuracy of its information. The "fan magazine" style can be a little cloying at times, but for those who want the NHL story as well as the facts, this guide should do nicely. At less than $20, the price is certainly right.
—**Samuel Rothstein**

TENNIS

750. **Bud Collins' Tennis Encyclopedia.** [3d ed.] Bud Collins and Zander Hollander, eds. Detroit, Visible Ink Press/Gale, 1997. 698p. illus. index. $19.95pa. ISBN 1-57859-000-0.

The 2d edition of *Bud Collins' Modern Encyclopedia of Tennis* (see ARBA 95, entry 825) came out in 1994, 14 years after the 1st edition. The new 3d edition, under the revised title *Bud Collins' Tennis Encyclopedia*, is out 3 short years after the 2d. This may be because Gale assumed publication of the 2d edition, and Gale regularly updates many of its titles. Frequent updates can tax a library's budget, although the title under review is cheap by reference book standards (only available in paperback).

Except for a few minor changes, such as the exclusion of the chapter on equipment and technology, the 3d edition simply adds 4 more years of tennis history, taking the reader through 1996. Consequently, it includes a small percentage of new information. The absence of a hard cover and acid-free paper should not be a problem if the publisher issues editions every few years. Libraries that own the 2d edition and subscribe to the *USTA Official Yearbook* (published by the U.S. Tennis Association) can wait for a future edition. Libraries that are looking for a low cost, up-to-date tennis encyclopedia should acquire the 3d edition.—**John P. Stierman**

TRACK-ATHLETICS

751. **National Road Race Encyclopedia.** Michael Weddington and Barry Perilli, eds. Santa Rosa, Calif., Weddington's Running Series and Glendale, Calif., Griffin Publishing, 1997. 1v. (unpaged). illus. maps. index. $24.95pa. ISBN 1-882180-73-9.

This is the first in what is planned to be an annual series listing running road races in the United States. One hundred races in thirty-three states are included. The races were selected primarily because of the fact that they had the largest number of finishers, as reported by U.S.A. Track and Field's Road Racing Information Center. Although the editors call this an "encyclopedia," "directory" is the more accurate term. The listing for each race is four pages in length and includes all pertinent race information: location, date, distance, size, age of race, altitude, weather, start time, course description and map, registration information and fees, age divisions, awards, special and concurrent events, lodging, results, who to contact, sponsors, and who benefits from the race proceeds. Lists of top 100 finishers by gender and top 20 divisional finishers are also provided with times and year of record.

This directory is organized alphabetically by race name. There is an index by state, but an index by city would be helpful, especially in the case of such overrepresented states as California (18 races) and Texas (10 races). The two main reference values of the directory are the top finisher statistics for each race and descriptive information that could be used by runners to plan travel to and entry into the races. This fills a void in the literature in that the only other way to find this information currently involves using the monthly "Calendar: Races in All Places" section in *Running Times*, or the "Race Calendar" section of *Runner's World*, and those give only sketchy information. Weddington and Perilli plan to publish regional directories as well (on Southeast top 100 road races, world ultra marathons, and Northern California races, for example), and these should also be useful reference sources. The title at hand is recommended for large public and academic libraries.—**Thomas K. Fry**

WRESTLING

752. Lentz, Harris M., III. **Biographical Dictionary of Professional Wrestling.** Jefferson, N.C., McFarland, 1997. 373p. index. $55.00. ISBN 0-7864-0303-9.

Lentz has done a thoughtful job of assembling brief biographical information about virtually every professional wrestler of any note who plied his or her trade in the twentieth century. Entries are arranged alphabetically by the wrestler's best-known name, with ample cross-references to the many other names he or she may have used, and start with basic information about the person's life. Lentz is careful to point out how unreliable much of that information, which is supplied by promoters, may be. He also provides detailed information about each person's professional career, including titles; affiliations with other wrestlers (which shift frequently); major bouts; and, in some cases, other activities such as appearances in films.

As the first standard biographical dictionary dealing with this sport/entertainment, the dictionary is a major contribution to knowledge in the field. The volume can, in most respects, serve as an abbreviated history of professional wrestling until such a badly needed history is finally written. It would be all too easy for public and school librarians to dismiss this biographical dictionary as not worthy of being added to their collections whether for snobbish reasons or because they feel that library users are not likely to be wrestling fans. That judgment would be a mistake because, for all of its flaws, professional wrestling does attract wide audiences, including many young people, from a diverse range of backgrounds. Because there is a real shortage of serious and useful books on professional wrestling, this biographical dictionary deserves a place in public and school libraries.—**Norman D. Stevens**

16 Sociology

GENERAL WORKS

753. Aby, Stephen H. **Sociology: A Guide to Reference and Information Sources.** 2d ed. Englewood, Colo., Libraries Unlimited, 1997. 227p. index. (Reference Sources in the Social Sciences Series). $42.00. ISBN 1-56308-422-8.

This 2d edition describes 576 of the major references sources in sociology and related social sciences and includes indexes, bibliographies, handbooks, databases, dictionaries, Websites, and other electronic sources. These materials were, for the most part, published between 1985 and 1996, therefore supplementing, rather than replacing, the first edition (see ARBA 88, entry 808), which covered 659 sources published from 1970 through early 1986. There are a few works that precede this period that are included because they are "considered classics"; however, no explanation is given as how these sources were chosen.

This work is divided into four parts—starting with the general and ending with the specific. Part 1 covers general social science reference sources. Broad social science disciplines are presented in part 2. Part 3 covers sociology general reference sources, and part 4 includes specific sociological fields, each in a separate chapter. Topics include clinical and applied sociology; criminology, law, and deviance; gerontology and aging; industrial sociology; marriage and the family; medical sociology; population and demography; race and ethnic relations; research methods and statistics; rural sociology; social change, movements, and collective behavior; social indicators; social problems; socialization, gender roles, and social psychology; sociology of education; sociology of organizations and groups; sociology of religion; sociology of sport and leisure; stratification and inequality; theory; urban sociology; and women's studies. The annotations are generally descriptive, yet concise.

Websites are a new feature of this edition. Unfortunately, some of the addresses are no longer current. By using many of the Internet search engines, however, the new addresses of the pages were found. This is a good starting point for looking at sociological resources, both electronic and Web-based.
—Robert L. Turner Jr.

ABORTION

754. **Abortion: An Eternal Social and Moral Issue.** 1996 ed. Alison Landes, Mark A. Siegel, and Nancy R. Jacobs, eds. Wylie, Tex., Information Plus, 1996. 212p. index. $13.95pa. ISBN 1-57302-012-5.

Abortion is an $8\frac{1}{2}$-by-11-inch, softbound volume in an inexpensive, open-ended series on social problems. Two of the three editors, who also appear to be the authors of the text, hold advanced degrees, but there is no information about their areas of expertise. The book is clearly meant to be a source of factual information for young students doing research reports. The editors draw from information sources and studies listed in the back of the book, and the statistical charts and graphs have source documentation in the body of the text. The not-very-clear authority of this series has influenced this reviewer not to purchase its titles. Yet the editors insert in-text documentation and make a solid attempt to present all sides of an emotional issue. They include historical material, a chronology of major abortion-related court cases, the positions taken by various religious groups, the status of abortion in other countries, plenty of official statistics, and the position statements of spokespersons and groups. The editors pay attention to ethics, events, public response, and legislation, and they endeavor to be thorough and sensitive. First published in 1980, the book has been revised every two years since 1988. The next scheduled update is for spring 1998. *Abortion* is a student-friendly secondary source.—**Edna M. Boardman**

755. **Abortion & Reproductive Rights: A Comprehensive Guide to Medicine, Ethics, and the Law.** [CD-ROM]. By J. Douglas Butler. Phoenix, Ariz., Oryx Press, 1997. Minimum system requirements: IBM or compatible, MPC-II compliant 486/20MHz. CD-ROM drive with Microsoft CD-ROM Extensions 2.2. Windows 3.1. 8MB RAM. SVGA 640 x 480, 256-color monitor. SoundBlaster or compatible sound card. Mouse. $495.00. ISBN 1-57356-112-6.

This CD-ROM installs easily using Windows 95. The program is found installed under "Start, Programs, Dr. Butler." Butler is the author of this excellent resource for those researching human reproductive rights. The disc provides more than 20,000 pages of text, including 65 full-text Supreme Court cases as well as important books and articles, 200-plus slides, an ultrasound video, and an unabridged audio of *Roe v. Wade* Supreme Court arguments (which gives a real "you are there" feeling). Boolean searching, hyperlinks between entries, printing all or a portion of an article, bookmarking, and annotating entries are all possible. The cases, books, and articles are not listed in either alphabetic or chronological order.

The three main categories, medicine, ethics, and law, may be selected from the table of contents page or from the tool bar. Yet sometimes the two lists do not match; for example, medicine on the tool bar lists ultrasound *videos*, but the table of contents reads *video*. Medicine subdivides into Centers for Disease Control, National Institute of Health, population control, the Alan Guttmacher Institute, normal and abnormal embryology, medical journals, ultrasound videos, slides, and books and articles. Ethics covers the Hastings Center, U.S. Congress, and books and articles. A copy of the Constitution appears under "Congress."

This disc will be welcomed by libraries whose patrons research reproductive rights. Students in high school and college will love the one-stop shopping at research time.—**Esther R. Sinofsky**

756. Blanchard, Dallas A. **The Anti-Abortion Movement: References and Resources.** New York, G. K. Hall/Simon & Schuster Macmillan, 1996. 378p. index. (Reference Publications on American Social Movements). $45.00. ISBN 0-8161-7258-7.

Blanchard has written two books and numerous articles on the subject of the antiabortion movement. This 3d book is primarily an annotated bibliography of more than 2,000 books, articles, and media stories about this movement. Blanchard begins with a survey of the antiabortion movement in the United States. In reading this history, it is clear that Blanchard is biased against the pro-life movement, which he calls "... primarily a protest against social change, a movement seeking return to the medieval hegemony of religion over all social institutions." This bias continues to be evident throughout the main section of the book, where an overwhelming majority of citations to articles condemn the pro-life movement.

This work is limited to the topics of medicine, history, sociology, political science, psychology, and social work. The bibliography is divided into 15 chapters with the longest concentrating on 39 major organizations in the movement. The other chapters deal with topics such as political activities, movement tactics, the movement and the media, and the religious basis of the movement. Considering that the introduction states that works centering on ethical, philosophic, theological, or moral issues were omitted, one wonders why a chapter on the religious basis of the movement was included. Blanchard accomplishes this by including citations primarily from secular sources. In the interest of balance, this book would be a more valuable resource had the pro-life movement been better represented.—**Michele Russo**

757. Fitzsimmons, Richard, and Joan P. Diana. **Pro-Choice/Pro-Life Issues in the 1990s: An Annotated, Selected Bibliography.** Westport, Conn., Greenwood Press, 1996. 284p. index. (Bibliographies and Indexes in Sociology, no.24). $59.95. ISBN 0-313-29335-4.

This volume is a supplement to a bibliography published in 1991 that covered the years 1972-1989 (see ARBA 92, entry 834). There has certainly been enough publishing activity to make a supplement useful: There are only 125 fewer entries than the previous volume, although the period covered (1990-1994) is much briefer. That said, however, the value of this bibliography in the current electronic environment is questionable. The authors have, in this case, repeated the introduction from the 1991 edition almost word for word; as before, there is no effort to provide any kind of topical organization or analytic framework. The bibliography is geared toward, again, both the academic and professional; no mention is made of women. Monographs, periodicals, legal decisions, and congressional hearings are included.

The bibliography claims to be selective in the aspects of the topic covered (contraceptive devices and clinic bombings, for example, are excluded) but otherwise comprehensive in its coverage of the abortion issue in U.S. society. However, a review of the entries shows several articles on Japan but the omission of works more appropriate to the stated topic, such as Stephen Presser's *Recapturing the Constitution* (Regnery, 1994); *Ethics of Abortion: Pro-Life vs. Pro-Choice* (Prometheus, 1993); or *Freedom of Choice Act of 1989: Hearings Before the Subcommittee on Civil and Constitutional Rights . . .* (U.S. Government Printing Office, 1992). A quick search of a local online catalog and of such online databases as Social Sciences Index showed numerous items not included in the print bibliography, especially, but not exclusively, from movement organizations. More directed bibliographies such as Dallas Blandard's *The Anti-Abortion Movement* (G. K. Hall, 1996) seem more interesting and useful.—**V. W. Hill**

AGING

758. Aday, Ronald H., and Kathryn L. Aday. **Group Work with the Elderly: An Annotated Bibliography.** Westport, Conn., Greenwood Press, 1997. 170p. index. (Bibliographies and Indexes in Gerontology, no.33). $69.50. ISBN 0-313-29845-9.

This timely and useful bibliography addresses the use of group process as an instrument to achieve multiple benefits for the aging and elderly. Groups offer a cost-effective means to stimulate and maintain social skills and to provide a sense of belonging and support. More specifically, they offer opportunities for intervention, stimulation, communication, and maintenance of social skills and aid in reducing feelings of loneliness and isolation. These benefits can improve interpersonal relationships and enhance overall social and psychological well-being. Group work is used to advantage in most community and institutional settings, such as senior centers and day care, retirement and nursing homes, and mental health settings.

Citations in this bibliography include 451 sources from 1970 to 1996, including journals, books, theses, dissertations, and research reports. Access to these citations provides social workers, counselors, group facilitators, activity directors, researchers, and mental health professionals with materials that reflect program designs, techniques, standards, leaders, and ethics in the field. The entries offer full citations and a one-paragraph review noting the scope, content, and format, where relevant. Entries are indexed by author and by topic. This assemblage of material takes full advantage of the recent increase in articles and books from gerontological professionals who work with older adults. Chapters address general group issues and the use of groups for counseling, caregiver support, expressive therapy, psychotherapy, remotivation, reality orientation, reminiscence, and life review.

The authors are qualified by experience and position. Ronald Aday is executive director of the Tennessee Association of Gerontology/Geriatric Education and director of aging studies at Middle Tennessee State University. Kathryn Aday is a geriatric group therapist.—**Barbara Conroy**

759. **Funding in Aging: A Guide to Giving by Foundations, Corporations, & Charitable Organizations.** Elizabeth H. Rich, ed. New York, Foundation Center, 1996. 294p. index. $95.00pa. ISBN 0-87954-663-8.

This book is published by the Foundation Center. It is similar to the *Foundation Directory* (see entry 787), a descriptive directory of grant-makers, with information on those organizations and agencies that provide funding to the aging. *Funding in Aging* also includes a bibliography and lists of publications and services of the Foundation Center and the Foundation Center Cooperating Collections. The 2d section of the book includes voluntary organizations, including academic and research centers, denominational organizations, gerontological organizations, and professional and service organizations. This section is a useful addition for those who need this type of information. An index is provided for easy access. The recommendation for purchase of this book is limited to those agencies who deal primarily with the aging. For public and academic libraries with limited funds, the same information is available in the *Foundation Directory*, which includes all subject fields.—**Theresa Maggio**

760. Kausler, Donald H., and Barry C. Kausler. **The Graying of America: An Encyclopedia of Aging, Health, Mind, and Behavior.** Champaign, Ill., University of Illinois Press, 1996. 356p. index. $39.95. ISBN 0-252-02159-2.

Co-authored by a noted gerontologist and his copywriter son, this utilitarian encyclopedic work about aging, health, mind, and behavior is a recommended purchase for academic, medical, and public libraries and nursing homes. Using an A to Z approach, the authors have taken great care to define and expound upon approximately 300 age-related terms, concepts, and diseases that range from health problems, such as cardiovascular disease and cancer, to psychological issues concerning sibling rivalry and wisdom. Entries vary from one-half to four pages in length and the, and their contents reflect the authors' commitment to sharing salient research results in appropriate, layperson's terms. The book concludes with a 10-page index and a shorter index that lists subjects within broader topics.

Every topic is treated from a gerontological perspective. Diabetes, for example, is discussed from the standpoint of aging and its possible concomitant symptom of blurred vision. The most puzzling entry, however, is entitled "Hiding Your Age." This entry contains the statistic that 34 percent of the female population older than 65 use hair dye, but nowhere does it cite the growing recourse to plastic surgery by aging citizens to slow the gerontological external clock. Devoting a full paragraph to "tear secretion" while omitting a bewildering array of cosmetic surgery treatments, such as face and neck lifts, skin peels, and tummy tucks, will surely frustrate aging Baby Boomers who are searching for simple definitions and explanations about these treatments to combat the visages of aging. Unfortunately, this fast-growing solution to the inexorable ravages of time and gravity is given nary a sentence.

A second flaw concerns the absence of hotline numbers for many of the organizations, programs, and services cited. These numbers, coupled with appropriate Internet site addresses, would have improved this work considerably. Despite these caveats, *The Graying of America* will make a useful addition to any collection in need of gerontological works.—**Kathleen W. Craver**

761. Miletich, John J. **Depression in the Elderly: A Multimedia Sourcebook.** Westport, Conn., Greenwood Press, 1997. 226p. index. (Bibliographies and Indexes in Gerontology series, v.36). $69.50. ISBN 0-313-30113-1.

As more and more elderly persons continue to live longer, it is likely that the problem of depression in the elderly will continue to increase. As part of the Bibliographies and Indexes in Gerontology series, this multimedia sourcebook, covering the period from 1970 to 1996, provides lists of materials relating to all aspects of the problem. Chapters include such topics as diagnosis, physical illness, institutional and home environments, nationality and race, bereavement, suicide, religion, and various treatments. Most of the materials in each chapter are journal articles, but there are also some books, audio- or videocassettes, conference papers, and theses and dissertations. Approximately half of the entries have annotations, but it is not clear why some items are annotated and others (even from the same journal) are not. Three appendixes contain lists of information providers, related associations, and television programs. There are indexes for both authors and subjects, the latter being especially helpful when seeking information on a subject that could span several chapters, such as Hispanic elderly.

Many of the articles listed could be found in databases available in most academic libraries today, but the advantage of this sourcebook is in having all of the different types of materials together. It is perhaps unfortunate that the move toward alternative medicine has not been reflected to any extent in the work. There is a chapter on nonpharmacological treatments, but most of the treatments tend to be in the areas of psychotherapy, electroconvulsive therapy, or other behavioral therapies.

The work is designed for health care and other professionals, including gerontologists, psychiatrists, psychologists, social workers, nurses, and even paramedics and students. For these professionals who are working with the elderly, the volume should be useful. It is recommended for academic and large public libraries with such clientele.—**Lucille Whalen**

762. Shuldiner, David P. **Folklore, Culture, and Aging: A Research Guide.** Westport, Conn., Greenwood Press, 1997. 283p. index. (Bibliographies and Indexes in Gerontology, no.34). $69.50. ISBN 0-313-29897-1.

Designed to aid researchers and teachers of folklore, culture, and gerontology, as well as for those seeking information on the value of folklore in providing culturally sensitive services to the elderly, this volume fills not only a niche in the Greenwood Press series of Bibliographies and Indexes in Gerontology but a much larger gap in the literature on aging research. The well-qualified author provides a substantial representation of the English-language materials by and about the expressive behavior and culture of aging adults. The focus is on the peoples of North America, and the concentration is on literature published since 1970.

An excellent introduction precedes eight chapters on research tools, general works, beliefs and customs, narratives, traditional arts, health and healing, applied folklore, and films. Each chapter is subdivided by ethnicity, region, gender, folklore genre, and social practice. Topics extend from broad cultural areas to works that are specific in both time and space, and entries range in format from books and periodicals to theses, oral histories, and motion pictures. Brief annotations provide insights into, as well as descriptions of, each entry. Author and subject indexes provide some access to the entries; however, long lists of entry numbers under some subjects are difficult to follow. Adding the subheadings of each chapter to the table of contents would have enhanced access to the entries.

Although not intended to be an exhaustive compilation, the inclusiveness and careful organization of this research guide make it a valuable tool for anthropologists, folklorists, gerontologists, and community workers. This resource would be an important addition to any research library.—**Debra S. Van Tassel**

763. Wheeler, Helen Rippier. **Women & Aging: A Guide to the Literature.** Boulder, Colo., Lynne Rienner, 1997. 259p. index. $65.00. ISBN 1-55587-661-7.

Nearly 2,000 journal articles, books, book chapters, and doctoral and master's dissertations that reflect how aging women are viewed in social and behavioral sciences and humanities literature are the focus of this guide. Entries cover the period from 1980 to 1994. The majority are nonfiction, but fiction and poetry are included.

There are 13 chapters representing broad areas such as psychological and sociological perspectives on women's aging, ageism and sexism, economic issues, biography, and living arrangements. Each chapter has a table of contents outlining the alphabetically arranged topical subsections. There are *see also* references to related entries and topics. Sequentially numbered entries include the author's full name, the full title of the work, the publication date and, in the case of books, an analytical annotation. Dissertation entries include a locator number for *Dissertation Abstracts International*. Document numbers are given for ERIC documents.

The works cited were chosen for their usefulness to scholars and educators in the fields of gerontology and women's studies. The scope of the guide is broad and encompasses a variety of subjects, from scholarly research articles to Jane Fonda's workout book. Excluded are comprehensive reference works, most popular life skills guides, directories, handbooks, and manuals. Subject and author indexes provide access to specific areas of interest.

Although there are citations with post-1990 publication dates, they are in the minority, and most entries date from the 1980s. With the growth of the female aging population, much more has been and will be written on the subject. The guide's final chapter on locating additional sources will prove beneficial to researchers looking for current information.—**Marlene M. Kuhl**

COMMUNITY LIFE

764. Axelrod, Alan. **The International Encyclopedia of Secret Societies and Fraternal Orders.** New York, Facts on File, 1997. 287p. index. $40.00. ISBN 0-8160-2307-7.

Primarily a short-entry list of all sorts of secret societies and similar groups from all over the world, this volume also contains some entries for important concepts and people. Organizations listed must require conscious application for membership; have some sort of rite/oath of initiation; and either claim to transmit some secret knowledge, support members against others, or behave fraternally or benevolently toward others. These criteria include listings for insurance societies; political and labor groups, such as the Molly Maguires and the Carbonari; and "friendly societies" like the Elks, as well as groups like the Freemasons. The criteria exclude such groups as the Mafia, the Irish Republican Army (although the Fenians are listed), and most religious sects. Entries, arranged alphabetically, vary in length from about 25 words to several thousand, apparently depending on the importance of the group, and include addresses for currently active groups. A useful introduction provides a brief historical and philosophical discussion.

This is the only recent book of its type, other similar titles being reprints from 20 to 50 years ago. Unfortunately, although there is an unannotated bibliography (listing only books), individual entries lack any documentation at all, the index is incomplete, and cross-referencing is spotty. Given the number of arcane terms, misspellings are downright confusing (a reference to "key lines," for example, really refers to "ley lines"), and too many technical terms are used without either indexing or cross-references to the definition often concealed in one entry. Given the lack of other current information, the worldwide inclusiveness of this title, its reasonable price, and the good writing (although some groups may take offense at what this reviewer felt was humor and frankness), this source is worthy of consideration. It is most unfortunate that the editing is so poor—the author deserves better.—**James H. Sweetland**

765. **Guide to Federal Funding for Housing & Homeless Programs.** 3d ed. Elizabeth A. Bernhard, ed. Arlington, Va., Government Information Services, 1997. 1v. (various paging). $267.95/yr. looseleaf w/binder. ISBN 0-933544-92-8.

A private-sector publisher provides a guide to government funding for private groups and government entities who seek to fulfill the needs of low- and no-income persons. The editors, who pull together information from a variety of departments and agencies, draw from government sources, including interviews with officials. This guide includes housing, food stamps, energy assistance, and many other services that, the publisher says, are not included in the government's own materials that purport to parallel this one.

The 14 sections are labeled by target population and type of service. Each section is set up in a uniform format so the user can readily identify such items as the program purpose, flow and uses of funds, eligibility for receiving funds, type of aid, likelihood that an applicant will be funded, and whom to contact. Applicants must still get material from the specific grant-awarding agency but will find this an excellent place to start. This is an expensive resource, however it includes the looseleaf binder, four annual supplements, and access to a password-protected Internet site that informs users of deadlines and new rules and programs. A regional library in an economically-depressed area will find it valuable. Libraries will need to advertise it specifically to contractors, housing developers, issuers of food stamps, veterans groups, managers of homeless shelters, and others who serve disadvantaged populations. The publisher promises money back if not satisfied.—**Edna M. Boardman**

766. **Homelessness in America.** Jim Baumohl, ed. Phoenix, Ariz., for the National Coalition for the Homeless, Oryx Press, 1996. 291p. index. $39.50. ISBN 0-89774-869-7.

The phenomenon of homelessness has reached almost epidemic proportions in many U.S. cities. *Homelessness in America* was compiled under a grant from the National Coalition for the Homeless in its pursuit of enlightening the public about homelessness and bringing about change in a social policy that allows such a devastating situation. Specifically, the book attempts to answer the questions of what are the underlying causes of homelessness and what steps can be taken to alleviate the problem. Divided into three main sections—"History, Definition, and Causes"; "Dimensions of Homelessness"; and "Responses to Homelessness"—each of which consists of six chapters, the work explores such areas as housing policies, homeless families, survival strategies on the street, public attitudes toward the homeless, and antihomeless movements.

Under the editorship of Baumohl, an associate professor in the Graduate School of Social Work and Social Relations at Bryn Mawr, each chapter is presented by an expert in the field in a serious, well-written style that attempts to counteract the oftentimes oversimplified writing on the subject found in newspapers and popular magazines. Extensive notes are given for each chapter in addition to a 22-page bibliography found in the appendix. The inclusion of tables throughout the text, a list of organizations and clearinghouses related to homelessness, and a detailed index add to the value of this excellent volume. It should appeal to a wide audience: academics, including both faculty and students; administrators and those working in social service areas related to homelessness; and the general public who are becoming increasingly vocal in their criticism of the problems related to the homeless in their cities. *Homelessness in America* is recommended for academic and public libraries.—**Lucille Whalen**

DEATH

767. Jones, Constance. **R.I.P.: The Complete Book of Death and Dying.** New York, Stonesong Press/HarperCollins, 1997. 328p. index. $25.00. ISBN 0-06-270140-1.

A question this title inspires is, Can a book with *Complete* in the title really be complete? This one attempts to be. It is divided into 2 major sections. The 1st section surveys the practices and attitudes surrounding death and the process of dying. A chapter is devoted to each of the following: the cultural tradition; scientific studies of dying; demographic statistics; funeral customs; religious beliefs; creative expressions about death; and historical anecdotes, including such things as famous last lines. The 2d section contains practical information on preparing for death, the financial concerns, funeral arrangements, and the mourning process. This section will be a valuable resource for those who are coping with the issue, because it deals with practical items, such as fraud in the funeral industry and what to look out for. There is a resource list that includes organizations and government agencies and a section on mail-order caskets and plans. An extensive bibliography and a useful index appear as well.

This book has enough interesting information to be read straight through, or it can be used as a helpful reference source. Some parts are even humorous. Some sections, such as what happens to the body after death occurs, more sensitive readers may want to skip because of the graphic descriptions. *R.I.P.* will be useful in most libraries.—**Robert L. Turner Jr.**

768. Lester, David. **An Encyclopedia of Famous Suicides.** Commack, N.Y., Nova Science Publishers, 1996. 149p. index. $59.00. ISBN 1-56072-240-1.

This work contains 334 entries for people who, according to the author, committed suicide. There is no indication of selection criteria, and there appear to be some questionable entries for the marginally famous (e.g., many Roman generals, Ernest Hemingway's brother Leicester); some whose suicides are uncertain (e.g., Thomas Clifford, whose "death is thought to have been from suicide"); some who can only be considered to have committed suicide through a very broad definition of the word (e.g., George Armstrong Custer, Alexander Hamilton); and some whose deaths are officially listed as other than suicide (e.g., Brian Epstein, Jack London). All entries appear to be for actual people, with the exception of an entry for the mythological Oedipus and Jocasta.

Entries include the birth and death places and dates of the subjects, when known, and brief, superficial descriptions of the subjects' lives and deaths. There is an alphabetic index (which does not include a separate entry for Jocasta), which is unnecessary because the entries are arranged alphabetically.

It is difficult to imagine to what reference use this book could be put. It is more of a curiosity than a reference work—and an expensive curiosity at that.—**Gari-Anne Patzwald**

769. **The National Directory of Bereavement Support Groups and Services, 1996.** Mary M. Wong, ed. Forest Hills, N.Y., ADM Publishing, 1996. 484p. index. $29.95pa. ISBN 0-9645608-7-9. ISSN 1086-8976.

Death educators have seen an outpouring of books by new authors who come into the field with grief and a desire to share their story as their primary credentials. Although Wong found the motivation for this book in her own grief for her stepdaughter who died in 1984, what she has accomplished is out of the ordinary. This is a book that needed to be written.

Most of Wong's directory (75 percent) are the names, addresses, and telephone numbers of bereavement support groups categorized by type of death. The remaining 25 percent is devoted to articles on the types of death Wong references. Parents of a teen killed in a car accident, for example, will find 35 groups in 24 states, 5 at the national level, and an article on vehicular homicide. The other categories are AIDS; murder; suicide; and the death of a child, infant, spouse, and pet. In addition, there are references to groups that help those who mourn the loss of an organ donor, a police officer, or someone killed in an aircraft accident. Wong has found a group for every type of grief imaginable.

Wong's goal was to compile the definitive reference guide for persons beset by grief in all its manifestations. Although she has succeeded admirably, there are some limitations to this book. The support groups chosen for inclusion are those open to the general community. This criterion excludes those hospices, for example, who work only with bereaved survivors of their patients. Wong includes a contact person with each group—a nice touch, but such lists need to be updated regularly in order to be current. The date in the title, 1996, gives the impression that new directories would be published annually. Although annual revisions were what Wong intended, the next issue is scheduled for March 1998 and will be the 1998-1999 directory. Because Wong has said it will add 1,000 new entries to the 1,600 in the 1996 edition, librarians may decide to wait until then to order.

This book is recommended for all libraries. To this reviewer's knowledge, there is nothing else like it.

—Pete Prunkl

770. Wright, Russell O. **Life and Death in the United States: Statistics on Life Expectancies, Diseases, and Death Rates for the Twentieth Century.** Jefferson, N.C., McFarland, 1997. 139p. index. $28.50pa. ISBN 0-7864-0320-9.

By utilizing charts and tables, the author presents a statistical overview of life expectancy and death rates in the United States in the twentieth century. This reference consists of five major parts and an excellent index. In part 1 significant advancements in life expectancy from birth are provided. Included are life expectancies at various ages. Part 2 focuses on death rates at different ages and is broken down by gender and cause of death. Because death rates for both cardiovascular disease and cancer dominate today's statistics, part 3 and part 4 address these diseases in depth. Part 5 concludes with a statistical basis for predicting future factors that will impact the overall death rate, and provides steps to prevent premature death and reach full life expectancy.

The primary source for the data in *Life and Death in the United States* was the U.S. Census Bureau's *Statistical Abstract of the United States*. Data from the American Cancer Society and the American Heart Association were also used to highlight trends pertaining to cancer and cardiovascular disease.

Wright provides the individual with myriad statistics and analysis pertaining to life and death rates. The information is presented in a manner that is easily understood. The data are not only informative but, in the case of part 5, which concludes with information on how to avoid premature death, practical.

—Earl Shumaker

DISABLED

771. **The Complete Directory for People with Disabilities, 1997-98.** Leslie Mackenzie, comp. Alexcia Fales and Nicholas Gottlieb, eds. Lakeville, Conn., Grey House Publishing, 1997. 832p. index. $145.00. ISBN 0-939300-86-9.

With 3,000 more entries than the previous edition, this work shows its increased comprehensiveness in including products and services available for the disabled. Entries are arranged alphabetically under subject listings. The table of contents and three indexes—disability, geographic, and title/entry name—are the means of further accessibility. Unfortunately, entry listings in the disability and geographic indexes are not arranged in alphabetic order; therefore, the user must read through the entire list even when looking for a known item. This caveat aside, the directory, while not complete, provides valuable information for anyone in search of products or services in this area and is recommended for its intended use.

—Jo Anne H. Ricca

772. **Directory of Agencies and Organizations Serving Individuals Who are Deaf-Blind.** rev. ed. Compiled by the Helen Keller National Center. Sands Point, N.Y., Helen Keller National Center, 1996. 1v. (unpaged). index. $25.00 looseleaf w/binder.

This directory lists agencies and organizations that work with people who are deaf-blind. Its intention is to serve as a resource and aid for securing services for that audience. The information in the directory is based on a survey conducted by the Helen Keller National Center. The publisher does not claim to be inclusive or current in listing all organizations and agencies. However, the continuing invitations for updates and additions have made the 1996 edition a more complete resource than the 1987 edition (see ARBA 89, entry 760).

The volume begins with an alphabetic listing of more than 450 organizations and agencies. Their names lead readers to the city and state where the organizations are located. The descriptive information on each organization can be found under its geographic location. Each entry gives the address, telephone and fax numbers, homepage address, names of the administrator and the contact person, age range of the person who may be served, types of programs and services provided, availability of publications, and the staff communication skills reported. The information on service programs is of special interest and relevance to readers. Some of the services listed are placement, job skills training, Braille classes, computer training, counseling, independent living skills, physical therapy, recreation, referrals, socialization groups, family training, and support.

The directory is valuable not only to individuals who are deaf-blind but also to the organizations and agencies interested in expanding and improving their services and in establishing support and cooperation with other organizations. The resource would be even more useful if published in Braille or other audio or visual formats, so that it can be fully used by the intended audiences. The work is recommended for social service organizations, public libraries, and academic and research institutes supporting programs in deaf-blind services.—**Eveline L. Yang**

773. **Directory of College Facilities and Services for People with Disabilities.** 4th ed. Compiled by Modoc Press. Phoenix, Ariz., Oryx Press, 1996. 423p. index. $125.00pa. ISBN 0-89774-894-8. ISSN 1085-9411.

Because of the rise in the number of students with disabilities and because of such legislation as the Americans with Disabilities Act of 1990 and the Rehabilitation Act of 1973, there has been a dramatic increase in disability issues and disability services offered on college and university campuses since the late 1970s. The 4th edition of the *Directory of College Facilities and Services for People with Disabilities* reflects changes and improvements to structures and services listed in the 3d edition (see ARBA 92, entry 321), as well as institutions not listed in the prior edition. Excluded are institutions that requested exclusion and those institutions that do not accommodate persons with disabilities for professional, military, or religious reasons. Also, only those schools that responded are listed. The purpose of the 4th edition has not changed since the earlier volume: "to serve as a basic guide for individuals with disabilities, as well as counselors in high schools, rehabilitation agencies, and colleges who assist this population."

Information pertaining to programs and services available for students in more than 1,500 postsecondary institutions within the United States, outlying areas, and the Canadian provinces is provided. Arrangement is by state or province. Each entry includes the institutional address and, if possible, a resource person. A general description of the institution, including the number of students with disabilities and disability types, is included, along with information about grounds and facility accessibility. Incorporated into the entry are services available to the students and restrictions or special service emphases.

The main entries are followed by two indexes. The first index, "Number of Students Currently Being Served, Arranged by Disability," is arranged alphabetically by disability category. The institutions are arranged alphabetically by state or province, then by institution. Following the state or province abbreviations is the number of students served for each category. Disabilities included are attention deficit disorder, autism, blind or visual impairment, brain injury, chronic health disorder, deaf or hearing impairment, developmental disability, dwarfism, learning disability, mobility/orthopedic impairment, multiple disability condition, neurological disorder, obesity, psychiatric disorder, seizure disorder, speech/language disorder, substance abuse, and miscellaneous disorders. The second index lists institutions alphabetically with a designation for those institutions providing special financial aid programs and resident facilities. One section that is missing from the 4th edition is a list of associations, centers, organizations, and societies concerned with the disabled and disability issues. Also, the 3d edition included lists of print sources, grant resources and clearinghouses, and various databases pertaining to the disabled and disability issues. This feature was an enhancement to that edition; likewise, it would have added to the usefulness of the 4th edition.
—**Earl Shumaker**

774. **Directory of Grants for Organizations Serving People with Disabilities: A Reference Directory Identifying Grants Available to Nonprofit Organizations.** 10th ed. Loxahatchee, Fla., Research Grant Guides, 1997. 152p. index. $59.50pa. ISBN 0-945078-17-X. ISSN 0777-3282.

The expectations for the quality of social and educational services to the disabled have been raised in recent years, thanks in part to political organizing, concerns for social equality, and the law. For nonprofit organizations serving the disabled, there is an ever-present need for funding to provide this quality service. This directory aids in that process by identifying over 800 foundations that award grants to organizations providing services to the disabled.

The directory entries are arranged alphabetically by state and foundation name and typically include an address and telephone number, the dollar amount range of funded grants, geographic restrictions on the awarding of grants, and recent recipients of grants. If specific recipients of grants are not listed, the categories for the preferred disabilities served (e.g., hearing impaired) are listed. Additional access to the entries is provided by a subject index, which includes 16 categories: accessibility projects, blind, cultural programs, deaf, developmentally disabled, education, independent living, learning disabilities, mentally disabled, physically disabled, recreation, rehabilitation, research, speech impaired, vocational training, and youth. There is also a foundation name index as well as appendixes describing the Grantsmanship Center (a training organization) and the Foundation Center (a network of information providers with locations nationwide).

As a lead to potential funding sources, this directory has value. However, although it identifies recipients of grants, it does not identify the specific proposals that were funded. This is a valuable feature of *The Foundation Grants Index* (see ARBA 96, entry 883) that would improve the utility of this source. Furthermore, and maybe as a result of the above limitation, the subject index includes far too many entry numbers under each broad subject category. Subheadings would have been more helpful. These limitations aside, libraries supporting collections in grant-seeking will want this directory.—**Stephen H. Aby**

775. **A Man's Guide to Coping with Disability.** Lexington, Mass., Resources for Rehabilitation, 1997. 256p. index. $42.95pa. ISBN 0-929718-18-6.

Nearly 20 percent of the male population in the United States is living with some type of disability or chronic disease. Recent reference tools examining available resources for the disabled have focused either on the specific needs of women or the public at large. The compilers of this volume seek to provide a companion guide to these reference works, emphasizing the unique needs of men living with disabilities or chronic diseases.

The 10 chapters in this volume fall into 2 categories. The first three chapters present broad overview discussions covering how men attempt to cope with disabilities and the laws that can assist them in these efforts. The last seven chapters provide information on specific diseases/disabilities (e.g., diabetes, stroke, prostate conditions, and spinal cord injuries). Each chapter contains introductory text describing the impact of these conditions on men, with special attention to problems created for sexual functioning and the psychological aspects caused by these ailments. Following the text, the compilers present a briefly annotated listing of organizations; publications and tapes; assistive devices dealing with specific conditions when available; and the types of health professionals who work in that health specialty. Addresses, telephone numbers, and URLs are provided for these resources, when available.

Although there is a limited amount of new material in this reference work, much of its content is already available in *Resources for People with Disabilities and Chronic Conditions*, published by the same firm (3d ed.; see ARBA 97, entry 673). Additional resources for the disabled can be found in *The Complete Directory for People with Disabilities* from Grey House Publishing (see ARBA 93, entry 862).—**Jonathon Erlen**

776. Pelka, Fred. **The ABC-CLIO Companion to the Disability Rights Movement.** Santa Barbara, Calif., ABC-CLIO, 1997. 422p. illus. index. (ABC-CLIO Companions to Key Issues in American History and Life). $60.00. ISBN 0-87436-834-0.

The history of how U.S. society has treated the physically disabled and the mentally handicapped is a long, sad story of disinterest, ridicule, and pity. Despite these obstacles, there have been fragmented efforts during the past century to assert the rights of this disenfranchised portion of the public. This valuable reference guide compiles the stories of many of the leading people, organizations, court cases, and federal laws that have led the fight to enable disabled citizens in the United States to function at their fullest possible capacity. The companion covers aspects from access to transportation to the right to vote.

Pelka presents an alphabetically arranged series of nearly 500 entries that comprise the history of the U.S. disability rights movement, from the 1817 founding of the American School for the Deaf through the 1996 election of the disabled candidate Max Cleveland to the U.S. Senate. These entries range from a few paragraphs to several pages in length. Whereas some of the biographical entries cover such well-known figures as Franklin D. Roosevelt and Helen Keller, most of the individuals profiled are relatively unknown to the general public (e.g., Mark Johnson, the founder of ADAPT; Harlan Lane, a sign-language expert; and Edward V. Roberts, "the father of the independent living movement"). Major coverage is presented of significant court cases that have upheld the rights of the disabled (*Buck v. Bell* in 1927; *Honig v. Doe* in 1988) and key federal legislation promoting and protecting these rights (the 1918 Smith-Sears Veteran's Vocational Rehabilitation Act; the 1990 Americans with Disabilities Act). There are also entries for broader categories of concerns for the disabled: alcohol and drug dependence, religion, and women with disabilities. Interesting illustrations, a succinct chronology of major events, a useful bibliography, and an in-depth subject index enhance this volume's value. This major reference tool covering the history of the U.S. disability rights movement is an important addition to all public, academic, and health-related libraries.—**Jonathon Erlen**

777. **A Woman's Guide to Coping with Disability.** 2d ed. Lexington, Mass., Resources for Rehabilitation, 1997. 256p. index. $42.95pa. ISBN 0-929718-19-4.

This is the 2d edition of a publication that originally appeared in 1994 (see ARBA 96, entry 859). The general format and the information provided remain essentially the same. The guide continues to deal with the needs of women who have chronic conditions. Three introductory chapters discuss how disabilities affect women in regard to self-image, age, sexual function, and childbearing. There are also discussions dealing with the health care system, caregivers, and laws that relate to disabilities. A new section reveals how computers can aid the disabled to help perform tasks and as a source of medical information and listserv support groups.

The conditions covered are arthritis, diabetes, epilepsy, lupus, multiple sclerosis, osteoporosis, and spinal cord injury. For each condition there is a discussion about the nature of the illness, the impact on life-style, and the treatment. Each chapter concludes with a list of books, articles, and government documents about the condition and list of organizations where support and information can be found. Each organization has complete directory information that now includes Internet and e-mail addresses wherever they are available. Bibliographies contain information as late as 1996, and obsolete organizations have been removed and new ones added. The information is well arranged and easy to access with a table of contents and an index of organizations.

This kind of information is always welcome, and the number of addresses of organizations and resources makes the directory particularly valuable. It would be helpful in the future if other conditions affecting women could be included, such as AIDS, chronic fatigue syndrome, and fibromyalgia. These conditions are also disabling and should not be ignored.—**Marilyn Strong Noronha**

FAMILY, MARRIAGE, AND DIVORCE

778. Lilly, Teri Ann, Marcie Pitt-Catsouphes, and Bradley K. Googins, comps. **Work-Family Research: An Annotated Bibliography.** Westport, Conn., Greenwood Press, 1997. 315p. index. (Bibliographies and Indexes in Sociology, no.25). $69.50. ISBN 0-313-30322-3.

This bibliography provides 934 citations to research on the work-family field. The compilers are affiliated with Boston College's Center for Work & Family, which was founded in 1990. The focus is on a sample of classic studies in the field, selected papers, reports from independent research groups, and research articles written in the past eight years.

Development perspective, the work and the family focus, and work-family interaction are the three predominant perspectives of the work-family field that this source covers in nine chapters. Though the compilers apologize for the many works not listed because of the prodigious amount of literature being written on this topic, the attempt to narrow the massive research on the subject of work and family is commendable. Each entry provides a bibliographic citation and the majority of the entries are annotated. Because of space limitations, however, the compilers did not annotate some items, usually books. An author index is provided, but the value of this work could be enhanced by a subject index. Because so many people are affected by work and family issues, this bibliography will provide an excellent starting point for anyone interested in work-family research.—**Diane J. Turner**

779. **POPLINE: Through December 1996.** [CD-ROM]. Baltimore, Md., National Information Services Corporation, 1997. Minimum system requirements: IBM or compatible 386. CD-ROM drive. 3MB RAM. 480K conventional memory. 2.5MB hard disk space. Color or monochrome monitor. $695.00/yr.

POPLINE is a comprehensive information service on CD-ROM that covers population, family planning, and related health issues. There are 235,000 citations with abstracts from published and unpublished sources. *POPLINE* is supported by the United States Agency for International Development and the United Nations Population Fund. Sources of the information come from U.S. government documents; international agency documents; family planning organizations; and databases on sociology, clinical medicine, and health. The disc indexes and abstracts government reports, books, journals, monographs, technical reports, laws, court decisions, theses, dissertations, conference papers, unpublished reports, newspaper articles, and training manuals. The major topics under the previously mentioned three categories are more concerned with public health issues: family planning, technology, maternal and child health care, family planning programs, health care instruction, AIDS, population dynamics, primary health care, overpopulation issues, child immunization, reproductive performance, law and policy on reproduction, migration trends and policies, fertility regulation, infant and maternal mortality, sexually transmitted diseases, health care training materials, and population and natural resources ecological affects.

This service uses the standard CD-ROM product technology. A quick guide helps the user learn the search operators and searching techniques. A detailed user's guide for the librarian offers ways in which to make the software more conducive to local needs and local setups. The quick guide is clear, concise, and direct, and most PC operators using CD-ROM products will find it sufficient to operate the database.

Users can identify consultants in specific fields or locations and compile lists of publications by organization or any of the major topic and other criteria. Background information by country or region can be found, although many libraries have this information in other formats. *POPLINE* is an important reference resource for libraries serving public health settings and comprehensive social work and sociology clientele.—**Gerald D. Moran**

780. Strauss, Carol Ann. **Grandparents: An Annotated Bibliography on Roles, Rights, and Relationships.** Lanham, Md., Scarecrow, 1996. 507p. index. $84.00. ISBN 0-8108-3135-X.

The population is aging. This means that some people are lucky enough to have grandparents still with them. This volume, compiled by Strauss, is in response, she says, to the "increased interest in the study of grandparenthood" (introduction). The annotated bibliography emphasizes research literature in English-language publications, including books, chapters of books, journal articles, and theses and dissertations. The 1,054 annotations are divided into sections, including demographics and surveys of how the family is changing, grandmothers, grandfathers, divorce and grandparents, legal rights, perceptions and portrayals, and others. The indexes include author, subject, and legal cases involving grandparents.

This is an unusual compilation of articles. A brief look at some of the titles shows the range of material: "Role of Grandparents in Transsexualism," "Intergenerational Family Therapy," and "Extended Family Support and Problems." It is easy to see that this volume could be useful to the social scientist interested in studying the role that grandparents play in society. The bibliography is recommended for college libraries and public libraries with a large research collection.—**Barbara J. O'Hara**

GAY AND LESBIAN STUDIES

781. Dawson, Jeff. **Gay & Lesbian Online.** rev. ed. Berkeley, Calif., Peachpit Press, 1997. 389p. illus. index. $16.95pa. ISBN 0-201-68861-1.

That the revised edition of this title was published only a year after the 1st edition appeared (see ARBA 97, entry 676) attests to both the popularity of the World Wide Web and its phenomenal growth. The subtitle "The Travel Guide to Digital Queerdom on the World Wide Web," which appears on the cover of the present edition, differs from the original by excluding references to commercial online services, such as America Online and CompuServe. The author bemoans the reduction of gay-related information available on the commercial networks, but contrasts this loss with the expansion of the Web and its current status as the richest source of gay online life. Consequently, nearly all resources included in this edition are freely accessible Websites, which improves the guide's usefulness.

The format remains unchanged: chapters begin with a brief discussion of the most relevant sites followed by a more extensive, unannotated listing of Web pages and their URLs. The content is also similar to the 1st edition. Many chapter titles are identical to the previous edition and range from "AIDS" and "Opera" to "Sex." Clearly there are more sites referenced in the 2d edition, and, with the aid of a subject index, this "Webliography" provides access to a broad range of gay resources online.—**Michael Weinberg**

782. **Gay & Lesbian Biography.** Michael J. Tyrkus, ed. Detroit, St. James Press, 1997. 515p. illus. index. $90.00. ISBN 1-55862-237-3.

Information regarding the sexual orientation of prominent individuals has long been a neglected aspect of biographical data presented by standard reference works. *Gay & Lesbian Biography*'s unique value lies in its offering of a more balanced evaluation of 275 prominent and lesser-known individuals and in its expanding of the range of personal identity elements viewed as significant to biography to include sexual orientation. Both recognized historical figures (a group ranging from Sappho of Lesbos and Hadrian through Leonardo da Vinci and Frederick the Great) to contemporary men and women whose lives are or were openly gay or lesbian are included. For some of the latter, their essays are the first extended biographical coverage available in any reference source. Information is provided on the individual's life and creative accomplishments, their relationship to the larger gay and lesbian community as a whole (of whatever era), a list of references cited, and photographs or portraits when available. Indexes provide access by nationality, occupation, and general subject categories. The work is recommended for all public, college, and university libraries.—**Robert B. Marks Ridinger**

PHILANTHROPY

Bibliography

783. Johnson, Jean E., Elisa Cho, and Jacqueline Tyson. **The Literature of the Nonprofit Sector, Volume 8: A Bibliography with Abstracts.** New York, Foundation Center, 1996. 133p. index. $45.00pa. ISBN 0-87954-702-2.

This is the 8th volume in a series of printed bibliographies based on the collections of the Foundation Center's five libraries in the areas of philanthropy, foundations, and other nonprofit organizations. The entire retrospective bibliography of 15,196 entries is also available on the center's Website. Much of the material covered relates to scholarly research on philanthropy, but practical and "how-to" materials are also included; coverage includes local as well as national publications. About 70 percent of the entries represent articles in philanthropic and general periodicals, but books, dissertations, and audiovisual works are also listed. The entries for books and pamphlets do not give pagination, which would have been helpful. Of the 1,036 entries, 759 have abstracts; in many cases the abstracts include substantive information such as statistics. Entries are organized under 12 topical areas in such areas as corporate philanthropy, proposal development, tax and legal issues, and government funding and the nonprofit sector. There are also detailed subject, author, and title indexes. A final section lists publications and services of the Foundation Center. This book would be helpful to any library interested in nonprofit organizations or fund-raising and essential for any collection relating to philanthropy.—**Marit S. MacArthur**

Dictionaries and Encyclopedias

784. **The NSFRE Fund-Raising Dictionary.** By the National Society of Fund Raising Executives. Barbara R. Levy and R. L. Cherry, eds. New York, John Wiley, 1996. 201p. (The NSFRE/Wiley Fund Development Series). $29.95. ISBN 0-471-14916-0.

The NSFRE Fund-Raising Dictionary is a comprehensive guide that provides nearly 1,400 definitions exclusively from the fund-raising perspective. The primary reason for developing the reference was to demystify fund-raising so that donors would feel greater trust, and the public would better understand the process. The dictionary is a source of information for those involved in philanthropy: donors, volunteers, staff, administrators, legislators, and the public.

The National Society of Fund Raising Executives (NSFRE) is a professional organization whose 16,000 members work for the causes represented in the not-for-profit sector. In 1976 the group compiled a glossary of fund-raising terms with 355 entries. The glossary was updated in 1986, tripling its size. An NSFRE task force was appointed in 1993 to expand the publication into a dictionary.

Each full listing in the resulting dictionary includes three sections: a headword, the part of speech, and a definition. Cross-references abound. The words chosen encompass the English-speaking world and identify those special to Great Britain, Australia, or South Africa, such as *inland revenue*. Included are terms relating to fund-raising but taken from law (*ademption*), business (*chair*), mailing services (*nixie*), accounting (*endowment*), printing (*bleed*), and the computer world (*Gopher*). Specialized terms from fund-raising (*hanger*, *lybunt*) are also listed.

Looking for a particular definition can be educational, such as finding the precise meaning of *charitable remainder unitrust*. Just browsing can also be entertaining, for one may discover *gazoomph*.

—Jerri Spoehel

Directories

785. **Corporate Foundation Profiles.** 9th ed. Francine Jones, Katie Lewis, and Georgetta Toth, eds. New York, Foundation Center, 1996. 778p. index. $155.00. ISBN 0-87954-653-0.

According to the editors, every effort has been made to include the most current data on the 235 company-sponsored foundations profiled in this book by using "direct information from the foundations, published foundation annual reports, news releases, newspaper and periodical articles, and tax information." However, with a 1996 copyright, the book's information should be used as a guide only unless the user is seeking historical data.

The 1st part of the book features the profiles, which are made up of 2 sections. One provides basic information and the other a grants analysis. Basic information includes address; telephone number; contact; purpose; limitations; support areas; program areas; financial data; officers, governing board, and principal staff; number of staff; sponsoring company; background; policies and application guidelines; and foundation publications. Subject area, recipient type, type of support, population group, geographic distribution, and sample grants are covered in the second section. In part 2 the foundations are listed first in descending order by total annual giving, with additional information provided. They are then listed in alphabetic order with the same information as found in the first listing. Five indexes that provide access to the profiles conclude the work.—**Jo Anne H. Ricca**

786. **Directory of Operating Grants: A Reference Directory Identifying General Operating Grants Available to Nonprofit Organizations.** 3d ed. Loxahatchee, Fla., Research Grant Guides, 1997. 144p. index. $59.50pa. ISBN 0-945078-16-1. ISSN 1071-6726.

This book is intended to advise officials at nonprofit organizations on how to maximize their chances of obtaining general operating grants. Such grants come with fewer restrictions than do project and restricted core support grants, and thus they are highly coveted. The directory consists mostly of lists and contains little continuous text. The core of the book, occupying almost 75 percent of its pages, is a list (in alphabetic order by state) of 672 foundations that make grants for general operating costs. The volume also contains much shorter lists of all 672 foundations, in alphabetic order. The areas for which each foundation makes grants—cultural organizations, higher education, hospitals, and libraries that stock materials about foundations distributed by the Foundation Center—are treated as well. The continuous text material consists mostly of three brief essays on how to apply for a general operating grant.

This book can serve as a useful starting point for those seeking such a foundation grant. It could be more helpful than it is now, however, if the compilers of future editions did the following: included not only each foundation's telephone number, but also its fax number and e-mail address; included more and longer essays on how to obtain a grant; and set most of its lists in a larger typeface.—**David S. Webster**

787. **The Foundation Directory 1997.** 19th ed. Compiled by the Foundation Center. Michael N. Tuller and Gina Marie Cantarella, eds. New York, Foundation Center, 1997. 2173p. index. $190.00pa. ISBN 0-87954-706-5. ISSN 0071-8092.

This standard reference book has been around since 1960, and each year it grows in the number of entries. The 1997 edition contains 7,960 entries, a gain of 780 foundations from the previous edition. For inclusion in *The Foundation Directory*, a foundation must meet the criteria of at least $2 million in assets or $200,000 in annual giving. The Foundation Center staff identifies organizations for inclusion in the directory by monitoring IRS information, journal and newspaper articles, and foundation publications such as annual reports and news releases. After the entries are prepared, they are sent to the foundation for verification. There is an extensive introduction provided to inform and guide the grant-seeker.

For each foundation, the entry provides the street address, the name of the contact person, when it was established, the areas of giving, types of grants and support, geographic and subject area limitations, application information, number of staff members, financial information or assets, total expenditure figures, and amount and number of grants paid. When provided by the foundation, there is a selected list of grants reported for the previous fiscal year. There are seven indexes: geographic; types of support; a list of donors, officers, and trustees; international giving; subject; a list of foundations new to the edition; and a name index to identify potential funding sources. This directory is an essential reference tool that should be in all public and academic libraries.—**Sue Brown**

788. **The Foundation Directory Supplement.** 1997 ed. Michael N. Tuller and Amy Horowitz, eds. New York, Foundation Center, 1997. 718p. index. $135.00pa. ISBN 0-87954-720-0.

The Foundation Directory (see entry 787) and *The Foundation Directory Supplement* are the standard reference sources for information on the nation's 12,823 largest foundations. Six months after *The Foundation Directory* (parts 1 and 2) are published, the *Supplement* updates this information. It provides complete, revised entries for foundations that have reported substantial changes in personnel, names, addresses, program interests, limitations, application procedures, or other areas by the midpoint of the yearly directory cycle. Libraries that have the parent works will want to consider whether or not patron use warrants its purchase.—**Bohdan S. Wynar**

789. **Guide to U.S. Foundations, Their Trustees, Officers, and Donors.** 1997 ed. Compiled by the Foundation Center. Elizabeth H. Rich and Joan Seabourne, eds. New York, Foundation Center, 1997. 2v. index. $225.00pa./set. ISBN 0-87954-707-3.

Foundations are big business, with assets that total more than $226 billion. The 1997 *Guide to U.S. Foundations* is an enormous compilation of information about these foundations. The 1st of the 2 volumes includes 3,436 pages with 40,379 entries, 27,500 of which are not covered in any other reference source. The 2d volume has 1,302 pages, with an alphabetic guide to all foundations in volume 1, as well as an index of trustees, officers, and donors. Together, the volumes are 4 inches thick and weigh more than 11 pounds.

An entry generally includes the foundation's legal name; contact person; address; establishment data; donors; accounting period; financial data (grants paid, assets, expenditures); application information; limitations on giving (especially geographic); and available printed material. Listings are alphabetic by state, in descending order by total grants paid. More information ranges from a bibliography of state and local foundation directories to sophisticated analyses of fiscal data. An appendix has 1,244 foundations no longer qualifying and others that award grants only to specified beneficiaries.

The guide is designed so that grant-seekers can easily do preliminary research on funding sources. It gives excellent basic descriptions of the nation's largest foundations as well as small, local funders and newly established grant-makers. Help includes suggestions for research methods. The most important information is under "Limitations": The strongest admonition is "if you don't qualify, don't apply."—**Jerri Spoehel**

790. **National Directory of Corporate Giving.** 5th ed. Jeffrey A. Falkenstein, ed. New York, Foundation Center, 1997. 1224p. index. $225.00. ISBN 0-87954-722-7.

An important reference work for grant-seekers, this edition profiles 2,532 companies whose giving history has been "verified by the corporations themselves or compiled from reliable public records." These criteria, while limiting comprehensiveness of the subject, ensure the most up-to-date information available at the time of publication. The alphabetically arranged entries have a descriptive overview of a company and a description of the type or types of giving programs—direct giving, private foundation, or both. Each program is a full entry within itself. A main entry can have up to 68 elements, depending on the size of the company's giving program and the availability of substantiated information. Seven indexes that provide access from a variety of means (e.g., geographic information, types of business) conclude the directory.—**Jo Anne H. Ricca**

Handbooks and Yearbooks

791. Clough, Leonard G., David G. Clough, Ellen G. Estes, and Ednalou C. Ballard. **Practical Guide to Planned Giving 1998.** Detroit, Taft Group/Gale, 1997. 930p. index. $130.00pa. ISBN 1-5699-5054-7. ISSN 1053-0436.

Practical Guide to Planned Giving 1998 is a guide to all aspects of planned giving written in lay terms; it is really for the noninitiated and beginning professional. The guide is a handy compendium for the multitasked nonprofit organizational leader who has to take on fund-raising responsibilities. Written by a certified financial planner and a registered investment adviser, among others, this guide would be essential to most organizations' advancement.

The 1st section establishes how to start a successful planned giving program, with details on defining planned giving for an organization; setting up a structure, philosophy, and mission; definitions and descriptions of the various aspects of planned gifts; asking for the first gift; and marketing a planned giving program. The 2d section has several how-to essays on managing a planned giving program, including methodology, marketing, evaluation, and how to manage when planned giving is one of the other responsibilities of the leader. Section 3 provides a simplified explanation of the federal tax aspects of planned giving. This may be too simplified; therefore, the reader should be careful before advising clients based solely on the handbook. The 4th section has chapters on the roles of financial planners, insurance professionals, attorneys, and accountants in a planned giving team. The appendixes include a glossary of planned giving terms, tax forms, educational resources, ethics, and IRS forms and publications.

Practical Guide to Planned Giving 1998 contains numerous case studies, checklists, and sample documents that can be used as guidelines. The true beginner planned giving professional will find wisdom in the hypothetical case study that illustrates exactly how a planned giving team of professionals solicits and secures a planned gift.—**Gerald D. Moran**

792. **Guide to Federal Funding for Governments & Nonprofits, 1997.** 19th ed. Elizabeth A. Bernhard, Jody Feder, and Alvin C. Lin, eds. Arlington, Va., Government Information Services, 1997. 2v. index. $389.95/yr. looseleaf w/binder. ISBN 0-933544-91-X.

This immense set, weighing more than 12 pounds, provides information about more than 550 federal grant programs that give money to one or more of these groups: community nonprofit organizations, local governments, and state governments. The heart of the work is the descriptions of each funding program, most of them from one to five pages in length. These descriptions include, in addition to other information, who is eligible for the grant, how to apply, criteria for selecting grant-winners, and the amount of money Congress has appropriated to the program. A particularly helpful feature is a rating system that shows whether it is easy or difficult to be funded by the various programs.

According to promotional material the publisher makes available to reviewers, this set has several advantages over other books that cover the same territory. For example, instead of being based on the U.S. government's *Catalog of Federal Domestic Assistance* (CFDA), this title is based on original research. Also, it covers programs that are found in no other reference book on the same topic. Finally, the set is published more promptly than CFDA and similar books.—**David S. Webster**

793. Meiners, Phyllis A., and Hilary Henri Tun-Atz. **Corporate and Foundation Fundraising Manual for Native Americans.** 3d ed. Kansas City, Mo., CRC Publishing, 1996. 294p. $129.95 spiralbound. ISBN 0-9633694-6-6.

Although this work is written with Native Americans in Mind, this *Corporate and Foundation Fundraising Manual* is an excellent resource for everyone. Non-Native Americans can easily overlook the comments on tribal government or funding for Native American programs. The spiral binding allows access to all material, and tabs list areas from the table of contents. Excellent advice is given on incorporation and by-laws, with plenty of examples. Helpful, too, are suggestions for the establishment of priorities, including what is too much money to be raised and how to prepare a wish list.

One popular section is sure to be "Public Relations," which lists "114 PR possibilities for under $114," along with a checklist for materials with the admonition "Don't look too expensive." Instructions on preparing a prospectus give a complete overview, even suggesting that it not be on white paper.

Guidance on seeking future donors tells where to look, free information centers (listed by state), and even Internet sites. Counsel includes how many prospects to identify at each stage and what to include in a prospect profile. Directions on asking for money have tips on writing request letters, conducting prospect interviews, methods of rehearsal, and the contents of a presentation packet. A final reminder is that follow-up is as important as preparation. Even the upgrading of skills is considered: memberships in professional organizations, attending conferences and seminars, and seeking evaluation services.

The manual is complete, well organized, and practical. All that remains for success is to follow its instructions. [R: Choice, Oct 97, p. 266]—**Jerri Spoehel**

794. Renz, Loren, Crystal Mandler, and Trinh C. Tran. **Foundation Giving: Yearbook of Facts and Figures on Private, Corporate, and Community Foundations.** 1997 ed. New York, Foundation Center, 1997. 133p. index. $24.95pa. ISBN 0-87954-719-7.

Foundation Giving analyzes and interprets in one slim volume all the data collected by the Foundation Center on 40,140 active grant-making foundations. The statistics here are from 1995. The yearbook's purpose is fourfold: (1) to measure the dimensions of U.S. grant-making foundations by number, assets, grants, and gifts received and thus document their capacity for supporting the nonprofit sector; (2) to monitor new foundation formation; (3) to track growth and spot changes in the largest foundations; and (4) to analyze grant distribution patterns and report changes in giving trends.

The excellent written text is augmented by 81 tables and 39 figures. The headings are rather like headlines, giving a summary of the information to come. Useful tables or pie charts show funding amounts given to education, health, human services, the arts, culture and humanities, the performing arts, museums, the environment, animals and wildlife, science, social science, development, international affairs, and peace. Special information is given on grants of $20 million or more; the giving trends of the 100 largest foundations; and the giving trends of independent, corporate, and community foundations. Although foundations represent only 12.4 percent of all private giving, the grants they make total $17.84 billion, so they are certainly an important part of national philanthropy.—**Jerri Spoehel**

795. **Volunteer America: A Comprehensive National Guide to Opportunities for Service, Training, and Work Experience.** 4th ed. Harriet Clyde Kipps, ed. Chicago, J. G. Ferguson Publishing, 1997. 656p. index. $89.95. ISBN 0-89434-169-3.

Volunteer America is a directory guide to volunteer organizations and training programs. Previous editions were titled *Community Resource Tie Line* (1st ed.); *Community Resources Directory* (2d ed.; see ARBA 85, entry 706); and *Volunteerism* (3d ed.; see ARBA 92, entry 829). The present work begins with directory listings and information on volunteer centers (centers that help match up volunteers to organizations who need them), an explanation of rights and responsibilities in volunteer relationships, and a discussion on the diversity of roles for the volunteer.

The next section is a list of volunteer organizations. It is divided into two large segments: "Administrative/Organizational Resources" and "Programs," each containing several subject subdivisions. The entries are listed alphabetically under each subdivision and include directory information, a description of the program's objectives, and an overview of its scope and history. The final section lists training programs for volunteers. Entries are listed alphabetically under each state and contain directory information, credit for event, program description, and publications offered through the event. Organizational and geographic indexes further assist in locating information.

This volume stands alone in its attempt to cover volunteer organizations nationwide. The first 2 sections are helpful in getting an overview of volunteering opportunities and training courses that are available, but are not thorough enough to be of help to many prospective volunteers. The 1st section, however, would help individuals find a volunteer center that could assist them in finding the right organization. *Volunteer America* is recommended for large public libraries and organizations assisting in volunteer efforts.—**Laura K. Blessing**

SEX STUDIES

796. **The Black Book.** 4th ed. Bill Brent and Steve Omlid, eds. San Francisco, Calif., Black Books, 1996. 187p. illus. index. $15.00pa. ISBN 0-9637401-3-X.

This compact and valuable resource guide is a problematic library purchase because its subject matter is on the outré edges of sexual expression and activity. The routine category listings are here, from mail order catalogs to computer bulletin board services and from bookstores to equipment vendors, but the subject matter is far outside the realm of what most librarians and library users would define as tasteful (if not legal).

Entries are arranged A to Z by corporate name. There are indexes by topic (clubs and organizations, services); by service category (archives/libraries, travel agencies); and by geographic location (United States, Canada, Australia, Brazil). Descriptive blurbs accompany each directory listing, which give mailing address; telephone number; e-mail address; intended audience (e.g., gay men); hours of operation; and types of payment accepted. Incomplete information is given for many of the entries. The directory listings are interspersed with vendor advertisements, the text and graphics of which will offend almost everyone.

Why include this small paperback in *American Reference Books Annual*? This reviewer, admittedly not an expert on the matter, knows of no other monographic source for this kind of information. The listings appear to be current and are presented in a usable format. *The Black Book* is recommended for sex studies collections and adventurous general collections.—**Ed Volz**

797. **The International Encyclopedia of Sexuality.** Robert T. Francoeur, ed. New York, Continuum Publishing, 1997. 3v. maps. index. $255.00/set. ISBN 0-8264-0841-9.

Comprehensive without being exhaustive, this 3-volume set presents the reader with unique and valuable information regarding the status, patterns, and trends in the sexual behaviors and attitudes of 32 countries. Each study is written by a scholar or team of scholars familiar with the country and its culture. Credentialed in their disciplines, most of the contributors are psychologists and physicians, with many sociologists and anthropologists making contributions as well. Most contributors also have membership in the Society for the Scientific Study of Sexuality or the World Association of Sexology.

Essays vary in length and are arranged alphabetically by country. The basic structure of treatment is maintained throughout, allowing for greater ease of comparison. For each country, basic demographics and a historical perspective are presented, followed by these major divisions: "Basic Sexological Premises," including a discussion of the character of gender roles, the sociological status of males and females, and the general concepts of sexuality and love; "Religious and Ethnic Factors," treating the sources and character of religious values and the character of ethnic values; "Sexuality Knowledge and Education," discussing government and other formal and informal sources of knowledge; "Autoerotic Behaviors and Patterns," examining differences between children/adolescent and adult populations; "Interpersonal Heterosexual Behaviors," with subtreatments by age groups and behaviors; "Homoerotic, Homosexual and Ambisexual Behaviors"; "Gender Conflicted Persons"; "Significant Unconventional Sexual Behaviors," including coercive sex, child sexual abuse, incest, pedophilia, sexual harassment, rape, prostitution, pornography and erotica, and paraphilias; "Contraception, Abortion, and Population Planning"; "Sexually Transmitted Diseases"; "HIV/AIDS"; "Sexual Dysfunctions, Counseling, and Therapies"; "Research and Advanced Education," indicating graduate programs and other sexological research initiatives, organizations, and publications; "Aboriginals, Important Ethnic, Racial, and/or Religious Minorities"; and a concluding list of reference and suggested reading. Supplementing the 32 essays are a list of contributors, acknowledgments, maps of coverage locations, a directory of sexuality organizations, and a "Comparison-Facilitating Index."

Coverage and depth of treatment varies by country, in large part due to the nature of available information regarding the populations and cultures. Some chapters rely heavily on statistics, whereas others read more like a sociological travel guide. However, there is no other single source of compiled information to rival this encyclopedia. Information presented here will need to be supplemented by journal literature and other current sources. The work is most likely to be used by students and other researchers investigating a particular aspect of sexuality, either within a country or from a cross-cultural perspective. For this purpose, the set provides a sound base of knowledge and discussion of its subject. It is recommended for addition to academic and large public library reference collections. [R: LJ, 15 June 97, p. 62]

—**Edmund F. SantaVicca**

798. Walker, Bonnie L., comp. **Sexuality and the Elderly: A Research Guide.** Westport, Conn., Greenwood Press, 1997. 301p. index. (Bibliographies and Indexes in Gerontology, no.35). $75.00. ISBN 0-313-30133-6.

This work, consisting of 457 entries that include books, book chapters, and articles, is part of an annotated bibliography series. The purpose of the series is to provide comprehensive reviews and references for the work done in the various fields of gerontology and to provide caregivers with important information regarding the elderly. Empirical studies were given the first priority for inclusion in this bibliography; however, popular titles, such as *The Joy of Sex*, were also included because they influence the way society thinks about sexuality. The book is divided into 18 chapters that explore every aspect of the topic, from sexual behavior of the elderly and AIDS and the elderly to caregiver attitudes about sexuality. Each chapter has an introduction, and each citation is annotated.

Because of the thoroughness of this work, the compiler feels that researchers can check it first and be assured that they are not duplicating past research efforts. The information begins in 1971 and goes forward to 1996. The guide is most useful for a historical review of the literature and the annotations. Computer indexes may not go back as far as this and do not always provide annotations. The books listed here may now be out of print and could be overlooked if many sources were not searched. The work fulfills its purpose in presenting an overview of some of the major literature written to date on this topic and would be an important acquisition for institutions and libraries where research is done on the elderly.

Although the work fulfills its purpose as the first source to check when beginning research, the serious scholar must continue to search computer databases for the burgeoning amounts of new information that increasingly may be annotated and available in full text. Dissertations and theses have not been included here, and *Dissertation Abstracts* and other sources must also be searched for these. The researcher's job is never done, an; researchers will need to use this information and expand upon it.

—Marilyn Strong Noronha

SOCIAL WELFARE AND SOCIAL WORK

799. Hombs, Mary Ellen. **Welfare Reform: A Reference Handbook.** Santa Barbara, Calif., ABC-CLIO, 1996. 165p. index. (Contemporary World Issues). $39.50. ISBN 0-87436-844-8.

Welfare reform is not a new issue, but it has been newly politicized in the current congressional climate. The political debate rages over such issues as the causes and consequences of welfare, the most efficient source and methods of control of welfare programs, and the form such programs should take. This handbook provides information on the history of welfare, on the current debate, and on sources of information for delving further into the topic.

The volume is divided into 9 chapters covering various aspects of the subject or different types of resources. Chapter 1 provides a brief history of welfare as well as an overview of recent policy positions, legislation, and related survey and statistical data. It also defines welfare and includes a statistical profile of welfare recipients. Chapter 2 is a chronology of key historical events related to welfare programs, from 1932 through August 1996. Chapter 3 provides brief biographies of 14 key individuals, past and present, in the history of welfare. Chapter 4 presents facts and statistics on welfare programs, with most of the data drawn from government sources. Included are facts on poverty, Aid to Families with Dependent Children, the JOBS Training Program, Supplemental Security Income, food stamps, and more. Chapter 5 includes excerpts of current and historical documents and speeches dealing with welfare; these are taken from government and nongovernment sources, and they span the political spectrum. Chapter 6 provides an overview of the 1996 welfare reform bill that was signed by President Clinton. Chapters 7, 8, and 9 are annotated guides to organizations, print sources of information, and nonprint sources of information, respectively. The nonprint sources include World Wide Web addresses for relevant government agencies, political parties, and Congress. A glossary of key terms is also included, as is a subject/name index.

The clear writing and concise overview of the topic make this handbook an excellent starting point for those beginning to research welfare reform. Furthermore, the book features a variety of political positions, thus allowing the reader to gain more insight into the ideological aspects of the policy debates. Public, school, and academic libraries should find this volume a valuable addition to their reference collections.

—Stephen H. Aby

800. Metz, Allan, comp. **National Service and AmeriCorps: An Annotated Bibliography.** Westport, Conn., Greenwood Press, 1997. 269p. index. (Bibliographies and Indexes in Law and Political Science, no.26). $69.50. ISBN 0-313-30267-7.

President Clinton's brainchild, the AmeriCorps program was passed into law in 1993. This bibliography cites 1,300 sources on AmeriCorps and national service in general, covering the 1960s through 1995. Included are books, dissertations, government documents, and journal and newspaper articles. Useful Internet sites are listed separately at the end. Except for newspaper articles, each entry has a nice, sometimes lengthy, abstract, allowing the bibliography to serve as a source in itself. Author and subject indexes refer to entry numbers. Some background on AmeriCorps and national service would have been welcome in the book's introduction. That omission aside, the bibliography is a thorough, handy guide to its subject.—**Cathy Seitz Whitaker**

801. **Refugees in America in the 1990s: A Reference Handbook.** David W. Haines, ed. Westport, Conn., Greenwood Press, 1996. 467p. index. $79.50. ISBN 0-313-29344-9.

U.S. refugee and immigration policies are, historically, an intriguing mix of politics, ideology, and world events. This edited collection brings together essays that deal with refugee policy from a variety of analytic perspectives, including historical research, comparative research, and case studies. The chapters are organized into 3 parts. Part 1 includes 2 chapters detailing the history of and patterns in refugee settlement in the United States. Part 2 is composed of 12 chapters that are case studies of refugees from particular countries or regions, including Afghans, Chinese from Southeast Asia, Cubans, Eastern Europeans, Ethiopians and Eritreans, Haitians, Hmong, Iranians, Khmer, Laotians, Soviet Jews, and Vietnamese. Although the political events that precipitated these refugee movements are often fairly recent, these case studies nonetheless provide the necessary historical context to fully appreciate the more recent developments. In addition, coverage of these refugee movements typically extends well into the 1990s. Part 3 consists of chapters primarily addressing comparative aspects of refugee movements, including public and political opinion, the global refugee problem, resettlement patterns in the United States, documentary films about refugees, and an annotated bibliography of the literature.

This is an excellent and instructive volume, dealing as it does with critical and timely policy issues. The historical analyses provide needed balance to and perspective on what can be a heated subject. Furthermore, the case studies address the most well-known refugee populations of recent decades. Finally, as an added bonus, the essays are written in a straightforward manner and therefore suitable for a wide range of audiences. This handbook is recommended for large public and academic libraries.—**Stephen H. Aby**

YOUTH AND CHILD DEVELOPMENT

802. Fenwick, Elizabeth, and Tony Smith. **Adolescence: The Survival Guide for Parents and Teenagers.** New York, DK Publishing, 1996. 286p. illus. index. $14.95pa. ISBN 0-7894-0635-7.

Attempting to write a "survival guide" designed for use by both parents and teenagers is an ambitious goal, yet this work has potential for helping many parents and adolescents find their way through the teen years. Several features help set this book apart from others with a similar goal. The authors obtained input from adolescents; the results of a questionnaire sent to 100 high school students helped determine the content of this book. As a result, the volume deals with such concerns as "The Milestones of Adolescence" (including physical development); "Learning to Live Together" (talking to teenagers, rebellion, the quest for freedom); "The Adolescent and the Outside World" (friends, social life, sexuality, sexual abuse, school, money matters, facing up to adulthood); and "The Adolescent in Trouble" (drugs, running away, emotional problems). Another advantage is that within each chapter is a section designed for parents as well as a separate section for adolescents, very obvious because it is printed in blue. Real-life case studies are presented that give both the parent's and the youth's viewpoint. Through these case studies, the authors help the reader to see a situation from the other person's perspective.

Both adult and teen readers may browse through this book at the library or even check it out. Although it may not necessarily serve as a focal point for discussion among members of the same family, its strength may be that it helps teen readers to see common situations through their parents' eyes (even if the parent has not read the book), and thus helps the teen communicate with parents. It also gives teens—especially those who are uncomfortable with discussing certain situations—practical suggestions as to where they can get information, help, or advice beyond the family. In other families, it may be only the adult who receives insight and guidance. Ideally, several members of the family will read the guide and use it as a jumping-off point to solve problems jointly. This book may be especially useful in larger group discussions where both parents and teens are willing to open up communication avenues.

This book has reference value because of the index and because the independent—yet integrated—nature of the chapters allows readers to consult just those pages that would be most useful at a given time. A cautionary note for librarians: Not all parents will want their adolescents to have access to the frank discussions of some issues, especially those dealing with sexuality. On the whole, this is a well-intentioned and well-designed reference that most libraries serving adolescents and their families will want to have in their collection.—**Jan Bakker**

803. Franck, Irene, and David Brownstone. **Parenting A to Z.** 2d ed. New York, HarperCollins, 1996. 728p. index. $32.50. ISBN 0-06-271598-4.

The subtitle of this book is indicative of the authors' stated goals—providing a guide to parents concerning everything about children from conception to college. Franck and Brownstone arranged the material alphabetically to enable parents to quickly and easily find their intended subject matter. Although this format should make the book simple and easy to use, such is not always the case. A parent trying to find trisomy 21 disorder would not find it in the index and would have to know that the disorder is a form of mental retardation. The index is not nearly as well cross-referenced as it should be for a text of this type. This volume also suffers from offering too little about too much. It could be likened to a tapas bar—little tidbits of information about a great deal of subject matter without significant substantive content. However, the authors do provide a fairly extensive list of groups—governmental, professional, and self-help—that would be a useful source of detailed information for those parents requiring it.

At the conclusion of the text is a special component on parenting resources. Included in this section is information about exercises during pregnancy, a chart of normal child development, a list of organizations offering general information about parenting, information about choosing a school, child abuse and neglect, children with special needs, and resources about substance abuse. Additionally, many fine charts and diagrams with simple-to-follow instructions have been included. *Parenting A to Z* can be recommended as a general reference on child care for parents.—**Celia J. Wintz**

17 Statistics, Demography, and Urban Studies

DEMOGRAPHY

804. **Demographic Yearbook, 1995. Annuaire Demographique.** 47th ed. By the Department for Economic and Social Information and Policy Analysis, Statistics Division. New York, United Nations, 1997. 1087p. index. $125.00. ISBN 92-1-051086-0. S/N E/F.97.XIII.1.

The *Demographic Yearbook, 1995* is a welcome addition to the statistical data and information provided by the United Nations. This work focuses on households and family characteristics for approximately 233 countries or areas throughout the world. For demographic purposes, 1995 is used as a baseline year for common reference. This work is basically in 2 parts. The 1st includes tables that provide a world summary of basic demographic statistics, followed by data on the size, distribution, and population trends in such topics as infant and maternal mortality, general mortality, marital status, and divorce. The 2d part updates the household and family characteristics featured in the 1987 issue.

An important aspect of this work is its attempt to be comprehensive and to cumulate pertinent statistical data on different countries and parts of the world, thereby enabling the serious researcher and informed layperson to access this material. Moreover, the United Nations Statistics Division has devoted considerable time and energy to validate data used and the integrity of information provided in these compilations. Although many statistical abstracts that provide a population snapshot for different countries or major regions of the world are available, this work builds on and continues to update previous cumulations, assisting the user to identify and monitor international trends in population. For those who prefer a more rapid form of access to these data, magnetic tape is available at a cost of $320. At the moment, a database accessible by a system that runs on an IBM-compatible microcomputer is under development. Users wanting to conduct their own research can do so by obtaining the database on diskette. The establishment of a computer access system to the United Nations's demographic databases will be an important improvement in doing research and study on worldwide population characteristics and trends. This work is recommended for purchase by large public libraries, specialized libraries that require reliable demographic data and statistical information, and most four-year colleges and universities.—**Roberto P. Haro**

805. **Handbook of Population and Housing Censuses. Part IV: Economic Activity Status.** By the Department for International Economic and Social Information and Policy Analysis, Statistics Division. New York, United Nations, 1996. 98p. (Studies in Methods, Series F, no.54 [pt.4]). $25.00pa. ISBN 92-1-161387-6. S/N E.96.XVII.13.

This is a publication by the United Nations and forms part 4 of its series, Handbook of Population and Housing Censuses. It is a relatively thin volume treating, as its subtitle explains, the status of the economic activity of member nations and their major colonies and possessions. The book is divided nearly equally between tables showing the results of censuses of each of 216 lands and explanatory notes and references.

Although the book was published in 1996, there appear to be no census data later than 1984. The census data themselves are not provided, only the kinds of information sought. Thus, the report has a limited potential readership. Sociologists and economists interested in comparative or international studies may find the book useful, but not much is here for other readers.—**Arthur R. Upgren**

806. **Key Indicators of County Growth 1970-2025.** 1996 ed. Washington, D.C., NPA Data Services, 1996. 1v. (various paging). maps. $195.00 spiralbound. ISBN 0-936555-30-0.

As an overview of economic and demographic trends for U.S. counties, this edition follows the format and content of the previous one (see ARBA 89, entry 166). Historical and projected data for 12 key indicators of population, income, and employment are offered for 8 years (since 1970), with 11 county maps. The data report 1995 figures, with projections to 2025 and three annual growth rates. Data collection methods and analysis techniques explained in the previous edition are unspecified here.

Organized in 3 parts, 2 brief chapters summarize economic and demographic characteristics (e.g., jobs, average earnings) and growth trends (e.g., household income). Part 2, the main part of the volume, consists of 1 table for each county or unit. There are no table headings, leaving users to refer to the technical information (chapter 1) to determine which figures are dollars.

Intended for use in both short- and long-term analyses, the disk version of this title is capable of more extensive comparisons. With the trend toward electronic statistical products from U.S. agencies, the value-added nature of this work is less obvious. The publisher has missed an opportunity to craft a separate analysis for each state, adopt the newer technologies, and add comparative data. Larger libraries now have these data in alternate formats, and patrons, most notably students, crave more detailed analyses.
—**Sandra E. Belanger**

807. **The Penguin Atlas of Diasporas.** By Gerard Chaliand and Jean-Pierre Rageau. New York, Penguin Books, 1997. 182p. illus. maps. $22.95pa. ISBN 0-14-017814-7.

This book begins with a brief explanation of the key characteristics of a diaspora, followed by maps and narrative for 12 cultural dispersions. The maps show the historical movement of each displaced people. Tables illustrate the population effect on the receiving countries during the course of the expulsion.

The authors take a broad definition of diaspora and acknowledge in their introductory essay that they expect to be challenged on their selections. Indeed, one does question putting a migration for economic benefit on the same par as an expulsion by brute force, such as those experienced by the Jews, the Gypsies, or the Armenians.

The book focuses primarily on the Jewish Diaspora, and the remaining 11 dispersions are only superficially discussed. For example, the Korean and Vietnamese movements are grouped together in two pages of text with one map. Cataclysmic events are dispassionately sketched with barely a hint of the suffering underlying the cold statistics shown on the maps and population tables. More depth would make this general reference more useful.—**Adrienne Antink Bendel**

808. Wright, Russell O. **A Twentieth-Century History of United States Population.** Lanham, Md., Scarecrow, 1996. 203p. $44.00. ISBN 0-8108-3182-1.

This small book is appropriate titled, as it presents the populations of the states and some major cities for each census between 1900 and 1990, with estimates for the year 2000 and projections for the year 2050. Along with data for each state, the District of Columbia, and 24 large cities comes a brief analysis of the history and factors influencing population change. Considerable discussion is given for regions of the United States (Northeast, Central, West, and South) and in particular for the Sunbelt as such (comprising most of the South and some of the West). Even though the projections were compiled only a year or two ago, discrepancies begin to surface; it is inevitable that some predictions become quickly out of date. The emphasis on Sunbelt growth may need toning down, as Massachusetts has resumed a healthy growth and some western states show signs of slowing down. Predictions for the year 2050 may already be too optimistic for many places. Population figures for the cities are next to useless for most purposes, because they are for the core city only. Thus, Jacksonville's annexation of many suburbs in the 1960s leads to a problem when comparing it to large-area cities (Dallas, Los Angeles) or small ones (Boston, San Francisco). Such demographics would be improved by considering metropolitan area, not now available on a uniform system. Nonetheless, this compact volume makes a valuable reference for its subject for any level of readership.—**Arthur R. Upgren**

STATISTICS

General Works

809. **Encyclopedia of Statistical Sciences: Update Volume 1.** Samuel Kotz and others, eds. New York, John Wiley, 1997. 568p. illus. index. (A Wiley-Interscience Publication). $195.00. ISBN 0-471-11836-2.

Despite some protesting to the contrary, the purpose of this new *Encyclopedia of Statistical Sciences*'s first supplemental volume is to add to the statistical sophistication of the encyclopedia as a whole. For example, in the area of total quality control, the untimely passing of William Edwards Deming on December 20, 1993, permits that entry in the volume to dwell on Deming's contributions to Japan's postwar production goals and his connections with the graduate school of the U.S. Department of Agriculture, Washington, D. C.

The areas of emphasis include such topics as computer-intensive statistical methodologies, genetics, medicine, and the environment. Another breakdown is: statistics, biostatistics, quality control, economics, sociology, engineering, probability theory, computer science, biomedicine, and psychology.

—**Eugene B. Jackson**

810. **Numbers: How Many, How Far, How Long, How Much.** Andrea Sutcliffe, ed. New York, HarperPerennial/HarperCollins, 1996. 630p. maps. index. (A Stonesong Press Book). $20.00pa. ISBN 0-06-273362-1.

This volume is yet another one of those handy books that gets shelved next to *The New York Public Library Desk Reference* (2d ed.; see ARBA 95, entry 80) and other vade mecums. The focus of the book at hand is numbers and general numerical data, so it differs from the more general desk references, but there is some overlap. The scope is more general and inclusive than other numerical resources, such as *The Economist Desk Companion* (Henry Holt, 1994). *Numbers* is arranged by topic into 11 chapters—money, time, universe, travel, weather, and daily life, to name a few. Often the editor provides brief explanations of the numbers. Each category has a significant set of oddities, such as how to find out a cholesterol ratio, prime numbers, monthly mortgage tables, caffeine content, everyday math, explanation of the Universal Product Code, conversions, how long foods will keep if the power fails, thickness of mulch needed to control weeds, relative sizes of the planets, a 15 percent tipping table, standard tipping practices in restaurants by country (39 countries are listed), and 9 ways numbers can lie. A detailed table of contents and a sufficient index make the data in this book easily accessible.

Much of the information in this eclectic compilation has been gleaned from a variety of standard government documents, but some is cited as coming from specific trade associations. Not all items listed mention the originating source. A brief list of recommended resources mentions standard almanacs and statistical works. This volume is the type of reference that would need to be updated every few years, because some of the information, such as area codes and population figures, are already outdated. If anything, *Numbers* is fun to browse and, for those who can afford the reasonable price, worth the convenience for public or personal libraries.—**Christine Drew**

International

811. **Asia-Pacific in Figures.** 10th ed. By the Economic and Social Commission for Asia and the Pacific. New York, United Nations, 1997. 56p. $10.00pa. ISBN 92-1-119732-5. ISSN 1014-3750. S/N E.96.II.F.38.

This compact publication, like its predecessors, provides essential statistical data on the social and economic aspects of the countries in this region from 1980 to 1996. In all, 56 countries or areas are covered. The volume includes some of the major countries, such as China, India, Japan, and Russia, as well as some less recognizable countries or areas, such as Kiribati, Nauru, and Tuvalu.

The major topics included are statistics on population, social aspects, employment, energy, national accounts, external trade, central government expenditure by function, finance, production, prices, land use, transportation, and tourism. Each of these subjects is further divided into several categories. For example, under population statistics, one can find statistics on total population, age distribution, rural residence, annual crude rates of live births and deaths, rate of increase, and density. The statistics, for the most part, come from governmental official publications and the United Nations. In many cases, no statistics are provided for some categories (e.g., central government expenditure by function) because of secrecy or nonexistence.

The information provided seems to be consistent with the information found in other sources, such as *Statistical Indicators for Asia and the Pacific* (United Nations, 1997), *Statistical Yearbook for Asia and the Pacific* (see entry 815), and others, which are more comprehensive. However, as with many other statistical sources that rely on governmental official statistics, users should use this work with caution because some of the statistics provided by governments are not always reliable.

Political science and international business students will find *Asia-Pacific in Figures* useful. Large public and college libraries should purchase this work.—**Binh P. Le**

812. Kurian, George Thomas. **Global Data Locator.** Lanham, Md., Bernan Associates, 1997. 375p. index. $89.00. ISBN 0-89059-039-7.

This volume is a guide to sources of statistical information on a worldwide or regional level—as opposed to a national or subnational level—and, with 240 titles, is an updated and slightly expanded version of the *Sourcebook of Global Statistics* (New York: Facts on File, 1987). It provides annotated and descriptive reviews as well as tables of contents of the source materials. The sources covered are those published in English, which are available from both official and commercial organizations.

The 1st part of this volume deals with printed statistics and includes both serials and monographs. Certain types of publications that reprint statistics from primary sources are excluded, and as a result, such titles as *World Almanac* and *Europa Yearbook* are not listed. The 2d part of this publication, which has been added since the earlier edition, deals with electronic databases. This section lists sources available via batch access products, CD-ROMs, diskettes, magnetic tapes, and online access. Entries include bibliographic information, purpose and scope, data organization, methodology (where or how the data are collected), and contents.

Unlike the 1st edition, the entries are now arranged by subject to make it easier for users to locate publications if they know the topic they want. Examples of the topics included are agriculture in Asia, cocoa, external debt, energy, motor vehicles, and population. A title index is included, and three appendixes are attached, including a directory of publishers, the international statistical system and the international statistical series, and a list of publications by publisher.

Reference librarians and researchers looking for appropriate places to find needed statistical information at the global or regional level ought to find this book useful and quite a time-saver.
—**Paul H. Thomas**

813. Kurian, George Thomas. **The Illustrated Book of World Rankings.** rev. ed. Armonk, N.Y., Sharpe Reference/M. E. Sharpe, 1997. 403p. index. $99.00. ISBN 1-56324-892-1.

This book provides comparative rankings for up to 190 nations on 300 performance measures. The tables are arranged by 25 categories ranging from geography, population, and agriculture to military power, communications, and more. A short explanation is given before each entry to define the variable and to explain its relevancy. In many cases, pie charts and bar graphs are used to visually portray differences. The origin of the data is cited for each table. In addition to the United Nations and World Bank data, material is pulled from other sources, such as the *Demographic Yearbook* (see entry 804), the *World Factbook* (Claitor's Publishing, 1997), INTERPOL, and such lesser-known agencies as Transparency International. An extensive list of organizations collecting global statistics is provided as an appendix. Unfortunately, addresses are not included. This is the 4th revision of this reference, and it gives primarily 1994-1995 data. For statistics more difficult to collect, older data may be provided from the early 1990s.

The purpose of this publication is to enable the general reader to evaluate individual national standings and use these insights to make business decisions and understand socioeconomic trends. Although many of the statistics are no surprise, others are. For example, Belgium leads the world in the number of periodicals published, at 13,706. The United States comes in second, with 11,593. This is a user-friendly reference with a broad variety of world statistics. Its detailed index makes it easy to determine quickly if the fact sought is to be found in this volume. [R: LJ, 1 Mar 97, p. 70]—**Adrienne Antink Bendel**

814. **A Matter of Fact: Statements Containing Statistics on Current Social, Economic, and Political Issues. Volume 24.** Ann Arbor, Mich., Pierian Press, 1996. 721p. $70.00; $129.00/yr. ISBN 0-87650-321-0.

Scholars who follow current events, public officials who want to stay abreast of economic and political issues, or students who are seeking information on almost any topic of contemporary concern will find this volume of *A Matter of Fact* most helpful. It is literally a treasure trove of statistical data on the social, economic, and political issues of today. Interested in baseball attendance in the United States, violence on television, the cigar industry, the salaries of college teachers, the decline of Catholic nuns and priests since 1960, bats in the United States, the percentage of African Americans presently serving in the U.S. military, or the number of medically uninsured Americans in 1996? If so, *A Matter of Fact* is the book to consult. However, there is a word of caution. The statistical material herein—of which approximately a third comes from congressional hearings and the *Congressional Record*, and the remainder from major newspapers and journals—is only as accurate as the sources cited. The editors of *A Matter of Fact* do not verify information but merely print excerpts from statements of influential people.

Organized alphabetically, the entries are readily accessible. Moreover, for major topics there usually are several subtopics. Under abortion, for instance, are subsumed items on abortion in Egypt, Brazil, Russia, and the United States. Cross-referencing assists the location of related material. Particularly significant to volume 24 is the inclusion of Uniform Resource Locators (URLs), which provide access to the Internet. Researchers will find this feature invaluable. High school, college, and university libraries should have *A Matter of Fact* in their reference collections.—**John W. Storey**

815. **Statistical Yearbook for Asia and the Pacific 1996. Annuaire Statistique pour l'Asie et le Pacifique.** By the Economic and Social Commission for Asia and the Pacific. New York, United Nations, 1997. 635p. $80.00pa. ISBN 92-1-119737-6. ISSN 0252-3655. S/N E/F.97.II.F.1.

Statistical Yearbook for Asia and the Pacific 1996 is the 28th edition published by the Economic Commission for Asia and the Pacific, a statistical division of the United Nations. The statistical data begin in 1985 and give an annual summary through 1995. The yearbook is a compilation of statistics from the 56 regional members, including Australia, Japan, New Zealand, and the Russian Federation.

The information is arranged alphabetically by country, Afghanistan to Vietnam. The statistics cover population; workforce; national accounts; agriculture; forestry and fishing; industry; energy; transport and communications; external trade; wages; prices; and consumption, finance, and social statistics. Annex 1 contains the sources of information. Annex 2 has the imperial British and American equivalents of the principal metric weights and measures, derived coefficients, and other conversion factors used in compiling the statistical tables. There is no index, but the alphabetic by country arrangement and the consistent format of the tables are efficient for locating specific statistics. The yearbook is recommended for large business collections or libraries that have a special interest in Asian and Pacific Rim countries.
—**Kay M. Stebbins**

816. **Statistical Yearbook 1994. Annuaire Statistique.** 41st ed. By the Department for Economic and Social Information and Policy Analysis, Statistics Division. New York, United Nations, 1996. 886p. index. $120.00. ISBN 92-1-061167-5. ISSN 0082-8459. S/N E/F.96.XVII.1.

This edition continues to reflect a phased program of changes in the yearbook's organization and presentation, which began in 1990, in response to the continuing long-term expansion of international data available and demanded by users (in terms of country and subject matter coverage and level of detail) and the impact of electronic data processing technologies on data compilation and typesetting. The total number of tables continues to decrease because of extensive revisions to the list of basic commodity tables, deleting some and adding some of more contemporary importance in agriculture and manufacturing and excluding tables for which new data are not available. The yearbook's concern for data comparability is unchanged, and readers continue to be reminded of the importance of consulting footnotes and technical notes appended to the tables.

This issue provides data for a 10-year period from 1984 to 1993 or 1985 to 1994, depending on the statistics available as of December 31, 1995. Yearbook tables are grouped, as in each volume since 1988-1989, into four broad groups: world and regional summary, population and social statistics, economic activity, and international economic relations. The work, which is updated by *Monthly Bulletin of Statistics*, concludes with "Annex III: Statistical Sources and References" and an index (restored with the 38th edition). Libraries, except for the smallest, will find it a valuable and reliable source.—**Wiley J. Williams**

United States

817. **CQ's State Fact Finder 1997: Rankings Across America.** By Harold A. Hovey and Kendra A. Hovey. Washington, D.C., Congressional Quarterly, 1997. 408p. index. $78.95; $44.95pa. ISBN 1-56802-296-4; 1-56802-297-2pa. ISSN 1079-7149.

CQ's State Fact Finder 1997 represents a 3d edition of a comparative data reference tool for people interested in economic, political, and social developments as well as trends in United States' 50 states and the District of Columbia. The tables in this work are grouped in 12 subject categories: population, economics, geography, government, federal impacts, taxes, revenues and finances, education, health, crime and law enforcement, transportation, and welfare. States are listed alphabetically in each table, then ranked according to their position in each subject area.

In addition to the specific subject tables, an essay on frequently asked questions is featured. This section is divided into three parts. The first part covers personal and family decisions, such as finding the best state to find a job, which state has the best public schools, and others. The second part covers business decisions. Questions relating to best locations for locating businesses and taxes on businesses are addressed here. And the third part looks at information about government and public policy. The intent of this essay is to help readers understand the scope of information available to them. The third component of *CQ's State Fact Finder*, "State Rankings," gives a composite view of each state. The rankings for each state are brought together, giving the researcher a summary of each state's position in each subject area.

This resource has an excellent index and carefully documented sources following the tables in each section so that readers can understand the usefulness of and any caveats about, the subject data.

In general, the table headings and data definitions in this edition parallel those of the 1996 edition. This edition, however, reflects new data for more than 90 percent of the statistics covered in the 1996 edition. Also, the actual number of individual statistics about the states has been increased by nearly 20 percent in this edition. Not only is this resource a useful and reliable source for comparing statistics of the states, it is also a good analytical tool for reviewing economic, political, and social trends in the states and the District of Columbia.—**Earl Shumaker**

818. **A Geographic Database for U.S. Economy, Technology, and Growth.** [CD-ROM]. Washington, D.C., NPA Data Services, 1996. Minimum system requirements: IBM or compatible. CD-ROM drive. Windows 3.1. 8MB RAM. 7MB hard disk space. $175.00.

This CD-ROM contains the geographic database for the *Atlas of U.S. Economy, Technology, and Growth* (see ARBA 97, entry 714), a 484-page reference book. Both items are published by NPA Data Services and are sold as a set ($275) or separately ($175 for the disc, $225 for the print version). The disc allows a user to view 227 statistics in 8 categories for every U.S. county as well as 614 statistics in 12 categories for the 50 states and the District of Columbia. Drop-down menus are available for counties, states, and categories. Projections to the year 2015 are included for some categories. Most categories include data for 1970, 1980, 1985, 1990, and 1994.

Installing the CD-ROM for Windows 95 required a call to the publisher. Installation instructions are minimal. A press release states, "The CD-ROM has a software feature for interactive viewing or printing of data for individual counties or states." Printing the data was available on the CD-ROM under review; there were no instructions for interactive viewing. Files can be exported. To do so requires a "map number," which was available only by consulting the print atlas. Without the atlas, this feature may create user confusion. Data are in "thousands" or "percents" and identified to the right of the screen.

By accessing "all counties" or "all states," various statistics can be quickly compared within and between states, a neat feature, but one hampered by the absence of a scroll bar or instructions for accessing data in the category but not on the screen. The title is recommended for graduate programs.—**Pete Prunkl**

819. **Historical Statistics of the United States.** bicentennial ed. [CD-ROM]. New York, Cambridge University Press, 1997. Minimum system requirements (Windows version): IBM or compatible 386. Double-speed CD-ROM drive. Windows 3.1. 8MB RAM. Minimum system requirements (Macintosh version): Double-speed CD-ROM drive. System 7. 4MB RAM. $195.00. ISBN 0-521-58541-4.

The electronic version of this standard reference work includes all 57 chapters of the 1975 print version (see ARBA 77, entry 753) and contains statistics from colonial times to 1970 on population, labor, income, agriculture, minerals, manufacturing, energy, government, and much more. Most data are organized by year for as far back as reliable statistics allow. Introductory text describes the sources of data plus concepts and historical backgrounds. With a few exceptions, the print and electronic works are the same in content and presentation. The latter version, however, does not tap the potential resources of an electronic format. The most common use of this resource likely will be for exporting raw statistical data; the print version remains more approachable for browsing.

Although the DynaText software makes simple and complex text searches easy, it also limits the work's utility. The tables must be viewed with care: Although table borders imply that the entire table is visible, in fact much of it is not. Data series must be downloaded as Lotus 1-2-3 or text files and then imported into other programs before they can be compared with one another; one cannot combine such series within the program. The user can create notes and hyperlinks within the document, although these annotations are stored on the user's computer and will not transfer if the disc is moved from one machine to another. In a networked environment, however, one can create both "public" and "private" notes. A journal option allows one to record a series of steps through the book, which can be replayed or edited at a later time.

DynaText runs on both Macintosh and Windows-based machines. Printing is difficult, but possible. A helpful User's Guide accompanies the disc; it is clear, concise, easy to follow, and includes specific details on SGML encoding and the DynaText query language. For those who regularly use data from this source, the disc will be quite useful. For most users, however, the electronic version will not replace the printed version.—**Peter H. McCracken**

URBAN STUDIES

820. **America's Top-Rated Cities 1997: A Statistical Handbook.** 5th ed. Rhoda Garoogian, Andrew Garoogian, and Patrice Walsh Weingart, eds. Boca Raton, Fla., Universal Reference, 1997. 4v. $145.00pa./set. ISBN 1-881220-31-1.

This 4-volume statistical handbook, now in its 5th edition, is intended for individuals and businesses considering relocation, market researchers, real estate consultants, and others needing detailed information on some 75 top-rated cities. The volumes are divided geographically into the southern, eastern, central, and western regions of the United States, with the cities in each volume alphabetically arranged and conveniently listed on the cover. The choice of cities considered top-rated is based on size—more than 100,000 in population—and rankings in various surveys (*Fortune, Money, Entrepreneur*, and so on) that designated them as "best" in 1996. Rankings and evaluative comments are further given as part of the information for each city, so it is possible to determine more specifically how a particular city was ranked in different surveys.

Introducing the material on each city is a background statement giving some history and an overall view of the city and its environs. The information for each city is divided into two main sections: the business environment, including such items as income, employment, taxes, and businesses; and the living environment, including cost of living, health care, education, public safety, and the like. For each of the tables and charts detailing the information, the source is always given, and frequently there are helpful notes added. At the end of each volume is a section on comparative statistics, showing comparisons of statistical data for the cities described in that volume. Also included as appendixes are a list of the metropolitan statistical areas for the region, a list of the chambers of commerce and economic development organizations, and the addresses of the state departments of labor and employment for the states included.

Although there is no index, the table of contents for each volume includes a page for each city, with all the sections and subsections clearly indicated with a page number, making it possible, for example, to find statistical information on teacher salaries in Abilene, Texas, quickly and easily. Much of the material in these volumes is available in other sources, but there is no other work that brings all of the statistical information together in one place. For this reason and because it is easy to use (largely because of its format and reader-friendly page layout), *America's Top-Rated Cities* should be useful to its intended audience.—**Lucille Whalen**

821. **America's Top-Rated Smaller Cities 1996-1997: A Statistical Handbook.** 2d ed. Rhoda Garoogian, Andrew Garoogian, and Joy Fromm, eds. Boca Raton, Fla., Universal Reference, 1996. 732p. $75.00pa. ISBN 1-881220-26-5.

The 2d edition of *American's Top-Rated Smaller Cities* is nearly identical to the 1st edition, published in 1994 (see ARBA 96, entry 926). Of the 60 top-ranked cities, with populations between 25,000 and 100,000, 22 cities are new to this edition. New entries include Albany, Georgia; Fort Myers, Florida; Hagerstown, Maryland; Lafayette, Indiana; and Santa Barbara, California. Asheville, North Carolina, and Scranton, Pennsylvania, were among the places dropped. The statistical categories have only been slightly modified; new data are provided for state bond ratings and for means of transportation to work. All of the previous categories have been updated and continue to draw upon a variety of statistical sources (including publications from the U.S. Census Bureau, the Bureau of Labor Statistics, the *American Cost of Living Survey*, and the *Editor & Publisher Market Guide*). This handbook continues to be a useful comparative guide for public and academic libraries, although patrons will need to consult additional sources for a fuller comparison.—**Thomas A. Karel**

822. **Annual Bulletin of Housing and Building Statistics for Europe and North America 1996.** By the Economic Commission for Europe. New York, United Nations, 1997. 97p. $25.00pa. ISBN 92-1-016304-4. ISSN 0066-3840. S/N E/F/R.97.II.E.3.

Increasingly, the world's problems are urban problems, and existing tools for monitoring and managing the city are inadequate. This volume attempts to remedy the situation by providing the "appropriate" statistical information at the city level to aid in the development of human settlement policy in both developed and developing countries. Published by the United Nations Economic Commission for Europe (UN/ECE), this annual bulletin is an invaluable source for up-to-date comparative housing and building statistics. In most cases, data do not predate 1990, and the most recent data are typically for 1994.

The volume provides trend data for European countries, Canada, and the United States. In 32 tables, the scope of the data covers population and households, dwelling stock, new dwellings, construction of nonresidential buildings, value of construction, building firms, building materials, gross domestic product and gross fixed capital formation, prices, costs, and rents. Also included are appendixes for national currency units; definitions and general notes; and a list of ECE reports concerning housing, building, and planning issues published since 1985. Although intended for specialized use by policy researchers and academic audiences, this volume would be a welcome addition to any research library in North America.
—**David V. Waller**

823. Carpenter, Allan, with Carl Provorse, comps. **Facts About the Cities.** 2d ed. Bronx, N.Y., H. W. Wilson, 1996. 653p. $55.00. ISBN 0-8242-0897-8.

Organized alphabetically by state, and city within the state, the 2d edition of this concise reference work offers quick access to profiles and statistical data on 373 U.S. communities, 40 more than the 1st edition (see ARBA 93, entry 918). Information on each city is introduced by a one-paragraph description of the community's history, economy, attractions, and notable features. The 2-page section devoted to each city continues with factual and statistical data presented under 19 categories: general information, climate and environment, population, economy, cost of living, personal finance, households, housing, education, libraries, government and politics, taxes and revenue, crime, transportation, health, conventions and tourism, communication, cultural resources, and sports. New in this edition is a 30-page overview chapter in which tabular data show the comparative standing of the cities on key factors within several categories. For example, the overview's education section ranks 50 cities on per pupil expenditure; pupil-teacher ration; and percentage of people completing high school, college, and so on.

Selection criteria allows for the inclusion of some cities that are omitted from the popular *Places Rated Almanac* (see ARBA 91, entry 908). Whereas the latter focuses on metropolitan areas, *Facts About the Cities* includes cities with populations exceeding 75,000 as well as all state capitals, even those with fewer than 75,000 residents. Other smaller cities are also included to ensure that each state and territory is represented by at least three cities. New in this edition is the inclusion of census designated places with a population greater than 75,000. The importance of these selection criteria to library staff and patrons is illustrated in the coverage of Illinois; cities such as Elgin, Joliet, and Naperville are included in *Facts About the Cities*, whereas in *Places Rated* they are indistinguishable as part of the Chicago metropolitan area. On the other hand, Kankakee is profiled in *Places Rated* but not found in *Facts About the Cities*.

Librarians will find the volume under review complements rather than substitutes for the popular *Places Rated* with its more in-depth treatment of cities and its focus on comparative ratings. Although they include many cities in common, each reference tool contains some cities omitted by the other. Also with *Facts About the Cities*'s consolidation of all information about a city in one place and its attention to ranking cities in the new overview chapter, it definitely should have a place on the reference shelf in most libraries.—**Jan Bakker**

824. **The Comparative Guide to American Suburbs.** Milpitas, Calif., Toucan Valley, 1997. 800p. index. $89.00pa. ISBN 1-884925-61-8.

Around every large U.S. city, rings of suburbs extend for miles in all directions. It has been remarked that inside each First World city lies a Third World city, the implication being that all have an inner region of decay, slums, and extreme poverty. In any event, perceptions like this have driven the upper and middle classes into suburbs created and incorporated for their use. This volume incorporates this truism in that it is a statistical study of the suburbs of the largest cities in this country but not the core city itself. Its purpose appears to provide the grounds for the selection of suburbs for business or residence. As such, it achieves its aim. It is thus not so much a reference for urban life but rather a guide for making such choices. Because core cities vary widely in their areal extent from small, true urban cores to cities that have annexed many former suburbs, their absence here deprives the book from providing a comparison study between one urban agglomeration and another. It is recommended only for detailed comparison between suburban communities with a population of more than 10,000 in each of the 50 largest metropolitan areas in the United States.—**Arthur R. Upgren**

825. Rodger, Richard. **A Consolidated Bibliography of Urban History.** Brookfield, Vt., Ashgate Publishing, 1996. 1173p. index. $154.95. ISBN 1-85928-113-3.

The content of this work is informed by the consolidation of 18 volumes of the *Urban History Yearbook* (see ARBA 90, entry 846) and the bibliographies contained in the earlier *Newsletters of the Urban History Group*. The unannotated bibliography includes almost 20,000 citations to scholarly journal articles; books listed in the British National Bibliography; local history publications; and non-British works, primarily French and U.S. imprints, although other languages are represented. The entries are divided into 10 chapters, each representing a broad subject category, such as "Planning and Environment." These chapters are then further subdivided into more precise topical headings, such as "Housing Improvement." The author index and place-name index are useful in locating specific entries, although the lack of a keyword index forces the reader to rely upon the heading classification for subject access. There is no cross-referencing or *see also* references.

As noted in the book's introduction, the greatest concentration of entries is under the "General" heading, reflecting the large number of local history works. A review of the entries indicates that the broadest possible definition of urban history has been applied to the bibliography's scope, making this a useful cross-disciplinary research tool. However, as the author points out in the introduction, the geographic focus of the bibliography is the British Isles and London, representing almost 60 percent of all entries; only 18 percent of the entries are associated with the United States and Canada. This renders the bibliography of limited value to North American urban planning historians, who should consult *America: History and Life* and the *Journal of Planning Literature* for more thorough coverage of the United States and border countries. Given the book's cost and geographic focus, this resource should only be purchased by institutions with comprehensive urban planning programs. [R: Choice, May 97, p. 1480]
—**Robert V. Labaree**

18 Women's Studies

ALMANACS

826. **The American Women's Almanac: An Inspiring and Irreverent Women's History.** By Louise Bernikow, with the National Women's History Project. New York, Berkley, 1997. 388p. illus. index. $16.95pa. ISBN 0-425-15616-8.

Bernikow has put together a fascinating mosaic of quotations, facts, and vignettes about women's history in the United States in *The American Women's Almanac*. The book is ideal for random browsing. Chapters cover nine topics: politics, the female body, the female body in motion, the female mind, writers and artists, entertainers, media, domestic life, and work. Each chapter begins with a two- to three-page introductory essay followed by a diverse collection of one- to four-paragraph features highlighting specific people, events, or ideas. A brief introduction, an epilogue focusing on cooperation between women, and a bibliography of suggested readings round out the work. Perhaps its strongest points are the plentiful illustrations and photographs and the pithy quotations.

Aside from being "inspiring and irreverent," this volume is not really a useful reference book. The short feature paragraphs may whet one's appetite (or provide color for a speech), but they lack attribution or references for further research. The bibliography is general and gives no clue as to from where the facts and sayings in the text came. The index is remarkably poor on any topic except personal names. Trying to find specific events or concepts is usually a matter of luck.

This book's low cost and excellent illustrations make it attractive despite its weaknesses. It would be a suitable purchase for a public or school library or as a popular addition to a collection already strong in women's history. [R: RBB, 15 April 97, p. 1447]—**Susan Davis Herring**

827. **Women's Almanac.** Linda Schmittroth and Mary Reilly McCall, eds. Detroit, U*X*L/Gale, 1997. 3v. illus. index. $85.00/set. ISBN 0-7876-0656-1.

Women's Almanac is a 3-volume collection of assorted information about women that is designed primarily for youthful readers. The set is an independent component of U*X*L's projected 13-volume "Women's Reference Library." Although the 3 volumes are subtitled, respectively, *History*, *Society*, and *Culture*, the focus of each volume is not as narrow as the subtitles imply. Each volume contains a wide assortment of material about women of the past and present, about gender roles in various cultural settings, and about critical issues that have had significant impact upon women of different times and places. The volumes cover a wide range of topics, including essays on women in politics, education, sports, science, medicine, the military, music, the arts, religion, and the family. The almanac also includes more than 200 black-and-white photographs and illustrations of people and events, scores of excerpts from important historical documents, dozens of charts of pertinent statistics depicting the place of women in society, a glossary of words readers need to know, and a comprehensive index.

Academic historians will quiver at the frequent oversimplifications and erroneous historical facts scattered throughout the volumes. These imperfections notwithstanding, *Women's Almanac* is an appealing and readable introduction to a large number of pertinent topics relating to women worldwide. The set is recommended for high school libraries.—**Terry D. Bilhartz**

BIBLIOGRAPHY

828. Blair, Karen J. **Northwest Women: An Annotated Bibliography of Sources on the History of Oregon and Washington Women, 1787-1970.** Pullman, Wash., WSU Press, 1997. 134p. index. $32.95pa. ISBN 0-87422-145-5.

Blair, a history professor at Central Washington University, compiled this bibliography because of the dearth of information she encountered while attempting to familiarize herself with women's contributions to the area's history. She does not claim that the bibliography is a comprehensive guide to Northwest women, but calls it a "keyhole to a large unexplored history" (p. x). The bibliography focuses on English-language books and articles published before 1995 that examine women's experiences through 1970, the year the state of Washington passed the Equal Rights Amendment. Thus, oral history transcripts, fiction, memoirs, and primary sources are excluded.

Arranged alphabetically by author, each entry provides complete citations, including brief but useful descriptions of photographs and an annotation detailed enough to give researchers a clear idea of what information the material contains. An excellent name, title, and subject index includes entries for such topics as African Americans, Japanese American internment, Native Americans (subdivided by tribe), lesbianism, suffragists, homesteaders, and various occupations.

Researchers concentrating on women's history in Oregon and Washington should find this bibliography helpful, and it fills a gap in the literature. The volume is recommended for comprehensive, regional, and women's studies collections in academic libraries.—**Linda A. Krikos**

829. Cox, Elizabeth M. **Women in Modern American Politics: A Bibliography 1900-1995.** Washington, D.C., Congressional Quarterly, 1997. 414p. index. $129.00. ISBN 1-56802-133-X.

This volume is a comprehensive bibliography of writings on women in U.S. politics in the twentieth century. It contains 6,000 entries of articles and books on numerous topics that are relevant in documenting the evolution of people in politics. Some of these topics include women in public institutions, political participation and behavior, running for elective offices, the gender gap in political attitudes, voting behavior, the advocacy movement, and historical trends in women's political attitudes and opinions. Also included are writings about the pioneering women who first ventured into politics back in 1894. Women exercised their influence by organizing political clubs, speaking, and writing campaign literature despite the fact that they could not vote. By 1996, women held 20 percent of state legislative offices and 10 percent of congressional seats. Women are not equal players in U.S. politics, but they are no longer outsiders, either.

This book contains selections from magazines, journals, books, dissertations, and papers delivered at professional conferences. Newspaper articles are not included. The entries are organized by subjects: movement and advocacy, mass behavior, participation and voting, running for elective office, public institutions, public policy, attitudes and opinions, and political theory. Under most of these subjects, the entries are organized by appropriate subtopics, such as feminism from 1920 to 1965, the Equal Rights Amendment, lesbian rights, women of color, affirmative action, crimes against women, reproductive and abortion rights, sex discrimination, and so on. They are also organized by the level of government and individual states. The entries are listed only once and give no cross-references to other related writings.

The publication dates and the amount of writings included in this bibliography reveal the historical emergence and decline of women's political role in U.S. history. Most of the entries were published in the 1970s, when the women's movement in politics made significant gains. Compared to a similar work, Barbara Ryan's *The Women's Movement: References and Resources* (G. K. Hall, 1996), the bibliography at hand is more focused on the women's movement and participation in politics than in social movements. The work under review focuses on women in U.S. politics, whereas Ryan's work includes writings on women in other countries as well. There is merit in using both as companion volumes in doing research on women's issues.

This volume is a well-organized and substantial reference source. As a resource guide for women's studies, it is recommended for academic libraries and for any type of library collecting books on women's studies.

—**Eveline L. Yang**

830. Kimball, Michelle R., and Barbara R. von Schlegell. **Muslim Women Throughout the World: A Bibliography.** Boulder, Colo., Lynne Rienner, 1997. 309p. index. $75.00. ISBN 1-55587-680-3.

There is much to love about this book. The organization is easy to comprehend, the subject coverage complete, and the indexing thorough. It is obvious that Kimball, an Islamic studies scholar, and von Schlegell, assistant professor in the Department of Religious Studies at the University of Pennsylvania, really understand the issues surrounding Muslim women. Undoubtedly financial support from the Andrew Mellon Foundation, the University of California at Berkeley, and the University of California at Santa Barbara enabled the authors to dedicate their energies toward this project.

Covering nearly 3,000 books and articles published in English through 1995, the publication includes bibliographic listings for anything related to women in the Muslim world. Sorted alphabetically by author and title, each entry has a number to which the meticulous index refers. Although the subject coverage addresses areas of concern common to all women, it also includes issues specific to Muslims, such as female circumcision, seclusion, and veiling. Major geographic influences include, but are not limited to, the Middle East, South Asia, Indonesia, Africa, and North America. A few prominent people, such as Benazir Bhutto, Jihan Sadat, and Nawal El Saadawi, appear as both an author and a subject heading in the index.

Based on recommendations from Muslim and Middle Eastern women's studies specialists, Kimball and von Schlegell compiled a list of 50 "must-read" books; concise annotations capture their themes. Some of this reviewer's personal favorites include El Saadawi's *The Hidden Face of Eve: Women in the Arab World* (London, Zed Books, 1980); Fatima Mernissi's *Beyond the Veil: Male-Female Dynamics in Modern Muslim Society* (Schenkman Publishing, 1975); and Edward Said's *Orientalism* (Pantheon Books, 1978). A few pertinent content omissions do appear. The authors omitted articles in newspapers and popular magazines, probably because these can be readily obtained through various online services and printed indexes. For a complete listing of biographies, hadiths, Koranic commentaries, and collections of prophetic traditions, the authors refer readers to bibliographies listed in the book.—**Susan D. Baird-Joshi**

831. Nordquist, Joan, comp. **Feminism Worldwide: A Bibliography.** Santa Cruz, Calif., Reference and Research Services, 1996. 64p. index. (Contemporary Social Issues: A Bibliographic Series, no.44). $15.00pa. ISBN 0-937855-86-3.

This selective bibliographic guide to resources on feminism is the most current offering in the Contemporary Social Issues: A Bibliographic Series. The bibliography offers a convenient sample of books, periodical articles, pamphlets, government documents, and the like, from a wide range of international feminist literature.

The 10 sections in the bibliography are divided into 9 geographic subject areas and 1 section of bibliographies. The geographic subject areas cover international feminism and feminism in Europe, England, Canada, Australia and New Zealand, the Third World, Latin America, the Middle East, and Africa and Asia. The majority of the 541 entries range from the early to mid-1980s to 1996. Full bibliographic citations are provided, together with brief country indexes that appear at the end of appropriate sections. The indexes group the entries for individual countries in a particular geographic area. Although these resources have been indexed in other publications, this short, inexpensive bibliography is an alternative to locating often difficult to find material. It is recommended for all academic libraries.
—**Jane Jurgens**

832. Nordquist, Joan, comp. **French Feminist Theory (III): Luce Irigaray and Helene Cixous: A Bibliography.** Santa Cruz, Calif., Reference and Research Services, 1996. 72p. index. (Social Theory: A Bibliographic Series, no.44). $15.00pa. ISBN 0-937855-87-1.

This volume is a supplement to Nordquist's 1990 bibliography, *French Feminist Theory: Luce Irigaray and Helene Cixous* (see ARBA 92, entry 858), and brings the earlier edition up-to-date. Like the original, the bibliography is arranged in four sections. The first section lists books by Irigaray and Cixous, along with critical articles on those books. The second section lists essays and interviews that have been translated into English and criticism of the essays. The third section lists books, dissertations, and theses about Irigaray and Cixous, and the fourth section lists articles about Irigaray and Cixous published since 1990. There is no author index, but convenient keyword-in-context indexes are given at the end of each section. The bibliography is remarkably complete in its list of works by the two authors, but a quick search of the *MLA International Bibliography* shows that many critical articles have been missed, especially those published in collections. However, one major improvement over the 1st volume is the addition of a brief biographical and interpretive introduction to the two authors and their work. Overall, Nordquist's work is a valuable and useful resource for academic libraries.—**Susan Davis Herring**

BIOGRAPHY

833. Kaptur, Marcy. **Women of Congress: A Twentieth-Century Odyssey.** Washington, D.C., Congressional Quarterly, 1996. 256p. illus. index. $23.95. ISBN 0-87187-989-1.

Since the founding of the United States, fewer than 200 members of Congress have been women. Of these, only 42 served longer than a decade. Presently only 11 percent of the members of Congress are women. It is interesting to note that twice as many of these women have been Democrats as Republicans. This book was written to pay homage to these women and their perseverance over adversity in politics. They are trailblazers and pioneers in U.S. politics. The author, a congresswoman herself, includes the profiles of 15 tenured congresswomen and overviews of other women lawmakers during 3 periods of the twentieth century. The first period, covering 1917 to World War II, includes such pioneers as Jeannette Rankin and Mary Teresa Norton. The second period, called "The Greening Years," covers World War II through the 1960s and features long-serving Frances Payne Bolton and Margaret Chase Smith. The third period, "The Modern Era," profiles some contemporary leaders, such as Shirley Chisholm, Pat Schroeder, and Nancy Kassebaum. These congresswomen's legislative records are sufficiently rich and significantly influential in U.S. society. The overviews in each section are particularly informative because they summarize and assess the triumph and struggle of women politicians in that era. The articles provide biographical information, data on the political career, and some of the notable issues and viewpoints of these congresswomen. The entries end with a brief evaluation of their contributions to Congress and society.

As one can expect, the roles that women have played in Congress have varied widely and have assumed greater significance over time. Only a few women rose to positions of seniority and chaired important committees—Julia Butler Hansen and Barbara Vucanovich are still the only women to have chaired House Appropriations subcommittees. Barbara Mikulski of Maryland is the only woman to have chaired a Senate Appropriations subcommittee. The pattern of few women in leadership positions in Congress is slowly changing. The influence of women in Congress has been mostly in the traditionally feminine areas of interest, such as family, children, health, and literacy. Overall, these women are often less concerned with the attainment of a position and more concerned with the well-being of the nation than are their male counterparts. The author predicts that in the twenty-first century, more U.S. women will be unleashed from the previous conventions and commit their potentials and energy to ensure the survival and advancement of the United States.

The reference materials section presents charts and tables that list the women in Congress by their names, dates and length of service, a brief profile, professional background, key committees they served on, and political interests. This is not only an informative resource book about congresswomen in the United States but is also remarkably entertaining reading for those who are interested in the personal biographies of these remarkable women. The volume is highly recommended for libraries supporting women's studies and political science programs. [R: RBB, 15 Feb 97, p. 1043]—**Eveline L. Yang**

CHRONOLOGY

834. **Women's Chronology: A History of Women's Achievements.** Peggy Saari, Tim Gall, and Susan Gall, eds. Detroit, U*X*L/Gale, 1997. 2v. illus. index. $55.00/set. ISBN 0-7876-0660-X.

This two-volume chronology of women's history includes prehistory to 1996 in a series of short (one- to two-paragraph) entries. Volume 1 covers approximately 4000 B.C.E. to 1849, and volume 2 covers 1850 to the present. Other than the first few entries, which deal with Sumerian, Greek, and Chinese gods, the book covers individual women who are notable for their accomplishments and achievements. The entries are brief, simple, aimed at middle and high school-level readers, and provide minimal information about the people, events, and historic or social context. The 10-page introduction gives a sketchy overview of women's history since the Bronze Age.

Like any chronology, this book is selective and misses many interesting people. For example, a random check showed no entries for Josephine Baker, Rachel Carson, or Lucretia Borgia. However, it does provide more international coverage than many women's chronologies, especially of Asian and Middle Eastern women. It is also well illustrated and includes a useful glossary. Words not normally within a middle school vocabulary are defined parenthetically within the entries.

The major weakness of this set is the inaccessibility of the information. The entries are in chronological order, and the index is limited to proper names and titles. It is impossible for a user to look up women by country, profession, contribution, achievement, or any other general category of interest, which turns an otherwise useful reference source into a source of great potential frustration. In addition, it lacks a bibliography.

Women's Chronology is clearly aimed at general use by middle school and high school students or public library patrons looking for introductory information. It is not suitable for academic or research libraries or for anything beyond simple reference use.—**Susan Davis Herring**

835. **Women's Firsts.** Caroline Zilboorg, ed. Detroit, Gale, 1997. 564p. illus. index. $44.95. ISBN 0-7876-0151-9.

Christine Todd Whitman, first female governor of the state of New Jersey, proclaims in the foreword to this volume, "*Women's Firsts* offers a tribute to women of achievement whose stories can inspire, enlighten, and motivate." After careful review of the text, most would probably agree.

This reference source covers many fields of endeavor and is arranged by subjects that include activism, the arts, business, education, literature, religion, science, and sports, to name only a few. It is further arranged by date, with special emphasis on the nineteenth and twentieth centuries. Each entry identifies the achievement, describes it, summarizes its content, and is immediately documented by its source. The more than 150 illustrations of clear photographs and reprints are impressive. Other features include a timeline of events in women's history; an index by day of the month; an index by year; a keyword index listing women, important events, issues, and locations; and a bibliography.

With the growing interest in women's history, this volume should prove useful to scholars, historians, students, and all who seek information on women's concerns. This addition would be great for academic, public, and school libraries. [R: RBB, 15 Mar 97, p. 1261]—**Mary L. Bowman**

DICTIONARIES AND ENCYCLOPEDIAS

836. **Scholastic Encyclopedia of Women in the United States.** By Sheila Keenan. New York, Scholastic, 1996. 206p. illus. index. $17.95. ISBN 0-590-22792-0.

Scholastic Encyclopedia of Women in the United States is a valuable illustrated profile of women who have made a difference in U.S. history, from Pocahontas to Hillary Rodham Clinton. The biographies are brief and represent a broad range of women's lives. Women treated are from every walk of life and from every ethnic group. A significant number are included because they filled nontraditional roles.

Entries are divided into six broad categories covering a period from the 1500s through the 1990s. Most entries are biographical, but a significant number of cameos are included that highlight women whose broader lives are not detailed. A section called "Women's Words" presents quotations by and about women. A section entitled "Women's Sphere" is a sidebar that provides information on what women's lives were really like during a certain period.

This source contains both a topical and an alphabetic index. It is recommended for both public and school libraries.—**Mary L. Bowman**

837. **Women's Issues.** Margaret McFadden, ed. Pasadena, Calif., Salem Press, 1997. 3v. illus. maps. index. (Ready Reference). $270.00/set. ISBN 0-89356-765-5.

What does it mean to be female in the United States? *Women's Issues*, a 3-volume publication of the editors of Salem Press, provides multiple insightful answers to this central question. This ready-reference encyclopedia includes 696 entries that range in length from 100 to 4,000 words and are presented in an easy-to-access, alphabetic format. The entries cover a wide range of topics, including 48 entries on pertinent U.S. Supreme Court cases and federal legislation; 50 entries describing the role of women in literature and the arts; 48 entries on marriage and the family; 37 articles dealing with issues of women and race; 66 pieces discussing concepts in feminist theory; 84 entries covering questions of health, sexuality, and reproductive rights; and 74 biographical entries on notable women of special achievement.

In addition to the content of each article, each entry contains a "Relevant Issues" section that places it into a thematic context, a "Significance" statement that summarizes its importance, and a cross-reference link to related topics of interest in the encyclopedia. The longer articles include an annotated bibliography of major sources. More than 200 photographs as well as dozens of graphs and charts also fill the volumes. Volume 3 concludes with 5 appendixes that list, among other items, important research centers for women's studies; the names and addresses of women's organizations; and a 21-page timeline of key events in U.S. women's history, from Pocahontas's marriage to John Rolfe in 1614 to the gold medals won by U.S. women in the 1996 Olympic Games in Atlanta.

This well-indexed, 3-volume set was prepared by more than 200 contributors, most of whom are instructors at institutions of higher education across the United States. Together they have produced an attractive, comprehensive, readable, and easy-to-use reference guide that will be a valuable addition to any college or community public library. It is highly recommended.—**Terry D. Bilhartz**

HANDBOOKS AND YEARBOOKS

838. **Contemporary Women's Issues 1992-July 1997.** [CD-ROM]. Beachwood, Ohio, Responsive Database Services, 1997. Minimum system requirements: IBM or compatible 386. CD-ROM drive. 2MB hard disk space. 180KB conventional memory (512KB if no extended memory is available). 1.5MB extended memory. Color or monochrome monitor. $300.00/single user (high schools); $600.00/single user (public and academic libraries).

Contemporary Women's Issues provides a valuable CD-ROM index and full-text access to material on a broad array of women's concerns—material that is otherwise not easily found. Content is selected for the quality and relevance of information as well as for unique perspective; however, all articles and reviews refer to nonfiction current women's issues (i.e., historical articles are only included when they refer to contemporary issues). The extensive subject coverage—education, employment, health, environment, rights, and religion—reflects the international scope and wide interest range of the compilers. With over 600 sources, the database gives access to journals, such as *Off Our Backs, International Midwife*, and *Tradeswoman*; newsletters, such as *Asian Women, Newsletter on International Buddhist Women's Activities*, and *USAID Developments*; and reports, such as *Assisting Rural Battered Women* and *Impact of Technological Changes on Women's Employment*. For the most part, these are not widely circulated publications, which makes the compilation of them into *Contemporary Women's Issues* even more valuable. The perspective of the materials collected here tends to be liberal, feminist, and activist.

The DOS-based CD-ROM uses straightforward search screens and allows for thesaurus searches, Boolean combinations, and application of date limits. The advanced search mode seems preferable for more than a single concept search. The full-text display always provides a full bibliographic description, and sometimes provides useful annotations, such as author notes. The CD-ROM is updated quarterly with a cumulative disc.

Contemporary Women's Issues gives excellent, timely access to primary source material on women's concerns, and is highly recommended for academic and public libraries as well as women's centers with an interest in research. [R: Choice, May 97, p. 1482; LJ, 15 May 97, p. 111]—**Jean C. McManus**

839. Kinnear, Karen L. **Women in the Third World: A Reference Handbook.** Santa Barbara, Calif., ABC-CLIO, 1997. 348p. index. (Contemporary World Issues). $39.50. ISBN 0-87436-922-3.

This book is one of the volumes in the Contemporary World Issues series. The volume describes how issues such as family relations, violence, health care, work, and politics affect the status of women in developing countries. It provides a survey of the available literature and other resources on the topic of women in the Third World. Kinnear—a professional researcher, editor, and writer with more than 20 years of experience in sociological, economic, statistical, and financial analysis—strives to offer sources for further research and opportunities to learn more about women in the Third World, their lives, and the challenges many of them face from day to day.

The book contains seven chapters: an overview of the subject including aspects of education, health, the family, work, and politics; a detailed chronology of significant events; biographical sketches of the women who have played key roles in politics, social activism, education, and other important areas; facts and statistics concerning women's lives and status in developing countries; a list of international agreements; a directory of organizations and agencies; and an annotated list of print and nonprint resources, including Internet sites. A glossary and an index also appear. The book is for students, writers, educators, researchers, professionals in the field, and women's advocacy groups.—**Vera Gao**

840. **Women's Voices: A Documentary History of Women in America.** Lorie Jenkins McElroy, ed. Detroit, U*X*L/Gale, 1997. 2v. illus. index. $55.00/set. ISBN 0-7876-0663-4.

Women's Voices, geared toward the secondary-school library market, provides students with an opportunity to read firsthand the words of many of the women who have helped shape social issues during the past two centuries. The set's 32 documents are organized by topic: education, abolition, suffrage, property and labor, civic and social equality, and reproductive rights. Coverage includes many classics, such as Virginia Woolf's "A Room of One's Own," Sojourner Truth's "Ain't I a Woman?," and excerpts from Simone de Beauvoir's *Second Sex*, as well as more contemporary writings by Gloria Steinem and Betty Friedan. Emphasis is on the expansion of women's rights and the speeches, writings, and documents (such as the Supreme Court's *Roe v. Wade* decision) that have supported this trend.

Each excerpt includes biographical information about the speaker or writer plus historical overviews that place the issue in a broader context. Words students may not understand are explained in sidebars throughout the 32 sections. Other teaching points include "What Happened Next" and "Did You Know" sections that highlight interesting information. More than 100 photographs and portraits, a glossary, an index, and a timeline supplement the text.

The speeches, diary entries, newspaper articles, poems, and reminiscences recounted in these two volumes provide a fascinating overview of women's halting but irresistible progress toward a society that embraces equal rights for both sexes. It should be in every secondary school library.—**G. Kim Dority**

INDEXES

841. **An Index to Women's Studies Anthologies: Research Across the Disciplines, 1985-1989.** By Sara Brownmiller and Ruth Dickstein. New York, G. K. Hall/Simon & Schuster Macmillan, 1996. 725p. $165.00. ISBN 0-7838-1531-X.

Reflecting the growth of works by and about women, this compendium is an unusual source—a thorough bibliography of woman-centered articles. Trimmed to a manageable five-year period, the text covers essay collections and published proceedings to provide convenient and readable access to resources. The work opens with a straightforward explanation of purpose, working method, criteria for selection, discussion of software, and explanation of organization in 5 sections. The 1st, "Anthologies and Tables of Contents," covers data by chapter title, author, and page number. The subject index contains 38 categories: agriculture, geography, television, film, theater, and music. An alphabetic editor index lists title and entry number from section 1. An author index covers full titles of authored chapters and samples a fair balance of entries by male and female authors. The largest section, the keyword index, identifies subject areas and catalogs each significant word under 13 umbrella terms: abuse, age, child, class, crime, discrimination, education, employment, family, law, pay, reproduction, and religion.

Several aspects of this compendium recommend it to university and research libraries. The tricolumned layout is clear, the typefaces well balanced, and the notation unencumbered by excess. Comprehensive listings and cross-referencing aid research in multiple disciplines, for example, human mating, sacred images, violence against women, empowerment, girls and math, films for women, women in the African Diaspora, psychotherapy with lesbians and gay men, and social science and public policy. The scope is global but heavily skewed toward North America.—**Mary Ellen Snodgrass**

842. **Women's Studies Index 1995.** New York, G. K. Hall/Simon & Schuster Macmillan, 1996. 683p. $175.00. ISBN 0-7838-2109-3. ISSN 1058-8369.

The 6th volume of this index maintains the improvements made to the source after the inaugural volume, published in 1991 (see ARBA 92, entry 869): It lists specific journal/magazine issues indexed, includes subscription addresses for the periodicals covered, articulates indexing criteria, and includes guide headings at the top of each page. Additionally, the scope of coverage remains broad, including literary, core women's studies, lesbian, radical, and international titles. It is still the only index in the field to include citations for creative works. The biggest drawback of the early volumes, the two-year publishing lag, has improved, but annual updates are not timely enough for an index. The electronic version of this index, *Women's Studies on Disc* (see ARBA 97, entry 742), released twice a year, began including abstracts for major articles in 1995, an improvement that will not be mirrored in the print product because of size considerations.

Women's Studies Index is suitable for community colleges, large public libraries, and universities with undergraduate women's studies courses. Research institutions and schools with established women's studies programs should consider *Women Studies Abstracts* (WSA) (see ARBA 73, entry 744) or *Women's Resources International* (WRI), an electronic index that includes WSA and several other indexes and bibliographies. Coverage of the literature in both WSA and WRI begins in 1972, compared to the 1989 starting date of the G. K. Hall products.—**Linda A. Krikos**

Part III
HUMANITIES

19 Humanities in General

HUMANITIES IN GENERAL

843. **Benét's Reader's Encyclopedia.** 4th ed. Bruce Murphy, ed. New York, HarperCollins, 1996. 1144p. $50.00. ISBN 0-06-270110-X.

William Rose Benét's legacy lives on with this 4th edition of a classic work. Touted as "the single most complete one-volume encyclopedia" of world literature (jacket flap), this edition reflects a more diversified canon, with greater focus on African, African American, Eastern, Eastern European, Middle Eastern, South American, and women's literature. Last updated in 1987 (see ARBA 89, entry 816), the structure and type of entries remain virtually the same in the new edition. Entries cover more than just writers and works of literature—musical composers, philosophers, artists, historical and political figures, literary characters, terms, locales, folktales, mythology, and more are treated between these covers. New additions include John Cage, the Frankfurt School, and Jaime Salom. Toni Morrison's entry has been updated to reflect her winning of the Nobel prize and the publication of her latest novel, *Jazz* (1992). That said, one must also note the entries that have not been updated. For example, Louisa May Alcott's entry does not mention the recent publication of *A Long Fatal Love Chase* (published in 1995 by Bantam Doubleday Dell). One must wonder what other recent developments in the literary world have not been recorded here. Obviously, no one-volume encyclopedia can be entirely comprehensive on such an enormous topic. However, a casual browse reveals more entries not carried over from the 3d edition than entries added to the 4th edition. Perhaps this reviewer merely looked on the wrong pages, but a perusal of several letters of the alphabet within the encyclopedia should have yielded better results. Essentially, the encyclopedia is an important work, but this long-awaited new edition could have gone even further in promoting the diversity of world literature in the 1990s. [R: C&RL, Sept 97, p. 478]

—Melissa Rae Root

844. **Comprehensive Dissertation Index 1996 Supplement.** Ann Arbor, Mich., UMI Research Press, 1997. 5v. $2,140.00/set. ISBN 0-8357-2467-0.

This comprehensive inventory of doctoral dissertations contains bibliographic entries on 55,467 dissertations from 250 U.S. and Canadian institutions. Published by University Microfilms International, this annual supplement covers the calendar year 1996 and is part of a series of CDIs that have been published since 1973. Since 1988, UMI has published annual supplements similar to this 1996 set. Dissertation abstracts and copies of the dissertations themselves are also available through UMI, with this index being a key publication to locate dissertations. There are five volumes to this work. Volumes 1 and 2 contain information on dissertations in science and engineering; volumes 3 and 4 contain information on dissertations in social sciences and humanities; and the 5th volume contains an author index for the entire 1996 set. This index is organized by keyword, with each dissertation being listed under an average of four keywords. In addition, the volumes contain a subject cross-reference list and a list of the 250 schools covered by the index.

Although these volumes are important purchases for research libraries, especially academic libraries, it should be noted the UMI's database is available in several electronic formats, including CD-ROM and a Website. Using these electronic sources, a person could do more exact keyword searches that do not depend on the indexers' choices for keywords. In addition, an electronic search could cover the entire database, not just a single year. Although these hard copy versions of the database are important for those unfamiliar with electronic database searching or for historical purposes, a book copy of this index is probably no longer the best way to locate information in dissertation research.—**Kay Mariea**

845. **Humanities Abstracts Full Text.** [CD-ROM]. Bronx, N.Y., H. W. Wilson, 1997. Minimum system requirements (Windows version): IBM or compatible 386SX. CD-ROM drive. DOS 3.1. Windows 3.1. 4MB RAM (8MB recommended). 14MB hard disk space. Printer (optional). Hayes or compatible modem (for online capabilities). Minimum system requirements (Macintosh version): 68020 or Power PC. CD-ROM drive. System 7.0. 2MB RAM. 10MB hard disk space. $2,995.00/yr.

The broad range of topics addressed by the disciplines of the humanities is well represented in this CD-ROM resource that uses a standard H. W. Wilson interface. Although search options are provided for keywords and free-text browsing, it is the subject access that will be of the most value for reference queries. This is due to the level of detail provided by the topical headings, which cover reviews of ballet, dance, drama, exhibitions, fiction, motion pictures, musical comedies, opera, operettas, oratorios, and poetry and radio programs in addition to more generic subjects, such as interviews and biography. Being able to access the full text of major humanities periodicals will be most useful for libraries with limited serials collections, although the cost of this product makes it more suitable for placement on a network server for larger public and academic collections.—**Robert B. Marks Ridinger**

846. **Humanities Index. April 1995 to March 1996.** Joanna Greenspon and others, eds. Bronx, N.Y., H. W. Wilson, 1995, 1996. 1526p. priced on a service basis rate. ISSN 0095-5981.

Two factors must be weighed when assessing any of the indexes published by H. W. Wilson Company: content and format. Arranged by author and subject by the *Humanities Index* currently indexes more than 400 English-language periodicals covering archaeology, art, classics, film, folklore, journalism, linguistics, music, the performing arts, philosophy, religion, world history, and world literature. Of course, by extension, it also covers the many interdisciplinary fields that today mingle with the traditional humanities disciplines. Since it split from the current *Social Sciences Index* (see entry 93) more than 20 years ago, *Humanities Index* has been a basic periodical index for students in the humanities, supplemented by the various comprehensive single-discipline indexes published by other publishers or scholarly organizations. The print form of this resource has the advantage of sharing the format made familiar to generations of students through their use of the *Readers' Guide to Periodical Literature* (New York: H. W. Wilson, 1901-). That format served well in the print world but now is dated. The use in the print product of periodical title abbreviations in citations is a mystery to most students, even though a key to these appears in the volume's front matter. The electronic format (e.g., as Humanities Abstracts on OCLC's FirstSearch) uses full titles and provides informative abstracts. This means that libraries today should do all they can to provide user-friendly online or CD-ROM access to this and other H. W. Wilson indexes. Libraries should rely on subscriptions to the print versions only as a last resort.

H. W. Wilson has done a fine job of maintaining the quality of the contents of *Humanities Index*, but it has violated Ranganathan's Fourth Law of Library Science—"Save the time of the reader"—by clinging to outdated practices designed long ago to conserve lead type rather than reader's time.

—**James Rettig**

847. **Lives and Works in the Arts from the Renaissance to the 20th Century.** Armonk, N.Y., Sharpe Reference/M. E. Sharpe, 1997. 9v. illus. index. $450.00/set. ISBN 1-56324-817-4.

This handsomely produced set, appropriate for high school and undergraduate students, profiles a variety of artists, writers, and musicians beginning with the Renaissance and continuing up through the twentieth century, with an emphasis on Western Europe and the United States. Starting with the Renaissance in volume 1, each of the volumes begins with an introductory overview of the period, followed by 21 entries on selected painters, sculptors, novelists, poets, dramatists, composers, and architects from the time period. Each well-written essay outlines biographical milestones for that individual and emphasizes the significance of that person in the time period; for example, in twentieth-century Europe, James Joyce's avant-garde contributions to the development of the novel, or, in the seventeenth century, Nicolas Poussin's classicism, which formed the basis of French academic painting for the next two centuries.

Interspersed with the biographical text is a boxed timeline noting key dates for the individual, as well as a "background" box on a person, historical movement, or philosophy relevant to the biographee and the time period. Additional essays note the importance of the biographee to the arts of the period. Most helpful is the glossary of terms concluding each volume and a brief bibliography for further reading. A timeline for the century lists major historical and political events by decade, followed by an outline of the biographees in the volume arranged chronologically by birth and death dates. On their covers, volumes reproduce in color a major artwork. Individual entries feature a portrait of the biographee, often a painting, line drawing, or charcoal, as well as additional reproductions of artworks, such as Joseph Severn's depiction of *Keats and the Nightingale* for the entry on John Keats.

For ease of use, each volume has its own index. The last volume indexes the entire set and provides additional indexes of ethnic minorities and women and writers, artists, and composers by nationality. Again, the timelines for the individual volumes are reproduced, and the glossaries are cumulated. Although it is expensive, and smaller libraries may not be able to afford it, the set merits purchase because of its content and quality.—**Bernice Bergup**

848. Schlachter, Gail Ann, and R. David Weber. **Money for Graduate Students in the Humanities 1996-1998.** San Carlos, Calif., Reference Service Press, 1996. 296p. index. $37.50. ISBN 0-918276-31-4.

With today's tremendous cost of graduate study, here is a guide to financial support for those with an interest in the humanities. Some of the funding sources covered include awards, fellowships, grants, loans, and traineeships. This most helpful book has an easy-to-understand explanation of the organization of the contents and how to make use of the directory. A well-organized guide, clearly written with a generously sized typeface, this volume also has a list of state sources for information on financial aid and student loans and an annotated bibliography of materials on financial aid. There are helpful indexes on such topics as program titles, sponsoring organizations, and tenability (funding that is restricted to a certain geographic area).

Schlachter is an experienced author in the field of financial aid, as is Weber, a noted social scientist. Together they have co-authored several books dealing with the various facets of financial assistance. This comprehensive directory of financial aid available to students in the humanities will be useful in public and academic libraries, as well as other collections on campus that serve potential graduate students. [R: Choice, Mar 97, pp. 1140-41]—**Bruce H. Webb**

849. **World Databases in Humanities.** C. J. Armstrong and R. R. Fenton, eds. New Providence, N.J., Bowker-Saur/Reed Reference Publishing, 1996. 1060p. index. (World Databases Series). $250.00. ISBN 1-85739-048-2.

With more and more electronic information sources becoming available, it is often difficult to tell which are best suited to particular reference needs. *World Databases in the Humanities* is the latest addition to Bowker-Saur's World Databases Series. The volume is an evaluative directory to the world's databases for the humanities, accessing all electronic products currently available on the Internet, CD-ROM, magnetic tape, or diskettes; online; or via fax, wire, or data broadcast. Subjects included as humanities are fine arts, music, performing arts, language, literature, religion, philosophy, and crafts. The directory is divided into these respective subject areas, and then entries are listed alphabetically within each section.

The entries are highly detailed, providing names of databases, a complete description, years of coverage, number of records held, geographic area, language, search software used, search aids and manuals, type of database, and host or provider information. Particularly useful is the evaluative information provided in the entries; most compare the same databases held by different hosts or in different formats to help users assess the sources best suited for their needs. This volume is a useful and necessary addition to any humanities collection.—**Jennifer Comi Ellard**

20 Communication and Mass Media

GENERAL WORKS

Bibliography

850. Asante, Clement E., comp. **Press Freedom and Development: A Research Guide and Selected Bibliography.** Westport, Conn., Greenwood Press, 1997. 216p. index. (Bibliographies and Indexes in Mass Media and Communications, no.11). $75.00. ISBN 0-313-29994-3.

The complex relationships between mass media and government, particularly in the areas of press freedom and development, are the focus of this guide. Asante, the director of several nonprofit organizations and author of a book on the press in Ghana, divides his work into 2 parts. The 1st part explores and synthesizes the literature pertaining to the issues surrounding freedom of the press, and the 2d part is devoted to the role that the media and other communication networks play in bringing about change and in promoting national development, especially in Third World countries. Each part includes an essay that offers both a historical overview and a review of the literature pertaining to these areas of study, a bibliography of works cited in the essay, and a selective annotated bibliography of sources that the compiler has judged most significant. Surprisingly, only a small percentage of the 518 entries in the annotated bibliographies repeat works covered in the literature reviews, an anomaly that may be problematic for unsuspecting users who do not read the introduction carefully.

Asante's selections, which include imprints through 1996, encompass books, journal articles, dissertations, and other publications. However, some significant omissions spark concerns about the consistency and reliability of his bibliographic methods. For example, he overlooks David Linton's *The Twentieth-Century Newspaper Press in Britain: An Annotated Bibliography* (see ARBA 96, entry 972), but he includes the companion volume *The Newspaper Press in Britain: An Annotated Bibliography* (see ARBA 88, entry 927). Moreover, he does not cite Ralph McCoy's *Freedom of the Press: An Annotated Bibliography* (Southern Illinois University Press, 1968), although he lists the first and second supplements to this monumental compilation.

An author index provides references to names in the literature reviews as well as in the bibliographies. However, the subject index inexplicably covers only the literature reviews. Thus, there is no subject access (other than broad geographic categories) to the sources described in the annotated bibliographies. This leaves users with no efficient means of identifying works on such topics as development communication in Jordan or the use of television in political campaigns in Argentina.

This volume has some serious flaws that greatly detract from its usefulness. It will be of interest primarily to academic libraries that collect extensively in the areas of international mass media, political communication, or development communication.—**Marie Ellis**

851. Cates, Jo A. **Journalism: A Guide to the Reference Literature.** 2d ed. Englewood, Colo., Libraries Unlimited, 1997. 317p. index. (Reference Sources in the Humanities Series). $45.00. ISBN 1-56308-374-4.

Covering the English-language reference literature on print and broadcast journalism, this annotated bibliography includes sources from the late 1960s through 1995, with a few 1996 volumes. More than one-third of the entries are new and about 90 percent have been either substantially or completely revised since the 1st edition (see ARBA 91, entry 958). In addition, there is a new chapter on electronic databases and Internet sources. The entries are descriptive and evaluative and include basic bibliographic information, including author, title, place of publication, copyright date, ISBN/ISSN information, etc. The compiler explicitly limits the coverage to journalism sources, which she defines as the sources that focus on the "gathering, evaluating, displaying, or disseminating (of) news, opinion, or information."

Cates, a former librarian at the Poynter Institute for Media Studies, is obviously knowledgeable on the reference literature of journalism, which she amply demonstrates in this outstanding bibliography. Some suggestions for entries in future editions: *American-Jewish Media Directory*, *Boston University Media Guidebook*, and the *Asian American Journalists Association*. This work is highly recommended for public and academic libraries.—**Donald Altschiller**

852. **U.S. News Coverage of Racial Minorities: A Sourcebook, 1934-1996.** Beverly Ann Deepe Deever, Carolyn Martindale, and Mary Ann Weston, eds. Westport, Conn., Greenwood Press, 1997. 387p. index. $85.00. ISBN 0-313-29671-5.

This reference provides a chronology of how Americans of African, Asian, Hispanic, Native American, and Pacific Rim descent have been portrayed in U.S. mainstream media. The focus is primarily on press coverage, with limited discussion of the broadcast venue. This longitudinal study brings together the research of many scholarly works from a broad range of disciplines. Each chapter addresses an individual minority and ends with full citations to the original research and a comprehensive bibliography.

By consolidating information on five minorities in one volume, the reader is able to identify common themes in the United States' uneven movement to integration. This book provides a valuable historical framework for understanding the current racial tensions our society faces and the power of the press to mold public perceptions.—**Adrienne Antink Bendel**

853. Walsh, Gretchen. **The Media in Africa and Africa in the Media: An Annotated Bibliography.** New Providence, N.J., Hans Zell/Reed Reference Publishing, 1996. 291p. index. $100.00. ISBN 1-873836-81-3.

This book is a comprehensive annotated bibliography listing 1,755 references. Walsh combines entries from African journals with publications from the West. Divided into four categories—press, broadcasting, film, and general—the cited articles cover African cultural and current events, censorship, and the training of African communications professionals. Significant attention is also given to development journalism. This term refers to the media's role in the shaping of social and political policies, their part in the formation of national identity and unity, and how Western reporting has influenced African perceptions of their own national cultures. The material is indexed by author, by subject, and by geographic location. A list is given of all the journals used in the bibliography, but without addresses.

All citations are available in American and European libraries. They range in date from the 1960s to 1996. This bibliography focuses on print sources and only in passing tacks on a few Internet sites. Walsh has compiled a valuable research tool with an impressive array of African works by African scholars. She has recognized that all too often inaccuracies are interjected by writers seeing Africa only from a Western cultural bias.—**Adrienne Antink Bendel**

Dictionaries and Encyclopedias

854. Gardner, Robert, and Dennis Shortelle. **From Talking Drums to the Internet: An Encyclopedia of Communications Technology.** Santa Barbara, Calif., ABC-CLIO, 1997. 355p. illus. index. $60.00. ISBN 0-87436-832-4.

This is a concise encyclopedia of communications technologies suitable for high school students. Gardner and Shortelle are experienced educators and have co-authored other books on historical or scientific topics. For this encyclopedia they define "communication technologies" as anything involved in the transfer or receipt of information.

This volume avoids the inevitable problem of obsolescence that plagues technical dictionaries and encyclopedias by defining only established terms and including biographies. Thus, the newest technologies, such as ISDN and multimedia, are not included; however, Walt Disney, the Goodyear Blimp, Helen Keller, and the information superhighway are. Each entry contains *see also* and *source* references, and there is a helpful bibliography as well as an index. Black-and-white photographs are interspersed in the text.

Libraries owning *International Encyclopedia of Communications* (see ARBA 90, entry 887), or a general science encyclopedia such as *The New How It Works* (Westport: Stuttman, 1993), can forgo this one. However, if you cannot afford a good science biography source, a general science encyclopedia, or a communications encyclopedia, this is a way to get all of those in one.—**Glynys R. Thomas**

855. Newton, David E. **Encyclopedia of Cryptology.** Santa Barbara, Calif., ABC-CLIO, 1997. 330p. illus. index. $60.00. ISBN 0-87436-772-7.

Intended as an introduction to the basic concepts of cryptology, the science and art of secret writing, this encyclopedia consists of more than 550 alphabetically arranged entries, ranging in length from a one-line definition to a three-page biography. All aspects of cryptology are covered, including the use of cryptology in military and political affairs, contemporary computer encryption systems, technological developments associated with cryptology throughout history, biographies of individuals important in the field, and the use of cryptology in literary works. Many of the entries also list sources for further study. The text of the federal Data Encryption Standard is provided in an appendix. There is also a short bibliography of general books, articles, and electronic sources. An index provides access to information contained within entries as well as to the entries themselves.

The entries are clearly written and well geared to the nonspecialist. Examples of the many different types of codes and ciphers help to clarify the explanations. Copious illustrations also enliven the text. Like the bibliography, the lists of further readings include both print and electronic sources. Not unexpectedly, a random check shows that some of the URLs already have moved or are no longer active. Because only the addresses and not the names of the sites have been given, it will be difficult to try to track down such sites in the future. The index is generally adequate, but there are some unexplained inconsistencies, such as the indexing of some publication titles but not others. These are relatively minor problems, however, and do not detract from the overall usefulness of the work. This will be a helpful reference in both public and academic libraries.—**Barbara E. Kemp**

856. Silverblatt, Art, and Ellen M. Enright Eliceiri. **Dictionary of Media Literacy.** Westport, Conn., Greenwood Press, 1997. 234p. index. $65.00. ISBN 0-313-29743-6.

The *Dictionary of Media Literacy* is a useful reference, especially for those exploring media studies and media literacy who specialize in other disciplines. It will also prove useful for students new to the critical study of mass media. It provides brief descriptive definitions of concepts (e.g., "emancipatory programming"), brief biographies of major figures in the field, and descriptions of and contact information for organizations of interest to those engaged in media-related scholarships. The entries are cross-referenced, and most end with a list of references for further reading. It is a useful volume to be used as a starting point. More problematic for many readers will be the reductive treatment of complex concepts and theories as they are harnessed to "media literacy." Although this fault may be unavoidable in a work that aims for both brevity and broad coverage, those using it should be aware that further research will reveal far greater complexity of some concepts than the *Dictionary of Media Literacy* acknowledges. [R: LJ, 15 April 97, p. 74]—**Marcus P. Elmore**

857. Watson, James, and Anne Hill. **A Dictionary of Communication and Media Studies.** 4th ed. London, Arnold; distr., New York, St. Martin's Press, 1997. 251p. illus. $18.95pa. ISBN 0-340-67635-3.

Since its appearance in 1984, this compendium of information—it is far more than a simple dictionary of terms—has been a reliable source of knowledge for professionals in the mass media. The current edition has been enlarged in the area of cultural terms, although this has been achieved at the expense of terms related to print. For example, *linotype* is included, while *signature*, *forme*, and *casing* are excluded; likewise, *gramophone* is retained, even though *compact disc*, *78*, and *cassette* are omitted. Yet the shortcomings are few and may not be significant. (Does anyone need a definition of *3-D* these days?) In most cases there are succinct quotations from original sources of terms, although the country rather than the city of publication is provided in bibliographic entries. Cross-references are not only helpful but extensive.

Some entries could be expanded more thoroughly: *head nods*, under the section "Non-verbal behaviour," could note the significant difference between western and Indian gestures as they relate to intercultural communication; *hermeneutics*, a much-used term at present, is briefly explained without current allusions to media theory. The style of composition is commendable. The authors agree that "TV appears to work on the principle that culture is basically communication and that popular culture is essentially interactive" and use this as the premise for selecting terms. It would be useful to include more United States (and perhaps European) television/radio series to exemplify terms, for not all readers outside Great Britain are familiar with even the most popular British programs. Notwithstanding these several small matters, this is an essential reference book for those in mass communications.—**Marian B. McLeod**

858. **Webster's New World Dictionary of Media and Communications.** rev. ed. By Richard Weiner. New York, Macmillan Library Reference/Simon & Schuster Macmillan, 1996. 676p. $27.95pa. ISBN 0-02-860611-6.

A rather odd addition to the "kitchen sink school" of reference publishing, *Webster's New World Dictionary of Media and Communications* attempts to cover a dizzying lot of territory in its 676 pages. Entries are taken from a plethora of sometimes tenuously related fields, including advertising, publishing, broadcasting, journalism, marketing, public relations, library science, printing, film, television, theater, and graphic arts. Although there is undeniably much that is useful and unique about this work (including specialized industry slang and jargon), the claim that this edition "has more definitions than you'll find in any one . . . media or communications dictionary" is laughably hyperbolic.

As may be expected in a work this lexographically ambitious, there is a fair amount of editorial quirk and idiosyncrasy to be found. The rationale for inclusions or exclusions is often disarmingly unclear: There is reference to Dada, presumably because of the movement's relation to film, but not to surrealism, decidedly the more cinematically influential movement. Entries appear for two of the three primary international video standards (NTSC and PAL), but not the third—SECAM. Despite these weaknesses, the *Dictionary of Media and Communications* does pack ample information between its covers, and it would probably be a useful addition to smaller general reference collections.—**Gary Handman**

Directories

859. **Hoover's Guide to Media Companies.** Austin, Tex., Hoover's, 1996. 522p. index. $29.95pa. ISBN 1-878753-96-7.

According to the introductory industry summary, during the period between 1995 and 1999, media will become the fourth fastest growing industry in the United States, with each adult spending 113 hours a year in new media-related activities ("new" meaning not television, radio, magazines, or books), up from 55 hours in 1990. Certainly such impressive statistics easily argue for the production of special industry guides such as this one. In addition to an introduction containing industry-related statistics and tidbits, the guide includes data complied on the top media companies. Each company entry contains an overview of the company; who the important officers are; where (both geographically and electronically) the company is located; what its products and services are; a list of its key competitors; and a variety of types of financial information, possibly including earnings, growth, salaries, stock pricing, and the like.

There are actually two substantive lists, the first defined as companies with "two-page entries," the second as companies with "one-page entries." Although there is probable legitimacy to expressing a company's size and importance this way, it sounds a little peculiar in the reading. There is then a more inclusive third list that briefly lists many more media-related companies, often referring back to the previous lists for those entries with more complete listings. The material in the three lists is indexed by a headquarters location index and an index in which brands, company names, and key people are interfiled. Both public and private companies are included, and many major foreign companies are also listed.

Business information published in book format can always be critiqued for being outdated as soon as (or perhaps before) it appears in print. That fact is certainly true of a guide that includes as many World Wide Web references as this one does. However, the advantage of an easy-to-use collection of industry profiles is that it can quickly steer readers to where or to what they should turn next. Both comments can be made about this recent entry into Hoover's growing collection of industry overviews. All in all, it is a handy directory that deserves a place in any relevant collection. It would prove to be equally useful for people looking for industry information or for job-hunters. Any academic or public library serving a population needing communications and media-related materials should consider this publication. Certainly, any business library should include this title in its collection.—**Caroline M. Kent**

860. **Media Courses UK 1997.** 4th ed. Lavinia Orton, ed. London, British Film Institute; distr., Bloomington, Ind., Indiana University Press, 1996. 231p. index. $14.95pa. ISBN 0-85170-587-1.

This volume is a guidebook to courses about media in the United Kingdom, which consists of England, Northern Ireland, Scotland, and Wales. The book is divided into four parts; it also contains two appendixes. The first part covers media courses in adult education; the second, undergraduate courses; the third, graduate-level courses; and the fourth, "short courses," ranging from one day to several weeks in length.

Each part contains information about a particular kind of media course. The section on short courses lists the name of each institution offering such a course, its address and telephone number, and a contact person. The segment on adult education includes this information and also contains information on how long a program takes to complete, how practical it is, and whether students attend full-time or part-time. The parts on undergraduate and graduate programs list the degree one earns after completing the program and offer a brief narrative description of each one.

Appendix 1 lists the wide variety of subjects taught in 1 or more media programs, including acting, communication, drama, film, journalism, and many others. Appendix 2 lists the media programs, county by county. Most U.S. readers will probably not be familiar with some of the book's words, phrases, and acronyms.—**David S. Webster**

861. Whisler, Kirk, and Octavio Nuiry. **The National Hispanic Media Directory, 1997.** Carlsbad, Calif., with Newport Beach, Calif., ADR Publishing, WPR Publishing, 1996. 315p. $95.00pa. ISBN 1-889379-06-9.

Primarily for locating Hispanic media, this directory may be useful to media buyers, advertisers, and conceivably job hunters. Whisler's National Association of Hispanic Publications and its "official sales team," the Latino Print Network, get their own section in the directory. Listed media are for a Spanish-speaking audience but are not necessarily owned and operated by Hispanics.

The main body of the directory (which is mercifully tabbed with boldfaced margin guides) includes introductory state-of-Hispanic-media articles followed by sections covering media formats and services: print, television, radio, online, advertising and public relations agencies, news services, and distributors. Issues per year, circulation, and MSA are given for each type of print media along with statistics, such as how many publications accept advertisements and total annual advertisement revenues for that media type. All other sections are organized geographically with contact names, addresses, and telephone numbers listed.

This directory fulfills its purpose, if not very elegantly. Minor typographic errors, combined with Susana Rendon McHugh's name on the cover even though her affiliation with the publication is unexplained, give this volume a slapdash feel. The authors acknowledge how quickly media information becomes outdated—even for an annual volume—suggesting that a looseleaf format may have offered greater accuracy. If a collection has *Hispanic Media and Markets* from Standard Rate and Data Service (quarterly), it will not need this volume. The directory under review is for comprehensive media collections only.—**Glynys R. Thomas**

Handbooks and Yearbooks

862. Nimmo, Dan, and Chevelle Newsome. **Political Commentators in the United States in the 20th Century: A Bio-Critical Sourcebook.** Westport, Conn., Greenwood Press, 1997. 424p. index. $95.00. ISBN 0-313-29585-9.

In 40 essays, the life and contribution to U.S. political commentary of 42 key personalities—2 essays treat 2 persons each, Robert MacNeil and James Lehrer and Martha Rountree and Lawrence Spivak—are set forth. The entries are alphabetic by the names of the commentators, one-half of whom are deceased. As explained in the introduction, the book traces political commentary through four phases: that of newspaper columnists, 1914-1928; radio commentators, 1929-1946 (the "golden age of radio"); the entertainment phase of television, 1949-1980; and the era of "opinionated commentary that invites expressive behavior among audiences," 1981 to the present. The introduction also points out the highly selective nature of the work—a selection (Walter Cronkite, Larry King, Rush Limbaugh, Dan Rather, and

Bernard Shaw are among the living ones included) from the hundreds of commentators this nation has produced in this century—as well as listing standard, general biographical and media-specific biographical sources consulted.

Coverage is current enough to include John Chancellor's death on July 12, 1996, but not David Brinkley's departure as anchor of "This Week" the following November. Each well-written essay usually concludes with three types of selected reference material: works by the commentator, critical works about him or her, and general works. A selected bibliography and an index of persons; newspapers and periodicals; radio and television shows; radio and television stations and networks; government agencies; places; and historic events, such as the Vietnam War, Watergate, and the two World Wars, conclude the book.

The authors—a political scientist at Baylor University and a communications teacher/researcher at California State University, Sacramento—state that the purpose of *Political Commentators* is to "portray the careers of key political commentators of the era and, through their lives and works, to illustrate the rise and decline of political commentary across the century." In this goal they have succeeded. This book can be recommended for medium-sized and large public and academic journalism/mass communications collections. [R: LJ, 15 Mar 97, p. 57]—**Wiley J. Williams**

AUTHORSHIP

General Works

863. **Freelance Editorial Association Yellow Pages and Code of Fair Practice, 1997-98.** Cambridge, Mass., Freelance Editorial Association, 1997. 131p. index. $47.50pa. ISBN 0-9628636-9-1.

The Freelance Editorial Association is a nonprofit organization, run by volunteers, that is designed to provide professionals in the editorial business with up-to-date information on trends in the publishing industry. This guide is designed with both freelance professionals and publishers looking for editorial assistance in mind. The introduction provides details on how to join the organization and mentions the benefits of membership, such as newsletters with current information on the industry, invitations to meetings with other freelance professionals, and contact information for the Members' Network (a telephone service that answers editorial questions).

The main focus of this directory is to provide a compilation of the contact information of association members, including name, address, telephone and fax numbers, e-mail address, and Website address. The book is separated into 10 different professions: copyeditors, desktop publishers, developmental editors, illustrators, indexers, project managers, proofreaders, researchers, translators, and writers. Many of the members of the association are listed under more than one of these headings. Some of the entries include additional information about the professional such as areas of expertise, how many years in the business, and technical skills. Three indexes are provided at the end of the directory to assist in locating freelance professionals: a specialties index, a geographic index, and a name index.

The directory also provides a 17-page reproduction of the Freelance Editorial Association's Code of Fair Practice. This contains valuable information for both those interested in hiring editorial freelancers and the freelancers themselves. Explained are the details involved in setting fees, establishing a professional relationship with clients, drawing up contracts for specific projects, and advice on how to resolve conflicts between clients and freelancers. A helpful chart is provided as well, which aids both freelancers and publishers in establishing scheduling and fee guidelines. An index to the Code of Fair Practice concludes this section.

This directory will be useful to both publishers looking for freelance editorial professionals and editorial freelancers looking to advertise their skills and meet others in their profession.

—**Shannon M. Graff**

Handbooks and Yearbooks

864. **The Avisson Book of Contests and Prize Competitions for Poets.** 1997-98 ed. M. L. Hester, ed. Greensboro, N.C., Avisson Press, 1997. 110p. index. (Avisson Writers Reference series). $27.50; $15.00pa. ISBN 1-888105-25-9.

More writers than ever are experimenting with poetry today, while at the same time many traditional avenues of publication no longer exist. One way poets can perhaps achieve both publication and financial remuneration is by entering their work in contests. According to the editor, *The Avisson Book of Contests and Prize Competitions for Poets* is the first and only reference work to gather together in one volume all of the many contests and prize competitions available to individual poets and authors of book manuscripts of poetry in the United States, as well as some Canadian and international entries.

The introduction defines terms and gives the novice writer sample guidelines, along with valuable tips about entering contests. The body of the book lists over 300 contests, with separate chapters for book competitions, chapbook contests, and single-poem contests. Also included is a bibliography of publications offering information about poetry contests. For quick reference, the index has three divisions: all contests, restricted contests, and a listing of sponsoring publishers and organizations.

The Avisson Book of Contests and Prize Competitions is easy to use and contains a great deal of information. Although its listings will quickly become outdated, this small volume will be popular with both published and unpublished poets, whether hobbyists or professionals. [R: LJ, 15 Sept 97, p. 60]
—**Kay O. Cornelius**

865. Grant, Daniel. **The Writer's Resource Handbook.** New York, Allworth Press, 1996. 261p. index. $19.95pa. ISBN 1-880559-58-7.

Writers looking in *The Writer's Resource Handbook* for assistance with their writing skills will not find help here. Rather, the book facilitates writers' relationships with the "middlemen" who make their works available to readers. Grant pulls together helpful information that writers often search for in vain. The names and addresses of legal assistance groups, writers' organizations, awards, editorial services, agencies that provide public and private support for writers, writer-in-residence programs, creative writing courses, and other sources of career assistance are provided. Chapters tell how to locate and deal with writers' groups and services, including arts groups. The books target audience will find far more information here of this type than most such sources offer. It will be best used as a complement to *Writer's Market, 1998* (see entries 869 and 870).—**Edna M. Boardman**

866. **Guide to Literary Agents, 1997.** Donald M. Prues, ed. Cincinnati, Ohio, Writer's Digest Books/F & W Publications, 1997. 300p. index. $30.00. ISBN 0-89879-766-7. ISSN 1078-6945.

Getting an inside peek at the world of literary agents has got to be fascinating for writers trying to sell their work. That fascination is why this annual is not only a reference book but also a fun read. Expanded and improved every year, the guide leads off with articles by literary agents and published authors giving their views and tips about the industry and how writers can choose and get accepted by the right agent. The main listings follow, divided according to nonfee- and fee-charging agencies with explanations of the pros and cons of each, and further separated into literary (fiction and nonfiction books) and script (screenplays for television and movies and stage plays) sections. A thorough index section allows the reader to search for an agent by subject, geography, individual agent names, or agency. There are also a glossary, a bibliography, a resource list, and even a ranking of agencies according to how likely they are to accept submissions.

Previous editions (see ARBA 93, entry 961, for example) are worth consulting both for the insider articles and for dropped listings (given with a coded explanation) that are still viable prospects. Aspiring writers may also want to consult competing guides, including *Literary Agents of North America* (4th ed.; see ARBA 92, entry 896) and *Writer's Guide to Book Editors, Publishers, and Literary Agencies, 1997-98* by Jeff Herman (a contributing writer to the present guide). However, libraries should not be without *The Guide to Literary Agents*, made invaluable by virtue of its annual updating and by Writer's Digest Books's longtime demonstrated commitment to and expertise in assisting writers in finding their way around the literary maze.—**Larry Lobel**

867. **Guidebook for Publishing Philosophy.** 1997 ed. Eric Hoffman, ed. Bowling Green, Ohio, Philosophy Documentation Center/Bowling Green State University, 1997. 255p. $30.00pa. ISBN 1-880559-15-3.

The present volume serves as a warning label on the tenure-hoping product called "New Author." Indeed, the first essay by Samuel Gorovitz ("Perils of Publishing") is a diatribe against Macmillan, Random House, and Prentice Hall, with one happy ending thrown in. The book is at once a combination of "misery loves company" and practical advice. Because publishing is a form of perishing, professors seeking publication will want to use, if not purchase, this volume even if they are not philosophy professors. Although most of the volume's practical advice focuses on philosophy, the essays dealing with publishing and manuscript preparation (six in number) are excellent advice for anyone who seeks to see his or her name in print. The majority of the book contains listings of United States, Canadian, and United Kingdom journals and publishers in philosophy and a listing of selected international philosophy journals.—**Mark Y. Herring**

868. **Poet's Market, 1998: 1,800 Places to Publish Your Poetry.** Chantelle Bentley and Tara A. Horton, eds. Cincinnati, Ohio, Writer's Digest Books/F & W Publications, 1997. 603p. index. $22.99pa. ISBN 0-89879-796-9. ISSN 0883-5470.

Since its inception in 1986, this annual guide has become a standard source for poets seeking to publish their work. In addition to offering more than 400 new listings, the 1998 edition also introduces several new features, among them a chapter on Internet opportunities for poets, a list of Websites of interest to poets, a one-page glossary of poetic terms, and the use of symbols to readily identify Canadian and overseas markets.

The heart of the work is an alphabetic directory of approximately 1,800 publishers and publications that accept poetry. Each entry provides basic information about the publication, including a brief description of its purpose, contents, and format, as well as an outline of the submission requirements and the selection process. Many entries include sample lines from a recently published poem. Additional directories list poetry contests and awards, conferences and workshops, and writing colonies and organizations of interest to poets, and other sections offer advice on submitting poetry and interviews with selected poets and publishers. Supplementing the general index to titles and publishers are geographic and subject indexes.

Poet's Market is similar in purpose and scope to another annual publication, the *Directory of Poetry Publishers* (see entry 599). Although the 1997-1998 edition of the latter guide includes 2,200 listings (approximately 400 more than *Poet's Market*), its entries generally are not as full as those in *Poet's Market*. However, its subject index, with almost 200 categories, is much more precise than the 30-category index in this work. Because each compilation has unique features and listings, most larger libraries will want to acquire both.—**Marie Ellis**

869. **Writer's Market, 1998: 4,200 Places to Sell What You Write.** electronic ed. [CD-ROM]. Cincinnati, Ohio, Writer's Digest Books/F & W Publications, 1997. Minimum system requirements: IBM or compatible 486DX/66MHz. Double-speed CD-ROM drive. MS-DOS 5.0. Windows 3.1. 8MB RAM. 15MB hard disk space. 640 x 480, 256-color monitor. Mouse. $49.99. ISBN 0-89879-802-7.

In the CD-ROM edition of *Writer's Market, 1998*, most of the information from the print edition has been transferred into the electronic medium; exceptions include the glossary and indexes. The CD-ROM tool also contains a "Submission Tracker" and "Writer's Encyclopedia," which is apparently an electronic version of the print publication of that name (no further explanation is given). Besides the print version itself, which makes no reference to the CD-ROM version except on a jacket cover, the CD-ROM has limited instructions on how to install and run the programs in Windows. Users conversant with Windows applications and procedures will find accessing individual markets in the electronic version straightforward, provided they are looking for a known market present in the database. However, access is for the most part neither simpler nor easier than in the print version. Furthermore, the CD-ROM has a number of disconcerting features, so much so that an attempt to present the CD-ROM's merits is hard to separate from its demerits.

For example, indexing is integral to the concept of the printed work. Entering text in the text finder box is the electronic analog to using a printed index; however, the CD-ROM omits some information that the print index contains. Thus, in a search for *Oxford*, no result was given for Oxford University Press—for which the print version's general index has a note indicating that the market is not receiving submissions (and therefore has no entry). An additional flaw is that clearing the dialog box in order to enter new data is a procedure that takes several seconds to perform.

The section introductions are designed to explain the market entries that, in print, follow immediately. In the CD-ROM version, the section introductions and the markets have been separated into different data areas. Here, hypertext links between the two are wanted, and the text needs redrafting. For example, the section introduction "Humor" (a subsection of Consumer Magazines), states "Publications listed here . . ." but no publications are displayed and one cannot click on a button to access them. Moreover, when viewing a section introduction, there is no way to get from section introductions to other functions without exiting to Windows and reentering. Within the dialog box that serves as principal mode of access to individual markets, finding consumer magazines that specialize in humor is not difficult, provided that the user correctly identifies the various elements of the dialog box and makes appropriate selections. To do so, one clicks on "Criteria" and selects consumer magazines. Next, the dialog box is reconfigured to show a list of subjects (the subsections of the print edition), as well as other limiting options. Selecting "Humor" will result in the same listing of markets as in the print version. One can save the list or customize it, but a button to access the section introduction is wanting. On the other hand, the CD-ROM user has another option: to enter the word "humor" in the text finder box. Doing so will result in a list of those markets containing that word in the data record. In this respect CD-ROM technology does have an advantage over print, provided that appropriate keywords are present in the pertinent records. The capacity to add markets is available, but is not necessarily appropriate in a context where multiple users will access the tool.

Accessing the help files is also problematic. This can be done from the Windows Start menu or by clicking on "Learn to Use Writer's Market." This option does not, however, present the much needed tutorial one expects. Neither does clicking on "How to Use Writer's Market: The Electronic Edition." Instead a document containing a maze of hypertext links comes up, each of which leads to another document with yet more links (including *see also* references).

The "Submission Tracker" allows users to keep records of their interactions with potential publishers. This facility will serve prolific writers well. Again, for multiple usership considerable administration is required. For library usage, it is recommended that the CD-ROM be installed as "read only," which will prevent any access to "Submission Tracker." In short, the tool has not been transferred to the electronic medium in a fully satisfactory manner. The producers should note that certain sections in the print version are integrally bound with other types of information, and should reconceive the electronic tool fully in its own terms. A de-installation option would be a welcome addition to the programs. The CD-ROM version can provide additional and enhanced access, but the print version remains a much-needed reference tool in libraries.—**Ian Fairclough**

870. **Writer's Market, 1998: Where & How to Sell What You Write.** Kirsten C. Holm and Don Prues, eds. Cincinnati, Ohio, Writer's Digest Books/F & W Publications, 1997. 1114p. index. $27.99. ISBN 0-89879-792-6. ISSN 0084-2729.

For most of this century, *Writer's Market* has been the preeminent tool for authors publishing their work. This 1998 edition, the first to be issued in paperback, is 10 percent larger than the previous year's, which was the first to appear in CD-ROM format as well as in print. The 1998 edition is also the first to include a section on online markets for writers aspiring to be published in electronic format.

Entries are arranged in chapters by categories such as book publishers (with Canadian and international publishers listed separately), small presses, consumer magazines and trade journals (each with numerous topical subdivisions), scriptwriting, screenwriting, greeting cards, and contests and awards. Each entry contains contact information (for this edition, Websites and e-mail addresses are included), a brief summary of the scope and format of materials accepted, payment and publication arrangements, and other valuable information. Although much material is carried forward from the previous edition, the editors have updated information wherever possible and have added numerous mission statements from U.S. publishers, which are identified by quotation marks. Noticeable also are several changes in layout and typography.

What makes this tool particularly attractive to peruse are the numerous explanatory chapters and side-bar essays (called "Insider Reports") that occupy the first 70 pages, plus the descriptive paragraphs that precede each section. The introductory chapters are specially written for this edition; however, the chapter titled "Getting Published" is a repeat. The four-page contents listing provides easy access to any section. In back are a glossary and lists of other resources—organizations, publications, and Websites—and two indexes. One index is to book publishers, arranged by broad subject categories. The general index intersperses topics with markets. It identifies new entries and includes references to markets not carried forward from the previous edition, with coded explanations such as "not accepting submissions" or "unable to contact."

The editors state that librarians report this work is frequently stolen. Such popularity suggests that the work should be considered for the circulating collection rather than just for reference. Publishers can use *Writer's Market* to compare their standing with the competition; they are also urged to cooperate by providing as full information as possible to the editors. High school librarians can use the tool to promote writing as a career to advanced students. With the growth of home-based self-employment in today's society, it is desirable that *Writer's Market* be made widely available.—**Ian Fairclough**

871. **The Writer's Resource: The Watson-Guptill Guide to Workshops, Conferences, Artists' Colonies, Academic Programs.** By David Emblidge and Barbara Zheutlin. New York, Watson-Guptill, 1997. 208p. illus. index. (Getting Your Act Together). $19.95pa. ISBN 0-8230-7651-2.

The Writer's Resource fits nicely into Watson-Guptill's Getting Your Act Together series. In the foreword, mystery writer Sue Grafton comments that "a writer is always learning, and a good writer is always seeking ways to extend the range of his or her talent." This slim volume is a veritable supermarket of opportunities, offering current and detailed information about nearly 300 workshops, conferences, and artist's colonies.

The work is divided into 3 parts. The 1st section deals with writing as a vocation. Short essays discuss a career in writing, touching upon the many different forms of the art: children's stories, journalism, playwriting, academic writing, and so forth. The 2d part, which makes up most of the book, opens with a list of national organizations and associations for writers. This is followed by a gazetteer listing residential programs, workshops, and conferences for writers. Entries are arranged alphabetically by state, followed by a list of academic programs. Simple icons identify each program as either residential, workshop, conference, or academic. The accompanying text lists basic contact information, such as name, address, and telephone number, plus information on admission requirements, deadlines, costs, class sizes, and financial aid. A few entries also indicate that the program is disability-accessible.

The final section deals with the "business of writing," offering a bare-bones overview of such basics as financial aid, getting started as a writer, how to submit a manuscript, and dealing with copyright. *The Writer's Resource* includes a brief bibliography and a topical index.—**Steven J. Schmidt**

Style Manuals

872. **The ACS Style Guide: A Manual for Authors and Editors.** 2d ed. Janet S. Dodd, ed. Washington, D.C., American Chemical Society, 1997. 460p. index. $26.95pa. ISBN 0-8412-3462-0.

The coverage of this book is much broader than the title might suggest. In fact, it covers almost every aspect of scientific communication, not just traditional activities like writing articles and giving technical papers, but even scientific poster presentations, letters to the editor, and press releases. There are even two sections to help those who review scientific manuscripts. This latter material discusses ethical guidelines and offers comments from experienced reviewers about how they work.

The conditions of scientific publication have changed significantly since the prior edition of this book (see ARBA 87, entry 872). Various types of electronic communication have become widely used, there have been changes in copyright law, and there is a greater tendency for individual scientists to word process their own papers rather than use a typist. The authors have responded effectively to each of these innovations. The only oversight noted was that computerized presentation software, which is becoming increasingly popular, was not covered in the section on oral presentations; however, many of the comments about traditional methods of giving oral presentations can be applied equally well to this new technology.

The 1st edition of this manual has been widely used, not only by chemists but also by scientists in related fields. This new edition should be equally popular. Overall, the range of information provided here is so extensive and so useful that the book will be helpful to a broad range of scientists, from experienced authors to graduate students who are doing their first professional writing. It can also be read profitably by well-prepared undergraduates. This work is strongly recommended.—**Harry E. Pence**

873. **The AMA Style Guide for Business Writing.** By the Editors at the American Management Association. New York, AMACOM, 1996. 326p. index. $29.95. ISBN 0-8144-0297-6.

Written by the editors at the American Management Association, this style manual addresses the special needs of business managers. It does not replace a good secretarial handbook, which should provide more thorough coverage of grammar, punctuation, and even letter composition. However, it explains the how-to of various business documents: goals and objectives, organization charts, procedures manuals and flowcharts, proposals, budget forecasts and financial reports, and basic writing guidelines. The guide's alphabetic arrangement of topics is intended to provide a quick reference source for those involved in preparing business communications, and it includes some sample forms. [R: RBB, 1 May 97, p. 1514]

—**Jean Engler**

874. **The Associated Press Stylebook and Libel Manual.** 6th ed. Norm Goldstein, ed. New York, Addison-Wesley, 1996. 332p. $14.00pa. ISBN 0-201-40717-5.

The Associated Press Stylebook and Libel Manual is the self-proclaimed "journalist's bible" (back cover), but it can also serve other writers and editors. Covering not only rules on spelling, grammar, and usage, the AP guide also gives information on country names, language to avoid, and other information for a changing world. After the foreword, nine sections make up the guide: the stylebook, the libel manual, copyright guidelines, details on the Freedom of Information Act, information on captions for photographs, guidelines for filing on the wire, filing practices, a list of proofreaders' marks, and information about the Associated Press. The stylebook and libel manual make up the largest portions of the text. The stylebook is A to Z in format and provides explanations, examples, and cross-references for many words and phrases. Separate alphabetic subsections on sports guidelines and style, business guidelines and style, punctuation, and bibliographies complete the stylebook. The libel manual gives pertinent information on how to avoid legal problems because of libel.

Last reviewed in ARBA 79 (see entry 127), little has changed in this guide to AP style in terms of format. When it comes to content, however, changes reflect updates in spelling, usage, and context for words and phrases. Examples of new terms include those relating to the Internet (e.g., URL, Website). Many things have changed during the past few years, and anyone wanting to keep abreast of changes in AP style and who does not have access to changes announced on the wires should purchase this latest edition. [R: RBB, 1 May 97, p. 1514]—**Melissa Rae Root**

875. Li, Xia, and Nancy B. Crane. **Electronic Styles: A Handbook for Citing Electronic Information.** 2d ed. Medford, N.J., Information Today, 1996. 213p. index. $19.99pa. ISBN 1-57387-027-7.

Obsolescence, like almost everything else, has been accelerated by the computer revolution. The authors of this handbook had to begin work on this revised edition almost immediately upon publication of the 1st edition (see ARBA 94, entry 1002), shortly before the World Wide Web's public debut made immensely greater sources of electronic information available to a vastly expanded audience. Feedback from users of the earlier guide—librarians, scholars, and students—showed their need for uniform formats to follow when citing sources of electronic information that had not existed just a short while earlier: the URLs that have become unavoidably familiar even to those who are entirely computer illiterate. Comments from users also convinced the authors that the widely emulated citation style of the *Publication Manual of the American Psychological Association* (4th ed., 1994), on which the 1st edition was based, is not amenable to all users. This accounts for the tripling in size of the present edition, which now includes an alternative citation format based on the also-popular *MLA Handbook for Writers of Research Papers* (4th ed., Modern Language Association, 1995) and the title's pluralization.

Two recent books in this new subspecialty, *Wired Style* (see ARBA 97, entry 758) and *The High-Technology Editorial Guide and Stylebook* (see ARBA 93, entry 969), designate themselves as stylebooks, but both seem to address usage (spelling and terminology) rather than style and are geared to a less academic audience. Readers should be aware of these different emphases, so they can refer to *Electronic Styles* for its intended use of "scholarly interaction." Attractive design, high-quality paper, and readability of typeface and format combine to make this book easy and pleasant to use.—**Larry Lobel**

NEWSPAPERS AND MAGAZINES

876. **Bacon's Magazine Directory 1998.** 46th ed. Chicago, Bacon's Information, 1997. 1616p. index. (Bacon's Media Directories). $275.00pa. ISSN 1088-9663.

Bacon's Magazine Directory 1998 is a comprehensive media guide to more than 11,600 business, trade, professional, and consumer publications in the United States and Canada. It is designed to provide the media and editorial contacts needed for preparing accurate, effective news release lists for organizations. This goal differentiates the tool from other directories, providing it with a distinct voice in serial bibliography. The publishers have issued other tools of similar purpose: *Bacon's Newspaper Directory* (see entry 877), *Bacon's Business Media Directory* (see ARBA 95, entry 933), and *Bacon's TV/Cable Directory* (see entry 886). Of these, the newspaper directory is mentioned in the introduction; indeed, they are integrally linked together. An earlier title was *Bacon's Publicity Checker* (see ARBA 92, entry 899), which was succeeded by *Bacon's Newspaper/Magazine Directory* (see ARBA 94, entry 1004).

Yet another tool is identified as "Bacon's Media Bank, the print media database for Bacon's Mailing Services and Bacon's Clipping Bureau." Unfortunately it is not clear whether this database is electronic or manual in format or to whom, outside of the publishing house, this database is made available. Thus, the bibliographic history as well as current availability of these tools is unclear and makes the task of retrieving and identifying them in an index or database somewhat onerous. A precise statement of the relationship between them would alleviate this situation. Librarians considering the work under review for acquisition may want to ponder whether users who find this work in the collection will also expect it to hold the other titles from Bacon's Information. Despite this confusion, *Bacon's Magazine Directory* stands alone and gives access to the kind of data that advertisers and publicity agents can use to place their news releases with magazines that are likely to find them of interest to their readership.

This guide is clearly written and laid out and is followed by indexes of market classifications into which entries are organized. Entries include addresses, telephone and fax numbers, e-mail addresses, circulation figures, frequency, and subscription and advertising rates, with a brief profile. (One entry includes the admonition, "Do be patient while waiting for a response.") Agents such as publishers and editors are listed by name. All publications are indexed by title. Those oriented to the Black and Hispanic communities and newsletters are listed separately. A list of publishers issuing three or more listed publications is provided. There is a wide scope of magazines included: Section 10A includes *Book Trades & Libraries*, *Library Journal*, and *Reference and User Services Quarterly*, as are some state library associations' publications. The criteria for inclusion are not stated. Thus, the work's claim to be comprehensive should not be taken as approaching exhaustiveness. This tool is required in libraries specializing in journalism and publishing. Others will find it useful to assist users whose goal is to find the most suitable magazine in which to seek publicity. The publishers have provided cards for submission of contributions of additional entries.—**Barbara B. Goldstein**

877. **Bacon's Newspaper Directory 1998.** 46th ed. Chicago, Bacon's Information, 1997. 1346p. index. (Bacon's Media Directories). $275.00pa. ISSN 1088-9639.

A critical scrutiny of the listings in this directory yields interesting, and sometimes alarming and disturbing, information. Although more than 27,000 newspapers are listed for the United States and Canada, only 1,550 of those are dailies in the United States, down from the long-held total (until recently), of 1,750. Slightly more than one-third of those are concentrated in California (98), Illinois (95), Texas (89), Pennsylvania (85), and Ohio (84); Delaware only has 2 dailies listed. When dailies and weeklies are combined, Delaware and Hawaii have a mere 19 and 20 newspapers total. Circulation also shows a wide range, with only 4 dailies topping 1 million and 106 over 100,000; in fact, the 250th newspaper in circulation has 41,467 purchasers. Many hang on with circulations under 10,000, even as low as 2,400. Most North American dailies are a part of 94 listed chains (called multiple publishers by *Bacon's*), with

American Publishing (102), Gannett (78), Thomson (69), and Donrey (49) leading the way in number of outlets. Very few newspaper-distributed magazines (only 7, led by the Newhouse-owned *Parade* with 37.7 million circulation) and Sunday supplements (28 in 17 states) remain.

Yet, *Bacon's Newspaper Directory* was not intended for this type of analysis, designed, as it has been for 46 years, for those seeking places for their public relations releases. The book serves that clientele well with names (and some e-mail addresses) of more than 156,000 editorial contacts. Divided into three sections, *Bacon's* provides detailed data, including names of personnel (down to the reporter level in many cases) on United States and Canadian dailies, alphabetically arranged by state/province and then by city. A 2d section is less comprehensive for community weeklies, whereas the 3d part is full of valuable information on news services/syndicates, a syndicated columnist index, newspaper distributed magazines/Sunday supplements, black and Hispanic newspaper indexes, multiple publishers, top 250 dailies, dailies over 50,000 circulation, state publisher associations, and daily and weekly newspaper locators.

Bacon's Newspaper Directory is the most thorough and accessible directory of its type that this reviewer has seen. It is a must for all research libraries (assuming they can afford its price).—**John A. Lent**

878. **The Desert Magazine Subject Index: All 534 Issues....** By Tom Budlong and Joan Brooks. Spokane, Wash., Arthur H. Clark, 1997. 525p. $65.00. ISBN 0-87062-281-1.

The Desert Magazine, founded and edited for many years by Randall Henderson, was published 534 times between 1937 and 1985. Its short-lived successor, *The American Desert*, appeared five times during 1992 and 1993. These two magazines, spanning 50 years, contain a wealth of information about the southwestern United States and other far western localities; not only providing information about the desert, but covering social and natural history as well.

The work reviewed here is a comprehensive, cross-referenced index to these two magazines. A listing of every author, article title, map, cover picture, book review, mining notice, editorial, and advertisement, as well as some letters to the editor is presented in a single alphabetic sequence. Titles appear in bold, italicized typeface, and a short synopsis has been added when a title was cryptic or uninformative. The nature of the entry is also identified. Subject entries can be precise (e.g., Lost Mine; Lost Mines; Lost Mines and Treasures) but many entries have been collected into 36 general categories (e.g., Archaeology; Bottles; Ghost Towns; Maps; Missions; Railroads; and Weather, as well as seven inverted headings under Indians).

The work is beautifully produced. Headers appear at both sides of a page—at the inner and outer edge. The work is bound in a textured, gold-embossed buckram cover. The work is an essential addition for any library holding *The Desert Magazine* or maintaining substantive collections about the southwest.—**Glenn R. Wittig**

879. **Magazines for Kids and Teens.** rev. ed. Donald R. Stoll, ed. Newark, Del., International Reading Association and Glassboro, N.J., Educational Press Association of America, 1997. 118p. $19.95pa. ISBN 0-87207-243-6.

A parent-oriented introduction and an appealing essay begin this superb resource designed for the people selecting magazines for young people. The editor of this 4th edition believes that periodicals invite children and youth to read more and can serve as a venue for budding writers. The body of the book consists of an alphabetic listing of 200 periodicals, including religious and foreign publications, each with an annotation provided by the publishers as well as its full address and telephone number. The editor has sought out newly published titles and has deleted (or marked) those no longer available. A note in the alphabetic listing helps readers identify audience, subject, circulation, cost, availability of samples, and whether the magazine accepts reader submissions. Appended title indexes group magazines by age, subject, and whether they publish reader work exclusively, regularly, occasionally, or not at all. This work will help adult writers locate outlets in the youth market, though this is not its overt purpose and parents wanting to stimulate literacy in their children will appreciate having it made available to them. This resource is far superior to computer-printout listings.—**Edna M. Boardman**

880. **Newsletters in Print 1998: A Descriptive Guide to Subscription, Membership, and Fee Newsletters....** 10th ed. Louise Gagne, ed. Detroit, Gale, 1997. 1600p. index. $245.00. ISBN 0-7876-1117-4. ISSN 0899-0425.

The life of a newsletter can be quite short or the information concerning it can change quickly; these facts acknowledged, the editor is to be applauded for this excellent compilation of more than 11,500 entries. Included are serials published in the United States or Canada, which are readily available to the public and have national or broad regional interest on specialized interests. The descriptive entries generally give publisher; editorial, subscription, and e-mail addresses; telephone and fax numbers; and editors. In addition, an entry may include the subtitle, description, audience, editorial policies, circulation, price, and additional information (e.g., available on microfilm or online).

Entries are arranged into 33 subject sections, which are divided into the 7 categories of business and industry, family and everyday life, information and communications, agriculture and life sciences, community and world affairs, science and technology, and liberal arts. Six indexes provide the user with easy access. The subject index is especially helpful, with more than 4,000 terms and myriad cross-references. The publisher, title, and keyword indexes note newsletters that the editor was unable to locate or that have ceased publication. This volume is recommended to the appropriate personnel in marketing, advertising, communications, and public relations as well as public libraries.—**Jo Anne H. Ricca**

881. Roth, Mitchel P. **Historical Dictionary of War Journalism.** Westport, Conn., Greenwood Press, 1997. 482p. index. $85.00. ISBN 0-313-29171-3.

Most general or military history encyclopedias give little space to war correspondents, unless they are well known (such as Edward R. Murrow), so this primarily biographical reference book should be appreciated. Although international in scope, most of the biographical entries are for those from the United States or the United Kingdom, reflecting in part the greater availability of information from these countries. In addition to reporters and photographers, artists who represented news organizations are also included, along with terms or important events and publications relating to the topic.

The period covered is 1846 to the Persian Gulf War. Cross-references within an entry are indicated by asterisks. Although the birth and death years for individuals are provided (if available), one wishes that the day and month had been included as well, along with some detail as to how and where the person died. There is only space for highlights of a person's career; one is left wanting more. The entries for wars mention the main journalistic personages. At the end of each entry are one or two references for further reading; however, they are incomplete, providing only the author, title, and date. Some of these individuals received longer entries in the earlier *Biographical Dictionary of American Journalism* (see ARBA 90, entry 905).

The valuable appendixes list correspondents for major wars from the Mexican-American War to Vietnam, those who died covering war zones, and Pulitzer prize-winners. A five-page selected bibliography rounds out the book. Roth is a professor of history and criminal justice at Sam Houston State University and has done much writing on the subject of the Texas Rangers. This volume is recommended for the reference collections of public and academic libraries.—**Daniel K. Blewett**

882. **Samir Husni's Guide to New Consumer Magazines.** 1997 ed. Samir A. Husni, ed. New York, Oxbridge Communications, 1997. 306p. illus. index. $95.00pa. ISBN 0-917460-84-7.

Husni, professor of journalism at the University of Mississippi, began this annual guide to new U.S. consumer magazines 12 years ago. This latest edition, covering magazines that began in 1996, describes 933 titles. They are arranged in 49 subject categories, such as arts and antiques, computers, gay and lesbian, music, pop culture, travel, and women's. Along with a black-and-white picture of one issue's cover (except for titles in the "Sex" category), information for each title includes publisher and editor, with address and telephone number; starting date; frequency; price; total number of pages; number of advertisement pages; and a brief comment on its editorial concept. An introductory essay provides a summary of the year's production; a title index concludes the volume. Anyone interested in trends in U.S. magazine publishing can profit from the guide. It should be in libraries with extensive journalism collections.—**Evan Ira Farber**

883. **Twentieth-Century American Sportswriters.** Richard Orodenker, ed. Detroit, Gale, 1996. 439p. illus. index. (Dictionary of Literary Biography, v.171). $140.00. ISBN 0-8103-9934-2.

Although biographies of sportswriters have been published separately or have appeared in other compilations, this book is devoted entirely to the genre. Forty writers, flourishing from the early part of the twentieth century to 1970, have been chosen to represent various styles and decades. Some, such as Roger Kahn and Grantland Rice, are well known in the field. Others, such as Paul Gallico and Damon Runyon, are perhaps better known in other genres. The majority, however, will be unfamiliar to most readers.

The alphabetic entries follow the familiar Dictionary of Literary Biography (DLB) format: birth and death dates as appropriate; references to entries in other DLB volumes; major positions held; a bibliography of the individual's publications; the biographical essay; a list of further readings, if available; and the location of the individual's personal papers, if appropriate. The entry focuses on the sportswriting career and achievements of the subject. Additional features, which enhance the value of the work, include a brief introduction that gives an overview of sports literature and sportswriting in general and a checklist of further readings. Combining convenient access and readable essays, this is a welcome addition to a major reference work that is a standard in libraries of all types and sizes.—**Barbara E. Kemp**

RADIO, TELEVISION, AUDIO, AND VIDEO

884. **AV Market Place 1997: The Complete Business Directory of Products & Services for the Audio Video Industry....** New Providence, N.J., R. R. Bowker/Reed Reference Publishing, 1997. 1519p. $159.95pa. ISBN 0-8352-3818-0. ISSN 1044-0445.

The 25th edition of this guide to the audio/visual (AV) industry should be well known to all but the smallest libraries. As with previous editions, this volume has been designed to permit easy access to vendors in the AV industry, computer systems, and film. An index of products and services at the front of the book lists the more than 1,250 categories used to classify industry entries. Most of the directory is comprised of an 800-page combined listing of audio-visual products, services, and companies. Various listings follow, including companies, trade association, film/television commissions, awards and festivals, and relevant books and periodicals. An activities calendar for trade shows in included; the resource closes with an industry yellow pages directory to people and organizations.

Bowker is respected as a publisher of exhaustive and reliable directories that are models of information organizations. This title is no exception, and as such is recommended to all libraries offering AV services or information about such services.—**Bohdan S. Wynar**

885. **Bacon's Radio Directory 1998.** 12th ed. Chicago, Bacon's Information, 1997. 2v. index. (Bacon's Media Directories). $275.00/set. ISSN 1088-9647.

886. **Bacon's TV/Cable Directory 1998.** 12th ed. Chicago, Bacon's Information, 1997. 2v. index. (Bacon's Media Directories). $275.00/set. ISSN 1088-9655.

These are the most recent editions of these standard media directories (see ARBA 95, entries 961 and 962 for a review of the 1994 edition). The 1st volume, *Bacon's Radio Directory*, provides information about more than 11,200 commercial and noncommercial radio stations in the United States. The majority of the work is devoted to a list of these stations. Arranged first by state and city, information is given about the market area (location, population, and the like). Under each city, the stations are listed alphabetically by call letters. Each entry indicates the AM or FM frequency; contact information (telephone and fax numbers, address, and e-mail and homepage addresses, if available); the owner; network affiliation; and management/news executives. Noncommercial, Hispanic, and black stations are also designated.

A station profile gives the target audience, the power in watts, news/talk show data, how guests appear (live/telephone/taped), sports play-by-play programming, use of releases or scripts for news segments, Arbitron rating, advertising lead time, and policy on public service announcements. The airtime, profile, and format of programs, including syndicated programs, are also given. Other sections give similar information about national and regional radio networks and radio syndicators. Additional helpful information includes counts of radio stations by state and format and listings of multiple radio owners. A call letter index and indexes to programs by title, topic, and syndicated programs all increase access to the abundant information found in the work.

The 2d volume, *Bacon's TV/Cable Directory*, deals with television and cable networks and stations in the United States. The body of the work is in three parts: national and regional television and cable networks and syndicators; individual television stations; and cable satellite systems. In the 1st section directory information is given for each network, including names of top executives, producers, and correspondents and their telephone numbers, with similar information for each program produced. The 2d and largest section of the volume supplies information on each television station in the United States and is arranged alphabetically by state and then by city. Again, general directory information precedes coverage for each television program produced locally. Coverage for both national and local programs includes lead times, guest information, product usage, and contact preferences. The 3d section is devoted to a geographically arranged run-down on cable satellite systems (e.g., Time Warner Cable of New York City) and the programs they produce. A total of more than 25,000 network, station, and show outlets are listed in this volume and it provides almost 138,000 contact names, with telephone and fax numbers and e-mail addresses. The listings appear to be accurate and up-to-date, although in this industry changes are rapid and frequent.

Much of the data provided in these two volumes will be of particular interest to those working in advertising, public relations, and similar fields who want to identify appropriate advertising outlets for their products or clients. However, anyone doing research in the field will find this a solid source of information. This directory will be a welcome addition to any general or subject reference collection.

—**John T. Gillespie and Barbara E. Kemp**

887. Buxton, Frank, and Bill Owen. **The Big Broadcast, 1920-1950.** 2d ed. Lanham, Md., Scarecrow, 1997. 294p. index. $59.50. ISBN 0-8108-2957-6.

This is actually the 3d edition of this work by Buxton. The 1st edition came out in 1966 under the title *Radio's Golden Age*. The "2d edition," actually the 1st under the title *The Big Broadcast*, was an expanded version that came out in 1972 and is now 17 years old (see ARBA 73, entry 1082). The 1997 edition is a further expansion and elaboration of the topic of what the authors call "real radio." "Real Radio" is not to be confused with current-day radio, which is "primarily talk and music without a single sound effect." In the 20-some years since the 1st edition of this work appeared, the old time radio (OTR) field has gone from what was fast becoming a lost art to a collecting passion for many individuals. Although most of the radio greats of the past have passed on, interest in collection and listing to these old radio programs reaches a new high each year. This interest is reflected in a number of collector groups currently active, the largest of which are the OTR Society of Newark, New Jersey, and the California Society for the Preservation of Radio Drama, Comedy, and Variety.

Buxton and Owen's work is arranged alphabetically by program name, such as *The Abbott and Costello Program*, *The Buster Brown Gang*, *The Line-Up*, and *When a Girl Marries*. Program entries are interspersed with factual articles about radio themes, such as "Sound Effects Men," "Announcers," "Musicians," and "Religion." No list of these topics is provided, nor are they in the index. A typical radio program entry consists of program name, cast, announcer, producer, writers, musical director, opening text, catch phrase, alternate version information, closing, notes, themes, and sometimes a brief narrative by the authors about the program. Some entries, such as the ones for *Hopalong Cassidy* and *Uncle Wiggily*, are rather brief. The authors have provided an excellent five-page bibliography. A personal name index (no topics or program names listed) and vitas for the authors are provided. An excellent introduction by Henry Morgan, a "radio personality," talks about the old days. Both Buxton and Owen are well qualified, with long histories in the radio field, to write this book. The book is bound in a sturdy library binding. There are no illustrations, which detracts somewhat from the book. Also not provided is a table of contents.

This volume is highly recommended for purchase by most general library collections. Libraries that have patrons with an interest in nostalgia radio will find this work a delight to read.—**Ralph Lee Scott**

888. **Encyclopedia of Television.** Horace Newcomb, ed. Chicago, Fitzroy Dearborn, 1997. 3v. illus. index. $250.00/set. ISBN 1-884964-26-5.

The Museum of Broadcast Communications was founded in 1987. It aims to document the moving target the television arena represents and to provide a forum for education and study of media issues. To that end, it makes its vast archive available to researchers and the general public alike. This admirable encyclopedia—1,948 elegant pages in 3 massive volumes—is an extension of that effort.

Newcomb and his 14-member advisory board have employed both ends of the telescope to concoct a worthwhile portrait of the medium. Important shows and individuals (actors, writers, producers, journalists, network executives) rate their own entries, along with general topics and corporate entities. The English-speaking countries get most of the attention, but there are essays on television developments in many other places. However much one may quarrel with isolated choices (is *The Outer Limits* less significant than *Honey West*?), the thousand-subject format contains no glaring omissions.

Contributors number in excess of 300, so a unified viewpoint (or singular prose) is out of the question. From *My Little Margie* to *The Forsyte Saga* to *Beavis and Butt-Head*, everything is viewed as equally deserving of one's time. No hierarchies or discouraging words need apply. Still, an enormous mass of material has been brought together, in a useful and attractive presentation. The alphabetic arrangement encourages browsing as much as serious endeavors; all names are indexed. This set is a must for reference libraries, but it also affords the casual reader much pleasure.—**Walt Mundkowsky**

889. Shiers, George, and May Shiers, comps. **Early Television: A Bibliographic Guide to 1940.** New York, Garland, 1997. 616p. index. (Garland Reference Library of Social Science, v.582). $95.00. ISBN 0-8240-7782-2.

George Shiers planned *Early Television* as a comprehensive, annotated bibliography of the entire literature on television—books, journal and newspaper articles, and patents—in English, French, German, and occasionally Italian, starting as far back as the basic discovery of the light-sensitive metal selenium in 1817. The work is divided into chronological chapters (annual after 1926), each introduced by an essay surveying developments, patent applications, and publishing trends and a chronology of events. Unhappily, the death of Shiers occurred before completion of so tremendous a task, and the work is as stated above only down to 1931. The chapters for the years 1932 to 1935 lack their introductory essay, those for 1936 to 1939 lack their chronologies as well, and the final chapter 20, "Distant View, 1940-1995," has only 250 citations—of books and just a few of the more important journal articles. In offering this necessarily truncated version, Shiers's wife and friends who edited his manuscript have added *Early* to the title as a cautious delimiter. Nevertheless, what readers have is a good overview of the entire development of the invention to 1995, and a most detailed, definitive resource (8,633 citations) for the pioneering first century and a quarter.

The work opens with an introduction by Tony Bridgewater, former chief engineer for BBC Television, and another by George Shiers ("Understanding a Century of Television"). The volume closes with a name (including country and institution name) index and a subject index (which includes individual transmitting stations). These indexes, although adequate, are to item numbers only, resulting sometimes (e.g., under "Baird Television" and "Cathode-Ray Tube") in as much as a column-long phalanx of undifferentiated reference numbers.—**L. Hallewell**

21 Decorative Arts

COLLECTING

General Works

890. Andacht, Sandra. **Collector's Value Guide to Oriental Decorative Arts.** Dubuque, Iowa, Antique Trader Books, 1997. 250p. illus. index. $24.95pa. ISBN 0-930625-80-3.

This book is not meant for the top bidders at high-level auction houses with advanced expertise and pocketbooks to match, but rather for mid-level collectors, regular shoppers of antique fairs and upscale flea markets, and knowledgeable amateur collectors of fine decorative wares. The author, a dealer in these works and the publisher of *The Orientalia Journal*, has compiled many fine examples of the various genres and given lucid descriptions as well as offered brief explanations of techniques and styles for a variety of Oriental decorative objects. The prices given must all be taken as approximations due to the wide variance found in changing tastes and the market at any given time. Illustrations, in both color and black-and-white, are helpful, and the work includes a useful set of appendixes that detail Chinese and Japanese dynasties, snuff bottle marks, various themes frequently used in decorations, and woodblock artists' signatures. All of these are important reference tools for the collector and dealer and make this book a worthwhile purchase for a collector's private library.—**Paula Frosch**

891. **Antique Trader's Guide to Games & Puzzles.** By Harry L. Rinker. Dubuque, Iowa, Antique Trader Books, 1997. 256p. illus. index. $17.95pa. ISBN 0-930625-62-5.

This price guide to more than 3,000 games (board, skill, and cards) and jigsaw puzzles is evidence that some collectibles are still affordable. The focus is on commercial products from the mid-1800s to the present. Patrons should consult *Kovels' Antiques & Collectibles* (Crown Publishing Group, 1997) by Ralph and Terry Kovel, or a similar title for the value of generic antiques, such as playing cards, checkerboards, and chess sets. Informative introductory chapters discuss the history of games and puzzles, how to collect and care for them, and the "state of the market."

Games, listed alphabetically by title, make up the greatest part of the guide. Each entry gives the manufacturer's name, type of game, and a brief description of distinguishing features, such as cover art, year, and value. Some note number of game pieces, movie and television tie-ins, and international editions. The fairly small section on puzzles is divided into a number of categories, including adult hand cut, adult die cut, juvenile by year range, juvenile frame tray, and advertising. Puzzle entries are arranged by manufacturer, and provide description of image, artist name, finished dimensions, number of pieces, approximate date, and price. Many also note a puzzle number and whether or not the original box is included. All prices are retail, from venues such as flea markets. Black-and-white illustrations are a nice addition on most pages. A subject index to games and a title index to puzzles allow access for "crossover" collectors (e.g., those who collect aviation or holiday-related stuff).

Public libraries that purchase titles on antiques and collecting should consider this guide for the reference or circulating collection.—**Deborah V. Rollins**

892. **Black Americana Price Guide.** Kyle Husfloen, ed. Dubuque, Iowa, Antique Trader Publications, 1996. 178p. illus. $17.95pa. ISBN 0-930625-34-X.

The richly illustrated *Black Americana Price Guide* is both a collectors' and a historical tool. The guide includes pricing of popular culture items, such as trading cards, political and sports memorabilia, and kitchen goods, among other items. Items listed provide reminders of segregation, civil rights campaigns, notable African Americans, and achievements in music. The guide is introduced by Julian Bond, noted activist and academic, who is an avid collector of black Americana. Entries are grouped by type of object, and each listing gives a description and date, along with a price. The guide features numerous clear illustrations in color and black-and-white. This volume would be valuable to libraries with an interest in collectible guides or African American studies and history.—**Lynne M. Fox**

893. Brecka, Shawn. **Collecting in Cyberspace: A Guide to Finding Antiques & Collectibles On-Line.** Dubuque, Iowa, Antique Trader Books, 1997. 154p. $14.95pa. ISBN 0-930625-69-2.

This topical guide to cyber addresses lists approximately 2,000 Internet locations and Websites for 82 types of antiques and collectibles, including quilts, musical instruments, art glass, movie memorabilia, and pottery. Provided within each broad category are the URLs of useful Websites; Web addressses for related publication sites; club, association, and organization sites; and chat lines on America OnLine, CompuServe, and Prodigy. Content for each Website is explained by such terms as FAQ, general information, pictures, buy/sell/trade, links, price guide, or auction. For this type of guide, it would be useful if the contents provided a more detailed explanation. The 11-page introduction to using the Internet for collecting is clearly written, accurate, and understandable to the neophyte. The publisher, Antique Trader Books, is an experienced, authoritative, and respected information provider in the antiques and collectibles field. On its own, this slight volume is a reasonably priced, acceptable purchase for libraries seeking a comprehensive collection for antiques and collectibles. Nonetheless, with the effectiveness of Web search engines, such as Altavista or Yahoo, and the rapidly changing nature of the Web, libraries must question the need for the title.—**Patrick J. Brunet**

894. **Country Americana Price Guide.** Kyle Husfloen, ed. Dubuque, Iowa, Antique Trader Publications, 1996. 380p. illus. $16.95pa. ISBN 0-930625-26-9.

As important cultural artifacts, American country antiques have continued to be popular with the antique-loving public. *Country Americana Price Guide* is a fairly comprehensive pricing guide for collectors of "country Americana." This guide focuses on a diverse range of topics that reflect a wide range of collecting tastes. Exploring a captivating part of evolving heritage, the guide has almost 400 pages of collectible treasures from the United States, past and present.

The book is generously illustrated with more than 800 black-and-white photographs to aid in dating and identifying items of country furniture, decorated stoneware, graniteware, and more. The guide covers 30 of the most important categories of country collectibles. Categories are listed alphabetically by primary classification (e.g., ceramics) with subclassifications (e.g., blue and white, redware, stoneware) following. Addresses and telephone numbers of collector clubs, organizations, newsletters, and auction houses are in a special appendix at the back of the book. There is also a list of suggested further readings. Unfortunately, no detailed index supplements the table of contents.

Drawing on the experience and expertise of many of the nation's specialist collectors, dealers, authors, and auctioneers, this book offers up-to-date value information. In the introductory article, Tom Porter of the highly respected Garth's Auctions shares insights gathered during his career as auctioneer and collector. This work is reasonably priced and easy to read, particularly in a semibrowsing mode. The guide is recommended for public libraries that want to provide a user-friendly resource for the antique-loving public.—**Vera Gao**

895. Coykendall, Ralf, Jr. **Coykendall's Complete Guide to Sporting Collectibles.** Radnor, Pa., Wallace-Homestead/Chilton Book, 1996. 294p. illus. index. $22.95pa. ISBN 0-87069-736-6.

This useful survey covers four areas of sporting collectibles: (1) paper, including duck stamps, books (with a special section on Derrydale's), ephemera, magazines, periodicals, calendars, and posters; (2) fishing, including split cane rods, flies, lures, and accessories; (3) hunting and shooting, including antique firearms, cartridges, and knives; and (4) decoys, including birds and carved fish. Each category and subcategory has a brief one- to three-page introduction explaining history and pointers to consider when collecting, followed by the entries complete with an estimated value. Informative sidebars are interspersed throughout the volume and add greatly to its utility. The work is well illustrated with mostly black-and-white photographs.

This is Coykendall's third price guide for sporting collectibles; he has also written extensively on wildfowling and duck decoys in addition to being a regular columnist for *Antique Week*. With the many topics listed, the work cannot cover any area in much depth, and serious collectors will be better served by the specialist volumes in their area, such as *Fishing Lure Collectibles* (Collector Books, 1995) or *Fishing Tackle Antiques and Collectibles* (Holli Enterprises, 1992). Still, as a one-volume overview, this guide is a good purchase for any library looking to stretch its collectibles dollar.—**Patrick J. Brunet**

896. **Flea Market Trader: Thousands of Items with Current Values.** 11th ed. Sharon Huxford and Bob Huxford, eds. Paducah, Ky., Collector Books, 1997. 447p. illus. index. $9.95pa. ISBN 0-89145-779-8.

This price guide to hundreds of commonly found flea market items has few competitors. The editors provide background information on each category of collectible and suggest general values for particular items. These values are based on personal experience and assume mint condition, unless otherwise noted. The point is also made that prices will vary somewhat throughout the United States. The book is alphabetically arranged, beginning with "Advertising Collectibles" and ending with "World's Fairs and Expositions." One or two black-and-white photographs appear per page. A state-by-state directory of specialist dealers is included, as is a list of clubs and newsletters. These added features will help collectors expand their expertise and locate hard-to-find items. The index is useful, even though such categories as ashtrays, banks, and dolls have 40 or more citations to look up. At the reasonable price, public libraries may want a circulating as well as a reference copy for their shelves.—**Gary D. Barber**

897. **Garage Sale & Flea Market Annual: Cashing in on Today's Lucrative Collectibles Market.** 5th ed. Paducah, Ky., Collector Books, 1997. 463p. illus. index. $19.95. ISBN 0-89145-786-0.

This annual publication is a guide to the collectibles market of newer items, that is, items produced from the 1930s on. The compilers, Sharon and Bob Huxford, propose to help the reader identify valuable collectibles found at garage sales and flea markets. Introductory sections cover information on holding a garage sale, finding bargains, identifying what is hot, and deciding where to sell finds. Arrangement within the text is by manufacturer or broader headings, such as cat collectibles, napkin dolls, or cookie jars. Headings for manufacturers are followed by a short description of the company or producer and lists of clubs or related books. The collectibles are listed in alphabetic order following the headings.

Each entry includes the "book" value of the item, usually a high average retail price. Lists at the end of the book cover auction houses, clubs, special interests (persons), and a topical index. The arrangement of the entries and the breadth of coverage means that locating a specific item can be time-consuming. There is no table of contents, but the index is somewhat useful. Because the compilers attempt to cover all major categories of collectibles since 1930, some areas receive limited coverage, such as Depression glass or Coca-Cola collectibles. These are better served by books devoted solely to them. However, for the novice or the amateur collector, this can be a valuable resource. The annual guide contains many black-and-white illustrations in addition to the hundreds of entries. This publication is a useful addition for libraries serving patrons interested in collectibles and garage sale finds.—**Ingrid Schierling Burnett**

898. Henriques, Gary, and Audre DuVall. **McDonald's Collectibles: Identification and Value Guide.** Paducah, Ky., Collector Books, 1997. 351p. illus. index. $19.95pa. ISBN 0-89145-783-6.

Going to McDonald's is as American as apple pie. In 1948, the McDonald Brothers opened their first drive-in restaurant in San Bernardino, California, selling 15 cent hamburgers. Today there are more than 15,205 restaurants worldwide, and McDonald's has exceeded $25.9 trillion in sales. The McDonald brothers appealed to the kids' market with special promotions and giveaway items.

This book is a guide to the McDonald collectibles. The prices shown in the book are not intended to set prices in the marketplace. They are for items in average to mint condition, unless otherwise noted. This book recalls for the reader the fun and nostalgia of McDonald's. It will also make one ask the question, "Why did I throw that away?" about the many items one had as a child. The book begins with the McDonald's story, followed by the cast of characters. The pictures are in color and include a brief description. There is a 17-page chronological history of the McDonald's Corporation from 1948 through 1994. Following are the giveaways from the early days, including coloring books, postcards, games, and so forth.

In 1977, the Happy Meal was introduced with test items such as riddles, secret decoders, puzzles, and patches, to name just a few. The book continues with Happy Meals giveaways; dolls; jewelry; and miscellaneous items, such as yo-yos, watches, and trading cards. There are also pages of tableware. An extensive index is found on pages 345-51. A list of regional clubs is included for all the McDonald's collectible collectors.

Readers of all ages will derive pleasure from this guide, an informative book. It will satisfy the beginning collector and the older, more serious one.—**Barbara B. Goldstein**

899. Kerr, Ann. **Fostoria, Volume II: Identification and Value Guide to Etched, Carved & Cut Designs.** Paducah, Ky., Collector Books, 1997. 357p. illus. $24.95. ISBN 0-89145-726-7.

Volume 2 of this collector's guide is a companion to *Fostoria: An Identification and Value Guide of Pressed, Blown, and Hand Molded Shapes* (Collector Books, 1994). Like the first volume, this book includes an introduction to fostoria glass and a glossary of terms for describing items. The majority of the book is an alphabetic guide to the designs; under each is a list of items with identification number, dimensions or weight capacity, and price in today's collector's market. For most designs, there is a black-and-white reproduction or drawing. Sixteen pages of color photographs, nicely reproduced, show glass colors. At the end of the book is an update to volume 1, consisting of item names; shape numbers; item numbers (which were absent from the earlier volume, thereby confusing the reader); and pictures of plain shapes listed therein. *Fostoria, Volume II* is recommended for collectors, public libraries, and any collection possessing the first volume.—**Lori D. Kranz**

900. **Standard Catalog of Football Cards, 1998.** By the Editors of Sports Collectors Digest. Iola, Wis., Krause Publications, 1997. 399p. illus. $24.95pa. ISBN 0-87341-550-7.

This 400-page book by the editors of *Sports Collection Digest* is one of the most complete guides to football cards ever published. Patterned after the highly successful *Standard Catalog of Baseball Cards* (see entry 906), the book contains information on 175,000-plus football cards and more than 1,500 sets. Collector issue cards, such as those from bubble gum packs, are not included because they have little value to collectors.

The book opens with a concisely written introduction that describes how the volume is organized and how to identify a card's age, how to grade a card's condition and determine its value, and how to identify counterfeit and reprint cards. The histories of different football cards, such as Bowman, Topps, Fleer, Upper Deck, Play-off, and Philadelphia, are also reviewed. Careful research is evident in the compilation of a tremendous variety of cards from 1894 to the present. In addition to football cards, prices are listed for selected college football sets and specialty memorabilia and figurines. A photograph of a representative card from each set and a detailed description of how the card looks are useful aids for identifying cards.

Because of the huge numbers of players, individuals are not indexed by name. Therefore, to find an individual player his team must be known. The history section could have benefited from a list of the top 100 cards and why they are valuable.—**Mark J. Crawford**

901. **Wanted to Buy: A Listing of Serious Buyers Paying CASH for Everything Collectible.** 6th ed. Paducah, Ky., Collector Books, 1997. 368p. index. $9.95pa. ISBN 0-89145-791-7.

Wanted to Buy lists collectors and dealers of all types of objects. The subtitle promises that the listings include "serious buyers paying cash." The directory is arranged by type of collectible. Predictable categories appear, such as pottery, china, and glassware. Also included are less common collectible categories, such as back scratchers, pocket calculators, or chewing gum wrappers.

Although *Wanted to Buy* is not a comprehensive source, it does provide valuable information for patrons who wish to dispose of collectibles to reputable dealers and collectors. Entries include descriptions for each dealer's collection interest and provide specific examples with prices that dealers are willing to pay. This makes the book a price guide as well as a directory of dealers. It would be a valuable addition to any library where patrons need information on buyers or dealers of collectibles.—**Lynne M. Fox**

902. Wisniewski, Debra J. **Antique & Collectible Buttons: Identification & Values.** Paducah, Ky., Collector Books, 1997. 168p. illus. index. $19.95. ISBN 0-89145-711-9.

Although the title identifies this work as a guide to identification and values of antique and collectible buttons, the purpose, as stated in the introduction, is to provide general information about the different materials and range of subjects that buttons represent. This work is not so much a reference book as it is a personal scrapbook. Aimed at sharing her knowledge with beginning collectors, the author's joy of button collecting is evident throughout the work.

Sections are devoted to buttons made from particular materials: glass, plastic, pearl, shell, metal rhinestone, and enamel, as well as to particular types or sizes of buttons: goofies, realistics, diminutives, studio, uniform, and commemorative buttons. Beautiful, full-color photographs of carefully selected and arranged buttons fill the glossy pages. Button values for each photograph are helpful, despite the early disclaimer that dealer and auction prices vary greatly depending on condition, demand, and locale.

The conversational language contains useful tips on how to get started, button cleaning, shanks, mounting boards, and material identification. The text, however, contains numerous grammatical, punctuation, and typographic errors, and the organization is haphazard (e.g., paragraphs covering storage, condition, and pricing are discussed under the larger heading "Button Cleaning Tips"). The inclusion of introductory paragraphs for some chapters but not others is disconcerting, and the significance of several unlabeled photographs is puzzling. Of interest to beginning as well as avid button collectors, this volume may be a useful addition to the collections of public libraries. However, scholars and academic libraries would be better served by Diana Epstein and Millicent Safro's *Buttons* (Harry N. Abrams, 1991) or Nancy Fink's *Buttons: A Collector's Guide to Selecting, Restoring, and Enjoying New and Vintage Buttons* (Courage Books, 1994).—**Debra S. Van Tassel**

Antiques

903. **Miller's International Antiques Price Guide 1997.** 18th ed. Judith Miller, Ian McKay, and Elizabeth Norfolk, eds. Wappingers Falls, N.Y., Antique Collector's Club, 1996. 808p. illus. index. $35.00. ISBN 1-85732-892-2.

Now one of the standard tools in its field, *Miller's International Antiques Price Guide*, which continues to show its British origins, has now established itself as a long-term, reliable price guide to high-quality antiques. It has undergone little, if any, change in its basic approach since its last review (see ARBA 88, entry 969). That in itself contributes to its lasting quality. Unlike many antique guides that seem to establish their pricing based largely on the "expertise" of the author, *Miller's* relies on established sales prices either at auction sales or in antique shops, markets, or fairs. This edition, like its predecessors, lists approximately 10,000 items, each accompanied by a black-and-white photograph, a concise description, and a fairly narrow price range based on sales. Each entry also includes an abbreviation that refers to the list of auctioneers and dealers who contributed the information. In addition, there are, as usual, several review sections that provide color photographs of some of the more important pieces in a number of categories. The items are arranged in approximately 60 categories that range from the broad (e.g., "furniture") to the narrow (e.g., "card cases"). Within each category, like items (such as stools) are loosely grouped together. The arrangement and the availability of a detailed 13-page index make it easy to locate a particular item.

Although this guide lists a large number of items, it is not always possible to find in a particular edition a piece that matches an item for which information is being sought. The real value of this guide is that, taken as a whole, the various editions do provide, over time, comprehensive information about a wide range and variety of antiques. Its large format ($6\frac{1}{2}$ by 11 inches) and hefty size (808 pages) do not lend themselves to carrying this volume around to auctions, shops, or sales. The guide does represent one of the best purchases in the field for libraries whose patrons have a strong interest in high-quality antiques.

—**Norman D. Stevens**

904. Raycraft, Don, and Carol Raycraft. **Wallace-Homestead Price Guide to American Country Antiques.** 15th ed. Iola, Wis., Krause Publications, 1997. 256p. illus. $19.95pa. ISBN 0-87069-721-8.

This publication, written by Don and Carol Raycraft, contains aspects of American antiques that are necessary for present and future collectors to be aware of and covers the 1700s through the early part of the nineteenth century. Price guides, trends and predictions, a collector inventory, and market and auction houses are all part of this spectacular visual and textual publication. Included in this 15th edition are more than 750 photographs of a variety of country antiques with comprehensive descriptions and current values—for example: "Oak wall telephone, working condition, original finish, c1930s ($275–$325)." One can learn much with this publication on American antiques through photographs and written words. This guide is a valuable and well-researched work that is highly recommended for academic, public, or special libraries interested in the antiques field and other institutions.—**Lisé Rasmussen**

905. **Schroeder's Antiques Price Guide.** 15th ed. Sharon Huxford and Bob Huxford, eds. Paducah, Ky., Collector Books, 1997. 602p. illus. index. $12.95pa. ISBN 0-89145-734-8.

Prices and descriptions of some 50,000 antiques and collectibles can be found in *Schroeder's Antiques Price Guide*. Nearly 500 categories, from "A B C Plates" to "Zsolnay," are arranged alphabetically. Each entry begins with a short historical explanation of the collectible and its manufacturer(s), followed by a descriptive list of specific items and their current prices. These prices were obtained from collector's clubs, auctions, dealers, appraisers, advertisements, and other authorities. Small black-and-white photographs of some objects are included. Completing this book are a list of the more than 400 advisers on the publisher's board; directories of auction houses and contributors to the guide; a list of clubs, newsletters, and catalogs; and an index by category and manufacturer. This is a good price guide for the generalist, but collectors and dealers who specialize will also want more specific guides, such as those concerned with toys, glassware, dolls, pottery, and so on.—**Lori D. Kranz**

Baseball Cards

906. **Standard Catalog of Baseball Cards, 1998.** 7th ed. Bob Lemke, Joe Clemens, and Steve Bloedow, eds. Iola, Wis., Krause Publications, 1997. 1568p. illus. index. $39.95pa. ISBN 0-87341-529-9.

Baseball legend Bill Veek's definition of baseball as "an island of surety in a changing world" could as well apply to this collegiate dictionary-sized volume. As the editor of the less comprehensive *Sports Collectors Digest Baseball Card Price Guide* (see ARBA 88, entry 990), Lemke includes in this book the market values for 330,000 baseball cards and for more than 7,000 sets. With this latest edition, Lemke has reorganized and split the main body of the catalog into two sections: the first provides valuations for cards (and other collectibles of pulp manufacture) issued from 1869 through 1980, and the second provides valuations for such items issued from 1981 to 1997. Each of these two lengthy listings is organized alphabetically by each collectible series' title and, except for the most obscure series, a 50-to-100 word overview precedes the item-by-item valuations. Appraisals for major league items issued after 1980 that are in mint condition are no longer accompanied by near mint (NM) and excellent (Ex) condition valuations in this edition. Also, the grade of good (G) has been dropped for items of any vintage, which is understandable, given the highly competitive world of serious collectors. Additional sections in this reference give price quotations for collectors' issues, foreign cards, and minor league cards. A glossary of 200 terms (e.g., "autograph guest," "cabinet card," and "Goudey") supplies succinct yet helpful definitions. Useful alphabetic and chronological indexes complete the catalog. Unfortunately, a masterful survey essay from the 7th edition has not been carried over to the current edition. Also, renderings of the reverse sides of many items have been omitted from this edition, in favor of inconsequential enlargements depicting the obverse sides of said items. Although some collectibles (e.g., Stein Market Red Sox cards) have been dropped from this edition, others such as Futera Australian Baseball League cards are included. For the first time, each of this work's sections is preceded by a brief but satisfactory introduction. In scope and reliability, this international price guide remains the uncontested champion in its field.—**Jeffrey E. Long**

Books

907. **Comics Values Annual: The Comics Books Price Guide.** 1998 ed. By Alex G. Malloy. Stuart Wells III, ed. Dubuque, Iowa, Antique Trader Publications, 1997. 675p. illus. index. $14.95pa. ISBN 0-930625-85-4. ISSN 1062-4503.

This book took years to evolve to its present stage, a listing of more than 6,600 comic book titles in 74,000 or more entries, with 30,000-plus updated prices. For the comic book collector, it is one of a few useful guides, providing the near-mint prices of comic books, organized by company, title (alphabetically), and issue number. Each entry provides the initials of the creator and a two- or three-word identification of the contents. The sections are DC Comics, Marvel, Golden Age, Acclaim (Valiant), Dark Horse, Image, Malibu, Color Publishing, B&W Publishers, Classics Illustrated, and Underground.

Difficult to fathom is why Malloy would take such an enormous amount of time to compile such a comprehensive volume and then fail to tell the reader his parameters, intentions, and rationales, as well as the most effective way to use the data. For example, why does he mix corporate names with types of publishing (color and black-and-white), genre (underground), period (golden age), and a title (*Classics Illustrated*) in his main headings? Why list only near-mint condition? Why abbreviate creators' names and include them separate from the main body of the book, making for difficult cross-referencing?

The place for answers to these and other questions (such as, how does Malloy's book differ from others?) is the preface, which Malloy uses to provide an extremely superficial, brief, and folksy overview of the comics market, industry, and collecting. An essay called "The Rise and Fall of Atlas Comics," an interview with Jeph Loeb, a comics grading guide, and a miserably weak bibliography round out the book. Because the text is laced with poor grammar, spelling and typographic errors, and other marks of poor editing, one must wonder also about the validity of the main data. This guide is recommended only if it is used with caution and in conjunction with other listings.—**John A. Lent**

908. Thompson, Maggie, and Brent Frankenhoff. **Comics Buyer's Guide 1998: Comic Book Checklist & Price Guide, 1961 to Present.** 4th ed. Iola, Wis., Krause Publications, 1997. 600p. illus. $16.95pa. ISBN 0-87341-527-2.

This 600-page guide is complete and easy to follow. It opens with a section entitled "Are There Any Questions?" in which the authors answer some of the most common questions pertaining to the book. Some are actual letters sent in by collectors and others are merely tips the author feels may help readers get the most out of their collections. Following this is a "Photo Grading Guide" that explains the different levels of quality that determine the worth of these collectibles. Examples of mint condition and very fine condition, to good and poor condition will give readers information as to what to look for when building a quality collection. There is also a "Guide to Defects," which explains common defects found in comic books, such as off-center printing, subscription crease, rusty staple, water damage, and multiple folds and wrinkles, which can decrease the value of a comic book.

After scanning the "Abbreviations" section, which defines the many abbreviations found in the book, readers can concentrated on the bulk of the guide. The next 291 pages provide an alphabetic listing of more than 75,000 comics, with more than 200,000 current prices. Each entry shows numbers of issues; dates; original sale price; and current market value for good, fine, and mint condition. This is both a useful guide to determine the worth of a current collection and a must in the trenches of the comic booksellers market. It lends the power of knowledge and experience in a field of collectibles where many time it is buyer beware.—**Michael Florman**

Coins (and Paper Money)

909. Carlton, R. Scott. **The International Encyclopaedic Dictionary of Numismatics.** Iola, Wis., Krause Publications, 1996. 444p. illus. $39.95. ISBN 0-87341-443-8.

The field of numismatics seems to invite specialization; most of its texts deal with a specific area of collecting, coinage of a particular country, or are simple price guides. This book is distinguished by its broad overview, which includes all forms of money used around the world throughout history, from cowry shells to digital currency. The only similar book published in the past 15 years seems to be *The Macmillan*

Encyclopedic Dictionary of Numismatics (see ARBA 83, entry 871). Although that volume had more illustrations and a larger section of color photographs, the present work features a useful pictorial section that illustrates numismatic terms using actual coins, a dictionary section of non-Roman alphabets (Greek, Cyrillic, and Hebrew), and a "multi-language matrix" (English terms translated into 20 languages). The usefulness of these last two features is questionable and redundant. The foreign-language terms in the dictionary section also appear as entries in the encyclopedic section. Although this might be useful for non-English-speaking readers, it clutters the encyclopedia and steals space that might have been used for more informative material. Other flaws noted are excessively long biographical articles (it's easy to find information on Franklin D. Roosevelt elsewhere) and lack of cross-references in the encyclopedia section—for example, the Hebrew term *bilti m'zoheh* is simply defined as "unattributed." Looking it up in the dictionary section gives the same definition. Looking up "unattributed" in the encyclopedia section, one learns that the Hebrew word probably refers to a coin that is "not fully identified." Curiously, although the matrix section translates into Korean, Japanese, and Chinese, none of the Oriental languages are included in the alphabets section. Another criticism is that the paper used is nonopaque, which readers will find distracting when an illustrations bleed through on the opposite side of the page.

Those interested in the subject will find it fun to browse the articles, illustrations, and beautiful glossy color photographs. Despite its flaws and because of its coverage of neglected areas, it is recommended for public libraries. [R: RBB, 15 May 97, pp. 1613-14]—**Larry Lobel**

910. **Handbook of United States Coins, 1998.** 55th ed. R. S. Yeoman and Kenneth Bressett, eds. Racine, Wis., Whitman Coin Products/Golden Books Publishing, 1997. 208p. illus. index. $6.95pa. ISBN 0-307-19906-1.

Both the *Handbook of United States Coins* and *The Guide Book of United States Coins* (see ARBA 96, entry 1008) have been indispensable to generations of coin collectors, but their value as price guides has diminished as the electronic revolution has spawned the development of more current sources of information about coin market prices and conditions, most notably the weekly *Gray Sheet*, newspaper financial sections, and Internet sources. Much of the pricing information in these books is out of date upon publication, because fluctuating gold and silver values have an effect on the more common collector coins.

Although this handbook shows wholesale prices paid by dealers, and the *Guide Book of United States Coins* lists retail prices paid by collectors, much of the remaining historical, photographic, and mintage information is identical. The latter, however, is consumer-targeted and contains more introductory and expository material, featuring short essays about the rare coin market, how to detect counterfeits, and other material of interest to collectors.

Other price guides list buy and sell prices side by side—what dealers will pay for an item and what they will sell it for. Buyers realize there must be a spread between these to allow dealers to make a profit, and publishing dealer prices in a separate book has never succeeded in keeping this knowledge from the public. Because both books are acquired by coin dealers and collectors primarily for the excellent numismatic information they contain rather than as price guides, it seems sensible to consolidate them. This would simplify and reduce the cost of acquiring information that neither libraries nor individuals can afford to do without.—**Larry Lobel**

911. Krause, Chester L., and Clifford Mishler. **Standard Catalog of World Coins, Eighteenth Century 1701-1800.** 2d ed. Iola, Wis., Krause Publications, 1997. 1136p. illus. $65.00pa. ISBN 0-87341-526-4.

This volume, covering 1 century of the world's coinage, resulted from the gathering of 25 years of continuous data and expands the scope of the original 1-volume version of this authoritative reference. This necessitated subdividing the work into 2 volumes in the late 1980s, and into 4 volumes (one for each century since 1600), with the publication of the 1st edition of the present work in 1996 (see ARBA 97, entry 780).

Although numismatists will appreciate the thoroughness of the coverage, the unwieldiness and expense of purchasing 4 volumes annually will present a problem for many collectors, and could be handily remedied by making this work available on CD-ROM. This would also avoid duplication of much of the prefatory and supplementary material found in each of the four annual volumes, which includes conversion charts, maps and geopolitical data, glossaries, charts, grading criteria, and more.

This volume, covering the interesting period of European expansion, compares well with the *Standard Catalog of World Coins, 1998* edition (see entry 912). All the useful formats and features found in the other volumes in the series are retained. Among these are arrangement alphabetically by country of origin, then by denomination, then by year of issue; illustration by actual-size photographs of coins (nearly 18,000 shown); Instant Identifiers (for quick determination of the origin of coins bearing unfamiliar alphabets and numerical systems); four-level pricing; and much else. This guide is recommended for collections with larger numismatic holdings.—**Larry Lobel**

912. Krause, Chester L., and Clifford Mishler. **Standard Catalog of World Coins, 1998.** 25th ed. Iola, Wis., Krause Publications, 1997. 1792p. illus. $47.95pa. ISBN 0-87341-497-7.

This year's edition of *Standard Catalog of World Coins* celebrates the 25th anniversary of what is the most comprehensive reference work for identifying coins of all the world's nations. As each new edition has brought expanded coverage and knowledge of world coinage (see ARBA 87, entry 915, ARBA 85, entry 815, and ARBA 81, entry 968), it became necessary to divide the original single volume into four separate volumes; one for each century, beginning with the year 1600. This portion of the set, covering only those coins issued in the twentieth century, adds to the useful formats and features that have been developed over the years, including actual-size photographs of the more than 45,000 cataloged coins, glossaries, charts, maps and geopolitical information, four-level pricing, grading criteria, and much more.

It is the aim of the authors to be as comprehensive as possible. Thus, the inclusion of NCLT (non-circulating legal tender) or commemorative coins, issued by governments to market to collectors, has contributed significantly to the explosive growth of this reference. Because it has become unwieldy and expensive to acquire, it is hoped that this guide will be converted to CD-ROM format, enabling collectors and libraries to update annually at a savings to both buyers and publisher. Until a CD-ROM is available, however, libraries will want to purchase this indispensable guide for those interested in the numismatic field.—**Larry Lobel**

913. Olsen, Margaret, with Alison Matthews. **The Platinum & Palladium Buyer's Guide.** Westminster, Colo., Westminster Publishing, 1997. 266p. illus. index. $24.95pa. ISBN 0-9630498-2-8.

At first glance, one may think that this book has limited appeal. In fact, the authors have presented the topic in such a way that it makes for interesting reading whether one collects in this very specialized field or not. The elements, platinum and palladium, are rarer than gold and were only refined in the last century.

The book is divided into three parts. In the 1st part, the authors give a history of the metallic art and tips on the buying, selling, and care of precious metals. Part 2 is a catalog of coin and metallic issues. First, platinum issues are listed by country of issue, followed by platinum refineries and mints. Next comes palladium issues, listed by county, concluding with refineries and mints of palladium issues. Each issue or series is described by 13 different parameters, including weight, size, and fineness. Most are illustrated by photographs shown to actual size. The final section contains various tables of weight equivalents, recent high and low prices for platinum, palladium, gold, and silver. There are also a glossary and a bibliography.

Although the business of buying and selling coinage of such rare metals is beyond most collectors, this book offers insight into the beauty and the art produced in these metals. The guide is recommended for any collection with an extensive coin collecting section.—**Margaret F. Dominy**

914. Rulau, Russell. **Standard Catalog of United States Tokens 1700-1900.** 2d ed. Iola, Wis., Krause Publications, 1997. 944p. illus. index. $47.95pa. ISBN 0-87341-479-9.

The collecting of tokens has a long history, but general reference resources devoted to this specialty have not existed until now. Tokens have been around since colonial times and were used when the availability of coinage or currency (legal tender) was limited, as promotional items, or as wages of a kind. Tokens were made from a variety of metals, wood, cardboard, or plastic. This work, a cooperative effort of Krause Publications and the Civil War Token Society, has brought together the rich arena that is token collecting. More than 500 individuals and numerous token and historical societies contributed to this catalog.

The catalog is arranged chronologically. Varieties may be arranged geographically, by use, or by composite material. The photographs are generally of high quality but ultimately can only be as good as the condition of the original object allows. Special note should be made about the extensive use of anecdotal information provided for some issues. The background stories about the origin or use of certain tokens deliver wonderful insights into history and even the human condition.

The catalog has a comprehensive index and information about token societies. It is highly recommended for public and academic collections.—**Margaret F. Dominy**

915. **Warman's Coins & Currency.** 2d ed. By Allen G. Berman and Alex G. Malloy. Radnor, Pa., Wallace-Homestead/Chilton Book, 1997. 211p. illus. index. $19.95pa. ISBN 0-87069-747-1.

Virtually everyone, at one time or another, has set aside a special coin or paper money just because it was interesting beyond its buying power. For some, this turns into a lifelong, extensive, and intensive avocation. For most, coin and currency collecting goes no farther than the jar in the back of the closet.

The novice or the mildly interested collector will find this book a useful resource. It covers ancient to modern coins and currency, including medals, commemoratives, tokens, and more. The authors have provided a well-organized and easily accessible reference work. Large, boldfaced headings for each series make for easy finding. An illustration typical of the series, a brief history, and additional references are provided. A unique service the authors have included is the "Counterfeit Alert" for each series. The authors should be commended for including this feature to alert the casual collector to any history of counterfeiting a particular series may have had. The "Hints" section attached to each series is evidence of the mentoring attitude of the authors. Here, they may provide advice on the storage of proof sets, a statement about the typical condition of a particular series, or a series that is kind to one's budget. Selected retail price guides are given as a frame of reference to determine valuation, and no attempt was made to include multiple grades or rare types.

Finally, Berman and Malloy frankly discuss the process of selecting a dealer. This advice alone is worth the price of the book, which is highly recommended for public, school, and academic reference collections.—**Margaret F. Dominy**

Dolls

916. Herlocher, Dawn. **200 Years of Dolls: Identification and Price Guide.** Dubuque, Iowa, Antique Trader Publications, 1996. 276p. illus. index. $17.95pa. ISBN 0-930625-29-3.

Doll enthusiasts and antique dealers will not be disappointed with the abundance of information provided by this book. The dolls covered are primarily from the United States, Great Britain, France, Germany, and Japan. Arranged alphabetically by manufacturer or type, the entries include photographs of typical specimens (in the author's opening notes, she mentions how difficult it was to track down examples for visual documentation); production history; a description of characteristic markings (as well as variations); current values; and comments on flaws or damage that may affect the price. Sometimes there are hints on how to recognize reproductions. Other features are advice on how to care for dolls, a glossary of terms, and a listing of manufacturers' mold numbers.

Because Herlocher, a recognized doll expert, provides concise but surprisingly detailed entries for each type of doll, this book is ideal as a library reference tool. Readers will find information not only on such classic products as Effanbee, Madame Alexander, and Barbie dolls but also on such categories as Japanese dolls, kewpies, mechanical dolls (sometimes referred to as "automata"), Cabbage Patch dolls, and contemporary collectible dolls.—**Margarete Gross**

917. King, Constance. **Collecting Dolls Reference and Price Guide.** Wappingers Falls, N.Y., Antique Collectors' Club, 1997. 279p. illus. index. $49.50. ISBN 1-85149-254-2.

This well-designed, highly useful, and handsome British publication is a new addition to the series of price guides published through the auspices of the Antique Collector's Club. Like the others, it is copiously illustrated, with black-and-white and color photographs provided for each doll. These photographs are of excellent quality, many of them procured from the auction houses and sales rooms where the dolls were sold. Hundreds of high-quality vintage dolls are presented, dating from 1600 to the late

1930s, with the emphasis being on those most frequently found in good salesrooms or in the stock sold by specialist dealers. The dolls are organized under 10 categories: wooden and early dolls, wax dolls, papier-mâché dolls, fabric dolls, and indestructible dolls. Each category is provided a full-page introduction, which gives a historical description relating to the origin and production as well as collecting and pricing. Entries are given for each doll described in terms of construction and appearance; makers, dates, marks, and country of origin are enumerated, along with a valuation given in pounds. Valuations range from 10 pounds to 30,000 pounds. An informative introduction gives advice on collecting and explains the possible variations in pricing, which occur due to geographic location of the sale, condition of the doll, or even provenance. In addition to a general index, access is facilitated by brief indexes of marks and of numbers.—**Ron Blazek**

918. Moyer, Patsy. **Doll Values Antique to Modern.** Paducah, Ky., Collector Books, 1997. 383p. illus. index. $12.95pa. ISBN 0-89145-778-X.

919. Moyer, Patsy. **Modern Collectible Dolls Identification & Value Guide.** Paducah, Ky., Collector Books, 1997. 215p. illus. index. $19.95. ISBN 0-89145-785-2.

Both of these books help doll collectors identify and assign a value to many types of dolls. Each book is arranged in alphabetic order by manufacturer or, in some cases, by type of doll (china, cloth, wooden, advertising dolls, and so forth). Each book features a short bibliography and index, and both offer lists of collectors' groups where the reader can find out more information about particular dolls. In scope and purpose, however, the two titles differ somewhat.

Modern Collectible Dolls describes only dolls manufactured within the past 70 years. Although definitions differ, most collectors generally agree on that period for the term *modern*. In contrast, *Doll Values Antique to Modern* lists prices for dolls manufactured during a longer period of time, with the earliest examples dating from the 1820s. *Modern Collectible Dolls* is aimed at novice doll collectors. In her introduction, Moyer defines terms, explains where to look for identifying marks on the doll, advises readers on how to start a collection, and recommends keeping track of one's purchases using a computer program. The introduction in *Doll Values* assumes most of this information. Instead, Moyer presents here an informative essay on the qualities that influence the price a doll can command. Every doll in *Modern Collectible Dolls* is illustrated with a color photograph, captioned with the doll's height; the composition of its head (dolls are identified by their heads: A vinyl doll has a vinyl head, regardless of its body composition); and a suggested value. Moyer describes approximately 600 to 700 dolls. *Doll Values* is less heavily illustrated but offers more prices—more than 500 prices for Madame Alexander dolls alone. In *Doll Values*, Moyer often lists two prices for a particular doll, one for good but not perfect condition and the other for mint condition. She averages prices taken from her database of sales recorded at auctions and doll shows, published in doll publications, and reported by collectors.

Despite the overlap in the dolls covered, surprisingly few photographs appear in both volumes. Both books will be helpful to the collector. No one doll identification book can serve all needs, but by consulting a number of works collectors can increase their chances of finding some information on unknown purchases.
—**Linda Keir Simons**

Firearms

920. **Gun Digest, 1998.** 52d ed. Ken Warner, ed. Iola, Wis., DBI Books/Krause Publications, 1997. 542p. illus. $24.95pa. ISBN 0-87349-191-2.

The most recent edition of this standard work continues the tradition of comprehensive coverage of guns and gun topics for all shooters—hunters, handgunners, collectors, handloaders, and those interested in the history of firearms. The volume is broken into three sections: feature articles, departments, and the catalog itself. The feature articles include both articles on the history of firearms and their production as well as current topics of interest to today's shooters. Biographies of several individuals are also included in this section. In the departments section, users will find informative articles on the current state of the shooting industry with product development discussions concerned with presenting information needed by the consumer in making purchasing decisions. An example of this type of article is the one authored by Holt Bodinson entitled "Ammunition, Ballistics and Components." Other articles include such topics as scopes, handloading, and a blackpowder review.

The main section of the volume is the catalog of currently produced and available guns of all types—rifles, handguns, shotguns, blackpowder, and air rifles. Each entry in this section includes an illustration of the firearm listed as well as other useful information: caliber, barrel length, weight, overall dimensions, stock composition, type of sights, any special features, and an estimated price. If there is an alternate price for added features, models, or left-handed version, that price is listed as well. The volume concludes with several indexes and appendixes, among those listed are periodicals devoted to firearms, books on the subject, and a manufacturers directory.

This work will find many users in public libraries and libraries specializing in firearms, hunting, or collecting topics. To be most useful to researchers, this volume needs to be purchased for each edition published because of the changing nature of the subject matter. This will not present a burden to most libraries because of the reasonable price of the work.—**Gregory Curtis**

Memorabilia

921. Augsburger, Jeff, Marty Eck, and Rick Rann. **The Beatles Memorabilia Price Guide.** 3d ed. Dubuque, Iowa, Antique Trader Publications, 1997. 227p. illus. $24.95pa. ISBN 0-930625-68-4.

The 3d edition of *The Beatles Memorabilia Price Guide* is a useful tool for collectors and a walk down memory lane all rolled into one. Those old enough to remember Yellow Submarine bulletin boards, Beatles sneakers, Beatles candy or gum, or Beatles hair spray they may now be owners of valuable collectibles. The guide divides items by type, including jewelry, pins, posters, books, magazines, music, movies, promotional items, trading cards, and performance-related items. Special chapters are set aside for Yellow Submarine items and Apple Records memorabilia. Each entry includes an item number, name, detailed description, value, and original country where sold. All items are priced according to grades of good to near-mint condition. Special notes identify factors that affect price, such as original packaging. The guide is heavily illustrated and includes recommendations for purchase by beginning collectors. One chapter provides tips and information on spotting reproduction items and counterfeits. A glossary and abbreviations list completes the guide. The guide does not provide an index. *The Beatles Memorabilia Price Guide*, is a nicely produced resource although it will not be a required addition to most libraries' collections.—**Lynne M. Fox**

922. Davis, Greg, and Bill Morgan. **Collector's Guide to TV Memorabilia, 1960s & 1970s.** Paducah, Ky., Collector Books, 1996. 277p. illus. index. $24.95. ISBN 0-89145-705-4.

The intention of this price guide to television memorabilia is to give a range of values for a comprehensive list of merchandise produced for television shows of the 1960s and 1970s. The guide highlights items marketed for the purpose of promoting a television show during its original run. These include toys, books, games, posters, school supplies, and other items that bear the name of the show. The guide is divided into 46 sections. Presented alphabetically (from *The Beverly Hillbillies* to *Wonder Woman*), each section contains full-color photographs and suggested price ranges for each item. Of particular note are the television icons appearing at the heading of each show's section. The icons contain much information on the series, including its run dates, the number of episodes produced, the show's peak rating position, and a list of main characters and cast members.—**Jennifer Comi Ellard**

923. Petretti, Allan. **Petretti's Coca-Cola Collectibles Price Guide.** 10th ed. Norfolk, Va., Antique Trader Publications/Landmark Specialty Books, 1997. 648p. illus. index. $42.95. ISBN 0-930625-76-5.

Petretti's price guide is an authoritative volume, or, as the author states in the introduction, the "text book" of Coca-Cola collectibles. Containing more than 6,000 illustrations and many colored plates, this is the complete source for both the serious collector and the amateur.

An excellent table of contents preceding the entries and an index at the end of the guide provide good access to the sections of this volume. The collectibles are grouped by type, including calendars, Santas, cardboard signs, watch fobs, and others. Especially valuable is the section on illegal and unauthorized reproductions and the warnings against fraudulent usage of logos and names.

In addition to the hundreds of pages of illustrations, there are informative sections on the history of the company and the history of collectibles as well as on tips for the collector, the art of the company, the competition, the script trademark, slogans with their date of use, a chronology of important years, suggested books for collectors, sources of related organizations, and a glossary. Petretti has been a devoted collector for many years. He often appears on radio and television shows and writes regular columns and feature articles in collecting publications.

This is the volume all serious collectors of Coca-Cola memorabilia must own and a valuable reference book for libraries with an interest in collectibles.—**Ingrid Schierling Burnett**

Pottery

924.   **The Charlton Standard Catalogue of Chintz.** 2d ed. By Linda Eberle and Susan Scott. Toronto, Charlton Press, 1997. 230p. illus. index. $24.95pa. (U.S.). ISBN 0-88969-188-0.

Who can predict how collecting trends will develop? At the beginning of 1996, books on this year's hot new collectible—chintz ceramics—were nonexistent. This year, there are several. In addition, Christie's auction house in London recently conducted an all-chintz sale. But what exactly is chintz? It is flower-print English pottery—reminiscent of old wallpaper and cozy cottages—that first made its appearance in the 1820s. Many potteries manufactured it, and patterns abound. Because it was considered a poor person's pottery, no records were maintained on its history. The authors (one from the United States, one from Canada) resorted to advertising in British newspapers in order to find documentation on the subject. In the United States, chintz-ware reached its heyday, ironically, during the art deco period of the 1920s, but Canadians, Australians, and New Zealanders were importing it until the early 1960s. As recently as 1980, Mikasa was turning out its own line.

This book provides advice on collecting (as with anything, never collect for investment purposes alone), as well as classified advertisements for dealers worldwide whose specialty is chintz-ware. There are separate sections on the 18 major manufacturers of chintz-ware, with a brief profile of each company; current prices of individual items (e.g., cake plates, cheese keeps, teapots) in American, Canadian, and British currencies; and full-color illustrations of various patterns and makers' marks. Because it can be difficult to be precise with word descriptions of pottery shapes, one section itemizes "shapes" by means of dozens of photographs of ceramic objects, such as teapots and nut dishes. This catalog is recommended for all decorative arts collections.—**Margarete Gross**

925.   **The Charlton Standard Catalogue of Royal Doulton Beswick Figurines.** 5th ed. By Jean Dale. Toronto, Charlton Press, 1996. 444p. illus. index. $19.95pa. (U.S.). ISBN 0-88969-161-9.

926.   **The Charlton Standard Catalogue of Royal Doulton Beswick Jugs.** 4th ed. By Jean Dale. Toronto, Charlton Press, 1997. 626p. illus. index. $24.95pa. (U.S.). ISBN 0-88968-202-X.

These guides provide much of the information beginning collectors need to identify the most interesting forms and subjects. Indexes provide ready access to manufacturer's identification number, series (such as figurines in the Colonial Williamsburg series), and names for individual pottery pieces. An important consideration for the beginning as well as the experienced collector is price. Prices are given in three currencies: United States, Canada, and the United Kingdom (sterling). There are few items not pictured for either jugs or figurines. The black-and-white photographs of the figurines show enough detail for quick identification. The photographs of some early jugs do not enable users to identify type of handle or details of dress; for example, vests, tankards, shoes, or hands. Photographs of the twentieth-century Toby jugs are excellent (handles are always shown).

Pottery marks are given for many of the jugs pictured. Marks associated with Doulton figurines are in that guide's introduction. The information given on editions (number made, years produced) is easily understood. Jugs were often produced in limited editions, but most figurines were produced for a number of years, and starting and ending dates are given.

These guides provide collectors—especially beginners—useful identification information that should help them understand the marketplace. Both guides contain further reading lists; however, bibliographic information is incomplete.—**Milton H. Crouch**

927. **Pottery and Porcelain Ceramics Price Guide.** 2d ed. Kyle Husfloen, ed. Dubuque, Iowa, Antique Trader Books, 1997. 406p. illus. index. $14.95pa. ISBN 0-930625-73-0.

This price guide is one of many publications from Antique Trader Books, the company that also publishes *Antique Trader Weekly* and maintains the Antique Trader Online database on the World Wide Web. Husfloen, editor of many similar publications, presents a substantial listing of the major ceramic and pottery collectibles that are on the market today. The volume is an alphabetic listing of companies and pottery types, with detailed descriptions of thousands of pieces and hundreds of black-and-white photographs. Each section includes a brief description of the company with drawings of identifying marks, as appropriate.

As in the 1st edition, the coverage of this volume includes ceramic pieces dating from the early eighteenth century through the middle of the twentieth century from the United States and Europe. In addition, there are a greater number of entries for popular twentieth-century U.S. pottery and china, particularly those pieces currently of interest to collectors. Each entry includes a price. The editor does not indicate the basis for the prices shown.

The guide includes useful introductory chapters on collecting; descriptions and drawings of typical ceramic shapes; a glossary of selected ceramic terms; and helpful appendixes on clubs, associations, museums, and English registry marks.

More and more of this kind of information is available in various formats on the Internet from collectors and vendors of antiques and collectibles. However, for the library looking for an inexpensive one-volume guide, this book is recommended.—**Ingrid Schierling Burnett**

Stamps

928. **Brookman United States, United Nations, & Canada Stamps & Postal Collectibles, 1998.** Iola, Wis., Krause Publications, 1997. 250p. illus. $15.95pa. ISBN 0-936937-41-6.

Brookman provides illustrations, descriptions, denominations, and values of the principal stamps, used and unused, of the United States, the United Nations, and Canada. The guide also refers users to *Scott*'s numbers (the *Scott Standard Postage Stamp Catalogue* [Wehman] covers the world's stamps in seven volumes). An introduction to the volume was prepared by the American Philatelic Society. This catalog has 4,000 pictures and prices for 35,000 stamps and covers issued from 1847 to 1997. This edition contains 10,000 price changes and added hunting permit stamps, first-day covers, and sections for self-adhesive plate number coil strips, panes, and booklets. The book's strengths are in historical and technical information, and it is most appropriate for personal or small collections and in support of the *Scott Catalogue*, a more complete work.—**Susan C. Awe**

Toys

929. Johnson, Dana. **Matchbox Toys 1947-1996: Identification & Value Guide.** 2d ed. Paducah, Ky., Collector Books, 1997. 190p. illus. index. $18.95pa. ISBN 0-89145-730-5.

This is the 2d edition of *Matchbox Toys 1947-1996: Identification and Value Guide* for miniature vehicle collectors. This guide includes model matchbox toys from a variety of series. The bulk of this work is devoted to listings by series. Entries include model number, description, and valuation. Separate indexes provide access by model number and description. There is a section listing Matchbox catalogs offered over the years and the estimated current prices for obtaining catalogs when they can be found. Typical caveats for collector valuations should be applied to this publication—prices are for guidance only and may vary by region and transaction. This guide is a modestly priced tool recommended for purchase in any library where this niche of collecting is popular.—**Lynne M. Fox**

930. Kelly, Douglas R. **The Die Cast Price Guide. Post-War: 1946 to Present.** Dubuque, Iowa, Antique Trader Books, 1997. 260p. illus. index. $26.95pa. ISBN 0-930625-27-7.

With a foreword written by John Hall, the founder of Brooklyn Models, this 260-page book looks at the world of die cast collectibles. The guide begins with an introduction, which, through the use of both text and illustrations, explains the making of die cast models. A section on smart collecting and a brief market report leads the reader into the company histories and listings section. The listings section is an alphabetic listing of die cast model makers, including a brief history and description of the line of models they represent, followed by a list of die cast models that depicts their current market value, a description and model, or part number. This helps take the guess-work out of deciding whether a piece is genuine or a re-creation. Many full-color photographs accompany the book, giving examples of everyday die cast models and also those hard-to-find treasures that would be a welcome addition to any collection.

There is a section of additional resources that lists other related books on die cast models, followed by addresses and telephone numbers of many die cast book dealers, magazines, and collectors clubs. Also offered is a list of annual shows and auctions to help launch a collection or give avenues to die cast trading. A short bibliography and index are also included.—**Michael Florman**

CRAFTS

931. Boyd, Margaret A. **The Crafts Supply Source Book: A Comprehensive Shop-by-Mail Guide for Thousands of Craft Materials.** 4th ed. Cincinnati, Ohio, F & W Publications, 1996. 281p. index. $18.99pa. ISBN 1-55870-441-8.

The 4th edition of this sourcebook includes hundreds of new suppliers as well as updated information. The listings in this work are divided into 3 sections: section 1 contains general arts, crafts, and hobbies and section 2 has needlecraft, sewing, and fiber arts. Section 3 offers resources that include associations, books and booksellers, general craft business, publications, and supportive materials and aids. Within these sections are 64 categories of supplies, starting with art instruction and ending with woodworking. If there is a store location in addition to the mail-order services, the entry may include an address along with hours open to the public. Most listings have telephone numbers, many include a fax number, and some provide an e-mail address. There are entries, such as for Steebar, that contain the bare information of a post office box and a sentence on their offerings. Many listings offer a free catalog or those available for a nominal charge. Listings include how one can obtain contact information.

Most suppliers listed are retailers who offer wholesale prices to businesses. In such cases, there is a note following the "Discount" heading. A few of the suppliers listed are manufacturers and sell wholesale only. The entries were compiled and verified by mail; however, the information is limited to what was provided by the individual businesses. There are some misspellings, such as Zum Bali Bali Rubber Stamps, which should read Zum Gali Gali Rubber Stamp. This volume is a good general catalog for beginners. A more seasoned collector would want more than an enumerated list of designs and images, such as people, plants, cupids, birds, buildings, and so on.—**Magda Želinská-Ferl**

932. Hamer, Frank, and Janet Hamer. **The Potter's Dictionary of Materials and Techniques.** 4th ed. Philadelphia, University of Pennsylvania Press, 1997. 406p. illus. $49.95. ISBN 0-8122-3404-9.

Some of the new articles in this updated edition of the only all-around potter's reference include soda firing, paper clay, computer glaze calculations, and fuming. Revisions were made to the "potter's periodic table," raku, instrumentation, and more. Alphabetically arranged entries range in length from a brief paragraph or half-page (Martin brothers, neriage, fettling, phosphorous oxide) to longer essays on subjects such as formulas, health hazards, and cones. Subject matter ranges widely, covering all the processes and materials involved in pottery formation, decoration, and firing. The authors continue to omit captions on the 600-plus excellent black-and-white photographs, charts, and diagrams, which can mean a frustrating search for an explanation or artist name in the text. But the 69 gorgeous color plates of pots and glaze effects are captioned and credited.

Readers seeking practical information for use in the studio will sometimes be disappointed. For instance, it would be nice to have a drawing of a roulette wheel next to the photograph of the decorative effect it creates. There is no simple formula for kiln wash to be found—either under the essay on kiln furniture or in the recipe appendix. However, more detailed physical and chemical analyses of materials and processes (fluidity, glaze, iron oxide) provide clear explanations to the working potter who wants to know the science behind the art. Although there are numerous cross-references embedded in entries, the book's comprehensive coverage would be completely accessible with the addition of a good index and better cross-references to alternate terminology. "Americanisms" of the pottery world—we often use "trimming" instead of the authors' more British "turning," or "kiln posts" for "props"—are also hard to find unless one already knows the right British synonym. An appendix of 42 tables is handy for data on temperatures, cones, equivalencies, conversions, and ratings of materials and amounts. The supplier appendix emphasizes United Kingdom sources.

Despite the minor access problems noted above, the Hamers' thorough treatment of the diversity of pottery concepts makes *The Potter's Dictionary* a must for the art and science reference collections of most academic and public libraries.—**Deborah V. Rollins**

FASHION AND COSTUME

933. Conway, George L. **Garment and Textile Dictionary.** Albany, N.Y., Delmar, 1997. 261p. $33.95pa. ISBN 0-8273-7986-2.

Conway has compiled an alphabetic listing of more than 3,500 terms that are commonly used in the garment and textile industry. A brief definition, one sentence to a paragraph in length, is given for each term, combined with its phonetic pronunciation. At the end of each letter, Conway has given a chart of the most common fabric defects associated with that letter. The chart includes the fabric defect, an explanation of the problem, and a rating of its severity when producing a fabric. The book closes with an appendix of textile and textile-related associations and a list of selected Internet sites related to garments, fabrics, and textiles.

The *Garment & Textile Dictionary* includes a collection of definitions that are clear, concise, and easy for the general public to understand. The presentation of the text is direct, and the definitions are to the point, even though they are brief. One problem does arise in this dictionary format when some terms are listed under the descriptive adjective rather than the specific subject matter. For instance, brushed rayon is filed under "B" rather than "R." Otherwise, this volume would be a valuable addition for ready-reference work in a public library or for a personal collection.—**Bridget Volz**

934. Seligman, Kevin L. **Cutting for All! The Sartorial Arts, Related Crafts, and the Commercial Paper Pattern: A Bibliographic Reference Guide for Designers, Technicians, and Historians.** Carbondale, Ill., Southern Illinois University Press, 1996. 351p. illus. index. $59.95; $34.95pa. ISBN 0-8093-2005-3; 0-8093-2006-1pa.

This specialized bibliography focuses on published works in English covering flat patterning, draping, grading, and tailoring techniques. The chapters include an extensive chronological listing, a list of professional journals, and a selected list of journal articles that contain pattern diagrams. They cover general sources from the late sixteenth century through 1989 as well as related fields, such as accessories, armor, fur and leather, military and academic garments, and undergarments. Other chapters list sources for costume and dance (references to historical garments and theatrical costumes); dolls; folk and national dress; footwear; millinery; wigmaking and hair; and commercial pattern companies, periodicals, and catalogs. Index terms are listed under logical headings, with a generous number of cross-references. The introductory chapter provides a useful summary of the history of the paper pattern and published pattern drafting systems. The brief passages heading each section offer advice on tailoring and pattern-making, and selected illustrations are useful and delightful adjuncts to the text.

This highly focused bibliography would be a good resource for libraries with clientele active in theater production, costume design, living history organizations, and reenactment groups because works listed contain cutting diagrams or patterns for garments of the times. Social and cultural historians may form a broader audience. However, the practical value—especially of the chronological section—will be limited for interested amateurs because a high proportion of the older original sources and periodicals indexed are unavailable in most public and university libraries. This book is valuable, however, for it publicizes little-known works, particularly from the nineteenth century, that may lead designers and historians toward sources for further research. [R: Choice, July/Aug 97, p. 1786]—**Lizbeth Langston**

INTERIOR DESIGN

935. **Encyclopedia of Interior Design.** Joanna Banham, ed. Chicago, Fitzroy Dearborn, 1997. 2v. illus. index. $250.00/set. ISBN 1-884964-19-2.

This work represents the first attempt to combine all those disparate entities existing in a variety of categories from interior decoration and decorative arts to architectural design and furniture history. While acknowledging the Eurocentric and North American emphasis, as well as the high concentration of nineteenth- and twentieth-century topics and personages, one must still admire the breadth of scope and the excellence of information achieved in the volumes at hand. Here one can find a variety of topics, all in signed essays that include historical perspectives and critical evaluations. These are followed by biographical data and selected works, where appropriate, publications, and a short bibliography providing guidance for further, fuller investigation. The brief sections on various countries offer an overview of the changing styles of interiors, nothing extensive but interesting as a starting point.

The illustrations are all, sadly, in black-and-white, which does lessen the impact of a Rococo salon or a Herter interior. Yet this is, after all, an encyclopedia rather than a coffee-table book. The work is an attractive publication with a neat, simple typeface and clearly defined headings. The organization and content make this well worth its price with but one caveat: The covers are quite flimsy for a work of this size, and one must wonder how long they will last through frequent use.—**Paula Frosch**

PHOTOGRAPHY

936. **Photographer's Market, 1998: 2,000 Places to Sell Your Photographs.** Michael Willins, Alice P. Buening, and Barbara Kuroff, eds. Cincinnati, Ohio, Writer's Digest Books/F & W Publications, 1997. 614p. illus. index. $23.99pa. ISBN 0-89879-793-4. ISSN 0147-247X.

Photographer's Market, 1998 continues the tradition of being geared primarily toward the photographer with little experience in the business side of photography. The first 40 pages deal with such topics as the basics of business knowledge, putting together and presenting a portfolio, pricing, and understanding copyright. Some chapters in this first section appeared in the previous edition, while others are new.

The categories in the "Markets" section have been reorganized to bring the most used markets to the front of the book. Each category is again introduced by an essay with information relevant to that category. The character of the individual market entries has not changed from the previous edition, being packed with such valuable information as contact name and address, market needs, how to make contact, terms, and tips. Categories in the "Resources" section have not changed, but some include more listings. The subject index has been expanded to include references to entries in five categories, rather than just the "Publications" category as in the past, and the number of subject categories has nearly doubled. The digital markets index, new in the 1997 edition, has been expanded, and the general index includes markets that were listed in the previous edition but not in the current one, with a code to indicate why the listing does not appear.

This is a valuable reference source for both novice and experienced photographers, dealing as it does with companies that actively welcome submissions from freelance photographers. Individual entries are rich in information, essays provide useful introductions to business topics, the resource section points toward other helpful sources, and the various indexes are quite useful. One problem is that the citations in the bibliography do not include dates of publication, leaving the reader to research the most up-to-date sources. Because each edition contains some unique text chapters, it is recommended that libraries with enough space retain older editions (see ARBA 95, entry 989).—**Kristin Doty**

937. **Photographers on Disc: An International Index of Photographers, Exhibitions, and Collections.** [CD-ROM]. New York, G. K. Hall/Simon & Schuster Macmillan, 1996. Minimum system requirements: IBM or compatible. CD-ROM drive with Microsoft CD-ROM Extensions 2.0. 512K RAM. $495.00.

Price is the first detail one notices about this CD-ROM. To pay $495.00 for a DOS-based CD-ROM is perhaps a bit disconcerting for most librarians. The product itself is straightforward. It contains three files: an alphabetic list of photographers, with birth and death dates and nationality noted, as well as address if applicable; a list of institutions with collections in photography; and a list of exhibitions of the photographer's work. Searching is also straightforward and typical of CD-ROM products. One can search using Boolean techniques—combining terms and using Boolean limiters. Thus, a search on Ansel Adams can be done and combined with a term such as Yosemite. The result is a list of places that house those works by Adams. One can also directly search any index. Thus, one can go into the institution index, search directly for the name of a particular institution, and retrieve its name and address. Display and print functions are easily learned.

Some of the information on this disk is available in other standard sources such as *The Photographers Market, 1998* (see entry 936) for biographical information on contemporary photographers, or *Index to American Photographic Collections* (G. K. Hall, 1995) for information on photography collections. This CD-ROM, however, also lists historical photographers in addition to ones currently active.

More unusual, and perhaps more helpful, is the list of exhibitions. The standard way to identify exhibitions that have been held on a photographer's work is to look through past editions of photography magazines and newsletters. Similarly, to locate upcoming exhibitions, one has to subscribe to or have access to these same publications and be willing to keep them up-to-date. This list of exhibitions, if updated on subsequent disks, should prove helpful. This brings us back to the original question: Is $495 too much to pay to have organized access to this information? It is a question that librarians will have to answer for themselves, considering their own situations, needs, and budgets.—**Terry Ann Mood**

938. Roosens, Laurent, and Luc Salu. **History of Photography: A Bibliography of Books, Volume 3.** Herndon, Va., Mansell/Cassell, 1996. 444p. index. $150.00. ISBN 0-7201-2310-0.

Volume 3 of the *History of Photography* is similar to volumes 1 and 2 (see ARBA 90, entry 943, and ARBA 96, entry 1019). Volume 1 covered up to 1914, volume 2 up to 1936, and volume 3 up to 1950. Also included are some general works about contemporary photography. These "contemporary" artists use a variety of media; therefore, some of the entries are not strictly "photographic."

This volume lists 5,092 books under 2,500 alphabetically arranged subject headings and subheadings. The literature is then arranged chronologically, whereas subheadings are geographic or chronological. Volume 3 picks up where volume 2 left off, at number 16,463, and goes to 21,555. The entries include name of author(s), editor(s), contributor(s), translator(s); title and place(s); year(s) of publication; publisher(s); number of pages, number of illustrations in black-and-white and color; language(s); new editions; and sometimes a short commentary to clarify the content. The index lists 17,000 names cited in the entries of all 3 volumes and includes authors, photographers, introducers, translators, editors, and inventors.

Libraries that purchased volumes 1 and 2 will certainly want to purchase volume 3, even though the price is rather steep. [R: Choice, Mar 97, p. 1146]—**Kathleen J. Voigt**

22 Fine Arts

GENERAL WORKS

Bibliography

939. **Annual Bibliography of Modern Art, 1995.** By the Museum of Modern Art Library, New York. New York, G. K. Hall/Simon & Schuster Macmillan, 1996. 464p. $245.00. ISBN 0-7838-1530-1. ISSN 0898-7300.

Many people know that the problem of how to record books has been experimented with for at least 200 years. Perhaps the librarians of ancient Pergamon, Alexandria, and Buddhism had to struggle with what to include in a list on a scroll or codex. Now most big libraries are changing from books to computers. *Art Index* (see entry 968) is being replaced, for example, by *ArtModernBibliographies*, a CD-ROM. Yet the issue of what to include in each entry is still present. No matter how much cross-referencing and categorizing a bibliography has, what a seeker can find is typically a matter of persistence and luck. Moreover, in reading a bibliography, one often experiences inexplicable elements and redundancies. To eradicate the latter problem, some bibliographers label every author, title, subject, publisher, and date; second best is a user's guide. Unfortunately, the 1995 Museum of Modern Art (MOMA) Library's annual acquisition bibliography's user's guide does not clearly identify the data and has some errors. Floundering will be inevitable except for the trained until a correction is distributed. This compilation does no categorizing, but items are entered alphabetically under title, author, and subject, which ensures some success. Since 1986, MOMA has annually put in print a list of its exemplary international acquisitions. Making this reading available to people who can get to New York as well as to those who want to see if their own libraries have what MOMA has is a valuable social service.—**Elizabeth L. Anderson**

940. **Art Books: A Basic Bibliography of Monographs on Artists.** 2d ed. Wolfgang M. Freitag, ed. New York, Garland, 1997. 542p. index. (Garland Reference Library of the Humanities, v.1264). $95.00. ISBN 0-8240-3326-4.

This updated bibliography (see ARBA 86, entry 1002, for a review of the 1st edition) is designed primarily for graduate students, but it is equally useful for the acquisition librarian or art book dealer. The book is a reasonably comprehensive and compact tool that reflects what is in vogue in art history scholarship. As with the 1st edition, there is a selected list of biographical dictionaries and reference works listed by country. This list is followed by a substantive, alphabetically arranged list of international artists primarily from North America and Europe of all periods. An author, editor, and compiler index follows the main list. Unfortunately, there is still no title index.

Freitag has added a new preface. The 13,937 bibliographic citations reflect an increase of roughly 32 percent over the previous edition and a 15 percent increase in artists (including architects and designers). Titles cited are in many languages and have publication dates as late as 1996. It is still refreshing to see a bibliography that has been personally examined by the editor rather than created by a computer program. For many more years, this book will continue to serve as an authoritative source.

—**Nadine Salmons**

941. **Bibliographic Guide to Art and Architecture 1996.** New York, G. K. Hall/Simon & Schuster Macmillan, 1997. 2v. $395.00/set. ISBN 0-7838-1740-1. ISSN 0360-2699.

The fine arts entry in G. K. Hall's subject bibliography series (see entry 109 for a complete review) is a 2-volume set. It contains cataloging records compiled from the Library of Congress and the Research Libraries of the New York Public Library. Material in this edition represents titles processed from January 1, 1996, through December 31, 1996. Works in all languages and from a variety of formats (books, serials, nonbooks) are included. Full bibliographic information is given for each entry. Subjects emphasized are architecture, decorative and applied arts, drawing, painting, printing, sculpture, and the visual arts in general. This is a fundamental resource for fine arts collection development and reference work.

—Ed Volz

942. **Key Guide to Electronic Resources: Art and Art History.** Martin Raish, ed. Medford, N.J., Information Today, 1996. 128p. index. $39.50pa. ISBN 1-57387-022-6.

This guide aims to provide a descriptive list of art-related electronic resources to the scholarly community. The explosion of resources, especially CD-ROM and World Wide Web, at the time of compilation precluded an exhaustive listing of all those available, but the editor has provided a reasonable and wide-ranging guide. He has given "a panorama—of the landscape of art-related electronic resources as it was in mid-1995," the most anyone may hope to do with such a volatile information format. The editor deals with three major categories—optical, magnetic, and network—followed by three sections of miscellaneous resources. He has excluded several types of resources, such as videotapes, resources on commercial networks, and academic library online catalogs. He also excluded Gopher sites, reasoning that it had become a stale technology, and many Websites, choosing to provide a few good examples and then identify sites that keep track of the enormous number of other sites.

The guide is well organized, with two of the three categories broken down into logical subcategories, and entries alphabetized by title within the subcategory. Each category or subcategory begins with an introduction that discusses the format, type of usual content, and format of the entries. The introduction for laserdiscs is extensive, listing the titles arranged by the four major producers/distributors. The entry format is clear and generally uniform, with some tailoring in categories and subcategories to provide information appropriate to the individual format. Entries include title; producer; description (many verbatim from the resource itself or promotional material); price; equipment requirements when applicable; and for laserdiscs, the interactivity potential. Approximately half of the entries include a cogent evaluation, either on its own or within the description of the resource. Entries for Internet discussion groups include information on the number of subscribers, amount of traffic, whether the list is moderated and messages archived, how to subscribe, and a contact person.

The guide is well indexed, with separate title, artist, and subject indexes, and two useful features. The artist index includes only those specifically named in a title or description, and the editor provides suggestions of other ways to use the indexes to find a specific artist if he or she is not listed. The subject index begins with a list of titles that are impossible to categorize by a few terms and because of their comprehensiveness are not listed in the body of the index. The editor has produced a usable guide that provides both an excellent introduction to and entry into the world of electronic resources for art and art history, making manageable a complex and fast-changing information environment.—**Kristin Doty**

943. Michael, Erika. **Hans Holbein the Younger: A Guide to Research.** New York, Garland, 1997. 749p. index. (Artist Resource Manuals, v.2; Garland Reference Library of the Humanities, v.1480). $95.00. ISBN 0-8153-0389-0.

As the most recent contribution to Garland's Artist Resource Manuals series, *Hans Holbein the Younger* fulfills all the conventional expectations of a scholarly guide to the literature. Compiled and annotated by Michael, an acknowledged Holbein expert, the main body of this work gathers together 2,500 bibliographic citations to primary and secondary sources focusing primarily on Holbein's individual paintings, collected drawings, and prints. However, the truly innovative aspect of the work is found in the bibliographic essay that precedes the annotated bibliography.

Organized as a series of thematically related vignettes, this work traces the reception of Holbein's work not only by painters and art critics, but by dealers, curators, poets, and fiction writers. Thus, groundwork is laid for new directions in Holbein scholarship emphasizing a multifaceted approach to the perception of the artist's work. The annotated bibliography contains references to items from the popular press, magazines, and newspapers as well as citations to literary studies that document the impact of Holbein's artistic achievement on poetry, fiction, and even literary theory. Consequently, this guide will be particularly valuable as a research tool for scholars and graduate students committed to a cross-disciplinary approach to academic studies. Of special interest are the final two sections of the guide, which present a synopsis of Holbein scholarship since 1980, with a critical assessment of the most significant monographs, catalogs, and exhibitions. For quick reference this work contains an index to personal authors of works cited in the annotated bibliography. *Hans Holbein the Younger* is strongly recommended for college and university libraries supporting graduate programs in the humanities and fine arts.—**David G. Nowak**

Biography

944. Houfe, Simon. **The Dictionary of 19th Century British Book Illustrators and Caricaturists.** rev. ed. Wappingers Falls, N.Y., Antique Collectors' Club, 1996. 367p. illus. $79.50. ISBN 1-85149-193-7.

Although *The Dictionary of 19th Century British Book Illustrators and Caricaturists* remains an important reference tool, the publishers missed the opportunity of creating a visually interesting as well as useful tool worthy of the subject. This 2d and "extensively revised" edition adds 250 new artist entries, but for a subject wealthy in color and imagination, one would expect to see more samples of the artists' work. The 30 color plates, placed within the informative opening essay, "A Century of Illustration," fall short of what one would expect to see for the price asked. Another aggravating feature is the lack of information provided for the "minor artists and amateurs." Some of the artist entries are of limited use because the only information provided is the year the artist contributed to a certain publication.

The appendix of monograms in interesting and pertinent, but the other appendixes seem to be an afterthought. For example, appendix B lists "Specialist Illustration" yet divides the artists into only two subjects, "Fairy Artists" and "Special Artists." "Special Artists" seems to refer to those artists who provided art for specific publications and repeats information already given in the artist's biographical sketch. Despite these bothersome idiosyncrasies, the dictionary remains the only source available on the subject. One hopes that the 3d edition will include more samples of the artists' illustrations. The title is recommended for most library reference collections.—**Elizabeth A. Ginno**

945. **St. James Guide to Black Artists.** Thomas Riggs, ed. Detroit, St. James Press, 1997. 625p. illus. index. $155.00. ISBN 1-55862-220-9.

The *St. James Guide to Black Artists* contains biographical and career information on 400 of the most well-known black artists worldwide. Approximately 75 percent (around 300 artists) were alive at the time of publication, and the remainder were active in the early part of the twentieth century. The research for the volume was done with the assistance of the New York Public Library's Schomburg Center for Research in Black Culture. A few of the artists included were active in the nineteenth century. Although the entries vary from a few remarks about the individual to complete essays detailing his or her life, the coverage is generally adequate, and in some cases extensive. In addition, there are more than 300 illustrations (mostly portraits of the artists covered).

Even though there is no shortage of biographical dictionaries of black artists in print, the *St. James Guide* is unique not only in its depth of coverage but its inclusion of a number of artists from Africa, the Caribbean, Brazil, and other countries that have not had good coverage. Several works already available will complement this work, including Robert Doty's *Contemporary Black Artists in America* (Whitney Museum of American Art, 1971); David Driskell's *Two Centuries of Black American Art* (Los Angeles County Museum of Arts, 1976); and the Albany Institute of History and Art's compilation entitled *The Negro Artist Comes of Age: A National Survey of Contemporary American Artists* (1945). In addition, there have been some notable works covering black women artists, including *Gumbo YaYa: Anthology of Contemporary African-American Women Artists* (Midmarch Arts Press, 1995).

Each entry in the present publication includes a brief biographical sketch; a timeline showing exhibitions, collections, and publications; and a biographical essay covering the individuals' life and work. Some of the essays are "critical" in the sense of critiquing some of the works of the artists. The illustrations, even though all black-and-white, are nicely produced and generally quite interesting. The *St. James Guide to Black Artists* is highly recommended for all larger academic and public libraries with specialized collections, and at the same time it should be of value to smaller academic, public, and school libraries that wish to select a good biographical source for black artists. [R: RBB, 15 Oct 97, pp. 429-30]—**Robert L. Wick**

Catalogs and Collections

946. Bremer-David, Charissa. **French Tapestries & Textiles in the J. Paul Getty Museum.** Los Angeles, Calif., J. Paul Getty Museum; distr., New York, Oxford University Press, 1997. 187p. illus. index. $85.00. ISBN 0-89236-379-7.

Bremer-David's catalog of the French tapestries and textiles contained in the J. Paul Getty Museum represents a significant contribution to the study of textiles. Because of the size of individual pieces and the volume of the entire collection as well as the sensitivity of the dyes in pieces when exposed to light, only parts of the collection can be displayed for a limited time at the museum. Therefore, this book is the only complete overview of the collection that is available to the public, to textile students, and to art historians studying seventeenth- and eighteenth-century French textiles. *French Tapestries & Textiles* is the 4th volume in a series of books that catalog specific collections in the museum. It is preceded by *Mounted Oriental Porcelain* (1982), *Vincennes and Sevres Porcelain* (1991), and *European Clocks* (1996). The pieces included in this new volume are systematically arranged for easy access. They are initially grouped by the technique used in production: tapestry, knotted pile, and needlework. Then the pieces are subdivided by the place of manufacture, and finally arranged in chronological order so that changes in production over time are readily apparent.

The information on the tapestry collection the Getty Museum is not only thorough in its explanation but attractive in its presentation. The description of each piece includes the manufacturing dates, the artists and weavers, the materials used, the dimensions of the piece, and even the number of warp threads or knots and weft threads that were used per inch in production. This is followed by a description of the design, the condition of the piece, and efforts that are being taken for its preservation. The catalog includes 55 full-color and almost 150 additional black-and-white photographs of the collection, displaying complete tapestries and close-up views of specific areas in each piece. Bremer-David's catalog is both a valuable resource for large libraries with strong art and textile collections, and a feast to the eyes for anyone interested in viewing beautiful tapestries. It would be a significant addition to a large library or to an individual's collection.—**Bridget Volz**

Dictionaries and Encyclopedias

947. **The Dictionary of Art.** Jane Turner, ed. New York, Grove's Dictionaries, 1996. 34v. illus. index. $8,800.00/set. ISBN 1-884446-00-0.

The 34 volumes of *The Dictionary of Art* contain much of the knowledge of art compiled over the centuries. Approximately 6,700 scholars contributed essays on their areas of expertise, which comprise the 41,000 articles illustrated with 15,000 reproductions and documented with 300,000 bibliographic citations. The dictionary includes biographical essays on artists, architects, designers, craftspeople, collectors, dealers, art historians, critics, and art museum professionals. The entries on sites are impressive because of the comprehensive manner in which they are handled and because of the numerous cross-references furnished for related subjects. It is a delight for the reference librarian to have a single source to consult that provides terms and techniques, mythological subjects, institutions, art movements, and archaeological sites.

The dictionary must be consulted through its index volume; otherwise, one would miss such esoteric topics as "Syriac manuscripts," which is part of a larger entry on early Christian and Byzantine art. The index is somewhat cumbersome when dealing with institutions, which are listed by city—a tedious and outdated research method. The dictionary does have some minor flaws; however, these are far outweighed by the comprehensive nature of the work as a whole, which makes it the most important art source published in the past few decades. Although there is room for improvement in the index and in the number of illustrations included, all university libraries, major public libraries, and art libraries must have this reference source in their collection.—**Lamia Doumato**

948. **Dictionary of Women Artists.** Delia Gaze, ed. Chicago, Fitzroy Dearborn, 1997. 2v. illus. $250.00/set. ISBN 1-884964-21-4.

Another star is born in the fields of art research and women's studies with the publication of *The Dictionary of Women Artists* from Fitzroy Dearborn. This two-volume reference work is a welcome addition to the above-mentioned fields.

Arranged alphabetically by name of artist, each article is a scholarly overview of the artist's life, including training/biographical information as well as critical and stylistic interpretations of her works. Two indexes enhance this alphabetic arrangement. One is an alphabetic list of all artists (name only), and the other is a chronological list. These lists are included at the front of both volumes. As stated in the foreword, no one born since 1945 is included; this dictionary is a historical survey. The dictionary is also international in scope. Several factors were used in determining what artists were to be included, which are detailed in the foreword as well. However, the concentration is on the fine arts (painting, sculpture, photography, and the like) as opposed to the applied arts. Even though the volume presents scholarly entries, many different users, from high school age through graduate-level researchers, can use it.

In comparing this title to the recently published *Dictionary of Art* (see entry 947), it becomes obvious that the two works complement each other. For example, the bibliographies are quite different. The bibliographies in *Dictionary of Women Artists* are arranged chronologically and are composed of the key works relating to the entry. They vary in comprehensiveness. For example, the bibliography for Frida Kahlo contains 25 items. The bibliographies in the *Dictionary of Art* are alphabetic by main entry, are selective, and tend to focus on the core primary sources. The Kahlo bibliography here consists of seven items, three of which are not included in the formerly mentioned bibliography.

There are 11 introductory surveys that cover the full range of art history, beginning with an essay entitled "Women as Artists in the Middle Ages" and ending with "Feminism and Women Artists." All of these are comprehensive and add immense value to this work. The only noticeable flaw is the illustrations, which appear only in black-and-white. Also, there is a wide range in the quality of the illustrations. Some are clear and well reproduced; others are dreadful. This difference in reproduction quality may have to do with the originals used at the source. This flaw is minor given the overall excellence of the work, especially because there are many sources for illustrations. *Dictionary of Women Artists* is highly recommended for most academic and larger public libraries.—**Roland C. Hansen**

949. **Dutch Art: An Encyclopedia.** Sheila D. Muller, ed. New York, Garland, 1997. 489p. illus. index. (Garland Reference Library of the Humanities, v.1021). $125.00. ISBN 0-8153-0065-4.

Dutch art, from the luminous flesh tones of a Rembrandt portrait to the meticulous detail of a Gerrit Dou genre painting, from the mathematical precision of a Piet Mondrian painting to its equivalent in a Gerrit Rietveld chair, has always held a special place in the canon of art history. This work, a compilation of essays by more than 100 recognized scholars in the field, offers a tripartite approach to the vast topic, one part devoted to biographies (Pieter Aertsen through Lambertus Zijl); one to a historical narrative; and the other to specific concepts, both stylistic and developmental. The arrangement appears to be a simple alphabetic format, but the reader must be aware of the somewhat hierarchical organization peculiar to this work: There are preliminary lists of themes in a variety of groupings, which include asterisked items suggested as an introduction to a topic. It is therefore of primary importance to thoroughly read the "Reader's Guide and Bibliographical Note" to understand just how best to proceed in using this reference.

Each entry ends with a *see also* reference that leads to further information on specific topics. Many of the artists for whom biographical information appears to be lacking can be located in topical articles by consulting the index. The bibliographies provided contain literature in a variety of languages, reflecting the current spate of Netherlands research arising from sources closer to both the origins as well as the sites of the current collections. The plates, with a small number in color, are quite good. However, they are gathered in three groupings that require a bit of referring back and forth, but this may well be secondary to useful book design and practical binding.

The work is a sound survey of a profoundly important and enormously interesting topic; its comprehensive coverage, essentially from the mid-fifteenth century to the present, makes it a valuable addition to any research library. The volume is highly recommended with one caveat—access is neither as quick nor as simple as is suggested in its press release; but the extra effort proves worthwhile.

—**Paula Frosch**

950. Murray, Peter, and Linda Murray. **The Oxford Companion to Christian Art and Architecture.** New York, Oxford University Press, 1996. 596p. illus. $45.00. ISBN 0-19-866165-7.

One of the obstacles to understanding and appreciating some of the greatest art ever produced is a lack of knowledge of the Bible and of Christian doctrine. This is the premise behind the encyclopedic volume on Christian art and architecture written by the highly respected art historians Peter and Linda Murray. As stated in the introduction, this book is intended to demonstrate the inspiration and creative drive provided by the Christian religion from its beginnings to the present century. Lavishly illustrated and including numerous color plates, the volume contains hundreds of entries that explore the Christian tradition in Western art. The authors do not claim to treat the subject fully but have chosen to cover Christian art and architecture from the early Christian and Byzantine periods through the Counter-Reformation and into the twentieth century. The emphasis is heavily on the European tradition, with only scant references to the remainder of the world.

Biblical symbols, people and references and religious buildings are some of the types of entries in this volume. The entries are listed alphabetically and vary in length from a few lines to several pages. Some are quite exhaustive, as for example "Early Christian Art and Architecture," which is described in seven pages with subheadings on architecture, mosaics, and sculpture. Others are shorter, such as "Deadly Sins, The Seven," described in one paragraph. Although cross-references direct the reader to appropriate entries, an index would have greatly increased the usefulness of this tool. Locating an appropriate entry can be difficult. For example, this reviewer could not locate any reference to the architecture of Spanish mission churches in the southwestern United States or Mexico. The entries do not contain bibliographic references, but a comprehensive bibliography is listed at the end of the book. A helpful eight-page glossary of architectural terms is also included.

This is a valuable book for libraries serving students of art and architecture. The cost is modest for the size and depth of this one-volume aid to Christian art and architecture. [R: RBB, 15 Feb 97, p. 1043]
—**Ingrid Schierling Burnett**

951. Patin, Thomas, and Jennifer McLerran. **Artwords: A Glossary of Contemporary Art Theory.** Westport, Conn., Greenwood Press, 1997. 153p. index. $65.00. ISBN 0-313-29272-8.

Many a guidebook to the transdisciplinary vocabulary of cultural studies has been published of late. *Artwords* is unique among them because it centers on contemporary art theory and criticism; in turn, it is unique among visual arts dictionaries in documenting the newer, "imported" vocabularies of philosophy and social/political/literary theory rather than the traditional terminology of periods, movements, forms, styles, and techniques. Following a short preface explaining the volume's scope and purpose, a helpful introductory section lists terms (there are no entries for persons) in thematic groups; the 400 glossary entries, many of them *see references* to longer articles, vary in length from a sentence to a few pages. A cumulative bibliography of approximately 125 titles and an index of names and major topics conclude the volume.

Granted that many of the terms are controversial and otherwise resist 25-words-or-less treatment, *Artwords*'s definitions too often waste words saying that something is important; fail to categorize the term in the first sentence of the entry; or reach oversimplified, vague conclusions; furthermore, the authors do not systematically enough relate terms to artistic practice and art scholarship. Inconsistent, often trivial use of the cross-reference system, typographic errors, wordiness, and anemic or imprecise definitions suggest a need for stronger editing. Although the right kind of effort, the book does not satisfy, which means that those who customarily use other resources would be well advised, until a cleaned up, tightened up version of *Artwords* appears, to continue to use the better-written literature/cultural studies works cited in the preface; for example, *A Glossary of Contemporary Literary Theory* (see ARBA 93, entry 1113); *A Dictionary of Cultural and Critical Theory* (see ARBA 97, entry 746); and the long, thematic essays contained in Robert S. Nelson and Richard Shiff's *Critical Terms for Art History* (University of Chicago Press, 1996).—**Robert H. Kieft**

952. **Spanish Artists from the Fourth to the Twentieth Century: A Critical Dictionary.** New York, with Frick Art Reference Library, G. K. Hall/Simon & Schuster Macmillan, 1993, 1996. 4v. index. $140.00/volume. ISBN 0-8161-0164-2 (v.1); 0-8161-0656-8 (v.2); 0-8161-0657-6 (v.3); 0-7838-8037-5 (index); 0-8161-0614-2 (set).

Spanish Artists, produced in conjunction with the Frick Art Reference Library, lists approximately 10,000 painters, sculptors, draftspeople, printers, architects, and applied artists, covering 1,600 years of Spanish art. The artists included were either born in Spain or worked chiefly in Spain. Artists born in

1920 and after are not included. The original project began as a 3-volume annotated checklist with a chronological list of artists and a complete bibliography of all sources used in the compilation. The completed project includes 3 volumes from A to Z and the 4th volume, the bibliography. It is based on the Authority File of Artists, an internal resource of the Frick Art Reference Library.

This critical dictionary is more comprehensive in scope than any other record in English of Spanish art. The introduction and guide to use are given in English, Spanish, French, and German. Entries are listed under authority names and include all the alternative names used by the artist. Each entry contains authority name, alternate names, dates of birth or death or documented activity, national school when nationality is questioned, fields of artistic endeavor when not exclusively a painter, notes when clarification is necessary, and bibliographic references. Volumes 1 and 2 are divided into 2 parts—artists' records and bibliography—and volume 3 contains artists' records only. Volume 4 consists of the general bibliography, a chronological index, and a comprehensive index of authority and alternate names. This set is a must for every public library art collection and art museum, even though it is an expensive title.

—**Kathleen J. Voigt**

Directories

953. **Art Diary 97/98: Art Directory International.** Milan, Italy, Giancarlo Politi Editore, for New York, Flash Art, 1997. 563p. illus. $30.00pa. ISBN 88-7816-097-0.

This compact directory focuses on the international contemporary and avant-garde art scene, providing users with the names and mailing addresses (and sometimes fax numbers and e-mail addresses) of current artists, art businesses, art organizations, and other individuals or groups involved in the business of art. A 1997/1998 calendar of major international art events is also included. Arranged alphabetically by country, the book also includes subsections for some major metropolitan areas. Within these sections, names are grouped in categories—artists, critics, galleries, museums, and so forth. Names and addresses are given, but no further information. One may assume the book is intended for those with some prior knowledge of the field because there is no index or guidelines for use.

Although fairly comprehensive, coverage is uneven. For example, the section for New York is far larger than that for Los Angeles—and many countries and even continents are not covered at all (e.g., Australia, Africa). The reader may also wonder why Asian countries are lumped together in a separate section or why there is a category called "World Others." The editors do not explain their purpose, scope, methodology, or criteria for selection, so one can only guess why such well-known artists as Eric Fischl, Andy Goldsworthy, and Ellsworth Kelly are not included. This is not to say that there is not a great deal of information in the book. Indeed, those seeking information on the business of art (e.g., artists, gallery owners and museum personnel, critics and reviewers) will find it immensely helpful. Those wanting more detail on the galleries of New York City should consult *New York Contemporary Art Galleries: The Complete Annual Guide*, published by Manhattan Arts and now in its 2d edition. It offers such particulars about galleries as the name of the owner or director, type of art shown, gallery size, artists represented, and markets.—**Barbara Ittner**

954. **Artists Communities: A Directory of Residencies in the United States Offering Time and Space for Creativity.** By the Alliance of Artists' Communities. New York, Allworth Press, 1996. 222p. illus. maps. $16.95pa. ISBN 1-880559-65-X.

Artists Communities offers libraries a unique resource for locating institutions offering refuge from everyday concerns for serious artists. Produced by the Alliance of Artists' Communities, this source provides a fast and easy way to locate an artist residency program. Seventy artist community sites in the United States are described in full. Each entry provides information on the deadline to apply for residency; focus of the institution in terms of type of creative effort supported (painting, sculpture, writing, and so forth); how long the average stay lasts; and how each applicant is selected. The five chart indexes provide a quick method of cross-referencing residencies based on artistic category, geographic location, season, administrative deadline, costs, available stipends, or disability accommodations. A separate list of addresses and telephone numbers is given for artist residency programs that do not provide the same services but offer other venues to artists. Also included is a list of international artists communities.

Artists Communities fills a void in art reference. It collects hard-to-find information on an ephemeral subject in a utilitarian yet artistic way. One hopes that it is updated each year by the Alliance. From the introductory essay by Stanley Kunitz to the photographs of each community, this resource reflects its artistic origins and is appropriate for any library.—**Elizabeth A. Ginno**

955. **Contemporary Latin American Artists: Exhibitions at the Organization of American States 1941-1964.** Annick Sanjurjo, ed. Lanham, Md., Scarecrow, 1997. 506p. index. $75.00. ISBN 0-8108-3281-X.

This is the 2d volume of a 2-volume set that together records some 750 exhibitions by more than 2,000 artists covering the years 1941 to 1985 at the Museum of Modern Art of Latin America of the Organization of American States in Washington, D.C. The volume under review here deals with about 320 exhibitions of the work of approximately 950 artists between the years 1941 and 1964.

Information on the exhibits is inserted in chronological order, including professional résumés and curricula vitae of those artists whose information was available to the editor. Recognizing that the chronological scheme for the entries alone would make it difficult and even tiresome to look up individual artists or works from any given country, the editor included two useful indexes: an index of artists and an index of exhibitions by country.—**S. D. Markman**

Handbooks and Yearbooks

956. **African Art.** By William R. Rea. New York, Facts on File, 1996. 64p. illus. maps. index. (International Encyclopedia of Art). $18.95; $121.00/set. ISBN 0-8160-3330-7; 0-8160-3327-7/set.

957. **Art of the Ancient Mediterranean World.** By Bernice Wilson. New York, Facts on File, 1996. 64p. illus. maps. index. (International Encyclopedia of Art). $18.95; $121.00/set. ISBN 0-8160-3331-5; 0-8160-3327-7/set.

958. **European Art Since 1850.** By Nancy Malloy. New York, Facts on File, 1997. 64p. illus. maps. index. (International Encyclopedia of Art). $18.95; $121.00/set. ISBN 0-8160-3334-X; 0-8160-3327-7/set.

959. **European Art to 1850.** By Tony Lucchesi and Fulvio Palombo. New York, Facts on File, 1997. 64p. illus. maps. index. (International Encyclopedia of Art). $18.95; $121.00/set. ISBN 0-8160-3333-1; 0-8160-3327-7/set.

960. **Far Eastern Art.** By Charles Doherty. New York, Facts on File, 1997. 64p. illus. maps. index. (International Encyclopedia of Art). $18.95; $121.00/set. ISBN 0-8160-3335-8; 0-8160-3327-7/set.

961. **Mexican, Central, and South American Art.** By John F. Scott. New York, Facts on File, 1996. 64p. illus. maps. index. (International Encyclopedia of Art). $18.95; $121.00/set. ISBN 0-8160-3329-3; 0-8160-3327-7/set

962. **North American Art Since 1900.** By C. M. E. P. Turner. New York, Facts on File, 1996. 64p. illus. maps. index. (International Encyclopedia of Art). $18.95; $121.00/set. ISBN 0-8160-3328-5; 0-8160-3327-7/set.

963. **North American Art to 1900.** By Arleen Pancza-Graham. New York, Facts on File, 1997. 64p. illus. maps. index. (International Encyclopedia of Art). $18.95; $121.00/set. ISBN 0-8160-3332-3; 0-8160-3327-7/set.

The purpose of these volumes is to show world art in both a cultural and a social context. They accomplish this goal by relating the art to history and events of the time, focusing on the culture that created the art. There are two volumes on both European and North American art and single volumes on ancient Mediterranean; Far Eastern; African; and Mexican, Central, and South American art. The volumes are arranged chronologically into brief, two-page chapters that cover key aspects of the art under discussion. An example of what a chapter treats can be seen in the entry on Mexican mural paintings, which describes Latin American communism, the Mexican nation, and pre-Columbian history in addition to offering an overview of mural painting.

The format is user friendly, with an excellent layout that allows users to quickly access essential information. White space, graphics, illustrations, and text are used effectively, allowing users to quickly digest information. Each entry is amply illustrated with both black-and-white and color images. Individual volumes include a timeline, a brief bibliography, and a glossary of terms. The bibliographies could be more current; the latest citations are from 1994.

Unlike Grove's *Dictionary of Art* (see entry 947) or the *Encyclopedia of Art* (Greystone Press, 1967-), this source is not comprehensive, providing only basic-level information. However, the low cost of the set makes this source an attractive purchase. The encyclopedia would be most effectively used by grammar or high school students beginning research in a particular area because it provides basic, brief, and introductory information. The set is recommended for both school and public libraries.—**Monica Fusich**

964. Grant, Daniel. **Artist's Resource Handbook.** rev. ed. New York, Allworth Press, 1996. 247p. index. $18.95pa. ISBN 1-880559-58-7.

This revised edition of Grant's 1994 handbook (see ARBA 96, entry 1040) is again intended to fill the gap in career development assistance experienced by the approximately 11,000 graduates of art schools and university art departments. According to the author, three factors cause a need for this type of handbook: a lack of preparation for career development in most schools; the diffuse nature of information for artists, with few organizations sharing their research with others; and the fact that most career and business workshops for artists focus on applying for grants, although public and private grant funding has declined dramatically in the past two decades. The handbook provides information and advice on a wide range of topics dealing with survival as a working artist, including career assistance, working with organizations, health and safety issues, and ethical conduct. Half of the chapters have been enhanced with additional sections, bringing the information up-to-date and making the handbook approximately 70 pages longer than the 1st edition.

The chapter format is the same as in the 1st edition, consisting of narrative sections followed by listings of organizations and individuals. Some narratives are extensive and give useful information on the background of the topic, such as history, trends, and apparent current directions. Others are minimal, serving mainly to introduce a list of resources. In the bibliography, section names are the same, and all but one section have had titles added. There are 15 new titles, most published since the appearance of the 1st edition; 9 citations list newer editions, but at least 1 citation did not get updated. The index primarily lists the organizations and individuals cited in the resource listings, with a small proportion of subject listings. This lack of subject indexing is offset by the detailed list of chapter sections in the table of contents.

This revised edition, appearing just 2 years after the 1st edition, provides much-needed advice and resources to art graduates. Although many arts organizations and publications are stable, others appear and disappear in a short time span, so this revision helps artists to stay up-to-date in a constantly changing field. Used in conjunction with others of the myriad self-help business books available for artists, this handbook can make the business of being an artist less frustrating for the beginner, as well as assisting more experienced artists to stay current.—**Kristin Doty**

965. Janson, H. W., and Anthony F. Janson. **History of Art for Young People.** 5th ed. Bergenfield, N.J., Harry N. Abrams, 1997. 632p. illus. index. $49.50. ISBN 0-8109-4150-3.

Three decades of university students have learned about art history using an imposing textbook called *History of Art*, written originally by Horst Janson in 1962 and now continued by his son Anthony. Just as the university textbook has undergone periodic review, so has a shorter version for high school and junior college audiences called variously the *History of Art for Young People* or *Basic History of Art*. This new edition includes revisions to the treatment of art before the Renaissance as well as an extended look at the art of the twentieth century, including postmodernism.

Every public or school library needs a basic survey of art history in its reference collection. This one continues to be a popular choice because of the clarity of the prose, useful tables and maps, and the ever-increasing number of spectacular color illustrations. Several editorial changes have increased its value as a library reference book. An attractive redesign has simplified the process of identifying key artists and their works in the text. The reformatting also allows for extensive explanatory marginalia defining terms (*silkscreen* or *Augustine of Hippo*, for example) and line drawings illustrating key concepts. In addition, new boxed sections relate art historical movements to contemporary developments in music and theater. The changes continue to improve a good thing and update a valued intellectual guidebook for a new generation.—**Stephanie C. Sigala**

966. **National Museum of American Art.** [CD-ROM]. New York, Macmillan Digital, 1996. Minimum system requirements (Windows version): IBM or compatible 486/33MHz. Double-speed CD-ROM drive. Windows 3.1. 8MB RAM. SVGA, 256-color monitor with 640 x 480 resolution (24 bit recommended). Minimum system requirements (Macintosh version): Performa/33MHz. Double-speed CD-ROM drive. System 7.0.1. 8MB RAM. 256-color monitor (24 bit recommended). $20.00. ISBN 1-57595-013-8.

The most powerful feature of this CD-ROM, jointly created by the Smithsonian Institution and Macmillan Digital, is the rich web of hypertext linkages between its different sections. Viewing of 763 works from the National Museum of American Art's (NMAA) permanent collection forms the core of the NMAA CD-ROM. Detailed commentaries on each work include artist annotations and biographies, links to the glossary, bibliographies, and multimedia components, including video, audio, and slide show. Other features include a timeline tracing the creation dates of the pieces in the collection, clickable maps of the birthplaces of artists and works, a "Datadisc" identifying other pieces related to each work, and the full text of six museum exhibition catalogs. Elizabeth Broun, the Museum's director, narrates a multimedia tour, focusing on her 13 favorite pieces.

The interface is amazingly appealing and fluid. Eight ever-present navigational buttons ease movement between sections: Exit, Copyright, Help (pop-up explanations appear as the cursor hovers over parts of the screen), Navigate, Go Back, Search, Catalog, and Options (which controls the speed, size, order, and categories of items displayed). However, the user must remember to click the Catalog button to return to the index (where works are listed by author and title) from a specific entry.

There are so many details to this complex collection of art, history, and biography that viewers could become lost without the powerful Portfolio feature. This allows users to select, organize, and annotate a multimedia collection of any of the materials included in the CD-ROM into one or more personal portfolios for downloading, printing, or viewing as a slide show.

The viewer may wonder why these particular pieces were selected from the more than 37,000 items in the museum's collection. The clues as to which items are genuine masterpieces, which are normally evident in written guides and through placement within an actual museum, are lacking in the computer medium. Some weighting or ranking system would benefit novice users. But the limitation of not viewing each artwork firsthand is more than offset by the wealth of background information provided about each work.

A companion book, *The National Museum of American Art* (Bulfinch Press, 1995), is available for $28.50. Consult the museum's equally notable Website for further information, http://www.nmaa.si.edu. It takes several hours of practice to master the depth of resources available here, but the rewards are worth the time invested. Librarians will appreciate the flexibility and interconnectedness of its content. This is a vital tool for any library.—**Anne C. Moore**

967. Sullivan, Michael. **Art and Artists of Twentieth-Century China.** Berkeley, Calif., University of California Press, 1996. 354p. illus. index. $65.00. ISBN 0-520-07556-0.

In this book, Sullivan, a world-recognized leading scholar of Chinese art with numerous publications on the subject, provides an in-depth look at the development of modern Chinese art. The theme of the book is "the rebirth of Chinese art in the twentieth century under the influence of Western art and culture" (p. xxvii), and he aptly demonstrates how Western influence was necessary to revitalize Chinese art. Although the author offers the book as a personal view developed during 50 years of observation, his scholarship is evident throughout the work, making this an essential work for advanced undergraduates, graduate students, and faculty in this area of art history. Despite the difficulties of finding accurate, unbiased information and gaining access to historical documents, Sullivan's knowledge of the country and its art enables him to make sense of its complexly intertwined history and art from the late 1800s into the 1990s. The book received a special mention from the 1997 George Wittenborn Memorial Book Award Committee of the Art Libraries Society of North America.

Sullivan provides a fascinating panorama of modern Chinese art, primarily painting and sculpture, from the early intense debates between traditionalists and reformers through the struggles of the Cultural Revolution to the exodus in the 1980s of young artists seeking the greater freedom of the West, to attempts by those who remained in China to push back the limits of the Communist Party's tolerance, and to the new challenges faced after Tiananmen Square. His insights are profound and so well formed that they seem to flow quite naturally through the historical discussions. The book is well written, with events lucidly set out in logical progression and well placed in context. From the beginning, the reader is aware of the depth and breadth of the author's knowledge and understanding of his subject, an awareness that enriches the experience of reading the book.

The high quality of the text is maintained in and complemented by the supplementary material. In the 94 color plates and 278 black-and-white illustrations, the author has included not only recognized major works but also works that illustrate an unfolding historical process. The extensive endnotes provide rich supplementary information in addition to citations of sources and are complemented by the selected bibliography that organizes both Chinese- and Western-language sources for ease of access. Although the author points out the impossibility of the biographical index being either complete or completely accurate, it is nonetheless an important and much-needed resource, with numerous cross-references, that may be used on its own as well as with the text. The 20-page index to the text includes names of artists and institutions as well as subjects and is well supplied with cross-references, a necessity considering the several different ways it is possible to romanize a name. This substantial work likely will be a standard reference for years to come, coming as it does before the amount of material becomes too unwieldy to allow for a comprehensive general survey.—**Kristin Doty**

Indexes

968. **Art Index. November 1995 to October 1996.** Alison Adams Dickey and others, eds. Bronx, N.Y., H. W. Wilson, 1995, 1996. 1556p. priced on a service basis rate. ISSN 0004-3222.

Like all of H. W. Wilson's bibliographic titles, *Art Index* is a solid, easy-to-use volume. Most of the publications indexed are periodicals (276 titles), but some yearbooks and museum bulletins have also been included. The coverage is international, although there is an obvious English-language bias. Wilson accepts nominations for new titles from its indexes' users, and the included titles are periodically reviewed. *Art Index* remains an important, basic indexing tool for researchers in art and architecture.

The index covers a broad range of art and art-related topics, including archaeology, architecture, motion pictures, city planning, crafts, graphic arts, industrial design, interior design, landscape architecture, museology, and so forth. The volume does not include some of the more specialized sources, such as large numbers of exhibition catalogs. For additional coverage of specialized subjects or materials in specialized formats, one may consider the purchase of such titles as *ARTbibliographies MODERN* (see ARBA 86, entry 1024) or *The Architectural Index* (see ARBA 85, entry 902). Subjects and authors are interfiled in one alphabetic sequence, and there is extensive cross-referencing. *Art Index*'s citation style is unusual in that if an article is illustrated by an artist's work, up to 10 titles of those works follow the citation. Each volume also contains a separate listing of the book reviews found in the indexed periodicals.

Any college, university, or large public library should have this title in its collection. In addition, any special museum library should purchase it. It is a basic art and architecture reference tool. *Art Index* is also now available on CD-ROM (see ARBA 93, entry 1030), and the purchase of that title should be considered if a library wants increased bibliographic access or wants to distribute the information more widely than its own reference room.—**Caroline M. Kent**

969. **Twentieth-Century Artists on Art: An Index to Writings, Statements, and Interviews by Artists, Architects, and Designers.** 2d ed. By Jack S. Robertson. New York, G. K. Hall/Simon & Schuster Macmillan, 1996. 834p. $95.00. ISBN 0-8161-9059-3.

Robertson has once again provided access to primary materials by twentieth-century artists in this updated edition of his 1985 work (see ARBA 86, entry 1025). The contents of more than 930 publications—such as anthologies of interviews, essays, manifestos, and group exhibition catalogs—have been indexed. Since the last edition, the number of citations has increased from 14,000 to 27,500-plus, and the number of artists listed has almost tripled. This source continues to provide coverage to artists of more than 60 nationalities and covers the media of painting, sculpture, architecture, photography, video, performance art, and earthworks. The 2d edition provides increased entries for the media of architecture, commercial and industrial design, and crafts.

This index is crucial to researchers because it provides access to information otherwise unindexed. This excellent and important reference work is highly recommended and should be in the reference collections of all art and museum libraries as well as public libraries with a strong interest in twentieth-century art and artists.—**Monica Fusich**

ARCHITECTURE

970. **Avery Index to Architectural Periodicals at Columbia University.** [CD-ROM]. New York, G. K. Hall/Simon & Schuster Macmillan, 1996. Minimum system requirements: IBM or compatible. CD-ROM drive with Microsoft CD-ROM Extensions 2.0. 512K RAM. $995.00.

The *Avery Index* on CD-ROM is based on the collections at the Avery Architectural and Fine Arts Library at Columbia University. The index is a comprehensive list of journal articles, interviews, obituaries, book reviews, and exhibit reviews on architecture. Providing bibliographic description and indexing for 15,000 citations per year, the index covers approximately 800 journals from more than 40 countries. The publishers indicate that 80 percent of the journals are non-U.S. publications, and 75 percent of the journals in this index are not covered elsewhere.

The CD-ROM requires the use of an IBM or compatible. The disc comes with easy instructions for installation, brief explanations on how to modify the disc for customizing, and a brief troubleshooting guide. The packet also includes a one-page flyer describing the functions the CD-ROM will perform—keyword searching, display formats, sorting, printing, and so on. The database is relatively easy to use. A significant amount of data can be retrieved with no previous experience. The default search method is keyword. Type the keyword, hit Enter, and the number of citations retrieved appears. To see the brief citation (title, illustrative materials, journal citation), the user presses F4. The list of citations comes up quickly. This list can be manipulated in various ways. "F" will change the display to a full format (ID number, title, author(s), illustrative materials, language, journal citation, ISSN, notes [brief abstract], subject headings, and Avery call number). Citations in either format may be sorted, tagged, downloaded, or printed. Sorted lists may be displayed, printed, downloaded, and so on.

Boolean operators and truncation are acceptable in this database. The database can be customized to add local information on the start-up screen; add a new help chapter with information on local holdings; customize the brief and full displays; change the color, size, and text of most screens; and change the error and help messages. One can also search specific indexes: author, title, subject, journal, title keyword, subject keyword, Avery call number, country, language, ID number, and illustration. The index tag (AU=author) can be typed at the search prompt, or the author index may be searched. Searches can be conjoined (S1 and S4) to create hybrids. Speed keys are listed in the Help section for simple operations, such as jumping to a specified citation in the list or going to the first record. Technical support telephone numbers and an e-mail address are listed in Help and on the installation guide. All articles are available at the Avery Library through interlibrary loan.

There is nothing to tell the user what period is covered by this CD-ROM. It appears that the disc covers 1996 and back to 1970 for most current titles. There is then a gap until citations for long-standing journals begin again in about 1890. Citations to articles as old as 1873 were found. The journal index indicates title and number of citations, but not dates covered.

For a novice user, this database is relatively easy to use. Some useful citations will be generated with little effort. However, the more sophisticated user may find this CD-ROM somewhat frustrating, as not enough information is given "up front." Although it is relatively expensive, the disc should be in most libraries that support an architecture program.—**Joanna M. Burkhardt**

971. **Avery's Choice: Five Centuries of Great Architectural Books: One Hundred Years of an Architectural Library, 1890-1990.** Adolf K. Placzek, ed. New York, G. K. Hall/Simon & Schuster Macmillan, 1997. 292p. illus. index. $175.00. ISBN 0-7838-1597-2.

The Avery Architectural and Fine Arts Library of Columbia University, in celebration of the centennial of its founding, has selected and described 427 of its treasures from its collections in a volume that will be wanted by every architectural school and library. Although the volume mostly reflects printed Western literature, it covers the entire gamut of the history of architecture, from the rise of the Renaissance and its spread, through Classicism and Baroque in the seventeenth and eighteenth centuries, to North America before 1800, revivalism, eclecticism, and innovation in the nineteenth century, the twentieth century, and finally a look toward the future. Each chapter has an introductory essay by an expert educator in the field, followed by the bibliographic description and a short essay on each of the selected books by one of 15 contributors. There are 406 illustrations, almost 1 for every cited volume. Also appearing are 16 color plates, an author index, a title index, and a date of publication index. Even though the book is expensive, it will receive much use, have long value, and serve as a guide to an ideal architecture library collection.
—**Robert J. Havlik**

972. Johnson, Donald Leslie, and Donald Langmead. **Makers of 20th Century Modern Architecture: A Bio-Critical Sourcebook.** Westport, Conn., Greenwood Press, 1997. 387p. illus. maps. index. $89.50. ISBN 0-313-29353-8.

Frank Lloyd Wright said that architecture must always be in transition. This sourcebook, intended for a wide audience, combines biographies with extensive but selective bibliographies. "Whither We Went," an introductory philosophical and historical essay on the evolution of modern architecture, explores how late nineteenth-century architecture influenced the twentieth century. Central to the avant-garde movement was Wright. Accordingly, he is given a lengthy biography and is discussed in more than half of the introduction, linking him to several other architects.

The dictionary includes several concepts and groups, such as Archigram, Congrès Internationaux d'Architecture Moderne (CIAM), Coop Himmelblau, futurism, and metabolism, and major firms like Skidmore, Owings, and Merrill. Coverage is worldwide, including Hassan Fathy (Egypt), Arata Isozaki (Japan), Ieoh Ming Pei (China), Denise Scott Brown (Zambia), and Luis Barragán (Mexico). Each of the more than 80 architects' biographies addresses his or her life and works, followed by a 3- to 5-part bibliography: writings by the architect, biographical works, assessment articles about their work, and bibliographic and archival sources for further research. Fifty-two plates, from drawings to photographs, illustrate the varied styles.

A chronology and list of founders provide further links between contemporary architects. Two indexes complete the book, one by personal names/concepts and one by place-names. Both authors, with previous contributions to the scholarship of architecture, have created a source essential for architecture libraries and interdisciplinary collections.—**Ralph Hartsock**

973. Keister, Douglas. **Going Out in Style: The Architecture of Eternity.** New York, Facts on File, 1997. 150p. illus. index. $29.95. ISBN 0-8160-3649-7.

Photographer Keister, famous for his Painted Ladies series of Victorian homes, takes a look at mausoleum architecture in this book written with Xavier Cronin, author of *Grave Exodus: Tending to Our Dead in the 21st Century* (Barricade Books, 1996). This collaboration begins with a lengthy and fascinating introduction describing the evolution of burial practices, from King Mausolus's elaborate tomb in 353 B.C.E. Turkey to the $4 billion cemetery industry in the United States, noting the world's largest Catholic mausoleum in Chicago with more than 33,000 crypts. The major portion of the book is devoted to photographs of some of the most extraordinary cemetery structures in such locations as New York, Boston, Chicago, New Orleans, Philadelphia, Los Angeles, and San Francisco.

The book is divided into sections that cover the revival architectural style popular in the nineteenth century; replicas of classic architecture, such as the Parthenon and the Sainte-Chapelle in Paris; unique structures that do not fit a particular architectural style; mausoleum interiors that feature stunning stained glass windows and elaborate altars; exterior statuary; chapels, columbaria, and other cemetery buildings; and finally modern architecture. Each site pictured includes a description of the architectural style, information about the person or family memorialized, anecdotes and any special background information, and its location. *Going Out in Style* is recommended for its entertaining treatment of a somewhat morose subject and for the quality full-color photographs.—**Jean Engler**

974. Langmead, Donald. **Willem Marinus Dudok, a Dutch Modernist: A Bio-bibliography.** Westport, Conn., Greenwood Press, 1996. 265p. illus. index. (Bio-bibliographies in Art and Architecture, no.4). $79.50. ISBN 0-313-29425-9.

The self-taught architect Willem Dudok spent most of his professional career serving as a parochial municipal architect in the provincial town of Hilversum, Holland, yet he is arguably one of the most widely copied architects of the 1930s and 1940s. This volume begins with an introductory essay describing his life and work, followed by an annotated bibliography of the international literature. The more than 1,200 bibliographic entries in this work are presented alphabetically by decades and are further divided by genres. Each entry is summarized, described, and evaluated in the context of a critical overview of Dudok's career. The last two sections of the book provide a guide to the major archival sources and a chronological list of Dudok's architectural work. The volume includes black-and-white photographs and drawings.

—**Jennifer Comi Ellard**

975. **Preservation Yellow Pages: The Complete Information Source for Homeowners, Communities, and Professionals.** rev. ed. By the National Trust for Historic Preservation. Julie Zagars, ed. New York, Preservation Press/John Wiley, 1997. 277p. illus. index. $24.95pa. ISBN 0-471-19183-3.

Originally published as *The Brown Book: A Directory of Preservation Information* in 1983 (see ARBA 85, entry 490), this handbook has undergone revision and addition in 1990 and 1993. Under the direction of the United States Committee of the International Council on Monuments and Sites for the 1st edition and now written under the direction of the National Trust for Historic Preservation, the work attempts to convey basic preservation knowledge to home owners and concerned preservationists.

The work is divided into 4 sections. The 1st is a preservation primer that places current preservation activities in a historical perspective and attempts to answer the question, "Why Preserve?" The next section is a sort of mini-handbook consisting of a series of essays and lists of architectural styles, the National Register, the Department of the Interior Standards for Rehabilitation, tax credit information, historic preservation law, a glossary, degree programs in historic preservation, a bibliography, and a U.S. preservation chronology from 1812 (founding of the American Antiquarian Society) to 1996. Section 3 consists of "Preservation Partners," an overview list of national, regional, and international preservation organizations and programs. The final section has proved to be for many the most valuable: a state-by-state list of local and statewide preservation contacts.

The volume is an attractively designed paperback, illustrated with a fair number of line drawings of historic structures. The text is readable and provides sufficient background for the novice and an excellent refresher for the professional. The local state lists are correct and up-to-date, including Internet addresses for many. A minor quibble here is that the state National Trust Officers are listed only by their city of residence, which for such places as New York City is not much of a locator. If there is some reason for not including their addresses (such as privacy), why then include the name at all? Individual city listings seem haphazard and incomplete. For example, for Raleigh, North Carolina, the secretary of state is listed (but not explained), and at least two local historic preservation groups are not, even though a stained glass company is. One can only assume that similar omissions and oddities occur elsewhere in other state listings.

Overall, the book is a useful place to start reviewing the topic. Although numerous gaps plague the local state sections, and admittedly the accumulation of local information is an expansive task, one hopes the next edition will be more inclusive in this regard. The work is recommended for all general reference collections.—**Ralph Lee Scott**

976. Stevenson, Neil. **Architecture.** New York, DK Publishing, 1997. 112p. illus. index. (Annotated Guides). $24.95. ISBN 0-7894-1965-3.

Architecture is both a catalog of outstanding buildings around the world and a chronological analysis of the use of materials, architectural features, and the way architectural design reflects function and society. The volume is primarily a large-format pictorial essay of 50 of the world's architectural icons studied in chronological order, beginning with the Egyptian Temple of Amun at Karnak and concluding with the Kansai International Airport Terminal in Japan. Expected inclusions, such as the Pantheon and the Empire State Building, are shown among others less frequently studied, such as Angkor Wat in Cambodia and the Ark Office Complex in England. Although the photographs dominate the book, the supporting text describes architectural, engineering, and construction details that may be overlooked during a casual perusal of the pictures. An introduction explains what architecture is and how it can be studied. The text helps the reader focus on variations in style, materials, site influence, and function that allow each building to reflect its time. Buildings are displayed on a two-page spread, and the uniform presentation format includes background information about the building, the architect or builder, a small box of specification details, and some information about how the building related to the society it served. A short glossary is also provided.

Despite the general excellence, there are some details that could have been improved. The placement of some of the photographs on the pages disturbs the aspect of the building being illustrated. The crease bisects the verticality of the Durham Cathedral and Empire State Building as well as the lateral extension of the façades of the Altes Museum and Castle Howard. A list of references or additional reading would have been helpful for those looking for more information. Overall, however, the book is an excellent architectural study and a value. It would serve well as an architectural reference, a reminiscence of architectural sites visited, or as a coffee-table volume.—**Craig A. Munsart**

977. Wayne, Kathryn M. **Architecture Sourcebook: A Guide to Resources on the Practice of Architecture.** Detroit, Omnigraphics, 1997. 417p. index. (Design Reference Series, v.2). $45.00. ISBN 0-7808-0024-9.

Wayne, architectural librarian at the University of California at Berkeley's Environmental Design Library, has been a member of the Art Library Society of North America (ARLIS) and the Association of Architectural Librarians (AAL) for a number of years. This experienced librarian's new book should prove valuable to a variety of researchers, including other librarians and academics as well as practicing architects and designers.

Part 1, the majority of the work, consists of 14 chapters arranged by building type. When bidding a project, an architect wants all material about a building type easily available and does not want to wade through numerous alphabetic lists of dictionaries, encyclopedias, and bibliographies. In each chapter, Wayne introduces a building type, such as religious buildings. She then lists and annotates such topics as associations, bibliographies, books, and periodicals pertaining to the building type. Uniformly formatted chapters make finding things easy. Part 2, "Additional Reference Sources," follows a more traditional format: dictionaries and encyclopedias, indexes, handbooks and manuals, and periodicals. Librarians will find this classification useful in developing and maintaining a core collection of architectural reference collections. Following the 2 major sections are appendix 1, "Architecture Collections in the United States," and appendix 2, "Publication Sources." Thorough author/title and subject indexes round out the work.

The timing of this architectural resource is good. Other than the 1996 2d edition of *Information Sources in Architecture and Construction* (see ARBA 97, entry 1299), Wayne's work has little competition. The 1996 book is heavily slanted toward international and especially British resources, so overlap between the two books is minimal. A comparable work from 1984, *Design Resources* (see ARBA 85, entry 903), is too old for up-to-date research.

Architecture Sourcebook is the second volume in the Design Reference Series by Omnigraphics. The first volume in the series treats landscape architecture (see entry 1438); the third will cover interior design. In spite of the impression that two typographic errors in the series editor's preface may create, *Architectural Sourcebook* is a generally well-edited and valuable resource. The volume is recommended for use by public, academic, and appropriate special libraries, as well as in the offices of practicing architects and designers.—**Linda D. Tietjen**

DRAWING

978. Feher, Gyorgy. **Cyclopedia Anatomicae: More than 1,500 Illustrations of the Human and Animal Figure for the Artist.** New York, Black Dog & Leventhal; distr., New York, Workman Publishing, 1996. 603p. illus. $24.98. ISBN 1-884822-87-8.

This oversized, fully illustrated work details human anatomy as well as the anatomy of a handful of animals. As the introduction says, "Anatomy is an applied science which underpins fine art; the study of structure is essential for artistic representation." This book assists in acquiring the knowledge of anatomy in order to draw the human and animal figure. It illustrates skeletal form, joints, muscular systems, sensory organs, and surface structures (skin, fur, and the like), and, at times, compares human anatomy with the anatomy of animals, including horses, dogs, cats, and others.

In reviewing reference sources such as this, certain factors are evaluated in determining whether the piece is a useful resource (one to be recommended), or an invaluable resource (one not to be without). I wish I could place this source in the latter category, but there are several books out there that already carry the same information—*Gray's Anatomy of the Human Body* for one—and, with this book specifically targeted to artists, the work could have offered more of what an artist (particularly the beginner and student) would be interested in seeing. If the author and illustrator had concentrated on human anatomy only and showed more of the whole muscular body in multiple positions; appendages extended and graduating to folded positions; extensive views of foreshortening of limbs and fingers; all sides and angles of the head; perspective and dramatic perspective; and so on, then it would have been an invaluable resource.

As a stand-alone cyclopedia, the quality of the art is excellent, and the 1,500 illustrations amply satisfy. With its reasonable price, this is a useful reference source that can be recommended for any library.—**Joan Garner**

GRAPHIC ARTS

979. Barlowe, Wayne Douglas, with Neil Duskis. **Barlowe's Guide to Fantasy.** New York, HarperPrism/ HarperCollins, 1996. 100p. illus. $35.00. ISBN 0-06-105238-8.

Barlowe's Guide to Fantasy provides Barlowe's colorful renditions of 50 fantastic beings. These beings include an epic creature (Grendel); several mythical creatures (Griffin and Tengu); and several beings from the nineteenth century (Lewis Carroll's Caterpillar, Richard F. Burton's Baital, Edgar Allan Poe's Red Death). Yet the majority of the renditions are of figures created by such twentieth-century writers as Peter S. Beagle (Unicorn), Gene Wolfe (Alzabo), Marion Zimmer Bradley (Morgaine), Robert Holdstock (Elemental), and Jack Vance (Nissifer), to name but a few. Accompanying each illustration are a description of the being's world, the history of that world, and the character's physical characteristics; in addition, there is an additional detail of the character. Also available is a comparative size chart. The book concludes with a selection of pencil sketches, some of which prefigure the illustrations of this book and some of which will appear in Barlowe's next project. There is no index.

The success of such a book as this depends upon the artist's ability to create a vision that will supplant or enhance the vision originally formed by the reader, and in many cases, Barlowe's vision falls flat, conveying neither mystery, menace, nor a sense of the ineffable made tangible. This lack is in part because Barlowe has drawn his characters in isolation rather than showing them in situ and in part because many of the illustrations are no more than competent commercial art: The female characters rendered here are reminiscent only of the tall bosomy women appearing on the covers of innumerable fantasy series. On a slightly different note, Barlowe's portrait of Carroll's Caterpillar is inferior to that drawn first by John Tenniel, and his interpretation of Gideon Winter is a mere caricature of Peter Straub's sexually magnetic figure. In addition, there are occasional misspellings (Poe's middle name), and Barlowe's prose is occasionally clumsy. Nevertheless, Barlowe's ursine rendition of Ursula Le Guin's Shadow is powerful, reminiscent of Japanese woodblock illustrations; his depiction of L. Frank Baum's Saw-Horse is properly whimsical; and there are other illustrations that demonstrate significant artistic ability. Whether these successes justify the volume's purchase price, however, is debatable.—**Richard Bleiler**

PAINTING

980. Castagno, John. **Old Masters: Signatures and Monograms, 1400-born 1800.** Lanham, Md., Scarecrow, 1996. 379p. $110.00. ISBN 0-8108-3082-5.

Art histories and collectors will find this volume of artists' signatures of value in researching the artwork of the Old Masters. Included are signature examples for artists dating from the fifteenth century through those born no later than 1800. The signature examples were personally reproduced by the author from many sources. Unlike similar volumes, this work focuses on signature examples not only from oil paintings but also from watercolors, pastels, drawings, prints, and other works.

The volume is divided into several sections, the main body of which contains 2,700 signature examples of 1,700 artists. Nationality and birth and death dates are given as well as bibliographic references, including auction record catalogs. Three sections follow the main body of the volume: monograms and initials, symbols, and alternate names. These sections provide for easy cross-reference with the main body of the volume. Supplemental signature information on additional artists whose actual signatures were not available to the author is given in the final section of the volume.—**Jennifer Comi Ellard**

981. Harris, Elree I., and Shirley R. Scott. **A Gallery of Her Own: An Annotated Bibliography of Women in Victorian Painting.** New York, Garland, 1997. 373p. index. (Women's History and Culture, v.12; Garland Reference Library of the Humanities, v.1414). $68.00. ISBN 0-8153-0040-9.

This resource guide covers primary and secondary contemporary sources of women contributing to art in nineteenth-century Great Britain. References include books, articles, essays, exhibition catalogs, dissertations, advertisements, newspapers, and general studies of women painters and images of women.

The volume is divided into 4 chapters: on Victorian women painters ("Escape into Allegory"); exhibitions ("Going Public"); models ("The Tyranny of the Ideal"); and criticism, art schools, and reviews ("Integration and Commitment"). The division is not always distinct because some painters were also models and may be mentioned in several chapters. The annotations cover 1,003 entries, with each chapter being arranged chronologically so one can follow an artist painting and exhibiting at the same time. Three useful indexes by name, subject, and reproduction are included.

This bibliography will be used by art historians, students of women's studies, and interdisciplinary researchers. It would be a useful addition to art museum libraries as well as art collections in public libraries.
—**Kathleen J. Voigt**

982. Stewart, Brian, and Mervyn Cutten. **The Dictionary of Portrait Painters in Britain up to 1920.** Wappingers Falls, N.Y., Antique Collectors' Club, 1997. 502p. illus. $89.50. ISBN 1-85149-173-2.

More than 5,000 portraitists in Britain from the early 16th century to the early 20th century are listed in this biographical dictionary. Entries range from the virtual unknowns, with little more than a line of information, to luminaries such as Gainsborough, who merits one column. A standard entry includes details of the artist's training, such as where he (most listings are male) studied and under whom. Career highlights are covered, including elements of style and what other artists or movements influenced the painter as well as who the painter himself taught or influenced. Engravers employed by the artist are listed. Galleries and salons where the artist exhibited during his lifetime are noted. Modern museums where the painter is represented are listed followed by a bibliography of works on the artist. There are 75 color plates arranged alphabetically by artist at the front of the volume. Other black-and-white plates are liberally located throughout the text along with the alphabetic sequence of entries. A short introduction, a bibliography, and a list of abbreviations round out this book.

Stewart, formerly of Christie's, and now an art consultant and author, and Cutten, a genealogist and archivist, have created a much needed reference source in art history. Portraiture is a particularly British preoccupation making this dictionary a significant contribution in an area that has had little attention over the years. This work is recommended for college and larger public libraries. [R: LJ, 15 May 97, p. 73]
—**Gerald L. Gill**

SCULPTURE

983. Bassett, Jane, and Peggy Fogelman. **Looking at European Sculpture: A Guide to Technical Terms.** Los Angeles, Calif., J. Paul Getty Museum; distr., New York, Oxford University Press, 1997. 103p. illus. (Looking at). $11.95pa. ISBN 0-89236-291-X.

Brief alphabetic definitions in this easily portable dictionary help clarify meanings and applications of terms relating to European sculpture from the Renaissance through the nineteenth century. The terms that appear in the book are those most often found in catalog texts or on labels in museums and particularly reflect the holdings of the Department of Sculpture and Works of Art of the J. Paul Getty Museum in California and the Victoria and Albert Museum in London.

From *aftercast* to *zinc*, keywords appear in bold typeface with generous annotations. *See* references are abundant. Sixty-five color and thirty-four black-and-white photographs grace the volume. Reproductive printing and color separations of the photographs are crisp and carefully registered. All photograph captions include artist, birth and death dates, title, size, and location in the Getty Museum or the Victoria and Albert Museum. Key headwords in photograph captions that have their own entry are in capital letters. A 16-entry bibliography completes the book; no entries date after 1993.

What is a *herm*? How are death and life masks prepared? Does the word *tomb* belong in a book on sculptural terms? Find the answers to these questions and many tidbits about postclassical European sculpture in this concise and readable guide. Museum-goers, particularly for the two museums featured here, will appreciate this slim volume.—**Judy Gay Matthews**

23 Language and Linguistics

GENERAL WORKS

Bibliography

984. **A Bibliography on Writing and Written Language.** Konrad Ehlich, Florian Coulmas, and Gabriele Graefen, eds. New York, Mouton de Gruyter/Walter de Gruyter, 1996. 3v. (Trends in Linguistics: Studies and Monographs, no.89). $962.00/set. ISBN 3-11-010158-0.

This immense, unannotated philological bibliography includes 27,500 entries published from 1930 to 1992 on the interdisciplinary field of writing and written language, defined by the editors as what writing is, what it does, and what function writing systems serve. According to an introductory section, the three-volume work is intended to facilitate "out of area studies," and is not a comprehensive bibliography of any field encompassed. Although with 94 subject indexes (ranging from runes and Esperanto to Braille and adult literacy programs) and no restriction as to country of publication or language, it may prove to be the closest thing to a single, international bibliography since the publication of a seminal 1935 bibliography mentioned in the introduction. Volume 1 includes an exhaustive user's guide that details the techniques used to transliterate entries and arrange and file entries; an index of subject indexes and the abbreviations used in volume 2's bibliographic entries to indicate a publication's inclusion in those indexes (for example, LITE for literacy); and lists of scripts covered and of bibliographic abbreviations used, such as Ed. Most of volumes 1 and 2 consists of the bibliography, arranged alphabetically by author name. In addition to usual information such as author, title, or journal name, short references to reviews, reprints, and translations are listed, followed by the uppercase abbreviation(s) of the subject indexes in which the item is included. German and French titles are not translated into English; nearly all titles are given in their original languages, followed by the English translation. Finally, volume 3 comprises of subject indexes, each listing short author-year entries referring to the complete citations in volumes 1 and 2.

Forty to fifty percent of the works included were not examined or verified by the editors, and the lack of annotations, sometimes confusing bibliographic information, and occasional absence of helpful English-language translation for the monolingual may not make this the first choice of some researchers. However, its ambition, size, and breadth of subjects covered makes this an important work for large academic collections.—**Jennie Ver Steeg**

985. **Key Guide to Electronic Resources: Language and Literature.** Diane K. Kovacs, ed. Medford, N.J., Information Today, 1996. 120p. index. $39.50pa. ISBN 1-57387-020-X.

This work's introduction says that the rationale for the book came from Constance Gould's *Information Needs in the Humanities: An Assessment* (Research Libraries Group, 1990), in which she first called for more—and better organized—electronic sources that would cater to the information and research needs of scholars in the humanities. This book is a response to that call: an attempt to organize and present selected electronic-format source material in language and literature as a finding guide for those scholars.

The body of the work consists of lists of online databases (both dial-access and Internet), CD-ROM databases and online catalogs, and other Internet resources having to do with language and literature, but broadly cross-referenced to (and from) other humanities disciplines and a few of the social sciences.

"Researchers need primary sources on which to base their work and secondary sources to support their findings. After identifying the material, scholars must then be able to locate these resources as efficiently as possible," the editor says in her introduction. There follows several lists of such materials, Kovacs noting that "the shift to use of these resources is changing libraries from places that own or hold information materials to sources for accessing information materials." Even though that assertion is unarguably true, it seems rather obvious.

Creditably, the book presents selected sources of information that can be used to identify and locate electronic resources in language-related subject areas. Organization is divided into two broad categories, online and CD-ROM, and then subdivided within them. For each source, the format is consistent: database producer (with address and telephone number); vendor; (brief) description of contents and coverage; review citations (where found); other formats available; equipment and software requirements (e.g., IBM PC-compatible, MS-DOS); and reported current price per year.

There is something jarring about a collection of citations to electronic resources marketed as a pricey paperback, especially considering the frequent changes that can occur in source material, formats, features, and prices. The editor's introduction says that "this reference book will make an excellent text for use in advanced and intermediate reference courses in library and information science programs." Possibly, but what would have been more welcome would be a World Wide Web homepage containing the same information in electronic (and thus revisable) format, keeping itself up-to-date at the same time as saving libraries the inordinate price of yet another print source that has begun to decay as (if not before) it is published.—**Bruce A. Shuman**

986. **Southeast Asian Languages and Literatures: A Bibliographical Guide to Burmese, Cambodian, Indonesian, Javanese, Malay, Minangkabau, Thai, and Vietnamese.** E. Ulrich Kratz, ed. London, Tauris Academic Studies; distr., New York, St. Martin's Press, 1996. 455p. $95.00. ISBN 1-86064-114-8.

Standing at the crossroads of the world, Southeast Asia was exposed to diverse cultural, religious, and linguistic customs even prior to colonial rule. Although the region has gained prominence as a growing center of production and trade, its languages and literatures remain unknown to much of the world. Although attention has been paid to English-language literatures of the region in G. L. Anderson's *Asian Literature in English* (see ARBA 82, entry 1381) and Mark Williams's *Post-Colonial Literatures in English: Southeast Asia, New Zealand, and the Pacific, 1970-1992* (see ARBA 97, entry 1013), guides to the indigenous languages and literatures are considered highly specialized. This guide to eight of the region's languages and literatures is intended to simplify access to reference materials, source texts, and translations as well as offer different comparisons and insights that may stimulate reading and research.

The 13 language and literature sections were compiled by experts at the School of African and Oriental Studies in London. Although a useful section on translations from vernacular languages is included, important languages of the Philippines were excluded. Authors begin each section with a broad survey of research and publication in the field. The dictionaries, grammars and other language resources, and surveys of the literary history included in the bibliographies that follow are both historical and current—up to 1994.

The bibliographies are not annotated, and the typeface makes them difficult to read. This combined with the absence of a general subject index to major types or categories of publications diminishes the value of the guide, especially to those interested in comparative aspects or not familiar with the region's culture and history. The title is recommended for collections with an interest in language and linguistics or Asian studies.—**Carol L. Mitchell**

Dictionaries and Encyclopedias

987. Trask, R. L. **A Student's Dictionary of Language and Linguistics.** London, Arnold; distr., New York, St. Martin's Press, 1997. 247p. $49.95; $16.95pa. ISBN 0-340-65267-5; 0-340-65266-7pa.

Reference guides to any topic should be concise but at the same time sufficiently detailed to satisfy the curiosity of the layperson, and yet not disappoint the knowing gaze of the specialist. Trask's *A Student's Dictionary of Language and Linguistics* succeeds in attaining both of these two somewhat conflicting goals. Targeting the introductory linguistics course at the undergraduate as well as the postgraduate levels, the guide is especially useful in its ability to define such basic terms as *morphology* and *typology* in easy-to-understand language. Extensive cross-referencing further eases the process of explaining the seemingly more esoteric terms. The examples given of various linguistic phenomena are precise and appropriate.

This useful guide concludes with a brief section devoted to further readings on some of the broader topics, such as pronunciation, grammar, and meaning. Professional organizations devoted to linguistic study are also mentioned. Also, a sign of the times, electronic resources are referred to, but no specific Internet addresses are given. Perhaps a future edition could list starting points for Internet research on some of the topics mentioned in the book. *A Student's Dictionary of Language and Linguistics* is the perfect supplementary text for university-level introductory linguistics courses. It is also a nice reference tool for people who are fascinated by how language works.—**John B. Romeiser**

Directories

988. **English Language & Orientation Programs in the United States: Offered by U.S. Institutions of Higher Education and Private Language Schools.** 11th ed. Carl De Angelis and Sara J. Steen, eds. New York, Institute of International Education, 1997. 359p. index. $42.95pa. ISBN 0-87206-238-4.

The 11th edition of this standard reference tool for identifying 800 preacademic, intensive English programs and English as a Second Language (ESL) courses is a significant improvement over the 1992 edition (see ARBA 93, entry 1053). Compiled by the respected Institute of International Education, *English Language & Orientation Programs in the United States* (ELOP) provides users with an alphabetized state listing of higher educational institutions that offer intensive English programs for international students wanting to apply to U.S. colleges and universities. Intensive English programs are defined by ELOP as full-time, educational programs that include a minimum of 15 hours of class instruction each week. ESL courses, in contrast, offer less than 15 hours of weekly language instruction and are taken by currently enrolled students desirous of improving their English proficiency while studying for a degree.

Several helpful introductory pages give detailed information about the numerous abbreviations and acronyms used in various entries. Alphabetically grouped by state, each entry contains the following components: educational institution name; intensive English and ESL offerings; telephone, fax, e-mail, and URL particulars; number of class laboratories and computer-assisted instructional hours offered; levels of language instruction, ranging from beginner to advanced; longest break or vacation period; average class size; degree of student ethnic diversity; eligibility; faculty backgrounds; academic credit; required tests; costs; housing; board; and sponsoring institution's accreditation status.

This edition also includes extensive indexes for "specific purposes English programs," such as law, business, and science; an extensive bibliographic guide to funding for U.S. study sources; and a list of start dates for intensive English programs. Four appendixes furnish users with various international accrediting agencies' standards and sponsoring organizations' principles for self-study.

U.S. libraries whose institutions sponsor or counsel international students should consider ELOP a mandatory purchase. It is replete with information that many aspiring English-speaking students will want to access.—**Kathleen W. Craver**

Handbooks and Yearbooks

989. **The Cambridge Encyclopedia of Language.** 2d ed. By David Crystal. New York, Cambridge University Press, 1997. 480p. illus. maps. index. $69.95; $29.95pa. ISBN 0-521-550505; 0-521-559677pa.

The fascination with words, their meanings and implications, their origins and transformations is an integral part of an examination of the world, an effort to make sense of what is seen and heard. The development of language as a tool and the problems of communication—physical, psychological, and cultural—are of paramount importance in a world in which the transmission of information is almost instantaneous.

The Cambridge Encyclopedia of Language is an ambitious but flawed work. Its aim is to describe the history of language and the scientific area of linguistics, but it is neither a simple examination of the myriad of human languages nor a technical investigation of linguistic origins and developments. The chapter descriptions promise valuable content, but the overall effect is a series of information bites. The format, somewhat like MTV in print, offers little ease to the eye, with many different colored insets, disruptive sidebars, and illustrations that do not always have labels or explanations for their inclusion. Perhaps the most interesting and potentially useful section is that dealing with the languages of the world, but the failure to include a reasonable number of samples of those languages discussed is a major deficit.

It is not clear for whom this work is intended, but it is certainly not the beginning adventurer into the linguistic jungle or the highly sophisticated scientific researcher. One would imagine that the encyclopedia is aimed at the college and early graduate school level, including as it does an extensive glossary and bibliography. The cost of the book, particularly in paperback, would make it a useful purchase for libraries serving this population and for large public collections.—**Paula Frosch**

990. Parker, Philip M. **Linguistic Cultures of the World: A Statistical Reference.** Westport, Conn., Greenwood Press, 1997. 435p. index. (Cross-Cultural Statistical Encyclopedia of the World, v.2). $95.00. ISBN 0-313-29769-X.

Linguistic Cultures of the World is a comprehensive guide to the cultural, economic, and geographic circumstances of the planet's 460 main language groups. Its goal is to contextualize the world's language groups, thereby providing precious information for such fields as business, economics, sociology, ethnography, and geography. This is not so much a book about language as it is a statistical reference manual on the interplay between language and place.

Organized into 11 chapters, *Linguistic Cultures of the World* provides abundant quantitative comparisons across language groups in multiple countries located in multiple continents. The work asks such fundamental questions for transnational languages like English, French, and Spanish as: What is the rank order of languages by income per capita and which language groups have the highest (and lowest) consumption levels of food, goods, and services? There are many surprises in this reference guide that defy conventional wisdom, including adult literacy rates (English-speaking countries are not in the top 20) and economic affluence (English comes in 14th after Danish, Icelandic, and German, and just ahead of Indochinois and French).

The primary divisions of this guide are as follows: economics (gross national product, saving rate, inflation rate, and others), demography and sociology (death, birth, and crime rates), cultural resources (ethnic groups and religions), mineral resources (percentage of world reserves of key minerals), as well as land, marine, and climatic resources. The book is thoroughly indexed and contains a select bibliography of research works focusing on the relationship between language and physioeconomic factors, especially climate.

Linguistic Cultures of the World is an essential reference work for educators and professionals who need hard data to make informed research or business decisions.—**John B. Romeiser**

991. Sofer, Morry. **The Translator's Handbook 1997.** Rockville, Md., Schreiber Publishing, 1996. 475p. index. $24.95pa. ISBN 1-887563-22-9.

Unlike other fields suffering from an overabundance of professional literature, the field of and the professionals in translation have long lacked professional recognition. Sofer's first publication, *Guide for Translators*, was viewed as the one and only handbook published exclusively for professionals in the translation field. This book is an expanded, improved version of the guide. The new book contains new materials for both experienced and aspiring translators and is four times the size of the guide. The handbook is designed to cover all aspects of translation, both theoretical and pragmatic. It is meant to serve as a sourcebook for all translators in all languages, both in and outside of the United States.

The author begins by making clear the work of translation. It takes not only language skills but also an innate aptitude for translation to bring forth the full intent and flavor of the original language. Even the best translators can only hope to provide a rendition close enough to the original, and they still risk altering the original's stylistic character. Translation involves both words as well as ideas. "The Requisites for Professional Translators" in this book specify the important quality and talents that a good translator possesses. "The Self Evaluation" can be helpful to aspiring translators in gauging their skills and identifying the needed improvement. Other chapters are devoted to practical suggestions and solutions to problems in the translation profession, such as legal and financial issues, the freelance market, record keeping, the translator/client relationship, and reference literature for various languages. The appendixes provide useful information, such as foreign-language software sources, translation agencies, translation accreditation, and continuing education programs.

The Translator's Handbook can be an invaluable tool for professional as well as occasional translators. An annual update of the handbook will meet expectations and become a standard tool for translators for years to come.—**Eveline L. Yang**

ENGLISH-LANGUAGE DICTIONARIES

General Usage

992. Brownstein, Samuel C., Mitchel Weiner, and Sharon Weiner Green. **Basic Word List**. 3d ed. Hauppauge, N.Y., Barron's Educational Series, 1997. 274p. $6.95pa. ISBN 0-8120-9659-5.

More than 2,000 vocabulary words likely to appear on college-level standardized tests are presented in this 3d-edition volume (the 1st edition was published in 1981, the 2d in 1990). Apparently for easier digestion, the words, although remaining in one alphabetic sequence, are now divided into 50 lists. For each word, the authors include its part of speech, a short definition, and a sentence showing how it is used. There are also sample tests, an answer key, a section on common prefixes and roots, and an introduction with clever tips on improving study skills.

Many of the other Barron's guides include similar vocabulary lists. For instance, *How to Prepare for the GRE* (11th ed., Barron's Educational Series, 1994) has a "Master Word List" of some 3,500 words, also with definitions and sample sentences. Someone taking a specific test would probably be better off with one of these. However, adults interested in improving their vocabulary or students wanting a basic list of words to learn over the summer would like the book at hand. The binding and paper would not stand up to heavy library use, and the pages beg to be written on. For these reasons, although libraries may also choose this lightweight, inexpensive volume, it is more appropriate for bookstores.—**Hope Yelich**

993. **The Oxford Desk Dictionary and Thesaurus**. American ed. Frank R. Abate, ed. New York, Oxford University Press, 1997. 972p. $15.95. ISBN 0-19-511214-8.

In a handy, portable format, this reference tool provides more than 150,000 entries, synonyms, and senses for words in American English. The typical entry indicates pronunciation (based on a simplified key), part of speech, inflected forms, senses or meanings of words, idioms and phrases, derivatives, and finally synonyms. Not all entries have synonym lists, and in some cases there is one simple synonym list that covers multiple meanings of a word. Cross-references are given when appropriate. Etymology, however, is completely absent from the volume, as are illustrations. Supplemental reference appendixes include guides to signs, symbols, weights and measures, chemical elements, time periods, wedding anniversary gifts, books of the Bible, U.S. presidents, area codes, and other typical lists.

From one of the foremost publishers of English-language reference tools, this volume should enhance most personal libraries for its simplicity of design and use. Its primary value is found in the integration of dictionary and thesaurus formats. Although not exhaustive, it is comprehensive in scope. Public and academic libraries will likely find some duplication here with other reference works. However, the work is affordable and visually pleasing to use, which may give it an edge over similar products.
—**Edmund F. SantaVicca**

994. **The Oxford Dictionary and Thesaurus**. American ed. New York, Oxford University Press, 1996. 1828p. $30.00. ISBN 0-19-509949-4.

This new dictionary from Oxford University Press successfully combines material found in two previous publications, *The Concise Oxford Dictionary of Current English* (8th ed.; see ARBA 91, entry 1048) and *The Oxford Thesaurus* (see ARBA 94, entry 1107). The result is a useful abridgment that integrates standard dictionary information with synonyms for keywords. The present volume has approximately 100,000 entries, each of which contains standard dictionary information (e.g., pronunciation, part of speech, irregular plurals and tenses, brief etymologies), followed by clear, succinct definitions that are numbered and arranged by order of importance and familiarity. Keywords (approximately one-third of the entries) contain synonym entries that are also arranged numerically to correspond to the definitions. Plentiful *see* references guide the reader to related main entries and synonym entries. A total of more than 300,000 synonyms are listed, but there is no coverage of antonyms.

Entries are up-to-date (e.g., *downsize* and *grunge* are defined), and current slang expressions, such as *nerd* and *cool*, are also included. There are no illustrations, nor are there entries for people or places; however, coverage encompasses many entries for abbreviations (e.g., *DOE* for the Department of Energy). American spelling, usage, and idioms are stressed. The pronunciation key is found only in the prefatory material, along with a list of abbreviations used in the text and directions for using the volume efficiently. Copious appendixes feature lists of proverbs, signs and symbols, technical terms, countries, U.S. presidents, and a brief history of the English language.

This volume is ideally suited for the home market (it was originally published as *Reader's Digest Oxford Complete Wordfinder*). However, many high school, public, and college libraries will find it a handy single volume that effectively integrates basic material from an abridged dictionary with that found in a thesaurus. [R: LJ, Jan 97, p. 90]—**John T. Gillespie**

995. **Pockets: English Dictionary A to Z.** New York, DK Publishing, 1997. 512p. (DK Pockets). $6.95 flexibinding. ISBN 0-7894-1497-X.

This dictionary lives up to its advertising blurb that it has more than 50,000 entries, including many current words; that its definitions are concise and easy to understand; that abbreviations and acronyms are spelled out; and that it includes many word variations. Unfortunately, that is all the description the editors provide; there is no foreword, introduction, or usage notes, just a one-page list of abbreviations (such as "Brit" for British) to help the user understand what this dictionary includes and omits. This volume is the first American edition; nevertheless, some entries, even in a source as concise as this one, are primarily of interest to British readers (e.g., *privy purse*: "allowance for sovereign's personal use").

Very current words and phrases are defined, such as *political correctness* and *ethnic cleansing*. Definitions are clear and concise; for example, *doggy bag*: "bag for taking home uneaten food from restaurant." Numerous obscene words (but not the "F" word) are included, as are other forms of slang. When more than one meaning of a word is listed, it appears that the most common meaning occurs first. Occasionally the old-fashioned usage prevails over a contemporary meaning (*disinterested* is defined as meaning "without selfish motives; impartial"; the sense of "uninterested" is not given). Some definitions are questionable (is it really true that a senior citizen is a "person beyond the age of retirement"?).

Although the typeface is clear, two typographic errors were found in just a few minutes of browsing: "charletan" as a definition of *quack* and "multididinous" as a spelling of *multitudinous*. Despite some careless proofreading, this dictionary is bargain-priced for personal reference use. The flexibinding is durable, and the small size means it will literally fit into (large) pockets. This book will not, however, be needed in most reference departments.—**David Isaacson**

996. **The World Book Dictionary.** Robert K. Barnhart, ed. Chicago, World Book, 1996. 2v. illus. $87.00/set. ISBN 0-7166-0296-2.

More than any other book that one uses regularly, one's dictionary seems like a valued companion. People know its strengths and weaknesses, but most of all, its peculiarities. When people use another dictionary, it is easy to feel uncomfortable or insecure with its different approach to definitions, etymologies, and synonyms, as well as its unfamiliar format. In turning to the latest revision (called neither a new edition nor a new printing) of this dictionary, this reviewer found that he had easily made a new friend both comfortable and uncomplicated. *The World Book Dictionary*'s intended user group is students; this shows by the simplicity and clarity of its style. The dictionary will serve them well, as well as make a good, basic dictionary for any household in need of one. Designed to be practical, the dictionary omits obsolete and unusual words to concentrate on the 225,000 terms in the working vocabulary of English. Desiring that the dictionary will be used in conjunction with *The World Book Encyclopedia*, this volume also omits biographical and geographic entries, but this is not of great importance.

Every definition is clear and straightforward but achieved with simple language. The most commonly used meaning is given first. Illustrative phrases and sentences, given with sources ranging from popular magazines to the Bible and Shakespearean works to show how the word is properly used, come from quotation files maintained by the publisher of more than 3 million quotations assembled in a period of more than 35 years. Etymologies are bracketed and placed near the end of the entries. Synonyms are as specific as possible and clearly given for each use of a word with multiple meanings.

The illustrations are the usual dictionary drawing type but are especially skillfully used. In comparing this dictionary with many others of similar size and scope, it is striking to see the way in which this lexicon uses illustrations to show the many different meanings of some words. For example, this dictionary shows specifically that a barb can be the tip of an arrow; part of a fishhook, a feather, or a catfish; and a part of a medieval woman's headdress. Claw illustrations show parts of birds, animals, furniture, and tools.

Introductory materials run to page 124, and in addition to the expected information on the use of the book, there are large sections on using the English language and different languages that cover such matters as prefixes, suffixes, spelling, capitalization, vocabulary, and punctuation as well as codes and ciphers, signs and symbols, measures, and metric conversions. A sizable section on writing effectively includes instructions for terms papers, book reports, outlines, letter writing, and forms of address. *The World Book Dictionary* is a fine, user-friendly reference. [R: RBB, June 97, p. 1748]—**O. Gene Norman**

Abridged

997. **The American Heritage Talking Dictionary.** [CD-ROM]. Cambridge, Mass., SoftKey, 1996. Minimum system requirements: IBM or compatible 386/25MHz (486 recommended). Double-speed CD-ROM drive. DOS 5.0. Windows 3.1. 8MB RAM. 22MB hard disk space (12MB for Windows 95). VGA 256-color monitor. Microsoft or compatible mouse. MPC-compliant 8 bit sound card. $59.95.

An electronic dictionary is not only faster, more convenient and versatile, and easier on the eyes than a print dictionary; it is also much more fun, especially with the advent of multimedia. The user friendliness of newer computers and software makes it a breeze to learn this program. All the features of the previous version (see ARBA 96, entry 1062) have been retained and some excellent new ones added, together with dazzling photographs, maps, and short video clips. These features include a "hide obscenities" password option that will be welcomed by parents, an automatic pop-up "Word of the Day" vocabulary builder, and a quick-view miniwindow to place on the electronic desktop and run concurrently with other programs; the latter function makes it wonderfully easy when reading or writing on-screen to access the dictionary and thesaurus.

The number of main dictionary entries has remained the same, but the addition of an entire new *Dictionary of Cultural Literacy* vastly increases the number of words defined, and thesaurus entries have been tripled. The 1,500 photographs and maps are attractive and well chosen, but the small number of video clips (50) forced some questionable choices: There are videos of Frank Sinatra, Marilyn Monroe, and Babe Ruth, but none for Martin Luther King Jr., Willie Mays, or George Gershwin. The megabytes devoted to an unmoving, hazy, black-and-white video of Mt. Fuji could have been put to better use showing a hummingbird in flight, a waterwheel, or flamenco dancing, none of which are illustrated with videos.

The compatibility problems of the earlier version seem to have been resolved, and the price has remained the same. The new version includes a free CD-ROM of the *Time Magazine Multimedia Almanac*, another useful and exciting program. This electronic dictionary is an excellent product and is highly recommended for libraries and individuals. [R: Choice, Mar 97, p. 1147]—**Larry Lobel**

998. **Merriam-Webster's Collegiate Dictionary, Deluxe Audio Edition.** [CD-ROM]. Springfield, Mass., Merriam-Webster, 1996. Minimum system requirements (Windows version): IBM or compatible 486SX. CD-ROM drive. Windows 3.1. 4MB RAM. 2MB hard disk space. VGA or SVGA monitor. Mouse. Sound card. Speakers. Minimum system requirements (Macintosh version): Motorola 68030. CD-ROM drive. System 7.0. 4MB RAM. 2MB hard disk space. Mouse. True-type font and foreign-file access. $49.95. ISBN 0-87779-460-X.

The dictionary publisher's latest spin-off is a moderately-priced CD-ROM developed for use in the personal computers of today's high school and college students. The disc includes the 10th edition of *Merrian-Webster's Collegiate Dictionary* and the publisher's *Collegiate Thesaurus*. The former contains more than 214,000 definitions; the latter includes more than 130,000 synonyms, antonyms, and related entries. The digital configuration offers features that the printed books, of course, cannot. The requisite search options with Boolean operators are present, users may hear audio pronunciation of 100,000 of the dictionary entries, and a single-click on a camera-shaped icon brings up one of 1,000 color illustrations.

The CD-ROM loaded flawlessly onto a Pentium/Windows 95 platform. The lack of on-screen "back" and "forward" buttons was the only impediment to immediate easy use. Users of CD-ROMs will not be disappointed by this product. It contains the text that one expects to see, and it features the searching options that one hopes to find. Priced more for library, rather than individual, purchase, this should be in demand in both camps. [R: Choice, July/Aug 97, p. 1789]—**Ed Volz**

999. **The New Shorter Oxford English Dictionary.** [CD-ROM]. New York, Oxford University Press, 1996. Minimum system requirements: IBM or compatible. 386SX/20MHz. Double-speed CD-ROM drive with Microsoft CD-ROM Extensions 2.21. DOS 5.0. Windows 3.1. 8MB RAM. 2MB hard disk space. VGA 16-color monitor. Microsoft compatible mouse. $95.00. ISBN 0-19-268302-0.

The New Shorter Oxford English Dictionary (NSOED) on CD-ROM is a scaled-down version of the *Oxford English Dictionary* on CD-ROM. Whether one is looking up slang or formal words they can be found here and quickly.

After installation and launch, a window opens with four tabbed sections: Simple Search, Index Search, Full-Text Search, and Special Search. Simple Search allows for a straight forward search of a word. Type it in and a list of headwords appears. Choose a headword from the list and double-click. The definition window appears giving pronunciation, part of speech, etymology, and then definitions and quotations. Green codes, at first cryptic, appear throughout, which it was discovered (thanks to the online help) are date entries of when the word(s) came into use. Cross-references from the definitions to other words in the dictionary are accessed if colored blue. Displays in Simple Search can be modified in three ways: (1) display sense and illustration of text in separate groups; (2) display sense and illustration of text adjacent; and (3) display sense of text only. Index Search allows searching by headword, derivatives, abbreviations, phrases and compounds, uses and references, and other forms. You may search by all of the above, but not specific combinations thereof. Full-Text Search allows searching by all text, etymology (plus dozens of foreign languages), definition, or quotation. It also allows for combinations of the above. Special Search allows for anagram searches, rhyming searches, or phonetic searches. The phonetic search seems limited in its usefulness as one would have to know how to pronounce something before being able to search for it.

Pull-down menus allow for all search functions located in the four tabbed sections. Use of the program is simple and well thought out. Buttons have pop up explanations of what the button does. A great online help menu allows a search for topics and "how-to" information.

A special macro feature allows access to the NSOED while in Word 6.0 or 7.0 as well as Word Perfect 6.0 and 6.1 and Ami Pro 3.1. If one chooses to install it, a button appears in the tool bar. Select from the document the unknown word or word that a definition is needed for, and click the NSOED button. NSOED opens and lists all parts of speech for that word. Select the word you want and the definition screen opens as usual. You can then stay in NSOED or switch back to your word processor.

Without all the full, academic information of the *Oxford English Dictionary on Compact Disc* (see ARBA 97, entry 843), the NSOED at its very accessible price would benefit all school library media centers.
—**Kevin W. Perizzolo**

Etymology

1000. Barnhart, David K., and Allan A. Metcalf. **America in So Many Words: Words That Have Shaped America.** New York, Houghton Mifflin, 1997. 308p. illus. index. $18.00. ISBN 0-395-86020-2.

Barnhart and Metcalf have created a rare volume: a reference book that compels one to read it from cover to cover. Using a chronological approach, the authors have selected one particularly American word from each year since the founding of Jamestown in 1607 and explain how each word has had an impact in shaping the nation's course. As the authors note, many of the words are not necessarily distinguished and are, in fact, very common. These words are included because they are "symptomatic of American thought and action."

With only about 300 entries, this book does not compare to such classics as the massive 4-volume *A Dictionary of American English on Historical Principles*, edited by William A. Craigie and James R. Hulbert (1938-1944), or the 2-volume *A Dictionary of Americanisms on Historical Principles*, edited by Mitford M. Mathews (1951). But it does not aim to compete with these extensive works. Instead, it gives the reader a series of comprehensive, literate, and entertaining entries that form a diachronic continuity across the whole book.

Barnhart is an editor, publisher, longtime student of lexicography and the American language; Allen Metcalf, professor of English at MacMurray College, is a specialist in American dialects. Their entries are well chosen and include such words as corn (1608), Thanksgiving (1621), boss (1635), frontier (1676), backlog (1684), settler (1695), cookie (1703), store (1721), barbecue (1733), mileage (1753), and Yankee (1765), to name a few.

This book is highly recommended, both as a reference book and as a good read.—**Richard W. Clement**

1001. **The Facts on File Encyclopedia of Word and Phrase Origins.** rev. ed. By Robert Hendrickson. New York, Facts on File, 1997. 754p. index. $65.00. ISBN 0-8160-3266-1.

If the complexity and variety of languages and related symbolic systems best distinguish human beings from other creatures, then lexicography is the science closest to what humans are and lexicographers the guardians of humanity's identity. In a way, therefore, no library can have too many dictionaries because, like human beings, no one of them will ever suffice for all purposes. Freelance writer Hendrickson competes in a market long dominated by lexical giants Brewer, Fowler, and Partridge, whose dictionaries, although not labeled "etymological," do offer the kind of information that Hendrickson does.

According to its preface, this new edition offers 25 percent more material than the 1st (see ARBA 88, entry 1066) and—at 15,000 cross-referenced eponyms; toponymns; phrases; coinages; colloquialisms; and slang, technical, and jargon terms—includes 3 times as many entries as "any previous collection of its kind." The new edition has also added an index of people mentioned in entries and of words not enjoying their own entries; the design remains the same, and the tone of the narrative etymologies remains learnedly chatty.

Along with the *Oxford English Dictionary*, Frederic G. Cassidy's *Dictionary of American Regional English* (see ARBA 93, entry 1062) and J. E. Lighter's *Random House Historical Dictionary of American Slang* (see ARBA 95, entry 1061) (the latter two both in progress) are the standard works for large libraries. Although no reference collection should surrender shelf space occupied by Brewer and Partridge, Hendrickson's dictionary would make a useful addition to most collections, if only for its reader-friendly design. There is *gee-whiz* here for the browser, *succor* for the puzzled, *clarity* for the confused, *information* for the ignorant, and *delight* and *instruction* for all.—**Robert H. Kieft**

1002. Flexner, Stuart Berg, and Anne H. Soukhanov. **Speaking Freely: A Guided Tour of American English from Plymouth Rock to Silicon Valley.** New York, Oxford University Press, 1997. 472p. illus. index. $39.95. ISBN 0-19-510692-X.

This is a book of social history in which words are the chief indicators of change. More than half of it is based on two of Flexner's popular earlier works, *I Hear America Talking* (see ARBA 78, entry 1031) and *Listening to America* (see ARBA 84, entry 1023). The rest is the work of lexicographer Soukhanov, who shows how aspects of American English have evolved over the past 20 years. Supplemented with up-to-date photographs, illustrations, and quotations from various sources, this is a beautifully designed and highly entertaining volume.

Soukhanov takes 39 subject groups, most highlighting aspects of everyday existence—health, fashion, politics, and others—and shows how specific words and phrases have reflected changes in American life and culture. Many of these words are woven into the text, whereas others appear in lists. When appropriate, she gives definitions and short histories of the words; interesting anecdotes abound. How many of us knew that Francis Bacon experimented with freezing chickens by stuffing them with snow in 1626 or that the word "tycoon" comes from the Japanese "taikun," which means shogun or military leader?

This is not a traditional dictionary of etymology, slang, or regional English. It does not claim to be comprehensive. Although an excellent index at the back increases the book's reference value, readers would savor the gems in *Speaking Freely* best by browsing. Recommended as a gift book and for the circulating collections of public and academic libraries.—**Hope Yelich**

Foreign Words and Phrases

1003. Evans, Toshie M. **A Dictionary of Japanese Loanwords.** Westport, Conn., Greenwood Press, 1997. 230p. $75.00. ISBN 0-313-28741-4.

Evans is a reporter for a journal on Japanese as a second language. She has published articles on language and language education. Her unique reference source contains more than 1,000 entries and includes explanatory notes, a pronunciation key, and a bibliography, in addition to the dictionary itself. The dictionary lists terms borrowed from Japanese, recently the second-largest source of foreign words adopted into English. Entries are accompanied by their pronunciation, alternatives, derivation, date of borrowing, and examples of use.

The coverage illustrates the richness of the use of Japanese terms in cuisine, sports, medicine, electronics, astronomy, politics, economics, and other areas. Many of the terms have specific applications, such as to some aspects of Japanese history, art, or religion. Others refer to such narrow areas as oceanography or botany. Still others may be useful to tourists when they read guidebooks on Japan or to general readers on subjects relating to Japan. The user of this dictionary will derive a greater appreciation for English-speakers' linguistic debt to the Japanese and will gain a precise understanding of some terms that are used but only loosely understood.—**Bogdan Mieczkowski**

Grammar

1004. Grossman, Ellie. **The Grammatically Correct Handbook: A Lively and Unorthodox Review of Common English, for the Linguistically Challenged.** New York, Hyperion, 1997. 235p. index. $9.95pa. ISBN 0-7868-8169-0.

Operating on the assumption that humor teaches as well as entertains, this book illustrates basic rules of English grammar, diction, and style with jokes, puns, limericks, and other forms of humor rather than "straight" examples. If the reader shares Grossman's sense of humor, this book achieves its purpose. However, old-fashioned experts on grammar or readers needing more explanation of grammar will not be well-served because humor sometimes substitutes for clarity. Declaring herself an advocate of common sense over obfuscation, Grossman's tone is sometimes decidedly anti-intellectual. For instance, she states in the introduction that she offers "No complicated rules. No dense explanations. No jargon. (If you didn't understand 'intransitive' back then, why should you have to try now?)" (p. 2).

This book has 3 sections: "Mistaken Identities," which consists of 31 brief essays distinguishing between easily confused pairs of words, such as "uninterested and disinterested"; "Mindbenders," which devotes 17 essays to difficult grammatical matters, such as the difference between "none" and "no one"; and "Miscellaneous Misunderstandings," which presents 18 more essays on a variety of stylistic considerations, such as the controversy over the appropriate use of the word "hopefully."

Grossman is not the first author to combine grammar with humor. Karen Elizabeth Gordon has written two witty handbooks, *The Transitive Vampire: A Handbook of Grammar for the Innocent, the Eager, and the Doomed* (New York, Times Books, 1984) and *The Well-Tempered Sentence: A Punctuation Handbook for the Innocent, the Eager, and the Doomed* (New Haven, Ticknor and Fields, 1983). Gordon's books are more straightforward than Grossman's; each rule is stated in clear, unambiguous prose and illustrated by an often mordantly witty rather than merely a humorous sentence. Although Grossman's book is somewhat useful as well as being occasionally amusing, Gordon's books are much more clearly organized for reference and written for a more literate audience. [R: LJ, Aug 97, p. 87]—**David Isaacson**

1005. Stilman, Anne. **Grammatically Correct: The Writer's Essential Guide to Punctuation, Spelling, Style, Usage, and Grammar.** Cincinnati, Ohio, Writer's Digest Books/F & W Publications, 1997. 328p. index. $19.99. ISBN 0-89879-776-4.

Does the world really need another handbook on English usage? The author of this one has added some largely cosmetic touches to the standard formula for such works in order to convince readers that hers indeed fills a gap. Nevertheless, she has produced a sensible, thoroughly up-to-date, and highly useful guide. Stilman shuns rigid and stuffy grammatical prescriptions (e.g., proscribing split infinitives), yet she wisely insists on maintaining useful distinctions (e.g., *imply* versus *infer*). When more than one form or usage is acceptable, she makes note of it. The book is divided into five sections—spelling, problem words, punctuation, grammar, and style—each of which is characterized by a no-nonsense approach, with emphasis on practicality. A useful and interesting feature of this handbook is its frequent use of quotations from all manner of authors to illustrate specific points. This is a guide for "individuals who already know English well and just want some specific answers on tricky topics."—**Jeffrey R. Luttrell**

Idioms, Colloquialisms, Special Usage

1006. **The American Heritage Dictionary of Idioms.** By Christine Ammer. New York, Houghton Mifflin, 1997. 729p. $30.00. ISBN 0-395-72774-X.

Idioms, those expressions impossible to explain from a literal translation of the individual words in the phrase, clause, or sentence, have long been the bane of nonnative learners of languages. English abounds in these often colorful expressions that are contributed to the language richness from all levels of society, from other languages, and from the earliest of times. Ammer's work is only the newest and largest of a number of dictionaries designed to make sense of these idiosyncratic figures of speech, interjections, formula phrases, emphatic redundancies, common proverbs, colloquialisms, and slang expressions of American English. Each entry is defined and illustrated by at least one sample sentence showing its use in context. When possible, the origin and date of its first appearance are included. Alphabetization and cross-references make finding an expression or its variants easy. Usage labels indicate the degree of formality or offensiveness associated with an expression, but no label indicates standard English.

Not just for those learning English but for anyone who enjoys learning more about American English, its idiosyncrasies, roots, and origins, this new dictionary is highly recommended. All libraries will find this a useful and authoritative addition to their specialized dictionary collections.—**Blaine H. Hall**

1007. Hendrickson, Robert. **Mountain Range: A Dictionary of Expressions from Appalachia to the Ozarks.** New York, Facts on File, 1997. 288p. index. (Dictionary of American Regional Expressions Series). $24.95; $14.95pa. ISBN 0-8160-2113-9; 0-8160-3692-6pa.

The 4th volume in Facts on File's Dictionary of American Regional Expressions Series, *Mountain Range* provides definitions for 2,000 discrete words and phrases that are traditionally associated with English speakers residing in Appalachia, the Ozarks, the Blue Ridge Mountains, the Smokies, and the Cumberlands. Hendrickson supplements several hundred of these entries with illustrative quotations, particularly drawing upon the writings of Kentuckian, Jesse Stuart.

Most entries contain fewer than 30 words, and most lack cross-referencing citations, as between "hearing" and "hurd." Etymological information appears irregularly as well. Entries whose length exceed 100 words, such as "sequoia," "Ozarks," and "you all," appear infrequently.

Although reliable and thorough in its lexical range, perspective, and presentation, this dictionary has more than its share of errors of commission and omission. For instance, Hendrickson's contention that "stand" typically denotes "beehive" among Appalachian speakers is suspect. The definition for "drammer" is circular, relying upon the undefined term "dram." Unaccountably absent from this volume is the common expression "like ta" (which means "nearly" or "almost," as in "He was like ta lose his temper"). The entries "volunteer" and "razorback" fail to allude to these words' associations with the residents of Tennessee and Arkansas. Entries for West Virginia and Mount Kephart appear in *Mountain Range*; however, entries for Virginia and for the Allegheny Mountains do not. Noteworthy, too, are the absences of entries for such terms as "hornswoggle" (to cheat), "sommers" (somewhere), "wooden overcoat" (coffin), and "rooster" (to cock a gun).

The lack of a keyword index is a serious omission. It is doubtful that users of this reference will easily locate such alphabetized entries as "have the big eye" or "I'm tellin' you right." Furthermore, a number of minor but irritating gaffes will do little to inspire confident use of this resource by serious researchers. For example, "dry grins" is misspelled as "dry gins."

Hendrickson's inconsistent means of indicating preferred pronunciations of problematic terms is often difficult to follow. In some cases, pronunciation is conveyed by the phonetic rendering of a headword's spelling, but in other instances it is communicated through a notation following the headword. Unintended ambiguity sometimes results.

Used judiciously, *Mountain Range* will be of some value to collections lacking the word lists and glossaries found in Vance Randolph's seminal *Down in the Holler: A Gallery of Ozark Folk Speech* (University of Oklahoma Press, 1953; reprinted 1979) and Cratis D. Williams's *Southern Mountain Speech* (Berea College Press, 1992).—**Jeffrey E. Long**

Juvenile

1008. **Scholastic Children's Dictionary.** rev. ed. By the Editors of Scholastic, Inc. New York, Scholastic, 1996. 648p. illus. maps. index. $16.95. ISBN 0-590-25271-2.

Perhaps if every variant of a word, defined or undefined, was counted, the 30,000 words claimed for this dictionary by some reviewers might be reached. Defined terms are closer to half that number; main entries are still fewer. This dictionary, designed for children in grades 3 through 6, and based on an English dictionary, provides its own pronunciation, which is given only once. The pronunciation helps are rather standard sounds such as "a" for the sound in "mad" and "ah" for the sound in "father" and should be fairly simple to follow.

Most entries provide pronunciation, part of speech, and definition. Many include more than one definition and related words, and some include sample sentences. Homophones are given when appropriate, introduced by the phrase "sounds like." Very little information is provided on the history of words—only 5 in the 1st 25 pages. Those provided are designed to catch the interest of the readers. For example, the word history of *girl* points out that *girl* used to refer to a child of either sex and *gun* came from a huge crossbow from the fourteenth century named a "Lady Gunilda." Many colorful drawings and photographs illustrate further some complex terms, such as *ice-skating movements*, and suffix and synonym notes expand some definitions.

Supplements include the Braille alphabet, sign language symbols, world and U.S. maps, flags, facts about the states and presidents, and an index of picture labels. These last appear to be words that are not otherwise defined in the dictionary, although this is not always true and all labels are not included.

The editors have made an effort to address newer terms. *Kwanzaa* is defined, as are *Islam*, *Christianity*, and *Catholic*. Although *Protestant* is included, individual denominations are not. More body parts are defined than has been typical of children's dictionaries, but there are functions that are not included. For example, *manure* is defined, but *human waste* is not. More notice is taken of inclusive terminology, but *mankind* is defined and *humankind* is not.

This is a physically appealing dictionary, probably best used as one of several children's dictionaries, such as *The American Heritage Children's Dictionary* (Houghton Mifflin, 1994) or the *Macmillan Dictionary for Children* (Macmillan, 1989), in school and public libraries.—**Betty Jo Buckingham**

1009. **Thorndike-Barnhart Junior Dictionary.** By E. L. Thorndike and Clarence L. Barnhart. New York, HarperCollins, 1997. 1024p. illus. maps. $19.00. ISBN 0-06-270161-4.

The *Thorndike-Barnhart Junior Dictionary* defines approximately 68,000 words, including a number of geographic terms and biographical entries; some basic scientific terms are also defined. Syllabication, part of speech, and pronunciation (including variants) are given; pluralizations of nouns and the participles and past tenses of verbs are frequently given. In addition, there are 1,200 photographs and illustrations; 34,000 illustrative examples; 900 usage notes and synonym studies; and a concluding section that contains world maps, a table of elements, and pictures and information about the U.S. presidents.

One does not expect a dictionary intended for middle school students to include obscenities, and this one does not. At the same time, one hopes for a dictionary to present information accurately, clearly, and concisely, and the *Junior Dictionary* again does not; its flaws are disturbing and manifest. There are persistent problems with names: Pseudonyms and birth names are rarely revealed, leading putative users to suppose that such figures as George Orwell, Houdini, and Boris Karloff had no other names. Full names of people are inconsistently given, and the first names of T. S. Eliot and F. Scott Fitzgerald remain mysterious. Also, the editorial decision to lump together all entries for people sharing a similar last name leads to some thoroughly misleading juxtapositions. One has the Franklins (Aretha and Benjamin), the O'Connors (Flannery and Sandra Day), and the Adams (Abigail, Ansel, John, John Quincy, and Samuel), to name but three examples.

Cross-referencing between entries is similarly weak: The entry for Buckminster Fuller mentions his role in creating the geodesic dome, but the entry for geodesic dome does not mention Fuller. Similarly, Karloff's entry mentions his role in *Frankenstein* (without providing the year of the motion picture), but the definition for *Frankenstein* provides an unidentified picture of Karloff, the caption stating only that it is the monster "as played by an actor." (Nor does the definition of *Frankenstein* provide the scientist's first name.) Finally, the quality of the definitions is poor. For example, to define *tzarina* only as *czarina* is of no help (and there is no cross-reference to the fuller definition given under *czarina*). This dictionary was also published as the *Scott Foresman Intermediate Dictionary*.—**Richard Bleiler**

New Words

1010. **The Barnhart Dictionary Companion: A Quarterly of New Words. Volume 10, Number 1, Summer 1997.** David K. Barnhart, ed. Springfield, Mass., Merriam-Webster, 1997. 90p. index. $98.00pa./yr. ISSN 0736-1122.

The Barnhart Dictionary Companion is a Merriam-Webster-backed continuation of a serial that has been in publication since 1982. The purpose of the companion is to bring to light changes in English vocabulary that have not found their way into a dictionary yet. The issue in hand (summer 1997) contains approximately 150 new words. To qualify as new, words must be completely new (*blooming onion*—a deep-fried appetizer) or must have picked up a new meaning (*boot camp*—which now indicates a type of juvenile prison as well as a military basic training facility) or must have undergone a change in usage (*touchpad*—which originated as *touch pad*). Each entry includes usage and frequency labels as well as multiple examples of written usage, many of which were located via Nexis searches.

As may be expected, terms from the fast-changing worlds of science and technology (especially computer technology) dominate the entries, but there are also examples from the arts, humanities, and popular culture (*dilberted*—to be mistreated by one's boss) as well as the social sciences (*learnfare*—public assistance based on school attendance). Book notices, an editor's page, and an index round out the issue. The strength of the companion is its ability to at least attempt to keep up with new words, something that standard dictionaries cannot do.

The title is recommended for libraries supporting programs in linguistics or for libraries that serve a significant number of users interested in new words and the social/scientific trends that give birth to them.

—**Donald A. Barclay**

Obsolete Words

1011. Durant, David N. **Where Queen Elizabeth Slept & What the Butler Saw: Historical Terms from the Sixteenth Century to the Present.** New York, St. Martin's Press, 1996. 342p. $24.95. ISBN 0-312-15688-X.

Described as a "treasure trove of historical trivia," Durant's book is aimed at history and literary buffs who made a popular success of Daniel Pool's *What Jane Austen Ate & Charles Dickens Knew* (Touchstone Books, 1994). Rather than an in-depth look at one segment of British life, Durant's slender volume presents a vast selection of terms from the sixteenth century to the present, with many definitions referencing earlier centuries. The result is an occasionally superficial coverage that often leaves the reader wishing the author had narrowed the scope. General readers would also appreciate some illustrations to enhance the briefer descriptions.

Nevertheless, Durant's work accomplishes its purpose to provide insight into the historical life of Britain. An author and lecturer on British social and architectural history, he is decidedly at his best in thumbnails of actual events (Civil War [1642-1649], the Reformation) and the development of architectural styles (Palladianism, the Renaissance style), even citing English castles, manors and country houses that contain the best examples. His entries on fashion (cravat) and social custom (shooting) are engaging, and the two-page survey of English garden design is very detailed.

Although neither comprehensive nor complete as a dictionary of historical terminology, this book is an accessible introduction to the field and would serve as a helpful study tool for British literature or history courses. The book is not indexed, but terms are arranged alphabetically and are abundantly cross-referenced to related topics.

General libraries and teachers will find this an entertaining addition to their English literature and history collections. [R: RBB, 1 Sept 97, p. 173]—**Cheryl J. Eckl**

Other English-Speaking Countries

1012. **Gage Canadian Dictionary.** rev. ed. By Gaelan Dodds de Wolf, Robert J. Gregg, Barbara P. Harris, and Matthew H. Scargill. Agincourt, Ont., Gage Educational Publishing; distr., Toronto, Macmillan of Canada, 1997. 1718p. illus. $29.95. ISBN 0-7715-7399-5.

Newly revised and expanded from the previous edition (1983), the *Gage Canadian Dictionary* features clear, concise Canadian English vocabulary reflecting current Canadian usage, terminology, and expression. Endpapers provide pronunciation and abbreviation keys as well as an example of a typical dictionary entry. The standard entry provides the generally accepted Canadian spelling and forms (with note of common variations), pronunciation using the standard International Phonetic Alphabet (especially helpful to those for whom English is not a first language), clear definition with examples in sentence context, and synonyms and homonyms (noted graphically by a "fistnote") as appropriate. A substantial guide to using the volume is included in the prefatory pages, with several appendixes providing less standard (for example, an air quality index) although potentially useful information. With more than 140,000 definitions and 13,000 new entries, this 1-volume standard reflects the pace and diversity of development in terminology and multicultural aspects of Canadian society.

Last in the Gage series of graded dictionaries, this reference is intended for high school, university, and general adult use. It compares favorably with other dictionaries of Canadian English, such as *ITP Nelson Canadian Dictionary of the English Language* (see entry 1013).—**Virginia S. Fischer**

1013. **ITP Nelson Canadian Dictionary of the English Language: An Encyclopedic Reference.** Scarborough, Ont., ITP Nelson, 1997. 1694p. illus. maps. $33.95. ISBN 0-17-606591-1.

The *ITP Nelson Canadian Dictionary of the English Language* manages, in a concise one-volume format, to provide an encyclopedic reference that also functions as a thesaurus for the English language as it is spoken, spelled, and written by Canadians. By presenting a uniquely Canadian viewpoint, this dictionary will be a standard Canadian reference source, featuring Canadian spellings, pronunciation, and phrases unique to English Canada. It provides as well the typical features found in any good dictionary—a comprehensive word entry with syllabication, place in speech, clear and concise definition, derivation, and usage notes. Illustrative materials, where applicable, are composed of photographs, drawings, maps, charts, and tables to supply additional explanatory information.

A substantial introductory section details a basic style and convention guide as well as a key to abbreviations and pronunciation. Appendixes of more than 100 pages augment the volume by inclusion of historical background relating to the national origins and symbols of the Canadian government, its provinces and territories, and current statistical profiles. The appendixes, which are prefaced by a separate table of contents, also include a substantive section on language and linguistic development. For Canadians and those interested in the English language from the Canadian perspective, this volume is highly recommended.—**Virginia S. Fischer**

Slang

1014. Dunn, Jerry. **Idiom Savant: Slang As It Is Slung.** New York, Henry Holt, 1997. 296p. $25.00. ISBN 0-8050-5094-9.

Unlike many other dictionaries of slang, this work is divided into approximately 75 different occupations or activities, such as nursing, bullfighting, sailing, gambling, and so on. The terms are all current, most of them being supplied by Internet users. In addition, the author gives credit to nearly 700 people, whose names he lists at the end. The definitions are terse and often include a synonym and sometimes an antonym. If derived from a proper name, such as a *Betty* (a pretty girl) or a *Madison* (a type of body piercing), the origin is given, but not always: The state of California begets the *California Special* (a coin doctored up to enhance its value), yet the connection is not made here. Many slang terms are obvious: a *T-bone* is a collision between two sailboats at right angles. A *windshield wiper* is a table tennis player who uses the same side of the paddle for forehand and backhand. *Waving a dead chicken* is pretending to repair a worn-out electronic unit.

The value of this volume to reference librarians is obvious. First, it will answer queries about unexplainable expressions (although the context or background may be necessary). Second, it will enable novelist and journalist patrons to use correct slang in their writings about fictitious or real truck drivers, bikers, boxers, skateboarders, or whatever. Best of all, the dictionary will be fun to browse. *Grandma's teeth* (an expression one will not find just anywhere) refers to a random group of pins left after an unlucky bowl; *hockey pucks* are the small sandwiches served on an economy air flight; and an *Arizona Windsor* is a furniture auctioneer's term for a phony antique.

Every reference desk should have a copy of *Idiom Savant*, if only for the pleasure it will give the staff during the quieter moments on their shift. Then they, too, will in sympathy turn their gaze in the opposite direction when the skipper of a small sailboat says that he has to go to the stern to check the tension of the backstay (see p. 165).—**Raymund F. Wood**

1015. **Random House Historical Dictionary of American Slang. Volume 2: H-O.** J. E. Lighter, J. Ball, and J. O'Connor, eds. New York, Random House, 1997. 736p. $65.00. ISBN 0-679-43464-X.

Reviewers heaped praise on the 1st volume, greeting it enthusiastically as "a landmark publication," "an absolutely astounding work of scholarship," and "the definitive work in the field." The 2d volume simply reinforces the impressiveness of this contribution to lexicography, and (no pun intended) its historical importance as a first of its kind. Users may want to reread Lighter's introduction to the field in the 1st volume, where he characterizes slang as informal, nontechnical, and nonstandard words or phrases that are novel-sounding replacements for standard terms.

The 2d volume repeats the "Guide to the Dictionary" with a few minor changes, mostly in the examples for slang words falling between "H" for *hell* and "O" for *Ozzie*, a mispronunciation of *Aussie*, meaning an Australian soldier. Here Lighter elucidates the structure of entries and the conventions used for their organization. With volume 3 projected for the year 2000, language aficionados will have cause to celebrate more than the millennium. This set is a reference work to savor as well as to consult.—**Bernice Bergup**

Synonyms and Antonyms

1016. **The American Heritage Children's Thesaurus.** By Paul Hellweg, with the editors of the American Heritage Dictionaries. New York, Houghton Mifflin, 1997. 279p. illus. $17.00. ISBN 0-395-84977-2.

In a kid-friendly format and size, Hellweg introduces young students to the concept and use of a thesaurus. An opening how-to chapter will be useful to the students and teachers designing first lessons in word-use reference books beyond the dictionary. Most two-page spreads have color pictures that relate in some way to a word on the page, and many have a color-border box that contains antonyms. (Antonyms are not mixed with the synonyms.) The author uses color, space, bold typeface, four-point stars, italics, and numbers to set apart groups of definitions and parts of speech. This reviewer prefers Roget's traditional thesaurus over dictionary formats such as this, but this is the best way for a young person to start. The grade-level recommendation is better at the high than at the low end of the grade spectrum. Schools will appreciate Houghton Mifflin's effort to keep down the price.—**Edna M. Boardman**

1017. Ehrlich, Eugene. **The Highly Selective Dictionary for the Extraordinarily Literate.** New York, HarperCollins, 1997. 192p. $16.00. ISBN 0-06-270190-8.

Although not acknowledged on the title page, on the verso of the title page, or in the introductory information, this appears to be a 2d edition of *The Highly Selective Thesaurus for the Extraordinarily Literate* published by HarperCollins in 1994, down in size from around 5,000 words on 209 pages (the ARBA 95 review [see entry 1066] says 50,000 words, which is probably a typographic error) to "more than 3,500" (dust jacket) on 192 pages in this edition. The book is, as the title says, a "highly selective dictionary." It gives pronunciation, a brief definition, and occasional comments about words with which the defined word may be confused. Ehrlich may have taken the comments in the ARBA review to heart, because this reviewer found few of the terms mentioned in 1995 discussed in this edition. Although many of the words chosen were familiar—for example, *abominate, anxious, argot, capricious,* and *fell*—many were not in this reviewer's normal usage vocabulary (e.g., *patulous, noctambulist, littoral,* and *smegma*).

The pronunciation key and the definitions are clear. The author acknowledges in the pronunciation notes that "some of the pronunciations supplied indulge the editor's own preferences." An example is the word *agape,* which Ehrlich pronounces [AH-gah-pay] and defines as "brotherly, unselfish love. (contrasted with erotic love)." *Harper's Bible Dictionary* (see ARBA 86, entry 1382), if one used Ehrlich's key, would emphasize the second syllable [ah-GAH-pay] and stresses "selfless and self-giving love." *Merriam-Webster's Collegiate Dictionary* (10th ed., see ARBA 94, entry 1076) gives the *Bible Dictionary* pronunciation first and Ehrlich's second. In regard to the definition, it appears the author continues the unfortunate practice of lexicographers of using such exclusive and sexist terms as "brotherly" when they do not mean affection between brothers or male human beings. Also, for someone interested in correct usage, which this book advocates, illustrating a term by use in one or more sentences would be helpful.

The Highly Selective Dictionary will appeal to people who wish to improve their vocabularies and who enjoy such titles as Fiske's *Thesaurus of Alternatives to Worn-Out Words and Phrases* (see ARBA 95, entry 1067); *The New Fowler's Modern English Usage* (see ARBA 97, entry 756); and other titles by Ehrlich and by Richard Lederer, the author of the preface of this book.—**Betty Jo Buckingham**

Terms and Phrases

1018. **Cassell Dictionary of Clichés.** By Nigel Rees. London, Cassell; distr., New York, Sterling Publishing, 1996. 288p. $24.95. ISBN 0-304-34698-5.

Despite the author's statement in the introduction that "Hitherto, the only major attempt to list examples of the breed [clichés] has been Eric Partridge's *Dictionary of Clichés,* first published in 1940 with the fifth edition appearing in 1978," there are several works aside from those written by Rees that at least purport to be about clichés. Two of those titles—*Methuen Dictionary of Clichés* (1992) and *Have a Nice Day—No Problem!* (NAL-Dutton, 1993)—Rees states, do not cover clichés but are books "of popular phrases and catch phrases" (p. ix). Others include *Catch Phrases, Clichés and Idioms: A Dictionary of Familiar Expressions,* compiled by Doris Craig (see ARBA 92, entry 1039), and James Rogers's *Dictionary of Clichés* (see ARBA 86, entry 1055). *Merriam-Webster's Collegiate Dictionary* (10th ed.; see ARBA 94, entry 1076) defines a cliché as "a trite expression . . . a hackneyed theme . . . overly familiar or commonplace." The authors of all of the books named agree with the definition but are not necessarily in agreement about what terms or phrases can be so defined.

Rees's book contains approximately 1,000 clichés, according to the book jacket. Entries include an explanation of where an expression was used, when and where the saying originated (if known), and (frequently) when the phrase became a cliché. Entries are in alphabetic order with many cross-references from keywords to the first word of a phrase. There is no index. Although many terms are definitely British, and most of the citations are British, a number, such as "no pun intended," "charmed life," and "buck stops here," are American in origin or widespread enough to address American usage. Although not limited to clichés, Craig's book includes 20,000 expressions, and Rogers's book includes 2,000 terms identified as clichés. The latter book is said by the Book Review Digest Database to overlap the Partridge book, although Rees did not feel inclined to list many of the clichés.

The dilemma is determining what is a cliché. Rees appears correct in his assumption that his—and by inference any—book of clichés will be highly subjective. Who, after all, determines when a term has been used for so long that it is trite or hackneyed? Can a term be hackneyed in one part of the English-speaking world and fresh and appealing in another? Many terms in Rees's volume will be totally new to American readers. The American student of language who wishes to avoid or rescue overworked terms may find *Cassell Dictionary of Clichés* useful but will want to consult other volumes as well, especially those with a more American flavor. Word buffs will of course enjoy another Rees book on language. [R: LJ, 15 May 97, p. 73]—**Betty Jo Buckingham**

1019. Kirkpatrick, Betty. **Clichés: Over 1500 Phrases Explored and Explained.** New York, St. Martin's Press, 1996. 207p. $19.95. ISBN 0-312-15494-1.

Kirkpatrick provides definitions, illustrative contexts, and etymological background for hundreds of British and American clichés, as well as occasional entries for terms having French, Latin, Greek, Italian, and Spanish derivations. Most entries range from 40 to 100 words in length, but approximately 2 dozen entries (e.g., "bottom line," "come home to roost," "fly in the face of danger") extend to nearly 200 words apiece. Page layout has been handsomely executed, with guide words and headwords appearing in bold typeface, and usage examples set in italics. Despite their scarcity, entries reflecting recent coinage are in evidence, for example, "drop dead," as in "drop dead handsome"; "quality time"; and "away from one's desk"). Also laudatory is Kirkpatrick's instructive yet entertaining introduction, in which clichés are usefully broken into 14 types—simile, euphemism, catchphrase, situational, and others.

Unfortunately, this work is not without its downside. Entry cross-referencing is sporadic at best; no cross-reference appears from "over the top" to "OTT," and although "die is cast" directs the user to "cross the Rubicon," this latter entry makes no mention of the former. Also, entries are too often arranged alphabetically by keyword in an inconsistent or unpredictable manner. For instance, "see the wood for the trees" is found among *s* entries, whereas "see the writing on the wall" is filed within the *w* listings. Because this volume has no keyword index, entries whose initial words are colloquially variable may be difficult to locate, such as the phrases "at one fell swoop," or "cut a long story short."

Clichés suffers much, as well, from its low entry count. Among many others, notable omissions include "a penny saved is a penny earned"; "make love, not war"; "spare the rod and spoil the child"; "burn the candle at both ends"; and "take a raincheck." Scholarship is at times suspect, too, as witnessed by one entry in which appears the misquotation "at this moment in time," rather than the genuine Watergate-generated cliché "at this point in time."

Most disturbing, however, is this resource's dustjacket declaration that Kirkpatrick "provides the origin of each cliché." In fact, perhaps 200 cliché entries appear without any theory as to what their origin may have been. British fiction devotees, Americans traveling abroad, and those engaged in British culture studies will be ably served by this book. Other researchers should opt for such superior dictionaries as Christine Ammer's *Have a Nice Day—No Problem!* (Plume, 1993), Eric Partridge's *A Dictionary of Clichés* (Routledge, 1993), Louis A. Berman's *Proverb Wit & Wisdom* (Perigee, 1997), or Doris Craig's comprehensive checklist *Catch Phrases, Clichés and Idioms* (McFarland, 1990). [R: LJ, July 97, pp. 77-78]—**Jeffrey E. Long**

Unabridged

1020. **A Dictionary of the English Language.** [CD-ROM]. By Samuel Johnson. Anne McDermott, ed. New York, Cambridge University Press, 1996. Minimum system requirements (Windows version): IBM or compatible 386. Double-speed CD-ROM drive. Windows 3.1. 8MB RAM. Minimum system requirements (Macintosh version): Double-speed CD-ROM drive. System 7. 4MB RAM. $145.00. ISBN 0-521-55765-8.

This electronic edition of the premier scholarly dictionary of the English language combines the text of the 1st edition of 1755 and the 4th edition of 1773. Users who may not care about differences between the 1st and 4th editions or who do not need sophisticated online searching features will probably be satisfied with any of the 4 print editions listed in *Books in Print*. However, students of the history of the English language and lexicographers will be pleased with the great variety of search options on this CD-ROM. The printed manual is user friendly, clearly explaining installation procedures on a PC or a Macintosh. After a short discussion of the historical significance of the dictionary, most of the manual is devoted to a step-by-step description of searching features, often accompanied by illustrations of sample computer screens. There is an advantage to the electronic version even for simple headword searches, because the text is easier to decipher than the facsimile printed versions of the original dictionary.

Yet the CD-ROM also simplifies a great many complex searches, such as quickly comparing the same entry viewed side by side in the two editions; easily accessing a facsimile of the original printed texts; making images smaller or larger with the zoom feature; limiting searches to quoted author, quoted work, words in the definition or words in the quotation; using proximity searching (specifying the number of words between search words); and implementing various wildcard searches, Boolean searches, and context searches using the keywords "containing," "directly," "in," "inside," "null," "with," or the "=" sign. A user may copy text into a clipboard, annotate copied text, create bookmarks or hyperlinks, and choose from a variety of print options. Some of these features require knowledge of SGML coding, which is explained in considerable detail in the manual.

Even if a library already owns a printed edition of either or both the 1755 and 1773 editions, the electronic text is easier to read. Scholars will definitely welcome the great range of search options. For an added price, the disc may be networked, thus proving 250 years later the usefulness of one of Samuel Johnson's most often quoted definitions: "Network: Any thing reticulated or decussated, at equal distances, with interstices between the intersections."—**David Isaacson**

NON-ENGLISH-LANGUAGE DICTIONARIES

General Works

1021. **Oxford 3-in-1 Bilingual Dictionary.** [CD-ROM]. New York, Oxford University Press, 1997. Minimum system requirements (Windows version): IBM or compatible 486SX (DX recommended). Windows-compatible CD-ROM drive with Microsoft CD-ROM Extensions 2.21. DOS 3.3. Windows 3.1. 4MB RAM. 0.6MB hard disk space. VGA monitor. Microsoft-compatible mouse. Minimum system requirements (Macintosh version): 68040 processor. CD-ROM drive. System 7.5. 6MB RAM (12MB recommended). 13-inch screen with 256 colors. $75.00. ISBN 0-19-268332-2.

This disc contains the full text and graphics of three popular dictionaries of European languages, *The Oxford-Hachette French Dictionary* (see ARBA 96, entry 1100); *The Oxford Starter Spanish Dictionary* (see entry 1051); and *The Oxford Duden German Dictionary* (see entry 1031). Access is via the clearly written Superlex software product, which is noted as being intended as the framework for a planned series of Oxford University Press electronic reference books. Both Windows and Macintosh versions are available on the CD-ROM. Basic general searching is by individual words (termed "headwords") and examples of usage (with the option of full text), idioms, phrasal verbs, and a valuable section on acronyms and abbreviations. Special search options are provided for background information, irregular verbs, correspondence, grammatical and lexical information, phonetic symbols, spelling changes, and maps. Given the constant demand for regularly available French, German, and Spanish dictionaries, libraries at all levels of education from elementary through graduate school will find this a valuable and affordable addition to locally networked resources.—**Robert B. Marks Ridinger**

Chinese

1022. Keuper, Jerome P. **Chinese 1000: Idiomatic and Colloquial Expressions. Mandarin Chinese/English.** Malabar, Fla., Krieger Publishing, 1997. 152p. illus. index. $32.00; $22.50pa. ISBN 1-57524-006-8; 1-57524-047-5pa.

Designed to be a ready-reference to Chinese idioms and colloquial expressions, this book contains 1,003 entries on customary phrases of courtesy, rude sayings, expletives, and slang words in Mandarin Chinese. The author, a nuclear physicist with a lifelong interest but no formal training in the Chinese language, based most of the selections on a review of 69 books published worldwide, which are listed in the bibliography section. The criteria for inclusion are terms that are useful, interesting, humorous, and popular in everyday speech. Each entry is numbered and arranged alphabetically using the pinyin romanization system, followed by simplified

Chinese characters, a translation of the literal meaning, and the figurative meaning in English. Translations are fairly accurate and, in some cases, the author also provides idiomatic equivalents of a familiar saying in English. A cross-indexing from English to Chinese is appended to provide a complete listing of English code words and entry number for corresponding Chinese expressions. Tone marks are placed over the vowel in the pinyin syllables to aid readers for correct pronunciations. Large print also makes the book easy to use. Beginning or intermediate students of Chinese as a foreign language will find this book a handy reference tool as many entries are built upon the basic vocabulary that they are expected to master. Although the price is a little high, this work is suitable for undergraduate collections. For those who wish to go beyond this supplemental source for more advanced and comprehensive coverage, the following are recommended for their quality and quantity: X. Heng's *A Chinese-English Dictionary of Idioms and Proverbs* (1988), T. Wang's *A Chinese-English Handbook of Idioms* (1987), and H. Chen's *A Collection of Chinese Idioms, Proverbs, and Phrases with English Translation* (1984).—**Karen T. Wei**

1023. Shou-hsin, Teng. **Chinese Synonyms Usage Dictionary.** Boston, Cheng & Tsui, 1996. 533p. index. $35.00. ISBN 0-88727-243-6.

This dictionary of some 700 entries of Chinese synonyms usage is intended for nonnative speakers of Mandarin Chinese with a minimum of three years of language training at the college level. Knowledge of approximately 1,500 Chinese characters and the pinyin romanization system is also assumed. Even though the preface indicates that knowledge of Chinese characters in the simplified form is needed, the entire dictionary uses traditional forms instead. The preface also lacks a clear explanation of how to use the dictionary, leaving readers to figure it out on their own.

A table of contents precedes the main body of the dictionary, which is organized alphabetically by pinyin romanization of the Chinese synonyms. The order in the table of contents is not necessarily followed in the body of the work, and occasionally some terms are missing from the main body. The synonyms are listed under each entry in Chinese traditional characters followed by corresponding pinyin pronunciations in parentheses. They are usually listed in groups of two to six so-called near-synonyms (as defined by the editor). Each term begins with a literary definition in English followed by descriptions and sample sentences provided to establish the contextual framework. A table listing the synonyms in each group and their various attributes are then compared and contrasted in actual frames of usage to allow for easy reference and comparison. The occurrences and nonoccurrences of specific sentences are clearly marked and are based on extensive surveys conducted in Taiwan among college-level native speakers of Mandarin Chinese.

The dictionary offers two indexes, a pinyin index and a character index. The character index is arranged by stroke count, which includes traditional character, simplified character, and pinyin romanization. Both indexes refer to page numbers for easy reference. Although there are many dictionaries on synonyms in Chinese, a bilingual dictionary such as this is uncommon. Advanced students should find this volume useful once they determine how to use it.—**Karen T. Wei**

French

1024. **Collins-Robert French-English, English-French Dictionary.** 3d ed. By Beryl T. Atkins, Alain Duval, Hélène M. A. Lewis, and Rosemary C. Milne. New York, HarperCollins, 1997. 1v. (various paging). $25.00. ISBN 0-06-275521-8.

This surprisingly inexpensive French dictionary is a good buy for academic libraries, but it may be a bit too intimidating for the average user at a branch of a public library. It has 465 pages of French-to-English translations and 71 pages in the center, forming a kind of compendium of verbs, numbers, dates, and even tips on how best to use the telephone. This is followed by 551 pages of the English-to-French section. Both sections go into extreme detail in explaining and translating words in their various meanings when joined to other words. The word "be," for example, takes up an entire column, including such expressions as "he has been and gone," or "the telegram was to warn us." The word getting the most pagination is the word "get," which has four full columns, including just about every known way of using "get" in English, with fairly close translations into French. Such phrases as "he gets to me" or "get along with you" are all given separate entries.

Despite its excellence and profusion of definitions, the casual user will be put off by the scholarly apparatus. Verbs in the past tense are said to be "pret" (for preterite), and abbreviations abound, requiring either a thorough acquaintance with the book or constant reference to the table of abbreviations at the front (not an easy task, given the weight of the book at four pounds). Few colloquialisms, such as "joy ride" or "hot dog," are found, although there is an entry for "popsicle" and another for "hamburger," which is translated as *Hamburger*. Strangely, the word "morne" in the sense of a small hill or rise on a mountainside is omitted, even though the term is common in French Martinique.

By reason of the excellence and completeness of its coverage of almost every possible use of both English and French words and idioms, this book is strongly recommended for collegiate and similar libraries. However, public libraries would probably do better to stick to an up-to-date edition of *Cassell's French Dictionary*, which has been a steady favorite since at least the 1940s.—**Raymund F. Wood**

1025. Ehrlich, Eugene. **Les Bons Mots: How to Amaze "Tout le Monde" with Everyday French.** New York, Henry Holt, 1997. 312p. index. $24.00. ISBN 0-8050-4711-5.

A rarity in the reference world, Ehrlich's handbook of French phrases and idioms escapes pedantry with wit, wisdom, and a light touch. Scholarly enough for the average reader, librarian, journalist, historian, or belletrist, the compendium opens onto a book flap that summarizes the style and content—a quick explanation of "have an affair" and "find the rest room," followed with four examples of familiar phrases found in modern literature and heard on television and in movies and conversation. Gracefully presented in a pleasing typeface, the work opens with a preface and acknowledgments, five pages of pronunciation notes, and a collection of thumbnail biographies of French literary masters cited in the work, such as Honoré de Balzac, Pierre Corneille, Victor Hugo, Jean La Fontaine, Jean-Baptiste Molière, Marcel Proust, François Rabelais, Jean Racine, Voltaire, and Émile Zola.

Entries appear alphabetically. Each is pronounced with the H-based system, for example, idée (ee-DAY), which avoids most diacritical marks, except the grave, acute, diaeresis, and schwa. Brief translations include one literal and one or more figurative explanations, including a near match of English idiom, as with *monter en amazone*, literally "ride in the style of an Amazon" and more familiarly, "ride sidesaddle." Ehrlich adds information about *amazone*, a synonym for "horsewoman," taken from the mythical female warrior and also a South American river. Appropriately, the text winds down to *zut alors!*, in other words "darn it," or "shut up," and concludes with a precise 18-page index.

Ehrlich, a proven linguist with his bestselling *Amo, Amas, Amat, and More* (HarperCollins, 1985), once more provides the discriminating reader and scholar with a reasonably priced volume of manageable size and scope, on topics from food to social graces. His wit never gets in the way of accuracy, nor does his learning belabor the point. *Les Bons Mots* is a must-have volume.—**Mary Ellen Snodgrass**

1026. **The Oxford-Hachette French Desk Dictionary.** Marie-Hèléne Corréard, ed. New York, Oxford University Press, 1996. 783p. $14.95. ISBN 0-19-860149-2.

Students, travelers, and international entrepreneurs often need a dictionary. This new bilingual desk dictionary contains more than 80,000 words and phrases and 115,000 translations taken from the *Oxford-Hachette French Dictionary* (1994). Because this work is a collaboration of two distinguished publishers using both French- and English-language databases, it reflects current usage of the two languages well. Formal, informal, and scientific and technical usages are included. Both British and American spellings of English words are given. The dictionary is designed for easy use by students of French.

The front matter contains instructions for using the dictionary, abbreviations, and information on French pronunciation. The main body of the text is arranged in two columns with adequate white space on the page. The typeface is clear and easy to read. Entry terms are in bold typeface followed by the pronunciation (French only) using the International Phonetic Alphabet. Alphabetization is letter by letter. Definitions are brief, often only one word, but accurate. Useful features include providing both masculine and feminine forms of adjectives and nouns and making idiomatic expressions independent categories within an entry. This means that users will find both *boulanger* and *boulangère* when looking up "baker." The entry for "foot" includes not only the anatomical part and the measurement, but also expressions such as "to foot the bill" and "to put one's foot in it."

Lexical and grammatical notes are one-page summaries found throughout the text. They deal with useful or confusing expressions in both languages, such as time (both telling time by the clock and expressing duration), forms of address, and the words should and not. Short notes within the body of the text explain simpler concepts, such as when to use *cela* and *ça*, and the fact that there is no French equivalent of the English multipurpose verb "to get." A supplement on writing business and social letters and classified advertisements in French, conjugation tables for French verbs, and a chart of French cardinal and ordinal numbers complete the text.

This is an excellent small dictionary with features that usually appear only in larger works. Although reference collections should purchase the full-size *Oxford-Hachette French Dictionary*, the desk dictionary is a fine addition to circulating collections or personal libraries.—**Barbara M. Bibel**

1027. **The Oxford Starter French Dictionary.** Marie-Hélène Corréard and Mary O'Neill, eds. New York, Oxford University Press, 1997. 399p. $8.95pa. ISBN 0-19-864527-9.

Organization, clarity, and coverage make this manual ideal for the beginning French student but can also be of substantial aid to one not yet totally fluent or one who wishes to brush up on forgotten matters. The preliminary pages tersely clarify the format and offer a pronunciation guide. The latter is a problem area with 19 delicately nuanced French vowels and semivowels, distinguished here by use of phonetic symbols but less helpful with the English equivalents (the English "cat" and French *basse* do not share the same vowel sounds, probably no matter what English dialect is selected). A most helpful quiz appears between the French and English dictionary sections, and exceptionally helpful grammatical explanations are inserted, such as the seven different uses of *en* in the French section and "languages and nationalities" or "using the subjunctive" in the English section. The vocabularies are practically limited, certainly providing the user with as much aid as one may need in more advanced applications. They both include lucid and multiple definitions as well as phrases, but (again the matter of practicality) they do not in all instances share the same words. Words of newer vintage are included (e.g., "remote control," but not "Internet"). Some recent slang appears ("cool" = *branché*), and symbols caution the user when the expression is too colloquial for formal discourse or may be offensive. Symbolic indications in still other applications readily guide one to pages where amplification is offered, to which auxiliary verb is needed for compound tenses, and to those adjectives that remain the same regardless of the noun's gender. The book is a pleasure to use.—**Dominique-René de Lerma**

1028. **Pockets: French Dictionary.** New York, DK Publishing, 1997. 509p. (DK Pockets). $6.95pa. ISBN 0-7894-2194-1.

This inexpensive but poorly conceived dictionary lacks a clear audience. It contains no explanatory preface, providing only a 37-word blurb on the back cover. (*Blurb*, by the way, is one of many common English colloquialisms the dictionary fails to render, despite its claim to perform such a service.) The work seems to be directed to those learning to read French who need certain basic vocabulary items. It has no value, however, for those learning to speak French: Instead of using the simple and precise International Phonetic Alphabet to indicate pronunciation of French words, it uses a strange system of its own that will help no one speak French intelligibly. So *je crois* is rendered as "sher kro'ah" and *chirurgien* as "she-rEEr-she-ang." No forms of irregular verbs are offered, despite the occasional need for them by even advanced speakers of French.

The shortcomings are many. One can only recommend instead the splendid 1995 *Oxford-Hachette French Dictionary* (see ARBA 96, entry 1100), twice the size and price but incomparably more accurate and useful.—**John B. Beston**

German

1029. Beaton, K. B. **A Practical Dictionary of German Usage.** New York, Clarendon Press/Oxford University Press, 1996. 921p. index. $153.00. ISBN 0-19-824002-3.

This dictionary is intended for advanced speakers of German. It addresses a need that is not properly met by even the best bilingual dictionaries. Whereas recent bilingual German-English dictionaries are fast becoming more focused, supplying different German equivalents of an English word from a frequency count of specific meanings, they do not give detailed and accurate explanations as this book does.

Commonly used English words often have a number of meanings, for example, *appreciate* has among its senses *estimate the value of*, *esteem*, *be aware of*, *be grateful for*, and *increase in value*, all needing to be rendered by a different word in German. This dictionary is invaluable for its elucidations of such difficulties and for its rendering of the big problem words of English, such as *get* (to which it devotes more than three pages), *put* (five-plus pages), and *take* (more than nine pages).

Understandably, there are omissions that one may regret (such as *pick, -at, -out,* and *-up*). The chief weakness of the book, however, comes from the author's apparent unawareness of recent changes in English constructions. The author makes little effort to deal with the explosive growth during the past 30 years of 2-part and 3-part verbs that often replace Latinate constructions. So one finds a number of translations for *run* but none for *run -down, -in, -off, -out of, -up,* and no entries for such expressions as *to zero in on.* Nonetheless, this dictionary does indeed justify its claim of being essential for advanced users of German.—**John B. Beston**

1030. **The Oxford-Duden German Desk Dictionary: English-German, German-English.** new ed. M. Clark and O. Thyen, eds. New York, Oxford University Press, 1997. 856p. $14.95. ISBN 0-19-860147-6.

The editors at Oxford University Press and Dudenverlag have turned to the widely praised 1990 *The Oxford Duden German Dictionary* (see ARBA 91, entry 1085) to produce an economical, smaller dictionary for English- or German-speaking students, tourists, and readers who do not need a full-scale dictionary. Although sacrificing some features of the original, the resulting volume succeeds within these limits.

The content has been halved, to 70,000 words and phrases. Entries still include guides to pronunciation (using the International Phonetic Alphabet) and stress, with irregular plurals noted. Valuable features, such as "sense indicators" to clarify meaning and subject labels for specialized vocabulary, have been retained. There are far fewer cross-references, illustrative phrases, or entries for idioms and proverbs. Few labels remain identifying Swiss or Austrian regionalisms, but variations in standard British and American usage are noted. The user can still sort out the relationship between "lawyer," "solicitor," and *Rechtsanwalt*, or between "chips," "French fries," and *pommes frites*. Compared to its parent volume, the desk edition is of limited help with colloquial expressions and slang, such as "joint" ("marijuana" versus "roast" or *Braten*), or the British and American use of "semi" ("semi-detached house" versus "semi-trailer").

Tables of abbreviations and irregular verbs remain, with an appendix on weights and measures. Other appendixes have been dropped, including several with potential value for travelers, such as guides to money and telling the time of day. This new work provides a 56-page list of words and phrases affected by the 1996 German, Austrian, and Swiss spelling reform, altering some capitalization and the use of the *scharfes ess* ("double-s"). Despite these compromises, *The Oxford-Duden German Desk Dictionary* represents a good value for anyone needing a convenient bilingual dictionary that will cover most everyday translating needs.—**Steven W. Sowards**

1031. **The Oxford-Duden German Dictionary: German-English/English-German.** rev. ed. Werner Scholze-Stubenrecht and J. B. Sykes, eds. New York, Oxford University Press, 1997. 1712p. $45.00. ISBN 0-19-860132-8.

The Oxford-Duden German Dictionary is a unique product of cooperation by two formidable dictionary makers, the Oxford University Press in England and the Dudenredaktion of the Bibliographical Institut in Germany. Unlike the production of most dictionaries, linguists from both target languages were parties in the making of this work. The visible benefit is that this volume is rich in idiomatic expressions. This revised edition contains more than 260,000 words and phrases. Although American English is not forgotten, one can detect, especially in translating idioms, a certain tilting toward British usage. In every respect, orthographically and in the usage of words, the dictionary is up-to-date. It includes the latest information on the new German spelling system. The appearance of the dictionary from the cover to the layout of the page is pleasing to the eye. The headwords are set in bold typeface, providing for an easy and clear visibility. The dictionary contains a variety of guides and tables, and a thumb index promotes its use.—**Andrew Ezergailis**

1032. **Oxford-Duden German Dictionary.** [CD-ROM]. New York, Oxford University Press, 1997. Minimum system requirements (Windows version): IBM or compatible 486SX (DX recommended). Windows-compatible CD-ROM drive with Microsoft CD-ROM Extensions 2.21. DOS 3.3. Windows 3.1. 4MB RAM. 0.6MB hard disk space. VGA monitor. Microsoft-compatible mouse. Minimum system requirements (Macintosh version): 68040 processor. CD-ROM drive. System 7.5. 6MB RAM (12MB recommended). 13-inch screen with 256 colors. $49.95. ISBN 0-19-268310-1.

Regarded by many connoisseurs as the definitive reference for grammar and suitable vocabulary, the *Oxford Duden German Dictionary* is now available on CD-ROM for the first time. Containing more than 260,000 words and phrases and 450,000 translations, it is apparently not based on the 1997 revised edition (see entry 1031) but rather on the 1st edition (see ARBA 91, entry 1085), if not the 1994 enlargement. This conclusion is drawn from the fact that the 1997 paper edition contains full details on the changes to German-language orthography ratified in 1996; the electronic version includes neither the overview of spelling changes, as the paper version does, nor the implementation of those rules, which neither one does. Such an omission renders real the possibility of obsolescence in the not-too-distant future.

The electronic version does incorporate, however, the helpful appendixes of the paper edition: detailed grammatical information, examples of letter writing, and other similar aids for the benefit of the uninitiated, conveniently available through taskbar buttons and drop-down menus. The vocabulary is remarkably comprehensive and up-to-date, including expressions in both American and British English (although with a marked bias toward the latter), and Swiss and Austrian dialects as well as East and West German. Style and usage labels make the dictionary the front-running arbiter in those areas. The CD-ROM interface and search engine are easy to use and require relatively little training, a benefit because users must rely exclusively on online documentation for search assistance.

The software supports cut-and-paste options to allow toggling and transferring entries into word processing documents, although it may be difficult to envision the practicality of this function in a library environment (but not, of course, on a scholar's workstation, for which it would be logical). In fact, one might indeed question the applicability of a stand-alone CD-ROM dictionary in a library at all—would it not often be easier to consult the paper version for the ready-reference type of information for which this source is best suited? Also, with a cost differential of only $5 between the 2 versions, acquisition of the disc certainly does not provide any economic advantage.—**Lawrence Olszewski**

1033. **The Oxford Starter German Dictionary.** Neil Morris and Roswitha Morris, eds. New York, Oxford University Press, 1997. 356p. $8.95pa. ISBN 0-19-860033-X.

For anyone used to classic Oxford dictionaries, this title will be a significant departure. This work is a "starter" dictionary, suggesting that it focuses on beginners and those just starting a foray into the German language. The editors indicate in their introduction that this is a different dictionary in three main ways.

First, the dictionary looks different. There is no argument there. This volume does not consist of a staid presentation. The first thing that the user will notice is the typography of the book. The layout is clean, and it works. A nice touch is the use of a bomb icon for those entries that may be sensitive. Second, the dictionary provides information in a new way. The major point here is that the editors have made an excellent attempt at focusing on presentation from the beginner's level. For the most part, they are successful. Third, the German-English and the English-German sections are different. The English-German section is longer, focusing on the context and adding more points of grammar. The German-English section assumes a familiarity with English syntax and grammar and is shortened by the omission of this material. A "Dictionary Know-How" section separates the two sides of the dictionary. This section is an innovative compilation of information, such as when one can and cannot separate verb prefixes and the "time-manner-place" construction of standard German.

This title is a radical departure from the well-thumbed foreign-language dictionaries found in most reference collections. *The Oxford Starter German Dictionary* is highly recommended for multiple-copy purchase in any collection, from high school through university and specialized collections.—**C. D. Hurt**

Hani

1034. Lewis, Paul W., and Bai Bibo (Pui Bo), comps. **Hani-English/English-Hani Dictionary.** New York, with the International Institute for Asian Studies, Kegan Paul International; distr., Columbia University Press, 1996. 837p. $161.50. ISBN 0-7103-0564-8.

The Hani, a minority ethnic group, live in Yunnan Province in the extreme southwest of China and in Vietnam. They are closely related to Akha neighbors in Myanmar, Thailand, and Laos. The Hani and Akha populations consist of 2 million people, approximately 1.3 million of whom live in China. Their language is a member of the Loloish (Yi) branch of the Lolo-Burmese subgroup of the Tibeto-Burman family of languages. This 30,000-entry, 837-page dictionary is the first of the Hani language ever published. It took two scholars five years to complete this monumental work.

The main body of the dictionary is divided into two parts: Hani-English and English-Hani, both arranged in roman alphabets. Additionally, an introduction provides a basic description of Hani culture and the language with an extensive bibliography of English, Chinese, and Hani sources. Appendixes offer a comparison of the Hani and Akha orthographies; a story of the dragon and the son-in-law (in Hani and in English translation); Hani genealogies; Hani names of provinces, municipalities, and autonomous regions; words for sounds as the Hani hear them; Hani terms of endearment; set negative phrases; a sample of Hani proverbs and riddles; the Hani concept of time; and four-syllable elaborate expressions.

This highly specialized dictionary is a significant contribution to the study of the Tibeto-Burman languages in general, and to the Loloish (Yi) in particular. It will also be an important addition to linguistics, anthropology, and Asian studies collections in major research libraries.—**Hwa-Wei Lee**

Hebrew

1035. Harduf's Transliterated English-Hebrew Dictionary. Fourth Volume: L-M. Willowdale, Ont., Harduf Books, 1996. 1v. $45.50pa. (U.S.). ISBN 0-920243-75-4.

This work, part of an ambitious larger project, is a listing of English words beginning with "L" and "M," with their Hebrew equivalents, written in both Hebrew script (with vowels) and a transliterated English version. Entries include the part of speech and, in some cases, explanatory notes. The words are presented in two columns with wide inner and outer margins to simplify rebinding if necessary. The typeface is large, clear, and easy to read, with the transliteration in italics. Although the paper is classic linen (25 percent cotton fiber), the type impression shows through from one side to the other. However, this does not noticeably affect the readability of the work.

David Harduf, the author of this series, is a recognized Jewish scholar, linguist, and lexicographer. He has compiled a complete A to Z Yiddish-English dictionary (see entry 1055) and is the author of several works dealing with biblical names, a thesaurus and lexicon of literary names, and Talmudic works. This book is an important contribution to Hebrew lexicography and a useful tool for academic and research libraries, particularly those with strong religion, philosophy, or Jewish studies departments. It would also be a valuable addition to reference collections in religious and theological libraries and Jewish day school and public libraries.—**Susan J. Freiband**

Italian

1036. The Oxford Color Italian Dictionary: Italian-English, English-Italian. By Debora Mazza. New York, Oxford University Press, 1997. 504p. $8.95pa. ISBN 0-19-860135-2.

The year 1997 has been a busy one for Oxford University Press's lexicographers, as they have published almost simultaneously a new, revised edition of the *Oxford Italian Minidictionary*; a larger-sized *Oxford Italian Desk Dictionary*; (see entries 1037 and 1038), and now this one, containing more than 50,000 words and phrases and 70,000-plus translations. This leaves the present work (although nowhere near pocket-sized) having more in common with *il Mini* than with *il Desk*, but it incorporates two new and pleasant features that make it an improved hybrid of its relatives. Why Oxford found it necessary to rush out in small paperback bilingual dictionaries in Italian and English this year is not explained, but the most salient feature of the color version is the introduction of entries in bold color, making every page far more convenient to scan. Yet whereas the cover features the word "Color" in large, bright orange script, the only use of color throughout the work is that all entry words are printed in medium blue, and definitions, pronunciation, and usage notes are in traditional black print.

The English preface to this work says that "This new edition is an updated and expanded version of the *Oxford Italian Minidictionary*.... Colloquial words and phrases figure largely, as do neologisms. Noteworthy additions include terms from special areas such as computers and business that become a familiar feature of everyday language." That's true enough, even though Italian borrows liberally from English in giving names to new terms (e.g., *software, hardware, computer, dischetto* [diskette], *modem, Internet, pagina Web* [Webpage], and *sito Web* [Website]). Curiously, the term *Internet* is nowhere to be found in the *Minidictionary*, in either language, so users do get something extra besides blue-tinted entries in this version.

As a close relation to the other two dictionaries, this one carries along with it both the great strengths and the occasional weaknesses of its cousins. However, to give credit where credit is due, someone should have thought of this before: bold color on dictionary pages does set entries off from accompanying material nicely, making for ease of usage. A library that has already purchased *il Desk*—or even *il Mini*—however, can probably get along without this one.—**Bruce A. Shuman**

1037. **The Oxford Italian Desk Dictionary: Italian-English, English-Italian.** Debora Mazza and others, eds. New York, Oxford University Press, 380p. 1997. $15.95. ISBN 0-19-860158-1.

Earlier this year saw the publication of a new, revised edition of the *Oxford Italian Minidictionary* (see entry 1038), containing more than 50,000 words and phrases, with upwards of 70,000 translations and examples, all in a convenient pocket format. The present work—styled a "desk" dictionary—ups the ante on its kid brother, boasting more than 80,000 words and phrases, with 100,000-plus translations. The tradeoff is the size and number of inclusions at the cost of convenient portability. This dictionary also features a larger typeface, although the familiar Oxford University Press two-columns-per-page format is retained. The publishers tout this work as "the most authoritative, comprehensive, and up-to-date dictionary of its size, offering full coverage of contemporary idiomatic Italian and English at a remarkably affordable price." *E davvero* (in truth), the price is reasonable, and most of its definitions are set off by commendable pronunciation and grammar guidance.

Like the smaller work, this one includes some of the more common vulgarities (marked *vulg.*), which could lead to some colorful (and possibly dangerous) new forms of expression among those learning a new language prior to foreign travel. A few of the problems of the smaller work persist, however. For example, suppose a traveler wanted to buy some limes in Rome. Look up "lime" in the English section, and one gets "fruit: *cedro*; tree: *tiglio*." However, check *cedro* in the Italian section, and one gets "*albero*: cedar; *frutto*: citron." *Tiglio* is rendered simply as "lime" (referring to tree, fruit, or calcium compound?). Also *citron* (the fruit) has no English entry whatsoever. One can imagine some confusion in the mind of the reader seeking an explanation for such a term out of context. A traveler may have to try "*Cerco un frutto come un limone ma del colore verde*" ("I'm looking for a fruit like a lemon, but it is green") and just hope the grocer understands.

In the long, proud Oxford tradition, there is a decidedly British flavor to the definitions from Italian that could puzzle an American user. *Camion*, for example, is rendered first as "lorry" and then as "truck." *Ascensore* is "lift" and then "elevator, Am." Taking one consideration with another, this handsome dictionary is extremely easy to use, with good-sized, dark typeface on well-bordered pages. It is also commendably up-to-date, important in any work attempting to keep up with fast-changing international linguistic usage. By comparison with similar works, this dictionary shines because of its coverage, readability, currentness, and price.—**Bruce A. Shuman**

1038. **The Oxford Italian Minidictionary. Italian-English, English-Italian/Italiano-Inglese, Inglese-Italiano.** 2d ed. By Joyce Andrews. New York, Oxford University Press, 1997. 630p. $6.50pa. ISBN 0-19-860009-7.

The principal attraction of this bilingual travel dictionary is its size, and even though it is too thick (at 3 centimeters) to fit comfortably in a standard pocket, it is small enough (at approximately 8 by 12 centimeters) to fit nicely in a travel bag. The back cover boasts that this is the most up-to-date Italian-English dictionary of its size, extensively revised and updated (since the 1st edition in 1986). This abridgment now tops out at 50,000-plus words and phrases and more than 70,000 translations, many with examples, set off by a commendable amount of pronunciation and grammar guidance. British dictionaries have come a long way; in years past, the only way they could include dirty words was to substitute asterisks for certain critical vowels, but this dictionary has some of the more common vulgarities, (marked *vulg.*), which is both refreshing and useful.

Many English words have crept into Italian since the end of World War II, resulting in such terms as *computer, lobby, pub, pullman*, and even *slot-machine* being rendered the same in both languages. Americans will, however, quickly note numerous differences between British and American usage. Oxford's work (as one might expect) favors British usage, meaning that even in the English word list, Americans may have trouble locating a word because it is spelled differently (e.g., *kerb, offence*); has a different meaning (*braces, banger, lift*); or is a term not commonly used in the United States, such as *spanner* [chiave inglese]: "wrench," *petrol* [benzina]: "gasoline," *kip* [pisolino]: "nap," or *cheek* [sfacciataggine]: "impudent."

When a large dictionary is abridged, condensed, and squeezed into a compact format, something's got to give. In this case, there are instances in which precision seems to have been sacrificed for conciseness. As examples, both *puppy* and *cub* are translated as [cucciolo], and even though [limone] refers to both the lemon tree and its fruit, in looking up *lime*, one finds [tiglio] for the tree and [cedro] for its fruit. Cross-checking [cedro], however, gets users to *cedar* (tree) and *citron* (fruit), and *citron* has no entry whatsoever in the English section. These minor quibbles aside, however, Oxford has done a remarkable job of rendering two extensive parallel vocabularies into mutual intelligibility, all in a convenient, palm-sized format with adequate, dark typeface and a price that makes this dictionary appealing.—**Bruce A. Shuman**

Latin

1039. Stone, Jon R. **Latin for the Illiterati: Exorcizing the Ghosts of a Dead Language.** New York, Routledge, 1996. 201p. index. $55.00; $15.95pa. ISBN 0-415-91774-3; 0-415-91775-1pa.

Stone, in producing this book, has combed through *Cassell's Latin Dictionary*, which has been a standard for academic and public libraries for more than half a century, and has selected from it, and from a few other works, several thousand words and phrases, with their translations into English but not their etymologies. In addition, he has compiled a long list of sentence-length phrases, mottoes, wise sayings, and the like, such as *Pro rege at patria*, *De mortuis nil nisi bonum*, and *Urbs in horto* (Chicago's motto). An appendix, entitled "Miscellaneous," contains a list of Roman months (headed by *Mensis*, instead of *Menses*); the days of the week; colors; the seven hills of Rome; a long list of the classical names of places in Europe; the Roman numerals (both in words and symbols); and an English-Latin index to words and expressions, such as "and wife" (*et uxor*), "Behold the Man!" (*Ecce Homo*), and "by itself" (*per se*).

The author suggests in his preface that despite care to check tenses and spelling, some errors may yet be found. They may. Most egregious is the error in the words used to divide the whole book into its two primary parts, "Words" and "Sayings." These divisions are headed, in large typeface, *Verbi* and *Dicti*, whereas both are neuter, and should read *Verba* and *Dicta*, in the plural. Most other defects are obvious typographic errors, oversights, or just plain goofs, such as the translation of *Sursum corda*! as "Lift up your heads." Minor errors are *tyrannis* for *tyrannus*, *nervos* instead of *nervi* ("taxes are the essential—nerves—of the republic"), and *erubit* for *erubuit* (in the famous summation of the Miracle of the Wine at Cana: "the modest water saw its God and blushed").

These unfortunate glitches aside, is the book desirable for the reference desk? Perhaps not. It definitely would be useful in the home of the writer, the lawyer, the reader of learned journals, the historian, and the graduate student doing a paper on ancient Rome. But almost all of the *Verbi* can be found in Cassell's still-in-print dictionary, with a paperback edition selling for less than $5. The *Dicti* are largely duplicated in *The Harper Dictionary of Foreign Terms* by C. D. Sylvester Mauson and revised by Eugene Ehrlich (3d ed.; Harper & Row, 1987) or in A. J. Bliss's *A Dictionary of Foreign Words and Phrases* (Dutton, 1966). These two are fairly standard sources in most libraries.

For the above reasons, the work is recommended only to those libraries that have almost no classical dictionaries or those of foreign terms. Even for these, a cheap edition of Cassell's would probably be a better choice.—**Raymund F. Wood**

Mayan

1040. Hofling, Charles Andrew, with Félix Fernando Tesucún. **Itzaj Maya-Spanish-English Dictionary. Diccionario Maya Itzaj-Español-Ingles.** Salt Lake City, Utah, University of Utah Press, 1997. 910p. maps. index. $75.00pa. ISBN 0-87480-550-3.

This dictionary is the product of a successful cooperation of the linguistically trained main author with a native speaker as coauthor. There are few speakers of Itzaj Maya (in northern Guatemala), so even if there is—for now—no danger of the language disappearing, one can undoubtedly expect its future increasing acculturation to Spanish; these circumstances, of course, increase the value of this detailed dictionary. It is true that this work does not contain various ethnographic excursus (e.g., those in the *Batad*

Ifugao Dictionary with Ethnographic Notes by Leonard E. Newell [Manila, Linguistic Society of the Philippines, 1993]), but the vocabulary is so detailed that at least the material culture of the area is described. The front matter also contains long appendixes on the taxonomy of flora and fauna by Nancy L. Adamson and on body parts by the two authors.

The most important part of the front matter is the grammatical description of Itzaj Maya: It is a language with rich morphology; with many categories of tense, aspect, mood, voice, and "status"; and with some incorporation of the clitic objects into the verbal form. However, morphophonology seems not to have strong effects on the underlying forms, and there is not a rich derivational system operated through prefixation. There are tables that contain the paradigms of the grammatical forms and lists of (quite complicated) abbreviations by which the forms are identified in the main section of entries. All the front matter is offered twice, in English and in Spanish.

The meaning of the entries is also glossed by Spanish and English equivalents. This decision to make the dictionary trilingual increases its usefulness, or rather, the area of its usefulness. The equivalents are dealt with adroitly. For instance, the adverb *jet* is glossed as "mucho, demasiado" and [very, too much], but the illustrative example *jet ma'lo'* is glossed "muy, demasiado bueno" and [very good] ([too good] would be infelicitous). Yet sometimes the two equivalents given side by side invite a little thought. For instance, *jel-suma'an* is classified as a participle and glossed as "persogado" [haltered]. Because the participle, both in Spanish and in English, can be used either as a component of periphrastic verb forms, particularly of perfect tenses, or can be used attributively, there is a danger that the entry as it stands is not without ambiguity. With the help of the abbreviations and the passages in the grammatical description referred to by them, it is always possible to understand the passage. Last but not least, few people will read both the Spanish and the English glosses.

In any case, any student of a language with rich morphology, such as Arabic, Greek, or Sanskrit, will appreciate what a help it is to have not only the roots but also the concrete morphological forms, indicated as headwords of short, easily manageable entries. The author mentions in the preface that he used various sources when deciding what format to give to his dictionary, but that ultimately every dictionary must create a character of its own. This view is correct, and the character created for this dictionary is a highly useful one. The theoretical, professional linguist would probably prefer longer entries describing the generative possibilities of each root indicated as headword, but the authors of this dictionary have a broader public in mind, so the present format is probably more useful.—**L. Zgusta**

Portuguese

1041. **HarperCollins Portuguese Dictionary: English-Portuguese, Portuguese-English.** college ed. By John Whitlam, Vitoria Davies, and Mike Harland. New York, HarperCollins, 1997. 1v. (various paging). $13.00pa. ISBN 0-06-273489-X.

This volume updates the *Collins Portuguese Dictionary*, first published in 1991. In this revised edition, there are 382 pages of entries in the English-Portuguese section and 367 pages of Portuguese-English listings, for a combined total of more than 80,000 entries and 110,000 translations. By way of comparison, the pocket-sized *Collins Gem Portuguese Dictionary* (1993) has more than 40,000 references and 70,000 translations. Supplementary materials in the HarperCollins dictionary, although not exhaustive, do provide essential aids to understanding the language and identifying correct usage. These aids consist of separate pronunciation guides and verb form listings for Portuguese and English, a chart outlining the basic orthographic differences between European Portuguese and that of Brazil, and sections on abbreviations and numbers. Distinctions between Brazilian and European usage are clearly marked, as in the following examples: "girl" *menina* (BR), *rapariga* (PT); and "train" *trem* (BR), *comboio* (PT). The market of softbound Portuguese bilingual dictionaries aimed at English-speaking college students is not a crowded one. One of the major competitors of this handy, easy-to-use volume will be the compact gem edition described above. Both will serve students of Portuguese well.—**Melvin S. Arrington Jr.**

1042. **The Oxford Paperback Portuguese Dictionary: Portuguese-English, English-Portuguese.** John Whitlam and Lia Correia Raitt, comps. New York, Oxford University Press, 1996. 436p. $6.95pa. ISBN 0-19-864528-7.

There are a number of language dictionaries on the market, with a range of quality. *The Oxford Paperback Portuguese Dictionary* carries the reputation of the Oxford University Press name with an extremely affordable price. The dictionary is directed at speakers of both Portuguese and English, and it purports to have assembled the most useful words and expressions in use today, about 40,000 words and 65,000 translations. It is primarily a reference for tourists, students, and businesspeople who use the language, rather than a translation or scholarly dictionary.

The dictionary has the necessary pronunciation guide for both languages, as well as an addition for European Portuguese (spoken Portuguese varies somewhat in Portugal, Brazil, Africa, and scattered smaller locations). The back of the book also has a sample list of Portuguese verbs and tenses, a critical need for most English speakers. Unfortunately, Portuguese speakers are not treated to the same courtesy for English verbs and tenses. The form and meanings of word entries are clear and readable and seems to be accurate within the limitations of a small dictionary.

The book is recommended for any library as a useful and recent tool for patrons. Its low price makes it an affordable and practical update for any library, but most likely it should be an addition to other Portuguese dictionaries and not stand alone as the only available resource.—**Luiz Alberto Cardoso**

Russian

1043. Arany-Makkai, Agnes. **Russian Idioms.** Hauppauge, N.Y., Barron's Educational Series, 1996. 382p. illus. index. $6.95pa. ISBN 0-8120-9436-0.

This is a carefully thought out dictionary, even to the convenient format (5 by 3 by 1 inch). It has the special merit for the United States of being directed toward users of American rather than British English. The entries are from Russian to English, arranged according to the Russian alphabet. There is also an index arranged according to keyword (usually, but not always, a noun). Because the volume is not a dictionary of Russian but of Russian idioms, English speakers will at times need to use a Russian-English dictionary in conjunction with this work in order to look up the meaning of Russian words.

The introduction discusses the concept of *idiom* with unusual clarity. Considering abbreviations to be part of a language's idiom, the author includes a section on Russian equivalents of American abbreviations (e.g., *Gpzha* for "Miss" or "Mrs.," *SPID* for "AIDS") and American equivalents of Russian abbreviations (e.g., "UFO" for *NLO*, "cf." for *sr.*). When at times no equivalent exists (as for "RSVP"), she indicates that fact.—**John B. Beston**

1044. **Barron's Russian Dictionary.** By Nikolai Babiel and others. Hauppauge, N.Y., Barron's Educational Series, 1997. 331p. $10.95pa. ISBN 0-8120-9825-0.

Making dictionaries, especial bilingual dictionaries, is an expensive proposition. One of the ways publishers try to minimize their costs is to buy the rights for, say, Russian-English dictionaries designed and made in Russia, and then republish them for the English-speaking market. This enables the publisher to put out an inexpensive dictionary, but one that is ill-suited to the needs of U.S. users. Another ploy is to package the volume as both Russian-English and English-Russian—a procedure that expands the potential market but effectively serves neither.

Barron's Russian Dictionary, a volume modest in both price and word count (25,000), achieves a good compromise for popular use. First done in Germany, the definitions have now been replaced by their English equivalents. The dictionary is supplemented by a user's guide; a potted survey of Russian grammar; and a short list of idioms, antonyms, and a handful of brief "thematic" vocabularies—kinship, cloths, days of the week, time, and the like.

On the whole, the vocabulary is well chosen, although one can find quibbles. It is good to find current terms such as *varenka*, "stone-washed jeans," or *prixvatizatsila*, a punning play on *privatizatsiia* with the added (nefarious) meaning of "privatize to the advantage of a former high-ranking official." More questionable entries include such items as *grog* and *dvoebor'e*, an archaic word for "duel." *Krysha*, "roof," is defined in its transferred meaning, "a disguise" or "pretext," but omits its popular meaning of "bodyguard." Additional virtues are the dictionary's completeness of grammatical information accompanying each entry and its clear differentiation of homonyms and fields of usage.—**D. Barton Johnson**

1045. **NTC's New College Russian and English Dictionary.** By V. D. Arakin and others. Lincolnwood, Ill., National Textbook, 1996. 1v. (various paging). $27.95. ISBN 0-8442-4280-2.

Printed in Moscow, this dictionary is intended for students of either English or Russian, both groups assumed to be at an intermediate or advanced level. The English-language usage recorded is exclusively British, not American: such verbs as *dive, plead, shine,* and *strive,* for instance, have their past forms given in their British versions.

The vocabulary is selected from the most frequently used words of both languages, recent vocabulary said to be taken from newspapers. Yet whereas the vocabulary of space technology, an area of Russian expertise, is indeed up-to-date, the vocabulary of computer technology, an area of U.S. expertise, is entirely absent. Nor do such common recent words as *wimp, nerd,* and *gridlock* appear. One is constantly reminded of the Moscow origins of the work and the distance from English-speaking countries. Levels of usage are not indicated, whether colloquial, slang, or vulgar; in fact, English vulgarisms are entirely excluded, even the now fairly innocuous *shit*. Whatever one's attitude to these terms, they are an integral part of the language and need to be acknowledged.

Nothing is told to users about the seven authors of the dictionary, and the date of first publication is not indicated. However, this is a serviceable dictionary, even if not the most up-to-date, as claimed. At its modest price, the dictionary is a bargain. [R: Choice, Jan 97, p. 772]—**John B. Beston**

1046. **The Oxford Starter Russian Dictionary.** Della Thompson, ed. New York, Oxford University Press, 1997. 301p. $8.95pa. ISBN 0-19-860032-1.

This dictionary lives up to the jacket claims, especially that of being user friendly: "Help every step of the way" is indeed provided, and the layout is exceptionally clear. Words with multiple meanings, prolific in English, have their meanings precisely differentiated and illustrated with clear examples. Although the dictionary is designed especially for beginners (there are even exercises on how to use the dictionary, with answers to the exercises), it will also prove invaluable to advanced users in many ways. It is a "starter dictionary" in the sense that the vocabulary is limited and is related to such pragmatic areas as the family and home; the school or working day; dates, time, and weather; traveling on public transportation and finding one's way around; and shopping.

A particularly valuable feature of the dictionary is the series of boxed notes on both usage and grammar. (There is even an index to the Boxed Notes at the end of the book.) Notes on usage cover such topics as time and dates and the forms of Russian names and manner of addressing Russians. Grammatical notes, useful even for advanced speakers of Russian, cover such aspects as *to* as a preposition and an infinitive marker; verbs like *do, go, get,* and *have* in their many usages and in phrasal combinations; the relatives *which* and *what*; and the use of the impersonal *you*. Also, there are long and helpful entries for verbs like *leave, let, put,* and *take*.

The dictionary is indeed groundbreaking. It is quite simply the basic Russian-English dictionary that students should own.—**John B. Beston**

1047. **Russian-English Comprehensive Dictionary.** Oleg P. Benyukh, ed. New York, Hippocrene Books, 1997. 814p. $60.00; $35.00pa. ISBN 0-7818-0506-6; 0-7818-0560-0pa.

The volume at hand is a companion to editor Benyukh's 1995 *English-Russian Comprehensive Dictionary* (see ARBA 96, entry 1122). Designed and compiled in Russia, both volumes suffer from several defects from the point of view of English users. The greatest is the paucity of grammatical information on Russian words. The Russian scene has changed radically in recent years, and special attention is supposedly devoted here to business terminology, media and communications technology, and religion. Perhaps so, but the vocabulary of e-mail and the Internet seems to be almost entirely lacking. The volume does contain a number of appendixes: a table of numbers, metric measurements and conversions, world monetary units, world time zones, and lists of Russian proverbs and Latin words and phrases. The last are of dubious utility (e.g., the Russian proverb literally meaning "If it doesn't thunder, the muzhik won't cross himself" finds its "equivalent" in "Don't have thy cloak to make when it begins to rain"). Equally quaint is the Latin glossary that translates the Latin into Russian.

At nearly 40,000 entries, the volume under review is roughly equivalent to the second section of Kenneth Katzner's *English-Russian, Russian-English Dictionary* (see ARBA 96, entry 1124). Given that the latter, at roughly the same price, is a "two-way" dictionary in one volume, it is a much better buy in both quantity and quality.—**D. Barton Johnson**

Spanish

1048. **NTC's Dictionary of Spanish Cognates Thematically Organized.** By Rose Nash. Lincolnwood, Ill., National Textbook, 1997. 297p. $16.95. ISBN 0-8442-7961-7.

Designed as a combination reference/textbook, this dictionary lists approximately 20,000 American English words with their Latin American Spanish cognates. These words are similar in appearance and meaning in the two languages and serve as a resource for building vocabulary. Yet the entries as they are arranged, in parallel columns under theme headings and topical subheadings, limit the book's usefulness as a reference work: Translators attempting to locate a particular term must find it by trial and error among various topics and themes, in the absence of an alphabetic index. However, students seeking to develop a quick cognate vocabulary in Spanish can simply choose to focus on learning cognate words within a particular theme or topic. For example, in the "Putting Science to Work" theme, the topic "Technology Overview/Important Inventions," one finds *computer/computadora nj*.

The book includes a list of symbols and abbreviations that follows appendixes of equivalent British English spellings, irregular English and Spanish plurals, and supplemental vocabulary—terms that do not fit into any of the theme categories. The introduction provides helpful information, along with examples, of spelling patterns of cognates in each language, followed by an alphabetic list of topics and more than 100 commonly used cognates, such as *bank/banco nm* and *practical/práctico aj*. This book could serve as a useful circulating supplementary text and personal resource for teachers and translators, but it is of limited value in a library's reference collection.—**Joanna F. Fountain**

1049. Oliveres, Raphael A. **NTC's Dictionary of Latin American Spanish.** Lincolnwood, Ill., National Textbook, 1997. 375p. index. $19.95. ISBN 0-8442-7963-3.

The purpose of this dictionary is to define more than 6,000 Spanish words that are unique to one or more Latin American countries. It does not include words that are a part of the common Spanish lexicon. Words borrowed from English, commonly referred to as Spanglish, are included. The borrowed English words that are recognized by the Real Academia de la Lengua Española are noted by the initials "R.A.E."

Each entry includes the word followed by the country or countries of origin in italics. Definitions are provided in both English and Spanish. If there is no equivalent translation in one of the languages, it is noted with the abbreviation "N.E." Vulgarities are included within the entries but are clearly identified. Access to the entries is provided by four indexes. The first index is the "English Index," which lists the term in English and provides the Spanish equivalent. This is followed by the "Spanish Index," which does the same thing in reverse. The 3d index, entitled "Country Indexes," is really a collection of 19 extremely useful indexes. It lists each term in the dictionary under its country of origin. The final section is the "Index of Words Borrowed from English." The previously mentioned R.A.E. notation is also used in this index.

This is an excellent title that would be of use to anyone interested in the Spanish language. It could also save the user from embarrassment. For example, in countries such as Argentina, Colombia, Nicaragua, and Chile, the term "chicha" refers to an alcoholic drink. In Puerto Rico, the same word is a vulgar term for vagina. In Chiriqui, Panama, "chicha" also refers to a nonalcoholic fruit drink, which is a definition not included in this title. This dictionary belongs in all libraries with clientele interested in the Spanish language.—**John R. Burch Jr.**

1050. **The Oxford Paperback Spanish Dictionary and Grammar.** By Christine Lea and John Butt. New York, Oxford University Press, 1997. 1v. (various paging). index. $11.95pa. ISBN 0-19-860079-8.

This rather unhandy volume—827 pages in a 4-by-7-inch format—is really 2 books glued together into a common spine. The dictionary has 477 pages, whereas the grammar, separately paginated, has 350, set in a different typeface. The advantage or disadvantages of this system relate more to pedagogy than to librarianship. Does having a grammar in the same volume as a dictionary make learning a language easier? The primary purpose of a dictionary is to give the meaning of words. If one has discovered in the dictionary that *retretar* means to "paint a portrait," is there any immediate urgency to find out what form the verb might take in the subjunctive? As far as librarianship is concerned, there is the minor problem of where to shelve the volume—with dictionaries or with grammars?

The above problems aside, how does the dictionary under review compare with similar offerings on the market? From the dozen or more available, two were selected as typical and well known: *Larousse English-Spanish, Spanish-English Dictionary* (see ARBA 97, entry 873) and *The University of Chicago Spanish*

Dictionary. In general, the definitions in the Oxford University Press title were clear and differed little from the two other dictionaries. Yet in many cases, the number of definitions was less in the Oxford than in the other two. Here are some examples: The word *jaque*, meaning "check" (as in chess), has one definition in the Oxford dictionary. Larousse gives two, adding "to pester," and Chicago adds "a braggart; a bully." A more striking example is the word *fiel*, given in Oxford as "faithful; reliable; a believer," and also "needle (*de balanza*)." Larousse adds "exact; accurate" and also "the pin of a pair of scissors." Chicago has all the Larousse additions and also adds the plural form, *los fieles*, "the congregation." However, both the Oxford and the Larousse dictionaries do include the word *sancocho*, but Oxford defines it in only one word, "stew," whereas the more culinary-oriented Larousse tells readers that it is "a stew containing parboiled meat, yucca, and bananas."

The work under review is not recommended for those libraries that already have an adequate supply of dictionaries and grammars of Spanish. However, for libraries on a limited budget, the notion of getting two books for about the price of one may be a sufficient incentive for purchase.—**Raymund F. Wood**

1051. **The Oxford Starter Spanish Dictionary.** Ana Cristina Llompart, Jane Horwood, and Carol Styles Carvajal, eds. New York, Oxford University Press, 1997. 352p. $8.95pa. ISBN 0-19-860035-6.

For the beginning Spanish student, this dictionary provides an excellent reference source to look up basic vocabulary. Words are nicely spaced, printed in blue boldface, and are illustrated in a wide variety of examples to guide students to the correct meaning. The editors have included words with different meanings in parentheses (e.g., shower [rain] and shower [for washing]), which has created a built-in thesaurus. The editors have also made an effort to point to words used in different regions of both the Spanish- and the English-speaking world, for example, *tire* and *tyre* in English; *ducha* and *regadera* for shower. There are many encyclopedic components, such as an entire page dedicated to telling dates, with lists of the months, years, decades, and how to ask and give the date. When appropriate, words are cross-referenced to sections that have grammatical explanations. A useful appendix of verb tables and a glossary of grammatical terms are included. There is also a section of exercises, which seems out of place since a beginning student could not understand the required concepts by using only the dictionary. However, this is a user-friendly, handy, and reasonable reference tool for beginning students in all academic settings.—**Stella T. Clark**

1052. **Pockets: Spanish Dictionary.** New York, DK Publishing, 1997. 511p. (DK Pockets). $6.95pa. ISBN 0-7894-2195-X.

This volume is a handy pocket dictionary, meaning it is just the right size for a backpack, coat pocket, or purse. However, older users may find the typeface size painfully small. For the beginning English-to-Spanish user, the "imitated pronunciation" guide provides a quick and simplified course of instruction and includes explanations of stress and accents and other punctuation signs. Although this work basically follows Castilian Spanish, as being the "most correct Spanish," it does offer an explanation of variations found in certain areas of Latin America. Likewise, the Spanish-to-English pronunciation guide is a start at speaking English well enough to be understood. Each entry is followed by the pronunciation and then the translation. Note should be made of the binding—it is highly flexible yet, surprisingly, springs back after use with no damage.

Containing more than 50,000 words and phrases with coverage of colloquial and technical words, this dictionary is definitely more than adequate for most travelers. The convenient size and format encourages its use by students and those tourists or workers in a situation where Spanish or English is not their native tongue. Bookstores in general and especially campus bookstores will want to stock this dictionary.—**Louis G. Zelenka**

Swedish

1053. **NTC's Compact Swedish and English Dictionary.** Lincolnwood, Ill., National Textbook, 1997. 711p. $24.95. ISBN 0-8442-4959-9.

The natural competitor of this dictionary is *Prisma's Abridged English-Swedish and Swedish-English Dictionary* (see ARBA 96, entry 1138). Hence, it may be useful to compare the two works. *Prisma's* consists of 454 English-to-Swedish and 467 Swedish-to-English pages, with 18 pages of front matter. *NTC's* consists of 430 English-to-Swedish and 278 Swedish-to-English pages, with 84 pages of front matter. In respect to the front matter, the NTC dictionary offers more information. The descriptions of both Swedish and English grammar are somewhat more detailed. However, the NTC dictionary obviously targets as its readership people without any contact with linguistics. For instance, the forms of the nouns are given in *Prisma's* by the number of the paradigm indicated in the front matter; thus "s1" represents the class of nouns with forms such as *flicka - flickan - flickor*, "s2" nouns with forms such as *pojke - pojken - pojkar*, "s3" *rad - raden - rader*, and so forth up to "s9." The adjectives and verbs are treated in the same way. By contrast, in the NTC dictionary, the cardinal forms (i.e., singular indefinite, singular definite, plural indefinite for nouns) are given in the lemma of each entry for every noun—*flicka -an -or*. However, these indications are not always given in the case of adjectives and verbs; there the readers must rely on their memories to recollect what is stated in the front matter.

The NTC dictionary's front matter offers the reader what is called *Amerikansk Reseparlör*, in other words, a collection of expressions and phrases useful to the traveler. They are arranged topically, as is usual. Most of them give Swedish originals with English equivalents; only typically American dishes and drinks go from English to Swedish. The selection of the phrases is good, with some conspicuous gaps. For instance, the reader will find the English expressions "thank you," "thanks for the help," "thank you very much," and "thanks so very much," but not the instruction that a usual answer to such phrases is "you are welcome"; to give the reader the Southern variety "you bet" would also be useful, because it is indeed a mind-boggling idiom.

The body of the NTC dictionary is printed in a typeface several points larger than the Prisma text. Combined with the smaller number of pages, this means that the NTC work cannot offer as much information. Indeed, one gets in NTC the pronunciation of English (in the English-Swedish part); the forms of Swedish nouns (in the Swedish-English part); the equivalents for the most important or frequent senses in case of polysemy; and the most basic grammatical indications in both versions (irregular verbs, word classes). The English equivalents are accompanied by sense discrimination. However, there are next to no collocations or idioms. The information offered is solid and modern. Obviously, this is a dictionary for beginners or for users interested in the basic data only.—**L. Zgusta**

Yiddish

1054. Harduf, David Mendel. **English-Yiddish, Yiddish-English Dictionary.** [rev. ed.] Brookline, Mass., Israel Book Shop, 1997. 1v. (various paging). $10.00pa. ISBN 0-920243-10-X.

1055. Harduf, David Mendel. **Harduf's Transliterated English-Yiddish, Yiddish-English Dictionary.** [rev. ed.] Brookline, Mass., Israel Book Shop, 1997. 1v. (various paging). $24.95pa. ISBN 0-920243-77-0.

"Farshtasht Yiddish?" If someone asked that question, and a person knew neither the Yiddish language nor the Hebrew alphabet in which it is written, he or she could look it up in the transliterated version of these dictionaries, in which Yiddish words are spelled as they sound in English. This transliterated dictionary is a useful tool for the many users of the Yiddish language who cannot read Hebrew. The pocket-size version of the dictionary, which is not transliterated, will serve those who are familiar with Hebrew orthography. Both the pocket-size, originally published in 1983, and the large-format transliterated version derived from it, first published in 1991, have been through several editions (see ARBA 94, entry 1137, and ARBA 93, entry 1106).

Both dictionaries seem designed for the layperson or student; they look simple and easy to use. Typeface is large, with generous spacing for easy reading. The volumes are devoid of an introduction, preface, foreword, notes, or other trappings of academia, aside from a short list of abbreviations. The transliterated version has a basic pronunciation key, but this is eliminated in the pocket version (probably on the assumption that those using the nontransliterated version are already familiar with Yiddish pronunciation). If one looks up the word "perfection" in the English-Yiddish section of the transliterated dictionary, one will find the Yiddish equivalents *fulkomenkeit* and *shleimes*; however, in turning to the Yiddish-English (transliterated) section, neither word is found. This section appears improvised and abbreviated; instead of typography as in the first section, it looks typewritten and photocopied, and page numbers are hand-lettered. There are only half as many pages as in the first section and spacing is even more generous, so there must be far fewer definitions included. In the smaller dictionary, you also find the word "perfection" in the English-Yiddish section, but again the Yiddish equivalents are lacking in the Yiddish-English section. The serious scholar may be better served by Uriel Weinreich's *Modern English-Yiddish, Yiddish-English Dictionary* (see ARBA 79, entry 1156), but for the casual user, Harduf's dictionaries have many advantages.—**Larry Lobel**

24 Literature

GENERAL WORKS

Bibliography

1056. Newman, John, and others. **Vietnam War Literature: An Annotated Bibliography of Imaginative Works About Americans Fighting in Vietnam.** 3d ed. Lanham, Md., Scarecrow, 1996. 667p. index. $68.00. ISBN 0-8108-3184-8.

Why are Wendell Berry's poems "Dark with Power" and "Against the War in Vietnam" considered the most authentically conscientious responses to the Vietnam War? In "Poem for the Death of an American Serviceman in Vietnam," how does Charles Bukowski use surrealistic imagery to dramatize the shooting of a soldier through the bellybutton? In the musical *Miss Saigon*, do Alain Boublil and Claude-Michel Schoenberg succeed in updating Giacomo Puccini's opera, *Madame Butterfly*, by placing the story in 1970s Saigon? Such thoughts are generated by the thousands as one reads through the brief but informative bibliographic annotations in *Vietnam War Literature*.

Collecting the efforts of 5 compilers (as opposed to 1) and drawing on scholars most knowledgeable in Vietnam literature, this 3d edition is greatly expanded to reflect the growing numbers of imaginative writings about the war. Novels, short stories, poetry, drama, fiction, and miscellaneous works—the published writings covered include Vietnam War imaginative literature from its inception in 1964 to 1995. The most complete and authoritative bibliography of this violent struggle in Southeast Asia, the 3d edition of *Vietnam War Literature* is an essential reference for students, scholars, writers, book dealers, collectors, and others interested in the imaginative literature on the Vietnam War.—**Colby H. Kullman**

1057. Rosow, La Vergne. **Light 'n Lively Reads for ESL, Adult, and Teen Readers.** Englewood, Colo., Libraries Unlimited, 1996. 343p. index. $40.00pa. ISBN 1-56308-365-5.

Rosow calls *Light 'n Lively Reads for ESL, Adults, and Teen Readers* a thematic bibliography, which is certainly true, but it underplays the importance and usefulness of this volume. Rosow introduces her bibliography with an inspirational statement on her own successes and failures while teaching many different kinds of learners to read. In addition, she clearly delineates the pedagogical underpinnings of her strategy. A follower of Stephen Krashen's theories on "affective filters" (the emotional barrier to learning) and "comprehensible input" (presenting information in small increments so that it can absorbed more easily), Rosow succeeds in putting these principles into practice in her choice of books that she believes will appeal to readers from first graders to adult and ESL students. She also calls for a revival of the tradition of reading aloud, contending that it is a practice that is as beneficial for younger readers as it is for adults.

Light 'n Lively Reads for ESL, Adults, and Teen Readers is organized into a series of thematic units such as the arts, sports, parenting, and science. Within each chapter, the recommended titles are listed according to level of reading proficiency—first readers, "thin" books, and more challenging materials. Rosow does not limit herself to books alone. She includes newspaper and magazine articles as well as book chapters. Each recommended title is followed by a detailed and informative annotation. It is clear that Rosow has done her homework on these selections. Her annotations are written with warmth and critical penetration.

Rosow's thematic bibliography concludes with an index to her titles. The index is arranged by author/title/illustrator and by subject. *Light 'n Lively Reads for ESL, Adults, and Teen Readers* will appeal to both educators and parents. It succeeds admirably in its announced objectives in that it is both informative and inspirational.—**John B. Romeiser**

Bio-bibliography

1058. **Contemporary Popular Writers.** Dave Mote, ed. Detroit, St. James Press, 1997. 528p. index. (Contemporary Writers Series). $130.00. ISBN 1-55862-216-0.

No longer simply entertaining and diverting, contemporary popular literature has become serious, instructive, and important, even as it continues to please readers on a large scale. From Cleveland Amory, Isaac Asimov, and Margaret Atwood to Barbara Tuchman, Alice Walker, and Tom Wolfe, this useful reference tool provides copious information about 309 writers of popular fiction and nonfiction. Primarily American and British in its coverage, this volume includes novelists and short story writers, biographers, historians, humorists, playwrights, poets, social commentators, and psychologists who have been active in the field of popular literature since the early 1960s.

Each alphabetized author entry begins with nationality; birth and death dates; education; military service; family; career; awards; memberships; agent; and address followed by a list of publications (with publishers and dates), divided into genres. In many entries, bibliographies and critical studies are also listed. Concluding each entry is a signed, well-written critical commentary of varying length, usually a half-page, addressing various personal and professional highlights. A helpful preface outlines the raison d'être, content, and progress of popular literature from its beginnings in mid-century to the present. Nationality, genre, and title indexes, along with notes on advisers and contributors, conclude the volume.

Although the price is high, this well-bound, typographically pleasing text will be sought after frequently by users of public, academic, and, perhaps, high school libraries. It will have a long shelf life until the revised edition arrives. [R: RBB, 1 Mar 97, p. 1183]—**Charles R. Andrews**

1059. **Cyclopedia of World Authors.** 3d ed. Frank N. Magill, McCrea Adams, and Juliane Brand, eds. Pasadena, Calif., Salem Press, 1997. 5v. index. $350.00/set. ISBN 0-89356-434-6.

This 5-volume encyclopedia of more than 2,000 authors from Aesop (3d century B.C.E.) to Sherman Alexie (born 1966) has dual purposes: to combine, revise, and expand the 2 previous sets, *Cyclopedia of World Authors* (1974) and *Cyclopedia of World Authors II* (see ARBA 91, entry 1105); and to complement *Masterplots* (2d ed.; see ARBA 97, entry 906). The revisions are substantial: 25 percent of the entries are new to this edition. Although the greatest number of entries still come from the anglophone world, this edition includes new essays in major ethnic areas—African American, Latino, Asian American, Native American—and women's literature. The sketches consistently average a page in length, regardless of the writer's reputation, stressing biography over literary criticism.

Unlike other sources of this type, the *Cyclopedia* includes two unique aspects: writers whose primary claim to fame is not literary (Thorstein Veblen and Elizabeth Cady Stanton, for example), information about whom this source may not be the most obvious or intuitive choice, and one-hit wonders, such as Shelby Steele, Harriet Wilson, and Darryl Pinckney. The searcher is furthermore rewarded with ready access to contemporary writers (approximately 25 percent of the authors are still living). The 1997 copyright date, furthermore, reflects current biographical data, such as the recent death of Jose Donoso. In addition, most of the authors' works lists and bibliographies have been updated, if not expanded. As previously, the works lists are sorted by the genre in which the writer is best known; the bibliographic sources were selected on the basis of availability, timeliness, and usefulness, with a heavy slant toward English-language materials. The lack of page references for periodical citations, however, inhibits the effectiveness of the tool somewhat.

New to this edition are two indexes, one by a birth date timeline and one by where the writer flourished or was born. The geographic index inspires some caveats; for example, the cases of Albert Camus and Jacques Derrida, who are listed under both Algeria and France, are symptomatic of several duplications. Galicia, Silesia, and Numidia are designated as separate geographic entities. The master list of authors in volume 5 merely replicates the table of contents from each of the individual volumes; there is no additional index to names embedded within entries. All entries are signed, but an unusually high proportion of the contributors to this edition (nearly 15 percent) are designated as "independent scholar" under affiliation.

Although the set is almost beyond comparison in terms of sheer numbers of entries, its coverage is more superficial than that of Scribner's European, Ancient, British, American, and Latin American Writers sets (see ARBA 97, entry 961). *Cyclopedia*'s approach is more biographical and less interpretive than *Contemporary World Writers* (2d ed.; see ARBA 94, entry 1144). Its style is less colorful, but scholarship is more current than all but the most recent Wilson Authors series (see ARBA 97, entry 887). All in all, the set is a useful stepping-stone for works by and about the most influential and studied writers in today's curriculum.—**Lawrence Olszewski**

1060. **Major Tudor Authors: A Bio-bibliographical Critical Sourcebook.** Alan Hager, ed. Westport, Conn., Greenwood Press, 1997. 514p. index. $95.00. ISBN 0-313-29436-4.

The Tudor era in Great Britain (1485-1603) is known as a time of political and intellectual radicalism, complexity, and ambiguity. The authors of this period are among the most creative and challenging in British literary history, including such greats as Edmund Spenser, William Shakespeare, John Donne, and Elizabeth I. This new bio-bibliography provides a wide-ranging introduction to almost 100 authors, including dramatists, poets, religious writers, political figures, science writers, and music composers. They are primarily British, but many Irish, Scottish, and influential Europeans are also covered. A good collection of women authors is included.

Each author entry gives a brief biography, a discussion of major works and themes, a summary of the critical reception, and a bibliography of primary and secondary works. Entries vary in length from 3 to 10 pages, depending upon the importance of the figure. Bibliographies range from just a few entries to two to three pages. A brief, general bibliography and an index complete the volume.

The entries were written by over 50 contributors, primarily academics. As is typical in such a compilation, the writing is somewhat inconsistent, but the treatments are generally comprehensive and well written, providing interesting introductions and summaries. With few exceptions, the discussions of works, themes, and criticism are nicely balanced. One major exception is the "Critical Reception" section on John Donne, which, unfortunately, devolves into a critique by the author of the entry. The book could also be strengthened by the inclusion of a single, comprehensive listing of all authors, internal cross-references from variant forms of authors' names, and improved subject entries in the index.

Overall, Hager has compiled an important reference source on this exciting period in British literary history. This book will be a valuable addition to any academic library or public library and to larger high school collections.—**Susan Davis Herring**

Biography

1061. **Contemporary Authors Autobiography Series, Volume 25.** Shelly Andrews, ed. Detroit, Gale, 1996. 505p. illus. index. $140.00. ISBN 0-7876-0115-2.

1062. **Contemporary Authors Autobiography Series, Volume 26.** Shelly Andrews, ed. Detroit, Gale, 1997. 440p. illus. index. $140.00. ISBN 0-7876-0116-0.

1063. **Contemporary Authors Autobiography Series, Volume 27.** Shelly Andrews, ed. Detroit, Gale, 1997. 440p. illus. index. $140.00. ISBN 0-7876-1142-5.

Three new volumes have been added to the *Contemporary Authors Autobiography Series*. Each volume contains 16 or 17 autobiographies of approximately 10,000 words in length by mostly lesser-known writers. Although all genres are included, poets make up a large majority. There are also fiction writers, biographers, translators, and screenwriters, and many, of course, have published in more than one form. Photographs of the contributors at different ages and family pictures add interest.

The volumes make good browsing, especially as each book contains a brief sample of anecdotes or musings from five or six of the lives. There are a bibliography of published works at the end of each full-length entry and a cumulative index listing volume and page numbers of writers and their subject matter. The latter is essential, because although authors within a particular volume are listed alphabetically, there is no other system that would indicate in which volume a writer would be found. The volumes are too expensive and limited in scope to be purchased by any but the largest libraries, but they do contain information about published writers that may be difficult to find elsewhere.—**Charlotte Lindgren**

1064. **Contemporary Authors on CD.** [CD-ROM]. Detroit, Gale, 1997. IBM or compatible 286 (386 or faster recommended). ISO 9660-compatible CD-ROM player with cables, interface card, and MS-DOS CD-ROM Extensions 2.1 (double speed or faster recommended). MS-DOS 3.3. 640K RAM. 10MB hard disk space. VGA monitor and graphics card. Mouse (optional). Printer (optional). $795.00/yr. ISBN 0-7876-0670-7.

This CD-ROM version of a library standard includes the roughly 100,000 entries printed in the first 150 volumes of *Contemporary Authors* (CA); it is updated semiannually with new entries and amended entries from CA's New Revision Series. The main menu offers 5 buttons for name; nationality/ethnicity; personal data (17 categories for dates, affiliations, awards, and the like); title (word/phrase); and genre searches, with a 6th Advanced Search button for full-text searching of entries' narrative sections. Help, Exit, and About buttons also appear on this screen, the last uselessly presenting a nonsearchable list of all authors entered. Results displays helpfully drop searchers into index lists for choosing desired entries. Phrase, proximity, and Boolean searching as well as truncation are available for the advanced search.

Thoughtfully designed, the database is graphically and verbally adequate at reporting what it is doing and at telling searchers about options; online helps and tutorials are succinct and clear. Searchers can manipulate the database by mouse or keystrokes. Print/Save screens count the number of pages in each segment of the entry, an aid where searchers pay for printing, and entries print with citation and copyright information. One complaint: Searchers will be confused by the lack of authority control in the nationality/ethnicity list, which uses authors' self-reported identifications. Thus, searchers see "African American," "African American/Black," and "Afrikan" when the vast majority of black authors are found under "Black," or such useless designations as "All American" and "Mongrel."

CA in print has always been important for the wide variety of authors covered, but CA on disc is a superior product in that libraries serving large, dispersed populations can network it, and small or new libraries that do not wish to house or do not already own the print set can offer it on a workstation. In that the CD-ROM enjoys search capabilities that the print version does not (one can, for example, look for black authors born in Michigan in 1948), it will assist reader's advisory and collection development librarians as well as users developing book club or course reading lists.—**Robert H. Kieft**

1065. **DISCovering Authors: Biographies & Criticism on 400 Most-Studied Canadian & World Authors.** Canadian ed. [CD-ROM]. Toronto, Gale Canada, 1996. Minimum system requirements: IBM or compatible 286 (386 or faster recommended). ISO 9660-compatible CD-ROM drive with cables, interface card, and MS-DOS CD-ROM Extensions 2.1 (double speed or faster recommended). MS-DOS 3.3. 640K RAM. 10MB hard disk space. VGA monitor and graphics card. Mouse (optional). Printer (optional). $750.00. ISBN 0-8103-9955-5.

DISCovering Authors provides fast access to biographical, bibliographic, and critical information on the most well-known authors from ancient times to the present. More than 400 writers from all over the world have been included in the database. This version of *DISCovering Authors* includes biographies and criticism of more than 70 Canadian authors. In addition, 250-plus portraits are included.

Each entry in the biography section provides an introduction to the author; a portrait (if available); a full-text biography (usually approximately 1,000 words); personal background data including family, education, awards received, and so forth; a bibliography of the author's work; any media adaptations of the author's works (i.e., movies, television programs, books on tape); and any additional sources of information. In addition, there is a criticism section that consists of selected critical essays on the author's best-known works. These criticism entries supply subject headings that make it possible to search them and the bibliographic citation indicating the source. Additional features of the CD-ROM include a copy of the 10th edition of *Merriam-Webster's Collegiate Dictionary*, a glossary of literary terms, research paper topics, a timeline of literary and world events, and something called a "notepad editor" that allows the user to personalize the search to some extent. Much of the information included on this CD-ROM has been obtained from the Gale literary and biography series entitled Contemporary Authors, Contemporary Literary Criticism, Twentieth-Century Literary Criticism, the Dictionary of Literary Biography, Black Literature and Criticism, and others. The publisher contends that this information has been updated and corrected when necessary, but it appears that much of the material has been entered as it was in the original Gale publications.

The database is easily set up and used. It is possible to use it on local area networks with multiple users or as a stand-alone system. Search times are quick, and the printing setup is adequate. (The number of pages printed in one search session can be limited when the program is set up.) This disc is recommended for larger public and academic libraries (especially ones in Canada), and for libraries that do not already own many of the Gale biographical publications that provide the basic information. It is not recommended for smaller public and academic libraries because of the cost.—**Robert L. Wick**

1066. Kamm, Antony. **Biographical Companion to Literature in English.** rev. ed. Lanham, Md., Scarecrow, 1997. 614p. $60.00. ISBN 0-8108-3319-0.

Biographical Companion to Literature in English is the revised and updated edition of Kamm's earlier work, *Collins Biographical Dictionary of English Literature* (United Kingdom, 1993). Published in the United States, this new edition has been compiled with a North American audience in mind. A total of 1,544 authors from Britain, Ireland, the United States and other nations, as well as past and present members of the Commonwealth and authors from the classical world are included. The intent is to include a representative selection of authors who have made significant contributions to literature in English. Writers whose works are in languages other than English but have been widely read in English are also included. Thus, the reader can expect to find entries for Marcel Proust, Fyodor Dostoyevsky, Gabriel García-Marquez, Umberto Eco, and others who might not immediately come to mind when considering literature in English. Poets, novelists, dramatists, biographers, and others have been selected to provide a balance of works from different genres, cultures, regions, and nations.

Articles are long enough to provide substantive information, yet the volume remains usable as a quick reference source and can be easily scanned for key facts. Authors are simply arranged in alphabetic order and entries focus on brief outlines of lives and literary achievements. Prefacing the volume is a useful section informing the reader about the specific terminology, abbreviations, typefaces, and punctuation used in each entry. The book is well bound and is printed in an easily read typeface. Bibliographic references are given at the end of article entries.

The author has avoided the temptation to include many more names in this collection, and the result is a solidly balanced work. An index of writers by genre, and perhaps another by region or culture, would have provided even greater access to these well-chosen literary representatives.—**Lynn K. Sorenson**

1067. **Women Writers of Great Britain and Europe: An Encyclopedia.** Katharina M. Wilson, Paul Schlueter, and June Schlueter, eds. New York, Garland, 1997. 571p. illus. (Garland Reference Library of the Humanities, v.1980). $95.00. ISBN 0-8153-2343-3.

This impressive collection of essays provides a rich resource for readers interested in short introductions to the histories of hundreds of British and European women writers. Reaching back in time to Sappho in the seventh century B.C.E., the encyclopedia discusses women writers through the years, such as Nossis (third century B.C.E.), Héloïse (twelfth century), Dames des Roches (sixteenth century), Jeanne-Marie Leprince de Beaumont (eighteenth century), and Virginia Woolf (twentieth century).

The entries begin with the vital statistics: pseudonym (if applicable), birth date, birthplace, death date, place of death, genres, and languages. After a discussion of the writer, the entry concludes with a list of the author's works. The entries may be written by one of the editors or by one of more than 100 contributors. Because of this, the style varies widely, with some entries quite intriguing and others merely factual.

Occasional photographs and drawings enliven the text; more photographs would have been appreciated. Useful indexes include pseudonyms, a list of entries by countries, and a list of entries by centuries. Historians, women writers, students, and general readers will enjoy browsing this resource.—**Suzanne I. Barchers**

Handbooks and Yearbooks

1068. **Contemporary Literary Criticism: Excerpts from Criticism of the Works of Today's Novelists....Volume 90.** Jeff Chapman, Christopher Giroux, Brigham Narins, and others, eds. Detroit, Gale, 1996. 541p. illus. index. $129.00. ISBN 0-8103-9268-2.

Since 1973, the Contemporary Literary Criticism (CLC) series has provided readers with critical commentary on more than 2,000 authors now living or who died after December 31, 1959. The series was the first ongoing digest monitoring scholarly and popular sources of critical opinion and explication of modern literature. Each of the CLC volumes "presents significant passages from published criticism of works by creative writers. Authors are selected for inclusion for a variety of reasons, among them the publication or dramatic production of a critically acclaimed new work, the reception of a major literary award, revival of interest in past writings, or the adaptation of a literary work to film or television" (preface). Entries include the author heading, a portrait, a brief biographical and critical introduction, a list of the author's principal works, and excerpted criticism. Each CLC volume usually contains about 500 individual excerpts taken from book reviewing periodicals, general magazines, scholarly journals, monographs, and books. The critical excerpt section includes evaluations from the beginning of an author's career to the most current commentary. Entries also frequently include author interviews and a "Further Reading" section.

Volume 90 of CLC presents 14 authors from 6 countries; 13 of these are full critical presentations of each author's career. That is, the editorial staff attempts to include excerpts of seminal critical articles on all or most of the author's publications listed in the "Principal Works" section. James Baldwin's article, however, is devoted entirely to critical consideration of one work, *Sonny's Blues*. The authors featured in this volume are Baldwin, American novelist and short story writer; T. Coraghessan-Boyle, American novelist; Michael Crichton, American novelist; Saul Friedländer, Israeli historian; Barry Hannah, American novelist; Sébastien Japrisot, French novelist; Laurie Lee, English memoirist; Brian Mo Alice McDermott, American novelist; Brian Moore, Canadian novelist; Carol Muske, American poet and novelist; Luis Omar Salinas, American poet; Vikram Seth, Indian novelist; Jane Urquhart, Canadian novelist; and Wendy Wasserstein, American playwright.

The critical excerpt section of each entry provides the reviewer's name, the publication date of the review, and the full bibliographic citation. A brief summary statement by CLC's editorial staff is presented immediately before the text of the excerpted article. Usually, this statement provides brief biographical information on the reviewer and informs readers whether the review is favorable or unfavorable. The work or works reviewed in each excerpt are printed in bold typeface for ease of reference. In reviews of the author's best-known works, a significant sentence or paragraph from the excerpt is presented in bold typeface, followed by the reviewer's name. Occasionally, an excerpt from an author's work is presented for emphasis.

This volume of CLC is a worthy addition to the series based on its variety of authors and genres and the quality of excerpted criticism. The volume is recommended for both college and university libraries with strong literature programs.—**Mark Padnos**

1069. **Epics for Students: Presenting Analysis, Context, and Criticism on Commonly Studied Epics.** Marie Lazzari, ed. Detroit, Gale, 1997. 440p. illus. maps. index. $65.00. ISBN 0-7876-1685-0.

Gale has performed a service for librarians, literature teachers, and students, who will benefit from this elegant and useful compendium. Designed with Gale's usual attention to detail, it covers the most popular world epics: *The Aeneid, Beowulf, El Cid, Song of Roland, The Divine Comedy, Gilgamesh, The Iliad, Kalevala, Mahabharata, Niebelungenlied, The Odyssey, Omeros, Paradise Lost,* and *Sundiata,* the epic of Mali. The work opens with a superb essay by Helen Conrad-O'Briain of University College, Dublin, in which she celebrates the action, tension, passion, and thought of the epic. An introduction to the text enumerates each entry's focus, including introduction, author biography, book-by-book plot summary, characters, themes, style, historical and cultural context, critical overview, criticism, sources for further study, media adaptations, comparisons and contrasts, list of complementary readings, and study questions. A literary chronology precedes the body of entries. A glossary covers 161 literary terms, most without models. Indexing covers author/title, nationality/ethnicity, and subject/theme.

Every turn of the page of this monumental reference work is a treat. The cover, layout, icons, and illustrations are appealing. Phrasing is informative, direct, and neither overly literary nor dumbed-down. Useful information includes chronological lists of media adaptations, uncomplicated definitions of literary terms, and brief discussions of historical context; for example, the Bronze Age, the Dark Age, and the Iron Age in the entry on *The Iliad*. The book would have profited from a comprehensive list of world epics, but, overall, the coverage, tone, and appreciation for student difficulties in reading world epics make this work a must-have for public and school libraries.—**Mary Ellen Snodgrass**

1070. **Identities and Issues in Literature.** David Peck, ed. Pasadena, Calif., Salem Press, 1997. 3v. illus. index. $225.00/set. ISBN 0-89356-920-8.

This three-volume set attempts to treat identities and issues associated with literature. The set focuses on North America and the social issues that affect the vast melting pot that is the United States. More than 800 articles cover authors, titles, and topics. Author and title articles are approximately 500 words in length; subject articles may be up to 4,000 words in length. Some topics discussed include various aspects of American identity (life on the sea, West and the frontier); the black church; food and identity; Japanese American internment; rural life; and women and identity.

Articles on specific written works start by giving the author (with dates); year first published; and the identities associated with the title (e.g., adolescence and coming-of-age, religion, European American, and women). Works of fiction and nonfiction are both included in the set. The title articles provide details on the plot, a contextual framework, and information on the author. Author articles supply pertinent biographical details, including date and place of birth and principal works, as well as the identities associated with that author and his or her writings. The main articles then outline the significant achievement of the author in question. Articles on topics give the specific identities for which they are appropriate and an in-depth discussion of the topic, sometimes divided into subtopics if the article is a long one. All articles end with a list of suggested readings and *see also* references to other articles.

The editor and contributors have endeavored to avoid sexist and racist language and to use acceptable terms for group names in an effort to reduce pigeonholing. The choice of topics, writers, and works is broad and is as inclusive as a resource within the set parameters can be. However, the content and language of the articles are often rudimentary, suggesting that this tool would be most suitable for high school students or beginning undergraduates. Unfortunately, the binding of the volumes is somewhat flimsy for that particular audience.—**Melissa Rae Root**

1071. **The Literary Almanac: The Best of the Printed Word 1900 to the Present.** Kansas City, Mo., High Tide Press/Andrews McMeel Publishing, 1997. 288p. illus. $16.95pa. ISBN 0-8362-3701-3.

The Literary Almanac by High Tide Press covers twentieth-century North American writing from 1900 to the present. The book is arranged by year in an easy-to-read format and features poets, playwrights, and writers of fiction and nonfiction. Each year's entry includes notable births and deaths, excerpts from reviews, and two or three short biographies.

This work is most useful as a quick reference handbook for locating notable literary events year by year. Bestsellers, both hardcover and paperback; Pulitzer prize-winners for fiction, biography or autobiography, poetry and drama, and Newbery and Caldecott Medal winners are included. The National Book Award winner, the Booker Prize winner, and the National Book Critics Circle Award winner are all listed for each year the prize has been awarded. A section describing criteria for awarding the various prizes is included, as are several other sections that are mostly for fun. Some of these lighter sections are titled "Literary Love Affairs," "The Astrological Author," and "Alternate Occupations."

The almanac is most useful for high school and public libraries, as the presentation of information is informal and is not comprehensive. One serious flaw is the lack of indexing. The only guide for using this book as a reference work is a chronological approach. To find whether it includes an entry for Pearl S. Buck, for instance, one must almost read the book from cover to cover.—**Lynn K. Sorenson**

1072. Moss, Joyce, and George Wilson. **Literature and Its Times: Profiles of 300 Notable Literary Works and the Historical Events That Influenced Them.** Detroit, Gale, 1997. 5v. illus. maps. index. $395.00/set. ISBN 0-7876-0606-5.

No work of literature appears in a vacuum; every piece reflects its time in some form or another. Even works that portray an earlier period in history can resonate a contemporary context. This 5-volume set discusses the historical background of 300 of the most studied works of literature, including novels, poems, plays, short stories, and even speeches. The set attempts to address both the period in which the piece is set and the period in which it was written in order to give a total contextual framework. The volumes are arranged chronologically; for example, volume 1 covers ancient times to the American and French Revolutions (or prehistory-1790s). The last 3 volumes include parts of the twentieth century (1890-1930s, 1940-1950s, and 1960-2000), reflecting the proliferation of works written as time marches on. Within each volume, entries are arranged alphabetically by title. Timelines in each volume cite historical events for the period covered and the literary works set in that period. Contents both by title and by author introduce the individual volumes, as does an introduction tailored for the period treated. A combination author/title/subject index to the entire set appears in each volume, providing reference to volume and page number.

Entries contain a biography of the author, a brief synopsis and setting explanation, events in history at the time of the work, events in history at the time the work was written, and a bibliography for further information. If the work was written at the same time as it is set, the events sections are combined. Entries also discuss the work in focus, giving plot details and how they reflect the contemporary situation; possible sources; details on reviews of the work; and other information that places the writing in context. Although one can always quibble with the selection in such a set as this one, it is apparent that the authors strove to include women and world writers in addition to canonical classics. The titles are focused toward a high school or undergraduate audience.

The problems with the set arise from its format; unfortunately, said problems may be unavoidable in a work such as this one. The chronological arrangement places pieces of literature in the period in which they are set rather than that in which they were written. For example, *The Crucible* by Arthur Miller and *The Once and Future King* by T. H. White appear in the first volume, even though written in the twentieth century. Toni Morrison's *Beloved* is found in the second volume; George Orwell's *Nineteen Eighty-Four* and Aldous Huxley's *Brave New World* are analyzed in the last volume (and the latter should boost the coverage of the volume well beyond the year 2000). Also, some works extend beyond the parameters set by the volume's coverage; for instance, *One Hundred Years of Solitude* by Gabriel García Marquez covers a large period, from the 1830s to the 1930s, but it is found in the second volume, whose coverage only goes to the 1880s. Obviously, the authors had to make a judgment call as to in which volume to include the work, but some guidelines would have been helpful. In addition, certain works are set in an indeterminate period, such Greek tragedies and Arthurian legends, which are based on mythology, not necessarily actual events. Apparently the authors chose to classify Greek tragedies as the time they were written and Arthurian tales as ancient times. This arrangement is not inherently a problem unless a user does not know the correct period. The index simplifies access to the set somewhat, but a table of contents for the entire set or a separate title index would have been welcome.

Aside from the access issue, the only problem is one of occasional lapses in editing. Orwell's *Nineteen Eighty-Four* is spelled out in its entry, but mention of the title in the entry on Margaret Atwood's *The Handmaid's Tale* writes the numerals (*1984*). The entry on Herman Melville's *Moby-Dick* is missing its hyphen throughout. However, the content of the entries is sound, interesting, and useful. This set will be used in public, school, and academic libraries.—**Melissa Rae Root**

1073. **The Oxford Companion to Twentieth-Century Literature in English.** Jenny Stringer, ed. New York, Oxford University Press, 1996. 751p. $45.00. ISBN 0-19-212271-1.

This publication surveys the works of major anglophone writers of the twentieth century. Biographical profiles account for approximately 2,400 entries, and some 650 other entries target specific works, movements, genres, and other literary concepts. Presented in an attractive bicolumn layout, entries average approximately 270 words in length; essays of more than 1,000 words are accorded such giants as D. H. Lawrence, James Joyce, and T. S. Eliot. (Mark Twain has no entry because none of his significant writings were published in the twentieth century.) The text's entries are unsigned; a roster of nearly 100 contributors' names—without credentials—appears in the front matter.

Articles on the lives and works of novelists, poets, and dramatists from the United States, Canada, Great Britain, the Caribbean, Australia, New Zealand, and South Africa predominate, with fewer entries allotted to such scholars and other nonfiction writers as historians, art historians, biographers, philosophers, journalists, travel writers, sociologists, economists, and scientists. With its discursive style, this *Oxford Companion* often provides more extended and in-depth analysis of literary works than its forebears, *The Oxford Companion to English Literature* (see ARBA 86, entry 1162) and *The Oxford Companion to American Literature* (see ARBA 97, entry 966). A number of authors whose twentieth-century accomplishments were overshadowed by the quality and quantity of their earlier works have generously been granted entries, such as Joseph Conrad, Thomas Hardy, and Charlotte Perkins Gilman. Authorial entries often include titles of recent, acclaimed biographies.

Unfortunately, occasional gaffes in scholarship mar this compendium. Truman Capote's posthumous *Answered Prayers* is referred to as *Unanswered Prayers*, and Daphne du Maurier's story "Don't Look Now" is called "Don't Look Back." Also, the novel *Timequake* by Kurt Vonnegut (who no longer appends "Jr." to his surname) is said to have been published in 1994, although it actually appeared in 1997. Many librarians will be frustrated by the absence of a "Mystery Fiction" entry, as well as the absence of any cross-reference to the existing entry of "Detective Fiction." Neither is there an entry for "Gothic Fiction," nor a *see* note to "Romantic Fiction." Also, the article on "Realism" serves up examples only from the 1800s, saying nothing about twentieth-century embodiments of this literary technique, such as Upton Sinclair's *The Jungle*. Troubling, too, are the pinched definitions that accompany "Anthologies" and "Pulp Magazines." The former suggests that anthologies are gatherings of poetic works only, whereas the latter limits discussion to those periodicals of the 1920s and 1930s that carried lurid crime fiction.

Problems with birth and death dates are also evident. Although it is noted that Irish novelist Mary Lavin died in 1996, at least seven writers who passed away between 1992 and 1995 are recorded as living: Kay Boyle, John Hersey, Wallace Stegner, Margaret Millar, Ralph Ellison, and Stanley Elkin. Among typographic errors discovered are the misspellings "Le Clos" (for "De Laclos," p. 7); "Willima" (for "William," p. 490); and the omission of the final "s" from Carl Sandburg's title *Always the Young Strangers*. In a work of such ambitious scope, one can forgive the inevitable overlooking of certain deserving writers. However, how can one justify the scanting of a major field of writing, historiography? Because of its numerous flaws, *The Oxford Companion* to *Twentieth-Century Literature in English* must be used most guardedly.—**Jeffrey E. Long**

1074. **Twayne's Masterwork Studies on CD-ROM: The Student's Companion to Great Literature.** [CD-ROM]. New York, G. K. Hall/Simon & Schuster Macmillan, 1996. Minimum system requirements (Windows version): IBM or compatible. CD-ROM drive. Windows. 4MB RAM. 2700K extended memory. 256-color video driver. Minimum system requirements (Macintosh version): CD-ROM drive. 2MB RAM. 2000K memory. $495.00/single user; $595.00/networks.

Twayne's Masterwork Studies on CD-ROM contains the full text of 103 of the popular series' titles, which can be searched using the context-sensitive, pull-down menu options or icons provided. The text can be searched by author, title, keyword, genre, nationality, or period, and Boolean searching and truncation are supported. Typing in "pastoral," for example, results in a set of discrete paragraphs from Masterworks titles, each paragraph considered one "hit." The screen can be customized to view the results of two searches simultaneously. Using advanced options, the text can be saved with one's own notes or annotations, and the searches execute quickly. The searcher can look at the full text or table of contents of any title by clicking on the "Contents" icon, double-clicking on headings and subheadings, and "tunneling" until the full text is displayed. Aside from speed and the ability to customize, the novice user might have a difficult time executing even simple functions at initial try. Tagging a record to print requires going into "Edit" on the pull-down menu; clicking on "Query" in the same menu results in a message to use the magnifying glass icon instead. Some functions, such as the one noted, are not yet available or available only on Windows or Macintosh versions.

Academic and school libraries owning few Masterworks titles may find this an inexpensive and space-saving alternative to buying all the titles separately, but however impressive the added features on CD-ROM, the comparative difficulty in using these features makes purchase unnecessary for libraries holding the paper titles.—**Jennie Ver Steeg**

Indexes

1075. Index to the Wilson Authors Series. Bronx, N.Y., H. W. Wilson, 1997. 136p. $27.00. ISBN 0-8242-0900-1.

This 1997 edition of the *Index to the Wilson Authors Series* replaces the 1991 edition (see ARBA 92, entry 1112). Biographical dictionaries in the Wilson series include *Greek and Latin Authors 800 B.C.-A.D. 1000* (1980), *European Authors 1000-1900* (1967), *British Authors Before 1800* (1952), *British Authors of the Nineteenth Century* (1936), and *American Authors 1600-1900* (1938), as well as volumes on the twentieth century, world authors, and Spanish American authors. The Junior Authors and Illustrators series is also indexed.

This name index provides each author's dates or the years during which the author flourished. A code keyed to the particular volume in which the main biographical essay appears is also provided. This index is highly recommended for reference collections in school and public libraries.—**Mary L. Bowman**

CHILDREN'S AND YOUNG ADULT LITERATURE

General Works

Bibliography

1076. Berman, Matt. What Else Should I Read? Guiding Kids to Good Books, Volume 2. Englewood, Colo., Libraries Unlimited, 1996. 215p. illus. index. $24.00pa. ISBN 1-56308-419-8.

This is a useful cookbook of ideas for implementing a whole language approach in the middle grades and beyond. The introduction includes a brief summary of 15 to 20 types of activities that round out the literature program, whether implemented in the classroom or the media center, and discusses in more depth the elements of a good book discussion group. The substance of the book is composed of 30 book webs. They include such titles as *Brady*; *Captains Courageous*; *Charlotte's Web*; *A Day No Pigs Would Die*; *A Fine White Dust*; *Harriet the Spy*; *The Hundred Dresses*; *Incident at Hawk's Hill*; *Sarah, Plain and Tall*; *Stone Fox*; *Weasel*; and *The Yearling*. Each web contains reproducible bulletin board materials, including 9 to 12 topical bookmarks that have 4 to 8 more titles on the topic, with a brief review for each. The 45 to 50 bookmark titles include both current publications and backlisted standard titles, providing a nice blend. A feature for the user is that the title, author, and topic indexes indicate where the book is a featured web, found on a bookmark, or only listed on a web. This allows the professional to find the review easily to add it to another web where it applies, greatly expanding the potential scope of the material.

—**Elizabeth McClure Rosen**

1077. DeLong, Janice A., and Rachel E. Schwedt. Core Collection for Small Libraries: An Annotated Bibliography of Books for Children and Young Adults. Lanham, Md., Scarecrow, 1997. 229p. index. $29.50. ISBN 0-8108-3252-6.

The purpose of this book is to help parents and librarians select "essential books for their collections . . . [which are] deemed appropriate for children and young adults." The books range in age audience from kindergarten to high school. The subjects covered are picture books, traditional literature, modern fantasy, multicultural books, historical fiction, contemporary fiction, nonfiction, and poetry. The 494 titles are annotated with the added information of classroom applications for and values found in each book.

The chapter on "Multicultural Books" is an example of a typical chapter. A brief introduction to the genre provides a sufficient overview of the subject. The annotations are then listed alphabetically by author and include titles such as *Sounder* by William Armstrong, *Letters from Rifka* by Karen Hesse, *To Kill a Mockingbird* by Harper Lee, and *Knots on a Counting Rope* by Bill Martin. Sixty-four titles are listed in this chapter, and the oldest publication year is 1932, for *Young Fu of the Upper Yangtze* by Elizabeth Fore Lewis. The newest publication year is 1994, for *Pink and Say*. Of the 64 titles, 60 are still in print.

The appendixes at the end of the book offer additional valuable information. Appendix A lists 93 recommended authors, such as Louisa May Alcott, Margaret Wise Brown, James Daugherty, and Charlotte Zolotow. Appendix B describes various awards for children's literature. Two indexes at the back are by subject and author/title.

The authors have worked many years with children and children's literature. Because of their experience, they have created a balanced and useful selection of books. However, the name of their book is misleading. It is called a *Core Collection*, but the reader is left to wonder if the titles in this book are considered "core" because a library accreditation team would ask for these titles or because the authors like the books listed. Such popular authors as Roald Dahl, Robert Cormier, Judy Blume, and Lois Duncan were not included. A library would not regret having the 494 books listed in this bibliography on its shelves. However, libraries should look at this bibliography as a starting point for collection development. As such, the book is recommended for public, school, and university libraries that would like a useful children's literature bibliography.—**Suzanne Julian**

1078. **The Horn Book Guide to Children's and Young Adult Books. Volume VII, Number 2.** Boston, Horn Book, 1996. 463p. illus. index. $35.00pa./yr. ISSN 1044-405X.

The purpose of the *Horn Book Guide to Children's and Young Adult Books* is to offer brief, critical annotations of all hardcover trade children's and young adult books that have been published in the United States during the six months prior to the guide's publication. This particular issue reviews the books published from January to June 1996. The contributors to the publication, who are listed at the back of the volume, are made up of a wide variety of professionals, including members of the Horn Book staff, teachers, educators, librarians, booksellers, and freelance writers from around the country who are interested in finding good books for young people. The audience for the publication includes school librarians, public librarians, and any others working on book selection and collection development for the young.

The reviews in the volume are arranged logically for easy use and are initially divided into fiction and nonfiction categories. These categories are then arranged by age level for the fiction, and by subject according to Dewey Decimal Classification for the nonfiction. Finally, the reviews are arranged alphabetically within each area and evaluated according to quality—with a rating of 1 being outstanding to 6 being unacceptable in either style or content. All reviews that have been rated either 1 or 2 have been further flagged by a darkened triangle in the margin for easy identification.

The material in *Horn Book Guide* may appear dated, but it still serves as an excellent qualitative summary of the books published for children in the previous six months. This title is important for evaluating collections and for making added copy or paperback purchases for popular titles. It will be useful to those working in collection development.—**Bridget Volz**

1079. Schon, Isabel. **Recommended Books in Spanish for Children and Young Adults, 1991-1995.** Lanham, Md., Scarecrow, 1997. 327p. index. $42.50. ISBN 0-8108-3235-6.

This reference includes entries for 1,055 books in print (as of May 1996) that are recommended for Spanish-speaking children and young adults, or for those who wish to learn Spanish. Selected because of their quality of art and writing, presentation of material, and appeal to the intended audience, these are books that are intended to support the informational, educational, recreational, and personal needs of Spanish speakers from preschool through the 12th grade.

The book is arranged in sections, such as reference, nonfiction (which is divided into subjects following Dewey subject divisions), publishers' series, and fiction (including easy books and general fiction). Each book is listed under its main entry, with each title also translated into English. Complete bibliographic information, ISBN, price, and grade levels are given. Each entry includes a detailed annotation. Author, title, and subject indexes furnish additional access. Useful information is also provided in an appendix of dealers of books in Spanish.

This selection guide will be welcomed by libraries serving Spanish-speaking children and youth. It will be useful for selection of reading materials for beginning Spanish speakers.—**Dana McDougald**

Biography

1080. Something About the Author Autobiography Series, Volume 24. Gerard J. Senick and Joanna Brod, eds. Detroit, Gale, 1997. 387p. illus. index. $100.00. ISBN 0-7876-0117-9. ISSN 0885-6842.

This is the newest volume of the Autobiography Series (AS), which is an offshoot of the parent series, Something About the Author (SATA). Like its predecessors (see ARBA 92, entry 1125, and ARBA 91, entry 1119), it consists of autobiographical essays by well-known writers and illustrators of books for young people. Volume 24 features 15 authors. Each essay is approximately 10,000 words in length, illustrated by black-and-white photographs submitted by the writer. There are bibliographies of each author's full-length works and a useful cumulative index to the entire series, including references not only to the authors themselves but to major topics addressed in their essays.

The authors were given free rein in making their presentations. Geared to readers from upper-elementary through senior high school, the essays are well-written, relating experiences with which young people can identify. Of special interest are the authors' frequent discussions of the process of becoming a writer.

AS is recommended as a supplementary source to SATA, but it does not replace the more comprehensive, concise information found in the parent series. Although most useful as a set, that would be an expensive purchase for libraries with limited budgets. Individual volumes may be considered by institutions with a particular interest in one or more of the authors featured therein.—**Patricia A. Eskoz**

Handbooks and Yearbooks

1081. Booktalking the Award Winners: Children's Retrospective Volume. Joni Richards Bodart, ed. Bronx, N.Y., H. W. Wilson, 1997. 278p. index. $32.00pa. ISBN 0-8242-0901-X.

1082. Booktalking the Award Winners 3. Joni Richards Bodart, ed. Bronx, N.Y., H. W. Wilson, 1997. 179p. index. $32.00pa. ISBN 0-8242-0898-6. ISSN 1083-608X.

1083. Index to the Wilson Booktalking Series: A Guide to Talks from Nine Volumes. Joni Richards Bodart, ed. Bronx, N.Y., H. W. Wilson, 1997. 248p. (Booktalk! Series). $27.00pa. ISBN 0-8242-0905-2.

The name Joni Bodart and booktalking are nearly synonymous in the library world. These three volumes build on five titles in the Wilson Booktalk! series and five titles in the Booktalking the Award Winners series. The booktalks were written by a staff of experienced booktalkers, primarily librarians and teachers. They are complete and ready to use, with readers for both the inexperienced but motivated booktalker and for those for whom booktalking is an everyday experience. They can be used as they are written or can provide a frame of reference for those who would like to improve their own booktalking skills. The booktalks are brief, as they should be, ranging from three to five paragraphs, and provide a wide variety of styles and genres.

The *Index to the Wilson Booktalking Series* in an invaluable tool to provide access to nearly 3,000 talks on children's and young adult titles. The booktalks are indexed by title, author, age level of reader, booktalker, theme, and genre. All nine volumes in Bodart's booktalking series are currently in print and are included in this index. *Booktalking the Award Winners: Children's Retrospective Volume* contains more than 365 booktalks on award-winning children's books published before 1992. *Booktalking the Award Winners 3* contains approximately 200 booktalks on titles receiving awards from 1994 through 1995.

The volumes in this review, as well as previous and future volumes in both series, provide a valuable tool for teachers, reading specialists, and children or young adult librarians. The only drawback is their expense. The price of about $30 per volume will make it difficult for many libraries to afford.—**Lynda Welborn**

1084. Helbig, Alethea K., and Agnes Regan Perkins. **Myths and Hero Tales: A Cross-Cultural Guide to Literature for Children and Young Adults.** Westport, Conn., Greenwood Press, 1997. 288p. index. $49.95. ISBN 0-313-29935-8.

Compiled for use by both teachers and students, this work annotates 189 volumes, representing 1,455 retellings of myths and hero tales, published from 1985 through 1996. A majority of the entries are from Native American or African sources, although tales from most cultures are included. Short, critical reviews cover both single-tale books and multistory collections ranging from children's picture books to scholarly publications suitable for the high school reader. The guide has seven indexes that organize the works by writer (meaning the reteller or editor); story type; culture; characters, places, and other significant items; grade level; and illustrator. All entries are keyed to the review section.

A general index lists all works by individual authors who are annotated in the guide, the titles for each story within any collected works, and the cultural source for most individual tales. Preface matter defines and differentiates between myths and hero tales, and the "stories by type index" organizes the reviewed works in this manner. The authors provide a list of standard and classical books of myths and hero tales still available. The annotated entries summarize individual stories and either summarize or categorize all stories included in anthologies. These annotations evaluate the bibliographic and source information as well as the overall effect of the work, including illustrations. Particularly useful is the comparison of works when more than one book on the same subject is reviewed.

This bibliography should prove itself a valuable tool for teachers and librarians as well as for the serious student. Its extensive and complete coverage of works for children and young adults from kindergarten through high school provides concise and easily accessed information.—**Janet Hilbun**

1085. **Masterplots II: Juvenile and Young Adult Literature Series Supplement.** Frank N. Magill, ed. Pasadena, Calif., Salem Press, 1997. 3v. index. $275.00/set. ISBN 0-89356-916-X.

With well-written articles on 377 titles, the *Masterplots II: Juvenile and Young Adult Literature Series Supplement* is a welcome addition to an excellent series focusing on literature for children and young adults between the ages of 10 and 18. The supplement follows *Masterplots II: Juvenile and Young Adult Fiction Series* (see ARBA 92, entry 1128) and the *Masterplots II: Juvenile & Young Adult Biography Series* (see ARBA 95, entry 1150).

Titles included in this supplement represent a broad range of genres, periods, cultures, and countries of origin. For the first time, poetry collections (23 titles), plays (25 titles), short story collections (41 titles) and nonfiction books on the arts (4 titles), history (30 titles), sociology (4 titles), and science (22 titles) are included in addition to fiction. This work extends the Biography series by including 21 additional titles of autobiography and biography. Also represented are 53 Newbery Medal and Newbery Honor Books. Titles in the supplement are arranged alphabetically for easy access. Each article begins with informative ready-reference information about the title, followed by three subsections on "Form and Content," "Analysis," and "Critical Context." Four cumulative indexes in volume 3 allow the user to quickly locate articles in the series by title, author, subject, or name of an individual profiled in an autobiography or biography. A helpful annotated bibliography of general works about children's literature, selection aids, and further sources for finding information about some of the important children and young adult authors precedes the indexes. This work is highly recommended. [R: RBB, 15 Oct 97, pp. 428-29]
—**Elizabeth B. Miller**

Children's Literature

Bibliography

1086. **Choices for Young Readers: A Comprehensive Selection of the Best Children's Books....** [CD-ROM]. Evanston, Ill., John Gordon Burke, 1997. Minimum system requirements: IBM or compatible 386SX. 4x CD-ROM drive. MS-DOS 5.0. Windows 3.x. 8MB RAM. Hard disk space. Mouse. $89.50. ISBN 0-934272-49-2. ISSN 1089-8018.

This is a searchable annotated bibliography of 1,178 children's book titles previously included in volumes 1 through 3 of the reference series *Choices* (see ARBA 92, entry 330 for a review of volume 2). Both the CD-ROM and book format are resources for professionals and parents who encourage kindergarten through sixth grade reluctant readers through reader's advisory. The titles were published or in print between 1983 and 1996 (with slightly over half currently in print) and have been identified as the best books by consulting children's librarians. Like previous *Choices*, a database of book titles arranged alphabetically by author is provided, and each title indexed by subject, interest level, and reading level.

Excellent, sometimes exhaustive, descriptive annotations are also included, some with recommendations for curricular or individual use. Printed information included with the CD-ROM focuses primarily on installation and how to use the menus and mouse. Information on how the grade-based interest and reading level designations are derived and what criteria are used for title selection, which are included in the paper versions, are not provided in the CD-ROM. The inclusion of the phrases "Read Aloud," "Best Sellers," and "Group 2" as subject headings are confusing, because the definition of these terms is given only three sentences in the introductory material. Installation is straightforward; however, the search software and database itself must load initially, making for an unusually long wait before being able to search. Most functions execute far more slowly than librarians have come to expect. Also, the menu uses terms that might confuse those used to de facto standard CD-ROM terms, such as "search" or "start." For example, to move through the alphabetic list, one clicks a button marked "Segment," which moves the searcher to the beginning of the next letter display. To search for books by title, author, subject, or reading level, one selects "Filter," but the somewhat confusing three-step procedure to get out of filter mode makes such an option less attractive. The searcher cannot combine these search types, using Boolean logic or otherwise.

The bibliographic information and fine annotations will be useful for anyone involved with children and reading, as a supplement to other sources. However, the product lacks important information its paper predecessors have supplied, while failing to provide the value a CD-ROM format can add.—**Jennie Ver Steeg**

1087. **Kaleidoscope: A Multicultural Booklist for Grades K-8.** 2d ed. Rosalinda B. Barrera, Verlinda D. Thompson, and Mark Dressman, eds., with the Committee to Revise the Multicultural Booklist of the National Council of Teachers of English. Urbana, Ill., National Council of Teachers of English, 1997. 215p. illus. index. (NCTE Bibliography Series). $12.95pa. ISBN 0-8141-2541-7. ISSN 1051-4740.

The 1st edition of *Kaleidoscope: A Multicultural Booklist for Grades K-8* (see ARBA 96, entry 1182), is an annotated bibliography of over 400 titles that were published from 1990 to 1992. This 2d edition adheres to the selection criteria, arrangement, and purpose of the 1st, but provides annotated entries for about 600 titles that were published from 1993 to 1995. Both titles are intended as a resource for teachers.

Changes in this edition include the addition of a nonfiction section titled "Social and Environmental Issues." The "Potpourri of Resources" chapter of the 1st edition has been updated and expanded but is now an appendix called "Suggested Resources." The "Directory of Publishers" appendix of the 1st edition has been replaced with a "How to Order Books" appendix that lists addresses and telephone numbers for 8 distributors. The "Award-Winning Books" section of the 1st edition was an annotated list, subdivided by audience age, of the winners. It now explains what certain awards recognize and provides a list of the winners from 1993 to the most recent. Also included in this section is information on organizations that create recommended booklists and how to obtain copies. This publication continues to be a valuable resource for teachers, public and grade school libraries, and academic libraries with children's literature or education courses.—**Susanna Van Sant**

1088. Young, Philip H. **Children's Fiction Series: A Bibliography, 1850-1950.** Jefferson, N.C., McFarland, 1997. 301p. index. $55.00. ISBN 0-7864-0321-7.

Young has successfully achieved his purpose: to provide a comprehensive bibliography of fiction series written for children, published from the 1850s to the 1950s and beyond. Targeting book collectors, book dealers, librarians, and researchers, he has located and listed 1,243 series titles, a truly monumental task. The number of book titles within a series ranges from a single title to more than 200 titles. As an example, the Merriwell series of adventure books, published between 1901 and 1915, has 245 titles. Names well known to the senior population from when they were children include Oliver Optic, Edward Stratemeyer, and Horatio Alger. Readers of the ever-popular Bobbsey Twins series by Laura Lee Hope (a pseudonym of the Stratemeyer Syndicate), which first appeared in 1904, will learn that the 87th book was added in 1985.

Young's introduction to the bibliography presents an interesting historical overview of how and when series books developed as a genre of literature for children. It makes enjoyable reading for the casual reader as well as the professional. The bibliography, arranged alphabetically by series title, author (many of whom used pseudonyms), and publisher, is descriptive only; no annotations are provided. With a few exceptions, when publishing dates were available, books within each series are entered chronologically.

Author, illustrator, and title indexes are provided. Because the contents of the bibliography are targeted for the serious collector and researcher, a bibliography of the sources used to locate the information would have been of special interest.—**Margaret Denman-West**

Biography

1089. **Dictionary of Literary Biography Documentary Series: An Illustrated Chronicle. Volume Fourteen: Four Women Writers for Children, 1868-1918.** Caroline C. Hunt, ed. Detroit, Gale, 1996. 329p. illus. index. $140.00. ISBN 0-8103-9365-4.

The Documentary Series, a supplement to the Dictionary of Literary Biography series, is a bio-bibliographic guide to significant literary documents not easily accessible elsewhere. Volume 14 of the Documentary Series presents 4 North American women writers whose books, published in the late nineteenth to early twentieth centuries, achieved financial success in a profession dominated by men. The continuing popularity of Louisa May Alcott's classic *Little Women*, Frances Hodgson Burnett's *The Secret Garden*, and L. M. Montgomery's *Anne of Green Gables* is evidenced by recent versions at movie theaters, on Broadway, and on television. Will Gene Stratton Porter's *A Girl of the Limberlost* be next? The lives, careers, and writing styles of these four talented, independent, and creative women are quite different; nonetheless, the women were analogous in their refusal to let nineteenth-century society dictate their roles as women, impede their literary pursuits, or dim their creative enthusiasm.

The materials furnished reflect the personality of each writer and bring a broader understanding of the themes, characters, and settings of her books. The entries are an expansion of the biographical coverage in earlier Dictionary of Literary Biography volumes. Each section opens with a bibliography of the author's writings; a list of biographies; and, where appropriate, the location of archival materials. Essays on their lives and works, facsimiles of manuscripts, letters, reproductions of book covers, published reviews of their works, and other archival documents provide fascinating glimpses into the personal, as well as professional, lives of these four highly regarded writers. The intellectual and creative achievements of these women who paved the way for future authors of children's books attest to their worthiness of representation in the Documentary Series. Of concern are several mistakes that occur in date citations; however, they appear to be editorial oversights rather than author errors.—**Margaret Denman-West**

Handbooks and Yearbooks

1090. Ammon, Bette D., and Gale W. Sherman. **Worth a Thousand Words: An Annotated Guide to Picture Books for Older Readers.** Englewood, Colo., Libraries Unlimited, 1996. 210p. index. $26.50pa. ISBN 1-56308-390-6.

Picture books are one of the many staples of school libraries, but while there are good reviewing and selection tools to assist with their purchase, there are relatively few comprehensive guides to assist librarians and teachers with the effective use of those books. *Worth a Thousand Words* is an outstanding aid to the selection and use of such books for older readers. It demonstrates that picture books are not just for preschoolers and younger students. The 645 books that are listed and annotated are a fine representative example of the best of contemporary picture books, although there are a few omissions. As is often the case, older established authors and illustrators are more widely represented, and new and emerging contributors who are equally good, like E. B. Lewis, receive less attention. The books are arranged alphabetically by author, but there is an author/illustrator index as well as a detailed subject index for further assistance. Each entry includes the usual bibliographic data along with a brief descriptive annotation. The subjects used in the index, up to as many as a dozen for each book, are highlighted in a column parallel to the entry. Each entry is also accompanied by a list using 1 or more of 15 visual symbols that indicate the subject (e.g., history) or uses (e.g., read-aloud) for the book. Alongside the visual symbol are excellent suggestions about appropriate uses of the book, other books that may be of interest, and activities that students might undertake.

This is an important guide for the use of books that deserves to be in all school libraries and that librarians should encourage teachers to make widespread use of.—**Norman D. Stevens**

1091. Gillespie, John T., and Corinne J. Naden. **The Newbery Companion: Booktalk and Related Materials for Newbery Medal and Honor Books.** Englewood, Colo., Libraries Unlimited, 1996. 406p. index. $48.00. ISBN 1-56308-356-6.

The Newbery award honors the most distinguished children's book published in the United States during the year preceding the award. Runners-up to the award are known as Honor Books. This chronologically arranged companion gives information on the Newbery award-winners and Honor Books through 1996. For each winner, there is a paragraph that introduces the author, including material on the author's other literary works. In many cases, the origins of and inspiration behind the writing of the prize-winner are related.

Following the author information are a plot summary, which covers all key incidents and identifies all of the important characters; a section on themes and subjects, which identifies major themes covered in the story; a section that identifies passages suitable for reading aloud or retelling to stimulate interest in the book; a bibliography of related titles with brief annotations; a bibliography of sources for additional author information; and plot summaries for each of the year's Honor Books. Appendixes include a bibliography of works about John Newbery, the prize, its recipients, and the award-winning books, and author, title, and subject indexes.

Presented in a pleasing format with generous margins, clearly marked separations between sections, and boldface headings to introduce each section, this easy-to-use companion provides the kind of information that librarians and teachers need to present worthy literature to students. The detailed plot summaries of each award-winner and Honor Book would be enough to justify making this a part of any children's library collection; the additional information serves as an added bonus.—**Dana McDougald**

1092. **The Phoenix Award of the Children's Literature Association 1990-1994.** Alethea Helbig and Agnes Perkins, eds. Lanham, Md., Scarecrow, 1996. 282p. $45.00. ISBN 0-8108-3191-0.

The Phoenix Award of the Children's Literature Association is presented to an author or the author's estate for a children's book that was published 20 years earlier. The award-winning book must not have received any awards at the time of publication and may have fallen into obscurity since that time. Twenty years later, though, and with the new perspective of time, the book is considered to have high literary quality and lasting merit in today's society. This award notifies both the audience for, and the publishers of, children's literature that this book has lasting merit and should continue to be available. This title is a sequel to *The Phoenix Award of the Children's Literature Association 1985-1989* (Scarecrow Press, 1993), and covers the next five years that the award has been given by the Children's Literature Association.

The work is divided into five chapters, representing each year between 1990 and 1994. The chapters contain the acceptance speeches of the award-winning authors that were given at the annual banquets, papers by other authors about the winning books that were presented throughout the year, biographical sketches of the winning authors, and a listing of the honor books for that year, if any were named. Fashioned after the fabled bird, the phoenix, this award distinguishes noteworthy books that were previously published in the field of children's literature. These books deserve to be brought back into the limelight for the publishing industry, and back to the attention of scholars, librarians, and teachers working in the area of children's literature, so they can once again be both recognized and distinguished in the field. A book commemorating these titles is a necessary addition to any inclusive children's literature collection. [R: BR, May/June 97, p. 51]—**Bridget Volz**

1093. Thomas, Rebecca L. **Connecting Cultures: A Guide to Multicultural Literature for Children.** New Providence, N.J., R. R. Bowker/Reed Reference Publishing, 1996. 676p. index. $40.00. ISBN 0-8352-3760-5.

In recent years there has been a lot of interest in literature featuring the experiences of people from many cultures. *Connecting Cultures* is organized into six sections: annotated bibliography (the main part of the book), subject access, title index, illustrator index, culture index, and use-level index. The author consulted a number of standard sources such as *Children's Catalog*, *Elementary School Library Collection*, *Beyond Picture Books* as well as other similar titles listed in the preface. Entries in the annotated bibliography include standard bibliographic description, use-level symbols, cultural/regional designation, and brief annotations. Unfortunately, not all countries are represented in this professionally prepared collection; for example, European countries. Regarding Asia or Africa, the coverage is occasionally sketchy. All in all, this is a useful publication that should be of interest to all school and public libraries.—**Bohdan S. Wynar**

Young Adult Literature

Bibliography

1094. **Best Books for Young Adult Readers.** Stephen J. Calvert, ed. New Providence, N.J., R. R. Bowker/Reed Reference Publishing, 1997. 744p. index. $59.95. ISBN 0-8352-3832-6.

Bowker's The Best Book series was established to assist librarians and teachers in meeting both the curriculum-related and recreational reading needs of their students. The present volume covers recommended titles for readers in grades 7 through 12 and supplements the previously published titles *Best Books for Children* (5th ed.; see ARBA 95, entry 1130) and *Best Books for Junior High Readers* (see ARBA 92, entry 1116). The main part of the book is arranged by subject with three indexes—author, title, and subject/grade level. Annotations are brief and provide citations to published reviews in several standard sources. All in all, this well-balanced and professionally prepared volume should be in the hands of all juvenile libraries and most public libraries.—**Bohdan S. Wynar**

1095. **Books for You: An Annotated Booklist for Senior High.** 13th ed. Lois T. Stover and Stephanie F. Zenker, eds., with the Committee on the Senior High School Booklist of the National Council of Teachers of English. Urbana, Ill., National Council of Teachers of English, 1997. 451p. index. (NCTE Bibliography Series). $16.95pa. ISBN 0-8141-0368-5. ISSN 1051-4740.

A standard tool on school library and departmental reference shelves, this overview of the published works during the period 1994 to 1996 suited for secondary readers maintains the National Council of Teachers of English's criteria for print matter. Pleasantly laid out and easy to use, the book opens with a table of contents that divides the text into 40 categories of selections, totaling nearly 1,400 works of fiction and nonfiction, reference, self-help, and collections. Following a prefatory note by senior editor Michael Greer, the usual acknowledgments, and a foreword by Chris Crutcher, editors Stover and Zenker speak directly to young readers, suggesting how to locate works by favorite authors and how to apply the codes ER, WL, and MC, which stand for easy reading, world literature, and multicultural. Each chapter contains numbered entries followed by additional titles incorporated under other listings. Appendix A names award-winners in 14 listings of the Coretta Scott King Award and IRA Children's Book. The 2d appendix presents 12 pages of multicultural titles; the 3d follows the same procedure for 3 pages of titles from world literature. Appendix D names eight of the most common dealers: Econo-Clad, Houghton Mifflin, Penguin Books, Perma-Bound, Random House, Scholastic, Sundance, and William Morrow. The final 44 pages are the most helpful—indexes by author, subject, and title.

Weaknesses in this reference work are few. The editors could have included Internet addresses and advice on accessing online distributors and reviewers of young adult literature. The list of 57 committee members who made the choices for this work names 45 from Maryland. The fact that there is one lone southwesterner from Colorado and a sprinkling from Ohio leaves in doubt the fairness of the final call on titles to be included, especially works that address concerns and interests of readers along the Pacific Coast and in Hawaii. A final question that hovers over the work is the absence of explicit commentary on Random House's 1996 edition of Mark Twain's *The Adventures of Huckleberry Finn*, one of the most significant alterations in the high school canon in recent years.—**Mary Ellen Snodgrass**

1096. Herald, Diana Tixier. **Teen Genreflecting.** Englewood, Colo., Libraries Unlimited, 1997. 134p. index. $23.50. ISBN 1-56308-287-X.

Following the format established in *Genreflecting: A Guide to Reading Interests in Genre Fiction* (4th ed.; see ARBA 96, entry 1186), Herald has collected works popular with teen readers and grouped them for easy access in *Teen Genreflecting*. The purpose of this work is to provide a guide for those helping teen readers identify authors and titles of genre books in libraries and bookstores. This book is a springboard for reading guidance and possible collection development.

Seven genres are discussed—historical novels; science fiction; fantasy; mystery, suspense, and horror; adventure; contemporary; and romance. Within each of the classifications Herald adds subgenres, such as survival, war, technothriller and espionage, exploration, and heroism, under adventure. Each chapter follows the same pattern: an introduction to the genre, lists of titles under each division, genre lists from the Young Adult Library Services Association (YALSA), and Herald's favorites. Most titles are accompanied by a one- or two-sentence summary of the plot of the work. Little publication information (except for the YALSA lists) is provided. A combination author, title, and subject index that concludes the book aids in the cross-referencing of titles.

The usefulness of this work will be limited by the size of the library collection and the type of library. Small libraries may not have many of the titles. A librarian choosing to use *Teen Genreflecting* as a guide to collection development may find the lack of pricing information, publication dates, and evaluative criteria or literary criticism a problem. Public school media specialists who have specific audiences based on age and grade need to be aware that adult titles are mixed in with young adult titles. For example, Russell Banks's *Rule of the Bone* is listed alongside Felice Holman's *Slake's Limbo* in the homeless section.

As previously stated, Herald's book is a springboard, providing suggestions to help libraries reach and engage an audience that is often reluctant to read. This work serves as a guide, but not a replacement, to knowing the audience, community, and books before making recommendations.—**Michele Tyrrell**

1097. Matulka, Denise I. **Picture This: Picture Books for Young Adults: A Curriculum-Related Annotated Bibliography.** Westport, Conn., Greenwood Press, 1997. 267p. index. $39.95. ISBN 0-313-30182-4.

Matulka defines "young adults" as students between 8th and 12th grade, and "picture books" as having 100 to 3,000 words, plus strong use of illustrations in storytelling or presentation of information. Categories included are the arts, health, literature (longest list), mathematics, science, and social science (second longest). The selections are billed as curriculum-related, but the author does not include reviews of popular (and often excellent) series by publishers, such as Dorling-Kindersley, the Diagram Group, and Time-Life. Absent also are colorful travel, nature and wildlife books, and pricey "coffee-table books." The author says it is intended as a useful guide, not a critical study, and is designed for the library looking for quality materials. Most of the books mentioned can be used to spark interest, not provide core content; many can be used to introduce a unit, concept, or course, or to anchor a display. Matulka reviews each book individually in a descriptive paragraph, and suggests several related titles. She is sensitive to the traditional association of picture books with children, so suggestions for librarians and teachers wishing to promote them to older youth are provided. No prices are listed with entries; however, the work is thoroughly indexed.—**Edna M. Boardman**

1098. Spencer, Pam. **What Do Young Adults Read Next? A Reader's Guide to Fiction for Young Adults, Volume 2.** Detroit, Gale, 1997. 692p. index. $60.00. ISBN 0-8103-6449-2.

This is the 2d volume of *What Do Young Adults Read Next?* Originally published in 1994 (see ARBA 95, entry 1139), the 1st volume covered 1,500 titles published from 1988 to 1992. Volume 2 covers 1,169 titles published from 1993 to 1996. Contained within this volume and the 1st volume are "hundreds of current titles and titles from previous years" (p. vii). This explains why both volumes contain entries that are outside the stated dates of coverage.

The basic focus of this volume is the same as the original's, to answer readers' (parents, young adults, and librarians) questions concerning choosing books: following a certain series, choosing those on a certain subject, finding books in particular periods, following a character's story line, choosing books on a character's occupation, selecting books for certain ages or grades, following an author's works, finding other books on the same subject, choosing a geographic setting, and selecting award-winning books. The presentation is done in the form of 10 detailed indexes. This volume provides a particularly useful introduction that summarizes by year what was happening in the field of young adult literature in the areas of publishing, prices, trends, authors, censorship issues, awards, and notable books. The main section of the book is composed of entries arranged alphabetically by the author's last name and by title of the book. Included in each entry are subject headings, grade or age level, major characters, period, geographic locale, a descriptive summary, where reviews can be found, and other books by the same author. The 2d volume's entries feature different typefaces for author and title, and the centering of the headings makes them more readily identifiable.

Both volumes complement each other to present a fuller picture of an author's works and total subject coverage. There appears to be no duplication of entry titles between the two volumes. References to other titles contain books that were published outside the stated years of coverage, which does help in linking contemporary and older titles. This is certainly a worthy volume to be added to any collection that serves young adults or assists teachers and librarians in collection development and use of literature in the classroom.
—**Jan S. Squire**

1099. Totten, Herman L., Carolyn Garner, and Risa W. Brown. **Culturally Diverse Library Collections for Youth.** New York, Neal-Schuman, 1996. 220p. index. $35.00pa. ISBN 1-55570-141-8.

This work consists of mostly annotated bibliographic entries for biography, nonfiction, fiction, reference works, and videos concerned with ethnic Americans. The volume is divided into five sections, one each for African Americans, Native Americans, Hispanic Americans, Asian Americans, and a final section devoted to multiethnic materials. Each section is subdivided by genre. The descriptive annotations provide suggestions for integration of the material into curricula, and the bibliographic citation gives a recommended grade range. Coverage is sufficient, including both recent and older materials, although a majority of the books cited have been published within the past five years. The volume contains title, author, and subject indexes.

This resource should prove valuable for librarians seeking ethnically and culturally diverse acquisitions, as well as for teachers attempting to integrate such materials into their curricula. The guide will prove somewhat less useful for most scholarly purposes, given the emphasis upon recent primary materials, although the reference subsections do provide wide coverage of their respective fields.
—**Marcus P. Elmore**

Biography

1100. **Authors & Artists for Young Adults, Volume 20.** Thomas McMahon, ed. Detroit, Gale, 1997. 261p. illus. index. $79.00. ISBN 0-7876-1136-0.

1101. **Authors & Artists for Young Adults, Volume 21.** Thomas McMahon, ed. Detroit, Gale, 1997. 239p. illus. index. $79.00. ISBN 0-7876-1137-9.

This set of books is arranged in the same format as the Something About the Author (see ARBA 97, entries 926-930) and Contemporary Authors (see entries 1061–1063) series. The 20 to 25 authors in each volume are listed alphabetically, and entries include personal information, addresses, career data, awards and honors, writings, adaptations, and sidelights. Pictures of the authors and their work add interest to the entries. The information is written for young adults and is intended to entertain and inform them. The unique part of this series is the variety of artists, such as cartoonists, photographers, music composers, and playwrights, that are included. The people in these volumes range from children's authors, such as Louisa May Alcott, to young adult authors, such as Janet Bode, to adult authors, such as Dick Francis. However, it does not stop with just authors. Artists such as Kenneth Branagh, Mike Judge (creator of *Beavis and Butt-Head*), and Georgia O'Keeffe are also included.

The index in this set is similar to that in Something About the Author. However, it does not include references to the other Gale author series. In comparing 29 authors in *Authors & Artists for Young Adults* to the authors included in Something About the Author, only 9 were not included in the latter. Those 9 were actors, artists, and adult authors.

Authors & Artists for Young Adults offers the same great information found in other Gale publications. For those who serve young adults and do not own many biography sources, this set would be an excellent purchase. However, if the budget is tight and the library already owns Something About the Author and Contemporary Authors, *Authors & Artists* would be a nice purchase, but not a necessity.—**Suzanne Julian**

1102. Drew, Bernard A. **The 100 Most Popular Young Adult Authors: Biographical Sketches and Bibliographies.** rev. ed. Englewood, Colo., Libraries Unlimited, 1997. 531p. index. $55.00. ISBN 1-56308-615-8.

This collection covers 100 popular contemporary and classic young adult authors. Novelists are predominately American, with several British and other nationalities represented. It includes a few upper middle school authors, such as Judy Blume, Betsy Byars, and Phyllis Reynolds Naylor and several adult authors read by young adults—V. C. Andrews and Stephen King. The genres covered range from science fiction and historical fiction to recent horror authors like Christopher Pike and R. L. Stine.

The entries are listed alphabetically by surname of the writer. Each author's entry is listed with a genre type, birth date, date of death, birthplace, and most recognized works of fiction. The text includes a brief biography of the author; critical comments on his or her works from magazines, interviews, and other reference sources; a list of titles written; series information; and bibliographic information suggesting further reading about the author.

The entries represent an adequate list of authors read by the designated age group, but as a reference tool it is lacking in consistency and organization. The biographical information is too brief and lacking in substance. The writing careers of the individuals portrayed through interviews and critical sources are not organized chronologically and are difficult to follow. Criticism of specific works by the novelists is not mentioned uniformly or skillfully. The title contains some useful, concise information about the authors, but a more complete source such as the Something About the Author Autobiography series (see entry 1080) would be a more helpful tool.—**Marlene M. Kuhl**

Handbooks and Yearbooks

1103. Gillespie, John T., and Corinne J. Naden. **Characters in Young Adult Literature.** Detroit, Gale, 1997. 535p. illus. index. $60.00. ISBN 0-7876-0401-1.

This compendium of more than 2,000 characters from 232 works by 148 authors is a must for reviewers, school and public libraries, teachers, and college and university education departments. The text is illustrated with cover and movie art from 70 titles, for example, Gregory Peck in the role of Atticus Finch arguing his case before the jury in the entry for *To Kill a Mockingbird*. The layout is neatly marked with icons indicating plot and characters and includes birth and death dates of authors, genre and publication date of each work, and an extensive list of critical commentaries for additional data. Guide words and pagination are clearly marked. The preface explains the plan of each entry and of sequels, series, and trilogies. The text precedes a 57-page character and title index.

The appeal of this reference work begins with its manageable size and a colorful, intriguing cover, which duplicates the illustration on page 145, an action shot of Alexandre Dumas *pere*'s Three Musketeers dueling their challengers. The writing style of plot summaries and character studies is also upbeat and accessible to young researchers. Coverage is perhaps the major strength of this volume, which features standard works by J. R. R. Tolkien, Arthur Conan Doyle, Louisa May Alcott, and Hermann Hesse as well as significant young adult favorites by Cynthia Rylant, Gary Paulsen, Lois Lowry, Anne Rice, Avi, and Scott O'Dell. Science fiction buffs will find Jules Verne, Ursula K. Le Guin, H. G. Wells, Madeleine L'Engle, and Isaac Asimov. Nonwhite authors include Amy Tan, Walter Dean Myers, Alice Walker, Alice Childress, Toni Morrison, and Ernest Gaines. All in all, this volume deserves attention from the book world.—**Mary Ellen Snodgrass**

1104. **Writers for Young Adults.** Ted Hipple, ed. New York, Scribner's/Simon & Schuster Macmillan, 1997. 3v. illus. index. $235.00/set. ISBN 0-684-80474-3.

This 3-volume set is a great addition to secondary school libraries and the young adult section of public libraries, especially those that cannot afford Gale's *Authors & Artists for Young Adults* (see entries 1100 and 1101). Robert Cormier's foreword should be read. Signed articles cover 129 classical and contemporary authors, with the emphasis on the latter category. Teachers and students looking for background information will vie to use this set. It is also a browser's delight.

Each article includes the author's picture or illustrations, biographical information, critiques or interpretations of the author's important books, a selected bibliography of the author's works, works about the author, and how to contact the author. Many articles include a note indicating quotations are from current correspondence with the writer. Even though the articles provide typical information about the authors, each article is slightly different. This gives each entry a unique feel and lets the author discussed shine. The articles are written with young adults in mind.

The easy-to-read page layout includes outside margins used for definitions, brief explanations, suggestions for other authors to read who write in a similar vein, and so on. The list of contributors gives affiliations and articles written. The category index lists titles alphabetically by genre and theme; it certainly aids in reading list preparations. The general index lists authors and titles. In typical Scribner's fashion, the authors' names are listed on the spine of the book. There is a similar list on the back cover. These user-friendly additions ensure no fumbling with a table of contents, although the one for this set is well laid out. This set will definitely be requested at report-writing time. [R: RBB, 15 Oct 97, p. 430]—**Esther R. Sinofsky**

DRAMA

1105. Carpenter, Charles A. **Modern Drama Scholarship and Criticism 1981-1990: An International Bibliography.** Toronto and Buffalo, N.Y., with *Modern Drama*, University of Toronto Press, 1997. 632p. index. $90.00. ISBN 0-8020-0914-X.

The successor to *Modern Drama Scholarship and Criticism 1966-1980* (see ARBA 87, entry 1109), this massive new work will be widely used by teachers and students alike. It is sensibly organized in such familiar categories as "World Drama," "American Drama," "Hispanic Drama," "African and West Indian Drama," and "Asian Drama." The subcategories are also familiar—for example, under the "Hispanic" heading one finds Spanish, Portuguese, Brazilian, and Spanish-American drama. Also, there are "intellectual" categories, such as "Feminism," "Political Drama," and "Contemporary Theory." Thus, although the volume contains literally thousands of entries, it is relatively easy to find one's way around. Even though space does not permit Carpenter to annotate the entries, he offers instead an inclusiveness not often found in scholarly guides of this sort. However, it should be noted that the selections in this work are limited to material in Roman-alphabet languages in order to keep the project to a manageable size in one volume.

Virtually all the important playwrights of the modern period are included, along with many lesser-known artists who are worth knowing about, such as, in the Swedish section, Kjell Abel and Victoria Benedictsson next to such giants as August Strindberg and Ingmar Bergman. In the U.S. section, one finds Ted Shine and John Steppling as well as Tennessee Williams and Wendy Wasserstein. Carpenter tries to strike a reasonable balance between the major figures and the minor ones, without going too far into obscure writers or those who have had only a brief, flash-in-the-pan kind of fame. It seems clear that this long bibliography is predicated on careful consideration and seasoned literary judgment. Carpenter maintains a flexibility in his choices; thus, a number of nondramatic authors are included—people like Robert Penn Warren and John Steinbeck, novelists who have also proven themselves in the field of drama. The overall result of this judicious choosing is a 632-page research tool that is comprehensive without quite being exhaustive.

To anyone browsing Carpenter's project, a significant question automatically comes up: Why would a researcher need this large book of lists, when the *MLA International Bibliography* already does the job? The answer, according to Carpenter, is that his own lists have a "much greater comprehensiveness" and "somewhat greater selectivity" than the traditional MLA listings. Carpenter also points out that his volume, unlike the MLA, includes parts of "composite books" (even though the MLA does include "Festschriften"—collections of essays by various authors). Summing up, Carpenter declares that his bibliographies include "several thousand book titles that MLA does not include." He also says that, for example, of 156 books on Bertolt Brecht that he includes, only 33 are listed in the MLA annuals. Regarding periodicals, he states that of the "more than 1400" that he examined, approximately 30 percent are not on the MLA list. Carpenter suggests that much of the success of his searches for bibliographic material is because of TELNET, which of course is a branch of the Internet. [R: C&RL, Sept 97, p. 479]—**Peter Thorpe**

1106. Peterson, Jane T., and Suzanne Bennett. **Women Playwrights of Diversity: A Bio-bibliographical Sourcebook.** Westport, Conn., Greenwood Press, 1997. 399p. index. $79.50. ISBN 0-313-29179-9.

This work includes more than 100 women playwrights writing from and about the ethnic and cultural diversity in the United States in the 1990s, encompassing African American, Asian American, Latina, and lesbian/bisexual writers, both established and emerging. The sourcebook was produced as a resource for theater practitioners and teachers of dramatic literature and women's studies courses. The works included here have been written since 1970. Recommendations for inclusion were from community theater groups, drama critics, and selected scholars and teachers of marginalized women playwrights. The criteria for selection were existing production records of the writers and the potential for production on and off Broadway. Production values, such as appeal to a diverse audience; audience response to characters; the writer's understanding of the stage; the attraction of the works by directors, designers, and actors; the worth of the dramatic piece; and the piece's distinctive voice were considered in the selection process. The authors were particularly drawn to plays that would have an attraction for performance by other than the original creators. The list of playwrights is a selective one and thus does not include all ethnic and lesbian writers of import today, but it is representative of a broad and growing diversity in theater productions.

The volume includes an introduction by Bennett, followed by critical essays, the first on African American women playwrights by Sydne Mahone; the second on Asian American women playwrights by Chiori Miyagawa; the third on Latina drama by Tiffany Ana Lopez; and the fourth on lesbian playwrights by Jill Dolan. The major section of the book is devoted to separate entries about each playwright, arranged in alphabetic order by dramatist's surname. The entries include a brief biographical note, descriptions of important plays, a selected production history of each work, grants and awards won by the playwright, and a selected bibliography of critical works. Some of the playwrights included are Sydne Mahone, who wrote *for colored girls*; Wakako Yamauchi, who wrote *And the Soul Shall Dance*; Caridad Svich, who wrote *Any Place but Here*; and Jane Chambers, who wrote *Quintessential Image*.

There are 4 appendixes to the volume, the 1st with listings of key playwrights' names by cultural/ethnic grouping, the 2d a list of additional playwrights by the same cultural/ethnic group; the 3d a list of nominators associated with theaters from San Francisco to New York; and the last a list of nominators' names. A brief but important selected bibliography for further research is provided. It includes general reference works, collections of plays, and critical works. An index, arranged alphabetically by dramatist and title of work, leads back to the entries with page numbers in bold typeface referring to main entries.

The introduction, the essays, and the entries are well written and provocative, leading one to a greater understanding of the impact and importance of women dramatists of color and varying sexual orientation. Much of the information presented is difficult to identify and locate in traditional reference resources, thereby bringing new works to light and highlighting many others that have or will have a major impact on valuing cultural and ethnic diversity in the theater. [R: LJ, 1 April 97, p. 84]—**Maureen Pastine**

ESSAYS

1107. **Encyclopedia of the Essay.** Tracy Chevalier, ed. Chicago, Fitzroy Dearborn, 1997. 1002p. index. $125.00. ISBN 1-884965-30-3.

Though the genre may be somewhat secondary from a literary point of view, this encyclopedic treatment of it is certainly not. This impressive collection of essays on the "essay" is the collaborative effort of scholars worldwide. Defined broadly as "nonfictional prose texts," the essays fall into four categories: generic, based on the variety of the form; national, addressing major traditions and classical influences (British, French, German, Chinese, Japanese); and individual, on practitioners of the genre. The fourth group covers important periodicals that have influenced the market for essay writing, such as the *Edinburgh Review*, *Revue des deux mondes*, and the *New Yorker*. A few entries discuss essays of singular importance, including some on literary theory, such as Horace's *The Poetic Art*. Separate entries testify to the flexibility of the form, which may be autobiographical, critical, historical, sociological, or humorous. Other expressions appear in the essay film, character sketch, pamphlet, meditation, and satire.

Biographical entries represent not only literary figures but essayists in other disciplines. Together with the entry on the medical essay is one on the British physician Oliver Sacks. The religious essay is complemented by entries on Thomas Merton and Simone Weil. These examples merely hint at the richness of this collection. Geographic coverage is worldwide, represented by the scholars themselves and by the limitations of the genre in particular literatures. Development of the form is traced from classic literatures to the contemporary. More women essayists are included from the modern period as they gained prominence in the genre. Based on the kind of entry, there are references to selected writings, editions, bibliographies, biographical sketches, and suggestions for further reading.

A substantive reference, this work is highly recommended for all collections with a serious interest in literature.—**Bernice Bergup**

FICTION

General Works

1108. Adelman, Irving, and Rita Dworkin. **The Contemporary Novel: A Checklist of Critical Literature on the English Language Novel Since 1945.** 2d ed. Lanham, Md., Scarecrow, 1997. 666p. $125.00. ISBN 0-8108-3103-1.

Even the "clickeratti" generation will be impressed with the prodigious efforts of Dworkin, former Head Adult Services Librarian and Adelman, Head Reference Librarian at East Meadow Public Library, Long Island New York. Their bibliographic citation listing of critical literature on contemporary English-language novels published since 1945 is so comprehensive that online database searchers would have to log on to Arts and Humanities Citation Index, Humanities Index, Humanities Abstracts, MLA Bibliography, ArticlesFirst, and World Cat just to retrieve the degree of inclusion in this single-volume work.

It is a significant improvement over the 1st edition published in 1972 (see ARBA 73, entry 1246), which covered only contemporary British and U.S. authors, because it features criticism to works by writers in English anywhere in the world. An examination of the alphabetized listing of approximately 600 authors yielded, for example, Chinua Achebe, Arthur Koestler, Nadine Gordimer, Ngugi Wa Thiong'O (formerly James Ngugi), Alice Munro, V. S. Naipaul, and Ezekiel Mphahlele.

The authors have collected this literary criticism through 1982. More than 700 literary criticism journals, newsletters, books, and series were consulted to produce a comprehensive listing of criticism for these authors. Entries are arranged alphabetically by author with a listing of general criticism followed by literary criticism citations for individual novels. An abbreviations list prefaces the entries and a list of sources consulted concludes the text. This essential humanities reference source will be used by college preparatory high school, public, and academic libraries. It is especially helpful to users who need to research more than excerpted criticism in, for example, Gale's Contemporary Literary Criticism series.

With only a few exceptions, the authors have succeeded admirably in listing authors whose works have contributed to the literary canon. There are, however, several outstanding omissions. The absence of authors Salman Rushdie, Tom Wolfe, Ray Bradbury, Robert Cormier, and Isaac Asimov is somewhat disconcerting. In the case of Salman Rushdie, the literary criticism, especially for *Midnight's Children* (1980), is considerable. Yet Stephen King and Joseph Wambaugh, whose works lie clearly in the popular fiction genre, are included. Author Ray Bradbury, whose works are required reading in many secondary and college English curricula, is also absent; however, Kurt Vonnegut is not.

These omissions are indeed minuscule when this outstanding contribution to the field of literary criticism is considered as a whole. It is unsurpassed in its breadth and depth of scope. Consider this superb resource a mandatory purchase for all high school, public, and academic library collections.—**Kathleen W. Craver**

1109. **Novels for Students, Volume 1: Presenting Analysis, Context, and Criticism on Commonly Studied Novels.** Diane Telgen, ed. Detroit, Gale, 1997. 350p. illus. maps. index. $55.00. ISBN 0-7876-1686-9.

1110. **Novels for Students, Volume 2: Presenting Analysis, Context, and Criticism on Commonly Studied Novels.** Diane Telgen, ed. Detroit, Gale, 1997. 350p. illus. maps. index. $55.00. ISBN 0-7876-1687-7.

Intended for high school students, undergraduates, and teachers, this work can also be used by anyone seeking further information on selected novels. Various sources on teaching literature and analyses of course curricula were used to obtain the titles, which include a mixture of classics and contemporary works. Each 20-page entry includes an introduction, an author biography, a plot summary, character descriptions, themes, style, historical context of the work, a critical overview, and three critical essays. Rounding out the entries are mentions of media adaptations, topics for further study, "Compare and Contrast" and "What Do I Read Next?" sections, and a list of books for further study. Other useful features include a literary chronology, a subject/theme index, and cumulative indexes covering authors, titles, nationalities, and ethnicities.

The biographical information is more detailed than that found in *Something About the Author* (see entry 1080) and *Contemporary Authors* (see entries 1061-1063). Although *Twentieth Century Literary Criticism* (see ARBA 97, entries 919, 920, 921, and 922) is more sophisticated, it groups criticism of the major works of an author together, thus offering less coverage on each book. The advantage of this reference work is that by concentrating on one book per entry, it can provide a comprehensive overview of each work, its author, and its place in literature in an inviting format that encourages further research. A minor quibble concerns the distracting typeface used for the headings. At $55 these works will be a nice addition to public and academic reference collections.—**January Adams**

1111. Saar, Doreen Alvarez, and Mary Anne Schofield. **Eighteenth-Century Anglo-American Women Novelists: A Critical Reference Guide.** New York, G. K. Hall/Simon & Schuster Macmillan, 1996. 664p. index. (A Critical Reference Guide). $65.00. ISBN 0-8161-9085-2.

This annotated bibliography presents a comprehensive overview of the critical work that has been done in this century on eighteenth-century women novelists. A useful introduction summarizes the lack of critical interest in these writers before the 1970s and the growing attention paid to them by feminist critics since then. More than half of the alphabetically arranged entries were written by the two authors. Because the focus is on criticism, each entry lists the writer's novels but omits biographical information beyond dates of birth and death. A chronological, briefly annotated bibliography of critical work published between 1900 and 1992 follows. Works not seen by the authors or in a foreign language are marked. The list is intended to be complete, and a spot check uncovered no important omissions or errors.

However, the principles by which these 35 authors were chosen are not entirely clear. Except for two or three who spent part of their lives in the United States, they are unquestionably British, not "Anglo-American." Some are "quasi-canonical" writers like Frances Burney others are little known. Common sense apparently dictated the complete omission of Jane Austen, the extensive writing about her being too overwhelming, and the limitation of Mary Wollstonecraft criticism to that published since 1976, when Janet Todd's excellent bibliography ended. Yet it is confusing to learn that some writers were selected because they "worked in a variety of genres" when only their novels are listed and then to find their drama or poetry is mentioned in the criticism.

Nevertheless, researchers and advanced students will find this bibliography both useful and accurate. University libraries with collections of feminist and eighteenth-century literature will wish to purchase it.
—**Lynn F. Williams**

Crime and Mystery

1112. Green, Joseph, and Jim Finch. **Sleuths, Sidekicks, and Stooges: An Annotated Bibliography of Detectives, Their Assistants....** Brookfield, Vt., Scolar Press/Ashgate Publishing, 1997. 874p. $110.95. ISBN 1-85928-192-3.

At nearly 8,000 entries, *Sleuths, Sidekicks, and Stooges* contains significantly more entries than would a cumulation of *Trouble Is Their Business: Private Eyes in Fiction, Film and Television, 1927-1988* (see ARBA 91, entry 930); *Female Detectives in American Novels* (see ARBA 94, entry 1208); *Heroines: A Bibliography of Women Series Characters in Mystery, Espionage, Action, Science Fiction, Fantasy, Horror, Western, Romance, and Juvenile Novels* (see ARBA 91, entry 1129); and *Silk Stalkings: When Women Write of Murder* (see ARBA 90, entry 1107). Despite its monumental size, *Sleuths, Sidekicks, and Stooges* is simple in concept, being essentially a dictionary with entries on the detectives, their sidekicks, and rivals that appeared in English and American fiction published between 1795 and 1995. Unfortunately, the book is often muddled in presentation and is not particularly reliable as a reference work.

The majority of the volume is alphabetic by detective: A prose description of the character is given, as are his/her nationality, sex, location of operations, and professional status. Following this description, the name(s) of the sidekick(s) and stooge(s) are given, occasionally accompanied by a description of their relationship to the detective. Next, the author's name and a brief biography are provided; the names and biographies of other authors who have used the same character are also given. Other bylines of the primary author are listed, with reference made to other detectives created by that author. In addition, a "citation record" lists the number of the detective's book appearances, and the title, publisher, and year of publication of the first and last books in which the detective appeared are noted, occasionally accompanied by an explanatory narrative. Teams and multiple detectives are listed under the detective's name for which the most biographical information can be given; numerous cross-references are provided. The volume concludes with author/character, book title/character, and stooge/character indexes, and there are appendixes listing and annotating the sources from which Green and Finch derived their information, an annotated list of discrepancies among these sources, and a list of Sherlock Holmes parodies.

Although pages are numbered, letter-tabbed, and have the name of the detective given in the upper right-hand corner, the layout of entries is frequently unclear, and their arrangement is often confusing and repetitive. One may take Green and Finch to task for equating dime novels and pulp magazines and for demonstrating knowledge of neither. The cross-referencing system is often frustrating: A user looking at James Bond finds an entry for Robert Markham, author of a Bond pastiche, and is referenced to Peter Furneaux, and only in Furneaux's entry can it be learned that Markham was a pseudonym used by Kingsley Amis. Worst of all, there are numerous egregious errors: Jacques Futrelle's *The Diamond Master* does not feature The Thinking Machine; Nevada Alvarado, sidekick to Cleve Adams's Violet McDade, is not a Hispanic male; Chester Himes did not graduate from Ohio State University; T. S. Stribling's Henry Poggioli is a character in 36 short stories, not 20; Carroll John Daly's Race Williams did not surface in 1927, nor was "he fairly moderate in his activities and not widely imitated"; the correct identity of The Shadow is not revealed; Doc Savage's full name is not given (nor are the names of his sidekicks); Hannibal Lecter appears in more than one novel by Thomas Harris; and so forth.

None of this is to say that *Sleuths, Sidekicks, and Stooges* cannot be used. However, too often it cannot be used with confidence or relied upon to provide valid data.—**Richard Bleiler**

1113. Stilwell, Steven A. **What Mystery Do I Read Next? A Reader's Guide to Recent Mystery Fiction.** Detroit, Gale, 1997. 545p. index. $69.00. ISBN 0-7876-1592-7.

This volume is not an original guide but the cumulation of the lists that appeared in the first seven editions of Gale's annual *What Do I Read Next?* Like its parent publication, *What Mystery Do I Read Next?* attempts to serve as a reader's adviser, "pointing the way to the best fiction in the genre published in the 1990s." The volume begins with lists of the winners (since 1990) of the Edgar Allan Poe Awards, the Shamus Awards, the Agatha Awards, the Anthony Awards, and the Macavity Awards; the entries in these lists are, alas, segregated from the contents of the volume.

The 1,799 entries in *What Mystery Do I Read Next?* are arranged alphabetically by author. Each entry is separately numbered, and the data presented include the book's title, place of publication, publisher, date of publication, the series name (if any), the story type within the genre, the names and descriptions of up to three characters in the work, the period of the story, the locale, a brief (three or four sentences) plot summary, and a list of up to five books that use similar themes. Pseudonyms and co-authors are identified. A series of indexes provide access to the stories by series name, period, geographic setting, story type, character name, character description, author, and title. It should be mentioned that the index to story type uses some 16 different genres, ranging from "action/adventure" to "traditional" to classify its fiction; that the index to character description includes occupation (actress, librarian, publisher, and so on) as well as a plot function (e.g., counselor, cowboy, criminal); and that the index to geographic location offers reference not only to countries and continents but also to specific cities and even to imaginary and fictional places.

There is much to criticize here. The public library focus of the *What Do I Read Next?* family makes this volume perhaps unduly positive in its descriptions and unnecessarily chatty in the presentation of data. Similarly, the limitations of the series entails that only works published after 1990 are described, making the lists less comprehensive than those found in such works as Willetta Heising's *Detecting Women 2* (see ARBA 97, entry 947) and *Detecting Men* (Purple Moon, 1997). Furthermore, books that neither feature detectives nor contain mysteries (e.g., the techno-thrillers of Tom Clancy) are occasionally described, and works that should have been referenced (e.g., Sharyn McCrumb's 1988 *Bimbos of the Death Sun*) have been ignored. Finally, there has not been sufficient proofreading: Readers curious to find mysteries set in the Deep South will be partially disappointed, for the section devoted to Alabama has been omitted from the geographic index. Public and academic libraries that do not hold the works of Heising will find *What Mystery Do I Read Next?* generally useful, but it is best used in conjunction with other works, for it is not the last word on its subject. [R: LJ, 1 April 97, p. 86]—**Richard Bleiler**

Historical Fiction

1114. VanMeter, Vandelia L. **America in Historical Fiction: A Bibliographic Guide.** Englewood, Colo., Libraries Unlimited, 1997. 280p. index. $38.50. ISBN 1-56308-496-1.

Directed toward secondary students or adults who are seeking fiction dealing with the history of the United States, this book is also useful to media specialists who are building historical fiction collections. The author sought to support the National Standards for United States History and specifically addressed the need to more fully understand society by looking at its social history, which includes economic, religious, cultural, and political changes affecting social life.

The 1,168 titles listed here are divided into 8 chronological sections, a section on epic novels, and additional titles arranged by state. The coverage begins with Christopher Columbus's voyage and concludes in 1995. Selection criteria required the selected books to be in print, to be well written and well researched, to support the study of history, and to encourage historical understanding. No story collections are included. Each entry provides normal bibliographic information: author, title, original publisher and date, current publisher and date, ISBN, and cost. Dates, ISBN, and cost of 2d editions are given, as are notes if 3 or more editions are available in print. Annotations give the period, subject, location, and any known research base. Titles with more complicated plots are identified for mature readers; titles with a lower reading level and less complicated plots are suggested for younger readers. Prequels and sequels are also noted. The term *lengthy* is used to distinguish titles exceeding 600 pages. The additional titles section includes all basic bibliographic information for each entry, time of setting, and appropriate subject headings, but no annotations. All headings are compatible with those in the *Sears List of Subject Headings* (14th ed.; see ARBA 92, entry 585). More than 500 entries have the subject heading of "Social Life and Customs." The three indexes, by author, title, and subject, are thorough and include place of primary action, regional names, events, people, and broad subjects.

It is evident that much research was completed to include both valuable older titles and quality recent ones. There is an equitable amount of entries for each section and each state. *America in Historical Fiction* will be useful for a reading guide and for collection development.—**Elaine Ezell**

Romances

1115. Jaegly, Peggy J. **Romantic Hearts: A Personal Reference for Romance Readers.** 3d ed. Lanham, Md., Scarecrow, 1997. 915p. illus. index. $27.95pa. ISBN 1-57886-000-8.

More useful as a reader's checklist than a reference book, *Romantic Hearts* has three major sections: author profiles, an author pseudonym index, and author/title entries. There are only 70 profiles, in contrast to the many hundreds of authors listed in the author/title section. Some well-known past and present authors for whom biographical information is readily available, such as Georgette Heyer and Diana Gabaldon, are not profiled. Jaegly does not state criteria for inclusion. Many entries are written in the first person by the authors themselves, who talk about their personal lives, how they develop ideas for stories, and professional achievements. Profiles are two pages in length, including a full-page black-and-white photograph for most.

Actual names appear in bold in the pseudonym index, followed by pseudonyms used; pseudonym cross-references are italicized. Some names in the pseudonym index are not found in the author/title section (e.g., Elizabeth Bolton appears under only one of her seven pseudonyms there). The reason for the discrepancy is not stated. Authors and pseudonyms in the author/title index are followed by book titles, which are "usually listed in chronological order." More than 10,000 titles are listed. Publisher or publisher series (e.g., Harlequin Shadows), series number, and publication dates are provided for some, but not all, titles. It is unclear whether presence or lack of a publisher or date indicates in-print status. Reissued titles, such as Heyer paperbacks published by HarperCollins in the 1990s, appear at the end of the "chronological" list, which is misleading.

For more authoritative bio-bibliographic information for the more established writers, first try *Twentieth-Century Romance and Historical Writers* (see ARBA 95, entry 1163). For a reader's advisory on romantic subgenres (e.g., Gothic, Regency) or the most highly regarded authors, turn to *Genreflecting* (see ARBA 96, entry 1186); although *Romantic Hearts* includes titles from all sub-genres, it has no index to them by type. Public libraries and avid romance readers may want to purchase this book for its extensive lists of titles by author, which would be difficult to find anywhere else.—**Deborah V. Rollins**

Science Fiction, Fantasy, and Horror

1116. **The Encyclopedia of Fantasy.** John Clute, John Grant, and others, eds. New York, St. Martin's Press, 1997. 1049p. $75.00. ISBN 0-312-15897-1.

This outstanding reference volume is designed as a sibling to the critically acclaimed *The Encyclopedia of Science Fiction*, which John Clute and Peter Nicholls edited in 1993 (see ARBA 94, entry 1211). Using a "fuzzy set" definition of fantasy that includes all narratives involving impossibility, it covers everything from myths and movies. The encyclopedia's alphabetically arranged entries discuss genres, motifs, archetypes, traditional figures, authors, and more. Entries concentrate on achievements since the final decades of the eighteenth century. Refreshingly, they include illuminating discussions of children's books and authors. Cross-references appear both in context and at the end of entries. Many entries also conclude with a list of works providing additional information.

Most entries are thorough and informative. Author entries, for example, provide biographical information, descriptions of notable publications, and critical estimates of the author's achievement. Entries on motifs define the motif, explain its implications, and trace its uses throughout history. The brisk writing will lure most readers into following cross-references, providing hours of entertainment and many unexpected discoveries. Not the least of these is the critical vocabulary coined by the editors: Such terms as *polders* ("enclaves of toughened reality"), a metaphor derived from a Dutch term for land reclaimed by dikes, are useful critical instruments.

Naturally, a work of this scope has some limitations. Unlike the entry on Australian fantasy, for example, the discussion of Canadian fantasy neglects to mention any significant works for children. Nevertheless, this is one of the most important literary reference works published in the past decade. For a wide range of scholars and students, the encyclopedia will provide a useful starting point for research; for librarians, teachers, fans of fantasy, and general readers, it will be an indispensable source of information. This superb work is an essential purchase for all libraries.—**Raymond E. Jones**

1117. **Science Fiction and Fantasy Reference Index 1992-1995: An International Subject and Author Index to History and Criticism.** Hal W. Hall, ed. Englewood, Colo., Libraries Unlimited, 1997. 503p. $75.00. ISBN 1-56308-527-5.

This volume, the 3d in a series that began with *Science Fiction and Fantasy Reference Index, 1878-1985* (see ARBA 88, entry 1152) and continued with *Science Fiction and Fantasy Reference Index, 1985-1991* (see ARBA 94, entry 1213), cites some 10,627 books, chapters, dissertations, and newspaper and journal articles published between 1992 and 1995 that study aspects of science fiction, fantasy, and what Hall's preface refers to as the "related genres." These genres include horror fiction and utopian fiction. Despite its size, the arrangement of the *Reference Index* is simple: A subject index offers access by assigned subject headings, and an author index offers access by the authors and co-authors of the books, articles, and essays. Newspaper bylines, however, are not indexed by author. The majority of the citations are to English-language publications.

The *Reference Index* is easy to use; it is also, at times, oddly frustrating. Cross-references are not always provided. There are no linkages, for example, between the works of Michael Burgess and Robert Reginald, although Hall certainly knows that these names refer to the same man. Furthermore, the subject headings are not always usefully applied. Hall uses "Indians, American," to describe the works studying Native Americans in science fiction, but Shawn Reno's 1995 "The Zuni Indian Tribe: A Model for *Stranger in a Strange Land*'s Martian Culture" is indexed under the word "influence" and under the heading of "Zuni Indians"; it does not appear under "Indians, American."

None of this is to say that the index cannot be used—and it should be used—for Hall has made accessible an enormous number of publications that are elsewhere unindexed or at best poorly indexed. His efforts will save serious researchers enormous amounts of time and energy. This work belongs in all libraries holding the first two volumes.—**Richard Bleiler**

Short Stories

1118. Aycock, Wendell M. **Twentieth-Century Short Story Explication: New Series. Volume III: 1993-1994.** North Haven, Conn., Shoe String Press, 1997. 347p. index. $49.50. ISBN 0-208-02419-0.

This is a handy tool for those who need to research short stories. Arranged by author name, each story explicated is listed separately, with the citations to the explications listed alphabetically by the author's last name. Aycock has also provided checklists of the books and journals used in the project, which makes it easier to check the brief citations that are listed. Interestingly, one cannot help but notice the number of "Instructor's Manual" citations, meaning that collections and compilations designed for classroom use are included. This may mean more, ultimately, for faculty than for students, who would probably have a hard time laying hands on such a tome. Past and present stories and authors are featured, although the volume seems slanted toward the "canonical" authors and stays away from more cutting-edge writers. This exclusion may not be an editorial choice as much as a statement of the nature of the publishing business.
—**Bob Craigmile**

1119. Evans, Robert C., Anne C. Little, and Barbara Wiedemann. **Short Fiction: A Critical Companion.** West Cornwall, Conn., Locust Hill Press, 1997. 320p. index. $50.00. ISBN 0-933951-73-6.

This book serves two purposes: It is designed as an aid for the student faced with the "read and discuss" assignment as well as for general readers seeking greater dimension in their reading. Using a scheme devised by M. H. Abrams, a literary theorist, the first section of the work analyzes literary theories and forms of criticism, breaking them into the composite parts common to them all. It presents a discussion of various theories schematically according to writer, text, audience, "reality," and critic, and ranges from Aristotelian and Platonic ideas through formalism, psychoanalytic theory, Marxism, structuralism, feminism, deconstructionism, multiculturalism, and the new historicism. A vast array of literary commentary and widespread interpretations of life and letters are represented.

The practical aspect of the book is the "Companion," which takes familiar short stories, such as those by Ernest Hemingway and William Faulkner, as well as those by current authors, and presents critical analyses of each. This is followed by the abbreviation of the most closely tied critical approach as discussed in the introduction. Thus, "The Lottery" by Shirley Jackson is discussed in critical approaches varying from feminist to Marxist to thematic criticism. The final section takes a short story example and highlights sentences and discusses the work from a number of critical points of view. There are indexes, not exhaustive but substantive, of critical approaches, topics, and critics. The references to the stories are designated by the first three letters of the author's name and then sequential numbering.

This book should be useful in the teaching of literary theory, the interpretation of classic works, and the development of the reader's own ideas and interpretations. It should be used as a resource by students, not as a replacement for forming their own critical ideas.—**Paula Frosch**

1120. **Short Stories for Students, Volume 1: Presenting Analysis, Context, and Criticism on Commonly Studied Short Stories.** Kathleen Wilson, ed. Detroit, Gale, 1997. 333p. illus. index. $55.00. ISBN 0-7876-1690-7.

1121. **Short Stories for Students, Volume 2: Presenting Analysis, Context, and Criticism on Commonly Studied Short Stories.** Kathleen Wilson, ed. Detroit, Gale, 1997. 349p. illus. index. $55.00. ISBN 0-7876-1691-5.

A quick perusal of the first two volumes in this series, which are aimed at high school and early undergraduate students, might give one the initial impression of a deluxe version of Cliff Notes for short stories. Closer inspection reveals that although there are some basic similarities, the scope and depth of literary exposition and criticism provided here are much more extensive. There are approximately 20 carefully chosen classic and modern short stories included in each volume, including works by multicultural and female authors. An author biography, plot summary, and character and theme delineation are included in each entry as well as sections addressing style, historical and cultural contexts, and a critical overview (e.g., background on the authors' reputations and any controversies surrounding their work). Supplementing this latter feature is a "compare and contrast" section that notes differences between the author's time and current culture. Students are provided with lists of additional critical sources and supplemental reading as well as study questions for each story. Any media adaptations of the work are also noted. Of greatest value, perhaps, are the commissioned critical essays, written by academic experts, that follow each story. Although sometimes repetitious in content, these pieces are specifically geared toward student readers and serve to reinforce their comprehension of a story's significance and meaning. Additional useful features include a glossary of literary terms, a literary chronology of events, and author, title, and subject indexes, which are supplemented by a nationality/ethnicity index listing authors by background. The high quality and thorough coverage of significant short story literature provided in this series make it an excellent choice for purchase by high school and academic libraries.

—**Judith A. Matthews**

1122. **Short Story Index 1995: An Index to Stories in Collections and Periodicals.** John Greenfieldt, ed. Bronx, N.Y., H. W. Wilson, 1996. 248p. $115.00. ISSN 0360-9774.

The latest annual update to this venerable H. W. Wilson reference work indexes 4,619 stories published in 1995 in English or English translation appearing in 230 collections and 65 periodicals, about the same as the previous year. As is standard, the arrangement is by author, title, and subject in one alphabetic sequence. Stories in periodicals, however, are inexplicably indexed by author and title only. Author entries continue to provide the fullest information. Subject headings are loosely but not always exactly based on *Library of Congress Subject Headings* (see ARBA 97, entry 534) and include themes (drug addiction), locales (Russia), narrative techniques (story within a story), and genres (mystery stories). Both the subject and author entries supply cross-references when appropriate.

Three supplemental indexes furnish a list of collections indexed, a directory of publishers, and a directory of periodicals. The typically thorough Wilson indexing has a minor shortcoming, however, in the readers' advisory area. If readers like the Vargas Llosa story "On Sunday," for example, and want to find related stories, they can find them under the topics of "Swimming" and "Adolescence," but only if they know to look there; there is no listing of the assigned subject headings under each story title. If libraries have the entire run of the series, there is no reason to stop it now, unless usage is such that they want to wait for the next quinquennial cumulation, probably due ca.2000, if publication history is any indication.—**Lawrence Olszewski**

1123. **Short Story Writers.** Frank N. Magill, ed. Pasadena, Calif., Salem Press, 1997. 3v. illus. index. (Magill's Choice). $175.00/set. ISBN 0-89356-950-X.

Short Story Writers, a three-volume set, is the first title published under Salem Press's new series, Magill's Choice. This set surveys approximately 100 authors of short fiction whose inclusion is based on, according to the publisher's note, being "the most taught, most read, most acclaimed, and most researched in the American library." Essays in this work appeared first in the larger Salem Press reference, *Critical Survey of Short Fiction* (rev. ed.; see ARBA 94, entry 1215). The contents of this work focus primarily on the modern short story. However, earlier works, including Boccaccio's *Decameron*, Geoffrey Chaucer's *The Canterbury Tales*, and Jacob and Wilhelm Grimm's *Fairy Tales*, are treated as forerunners of modern short fiction. Although other countries are represented, more than half of the authors surveyed are from the United States.

Essays are arranged alphabetically in the 3 volumes, and pagination is continuous. The text is divided into four sections: other literary forms, achievements, biography, and analysis. The section on analysis examines several of the author's works. For the most part, the coverage is brief, but it is a good springboard for more serious and detailed examination. The sections are followed by a list of other major works and a bibliography. Each essay begins with the author's name, birth date and death date where appropriate, and a chronological list of major publications of short fiction. In many, but not all instances, a photograph of the author is included. Volume 3 contains both a glossary and an index. This is a useful reference tool for school, public, and undergraduate collections.—**Mary L. Bowman**

NATIONAL LITERATURE

American Literature

General Works

Bio-bibliography

1124. Barstow, Jane Missner. **One Hundred Years of American Women Writing, 1848-1948: An Annotated Bio-bibliography.** Pasadena, Calif., Salem Press and Lanham, Md., Scarecrow, 1997. 333p. index. (Magill Bibliographies). $42.00. ISBN 0-8108-3314-X.

This annotated bio-bibliography provides a valuable summary of the flood of critical attention paid to women writers since the beginning of the women's movement in 1970. Intended for a general audience rather than specialists, the work nevertheless contains ample useful information for the student or teacher embarking on a study of U.S. women's writing.

Barstow has chosen 66 representative writers who published most of their work between 1848, the year of the Seneca Falls Convention on Women's Rights, and 1948, when Simone de Beauvoir began her groundbreaking *The Second Sex*. Their work has been reissued in new editions and attracted considerable critical interest. The book is divided into sections by period, genre, and ethnicity (many categories overlap), each beginning with an introduction and an annotated list of general works. Individual entries, arranged in alphabetic order, contain a brief biography, a list of major works in modern reprints, and a selected and annotated bibliography of criticism since 1970. The annotations are economically written but provide a useful and generally accurate summary of the contents. Two appendixes, arranged by birthdate and by ethnicity, contain more names for further research.

Although this book does not claim to cover all U.S. women writers, it provides an excellent overview of well-chosen material. It will have a permanent place on this reviewer's reference shelf and belongs in every school and university library.—**Lynn F. Williams**

1125. **Contemporary Jewish-American Novelists: A Bio-Critical Sourcebook.** Joel Shatzky and Michael Taub, eds. Westport, Conn., Greenwood Press, 1997. 506p. index. $85.00. ISBN 0-313-29462-3.

With 63 alphabetic entries on novelists whose birth years range from 1874 to 1954, this volume focuses on works published after World War II. (The entry on Gertrude Stein, who died in 1946, is a curious exception.) Much earlier fiction by American Jews dealt with European experiences or trials of early immigrants rather than the subject emphasized here—problems resulting from assimilation into American culture. Except for Mordecai Richler, a Canadian, all the writers covered were born or are based in the United States. Most entries (the one for Lionel Trilling varies slightly) contain five sections: biographical sketch, analysis of major works and themes, summary of the writer's critical reception, listing of primary works, and bibliography of criticism. Discussion of major authors (Saul Bellow, Bernard Malamud, and especially Philip Roth) is thorough and incisive, but the editors choose to give slight attention to novels by authors of Jewish origin when those works reflect little ethnic concern (e.g., some popular novels by Norman Mailer). Potentially more useful, because they provide information not readily available elsewhere, are entries on lesser-known writers. Here the editors have included several women, some gay writers (Judith Katz and Lev Raphael), and one author, Art Spiegelman, whose narratives take the form of comic strips.

Directed toward both students and scholars of Jewish American literature, this work supplements and sometimes overlaps two earlier publications—*Jewish American Women Writers: A Bio-bibliographical and Critical Sourcebook* (Greenwood Press, 1994) and *Twentieth-Century American-Jewish Fiction Writers* (see ARBA 85, entry 1064). The book at hand contains a perceptive introduction to Jewish fiction by Sanford Marovitz, an appendix with minimal information about 25 Jewish women writers, and a general bibliography.—**Albert Wilhelm**

1126. **Nineteenth-Century American Women Writers: A Bio-bibliographical Critical Sourcebook.** Denise D. Knight, ed. Westport, Conn., Greenwood Press, 1997. 534p. index. $99.50. ISBN 0-313-29713-4.

This readable collection of essays profiles more than 70 U.S. women writers of the nineteenth century. Some names, such as Louisa May Alcott and Frances Hodgson Burnett, will be familiar. Other writers, such as Angelina Grimké, who addressed issues of slavery and abolitionism, are now generally unfamiliar. Yet, many of these writers held major roles through their writing. For example, Marietta Holley is credited by essayist Kate H. Winter as having helped gain the vote for women through her pen.

Although the essays are written by various (mostly women) authors, the underlying structure gives this resource cohesion and accessibility. Each essay begins with a biography that usually provides some family background; the writer's interests, activities, and accomplishments; and the context of the times. The next section, "Major Works and Themes," provides insights into the motivations of the writer. "Critical Reception" addresses the popularity, criticism, and general response to the writer's corpus of works. Some reviewers also address modern-day criticism when appropriate. The last sections detail the works cited, a bibliography of the author's works, and studies of the author. This is a particularly fine resource for those who are interested in a starting point for research or who simply want the pleasure of learning about some of the heritage of women writers.—**Suzanne I. Barchers**

Biography

1127. **American Expatriate Writers: Paris in the Twenties.** Matthew J. Bruccoli and Robert W. Trogdon, eds. Detroit, Gale, 1997. 378p. illus. index. (Dictionary of Literary Biography Documentary Series, v.15). $146.00. ISBN 0-8103-9971-7.

In 1980, *American Writers in Paris, 1920-1939*, the 4th volume of the Dictionary of Literary Biography (DLB) series, offered in-depth biographies of 99 writers, journalists, and publishers of the *belle epoque* of American letters in Paris. This volume, in the well-established companion documentary series, provides access (in facsimile or transcription, of course) to primary materials associated with the brightest stars of that incredibly creative expatriate society. Writers such as Ezra Pound, Ernest Hemingway, Gertrude Stein, F. Scott Fitzgerald, and John Dos Passos, whose works continue to provide pleasure and food for thought for new generations of readers, are included. It also covers the group's principal publishers—Sylvia Beach, William Bird, Robert McAlmon, and Edward Titusas well as lesser luminaries whose work still sparkles for scholars and others who seek out the era's fuller literary record. In addition, chapters treat the "Lost Generation's" key literary magazines—*The Little Review*, *The Transatlantic Review*, and *This Quarter*—and the milieu in which their café society flourished.

Typical chapters reproduce sample pages from drafts of major works as well as their book jackets or title pages. They also reprint letters, introductions to others' books, newspaper pieces, journal articles, and excerpts from books. The result is an inevitably incomplete mosaic—incomplete, that is, if viewed from the perspective of a scholar or a biographer who seeks to find and fit every piece together. However, this fragmentary view of these writers and publishers works, especially when multiple chapters are used to get a sense of the era rather than of just one writer, will look much more complete for the popular student audience for whom this is intended. Members of that audience will take from this book a richer, fuller understanding of the aesthetic ideas and ideals of these writers, the ways in which their personal interaction produced creative synergy, and the range of their work beyond the best known novels of Hemingway and Fitzgerald. Furthermore, the cumulative index covering both the Dictionary of Literary Biography Series and this documentary series will help them connect the in-depth critical biographies in other volumes with the selected documentary information in this volume.—**James Rettig**

1128. **American Novelists Since World War II, Fifth Series.** James R. Giles and Wanda H. Giles, eds. Detroit, Gale, 1996. 379p. illus. index. (Dictionary of Literary Biography, v.173). $140.00. ISBN 0-8103-9936-9.

Twenty writers are covered in this fifth installment in The Dictionary of Literary Biography's (DLB) *American Novelists Since World War II* sequence. Regrettably, only six of these writers are new to the DLB, the others having been treated previously—either in earlier installments of the *American Novelists* volumes (2 [see ARBA 80, entry 1237]; 6 [see ARBA 81, entry 1265]; 143 [see ARBA 96, entry 1204];

and 152 [see ARBA 96, entry 1203]) or in other DLB titles, such as its yearbook. Naturally in the case of such prolific, ongoing authors as Philip Roth, E. L. Doctorow, or Joan Didion, it is beneficial to have their entries brought up-to-date and their most recent work covered; however, it is less justifiable in the case of deceased authors, such as Carson McCullers and Jean Stafford. Also, it seems something of a stretch to treat Bobbie Ann Mason as a novelist when only three of her seven listed books are actually novels. Nevertheless, this volume has all the virtues of its predecessors in the DLB series: lucid, balanced writing; coverage of a wide range of authors; and a thorough primary and secondary bibliography. In addition, this volume has a particularly comprehensive and illuminating introduction.—**Jeffrey R. Luttrell**

Dictionaries and Encyclopedias

1129. **The Oxford Companion to African American Literature.** William L. Andrews, Frances Smith Foster, and Trudier Harris, eds. New York, Oxford University Press, 1997. 866p. index. $55.00. ISBN 0-19-506510-7.

African American studies has come into its own as a discipline. The establishment of a black literary canon is one aspect of the discipline's acceptance in academe, a fact indicated by the recent publication of such resources as *The Norton Anthology of African American Literature* (W. W. Norton, 1997) and the title at hand. The contemplation of the amount of work necessary to compile and edit a volume of this kind boggles the mind. The editors have done a superb job at this monumental task.

The Oxford Companion to African American Literature contains entries on more than 400 writers. Entries also appear for actual literary works and characters from those works, as well as stereotypical character types and icons of black culture not necessarily related to literature (e.g., Marcus Garvey, John Coltrane, Muhammad Ali, and Marian Anderson). Essays on such topics as jazz, dialect poetry, literary history (subdivided by periods), miscegenation, sermons and preaching, and violence establish this volume as not merely a literary but also a cultural work. As stated in the preface, "This *Companion* also serves as a primer on African American cultural literacy."

The entries are alphabetized in a letter-by-letter, not word-by-word, scheme, but this arrangement is not always consistent. For example, the entry for *Brown Girl, Brownstones* falls after the proliferation of writers with the last name of Brown, including William Wells Brown. The articles were written by a collaboration of more than 350 contributors and are signed. Asterisked words within entries indicate main headings elsewhere in the text. Most articles are followed by a bibliography. A comprehensive index at the end of the volume contains references to main articles as well as to mentions in other articles.

This amazing reference work will be a milestone in African American literary studies. The title is a must for academic libraries. High school and public libraries will also want to consider its purchase. [R: RBB, 15 Feb 97, pp. 1042-43]—**Melissa Rae Root**

1130. Snodgrass, Mary Ellen. **Encyclopedia of Frontier Literature.** Santa Barbara, Calif., ABC-CLIO, 1997. 540p. illus. index. (ABC-CLIO Literary Companion). $65.00. ISBN 0-87436-888-X.

Snodgrass defines frontier literature as the vast body of writing that focuses on the exploration and settlement of North America, and in this book she discusses the themes, genres, writers, and titles that define and exemplify this literature. The volume's main section consists of 94 alphabetically arranged essays covering persons (Owen Wister, Francis Parkman, Geronimo, Laura Ingalls Wilder); key concepts; literary motifs; and dominant themes (Native Americans in literature, short fiction of the frontier, the captivity motif, law and order, women on the frontier); and titles (*My Ántonia*, *The Last of the Mohicans*, *Roughing It*). Entries vary in length, but most are between two and four pages, with each containing textual commentary; historical background; literary analysis; and where appropriate, cross-references and a bibliography. Snodgrass, the author of numerous reference books, is an excellent writer, and each essay bristles with conciseness, clarity, detail, and a refreshing lack of academic posturing and pedantry. Researchers will find themselves browsing through the essays not only for their reference value, but simply because they are enjoyable to read.

Snodgrass also includes such valuable information as a timeline of frontier literature for the years 1532 to 1996, a list of major works from the frontier canon, a list of major authors and their works, and a timeline of films made from frontier literature (*The Virginian* in 1929 through Walt Disney's *Pocahontas* in 1994). A bibliography covers books, articles, audiocassettes, videos, CD-ROMs, and Internet sites. An exhaustive index notes all terms, names, and concepts examined in the book, whether they have their own entries or not. Handsomely illustrated and bound, this title is heartily recommended for school, public, and academic libraries.—**Jack Bales**

Handbooks and Yearbooks

1131. **Representative American Speeches 1995-1996.** Calvin McLeod Logue and Jean DeHart, eds. Bronx, N.Y., H. W. Wilson, 1996. 222p. index. (The Reference Shelf, v.68, no.6). $15.00pa. ISBN 0-8242-0891-9.

For libraries that subscribe to The Reference Shelf, this annual special issue of speeches culled from the contemporary media will arrive automatically. For all others, however, this anthology will promote access to a sampling of current U.S. political and sociological thought. The speeches are divided into eight categories—public discourse, government, environment, race, women's rights, media, religion, and continuing education. The speechmakers themselves also represent the spectrum of contemporary U.S. thought. Not only the Clintons—Bill twice and Hillary once—but also Janet Reno, Madeleine Albright, Vernon Jordan, and Bob Dole, among others, have their say. Because most of the speeches were not delivered at events with extensive media exposure (no States of the Union or inaugurals here), the volume provides samples of lesser-publicized but equally timely oratorical output from prominent dignitaries.

The retrospective invites comparison with its only real rival in the field, *Vital Speeches of the Day* (City News Publishing, 1934-), but no overlap was detected between the 26 speeches in this slender volume and the 400 or so that were published by the bimonthly periodical for the same period. Libraries requiring comprehensive coverage should subscribe to *Vital Speeches of the Day*, whereas the item under review will be adequate for others.—**Lawrence Olszewski**

Drama

1132. Dickey, Jerry. **Sophie Treadwell: A Research and Production Sourcebook.** Westport, Conn., Greenwood Press, 1997. 269p. index. (Modern Dramatists Research and Production Sourcebooks, no.12). $79.50. ISBN 0-313-29388-0.

Sophie Treadwell's play *Machinal* opened on Broadway in 1928 to mixed reviews. Most were impressed by the impressionistic style of the play, but some important critics remained unmoved by it despite their admiration for the strong cast, which included the young Clark Gable in a small role. The play is, however, the only of the nearly 40 plays written by the playwright to hold the stage. Productions in the past decade have been seen in New York, London, Chicago, and elsewhere. Only one of her other plays has ever been published, *Hope for a Harvest*. Treadwell certainly qualifies as a neglected woman in the history of the performing arts in the United States (with a career in the theater as actress, writer, and producer of nearly 60 years) overdue for study and evaluation. Her work as a journalist off and on in her life probably helped her to confront and be sensitive to the issues and conflicts facing people (especially women) of her time.

The contents of the book include a preface; a chronology; a biography; the plays (individual listings with detailed summaries and critical overviews); and primary and secondary bibliographies (annotated and with separate sections for reviews, books, and articles). A detailed list of productions and credits includes full casts for important performances of her plays. There are two indexes, for author and for subject.

The author of this impressive sourcebook is on the staff of the Department of Theatre Arts at the University of Arizona. The library of this university houses the collection of 53 cartons of Treadwell's papers. Dickey's guide to this woman and her life and works is flawlessly organized and presented. Any researcher with a need to know something about Treadwell will find using this book a joy and a reward.
—**George Louis Mayer**

Individual Authors

Stephen Crane

1133. Schaefer, Michael W. **A Reader's Guide to the Short Stories of Stephen Crane.** New York, G. K. Hall/Simon & Schuster Macmillan, 1996. 468p. index. (A Reference Publication in Literature). $50.00. ISBN 0-8161-7285-4.

Intending to distill "the large body of historical and critical information available as of the end of 1992" (p. ix) for 51 works by Stephen Crane that Schaefer defines as short stories, the guide's alphabetically arranged chapters present overviews of publication and composition histories, sources and influences, relationships with Crane's other works, and "significant critical interpretations" (p. xi) from the full range of perspectives, with "comprehensive" bibliographies for each story. Schaefer's most useful contribution is almost entirely synthetic. Details regarding composition and sources substantially derive from standard sources, especially *The Correspondence of Stephen Crane* (Columbia University Press, 1988), edited by Stanley Wertheim and Paul Sorrentino, and Thomas Beer's *Stephen Crane: A Study in American Letters* (Alfred J. Knopf, 1923). Although significantly relying on a core of major studies, such as Thomas A. Gullason's *Stephen Crane's Career: Perspectives and Evaluations* (New York University Press, 1972), Schaefer also recounts comments on Crane's short stories from the likes of Joseph Conrad, H. G. Wells, Harold Frederic, Willa Cather, and H. E. Bates.

Schaefer's most significant original assessments fill in critical voids, particularly in discussions of literary relationships with Crane's other works, and generally involve brief examinations of plots, characters, themes, and the like. The guide's most extensive chapters cover "The Blue Hotel" and "The Open Boat." In addition to an index of Crane's works, a general index references names, periodical titles, and selected topics, such as the Civil War, existentialism, impressionism, and the Spanish-American War. Like other volumes in G. K. Hall's series, Schaefer's provides an excellent starting point for research on an important portion of Crane's writings. Perhaps Stanley Wertheim's *A Stephen Crane Encyclopedia* (see entry 1134) will give details for Crane's sketches and other shorter, factually based prose works.
—**James K. Bracken**

1134. Wertheim, Stanley. **A Stephen Crane Encyclopedia.** Westport, Conn., Greenwood Press, 1997. 413p. index. $85.00. ISBN 0-313-29692-8.

Imagine having to write more than 400 pages on a figure whose public career spanned only 5 years and had only one well-known work. It almost seems laughable, yet that is exactly the life of Stephen Crane in a nutshell. Famous at the age of 23 for *The Red Badge of Courage*, Crane was dead before he reached his 29th birthday. Wertheim, an English professor at William Patterson University and a Crane expert (he has authored two other books and scores of articles on Crane, as well as served as president of the Stephen Crane society for 2 years), has brought to life Crane's true value.

The encyclopedia pulls together people, places, family members, close acquaintances, Crane biographers and bibliographers, and much more. Here is a treasure trove of Crane riches, and American literary studies are wealthier for it. Entries not only include the typical explanatory note but often cite other works, other readings, or provide historical background. The entries are delightfully well written, filled with witty asides and informative snippets. A helpful preface, a necessary chronology, and an extensive bibliography offer users of the volume a cornucopia of Crane memorabilia. It should also lay to rest the misguided notion that Crane was a one-hit wonder. Given its limited subject matter, the book is as good as its close relatives: *Mark Twain A to Z* (see ARBA 96, entry 1217); *A Herman Melville Encyclopedia* (see ARBA 96, entry 1212); and *The Poe Encyclopedia* (see entry 1137).—**Mark Y. Herring**

Emily Dickinson

1135. Bennett, Fordyce R. **A Reference Guide to the Bible in Emily Dickinson's Poetry.** Lanham, Md., Scarecrow, 1997. 500p. $49.00. ISBN 0-8108-3247-X.

Bennett's catalog of biblical references in the poetry of Emily Dickinson is an outstanding scholarly achievement. Using the edition of the poems edited by Thomas H. Johnson, Bennett links passages with biblical references keyed to the Authorized Version (King James) of the Bible. The references are quotations or allusions to words, phrases, or passages. Each numbered entry quotes the line number of the poem followed by the appropriate Bible reference. If practical, the verse is quoted in full. Many longer passages are abbreviated by the use of an ellipsis. Bennett notes the particular word or passage and its single, sometimes multiple, biblical referents. Not only does he tie together the biblical allusions, but he also comments on the significance of the poem as a whole and its relationship to the Dickinson corpus. Additionally, cross-references to her letters, her prose fragments, and standard reference works about her are abundant.

Bennett is quick to point out Dickinsonian echoes in other allusions, as, for example, when he notes the similarities to other writers: Dante (#337), John Donne (#430), Walt Whitman (#1099), Jonathan Swift (#1105), Henry Vaughan (#1241), and William Shakespeare (#1595). A brief appendix provides biographical information on key people in Dickinson's life. Bennett's familiarity with both the poetry itself and the Old and New Testaments is impressive, and his efforts have produced a major contribution to Dickinson studies.—**Bernice Bergup**

Lorraine Hansberry

1136. Leeson, Richard M. **Lorraine Hansberry: A Research and Production Sourcebook.** Westport, Conn., Greenwood Press, 1997. 175p. index. (Modern Dramatists Research and Production Sourcebooks, no.13). $65.00. ISBN 0-313-29312-0.

Although Lorraine Hansberry is best known for her play *A Raisin in the Sun* and the movie that was based on it, this book will help both beginning students and scholars find sources about the other works of this brilliant African American writer. Hansberry died of cancer at the tragically young age of 34, but a number of posthumous works, especially the play *To Be Young, Gifted and Black*, first produced in 1969 four years after Hansberry's death, have joined *A Raisin in the Sun* to make Hansberry a popular subject both for theater-lovers and scholars.

Leeson's book provides a useful chronology of key events in Hansberry's life, a brief essay on her life and career (which would benefit from some copyediting for style and punctuation), a substantial section providing generous plot summaries, a list of productions, and an overview of selected critical commentary on each of her seven major works. These sections are followed by a primary bibliography divided into drama, fiction and poetry, nonfiction, interviews, recordings and films, unpublished materials, and archival sources. Also, there are two briefly annotated, descriptive secondary bibliographies, the first consisting of reviews of the plays and the second listing books, journal articles, sections of books, and dissertations. Leeson also includes an author index to the secondary bibliographies and a general index. Because of the plot summaries, this book could serve as an introduction for first-time readers of Hansberry, but the detailed secondary bibliographies also provide ample resources for extensive research.
—**David Isaacson**

Edgar Allan Poe

1137. Frank, Frederick S., and Anthony Magistrale. **The Poe Encyclopedia.** Westport, Conn., Greenwood Press, 1997. 453p. index. $89.50. ISBN 0-313-27768-0.

Rumor has it that when one visits Edgar Allan Poe's graveside in January, a bottle of champagne and a rose are placed there in his memory. Guides will tell the curious that the gift-giver remains a mystery, adding yet more legend to the legendary writer of famous verse and infamous alcoholic excesses. The present volume stands equally as a gift and may, with age, prove as much claret as any bottle of wine. Alphabetic entries provide numerous trails through which layperson and scholar alike can trace Poe's influences throughout his career. Three indexes offer quick routes back through the text. An index of critics, editors, and acquaintances provides speedy passage to any critic, dreaded editor, or family friend. The index of authors, artists, and titles furnishes a more literary excursion, whereas the index to themes, subjects, and characters shows readers how to locate everything from the story of "The Tell-Tale Heart" to "humor" (a rather small entry) to "women" (considerably longer). A chronology of Poe's life, which begins the work, allows readers to see a picture of the whole man, his life, and work.

This work of more than 1,900 entries fills an important niche in Poe studies, being the first of its kind. All concerned will hope to see it regularly updated.—**Mark Y. Herring**

Eudora Welty

1138. Pingatore, Diana R. **A Reader's Guide to the Short Stories of Eudora Welty.** New York, G. K. Hall/Simon & Schuster Macmillan, 1996. 421p. index. (A Reference Publication in Literature). $50.00. ISBN 0-8161-7371-0.

People have long admired the elegant short stories of Eudora Welty (her novels, although worthwhile, are not as successful). Using the same order as in Welty's *The Collected Stories* (Harcourt Brace, 1980), Pingatore covers each of the 41 stories in minute detail. Publication history includes the date and place of first publication and the most important reprints, noting any changes made in later versions. A section on circumstances of composition, sources, and influences provides all information available, including that from critics and Welty herself. A section on relation to other Welty works again uses the comments of earlier researchers, and the interpretation and criticism segment summarizes chronologically in detail what every major and minor commentator has said about Welty's work. The last section on each story, "Works Cited," usually runs to several pages. The treatment of each story separately is convenient for the reader but results in a great deal of repetition.

Anyone wishing to study Welty will find this guide useful, if rather plodding. It is recommended for research libraries with collections in U.S. literature and women's studies.—**Lynn F. Williams**

Laura Ingalls Wilder

1139. Subramanian, Jane M. **Laura Ingalls Wilder: An Annotated Bibliography of Critical, Biographical, and Teaching Studies.** Westport, Conn., Greenwood Press, 1997. 115p. index. (Bibliographies and Indexes in American Literature, no.24). $55.00. ISBN 0-313-29999-4.

Laura Ingalls Wilder has joined the ranks of Ralph Waldo Emerson, Allen Ginsberg, and John Updike in Greenwood Press's Bibliographies and Indexes in American Literature series. This annotated bibliography concentrates on the areas of critical (including book reviews) and biographical materials and excludes primary materials; Wildereana (*Little House* songbooks, cookbooks, homesite information, and so forth); sequels written by other hands; and *Little House on the Prairie* television spin-offs, videos, Websites, and the like. Coverage is through mid-1995.

The bibliography contains 334 items divided into 6 sections arranged alphabetically by author: "Critical Works," "Biographical Works," "Teaching Studies & Materials," "Teaching Kits," "Serial Publications," and "Book Reviews." Author, source, subject, and "Younger Readers" indexes give multiple access points to the annotations. Descriptive annotations vary from several sentences in length to (in a few cases) "not available for review." Subramanian is a member of the library faculty at the State University of New York College at Potsdam.

The only other monograph devoted to a bibliography of Wilder is Mary J. Mooney-Getoff's out-of-date *Laura Ingalls Wilder, a Bibliography* (Wise Owl Press, 1980). The volume at hand seems complete within its prescribed limits. The annotations are usually detailed and helpful. The price seems expensive for a work of 115 pages, but large juvenile collections, college libraries supporting courses in children's literature, and curriculum centers will find it useful.—**Jonathan F. Husband**

Poetry

1140. **American Poets Since World War II, Fourth Series.** Joseph Conte, ed. Detroit, Gale, 1996. 377p. illus. index. (Dictionary of Literary Biography, v.165). $135.00. ISBN 0-8103-9360-3.

The 165th volume of the Dictionary of Literary Biography (DLB) is a recent addition to the ongoing series that records the achievements of the world's most influential literary figures. Each volume is devoted to a specific topic, period, or genre and is organized and written by experts in their respective fields.

The volume includes 20 poets (A. R. Ammons, John Ashbery, Robin Blaser, William Bronk, Gwendolyn Brooks, Hayden Carruth, Lyn Hejinian, Michael Heller, Robert Kelly, Li-Young Lee, Denise Levertov, Bernadette Mayer, James Merrill, George Oppen, Kenneth Rexroth, Stephen Sandy, Armand Schwerner, Gary Snyder, Charles Wright, and Louis Zukofsky) who represent 3 generations in this century. Zukofsky, for example, represents the first postmodernist generation (i.e., writers who dealt with the social, political, and personal concerns of their generation). The second generation—poets of the 1950s and 1960s—challenged the precepts of modernism, added new concepts to the encyclopedia of poetics, founded postmodern schools of poetry, and enjoyed the largest and broadest readership for poetry in the twentieth century. Finally, the third generation, the Baby Boomers, do not identify with postwar movements and feel only slightly indebted to former generations. They may be subdivided into four interest groups: traditional, experimental, identity politics, or personal lyricist.

In selecting the entries for DLB volume 165, the editor gave special consideration to its relation to prior volumes in the DLB series that treat U.S. poetry after 1945. He was particularly interested in the poets included in the two-volume *American Poets Since World War II, First Series* (see ARBA 81, entry 1264). In the years since the appearance of that set, a number of poets included in that volume have produced major new works or have since been the beneficiaries of extensive critical studies, providing grounds for a fresh appraisal. Finally, DLB volume 165 presents several poets whose work was still in a gestational stage in 1980 or who appear in the DLB for the first time.

The authors of articles on individual poets are themselves recognized authorities in the poetry field. Virtually all are well represented by contributions to scholarly journals listed in the *MLA International Bibliography*. This DLB volume is an indispensable critical appraisal of leading U.S. poets of the twentieth century and therefore belongs in every university or research library's Americana collection.—**Mark Padnos**

1141. **American Poets Since World War II, Fifth Series.** Joseph Conte, ed. Detroit, Gale, 1996. 404p. illus. index. (Dictionary of Literary Biography, v.169). $140.00. ISBN 0-8103-9932-6.

This 169th volume of the Dictionary of Literary Biography (DLB)—*American Poets Since World War II, Fifth Series*—is the latest entry in what began in 1975 as a way to develop a comprehensive biographical dictionary of persons who contributed to North American literature. The entries in DLB consist of career biographies, tracing the development of the author's canon and the evolution of his or her reputation. Each of these free-standing volumes is organized by topic, period, or genre and provides a biographical/bibliographic guide and overview for a particular area of literature. The chosen authors are listed alphabetically, and each volume includes a cumulative index of subject authors and articles. A comprehensive index to the entire series is not yet available.

Each entry begins with a chronological bibliography of the poet's works, followed by the poet's biography, along with excerpts from selected works and attendant literary criticism. Illustrations include material such as portraits, photographs, and even facsimile rough drafts of manuscript pages. The final portion of each entry lists critical references. Such volumes must always face the problem of which writers to include. Even though everyone would agree on many included authors, others are omitted who seem equally, if not more, critically acclaimed. One excellent service of a prestigious series such as this one could be introducing lesser-knowns (e.g., Jean Burden, Wyatt Prunty, Jean Valentine, Tom Rabbitt, and R. T. Smith) to a wider public, while including greats like Robert Lowell and Elizabeth Bishop. Certainly, every library that has earlier volumes will want to add *American Poets Since World War II, Fifth Series* to their collection.—**Kay O. Cornelius**

1142. **Index of American Periodical Verse 1995.** By Rafael Catala and James D. Anderson. Lanham, Md., Scarecrow, 1997. 650p. index. $69.50. ISBN 0-8108-3391-3.

The 25th annual volume of this easy-to-use index carries more than 19,000 entries for individual poems and some 6,900 entries for individual poets and translators. The poems indexed are those appearing in a broad cross-section of 300 popular, general, literary, scholarly, and "little" magazines, journals, and reviews published in the United States, Canada, and the Caribbean. Two indexes—by author and by title—comprise the volume. The 474-page author index is alphabetically arranged and sequentially numbered, with the title of each poem listed alphabetically under its author. Following each poem, the usual bibliographic information is given: journal title, volume, number, date, and page number. The poets range from the new to the long-established. The title index locates each poem by the number assigned to the poet in the author index. Included also are two lists of all periodicals indexed, one alphabetized by title acronym and one alphabetized by full title; a list of periodicals added since the last edition of the index; and a list of those periodicals dropped (with reasons why). The price of the index is high, but almost every mid-sized to large academic and public library will want to give it serious consideration for purchase.

—**Charles R. Andrews**

British Literature

General Works

Bibliography

1143. Beene, LynnDianne. **Guide to British Prose Fiction Explication: Nineteenth and Twentieth Centuries.** New York, G. K. Hall/Simon & Schuster Macmillan, 1997. 697p. (Guides to Prose Explication Series; A Reference Publication in Literature). $70.00. ISBN 0-8161-1987-2.

A useful reference for students and scholars of British literature, this volume lists critical essays and reviews of works for more than 140 writers, most of whom—such as Jane Austen, Charles Dickens, E. M. Forster, and Oscar Wilde—are easily recognized as having had considerable influence on the development of nineteenth- and twentieth-century British fiction. Others, such as Eric Ambler, Elspeth Barker, and Tanith Lee, are lesser-known but presumably have been productive and influential enough to merit consideration.

The authors' names, titles of primary sources, and bibliographic references for the explications (as secondary sources are called here) are all listed alphabetically. Authors' names also appear at the top of each page, making it easy to flip through the book to a particular writer and work. The headers are most welcome because the book does not include an index. Another useful feature of this book is the extensive list of English- and foreign-language journals and periodicals with abbreviations. Particularly for beginning graduate students, this list is an excellent guide to journal and periodical literature. The list of "Main Sources Consulted" is more specific to British literature but includes works that will be of interest to generalists in literature as well. This is a carefully documented book that should greatly simplify the task of researching and writing about British literature; it is highly recommended.—**Sandra Adell**

1144. Horwitz, Barbara J. **British Women Writers, 1700-1850: An Annotated Bibliography of Their Works and Works About Them.** Pasadena, Calif., Salem Press and Lanham, Md., Scarecrow, 1997. 231p. index. (Magill Bibliographies). $37.00. ISBN 0-8108-3315-8.

This modest but useful and readable volume begins with a short chapter that gives the reader an overview of the political and social setting of the times. The all-too-brief five pages only whet the appetite, which could be satisfied by consulting the works listed at the end of the chapter. Chapter 2 provides a thematic approach, "Literature Written by Women, 1700-1850." Topics range from anthologies of writing by women to guides to women's literature to the novel to drama by women. The majority of the book contains the annotations of the writings about British women authors. Entries begin with background information about the author. The bibliographies include various works about the authors, with thoughtful descriptions about the information contained in each article, book, or essay. Many annotations include works through 1996, making this a current resource.

The value of this resource lies not in what it provides but in the fact that it will serve as a beginning point for further research. The entries are brief, but they provide enough information that the user should generally know if the resource would be useful during extended research. Subject and writer indexes complete the book. The work is definitely a timesaving resource for the serious student of British women writers.
—**Suzanne I. Barchers**

1145. Letellier, Robert Ignatius. **The English Novel, 1660-1700: An Annotated Bibliography.** Westport, Conn., Greenwood Press, 1997. 448p. index. (Bibliographies and Indexes in World Literature, no.53). $85.00. ISBN 0-313-30368-1.

This ambitious bibliography focuses on a narrow but important period in English literary history. The Restoration saw the birth of the modern English novel. Crime stories, adventures, romances, and travel fiction all stem from this time.

Letellier has drawn together primary, secondary, and tertiary sources, along with works providing historical and social background, in this dedicated bibliography. The work is divided into two parts: part 1 lists bibliographies, anthologies, and general studies of the period, and part 2 lists works by and studies on the authors of the time. In addition to English authors, Letellier also includes authors, such as

Cervantes, whose translated work had an important impact on English prose fiction. A brief introduction provides historical background. Addenda include a chronological list of English prose fiction from 1660 to 1700, an index of scholars, and a subject index.

Although comprehensive, this bibliography is somewhat selective and misses some important scholarly studies, as comparison with the *MLA International Bibliography* (see ARBA 93, entry 1107) will show. The author claims coverage through 1993, but several major works from that year are not included, and his coverage of dissertations seems random. However, no bibliography of this type can ever be complete, and Letellier has done a remarkable and valuable job. One unfortunate and jarring feature is his method of entering anonymous works. In violation of all accepted standards of alphabetizing, he has listed these under the initial word even when this is an article, resulting in 3 entries under "A" and 79 under "The."

Despite its drawbacks, this is an important and valuable work that belongs in all academic libraries and larger public libraries.—**Susan Davis Herring**

1146. Mazzeno, Laurence W. **The British Novel 1680-1832: An Annotated Bibliography.** Pasadena, Calif., Salem Press, and Lanham, Md., Scarecrow, 1997. 247p. index. (Magill Bibliographies). $40.00. ISBN 0-8108-3249-6.

This eclectic collection of criticisms and analyses of significant novels written in Great Britain from the last decades of the seventeenth century and into the first four decades of the nineteenth century covers traditional research based in historical, social, and moral study as well as such poststructural scholarship as feminism and deconstruction. It accomplishes its stated goal of being designed to give scholars a review of this vast domain of twentieth-century criticism by calling attention in its introductory chapter to nearly 100 general studies; for example, Percy G. Adams's *Travel Literature and the Evolution of the Novel* discusses the blend of realism and romance that characterize both genres; Terry Castle's *Masquerade and Civilization* explores the carnivalesque in eighteenth-century culture and fiction; and Katharine Rogers's *Feminism in Eighteenth-Century England* focuses on the way new social relationships allowed women "to articulate the emotions and sanction the values that were important to them as women."

In 20 subsequent chapters, each devoted to a different author, the citations lead to the best modern criticism has to offer, whether highlighting the fiction of Aphra Behn or Daniel Defoe, Samuel Richardson or Henry Fielding, William Godwin or Mary Shelley, Jane Austen or Walter Scott. Concluding author and subject indexes are extremely helpful in exploring various associations of ideas inspired by the skillfully annotated critical theory. *The British Novel 1680-1832* is highly recommended for all scholars and enthusiasts devoted to the study of the British novel.—**Colby H. Kullman**

Biography

1147. **Sixteenth-Century British Nondramatic Writers, Fourth Series.** David A. Richardson, ed. Detroit, Gale, 1996. 377p. illus. index. (Dictionary of Literary Biography, v.172). $140.00. ISBN 0-8103-9935-0.

This fourth series follows the pattern established by the first three volumes (132 [see ARBA 95, entry 1201]; 136; and 167 [see ARBA 97, entry 983]) on sixteenth-century British nondramatic writers. Twenty-odd writers are treated, each writer receiving a two- to twenty-page entry that includes a sketch of the author's life, a publication history, a critical evaluation, and a primary and secondary bibliography. In this volume, 29 authors (ranging from the extremely obscure to such luminaries as Walter Raleigh and William Shakespeare) and one anonymous poem ("Zephyria") are treated. Entries typically begin with an account of the authors' lives, placing them in the social milieu of their time and expounding on contemporary influences on the authors' works. Then major individual works are given a balanced and succinct critical evaluation.

As always in the Dictionary of Literary Biography (DLB) series, these entries serve as an excellent introduction to individual authors, especially in the case of the lesser-known names, where the DLB entry may well be the only such modern critical overview available. In addition, this volume includes the texts of four contemporaneous documents on sixteenth-century literature, as well as a "Checklist of Further Readings" and an index to authors and works in all four series.—**Jeffrey R. Luttrell**

Catalogs and Collections

1148. **The Carl H. Pforzheimer Library, English Literature, 1475-1700.** 1997 ed. Los Angeles, Calif., Heritage Book Shop and New Castle, Del., Oak Knoll Press, 1997. 3v. index. $350.00/set. ISBN 1-884718-33-7.

John B. Thomas III, curator of the Pforzheimer Collection at the University of Texas, states in the foreword that only new preliminaries, a table of contents, and a list of books received in 1986, the year in which the university acquired the collection, were added to what he describes as William Alexander Jackson's "distinguished catalogue of the Pforzheimer Library." This catalog is a replica of that work. Containing more than 1,300 rare books and manuscripts, the significance of the collection may be noted by the authors, individuals, and publications cited throughout the 3 volumes. For example, the Gutenberg Bible, the first complete English Bible translated by Miles Coverdale in 1535, the first book printed in the English language, and the *Recuyell of the Historyes of Troye* (1473-1474) by Raoul LeFevre and translated and published by William Caxton are all listed. Also included are original publications of Francis Bacon, Geoffrey Chaucer, John Donne, John Dryden, Ben Jonson, William Shakespeare, Edmund Spenser, and Izaak Walton.

Each volume includes a list of plates. Volume 3 includes the following indexes: anonymous books, provenance, and bibliographies. These are followed by an addendum of books in the Pforzheimer Collection but not in the original catalog. Arrangement is alphabetic with each entry numbered consecutively. Descriptive entries appear to be extensive and may easily be a page or more in length. Thomas states that 10 years of use of the collection in conjunction with the catalog has confirmed that the descriptions including information on provenance and binding are remarkably complete and accurate.

In his 1940 introduction, Carl H. Pforzheimer discusses rare book collecting in the United States in the nineteenth century. Readers are reacquainted with the names of James Lenox, Henry E. Huntington, and Henry C. Folger and are given a brief history of book collection. This work makes the contents of this significant collection, which has been described as one of the finest American collections of English literature, more easily identifiable to the 750 institutions and libraries that will acquire the reproduction. Because the catalog itself is not available online, even though information about the collection is, this volume is especially significant.—**Robert M. Ballard**

Handbooks and Yearbooks

1149. **British Writers, Supplement IV.** George Stade and Carol Howard, eds. New York, Scribner's/Simon & Schuster Macmillan, 1997. 668p. index. $120.00. ISBN 0-684-80496-4.

This hefty volume surveys writers who were not represented either in the initial seven volumes of *British Writers* (1979-1984) or the three supplements (see ARBA 97, entry 982; ARBA 93, entry 1191; and ARBA 88, entry 1199). Even so, these are by no means left-over writers but writers who are not always or immediately recognized as British: Salman Rushdie, born in Bombay but a resident of the world; Roald Dahl, a native of Norway; Kazuo Ishiguro, born in Nagasaki, Japan; Thomas Kenneally and Christina Stead, both Australian-born; and the poet Paul Muldoon, born in Northern Ireland. Others are well known in their own right: Martin Amis, A. S. Byatt, Bruce Chatwin, Margaret Drabble, P. D. James, and D. M. Thomas, to name a few.

As in other volumes in this series, each author is accorded a substantial, well-researched essay of twelve to fifteen thousand words dealing with the writer's life and works, with emphasis on the works. Each essay concludes with a bibliography of the author's works as well as reviews and critical studies of those works. Aimed at "that mythical but inspiring figure, the general reader" (introduction), these essays are indeed readable and should be accessible to high school students and still valuable to college and graduate students.

A chronology of British history and literature from 1901 to 1997 opens the book. This particular volume concludes with a 107-page master index of the writers and their works that appear in the entire *British Writers* series through *Supplement IV*—a useful addition to a useful series.—**Edwin S. Gleaves**

1150. Nilsen, Don L. F. **Humor in British Literature, from the Middle Ages to the Restoration: A Reference Guide.** Westport, Conn., Greenwood Press, 1997. 226p. index. $75.00. ISBN 0-313-29706-1.

Nilsen's guide essentially excerpts or paraphrases selected critical assessments of the contributions of nearly 90 individual writers to British literary humor through the early eighteenth century. Drawing heavily on a core of historical sources, nearly every writer's bibliography cites one of the following: (1) Alfred G. L'Estrange's *History of English Humour* (London, Hurst and Blackett, 1878; reprinted by Burt Franklin, 1970), which Nilsen consistently cites as "New York: Burt Franklin, 1878"; (2) Louis Cazamian's *The Development of English Humor* (Duke University Press, 1952); or (3) Hugh Walker's *English Satire and Satirists* (London, J. M. Dent and E. P. Dutton, 1925), which Nilsen cites as "New York: Dent, 1925." Instead of bibliographies for individual writers, often amounting to solitary duplicative references to L'Estrange, Cazamian, or Walker for the likes of Henry Heywood, Gavin Douglas, John Penry, Thomas Coryate, Philip Massinger, and Thomas Fuller, among others, a single comprehensive list of analyzed sources could have served.

Nilsen's chapters for the medieval period through the seventeenth century—from Adhelm (ca.640-709) to John Wilmot, Earl of Rochester (1647-1680)—chronologically arrange entries for both major and minor writers, including many not identified in Steven H. Gale's two-volume *Encyclopedia of British Humorists* (see ARBA 97, entry 984). However, although providing an entry for Desidirius Erasmus, Nilsen does not offer specific entries for the *Beowulf* and *Pearl/Sir Gawain and the Green Knight* poets, both covered by Gale's encyclopedia. More significantly, Nilsen's guide neither summarizes nor indicates the humorous content of an individual writer's works. By comparison, Gale's encyclopedia gives both useful analyses of humor in individual works as well as critical assessments, with bibliographies of editions, biographical sources, and critical studies. Indeed, the bibliographies for George Chapman and Richard Tarlton in Gale's encyclopedia are fuller than those in Nilsen's guide. However, Nilsen identifies more works than Gale for both Geoffrey Chaucer and William Shakespeare. Nilsen's index of names and topics, such as "gender humor," "laughter," and "jokes," offers solid access. Although Nilsen's guide identifies critical responses to humor in more early British writers, Gale's encyclopedia is more generally useful both critically and bibliographically for the selection of early British writers.—**James K. Bracken**

Drama

1151. Mann, David D., and Susan Garland Mann, with Camille Garnier. **Women Playwrights in England, Ireland, and Scotland 1660-1823.** Bloomington, Ind., Indiana University Press, 1996. 417p. $57.50. ISBN 0-253-33087-4.

Prior to the mid-1980s when feminist scholars began in earnest to recover the works of women writers, women playwrights received scant attention from drama critics and theater historians alike. Now, with the publication of this volume, a more comprehensive picture of the role women played in the development of English drama begins to take shape. Covering the period from 1660 (when women were first allowed on London's and Dublin's theater stages) to 1823, the authors have compiled biographical information about more than 150 women playwrights and written summaries of many of their plays.

Arranged alphabetically according to the title of the plays and the authors' names, some of the entries are about plays whose authorship has not been established with certainty. As the authors explain in their introduction, women playwrights were rarely taken seriously and were often publicly ridiculed for their efforts to stage their works. To avoid criticism, they sometimes used pseudonyms or simply signed their plays with "By a Lady." Several of the playwrights included here wrote only a single play; others wrote "closet plays," that is, plays that were never intended for production. Also included are more prolific playwrights, such as Aphra Behn, Susannah Centlivre, Elizabeth Inchbald, Mary Pix, and Jane Scott, all of whom managed to sustain a fairly visible presence in English theater. The chronological list of plays in the appendixes helps to place the playwrights in a historical context, as does the authors' excellent introduction.

This groundbreaking book is filled with information on women who for too long have remained behind the scenes. Scholars, researchers, and general readers will all find this book easy to use and enjoyable to read. It is highly recommended. [R: Choice, Mar 97, p. 1140]—**Sandra Adell**

Fiction

1152. **Edwardian Fiction: An Oxford Companion.** By Sandra Kemp, Charlotte Mitchell, and David Trotter. New York, Oxford University Press, 1997. 431p. $39.95. ISBN 0-19-811760-4.

Emphasis in *Edwardian Fiction* is on some 800 mostly British writers of fiction from 1900 to 1914—the period between the Boer War (1899-1902) and the outbreak of World War I (beginning in 1914). Additionally, *Edwardian Fiction* contains concise plot outlines for about 250 carefully selected fictional works; longer entries for 20 selected topics (such as crime fiction, exoticism, feminist fiction, publishing, marriage problem fiction, and science fiction); brief, largely bibliographic entries for several periodicals, such as *Books*; an interesting chronology matching fiction with other books and cultural and historical events; and an index of pseudonyms and changes of name.

Although useful for information on major Edwardians (such as Arthur Conan Doyle, Joseph Conrad, E. M. Forster, and D. H. Lawrence), *Edwardian Fiction* is far more valuable for biographies of other equally prolific but more obscure writers. This coverage greatly surpasses that offered in Anthea Trodd's *A Reader's Guide to Edwardian Literature* (London: Harvester Wheatsheaf, 1991) and George M. Johnson's *Late-Victorian and Edwardian British Novelists. First Series* (see ARBA 96, entry 1235), volume 153 of the Dictionary of Literary Biography. Indeed, coverage of writers, works, and topics favorably compares with the *Oxford Companion to English Literature* (see ARBA 96, entry 1231), revised and edited by Margaret Drabble. *Edwardian Fiction* contains entries for Harold Bindloss, M. E. Brandon, Rosa Mouchette Carey, Mary Cholmondeley, Beatrice Harraden, Leonard Merrick, John Collis Snaith, and many other then-popular writers not included in the *Oxford Companion*. Whereas the *Oxford Companion* gives Eden Phillpotts a few lines, *Edwardian Fiction* offers a full page. Likewise, *Edwardian Fiction*'s entries for J. M. Barrie, Frank Harris, Robert Hichens, and "Fiona Macleod" are more factually and critically substantial than the *Oxford Companion*'s.

That entries for writers and topics at best inconsistently cite standard biographies and critical studies is perhaps *Edwardian Fiction*'s most notable shortcoming; in this even the *Oxford Companion* is generally bibliographically stronger. Nevertheless, scholars will find that *Edwardian Fiction* nicely complements existing sources for the period. In some public and academic libraries where the stacks seemingly swell with countless volumes of turn-of-the-century fiction by the likes of "Lady X," "Ouida," "Rita," and "Zack," *Edwardian Fiction* will prove to be an invaluable collection management tool. [R: RBB, June 97, pp. 1754-56]—**James K. Bracken**

Individual Authors

Jane Austen

1153. Gilson, David. **A Bibliography of Jane Austen.** [new ed.] New Castle, Del., Oak Knoll Press, 1997. 877p. index. $95.00. ISBN 1-884718-32-9.

Gilson has issued a facsimile edition of his bibliography originally published by the Oxford University Press in 1982 (see ARBA 83, entry 1216). This reprint is accompanied by several pages of corrections to the original work and 36 pages listing newly discovered or published materials. The researcher can locate all the new material in the introduction. In the new section on biography and criticism, Gilson has included books but excluded articles, theses, and parts of books. Although his decision is understandable because of space constraints, it is unfortunate given the recent critical interest in Austen. The reader will find articles, theses, and parts of books listed in the main body of the bibliography (works through 1978), but will have to consult another source, such as the Modern Language Association's *Annual Bibliography* or the Modern Humanities Research Association's *Annual Bibliography of English Language and Literature*, for post-1978 articles.

The main body of the work covers the editions of Austen's works thoroughly (original editions, first American editions, translations, later editions). Separate chapters describe collections of Austen's letters, dramatizations of her novels, continuations and completions of her unfinished works, and even a list of books owned by Austen. The last and largest chapter lists biographical and critical works. In many cases, Gilson describes the physical book and notes which copies he has examined. In the case of critical works, he lists reviews if available. An appendix provides a chronological listing of all editions, reprints, and adaptations of Austen's works from 1811 to 1978. The extensive index allows entry to the work by author, title, and subject. One is cautioned, however, that the index does not list any of the new introductory material. Gilson's work will be especially valuable to the reader who is studying Austen's work in some detail. Those interested in criticism, however, must augment use of this book with additional works as noted above.—**Linda Keir Simons**

Robert Browning

1154. Thomas, Charles Flint. **Art and Architecture in the Poetry of Robert Browning: An Illustrated Compendium of Sources. Appendix A.** Troy, N.Y., Whitston Publishing, 1996. 211p. illus. index. $35.00. ISBN 0-87875-467-9.

Some artists live and work in glorious isolation, their personal muse arising almost wholly from a fervid, internalized, and imaginative view of the world. However, that is not the road that most productive artists travel. Most artists' work is to a lesser or greater extent *derivative*, that is, they expose themselves to and are affected by the work of other artists. Art feeds art: A composer of opera is inspired by Norse myth, a painter is inspired by the grace of ballet dancers, and poet Robert Browning found inspiration in the places and art he saw in his Continental sojourns. Whole academic careers are based upon the determination and recording of particular artists' sources for inspiration.

From the time he started working on his dissertation, Thomas has traveled extensively, following in Browning's footsteps to locate the sources for his poetic inspiration. All of Thomas's observations have been made firsthand, and that fact distinguishes his work from that of many other literary historians. Some of Browning's sources are easily traced and identified; others Thomas has come across only through serendipity. Thomas has also analyzed many allusions as being composite and has developed lists of these "creative conflations" of sources.

In 1991, Thomas published the first part of his major study of the origins of Browning's visual allusions in his poetry, under the same title as the review volume. In the premier volume, Thomas listed 500 source notes on more than 70 of Browning's poems. Like its predecessor volume, *Appendix A* includes a Browning chronology, a list of illustrations, a "Citation and Notes" section, a summary of composite sources, indexes to artists and to sources with locations, and a key to bibliographic sources. In addition, the new volume contains a "Corrections and Revisions" section, updating some of the research in Thomas's first volume.

Interestingly, Thomas's introduction to *Appendix A* is much more illuminating than that which he wrote for the original compendium. In it, he outlines his work and that of other Browning "source hunters," putting those enterprises in clear research context. Therefore, a reader of the previous volume may well start with the introduction to the newer volume before proceeding into the body of the first volume. It should be noted that Thomas's research has continued and an *Appendix B* is currently being prepared. Any academic or large public library serving the needs of a population doing serious literary analysis of nineteenth-century authors should consider the purchase of this title and its preceding volume. Every major university research library should certainly own both titles and consider the continued purchase of future appendixes as they appear.—**Caroline M. Kent**

George Gordon Byron

1155. Goode, Clement Tyson, Jr. **George Gordon, Lord Byron: A Comprehensive, Annotated Research Bibliography of Secondary Materials in English, 1973-1994.** Lanham, Md., Scarecrow, 1997. 878p. index. $95.00. ISBN 0-8108-3186-4.

In 1812, Lord Byron, as he put it, "awoke and found himself famous." Publication of *Childe Harold's Pilgrimage* in that year launched his reputation, a reputation that has been mushrooming ever since. This comprehensive bibliography includes all secondary material on Byron in English, from the popular to the scholarly, for the years 1973 to 1994. Its almost 9,000 entries take up where *George Gordon, Lord Byron: A Comprehensive Bibliography of Secondary Materials in English, 1807-1974* (see ARBA 78, entry 1167) left off.

Goode's indispensable guide to everything written about Byron's life and work over the past 20 years provides a trove of such contemporary focuses as new historicism, Marxism, feminism, editorial method, text, and literary theory. All entries are briefly annotated and arranged chronologically, which allows for an understanding of the development of Byron scholarship. Six serviceable appendixes list dissertations and theses; sales, library acquisitions, and holdings; places and items associated with the poet; poetical tributes, attacks, and imitations; adaptations, parodies, and satires; and Byron in drama, fiction, and poetry. Three thorough indexes—by author, poem, and subject—permit ready access to all entries. This title is highly recommended for all college and university collections.—**G. A. Cevasco**

Geoffrey Chaucer

1156. **Chaucer's *Miller's*, *Reeve's*, and *Cook's Tales*.** T. L. Burton and Rosemary Greentree, eds. Toronto and Buffalo, N.Y., University of Toronto Press, 1997. 287p. index. (The Chaucer Bibliographies, no.5). $75.00. ISBN 0-8020-0874-7.

Volume 5 in The Chaucer Bibliographies focuses on published scholarship from 1900 to 1992 on the *Miller's Tale*, the *Reeve's Tale*, and the *Cook's Tale*, all part of Geoffrey Chaucer's masterpiece, *The Canterbury Tales*. The 755 entries have been selected and authoritatively annotated by a team of expert scholars and organized chronologically by the editors into 8 sections: "Editions, Translations, and Modernizations"; "Sources and Analogues"; "Items of Linguistic and Lexicographical Interest"; "The Narrators of the Tales Considered as Characters"; "The Tales Considered Together"; "The *Miller's Tale*"; "The *Reeve's Tale*"; and "The *Cook's Tale*." The editors provide a useful introduction to the volume that discusses the history of scholarship concerning these three tales during the period 1900 to 1992. A comprehensive index to names, titles of primary works, and subjects concludes the volume.

Like others in this excellent series, this volume is intended for several different audiences. This is a volume and series no Chaucerian scholar should be without. Likewise, graduate students will find it even more valuable as the authoritative annotations map out the contours of a dense and sometimes arcane scholarship. College instructors and high school teachers will also find an easy entrée into this dense literature that they may not otherwise approach. The Chaucer Bibliographies, and this volume in particular, are essential reference books for every college and university library.—**Richard W. Clement**

Charles Dickens

1157. **The Proverbial Charles Dickens: An Index to Proverbs in the Works of Charles Dickens.** By George B. Bryan and Wolfgang Mieder. New York, Peter Lang, 1997. 319p. $39.95. ISBN 0-8204-3837-5.

Rarely does the front matter of a reference book state the book's nature with the clarity that author Meider masters in explaining this one: "The work consists of an introductory essay on Dickens's use of proverbs, a list of the editions of his works consulted, and a key-word index, which is the heart of the book." The keyword index lists English proverbs and proverbial expressions in alphabetic order by their key elements, which are printed in bold typeface for easy and unambiguous navigation. Beneath each proverb one finds in chronological order dated, quoted passages showing every instance of Dickens's use of that proverb. As the complete citations for the quotations show, the book indexes proverbs in the complete Dickens corpus, including novels, stories, and letters. Following the quoted passages, citations indicate dictionaries of proverbs that explain the origin and meaning of the proverbs Dickens used. The introductory essay makes it abundantly clear that Dickens drew proverbs from literary and folk sources, but principally from the latter, befitting a novelist whose characters peopled the working and middle classes of Victorian England. It is not surprising that the source of at least one of the expressions in the index is Dickens himself; his "Barkis is willin'" from *David Copperfield* has become a proverbial expression for a man's readiness to marry.

Given the book's highly specialized nature, this is not, unlike the works it mines, a book for the masses, but one for scholars. They can take the raw materials of the proverbs in the index and use that material to build on the introductory essay's conclusions about the ways and reasons why Dickens wove proverbs into his works. Only in a very few libraries will this meet the definition of a reference book—one that is kept in the reference collection and does not circulate. It will go instead into the stacks where it will function nicely as what it is—a scholarly monograph, albeit one in which supporting evidence (i.e., the keyword index to proverbs) occupies far many more pages than the argument (i.e., Meider's introductory essay) it supports.—**James Rettig**

Arthur Conan Doyle

1158. **Good Old Index: The Sherlock Holmes Handbook.** By Thomas W. Ross. Columbia, S.C., Camden House, 1997. 171p. illus. $25.95pa. ISBN 1-57113-049-7.

Whereas the several standard companions to Authur Conan Doyle's Sherlock Holmes canon, most notably Orlando Park's *Sherlock Holmes, Esq., and John H. Watson, M.D.* (Northwestern University Press, 1962); Jack Tracy's *The Encyclopaedia Sherlockiana or, a Universal Dictionary of the State of Knowledge of Sherlock Holmes and His Biographer, John H. Watson, M.D.* (see ARBA 78, entry 1172); and Matthew E. Bunson's *Encyclopedia Sherlockiana: An A-to-Z Guide to the World of the Great Detective* (see ARBA 95, entry 1211), have tended to explain persons, places, and things, Ross's handbook approaches the same canon from a fairly unique and refreshingly novel perspective. Eschewing plot summaries, publication histories, and detailed character analyses (ably offered in Park, Tracy, and Bunson, among others), Ross's approximately 2,500 entries concentrate on the Holmes stories' facts and elementary details, particularly characters' physical features—the likes of beards, dress, eyes, feet, fingers, knees, laughter, lips, screams, and twitches. For example, Ross gives nearly two full pages of references to specific stories in the entry for hands. Similarly, he offers three pages of references for "money" and nearly one page for "keys." Like the handbooks of Bunson and Tracy, Ross notes Watson's appraisal of Holmes's knowledge of literature ("nil"). Yet surpassing Bunson and Tracy in detail, Ross additionally identifies and cross-references entries for some 20 writers whom Holmes quotes, paraphrases, or otherwise mentions. The result amounts to an index of features across Doyle's Holmes stories that affords an excellent aid for close reading.

The index's single glaring fault is commonly shared by other Holmes handbooks. Based on William S. Barin-Gould's two-volume *The Annotated Sherlock Holmes* (London, John Murray, 1968) and the two-volume American edition, *The Complete Sherlock Holmes* (Doubleday, 1936), with a preface by Christopher Morley, Ross fails to reference specific chapters or pages in the individual works (cited by acronyms). Doing what it does very well, Ross's index complements all yet supersedes none of the many other Holmes handbooks. Handbooks of the likes of Park's, Tracy's, and Bunson's remain valuable for information beyond Ross's scope. Likewise, Scott R. Bullard's and Michael Lee Collins's *Who's Who in Sherlock Holmes* (see ARBA 82, entry 1293) and Christopher Redmond's *A Sherlock Holmes Handbook* (see ARBA 95, entry 1212) complement these more traditional handbooks, as does John Hall's *I Remember the Date Very Well: A Chronology of the Sherlock Holmes Stories of Arthur Conan Doyle* (Players Press, 1993), which offers a useful chronological sequence of the published cases. [R: Choice, July/Aug 97, pp. 1785-86]—**James K. Bracken**

G. A. Henty

1159. Newbolt, Peter. **G. A. Henty 1832-1902: A Bibliographical Study of His British Editions....** Brookfield, Vt., Scolar Press/Ashgate Publishing, 1996. 710p. illus. index. $84.95. ISBN 1-85928-208-3.

British author George Alfred Henty (1832-1902) was best known as a writer of boys' books, popular works that combined adventure with history. Although not well known outside of England, Henty has, over the decades, inspired sufficient interest that in 1977 his nephew successfully launched The Henty Society, devoted to the study of his life and work. This bibliography, compiled with the Society's blessings, is intended for book collectors as well as Henty devotees and researchers. The 120 books (in 500 editions) included are described not by plot, theme, character, and the like, but instead by their physical characteristics. These include such attributes as size, binding methods and materials, contents, and other information of interest to booksellers and collectors. Newbolt also provides accounts of Henty's publishers, illustrators, and designers, as well as essays on the printing and binding methods of the day. Although obviously a specialized purchase, this comprehensive, exhaustively detailed "bibliographic study" will undoubtedly be welcomed by Henty enthusiasts.—**G. Kim Dority**

W. Somerset Maugham

1160. Rogal, Samuel J. **A William Somerset Maugham Encyclopedia.** Westport, Conn., Greenwood Press, 1997. 376p. index. $79.50. ISBN 0-313-29916-1.

This single-volume encyclopedia covers events relating to William Somerset Maugham (1874-1965) from the middle of the reign of Queen Victoria to that of Queen Elizabeth II. The work is organized into five sections: preface, chronology, encyclopedia, general bibliography, and index.

The preface briefly describes Maugham's life and prolific literary output: 20 novels, 31 plays, 9 volumes of short stories, and 7 volumes of nonfiction. His plots were used in seven movies. The chronology begins with 1788 and the birth of Maugham's paternal grandfather (unfortunately, his maternal grandfather is also mistakenly identified as paternal) and spans to the death in 1981 of his favorite nephew. Also listed are such historical dates as the passage of the Sexual Offense Act, the Copyright Act covering English works published in the United States, the Boer War, and the deaths of Queen Victoria and Winston Churchill.

The alphabetically arranged encyclopedic items include Maugham's works, friends, relatives, literary associates, places where he lived or visited, and such topics as Jews and homosexuals. Names mentioned within entries having a separate listing of their own are marked with an asterisk. Each entry is followed by a brief bibliography. More detailed reference sources are found under the general bibliography section. The index simplifies cross-referencing. This volume, which includes entries on such diverse people as Noël Coward, El Greco, Thomas Hardy, D. H. Lawrence, Clare Booth Luce, the Duke and Duchess of Windsor, and Virginia Woolf, provides useful and entertaining reading, even for those with only a peripheral interest in Maugham.—**Charlotte Lindgren**

William Shakespeare

1161. Clark, Sandra. **A Dictionary of Who, What, and Where in Shakespeare: A Comprehensive Guide to Shakespeare's Plays, Characters, and Contemporaries.** Lincolnwood, Ill., National Textbook, 1997. 291p. $12.95pa. ISBN 0-8442-5757-5.

This dictionary is a thumbnail guide to William Shakespeare's plays and characters. *Shakespeare A to Z* (see ARBA 92, entry 1209), which is also a dictionary treatment of all of Shakespeare, dwarfs this book in every way, and any library owning that book really does not need the one under review. However, for the price, Clark's dictionary makes a good circulating collection item or even a reference book for a small public library or personal collection.

This book does not cover all of Shakespeare's characters. For instance, the daughter of Antiochus in *Pericles* is missing, as are many of the historical figures who appear briefly in the history plays. Most entries are quite short (one to four lines in length), with no major character receiving more than a paragraph of discussion. The entry for Hamlet, as a character, is only 26 lines in length (the entry for Hamlet in *Shakespeare A to Z*, by comparison, is more than 8 times as long). The plays themselves receive anywhere from two to four pages of plot summary, textual background, and performance history. The entry for *Hamlet* the play is approximately 3.3 pages in length; the entry for *Hamlet* in *Shakespeare A to Z* would have run to more than 14 pages. There are also entries for important figures in Shakespeare's life (George Chapman, Nathaniel Field, Thomas Nash).

Despite its brevity, the dictionary is a current, useful little compendium. It is enhanced by a biographical essay, a short essay on Elizabethan theater and play production, and an unremarkable selected bibliography. A most useful 31-page essay on Shakespeare's nondramatic poetry is also provided. The book is a reprint of a 1994 volume entitled *The Shakespeare Dictionary* (see ARBA 96, entry 1241). It is printed in an unpleasant nineteenth-centuryish typeface that leads one to assume, initially, that it may be a photographic reproduction of a nineteenth-century work. However, the references show it to be current. All in all, this book is a secondary acquisition for academic libraries. It will add nothing new to the stock of knowledge, but it may help an occasional student.—**Bill Miller**

1162. **Exploring Shakespeare.** [CD-ROM]. Detroit, Gale, 1997. Minimum system requirements: IBM or compatible 386 (486DX/33MHz or higher highly recommended). CD-ROM drive with MS-DOS CD-ROM Extensions 2.2 (double-speed or faster recommended). DOS 5.0. Windows 3.1. 8MB RAM. 5MB hard disk space. SVGA monitor and graphics card (256 color). Windows-compatible mouse. 8-bit SoundBlaster-compatible sound card with Windows 3.1-compatible drivers and speakers or headphones (optional). Printer (optional). $300.00/stand-alone version. ISBN 0-7876-0914-5.

The rich content and enduring nature of William Shakespeare's work is ideal information for multimedia. Consequently, many Shakespeare CD-ROMs have come and gone as the technology has evolved. This year, Gale adds their version, *Exploring Shakespeare*, to the dozen or so CD-ROMs currently on the market. Users familiar with the DISCovering Program of CD-ROMs will recognize this product as a curriculum-driven resource designed primarily for high school students. The product is useful as well for adults seeking to expand their knowledge of Shakespeare and four of his more popular plays: *Hamlet*, *Julius Caesar*, *Macbeth*, and *Romeo and Juliet*. Full text of the 2d edition of *The Arden Shakespeare* for these plays is enhanced with explanatory notes from both Gale and Arden, which are easily accessed by clicking on quill-pen icons to the right of each line of text. Each play can be further explored through plot summaries, critical and interpretive essays, character studies, and historical information.

Other avenues of exploration consist of a biography of the playwright; descriptions of Elizabethan life and theater; and a list of additional resources, including books, journal articles, and media adaptations for each of the four plays. A timeline feature, integrating the life and works of Shakespeare with world events, sets the plays and their author in context. All of the paths of inquiry are interconnected with hypertext links and enhanced with black-and-white pictures, color maps and photographs, facsimiles of several primary documents, and excellent-quality audio clips. A number of interesting video clips of scenes from the plays and historical information from Shakespeare's England are unfortunately marred by the lack of synchronization between audio and video. Although most of the supporting information is taken from other Gale publications, such as *Shakespearean Criticism* (see ARBA 96, entry 1242, for a review of volume 26) and *Shakespeare for Students* (see entry 1163 for a review of *Book II*), much of the research has also been published elsewhere.

A comprehensive and well-indexed User's Manual, a concise Help Card, and on-disc Help screens provide excellent installation, navigation, and reference assistance. A thematically organized Teacher's Guide, designed to move the study of Shakespeare beyond the traditional, offers outcome-based activities that involve critical analysis, creative thinking, problem solving, and dramatic interpretation. As with any educational tool, much will depend on how it is used. With so many choices available, teachers, librarians, and individuals should take advantage of the free 30-day trial of this product and compare it to other titles, such as *Shakespeare: The Complete Works of William Shakespeare* (Creative Multimedia, 1989); *Much Ado About Shakespeare* (Bureau of Electronic Publishing, 1996); or *The Arden Shakespeare* (Thomas Nelson, 1997). Educators interested in a particular play may also consider G. K. Hall's *Shakespeare on Disc* (1989) for *Hamlet*, *Julius Caesar*, or *Romeo and Juliet*, and Voyager's *Macbeth* (1993). Users with Internet access may want to peruse the many Shakespearean sites available on the World Wide Web, and will be interested in Gale's intentions to make all the DISCovering Program CD-ROMs accessible via the Internet.—**Debra S. Van Tassel**

1163. **Shakespeare for Students, Book II.** Catherine C. Dominic, ed. Detroit, Gale, 1997. 549p. illus. index. $60.00. ISBN 0-7876-0157-8.

Shakespeare for Students, Book II complements an earlier volume, *Shakespeare for Students*. *Book II* offers critical interpretations of more popular, widely read Shakespearean plays that are often required reading for high school students and undergraduates. This volume treats *Henry IV, Part One*; *Henry V*; *King Lear*; *Much Ado About Nothing*; *Richard III*; *The Taming of the Shrew*; *The Tempest*; and *Twelfth Night*. *Book II* is similar in arrangement and content to the multivolume *Shakespearean Criticism* (see ARBA 96, entry 1242, for example). It provides further summarization of individual plays, background material, a list of principal characters, a plot synopsis, and a discussion of principal topics and themes, in addition to a selection of critical reviews reprinted from other sources. Many reviews reprinted in *Book II* are duplicated from *Shakespearean Criticism*; however, additional, more current reviews are included.

If a library cannot purchase *Shakespearean Criticism*, *Shakespeare for Students, Book II* and the earlier companion volume *Shakespeare for Students* are good values. This volume includes a chronology of Shakespeare's life and works, a glossary, and a short index to themes and characters.—**Jane Jurgens**

1164. **Shakespeare's Characters for Students.** Catherine C. Dominic, ed. Detroit, Gale, 1997. 537p. index. $65.00. ISBN 0-7876-1300-2.

The toughest and most frustrating part of reading William Shakespeare, especially for beginners, is keeping track of all the characters and little plot intricacies that determine the outcome of the play. *Shakespeare's Characters for Students* helps keep characters straight and provides basic plot summaries of the plays as well. This book is arranged alphabetically by play. Beginning each play's section is a synopsis of the play, followed by a "Modern Connections" section, then an explanation of each character and how he or she relates to other characters and to the plot. Naturally, the depth of this analysis depends on the character's importance in the story. The "Modern Connections" section, about a half-page in length, usually takes one theme that recent audiences have focused on when discussing the play. Although it does reference and quote the sources it draws from, the connections are limited and add little to help students understand the plays. The concept of connecting the play or parts of the play to the modern world is a solid one, but the execution leaves much to be desired.

This book would benefit from a heartier discussion of themes. Although Shakespearean themes could certainly fill a volume of books equal to an encyclopedia in number, it would do students some good to be more aware of their existence than this book will make them. A character list, such as those found at the beginning of the plays in almost every Shakespeare edition, would also be a helpful touch. What this work could do without is the quotations found on a majority of pages, which do nothing to draw the reader in, explain the text, or create appreciation for the poetry.

Shakespeare's Characters for Students is exactly what it claims to be. As a simple summary of the characters and plots, this book will suffice. Yet for themes, in-depth plot summaries, and criticisms, this book will leave the students it is aimed at looking for other books to consult.—**Tom Sullivan**

1165. **The World Shakespeare Bibliography on CD-ROM 1990-1993.** [CD-ROM]. James L. Harner, ed. New York, Cambridge University Press, 1996. Minimum system requirements (Windows version): IBM or compatible 386. Double-speed CD-ROM drive. Windows 3.1. 8MB RAM. Minimum system requirements (Macintosh version): Double-speed CD-ROM drive. System 7. 4MB RAM. $240.00. ISBN 0-521-55627-9.

This CD-ROM covers all important books, articles, book reviews, dissertations, theatrical productions, reviews of productions, audiovisual materials, electronic media, and other scholarly and popular materials related to William Shakespeare and published or produced between 1990 and 1993. The project is ongoing, and the publishers plan to take the coverage from 1900 to the present. It includes English- as well as other foreign-language publications. The CD-ROM omits obituaries of performers, abstracts of unpublished convention papers, operas not based on Shakespearean texts, and nonspeaking roles in Shakespearean productions.

The table of contents provides quick access with four subdivisions: "General Shakespeareana," "Play Groups," "Individual Works," and "Indexes." From the table of contents, it is easy to move to the entries that include complete bibliographic information, a summary of the material, and review citations. Hypertext links effortlessly connect the user to related works. Authors, actors, dramatists, and subjects have separate indexes with hypertext links to the text. Keyword searching and advanced features, such as Boolean, truncation, and proximity searching, provide quick access to information. Another nice feature available to the user is the ability to create annotations, add a bookmark, and even backtrack through the sources searched. Printing and downloading options are provided in the software.

The documentation is excellent. The information is accurate, clear, and easy-to-follow. The CD-ROM is easy to install and functioned without problems. The CD-ROM runs on both Windows and Macintosh platforms with no differences in functionality. However, the font size on the IBM is too small to read. An Enlarge button helps increase the font size, but every time a window is closed it reverts to the small letters. This becomes annoying when moving from one hypertext link to another. The font size on the Macintosh is large and easy to read.

For a research library with an interest in Shakespearean materials, this is an excellent resource. The CD-ROM provides quick, comprehensive bibliographic information on a variety of topics. Only three years of information are provided in this CD-ROM, but the access to information is incredible. It will be even better when the set is complete.—**Suzanne Julian**

William Butler Yeats

1166. McCready, Sam. **A William Butler Yeats Encyclopedia.** Westport, Conn., Greenwood Press, 1997. 484p. index. $95.00. ISBN 0-313-28371-0.

This compact, comprehensive encyclopedia is designed to appeal to scholars and amateurs alike. Written in a highly readable, no-nonsense style, it begins with a chronology of the chief events in William Butler Yeats's life and then provides more than 1,000 entries in alphabetic order. Topics include mythological and religious influences, Yeats's relatives and friends, his politics, writers who influenced him, and the organizations to which he belonged. Of particular interest are the entries concerning locations where the poet lived or the places he wrote about. For example, there is useful information about the county and town of Sligo, an area that Yeats looked upon as his spiritual home (although he was born in Dublin). It was here that he was enchanted by the "magical" hill, Ben Bulben, that figures prominently in his best verse, and it was here that Yeats as a young man drank in legends, songs, and myths as he listened to elderly servants or common working people. Yeats's profound attachment to Sligo is symbolized by his requesting to be buried in Drumcliff, at the foot of Ben Bulben (he died in France and was reinterred in 1948). Also useful in this encyclopedia is the information about Coole Park, the home of Lady Gregory, who with Yeats founded the renowned Abbey Theatre. Coole, where Yeats spent no fewer than 20 summers, is a place he saw as highly charged with feeling and meaning, as one can notice in several major poems, including "The Wild Swans at Coole." Yet there were many other locations that fascinated the poet—the Aran Islands, the village of Ardrahan, the town of Athenry—and the encyclopedia offers a "tour" through these, as well as through significant locations in England and on the Continent.

McCready has included literally hundreds of prominent person in this volume, most of them having strong connotations for readers of Yeats: Maude Gonne, Robert Gregory, Ezra Pound, Sean O'Casey, James McNeill Whistler, John Ruskin, and Lord Dunsany, to mention just a few. Each of these receives at least a paragraph, and even the lesser-known personages, such as Jeremiah Curtin or Rosa Mulholland, are treated in an interesting and responsible manner. James Joyce, first an enemy and then a friend, gets an entire page. The reader comes away with the impression that anyone who had any significance in Yeats's life is included in this volume. McCready's thoroughness is suggested not only by his extended treatment of the beautiful Gonne, whom Yeats loved for most of his life, but also by the discussion of her daughter (whom Yeats eventually tried to marry), and by references to other members of the Gonne family—Kathleen Gonne and May Gonne. McCready's tactics involve readers in the poet's life to the extent that they almost feel that they know him as a colleague and friend.

There are few errors or blemishes in this intriguing book. Although one could wish for more material concerning Yeats's "personal mythology" involving 2,000-year cycles of history (there is no entry for "gyre") and for more material on the poet's amorous excursions, this is still a successful, effective handbook, one that any serious reader or scholar of Yeats would want to own. It fills a large gap between heavy critical works about Yeats and the skimpy treatments that one finds in college outlines or the "companion" sorts of books.

McCready is professor of theater at the University of Maryland, Baltimore County. A longtime veteran of the theater and a practicing scholar, he is well qualified to write on a man who is perhaps the greatest poet of the twentieth century.—**Peter Thorpe**

African Literature

1167. **African Writers.** C. Brian Cox, ed. New York, Scribner's/Simon & Schuster Macmillan, 1997. 2v. index. $220.00/set. ISBN 0-684-19651-4.

This two-volume reference collection of essays offers an introduction to the richness and diversity of late-nineteenth- and twentieth-century literature from the African continent. The editor has chosen to feature those writers who were born or spent a good deal of their lives in Africa. He treats writers who have received international recognition for their achievement and made significant contributions to the literature of their countries. Although not entirely comprehensive, the editor's selection of 65 authors does include 4 writers awarded the Nobel prize in literature: Albert Camus (1957), Nadine Gordimer

(1991), Naguib Mahfouz (1988), and Wole Soyinka (1986). Not to be exclusionary, both women and men are represented in the collection. The diversity within the literature is shown by the inclusion of writers of everything from poetry to literary criticism.

The set is well organized. Following the table of contents, there is an index in which the authors are grouped according to the present-day African countries with which they are most frequently associated. In most cases, the countries are the lands in which the writers were born, grew up, and developed their reputations. This index includes a brief paragraph about the writer, which is quite useful. The writers discussed in this collection use many different languages. In general, those from Ghana, Kenya, Nigeria, and South Africa write in English; those from Algeria, Cameroon, Guinea, and Senegal write in French; those from Angola and Mozambique write in Portuguese; and Egyptian authors write in Arabic. A few write in indigenous African languages, such as Akan, Yoruba, and Kikuyu, and some write in more than one language. Most of the non-English works discussed in this collection are available in English translations. When this is the case, the published English titles appear in italics in parentheses following the original title.

A nice aspect of this set is a chronological table of African history from 1830 to 1996, which precedes the alphabetic essay entries. Biographical in nature and written by a number of contributors, these essays analyze the works of these world-renowned African writers. At the end of each entry is a selected bibliography of the publishing history of each writer and selected secondary sources. Volume 2 concludes with biographical sketches of the contributors and a comprehensive index for the set. This reference set is highly recommended for any library having a world literature collection or an explicit interest in global writers.—**Judith A. Valdez**

Argentine Literature

1168. Lichtblau, Myron I. **The Argentine Novel: An Annotated Bibliography.** Lanham, Md., Scarecrow, 1997. 1111p. $99.50. ISBN 0-8108-3242-9.

Lichtblau has succeeded in providing a useful reference work to a large body of literary work in one comprehensive tome. This bibliography of the novel in Argentina from 1788 to 1990 gives the reader a view of the rich novelistic production of two centuries and of its worldwide diffusion. The bibliography cuts a wide swath through genre and nationality as it includes translated editions, non-Argentinean writers residing in Argentina, and nonfictional works that have novelistic characteristics (Esteban Echeverría's *El Matadero*, a well-known critical semidocumentary on the Juan Manuel de Rosas regime, is an example). Moreover, Lichtblau includes *novela corta* (novella), as well as popular fiction, to demonstrate the fluidity of the genre in Argentina, where social commentary often prevails as the motivational force behind novelists' works. Entries are annotated with one or more quotations from previously published critical works on each particular novel. In its scope, therefore, this volume is a key reference tool that will guide readers to the many writers who deserve attention for their productivity and the quality of their work.—**Stella T. Clark**

Canadian Literature

1169. **Contemporary Canadian Authors, Volume 1: A Bio-bibliographical Guide....** Robert Lang, ed. Toronto, Gale Canada, 1996. 488p. $170.00; $125.00 (U.S.). ISBN 1-896413-08-0. ISSN 1203-2816.

Gale's premier volume of *Contemporary Canadian Authors* follows the same general principles and format of the Contemporary Authors series in providing bio-bibliographic information on writers of Canada from a wide range of fields, including media in numerous formats as well as more traditional literary publications. Entry sketches provide a nominal heading, including the most complete form of the author's name (with any variations or pseudonyms), personal information as available with pertinent points of contact, a career summary, and inclusion of awards/honors/memberships as appropriate. Writings are listed chronologically with date, edition, and adaptation notes and works in progress if known. A "sidelights" section furnishes a diverse blend of historical background, philosophy, and commentary by or about the author and may contain critical evaluations or interview materials. Concluding each entry is a list of source materials as a basis for further research.

Although not as comprehensive in coverage as individual inclusions in Gale's Dictionary of Literary Biography series, this initial volume provides a much broader framework of references and wider definition of authorship for Canadian writers. As a reference series, it will be an ongoing source of current information on Canadian literary endeavors. Access will be further enhanced if entries are to be included in Gale's Contemporary Authors cumulative index.—**Virginia S. Fischer**

East European Literature

1170. **The Modern Encyclopedia of East Slavic, Baltic, and Eurasian Literatures. Volume 10: Holub, Yurka—Ivanov-Paimen, Vlas Sakharovich.** Peter Rollberg, ed. Gulf Breeze, Fla., Academic International Press, 1996. 246p. $38.50. ISBN 0-87569-038-6.

This volume continues the previous nine volumes of *The Modern Encyclopedia of Russian and Soviet Literatures* that were issued by the same publisher from 1978 to 1989 (see ARBA 90, entry 1210, and ARBA 79, entry 1283). Because the Soviet cultural and political reality officially ceased to exist in August 1991, the changed title is a reflection of the solution to a problem faced by all East European, Baltic, and Eurasian scholarship. By using linguistic and geographic terms, the publisher has provided a respectable solution to this problem. In its new incarnation after a seven-year hiatus, heavier emphasis than before is now placed on the literature of the newly independent nations. The major literatures covered are Armenian, Azerbaijanian, Belarusian, Estonian, Georgian, Latvian, Russian, Udmurt, and Ukrainian. In total, about 80 literatures are eventually supposed to be represented.

In contrast to other encyclopedias issued by Academic International Press, in which many articles are translated by American and European scholars from the original sources, this present endeavor only includes original articles by qualified scholars. Most articles are attributed to the person writing them; those not so attributed are composed by the editorial staff. Each entry consists of a brief one- or two-sentence identifier and then goes on to include a more extensive essay, followed by bibliographic references to other English and vernacular sources.

The articles in this volume are well written and highly informative. Users could not ask for more in a reference work of this type. Articles on specific persons, for example, include prominent biographical details in addition to a critical appraisal and discussion of the author's work. Entries also exist for literary artifacts, literary schools, and other pertinent material. Relevant and useful bibliographies are included for most entries. What is not clear from the introduction by the editor is whether this and subsequent volumes will also cover émigré literatures (as the title page of previous volumes indicated), or whether coverage will be confined to literature only produced within the new national boundaries.

The only drawback to the use of these volumes is the decision of the editor not to use the Library of Congress (or another consistent and widely used) transliteration scheme. Because of this decision, names beginning with "IA" and "IU" will be spelled as "YA" and "YU," occasionally the initial letter "E" will be rendered "YE," terminal "YI" and "II" will be rendered as "Y," terminal "OI" as "OY," terminal soft signs dropped, and medial soft signs rendered as "I." This inconsistency is likely to confuse and frustrate any user (especially because no cross-references are provided from variant names). In spite of this minor stylistic flaw, this and subsequent volumes should prove to be useful and relevant to the needs of students and scholars alike.—**Robert H. Burger**

French Literature

1171. Harvey, Robert, and Héléne Volat. **Marguerite Duras: A Bio-bibliography.** Westport, Conn., Greenwood Press, 1997. 273p. index. (Bio-bibliographies in World Literature, no.5). $69.50. ISBN 0-313-28898-4.

Marguerite Duras (1914-1996) ranks among the most important postwar French writers. Her large (and strongly obsessive-compulsive) output found both popular success and critical esteem from the likes of Maurice Blanchot and Jacques Lacan. Since 1970, her oeuvre has inspired a flood of academic commentaries, giving the present volume its value.

Harvey and Volat here account for everything Duras published and nearly everything written about her in French and English. They begin with an elegant introduction ("Writing as Life") that touches Duras's themes and personal mythology. After a chronology of her life, readers get a catalog of writings (books and journalism); films; and interviews (print, radio, and television). Most of the space is devoted to Duras criticism. Every conceivable variant is addressed—monographs, collections of essays, single chapters in other books, special issues of journals, and individual journal articles. Each of these entries receives a (generally) objective summary of its contents. There are also listings of Ph.D. dissertations, book reviews arranged by subject, and miscellaneous magazine and newspaper articles. The titles of Duras's works, authors of criticism, and names referenced are all indexed.

If any category gets shortchanged, it is the series of remarkable films Duras made from her own texts; they form a more radical rejection of contemporary practice than her books and are little seen outside France. Some notes on the critical contributors may have helped, if only to separate, say, Blanchot from the scholar inching toward tenure. Still, this book is an invaluable achievement.—**Walt Mundkowsky**

German Literature

1172. **German Baroque Writers, 1661-1730.** James Hardin, ed. Detroit, Gale, 1996. 492p. illus. index. (Dictionary of Literary Biography, v.168). $140.00. ISBN 0-8103-9363-8.

This valuable addition to Gale's Dictionary of Literary Biography series covers 46 notable writers of the later German baroque period. Following the standard format of the series—consisting mainly of primary bibliography, illustrated bio-bibliographic essay, and secondary bibliography—its articles are clearly and concisely written and exhibit a high standard of scholarship. A sequel to *German Baroque Writers, 1580-1660* (see ARBA 97, entry 1006), it is the work of competent and distinguished specialists, including some of the contributors its predecessor. The choice of authors for coverage reflects an intelligently broad understanding of the term "literature"; in addition to persons known primarily as novelists, dramatists, and lyric poets, one finds the philosopher Gottfried Wilhelm Leibniz, the folklorist writer Johannes Praetorius, the polyhistorian Samuel Pufendorf, the educator and jurist Christian Thomasius, and the religious writer Nikolaus Ludwig von Zinzendorf. Perhaps in order to balance page counts, some "later" authors were covered in the earlier volume. This edition features all of the major literary figures of the latter part of the period, plus a balanced selection of others.

Dates of coverage for the individual bibliographies vary. Although some include matter published in 1994, others cease rather earlier. In several of the latter instances, important material from the early 1990s has been missed. Among the bibliographies whose usefulness has been compromised by this editorial decision are prominent writers such as Abraham a Sancta Clara, Daniel Casper von Lohenstein, and Johann Jacob Christoffel von Grimmelshausen. It is also unfortunate that either article author or editor failed to correct the opaque "Salluste" (p. 118) into "du Bartas" and the curious "Cassius Dion" (p. 277) into "Cassius Dio" or "Dio Cassius." Such errors detract from the high standard of editing established by earlier volumes in the series.

Despite the work's cost, which is about the same as that for obtaining similar books published in Germany, this volume is highly recommended for college and university libraries supporting strong programs in German literature, comparative literature, or German history. Major public libraries in German settlement areas of North America may also find it useful.—**John B. Dillon**

1173. **The Oxford Companion to German Literature.** 3d ed. By Henry Garland and Mary Garland. New York, Oxford University Press, 1997. 951p. $75.00. ISBN 0-19-815896-3.

This companion marks the 3d edition of a title first published by Henry and Mary Garland in 1975 (see ARBA 77, entry 1263), then revised by Mary Garland alone in 1986 (see ARBA 88, entry 1246). Mary Garland, who died shortly before the book went to press, has updated this work through the mid-1990s to reflect Germany's reunification, as well as the burgeoning crop of new authors, titles, and literary trends of the past decade. A further purpose is to increase representation of the neglected women writers of all periods.

Eighty new entries have been added and over two hundred existing ones revised. Among the new entries are those for contemporary authors such as Elfriede Jelinek, Monika Maron, and Gunter de Bruyn; and recent titles such as Thomas Bernhard's final novel *Ausloschung* (1986) and Gunter Grass's 1996 tome *Ein weites Feld*. Also new and welcome are articles on anti-Semitism and the Yiddish language. One wishes similar attention had been given to topics such as feminism or the flourishing literary output of Germany's new ethnic groups. Entries on living persons have been brought up-to-date and sometimes totally revised, such as in the case of Christa Wolf; new editions for writers of all periods have been duly noted. Geographic entries, such as Berlin or Potsdam, have been updated, and two current maps are included. The current period seems to have been slighted somewhat in order to retain almost all existing entries; important writers such as Sten Nadolny, Gerhard Roth, and Helga Konigsdorf receive no mention. However, enough new information is presented here to make the book's purchase worthwhile.—**Willa Schmidt**

Irish Literature

1174. Allison, Jonathan. **Patrick Kavanagh: A Reference Guide.** New York, G. K. Hall/Simon & Schuster Macmillan, 1996. 218p. index. (A Reference Guide to Literature). $40.00. ISBN 0-8161-7286-2.

The reputation of Patrick Kavanagh (1904-1967) stands higher now than during his lifetime: He has emerged as the most influential Irish poet since William Butler Yeats. Unlike that magisterial figure, Kavanagh was a poet of the ordinary, depicting local rural life realistically, eschewing both the subject matter and the style of the Irish Literary Revival. Allison's introduction offers an excellent account of the man and his work and graciously acknowledges Antoinette Quinn's book, *Patrick Kavanagh: A Critical Study* (Syracuse University Press, 1991), as the definitive study of the poems.

This book records and annotates some 1,500 items on Kavanagh from 1935 to 1995—books, articles, reviews, and radio and television broadcasts. Most of the writings on Kavanagh have been published in the Irish Republic and the United States. The items, listed chronologically by year, then alphabetically within the year, give clear evidence of Kavanagh's growing importance. Supplementary author and subject indexes are given. The book is a valuable resource for biographers of this truculent figure as well as for literary critics.—**John B. Beston**

1175. **Irish Playwrights, 1880-1995: A Research and Production Sourcebook.** Bernice Schrank and William W. Demastes, eds. Westport, Conn., Greenwood Press, 1997. 454p. index. $95.00. ISBN 0-313-28805-4.

The establishment of Irish drama as a recognized genre begins with the founding of the Abbey Theatre in 1897 as the Irish Literary Theatre by Lady Gregory, Edward Martyn, and William Butler Yeats. As the chronological limits in the title indicate, this reference book contains the 32 playwrights who were prominent at the founding of the theater and those who have emerged subsequently. The entries are arranged alphabetically from Samuel Beckett to Yeats. In addition to these two playwrights, other prominent names (e.g., Sean O'Casey, George Bernard Shaw, John Millington Synge, and Oscar Wilde) receive extensive treatment. Also included in the listing are lesser-known playwrights (e.g., Austin Clarke, Teresa Deevy, and Donagh MacDonagh). Perhaps it is the information on these latter figures that proves the greatest value of the volume.

Each entry is written by an expert contributor and includes a brief biographical sketch, production histories for major works, a critical assessment of the playwright's career, and extensive bibliographic information. Of particular usefulness is the list of archival sources for further reference. The sourcebook concludes with a selected, general bibliography that serves as an aid to locating general works on Irish drama. This reference book is characterized by careful scholarship and succinct, but thorough, entries. Its value to a reference collection in dramatic literature is apparent.—**Jackson Kesler**

1176. **Modern Irish Writers: A Bio-Critical Sourcebook.** Alexander G. Gonzalez, ed. Westport, Conn., Greenwood Press, 1997. 457p. index. $95.00. ISBN 0-313-29557-3.

Even though the "Irish Literary Revival" began ca.1885 and lasted through the Great Depression, the "Irish Renaissance" continues into the present. This creative surge has included some of the world's finest authors. The writers found in *Modern Irish Writers* range from familiar names, such as Padraic Colum and William Butler Yeats, to more exotic Celtic-language writers like Nuala Ní Dhomhnaill. Each of the book's 75 entries has been written by an expert on that particular author.

According to the editor, Irish scholar Gonzalez, this volume is intended as a reference for both the novice and more experienced researcher in the field of modern Irish literature. Each of the alphabetically arranged entries contains a brief biography; a concise, detailed discussion of the author's major works and themes; a review of the author's critical reception; and a bibliography of both primary and secondary sources. End matter includes an extensive bibliography, divided into "Literary History," "General," "Fiction," "Drama," and "Poetry," along with an index and an annotated list of the volume's 54 contributors.

An introductory essay makes the distinction between the terms "Irish Literary Revival" and "Irish Renaissance" and traces the history of scholarship on the subject. The editor cites the continuing interest in studying Irish literary culture as evidence that the subject is not soon likely to be exhausted. For that reason, this well-thought-out volume would be a valuable addition to any world literature collection.
—**Kay O. Cornelius**

Italian Literature

1177. **The Feminist Encyclopedia of Italian Literature.** Rinaldina Russell, ed. Westport, Conn., Greenwood Press, 1997. 402p. index. $79.50. ISBN 0-313-29435-6.

Intended to complement *Italian Women Writers* (see ARBA 95, entry 1235), also edited by Russell, this work has relatively little overlap with the earlier title. Most of the entries deal with topics and literary movements rather than individual writers. Those that do treat individuals (both men and women) do so from the standpoint of how their work deals with women and women's issues and are not intended to be comprehensive analyses of the authors' works. All the articles are signed (most, but not all, are written by women); the list of contributors gives their academic affiliations but no other information. The book includes an explanatory introduction, a selective bibliography, and a useful index.

The high level of scholarship and the lucid writing that characterized *Italian Women Writers* are again manifested in this title. Although the work does reflect, obviously, a particular point of view and tends to be more subjective than the earlier title (which focused largely on factual biographical and bibliographic information), the treatment of even the most controversial topics (e.g., "Abortion") is fair and reasonable, not propagandistic. Larger academic libraries supporting programs in Italian literature or women's studies will want to consider this work, especially if *Italian Women Writers* is being used. For general collections, the same publisher's *Dictionary of Italian Literature* (rev. ed.; see ARBA 97, entry 1010) is the basic work.—**Paul B. Cors**

Latin American and Caribbean Literature

1178. **Encyclopedia of Latin American Literature.** Verity Smith, ed. Chicago, Fitzroy Dearborn, 1997. 926p. index. $125.00. ISBN 1-884964-18-4.

This ambitious, one-volume reference covers the field of Latin American literature with authority and thoroughness. The reference is the work of more than 160 impressive contributors and advisers. Signed entries on genres, terms, countries, and authors, as well as other topics related to Latin American literature, each include a bibliography for further reading. Authors' entries also include biographies and selected works; some prolific authors (e.g., Carlos Fuentes and Gabriel García Márquez) even have a subentry of their selective, individual works. The layout arrangement of the book is in a generous two-column format. The introduction includes a general reading list, an alphabetic list of works, and an alphabetic list of the entries. In addition to the general index, there is a useful title index to quickly locate specific works. Professional notes on the team of advisers, contributors, and translators are also included.

This fine work is lacking in only a couple of minor aspects. So much material is put in one volume that the only way this was possible was to make the typeface quite small in the entries, and it is even smaller in the bibliographies. Users may need a magnifying glass to read the work. Pictures and illustrations would have made the text more interesting; only one map appears twice in the work, on the inside front and back covers of the book. This reference, however, is an ideal source for the most frequently asked questions on Latin American literature. It is highly recommended for all libraries.—**Edward Erazo**

1179. **Index to Translated Short Fiction by Latin American Women in English Language Anthologies.** Kathy S. Leonard, comp. Westport, Conn., Greenwood Press, 1997. 120p. (Bibliographies and Indexes in Women's Studies, no.25). $65.00. ISBN 0-313-30046-1.

This index will facilitate the process of locating English translations of short stories, short fiction, and novel excerpts written by Latin American women—a task that can otherwise be difficult because it entails going through the many anthologies that include English translations of these works from either Spanish or Portuguese. This index is actually five indexes in one, beginning with an anthology index with entries for 165 anthologies published between 1938 and 1996. These entries are arranged by editor or author and provide a complete bibliographic citation of the anthology as well as the titles of the short stories included in that anthology. Additionally, entries contain a note of other useful information included in the anthology (e.g., a foreword by a famous author or bio-bibliographic information on authors and translators that might be included in the particular anthology). The index uses a system of alphanumeric codes, which are assigned to each entry and cross-listed in other indexes in the work. These are especially useful for quickly locating various translations of the same work or of different works by the same author. The nationality of the authors is also included in parentheses after their names. Four other indexes finish the work: alphabetical author (more than 260 authors), author by country (19 countries), title (more than 1,100 titles), and authors and their works. Lastly, there is a bibliography of works cited, which includes 23 bibliographies of Latin American literature in translation.

This one-volume index of English translations of short stories, short fiction, and novel excerpts by Latin American women is well-organized and should prove invaluable for researchers, students, and instructors in Latin American literature and women's studies. This work is recommended for large libraries.
—**Edward Erazo**

1180. **Jewish Writers of Latin America: A Dictionary.** Darrell B. Lockhart, ed. New York, Garland, 1997. 612p. index. (Latin American Studies, v.9; Garland Reference Library of the Humanities, v.1794). $75.00. ISBN 0-8153-1495-7.

The editor states that this dictionary is the first that focuses on the contributions of Jewish writers as a category of Latin American literature. He points out that its purpose is two-fold: to provide greater recognition of the contribution made by Latin American Jewish writers and to stimulate further critical attention on their work. Fifty scholars contributed the approximately one hundred and twenty entries in the work, representing ten Latin American countries (although most are from Argentina, Brazil, and Mexico). Also appearing in the editor's introduction is a list of works cited, as well as a lengthy, selective bibliography.

The signed entries start with the name, year of birth, and country associated with the author (not necessarily his or her country of birth or residence). Each entry also includes a brief biography and a general overview—focusing on those details that pertain to Jewish identity—plus primary and secondary bibliographies. Entries vary in length; most are from 1 to 4 pages, but some are as long as 5 to 10 pages. An excellent index makes finding author entries and references easy.

This reference, a fine addition to Garland's Latin American Studies series, would make a solid addition to any library collection on Latin American and Caribbean literature. It fills a real void in reference material used in the study of the subject. The dictionary is recommended, especially for large public and academic libraries.—**Edward Erazo**

Russian Literature

1181. Davidson, Pamela. **Viacheslav Ivanov: A Reference Guide.** New York, G. K. Hall/Simon & Schuster Macmillan, 1996. 382p. index. (A Reference Guide to Literature). $60.00. ISBN 0-8161-1825-6.

Davidson, herself a well-known Ivanov scholar, has done an exemplary job of producing this annotated bibliography on the noted theoretician of symbolism and critic of culture. The majority of this scholarly work contains a selected, annotated, chronological list of works about Ivanov, beginning in 1903 with reviews of his collection of lyric verses, *Kormichie Zvezdy* (*Pilot Stars*), and ending in 1993 with some 57 items covering his entire oeuvre. Criticism in more than 10 different languages is represented, with 58 percent in Russian; 24 percent in English; and smaller percentages of Italian, German, French, Polish, Czech, Dutch, Hungarian, Lithuanian, and Serbian.

All but 2 of the 1,111 entries have been examined *de visu*; each consists of a full bibliographic citation (with English translation) and a descriptive annotation of the contents. When applicable, Davidson provides cross-references to other works cited. The volume also includes a lengthy introductory essay on Ivanov and his critics, which is divided into four periods: 1903-1924, 1925-1961, 1962-1985, and 1986-1993. In addition, a chronological list of works by Ivanov, as well as an author index and a detailed subject index to the entire contents, are provided. The annotations are models of clarity and informative exposition. Anyone interested in doing serious work on Ivanov cannot afford to ignore this book. [R: Choice, Feb 97, p. 942]—**Robert H. Burger**

Spanish Literature

1182. Scroggins, Daniel C. **20,000 Spanish American Pseudonyms.** Lanham, Md., Scarecrow, 1997. 1033p. $110.00. ISBN 0-8108-3364-6.

Anyone interested in this area of study will be pleased with this volume. Scroggins has collected into one book all verifiable identified pen names of Spanish American writers from colonial times to the present. Although he acknowledges this reference cannot be complete, his goal of providing a useful guide certainly has been realized. The first part of the book gives pseudonyms with real names, and the second part reverses this order. Included in each entry is reference to the author's source for those users who require additional information. A list of works cited completes the book. Scroggins even gives an annotated reference list (by country) of earlier collections of pseudonyms in his introduction as well as a list of additional useful references. This compilation should be a definite purchase for any library whose patrons need this kind of information.—**Jo Anne H. Ricca**

1183. Woodbridge, Hensley C. **Guide to Reference Works for the Study of the Spanish Language and Literature and Spanish American Literature.** 2d ed. New York, Modern Language Association of America, 1997. 236p. index. $18.00pa. ISBN 0-87352-968-5.

The 2d edition of what has become a standard bibliographic tool in Spanish literature has 2 improvements over the 1st edition (see ARBA 88, entry 1258). First, it added a much needed index to titles, while still maintaining the other two valuable authors and author bibliographies indexes. Second, it has added about 300 new items in addition to the earlier citations. New topics in this edition include historical syntax, sociolinguistics, lost medieval literature, literary theory and terminology, gay literature, and dissertations. The geographic dichotomy—works pertaining to Spanish language and literature, subarranged by time period, precede those referring to Spanish America—makes sense logically, although the breakdown may disorient nonspecialists unfamiliar with that standard division of the field. Most annotations are brief descriptions (rarely evaluative) of works in Spanish and English; as before, coverage begins from around 1950, but has been expanded to include a few works with a 1996 imprint. One may quibble over the padding of the total number of items as a result of cross-references and permutations of the same title as separate entries, for example, the 10 separate listings for El drama español under twentieth-century peninsular drama.

In short, Woodbridge's revised compilation constitutes a fine bibliographic overview for both Spanish and Spanish American language and literature. Its recent publication date makes it an attractive choice for public and academic librarians wanting authoritative information at a reasonable price and is recommended over Donald Bleznick's more idiosyncratic *A Sourcebook for Hispanic Literature and Language* (3d ed.; Scarecrow, 1996).—**Lawrence Olszewski**

POETRY

1184. **Exploring Poetry.** [CD-ROM]. Detroit, Gale, 1997. Minimum system requirements: IBM or compatible 386 (486DX/33MHz or higher highly recommended). CD-ROM drive with MS-DOS CD-ROM Extensions 2.2 (double-speed or faster recommended). DOS 5.0. Windows 3.1. 8MB RAM. 5MB hard disk space. SVGA monitor and graphics card (256 color). Windows-compatible mouse or pointing device. 8-bit SoundBlaster-compatible sound card with Windows 3.1.-compatible drivers and speakers or headphones (optional). Printer (optional). $300.00/stand-alone version. ISBN 0-7876-0921-8.

In this age of hypertextuality, the wall between the reference room and the stacks is crumbling. Print sources that represented texts with citations or summaries are now CD-ROMs or Websites incorporating those very texts, not to mention sound and lights and a whole lot more; index, bibliography, and guide conflate with monograph, archive, journal, and image collection, and the days of multiple lookups come to an end in multiple mouse clicks.

Gale's *Exploring Poetry*, addressed to the high school market, is a multimedia teaching and study anthology exemplary of this new reality. The CD-ROM offers roughly 500 frequently taught lyric poems by 140 predominantly Anglo-U.S. poets, richly linked explicatory and critical commentary written by Gale staff, a glossary of literary terms and allusions, biographical sketches, a timeline, and study questions, together with a "gallery" of pictures and audio/video clips. Poems are searchable topically according to a thesaurus of more than 1,000 terms. The Teacher's Guide provides lesson suggestions and a bibliography of relevant poetry books, CD-ROMs, Internet sites, and videos.

Loading the software proceeds as described; printing and downloading are available; and the interface works intuitively for those whose life experience includes the graphical, push-button, multiwindowed world of digital equipment. While *Exploring Poetry* could serve as a poetry reference collection in those very small libraries budgeted to support CD-ROM publications, its relatively brief repertory of poems will persuade most schools to offer it as a courseware "textbook."—**Robert H. Kieft**

1185. **Index of American Periodical Verse: 1994.** By Rafael Catala, James D. Anderson, and Martha Park Sollberger. Lanham, Md., Scarecrow, 1997. 617p. index. $67.50. ISBN 0-8108-3227-5. ISSN 0090-9130.

Reflecting the healthy state of poetry in the last decade of the twentieth century, the twenty-fourth volume of this annual index covers approximately 18,800 poems by 6,958 poets and translators. Although the vast majority of the 298 magazines, journals, literary reviews, and other periodicals indexed are published in the United States, 16 are Canadian and 2 are Caribbean. Ten of the publications are new to this edition, and nine titles indexed previously have been dropped, either because they have ceased or because the editors received no issues and no response to inquiries. Poets included range from Nobel prize-winners Seamus Heaney and Wislawa Szymborska; to Pulitzer prize-winners Rita Dove and James Tate; to former president Jimmy Carter; and to emerging poets such as Barbara Ras, recipient of the 1997 Walt Whitman award.

The major portion of the volume is devoted to the author index, in which each poet and translator is assigned an entry number. Titles of poems appear alphabetically under their authors, with the citation for each poem providing the abbreviated periodical title, volume and issue numbers, date, and pagination. The separate title index refers the user back to the appropriate entry number in the author index. Appearing at the front of the volume is a key to periodical title abbreviations that indicates the complete title, editor, address, subscription information, and issues indexed. Especially appropriate for larger academic and public libraries, this series continues to be a major resource for collections that support a strong interest in contemporary poetry.—**Marie Ellis**

25 Music

GENERAL WORKS

Bibliography

1186. **A Basic Music Library: Essential Scores and Sound Recordings.** 3d ed. Compiled by the Music Library Association. Chicago, American Library Association, 1997. 665p. index. $85.00. ISBN 0-8389-3461-7.

Now in its 3d edition, *A Basic Music Library* continues to be the best list of basic music books, scores, and recordings available for developing library collections. The volume is not only valuable for building music collections, but it is also an important source for evaluating present collections. The 3d edition lists more than 7,000 recordings and 3,000 printed scores as part of the more than 10,000 total entries. All of the entries are selected by experts in their areas. (A list of these contributors can be found in the prefatory materials.) An important new feature is a more detailed inclusion of popular and traditional music worldwide. It is pointed out in the preface that "the book is called a 'basic' music library primarily for two reasons: its listings are both systematic and selective; and it represents the musical world in a way that is balanced and diverse, culturally and geographically."

In order to help collection developers make selections appropriate for the various music collections, a three-tiered ranking system has been built into the book. Each entry contains two asterisks (indicating that the item is appropriate for the smallest, most selective, basic collection), one asterisk (indicating that the item is appropriate for a medium-sized public or small college library), or no asterisks (indicating that the item is appropriate for the most comprehensive music collection generally found in larger public libraries or university libraries supporting undergraduate music studies). The content and arrangement of the book (i.e., into "scores" and "sound recordings") points out an interesting reality in that there are many more sound recordings than scores listed. This is due to the fact that recordings are the primary documents for many of the musical genres (such as rock, jazz, and non-Western classical music) in which written notation plays no part in the creation or performance of the music. The format used for entries follows the *Anglo-American Cataloguing Rules* (2d ed., 1988) for the most part, but in order to conserve space, some of the elements found on library cards are omitted. Each entry does contain the name of the composer or creator of the music, the uniform title, any necessary notes, the publisher, and the price. No attempt has been made to indicate performers, conductors, and the like.

A Basic Music Library is highly recommended for all library music collections. It has been, and will no doubt continue to be, an important collection development tool for music collections of all sizes. At the same time, its usefulness as a guide to individual listening is probably limited because of the lack of detailed performance information. Yet as a guide to collection building, it is unequaled.—**Robert L. Wick**

1187. **Bibliographic Guide to Music 1996.** New York, G. K. Hall/Simon & Schuster Macmillan, 1997. 732p. $265.00. ISBN 0-7838-1772-X. ISSN 0360-2753.

The recent acquisitions of three research libraries are listed in this annual single-volume work last reviewed in ARBA 92 (see entry 1248): the American Music Center, the Library of Congress, and the New York Public Library. As is standard for the bibliographic series (see entry 109 for a complete review), materials are 1990 or newer and were cataloged during the 1996 calendar year. This list of cataloging copy includes works in all languages and all formats, with sheet music and recordings naturally well represented. Topical coverage is comprehensive: The literature of all musical genres is treated, as well as music study and teaching, record catalogs, Americana, and other subjects. Grouping similar titles (e.g., music with theater arts) of this trusted bibliographic series onto individual CD-ROMs would be a welcome acknowledgment of library space and financial constraints. Music libraries know this source is an essential one; others will purchase it as budgets allow.—**Ed Volz**

1188. Brook, Barry S., and Richard Viano. **Thematic Catalogues in Music: An Annotated Bibliography.** 2d ed. Stuyvesant, N.Y., Pendragon Press, 1997. 602p. index. (Annotated Reference Tools in Music, no.5). $68.00. ISBN 0-918728-86-X.

The use of the word *thematic* in the title of this work is somewhat problematic in that it may confuse many readers. *Thematic* in this case is referring to the "incipit" organization of the catalogs being listed. An "incipit" is the first series of notes at the beginning of a composition that are unique to each piece. Ever since the fifteenth century, music publishers have arranged their catalogs by incipit in order to positively identify the various pieces of music that often carry various titles and, at times, even more than one composer's name. Thematic catalogs are useful to the music trade because they provide mnemonic aids for identifying the music.

Thematic Catalogues in Music provides a complete list of thematic catalogs of music dating from 1645, when the first thematic catalog was published in London, through to modern listings (up to 1996). The book is arranged by composer or by compiler in the case of collections of compositions by more than one composer. A decimal numbering system is used to allow for future inclusions. Each entry provides the name of the compiler of the catalog if known, the title, the place of publication, the date, and an annotation that gives information concerning the catalog and its coverage. The annotations range from a few words in length to in-depth listings of all of the works in the catalog. In addition, the two introductions to the book provide a valuable history of the thematic catalog along with other information concerning music bibliography. Appendixes include a list of manuscript thematic catalogs published before 1830, a list of printed thematic catalogs before 1830, a list of catalogs recommended for use in uniform title references, examples of thematic catalogs including reproductions of covers, and a detailed index.

Thematic Catalogues in Music has already been established as a major, scholarly addition to music bibliographic research with the 1st edition (see ARBA 74, entry 1065), and this 2d edition only increases its importance. The bibliography is highly recommended for all larger academic and public library music collections where music historians and musicologists do research.—**Robert L. Wick**

1189. Duckle, Vincent H., and Ida Reed. **Music Reference and Research Materials: An Annotated Bibliography.** 5th ed. New York, Schirmer Books/Simon & Schuster Macmillan, 1997. 812p. index. $45.00. ISBN 0-02-870821-0.

To all who practice music bibliography, Duckle's work requires no introduction, for he has been the writer of the tools of first recourse for three decades. This edition, in which coauthor Reed's style is evident, follows the format of previous ones—one volume of annotated entries, arranged in chapters, with index access. This is a great improvement on its predecessor, the 1994 revision of the 4th edition (see ARBA 95, entry 1252).

Within the extensive annotations are critical commentary, bibliographic history, and references to reviews, including several from *American Reference Books Annual*. Chapters are now numbered, and entries are numbered by chapter position rather than continuously throughout. Reed provides a three-page introduction, with nearly two pages of credits to the many who have assisted. Duckle's introduction to the 1st edition is reprinted—those of intervening editions have been dropped. It contains clearly stated goals: to serve graduate students and music reference librarians. Reed's intentions are stated as a rationale rather than goals: "a bibliography selectively compiling titles from a wide array of available choices." Nevertheless, the work continues to serve Duckle's goals and will facilitate much music reference work in general libraries. In many cases, this book can and should be used to identify a secondary bibliographic tool. December 1995 is the cutoff date for inclusion. Several chapter headings have changed, and the former chapter, "Women in Music," has been dropped and its entries relocated. New entries are identified by asterisks, and cross-references no longer appear within the text. Individual composers now have their own chapter. Chapter 12, "Electronic Information Sources," is an entirely new concept, and departs from a previously established principle in that the entries for such resources as OCLC and RLIN represent general references sources, which were previously excluded. The 175-page index is especially commendable, and for many users (particularly those having a known author or title) will serve as the primary mode of access to the tool. Replacing the four indexes of previous editions, it has a page of introduction and incorporates authors, titles, and subjects in one sequence. Titles from the previous edition's Index of Selected Music Bibliographic Series no longer appear. Under authors' names, their titles are now listed rather than merely referenced by entry numbers, a most welcome addition. Some explanatory notes and *see also* references are included. Because many entries represent older tools that have not been revised and because most libraries will retain previous editions of the work, perhaps more such entries, if not all, should be weeded from each edition. The deselection rate for this edition is stated as about 15 percent. However, to have a completely current handbook as a single source is greatly desirable. Because so much time transpires between editions, perhaps an annual supplement (preferably with a cumulative index) is wanted. Or a future work might separate reference works from research materials—although this distinction is especially difficult for musicology. Separating tools intended for graduate students from those for librarians would be equally problematic. Consideration of such alternatives highlights the extraordinary achievement represented in this tool.

As a truly collaborative work, Duckle's and Reed's book now presents a healthy state of the art for music bibliography. Collection development officers would do well to compare its entries with their library's holdings. Users should take to heart Reed's repeated cautions that the work is selective, and avoid treating it as an exhaustive inventory of resources.—**Ian Fairclough**

1190. Hill, George R., and Norris L. Stephens. **Collected Editions Historical Series & Sets & Monuments of Music: A Bibliography.** Berkeley, Calif., Fallen Leaf Press, 1997. 1349p. (Fallen Leaf Reference Books in Music, no.14). $250.00. ISBN 0-914913-22-0.

This bibliography surveys more than 8,000 historically important collected editions of music found in major music collections at the Library of Congress and in other major music libraries throughout the United States. The work provides exhaustive coverage of most numbered monumental sets and composers' collected editions and at the same time gives listings of numerous significant publishers' series and anthologies. All entries have been derived from either a close examination of individual items or from library cataloging, not from publishers' catalogs. The bibliography is divided into two sections: catalogs and sigla, which is a list of catalogs, mostly thematic, referred to by abbreviation in the body of the bibliography; and a bibliography, which is an alphabetically arranged list of the works by composer, with each item numbered for reference to the original sets. The bibliography is filled with extensive cross-references from series titles and numbers in addition to names of editors and so forth. Each item includes composer, uniform title, instrumentation, thematic catalog numbers, original sources (when possible), editions, genres, and other information.

Collected Editions Historical Series & Sets is a monumental work of scholarship. The authors point out in the introduction that "this present volume almost certainly represents the last time the information it contains will be published in book format." Although not stated, the authors imply that future attempts at such compilations will undoubtedly be on CD-ROM or other computer-based media. Only one previous effort to compile such a bibliography comes to mind: Anna Harriet Heyer's *Historical Sets, Collected Editions, and Monuments of Music*, published by the American Library Association in 1938 and updated in more recent editions (see ARBA 82, entry 1018, for a review of the 3d edition). While Heyer's work is not as extensive as the bibliography under review, it does cover some works not represented in the current compilation. As is often the case in the publication of such scholarly works, the work of data collection was supported in part by funding from the National Endowment for the Humanities. If there is any omission in the work it would be that it lacks information as to where the individual items may be located. Because they were all examined directly or found in various catalogs around the country, it would have been relatively simple to code the entries to indicate which collections have them.

Collected Editions is highly recommended for larger public and academic libraries with extensive music collections. Its cost will make it an impossible purchase for smaller collections, and at the same time, it is a questionable purchase for small music libraries where few of the editions included will be available in any case.—**Robert L. Wick**

1191. Keeling, Richard. **North American Indian Music: A Guide to Published Sources and Selected Recordings.** New York, Garland, 1997. 420p. index. (Garland Library of Music Ethnology, v.5; Garland Reference Library of the Humanities, v.1440). $95.00. ISBN 0-8153-0232-0.

Considering the increased interest in world music and indigenous cultures, this is a timely volume. Keeling, whose academic credentials combine music and anthropology, has an impressive résumé for North American Indian music. Using Joseph Hickerson's 1961 work (*Annotated Bibliography of North American Indian Music North of Mexico*) as a base, Keeling has built a comprehensive bibliography with 1,497 sources. The book is divided into 10 sections arranged alphabetically by author: 1 general or interregional and 9 regional. The volume includes three indexes, by author, by tribes and languages, and by subject. Every aspect of music from dance to instrumentation is represented. The coverage spans 1535 to 1995 and also includes writings in different languages and sound recordings.

The volume needs to be more user friendly. Each entry is annotated, but the annotations are not consistent, ranging in length from one sentence to longer paragraphs. In some instances, Keeling uses Hickerson's annotations without having viewed the item. The subject index headings are too broad, often encompassing more than 40 citations per heading, and searching for a specific item or format, such as sound recordings, is difficult. Although the work is comprehensive and fills a gap in the literature, better access points and indexing would have improved its usability.—**Joshua Cohen**

1192. Morey, Carl. **Music in Canada: A Research and Information Guide.** New York, Garland, 1997. 283p. index. (Music Research and Information Guides, v.20; Garland Reference Library of the Humanities, v.1823). $45.00. ISBN 0-8153-1603-8.

Morey states in his introduction that the purpose of this guide is to provide ". . . a broad spectrum of specialized studies that include information on most topics of research, and that open pathways to further research." The study of the history of musical life in Canada is a recent development, according to Morey. In fact, the vast majority of the bibliography's carefully selected entries have publication dates from the past 40 years. The author states that the prolific amount of research on music in Canada since 1980 alone is cause enough for a new and selective guide.

The body of this bibliography contains more than 900 entries organized into 12 topic groupings. Some of these groupings, such as directories, catalogs, bibliographies, biographies, archives, and periodicals, are traditional fare. However, such groupings as commerce; media; and native, folk, and ethnic music materials contribute to the wide scope of inclusion that Morey alludes to in his introduction. The body of the bibliography is followed by an author/editor index, a title index, and a subject index. Articles and monographs make up the greatest portion of the bibliography. However, Morey also includes some electronic resources available through the Internet.

Entries in the bibliography mirror publication in a bilingual country. Items in French are listed by their French titles, but the annotations are in English. If a publication has both French and English titles, both titles are given in the main entry and are indexed separately in the title index. If one entry is a translation of the other, both titles are entered as separate publications with a single annotation.

This title will be of use to libraries of colleges and universities that offer music degrees. Because the guide includes materials about Canadian native, folk, and ethnic music, it can support anthropology and sociology curricula as well.—**C. Michael Phillips**

1193. Perone, James E., comp. **Harmony Theory: A Bibliography.** Westport, Conn., Greenwood Press, 1997. 254p. index. (Music Reference Collection, no.57). $69.50. ISBN 0-313-29593-X.

Perone's bibliography covers harmony as "chord theory, tonality, and harmonic usage" from 1700 to the present, in a wide range of European languages. Doctoral dissertations are included, but not master's theses. The body of the work lists harmony treatises by author and is divided into 2 chapters (A-L and M-Z); it consists of citations for individual works (identified with "T" numbers), followed when available by a list of books, articles, and reviews (identified with a separate sequence of "TB" numbers). A 3d chapter, called "General Bibliography," lists books and articles (identified with "GB" numbers) that deal either more briefly with harmony in general or with specific subtopics. The index is of personal names (for composers, subarranged by compositions) and refers to entry numbers.

This work is sadly deficient in several ways. No sense of history, which is critical to an understanding of the development of harmonic theory, can be gained by perusing its pages. General treatises are interspersed with those dealing with specific musical works. Reviews of treatises repeat the title and author of the treatise but omit the name of the reviewer. A title index is badly wanted. So is a subject index for such topics as the six-four chord, harmony for guitarists, and jazz. The intended readership is not stated; some entries are appropriate for advanced scholars, others for beginners. Some citations are articles of only one or two pages: furthermore, entry 37 under "General Bibliography" is in Polish. The preface covers some material that should serve as a user's guide, but does not state that, for access to treatises about a composer's compositions, one must consult the composer's name in the index. Thus, in the excellently chosen example of Arnold Schoenberg, the user is not advised that such treatises are entered, not under his name, but under the treatise's author. The absence of annotations—which would help some readers distinguish between primary sources, works of scholarship, and secondary and pedagogical works—is regrettable but understandable given the size of the publication.

Consequently, this work has met neither its objective nor its potential. The compiler has missed an opportunity to lay out the bibliography of a subject that is of fundamental significance to students of music theory in a manner that would assist beginners and scholars alike. One hopes that the next edition will be thoroughly rethought, with appropriate editorial guidance from the publisher.—**Ian Fairclough**

1194. Peters, Diane E. **Canadian Music and Music Education: An Annotated Bibliography of Theses and Dissertations.** Lanham, Md., Scarecrow, 1997. 476p. index. $62.00. ISBN 0-8108-3275-5.

It is always difficult to identify master's-level theses by subject. This bibliography is designed to help solve this problem, at least for music theses done in Canadian universities. The author points out in the introduction that she has become "aware of the limitations of *Dissertation Abstracts*, especially in uncovering works below the doctoral level." This book, at least in part, has been written to help fill in the obvious gaps found in *Dissertation Abstracts*. The bibliography identifies more than 1,200 theses or dissertations dealing with Canadian music or music education in Canada.

The bibliography is divided into 15 subject areas: analytic studies (general), analytic studies (instrumental music), analytic studies (vocal music), bibliographies, ethnomusicology and folk music, historical and biographical studies, music and literature, music education, music journalism and criticism, music recording and broadcasting, musical instruments, original compositions, psychology of music and music therapy, sacred music, and sociological studies. The entries are numbered, and each provides author, title, M.A. or Ph.D., college or university, date degree was conferred, number of pages, and an annotation. For the most part the annotations are detailed, but they do vary in length. Appendixes include detailed author, title, and subject indexes as well as an institutional index, which lists the Canadian universities where the theses and dissertations were submitted.

This work is highly recommended for all larger academic and public library music collections in both the United States and Canada and is recommended for all Canadian libraries with substantial music collections where musicologists and music historians may be doing research. The work probably has limited value for individual purchase.—**Robert L. Wick**

1195. Stubblebine, Donald J. **British Cinema Sheet Music: A Comprehensive Listing of Film Music Published in the United Kingdom, Canada, and Australia, 1916 Through 1994.** Jefferson, N.C., McFarland, 1997. 207p. index. $65.00. ISBN 0-7864-0313-6.

Stubblebine's work covers all sheet music published in the United Kingdom, Canada, and Australia that has been part of British films and British editions of music from American and foreign films. He points out in the preface that "more songs [in film scores] were published in the United Kingdom than were published in the United States." Each of the more than 2,400 entries listed includes the title of the film it is from, the title that appeared on the sheet music cover, the studio that recorded it, the date of the film's release, the main stars, the composers and lyricists, the publisher, and a description of the cover. It is assumed that a description of the cover is for bibliographic identification purposes. In addition, there are indexes by song and by composer and lyricist at the end of the book.

Although some of the items listed in this work appear in *Cinema Sheet Music* (see ARBA 93, entry 1272), the title at hand does provide additional source material for an area that has been neglected over the years. Another title that comes to mind is *Broadway Sheet Music* (see ARBA 97, entry 1069), which also includes some music later used in film.

Recently there seems to be renewed interest in film music research, and this work will, no doubt, provide additional source material. The book is highly recommended for all larger public and academic libraries that have specialized film collections and for smaller collections in the United Kingdom, Canada, and Australia.—**Robert L. Wick**

1196. Wick, Robert L. **Electronic and Computer Music: An Annotated Bibliography.** Westport, Conn., Greenwood Press, 1997. 198p. index. (Music Reference Collection, no.56). $79.50. ISBN 0-313-30076-3.

Wick's work is organized in nine chapters with four appendixes and name and subject indexes, as well as a preface and an introduction. The scope covers basic sources on the composition and performance of electronic and computer music and is restricted to titles in English. Today, Wick says, the distinction between "electronic" and "computer" music is no longer valid; his cited definition is "music which is produced or modified by electronic devices so that electronic equipment is required for it to be heard." Providing a definition of electronic music is a tricky proposition: Taken literally, the wording of Wick's definition embraces most recordings of acoustically created music! Nevertheless, his choice (taken from the *New Grove Dictionary of Music and Musicians* [see ARBA 81, entry 1016]) outlines the topic broadly, appropriately, and pertinently for his readership. Related topics such as sound engineering and computer programming are out of scope.

Running throughout the book is a strong historical theme. Electronic music is not new to the current generation but was an invention of the nineteenth century. Wick briefly covers the history in his introduction and lists 58 works in the first chapter, "Histories and General Works," many published decades ago. Entries 59 through 100, in a chapter headed "Electronic Music Synthesis and Synthesizers," continue this historical vein, as do the chapters "Electronic Music Instruments and Devices" and "Electronic Music Composition." Each chapter begins with an introduction. Educators will find the chapter on teaching electronic and computer music especially helpful, and all users will welcome the chapters "Bibliographies and Directories" and "Dictionaries." The chapter on electronic music conferences lists 20 sets of reports from conventions and is indicative of the central role of such meetings in the development and dissemination of electronic musical works, techniques, and technologies. The appendixes list theses and dissertations (including Xerox University Microfilms accession numbers); system manuals (for instruments); online sources; and periodicals; for works listed in appendixes, sparser annotations or none at all are provided.

The annotations, although Wick claims them to be as brief as possible, are actually substantial, in some cases (especially for proceedings) amounting to a page or more in length. Entries for anthologies contain a complete contents listing, to which access would be greatly enhanced by an index to the articles contained. A list of abbreviations would help, as would their inclusion in the subject index, as was done for MIDI (Musical Instrument Digital Interface). Regrettably, the chapters are not numbered for ease of reference.

Wick has provided a substantial work that serves as a starting point for all wishing to pursue study in this area, especially for those seeking a historical perspective. Librarians may wish to caution users to consult the publication dates in order to insure that the material they wish to consult is still pertinent to their needs.—**Ian Fairclough**

Biography

1197. **Baker's Biographical Dictionary of Twentieth-Century Classical Musicians.** By Nicolas Slonimsky. Laura Kuhn and Dennis McIntire, eds. New York, Schirmer Books/Simon & Schuster Macmillan, 1997. 1595p. $90.00. ISBN 0-02-871271-4.

This is the first single-volume work on twentieth-century classical composers and musicians. John Vinton's *Dictionary of Contemporary Music* (see ARBA 75, entry 1143) covered fewer composers although it treated terminology, but is becoming dated. *Contemporary Composers* (see ARBA 93, entry

1254) is selective in coverage. Editor Kuhn described the 8th edition of the more general *Baker's Biographical Dictionary of Musicians* (see ARBA 93, entry 1244) as "literally bursting its seams." *Baker's Biographical Dictionary of Twentieth-Century Classical Musicians* is physically husky, only 500 pages smaller than the more general work; 60 percent of its materials is new.

Kuhn, no stranger to lexicography, assisted the late Slonimsky with the biographical dictionary and the most recent edition of *Music Since 1900* (Schirmer Books, 1994). She and McIntire maintain the standards so ably set by the former editor. One visual improvement to the volume is bold typeface to highlight works and genre sections of the biographies and bibliographies. Limiting the volume to one century has allowed for more complete works lists for composers. Composers and performers who are known primarily for jazz but made a contribution to classical music are included, such as George Gershwin, Duke Ellington, Irving Berlin, Max Roach, and Wynton Marsalis. There are brief entries for Richard Rodgers and Frederick Loewe, but not George M. Cohan. For composers of band music, such as Henry Fillmore, *The Heritage Encyclopedia of Band Music* (see ARBA 93, entry 1283) still provides more information. Other entries have seen significant expansion from the 8th edition of *Baker's*, such as Morton Feldman, Samuel Barber, and Leonard Bernstein, with recent bibliographic entries. A glossary explains many of the forms and styles of avant-garde music, with links to specific composers. This volume will undoubtedly be an essential resource for study of twentieth-century classical musicians.—**Ralph Hartsock**

1198. Hoffmann, Frank, Dick Carty, and Quentin Riggs. **Billy Murray: The Phonograph Industry's First Great Recording Artist.** Lanham, Md., Scarecrow, 1997. 543p. index. $75.00. ISBN 0-8108-3105-8.

The reader is assured from the start that the subject may not be well known, but soon discovers that Billy Murray (1877-1954) was a major popular culture figure who, from 1903 to 1943, was one of the most recorded figures of his idiom (his discography here runs 152 pages). The trio of researchers on the project brings a total of more than 150 years of informational expertise and academic skills to their project. Because the authors provide a sober, scholarly treatment, they have offered a source for significant information on the last years of minstrelsy and the earlier days of the recording industry, with relevant excursions that may supplement local histories and biographies (e.g., George M. Cohan, Irving Berlin, Enrico Caruso, Eddie Cantor, Harry Von Tilzer, Victor Herbert).

The first 200 pages of the book provide a detailed biography, rich with usually expansive and valuable footnotes. The remainder of the study begins with the detailed and specific discography of titles (citing composers, text authors, participating musicians, record labels and numbers, and years of both recordings and issues). A dozen appendixes follow, providing supplementary notes on particular recordings, ratings by critics of Murray and his contemporaries, catalog longevity of the songs, notes on and addresses of archival and private record collections, texts of a few songs, and after other data, biographical sketches of other recording figures of the time. The concluding index of theaters, record companies, proper names, song titles, ensembles, and cities substantially adds to the reference potential of this important source on U.S. music from the first half of the twentieth century, but bibliographers will have to cull their information from the footnotes.—**Dominique-René de Lerma**

1199. Mender, Mona. **Extraordinary Women in Support of Music.** Lanham, Md., Scarecrow Press, 1997. 309p. index. $48.00. ISBN 0-8108-3278-X.

Occasionally, writers of reference books fill a slot that was not obviously gaping. Mender's *Extraordinary Women* is just such a filler. Opening with a preface explaining her intent to celebrate women in the secondary role of supporting the arts, she begins chapter 1 with a masterly capsulized history of music in the Western tradition that highlights the service of nuns, feudal homemakers, and the subdued objects of the troubadour's plaint. Specific supporters fall into roughly six categories: patronesses and salon mistresses, mates, teachers, administrators, family members, and choreographers. The addition of five pages of notes, more than six pages of sources, an index of proper names, and a brief author's biography undergirds the work with helpful scholarly connections. A more thorough index might have listed musical eras, genres, and individual musical instruments (e.g., baroque, hymnody, and pipe organ).

Entries are balanced biographies filled with insightful commentary and generous citations. Mender stresses the strengths, character, tastes, and passions of female music supporters, for example, Aspasia's wit, Diane de Poitiers's grounding in the arts, Eleanor of Aquitaine's intelligence, Alma Werfel's self-confidence,

Isabela d'Este's generosity toward Renaissance performers, and Maria Mozart's dedication to her brilliant brother. Some of the 63 subjects were themselves musicians, as is the case with opera diva Beverly Sills, cellist Marta Casals, vocalist Rildia Cliburn, conductor Sarah Caldwell, and composer Clara Schumann.

With compassion and regret, Mender expresses the yearnings of prefeminist music lovers and the philosophies of their eras that relegated them to the background of the art world. Of teacher Nadia-Juliette Boulanger, she notes that women were required to have a chaperone—preferably male—when attending public concerts. Counter to those who were muzzled by patriarchy, Mender celebrates the female love of life, as found in George Sand's embrace of public issues, Mary Louise Zimbalist's altruism, and Martha Graham's tribute to human reproduction through dance. Altogether, Mender's work is a surprisingly delightful compendium.—**Mary Ellen Snodgrass**

1200. **Musical Americans: A Biographical Dictionary 1918-1926.** Mary DuPree, ed. Berkeley, Calif., Fallen Leaf Press, 1997. 303p. index. (Fallen Leaf Reference Books in Music, no.23). $37.95. ISBN 0-914913-13-1.

Musical Americans consists of reprints of 414 biographies originally published in the magazine *Musical America* between February 1918 and January 1926. The editor provides an eight-page introduction describing *Musical America* and its relationship to the contemporary musical scene. She also describes the influence the magazine's editor, John Freund, had in selecting the chosen musicians. His selection features composers, singers, and instrumentalists, and he makes a point of including women in almost equal numbers with men. Many of the featured subjects are not found in standard music biographical tools. The biographies are arranged alphabetically, with two columns per page, and at the end of each entry the date of the original issue appears. In back are listings of musicians by date of article and by birthdate. A substantial index listing topics, corporate entities, musical works, and persons concludes the work.

The index comprises about one-third of the book and has a one-page introduction. It is unusual in that it refers directly to the names of the musicians (given in parentheses) rather than to pages. To users unfamiliar with this technique and who expect to see numerical references, either to pages or to article numbers, the absence of numbers may be mistaken for a production error. Actual errors found were the misspelling of Clough-Leighter and the misnumbering of footnotes 9 and 10 in the introduction.

Fallen Leaf Press has created a sturdy, attractive book, which will be a welcome source for historians of music and Americana as well as for those preparing program notes for concerts and recordings. The index itself constitutes a rich source of information and makes the work worthy of consultation for a wide range of historical topics. Because the original publication is likely to be difficult to obtain, this reproduction is welcome. The production format also lends itself to bedtime reading for avid connoisseurs of early twentieth-century American music. Users should bear in mind that the biographies are contemporary and that the subjects are still living, so further information may be available in other sources.—**Ian Fairclough**

1201. Steane, J. B. **Singers of the Century.** Portland, Oreg., Amadeus Press/Timber Press, 1996. 271p. illus. index. $34.95. ISBN 1-57467-009-3.

Connoisseurs of fine singing who have as much interest in the great artists of the past and their recordings as they do in those currently active in the opera house and concert hall must all know of Steane by now. As author of one of the great books on recorded voices, *The Grand Tradition: Seventy Years of Singing on Record 1900 to 1970* (the 2d edition is available in the United States from Amadeus Press), and as a regular contributor to *Gramophone* and other periodicals, the author has proven to have an exceptionally well-tuned ear for vocal quality and the mechanics of singing as well as uncompromising standards for musical interpretation. Steane helps the listener to hear what is important about a singer and to help place him or her among contemporary and historical performers of the same repertory. Because passing judgment on a fine singer is such a subjective enterprise, not everyone can always agree with Steane's verdicts, but one always knows what standards have been employed in presenting evidence and forming opinions.

Most of Steane's writings are about singers performing specific music. This book is something of a departure by its broader, more generalized discussions of singers' lives, careers, and performances. These are the first 50 articles of an ongoing series of 1,500-word pieces written for the periodical *Opera Now*. They are collected in the order in which they were published, which is to say haphazard, because the choice of a certain singer at any specific time may have been prompted by a timely event, such as a farewell recital or a death. The expected "golden age" singers such as Adelina Patti, Luisa Tetrazzini, and Fyodor Ivanovich Chaliapin are, of course, covered, as well as many mid-century singers, such as Kirsten Flagstad, Victoria de los Angeles, and Kathleen Ferrier, and some who came a bit later, such as Joan Sutherland and Birgit Nilsson. No young, currently active singers have yet made it into this series.

Although not designed as a reference book, the individual articles do present clear overviews of great singers' careers and help to explain them better than most reference books. A separate section, "Dates, Books and Records," has entries for each of the singers in the book, this time alphabetically arranged, adding facts not covered in the essays and making excellent suggestions as to what to read and listen to for further insights. Every singer in the book can be heard on recently issued historical CD-ROMs. *Singers of the Century* is highly recommended. [R: Choice, Jan 97, p. 776]—**George Louis Mayer**

Dictionaries and Encyclopedias

1202. Hoffman, Miles. **The NPR Classical Music Companion: Terms and Concepts from A to Z.** New York, Houghton Mifflin, 1997. 306p. index. $15.00pa. ISBN 0-395-70742-0.

Miles Hoffman is well known to listeners of National Public Radio's musical magazine program "Performance Today" for his weekly episode of commentary on music terminology, which is aptly called "Coming to Terms." *The NPR Classical Music Companion* is an embodiment in print of the essence of the conversational discussions with the program's host, Martin Goldsmith. It is a small, handy encyclopedia of articles oriented to musical laypersons needing immediate explanations of terms as they are encountered. "Terms" is understood in its broadest sense, and includes musical genres, styles, techniques, historical eras, and so forth. Those who consult this thoroughly readable book are likely to find themselves still reading it long after they have identified the information they sought. Not only are the entries informative and accurate, they also hit the mark for a readership that wants explanations to be self-contained rather than requiring further consultation elsewhere. For a dictionary of musical terminology, this objective is remarkably difficult to achieve.

The work is organized alphabetically, with an index of terms, musicians, works, styles of composition, and other topics. Some entries are just one paragraph, such as *Col Legno*, whereas others cover several pages, for example, *Percussion Instruments*, which describes several instruments together rather than in individual articles. The work contains no illustrations, and musical notation is given only when being explained as such. The presence of topics such as "Second Violin" and "Inner Voices" further emphasizes the work's orientation to the layperson. Nevertheless, this book is remarkably informative for the musically trained person as well. For example, this reviewer learned that harpists do not use their pinkies. The longer articles liberally include *see* references; in most cases these are actually *see also* references. The *see* references that occur independently rather than as part of an article could be incorporated into the index. This is, however, a minor technicality.

The work belongs close to the armchairs of listeners and is also suitable for public and school libraries and all collections specializing in music. Furthermore, it should be brought to the attention of teachers of music appreciation and introductory musicianship for consideration as a textbook. [R: LJ, Sept 97, p. 172]
—**Ian Fairclough**

Discography

1203. McBeth, Amy, comp. **A Discography of 78 RPM Era Recordings of the Horn: Solo and Chamber Literature with Commentary.** Westport, Conn., Greenwood Press, 1997. 210p. index. (Discographies, no.74). $69.50. ISBN 0-313-30444-0.

McBeth's highly specialized book is part of Greenwood's Discographies series and is an important contribution to horn bibliography. The author has concentrated on listing pre-LP recordings, thereby augmenting the work by Michael Hernon in his *French Horn Discography* (Greenwood Press, 1986).

McBeth admits that this is not an exhaustive list, but instead, carefully chosen from the following criteria: all recordings are from the 78 RPM era, the identity of the hornist is known or reasonably guessed, and the focus is on classical rather than popular music. However, there is a chapter on the horn in pop, big band, or jazz ensemble provided. Other chapters include hunting-horn music, solo horn with various accompaniment, chamber music, and horn in large groups. Information for each entry includes composer, title, hornist, other performers, record label, year of issue, and other relevant information. With some entries, McBeth includes her assessment of the performance, which unfortunately often shows her personal taste rather than giving objective comments.

Also included in this work are brief biographies of most of the hornists listed in the main section and a bibliography. These are both excellent and well-researched sections and will be of great interest to hornists. Information on both the well-known and the more obscure hornists are provided. There are also indexes for hornists, composers, and performers. This book will be useful to those libraries where there is a strong interest in discographies or horn playing.—**Michele Russo**

1204. Stuart, Philip, comp. **The London Philharmonic Discography.** Westport, Conn., Greenwood Press, 1997. 530p. index. (Discographies, no.69). $99.50. ISBN 0-313-29136-5.

The London Philharmonic Orchestra gave its first public concert in 1932. Stuart begins with a brief history of the ensemble, explanatory notes about the entries, and a chronological list of more than 1,100 recording sessions. Entries include record company and label, producer, engineer, location, conductor, soloists, and repertoire. Some compositions have not yet been released on compact disc, whereas others are LP issues and multiple reissues. Entries are numbered consecutively; videorecordings identified with "V" numbers, and live recordings with "L" numbers, are interfiled. Interspersed throughout are historical notes about the labels, highlighting contracts with the orchestra. The narrative about EMI Classics reveals label headings, trademark issues, and the numbering systems used by this manufacturer.

Four appendixes follow the main text. "Film Soundtracks" lists 29 additional sessions with "F" numbers (e.g., F29), and the "London Philharmonic Choir" adds 13 more recording sessions, with "C" numbers. In "Not the London Philharmonic," Stuart clarifies some of the confusion caused by the orchestra's names: LPO recorded as the Philharmonia Promenade Orchestra, but the Royal Philharmonic Orchestra, an entirely different orchestra, recorded under the pseudonym of the Philharmonic Symphony Orchestra of London. "The Players" lists principal and other performers throughout the history of the orchestra.

Stuart, an independent discographer, completes this book with four indexes: "Recording Locations" lists more than 60 venues, including Abbey Road Studios and Kingsway Hall. "Conductors" as varied as Zubin Mehta, Eugene Goossens, and Leonard Slatkin led the orchestra, as evidenced by that index. "Repertoire" includes the classic British composers as well as Dmitry Shostakovich, Igor Stravinsky, and Billy Strayhorn. The general index covers personal and corporate performers, record labels, engineers, and producers. Stuart has compiled a source that details the recordings of a major symphony orchestra, linked by useful indexes.—**Ralph Hartsock**

Handbooks and Yearbooks

1205. **Billboard 1996 Music Yearbook.** Joel Whitburn, comp. Menomonee Falls, Wis., Record Research, 1997. 261p. illus. $34.95pa. ISBN 0-89820-120-9.

Everything that charted on *Billboard*'s major music and videocassette listings for 1996 is contained in this yearbook. Chart ratings are obtained through monitoring radio airplay and by electronically collecting point of sale information from music retail outlets. The song title section lists all singles alphabetically, whereas top singles are broken into categories, such as "Hot 100," "Hot Country," "Hot R&B," "Adult Contemporary," and "Mainstream Rock." Albums are indexed by the top 200 pop, country, and R&B. Additional charts have complete listings for jazz, classical, reggae, religious, and Latin music. For those Number 1 hits not already covered in these charts, there are special chronological listings of 18 other *Billboard* charts, including "Hot Dance Music," "Hot Rap," "New Age," "Religious," and "Latin." Because 1996 was the year that the Macarena became the rage, the top 12 Macarena albums are given special listing. Top 25 video rentals and top 25 video sales are included, along with the *Hollywood*

Reporter's weekly Top 5 movie ratings at theaters. The all-inclusive coverage of the entertainment business is wrapped up with a list of obituaries for the year, and the abbreviated "time capsule" will help refresh users as to the year's events. Disc jockeys will find the arrangement of the pop annual section excellent, with ranking based on peak positions plus weeks in that position, total weeks charted in the Top 10 and the Top 40, and total weeks charted. Most charts also include debut date, playing time, and Recording Industry Association of America gold and platinum certifications. There is much information here for disc jockeys, music show hosts, and collectors.—**Louis G. Zelenka**

1206. Hill, Brad. **The Virtual Musician: A Complete Guide to Online Resources and Services.** New York, Schirmer Books/Simon & Schuster Macmillan, 1996. 257p. illus. index. $30.00pa. (with disc). ISBN 0-02-864583-9.

Hill points out in his preface that he has attempted the "impossible task" of surveying the entire landscape of online topics in music. To this end, he provides a basic discussion of the hardware needed to get online; how the Information Superhighway works; how to upload and download files; what sources are out there for musicians; and how to use World Wide Web providers, such as America Online, CompuServe, and Prodigy. Although what he has attempted is probably an impossible task to do in any detail, this book provides a fascinating introduction to the use of online sources in music. Sections cover what is needed to get online from the standpoint of hardware and software; using the Internet, e-mail, and commercial services; uploading and downloading information; a list of sources of information on the Web; an overview of services offered by America Online, CompuServe, and Prodigy; Usenet and the use of newsgroups; and how to use CD-ROMs for information concerning music.

In addition, lists are provided for online sources of interest to musicians, including online magazines, genre sites, music business sources, hardware and software, recordings, musical instruments, and others. These sources range from rock 'n' roll sites to classical music sources. The problem, of course, is the ephemeral nature of the Internet. Many of the sites listed are no longer available or have been moved and changed. In addition to the sources listed in the book, a CD-ROM is provided that lists the files referred to in the book and many additional sources. The CD-ROM will run on both PC and Macintosh platforms.

This book is a valuable resource for anyone who would like to access online information concerning music. It is especially valuable for the online beginner. *The Virtual Musician* is recommended for all libraries with music collections and for individuals who have an interest in online music sources and the equipment necessary for using CD-ROM technology. [R: Choice, June 97, p. 1640]—**Robert L. Wick**

1207. **Song Writer's Market, 1998: 2,000 Places to Market Your Songs.** Cindy Laufenburg, ed. Cincinnati, Ohio, Writer's Digest Books/F & W Publications, 1997. 519p. index. $22.99pa. ISBN 0-89879-795-0. ISSN 0161-5971.

A standard resource, the 1998 edition of this guide contains 400 new places to market music, including publishers; record companies and producers; managers and booking agents; advertising, audiovisual, and commercial firms; play producers and publishers; and classical music groups. Entries give the name of the contact person, address and telephone number, and e-mail and fax numbers if available. Submission guidelines and current needs as well as tips on marketing are provided as well. Subject and geographic indexes assist even further. As usual, the directory has a section of articles and interviews explaining the music business, and a listing of organizations, workshops and conferences, contests and awards, relevant periodicals, books, and Websites. Public libraries should own and replace this guide every year to provide current, accurate information for this ever-changing field.—**Jean Engler**

Indexes

1208. **International Index to Music Periodicals 1997:2.** [CD-ROM]. Alexandria, Va., Chadwyck-Healey, 1996. Minimum system requirements: IBM or compatible 386. CD-ROM drive and controller card with Microsoft CD-ROM Extensions 2.1. MS-DOS 3.1. Windows 3.1. 5MB hard disk space. 4MB memory. VGA or SVGA color monitor and card. Microsoft-compatible mouse. $1,095.00/stand-alone; $2,495.00/site license. ISSN 1087-6871.

The latest entry into the musical indexing field provides access to more than 400 international music periodicals from all aspects of music. The publisher furthermore claims exclusive coverage of 50 of those titles. Chadwyck-Healey hopes to have 350,000 retrospective records added by mid-1998, with additional ones continually added, and selective full text from 40 journals by the spring of 1998. The most obvious competitor in this field is *RILM Abstracts of Music Literature* (RILM, 1967-). Both contain abstracts, use thesauruses, and currently have about the same number of records (between 200,000 and 250,000). Furthermore, *RILM* is alternately available in print, online through OCLC's FirstSearch and EPIC, and on MUSE on CD-ROM. To test for subject coverage and overlap, a sample search was conducted on each database on three topics limited to 1995 and 1996: Sibelius, Te Deum, and the glockenspiel. *RILM* retrieved 22 for the 1st topic, 2 for the 2d, and 1 for the 3d. *International Index* picked up 28 for the 1st topic, with only 2 duplicates; 17 for the 2d with 1 duplicate; and 5 for the 3d, with only 1 overlap. Thus, for comprehensive searching both sources would be required. Part of the difference is one of coverage: *International Index* features music articles and obituaries appearing in *The New York Times* and *The Washington Post* as well as more popular titles, such as *Billboard*, *Rolling Stone*, and *Down Beat*, whereas *RILM* focuses exclusively on more scholarly journals.

The CD-ROM software, based on the publisher's Caravan product, is fairly straightforward for anyone used to the point-and-click navigation of a World Wide Web interface. The search engine is not without its minor irritations, however; for example, the default year of 1874 is rather disconcerting, because it forces users to either input the year desired or scroll through almost a century of dates if they want to limit their search to a current time frame only. The publisher's allegation that the product is "the only electronic index to current music periodicals" is questionable in light of the electronic availability of *Music Index* (Harmonie Park Press). Because all three are relatively equal in terms of price, the real decision boils down to expected usage: minimal access would render *RILM* the first choice; more widespread usage would make *International Index* the better deal. *Music Index* comes in third, mostly from its lack of currency.—**Lawrence Olszewski**

CHILDREN'S

1209. Murray, R. Michael. **The Golden Age of Walt Disney Records 1933-1988: Murray's Collectors' Price Guide and Discography.** Dubuque, Iowa, Antique Trader Publications, 1997. 246p. illus. index. $19.95pa. ISBN 0-930625-70-6.

In addition to full-color illustrations on nearly every page and price and identifying information on recordings of Disney music in shellac and vinyl record formats, this work provides information that has been absent from guides to Disney record album price guides. The introduction, the first three chapters, a history of recorded Disney music, and an explanation of condition and pricing explain Disney recordings' surprisingly complex, litigious, and entertaining history. It also explains the connection between price, condition, and market well enough to inspire even novice collectors. Over 50 records, including non-Disney labels, are listed alphabetically by label and in ascending numerical order. Described as the "collector's delight and archivist's nightmare," the numbering system is explained thoroughly because of Disney's habit of reissuing records in varying number sequences, on different labels, and with different cover art. Listings are further broken down by format, 78 rpm, 45 rpm, LP, EP, mono, and stereo. Title, artist, release date, and price are given. Finally, a filmography of full-length Disney animated films, a filmography of Disney musical composers, and an in-depth discussion of record-grading notation, along with an index, are included. The index to titles, performers, and composers should be the first stop for users unfamiliar with Disney's numbering system. Attractive and compact, this book will be useful and entertaining to collectors and civilians alike and a valuable resource in public or academic libraries with film and popular culture collections.—**Jennie Ver Steeg**

COMPOSERS

1210. Antokoletz, Elliott. **Béla Bartók: A Guide to Research.** 2d ed. New York, Garland, 1997. 489p. index. (Composer Resource Manuals, v.40; Garland Reference Library of the Humanities, v.1926). $75.00. ISBN 0-8153-2088-4.

Although the format of this work is the same as in the 1988 publication (see ARBA 89, entry 1193), its content has greatly expanded, with more than 40 percent of its material new to this edition. The guide begins with the history of Béla Bartók's musical development and then presents a comprehensive catalog of Bartók's published compositions. These sections are followed by 1,200 annotated bibliographic entries. Entries are arranged within one of four sections: "Primary Sources," "Biographical and Historical Studies," "Studies of Bartók's Musical Compositions," and "Discussions of Institutional Sources for Bartók Research and Essays in Collected Volumes." Each section includes several subsections. Only one new subsection has been added since the original edition, "Bartók's Editions and Transcription of Keyboard Works by Other Composers." Indexes include an author/title index; an index of Bartók's compositions, keyboard editions, and transcriptions; an index of proper names; and a subject index.

Information found in this work can be accessed by accumulating data from other sources, such as *Béla Bartók: A Complete Catalogue of His Published Works* (London, Boosey and Hawkes, 1970) and Gabor Kiss's "A Bartók Bibliography" in *Studia Musicologica* (1980-1989). However, the strength of this volume is in finding all the material in one easy-to-use edition. The guide is highly recommended for libraries collecting extensively in music. [R: Choice, Oct 97, p. 269]—**Laura K. Blessing**

1211. Craggs, Stewart R., comp. **Arthur Bliss: A Source Book.** Brookfield, Vt., Scolar Press/Ashgate Publishing, 1996. 366p. index. $99.95. ISBN 0-85967-940-3.

Master of the Queen's Music from 1953 to 1975, Arthur Bliss (1891-1975) is widely regarded as one of the most important twentieth-century composers, both in his native England and throughout the world. This sourcebook, based on the compiler's doctoral dissertation, "seeks to document and place in the public domain factual details concerning Arthur Bliss's life, career, and compositions which until now have only been available in scattered form and known only to those with access to the composer's private papers and composition manuscripts" (as stated in the acknowledgments).

To this end, Craggs brings together numerous elements that, taken together, provide an excellent map of Bliss resources. These include an alphabetic list of main compositions; a 35-page chronology; a list of manuscripts and 1st editions; a catalog of letters to and from Bliss with details of compositions mentioned, a discography; and a selective, unannotated bibliography.

As would be expected from what is basically a listing of information resources, what minimal prose exists in Craggs's sourcebook is academic and, at best, a bit dry. However, Giles Easterbrook's delightful, eloquent tribute to Bliss in the book's foreword helps explain the passion that drove Craggs to invest 20 years of research in this project. This will be a valuable resource for most music and academic libraries, as well as for large public libraries supporting strong music collections.—**G. Kim Dority**

1212. Dillard, Philip H. **Sir Arthur Sullivan: A Resource Book.** Lanham, Md., Scarecrow, 1996. 428p. index. $49.50. ISBN 0-8108-3157-0.

This helpful and user-friendly guide provides prose materials and lists of sources and resources enough to keep any fan of the music of Arthur Sullivan occupied for some time. The prose materials include a year-by-year account of Sullivan's life, capsule biographies of more than 80 people involved in some way in his career, descriptions of London theaters and halls in which his major works were performed, and descriptions of schools at which he studied and taught. Then comes an alphabetic list of Sullivan's theater works with such information as dates and places of premieres and names of librettists and cast members. Lists of his other works follow, by category, excluding his more than 70 hymns. Under the heading "Resources" are lists of published scores as well as compact disc, vinyl, cassette, and video recordings. Descriptions of major collections of source materials relating to Sullivan and a list of relevant Websites follow. The book closes with a bibliography of secondary sources in English and three indexes.

This book has clearly been compiled with dedication and care, and spot-checks indicate that the work is reliable. A particularly commendable feature is Dillard's policy of listing among his sources only items listed in the holdings of major libraries—hence accessible to researchers. The book's flaws relate more to Dillard's at times misapplied thoroughness, which results in much repetition of simple facts in his inelegant prose. Also, even though one is happy to read of the many Sullivan associates not now included in standard music reference books, one surely does not need one-paragraph biographies of such figures as Charles Dickens, Antonín Dvořák, Edward Elgar, or Queen Victoria, particularly because their relationships to Sullivan are covered in Dillard's biography. Regardless of these problems, however, this volume is sure to be welcomed by persons whose fascination with Gilbert and Sullivan operettas goes beyond just hearing and seeing them. [R: Choice, May 97, p. 1473]—**Karin Pendle**

1213. Dimond, Peter, comp. **A Mozart Diary: A Chronological Reconstruction of the Composer's Life, 1761-1791.** Westport, Conn., Greenwood Press, 1997. 231p. index. (Music Reference Collection, no.58). $65.00. ISBN 0-313-30131-X.

Not a diary in the strict sense of the word, this volume is a compilation of events in Wolfgang Amadeus Mozart's life, or as many as could be collected from various sources. The volume starts with Mozart at age 5, at which time the first precise dates begin to appear; it ends with the composer's death in 1791. In between, there are records of his travels and summations of his letters, as well as those written by others, particularly his father, an amazingly prolific letter writer. Letters are not quoted; the gist of each letter only is indicated, and the source for the complete letter is referenced, in this case Emily Anderson's *The Letters of Mozart and His Family* (2d ed., W. W. Norton, 1986).

Entries are also interspersed with names and numbers of Mozart's compositions, both as they were written and as they were performed. Regrettably, several typographic errors have crept into some of the composition titles in French and Italian, something that could easily have been avoided by comparing them with those in the Köchel catalog. Other inconsistencies include nonexistent cross-references and varied spellings of names. For instance, one can find (Jan) "Duschek" and "Dusek" referring to the same person, or "Constanze" and "Constanza" for Mozart's wife.

This book will be useful for music students and scholars, as well as writers of concert program notes, who frequently need to piece together events in Mozart's life relevant to a particular composition. The style of each entry is laconic, and the entire volume will be useful as a group of signposts from which a researcher can branch off to other publications, as needed, for additional details.—**Koraljka Lockhart**

1214. Holmes, Robyn, Patricia Shaw, and Peter Campbell. **Larry Sitsky: A Bio-bibliography.** Westport, Conn., Greenwood Press, 1997. 207p. index. (Bio-bibliographies in Music, no.65). $59.95. ISBN 0-313-29020-2.

This new addition to Greenwood Press's Bio-bibliographies in Music series is devoted to Larry Sitsky, an Australian composer, pianist, and scholar of Russian descent. The extensive biographical section that recounts Sitsky's absorbing life and career is valuable, because a substantial part of it is not available in any other single source. Other portions of the book follow the standard format for the series. Sitsky's more than 150 compositions are listed and described, as are his many writings. Sitsky is also a Ferruccio Benvenuto Busoni scholar, and he has published on a wide variety of music-related topics as well. The standard bibliography of writings about Sitsky and a discography are included. A list of performances and lectures by Sitsky and an appendix citing prizes that he has won are two supplemental features.

Sitsky is very well known in Australia—much less so in the United States. This well-executed and interesting book may remedy that situation.—**Allie Wise Goudy**

1215. **Minor Ballet Composers: Biographical Sketches of Sixty-Six Underappreciated Yet Significant Contributors to the Body of Western Ballet Music.** By Bruce R. Schuenenman. William E. Studwell, ed. Binghamton, N.Y., Haworth Press, 1997. 133p. index. $39.95. ISBN 0-7890-0323-6.

Schuenenman's compendium of brief biographies of composers of ballet music charges a steep price for the value offered. Featuring clear typefaces and attractive layout, the work opens with an adequate introduction to ballet history and purpose and follows with a note on *Les Six*, which introduces the members and time frame of this short-lived coterie of French composers. The selection in the main text is Eurocentric and stresses the contribution of female composers. Nationalities cover musicians from

England, France, Russia, Austria, Germany, Romania, Denmark, Scotland, Norway, Czechoslovakia, Hungary, Sweden, Italy, Egypt, and the United States. The 79-page text cites life span, places of birth and death, a terse summary of professional career, influence of mentors and collaborators, and titles and dates of significant ballet scores. The glossary of 20 choreographers is similarly spare. An index of ballet titles alphabetizes the 518 works covered in the text. A bibliography offers nearly six pages of notes, which establish the quality of the research. A 15-page index provides an additional list of titles along with composers and choreographers.

Schuenenman's style and depth are major stumbling blocks to the effectiveness of this work. Information is uneven in quality and coverage and is formatted and written at a grade-school level, for example, the 3-line summary of August Strindberg's *Miss Julie* on page 71 and the quick gloss of giants of the ballet world, notably Frederick Ashton, Agnes de Mille, George Balanchine, and Martha Graham. Overall, sentence structure is simplistic in the extreme and relies heavily on colorless verbs. The writer tends to omit or ignore causality, motivation, effect, and critical reputation and excludes commentary on awards and achievements. Information on the scoring of ballets for film is also skimpy. An index of entries by country would be a helpful addition.—**Mary Ellen Snodgrass**

1216. Schonberg, Harold C. **The Lives of the Great Composers.** 3d ed. New York, W. W. Norton, 1997. 653p. illus. index. $24.95. ISBN 0-393-03857-2.

This work was updated and enlarged in the 1997 edition. Some of the material in this book originally appeared in Schonberg's weekly *New York Times* column and as *New York Times Magazine* pieces and is presented here in a revised and amplified version. There are chapters on nationalistic schools and light classical composers such as Jacques Offenbach, Johann Strauss Jr., and Arthur Sullivan. Schonberg has not missed many composers. They are presented chronologically, and the *lives* of composers are stressed rather than their output. Detailed descriptions of the composers' works will not be found here, although a large bibliography (more than 400 items) is included so that the person who desires to look at a composer in more depth is given guidelines for a search. *The Lives of the Great Composers* is light reading and anecdotal in concept, but it does capture the interest of the readers so that they might read on and discover other composers.—**Robert L. Wick**

1217. Sonevyts'kyi, Ihor, and Nataliia Palidvor-Sonevyts'ka. **Dictionary of Ukrainian Composers.** New York, Union of Ukrainian Composers, 1997. 335p. index. $25.00pa.

As the only dictionary of Ukrainian composers published in English, this work fills a definite need. Presented in alphabetic order, all entries consist of 3 parts—biographical information; a comprehensive list of the composer's major works; and a bibliography of articles and books, if available, about the composer. Ihor Sonevyts'kyi, a noted composer in his own right, and his wife Nataliia spent many years on this important project, consulting all available sources published abroad and some reference sources published in the former Soviet Union (e.g., *Sovetskiie Kompozitory i Muzykovedy* [Moscow, 1978-1981] and *Spilka Kompozytoriv Ukrainy* [Kiev, 1968]). In addition, questionnaires were used as sources of information for those Ukrainian composers living abroad.

A spot-check of the entries listed under "A" and "B" was conducted to evaluate the coverage of this work. A number of names were found here that are not listed in standard Soviet sources (e.g., émigré composers and those composers who were censored under the Communist regime). Some examples of those covered in the Sonevyts'kyis' book are Mykola Arkas, Virko Baley, Volodymyr Boltarovych-Stone, Vasyl Barvins'kyi, and Maksym Berezovs'kyi. It is unfortunate that not all reference books published in the Soviet Union were available to the Sonevyts'kyis. For example, *Soiuz Kampozytoriv Ukrainy: Spravochnik* (Kiev, Musychna Ukraina, 1984) is not mentioned along with other sources consulted. A number of composers can be found in this Soviet publication that are not mentioned in the Sonevyts'kyis' work (e.g., S. Alekseeva, O. Arnautov, L. Archimovych, V. Ban'kevych, V. Barabasov, S. Bedusenko, M. Bilins'kaia, V. Borysov, and others). Obviously, not all of those omitted are prominent names; anyhow, it is difficult to trace the biographies of scholars, musicians, artists, or even politicians in Soviet reference works. One hopes this situation will improve over time.

In spite of the obstacles, these authors have performed a valuable service for Ukrainian scholarship. *Dictionary of Ukrainian Composers* is a scholarly and useful work that should be found in all music collections.—**Bohdan S. Wynar**

INSTRUMENTS

1218. MacAuslan, Janna, and Kristan Aspen, comps. **Guitar Music by Women Composers: An Annotated Catalog.** Westport, Conn., Greenwood Press, 1997. 202p. index. (Music Reference Collection, no.61). $69.50. ISBN 0-313-29385-6.

This catalog consists of two complementary parts: lists of works involving guitar alone or in conjunction with other instruments or voice(s) and thumbnail biographies of the composers whose works appear on these lists. Works are grouped according to instrumentation (e.g., flute and guitar, tape and guitar), and brief annotations for some of the pieces include information on length and difficulty, general style, and publisher. Appendix 1 provides addresses of many of the composers cited, whereas appendix 2 lists publishers and their addresses. There are indexes of composers and works (by title).

Judging this catalog can be frustrating. In general, it is both welcome and useful; more specifically, its many omissions and editorial problems keep it from being as helpful as it might be. The repertoire lists vary widely in the amount of information they provide. Many items are just titles, lacking anything further to help the reader find the work or even decide whether it is worth tracking down. In an effort to be thorough, the compilers have even listed items as "title unknown," which seems rather a waste of space. Some of the annotations are of dubious value: What, for example, is one to make of such vacuous judgments as "straightforward [sic] tonality," "lightly atonal," "almost tonal," "very atonal," or "geometrical"? Why could the compilers not find even basic information on works by such prominent living composers as Emma Lou Diemer, Violet Archer, Alice Parker, or Jean Coulthard? Yet even here there is a bright side: references to works by women of Spain, Portugal, and Latin America whose music is not well known in the United States.

The biographies are equally frustrating. Even though awkwardly written and necessarily inconsistent, many are accurate and informative. As a group, however, they contain too many spelling errors and are often out-of-date. For example, one never learns that Diemer and Coulthard have retired, nor that Miriam Gideon died in 1996. Again the attempt to be all-inclusive has a downside: the many names followed solely by "Looking for information about this composer." From a technical standpoint, it would seem that Greenwood Press has exercised little editorial control over this project. At the very least, a final proofreading would have put a better face on the product.—**Karin Pendle**

1219. Maroney, James F. **Music for Voice and Classical Guitar, 1945-1996: An Annotated Catalog.** Jefferson, N.C., McFarland, 1997. 146p. index. $42.50. ISBN 0-7864-0384-5.

This unique resource describes 576 art songs written for solo voice and guitar. Although the author has included a brief historical overview of songs composed for this combination, the bibliography focuses on music composed since 1945, reflecting a growth of musical works in this genre.

The book's main section contributes substantial information for each song. All entries include the type of voice the piece is for, the range/tessitura, and the difficulty level of the vocal part, as well as the publisher and the language and author of the text. Each entry includes an annotation that addresses specific characteristics of the piece and describes the vocal and guitar parts. Ample information has been included to enable performers to make knowledgeable choices when selecting literature. The author has also presented an interesting statistical analysis of these songs, in terms of voice distribution, difficulty, use of atonality, and other features of the songs.

Maroney has done an admirable job in compiling this bibliography. Its usefulness is entirely dependent on the needs of a collection's users.—**Allie Wise Goudy**

1220. Stoneham, Marshall, Jon A. Gillaspie, and David Lindsey Clark. **Wind Ensemble Sourcebook and Biographical Guide.** Westport, Conn., Greenwood Press, 1997. 432p. illus. index. (Music Reference Collection, no.55). $89.50. ISBN 0-313-29858-0.

"This sourcebook is intended for the many players and listeners who wish to gain a wider appreciation of wind music . . . [and] to fill a gap in musical history" (preface). The authors also point out that there are a number of guides to opera or the symphony in which the readers can obtain basic information on wind music, but that a single-volume source of this nature has not been previously available. The works included in this compilation are defined as music for wind harmony typically for an ensemble of four or more winds, usually in pairs. There are more than 12,000 works by 2,200 composers included. *Wind Ensemble Sourcebook and Biographical Guide* is actually the third volume of an unofficial series that also includes *Wind Ensemble Catalog* (Greenwood, 1997), which includes appropriate music from the late seventeenth century to the present, and *Wind Ensemble Thematic Catalog*, which gives incipits and lists of movements for works composed before 1900. These three volumes are designed to act in concert to provide details of the music, the composers or arrangers, a list of recordings, and where the music is to be found.

In addition to listing music for winds, the book provides much interesting information, including essays on wind bands worldwide, what wind harmony is and how it is scored, military and civil wind harmony, nationalism and ethnic issues, and a list of journals of music for winds. Also, there are chapters that provide information on wind music in English-speaking countries, France, German-speaking countries, Italy, Russia, Scandinavia, and Spain and Portugal and their empires. The section entitled "Composers and Arrangers: Biographical Information" gives alphabetic lists that include the composer or arranger's name, date of birth and death, city of birth, a brief (in some cases very brief) biography, and a few notes on his or her music for winds. The final chapter of the book is an essay on the development of wind instruments.

Also of interest is a short chapter on the methods used for determining the authenticity of interpretation and performance. A detailed index increases the value of the volume considerably. This important work is recommended for all larger public and academic libraries and for smaller libraries with special music collections. (The two companion volumes should also be considered.) Also, it would be an important purchase for musicians and musicologists interested in wind ensembles.—**Robert L. Wick**

MUSICAL FORMS

Classical

1221. **The Blackwell Guide to Recorded Contemporary Music.** By Brian Morton. Cambridge, Mass., Blackwell, 1996. 361p. index. (The Blackwell Guides). $47.00; $22.95pa. ISBN 0-631-18881-9; 0-631-20138-6pa.

The title leads one to expect a complete overview of contemporary recorded music, a feat that may be impossible to achieve in a relatively slim volume. Rather than offering lists, which are available elsewhere, the author offers a choice: He selected a highly and frankly personal selection of contemporary works, which he analyzes thoroughly. In doing this, he provided an overview of his subject, but also a vast body of omissions, some of them hard to explain. For instance, there is a sizable entry on John Corigliano but none on John Adams, certainly one of the present days' most respected, recorded, and performed composers. Virgil Thomson only exists as a mention in other composers' entries. The same fate befalls Philip Glass, Steve Reich, Lukas Foss, and so on. One also wonders about the thinking behind featuring Carl Orff and excluding Gottfried von Einem.

The book is divided into chapters, representing decades from the 1940s to the 1990s, the latter with only one entry: Corigliano. The author selected ten seminal twentieth-century compositions as a reference point for all his subsequent selections, and even these are highly personal, as he admits. No argument about Claude Debussy being a major innovator, but featuring his *Chansons de Bilitis* in this group rather than *Pelléas et Mélisande*, for instance, does raise the eyebrows. From this basic list, Morton branches off, choosing one work per composer for thorough analysis and a mention for selected other works. Even here, the author's personal preferences often seem odd. Leonard Bernstein's *Halil Symphony* is featured as the most representative of his non-Broadway output, seemingly an odd choice, as is Michael Tippett's "Four Ritual Dances" from *A Midsummer Marriage*, but not the complete opera. All in all, this is a decent attempt at covering a vast subject, but one that will be helpful only to persons whose personal preferences coincide with those of the author.—**Koraljka Lockhart**

1222. Nicholas, Jeremy. **The Classic FM Guide to Classical Music: The Essential Companion to Composers and Their Music.** London, Pavilion Books; distr., North Pomfret, Vt., Trafalgar Square, 1997. 375p. illus. index. $19.95pa. ISBN 1-86205-051-1.

Intended to aid those who want some guidance in what classical music to listen to, *The Classic FM Guide to Classical Music* includes a little bit of all kinds of information. Subtitled *The Essential Companion to Composers and Their Music*, the volume offers a brief chronological history of music, with terms defined within the text and composers placed in a timeline with concurrent musical and other events. A chronology of composers offers a sentence or two about many composers not covered elsewhere.

Most of the book is devoted to an alphabetic survey of more than 150 composers. Some of these are fairly obscure and known only for one work (such as Gregorio Allegri); others would be considered among the "greats." Many are fairly minor composers (Anton Arensky and Charles-Valentin Alkan, for example). The author's only criteria for inclusion are that they be born at least 50 years ago and that they have "stood the test of time."

Composers are covered to varying degrees. For those known only for a single work, often only the dates of the composer and something about the work are provided. Other composers receive more detailed treatment. For each, however, essential works have been selected. The author's measures for these are that the work(s) has been retained in the repertoire over time, that it is well written, and that it has had some influence in the musical world. Specific recordings of works are not recommended.

The review copy of this book contained errors in some appended lists included in the table of contents, but not actually in the book itself. Instead, the copy offers 100 pieces that are "The Classic FM Listener's Hall of Fame."

This guide is a fun and engaging book. Its focus on the nonmusician makes it most appropriate for public library and possibly general library collections.—**Allie Wise Goudy**

Operatic

1223. Goulding, Phil G. **Ticket to the Opera: Discovering and Exploring 100 Famous Works....** New York, Fawcett Columbine, 1996. 689p. illus. index. $25.00. ISBN 0-449-90900-X.

This is a far-ranging work about the opera world geared to the novice or, as the author writes, the "unwashed." The author is a retired journalist whose writing experience centered around national politics and security. In retirement, however, classical music and opera appear to be his consuming interests. His concise, often witty writing style reflects his journalist's credentials.

Primarily, 85 operas plus their composers are discussed, but the title says there are 100 operas covered. The several beyond the basic 85 are grouped as twentieth century or American. Goulding calls the first 25 operas "Warhorses," those that are deemed the most popular of the genre. It is not quite clear how these operas were chosen except perhaps for the number of performances given at the Metropolitan Opera. Each discussion basically includes biographical and creative information on the composer. This is followed by a plot summary that immediately moves to the section called "Highlights," a list of noteworthy parts of the work. The author also provides a critical commentary. An interesting snippet called "Keynote" gives brief subjective reactions to the opera. Finally, the reader can find the number of performances of the opera at the Met plus a listing of what may be considered a notable sound recording and video. Additionally, there are chapters that discuss the operatic voice and opera singers and opera in a historical context. One chapter carries the unique title of "Bleeding Hunks." The author takes 60 different operas and states what he feels to be the best segment (hunk) of each opera.

This book is reviewed with some significant mixed emotions. It is a delight to read, and it is jammed with information regarding opera. Yet from a scholarly point of view, it can be recommended only for a public library collection because of its near-total lack of documentation. There are no notes, and there is no bibliography of sources consulted or sources recommended. [R: RBB, 1 Mar 97, p. 1198]—**Phillip P. Powell**

1224. Summers, W. Franklin. **Operas in One Act: A Production Guide.** Lanham, Md., Scarecrow, 1997. 383p. index. $48.50. ISBN 0-8108-3222-4.

This production guide to one-act operas should prove to be of great use to performers, producers, directors, music educators, and others involved in selecting operas for performance in a variety of settings, from workshops to professional presentations. More than 275 operas are described in detail in the 2 parts of this book. Part 1 describes "Operas with English as the Original Language"; part 2 contains "Operas with English Translations." Works selected are considered to be within the reach of university programs and community organizations, with performance materials readily available. Most works are short and have English librettos or performable translations. Some classic works, such as *Gianni Schicchi* and *Cavalleria Rusticana*, are not included because they are well known and readily available.

The operas are listed in alphabetic order by composer. Title and subtitle, author and source of the libretto, and length of time for performance are given. Casts are listed with vocal range, and an indication of principal and secondary roles is provided. Chorus, dance, and orchestral requirements are explained in some detail, and the degree of difficulty of the piano accompaniment is furnished. An indication of style usually includes several descriptive phrases relating to the dramatic and musical character of the work. There are also a description of the setting of the work and a list of scenes. Then follows a summary of the plot. Entries conclude with production notes, the date and location of the opera's premier, and a source for performance materials. Indexes to composers and titles; a table of performance times (10 minutes or less, 26 to 30 minutes, and so on); and a directory of publishers and sources conclude the guide.—**Dean H. Keller**

Orchestral

1225. Arnold, Claude Graveley, comp. **The Orchestra on Record, 1896-1926: An Encyclopedia of Orchestral Recordings Made by the Acoustical Process.** Westport, Conn., Greenwood Press, 1997. 694p. index. (Discographies, no.73). $125.00. ISBN 0-313-30099-2.

The recordings made during the first 30 or so years of the industry were primitive and made with imagination and compromise before a simple horn that captured a narrow range of the sounds made by hovering performers on cylinders or discs. The sound of the solo voice and of instrumentalists were listenably and recognizably captured, but the attempt to record a whole orchestra—or the approximation of one—was a nearly impossible challenge during the earliest period of the decades covered by the acoustic process. Even the latest ones made before the advent of electrically made records from the mid-1920s onward, even though much improved, were what the compiler of this book calls "daring explorations," and these are what he has documented in this volume. Because orchestral recordings were so difficult to make and unsatisfactory to listen to, it was infrequent that large-scale works, such as uncut symphonies, were attempted. The body of truly important orchestral recordings made during this period is small but of great historical importance. In these days when all evidence of performance practices of earlier times is being evaluated, they are of unique value for study.

One of the great documents of this period is the recording of Ludwig van Beethoven's *Fifth Symphony* made by the great conductor Arthur Nikisch. The recording fascinates listeners to this day. Also of great importance is the first recording of a Gustav Mahler symphony. Oskar Fried recorded the massive *Symphony no. 2* with vocal soloists and chorus with the Berlin State Opera Orchestra in the early 1920s. Major conductors who did not live long enough to make recordings with vastly improved techniques include Eugène Ysaÿe. Some of the greatest conductors of somewhat later generations who did make wonderful sounding recordings still available in stores also, as very young men, made some early discs in this process. These youthful endeavors of Otto Klemperer, Arturo Toscanini, Leopold Stokowski, and Bruno Walter can still intrigue their admirers. Also of great importance are those of Richard Strauss, Maurice Ravel, Arthur Honegger, and Edward Elgar. Indexes provide good access to the material.

These orchestral recordings have long been neglected in comparison to those of the famous singers and instrumentalists (such as Enrico Caruso) of the same period. They have not had the glamour (or sonic satisfactions). However, this encyclopedia needed to be compiled to cover the field, and users are lucky that it has been done so well. Much detective work has gone into locating this information, and skill has been employed in its presentation.—**George Louis Mayer**

1226. Daniels, David. **Orchestral Music: A Handbook.** 3d ed. Lanham, Md., Scarecrow, 1996. 611p. index. $50.00. ISBN 0-8108-3228-3.

Daniels is a member of the music faculty at Oakland University and conducts the Pontiac-Oakland and Warren Symphonies in Michigan. He compiled the 1st edition of this work, published in 1972 (see ARBA 73, entry 1032), because he could not find a reference work on orchestral music meeting his needs. He has personally examined each score included here. The majority of each edition consists of an alphabetic list of composers and their orchestral compositions. Each composition entry includes a coded key to its instrumentation, approximate length, and publisher or publishers. New to this edition are lengths of individual movements (some taken from compact disc timings), as well as an index of nongeneric titles and significant composers' birth and death anniversaries through the year 2025.

The 1st edition consisted of all-uppercase computer printouts. The 2d edition of 1982 (see ARBA 83, entry 942) had grown from 301 to 413 pages, with a 35 percent increase in entries. It included new indexes by composers' nationalities or ethnic groups and by instrumental requirements. Vocal works were listed for the first time. The text was produced using a typewriter and, although more legible than the 1st edition, was not very attractive. The current edition has 1,100 additional entries and more than 200 new composers and uses a visually pleasing, thoughtful mix of typefaces. Other new features include available publishers' e-mail and Internet addresses, a list of resources, and an overview of the publishing morass of the Anton Bruckner symphonies.

Daniels makes no claim that the work is all-inclusive, but it is certainly wide-ranging and thorough. He states that numerous conductors, orchestra managers, and librarians worldwide contacted him with suggestions and corrections for this edition. Persons in these professional categories form the primary audience for this work. Libraries finding the first 2 editions useful will certainly want the new one, and large or specialized libraries not owning the earlier editions should consider acquiring this one.—**Richard S. Watts**

1227. Harris, John M. **A History of Music for Harpsichord or Piano and Orchestra.** Lanham, Md., Scarecrow Press, 1997. 473p. index. $69.50. ISBN 0-8108-3257-7.

This is an extremely comprehensive descriptive chronology of composers of piano or harpsichord music. Harris has included even the most obscure composers dating from the early 1700s up to the present. The chronology is divided geographically, with coverage stretching beyond Europe and North America to South America, Asia, and Oceania. Within these geographic subdivisions, the actual entries for the composers are arranged in a time sequence, which makes the detailed index very useful. Additionally, there is an extensive, but apparently selective, discography and a nearly 30-page bibliography including books, articles, and dissertations. For the user, the primary difficulty lies in the formatting of individual entries. There needs to be more of a distinction between entries beyond that of a paragraph indentation. This format is particularly disconcerting when the discussion of a composer goes beyond a single paragraph. The flow of reading would be greatly enhanced by the judicious use of spacing and a contrasting typeface.

Harris has aptly demonstrated the enormous number (3,600-plus) of composers of music for the keyboard. If there is a 2d edition, one could envision an expansion not necessarily of the number of entries but of the content within entries. Coverage varies widely, with first-level composers such as Wolfgang Amadeus Mozart, Ludwig van Beethoven, and Béla Bartók being analyzed beyond the cursory single paragraph and occasionally brief excerpts of scores. It is understood that the contributions of a vast majority of the composers are limited, but there are major composers aside from the aforementioned ones whose contributions to the literature could be more completely explicated. This is an excellent volume that offers much to the reader and could offer even more.—**Phillip P. Powell**

Popular

General Works

1228. **All Music Guide: The Experts' Guide to the Best Recordings....** 3d ed. Michael Erlewine, Vladimir Bogdanov, Chris Woodstra, and Stephen Thomas Erlewine, eds. San Francisco, Calif., Miller Freeman, 1997. 1499p. index. (All Music Guide Series). $27.95pa. ISBN 0-87930-423-5.

The *All Music Guide* reviews and rates more than 20,000 albums from 4,000 artists in a variety of musical categories. Readers will be hard-pressed to find a more comprehensive compilation of musical reviews in one reference source. The book's editor, Michael Erlewine, states that the main difference between this book and the 2d edition (see ARBA 94, entry 1314) is that the majority of the reviews have been rewritten in greater depth by experts in the music field. More than 150 reviewers contribute to this guide, most of which are well-known writers for such magazines as *Rolling Stone*, *Spin*, and *Billboard*.

The book is divided into 20 music categories, ranging from the familiar—rock and pop, country, and gospel—to the more obscure genres, including Cajun/zydeco, avant-garde, and gay music. Each chapter begins by defining the different styles within each music category. For example, the section titled "Rock, Pop, and Soul" has over 50 different styles listed within its category. The sections then go on to list artists and bands in alphabetic order, with annotations giving information such as name of artist(s), instruments of each performer, a biography of the artists career, and their major recordings. Albums that are deemed important contributions to the music field are symbolized with a clear star, meaning they are essential to any collection of the genre. All other albums are rated with diamonds—one being the lowest priority and five being the highest. Locating the artist of choice is made simple because artists are listed alphabetically within each musical category and there is a convenient index in the back of the book.

This guide will be a welcome addition to medium- and large-sized public libraries with substantial music collections or for personal libraries of music collectors.—**Shannon M. Graff**

Band

1229. **The Heritage Encyclopedia of Band Music: Composers and Their Music. Supplement (v. 3).** By William H. Rehrig. Paul E. Bierley, ed. Westerville, Ohio, Integrity Press, 1996. 1048p. index. $90.00. ISBN 0-918048-12-5.

When the author completed the two-volume *Heritage Encyclopedia of Band Music* in 1991 he knew that there was additional information that needed to be included. This volume is intended as a supplement to the original two volumes (see ARBA 93, entry 1283). It is neither a stand-alone book nor part of a series. The criteria for listings in this supplement are the same as in the original. This is a book of band music only. A composer's works for other media—piano, voice, and others—are not included unless they have been adapted for bands. As provided in the original, works are listed under the composer's name.

New works of composers are updated as well as biographical information. Included in this 1,056-page supplement are 5,279 new composers, 3,791 updates, and 52,738 entries in the title index. The supplement's format follows the same appearance as the 1st and 2d volumes. The same two-column format, typefaces, spacings, headings, and subheadings are used. Where updating information or errata are listed, instructions are given in italics, and readers are referred to the original page numbers. As in the original two volumes, the reader will find biographical sketches listed alphabetically, a list of works, pseudonyms, arrangers, publishers, dates, references, editions, a bibliography, and a glossary of publishers. However, there are changes in the 3d volume. The first is the addition of diacritical marks where available and the second is the addition of page numbers in citations.

This encyclopedia is unique in nature. It is the only publication of its kind and has come to be regarded as the most significant "band" document of the twentieth century. [R: Choice, Sept 97, p. 108]

—**Ian Fairclough**

Country

1230. **All Music Guide to Country: The Experts' Guide to the Best Recordings in Country Music.** Michael Erlewine, Vladimir Bogdanov, Chris Woodstra, and Stephen Thomas Erlewine, eds. San Francisco, Calif., Miller Freeman, 1997. 611p. illus. index. (All Music Guide Series). $22.95pa. ISBN 0-87930-475-8.

This most recent entry in the well-received All Music Guide series (e.g., *All Music Guide to Jazz* [see ARBA 95, entry 1304]; *All Music Guide to Rock* [see ARBA 96, entry 1330]; and *All Music Guide to the Blues* [see ARBA 97, entry 1072]) is devoted to one of the most popular genres of U.S. music today. Featuring concise career biographies of more than 1,000 performers, both individuals and groups, the guide covers the entire range of country music from the early trailblazers like Jimmie Rodgers and the Sons of the Pioneers to the newest stars like LeAnn Rimes. It also covers a broad array of subgenres, ranging from traditional country to contemporary alternative country. The alphabetically arranged entries vary in length but include basic vital statistics, an indication of instruments played, and style of music, followed by a career profile and critical assessment of the performer's work. A few of the entries include a photograph of the artist(s). After the profile, the artist's albums are listed in chronological order. Each is given a critical rating, and most have a brief critical review. Albums considered to be essential recordings for any good country collection and those recommended as a first purchase for the particular performer are separately labeled. More than 5,500 recordings are included, making this an excellent resource for collectors.

In addition to the individual entries, there are 23 essays tracing the development of country music, many of which include a list of recommended recordings. Fourteen "music maps" provide graphic illustrations of the development of many subgenres. A brief section of resources and a personal name index complete the features of the work. The information and critical reviews provided; the compact, easy-to-use format; and an affordable price make this a highly recommended purchase for personal collections and libraries of all sizes.—**Barbara E. Kemp**

1231. Freda, Michael D., comp. **Eddy Arnold Discography, 1944-1996.** Westport, Conn., Greenwood Press, 1997. 345p. index. (Discographies, no.70). $69.50. ISBN 0-313-30388-6.

As part of an ongoing discography series published by Greenwood Press, Freda's book is a complete listing of all the recordings by country singing artist Eddy Arnold. The work is based on information taken from the Country Music Foundation research center, record company archives, and personal interviews with Arnold.

Section 1 lists the 1,080 songs that Arnold recorded from 1944 to 1996 and includes other such data as the songwriters, musicians, engineers, vocalists, overdubbing sessions, formats, and catalog numbers. Various singles, extended-play recordings, albums, and compact discs with title listings, catalog numbers, and release dates are listed in sections 2 through 5. The compiler has also sorted out and documented different versions of single songs. The appendixes describe a variety of other collections and products. Of special interest is a listing of 104 Arnold recordings that have never been released.

The introduction gives a brief profile of Arnold. Even though most buyers of this book will know a great deal about Arnold, additional biographical information would have helped the less informed reader. Photographs, especially of early sessions, would have enhanced the sections. A statistical treatment of his recordings would also have been useful—for example, what were Arnold's biggest years and biggest hits? A drawback to the index is that it lists only song titles, which makes it difficult to determine which songwriters he worked with the most. Thoroughly researched and well organized, the book will be a valuable source for country music historians, libraries, or reference centers that specialize in music, and Arnold fans.—**Mark J. Crawford**

1232. Holtin, Alice Y., comp. **The Statler Brothers Discography.** Westport, Conn., Greenwood Press, 1997. 223p. illus. index. (Discographies, no.71). $65.00. ISBN 0-313-29663-4.

The Statler Brothers have been longtime country and gospel music singers; they made their first recordings in 1964 with Johnny Cash. Thirty-three years later they are still together, with only one personnel change, and have been recognized as "the most awarded act in the history of country music." The group, not brothers at all, recorded for Columbia from 1964 to 1970, which produced their biggest hit, "Flowers on the Wall," and then for Mercury. They also write most of their own songs. This discography is another in the excellent series that has already covered Waylon Jennings and Johnny Cash.

The first 120 pages cover the session and release information—master numbers, file identification numbers, overdub sessions, licensing data, and composer credits. Much of this includes the material devoted to their backup work with Johnny Cash and other performers. As in most compilations such as this, locations, dates, and vinyl and compact disk numbers are included.

The remainder of the book consists of chapters on their Billboard chart histories, a song listing for their television show (currently on the Nashville Network), and a long list of their awards. Three separate indexes cover song titles, musicians, and composer credits. This work is a recommended purchase for libraries with country music collections.—**Dean Tudor**

1233. **MusicHound Country: The Essential Album Guide.** Brian Mansfield and Gary Graff, eds. Detroit, Visible Ink Press/Gale, 1997. 642p. illus. index. $24.95pa. ISBN 1-57859-006-X.

MusicHound Country does not quite live up to its title, but it sure tries. Mansfield comes from *New Country* magazine, a recent country publication; Graff writes for *Country Song Roundup*, currently the oldest continuing country magazine (nearing 50 years). The emphasis, therefore, is on country icons (George Jones, Merle Haggard, and the like) and especially on alt.country (even country music has entered the Internet). Compilations are all but ignored, except for an index at the end, a glaring deletion. Entries consist of a short biographical sketch of the artist (members and years of membership for groups), "what to buy," "what to buy next," "what to avoid," and "the rest," rated on a system of WOOF! to five bones. Some also contain "worth searching for" for non-compact discs or hard-to-find works, and "influences"—both "influenced by" and "influencing." (Some of these can be quite loopy; i.e., comedian Jeff Foxworthy is listed as influencing President Clinton.)

Indexes are hit and miss. "Books" and "Magazines, Newspapers" are nowhere near thorough, and the magazine descriptions are pure, unhelpful public relations fluff. Really, these sections deserve a book of their own. Actually, except for "Five Bone Albums" (necessary) and the category index (some are silly, but fun), much better resources exist than all of these indexes. All in all, *MusicHound* is not a WOOF!, but it is not five bones either.—**R. S. Lehmann**

1234. Stambler, Irwin, and Grelun Landon. **Country Music: The Encyclopedia.** 3d ed. New York, St. Martin's Press, 1997. 708p. illus. index. $40.00. ISBN 0-312-15121-7.

The 3d edition of *Country Music: The Encyclopedia* suffers from the same malady the music does these days: it is not bad, but it is awfully bland.

Framed by a serviceable introduction and indexes (awards, etc.), the entries are not much more than compilations of quotes from interviews. Half of any given entry may be paragraphs of album titles, singles titles, and dates of release, which would have been better compiled into a list at the end of the entry. Unfortunately, most information only goes up to the end of 1995. Therefore, Faith Hill and Tim McGraw are not reported married and Pirates of the Mississippi are still together, to cite two errors of omission. Photographs are grouped into sections, instead of matched with their entry, and those of current stars are often outdated (George Strait's photo is at least 12 years old).

Many new acts have entries longer than their careers. This excess of length brings little depth. Country music is noted for being real, with its singers often living out the songs they sing. Rarely does the humanity of any act come through. There are better books out there containing more substance and less dirt. [R: LJ, July 97, p. 78]—**R. S. Lehmann**

Jazz

1235. Chilton, John. **Who's Who of British Jazz.** Herndon, Va., Mansell/Cassell, 1997. 370p. $29.95pa. ISBN 0-304-33910-5.

Chilton is a respected jazz researcher and historian whose previous work in this format, *Who's Who of Jazz—Storyville to Swing Street* (1970), is a standard reference work in the field. Chilton has also written books on such musicians as Billie Holiday, Sidney Bechet, and Coleman Hawkins. An Englishman himself, he devotes the present work exclusively to British jazz musicians, making it the first of its kind. Some 850 entries are presented here—covering all jazz styles and musicians who played in the 1920s, as well as the young players active today. At two or three entries a page, the information includes the musician's professional name and original name (if different), date and place of birth and death, instruments played, and a brief professional chronology. Despite the occasional and inevitable lapse—implying that pianist Derek Smith performed simultaneously on both the Johnny Carson Show (1967-1974) and the Tonight Show (1968-1975), when both names refer to the same program—Chilton is a knowledgeable and careful researcher. With the number of British musicians who are having an impact on jazz worldwide continuing to grow, this book is an important addition to reference shelves of most libraries.
—**A. David Franklin**

1236. Evans, Philip R., Stanley Hester, Stephen Hester, and Linda Evans. **The Red Nichols Story: After Intermission, 1942-1965.** Lanham, Md., Scarecrow, 1997. 746p. illus. index. (Studies in Jazz, no.22). $79.50. ISBN 0-8108-3096-5.

Loring "Red" Nichols, a celebrated jazz musician, performed with other jazz musicians from the 1930s to the early 1960s. His ensemble disbanded from 1937 to 1942. The authors call this an intermission and begin their coverage from 1942 to his death in 1965. The goal of this book is to document all known recordings, broadcasts, and live performances of Red Nichols as a sideman or leader. Arranged chronologically, it includes all recording formats—78s, 45s, 33s, cassettes, tapes, and compact discs. Even unissued tests are included. Brief biographical essays include quotations from fellow musicians and family members, which either dispel or clarify some of the myths associated with Nichols. The discography rectifies some inaccuracies about commercial discs. Dates in the discography are in military format: day number, alphabetic month, year, and day of week (e.g., 11 June 1952 [Wed]), and those in the index are the numerals for the month, day, and year (e.g., 06/11/52). The song title index lists all of the songs performed, with the surname of the composer or arranger. But this often leaves unanswered the questions, for example, which Williams composed *Darktown Poker Club*? (It was Bert Williams.)There is no composer index. Thus, access to *Blue Tango* by Leroy Anderson appears only in the title index. The musician and proper name index includes persons such as trumpeter Ziggy Elman, the Andrews Sisters, announcer Ken Carpenter, arranger Ned Freeman, host George Gobel, vocalist Dinah Shore, and violinist Joe Venuti. Each is identified by his or her function in the band.

The book includes 12 photographs and ends with a list of compositions by Red Nichols. Use of bold typeface for the headings makes this volume easy to read. With this tool, patrons can trace the careers of Nichols and several sidemen and soloists.—**Ralph Hartsock**

Rap

1237. Stancell, Steven. **Rap Whoz Who: The World of Rap Music.** New York, Schirmer Books/Simon & Schuster Macmillan, 1996. 339p. illus. index. $22.95pa. ISBN 0-02-864520-0.

This is a welcome addition to the relatively sparse literature on an influential genre of music. It contains basic data on many of the performers, producers, record labels, and promoters; data that should be easily available but has not been until the publication of this book.

Organized alphabetically, it contains articles on individuals as well as groups. Each article provides a brief history, a selected discography, and comments on their role in the world of Rap. The length of the articles reflects the importance of each topic. Afrika Bambaataa, Def Jam Recordings, Grandmaster Flash, and N. W. A., for example, are treated in greater depth. Scattered throughout the book are useful sidebars on various topics, including the definition of Rap terms; interviews with major figures, such as Afrika Bambaataa; performance and recording techniques, such as sampling and the art of MCŌing; and sympathetic discussions of political and moral issues, such as the relationship between violence and Rap. Photographs and a detailed index round out the book.

The author, who writes a regular column in the *New York Beacon on Rap*, introduces the book with a brief but informational and sympathetic history of the genre. The book is written in an informal and accessible style. This book is highly recommended for anyone who is interested in the history, people, techniques, and language of Rap. [R: Choice, Jan 97, p. 776]—**Howard Spring**

Rock

1238. **All Music Guide to Rock: The Experts' Guide to the Best Recordings....** 2d ed. Michael Erlewine and others, eds. San Francisco, Miller Freeman; distr., Emeryville, Calif., Publishers Group West, 1997. 1232p. index. (All Music Guide Series). $26.95pa. ISBN 0-87930-494-4.

This 2d edition of *All Music Guide to Rock*, like its predecessor (see ARBA 96, entry 1330), is an invaluable resource for identifying the best recordings of a rock artist or group. With information on over 1,800 artists and 11,000 recordings, the music covered in the guide spans all forms of rock and its subgenres, from rockabilly to techno. Arranged alphabetically by artist or group, entries include a concise biography and a listing of the most important recordings, nearly all of which are accompanied by a signed review. For less prolific artists, these listings may be complete discographies. All recordings listed are rated, and some are highlighted as suggested purchases. And as in the previous edition, the guide also includes a section consisting of essays on musical styles or periods, which are often followed by a list of recommended recordings. The volume concludes with an artist index.

Although this edition is again highly recommended, especially for its intended purpose as a resource for the rock music collector, the free online version at the All Music Guide Website (http://allmusic.com) is preferable as a reference tool. One can search here by artist as well as by album or song. A few quick searches shows that the printed edition, culled from this much larger database, contains less complete information on many artists.—**Michael Weinberg**

1239. ***Billboard*'s American Rock 'n' Roll in Review.** By Jay Warner. New York, Schirmer Books/Simon & Schuster Macmillan, 1997. 305p. index. $22.00pa. ISBN 0-02-872695-2.

Because it is hard to imagine classic rock and roll without the Beatles, the Rolling Stones, and other talent from the British Invasion of the 1960s, the scope of this work being only American artists is intriguing in itself. More than 100 top performers are profiled, from the pioneering days in the 1950s with Johnny Ace, the Moonglows, and Ritchie Valens through the early 1970s with Gladys Knight and the Pips. Included for each artist are knowledgeable, short biographies written by Warner, a six-time Grammy-winning music publisher well known for his *The Billboard Book of American Singing Groups* (see ARBA 94, entry 1359). Also furnished here are more than 3,000 reviews from *Billboard*, long the definitive news source for the music trade.

The reviews from *Billboard* offer fascinating new insights for the general public. The intended audience of *Billboard* has always been the people in the music business, so instead of the kind of critical, evaluative reviews appearing in mass market publications, these reviews assess the potential sales and success of new releases and serve to publicize them. For instance, Bob Dylan's "Leopardskin Pill-Box Hat" is judged by *Billboard* to "offer strong dance beats and compelling Dylan lyrics loaded with teen sales appeal" (p. 97). The Penguins's "Earth Angel" is described as having sensational success on the West Coast, followed by impressive sales in New York. Various rating systems used by *Billboard* to indicate success potential are included. This show business approach provides a new perspective for the typical fans who traditionally think in terms of the emotional, artistic value of songs, rather than their prospects for making big money.

Although the *Billboard* reviews are brief (most no more than one or two sentences in length), they appear to be remarkably accurate. By and large, the recordings for which huge success was predicted eventually achieved just that. This commercially oriented approach also pervades the biographical matter, as when it is noted that Ricky Nelson was the first teen idol to be promoted through television. *American Rock 'n' Roll in Review* is an extremely entertaining compendium, providing a viewpoint that many will find delightfully enlightening.—**Richard W. Grefrath**

1240. Dodd, David G., and Robert G. Weiner. **The Grateful Dead and the Deadheads: An Annotated Bibliography.** Westport, Conn., Greenwood Press, 1997. 423p. index. (Music Reference Collection, no.60). $75.00. ISBN 0-313-30141-7.

The abundance of written and recorded Grateful Dead material makes the band a terrific topic for an annotated bibliography. Divided into three parts, this thoroughly researched work addresses, by type, specific aspects of the Dead's ongoing legacy: books and articles, reviews of legitimate recordings, and fan magazines and band newsletters. The last is a key item in Dead studies, and this volume takes an important step in the bibliographic control of this sometimes ephemeral material. Films are not included per se (reviews are), nor are videos or bootlegs. World Wide Web sites are noted in the preface.

Within each section a chronological arrangement is followed, and it is a bit unwieldy for the nearly 2,000-item 1st section. Without a classification scheme, the excellent annotations will be most useful to those with prior knowledge of the extensive Dead realm. Comprehensive author, title, and subject indexes are included. *The Grateful Dead and the Deadheads* is certainly one of the better Greenwood Press titles, although this colorful topic suffers from Greenwood's no-frills book and page design. In all, this is an excellent work.—**Megan S. Farrell**

1241. Karnbach, James, and Carol Bernson. **It's Only Rock 'n' Roll: The Ultimate Guide to the Rolling Stones.** New York, Facts on File, 1997. 404p. illus. index. $40.00; $24.95pa. ISBN 0-8160-3035-9; 0-8160-3547-4pa.

This work is not a guide to "the world's greatest rock band" in the sense of a prosaic narrative, but is, instead, a factbook, containing the sorts of things truly rabid fans require. It contains sections listing the band's chronology (beginning with Bill Wyman's birth in 1936), tours and concerts (the largest section), a "Sessionography" (listing their recording sessions in the studio), a discography (through 1996), films, television appearances, and promotional films and videos. A section titled "Bootlegs" is provided as well, which offers added value in the form of commentary on what bootlegging is and which boots stand out in what is surely a crowded field that cannot be easily described, much less cataloged. An extremely short preface by ex-Stone Mick Taylor adds to the validity of the book.

Interested fans will note the full page dedicated to the infamous "Altamont" concert during which a fan was killed by the "security" force—otherwise known as the Hell's Angels biker gang. The book has many photos from all eras of the Rolling Stones' life, which may offer the best proof yet to younger readers that Keith Richards is indeed human after all. This book is appropriate for music libraries as well as those that collect popular culture titles.—**Bob Craigmile**

1242. Krebs, Gary M. **The Rock and Roll Reader's Guide.** New York, Billboard Books/Watson-Guptill, 1997. 445p. index. $21.95pa. ISBN 0-8230-7602-4.

This resource is a detailed annotated bibliography of materials published in print about rock bands and musicians. The question of who qualifies as a "rock artist" is defined as any influential name in the rock (e.g., Led Zeppelin) or pop (e.g., Michael Jackson) category from the 1950s to the present. Blues, country, and soul artists who have influenced rock music are also included, along with contemporary "crossover" artists, such as Dolly Parton and Garth Brooks. Barbra Streisand and Barry Manilow are among the musicians successful on the pop charts who are not found in this guide.

The first section lists general reference materials not devoted to any one artist, such as dictionaries and encyclopedias, essays, resources devoted to chart data and concert events, and special subjects, including women in rock and roll. A topical directory of magazines is included in this section as well. The main section consists of alphabetic entries for individual musicians and bands. The accompanying citations are organized under a variety of possible headings, depending on the nature of the materials published. Among the 21 headings used are "Biographies," "Chronologies," "Interviews," and "Books Solely About an Artist's Death." All bibliographic citations in the guide are accompanied by critical annotations with the exception of magazine titles for which the annotations are purely descriptive. Cross-references between musicians and bands as well as separate author and title indexes are included. Although the author's criticisms may be questioned as a matter of taste, this is a well-constructed, unique, and useful reference tool. [R: LJ, 1 May 97, p. 72]—**Michael Weinberg**

1243. **The Rock Song Index: Essential Information on the 7,500 Most Important Songs of Rock and Roll.** By Bruce Pollock. New York, Schirmer Books/Simon & Schuster Macmillan, 1997. 524p. index. $95.00. ISBN 0-02-872068-7.

Pollock's not-unworthy goal is to pare down the thousands upon thousands of rock 'n' roll songs recorded since the beginning of the era to a subset of the "most important" songs—arriving at the number 7,500 in order to allow for a wide variety of songs without being "indiscriminate." The question immediately arises, however: for whom is this book intended? Is it for the "awesome fantasy radio station" that Pollock posits every fan "carries around in his or her head" (p. vii)? Or is it for the "future generations of archaeologists" (p. vviii) who will be struggling to comprehend the phenomenon of rock 'n' roll? The book's goal is unclear. There is much good information here, but Pollock's inability to objectively state his criteria for inclusion casts the entire endeavor, which the author correctly characterizes as a "monumental project," in a dubious light.

Arranged alphabetically by artist, the work includes top hits and album tracks chronologically under each artist. Date, producer, album, record label, and songwriter are given for each song, along with a pithy and—surprisingly, given the author's obvious love of his subject—frequently cynical comment on the song. This blurb often serves to note important or unusual cover versions of a given song by other artists. Even though an extensive review of the book's factual accuracy is beyond the scope of this review, this reviewer did immediately consult the section on the Grateful Dead and found several errors. The song "Box of Rain" is inaccurately ascribed to the *Workingman's Dead* album, rather than to its actual source on *American Beauty*; the inclusion of Jerry Garcia's never-recorded "Days Between" is given the label of Arista, when in fact there can be no label for an unrecorded song; lyricist Robert Hunter is left out of the songwriting credits for "Casey Jones"; and to top it all off, "Franklin's Tower," from *Blues for Allah*, is blurbed as "recorded at the Sphinx in Egypt," which is completely off the mark. Such errors in one band's section makes one wonder about Pollock's reliability in his other entries.

Pollock provides only a song title index, when the work could have used indexes by producer, songwriter, and artist, as the author frequently notes other artists' versions of songs. All in all, this volume is a quirky and fun but flawed work.—**David Dodd**

Sacred

1244. **The Christian Music Directories: Printed Music 1997-98.** San Jose, Calif., Resource Publications, 1997. 1531p. index. $175.00pa. ISSN 0899-0115.

Formerly entitled *The Music Locator*, this directory contains more than 176,000 pieces of music. A broad range of Christian music is listed, including traditional hymns; contemporary titles; and voice, instrumental, inspirational, classical, folk, rock, and children's music. Individual titles can be accessed through three separate alphabetic indexes and one index by number. These indexes are the song title index, the composer index, the songbook index by title, and the songbook index by number. In addition, there are a list of publishers by name and a publisher code list. The song title index is the most comprehensive index and contains the song title; composer or arranger, year of publication, publisher code, and publisher's catalog number; and notes (these indicate type of arrangement, if permanently out of print and other information).

The main purpose of this book is to locate a specific piece of music needed in a songbook or a collection of Christian songs. The directory also can be used to help plan music for a Christian church service. Further, it can serve as an aid in identifying and locating the copyright owner to get permission to copy a particular song. Access to the directory could be improved by inserting a table of contents in the front of the volume. This is a comprehensive directory that would be especially useful for a music librarian, choir director, or performer of religious music.—**George Louis Mayer**

1245. Meyer, Ulrich. **Biblical Quotation and Allusion in the Cantata Libretti of Johann Sebastian Bach.** Lanham, Md., Scarecrow Press, 1997. 223p. index. (Studies in Liturgical Musicology, no.5). $48.00. ISBN 0-8108-3329-8.

It is refreshing to see a text such as this one. This book reminds the modern church that music once preached as well as the minister, if not better. Meyer has done everyone a favor by recounting, in alpha-subject fashion, all the quotations and allusions in the cantata libretti by the magisterial Johann Sebastian Bach. Although two-fifths of the sacred—and more of the secular—cantatas are considered lost, the volume is still an impressive one. Under such subjects as advent, Christmas, epiphany, and so forth, one finds the partial text along with its recitatives, arias, and more. The first index provides a list of the biblical texts in the order in which they are found in the Bible. The second index is an alphabetic listing of the cantatas. Subject headings are provided in English and German.

Bach's work is all the more splendid when one understands that he wrote these pieces, each week, throughout the year. When he applied for a job, he sent as his résumé the Brandenburg Concertos (oddly enough, he did not get the job). Moreover, he fathered more than a dozen children. When we hear Bach, especially in a majestic cathedral, perhaps even the most modern-minded people are tempted to say, as did Bach at the end of each work, *soli Dei gloria*!—**Mark Y. Herring**

1246. Music, David W. **Hymnology: A Collection of Source Readings.** Lanham, Md., Scarecrow, 1996. 235p. index. (Studies in Liturgical Musicology, no.4). $38.00. ISBN 0-8108-3148-1.

This volume is a compilation of basic documentary source material that reflects the historical development of hymnody in the Christian world from Rome (Pliny) through the twentieth century (*Vatican II*). With 72 sources arranged chronologically, the emphasis is on congregational singing as viewed by the songwriters, church leaders, and other commentators. Inclusion in this collection is selective with emphasis on such important names as Martin Luther, Isaac Watts, and Charles Wesley. Also, by the author's choice, there has been limited inclusion of twentieth-century sources.

Sources that are translations and English-language sources from the eighteenth century forward are relatively easy to read and comprehend. The usage is either present day or nearly so. English-language sources written in the sixteenth and seventeenth centuries are more challenging because the language is much less standardized and the word uses are archaic. Although these instances are few, some explanatory notes would increase the reader's understanding of these documents.

The book includes a bibliography designed to provide additional sources, plus it could be used for collection development purposes. Finally, there is an index detailing both names and works.—**Phillip P. Powell**

1247. Unger, Melvin P. **Handbook to Bach's Sacred Cantata Texts: An Interlinear Translation with Reference Guide to Biblical Quotations and Allusions.** Lanham, Md., Scarecrow, 1996. 776p. index. $95.00. ISBN 0-8108-2979-7.

The handbook under review contains the texts of more than 200 cantatas whose music was composed by Johann Sebastian Bach. The emphasis in this volume, however, is on the words that were written by various librettists, known and unknown, who collaborated with Bach. The texts are arranged in BWV (Bachwerkverzeichniss) numerical order rather than in a liturgical sequence.

These cantatas served as a teaching tool during Sunday services for an audience whose biblical knowledge was more sophisticated than the average twentieth-century churchgoer. The librettos were based upon biblical passages but were not necessarily direct quotations. This is where the two-column format is helpful to the contemporary reader: The left column is a direct German-English translation when possible. Adjustments are made accordingly whenever an interlinear translation cannot occur because of syntactic differences between the two languages. The right-hand column contains the exact verses of the Bible (Revised Standard Version) from which the verses in the libretto were drawn. The direct placement of the biblical verses next to the pertinent portion of the libretto allows the reader to more readily discern from where the allusions were derived.

The book concludes with numerous indexes. Examples include alphabetic indexes of movement summaries, librettists, and chorale stanzas; an index of scriptural quotations; and an index of first performance dates. Not all the indexes are easily decipherable to an inexperienced user, and there are not always adequate explanations.

There is no question about the highly specialized nature of the book. With a careful reading of the preface, however, it is a work that can give the reader a clearer understanding of the meanings of Bach's numerous sacred cantatas. Finally, the price is most reasonable for such a substantial work.—**Phillip P. Powell**

Symphonic

1248. Smoley, Lewis M. **Gustav Mahler's Symphonies: Critical Commentary on Recordings Since 1986.** Westport, Conn., Greenwood Press, 1996. 353p. index. (Discographies, no.66). $75.00. ISBN 0-313-29771-1.

The 1st edition of Smoley's *The Symphonies of Gustav Mahler: A Critical Discography* appeared a decade ago (see ARBA 87, entry 1253), and this new volume bears witness to the abundance of interest in recordings of Mahler's symphonies. Although the earlier work covers a span of 60-plus years, it is more than 100 pages shorter than the new volume, which covers only 10 years. The present volume also offers some improvements over the first. The typeface is much easier to read, and there is also an excellent introduction. Said introduction provides a readable discussion regarding Mahler's symphonies and the treatment different conductors and orchestras have given these masterworks.

Unfortunately, a few problems with Smoley's first work still remain. It appears that the preparation of the text was left mainly to the author. Spelling errors and typographic errors still hamper the text, but not to the degree they did in 1986. As with any critical discography, one must be prepared for the author's subjective comments to appear from time to time. Even though Smoley has done his homework with score in hand, and his opinions may be well informed, these are issues that are open to interpretation. In comparing Smoley's opinions with other reviews of the same recordings, some serious disagreements were found about tempo, interpretation, and technical production. Because this work is retrospective, it would have been a great benefit had the author cited references to other reviews or quoted them in the text.

Readers are told that Smoley has written and lectured extensively on Mahler, but the bibliography cites none of his works. Indeed, only nine discographical catalogs are listed in the bibliography. There are, however, five useful indexes that aid users in finding their favorite conductors, orchestras, soloists, and choruses, as well as a list of record company labels. The text requires more trust in the author than the evidence may merit. Readers are advised to beware and check other reviewers before rushing out to the record store to make a purchase on Smoley's recommendation alone.—**Gregg S. Geary**

26 Mythology, Folklore, and Popular Culture

FOLKLORE

1249. Berman, Louis A., with Daniel K. Berman. **Proverb Wit & Wisdom: A Treasury of Proverbs, Parodies, Quips....** New York, Perigree Books/Berkley, 1997. 522p. index. $16.95pa. ISBN 0-399-52273-5.

In *Proverb Wit & Wisdom*, Berman, a retired professor of psychology at the University of Illinois (Chicago), has compiled a book that many library workers will enjoy as a source for quotations. It is a pleasure to browse among the 10,000 entries—a selection of familiar proverbs ("Absence makes the heart grow fonder") and the related quotations that comment on the proverbs or give them a witty "twist" or parody ("Absence makes the heart go yonder" or "Absinthe makes the heart grow fonder"). The book includes traditional proverbs (e.g., "Experience is the best teacher"), quotations so familiar that they function as proverbs (e.g., "To err is human, to forgive divine"), and familiar sayings not found in other proverb dictionaries (e.g., "Everybody loves a fat man"). It is not Berman's purpose to provide a documented history of proverbs, which has already been done in books like Wolfgang Mieder's *Dictionary of American Proverbs* (see ARBA 93, entry 1299) and William Smith's *Oxford Dictionary of English Proverbs, 2d ed.* (1952). In many cases, however, brief documentation is provided. Under the proverb "A little knowledge is a dangerous thing" we learn, for example, that Robert Hutchins said, "The college graduate is presented with a sheepskin to cover his intellectual nakedness," and T. H. Huxley in *On Elemental Instruction in Physiology* wrote, "If a little knowledge is dangerous, where is the man who has so much as to be out of danger?" Some of the proverb "twists" are wonderfully entertaining—Under "Love conquers all" we are informed that Mae West once said, "except poverty and toothaches." Under "Plan ahead" an anonymous wit commented, "It wasn't raining when Noah built the ark." The keyword arrangement and the topical index of main entries make the book easy to use. Berman's book is a welcome and useful supplement to traditional proverb dictionaries. [R: LJ, 15 May 97, p. 70]—**Donald C. Dickinson**

1250. Cordry, Harold V. **The Multicultural Dictionary of Proverbs: Over 20,000 Adages....** Jefferson, N.C., McFarland, 1997. 406p. index. $47.50. ISBN 0-7864-0251-2.

A French proverb says, "Common sense is not so common," and a Polish one echoes the importance of common sense with the advice, "Ask the patient, not the physician, where the pain is." From the humorous to the profound, the more than 20,000 proverbs compiled by Cordry, a professor at Baker University, encapsulate observations of, comments on, and responses to common human experiences (e.g., friendship, truth, grief, tyranny, stupidity).

More than a collection of proverbs, this dictionary channels the reader's attention to the similarities in wisdom among the 120 languages, nationalities, and ethnic groups from which the proverbs are drawn. Each of the 1,300 alphabetically arranged headings includes short entries about the topic, complete with an attribution of its earliest source (e.g., English, Hindi, Latin). Numerous cross-references; multiple indexes (keyword, subject, source); and a chronologically arranged bibliography of the proverbs' sources (from 1530 to 1990) simplify access to the material.

This well-organized multicultural dictionary of proverbs not only illustrates the common insights that different cultures share but also provides a rich resource of wisdom that the casual reader can glean from perusing the proverbs in an entry. Writers, speakers, and scholars can benefit from referencing these gems of accumulated human knowledge that Cordry has so ably gathered together. As an English proverb about wisdom advises, "Wise men learn by other men's mistakes, fools by their own."—**Suzanne G. Frayser**

1251. **Dictionary of 1000 Jewish Proverbs.** David C. Gross, ed. New York, Hippocrene Books, 1997. 125p. $11.95pa. ISBN 0-7818-0529-5.

Yiddish, Hebrew, and Aramaic expressions are known for their expressiveness, and have become a part of the American repertoire. Hippocrene has released a collection of 1,000 Jewish proverbs, which are arranged by alphabetic and topical order, following the setup of their other Bilingual Proverbs series works.

Dictionaries of proverbs can provide leisurely reading or can be used as a writing tool. This book satisfies these needs. Unfortunately, unlike many of the publishers' offerings in more obscure languages, there are a number of other works in print that are far superior for the home or reference library. Foremost among these is Joseph L. Baron's *A Treasury of Jewish Quotations* (Aronson, 1996) and *The Talmudic Anthology* (Behrman House, 1978), the former of which is cited in the bibliography of this dictionary, as is the more celebrated *Treasury of Jewish Quotations* (McGraw-Hill, 1972). Another possible alternative is Alfred J. Kolatch's *Great Jewish Quotations* (Jonathan David, 1996).—**Andrew B. Wertheimer**

1252. **Dictionary of 1000 Polish Proverbs.** Miroslaw Lipinski, ed. New York, Hippocrene Books, 1997. 129p. index. $11.95pa. ISBN 0-7818-0482-5.

This dictionary contains only a small portion of the Polish proverbs published in the definitive, four-volume compilation by Julian Krzyżanowski: *Nowa Księga Przysłów I Wyrażeń Przysłowiowych Polskich* (Warsaw, Państwowy Instytut Wydawniczy, 1969). The present selection consists of commonly used proverbs and their English equivalents. As such, it is claimed to be the first and most numerous list of its type in the English language.

The arrangement is alphabetic by Polish keywords, with alternate words in the proverb listed in parentheses. Each proverb is translated and compared with a similar English proverb: Exact translations are printed in normal typeface, and their equivalencies (with similar meaning or context) are listed in italics. Entries are numbered, and an index is provided for the English keywords. There are approximately twice as many proverbs, both Polish and their English equivalencies, as the subjects they address; among the most numerous are the proverbs related to the concepts of friendship, fortune, and fools. The bibliography lists 19 works on proverbs, half of them in Polish and on Polish proverbs. Most translations of Polish proverbs into English are satisfactory, although occasionally a more literal rendition would better reflect their essence. There are only a few typographic errors; however, some of them may distort the meaning of the quotations. Most of the proverbs are formulated in colloquial Polish idioms, with some words not listed in standard Polish dictionaries, thus requiring a good command of the language to fully understand them.

The dictionary is intended and recommended for students of Polish language and culture. It would also serve readers interested in the proverbs themselves and the popular wisdom they express.
—**Danuta A. Nitecki**

1253. Galazka, Jacek, comp. **A Treasury of Polish Aphorisms.** Corwall Bridge, Conn., Polish Heritage Publications; distr., New York, Hippocrene Books, 1997. 139p. illus. $14.95. ISBN 0-7818-0549-X.

Treasury of Polish Aphorisms is both fun to read and mentally stimulating. All aphorisms and proverbs are rendered in the original Polish and in faultless English translation. The main part of the book consists of aphorisms garnered from the foremost works of Polish literature, from the sixteenth to twentieth century, while the remainder reviews selected Polish proverbs, omitting mainly those that have corresponding ones in English. However, even among the omitted proverbs the Polish version is at times strikingly evocative, as in the example quoted by the compiler of this book—"Man proposes, God disposes" becomes "Man shoots and God carries the bullets." In the main part of this work, some aphorisms that can be found in the Polish literature have been omitted in the inevitable process of selection. Some may seem suspect in the science-oriented world at the turn of the twenty-first century, such as "Love makes discoveries, dissipation makes inventions," perhaps correct when "inventions" are defined as related to inventiveness. But whether one agrees with a particular aphorism or not, thinking about them is fruitful for one's own understanding of the paradoxes of life. Some aphorisms can be used in particular situations, such as "Percussion wins every discussion"; some are a biting commentary on leaders—and not only the communist ones—as in "Illiterates have to dictate"; and some have at least double applications— political and personal—as in "It's difficult to fall from a pedestal slowly." There is much here for anyone willing to spend a little time on sampling the wisdom and wit of others.—**Bogdan Mieczkowski**

1254. Mieder, Wolfgang, and George B. Bryan. **Proverbs in World Literature: A Bibliography.** New York, Peter Lang, 1996. 305p. index. $42.95. ISBN 0-8204-3499-X.

Although heavily slanted toward Western literature by white males, Mieder and Bryan's bibliography is an impressive source work. The preface clarifies the focus: the use and function of proverbial language (expressions, comparisons, exaggerations, and Wellerisms) in multicultural literature. The introduction stakes out a sizable task—improving on previous works that merely list proverbs from belles lettres to the exclusion of a broader field from sermons, letters, diaries, travel journals, songs, and mass media. Because the authors intend their study for the use of folklorists and students, they have cited journal titles *in toto* and reduced the number of abbreviations to eight standard examples. The body of the book features 2,654 entries. The general studies section contains 284, with the major portion, 253 pages, allotted to an alphabetic arrangement of specific studies, followed by a generous list of scholars cited, heavily laced with works by Bartlett Jere Whiting and Mieder.

The test of this work is coverage. Although the book is slender, its range is ample, including Euripides, St. Augustine, George Bernard Shaw, Charles Dickens, William Shakespeare, J. R. R. Tolkien, Elisabeth Gaskell, Martin Luther, Thomas Hardy, George Eliot, and James Joyce alongside *Everyman*, *Beowulf*, *Sir Gawain and the Green Knight*, and the writings of Americans. There is a nod toward presidents (Harry S. Truman and Franklin Delano Roosevelt) and world authors, such as Immanuel Kant, Chinua Achebe, Michel de Montaigne, Gabriel García Márquez, Franz Kafka, and Miguel de Cervantes. Absent are numerous masters—Hans Christian Andersen, Nikos Kazantzakis, Charles Perrault, Anton Chekhov, Edmond Rostand, Lao-tzu, Elie Wiesel—as well as Native Americans and female authors, such as N. Scott Momaday, Willa Cather, Black Elk, Kate Chopin, and Jane Austen. [R: Choice, June 97, p. 1642]

—**Mary Ellen Snodgrass**

1255. Roth, John E. **American Elves: An Encyclopedia of Little People from the Lore of 380 Ethnic Groups of the Western Hemisphere.** Jefferson, N.C., McFarland, 1997. 329p. maps. $68.50. ISBN 0-89950-944-4.

Although different in format and approach, *American Elves* is an excellent companion piece to Katharine Briggs's *Dictionary of Fairies* (1976), subsequently published in an American edition as *An Encyclopedia of Fairies* (see ARBA 78, entry 1009), which concentrates on the little people of the British Isles. Whereas Briggs approached the subject from the standpoint of a traditional folklorist, Roth approaches it more from the standpoint of an anthropologist/sociologist. It should serve for many years to come as the standard guide to the little people of the Western Hemisphere.

Roth has done a careful job of condensing more than 3,000 stories from 380 cultures that he has collected from a wide variety of sources, including previous collections, oral histories, personal letters and memoirs, and other original resources. The material is organized into 53 ethnic or linguistic groups and, in most cases, is accompanied by a map that helps place the group in a geographic context. Within each entry, the material is organized into the following categories: shape-shifters; pygmies; dwarfs; individuals; habitat; techniques (e.g., speech, clothes, and food); social (e.g., play, politics); and magic (e.g., invisibility, origins, power). At the end of each entry there is a comprehensive, but abbreviated, list of sources that is tied to the extensive bibliography at the end of the book. There is also an extensive guide to ethnic and linguistic groups at the back of the book.

As fascinating and valuable as the copious information that Roth has collected is, this will be an extremely frustrating book for most users and many reference librarians to use effectively. The bibliography, which is primarily an alphabetic listing of sources, also includes cross-references—a number of which are blind—to ethnic or linguistic group names that appear to have been used in the titles of books or articles, but those cross-references serve little apparent useful purpose. In the same fashion, the long list of ethnic or linguistic groups provides numerous linkages, but those are not linked to the main arrangement of the material in any evident way. Most frustrating, however, is the lack of any sort of index to the names of the wide variety of little people who are described in the body of the text. The many users who may be looking for information about a specific type of little people, or an individual little person, but do not know what ethnic or linguistic group he or she may be associated with, will find it virtually impossible to find that information with any ease. Finally, the factual condensation of the tales takes away much of the true charm of the wonderful little people who populate so much of the world.

—**Norman D. Stevens**

1256. **Storytelling Encyclopedia: Historical, Cultural, and Multiethnic Approaches to Oral Traditions Around the World.** David Adams Leeming, ed. Phoenix, Ariz., Oryx Press, 1997. 543p. index. $69.95. ISBN 1-57356-025-1.

This encyclopedia of storytelling is diverse and intricate in its conception. The 1st part delineates historical, cultural, and multiethnic approaches to oral traditions globally. It analyzes fundamental storytelling elements, such as themes, motifs, characters, and places with tales from around the world. The introductory essays are well thought out and presented. The 2d section is an encyclopedic collection of entries, including tales, characters, and techniques. References are included in each entry, and all are cross-referenced.

One influence that the book lacks and would benefit from is a historian of religions' perspective. Much of the material is mythological and religious, and this perspective in the commentary is weak. The final bibliography and subject index are particularly helpful. The encyclopedia's use for reference in academic and general libraries is complemented by its use as a theoretical volume on oral tradition.
—Linda L. Lam-Easton

MYTHOLOGY

1257. Aghion, Irène, Claire Barbillon, and François Lissarrague. **Gods and Heroes of Classical Antiquity.** New York, Flammarion; distr., Abbeville Press, 1996. 317p. illus. index. (Flammarion Iconographic Guides). $45.00. ISBN 2-08013-581-3.

Gods and Heroes of Classical Antiquity is intended for readers who love art, as well as individuals simply curious about the subject. Originally published in French (in 1994) under the title *Héros et Dieux de l'Antiquité*, it is a handsomely presented iconographic guide to the most famous themes in Greek and Roman myth and history as represented in ancient and modern art since antiquity. *Gods and Heroes* provides ready if preliminary access to the narrative content of numerous works of art that readers are likely to encounter in either books or museums. Authors Aghion, Barbillon, and Lissarrague reach beyond the art—illustrated with beautiful color and black-and-white photographs—and back into the legends and tales that served as a source of inspiration for the artists themselves.

With that in mind, the tales are arranged alphabetically to assist readers looking for particular information. Latin spellings are used throughout, although some Greek names are retained when deemed absolutely essential. Cross-references are used where Greek names differ from Latin, as with Athena/Minerva or Dionysius/Bacchus. Translation of the names is also provided in the principal European languages. Multiepisodic legends with many characters are broken down, with episodes and characters receiving individual treatment. Each character entry entails a brief account of the relevant tradition, with particular attention paid to important features that help clarify the work of art. Mythic representation is discussed, with distinctions made between ancient and modern. In some instances, entries end with a list of attributes, cross-references to other entries, sources, and a concise bibliography. The section on sources, for example, notes the texts from which modern works of art derive, rather than all the texts that allude to a specific character and that the reader can find elsewhere in specific encyclopedias. Although books and articles about the iconography of a specific character are sometimes cited at the end of an entry, the principal iconographic repertories are placed in the general bibliography.

The authors of *Gods and Heroes of Classical Antiquity* have aimed for a modest and practical guide for the reader with a will to explore and learn something new. Their volume will clearly meet that goal. [R: Choice, May 97, p. 1471]—**Arthur Gribben**

1258. Monaghan, Patricia. **The New Book of Goddesses and Heroines.** 3d ed. Saint Paul, Minn., Llewellyn, 1997. 371p. illus. $19.95pa. ISBN 1-56718-465-0.

The stated purpose of this book is "to tell goddess myths and to describe goddess symbols." Monaghan pursues this goal with an alphabetic list of some 1,500 goddess figures and mythical heroines from around the world and throughout history. Written for the general reader, the entries provide basic information about the figures that is often presented in narrative, or story, form. Herein lies the weakness of the book, for the author does not pursue her subject in a detailed or scholarly manner. For example, the relatively lengthy entry on the Egyptian deity Isis summarizes a number of stories about the goddess, but does not convey her importance as creator of all things or her relationship to other mythologies and deities in ancient Mediterranean cultures (e.g., to the story of Mary's Egyptian journey).

A section new to this edition, "Culture of the Goddess," provides background material on the cultures from which the goddesses arose. Again, the material is very general, and one would be hard put to explain a practical application for the information. Another new section, "Names of the Goddess," cites some (but not all) of alternative spellings and names for many of the figures. There is also a list of "Feasts of the Goddess," a bibliography, and a topical section on "Symbols of the Goddess." Black-and-white photographs from Chicago's Field Museum of Natural History illustrate the text.

In a work this general, it would be helpful to cite sources for further study on each entry; however, that is not done. There is no index, nor are there cross-references. These omissions and the general nature of the book hamper its usefulness as a reference, but public libraries may want to consider it as a purchase for general readers interested in the topic.—**Barbara Ittner**

1259. Orchard, Andy. **Cassell Dictionary of Norse Myth and Legend.** London, Cassell; distr., New York, Sterling Publishing, 1997. 223p. illus. index. $29.95. ISBN 0-304-34520-2.

This attractively designed dictionary addresses the changing range of myths and legends current among the Germanic peoples of northern Europe during more than a millennium. Although the focus is mostly literary, ample coverage is given to historical figures (e.g., Bede, the Anglo-Saxon monk; Bishop Wulfstan; and the fierce warrior berserks); customs; traditions; artifacts (boat burials, oaths, runes); and place-names (Jelling, Sutton Hoo, Uppsala).

Each of the alphabetically arranged entries provides a translation of the Norse or Old English term—for example, *scyld* (shield), *valkyries* (choosers of the slain)—and then gives an extended definition, often including a quotation from the literary source where the term appears. Cross-references in the text are in small capital letters. At the end of the entry are references to individual listings in the bibliography of suggested further reading. Many of the well-known names and terms in translations of the Norse and Old English literature selections found in college survey texts are included, such as *Beowulf*, flytings, Herot, the Midgard-serpent, and trolls. The more advanced student or the reader of Germanic myths will find listings for Snorri Sturluson, the *Völsunga saga*, norns, Loki, Gunnar, and Fáfnir, among many others. The volume concludes with the above-mentioned bibliography; four appendixes (Odin's names and titles, dwarf names, giant names, and names of troll-wives, giantesses, and valkyries); and an index of passages and authors cited in the text. This reasonably priced dictionary should be welcomed in most academic and public library collections. [R: RBB, Aug 97, p. 1924]—**Charles R. Andrews**

1260. Room, Adrian. **Who's Who in Classical Mythology.** Lincolnwood, Ill., National Textbook, 1997. 343p. illus. $16.95pa. ISBN 0-8442-5469-X.

The title of this dictionary is somewhat misleading. Rather than discussing the feats or follies of classical gods and personages, the volume at hand is more reminiscent of a baby name book for Greek and Roman names. The acts perpetrated by the characters who embodied the names and the nonfamilial connections between them are for the most part left to other texts. This dictionary is etymological in nature, a study of classical name origins. The only discussion of deeds arises when relating an act to the etymology of the name; for instance, no mention is made of the Trojan War in the entry on Helen.

The volume begins with an introduction by Room, author of several other books, including *The Fascinating Origins of Everyday Words* (National Textbook, 1986) and *Literally Entitled* (see ARBA 97, entry 891). The introduction sets up a rather disconcerting problem that continues throughout the text: the inconsistency between use of Greek or Roman appellations (e.g., Heracles/Hercules, Odysseus/Ulysses). However, cross-references do appear within the dictionary, aiding users in finding the name they seek. The introduction is followed by a short list of technical terms defined.

The dictionary proper consists of more than 1,200 entries and is alphabetic. Main entries and cross-references to other main headings are boldfaced. Occasional black-and-white illustrations, taken mostly from vase paintings, break up the text. The body of the dictionary is followed by seven appendixes, which provide such information as common elements in Greek mythological names and corresponding names of characters (Greek versus Roman). A brief bibliography completes the work.

This dictionary is certainly unique and, as stated by Room in the introduction, fills a niche in classical studies. Those people searching for a dictionary that outlines Greek and Roman mythological stories will be better served by *Bulfinch's Mythology* (see ARBA 71, entry 1339). Those looking for the origins of mythological heroes' names should consult Room's dictionary.—**Melissa Rae Root**

1261. Sienkewicz, Thomas J. **Theories of Myth: An Annotated Bibliography.** Pasadena, Calif., Salem Press and Lanham, Md., Scarecrow, 1997. 227p. index. (Magill Bibliographies). $32.00. ISBN 0-8108-3388-3.

With the work of Joseph Campbell, interest in mythology has grown well beyond the classic Greek and Roman stories to include a vast array of world cultures. Anthropologists, psychologists, and other disciplines have begun to focus on myths as part of their subjects. This bibliography continues the work of Thomas Sienkewicz, who has published an earlier work, *World Mythology* (see ARBA 97, entry 1092), as part of the Magill series. The earlier work reviewed actual myths, whereas this newer work annotates books and articles that compare myths and search for structure or meaning in comparative mythology. Although the author states the intended audience is college students or advanced high school students, the work covers a more in-depth range of materials and could be of assistance to a serious researcher. This book is divided into chapters that group the following subjects: general studies, meaning of myths, comparative myths, anthropology, psychology, religion, and structure. Major influences in the field, such as Campbell, Levi-Strauss, and Cambridge School, are represented. The annotations are well written and provide a thorough understanding of what the book or article covers and the value of the work. This does seem to be a historical survey in that most of the citations are pre-1990 with few new titles. There is an attempt to cover more areas of the world, but many of the articles focus on western European stories or myths. This is a good companion piece to Sienkewicz's earlier work and a valuable tool for exploring the major theorists in the field.—**Joshua Cohen**

POPULAR CULTURE

1262. **Fiesta!** Danbury, Conn., Grolier, 1997. 16v. illus. maps. index. $259.00/set. ISBN 0-7172-9099-9.

Fiesta is a Spanish word whose meaning—festival—is understood worldwide. As this book points out, there is more than merrymaking to festivals. These occasions for worship and revelry show what different groups of people around the world find important. In this 16-volume set, students can learn what different cultures around the world find important by studying their public celebrations.

Students will learn from this set how people live, eat, talk, think, and worship. It introduces students to a nation's geography, culture, and legends. Along with a description of each festival, each volume provides recipes for food associated with the festivity, songs for the occasion, and at least two traditional stories surrounding a celebration. The names of the holidays and words for songs are not written phonetically, which could hinder student's pronunciation of these foreign words and phrases.

Titles in the set include Brazil, China, Germany, India, Ireland, Israel, Italy, Jamaica, Japan, Korea, Mexico, Nigeria, Peru, Russia, Turkey, and Vietnam. Each volume is 32 pages, for a total of 512 pages in the set. *Fiesta!* also offers special learning features, including colorful global and local illustrations throughout the set; a master set index and glossary in each volume as well as activities designed to help students experience new languages, food, crafts, religions, traditions, and values; and lessons promoting understanding and tolerance in our multicultural world.

This set is aimed at all students from elementary school to high school. It is easy to use, and students will benefit from the material included in each volume. For more than 100 years, the Grolier name has been respected worldwide for signifying excellence in printed reference and research material. *Fiesta!* is another example of Grolier's commitment to producing superior books for students.

—**Barbara B. Goldstein**

1263. **Holidays, Festivals, and Celebrations of the World Dictionary: Detailing More Than 2,000 Observances from All 50 States and More Than 100 Nations.** 2d ed. Helene Henderson and Sue Ellen Thompson, eds. Detroit, Omnigraphics, 1997. 822p. index. $84.00. ISBN 0-7808-0074-5.

This 2d edition follows much the same format as the 1st (see ARBA 96, entry 1358), providing an alphabetic annotated listing of national and international holidays and festivals covering cultural, ethnic, historical, popular, religious, and sports celebrations. Approximately 500 new entries are included, bringing the listing up to 2,000-plus entries. Each entry consists of the observant's name and variants, date(s) of celebration, a brief description of the origins and background of the event, and special activities and rituals associated with it. These listings now usually include one or more informational references and, where applicable, sponsoring organization names for further details. In addition to a general index and alphabetic name and keyword indexes, several new access points have been provided: an index to legal holidays by state and country and an ethnic and geographic index. As in the 1st edition, informative pieces on the calendar systems used around the world, a comparative table of calendar systems, and a list of words relating to periods of time are included.

New appendixes featured in this edition include a list of admission days for U.S. states and independence/republic/national days for the countries of the world, a special biographical section on U.S. presidents and relevant landmarks that commemorate them, domestic and international tourism information sources, an annotated topical bibliography on holiday- and festival-related books, and a short list of 12 Websites related to holidays. Also included is a brief overview on the concept and impact of the millennium.

Although some of the newer appendixes may be only generally related to the topic of holidays and festivals (such as the section on presidential biographies), students and researchers alike will continue to find this an easy-to-use ready-reference volume. With extensive indexing points to locate relevant entries, this work continues to prove a welcome companion to such helpful works as *Chase's Calendar of Events* (40th ed.; see ARBA 97, entry 5).—**Elizabeth Patterson**

27 Performing Arts

GENERAL WORKS

1264. **The A&E Entertainment Almanac, 1997.** Robert Moses, Alicia Potter, and Beth Rowen, eds. New York, Houghton Mifflin, 1996. 807p. illus. (An Information Please Almanac). $13.95pa. ISBN 0-395-82855-4.

This book is an information-packed compendium about many kinds of both popular and what used to be called "highbrow" entertainment. It contains sections on movies; popular music; radio and television; home entertainment (with coverage of home videos, the Internet and the World Wide Web, CD-ROMs, and video games); the performing arts (covering theater, dance, and opera); and book and magazine publishing. These sections are divided into two parts. The first section covers developments in 1997 and 1996; the second, or "reference," part covers past years and decades. Some of the reference part contains current material as well. New this year is a people section with biographies, averaging about 50 words in length, of famous people, living and dead, who influenced the entertainment industry.

The volume contains an abundance of information on what people and productions won major awards and prizes. The brief reviews of movies that were recently released in the United States are, as a group, excellent. The typeface in the reference section is very small; some people may find it difficult to read.—**David S. Webster**

1265. DuBoff, Leonard D. **The Performing Arts Business Encyclopedia.** New York, Allworth Press, 1996. 255p. $19.95pa. ISBN 1-880559-42-0.

Intended as a nontechnical resource for individuals, organizations, and such behind-the-scenes professionals as attorneys and advisers, this guide includes definitions and explanations of commonly used terms, concepts, and practices in the field of live theater. However, the author also makes it clear that the focus of this text is not on recorded music, movies, and television, which, he says, will be covered in other volumes of the series. The underlying purpose of this work is to provide an explanatory guide to the terms and practices used in the theater profession so that interested individuals and organizations may be able to better avoid time-consuming and costly litigation. Terms most often used in the field are arranged alphabetically with detailed explanations and definitions following each of the words and phrases. Cross-references are used extensively throughout the text.

Two brief but useful appendixes follow the text: A list of trade lists and associations, listed brokers, volunteer lawyers for the arts, and other resources is followed by a bibliography of publications useful to the reader. The relatively inexpensive cost of this resource, when combined with the easy-to-read language meant for a wide audience, indicates that many public libraries would find that this is a useful addition to their reference collections.—**James M. Murray**

1266. **Star Guide, 1997-98.** Ann Arbor, Mich., Axiom Information Resources, 1997. 184p. index. $12.95pa. ISBN 0-943213-22-3. ISSN 1060-9997.

If people are tired of playing "Six Degrees of Kevin Bacon," they can pick up a copy of this book and play "Who's Missing?" Being a bit put off by the hyperbole of the publishers ("The Definitive Guide" and the most unctuous "They're Not a Star Unless They're a Star in *Star Guide*"), this reviewer decided to play his own version of the game. In the world of television stars, for example, *ER*'s Anthony Edwards is in, but Bat-hunk and fellow *ER* star George Clooney is out. Roseanne is in; chunky television husband (and star of more movies) John Goodman is out. The cast of *Frasier* is one of the finest ensembles in television history, but only Kelsey Grammar made the cut; acerbic television brother David Hyde-Pierce did not. *Seinfeld*'s Jerry Seinfeld is listed; Julia Louis-Dreyfuss is not. And so it goes. Israel's leader, Benjamin Netanyahu, is not included, but people can still write to the deceased Spiro Agnew. There is a disturbing list of absent U.S. senators (Spencer Abrahams of Michigan, Missouri's John Ashcroft, Hawaii's Daniel Inouye, and the forceful Kay Bailey Hutchinson of Texas among them), but their addresses are far easier to obtain than any of the stars. Barney is accessible by mail, but forget about writing to the Bananas in Pajamas. Fuzzy Zoeller could be contacted about his statements concerning Tiger Woods, but one cannot get Woods's take, for his address is unavailable.

There are glaring typographic errors on virtually every page. Clint E.wood (p. 22), Medeleine Albright (p. 138), Emperor Akihoto (p. 138), and Steve Railback (p. 56) join legions who cry out for a spell checker. There are some interesting inclusions: many famous criminals are here (Timothy McVeigh, the Menendez Brothers, Charles Manson, and so on), but O. J. Simpson remains in the "Sports" category. This book is fluff, pure and simple, but every public library knows it is going to be a popular item. People who write to celebrities find out at their own peril that fame is as ephemeral as some of the addresses listed here. Anyhow, any book such as this one that does not list Doris Day has one strike against it, as far as this reviewer is concerned.—**Joseph L. Carlson**

DANCE

1267. **Bibliographic Guide to Dance 1995.** New York, G. K. Hall/Simon & Schuster Macmillan, 1996. 3v. $560.00/set. ISBN 0-7838-1316-3. ISSN 0360-2737.

The dance component of G. K. Hall's bibliographic series is a three-volume list of holdings at the New York Public Library's Research Libraries collection. It includes materials cataloged from September 1, 1994, to December 31, 1995. Works represent every style of dance, from ballet to burlesque, and document every aspect of dance, from the economic to the therapeutic. Only a small fraction of the items here are books; nonbook materials include clipping files, drawings, lithographs, motion pictures, periodicals, scrapbooks, scores (dance and music), videotapes, and various other media.

This publication is a partial annual supplement to the *Dictionary Catalog of the Dance Collection* (G. K. Hall, 1974). That collection is recognized as the most comprehensive of its kind. Such exhaustive coverage, matched with the clear and simple arrangement found in this bibliographic series, make this set an automatic purchase for dance and performing arts collections.—**Ed Volz**

1268. Billman, Larry. **Film Choreographers and Dance Directors: An Illustrated Biographical Encyclopedia....** Jefferson, N.C., McFarland, 1997. 652p. illus. index. $110.00. ISBN 0-89950-868-5.

Seeking to make the public more aware of the achievements and importance of dance directors and choreographers in U.S. cinema, Billman has compiled a biographical dictionary of the creators and directors of dance sequences in both musical and nonmusical motion pictures. The majority of this volume consists of an alphabetic listing of more than 900 choreographers. In his introduction, Billman writes of the difficulty of obtaining information on many choreographers. Indeed, many films do not even list the choreographer's name in the credits. The book's entries, therefore, vary in size and detail. Entries are much longer and more complete for such famous dance designers as Hermes Pan (creator of many dances for MGM and Warner Brothers musicals), Fred Astaire, Gene Kelly, and Agnes DeMille than for other lesser-known choreographers. When the information is available, Billman provides a short biography; a list of book-length biographies; and lists of credits for work in theater, ballet, television, video, and film.

Preceding the biographical entries is Billman's history of cinema choreography, arranged into chapter roughly by decade, and extending from 1893 to the early 1990s. Each chapter provides a quick overview of the decade, but no one film is covered in much detail. Each chapter concludes with a selected filmography (movie title, choreographer, studio name, date of release, video release information, and short annotation). Throughout the book, black-and-white photographs depict rehearsals, publicity shots, and other behind-the-scenes action. An appendix lists films alphabetically with their choreographers. Because choreography credits are hard to find, this part of the volume will be especially useful to librarians and dance historians. The book's index provides reliable access to people, films, plays, places, and selected subjects. Billman, a dancer and choreographer himself, has done the world of dance a service with the compilation of this book.—**Linda Keir Simons**

1269. **Dance on Disc: The Complete Catalog of the Dance Collection of the New York Public Library on CD-ROM.** [CD-ROM]. New York, G. K. Hall/Simon & Schuster Macmillan, 1996. Minimum system requirements: IBM or compatible. CD-ROM drive with CD-ROM Extensions 2.0. 512K RAM. $995.00.

Dance is an art passed from master to student. Eventually the student becomes the master, and a new student becomes the recipient of dance traditions that have been preserved by this apprenticeship over centuries. *Dance on Disc* offers new resources for the preservation of dance and for the study of dancers, choreographers, companies, music, staging, and works. This disk is based upon the collection of the New York Public Library's special collection of books, audiovisuals, periodicals, manuscripts, original artifacts, and other resources. In theory, a talented choreographer in Des Moines, Iowa, could stage a Balanchine work almost as if Balanchine had been the director, with the resources indexed in *Dance on Disc* and available from the New York Public Library. This CD-ROM has a simple and effective interface, allowing Boolean logic searching and specific field searching for authors, names, subjects, dates, and material type. Results can be displayed in both brief and full formats and sorted by fields such as author, material type, and date, among other fields. Printing and downloading options are available. The New York Public Library's special collection provides a treasure house of dance knowledge for the researcher and artist. This disk is a valuable and unduplicated resource for access to that collection.—**Lynne M. Fox**

1270. **Index to Dance Periodicals: 1995.** New York, G. K. Hall/Simon & Schuster Macmillan, 1996. 450p. $185.00. ISBN 0-7838-1533-6. ISSN 1058-6350.

Although this annual reference work is running about two years behind the calendar (the 1995 issue was published in 1997), it is a source worth waiting for. The *Index to Dance Periodicals: 1995* covers 85 dance and dance-related periodicals, 53 of which are from the United States. Citations appear in English and four other languages: French, German, Italian, and Spanish. This 450-page index is compiled by the staff of the New York Public Library for the Performing Arts who also publish the *Bibliographical Guide to Dance*, a catalog listing citations for more than 180,000 dance materials. These constitute the highest possible credentials for dance literature research.

Without this specialized dance index, a researcher would have to rely upon numerous indexes, from humanities to sports, to get the depth of coverage offered in this single resource. The *Index to Dance Periodicals* is arranged in a dictionary format with all entries falling under one alphabet. Subject headings are derived from Library of Congress subject headings and from the literature and reference works of the dance field, and conform to the New York Public Library for the Performing Arts dance collection authority file. Cross-references and *see also* references are also used.

There is no comparable index available for the field of dance. The *Dance Abstracts and Index* from UCLA's Dance Database Project covers more publication formats, such as theses, dissertations, and conference proceedings and reports, but for up-to-date periodical literature coverage the *Index to Dance Periodicals* stands alone.

The *Index to Dance Periodicals* is highly recommended for academic, large public, and specialized performing arts and humanities libraries. Researchers might also check the World Wide Web for a site entitled Dance Library Resources at http://www.artswire.org/Artswire/www.dance/resource.html.

—**Linda D. Tietjen**

FILM, TELEVISION, AND VIDEO

Bibliography

1271. Lerner, Loren. **Canadian Film and Video: A Bibliography and Guide to the Literature. Film et Video Canadiens.** Buffalo, N.Y. and Toronto, University of Toronto Press, 1997. 2v. index. $275.00/set. ISBN 0-8020-2988-4.

Lerner has produced a unique and major new reference resource for film researchers. *Canadian Film and Video* provides an excellent first step in finding information about Canadian film and filmmakers. The guide gives a bibliography on a wide range of topics in Canadian films, including listings for different genres (documentary, industrial, video, and animated) and area studies (Canada, Québec, British Columbia, and Atlantic Canada), as well as chapters on festivals, the Canadian film industry, and the people who make up that industry. One of the most interesting chapters is "Film and Censorship," in which the oldest citation dates back to 1913. The references for each subject are listed chronologically and go through 1989. The citations are from French as well as English sources, and the abstracts are either in one or both languages. The only drawbacks to this monumental work are the confusing flip-flop between languages and the fact that all references end in 1989.

The serious researcher will appreciate all the work that went into compiling such a collection of diffuse sources and will not mind updating the information. As Pierre Véronneau states in his foreword, "This bibliography will be an indispensable reference work for all cinema specialists in Canada." This reviewer would add that any library specializing in the study of film or video ought to own this source, as it will soon become a reference classic on the subject of Canadian film.—**Elizabeth A. Ginno**

Bio-bibliography

1272. Billman, Larry. **Fred Astaire: A Bio-bibliography.** Westport, Conn., Greenwood Press, 1997. 402p. illus. index. (Bio-bibliographies in the Performing Arts, no.76). $65.00. ISBN 0-313-29010-5.

Not many names are synonymous with grace, elegance, and style. Not many careers have spanned several performance mediums and served as models of excellence and as sources of inspiration. Fred Astaire's has. This bio-bibliography aims to extract and edit previously printed information regarding Astaire's life and career, thus presenting a well-rounded picture of his achievements. Further research is encouraged, starting from the extensive annotated bibliography provided here.

A biography and chronology precede sections chronicling Astaire's careers in stage, film, radio, and television. Entries list dates, credits, songs, the cast, a synopsis, reviews, and comments. The following chapters include a videography; a discography; lists of his musical compositions; collectibles; awards, honors, and tributes; and projects. The bibliography and an index, referring to pages in the previous sections, complete the volume. Several black-and-white photographs illustrate the volume. This reference work draws together the many aspects of Astaire's life and career and in doing so provides a balanced view of one of the most dynamic figures in U.S. entertainment.—**Anita Zutis**

1273. Frank, Sam. **Ronald Colman: A Bio-bibliography.** Westport, Conn., Greenwood Press, 1997. 294p. illus. index. (Bio-bibliographies in the Performing Arts, no.74). $65.00. ISBN 0-313-26433-3.

Ronald Colman's distinctive voice was the perfect embodiment of the suave, sophisticated, gentlemanly charm that he projected in such memorable silent films as *The White Sister* (1923), *Stella Dallas* (1925), and *Beau Geste* (1926). Therefore, with the coming of sound, his career went into high gear. He remained a popular star until the end of his life, making his mark first in films and then in radio and television. Colman won a Best Actor Oscar in 1948 for *A Double Life*, and in 1958, the year of his death, his was one of the first six stars inducted into the Hollywood Walk of Fame.

This volume, number 74 in Greenwood Press's Bio-bibliographies in the Performing Arts, follows the format established for the series. There are a biography; a chronology; an evaluation of Colman's career; and annotated listings with full credits and commentary of his work on stage, in films, and on radio and television. In addition, there is a discography, a listing of awards and honors, a 434-item bibliography, and an index. Little has been written about Colman since his death. This scholarly, readable volume, which the author describes as the product of 29 years of obsessive love and research, is a useful addition to this well-respected series.—**Joseph W. Palmer**

1274. Schultz, Margie. **Ann Sheridan: A Bio-bibliography.** Westport, Conn., Greenwood Press, 1997. 377p. index. (Bio-bibliographies in the Performing Arts, no.75). $65.00. ISBN 0-313-28482-2.

Ann Sheridan came to Hollywood in 1933 as a contestant in a studio-sponsored beauty contest. She subsequently appeared in dozens of minor films before achieving stardom in *Angels with Dirty Faces* (1938). During World War II, Sheridan's star burned brightest. Christened The Oomph Girl by the media, she became one of the United States' favorite wartime pin-ups and she appeared in her best-remembered film, *King's Row* (1942). During the 1950s and 1960s, Sheridan made numerous radio and television appearances, and she was starring in a prime-time television series, *Pistols 'n' Petticoats*, at the time of her death in 1967.

Schultz has exhaustively researched Sheridan's career. She presents her findings in a detailed reference book that includes a biography; a chronology; annotated listings with credits of her appearances on stage, screen, radio, and television; and, among other things, a discography, a list of awards and honors, a videography, a bibliography, and a directory of archival sources. Although the content of this book is certainly up to the high standards established by other titles in the series, the physical format is not. Other volumes contain illustrations. This one has only a portrait opposite the title page. Because Sheridan has not achieved the posthumous cult status of other stars and because her films are rarely seen today, a selection of stills and photographs would have greatly enhanced the book's effectiveness. Furthermore, the book appears to have been photographically reproduced from the output of a dot matrix printer. The darkness of the typeface varies, but much of it is too light. This flaw, together with unjustified margins, makes the book difficult to read without eyestrain. It is a shame that the publisher has allowed mediocre packaging to detract from the contents of this well-researched volume.—**Joseph W. Palmer**

1275. Schwartz, Donald Ray, and Anne Aull Bowbeer. **Lillian Russell: A Bio-bibliography.** Westport, Conn., Greenwood Press, 1997. 303p. illus. index. (Bio-bibliographies in the Performing Arts, no.77). $69.50. ISBN 0-313-27764-8.

This work treats a legendary stage personality, Lillian Russell, factually and with enough detail to present her human side. The resulting work is highly readable, whether as a general biography or as a reference providing historical documentation. This volume demonstrates careful research. Midwestern by birth (she was born in Iowa) and Victorian in her time frame, Russell's name today still conveys an image of a famous beauty and theater personality. With the inclusion of generous citations of national and international events happening during Russell's lifetime, the reader is provided with a broad awareness of the social and cultural picture of the late nineteenth and early twentieth centuries. By interweaving Russell's circle of friends and associates into the biography and chronology, the authors help convey her role as one of the great figures on the U.S. stage.

Divided into eight major sections and six appendixes, the work covers Russell's career by means of a biography, followed by a year-by-year and day-by-day chronology. Separate chapters pertain to aspects of her professional career and include stage and film appearances, a discography, and a list of sheet music items. Movies, radio, and television presentations about Russell are also highlighted. A comprehensive and annotated bibliography includes books, magazines and journals, newspapers, letters, and miscellaneous materials. Highly readable and well organized, this bio-bibliography will be a welcome addition as a reference source for the student of U.S. theater or for the general reader.—**Louis G. Zelenka**

Biography

1276. Aaker, Everett. **Television Western Players of the Fifties: A Biographical Encyclopedia of All Regular Cast Members in Western Series, 1949-1959.** Jefferson, N.C., McFarland, 1997. 576p. illus. index. $85.00. ISBN 0-7864-0284-9.

In *Television Western Players of the Fifties*, Aacker profiles actors and actresses who had regular roles in a Western television series from September 15, 1949, to December 31, 1959. Programs of this time included such series classics as *Gunsmoke; Have Gun, Will Travel; The Lone Ranger; Maverick; Bonanza; Rawhide;* and

Bat Masterson. Actors and actresses profiled range from those who already were or later became internationally known film stars to those who are now relatively obscure. Among the more prominent names featured are Clint Eastwood, Henry Fonda, Joel McCrea, Steve McQueen, Roy Rogers, Gene Autry, and James Garner.

Entries include a photograph, in most cases; a biographical profile; a filmography; a list of television series in which the individual appeared; and a list of references. Sources of biographical information cited by the author are encyclopedias and magazines, press releases, and (when possible) from the individuals themselves. Also provided are a television series catalog of the westerns that lists the original air dates, number of episodes, and plot synopses; a bibliography; and an index. This informative and fascinating source is recommended especially to public library collections.—**Lucy Heckman**

1277. Keller, Gary D., with Estela Keller. **A Biographical Handbook of Hispanics and United States Film.** Tempe, Ariz., Bilingual Press, 1997. 322p. illus. index. $49.00; $28.00pa. ISBN 0-927534-65-7; 0-927534-56-8pa.

This is the 2d volume of a 2-volume set by Gary Keller that began with *Hispanics & United States Film* (Bilingual Press, 1994). This work provides both biographical and filmographic information on Hispanic actors and filmmakers active in the U.S. film industry from 1894 to the present. The work at hand consists of biographical entries that include given and stage names, date and place of birth, and information about the films in which the individual participated. These entries are interspersed with 20 photographic themes that do little to enhance the usefulness of the work (e.g., "History as a Function of Interracial Sex" is not adequately explained by three photographs [p. 76]). The author uses Spanish-language diacritical marks within the majority of the text. He does make exceptions in those cases in which the American-style pronunciation is so common that adding diacritics would confuse the reader.

A weakness in this work's companion volume is addressed here by the inclusion of a comprehensive 43-page bibliography. The bibliography is divided into four sections: "Periodicals, Trade Journals, and Newspapers"; "Exhibition Programs, CD-ROMs, Videotapes, and Software Programs"; "Archival Materials at the Library of Congress and Elsewhere"; and "General Bibliography." The author includes two cumulative indexes that differentiate between the two volumes by using Roman numerals. There is an index for individual and group names and an index for film and television show titles. It is also noted in the introduction that spelling errors made in the 1st volume are corrected within the indexes. Keller has produced an excellent reference source that will be useful in both film collections and Hispanic studies collections. [R: LJ, 1 Mar 97, p. 70; RBB, 1 Mar 97, pp. 1183-84]—**John R. Burch Jr.**

1278. Moon, Spencer. **Reel Black Talk: A Sourcebook of 50 American Filmmakers.** Westport, Conn., Greenwood Press, 1997. 396p. illus. index. $79.50. ISBN 0-313-29830-0.

There are numerous general resources on films and directors, but most merely gloss over the contributions of African American filmmakers. Spencer Moon's *Reel Black Talk: A Sourcebook of 50 American Filmmakers* devotes long overdue attention to this neglected group of artists. This sourcebook is thoughtfully designed and well researched. Information was gathered from research, résumés, and interviews conducted by the author. Filmmaker's television, commercial, documentary, and feature films are given in the filmography. A helpful appendix lists distributors and sources for the films mentioned in the entries. A bibliography is an aid to researchers. The index incorporates listings by title, subject, and the proper names of individuals or groups.

Coverage is primarily contemporary, although pioneers like Oscar Micheaux or William Alexander are included. More than one-quarter of the entries are devoted to current and familiar feature filmmakers, such as the Wayans, the Hughes, the Van Peebles, Robert Townsend, Spike Lee, and John Singleton. One would hope that future editions will expand the list to include additional entries on less well known commercial and documentary artists. This sourcebook will be an excellent addition to any academic library that supports filmmaking programs or other libraries where interest in African American contributions to culture is present.—**Lynne M. Fox**

1279. Pickard, Roy. **The Oscar Stars from A-Z.** London, Headline; distr., North Pomfret, Vt., Trafalgar Square, 1996. 433p. illus. index. $29.95. ISBN 0-7472-1638-X.

As the author boasts in his all-too-brief preface, this is a "bright and breezy 'read and dip' " into Oscarland, listing all 717 nominees A to Z. Limited to performers only and to the period after the birth of sound (1929) to 1996, *The Oscar Stars* provides lively entries à la *Variety* that place nominations within the context of stars' careers. Pickard does not hesitate to make frank judgments about the winners and the professional impact of being a nominee. He also relates bits of fascinating trivia, among them oldest winner, Jessica Tandy at 82; youngest winner, Tatum O'Neal at 10; only director to direct his father and daughter to Oscars, John Huston; most honored Oscar actress and actors, Katharine Hepburn, 4 wins and 8 other nominations, Jack Nicholson and Laurence Olivier, 10 nominations each; only woman playing a man to win an Oscar, Linda Hunt in *The Year of Living Dangerously*; only star to win for a role where his face was behind a grotesque mask, John Hurt in *Elephant Man*; or only star to win without speaking a word of dialogue, Holly Hunter in *The Piano*.

Other interesting data can be gleaned from the entries, such as family nominees of the Fondas, the O'Neals, the Masseys, the Redgraves (father Michael and daughters Lynn and Vanessa), Paul Newman and Joanne Woodward, and Judy Garland and Liza Minelli; nominees with other claims to fame, such as Frank Sinatra, Robert Preston, Bobby Darin, Peggy Lee, Michael Chekhov (nephew of Anton Chekhov), and Melina Mercouri (Greek culture minister); or the hundreds of non-American nominees, 119 of whom hailed from the United Kingdom.

A chronology listing all nominees by year in the categories of best film, director, actor, actress, supporting actor, and supporting actress, and an index of films add to the book's usefulness. *The Oscar Stars* has something for everyone: film researchers, fans, and trivia buffs. [R: RBB, June 97, p. 1764]

—**John A. Lent**

1280. **Who's Who of Victorian Cinema: A Worldwide Survey.** Stephen Herbert and Luke McKernan, eds. London, British Film Institute; distr., Bloomington, Ind., Indiana University Press, 1996. 178p. illus. index. $59.95. ISBN 0-85170-539-1.

When Queen Victoria died in January 1901, just five years had elapsed since the Lumière brothers first exhibited a program of projected motion pictures to a paying audience. Although movies in 1901 were still a crude novelty found mostly on music hall bills and in cheap amusement arcades, they represented the culmination of decades of effort by investors and entrepreneurs who had worked first to perfect and then to exploit the new medium.

In order to provide a convenient and reliable source of information on persons who were involved with film prior to 1901, the British Film Institute commissioned 21 film scholars to research and compile this biographical dictionary. It includes short but well-written articles on more than 250 individuals, including inventors, camerapeople, businesspeople, and actors. There are even entries for prominent public figures who appeared in early films (e.g., President William McKinley) and for several individuals (e.g., the Sultan of Morocco and Winston Churchill) who were merely film aficionados. Portraits accompany articles dealing with persons who were especially significant in the development of film, and articles often debunk myths that have grown up about these individuals, thus correcting misinformation found in other sources.

Each entry has its own bibliography, but there is also an annotated bibliography at the back of the book that cites and describes the merits of 56 books dealing with nineteenth-century film. Indexes to personal names and to the names of inventions are available, but, alas, no indexes to corporate names, film titles, or geographic locations appear. The last is regrettable because the book is international in scope and there are articles (sometimes hard to locate) on pioneers in such diverse places as Russia, Denmark, Italy, Hungary, Japan, Venezuela, and Mexico. Authoritative and informative, this is a valuable addition to the film scholar's reference shelf. [R: Choice, Mar 97, p. 1144]—**Joseph W. Palmer**

1281. Wise, James E., Jr., and Anne Collier Rehill. **Stars in Blue: Movie Actors in America's Sea Services.** Annapolis, Md., Naval Institute Press, 1997. 316p. illus. index. $29.95. ISBN 1-55750-937-9.

Some of the names are quite familiar: Spencer Tracy, Kirk Douglas, Jack Lemmon, Henry Fonda. Some are fodder for crossword puzzles and trivia games: Wayne Morris, John Howard, Logan Ramsey. Others are real surprises: Jack Benny, Bill Cosby. What they all have in common is the fact that they led two lives. All of the people in this book were (or are) movie stars, and all served in the Navy or Coast Guard. Just about all of them portrayed military personas at some time in their careers, and after reading of their exploits, it is interesting to see how they applied their firsthand knowledge to their screen characters. Many of them won combat medals, and some of the stories are downright harrowing. Eddie

(*Green Acres*) Albert saved more than a dozen Marines on the bloody beaches of Tarawa, Tom (*The Seven Year Itch*) Ewell criss-crossed the Atlantic on merchant ships, and Kirk Douglas was a gunnery officer on a ship that saw frequent action in the Pacific.

Wise is a naval aviator who rose to the rank of captain and who has written several other military books. His coauthor is a writer, editor, and publisher. They have produced a well-researched, tightly written book on a unique subject, and their efforts to show readers the military career behind the movie star are successful. There are some omissions (Jason Robards, for example), and coverage of women's contributions to the war effort is confined to a chapter entitled "The Ladies Do Their Bit," but overall, this is a solid work that will prove popular in most public libraries and certainly in military history collections.—**Joseph L. Carlson**

Chronology

1282. **Chronicle of the Cinema.** rev. ed. Robyn Karney, ed. New York, DK Publishing, 1997. 941p. illus. index. $59.95. ISBN 0-7894-2249-2.

In the eye-catching manner reminiscent of *Chronicle of the World* and *Chronicle of the Year 1995* (see ARBA 97, entries 464 and 465, respectively), DK Publishing's survey of world cinema is flashily informative and casually educational. At 941 pages, a predictable increase of 21 pages from the original edition (see ARBA 96, entry 1371), and measuring approximately 10 by 12 inches, this is a coffee-table book in its physical dimensions. Is the content that of a reference book or a gargantuan movie magazine? It is difficult to decide.

The book is arranged in 17 chapters: 9 that are chronological (e.g., "The Silent Era 1920 to 1929"), and 8 that are thematic (e.g., "The Studio System"). The chronologies devote a few pages to each year's cinematic events, written about in a breezy, journalistic style. Items noted include births and deaths of film personalities, motion picture industry highlights, major film releases, personal and professional news about stars, and Academy Award winners. The last is given consistently in sidebars. News of other awards and festivals (e.g., the Cannes Film Festival) is sporadic and incomplete. Much of the text is composed of articles about individual films, accompanied by stills or poster reproductions. The book's editor consciously emulates the format of a newspaper here, and the success in doing so inspires browsing, not reference work. The thematic chapters are likewise written for the casual reader: The medium's New Wave movement (the topic of scores of books) is reviewed in two pages. There are two indexes, one for personal names and general topics and a second one for film titles. The book's coverage is from 1894 to early 1997, and Hollywood dominates the text. The films of other countries are given rudimentary attention: the avant-garde is neither ignored nor really addressed.

Astute reference librarians can use a coffee-table book as though it were a fact-filled resource and may be tempted to do so with a product so eminently readable, as books about movies tend to be. As crammed with information as it is, however, DK's take on the cinema is not actually a reference book. It is, however, an appealing survey of a topic of perennial interest to an increasing number of people. As such, it would appear to be a requisite purchase for circulating collections.—**Ed Volz**

Dictionaries and Encyclopedias

1283. Fulton, Roger. **The Encyclopedia of TV Science Fiction.** London, Boxtree with IPC Magazines; distr., North Pomfret, Vt., Trafalgar Square, 1997. 697p. illus. $19.95pa. ISBN 0-7522-1150-1.

Exhaustive may be an apt term to describe this British publication that claims to list in detail every science fiction television program, series, or movie that has been made in Great Britain, the United States, Canada, New Zealand, and Australia. The old favorites are here—*Dr. Who*, *The Twilight Zone*, *The Invaders*, all versions of *Star Trek*, *The X-Files*—but only true sci-fi buffs will recognize such offerings as *Terrahawks*, *Mission Eureka*, or *Chocky*. The 1st edition of this work appeared in 1990, followed by a 2d edition in 1995. Fulton claims that "a lot can happen in two years . . . new shows are born, live, and die in the blink of a Nielsen rating."

Fulton's entries reflect his love of the genre; beyond the bare essentials of title, production credits, number of episodes, and the like is a highly readable introduction to the elements that make a show great or cause it to spin quickly into a black hole. He credits good storytelling, plausible plots, and more than a dash of quirkiness with helping television science fiction rise above the usual schlocky mixture of monsters, mayhem, and cheesy special effects. Speaking of a British children's series entitled *Ace of Wands*, he writes, "the series wove magic, the supernatural and science fiction into a set of fantasy adventures that weren't afraid to send out a shiver or two." Failed series like *MANIMAL*, *Land of the Lost*, and *Galactica 1980* were dissected as well, providing insights into what makes one show a success when others become Dog Stars.

Library collections rich in television programming materials will find this a welcome addition, and at the price, a circulating copy will be a certain hit with sci-fi buffs. Fulton has come up with a winner in this entertaining, comprehensive, and exhaustive concordance to human efforts to explain the unexplainable. [R: LJ, Aug 97, p. 78]—**Joseph L. Carlson**

1284. Hayward, Susan. **Key Concepts in Cinema Studies.** New York, Routledge, 1996. 467p. index. $65.00; $17.95pa. ISBN 0-415-10718-0; 0-415-10719-9pa.

Hayward's excellent handbook of cinema terms is intended for film studies professors and students but can be read with interest by many filmgoers. The volume is actually several books in one, and the glossary-style entries come in alphabetic order. To move from the most easily observed to the most advanced, Hayward addresses terms used in film production (fade, shots), as well as genre (film noir, the Western) and long-term developments (black cinema, French New Wave). She also defines important concepts in academic (semiological) film discourse. That these separate disciplines keep bumping into one another indicates the book's wide range.

The entries often run to several pages but always strive to be allusive and terse. Many of these topics (feminist film theory, movie stars) could justify book-length examination. Hayward also maintains an ecumenical tone. In the section on postmodernism, for example, this results in some frantic back-and-forth shuttling. What she says is usually so perceptive and succinct that one wishes she would adopt a less neutral stance—more Samuel Johnson's dictionary than Webster's.

As befits its scholarly purpose, the entries are cross-referenced (every word that merits its own discussion is highlighted). All film titles, names, and subjects appearing in the text are indexed in separate categories, and the extensive bibliography amounts to 12 pages. This book can provide quick answers and also open doors to further study. It is heartily recommended for reference collections and film buff libraries. [R: Choice, Feb 97, p. 944]—**Walt Mundkowsky**

1285. Konigsberg, Ira. **The Complete Film Dictionary.** 2d ed. New York, Penguin Books, 1997. 469p. illus. $34.95. ISBN 0-670-10009-9.

This enlarged and updated dictionary of cinema terms covers an impressively wide terrain, even if it lacks a bit on aesthetic issues. A glance at the work reveals author Ira Konigsberg's triple focus—the motion picture as art object, technical process, and economic enterprise. Among the nearly 4,000 entries are every species of filmmaking equipment, often accompanied by excellent line drawings. Each task in the production stage is described, for example, the distinction between ADR and Foley, and fascinating movie-crew jargon is provided. Important studios, organizations, and periodicals are also granted attention, as are distribution strategies like four-walling. Konigsberg has a knack for presenting detailed information in entertaining, easy-to-understand language.

Portrayals of historic and stylistic trends are naturally more arguable. (It is easier to pin down a Mitchell BNC camera in a few words than film noir.) Part of the problem stems from the relatively brief texts; even so, certain omissions are galling—a Holocaust film account without Alain Resnais's *Night and Fog*, a horror film history that ignores Dario Argento and David Cronenberg. Now and then a judgment may inspire head scratching, as when *Blade Runner* is acclaimed as a key postmodern work.

Quibbles aside, the book stands as an indispensable reference tool for its factual aspects. The many black-and-white still photographs are small, but carefully reproduced. An index of film titles and individuals cited would strengthen the browsing potential. This book is recommended for all collections. [R: LJ, July 97, p. 77]—**Walt Mundkowsky**

1286. Phillips, Mark, and Frank Garcia. **Science Fiction Television Series: Episode Guides, Histories....** Jefferson, N.C., McFarland, 1996. 691p. illus. index. $75.00. ISBN 0-7864-0041-2.

Even though science fiction programs on television are perennially dismissed by many as a cult phenomenon, the present work clearly demonstrates the quality and depth of this popular genre. Comprehensive episode guides, production credits, and casts of characters are given for 62 science fiction series that aired from 1959 to 1989. In addition, each section includes a long introductory essay chronicling the making of the series and analyzing the issues and themes that it raises. For instance, discussing *The Prisoner* series, the authors observe that although many of the surveillance gadgets and other gizmos used seemed far-fetched at the time, most have come to exist, such as cordless phones, video cameras keeping an eye on customers in banks and stores, and plastic cards with numbers that identify people—all of which is tied into the pervasive sense of paranoia in the series. This degree of insight pervades the book, and the episode summaries are accurate and detailed. The overall sense is of a meticulously crafted work by authors with an awesome knowledge of the field. Of particular interest are the actors' observations about their roles, which are woven into the introductory essays.

Certainly there are some entrants that seem somewhat gimmicky and trivial in retrospect, such as *The Incredible Hulk* and *The Amazing Spiderman*, but serious television viewers reading this fine compendium will surely wish there would be rebroadcasts of such high quality shows as *Space: 1999* and *The Outer Limits*. Many readers will delight in simply reading the episode summaries of *The Twilight Zone* shows they have seen so often as to become a part of their psyches and the collective experience of a generation. Rounding out this excellent work is an extensive index listing every name in the multitude of cast entries, an appendix listing Emmy Award nominees and winners in Science Fiction TV, and a helpful bibliography. *Science Fiction Television Series* will quickly become the definitive guide in the field.
—**Richard W. Grefrath**

Directories

1287. Deivert, Bert, and Dan Harries. **Film & Video on the Internet: The Top 500 Sites.** Studio City, Calif., Michael Wiese Productions, 1996. 252p. illus. $26.95pa. ISBN 0-941188-54-X.

What began as a Usenet project of award-winning filmmaker Deivert and Harries, Webmaster of CineMedia, turned into an impressive resource for anyone—film buff to producer—interested in film. A useful introduction explains the vocabulary and landscape of the Internet for novices. The majority of the work consists of an annotated list of 500 Websites, organized by subject categories and illustrated with images of the homepages. Subjects covered include actors, directors, festivals/events, film and media schools, magazines and journals, organizations, research and databases, sound television programs, networks, listservs, studios, and videos. There is a list of film-related listservs and Usenet groups. The appendix functions as an extended cross-reference list.

Although there appears to be a 1 to 4 rating scale for the selected sites, the scale is not explained. No criteria are listed for inclusion of sites. The choices are a bit quirky. Readers may wonder why a Christina Applegate site was chosen over many sites devoted to far more famous actors. Several important video schools are missing as well. Annotations are engaging and offer subjective commentary. Even though the book contains ample active links of high quality, the 1996 copyright limits its usefulness. Newer sites like MSNBC are not listed. Many of the still-active sites continue to thrive, but the content described no longer exists. The authors are now soliciting additional sites, promising to forward a free copy of the next edition if the suggested site is usable.

Despite problems relating to currentness, the members of this reviewer's library's film department were impressed and looked forward to seeing an update. They thought a section on grants and financing would improve the usefulness of the book.

Film & Video on the Internet is recommended for film buffs and for libraries and schools with strong film or video departments. However, they may want to wait for the next edition.—**Joyce Kasman Valenza**

Filmography

1288. American Film Institute Catalog. Within Our Gates: Ethnicity in American Feature Films, 1911-1960. Alan Gevinson, ed. Berkeley, Calif., University of California Press, 1997. 1571p. index. $150.00. ISBN 0-520-20964-8.

Beyond the consistent goal of American Film Institute catalogs to "provide accurate and comprehensive information regarding the production, distribution, and exhibition" (p. xv) of films included, this volume adds another: to provide a "comprehensive source of information about every known American feature film made from 1911-1960 relating to ethnicity" (p. x). The 2,464 entries include traditional Hollywood studio films, independently produced films, films made by ethnic groups for specific audiences, and films made for non-English speakers. All share an emphasis on issues of American ethnic identity.

The alphabetically arranged entries include production information; the names and roles of actors; lengthy plot summaries; type of film (e.g., comedy, Western); and the major ethnic group(s) to which the film relates. Resources for understanding the films include five indexes (by film titles; subjects; ethnic categories; foreign languages; and personal names of all producers, directors, writers, and actors) as well as a selected bibliography of books relevant to ethnicity in film.

The utility of this volume derives from its compilation of films that document and portray the social and historical dimensions of ethnicity in the United States. The films serve as a reservoir of perceptions and memories that compose part of U.S. cultural heritage, cinematically reflecting and responding to the society out of which they arose. As such, the volume is useful not only for film enthusiasts but also for historians, social scientists, educators, and others interested in the challenge of exploring the implications of ethnicity in the United States. It is a unique and necessary compilation that will stand as a major reference work for anyone interested in ethnicity in film at the same time as it affirms the significance of all groups that contribute to the diversity of U.S. society.—**Suzanne G. Frayser**

1289. The British Co-operative Movement Film Catalogue. Alan Burton, comp. and ed. Westport, Conn., Greenwood Press, 1997. 234p. index. (Bibliographies and Indexes in World History, no.47). $79.50. ISBN 0-313-30565-X.

This is an exhaustive filmography enumerating more than 300 films made by the British Co-operative Movement. The movement was developed in the nineteenth century to reach out to workers and consumers. At its peak it controlled bakeries, dairies, laundries, mills, department stores, and even funeral services. The Co-operative Movement sponsored cultural activities, such as choirs, libraries, and clubs, and had an active publications program. As early as 1899, it began to produce films. Motion pictures were seen as an extension of the Co-operative's goals: publicity (or advertising) of Co-operative products and services, education, and propaganda. Always a target of commercial interests, the movement remained strong through the mid-1960s, when it became harder to compete with popular culture and glossy commercial megastores.

The volume is divided into several sections: an informative introductory essay giving the historical context of the Co-operative Movement; a chronological listing of extant films dating from 1909 through 1980; titles of known films yet to be found; reference prints waiting preservation and currently unavailable for viewing; appendixes with press articles illustrating the movement's response to film and its potential; and indexes by title, film archive, credits, product and industry, and location. Entries in the catalog give precise technical information about the print, as well as synopsis, description, and illuminating commentary. The majority of these films have been located by the author, and this work is obviously a labor of love. In 1992 the National Co-operative Film Archive was established, and this catalog was the second phase of that project. This is a highly specialized title that will be of interest to libraries with strong labor or film history collections.—**Ruth A. Carr**

1290. Day, David Howard. A Treasure Hard to Attain: Images of Archaeology in Popular Film, with a Filmography. Lanham, Md., Scarecrow, 1997. 203p. index. $42.50. ISBN 0-8108-3171-6.

This filmography examines the archaeological content of approximately 120 popular films, most of which have been produced in the United States since 1912. Part 1 deals with a historical overview of the depiction of archaeologists in popular film since the early 1900s. It describes what real archaeologists do and looks at screen archaeologists as they are shown in the classroom, in the laboratory, and in the field. There is also a collection of memorable quotations by archaeologists in popular films. Finally, the book compares the work of professional archaeologists with that done by those shown in films.

Part 2 includes a chronological listing of popular films featuring archaeologists and full reviews of each film. The reviews, in alphabetic order, list the title, production date, running time, distributor, and cast list. The reviews give a synopsis of the film plot, paying special attention to archaeological details and characters. The earliest review is of the 1912 feature *Vengeance of Egypt*. The most recent review is of *Stargate*, a 1994 film starring Kurt Russell. The book concludes with a bibliography and an index. The author is a professor of anthropology at Monroe Community College in Rochester, New York. *A Treasure Hard to Attain* would be a useful reference volume in popular culture and film collections.—**Francis Poole**

1291. Edwards, Paul M. **A Guide to Films on the Korean War.** Westport, Conn., Greenwood Press, 1997. 149p. index. (Bibliographies and Indexes in American History, no.35). $59.95. ISBN 0-313-30316-9.

A competent but thin and expensive book on a rather marginal subject, this is the kind of work that would never be printed if publishers could not depend on a captive market of academic libraries to buy almost anything that appears to be scholarly (which it more or less is). This book presents several short essay chapters that provide background on war films, the Korean War, Hollywood, Defense Department involvement, and the relationship of television to film. The heart of the book, annotations of 84 films about the Korean War, is curiously short. Each film receives approximately half-a-page, including the credits (year, studio, producer, director, screenwriter, actors, running time). The third-rate films (i.e., most of them) receive such short shrift that one learns almost nothing about them. The best-known films, such as *The Bridges at Toko-Ri* and *M*A*S*H*, receive only a few paragraphs.

There are indexes of actors, producers, directors, and screenwriters; a filmography of documentary and special films; and a three-page bibliography. Also included is a general index of film titles, actors, and subjects (such as "Communists" and "Cuban Missile Crisis"). Two lists also appear: one organizes the films in chronological order, and the other is a list of the author's nine personal "bests" (e.g., "Most Realistic: *Pork Chop Hill*") and one "Worst Film," which is *Operation Dames*.

It is unlikely that another book will be published exclusively on this same subject, so it is unfortunate that the treatment of the films here is not more extensive. If such treatment was really not warranted, why was the book necessary at all? Acquisition of this book is recommended only for the most comprehensive library collections.—**Bill Miller**

1292. Holston, Kim R., and Tom Winchester. **Science Fiction, Fantasy, and Horror Film Sequels, Series, and Remakes: An Illustrated Filmography....** Jefferson, N.C., McFarland, 1997. 601p. illus. index. $75.00. ISBN 0-7864-0155-9.

For film librarians or those simply obsessed with cinema, it would be difficult not to love and admire McFarland, a publisher that has discovered a pipeline into a seemingly bottomless well of specialized movie information and outright celluloid arcana. *Science Fiction, Fantasy, and Horror Film Sequels, Series, and Remakes* is a well-done and useful addition to this trove of cine-trivia.

Credit and production information and plot synopses are provided for over 400 English-language science fiction, fantasy, and supernatural horror films released between 1931 and 1995, including remakes, sequels, series, and cases in which a character or creature in one film appears in subsequent films (Frankenstein, Dracula, the Wolfman, and so on). Television movies are excluded. In addition to fairly elaborate and amusingly wry plot synopses, the authors have attempted to provide quotes from reviews contemporaneous with the release of the film. They also offer their own one- to four-star rating of films listed. This reviewer particularly liked their designation "awful but entertaining." Arrangement of titles is alphabetic, with remakes falling under the name of the original work. To inspect the thoroughness of the authors' research, I checked out the entry for *Jekyll and Hyde*—certainly one of the most remade and frequently mangled of all tingly classics. Using the Internet Movie Database as authority control, I found that not only did Holston and Winchester manage to include the obscure *Dr. Black Mr. Hyde* (featuring an African American physician experimenting with the cure for cirrosis of the liver, who finds the drug that turns black skin white), but they thought to include *Nutty Professor* and *Altered States*, as well. This work is highly recommended for larger film and popular culture collections. [R: RBB, 15 Oct 97, p. 429]—**Gary Handman**

1293. Julius, Marshall. **Action! The Action Movie A-Z.** Bloomington, Ind., Indiana University Press, 1996. 240p. illus. $35.00; $16.95pa. ISBN 0-253-33244-3; 0-253-21091-7pa.

This reference book is a guide to 250 mostly U.S.-made action movies ranging from 1938, *The Adventures of Robin Hood*, to 1996, *Broken Arrow*, *Eraser*, and *The Rock*. Arrangement of the unnumbered entries is alphabetic by title. Each entry consists of a standardized two lines, followed by the review section and the credits. The first line is the title, and the second lists the country of production, year, running time, and a graphic rating represented by the symbols for a big and a small gun. The scoring system ranges from one small gun depicting "boring rubbish," such as *Death Wish II* (1982), *Excessive Force* (1993), *King Solomon's Mines* (1985), and *Red Scorpion* (1989), to a fabulous five big guns for all-time action classics, the above-mentioned *The Adventures of Robin Hood*, *Die Hard* (1988), *Mad Max II* (1981), *Star Wars* (1977), and *The Terminator* (1984).

The movies are reviewed with detailed credit lists (director, producer, screenplay, production design, editor, photography, music, and cast) and behind-the-scenes information, including greatest one-liners, comebacks, and monologues in action film history; sequels; Top 10 lists; biographies of the biggest stars, entitled "Death Becomes Them" (Charles Bronson, Sean Connery, Chuck Norris, Bruce Willis, John Wu and the like); quotation favorites (under "Verbal Assaults"); a vast amount of trivia; and trivia quizzes called "Brainstorms." Illustrated with 68 black-and-white stills, this work is for movie buffs, not for serious scholars. There are no clear-cut criteria for establishing the genre, and consequently some important films are omitted. For example, none of Raul Walsh's adventure movies are listed. Missing is the seminal movie classic, *Point Blank* (1967), as is *The French Connection* (1971), which is best known for its chase scene. No adequate rating criteria are given, and one must ask why the low-budget, highly acclaimed *El Mariachi* (1992) and the all-time favorite *Robocop* (1987) received only two big guns and one small gun. Unfortunately, there is no index or bibliography. [R: LJ, 15 Feb 97, p. 128]—**Magda Želinská-Ferl**

1294. Kalat, David. **A Critical History and Filmography of Toho's Godzilla Series.** Jefferson, N.C., McFarland, 1997. 267p. index. $48.50. ISBN 0-7864-0300-4.

Contemporary audiences, now accustomed to the wide screen and special effects wizardry of science fiction films, have tended to regard the Godzilla series as simple. Crude effects—especially the monster, who is obviously an actor in a rubber monster costume, terrorizing cities that are obviously collections of toy buildings—all contribute to the low critical opinion of this famous film saga. Kalat, a Godzilla fan since childhood, is an independent filmmaker who has written several articles about his favorite monster for *G-Fan* (the premier magazine for Godzilla enthusiasts). In this book he attempts to round up some respect for Godzilla with this excellent and insightful filmography and critical history.

Toho studio produced the 25 films that comprise the Godzilla series. Here, they are thoroughly examined in their historical context (including the fear of atomic radiation as a recurring theme in the 1950s), as well as the intercultural context of the variations between the original Japanese versions and the U.S. versions. U.S. distributors frequently added and deleted footage in a way that changed the plot, and the original musical score was often inappropriately Americanized, which created a strange incongruity. Complete credits are provided for each film, including the actors' names who played the part of Godzilla, a screen credit they were often not given. Kalat's extensive knowledge of the subject enriches the text; his description of the day-to-day production of the films is detailed and entertaining.

Handy appendixes at the end of this book include a list of relevant Websites, Internet newsgroups, and a fine bibliography, which includes references to interviews with key filmmakers. This should become the definitive work on this important film series, easily eclipsing the rather slight *Godzilla Book* by Jim Harmon (Borgo Press, 1987). This is highly recommended for cinema and science fiction collections.
—**Richard W. Grefrath**

1295. Klotman, Phyllis R., and Gloria J. Gibson. **Frame by Frame II: A Filmography of the African American Image, 1978-1994.** Bloomington, Ind., Indiana University Press, 1997. 771p. index. $49.95; $29.95pa. ISBN 0-253-33280-X; 0-253-21120-4pa.

The concept behind this filmography is to credit African Americans who have contributed their talents to the film industry. An effort has been made to represent the totality of African American contributions. Representing more than 3,000 films are African American actors, screenwriters, musicians, directors, and producers. Each entry has been researched for the following: film title, series, cast, director, producer, music, screenwriter, and storywriter. Though the volume focuses on African Americans, the contributions of black Africans to independent as well as Hollywood films has also been acknowledged.

The filmography is organized by alphabetic listing of films and includes indexes of black cast, black directors, black executive producers, black music performers, and black screenwriters and distributors. There is also a selected list of archives, a selected bibliography, and a list of African American Oscar winners and nominees. The layout of the book is easy to follow, and the information in each entry is organized to be readily accessible. Of special interest and usefulness are the indexes to actors and directors. This volume builds on the earlier *Frame by Frame*, which includes productions through 1978 and should be a welcome addition to film studies scholars and students.—**Francis Poole**

1296. Marion, Donald J. **The Chinese Filmography: The 2444 Feature Films....** Jefferson, N.C., McFarland, 1997. 752p. illus. index. $125.00. ISBN 0-7864-0305-5.

The founding of the People's Republic of China in 1949 marked the end of an era for Chinese filmmaking. With Mao Tse Tung's pronouncement that "the purpose of art is to serve politics," an underlying principle was established for many years for the art, literature, and cinema of modern China. Therefore, the study of Chinese films of that era is really the study of the political history of modern China. From A to Z, this comparative reference work provides filmographic data on the 2,444 feature films released since the formation of the People's Republic of China. The films reflect the shifting dynamics of the Chinese film industry, from extensive epics to political docudramas. The author defines the scope of the reference work by setting the criteria to include only the feature films completed by 1995. Filmed operas and straight documentaries are not included. The entries treat titles in English, Chinese titles in pinyin romanization, year of release, studio, technical information, running time, technical credits, literary source, cast, plot summary, and awards won. The information in the entries was drawn mostly either from the Chinese source, or, when possible, from actual viewing of the film and recording of its criteria. The Western resources were used only as last resort.

To illustrate the role of films in modern Chinese political history, in the chapter on historical overviews, the author divided the films into three periods: 1949 to 1966 (pre-Cultural Revolution), 1966 to 1976 (post-Cultural Revolution or the "period of political disturbance"), and 1976 to the present (the "New Era"). There were a small number of films produced during the Cultural Revolution, when the industry was nearly destroyed by the political force. Not until the "New Era," after a series of economic reforms were announced as public policy, did the Chinese filmmaking industry begin to revive. The summarized review and assessment of filmmaking and the political condition is well researched and interesting to read.

The glossary lists and annotates the important political figures and historical events in modern China. The source list provides a bibliography that mainly consists of Chinese-language publications. The name index furnishes a quick reference to the filmmakers, directors, and performers. In view of the fact that it is impossible to separate films from politics in modern China, this comprehensive reference can serve a dual purpose as a tool to study cinematic arts as well as to study politics in modern China. *The Chinese Filmography* is recommended for inclusion in libraries that support performing arts and Chinese study programs.
—**Eveline L. Yang**

1297. Maxford, Howard. **The A-Z of Horror Films.** Bloomington, Ind., Indiana University Press, 1997. 302p. illus. $59.95; $29.95pa. ISBN 0-253-33253-2; 0-253-21107-7pa.

This guide to horror films is informative and for the most part a complete list of popular and not-so-popular films in the horror genre. The author opens the door to many releases that may have eluded even the most eager and watchful horror fan. The guide includes titles that have been released straight to video or those older titles that may be more readily found if a brother's cousin once knew someone who stayed up on a Friday night to tape the local fright night B-movie marathon. A short explanation of the film is followed by a reduced version of the final credits, including starring actors, producers, directors, and in many cases the effects and sound engineers. The release date for all the titles is listed, which can make the book a valuable guide in those times when one wishes to test the knowledge of a self-proclaimed expert. Many of the listings are, as the title suggests, horror films, but the author did not stop there. Offered also are many titles that may only center around a horror movie's theme, such as the classic *Abbott and Costello Meet the Mummy* or *Scared Stiff*, starring Dean Martin and Jerry Lewis.

There are also short annotations of many of the horror genres most-well-known actors and creators. The foreword to the book is written by B-movie Vampira (Ingrid Pitt), who offers a look at horror movies through the eyes of a veteran of the game. There is a short list of the author's favorites to open the book, which of course one may or may not agree with, but then again opinions of others are what carved the horror industry into the superpower it is today. Yes, it is a powerful medium, so do not forget to remind Aunt Sophie of that the next time she refers to horror films as mindless trash. If she wants proof to the contrary, just open this book and show her the error of her ways, from A to Z. [R: LJ, 15 Feb 97, p. 128]—**Michael Florman**

1298. Ness, Richard R. **From Headline Hunter to Superman: A Journalism Filmography.** Lanham, Md., Scarecrow, 1997. 789p. index. $89.50. ISBN 0-8108-3291-7.

This filmography provides detailed analyses of journalists as they have been portrayed in films. There are a total of 2,165 entries for feature films from the silent era through 1996. In addition to giving an extensive discussion of significant journalism films, this book includes lesser-known works, made-for-television movies, and the B-films made in the 1930s and 1940s. These films are identified as having helped reinforce the image of the journalist in films.

Because the goal of this filmography is to demonstrate changes in society's perception of journalists as reflected in films, the feature film entries are presented chronologically. With each year, the entries are listed alphabetically. Each decade is preceded by a discussion of significant developments during that time. The discussion essay summarizes the changes and development in society by relating the modification of images of media personnel in films. The essay addresses not only the significant characteristics in the movies but also the significant social issues, such as the role of women in the hierarchical structure of the journalism profession, the increasing influence of the foreign film market, and international orientation. The essay states that in recent years, films have reflected a mixed attitude toward journalists, especially those on television. Media professionals are viewed both with increasing fascination and mistrust and their responsibilities and roles with greater seriousness than in the early twentieth century.

The feature films included can be categorized into two groups: films that deal specifically with the practice of the journalism profession and films in which a journalist plays a contributing role in the events. When making selections, the author gave consideration to the importance of the journalist character in the film and to the emphasis given to their profession. The definition of *journalist* is for the most part confined to those who work in a news or editorial capacity. Films that feature photographers working outside the area of news reporting or working in a freelance capacity have been excluded. Also omitted are foreign films that were not released in the U.S. market. The exceptions are made for major foreign works, such as *La Dolce Vita* or *The Lost Honor of Katherina Blum*, as well as television miniseries, because these films have made important contributions to society's perception of journalists.

This filmography is the first and most comprehensive book of its kind, offering the listings to date on the subject of journalists in films. It is recommended for inclusion in libraries that support the study of filmography and journalism.—**Eveline L. Yang**

1299. Schwartz, Ronald. **Latin American Films, 1932-1994: A Critical Filmography.** Jefferson, N.C., McFarland, 1997. 294p. illus. index. $65.00. ISBN 0-7864-0174-5.

This is the season for reference books on popular culture. Encyclopedias, directories, and filmographies on almost every conceivable topic have made their rounds in the 1990s; increasingly, they have taken on international dimensions. Schwartz's work is of the latter type, filling a void he describes: "Latin American cinema, after Spanish cinema, is perhaps the second most neglected of the national cinemas by critics over the last thirty or so years." The book is an alphabetic listing of Schwartz's "personal selection" of more than 300 significant Latin American films from 1932 through 1994. Although he does not explain what makes them significant, Schwartz does claim, without supporting evidence, that they all reflect the diversity and mentality of Latin American countries. The beginning date of 1932 was chosen because that, according to Schwartz, was when "North American consciousness of Latin American cinema became prevalent in the United States."

Countries included are the top four film producers—Argentina, Mexico, Brazil, and Cuba—as well as Peru, Bolivia, Chile, Venezuela, Nicaragua, Uruguay, and Ecuador. A few Caribbean and Chicano films also make the list. For the most part, Schwartz analyzes films made exclusively in Latin America, in original languages, and produced and directed in their countries of origin by native filmmakers.

Features, made-for-television reports, documentaries, docudramas, and other film forms are included. Entries are made up of the usual—English title, director, year of release, running time, language, country, and detailed plot synopsis—but extend to background data on some film personnel and commentary on the films, the latter based on the author's viewings mixed with snippets from reviews.

A preface and an introduction provide a sketchy literature review and a history of Latin American film. Equally skimpy is a bibliography of only 17 sources. What Schwartz puts in the main part of the volume, "The Films: A to Z," seems thorough and accurate, and for that he is to be commended, because he has, no doubt, advanced scholarship on Latin American cinema. What he omits is a rationale for his selection and an overall setting in which to place these films, which gives the reader pause to reflect how valid this compendium is as a reflection of the Latin American cinematic experience.—**John A. Lent**

1300. Willis, Donald C. **Horror and Science Fiction Films IV.** Lanham, Md., Scarecrow, 1997. 642p. index. $89.50. ISBN 0-8108-3055-8.

Willis, the internationally recognized maven of monster and science fiction movies, has been happily and exhaustively compiling lists of these often-overlooked films since 1972, when he published his initial tome covering some 4,440 titles released through 1971 (see ARBA 73, entry 1099). Periodic updates have followed; the 2d in 1981 covers some 2,350 films released through 1981 (see ARBA 83, entry 1007), and the 3d, published in 1984, reports on some 760 titles released through December 1983 (see ARBA 85, entry 1252). The present update, in many ways the quirkiest and most useful, covers an additional 4,200 genre films through 1994. Here, Willis focuses on the deluge of heretofore inaccessible foreign films (e.g., the 1987 Taiwanese sex and horror quickie *Spooky Kama Sutra*) that are now available on video through specialist companies like Sinister Cinema. So-called "lost films," such as the 1931 Spanish-language version of *Dracula*, are also now out on video, and Willis includes them in his study.

As in the earlier volumes in the series, this supplement is alphabetically arranged by film title. Each entry contains information on the film's country of origin, production company, date of release, and detailed credits and cast lists. Annotations vary in length from a few lines (plot summaries taken directly from video box covers) to detailed references to "cult" magazine sources like *Fangoria* and *Video Watchdog* as well as to more traditional sources like *Variety* and *The New York Times*. Summaries are written in a lively, readable style that should appeal to fans of the genre. An index to films covered in the first three volumes is offered, as is a list of alternate film titles. Quite simply, *Horror and Science Fiction Films* is the most comprehensive, entertaining, and informative source for difficult-to-find films in these genres.—**David K. Frasier**

Handbooks and Yearbooks

1301. Baxter, Joan. **Television Musicals: Plots, Critiques, Casts, and Credits for 222 Shows....** Jefferson, N.C., McFarland, 1997. 204p. illus. index. $45.00. ISBN 0-7864-0286-5.

Baxter's book strives to provide information on original musicals written for and presented on television. She fills gaps but does not duplicate such sources as Vincent Terrace's *Television Specials* and George W. Woolery's *Animated Specials*. The musicals featured include musical episodes from nonmusical shows, animated specials, and operas.

Each entry provides air date, network, duration, cast, and credits. For animated programs, the cast named is the names of actors who provided the voices. There are also lists of songs and plots. Titles range from *Amahl and the Night Visitors* to the *Honeymooners* with Jackie Gleason and musicals by Danny Kaye. Several programs had multiple versions, such as *Aladdin*, *Cinderella*, and *Pinochio*. Represented are composers Ezra Laderman, Lukas Foss, and George Antheil and singers Liza Minnelli and Julie Andrews. Broadway musicals adapted for television are not included unless they are completely new versions. Excerpts of reviews from various periodicals include *Variety*, *The New York Times*, *Time*, and *Musical America*. There are several photographs of actors in costume for musicals, such as Steve Allen and Rick Nelson.

A chronology from 1944 to 1996; a bibliography; a song index; and a name index of composers, directors, and all performers complete the volume. The name index has a few minor oversights. It lists "Arthur Fiedler and the Boston Pops," but not as Fiedler or as the Boston Pops. Yet there are separate entries for "Namath, Joe" and for "New York Jets." In the text, *How the Grinch Stole Christmas!* is entered under "Dr. Seuss." The name index has no entry for "Dr. Seuss" or "Seuss, Dr." Oversights aside, Baxter has concisely presented an aspect of the medium that has shaped many lives in the late twentieth century—television.—**Ralph Hartsock**

1302. Bjorklund, Dennis A. **Toasting *Cheers*: An Episode Guide to the 1982-1993 Comedy Series....** Jefferson, N.C., McFarland, 1997. 407p. illus. index. $55.00. ISBN 0-89950-962-2.

It is easy to discern when an author approaches his writing tasks with an obvious affection for his topic. Attorney Bjorklund never tells the reader why he decided to write the definitive history of *Cheers*, but television viewer Bjorklund certainly demonstrates his love of this classic Boston bar sitcom. Lasting from 1982 through 1993, *Cheers* was one of the most beloved programs of all time, yet it had a rough and rocky start. Residing at the absolute bottom of the ratings chart for its first year, *Cheers* finally caught on with the public because of its commonplace approach to the foibles of people to whom everyone could relate. In an ensemble television program, casting is everything, and in *Cheers* a more congenial and talented group of performers could not have been found. Bjorklund relates some of the behind-the-scenes problems with the actors (especially with Shelley Long), but even in their most troubled times, the *Cheers* cast seemed to know that they were involved in something truly special and destined to be timeless.

Everything anyone could ever want to know about *Cheers* is found in this exhaustively comprehensive book: What Sam gave Norm for his 36th birthday, Coach's nickname, Frederick Crane's male nanny, and the play Rebecca was in during high school. Followers of the series will be in sitcom heaven as they read of the lives and loves of the actors as well as of the characters they portrayed. Despite some careless errors (George Peppard's crime show *Banacek* is listed as *Banazak*, actor Aidan Quinn's first name is spelled "Adrian"), this is a well-written, highly entertaining look at one of the premier television shows of all time. Even though it is officially a reference book, all public libraries would do their customers a favor by purchasing a copy for circulation. This will definitely be a popular item.—**Joseph L. Carlson**

1303. Case, Christopher. **The Ultimate Movie Thesaurus.** New York, Henry Holt, 1996. 1086p. (A Henry Holt Reference Book). $22.50pa. ISBN 0-8050-3496-X.

A viewer's advisory guide for film lovers, this versatile handbook is made up of four main parts: films by title, category entries, box office hits by year, and star ratings by year. More than 8,000 feature-length domestic and foreign movies, released from the silent era through 1995, are named, described, and rated by Case. Aside from providing such standard film directory data as running time, plot synopses, and principal actors for each movie, the author lists movie and television sequels, prequels, remakes, retreads, and flip sides for many films. Also, grouped beneath nearly every film title entry are the names of several movies that share similar theme or genre characteristics. From a pool of some 1,600 genre and theme categories created by the author, Case typically matches a dozen or more such descriptors to each film entry. Pithy but usually incisive asides also accompany many entries. In true thesaurus fashion, the second section of this volume reverses the first section's format, presenting an alphabetic roster of genre and theme categories, under which are listed representative film titles.

Rival sources are substantially inferior. *The Movie List Book* (see ARBA 95, entry 1389) indexes films according to approximately 550 terms, and *The Reel List* (see ARBA 96, entry 1400) uses fewer than 200. Examples of helpful categories in *The Ultimate Movie Thesaurus* are "Revisionist Films," "Boston," "1930s," "Southerns," and "Trail of a Killer." There are a number of minor, but annoying, flaws in this reference, however. The entry for *Casino Royale* fails to credit David Niven, although he portrays the character James Bond. Under *Raising Arizona*, *Fargo* is cited as having a genre kinship with it, but no main entry appears for the latter film. Finally, the film *PCU* appears out of alphabetic sequence in the first section. However, because of this resource's unparalleled breadth and depth of genre and theme indexing, as well as its affordable price, it remains a worthwhile acquisition for any library.—**Jeffrey E. Long**

1304. Einstein, Daniel. **Special Edition: A Guide to Network Television Documentary Series and Special News Reports, 1980-1989.** Lanham, Md., Scarecrow, 1997. 870p. index. $110.00. ISBN 0-8108-3220-8.

This work is a 2d volume that continues *Special Edition: A Guide to Network Television Documentary Series and Special News Reports, 1955-1979*, published in 1987 (see ARBA 88, entry 952). The guide covers network television documentary series programming and network television news specials and special reports broadcast on major commercial networks (ABC, CBS, and NBC). Entries describe documentary and magazine series programs and one-time-only news special reports covering the period January 1980 through December 1989. Excluded are news bulletins under 15 minutes, routine press conferences by presidents, routine space shuttle coverage, and political primaries and conventions, except in cases of historical significance. Also not covered are public television and cable programs.

For series programs, entries contain dates from first to (if applicable) final telecast, a brief history of the program, and a listing of each show, with dates aired. Each program provides a title and description of the subject, plus the name of the producer. The section on *60 Minutes*, for example, is comprehensive, listing dates when specific programs were first broadcast and later rerun. One-time news special reports (for example, the attempted assassination of President Reagan) are listed with the time of broadcast and a summary of what was reported. Several indexes are provided: "Index of Programs and Segment Titles," "Index of Personalities," "Index of Production/Technical Personnel," and "Index of Subjects and Places."

Special Edition is a reference tool of importance to academic and public library collections. Historians and researchers of television broadcasting should find it useful. One hopes that a new volume covering the 1990s is being planned. A recommendation would be to also include some, if not all, of the major cable and public television programs in the next volume.—**Lucy Heckman**

1305. **Halliwell's Filmgoer's Companion.** 12th ed. By Leslie Halliwell. John Walker, ed. New York, HarperPerennial/HarperCollins, 1997. 514p. $25.00pa. ISBN 0-06-273478-4.

This is an irreplaceable classic that has been on my personal bookshelf since its first edition in 1965. The 12th edition has been brought up to date by John Walker. This book has basic and vital information on everybody and everything connected with movies. There are some 10,000 entries on actors, directors, producers, writers, and others from behind the scenes, along with terms, definitive movies, fictional characters, and genres in film. Quotations from performers are liberally distributed throughout the book.

A typical entry has life dates, a brief description of their work, and a listing of their best movies, television work, or television series. All of the information is arranged on four columns across each page, with unavoidably tiny print in order to fit it all in. The book concludes with an extensive list of Academy Awards, British awards, Felixes (European awards), Golden Bears, Cannes, and Golden Lions awards. There are pages devoted to the top grossing films, CD-ROM versions of films, a history of the cinema, and a bibliography. No library with patrons interested in film should be without this book.—**Dean Tudor**

1306. Jones, Stephen, comp. **Clive Barker's A-Z of Horror.** New York, HarperPrism/HarperCollins, 1997. 256p. illus. index. $29.95. ISBN 0-06-105277-9.

In this colorful and oftentimes graphic book, the compiler takes readers on a macabre journey down that fine line separating art from reality. Or does it? As the title suggests, this is somewhat of an alphabetic joyride for those who are both fans of the horror genre and also for those who may prefer fact over fiction. Through countless examples, it may be concluded that they are at many times, and in many ways, one and the same. After perusing actual crime photographs, and news articles from criminal cases, that line may seem to blur a bit, leaving readers to look over their shoulder on their next exit out of the movie theater. From the terror of the *Texas Chainsaw Massacre* and *The Exorcist*, to the classics like *Strait Jacket* and *Psycho*, the compiler allows readers to take a sneak peak into the minds of their creators. Quoted accounts of the filming and also accounts of public reaction can help people to understand and appreciate a genre that is always pushing the audience to the limit of its own imagination.

There are many accounts by special effects technicians and animators into the secrets that make some of the most memorable scenes possible. Much like taking a look up the sleeves of great magicians, it gives the reader a chance to see the preparation and careful planning required to turn an ordinary scene into something both memorable and believable. Clive Barker has filled this book from cover to cover with his own personal thoughts and those of this colleagues about a constantly changing industry. The book would make a valuable addition to a collector's archive or would serve as a guide map to the world of horror that awaits the next generation of wide-eyed moviegoers.—**Michael Florman**

1307. Ledoux, Trish, and Doug Ranney. Patten, Fred, ed. **The Complete Anime Guide: Japanese Animation Film Directory & Resource Guide.** 2d ed. Issaquah, Wash., Tiger Mountain Press; distr., Gardena, Calif., SCB Distributors, 1997. 214p. illus. index. $19.95pa. ISBN 0-9649542-5-7.

Japanese animation (called *anime*) has enjoyed cult status in the United States since at least 1977, when the first fan club promoting it was formed. The remarkable success of the brilliant and soulful *Ghost in the Shell* (more than 200,000 copies were sold during the initial months of its U.S. release) may presage *anime*'s jump into the mainstream. New and old admirers of the form have needed a reliable guide to the entire landscape, and this volume fills that gap splendidly.

The book opens with a historical survey of animated series on Japanese television (since the mid-1980s, the most artistic efforts—and the worst junk—have been aimed at home video and theatrical markets). A lively discussion of *anime* genres follows. The noir/cyberpunk branch corners the critics' applause, but other modes also flourish: from romantic teen comedy to rape-oriented porn. The heart of the work is the directory listing every *anime* title available in the United States (a total of 1,300). An array of symbols provides content information, and the authors supply a critical sketch for each video. Fan clubs, fanzines, Websites, and conventions are set out in detail, as are complete ordering data for distributors and specialty shops. Creative credits are fully indexed.

Anime is, of course, a moving target, one that Ledoux and Ranney cover with authority and contagious affection. The softcover format and low price should appeal to every *anime* viewer, but libraries need not hesitate; this is an important sphere of activity.—**Walt Mundkowsky**

1308. Lentz, Harris M., III. **Television Westerns Episode Guide: All United States Series, 1949-1996.** Jefferson, N.C., McFarland, 1997. 568p. index. $95.00. ISBN 0-7864-0377-2.

Anyone growing up in the 1950s or 1960s must have watched their share of television westerns. This work covers all 180 series that were aired from 1949 to 1996 with cast, premise, network, day, time, and listing of each episode. The guide is arranged alphabetically by title with a personnel index and a story line index. Lentz, who also compiled *Western and Frontier Film and Television Credits 1903-1995* (see ARBA 97, entry 1130), suggests this work is intended to be a reference source but also to rekindle fond memories. As a reference work it succeeds admirably. For people who want to know that Ronald Reagan not only hosted *Death Valley Days* but also acted in eight episodes as well as in an episode of *Wagon Train*, the information is easy to find. The story line indexing, listing characters, locations, and other areas of plots, could be more extensive for people who can only remember fragments of a series. A helpful sorting that was not included would be a chronological listing for people who remember only that a series aired in the early 1960s. Reading through the book does rekindle fond memories, but leaves the reader hoping for pictures. Overall, this is a valuable work for any media library and for large reference collections.
—**Joshua Cohen**

1309. Morgan, Jenny, comp. **The Film Researcher's Handbook: A Guide to Sources in North America, South America, Asia, Australasia, and Africa.** New York, Routledge, 1996. 452p. index. $59.95. ISBN 0-415-15123-6.

An unfortunately misleading title is the least of the numerous problems that plague this curiously misguided and ineffectively realized work. What the publication seems to want to be is an international guide to institutions and commercial concerns from which stock footage and archival film resources can be purchased for incorporation into other film productions (research services and institutions without any material to sell are not included). Unfortunately, the publication falls short of realizing this goal. Take, for example, the perfunctory and inaccurate coverage of the United States. What happened to mention of the major university film and broadcast archives (e.g., Vanderbilt and Purdue) involved in selling footage? More amazingly, what happened to major commercial stock footage houses, such as Prelinger & Associates (the company that also produced what is still the best guide to U.S. stock footage sources)? One must also wonder why distribution companies such as Icarus Films (which is in the business of distributing well-produced documentary films but not stock footage) are included. To add more bibliographic insult to injury, Icarus's contact information was, at the time of this handbook's publication, well more than five years out of date. One cannot imagine that the accuracy of information for resources in Latin America and Australasia fares even this well. Organization of the handbook is by country and by broad subject/topical area. There is a separate list of national archives, which fails to mention the U.S. National Archives and Records Administration's National Audiovisual Center. Brief place, source, and subject indexes are provided. Routledge turns out some excellent film resources; this is not one of them. [R: C&RL, Mar 97, pp. 177-78]—**Gary Handman**

1310. Morris, Bruce B. **Prime Time Network Serials: Episode Guides, Casts, and Credits for 37 Continuing Television Dramas, 1964-1993.** Jefferson, N.C., McFarland, 1997. 841p. illus. index. $82.50. ISBN 0-7864-0164-8.

Prime Time Serials is a well made and complete guide to 37 prime-time television soap operas that appeared on the three major networks between 1964 and 1993. The book does not cover soaps that were produced for syndication (the most important being *Mary Hartman, Mary Hartman*) because the author was unable to obtain detailed information from the show's distributors or from sources such as *TV Guide*. The soaps are listed alphabetically by title, with detailed background information, cast lists, and plot summaries for each episode. The information was obtained from press releases, reviews, articles in entertainment magazines, and directly from the television screen. In fact, the author says that information on four soaps (*Dallas, Knots Landing, Dynasty,* and *Falcon Crest*) is even more complete because it was obtained "straight" from viewing the series.

Morris is listed as the author of what must be a related work, *Twenty-Five Years of Cliffhangers: The Complete Directory to TV's Night Time Soaps* (1989-). The question for libraries to consider before purchasing the reference book under review is whether there is enough interest in prime-time soaps to warrant the cost of the guide. Can most of the information be found elsewhere, perhaps as a Website? Standard reference works, such as Vincent Terrace's *Fifty Years of Television: A Guide to Series and Pilots, 1937-1988* (see ARBA 93, entry 998), provide less detail and do not contain plot summaries for each episode. Although the World Wide Web does provide information on some of the major soaps, including ones filmed since 1993, the information is also less complete.—**Jack E. Pontius**

1311. **The Motion Picture Guide: 1997 Annual (The Films of 1996).** Edmond Grant, Ken Fox, and Andrew Joseph, eds. New York, News America Publishing, 1997. 792p. index. $99.50. ISBN 0-933997-39-6.

The Motion Picture Guide: 1997 Annual is the 12th supplement to the original 12-volume *Motion Picture Guide* and has been reviewed in ARBA in past years (see ARBA 94, entry 1457). Its expanded coverage from years past includes critical reviews of films released in 1996—almost 700, including many more straight-to-video productions. It notes the Academy Award nominations and winners, contains a full section of detailed obituaries, and includes extensive indexes, including a master index of all films reviewed since 1984, and indexes of films by country of origin, distributor, star rating, genre, MPAA rating, and parental recommendation as well as a names index.

This annual contains a useful information key that helps the reader understand the structure of review entries. A helpful inclusion is the "Parental Recommendation" section, which rates movies according to their suitability for children, placed alongside the Motion Picture Association of America (MPAA) rating, as well as a star rating system. With these three guides and the detailed reviews, the reader will be able to make an informed decision whether to rent a particular movie. For research purposes this book contains a great deal of information, containing not only the movie synopses, but naming the many professionals who worked on the production. The annual opens with the editor's "Year in Review," a sweeping and readable look at what 1996 offered at the box office while the line between major production companies and independent producers blurred. *The Motion Picture Guide: 1997 Annual* is comprehensive and full-bodied in its writing. It will be an asset to any collection.—**Susan M. Sigman**

1312. Pitts, Michael R. **Poverty Row Studios, 1929-1940: An Illustrated History of 53 Independent Film Companies....** Jefferson, N.C., McFarland, 1997. 534p. illus. index. $75.00. ISBN 0-7864-0168-0.

During the 1930s, the public's demand for motion pictures was so great that many small independent production companies flourished, turning out low-budget "quickies" on rented soundstages, often in the section of Hollywood known in the industry as Poverty Row. Some of these films were dreadful, but others had merit, and many featured well-known actors or directors who were either on their way up or down the ladder of success. As Pitts notes, with the exception of the most famous Poverty Row independents—Monogram, Republic, Grand National, and Mascot—these companies and their films have received little scholarly attention.

Pitts remedies this by providing narrative histories and substantial filmographies for 55 (according to this reviewer's count) companies. Apparently, Pitts has personally viewed many of these films, and he enriches the book with numerous critical reviews that, like the histories, he fills with interesting anecdotes and revealing background information. Pitts is clearly an expert in this field, but, with the exception of acknowledging the help of eight individuals and the Library of Congress Motion Picture Division, he does not explain how this immense amount of information was gathered, nor does he provide a bibliography. These are curious deficiencies in an otherwise excellent reference book.—**Joseph W. Palmer**

1313. Rhodes, Karen. **Booking *Hawaii Five-O*: An Episode Guide and Critical History of the 1968-1980 Television Detective Series.** Jefferson, N.C., McFarland, 1997. 333p. illus. index. $45.00. ISBN 0-7864-0171-0.

If *Dragnet* paved the way for serious police television programs, *Hawaii Five-O* painted the centerline. Although previous police dramas gave viewers an inside look at solving crime, *Hawaii Five-O* showed that crime is battled by real people in real places. Sure, the Hawaiian background was attractive, but the show reminded viewers that crime happens somewhere; that *where* the cop works dictates *how* the cop works. Without *Hawaii Five-O*, there would be no *Miami Vice*, no *Hill Street Blues*, no *NYPD Blue*. The cop must know the territory, and viewers learned Hawaii through the eyes of Steve McGarrett and his faithful crew. On this show, the cops were cool because they caught the bad guys, and that is what good cop shows are supposed to be about. *Booking Hawaii Five-O* chronicles the success of this long-running police drama.

A major portion of the work consists of an episode guide for each of the 12 seasons. Each episode listing includes the air date; the production number; writing, directing, and musical credits; a list of guest stars; a two- to three-paragraph description; and critical assessment of the episode. Shorter chapters are dedicated to *Hawaii Five-O*'s inception and creation, the societal context of the show, and a brief critical analysis of the show's cultural elements. Appendixes include an essay on series collectibles and a glossary of Hawaiian words and phrases. The index is complete and useful. Several behind-the-scenes photographs are also provided.

Although Rhodes is admittedly a fan of the series, her approach is objective and often insightful. Many episodes are praised and others panned. Each episode entry offers the reader at least one interesting bit of background information. Most readers will find interest in the chapters that precede and follow the episode guide. Rhodes's prose is crisp and elegant, with a wry touch added for spice. Using her own exhaustive calculations, she deftly destroys the popular myth that *Hawaii Five-O* promoted racism by portraying people of Asian heritage as villains. Analytic essays on additional topics would improve the work.

Booking Hawaii Five-O succeeds in the task of cataloging, describing, and analyzing one of the most successful programs in television history. Colleges requiring research in television programming, as well as public libraries with patrons interested in such topics, will want to add this volume to their collections. Book 'em, Danno!—**Keith Kyker**

1314. Terrace, Vincent. **Experimental Television, Test Films, Pilots, and Trial Series, 1925 Through 1995: Seven Decades of Small Screen Almosts.** Jefferson, N.C., McFarland, 1997. 791p. illus. index. $99.50. ISBN 0-7864-0178-8.

Dazed and horrified by the current metastasizing progression of network sitcoms, specials, miniseries, cop shows, doctor shows, talk shows, soap and space operas? Just think about all those spawns of the vast wasteland that died aborning during the past 70 years—tests, short runs, pilots, and outright network missteps that either never made it to the small screen at all or died after a brief shot at mass media greatness. Terrace's excellent and unique reference work charts these television curiosities and ephemera, beginning with the low-resolution experiments of television's dim 1920s, 1930s, and 1940s prehistory and continuing to the present day.

More than 3,000 programs are listed alphabetically, each with air dates or production year, network, running time, complete cast credits (including guest appearances), and production credits. Pithy program descriptions are provided for each entry. Sixty-nine photographs—publicity stills and advertisements—are included. A thorough name index is furnished. This material is admittedly specialized; it would probably be most at home in libraries supporting large film, television, or popular culture collections. Then again, almost anyone with even a vague aesthetic sense would benefit from reading these entries and being thankful that these cathode-ray tube monstrosities never survived past infancy.—**Gary Handman**

1315. **Variety and Daily Variety Television Reviews. Volume 18: 1993-1994.** New York, Garland, 1996. 1v. (unpaged). index. $165.00. ISBN 0-8240-3797-9. ISSN 1064-9557.

This installment of *Variety Television Reviews* is the 3d supplement to the original 15-volume base set, which covered the years 1923-1988. Like the parent work, this volume provides reproductions of television show reviews from both *Daily Variety* (Hollywood) and its weekly New York counterpart, *Variety*, arranged in chronological order. Coverage includes a broad mix of network, cable, and PBS offerings and an odd sprinkling of recent home video reviews to boot. During the course of the last several releases of *Variety Television Reviews*, emphasis has increasingly been placed on reviews from *Daily Variety* (reviews in the weekly publication are frequently truncated versions of pieces originally appearing in the daily publication). When a review of a particular show appears in both publications, the longer of the two is reproduced; a brief entry is given for the shorter review, with a cross-reference to reproduced text.

Each column includes fairly extensive production and credit information at the head of the review. The reviews themselves are unmistakably show business in flavor—full of insider's smugness and peppered with *Variety*'s patently dingy jargon, Tinseltown neologisms, and vernacular nuttiness. For a stylistic example, one needs to look no further than the first paragraph of the review of *Beyond Control: The Amy Fisher Story*, which helpfully informs the reader that "the principals are physically attractive and in the right demo[graphic] range." A useful title index, including references to series' names, is provided. There is also a "Selected Name Index," which is considerably less than helpful. This volume is for academic and larger public library collections with strong mass communications or popular culture collections or with strong interests in the film and television industry.—**Gary Handman**

Indexes

1316. D'Agostino, Annette M., comp. **Filmmakers in *The Moving Picture World*: An Index of Articles, 1907-1927.** Jefferson, N.C., McFarland, 1997. 386p. $75.00. ISBN 0-7864-0290-3.

March 9, 1907, saw issue number 1 of *The Moving Picture World*, the first trade paper of the cinema industry, come into being. During its run, it featured various interesting articles on directors and producers; a plethora of stars, some of whom (such as Gloria Swanson, Bob Steele, Julie Faye, and Helen Hays) would make the not-so-easy move from the silent era to "talkies"; and also authors and writers (e.g., Booth Tarkington, Anita Loos, and Sinclair Lewis). It is surprising and pleasing to see a number of Asian and Latino stars of the day listed. Some stars went into such diverse areas as radio (e.g., Buddy Rodgers and Mary Pickford) or medicine (Richard Janeway, who played one of the infants in the *Our Gang* series, became chief of staff at the North Carolina Baptist Hospital in Winston-Salem). The journal ceased publication in 1927. A how-to-find information section on various personalities in this volume starts on page 7, and a brief history of the publication starts on page 11. The index is recommended for cinema historians and silent film fans.—**Lillian Jane Steele**

1317. **Michael Singer's Film Directors, 1997: A Complete Guide.** 12th ed. Michael Singer and Bethann Wetzel, comps. and eds. Los Angeles, Calif., Lone Eagle, 1997. 798p. index. $75.00pa. ISBN 0-943728-85-1. ISSN 0740-2872.

World film directors active in feature, documentary, and telefilm production are the focus of this hefty directory. Entries provide three distinct types of information: personal (date and place of birth); current contact information (agent, city, and telephone number); and film credits. The inclusion of contact information alone is worth the purchase price. "Active" directors are defined as those who have released a film in the past 10 years. Credits appear complete but concise, listing film title, distributor, and year. Supplementary materials include a section on notable directors of the past and indexes of foreign-based directors, guilds (worldwide), agents and managers (mostly from the United States), and a list of Academy Award nominees and winners.

With its emphasis on current directors (including documentary and television), the guide differs from other popular directories typically found in libraries, including the *International Motion Picture Almanac* (67th ed.; see ARBA 97, entry 770) and the *International Dictionary of Films and Filmmakers* (St. James Press, 1997). As such, its purchase complements existing holdings while providing a one-stop source for difficult-to-track information.—**Megan S. Farrell**

Videography

1318. O'Neill, James. **Sci-Fi on Tape: A Complete Guide to Science Fiction and Fantasy on Video.** New York, Billboard Books/Watson-Guptill, 1997. 301p. illus. $16.95pa. ISBN 0-8230-7659-8.

The introduction of this work captures the upbeat tone of this enjoyable compilation with its declaration that "science fiction and fantasy films make the impossible possible, the unimaginable into something that can be imagined and experienced over and over again like a favorite dream come true." More than 1,250 films are covered, including a good representation of silent films, such as Fritz Lang's 1926 classic *Metropolis*, though most are from the last 50 years.

Though unspecified, the criteria for inclusion appear quite liberal, encompassing such films as the Santa Claus favorite *Miracle on 34th Street*, and the entire James Bond series. Each entry features the expected data: year, film company, Motion Picture Association of America rating, running time, director, and a short cast. In addition, O'Neill, a Philadelphian who also published a similar guide to horror films titled *Terror on Tape* (Billboard, 1994), provides entertaining personal insights with a one- to four-star rating system and short synopsis for each film. Although his analyses are often less than profound (merely calling a film "controversial" [pp. 42, 43] is a typical maneuver to avoid probing inquiry), there is a comfortably casual, pleasantly unpretentious attitude throughout, and he is especially good when assessing genuine quality as opposed to high camp: *Jason and the Argonauts*, *A Clockwork Orange*, and *The Terminator* are among those singled out for the high praise of a four-star rating. By covering only those films available on videotape, this practical little paperback will be welcomed by the vast audience of videotape enthusiasts—a handy guide to have on the shelf to consult when wondering which tape to rent this weekend.

Although this is not really the definitive work on this genre, it does challenge the more scholarly, in-depth two-volume set *The Great Science Fiction Pictures* (see ARBA 91, entry 1382, and ARBA 78, entry 962), which tends to be overburdened with plot synopses.—**Richard W. Grefrath**

1319. **Roger Ebert's Video Companion.** 1998 ed. Kansas City, Mo., Andrews McMeel Publishing, 1997. 987p. index. $17.95pa. ISBN 0-8362-3688-2. ISSN 1072-561X.

Now in its 13th annual edition, Ebert's guide to over 1,500 videos currently in print continues to dominate the field of annual video guidebooks. Fans of his show with Gene Siskel, "At the Movies," or his *Chicago Sun-Times* review column know the quality of Ebert's criticism. This video companion serves as a guide to his personal best, significant, and worst films available for rent or purchase. However, users should note that, as with previous editions, this work is neither a comprehensive guide to everything on the market, as is *Leonard Maltin's Movie Encyclopedia* (see ARBA 96, entry 1377) with 19,000 selections, nor does it include every movie produced in 1997. Ebert is selective, and many of these reviews have appeared in earlier editions (new entries are marked NEW, although a list of the same would improve access); reviews are dropped as videos become unavailable, and old editions should be retained. Most of these reviews date from the last 25 years, although the occasional classic crops up. As an added treat, Ebert includes his interviews with celebrities, essays on Sundance and Cannes film festivals, and his opinion of the best films of the year. A companion pocket guide can be carted to video stores. The quality of any review collection ultimately rests on the intelligence and wit of the reviewer, and Roger Ebert is among the best in his field. Patrons might not always agree with his critiques, but they are never dull and are often incisive. No other critic approaches what Ebert does here, particularly for the low price. This guide is highly recommended as an annual purchase for most libraries.—**Anthony J. Adam**

1320. **VideoHound's Sci-Fi Experience: Your Quantum Guide to the Video Universe.** Detroit, Visible Ink Press/Gale, 1997. 445p. illus. index. $17.95pa. ISBN 0-7876-0615-4.

The VideoHound crew has consistently produced the best nonspecialist guides to movies available on videocassette, and this volume, dedicated to science fiction film, continues that tradition. Like the other VideoHound offerings, *Sci-Fi Experience* contains alphabetized reviews of all available videocassettes; extensive indexes allow for cross-referencing by cast members, directors, and categories (the latter consisting of clever inventions by the editors, such as "Alien Beings—Benign" or "Rampant Technology"). Short boxed articles scattered throughout the volume discuss generic conventions and the historical development of the genre, and the reviews themselves are both intelligent and marked by a wry sense of humor. A useful appendix lists the addresses and telephone numbers of almost every videocassette distributor in North America.

Because *Sci-Fi Experience* is intended for nonspecialist, nonacademic use, it fails to provide other resources. Although the listing of distributors, fan clubs, and magazines is impressive, there are no complementary lists of information for archives or scholarly organizations (even though a number exist). Reviews evaluate films almost entirely in terms of "enjoyability," and although the boxed articles provide a skeletal historical framework, there is little sense of how science fiction film has developed as a genre within the Hollywood system and been received in U.S. culture. These may be unfair criticisms of a work that makes no pretense of scholarly rigor, but potential users should be aware of the book's limitations. The only other disappointment (especially considering the generally high quality of the VideoHound series) is uneven copyediting.—**Marcus P. Elmore**

1321. **VideoHound's Vampires on Video.** J. Gordon Melton and the Transylvanian Society of Dracula, comps. Detroit, Visible Ink Press/Gale, 1997. 335p. illus. index. $17.95pa. ISBN 1-57859-002-7.

A century ago, Bram Stoker published his novel *Dracula*, and the world has not been quite the same since, as any Anne Rice fan will attest. As fascination with vampires continues to pervade the collective consciousness of Western civilization, this work, in the same vein as its popular companion volume, *VideoHound's Golden Movie Retriever* (see ARBA 95, entry 1399), specializes in a single genre of film available on video: the vampire flick. It would be shortsighted, however, merely to equate "vampire" with "Dracula." The book, primarily an alphabetic listing of the cinematic vampire oeuvre of all nations, lists and reviews more than 600 films having to do not just with Nosferatu and the notorious Transylvanian count but also with several varieties of spin-offs, such as comedy (*The Addams Family*), blaxploitation (*Blacula*), horror (*The Horror of the Blood Monsters*), science fiction (*Not of This Earth*), and alternative sexual preference (*Lesbian Vampires: The Heiress of Dracula*).

Not surprisingly, 26 of the listed film titles begin with the word "blood," 31 with "Dracula," and more than 50 of them with the six letters "Vampir." The book is profusely illustrated (in black-and-white), with Melton supplying joke captions (both funny and weak) for the characters or actions depicted. Several lengthier sidebars are provided on such engaging subjects as "best vampire films"; "vampires for children"; and one devoted entirely to Bela Lugosi, whose 1931 classic kick-started the pervasive interest in the genre that endures today.

Each title (many have been released under multiple titles) comes equipped with a description/review, a one-to-four-bones evaluation, and Melton's "Woof!" for what he deems real dogs. Also provided are the Motion Picture Association of America rating, running time, country, cast, director, format, producer, and distributor. Vampire movies are an acquired taste, but for those who like them, Melton is knowledgeable, witty, and not afraid to give strong opinions. This work is not only a reference source; it is also a fun read for those who only want to turn the pages and look at way cool pictures of Brad Pitt, Lugosi, and other monsters.
—**Bruce A. Shuman**

THEATER

Bibliography

1322. **Bibliographic Guide to Theatre Arts 1996.** New York, G. K. Hall/Simon & Schuster Macmillan, 1997. 231p. $215.00. ISBN 0-7838-1782-7. ISSN 0360-2788.

The cataloging copy for approximately 5,000 items on all aspects of theater arts is presented in this single-volume resource (see ARBA 92, entry 1375, for a previous review). The materials listed were those acquired by the Library of Congress and the New York Public Library Theatre and Drama Collection. Titles have imprint dates of 1990 to the present and were cataloged in 1996. Full bibliographic information is given, and the entries are filed in integrated main entry order. The geographic scope is international, and all formats of materials are included. The topical coverage extends from the performing arts (cinema, radio, stage, and television) into peripheral concerns (e.g., promptbooks and shooting scripts). Libraries seeking a full, authoritative source will want this title. (See entry 109 for a complete review of G. K. Hall's bibliographic series.)—**Ed Volz**

1323. Patterson, Michael. **German Theatre: A Bibliography from the Beginning to 1995.** New York, G. K. Hall/Simon & Schuster Macmillan, 1996. 887p. index. (The Motley Bibliographies, no.3). $240.00. ISBN 0-7838-1662-6.

This volume contains 17,537 citations that refer to publications pertaining to theater done in the German language. The subtitle to this tome claims that it covers the German theatrical literature from its beginning until 1995. The "beginning" is not clearly defined, but the earliest citations seem to be to publications that appeared in the middle of the eighteenth century. The author wishes to encompass the whole of German literature on the German theater. His entries include books, pamphlets, theatrical almanacs, exhibition catalogs, and dissertations. Journal articles are excluded. Only publications dealing with the spoken word are listed. Dance, opera, and non-theater-related music items are not discussed in this volume.

The entries are organized under 16 rubrics, including general references, legal and organizational aspects, religion, geographic locations, theatrical criticism, drama history, foreign influences, and music in the theater. Each of the topic areas has numerous subcategories. For example, "Theatre Practice" contains 10 subtopics ("acting," "directing," "stage design," and so forth). The entries are listed chronologically within the categories and subcategories. Each entry contains the author's name, the publication title, an enumeration of the number of illustrations (if any), the place of publication, the publisher, the date of publication, and an occasional bibliographic note. All citations are in German, while the bibliographic notes are in English. Separate subject and author indexes are provided. The indexes are indispensable for finding particular entries because the chronological organization of the citations does not make it easy for the reader to find items dealing with a particular writer or subject area.

This is a work that runs just under 900 pages; physically huge, it has a rather small typeface. The reference is exhaustive and would need to be so in order to accomplish its stated mission to encompass all of the German-language publications on the German theater. The size of the work would have multiplied to an unpredictable degree had the author decided to include journal articles. As such, it is already monumental and difficult to hold in hand. Also, users of this work will have to be able to read German because none of the citation material has been translated into English. Because the introduction, preface, and table of contents appear in both languages, the volume can be used by both German- and English-language speakers. This is a must-have reference work for all those interested in the status and history of German writings about the theater.—**Charles Neuringer**

Dictionaries and Encyclopedias

1324. Leiter, Samuel L. **New Kabuki Encyclopedia: A Revised Adaptation of *Kabuki Jiten*.** Westport, Conn., Greenwood Press, 1997. 823p. illus. index. $115.00. ISBN 0-313-29288-4.

The present volume is a greatly expanded and revised adaptation of the 1979 English version of a Japanese reference source entitled *Kabuki Encyclopedia* (see ARBA 81, entry 1067). This new publication contains approximately 1,750 entry headings, alphabetically arranged. Its usefulness is greatly enhanced by a double system of cross-referencing between Japanese and English terms. Boldfaced lettering is used to indicate items that have their own entries. Japanese characters are included for all main entry terms, titles, and names. There are approximately 130 figures, drawings, and black-and-white photographs. Included are five appendixes: a brief chronology of Kabuki, major plays, popularized or alternate play titles, actors' genealogies, and a list of Yago in use today. The highly selective bibliography contains both Japanese and English listings. A subject guide and a lengthy index increase the ease of using this research tool.

Kabuki, an essential part of Japanese heritage and culture for nearly four centuries, commands, for the most part, slight attention in the West. This reference book takes a major stride in closing this lapse of interest and knowledge. It is a major guide that any researcher in English would find valuable because of the ease in accessing its comprehensive information.—**Jackson Kesler**

Directories

1325. **Directory of Theatre Training Programs 1997-1999: Profiles of College and Conservatory Programs Throughout the United States.** 6th ed. Jill Charles, comp. and ed. Dorset, Vt., Theatre Directories, 1997. 244p. illus. $25.95pa. ISBN 0-933919-37-9.

The 6th edition of this directory is a valuable, easy-to-access reference tool for those starting a career in theatre. According to the publisher, 18 entries have been added and 85 percent of previous listings from the 1995 edition (see ARBA 96, entry 1419) have been updated. Listed alphabetically by state, with a limited number of specialized schools in Canada, Europe, and Great Britain, college and conservatory programs in all areas of theatrical studies are profiled, including all that are accredited by the National Association of Schools of Theatre and those that are members of the University/Resident Theatre Association. Each entry consists of data such as department contact person, enrollment statistics, admission, tuition, scholarship and faculty information, courses offered, as well as program description and philosophy. Three lively, interesting introductory essays present the realities and basics of a life in the theater for students and parents. A helpful chart at the end serves as an index to determine quickly which programs offer the desired degree. This is an excellent source for beginning an investigation of theatre programs on college and post-graduate levels.—**Marjorie N. Rosenthal**

Handbooks and Yearbooks

1326. Heuvel, Michael Vanden. **Elmer Rice: A Research and Production Sourcebook.** Westport, Conn., Greenwood Press, 1996. 242p. index. (Modern Dramatists Research and Production Sourcebooks, no.9). $69.50. ISBN 0-313-27431-2.

Second only to Eugene O'Neill among U.S. mid-twentieth-century playwrights, Elmer Rice (1892-1967) also achieved renown as a Pulitzer prize-winning director, theater owner, producer, and advocate for the U.S. popular theater. This sourcebook provides a good starting point from which to approach the Rice canon.

Heuvel leads off with a four-page chronology of Rice's professional achievements, followed by a four-page narrative biography. From here, the sourcebook moves into its main focus, the 1- to 3-page plot synopses and critical overviews of each of Rice's 35 plays. The summaries provide descriptions of central characters and outlines of significant events in the plot. Each overview includes sketches of the play's stage history, critical responses to it, and ensuing scholarly assessments. A "primary" bibliography of nondramatic primary works, dramatic publications, and unpublished collected materials (archival sources) supplements the play overviews, as do the book's annotated "secondary" bibliographies of reviews, books, articles, and sections. In addition, there is a listing of productions and credits, a feature that will be especially helpful to Rice researchers.

Although today Rice may be better known as a polemicist for his antifascist, anticensorship, pro-socialist political positions, he played a major role in the U.S. theater during its most vibrant developmental years. Because of that, students and others in need of information on the major influences in twentieth-century U.S. drama will welcome Heuvel's well-crafted sourcebook.—**G. Kim Dority**

1327. Hischak, Thomas S. **The Theatregoer's Almanac: A Collection of Lists, People, History, and Commentary on the American Theatre.** Westport, Conn., Greenwood Press, 1997. 287p. index. $45.00. ISBN 0-313-30246-4.

As the author confesses, much information in this work can be found in other standard theater reference sources (most of which are identified in the extensive bibliography), but no other work compiles the bits of information quite as this "almanac" does. It provides in one handy volume a wide range of information, descriptive but not evaluative. These tantalizing snippets deal with plays (both drama and musicals), playwrights, actors, producers, and awards. As the subtitle states, the emphasis is strictly American; the accent lies heavily on Broadway. Unfortunately, however, the information sometimes does not go far enough. For example, none of the directories of theater magazines, organizations, or regional theaters provides an address or telephone number. A seriously scaled-down glossary of "unusual theater terms" provides a questionable definition of *green room* and omits the term *break a leg*, about which the uninitiated may inquire. The so-called representative list of regional theaters includes the Indiana Repertory Theatre in Indianapolis but excludes the equally reputable and critically acclaimed Contemporary American Theatre Company in Columbus.

The compendium is not without its gems, however. Such highlights include a list of songs in productions that were almost cut from the final version and famous performances that did not win a Tony award, such as Ethel Merman's tour de force in *Gypsy*. The index provides sufficient access to information whose fast-food format is geared toward tracking down theater trivia and verifying simple facts. Hischak is an established contributor to the performance arts reference literature (e.g., *The American Musical Theatre Song Encyclopedia* [see ARBA 96, entry 1416] and *Stage It with Music* [see ARBA 94, entry 1473]).—**Lawrence Olszewski**

1328. Peterson, Bernard L., Jr. **The African American Theatre Directory, 1816-1960: A Comprehensive Guide....** Westport, Conn., Greenwood Press, 1997. 301p. index. $75.00. ISBN 0-313-29537-9.

Only a scholar with a deep love of the subject matter and a long-term commitment to it could have produced such a volume, which draws together much hard-to-find primary information about black theater from its earliest beginnings in the United States to the dawn of the Civil Rights era. The heart of the book is an alphabetic listing of approximately 500 theatrical troupes and theaters, the information having been ferreted out of a variety of books, dissertations, newspapers large and small, periodical articles, and library collections of archival material. Many of these acting troupes and theaters were of a fleeting and protean nature, changing names, going in and out of business, and laboring under hardships ranging from racial prejudice to more traditional economic and interpersonal strains. In addition to the professional and semiprofessional theater, the author stresses college troupes at traditionally black institutions and provides copious, hitherto virtually unavailable information about such groups.

Several appendixes increase the value of this work. Appendix A is a simple alphabetic list of the theaters included in the directory, along with dates for their existence, where available, and a second list of additional theaters not mentioned in the main body of the book, along with whatever scant information is known about them (mostly manager and circuit information). Appendix B classifies the troupes and theaters by type—minstrel companies; touring musical, dramatic, vaudeville, and variety companies; resident theater companies and stock companies; community little theater groups and dramatic societies; professional theatrical organizations; academic theater groups and dramatic associations; production and amusement companies; and nonacademic organizations that provided theater training. The first six of these categories, as in appendix A, are divided into two lists (those groups included in the main body of the work and a supplemental list of other troupes and theaters not discussed in the main entries but nevertheless of some interest or importance). Following the appendixes is a list of reference books and critical studies, dissertations and theses, and periodicals used in the work.

After the appendixes follows an extensive index of personal names, with variants of these names in parentheses. It is important to note that this book will be a companion volume to the author's as-yet-unpublished *Profiles of African American Theater People*, and the many names asterisked in this index are treated much more fully in the future companion volume. Other symbols indicate relative degrees of importance of the individuals, race (if not black), and nicknames, among other aspects. There are, finally, two major indexes: a list of predominantly black theatrical organizations and theaters, with extensive cross-referencing to variant names, and an index of titles of the theater productions cited in the directory.

This is the author's fourth major book on black theater. It deserves a place in every library that supports black studies or theater studies in any way. From the time that the African Company was founded in a tea garden in New York in 1816, there is a long and relatively unknown story to be learned about the precursors of modern black theater. Peterson's directory tells that story effectively through the depiction of the people and organizations struggling to bring forth art under the most trying of circumstances. [R: LJ, 15 Feb 97, pp. 128-29; RBB, 15 Feb 97, p. 1039]—**Bill Miller**

1329. Suskin, Steven. **More Opening Nights on Broadway: A Critical Quotebook of the Musical Theatre 1965 Through 1981.** New York, Schirmer Books/Simon & Schuster Macmillan, 1997. 1141p. illus. index. $45.00. ISBN 0-02-864571-5.

Picking up where Suskin's earlier edition left off (see ARBA 92, entry 1387), this sequel excerpts more than 1,500 first-night reviews of 210 musicals, provided by top newspaper critics. The aim here is to recreate the thrill of the Broadway musical, giving a feel for what the show was like, not just its plot. More than 100 black-and-white original poster illustrations accompany the entries. The new edition, although covering fewer years and productions, includes fuller and longer excerpts, necessitated by the increasing complexities of the latter-day musical. Individual entries run to several pages apiece in length.

Each entry contains production credits, opening date, theater, the reviews, and awards won. A scorecard lists the number of performances, reviews by category (from rave to pan), and the show's financial outcome. Following chapters include a list of shows that never made it to Broadway, a chronology of the musicals in the main section, overviews of 40 notable careers, and an all-inclusive index.

Although the Broadway musical has undergone many alterations since its "golden era," it can still generate a healthy dose of excitement and stardust. This informative and interesting book is proof of that statement. [R: LJ, 15 April 97, p. 74]—**Anita Zutis**

28 Philosophy and Religion

PHILOSOPHY

Bibliography

1330. Bynagle, Hans E. **Philosophy: A Guide to the Reference Literature.** 2d ed. Englewood, Colo., Libraries Unlimited, 1997. 233p. index. (Reference Sources in the Humanities Series). $38.50. ISBN 1-56308-376-0.

This 2d edition (the 1st appeared more than 10 years ago, in 1986 [see ARBA 87, entry 1334]) offers a critical, comprehensive survey of major reference works in philosophy (the survey includes a total of 572 entries in less than 200 pages). In comparison with the earlier edition, nearly 40 percent of the entries are either new (150 in all) or revised. Designed for professional philosophers as well as students, this volume is also intended to be of use to librarians and general readers as well. Annotations are designed specifically with the audiences most likely to find a given work of greatest use in mind. Although most books covered here are in English, a limited number of important elementary or comprehensive works in foreign languages have been included. Advanced studies in foreign languages, however, have usually not been listed. Emphasis has been given to recent publications and to readily available works.

A brief introduction provides a general discussion of both the scope and perspective adopted by the author in compiling this work. Bynagle provides a brief description of the major Western and non-Western philosophies covered in this reference work, as well as a shorter discussion of feminist philosophy. He also explains why two categories featured in the earlier edition, Marxist philosophy and neo-scholasticism, have been dropped from the new edition. Specific chapters are devoted to general bibliographic and research guides, including general dictionaries, encyclopedias, and handbooks. Later chapters concern more specialized reference works arranged according to branches and schools of philosophy, as well as by periods, countries, and regions. General indexes, abstracts, reviewing journals, and serial bibliographies are given a chapter of their own. A lengthy chapter covering bibliographies devoted to individual philosophers (77 in all) runs the gamut from Aristotle to Ludwig Wittgenstein and includes Simone de Beauvoir, Epictetus, Al-Farabi, Michel Foucault, Arthur Lovejoy, György Lukás, and Maurice Merleau-Ponty, among others. Unfortunately, no representative Indian or Oriental philosophers appear at all, and the index lists only seven entries for Indian philosophy and only four entries for Chinese philosophy, clearly the one serious weakness of this reference work in general.

Of special note in this edition are chapters devoted to electronic resources, basic journals, and professional organizations and research centers. Of the journals, those with particular reference value have been stressed, especially journals that include reviews of new books and lists of new publications. Likewise, organizations that emphasize publishing or that support research, reference, and referral services receive priority here. There is even a section devoted to philosophy in cyberspace. Directories and biographical sources are also covered briefly. Because the book is organized according to different types of reference works, the indexes are especially useful in providing access to specific subjects. These include author, title, and subject indexes. [R: Choice, Jul/Aug 97, p. 1776]—**Joseph W. Dauben**

1331. Casati, Roberto, and Achille C. Varzi. **50 Years of Events: An Annotated Bibliography, 1947 to 1997.** Bowling Green, Ohio, Philosophy Documentation Center/Bowling Green State University, 1997. 402p. index. $33.00. ISBN 0-912632-66-6.

No, this is not a bibliography on major happenings of the past half-century, nor even (taking a clue from the publisher's identity) on major philosophical happenings during that period. This misleadingly, maybe mischievously, titled work is concerned with the philosophical understanding of events as a conceptual and ontological category. This subject—encompassing also the analysis of specific types of events, such as actions, mental events, performances, and processes—has generated a remarkable volume of discussion spreading across many philosophical subdisciplines, especially metaphysics, logic, and the philosophy of language and spilling over into allied disciplines, such as linguistics and cognitive sciences.

Casati and Varzi offer this bibliography as an aid to tracking this wide and widely scattered literature, choosing as their starting point a seminal 1947 essay by Hans Reichenbach on the logical form of action sentences. Their 1,800-plus entries representing 900-plus authors include journal articles; books; collective works and individual contributions thereto; and a select number of reviews, dissertations, and technical reports that have figured prominently in the debates. Reprintings are extensively cited but with no pretense to exhaustiveness. Arrangement is by author, alphabetically, and secondarily by year of publication. To trace specific topics, connections, or strands in the debates, one must rely upon the subject and name indexes (the latter including names as subjects), which are admirably detailed for this purpose. Most entries include annotations, although these vary considerably in length and detail. Scholars and advanced students of its subject should find this specialized work a useful resource: ineptly titled, but aptly done.—**Hans E. Bynagle**

1332. **The Collaborative Bibliography of Women in Philosophy.** Noël Hutchings and William D. Rumsey, eds. Bowling Green, Ohio, Philosophy Documentation Center/Bowling Green State University, 1997. 375p. index. $39.50. ISBN 0-912632-65-8.

This is an unusual work. It is based on a database, NOEMA: The Collaborative Bibliography of Women in Philosophy, which is freely available over the World Wide Web (http://billyboy.ius.indiana.edu/WomeninPhilosophy/WomeninPhilo.html). This database was created by the editors of the work being reviewed, but it is set up so that others may collaborate by suggesting corrections or additions to the database. These suggestions are reviewed, and the database amended, with the initials of the collaborators appearing where appropriate. The database takes advantage of the communication possibilities inherent in the Internet—it is continually updated and corrected. The printed work being reviewed is, as is clearly pointed out in its preface, a "progress report" in print, and its editors hope it will serve not only as an aid to research but also as an invitation to collaborate in the continuing development of the database.

The printed work consists of a bibliography of more than 300 pages, a preface describing the database and the work in question, acknowledgments, and two appendixes: an index of subjects and names and a list of contributors. The bibliography is an alphabetic list of names under which are numbered entries, one for each work listed. The subject/name index refers to the entry numbers in the bibliography. *The Collaborative Bibliography* is an excellent project, providing access to works that would otherwise be difficult to locate using traditional reference works, such as the *Philosopher's Index* (see ARBA 91, entry 1408), which do not index materials by author's gender. As with Else Barth's *Women Philosophers: A Bibliography of Books Through 1990* (see ARBA 93, entry 1392), the bibliography at hand has a broad conception of its subject matter. It is carefully named to indicate that it covers "women in philosophy," not just women philosophers. Of course, such philosophers as Susanne Langer and G. E. M. Anscombe are included, but the majority of women included are contemporary academics who have written commentaries on philosophers. In addition, the bibliography treats such figures as Aspasia, who left no works and whose philosophical contributions are open to question, and others, such as Gale Schares, whose only listed work is "Should Eastern European Nations be Encouraged to Develop Free Market Institutions?" This broad scope only increases the value of the work. Most of the works listed are in English, but the bibliography does include works in many other languages, including non-European languages, and the database clearly aims to include as much as possible.

If the information in this work were available only in print, it would be easy to recommend it to every academic library. The book is useful, well organized, reasonably priced, and well produced. However, because it is really a snapshot of a dynamically expanding work on the Web, it is hard to recommend the print volume without reservation. Most people potentially interested in the content of this work will have access to a more up-to-date version of the same information via the Web. Libraries will have to judge for themselves whether their patrons are likely to use a static, print reference work when a dynamic version is available at no cost to anyone with access to the Internet.—**Richard H. Swain**

Dictionaries and Encyclopedias

1333. **Encyclopedia of Bioethics.** rev. ed. [CD-ROM]. New York, Macmillan Library Reference/Simon & Schuster Macmillan, 1996. Minimum system requirements: IBM or compatible 386. CD-ROM drive. Windows 3.1. 4MB RAM. 2MB hard disk space. $450.00.

It seems essential to mention at the outset the bonus that accompanies the text of the distinguished *Encyclopedia of Bioethics* on this CD-ROM, namely, the entire cumulated *Bibliography of Bioethics* from its inception in 1974 through the year 1995 (see ARBA 90, entry 1611, for the most recent review of the annual print version). Although this feature is surprisingly underpublicized—it is not mentioned on the disc label or on the cover of the accompanying documentation, for example—it adds considerable value to the package. As for the text of the recently revised print version of the encyclopedia (see ARBA 96, entry 1429), it is all here, including the extensive cross-references and bibliographies accompanying most articles as well as the appendixes comprising a wide-ranging collection of codes, oaths, and directives relating to ethical practice in the health professions and in biological, medical, and environmental sciences.

All of this is enhanced in the CD-ROM version by an impressive array of retrieval and navigational aids. The opening screen offers both an alphabetic list of articles, reproduced from the print version, and a synoptic (i.e., systematic) outline of articles, unique to the CD-ROM. Topics in each of these lists are hypertext-linked to permit jumping to the corresponding articles. Hypertext links are also provided from the cross-references at the ends of articles and, very usefully, from entries in the *Bibliography* to related articles in the *Encyclopedia*, although not in the opposite direction. (Within the *Bibliography*, hypertext linking permits jumping from a descriptor assigned to an entry to other entries sharing the same descriptor.)

Additional modes of access are afforded by a toolbar that can be customized. Among its features are a Query button for launching full-text word searches with ample capabilities for performing Boolean (*and/or/not*) operations, truncating terms, or specifying context (e.g., "find occurrences of heart and transplant, in that order, within a 10-word spread"). Another toolbar button initiates searches of a detailed table of contents at any of four hierarchical levels: main headings only, main headings plus first level subheadings, and so forth. Navigational tools include a Backtrack button for retracing one's steps and a Trail button that opens a window displaying all the places in the encyclopedia visited during the current session, with the opportunity to return instantly to any place. A toolbar option already active on installation but not explained either in the accompanying documentation or under the program's Help function is a template button ("Template 1") that permits specification of a word search to look for a word in the title of an article combined with other words occurring in the article's text. Additional template options listed under the toolbar preferences menu either could not be activated or produced inscrutable results. Presumably these are dummy options, or else their use requires more expertise or better documentation than that provided.

All in all, this product offers an attractive alternative to the print versions of both the *Encyclopedia* and the *Bibliography of Bioethics*, especially for those with frequent need to consult these major tools of the field. The ability to extract and save text for later review, manipulation, or printing is of course an extra benefit.—**Hans E. Bynagle**

1334. **Encyclopedia of Classical Philosophy.** Donald J. Zeyl, Daniel T. Devereux, and Phillip T. Mitsis, eds. Westport, Conn., Greenwood Press, 1997. 614p. index. $99.50. ISBN 0-313-28775-9.

Contained herein are those axioms known the world over that have been, in John Keats, fine phrase, "proved upon the pulses of the people." More than 250 entries cover what is generally referred to as classical philosophy, or philosophy before 600 C.E. Thus, Aristotle and Saint Augustine are here, but not Thomas Aquinas. Ninety scholars have contributed to the volume, making it both interesting and uneven. No attempt to reconcile conflicting opinions has been made.

Oddities occur in this volume, as one would expect. Yet some are more emblematic of the postmodern age than perhaps one may wish. Although Christianity is treated, it receives, for example, fewer pages than the obscure but interesting figure of Plotinus or the entry on Sophists.

It is unfair to compare this one-volume work with the magisterial *Encyclopedia of Philosophy* (see ARBA 75, entry 1237). That longer work covered the gamut of the mind. However, even where the two touch the same lines of thought, the present volume compares favorably. Not only are the entries equally informative, but this newer work has the added advantage of more recent research. A more accurate comparison to *The Oxford Companion to Philosophy* (see ARBA 97, entry 1166). Again, the volume under review stands up well. Even though the Oxford volume covers more ground with shorter entries (but is longer), *Encyclopedia of Classical Philosophy* provides more information. All libraries, educated laypeople, and scholars in the field would do well to purchase this important addition. [R: RBB, 15 Oct 97, p. 427]

—**Mark Y. Herring**

1335. **Encyclopedia of Phenomenology.** Lester Embree and others, eds. Norwell, Mass., Kluwer Academic, 1997. 764p. index. (Contributions to Phenomenology, v.18). $450.00. ISBN 0-7923-2956-2.

This is a work for the cognoscenti. Although the introduction includes an attempt to define phenomenology (giving one negative and five positive characteristics), it is an explanation that can be understood only by someone quite familiar with the history of philosophy and the peculiar vocabulary of phenomenology. Moreover, the entry on phenomenology in the body of the encyclopedia consists of nothing but cross-references to other entries covering aspects of phenomenology—constitutive phenomenology, constitutive phenomenology of the natural attitude, existential phenomenology, generative phenomenology, genetic phenomenology, hermeneutical phenomenology, and realistic phenomenology.

The encyclopedia consists of a single volume of approximately 750 pages. There is a preface explaining the nature of the work, the conventions used, the history and support of the project, and acknowledgments. The introduction is itself an essay briefly describing the philosophical antecedents of phenomenology and divided into sections entitled "What is Phenomenology?", "Evolution of the Phenomenological Agenda," "Contrasts with Phenomenology," and "Articulations of Phenomenology."

The body of the encyclopedia includes 166 signed entries averaging around 3,000 words in length, and each entry includes a bibliography. The entries discuss the work of Edmund Husserl, the founder of the phenomenological movement, and his "anticipators," including G. W. F. Hegel, Henri-Louis Bergson, Franz Brentano, Wilhem Dilthey, and William James. There are also entries on phenomenology in various countries around the world; on the relation of phenomenology to a variety of philosophical figures; and on the relation of phenomenology to various topics, such as education, music, religion, ethnic studies, feminism, political theory, architecture, theater, literature, dance, law, geography, ethnology, nursing, and psychology.

This encyclopedia is volume 18 in the series Contributions to Phenomenology and is published in cooperation with the Center for Advanced Research in Phenomenology. There is little or no attempt to clearly explain or justify phenomenology to the uninitiated, and all entries are written by and for phenomenologists. For example, the first sentence in the entry on education is: "Phenomenological theories of education have not so far achieved a consistent definition of their methodology and basic concepts." Although the work is well designed and well produced, it is fantastically overpriced, and it can only be recommended to libraries with large budgets that serve patrons already conversant in phenomenology.

—**Richard H. Swain**

1336. Grimes, John. **A Concise Dictionary of Indian Philosophy: Sanskrit Terms Defined in English.** rev. ed. Albany, N.Y., State University of New York Press, 1996. 366p. $78.50; $26.95pa. ISBN 0-7914-3067-7; 0-7914-3068-5pa.

For the beginning student of Indian philosophy who is not a specialist in Sanskrit, Grimes's concise dictionary is a next-to-indispensable study tool. No longer a living language, Sanskrit nevertheless provides the technical vocabulary of Indian philosophy. The dictionary covers many branches of philosophy: cosmology, epistemology, metaphysics, theology, and ethics. It encompasses as well the major schools of classical Indian philosophy; among them Buddhism, Jainism, Yoga, and Vedanta. This revision adds some 500 new terms and additional meanings to terms in the 1st edition, which numbered about 2,500 items.

Terms are entered in Roman transliteration and arranged according to the English alphabet, followed by the rendering in Devanagari script. Definitions, in English, elucidate terms, often delineating subtleties of meaning in different schools of thought. For example, the word *Jiva*, referring to "the individual soul," is defined according to 14 schools. The 15th definition extends the term's etymology and notes similar names, such as *bhotka* and *karta*. Although not substantially changed, this newer edition should be found in libraries that purchased the first edition. Students may want to purchase the paperback edition for personal use.—**Bernice Bergup**

1337. Reese, William L. **Dictionary of Philosophy and Religion: Eastern and Western Thought.** new ed. Atlantic Highlands, N.J., Humanities Press, 1996. 856p. $60.00; $25.00pa. ISBN 0-391-03864-8; 0-391-03865-6pa.

This new edition of a work first published in 1980 (see ARBA 81, entry 1128) not only updates the original with added or revised entries reflecting recent developments, but also expands its coverage, notably by increasing the number of entries relating to Eastern thought. By now, however, it has lost its formerly unique status as a contemporary single-volume, English-language dictionary encompassing both philosophy and religion, due to the entry in that category of Geddes MacGregor's *Dictionary of Religion and Philosophy* in 1989 (see ARBA 91, entry 1414). Yet whereas MacGregor's acknowledged focus is religious studies, with coverage of philosophy playing a subservient role, the reverse was and remains true in Reese's case.

Given his predominantly philosophical orientation, Reese's emphasis on the intellectual aspects of religion (as distinct from, say, its social or institutional aspects) is understandable, as is the relative paucity of entries for second-rank religious thinkers when compared with the generous inclusion of second-rank philosophers. What continues to disappoint most about Reese's dual orientation, however, is his frequent failure, largely uncorrected in this edition, to make connections between the philosophical and religious domains just on those topics where the connections are most important. One could read his article on ethics and never guess at the existence of a vast realm of religious (or, more specifically, Christian, Islamic, or Buddhist) ethics, let alone the extent to which philosophical and religious perspectives intersect, especially in recent years, in the flourishing field of applied ethics. Similarly, one can read Reese on the mind/body problem and find no hint of possible relationships of this philosophical topic to religious doctrines about the soul or an afterlife. This failure to capitalize on his cross-disciplinary opportunities does not render Reese's work valueless but leaves little to recommend it except as a supplement to more standard works in each field. Although solid enough, it is not in the forefront of philosophical, let alone of religious, dictionaries. If funds permit, libraries should acquire at least *The Oxford Companion to Philosophy* (see ARBA 97 entry 1166) or *The Cambridge Dictionary of Philosophy* (see ARBA 97, entry 1159) and a reasonably comprehensive dictionary of religion (e.g., *The Oxford Dictionary of World Religions* [see entry 1357]) before investing in Reese.—**Hans E. Bynagle**

1338. **The Shambhala Encyclopedia of Yoga.** By Georg Feuerstein. Boston, Shambhala, 1997. 357p. illus. maps. $30.00. ISBN 1-57062-137-3.

This one-volume encyclopedia is a revision of Feuerstein's excellent guide to terms and concepts used in Yoga, a major element of Hinduism over several thousand years (see ARBA 91, entry 1405). The author's goal is to provide a comprehensive but accessible reference work to this largely Indian tradition. He succeeds admirably, providing concise yet understandable descriptions of everything from abstract philosophical concepts to practical techniques of body manipulation. The entries, usually fairly brief, include the transliterated Sanskrit terms, their direct English translations, and a paragraph explaining how they relate to other concepts in Yoga. Extensive use is made of cross-references to other entries.

There are several improvements in the new work: More than 2,000 terms are now defined, an increase of nearly 400 entries; a substantial number of entries have been revised for greater clarity; the bibliography has been updated to reflect recent publications; and many of the black-and-white illustrations have been replaced with better-reproduced substitutes. In summary, this is a well-executed and inexpensive revision of a highly regarded reference tool.—**Christopher W. Nolan**

1339. Warburton, Nigel. **Thinking from A to Z.** New York, Routledge, 1996. 138p. $49.95; $9.95pa. ISBN 0-415-09685-5; 0-415-09686-3pa.

What is "humptydumpting"? What is the difference between an informal and a formal fallacy? Warburton answers these questions and others in *Thinking from A to Z*, a 138-page dictionary of critical thinking. Most of the 100-plus entries are at least a page in length, with abundant *see* and *see also* references. According to the author, most entries fall into one of the following four categories: common moves in argument, seductive reasoning errors, techniques of persuasion and avoidance, and psychological factors that are obstacles to clear thought. To his credit and for the reader's benefit, Warburton uses examples to illustrate concepts.

Although the work at hand is designed as a reference book, it can be read from cover to cover and would not be out of place next to monographs on this subject in the general collection. The book is ideal for students who want a quick overview of the subject. However, it also functions well as a reference book, aiding the user who needs to know, for example, the difference between a circular argument and a knockdown argument. To this reviewer's knowledge, *Thinking from A to Z* is the only critical thinking dictionary in or out of print. Librarians who help debate teams or lawyers hone their arguments will want a copy in the reference collection. Those who do not answer many logic, reasoning, or critical thinking questions should buy a copy for the main collection.—**John P. Stierman**

Directories

1340. **Directory of American Philosophers 1996-1997.** 18th ed. Archie J. Bahm and Richard H. Lineback, eds. Bowling Green, Ohio, Philosophy Documentation Center/Bowling Green State University, 1996. 488p. index. $119.00. ISBN 0-912632-57-7.

The 18th edition of this standard work, last reviewed in ARBA 95 (see entry 1430), continues its focus on all aspects of United States and Canadian philosophical education. The arrangement of the volume remains the same as previous editions: philosophy departments are arranged by state or province; followed by institutes, organizations, and societies; and finally by publications. Each entry includes names, addresses, and telephone and fax numbers. For philosophy departments, faculty names with credentials and research interest areas are provided. For the organizations and publications, purpose, activities, and publications or manuscript submission information are covered. Each section has a comprehensive index, which appears at the end of the volume. The brief statistical table mentioned in a previous review is retained in this edition. This directory remains a useful, up-to-date reference source. The primary users of this work will continue to be at colleges and universities.—**Gregory Curtis**

1341. Harris, Nigel G. E. **Professional Codes of Conduct in the United Kingdom: A Directory.** 2d ed. New York, Mansell/Cassell, 1996. 438p. index. $170.00. ISBN 0-7201-2235-X.

This 2d edition substantially revises and enlarges the 1st edition (see ARBA 91, entry 269). The number of entries has increased from 370 to 509, and a random sample indicates that the publisher is correct in stating that 80 percent of the entries have been updated. The entries are numbered and arranged alphabetically by the name of the professional organization. All entries include the address, telephone number, and fax number of the organization, and the professional code is given verbatim for approximately 200 organizations. For the remaining entries, the author has written a brief description of the subjects covered in the code. All codes are current as of 1995. A 20-page introduction discusses the organization and nature of the directory; the nature of professional codes; the differences between codes of ethics, codes of practice, and codes of conduct; and the recent growth in number of national and international codes. A comprehensive subject index refers users to entry numbers in the directory or page number in the introduction.

Harris is a senior lecturer in philosophy at the University of Dundee, Scotland, and he clearly aims beyond simply providing a single source in which one can find a large number of codes. The introduction covers general philosophical issues as well as more practical matters, and the work can be recommended to libraries supporting research in applied ethics as well as those supporting the work of one or more of the professions covered by the codes presented. The directory is well organized, well produced, and well written, and it provides convenient access to information not found in any other source. If a library needed the 1st edition, it will need the 2d edition. However, because the work is expensive, and because it covers only British professional codes, its appeal is limited for most United States libraries. Libraries needing information about professional codes in the United States should consider *Codes of Professional Responsibility* (3d ed.; see ARBA 96, entry 1431). Libraries supporting research in applied ethics should seriously consider purchasing both works.—**Richard H. Swain**

1342. **International Directory of Philosophy and Philosophers 1997-1998.** 10th ed. Ramona Cormier and Richard H. Lineback, eds. Bowling Green, Ohio, Philosophy Documentation Center/Bowling Green State University, 1997. 562p. $99.00. ISBN 0-912632-69-0.

The companion volume to the *Directory of American Philosophers* (see entry 1340), the *International Directory of Philosophy and Philosophers* is the most comprehensive guide to philosophers outside of the United States and Canada currently in print. It is divided into five main sections: universities, centers and institutes, societies, journals, and publishers. These are followed by an alphabetized list of the names and addresses of philosophers and indexes for each of the five sections. Entries for universities include department addresses and telephone numbers (and where applicable, fax numbers and e-mail addresses) as well as the alphabetized names of faculty members, their degrees, and areas of specialization. Entries for centers and institutes include a brief statement of purpose and a list of activities. The journals and publishers sections are the most useful, especially for junior faculty seeking publishing venues. Included in most entries is information on the kinds of manuscripts accepted for publication, the backlog of articles accepted for publication, and the percentage of accepted articles requiring significant revision. Most of the directory's entries are written in English. This highly recommended book is well organized and easy to use.

—**Sandra Adell**

RELIGION

General Works

Bibliography

1343. Arweck, Elisabeth, and Peter B. Clarke. **New Religious Movements in Western Europe: An Annotated Bibliography.** Westport, Conn., Greenwood Press, 1997. 380p. index. (Bibliographies and Indexes in Religious Studies, no.41). $89.50. ISBN 0-313-24324-7.

Intended as a companion volume to Diane Choquette's *New Religious Movements in the United States and Canada* (see ARBA 86, entry 1368), the Arweck and Clarke bibliography is an excellent addition to the study of an often-confusing and controversial topic. The introduction expertly discusses various explanations for the rise of new religious movements (NRMs), what constitutes an NRM, a brief historical overview of major NRMs in specific European countries, and the social impact of NRMs.

The body of the book is the annotated bibliography, in alphabetic order by main entry. Entries cover 1960 to the present and most Western European languages. All annotations are in English, and titles of foreign-language entries are given in the original language, with a bracketed English translation following. NRMs deriving from all sources are covered, whether from Christianity, Judaism, Eastern religions (the introduction has a particularly strong discussion of NRMs of Japanese origin), Paganism, New Age, or other origins.

Good indexing is vital to a bibliography. Arweck and Clarke have done a thorough job, providing a publications index, a periodicals index, a movements and personal names index, and a subject index. Although each entry has a unique number assigned to it, the index refers to page numbers. If a future edition is contemplated, it would be preferable to index by unique number, with a brief note at the beginning of the indexes stating that this is the case. A citation in the introduction listing two authors and a year was difficult to find because the bibliographic entry was by the second author's name.

The authors are experts in the field of NRMs and are coeditors of the *Journal of Contemporary Religion*. They have produced an excellent work of scholarship, and *New Religious Movements in Western Europe* is recommended for libraries with collections in religion or sociology.—**Mary A. Axford**

1344. Chidester, David, and others. **African Traditional Religion in South Africa: An Annotated Bibliography.** Westport, Conn., Greenwood Press, 1997. 462p. index. (Bibliographies and Indexes in Religious Studies, no.42). $79.50. ISBN 0-313-30474-2.

This collaboration by several faculty at the Institute for Comparative Religion in Southern Africa is the first of three proposed volumes. The two forthcoming will investigate Christianity and Islam, Hinduism, and Judaism, respectively (see entry 1345). This premier volume gathers 600 sources on indigenous religions and annotates them carefully. The books, articles, and theses included are introduced in excellent essays and annotations that carve out and delineate this emerging study. All relevant material on Khoisan, Xhosa, Zulu, Sotho-Tswana, Swazi, Tsonga, and Venda traditions are included. Each section can serve as a concise presentation of that tradition's history, experiences, practices, and beliefs. The index is particularly useful for tracking cross-tradition themes and issues. Copious information is found in this bibliography, and scholars and students of comparative religions and African religions will find much to induce further investigation.—**Linda L. Lam-Easton**

1345. Chidester, David, Judy Tobler, and Darrel Wratten. **Islam, Hinduism, and Judaism in South Africa: An Annotated Bibliography.** Westport, Conn., Greenwood Press, 1997. 295p. index. (Bibliographies and Indexes in Religious Studies, no.44). $75.00. ISBN 0-313-30472-6.

This collaboration by several faculty members at the Institute for Comparative Religion in Southern Africa is the second of three proposed volumes. The other two investigate Christianity and traditional African regions (see entry 1344). This study of three global religions—Islam, Hinduism, and Judaism—describes the immigrant origins, minority status, global connections, and strong local communities that each of the three developed. The books, articles, and theses included are introduced in excellent essays and annotations that carve out and delineate this emerging study. All relevant material on the traditions and their communities in various geographic regions of South Africa is provided. Each section can serve as a concise presentation of that tradition's history, experiences, practices, and beliefs. The index is particularly useful for tracking cross-tradition themes and issues. An abundance of information is found in this bibliography, and scholars and students of comparative religions and African religions will find much to induce further investigation.—**Linda L. Lam-Easton**

1346. Johnston, William M. **Recent Reference Books in Religion: A Guide for Students, Scholars, Researchers, Buyers, & Readers.** Downers Grove, Ill., InterVarsity Press, 1996. 318p. index. $34.99. ISBN 0-8308-1440-X.

Although Johnston's earlier books were in social and intellectual history, here he makes a foray into the field of religion with a guide to reference books for students, scholars, buyers, or simply readers in the discipline. He lists and assesses 318 reference works (most in English) published since 1970 that deal with ancient or modern religion. Introductory materials extol the value of reference works, explain recent developments in this genre, and set forth a typology for reference materials. The body of the volume organizes reference books under five headings: world religions; Christianity; other prophetic religions (i.e., Judaism and Islam); Asian religions; and alternative approaches (e.g., philosophy of religion). In each case, bibliographic information about the work and a summary evaluation bracket Johnston's assessment of its scope, strengths and weaknesses, and competitors. A list of the author's favorite reference books, descriptions of reference works that remain to be written, and five indexes conclude the book.

Although Johnston's effort is modestly successful, it attempts to do too much for too many. Its inclusion of important, scholarly reference works in French and German suggests that an audience of academic specialists is in mind, but the inclusion of extremely elementary "who's who in the Bible" publications and an introductory textbook to Bible study suggests first-year college students as readers. Serious students of the Bible will be disappointed to find that reference works for interpreting Hebrew and Greek biblical texts have been excluded, and only one-volume commentaries are treated. In addition, the most important English dictionary for the field of pastoral counseling was omitted. Even though the evaluations are often on target, sometimes the praise is too effusive, and the criticisms seem ill-founded. Finally, although the writing style is typically lively, it sometimes falters as the author tries to avoid the inevitable tedium of his genre. Even though the reference or acquisitions librarian or perhaps those scholars unfamiliar with reference resources in religion may find Johnston's work helpful, it seems less likely that the book will attract a strong following among beginning students in religion or those students and scholars who are more conversant with the field.—**M. Patrick Graham**

Biography

1347. Haught, James A. **2000 Years of Disbelief: Famous People with the Courage to Doubt.** Buffalo, N.Y., Prometheus Books, 1996. 334p. illus. index. $26.95. ISBN 1-57392-067-3.

As the end of the millennium approaches, society is struggling once again to reassess its values and institutions. Religion finds itself on a collision course with what Stephen Carter, in his best-selling book, calls *The Culture of Disbelief* (Basic Books, 1993). Thus, Haught's new book, *2000 Years of Disbelief*, seems an appropriate addition to the societal discourse. The book jacket, with its black-and-white portraits, suggests that the beliefs of historical figures will be examined. Its stated purpose is "to assure thinking people that they needn't apologize if they can't believe mystical claims" and purports to do so by using "the most reliable evidence," in other words, the words of notable figures.

Organized chronologically, with sections on ancient rationalism, the Renaissance, the European Enlightenment, American rationalists, and the nineteenth and twentieth centuries, each chapter presents a short biographical sketch of prominent philosophers, historians, politicians, writers, and artists of the era. Each biography, accompanied by a black-and-white portrait, is followed by a list of quotations taken from the individual's writings. The content of the volume does not, however, contribute significantly to an understanding of skeptical thought. The biographies focus less on the individual's beliefs and the historical context of their ideology than on the difficulties encountered because of their skepticism. The lists of quotations, with little effort to place them in context, offer only cursory insight into the individual's thoughts. The failure to provide complete bibliographic citations for either the author's claims or the subject's quotations is disturbing. The index, solely one of names, provides little access to ideas and prevents the reader from linking the ideas of one individual or era to another.

Although this work may lead readers to further investigate the beliefs of some of the world's greatest thinkers, *Be Reasonable: Selected Quotations for Inquiring Minds* (see ARBA 95, entry 1433) and *The Encyclopedia of Unbelief* (see ARBA 87, entry 756) provide more comprehensive biographical sketches, fuller quotations with complete bibliographic information, and well-documented discussions of the history of disbelief. [R: RBB, 1 April 97, p. 1358]—**Debra S. Van Tassel**

Dictionaries and Encyclopedias

1348. Breuilly, Elizabeth, Joanne O'Brien, and Martin Palmer. **Religions of the World: The Illustrated Guide to Origins, Beliefs, Traditions, & Festivals.** New York, Facts on File, 1997. 160p. illus. maps. index. $29.95. ISBN 0-8160-3723-X.

Facts on File's reputation for solid, well-produced basic reference works is exemplified with this illustrated introduction to world religion. Although not exhaustive, it presents an overview of the historical development and current state of religion, followed by chapters on each of the Abrahamic faiths (Judaism, Christianity, and Islam), the Vedic faiths (Hinduism, Buddhism, and Jainism), and four other major religious traditions (Shinto, Taoism, Sikhism, and Baha'i).

In introducing the sections on the Abrahamic faiths and the Vedic faiths, the authors highlight both the common heritage and the distinct developments of the traditions. The chapters on each of the particular faiths describes clearly and concisely their major beliefs, practices, and festivals. In addition, the authors have attempted to present each tradition as objectively as possible. Numerous photographs, drawings, maps, and charts illustrate what is presented in the text. Most helpful are the religious calendars (given for all groups but Jainism, Shinto, and Baha'i) and maps showing religious population distribution.

This work is authoritative enough for academic reference collections, yet it is presented simply enough for school libraries. It should be a welcome addition in libraries of all sizes.—**Craig W. Beard**

1349. Brockman, Norbert C. **Encyclopedia of Sacred Places.** Santa Barbara, Calif., ABC-CLIO, 1997. 342p. illus. maps. index. $65.00. ISBN 0-87436-830-8.

Containing 200 entries, this encyclopedia of sacred places provides a simple ready-reference to those who encounter place-names in their reading and study and need a concise understanding of them. It purports to contain both ancient and modern, grand and modest sites that humans have consecrated as special. Some sites are natural and sacred for their uniqueness, and some are historical or human-made. Along with the historical and cultural perspectives, the author offers firsthand descriptions and travel tips as a result of his personal visits to many of these places. A physical description of the site and details of its construction are also included, as well as the site's place in a larger context of religious activity, such as pilgrimage. Most valuable is the further resources section on each site, which cross-references as well as includes outside references. Appendixes group the sites by religion and geographic location, and this makes the volume even more useful for the traveler.—**Linda L. Lam-Easton**

1350. **Dictionary of Mission: Theology, History, Perspectives.** Karl Müller, Theo Sundermeier, Stephen B. Bevans, and Richard H. Bliese, eds. Maryknoll, N.Y., Orbis Books, 1997. 518p. (The American Society of Missiology Series). $50.00. ISBN 1-57075-148-X.

Though the title of this volume indicates that it is a dictionary, it is more typical of a one-volume encyclopedia. Based on a 1987 German work considered to be one of the highlights of mission theology literature, the present volume is not only a translation of the original but a fairly substantial revision, with deletions of outdated material, the addition of new materials within the articles, and entirely new articles. Such phenomena as the rapid advances in communications, the change to a global economy, and the burgeoning of Pentecostal and charismatic groups brought about significant changes in the social, political, and religious milieu in which missiology is studies. Thus, articles have been added on such topics as globalization, reconciliation, and ecology.

The English edition of this work was largely carried out by the editorial staff of the Catholic-sponsored Orbis Books; however, it was aided by the Chicago Center for Global Ministries, a group consisting of Catholic and Protestant institutions devoted to ecumenical theological education.

The scholarly, well-written articles are arranged alphabetically. Preceding each of the articles in bold typeface is a numbered list of the topics covered, making it easy to find a specific section in the text by number. Throughout the text, arrow signs are used to indicated cross-references. Each articles is signed by the author and followed by a lengthy bibliography of works in several languages, although the majority appear to be in English. Following the prefatory material in the beginning of the book is a list of more than 200 periodicals and documents that are referred to. The end of the volume provides a list of contributors with a brief identification statement and the titles of the articles written. This excellent work is a must for theological schools and seminaries but would be useful for academic libraries with religious studies programs as well.—**Lucille Whalen**

1351. **An Encyclopedia of Archetypal Symbolism, Volume 1.** [1997 ed.] Boston, Shambhala, 1997. 510p. illus. index. $125.00. ISBN 1-57062-250-7.

The Archive for Research in Archetypal Symbolism (ARAS), formed exclusively to collect, describe, and disseminate archetypal images, presents its long awaited reprint of its initial 1991 offering. Archetypal images, whether described by Carl Jung or Joseph Campbell, are images that stand for meaning in some cultures. Generally, these images are universally significant in the culture where they originated.

This ARAS volume is richly photographed, beautifully crafted, and well written. Nearly 100 images are included and categorized into 15 subdivisions, with Eastern influences predominating. Included are the "Colossal Wheel," "Brahma Offering Lotus," "Lion-man," "Ganesa," "Mushhush," "Sisiutl," and more. Fans of Campbell and Bill Moyers's program and accompanying book, *The Power of Myth* (Doubleday, 1988), as well as serious scholars of Jung and Mircea Eliade, will find valuable information in this work. Even small libraries serving only a few thousand patrons may want to consider the volume for its rich detail and exquisite renderings.

The accompanying text provides the right balance of scholarship and intrigue to meet the needs of every user. Usually full-color photographs are followed by four-page historical identifications, descriptive art historian comments, cultural context of the archetype, and the archetypal commentary. Given current New Age thinking, this may prove the perfect transition: a text that grants everything to believe in while requiring almost nothing by which to live.—**Mark Y. Herring**

1352. **An Encyclopedia of Archetypal Symbolism, Volume 2: The Body.** By George R. Elder. Boston, Shambhala, 1996. 452p. illus. index. $125.00. ISBN 1-57062-096-2.

The 2d volume from the Archive for Research in Archetypal Symbolism (ARAS) brings readers a picture trove filled with more than 13,000 symbols. This volume focuses on the body and each one of its archetypal appendages. Thus, in 12 chapters, readers will find meaning in body, bones, eyes, ears, hands, and more. There is even a chapter on the transformed or resurrected body.

The format of this volume is identical to its predecessor. The usually full-page symbol or archetype is followed by a two- to five-page summary that provides rich historical detail, cultural context, and the symbol's commentary from an art historian's point of view. Each entry has a short bibliography of cited and uncited sources. An expansive index follows.

Any patron will find useful information in this volume and its companion. The series resembles *Encyclopedia of World Art*, but in symbols alone. History, sociology, art, literature, and religion are examples of the subjects that are served by these volumes. Readers wishing to better understand any literature written before 1850 will want a set of their own.

Since the center's collection is available for viewing in only one place—the C. G. Jung Foundation of New York—this volume and its previous one now make available to any library (or patron) a private showing. If all subsequent volumes are as well done as this one and the 1991 reprint released this year, these sets will represent an important and perhaps soon-to-become standard source for the growing interest in symbols.—**Mark Y. Herring**

1353. **Encyclopedia of Religion.** [CD-ROM]. New York, Macmillan Library Reference/Simon & Schuster Macmillan, 1996. Minimum system requirements (Windows version): IBM or compatible 386. CD-ROM drive. Windows 3.1. 4MB RAM. 2MB hard disk space. Minimum system requirements (Macintosh version): System 6.0. CD-ROM drive. 4MB RAM. 2MB hard disk space. Color monitor. $325.00.

Back in 1987, when Macmillan's *Encyclopedia of Religion* was released in print format, it won the American Library Association's Dartmouth Medal, and *Booklist* called it "indispensable for students and schools in many disciplines." Originally published as a 17-volume set, the 8 million-word work is indeed comprehensive. The text is scholarly, yet approachable by high school students. At $325, the CD-ROM is far more affordable than the $700 selling price of the print version.

Users may search the entire database or by title entry, author, or abbreviations. Typing a word brings up a scrollable list of words contained in the encyclopedia. A keyword search may employ a variety of sophisticated functions: Boolean operators, nesting, wildcards, word stems, and phrase searching. A 12-button toolbelt runs along the left side of the screen, allowing users to access contents, search features, and previous or next records; display hits; or tag, print, save, backtrack, trail, or exit. The "Synoptic Outline" offers subject searching and a general view of the contents of the encyclopedia. It is divided into 2 parts: "Religions" (containing 44 sections) and the "History of Religion." By double-clicking on any of the subsections, users may jump to the corresponding articles.

Even though the CD-ROM has fine potential for the more patient or scholarly user, it is neither attractive nor easy to use. Aside from its one opening color image, the text of the database is presented in plain, rather unclear, black print on a white background. Search areas offer few user cues. The functions of the toolbelt icons are not obvious. An alphabetic search function allows users to double-click on a letter to browse for an entry, but this feature is clunky. Users must browse through every entry under the letter they are searching to get to the information they need. Users should be able to type an entire word to get closer to an entry, rather than browsing through all the "T" entries with the accompanying text to get from "Tabari" to "Towers." Text sections are divided into small discrete units, each with its own blue heading. These divisions distract the reader and make it difficult to read long passages of text. For example, the heading "Encyclopedia of Religion, TABOO, Vol. 14, p. 233" breaks up the article on taboo seven times before it changes to reflect a move to page 234.

Macmillan's *Encyclopedia of Religion* is an authoritative standard reference tool that belongs in most academic and many high school libraries in either its print or CD-ROM formats. The depth of research is not duplicated in other sources. Although keyword searching makes the information in this disc far more accessible, the product is seriously limited in attractiveness by the style of the interface and the facility of some of the search features, particularly the alphabetic function. The CD-ROM version of *Encyclopedia of Religion* is recommended, with reservations, for academic libraries and for high school libraries where religion is a major curricular component.—**Joyce Kasman Valenza**

1354. **Encyclopedia of Religious Controversies in the United States.** George H. Shriver and Bill J. Leonard, eds. Westport, Conn., Greenwood Press, 1997. 542p. index. $99.50. ISBN 0-313-29691-X.

The United States is a religiously pluralistic society that has experienced many religious controversies from its colonial origins in the seventeenth century through the present. Shriver and Leonard have conceived and edited a useful reference work that admirably surveys the main topics of U.S. religious controversies. It consists of 400 entries by 53 qualified contributors and covers people (Wallie Amos Criswell, Joseph Smith, Jr.), concepts (anti-Semitism, feminism), groups (Branch Davidians, Jehovah's Witnesses), and events (Antinomian Crisis, Scopes Trial). Individual entries range from about 250 to 1,500 words and include a bibliography for further reading. Cross-references are provided to related entries. A master bibliography of about 350 books on religious controversies and a general index concludes the volume. One slight flaw is the author of the "Branch Davidians" entry's use of the term "ATF Invasion." This fine encyclopedia belongs in any library with an interest in U.S. religion.—**Ronald H. Fritze**

1355. Guiley, Rosemary Ellen. **Encyclopedia of Angels.** New York, Facts on File, 1996. 214p. illus. index. $40.00. ISBN 0-8160-2988-1.

With all the references to angels in today's media, it was inevitable that an encyclopedia on the subject would be produced. *A Dictionary of Angels* by Gustav Davidson (Free Press, 1967) lacks the historical, philosophical, and biographical aspects that this encyclopedia provides. Guiley, who wrote *Angels of Mercy* (Pocket Books, 1994) and *Harper's Encyclopedia of Mystic & Paranormal Experience* (see ARBA 92, entry 765), was able to build on her knowledge and research for the volume at hand.

Some articles are short, but others extend to several pages. They cover individual angels, the beliefs of important philosophers who were concerned with angelology, and even extraterrestrial and near-death experiences. Included also are references to angels as they are found in various religions: Islam, Hinduism, Christianity, Judaism, Zoroastrianism, and Tantric Buddhism. Most articles conclude with "Further Readings," a bibliography that reflects the author's diligent research. Extensive cross-referencing and a separate index simplify the search for a specific fact. Illustrations are black-and-white, and some are quite dark, especially those reproduced from woodcuts, but each one's source is identified.

Several typographic errors and some minor factual errors were discovered. The article on Mormonism states that "it is better known as the Church of Christ of Latter-day Saints," omitting the "Jesus." *Choirs* is defined as "a band of singers," which Guiley states is too limiting when describing angel activities. Even a desk dictionary gives a second definition, "a division of angels." Although these are minor mistakes, of concern is that there may be larger ones that a nonspecialist may not detect. This encyclopedia is recommended for popular collections, not for theological libraries, which are better served by *The New Catholic Encyclopedia*.—**Sara R. Mack**

1356. **The Illustrated Encyclopedia of World Religions.** Chris Richards, ed. Rockport, Mass., Element Books, 1997. 256p. illus. maps. index. $34.95pa. ISBN 1-85230-997-0.

This volume is an excellent reference for those wanting to explore a variety of religious experiences. Unlike other one-volume reference works, such as the *Abingdon Dictionary of Living Religions* (1981) or the *HarperCollins Dictionary of Religion* (1995), which offer succinct, academic entries on a wide range of topics and concepts, this work is a compilation of 13 broad essays by various researchers examining the following faiths: primal religions, Hinduism, Judaism, Confucianism, Buddhism, Jainism, Christianity, Islam, Shinto, Sikhism, Taoism, the Baha'i faith, and Rastafarianism. There is a special section briefly defining 22 "Other Sects and Denominations" (e.g., Amish, Omotokyo, and humanism).

The essays, generally about 20 pages in length, are objective yet sympathetic summaries of key features of the history, tenets, and influence of each belief system. The introduction briefly explores the role of religion in addressing basic human questions and in world affairs today. Each essay is strengthened by many full-color paintings and photographs, excellently reproduced, which give glimpses of significant rituals, locales, and texts. As the general introduction points out, most of the contributors are believers of the religion; the essays occasionally present personal statements to clarify key points, but these never intrude on the evenhanded tone of the discussions. A guide to "Further Reading" offers a half-dozen additional books on each of the major faiths discussed. This volume would be a useful addition to church, public, high school, and undergraduate libraries.—**Christopher Baker**

1357. **The Oxford Dictionary of World Religions.** John Bowker, ed. New York, Oxford University Press, 1997. 1111p. index. $45.00. ISBN 0-19-213965-7.

Comprehensive one-volume dictionaries of religion have not been as plentiful as one may expect, but recent years have seen a minor proliferation in this genre. It includes *The Continuum Dictionary of Religion* (see ARBA 95, entry 1440); the *Larousse Dictionary of Beliefs and Religions* (see ARBA 95, entry 1443); the *HarperCollins Dictionary of Religions* (1995); and a revision of the 1984 *Facts on File Dictionary of Religions*, retitled *New Dictionary of Religions* (see ARBA 97, entry 1179). Now Oxford University Press weighs in with a contender whose 1,111 pages and approximately 8,200 entries probably justify its dust-jacket boast of providing "unrivalled coverage" (approached only by the HarperCollins title with a few more pages but far fewer entries). Many libraries, therefore, will want to find a place for this newcomer even if they already own one or more of the aforementioned works.

In the distinguished tradition of *The Oxford Dictionary of the Christian Church* (3d ed.; see entry 1389) and the Oxford Companion series, this dictionary offers concise encyclopedic coverage of its field: key concepts and doctrines; leading teachers and thinkers; sacred texts; sacred sites; submovements (sects, schools, denominations, and the like); and religious practices in all of the world's major religions, as well as general religious concepts (e.g., prayer, salvation, sin) and teachings and traditions, shared or diverse, regarding moral and behavioral issues (e.g., abortion, alcohol, just war, sex). The 7 consultant editors and the 80 or so contributors listed at the front bespeak a high level of authoritativeness for the volume as a whole. Their specific contributions, however, are not disclosed. Articles are unsigned, and chief editor Bowker, in his preface, appears to take a great deal of personal responsibility for their content. Be that as it may, a vast amount of solid and useful information is packed into the work's densely filled pages.

As for claims to impartiality (on the jacket) and unbiased treatment (on the publisher's flyer), these can largely be credited, although not without exception. On most matters, the teachings of particular religions are presented as they are, without judgment. Evenhandedness sometimes emerges in unexpected ways; for example, 30 percent of the article on Jesus is devoted to the Islamic view of him. Yet on some topics, sides are clearly taken. The article on feminine symbols and religion is a case in point, as is that on God, which is shot through with its author's own philosophizing, quite beyond what various religions have proclaimed on the subject. (Why, incidentally, are there no entries for either gods (plural) or goddesses?) The editor's self-confessed highly personal selectivity in the brief bibliographies accompanying most articles also raises some questions about balance and neutrality. These caveats aside, *The Oxford Dictionary of World Religions* undoubtedly merits wide distribution and frequent consultation.—**Hans E. Bynagle**

1358. **Westminster Dictionary of Theological Terms.** By Donald K. McKim. Louisville, Ky., Westminster/John Knox Press, 1996. 310p. $30.00; $20.00pa. ISBN 0-664-22089-4; 0-664-25511-6.

McKim, dean and professor of theology at Memphis Theological Seminary and editor of the acclaimed *Encyclopedia of the Reformed Faith* (see ARBA 93, entry 1422), has here compiled a collection of more than 5,500 definitions of terms in theology and related disciplines. The work is broad in its scope; terms cover biblical studies, church government, church history, ethics, evangelicalism, fundamentalism, liturgy, ministry, philosophy, social science, spirituality, worship, and religion in general. Terms representing many varieties of theology (e.g., Lutheran, Reformed, Roman Catholic, and Wesleyan, as well as liberation and feminist theologies) likewise appear; but proper names of persons—living or dead—are not included. The entries supply linguistic derivations of the term (where appropriate and within parentheses) and a one- or two-sentence neutral definition. The primary focus of what a term means is centered on its use in the Christian theological tradition but not all meanings of an item are always presented. Some *see* references from one form of a word to another are used, but cross-references per se are not. While the coverage of terms treated is exceptional, there are some words and expressions appearing in definitions that are not defined on their own (e.g., *meaninglessness* and *natural virtues*).

Westminster/John Knox Press has published a number of other dictionaries (e.g., *Christian Theology* [rev. ed., 1983]; *Christian Ethics* [1986]; and *Feminist Theologies* [see ARBA 97, entry 1177]); this new one concentrates on definition rather than exposition. The definitions are not encumbered with a theological angle, liberal or conservative. This dictionary is a superb work. It deserves praise for its conciseness, lucidity, and inclusiveness and should be a high-priority purchase for any theological—or theologian's—library.—**Glenn R. Wittig**

Handbooks and Yearbooks

1359. **Anthropology of Religion: A Handbook.** Stephen D. Glazier, ed. Westport, Conn., Greenwood Press, 1997. 542p. index. $99.50. ISBN 0-313-28351-6.

This reference book on new approaches to the anthropology of religion is presented in a case study format. It surveys some manifestations of religion in diverse cultural contexts by the use of themes but does not survey the various theoretical fields that interpret them. What is truly new in anthropological research is the striking array of new methodological approaches to themes. Although this thematic approach may be useful to some, this volume makes a selection of studies of themes that have been treated elsewhere in more full-blown form.

The themes presented are ritual, little and great traditions, shamanism, and an overview. The selections within each theme are too general to be of any more than introductory use. Most of the bibliographies stop in the late 1980s. The introduction and its discussion of other anthologies is helpful. The book, although it could serve as an addition to a complete library, should not be the only source on such a fascinating subject.—**Linda L. Lam-Easton**

1360. Barrett, David V. **Sects, 'Cults,' and Alternative Religions: A World Survey and Sourcebook.** London, Blandford/Cassell; distr., New York, Sterling Publishing, 1996. 320p. illus. index. $24.95. ISBN 0-7137-2567-2.

The author of this book is a graduate of religious studies and has taught, researched, and written in this field for a number of years. Here, Barrett examines the beliefs and practices of nontraditional religious groups, often viewed as "radical fringe groups." In an effort to provide unbiased material, he used a survey method to gather information directly from variant movements; thus he is able to present controversial issues in his text along with official responses. The book is organized in 5 sections, initially covering a brief history of world religions as a background for what follows: Christian origins and offshoots; Eastern movements, such as Hare Krishna and Divine Light; esoteric (Theosophical Society, Rosicrucians) and neopagan (Wicca, Shamanism) groups; and finally, personal development organizations, including Scientology and such psychology movements as Neuro-Linguistic Programming and Transcendental Meditation. In each case, Barrett gives a history of the movement and a summary of its beliefs and practices. He concludes with a lengthy essay on the general condition of religious movements, their public image, the concept of "brainwashing" indoctrination and deprogramming, and cult-watching organizations. A list of contact addresses follows the "Notes" section. This collection is representative rather than comprehensive, but still a useful resource for public libraries. (See also *The Illustrated Encyclopedia of Active New Religions, Sects, and Cults* in ARBA 94, entry 1529.) [R: RBB, July 97, p. 1838]—**Jean Engler**

1361. Bowker, John. **World Religions.** New York, DK Publishing, 1997. 200p. illus. maps. index. $34.95. ISBN 0-7894-1439-2.

DK Publishing has produced another eye-catching, informative volume in *World Religions*. The author won the HarperCollins Religious Book Award in 1993 for his work, *The Meanings of Death* (Cambridge University Press). Bowker served as dean of Trinity College, Cambridge, and is currently Gresham Professor of Divinity at Gresham College, London. In the United States, Bowker is an adjunct professor of religious studies at the University of Pennsylvania. At the end of the book, the publisher acknowledges experts consulted in each area.

World Religions looks at the beliefs and practices of many different religions, from the ancient Egyptians through Zoroastrianism and the major faiths practiced today—Christianity, Judaism, Hinduism, Buddhism, Jainism, Sikhism, and Islam. Each of the major faiths is examined through its sacred texts, imagery, key beliefs, and religious artifacts. The author's preface "What Is Religion?" successfully makes the transition to the subsequent chapters, each page generously illustrated with detailed annotations of superb reproductions of the symbolism and meaning of religious imagery and iconography. Of special interest is the section examining the Golden Rule as it exists in each of the religions. The appendixes contain useful religious timelines and maps. The work concludes with a bibliography on each religion's history, beliefs and practices, and art and architecture.

While the illustrations are stunning, the scope is somewhat limited. Macmillan's 16-volume *Encyclopedia of Religion* (see ARBA 88, entry 1392) is preferred for more in-depth discussion. DK's *World Religions*, however, is highly recommended for a colorful and informative overview of the topic and should be purchased both as a reference and as a circulating item for middle and secondary schools and all public libraries.—**Sharon Thomerson**

1362. **How to Be a Perfect Stranger: A Guide to Etiquette in Other People's Religious Ceremonies.** Arthur J. Magida, ed. Woodstock, Vt., Jewish Lights Publishing, 1996. 417p. $24.95. ISBN 1-879045-39-7.

1363. **How to Be a Perfect Stranger, Volume 2: A Guide to Etiquette in Other People's Religious Ceremonies.** Stuart M. Matlins and Arthur J. Magida, eds. Woodstock, Vt., Jewish Lights Publishing, 1997. 396p. $24.95. ISBN 1-879045-63-X.

What most impresses the reader of these two volumes are the endorsements from so many religious leaders. Leaders of Interfaith Alliances, Institutes of Christian-Jewish Studies, Muslim-Christian Studies, Centers for Jewish-Muslim Understanding, and the National Council of Churches all praise the work as groundbreaking.

Based on the responses of authorities in 37 traditions, the 2 books cover the pragmatic, not theological, aspects of the various practices. Each tradition is examined in terms of a short history and beliefs; the basic services (including proper guest attire, behavior, guidelines, and advice); special vocabulary; holy days and festivals (birth, marriage, initiation, funerals, and mourning); and home ceremonies and celebrations. The 1st volume was named best reference book of the year, and *Volume 2* is made with the same high quality. The handbooks are a pleasure to use.—**Linda L. Lam-Easton**

1364. Hubbard, Benjamin J., John T. Hatfield, and James A. Santucci. **America's Religions: An Educator's Guide to Beliefs and Practices.** Englewood, Colo., Teacher Ideas Press/Libraries Unlimited, 1997. 162p. index. $25.00pa. ISBN 1-56308-469-4.

This guide is offered to educators to help them avoid unknowingly offending the cultural and religious sensibilities of their students. The orientation of the book seems to be mainly for teachers in the primary and secondary grades of the public schools, and it is filled with admonitions regarding the separation of church and state and respecting the diversity of the classroom. The religious traditions treated include Baha'i, Buddhism, Chinese religions, Christianity, fundamentalism, Hinduism, Islam, Jainism, Judaism, Native American religions, New Age religion, secular humanism/atheism, Sikhism, and Unitarian Universalism. The section on fundamentalism is devoted primarily to Christian fundamentalism, but the broader aspects of this religious phenomenon are also recognized. In the chapter devoted to Christianity, five to seven pages are given to Protestantism and Roman Catholicism each, and similar amounts are given to such religious groups as Christian Science, Jehovah's Witnesses, Mormonism, and Adventism. Typically, each religion is treated in terms of its origins, sacred writings, practices, main subgroups, common stereotypes, classroom concerns, and population data, and suggestions are offered for further reading.

The book is clearly written, and the authors made use of appropriate authorities to review for accuracy their discussions of various religious groups treated. As with any work of this sort, the reader should not expect much more than a cursory and superficial treatment of complex religious beliefs. Although some Protestants may object to the short shrift that they receive, this is probably because they constitute the majority in the United States and their beliefs and practices are perceived by the authors as less problematic for public school teachers than those of the other groups, which often are at variance with common U.S. public practice. Sometimes this cursory treatment is confusing (e.g., Christian Church

[Disciples of Christ] is listed under the Baptist subgroup of Protestants [p. 60], but then "Churches of Christ, 3 million" appears under "Population Data" [p. 64]; the two are related, but the authors do not indicate how). The book is most appropriate for primary and secondary school libraries.—**M. Patrick Graham**

1365. Kellner, Mark A. **God on the Internet.** Foster City, Calif., IDG Books Worldwide, 1996. 308p. illus. index. $24.99pa. ISBN 1-56884-843-9.

Beginning users will find this book useful in that it discusses the basics of getting online, such as hardware, online services, etc. However, this makes it a little less appealing to the experienced online junkie.

Any book concerning the Internet has the distinct disadvantage of being hopelessly outdated within hours of its publication. This work is a good example. Sites such as Apple's "EWorld," which was eliminated last year, are given much coverage and make the book that much less useful. To its credit, the book covers areas such as the major online services and the major religions of the world. Much space is used on screen shots, which can best be described as filler. Why so many computer books do this is a mystery, especially when almost all of the screens pictured have changed several times since the book was published. This book serves a psychological purpose. There is at last a book about religion and the Internet, and this may give comfort to those uncomfortable with using computer-based reference tools. An unintended benefit of the book is that it documents the state of the Internet at a certain time. It serves as a snapshot of what was available online about religion in 1995 and 1996.—**Bob Craigmile**

1366. Melton, J. Gordon, Phillip Charles Lucas, and Jon R. Stone. **Prime-Time Religion: An Encyclopedia of Religious Broadcasting.** Phoenix, Ariz., Oryx Press, 1997. 413p. illus. index. $64.95. ISBN 0-89774-902-2.

"Religious radio programming is as old as radio itself" (p. xii), and there has been a religious presence in television since the early 1950s. Melton, who has been one of the most prolific investigators of the U.S. religious scene, turns his attention (along with Lucas and Stone) to religious broadcasting. This encyclopedia focuses on people (e.g., Billy Graham, Mother Angelica, Oral Roberts); programs (e.g., *Focus on the Family*, *Insight for Living*, *The 700 Club*); and organizations (e.g., Christian Broadcasting Network, National Religious Broadcasters, Trinity Broadcasting Network) that have had a major impact in the field. Although the emphasis is on Christian broadcasting in the United States (simply due to the realities of things rather than bias), non-Christian personalities, such as W. Deen Muhammad and H. Spencer Lewis, are included, as are ministers—Nora Lam and Dick Sheppard, for example—and ministries outside the United States. Following the alphabetically arranged entries are eight appendices and an index.

One of the hallmarks of Melton's works is objectivity. The writing tells it like it is, reporting the facts (although not in a dry, uninteresting way) and pulling no punches (but not in a hostile way). The same style infuses *Prime-Time Religion* as well. As with other books Melton has worked on, this one will likely appear in successive revised editions with updated information, new personalities, previously overlooked material, and more photographs of biographees. Yet even in its premier edition, this is a well-researched, well-written, and interesting work, recommended for academic and public libraries.

—**Craig W. Beard**

1367. **On Common Ground: World Religions in America.** [CD-ROM]. New York, Columbia University Press, 1997. Minimum system requirements (Windows version): IBM or compatible 486/33MHz. Double-speed CD-ROM drive. 8MB RAM. 640 x 480, 256-color monitor. 16-bit sound card. Speakers or headphones. Minimum system requirements (Macintosh version): 68030. Double-speed CD-ROM drive. System 7.1. 8MB RAM. Color monitor. $155.00/single user; $175.00/2-5 users; $195.00/unlimited networking. ISBN 0-231-10898-2.

An outstanding accomplishment that embellishes the true meaning of the phrase "multimedia reference," *On Common Ground* is a must-have for any library, school or organization needing resources about the religious diversity in the United States. The all-in-one compact disc makes it easy to install and use.

The information is divided into three sections: "A New Religious Landscape," "America's Many Religions" (presenting 15 religious traditions in the United States), and "Encountering Religious Diversity." There are cross-references to articles, sounds, music, graphics, and videos as well as glossaries, documents, and bibliographies. A directory showing locations of various religious centers around the United States is included, and an attempt is being made to update the information through the use of an online component connected to the Pluralism Project Website.

The presentation—using audio explanations and video images as well as text—makes the product seem more like an informative speech and gives the data an interesting documentary appeal. Developed from the work of Diana L. Eck and the Pluralism Project at Harvard University, *On Common Ground* will be an excellent resource.—**Mary L. Trenerry**

1368. Parker, Philip M. **Religious Cultures of the World: A Statistical Reference.** Westport, Conn., Greenwood Press, 1997. 144p. index. (Cross-Cultural Statistical Encyclopedia of the World, v.1). $69.50. ISBN 0-313-29768-1.

Recognizing that religion often plays a critical role in cross-cultural comparisons, the author, a professor at the European Institute of Business in Fontainbleau, France, has presented for the year 1994 some 120,000 statistics in various tables showing comparisons among religious cultures and some 300 variables for more than 400 ethnic groups. This is a work intended for those researchers who need to make quantifiable comparisons based on religious cultures of the world. The main part of the book (chapters 3 through 9) covers such areas as climatic resources, demography and sociology, land resources, and economics as they relate to various religious groups. The reader must rely on information in the first 2 chapters, however, to use the statistical material effectively. They detail the methodologies employed along with the caveats and limitations of estimation procedures used and a suggested physioeconomic framework that enables the user to overcome problems generally encountered in the use of cross-cultural studies. Included in the 1st chapter also are 4 appendixes. It is not clear why this type of material, which ordinarily would go at the end of the book, is placed here, but the appendixes contain valuable lists of religious groups, countries included, bibliographic references on religions of the world, and international statistics. The last 2 chapters of the book include further appendix material: a select bibliography on physioeconomic effects on religious culture and an index by country, religion, and general subject.

At the first volume of a four-volume work—the other three being devoted to linguistic cultures, ethnic cultures, and national cultures (see entries 90, 331, and 990)—this text makes a unique contribution to the world of scholarship. The book is not intended to be a ready-reference tool; indeed it should not be used without a careful reading of the introductory material. Of primary interest to researchers and graduate students in the social sciences, particularly in economics, this work should be a welcome addition to research libraries.—**Lucille Whalen**

Quotation Books

1369. **Divine Inspirations: Pearls of Bible Wisdom from the Old and New Testaments.** Anne Pierce, comp. John Mark Goerss, James R. Pierce, and Chestina Mitchell Archibald, eds. New York, HarperCollins, 1997. 211p. illus. $15.00. ISBN 0-06-270173-8.

Although a lovely little book, *Divine Inspirations* is more suitable for the circulating collection than the reference collection. A selection of quotations from the Bible is listed under more than 150 broad subject categories. Both Old and New Testament verses are represented from nine different English translations. The categories are arranged in alphabetic order, including such topics as family, adversity, leadership, and joy. *See also* references to alternate headings are also included.

This book is beautifully made, with designs of wood engravings by Old Masters down the center of each page. It is ideal for personal use or gift giving. It has deckled edges and an attached ribbon bookmark. However, as a reference tool indexing verses of the Bible it would be far surpassed by any standard handbook of quotations or a concordance or companion to the Bible. The contents lists the categories; there is no index.

The compiler is a freelance writer, and the editors are Lutheran pastors and educators. This work is recommended for personal and general collections, but not for reference collections.

—**Ingrid Schierling Burnett**

Bible Studies

Bibliography

1370. Mills, Watson E., comp. **The Acts of the Apostles.** Lewiston, N.Y., Edwin Mellen Press, 1996. 323p. index. (Bibliographies for Biblical Research New Testament Series, v.5). $99.95. ISBN 0-7734-2432-6.

The Book of Acts is already well represented by published bibliographies: *A Classified Bibliography of Literature on the Acts of the Apostles* (E. J. Brill, 1966); *An Exegetical Bibliography of the New Testament, Volume 2: Luke-Acts* (Mercer University Press, 1985); and *A Bibliography of the Periodical Literature on the Acts of the Apostles, 1962-1984* (E. J. Brill, 1986). (Mills includes only one of these—*An Exegetical Bibliography*—in his bibliography.) Therefore, a new bibliography has to have something to commend itself to potential users (and buyers) in order to merit consideration. The main thing this volume has to offer is currentness. It is more up-to-date by at least 10 years than the 3 bibliographies mentioned above (with few things later than 1994). In addition, Mills's bibliography includes items from the turn of the century until 1984 that did not make it into the others; it complements, but does not replace, them.

In keeping with the series format, entries are arranged in 3 parts: In part 1, entries are organized by chapter and verse, and in part 2, by subject; part 3 is a list of commentaries. As with the volume on Matthew (see ARBA 95, entry 1455), this one suffers from obvious omissions. In scanning part 3, the New International Commentary on the New Testament (William B. Eerdmans) was not found; Luke Timothy Johnson's *The Literary Function of Possessions in Luke-Acts* and Brian Rapske's *The Book of Acts and Paul in Roman Custody* are among the monographic items missing. There are also editorial oversights. Some sections in part 2 are out of alphabetic order ("Eucharist" and "literary criticism"); the section on the Septuagint is alphabetized as "LXX," which may cause it to be overlooked by users; and collective works are treated inconsistently (that is, some of them are analyzed and the constituent essays are listed separately, but others are not).

Because of its coverage of the past decade (and the gaps it fills from earlier years), this bibliography is recommended. However, tighter editorial control will certainly improve future editions and forthcoming additions to this series.—**Craig W. Beard**

1371. Mills, Watson E., comp. **Romans.** Lewiston, N.Y., Edwin Mellen Press, 1996. 205p. index. (Bibliographies for Biblical Research, New Testament Series, v.6). $89.95. ISBN 0-7734-2418-0.

As with the volumes on Matthew (see ARBA 95, entry 1455) and Acts (see entry 1370), this volume suffers from obvious omissions. Some standard works were omitted, for example, *The Romans Debate* (rev. ed., Hendrickson, 1991) and Krister Stendahl's *Paul Among Jews and Gentiles* (Fortress Press, 1976), which includes the essay "The Apostle Paul and the Introspective Conscience of the West." Also, some current works were overlooked: Anthony Guerra's *Romans and the Apologetic Tradition* (Cambridge University Press, 1995) and Stanley Stowers's *A Rereading of Romans* (Yale University Press, 1994). A comparison with recent volumes of *Religion Index One* (4th ed., American Theological Library Association, 1987) revealed that a number of current articles were not selected. In scanning part 3 ("Commentaries") of the work under review, more omissions were noted.

In the reviews of the volumes on Matthew and Acts, concern was expressed about the quality of the editorial work. That continues to be a problem with this volume. Arland J. Hultgren is cited as Arland J. Arland, Gunter Wagner as Guy Wagner, B. Noack as B. Moack, and D. L. Bock as D. L. Brock. Numerous entries are (or seem to be) listed under the wrong scripture heading in part 1: "Citations by Chapter and Verse." A major example is 20 of the 21 entries on Romans 13 being listed under "12:20." Several items in part 1 do not appear under the appropriate heading in part 2: ("Citations by Subjects"). For example, there are nearly 2 dozen sources that explicitly deal with baptism in the context of the first few verses of Romans 6, but only half-a-dozen are listed under "baptism" in part 2.

So far, this series has not realized its potential. More perspicacious selection and editing will be needed to make future volumes competitive with *An Exegetical Bibliography of the New Testament* (see ARBA 97, entry 1185) and worth the rather steep price.—**Craig W. Beard**

1372. Thompson, Henry O. **The Book of Amos: An Annotated Bibliography.** Lanham, Md., Scarecrow, 1997. 433p. index. (ATLA Bibliographies, no.42). $54.00. ISBN 0-8108-3274-7.

This bibliography of more than 1,700 entries from scholarly and traditional (mainly Christian) sources covers the general makeup of Amos: (1) first-person narratives, sayings by the prophet in carrying forth his mission, didactic questions, and hymnal poetry; (2) autobiographical narratives; (3) oracles against Tyre, Edom, and Judah and hymnic sections attributed to Deuteronomic circles; and (4) a postexilic message of consolation and hope (Amos 9:11-15) added by a cultic community in Jerusalem to assure a weeping remnant that redemption is near. On many of the books, articles, theses, and dissertations, Thompson contributes notes and explanatory paragraphs that illustrate their contribution to the history of Amos scholarship. However, Thompson's seemingly laissez-faire selection permits a number of mediocre, misconstrued, and misinterpreted references to slide through. Although the bibliography's mainly English listings are necessarily limited to scholars in the field, they do provide for others a useful guide to commentary and exegesis on the thought and times of an important eighth-century B.C.E. prophet.—**Zev Garber**

Dictionaries and Encyclopedias

1373. **New Bible Dictionary.** 3d ed. J. D. Douglas, ed. Revised by D. R. W. Wood. Downers Grove, Ill., InterVarsity Press, 1996. 1298p. illus. maps. index. $39.99. ISBN 0-8308-1439-6.

New Bible Dictionary was first published in 1962 and revised in 1982. Like the 1982 edition, this 3d edition covers all the major doctrines, people, and places associated with the Bible. However, more than 100 of the major articles have been rewritten to incorporate recent archaeological work and research in biblical studies. In addition, the bibliographies have all been updated and references to the New International Version of the Bible (where they were available) have been added. The Revised Standard Version of the Bible remains the main citation source.

The dictionary is arranged alphabetically with a comprehensive index. The contributors are highly respected biblical scholars from around the world. Each article has the initials of the author at the end. The list of contributors provides academic affiliations for the authors. All the major articles have thorough bibliographies. Cross-references are indicated by means of an asterisk followed by the title of the referenced article. Maps that are relevant to articles are included with the entries. The work is consistently produced throughout. The names of regions, provinces, and kingdoms are in large capital letters; tribes and large ethnic groups are in large italic capitals; and mountains, rivers, and lakes are in lowercase italics. Modern place-names are in brackets.

This is an excellent reference tool. The articles are clearly written and well researched. It is indispensable for serious biblical study. The dictionary will also be extremely useful in any reference collection for questions that may arise concerning the Bible or biblical times. For example, the section on writing contains comprehensive information on the development of the alphabet and writing tools. [R: RBB, 15 Mar 97, p. 1259]—**Linda Main**

1374. **New International Dictionary of Old Testament Theology & Exegesis.** Willem A. VanGemeren, ed. Grand Rapids, Mich., Zondervan Publishing/HarperCollins, 1997. 5v. index. $199.99/set. ISBN 0-310-48170-8.

For 20 years, the *New International Dictionary of New Testament Theology* (see ARBA 80, entry 1060; ARBA 78, entry 995; and ARBA 77, entry 1043) has served as a standard reference for students and scholars of the New Testament. Now, the long-awaited companion set for the Old Testament has appeared—all at one time rather than volume by volume. Unlike the New Testament version, this is not a translation, but a new work. The articles are written by an international team of more than 200 scholars. Though they recognize the Old Testament as part of the Christian biblical canon and they occasionally comment on the connection between the testaments, "their main concern lies with the interpretation and theological understanding of the Old Testament."

In some ways this work resembles the New Testament version. This can be seen primarily in the structure of the articles. They include related forms of the Hebrew words (with translations), the broader etymological context (the Ancient Near East), biblical (i.e., Old Testament) usage, and bibliographies.

There are, however, a few of notable differences between the two. First, in the 1st volume the dictionary itself is preceded by a book-length "Guide to Old Testament Theology and Exegesis," which shows how to integrate use of the Old Testament version into the exegetical and theological enterprises. Second, the entries in the dictionary are arranged alphabetically by the Hebrew words rather than by English equivalents. Because of this, users with little knowledge of Hebrew must depend upon the indexes in volume 5 to navigate the main part of the dictionary. Most helpful are the index of semantic fields, the scripture index, and the subject index. The last two indexes are self-explanatory. The index of semantic fields groups the Hebrew entries by their common themes—for example, assembly, deliverance, and land. In addition to the lexical articles that make up the bulk of the dictionary, volume 4 contains a section of topical articles that treat proper names, concepts, and the theology of the individual Old Testament books.

This is a work to be commended and will likely take its place beside the *New International Dictionary of New Testament Theology* as a standard. It certainly belongs in every seminary library and in academic libraries that support upper level biblical or Hebrew studies. Large public libraries will also want to consider adding it to their religion collections.—**Craig W. Beard**

1375. **Theological Dictionary of the Old Testament, Volume VIII.** G. Johannes Botterweck, Helmer Ringgren, and Heinz-Josef Fabry, eds. Grand Rapids, Mich., William B. Eerdmans, 1997. 560p. $45.00. ISBN 0-8028-2332-7.

This volume, along with others in the same series, represents a collaborative effort in ecumenical education and international scholarship. Seventy-six words and terms beginning with *lamed* and *mem* are carefully scrutinized, in architectonic fashion, for their linguistic and conceptual value in the Hebrew Bible and other writings (including Sumerian, Akkadian, Egyptian, Ethiopic, Ugaritic, Northwest Semitic, and Qumran, among others) and within the historical-cultural context of the Ancient Near East. The objective is to provide the necessary semantic (etymology and morphology, in particular) and exegetical foundation for the making of Old Testament theology, indispensable for the common interest of Christians and Jews.

Throughout, *Theological Dictionary of the Old Testament* is academic, recognizing the facts on and in the ground are more revealing than signs from the sky in imagining "Godtalk" while respecting ecclesiastical sensitivity; also, it separates responsible theories and opinions from doubtful hypotheses and research. Admittedly, there are restrictions and omissions. For Jews, the Hebrew Bible is *not* the "Old Testament," although both may report the same words; and for Christians, reading the Bible without the "Good News" is an exercise of mind without heart. Nonetheless, despite the divide in their religio-ethical thinking, both mother and daughter religions share the same Source. Why and how can be gleaned from the entries in this volume. This volume is a gallant attempt that helps point out how theology can talk to a complicated, secular age.—**Zev Garber**

1376. Waller, Lynn. **International Children's Bible Dictionary.** Dallas, Tex., Word Publishing, 1997. 128p. illus. maps. $12.99pa. ISBN 0-8499-4013-3.

This 128-page book contains more than 1,200 simple definitions of biblical words, phrases, people, and events. The definitions are arranged in alphabetic order to make the entries easy to locate. Entries include references to where the term can be found in the Bible as well as cross-references to other entries in the dictionary. Many words also have a pronunciation guide to help children pronounce unfamiliar words. In addition, the author has included approximately 100 realistic-looking illustrations and maps to help readers understand the terms defined and how they were used in biblical times. The two-page introduction suggests that this dictionary has been prepared for elementary school-age children; although the definitions are clear and straightforward, the typeface size would suggest that this book is not directed to younger elementary students. Parents and teachers who work with elementary or middle school children, however, will find this a useful resource that seems to address many terms and phrases that would be encountered in teaching the Bible to younger children.—**Kay Mariea**

Handbooks and Yearbooks

1377. **The Cambridge Companion to the Bible.** By Howard Clark Kee, Eric M. Meyers, John Rogerson, and Anthony J. Saldarini. New York, Cambridge University Press, 1997. 616p. illus. maps. index. $49.95. ISBN 0-521-34369-0.

The four authors generally follow the order of the biblical books with literary, historical, archaeological, and cultural background information and many sidebars with definitions or small articles on associated topics. (This is a contrast with *The Oxford Companion to the Bible* [Oxford, 1993], which has many contributors and entries that are alphabetic like a Bible dictionary.) The Cambridge title has appreciable coverage of the intertestamental books, the Apocrypha and pseudepigrapha, and projects after the New Testament period into the time of the early church founders and the New Testament Apocrypha. It contains an index of biblical references, a general index, and bibliographic and biographical essays. The latter does not include samplings of conservative scholars.

Most of the photographs are black-and-white, but there is a set of 26 color plates and 2 color maps, well chosen and of good quality, although a drawing of the Second Temple on page 173 is described as a depiction of the most ambitious Israelite water system ever discovered. The tone is set toward younger uninformed laity. The text does not elaborate controversies (such as whether there is an altar on Mt. Ebal), nor does it significantly explicate issues (such as myth and form criticism), and it lightly passes over some terms that are not self-evident (e.g., it refers to Codex Sinaiticus simply as a fourth-century C.E. Greek manuscript). The use of sidebars produces some redundancies. For example, Habakkuk, Son of Man, and Sanhedrin are explained both in the main text and in the separate sidebars.—**Robert T. Anderson**

1378. DeVries, LaMoine F. **Cities of the Biblical World.** Peabody, Mass., Hendrickson, 1997. 398p. illus. maps. index. $34.95. ISBN 1-56563-145-5.

The author describes the work as a text to introduce (presumably undergraduate) students of the Bible to the archaeology, geography, and history of important cities related to biblical study. Part 1 focuses on the Old Testament and is subdivided into the cities of Mesopotamia, Syria, Anatolia, Egypt, and Palestine. Part 2, focusing on the New Testament, is subdivided into Palestine and the rest of the Roman world. Descriptions of sites and historical narratives are general and rarely enter into scholarly controversies. The narrative is rather prosaic and not as detailed as entries in other Bible dictionaries. The two dozen small, black-and-white photographs include a plan of the palace at Mari, a drawing of the Yehimilk inscription (without explanation), maps locating the cities of each of the major areas, and a one-page historical chart. There are bibliographies listing mainly dictionary articles rather than monographs and an index of place-names and biblical and ancient sources.—**Robert T. Anderson**

1379. **The IVP Bible Background Commentary: Genesis-Deuteronomy.** By John H. Walton and Victor H. Matthews. Downers Grove, Ill., InterVarsity Press, 1997. 276p. $19.99. ISBN 0-8308-1406-X.

This reference work for nonprofessional adults proceeds chapter by chapter through the first five biblical books. References to nonbiblical documents reveal how ancient Near Eastern law, ritual and customs enhance the meaning of scripture, which has been obscured by time and changing culture. There is a brief introduction to each book and several one-page articles, charts, and maps on related aspects of ancient Near Eastern culture. The book parallels the center page, "Exegesis," section of the *Interpreter's Bible* (Abingdon, 1952), but focuses only on cultural aspects rather than including literary or historical criticism. It is built on the strength of the authors' previous books on the cultural context of the Old Testament and reflects here, as there, a rather apologetic conservative scholarly position. The authors do suggest that the Hebrews crossed a sea of reeds to the north of the Red Sea rather than the Red Sea itself, but they avoid many controversial issues. Most noticeable is the absence of any mention of the widely accepted documentary hypothesis, which argues that the Pentateuch was created in various layers dating from the tenth to the fifth century B.C.E., or any other theory of authorship or dating. Without including a proposed dating for the biblical material, it is difficult to assess the relevance of nonbiblical works that may be contemporary or separated by as much as a thousand years. The authors minimize explicit references and bibliography because they are writing for nonspecialists.—**Robert T. Anderson**

1380. **NIV Complete Bible Library.** [CD-ROM]. Grand Rapids, Mich., Zondervan Interactive/ HarperCollins, [1997]. Minimum system requirements: IBM or compatible. CD-ROM drive. Windows 3.1 (Windows 95 required for Windows 95-specific features). 3MB hard disk space. Windows-supported video card or printer. $129.95. ISBN 0-310-21220-0.

This Bible study library includes three Bible versions—New International Version (NIV), King James Version, and *New American Standard Bible*—as well as footnotes from the NIV, *NIV Study Bible Notes*, the *NIV Bible Commentary*, and the *Encyclopedia of Biblical Difficulties*, all of which can be displayed in individual windows and linked so that they can be scrolled simultaneously. Two additional text modules can be added: the Greek New Testament and the Apocrypha in the New Revised Standard Version. There are another five resources that cannot be linked to scroll with the others: the *NIV Bible Dictionary*, *NIV Study Bible Maps* (with captions), the *NIV Nave's Topical Bible*, the *Expository Dictionary of Bible Words*, and a collection of inspirational readings from the Bible.

This product makes it possible for users to search for keywords and phrases and specific citations (book, chapter, and verse) in the biblical text. An exhaustive concordance feature allows an original-language search, without requiring knowledge of Greek, Hebrew, or Aramaic. In addition, all the reference modules (including the latter, nonlinkable ones) have hot-links to the biblical citations included in them. By clicking on the highlighted citations, the corresponding passage of scripture can be displayed in context. However, unlike some more sophisticated programs, such as Logos Bible Software, there are no hot-links from words or topics in the biblical text to reference works.

This program is reasonably priced, installs quickly, and is easy to use. If the need is for a solid, basic Bible study package, this one will meet that need.—**Craig W. Beard**

1381. **Pockets: Bible Companion.** By Myrtle Langley. New York, DK Publishing, 1997. 128p. illus. maps. index. (DK Pockets). $6.95pa. ISBN 0-7895-1495-3.

DK Publishing has enlarged its original selection of 4-by-5-inch, full-color pocket book titles to include a handy, illustrated guide to the Bible. The choice of topics, pleasing layout, crisp-clear photographs, and labeled drawings and schematics are well worth the dollar increase in price over the original set, which sold for $5.95. The book follows a pattern: color-coded sections, illustrated text, running heads, and annotations. The reference section at the end stresses peripheral information with a who's who of Bible characters. The author anticipated the kinds of questions children will ask about events in the Bible. A glossary and index introduce readers to the types of data that quality reference works should include. The book respects the intelligence and anticipates the needs of children by challenging and enticing the reader to turn another page, read another fact, and add to a growing base knowledge of the subject (for instance, the locations of ancient Hebrew cities on a map of the eastern Mediterranean). The entries are brief enough but cover central facts and raise a few points that readers may not have encountered before.

Since the publication of the first set of pocketbooks, DK's editors have made no attempts to address weaknesses, particularly the lack of phonetic spellings of such daunting terms as *Apocrypha*. Also puzzling is the deletion of color in the reference section, particularly troubling on pages 104-05, a dull pair of pages in contrast to the main body of information. Still muddling the quality of DK reference works in the heyday of inclusion is the absence of important women, particularly the matriarchs Esther and Ruth as well as Hannah, Elizabeth, Bathsheba, Sarah, Rachel and Leah, and Mary and Martha.—**Mary Ellen Snodgrass**

Christianity

Bibliography

1382. Chidester, David, Judy Tobler, and Darrel Wratten. **Christianity in South Africa: An Annotated Bibliography.** Westport, Conn., Greenwood Press, 1997. 489p. index. (Bibliographies and Indexes in Religious Studies, no.43). $95.00. ISBN 0-313-30473-4.

This bibliography addresses three major areas: missions, denominations, and African-initiated Christian churches. An introduction provides a historical background. The authors describe the influence of language upon missionaries, who appropriated terms from an indigenous vocabulary. Important figures in history like Nelson Mandela are also mentioned.

This bibliography, containing over 600 entries, has a subject index. Bibliographic essays, which give references in scientific form of citation, without reference to the item number in the bibliography begin each section. The authors present additional historical details and highlight trends in research. Text in these essays, however, is not indexed.

The section on missions is subdivided geographically. The denominations section includes Dutch Reformed, Roman Catholic, Anglican, Methodist, and others, with an essay discussing the effect of apartheid on Christianity and research. The African-initiated churches section includes Ethiopians, Millenarians, Nazarites, and Zionists. Articles cited are principally in English, with some in Afrikaans, particularly in the denominations section. Annotations are thorough, and entries include scholarly journal articles, books, and dissertations. This is by far the most comprehensive and current source on Christianity in South Africa available.—**Ralph Hartsock**

1383. Magnuson, Norris A., and William G. Travis. **American Evangelicalism II: First Bibliographical Supplement, 1990-1996.** West Cornwall, Conn., Locust Hill Press, 1997. 273p. index. $40.00. ISBN 0-933951-27-2.

This work is a supplement to a larger work. As such, it is limited in its scope by the publication date of the original work (see ARBA 92, entry 1408). Coverage for the current work is 1990 to 1996. Regardless of these inherent limitations, its size is still remarkable. As is stated in the introduction, writing on the subject of American evangelicalism is seemingly without end. With more than 1,500 entries for the 7-year period, it appears that the authors' statement is nearly accurate.

The bibliography is especially useful because the subject divisions used are well thought out. Entries are well annotated and well written. There is a good representation of perspectives in the book, with works drawn from critics and proponents of evangelicalism, both from theological as well as political perspectives.

This bibliography is recommended for any library that either already owns the main volume or any library that is aspiring to build a collection on the subject of modern religion. In reference or collection development departments, the work will serve as both a useful and usable tool for collection development and as an excellent research tool.—**Richard A. Leiter**

Dictionaries and Encyclopedias

1384. Collinge, William J. **Historical Dictionary of Catholicism.** Lanham, Md., Scarecrow, 1997. 551p. index. (Historical Dictionaries of Religions, Philosophies, and Movements, no.12). $58.00. ISBN 0-8108-3233-X.

This reference on Catholicism provides more than 500 entries on its history, traditions, beliefs, and concepts. It covers the entire history—nearly 2,000 years—as well as the vast traditions, the key individuals, and the complex ideas that are all part of Catholicism. This is a remarkable and ambitious task given that it is the work of one person. The author holds a Ph.D. in philosophy from Yale University and is a professor of theology and philosophy at Mount St. Mary's College.

A sampling of entries includes celibacy, euthanasia, mysticism, Oscar Romero, the ordination of women, and Thomism. The only major omissions, the author explains, are biblical topics, persons, and places. Entries vary in length from less than 30 to more than 500 words. Cross-referencing makes it easy to find information quickly. The work also provides a chronology of events during nearly 2,000 years. An extensive bibliography runs 71 pages and even has its own outline. There are 5 appendixes: the 261 popes and the years of each papacy; the 21 Ecumenical Councils and their dates; the documents of Vatican Council II; 32 of the so-called more important Papal Encyclicals from the 289 issued between 1740 and early 1996; and the 7 best-known and most often used prayers.

With more than 1 billion members worldwide, Catholicism is the Christian religion with the most members; this easy-to-use, one-volume dictionary succeeds in capturing the important elements that are at its core. It is recommended for all libraries.—**Edward Erazo**

1385. **The Complete Book of Everyday Christianity: An A-to-Z Guide to Following Christ in Every Aspect of Life.** Robert Banks and R. Paul Stevens, eds. Downers Grove, Ill., InterVarsity Press, 1997. 1166p. index. $29.99. ISBN 0-8308-1450-7.

The Complete Book of Everyday Christianity seeks to connect life and religion by discussing hundreds of diverse topics. With a book of this title, one would expect to find listings for clergy, Sabbath, communion, and denomination. Other items listed represent a broad spectrum, such as coffee drinking, voting, zoning, credit card, information superhighway, backpacking, and chocolate. The intriguing collection has extensive cross-references.

This book is designed for several intended users: for those pursuing a particular interest (such as developing a simpler lifestyle); for those seeking help if passing through a troublesome period of life; for those preparing a talk, study, sermon, or workshop; educators using the volume as a classroom text; or for those browsing for enjoyment.

It was noted immediately the editors were not afraid of difficult subjects, witnessed by some of the listings under "A": abortion, abuse, addiction, adolescence, and aging. However, a conservative bias was quickly and easily observed after reading the entry under "homosexuality." Though certain judgments are favored, other opinions are presented satisfactorily.

The physical book itself was a problem to this reviewer. The binding broke immediately, although the book was opened with care, making the reader wonder about the quality of production. However, the adequate handling of subject matter is of far more importance.—**Jerri Spoehel**

1386. **Encyclopedia of Early Christianity.** 2d ed. Everett Ferguson, Michael P. McHugh, and Frederick W. Norris, eds. New York, Garland, 1997. 2v. illus. maps. index. (Garland Reference Library of the Humanities, v.1839). $150.00/set. ISBN 0-8153-1663-1.

The 1st edition of this work (see ARBA 91, entry 1442) appeared in 1990 to glowing reviews; it was even named a *Library Journal* "Best Reference Book" for 1990. The coverage has remained the same (both topically and chronologically), but the volume has been expanded by 230 pages (now in 2 volumes), 268 entries, and 32 writers. In addition, the entries that were carried over have been revised where necessary and the bibliographies updated. There are several new photographs, maps, and tables. The print quality has improved significantly. In the 1st edition, the text was sometimes faint, the italics difficult to identify, and the bold typeface in the index (used to refer the reader to main entries) nearly impossible to differentiate from the regular typeface. These deficiencies have been corrected, making the encyclopedia more user friendly and appealing.

A recent comparable work, Oxford University Press's *Encyclopedia of the Early Church* (see ARBA 93, entry 1406), is in some ways more extensive than the *Encyclopedia of Early Christianity*. The Oxford title's coverage extends into the eighth century and includes more people (even for the time both works cover). However, there also are entries in the title at hand that are not in the Oxford reference. For example, *Encyclopedia of Early Christianity* has separate entries for apocryphal acts, gospels, and so forth, whereas *Encyclopedia of the Early Church* has a single article, "Apocrypha." The set under review includes entries on funerary practices, games, healing, homosexuality, and numerous others that do not appear in the other set. Also, the prose in *Encyclopedia of Early Christianity* will in many cases be more accessible to nonspecialists. Both works should be afforded a place in the reference collection. The Garland set is highly recommended.—**Craig W. Beard**

1387. O'Donnell, Christopher. **Ecclesia: A Theological Encyclopedia of the Church.** Collegeville, Minn., Liturgical Press, 1996. 520p. index. (A Micheal Glazer Book). $65.00. ISBN 0-8146-5832-6.

The subtitle aptly describes this book, a theological encyclopedia of the Catholic Church. Although it is an outstanding work in its field, its narrow focus limits its usefulness for many libraries. The 389 entries are carefully chosen for their relevance to the Catholic Church with no trivial or unnecessary entries. A topical index refers the reader to appropriate articles and mainly serves to provide cross-references. A brief foreword describes the selection process for the entries and points to the relevance of this work for the specialist. The articles, while scholarly, are nonetheless extremely readable. Of special mention is the emphasis on current scholarship in the bibliographic references following each entry and the inclusion of references in languages other than English.

A library wishing to acquire a comprehensive one-volume encyclopedia of the Catholic Church will want to select another reference book, for example, *The HarperCollins Encyclopedia of Catholicism* (see ARBA 96, entry 1469). At the same time, *Ecclesia* is more current than a similar work, the *Handbook of Catholic Theology* (see ARBA 96, entry 1475), which is essentially a translation with some updated entries and bibliographies of a 1987 German work published by Herder. The author of the work under review is a senior lecturer in systematic theology at the Milltown Institute, Dublin, Ireland, and holds a doctorate in sacred theology from the Gregorian University in Rome. He is the author of 4 books and more than 200 articles. O'Donnell's writing style is personal and engaging, in this encyclopedia giving more than the official Church position and often focusing on the positive. The work is highly recommended for special libraries in the field and libraries with comprehensive collections in religion.

—**Ingrid Schierling Burnett**

1388. **Our Sunday Visitor's Encyclopedia of Catholic Doctrine.** Russell Shaw, ed. Huntington, Ind., Our Sunday Visitor, 1997. 751p. index. $39.95. ISBN 0-87973-746-8.

Publication of the *Catechism of the Catholic Church* in 1992, often adjudged one of the most important events in the life of the Church since the Second Vatican Council, has spawned countless articles and a multitude of books. This latest addition to an ever-increasing bibliography seeks "to enrich Catholics' understanding of the faith they profess and the morality that guides their lives." More than 400 entries treat virtually all aspects of the faith. Obviously not meant to take the place of the *Catechism*, this presentation of doctrine does make reading it a more fruitful enterprise, especially because this encyclopedia explains and expands upon matters the *Catechism* mentions without historical background or pastoral insights. Entries detail the perennial questions of penance, purgatory, indulgences, apostasy, and subsidiarity as well as providing up-to-date examinations of ensoulment, collegiality, capital punishment, environmentalism, and proportionalism. Appended to longer entries are cross-reference subjects and brief bibliographies. A 38-page index further enhances this informative and useful reference tool.

To the credit of its editor and 40 contributors—all of whom are highly regarded theologians and scholars—this volume is more than a popular Catholic digest. It is aimed at the serious-minded reader who wants to learn more about the profundities of Catholic doctrine. Of significance is the fact that this comprehensive work is fully in accord with the Magisterium of the Church, having been reviewed by an ad hoc committee on the catechism and judged worthy of the imprimatur of John M. D'Arcy, Bishop of Fort Wayne-South Bend.—**G. A. Cevasco**

1389. **The Oxford Dictionary of the Christian Church.** 3d ed. F. L. Cross and E. A. Livingstone, eds. New York, Oxford University Press, 1997. 1786p. $125.00. ISBN 0-19-211655-X.

This work has long held the top spot as the authoritative, one-volume reference on the Christian Church, and with the latest edition, the tradition continues. Some of the articles from the 2d edition (see ARBA 75, entry 1220) have been retained with little or no change except for an updated bibliography. (This statement is not intended as a criticism, as these articles are still quite good.) Other articles have been rewritten, revised, and expanded. The article on the Holocaust now includes as a definition the persecution and mass extermination of Jews by the Nazis. "Broadcasting, Religious" has been significantly expanded (from a half-page to two pages) to include the United States and Europe beyond Great Britain. Articles on Christianity in particular countries have been updated. For example, the article on Russia now covers Russia, the Soviet Union, and the Commonwealth of Independent States and reflects changes since the breakup of the USSR. In addition, there are new articles on Angola, Ghana, Indonesia, Kenya, Korea, Malawi, Nigeria, Sierra Leone, Vietnam, Zaire, and Zimbabwe.

Other new articles were added because of changes in the theological climate. Some of the most notable additions are "Feminist Theology," "Liberation Theology," "Homosexuality," and "Women, Ordination of." Also "Jews, Missions to the" has been replaced by an article with a different perspective: "Jews, Christian Attitudes to." Several new biographical sketches appear: Hans Kung, Thomas Merton, Jürgen Moltmann, Pope John Paul I, Pope John Paul II, and Oscar Romero. One would expect to find an entry for Desmond Tutu, but he was not included. Much has changed from the previous edition of *The Oxford Dictionary of the Christian Church*, and there is still much of value in both earlier editions. The 3d edition should take its place in all reference collections beside its predecessors.—**Craig W. Beard**

Directories

1390. DeRyan, Tim. **The Catholic Internet.** USA ed. Stroudsburg, Pa., Fabian, 1997. 163p. $14.95pa. ISBN 0-9660316-0-1.

The late Tim DeRyan (who passed away in August 1997) spent the last two years of his life compiling *The Catholic Internet* USA edition, advertised as the most comprehensive guide to Catholic information on the Internet. From the beginning, the worldwide Roman Catholic Church (998 million members in 1997) is connected more by allies in the sky and interpretation by the Vatican than by communication between Catholic communities. The Internet explosion has changed all this, and now loyalists, by using lists generated by computer telecommunications, can overcome restrictions of time and space and dialog one with another. The author's intention was not to list only database information by NCCB/USCC-approved Catholic organizations (dioceses, schools, parishes) and related ministries. His was a much-needed plea for pragmatism: curtail the chaotic outpouring of "Catholic" and "Catholicism" (195,700 as of July 1997) by mentioning the good and rejecting the bad. DeRyan alone will not stay the storm, but his directory is proof that Catholics "internetted" become a veritable *ecclesiae ecumenicae.*—**Zev Garber**

Handbooks and Yearbooks

1391. Fox, Thomas C. **Catholicism on the Web.** New York, MIS:Press/Henry Holt, 1997. 468p. index. $16.95pa. ISBN 1-55828-516-4.

There are any number of problems one can name with a book about World Wide Web sites; most come back to the inherent problems with Webpages, such as short life span, changing addresses, and infrequent maintenance. That being said, it is worth the effort to document, in nonelectronic form, the nature of the Web on a particular subject at a particular time. Why? For one thing, it gives a glimpse of Web life the way a time capsule might. Also, it gives beginners on the Internet a more familiar place to start.

Such is the case with the present work. This book features a fine structure, with sections on Catholic organization, ideas, activism, and "Transcendence" (meaning theology, spirituality, and the like). It also has a decent enough index, a surprise for books of its type. A list of online directories about Catholicism is useful as well. Why is the guide not on disk? Readers will be inconvenienced and need to type in URLs, when a disk-based version could be used (if it existed) within any standard Web browser. It need not have all the text but could simply be a list of the links in the book. This shortcoming aside, the book is worth having and can be more useful than relying on a search engine's always unpredictable (and often monstrous) results. The homepage for this book is http://www.mispress.com/catholicism/.—**Bob Craigmile**

Hinduism

1392. Sullivan, Bruce M. **Historical Dictionary of Hinduism.** Lanham, Md., Scarecrow, 1997. 345p. (Historical Dictionaries of Religions, Philosophies, and Movements, no.13). $79.50. ISBN 0-8108-3327-1.

This dictionary sets out to define Hindu terms in the context of their historic and social significance. The words described are from religion, schools, movements, rituals, doctrines, and sacred texts. Many of the 570 entries are biographies of religious leaders as well as social and political figures. Definitions range in length from a few words to a page. There are ample *see* references and almost every entry has a *see also* reference. The entries are well written and assume no knowledge of Hinduism. The most difficult concepts are explained with refreshing lucidity. Even areas of potential debate or negative notoriety (e.g., Madame Blavatsky, Transcendental Meditation, Bhagwan Rajneesh) are given evenhanded and impartial treatment.

In addition to defining terms, there are added features that make the source even more valuable. A 20-page introduction covering the history of Hinduism, doctrines, and Hindu community life is included. A chronology on the history of Hinduism is also provided. Next to the definitions of terms, the most valuable asset is the 79-page bibliography. This starts with a bibliographic essay of other, more comprehensive, bibliographies followed by the bibliographic entries broken down into 10 categories, such as historical development, texts, practices, sacred places, and others. Because the literature on Hinduism is so extensive, the author concentrates on modern, mainly English-language material, both books and articles. Included are many well-regarded and classic sources.

The author has his doctorate from the University of Chicago and is a professor of religious studies and coordinator of Asian studies at Northern Arizona University. He has created an excellent source of information on Hindu religion and culture. This source is recommended for all academic and medium and large public libraries. It is a significant contribution to religion and multicultural collections.

—**Gerald L. Gill**

Judaism

1393. **Encyclopaedia Judaica.** [CD-ROM]. Shaker Heights, Ohio, Judaica Multimedia; distr., Danbury, Conn., Grolier, 1997. Minimum system requirements: IBM or compatible 486. Double-speed CD-ROM drive. Windows 3.x. 4MB RAM. 256-color monitor. Sound card. $595.00/single user; $995.00/2-8 users; $1,595.00/9 or more users. ISBN 965-07-0665-8.

The release of the *Encyclopaedia Judaica* (EJCD) on CD-ROM is one of the most significant events in the development of reference tools in Jewish studies since the publication of the original 1972 printed edition (see ARBA 73, entry 274) or the publication of the *Jewish Encyclopedia* (1904).

This work contains all of the material from the original 16 volumes as well as the articles from the yearbooks and deciannial editions that updated *Encyclopedaedia Judaica*. In addition, several of the most important articles have been updated under the direction of Geoffrey Wigoder, who was the editor. One problem with this is that users cannot tell when an article was last revised. This will pose a problem if future releases of the EJCD are introduced.

Bohdan Wynar's 1973 review in ARBA (see entry 274) of *Encyclopaedia Judaica* praised it as a "monumental work" but pointed out the problems with its index. The index was every Judaica librarian's nightmare; cross-indexing was inconsistent and the work had introduced its own transliteration scheme for the large number of words from Hebrew and other Jewish languages, which are the primary access points. Although EJCD did not change the transliteration system or index, it has successfully allowed keyword searching of articles, and this is what makes it most worthwhile. The hypertext cross-references and definitions encourage users to spend hours surfing interesting secondary material. EJCD has also introduced a number of features to use the technology and appeal to both the home and school markets. Some of these are interesting, such as audio recordings of the Israeli Declaration of Independence or Jewish prayers and multimedia and video recordings of other major events in Jewish recent history.

EJCD is user friendly, and indeed the images make it seem almost more appealing to young adults than academics. With keyword access to ready reference and detailed information on all questions of Judaism and Jewish life, it is hard to think of many libraries that would not greatly benefit from this purchase. This is especially the case for libraries that often use the *Encyclopaedia Judaica* because of the updates and the significantly improved accessibility.—**Andrew B. Wertheimer**

1394. Grubel, Monika. **Judaism.** Hauppauge, N.Y., Barron's Educational Series, 1997. 216p. illus. maps. index. (Crash Course Series). $12.95pa. ISBN 0-7641-0051-3.

This concise, illustrated overview of Jewish history and religion begins with the patriarchs in Canaan and ends with the election of Benjamin Netanyahu as Israeli prime minister in 1996. Some chapters contains sidebar essays on the Jewish calendar; the Sadducees, Pharisees, Essenes, and Zealots; Maimonides; the mikveh; dietary laws; and Jewish life from cradle to grave, which are accurate, informative, readable (as is the whole book), and smoothly integrated into the historical narrative. The selective bibliography, useful glossary, accurate indexes, historical overview, list of Jewish museums, and abundance of tiny but clear illustrations all make this a reasonable—for its size—general reference. It also makes for an absorbing narrative when read from cover to cover.

As an inexpensive, beginning resource for someone wanting to learn about Judaism, Grubel's gem compares well with its competitors. To someone who has read a fair number of such surveys, *Judaism: An Illustrated Historical Overview* provides much new information and insights. Although her book is balanced and scholarly, Grubel's passion for her subject is clear and contagious (but her credentials are not listed). This book should keep the interest of Jewish students of many ages, the casual reader, and, perhaps, some of the various Christian groups seeking to learn about Judaism.—**Anthony Gottlieb**

1395. **The Jewish Year Book 1997.** Stephen W. Massil, ed. London, in association with the Jewish Chronicle, Vallentine Mitchell; distr., Portland, Oreg., International Specialized Book Services, 1997. 365p. index. $32.50. ISBN 0-85303-326-9. ISSN 0075-3769.

Now in its 101st year of publication, this British annual is similar in scope and objectives to the *American Jewish Year Book* (see ARBA 97, entry 1220, and ARBA 93, entry 439). The work at hand is loaded with information for and about Jewish people worldwide, with an emphasis on the United Kingdom and especially London, where this series is published and which has one of the largest Jewish populations in Europe. Starting with a half-dozen essays by prominent British Jews concerning Jewish culture and history, the remaining sections are in the form of statistics on Jewish population; lists of religious, cultural, and welfare organizations; an extensive who's who of British Jewry; obituaries and publications of the preceding year; Jewish events and holidays for the coming year; a detailed explanation of the complex Hebrew calendar with a 30-year calculator for civil and Hebraic dates; and an index.

The yearbook provides a feast for anyone with an appetite for Jewish matters. The opening essays offer historical information about Zionism, a topic often discussed by uninformed persons. The demographic section offers a fascinating look at Jewish communities worldwide, from the smallest (Pakistan's two families) to the largest (the United States' population of Jews exceeds Israel's by about one million) and includes the history of their founding and the persecution and expulsion of many of these communities. The lists of prominent Jews neglects those in sports and entertainment in favor of those in the fields of science, politics, and the arts. However, this information can be found elsewhere. On the whole, this yearbook provides a useful overview of the world of Judaism.—**Larry Lobel**

1396. **The Oxford Dictionary of the Jewish Religion.** R. J. Zwi Werblowsky and Geoffrey Wigoder, eds. New York, Oxford University Press, 1997. 764p. $95.00. ISBN 0-19-508605-8.

Although growing out of an earlier volume also edited by Werblowsky and Wigoder—*Encyclopedia of the Jewish Religion* (Holt, Rinehart, and Winston, 1966)—because of additional material and extensive rewriting of the articles that were brought over, this volume is for all intents and purposes a new work. The dictionary aims at covering the entire chronological and conceptual scope of the Jewish religion, but excludes so-called secular Judaism. For example, the major articles on the state of Israel are "Israel, State of, Religious Life in" and "Israel, State of, Theological Aspects." Thus, the Oxford title is more restrictive in its focus than *The Blackwell Dictionary of Judaica* (see ARBA 94, entry 1554) and *The New Standard Jewish Encyclopedia* (see ARBA 93, entry 448). The nearly 2,400 alphabetically arranged articles illuminate beliefs, practices, institutions, places, and people important in the development of the Jewish religion. Most of them are supplemented by brief bibliographies. The writing is clear and concise, and the coverage is thorough and generally balanced.

In its focus, *The Oxford Dictionary of the Jewish Religion* (ODJR) is comparable to *The Encyclopedia of Judaism* (EJ) (see ARBA 91, entry 1449), which was edited by Wigoder, although his latest work is more comprehensive. ODJR has approximately 1,400 more entries than EJ. Some of those entries—but by no means all—are biblical characters; individual apocryphal and pseudepigraphal works (for example, Baruch and the Assumption of Moses, respectively); and the major sectarian documents from the Dead Sea Scrolls (such as the Rule of the Community and the Genesis Apocryphon). There are also substantially more biographical entries. One feature that is missing in ODJR is illustrations. EJ is full of black-and-white and color pictures, but the Oxford title has none at all.

If there is a weakness here, it is in the cross-referencing. For example, the article on "Marriage" refers the reader to "Betrothal" and "Matrimony," and "Matrimony" refers to "Betrothal" and "Marriage," but "Betrothal" refers to neither of the other articles. However, this alone does not merit passing this work over. ODJR is recommended for academic, public, synagogue, and church libraries.—**Craig W. Beard**

Mormon Church

1397. Parry, Donald W., Jeanette W. Miller, and Sandra A. Thorne. **A Comprehensive Annotated Book of Mormon Bibliography.** Provo, Utah, Research Press, 1996. 643p. index. $99.95. ISBN 0-934893-19-5.

Coming as it does from the press of the Foundation for Ancient Research and Mormon Studies in Provo, Utah, this large bibliography is an "insiders" document. Focused exclusively on published items about the Book of Mormon, this immense volume appears exhaustive. What critical studies are omitted is left to the serious scholar to discern.

The book lists by author and by subject, making research easy. The bibliography was compiled from articles, book reviews, periodicals, books, monographs, pamphlets, reports, plays, and poems. It is categorized by five sections—general studies, religion, polemics, fiction, and book reviews—and copiously annotated. The annotations are descriptive, not critical. An addendum gives nonannotated materials for the 1994-1995 publications. The appendix of Book of Mormon editions and translations is valuable, as is the comprehensive index. This bibliography can serve as a starting point for research on the Book of Mormon as seen from within the church. [R: Choice, Mar 97, p. 1142]—**Linda L. Lam-Easton**

Part IV
SCIENCE AND TECHNOLOGY

29 Science and Technology in General

BIBLIOGRAPHY

1398. **Bibliographic Guide to Technology 1996.** New York, G. K. Hall/Simon & Schuster Macmillan, 1997. 2v. $375.00/set. ISBN 0-7838-1779-7. ISSN 0360-2761.

The source material for this two-volume set, previously reviewed in ARBA 92 (see entry 1450), is cataloging copy from the New York Public Library and the Library of Congress, as well as New York's Engineering Societies Library. Titles are imprints of 1990 or newer, are international in scope, and are in all languages and formats. They were cataloged during the 1996 calendar year. The disciplines represented include the various engineering fields, aeronautics, patents, trademarks, and food processing. Access is by integrated main entry, and the filing follows the Anglo-American Cataloguing Rules (AACR2). (See entry 109 for a complete review of G. K. Hall's bibliographic series.)—**Ed Volz**

BIOGRAPHY

1399. **The Cambridge Dictionary of Scientists.** By David Millar and others. New York, Cambridge University Press, 1996. 387p. illus. maps. index. $39.95; $16.95pa. ISBN 0-521-56185-X; 0-521-56718-1pa.

Approximately 1,000 short biographies (the claim in the preface for coverage of 1,300 scientists is misleading) of important scientific figures are included in this welcome update of Millar's earlier *Chambers Concise Dictionary of Scientists* (see ARBA 91, entry 1460). Coverage is especially good in the physical and biological sciences, but selected inventors, mathematicians, and social scientists are also included. The book also contains a number of diagrams and approximately 30 interspersed essays discussing various topics, such as the history of mathematics and the development of the computer. Although many biographical entries are essentially the same as in the previous work, others have been revised, and some entries are completely new. The most notable additions are those for female scientists, such as Hypatia of Alexandria and Rachel Carson. Most of the biographies are pithy and balanced (a notable exception being the strangely critical entry on Carson) and often are spiced with descriptions of idiosyncrasies and ironic events that make the book a delight to read. The portraits that accompanied the earlier dictionary have been eliminated, to no great loss.

Overall, this is a useful, quick reference to important figures in the sciences. Some scattered British usages may be enigmatic to those without a British background, however. Also, because the primary use of this volume will be for information on particular scientists, few will appreciate the interspersed essays. Although some of the sources used in the writing of the biographies are listed in the preface, the inclusion of a key reference for each biographee would have enhanced the reference use of this book.

—**Joseph Hannibal**

1400. **The Grolier Library of Science Biographies.** Danbury, Conn., Grolier, 1997. 10v. illus. index. $299.00/set. ISBN 0-7172-7626-0.

This 10-volume set of science biographies by Grolier contains 2,000 entries of basic biographical data on the world's most influential and well-known scientists. Intended for students from grade 7 to adults, each biography includes a portrait of the scientist, the period in which he or she worked, and the scientific field to which the person made a contribution. In addition, there are an index for the entire set, a glossary for the entire set, and a useful "Chronology" or timeline that places the scientists and their discoveries in order.

After comparing other well-known scientific biographies such as Scribner's *Dictionary of Scientific Biography* (see ARBA 91, entries 1461 and 1462), this set by Grolier is not as complete. Some famous scientists have been left out, such as Gottfried Leibniz, and eighteenth century physicist, and the entries are not as detailed and informative. Although there is a section called "Sources and Further Reading" in each volume, it would be more convenient to have this information at the end of each biography for faster and easier reference by students, especially because some entries are not very detailed. *The Grolier Library of Science Biographies* is useful for middle school, high school, and public library collections; however, it is not as scholarly as other available biography collections.—**Natalie Brower-Kirton**

1401. **Scientists: The Lives and Works of 150 Scientists.** Peggy Saari and Stephen Allison, eds. Detroit, U*X*L/Gale, 1996. 3v. illus. index. $99.95/set. ISBN 0-7876-0959-5.

This 1,000-page, 3-volume guide to the lives and works of 150 scientists is a highly selective, even arbitrary catalog of some well-known and a greater number of lesser-known scientific figures. The profiles range in time from Johannes Kepler to living scientists, many of them Nobel prize-winners. The tone is set by the "Reader's Guide," which notes that "budding scientists and those entering the fascinating world of science for fun or study will find inspiration in these volumes."

The preface states that the biographies range from Louis Pasteur to Bill Gates. Individual articles are meant to recount each scientist's upbringing, formative experiences, and major inspirations, details meant to "keep students reading." A timeline of scientific breakthroughs is provided, which begins with the industrial revolution (which many may argue does not reflect science but rather technology, and that a significant distinction ought to be drawn between the two) and ends with Mark Plotkin's ethnobotanical studies of the Amazon rain forest. Because most of the biographies of living scientists provide no sources concerning their lives, it is not clear how the research for this book was actually conducted. Nor is there any indication of what criteria were used in selecting the individuals presented here. Although all have made commendable contributions, not all are equally distinguished, and the biggest surprises are the omissions.

What should be emphasized is that the editors have gone out of their way to include women and minorities to a larger extent than is the case with most comparable reference works. Among women, for example, the biographies include women whose names are probably not so well-known outside their own circles, such as Angeles Alvariño, Elizabeth Blackburn, Helen Caldicott, Sylvia Earle, Dorothy Horstmann, Ruth Patrick, Berta Scharrer, and Florence Seibert. Why, if these relative unknowns are listed, were not such better-known women as Maria Gaetana Agnesi, Mary Cartwright, Sofia Kolaveskaya, Sophie Germain, Christine Ladd Franklin, Julia Robinson, Olga Taussky, Dorothy Wrinch, or Grace Chisholm Young?

As for bibliographies to "stimulate further reading," these seem inadequate in many cases. For example, the list for Albert Einstein does not recommend any of the major, authoritative biographies, including those by Jeremy Bernstein and Abraham Pais. Similarly, for the prominent mathematician Carl Friedrich Gauss, only one article from *Scientific American* is given. Despite the arbitrary selection of the scientists included in these three volumes and the unfortunate lack of substantial bibliographic references, this collection of biographies may still be a useful resource for high school students or for anyone in need of brief information about the scientific figures included here, especially lesser-known women, blacks, and other minorities.—**Joseph W. Dauben**

CHRONOLOGY

1402. Bruno, Leonard C. **Science & Technology Firsts.** Detroit, Gale, 1997. 636p. illus. maps. index. $65.00. ISBN 0-7876-0256-6.

This carefully edited tour through the events of scientific and technological history is bound to merit a favorable review: The author has had access to the unsurpassed collections of the Library of Congress in science and technology over the years and has exhibited the ability to explain in simple terms complex activities for the nonspecialist. Political correctness is in evidence—there are many sketches of female researchers, for example, and credit is given to indigenous peoples where appropriate. A sense of immediacy is provided by the consistent use of the present tense in entries.

The text is arranged in chronological order under 12 subjects, 4 of which were read in their entirety: "Agriculture & Everyday Life," "Communications," "Mathematics," and "Physics." The remaining subjects were covered since the 1980s for completeness. Cropping of photographs was done in a modern manner. The index is full in scope, but little editing had followed the machine sort. This volume is a must-purchase for every science/technology collection. [R: BR, May/June 97, pp. 54-55]—**Eugene B. Jackson**

DICTIONARIES AND ENCYCLOPEDIAS

1403. **Eyewitness Encyclopedia of Science.** [CD-ROM]. New York, DK Multimedia, 1996. Minimum system requirements (Windows version): IBM or compatible 486DX/33MHz. Double-speed CD-ROM drive. Windows 3.1. 8MB RAM. 22MB hard disk space. 640 x 480 pixels, 256-color monitor (16-bit colors preferred). Mouse. 8-bit sound card. Loudspeakers or headphones. Minimum system requirements (Macintosh version): 68LC040 25MHz. Double-speed CD-ROM drive. System 7.0. 12MB RAM. 25MB hard disk space. 640 x 480 pixels, 256-color monitor (thousands of colors preferred). Mouse. 8-bit sound card. Loudspeakers or headphones. $39.95. ISBN 0-7894-1230-6.

This CD-ROM product is a visually intriguing and entertaining attempt to deliver information about the sciences in a multimedia, encyclopedic format. Its major coverage includes mathematics, physics, chemistry, and the life sciences, with further subject breakdown for each area. Chemistry, for example, further refines into such topics as physical states and changes, reactions, chemical elements, organic chemistry, and so forth. Clicking on any of these categories offers the user another set of even more specific subcategories. Once at this level, a short hypertext article (with highlighted keywords to click on for further information) appears on the screen and is narrated. A "see also" box and a "find out more" list are also offered.

Complementing the core subject areas are other features. Biographical information about scientists, arranged alphabetically, is included in a "Who's Who" area. A "Virtual Molecule" program displays moving, 3-D images of a dozen different molecules, along with a short description and an opportunity to click on related articles. A "Matter Explorer" offers a chance to select and increasingly magnify a variety of objects—view an aphid with the naked eye, then at 10 times its size, for example. Forty different short, narrated videos on various topics are also available for viewing. "Earth and the Universe" offers information on astronomy. (One may wonder why astronomy was not included as a topic in its own right.) A "Quiz Master" feature gives users a chance to test their knowledge in the areas of scientific facts, principles, and people. Finally, indexes to videos, animations, and articles are offered, along with a search engine allowing keyword Boolean and other refined searches of the encyclopedia's contents.

There are some significant weaknesses to this multimedia tool, however. The most striking is that, although the graphics are attractive and the sound is of professional quality, there are no clear clues for navigation. The graphics are fun, but they are not terribly intuitive. From the initial screen the major options seem somewhat obvious at first, but closer inspection reveals much more going on in the background: a tiny "A-Z" icon for the index and an almost invisible question mark where one may click to find help information, for example. It is simply not clear which are clickable image areas versus simple illustrations, and what will happen when one does click. Beyond the main screen, it is not clear how to exit an area, return to an earlier screen, or close a text box. These problems detract considerably from ease of use.

It is a bit of a stretch to label this product an encyclopedia. For all its bells and whistles, the CD-ROM's scope and depth of topic coverage do not begin to approach that of a print encyclopedia—articles are brief and the content and language simplistic. Instead, it may be wiser to market this tool as simply an entertaining introduction to science. Finally, selectors would find it helpful if academic credentials had been included with the credits for the science information included on the disc.—**Judith A. Matthews**

1404. Graham, Ian, and Paul Sterry. **Questions & Answers Book of Science Facts.** New York, Facts on File, 1997. 80p. illus. maps. index. $19.95. ISBN 0-8160-3655-1.

Large typeface, nice color illustrations, and interesting information make this a great browsing book for a middle school-age student. It contains broad categories of information on space, the world, nature, and science and technology. "Space" deals with four topics related to stars and space exploration. "Our World" has five subjects that range from the Earth to habitats. "Nature" is a large section with 15 categories that start at evolution and work through pets into plant life. The "Science & Technology" category contains 14 subjects moving from physics to machines and structures. Each subject has six or seven questions and their answers. For example, in the category of science and technology, one of the subjects is "materials." Such questions as "What are materials?" and "How is paper made?" contain brief, general information. A color illustration accompanies each question and answer.

Some entries are simple, such as "What is gravity?" but can become complex, such as "What is an Archimedes' Screw used for?" Each question has a clear, understandable answer to a child with good reading skills and basic science background. It is not clear how questions were chosen for inclusion in the book. Surprisingly, computers are not included in the "machine" subject of "Science & Technology." The book contains an excellent index but does not include any other supplementary materials, such as a glossary or a bibliography.

The strength of this book is in the intriguing questions with a brief but clear answer that will encourage a student to explore a science topic in greater detail. Although the volume could not be used as a source for a science report, it can give students ideas for their reports.—**Suzanne Julian**

1405. **Illustrated Science Encyclopedia.** Austin, Tex., Raintree/Steck-Vaughn, 1997. 24v. illus. maps. index. $499.50/set. ISBN 0-8172-3943-X.

This encyclopedia is intended to be a student-friendly, comprehensive science reference work for middle school students. Most articles are illustrated with color photographs or drawings. Many article titles have phonetic pronunciation shown, with a pronunciation key at the beginning of each volume. Some articles include an "Activity Box" containing a simple project students can complete to enhance understanding of the subject. Articles often go beyond the clinical exposition of their title. "Agriculture" and "Plastic," for example, also include a subsection about the environment, important information for students. The encyclopedia contains a useful student bibliography annotated with the grade level appropriateness of the citations. It is arranged by subject and includes CD-ROMs. Many bibliographic citations are of other Raintree/Steck-Vaughn publications. The final volume contains 75 science projects, easily completed by students, that are tied to and reinforce articles in the main text. The index lists article titles as well as other locations of the keyword.

Overall, the encyclopedia is done well, but there are some areas that could have been improved. An occasional article contains misleading information. Under "Airplane," the *Concorde* is indicated as a French airplane; the information is corrected under "Aviation," where it is correctly described as being developed by the British and the French. Under "Astronautics," the caption of the space shuttle drawing describes the shuttle as being launched into orbit by two recoverable, solid rocket boosters; the description omits the large, nonrecoverable, external tank containing the liquid fuel for the *Orbiter*'s own engines. The "Engine" article omits the two-stroke type, a common, small engine students may know. Some articles without an illustration could benefit from one, such as "Plimsoll Line" and "Halibut." At other times, an illustration supports the article poorly, such as the photograph of a wild almond tree in bloom for "Almond," when students may be more interested in the edible nut of the plant and its products. The price of the set would preclude it from most classrooms, but, despite some editorial shortcomings, this set could be a useful addition to the middle school library.—**Craig A. Munsart**

1406. **Macmillan Encyclopedia of Science.** rev. ed. New York, Macmillan Library Reference/Simon & Schuster Macmillan, 1997. 12v. illus. maps. index. $375.00/set. ISBN 0-02-8645561.

Hailed as a revision of the 1991 edition of *Macmillan Encyclopedia of Science* (see ARBA 92, entry 1456), this set of 12 volumes presents science in the same topical arrangement, with the first 6 volumes devoted to life, physical, earth, and space sciences and volumes 7-12 covering applied science. This set is not a major revision but rather an updating of information in the areas of space technology, computer technology, and recent developments in industry. The new photographs and illustrations are also primarily in these areas. The majority of the articles, illustrations, and glossaries remain unchanged. Up to 15 "Spot Facts" now open each module, whereas the earlier edition averaged 5. Indexes and glossaries have been changed to reflect the recent information. The biographical section on key scientists at the end of volume 12 has also been revised. All of the bibliographic sections of suggestions for further reading were updated to include primarily titles since 1990; only five references were published prior to that date. The 1997 edition has a brighter and more colorful binding, with the titles of the 12 volumes identified on the front and back of each volume. The new set is recommended for grades 5-8.—**Elaine Ezell**

1407. **McGraw-Hill Encyclopedia of Science & Technology.** 8th ed. Sybil P. Parker and others, eds. New York, McGraw-Hill, 1997. 20v. illus. maps. index. $1,995.00/set. ISBN 0-07-911504-7.

The 8th edition of this encyclopedia, which is published on an approximate 5-year cycle, contains the significant revisions, increased current topic coverage, and advanced illustrations one would expect in an encyclopedia of this caliber (see ARBA 93, entry 1446, for a review of the 7th edition). The latest edition boasts 1,600 totally new or revised entries, 1,750 new illustrations, and 78 full-color pages. A larger typeface makes reading easier, and new color article dividers throughout the set replace dull gray. Approximately 80 major science and technology subject areas are covered, for a total of 7,100 entries.

There has been significant turnover in consulting editors and contributors, and the number of Nobel prize-winning contributors has decreased slightly. A new feature, an "Activity Guide" with notes for instructors, joins the study guides geared for the high school and college students that have accompanied the encyclopedia in the past. The format has remained unchanged in this set. Articles, all signed, include cross-references and are presented alphabetically by subject. Coverage within each article is pyramid style—each topic is given a basic definition and general overview, followed by more in-depth coverage. Index access is excellent, consisting of four parts: a list of contributors, scientific tables and style notations, a topical index, and an analytic index. A press release for the encyclopedia echoes kudos from library schools for "the perfect index," and the set is indeed extremely well done.

It must be especially daunting to try to keep up with the explosion of new topics in science. Unfortunately, this encyclopedia falls short in some cases. Although coverage of current food topics has increased by more than 20 pages, and other "hot" topics, such as chaos, nanotechnology, and the Mars *Observer* and *Mir* space missions are included, some others are not. Bovine Spongiform Encephalopathy or "mad cow disease" was identified as a possible human health risk in autumn 1995; this edition is completely silent on the topic. A student writing a term paper or a citizen looking up health risks would expect a resource dated 1997 to cover it. Also, coverage is sometimes uneven—a section on anorexia nervosa runs to almost three pages, but a section on Alzheimer's disease is comparatively brief. Coverage of AIDS has improved, in that it now better acknowledges perinatal, heterosexual, and blood product transmission risks, and the entry includes a chart of opportunistic infections associated with the disease. Yet, no bibliography is given for this popular topic of research.

Increasingly, multivolume print encyclopedias will face competition from electronic resources. Recognizing this fact, the publisher released a CD-ROM product in 1994, the *McGraw-Hill Multimedia Encyclopedia of Science & Technology* (see ARBA 95, entry 1494), with articles and illustrations from the 7th edition of the print encyclopedia, as well as scientific terms from the 5th edition of the *McGraw-Hill Dictionary of Scientific and Technical Terms* (see ARBA 95, entry 1493). Yet, if a future edition of the multimedia encyclopedia is merely a snapshot of the print edition, it will inherit its deficiencies. *Encyclopaedia Britannica* has, for example, chosen a World Wide Web-based edition that is continuously updated. The Britannica strategy blends the readability and permanence of a print edition with updated and new articles delivered via the Web.

Emblematic of the need for McGraw-Hill to embrace the Internet is the shocking paucity of information about that topic in the 8th edition of its encyclopedia. No mention is made of the explosion of network applications since 1992; the term *World Wide Web* does not appear in the index. The importance of the Internet in general and the Web in particular were understood by 1994; the omission is inexcusable. One hopes that McGraw-Hill will embrace the Internet fully, both in the actual content of any future editions and as a delivery mechanism for supplemental content in general. This is an expensive, well-respected set that should address such weaknesses to retain its reputation as a leading science encyclopedia.—**Judith A. Matthews**

1408. **Routledge Spanish Technical Dictionary. Diccionario Técnico Inglés.** New York, Routledge, 1997. 2v. $280.00/set. ISBN 0-415-11274-5.

This two-volume reference aids in the translation of technical terms between Spanish and English. Prepared with the help of more than 100 specialists from industry and academia as well as professional translators, it contains a broad base of terminology drawn from more than 70 areas of technology, such as mechanical engineering, the construction industry, electrical engineering and electronics, as well as newer subject areas, such as fuelless energy sources, safety engineering, and quality assurance.

Volume 1, Spanish-English, is arranged alphabetically by each term's first element. A list of elements under which Spanish terms are not entered is provided in the introductory material. Each entry is accompanied by a label indicating the term's part of speech, and the gender is given for every noun term. Every term also gives an indication of the technological area in which it is used. Other supplementary information about terms includes the typical subject or object of a verb, typical nouns used with an adjective, words indicating the reference of a noun, and a paraphrase or broad equivalent. Because both British and North American terms are covered, these are differentiated by regional labels. Both abbreviations and their full forms are covered in the main body of the dictionary in alphabetic sequence. Cross-references to the full form or abbreviations as appropriate are provided with such entries. Volume 2, English-Spanish, is also arranged alphabetically by each term's first element. A list of elements under which English terms are not entered is provided. Each entry furnishes the term's part of speech, an indication of the technological area in which the term is used, the gender for each Spanish noun, and other data as necessary and as described for volume 1.

The easy-to-use format includes two-columned pages, bold typeface for term entries and cross-references, and guide words at the top of each page. The typeface size is adequate for easy reading. Supplementary material includes a variety of conversion tables and a list of the chemical elements in both English and Spanish, along with their symbols and atomic numbers.—**Dana McDougald**

1409. **The World Book Encyclopedia of Science.** Chicago, World Book, 1997. 8v. illus. maps. index. $149.00/set. ISBN 0-7166-3394-9.

The World Book Encyclopedia of Science presents basic science concepts in 8 volumes: *Astronomy, Physics, Chemistry, The Planet Earth, The Plant World, The Animal World, The Human Body,* and *Men and Women of Science.* These volumes cover all areas of science in a clear and readable manner for children or adults with no science background. The purpose of this set is to demystify complex scientific information by explaining concepts in language accessible to the general reader. The many illustrations aid the set in the goal of avoiding the "often forbidding appearance of traditional science publications" (p. 6, v. 1). There are glossaries at the end of each volume (except v. 8), and these provide clear explanations of scientific terms.

Photography credits are listed in aggregate at the end of each volume, are very brief, and thus provide too little connection with the illustrations. For instance, Harold Edgerton's famous photograph of a bullet moving through an apple is shown in volume 2 but with no text relating the photograph to Edgerton except in the densely packed "Credits" at the end of the book. More information on the photograph itself and some background about Edgerton would have been welcome. Overall, the individual volumes would be improved with more integration of information about men and women in science, because the people behind science often make it more fascinating. The separate volume on men and women provides extremely useful but too few and too brief biographies.

These are relatively minor criticisms of an overall excellent and affordable effort to present science clearly to a wide range of ages and abilities. The set is recommended for children's collections and public libraries. [R: RBB, 15 Mar 97, p. 1262]—**Constance Rinaldo**

1410. **World Book's Young Scientist.** Chicago, World Book, 1997. 10v. illus. maps. index. $140.00/set. ISBN 0-7166-2796-5.

This series of reference books is designed to be a student-friendly science source for upper-intermediate and middle school students. Unlike encyclopedias, which have articles in alphabetic order, each of the 10 volumes addresses specific subjects, such as space technology and computers (volume 1) or the human body and communication (volume 7). The format makes the work well suited to student needs, such as researching basics of a particular subject for a report. Each of the volumes contains a detailed table of contents, a glossary, and an index. Keywords within articles are indicated in bold typeface and are included as the index entries. Articles are well illustrated with combinations of drawings and photographs, all in color. Students of multiracial backgrounds are included in many of the illustrations. Easily completed student activities are incorporated within the text, allowing students the opportunity to explore various concepts; when necessary, these include a logo that indicates the need for adult supervision. Cross-references within a volume indicate pages that provide additional information.

The final volume includes a comprehensive index to the entire series and a minimal glossary that includes words already defined in the individual volumes. Some questions are posed within the text, and the answers to these are given in volume 10. The remainder of the final volume is more of an introduction and might be more likely used by students if they were directed to it in volume 1 or if the information was in volume 1. General information about science and scientists, a guide for researching and using the set, methods and units of measurement, and helpful ideas about completing the activities in the book are included here.

Some opportunities were missed to make the books even more student-centered. Possible damage to hearing by listening to loud music is absent in both the discussions of the human ear (volume 7) and the discussion of sound energy (volume 8). In an effort to simplify text, some information provided is misleading. In volume 8, only wind and gasoline are indicated as energy sources for boats, omitting diesel fuel, other petroleum products, and nuclear energy. Minor editorial errors also exist. Materials listed for an activity on water level (volume 4) and the supporting illustrations indicate a can should be used; the description of the activity cites a glass jar.

Such minor errors detract only a little from the overall quality of these books. The price, format, and content make this set an excellent addition to either an elementary school, middle school, or home library.
—**Craig A. Munsart**

DIRECTORIES

1411. Schlachter, Gail Ann, and R. David Weber. **Money for Graduate Students in the Sciences 1996-1998.** San Carlos, Calif., Reference Service Press, 1996. 418p. index. $45.00. ISBN 0-918276-32-2.

This publication is 1 of 13 directories of financial aid sources published by Reference Service Press; it is 1 of 3 of the press's published directories listing opportunities for graduate students (see entries 91 and 848 for reviews of the other 2). The authors are well qualified, each having published other reference works, including other financial aid directories. Two of Schlachter's prior reference works have won awards. Entries support study, training, research, and creative activities and promote efforts in agriculture, astronomy, biology, chemistry, computer science, dentistry, engineering, environmental science, geology, genetics, mathematics, medicine, nursing, nutrition, pharmacology, physics, technology, and zoology.

This work, listing programs specifically supporting graduate students in the sciences, is a boon. It is not too inclusive, such as Daniel Cassidy's *The Scholarship Book* (5th ed., Prentice Hall, 1996), which lists entries that may or may not support graduate students and includes fields other than the sciences. Likewise, it is not too specialized, such as *Dollars for College: The Quick Guide to Financial Aid for Nursing and Other Health Fields* (Garrett Park Press, 1995). Other works listing support for graduate students, such as Daniel Cassidy's *Graduate Scholarship Directory* (see ARBA 94, entry 331), list fewer funding programs. The purpose, eligibility, financial data, and special features sections are complete enough to help users screen themselves in or out and thus avoid wasted time. This work is a must-have for library reference collections at colleges whose science graduates go on to advanced study and at graduate institutions offering degrees in the sciences. [R: Choice, Mar 97, pp. 1140-41]—**George L. Findlen**

HANDBOOKS AND YEARBOOKS

1412. **The Addison-Wesley Science Handbook.** By Gordon J. Coleman and David Dewar. New York, Helix Books/Addison-Wesley, 1997. 281p. illus. maps. $18.00pa. ISBN 0-201-76652-3.

In times past, everyone used to buy the *Handbook of Chemistry and Physics* produced by the Chemical Rubber Company (otherwise known as the "CRC Bible"). It is still useful from time to time to look up an odd formula. Coleman and Dewar have done the same thing on a reduced scale and have added some biology and geology. This means the volume at hand is the right size and is based broadly enough to be hauled off the shelf time and again by amateurs and professionals alike. Science graduates will recognize old friends they have not seen or used in a while. Those who work in the sciences can quickly find a half-remembered equation in a related field. The layperson can find interesting and informative tidbits. For the most part, this is a reference rather than a tutorial. There are some quick explanatory pieces, particularly in the sections on biology, chemistry, and geology. The dozen or so pages on the human body would be an excellent background for a first aid course—just enough material to have the procedures make sense, but not so much that it is bogged down in tons of detail. As with the "CRC Bible," disappointingly, certain entries did not appear. Overall, however, this handbook is quite good.—**Robert M. Slade**

1413. **DISCovering Science.** [CD-ROM]. Detroit, Gale, 1997. Minimum system requirements: IBM or compatible 386 (486 or higher recommended). CD-ROM drive. DOS 5.0. Windows 3.1. 8MB RAM. SVGA 256-color monitor. Mouse. Sound card. Speakers or headphones. $300.00/yr. ISBN 0-8103-7164-2.

This new entry in the DISCovering series from Gale offers a broad look at the history, people, inventions, discoveries, theories, life forms, and objects that make up the world of science. This work contains 2,500 essays on scientific theories and discoveries; 1,000 periodical article abstracts covering the latest scientific developments; more than 1,000 biographies of notable people in the history of science; glossary terms; a hyperlinked timeline; and multimedia features, including video and audio clips as well as photographs.

The disc is easily installed. The main menu screen is attractively designed and easy to read with menu choices clearly labeled. Off the main search menu, users can search by word or by phrase or use one of the categories provided: "Encyclopedia," "Subject," "People," "Timeline," "Full Text Search," "Custom Search," and "Multimedia Gallery." Expanded searching features are available in "Custom Search," where users can search key terms or categories and can limit to such features as occupation, gender, nationality, or document type. Boolean searching can be done at various categories. Many searching options are also provided within the categories, for example, in the "Subject" category, users can search either using an alphabetic list of subjects or switch to an outline form that lists broad areas of disciplines, such as topics in the mathematics, earth sciences, physical sciences, and so on. The documents retrieved from the search are informative and include photographs, hyperlinked *see also* references, multimedia, and bibliographies. Tool bar functions allow the user to save, print, access Help, return to the main menu, jump to a different search category, or even access Merriam-Webster's dictionary.

As useful as this product is, it does have its faults. No visible Help option is available on the main menu. An inexperienced user may not know to press F1 for Help. In some cases, the user is led to marginal or irrelevant material. A search for murres directs one to a document on auks in which murres are just mentioned in a sentence. In the "People" category, names appear on its browse list but lead nowhere. The absence of some well-known people, such as Isaac Asimov, Carl Sagan, or even John James Audubon, stands out. For good or bad, when viewing the results of a search, the document always begins at the beginning and not at the portion relevant to the search. The good news is that accessing a tool bar function will jump the user to the appropriate spot.

As an introductory tool to the subject, this product would be of use to college or university undergraduates or even high school students needing the level of information presented here. Libraries should take advantage of the trial period to evaluate the product for their specific needs.—**Julia Perez**

1414. **The Handy Science Answer Book.** 2d ed. Compiled by the Science and Technology Department of the Carnegie Library of Pittsburgh. Detroit, Visible Ink Press/Gale, 1997. 580p. illus. maps. index. $16.95pa. ISBN 0-7876-1013-5.

It is often said that this is an age of information explosion. That statement may be true, but there never was an age when a single human being could have absorbed all available human knowledge. Although it is accurate that the twentieth century has witnessed a mushrooming of knowledge and information such as never before in recorded human history, it is no less correct that never before was information more easily available or accessible.

The Handy Science Answer Book is one of hundreds of efforts to make knowledge and science easily available to anyone who will take the trouble of opening the pages of a book. The more than 1,400 questions have been culled from inquiries directed by the general public to the staff of the Science and Technology Department of the Carnegie Library of Pittsburgh. All are interesting questions, but not all of them truly pertain to science, even though they are presented under the broad headings of physics and chemistry, space, Earth, biology, and the like. Some questions are of purely historical interest (e.g., What is phlogiston?), while some have only terminological value (e.g., What is an adiabatic process?). Some are purely informative (e.g., What is the composition of air?) and some have no more than numerical significance (e.g., What are the relative gravitational pulls on planets?).

Despite the fact that many of the questions are not purely scientific, books such as this one can provoke the curious, inspire the young, or liven up conversations at the dinner table. At a time when the United States has become aware of how low the nation's level of scientific literacy is, this work can come in handy indeed.—**Varadaraja V. Raman**

1415. **Science on File.** [CD-ROM]. By the Diagram Group. New York, Facts on File, 1996. Minimum system requirements (Windows version): IBM or compatible 386/16MHz. Double-speed CD-ROM drive. Windows 3.1. 8MB RAM. 2MB hard disk space. Color monitor. Windows-compatible mouse. Windows-compatible printer. Minimum system requirements (Macintosh version): 68030. Double-speed CD-ROM drive. System 7.1. 2MB RAM. 1.3MB hard disk space. 13-inch, 256-color monitor. Macintosh-compatible printer. $149.95 ea. / $499.99 for 5. ISBN 0-8160-3408-7 (Windows); 0-8160-3496-6 (Macintosh).

This CD-ROM combines 1,200 images from 5 titles in the On File series: *Human Body on File*, *Animal Anatomy on File*, *Life Sciences on File*, *Earth Sciences on File*, and *Physical Sciences on File*. As with Facts on File print materials, the images are copyright-free for nonprofit educational uses. If users have seen any Facts on File binders, they will know what to expect here. Simple black-and-white images provide charts, graphs, cross-sections, bird's-eye views, step-by-step drawings, and all manner of images on a wide variety of topics. Coverage is broad rather than deep and is geared to topics normally taught in middle school and high school science classes. So, even though there are only two views of a dolphin (external view and skeleton), there are seven images each of the commonly dissected eyeballs and frogs.

The images can be saved to disk (.TIF files) or printed. The drawings can be printed with labels and captions in place (for teaching and lecture) or without them, for testing. There is only one option for print quality—300 dpi. This produces a fairly poor-quality print, especially if one is considering using it as an overhead. That may be a fair trade-off for the convenience of having all these images at one's disposal. Key terms and concepts are defined in articles of varying lengths. The articles can be found by first pulling up a drawing and then scanning it for the concept or term. If the concept or term accompanies the drawing *and* the term is underlined, users can click on it to link to the article. Users would probably find it useful to have direct access to encyclopedia articles.

The biggest challenge to the user will be figuring out how to use this CD-ROM. The jewel case liner, which serves double-duty as advertisement and installation guide, offers only vague promises and inaccurate instructions. The online Help is nearly nonexistent. It is not searchable; instead, each type of screen (image screen, menu screen) has a single Help page. If the few explanations on that page do not address a particular question, the user is out of luck. Even the simplest action—returning to a search screen after viewing a drawing—becomes a matter of trial and error, because there is no Back button, and the online Help does not offer any suggestions.

According to printed materials, "Title, Category, and Keyword searches allow the user to view images and encyclopedia entries, while Physical and Life Science indexes provide direct access to the drawings." This reviewer found buttons to initiate title and category searches, but none for keyword searches. An Advanced Search button allows Boolean searches, but those searches led only to drawings, as did the searches done by title and category. Even installing the disc is difficult because of poor instructions. The installation instructions direct the user to select a file named setup.exe. This file does not exist. The name of the file is install.exe. The instructions that accompany the CD-ROM submitted for review are written for "Windows 3.1 or higher" but do not address Windows 95. This omission creates problems, because Windows 95 presents program groups and icons differently than previous versions, so some of the instructions are incorrect. One disc includes both Windows and Macintosh files. The Macintosh files and instructions were not tested.—**Constance Hardesty**

1416. **Science Year 1997: The World Book Annual Science Supplement. A Review of Science and Technology During the 1996 School Year.** Chicago, World Book, 1996. 352p. illus. maps. index. $29.40. ISBN 0-7166-0597-X.

1417. **Science Year 1998: The World Book Annual Science Supplement. A Review of Science and Technology During the 1997 School Year.** Chicago, World Book, 1997. 352p. illus. maps. index. $29.40. ISBN 0-7166-0598-8.

At the end of each school year, a science supplement to *The World Book Encyclopedia* is issued. Each section of the supplement is keyed to a corresponding section of the encyclopedia. The 1998 supplement, covering the 1997 school year, deals with space probes (such as Cassini), fossils in amber, prion molecules, the deep ocean, and paranormal events. The treatment is evenhanded, and the quality of writing, the illustrations, and the authority are comparable to those of a magazine such as *Scientific American*. It is, of course, not possible to cover all the details of a year's science in a few hundred pages, but these are fine pieces of work.—**Robert B. McKee**

INDEXES

1418. **Applied Science & Technology Index 1996.** Joyce M. Howard and others, eds. Bronx, N.Y., H. W. Wilson, 1996, 1997. 2v. price on a service basis rate. ISSN 0003-6986.

H. W. Wilson indexes have long had the reputation of being high-quality guides to the journal literature for general and undergraduate user populations, and *Applied Science & Technology Index*, which dates back to 1958 under its present title, is no exception. The subject headings are well chosen and up-to-date, with appropriate *see* and *see also* references. If there are typographic errors, they must be very few, as this reviewer was unable to find any. The volumes are solidly produced for many years of hard use.

Some additions to the journals indexed would be nice to see—for example, *Electrochemical Society Interface*, *IEEE Potentials*, and MRS Bulletin of the Materials Research Society. However, journals are chosen by Wilson through a two-step process in which an American Library Association committee selects a list for consideration, which is then voted on by the subscribers. Perhaps it is unnecessary to remark that an increasing number of subscribers purchase an electronic version of this title rather than the print version, as indeed many institutions do with most indexes and abstracts. Printed indexes such as this handsomely produced set are the among the last examples of a vanishing world.—**Robert Michaelson**

30 Agricultural Sciences

GENERAL WORKS

1419. Wendel, C. H. **Encyclopedia of American Farm Implements & Antiques.** Iola, Wis., Krause Publications, 1997. 395p. illus. $24.95pa. ISBN 0-87341-507-8.

Imagine the family dog treading to power a butter churn; one nineteenth-century inventor saw the possibility. Horses were put on treadmills too, energizing even heavier agricultural equipment. From pig scratching posts and oilers to portable grain elevators, this volume shows—in nearly 2,000 photographs—that ingenuity in the industrial age was not confined to the factory; it arguably started on the farm.

Lightning rods; bone cutters (mashed bone was once a preferred fertilizer); and cement mixers and fence-making tools (e.g., "comealong" for pulling barbed wire, post diggers) have a history of form that is every bit as diverse as the designs of combines (i.e., combined harvester-thresher). Variety ruled, of course. For example, the many types of baling (originally, "pressing") machinery demonstrate many solutions to the same problem. Corn graders, which sorted kernels by size to garner the best for sowing, indicate how serious a business farming—including the dimension of crop improvement—has long been. By the 1880s, naming equipment became a serious business and by the beginning the twentieth century, trademarks from Daisy to Tornado proliferated. An array of trademarks complements the book.

Food for the mind is the stuff of this book, the culmination of 30 years of work. It is difficult to imagine a public library without a copy.—**Diane M. Calabrese**

FOOD SCIENCES AND TECHNOLOGY
Dictionaries and Encyclopedias

1420. Bennett, Bev, and Virginia Van Vynckt. **Dictionary of Healthful Food Terms.** Hauppauge, N.Y., Barron's Educational Series, 1997. 333p. $8.95pa. ISBN 0-8120-9751-3.

Including such topics as antioxidants, food safety, proteins, vitamins and minerals, and much more, this reference is a compilation of more than 1,000 diet, food, and nutrition terms. This volume is not a dictionary of foodstuff; the emphasis is on nutrition and encompasses the latest medicinal uses and combinations of foods, herbs, and supplements. Definitions are clearly written and easily understood; the volume is of use to the layperson as well as the health or food professional. Equally important is the appended information: an interpretation of the new food label; how to use the Food Pyramid; an explanation of serving sizes; recommended dietary allowances (RDAs) and foods that are high in nutrients and meet the daily RDAs; lists of food additives and their function; questionable food additives; and more. The dictionary is complete with cross-references, source notes, and a good bibliography. It complements the publishers' *Food Lover's Companion* (see ARBA 91, entry 1483) and is an excellent purchase for any person or library.—**Joy Hastings**

1421. Heaton, Donald D. **A Produce Reference Guide to Fruits and Vegetables from Around the World: Nature's Harvest.** Binghamton, N.Y., Food Products Press/Haworth Press, 1997. 244p. illus. index. $29.95. ISBN 1-56022-865-2.

A descriptive title is just one of this compact guide's many appeals. More than 400 fruits and vegetables are described, with entries providing such information as the history of each food item, the common and uncommon names, a description of the food's appearance and taste, its period of availability (e.g., "July through October"), and uses as a consumer product. A handy chart of fruit yields is presented (a pound of oranges creates a cup of juice), nutritional values are listed (vitamin content, calories per serving, and so on), and a liberally cross-referenced index is included.

It takes a moment to grasp the alphabetic arrangement of the food names. The category of food is listed first, with a modifier following (e.g., "nut macadamia," "nut peanut"). Once that minor oddity (actually a savvy arrangement) is understood, users will find this source to be a model dictionary. It's straightforward, clearly written, and quite informative. One caveat—a black-and-white sketch is used to illustrate each food item. Color photographs would have been an improvement but would also have dramatically increased production costs. In this time of increasing consumer experimentation with exotic produce, libraries should have on hand this economical guidebook. [R: RBB, 1 Oct 97, p. 357]—**Ed Volz**

1422. Lagua, Rosalinda T., and Virginia S. Claudio. **Nutrition and Diet Therapy Reference Dictionary.** 4th ed. New York, Chapman & Hall, 1996. 491p. $69.95; $37.95pa. ISBN 0-412-07051-0; 0-412-07061-8pa.

This 4th edition is still an excellent reference tool. The main text is the dictionary, with word descriptions; subentries; and *see*, *see also*, and *see under* cross-references. When a word has more than one meaning, the most accepted meaning is listed first, and other meanings continue to be listed in order of usage. The definitions are all related to nutrition in its various applications and are clearly and concisely written.

The 50 appendixes cover the nutritional contents on foods, vitamins, the food pyramid, U.S. nutrition labeling, the classification and utilization of carbohydrates, proteins, lipids, the digestive enzymes, selected hormones, the reference values for blood constituents and lipids, the fiber content of foods, and other nutritional data too numerous to name here. Three exceptional appendixes include the religious food practices chart, the public health nutrition programs and surveys in the United States and the administering agency, and the list of agencies and organizations with nutrition-related activities. This book also is a collection development resource for librarians, because one appendix lists sources of nutrition information broken down into the categories of books, journals, miscellaneous newsletters, pamphlets, videos, and tapes.

This book is highly recommended not only to medical libraries but to academic libraries where nutrition is taught as a major and as a part of other majors. The dictionary is also recommended to public libraries as an excellent source of information on the topic.—**Betsy J. Kraus**

1423. Morton, Mark. **Cupboard Love: A Dictionary of Culinary Curiosities.** Winnipeg, Man., Bain & Cox/Blizzard Publishing; distr., Buffalo, N.Y., General Distribution Services, 1996. 399p. $21.95 (U.S.). ISBN 0-921368-66-6.

Culinary terms have an interesting and colorful history. They come from many languages and cultures and describe foods or methods of preparation. This charming dictionary provides the etymology for 1,000 English-language words related to food and cooking.

A brief introduction includes an abbreviated history of the English language and a list of the major reference sources that the author used. He provides only authors and titles. They are standard works such as the *Oxford English Dictionary* (2d ed.; see ARBA 90, entry 1006) and the *Larousse Gastronomique* (see ARBA 89, entry 1373). Alphabetic entries range in length from a few sentences to one page. The content of the entry emphasizes the history of the word rather than the origin and preparation of the food. The terms covered include standard food items, such as cheese; more exotic dishes, such as haggis; and fanciful terms, such as *pingle* (to pick at one's food) and the infamous *spotted dick*. Perusing this book, one discovers that the term *soufflé* has the same Latin root (*flare*) as the word flatulence and that many gastronomical terms, such as *cappuccino* and *pope's nose*, target the clergy.

Although *Cupboard Love* is delightful reading, patrons who need to know more about culinary history will need other sources. John Ayto's *The Glutton's Glossary* (see ARBA 92, entry 1480) provides this information. For more depth, the *Larousse Gastronomique* is the standard source. *Cupboard Love* complements these works and offers additional information for gourmands and linguists. [R: Choice, July/Aug 97, p. 1782]—**Barbara M. Bibel**

1424. **The New Sotheby's Wine Encyclopedia.** By Tom Stevenson. New York, DK Publishing, 1997. 600p. illus. maps. index. $50.00. ISBN 0-7894-2079-1.

Originally published in 1988 as *Sotheby's World Wine Encyclopedia* (see ARBA 89, entry 1376), this book is now in its first U.S. edition. Over the years, it has proven to be an enormous seller as well as the winner of five awards. (Sotheby's is, of course, the British auction house, which, along with Christie's, offers wine auctions.) Stevenson himself has many awards, principally as three-time winner of Wine Writer of the Year (British).

The book is arranged geographically, with about 100 half-page maps. It covers 4,000 appellations or wine-growing districts and styles, as well as 2,000 producers. The top producers and regions are profiled, and some assessment of the wines is made. Stevenson adds a more rigorous listing of recommended wines after each country has been described, apart from the main text.

Each area has a history of the region and the styles of the wines, as well as a description of the grape varieties used and the climates. The author goes on to show the methods of cultivation and wine making unique to each area. Scattered throughout are color maps and reproductions of wine labels. The work concludes with guidelines, glossaries, tasting charts, wine and food pairings, and an extensive workable index.

The six pages devoted to Canada, a cool climate wine-producing area of modest distinction noted mainly for its Icewines, are adequate. But more stress could have been placed on the nature of Icewines; the best wines made in Canada.

Throughout the book there are a lot of sidebars with short notes. This makes the visual presentation a little choppy in style, but that is the impact of CD-ROM graphics and writing for one computer screen at a time. Although there are other books similar to this one (and other major sources on the Internet or on CD-ROM), here is a chance to acquire the latest up-to-date material in-print. It will serve nicely until the next wine encyclopedia comes along.—**Dean Tudor**

Handbooks and Yearbooks

1425. Berthold-Bond, Annie. **The Green Kitchen Handbook: Practical Advice, References, and Sources for Transforming the Center of Your Home into a Healthful, Livable Place.** New York, HarperCollins, 1997. 278p. index. $15.00pa. ISBN 0-06-095186-9.

The full title of this book aptly describes the intentions of the author: *The Green Kitchen Handbook: Practical Advice, References, and Sources for Transforming the Center of Your Home into a Healthful, Livable Place*. The handbook is excellent for the beginner and a good review for the advanced reader in sustainable living. It is an easily understood book that can be read chapter by chapter or used as a resource. Aside from the foreword by Meryl Streep, the preface by Wendy Gordon (executive director, Mothers & Others for a Livable Planet); acknowledgments; and six chapters with multiple subsections, there is an appendix of nutritional data, an extensive resource list, and an index.

Throughout the book are simple charts and tables with information on canning, drying, freezing, nutritional value of food items, root cellar storage details, fiber content of foods, and seasonal harvest calendars. Brief definitions and practical tips of all kinds include alternative ways of cleaning with nontoxic materials, cooking, and saving natural resources through recycling, as well as information on canning, composting, and gardening. The author is supportive of organic, local, sustainable farmers rather than industrial farmers. Chapter 3 lists individual food items and best choice (if any) of each. This chapter will be an excellent quick reference source for organically grown, unrefined, edible products.

At times, the author becomes too pessimistic about the environment and its future. Nonetheless, *The Green Kitchen Handbook* is recommended for public libraries.—**Nadine Salmons**

1426. Murray, Jim. **The Complete Guide to Whiskey: Selecting, Comparing, and Drinking the World's Great Whiskeys.** Chicago, Triumph Books, 1997. 256p. maps. index. $14.95pa. ISBN 1-57243-151-2.

This pocket-size book starts with the art of making whiskey, providing descriptions of the primary ingredients and the basic processes, which include malting, peating, milling, cooking, mashing, fermentation, distillation, and maturation. The next chapter covers Scottish malt whiskey and contains a map showing locations of distilleries along with a history of the area. The history of Scotch is followed by a list of regions that produce Scotch and their particular specialty, as well as the history of Scotch including the age, strength, and character description of the product. This format is repeated for Irish whiskey, bourbon, rye whiskey, and Canadian whiskey. The main text is followed by a glossary and an index. The maps add interest and help to locate the area of the world where whiskey is produced. The typeface is small but is in two colors, making the text easier to read. This work contains interesting historical facts and will be enjoyed by the connoisseur as well as being helpful to persons in hospitality management.

—**Herbert W. Ockerman**

1427. Onstad, Dianne. **Whole Foods Companion: A Guide for Adventurous Cooks, Curious Shoppers, & Lovers of Natural Foods.** White River Junction, Vt., Chelsea Green, 1996. 528p. illus. index. $29.00pa. ISBN 0-930031-83-0.

Despite an abundance of books written about natural foods, the author of this work has still managed to produce a unique offering. Onstad focuses on plant-based foods only, describing them in an encyclopedic format. Similar encyclopedias of whole foods, such as *The Whole Foods Encyclopedia* (Viking Penguin, 1997) and *The Wholefood Catalog* (Fawcett Columbine, 1988) also describe natural foods, but in much less detail than *Whole Foods Companion*. The two earlier works do, however, include recipes, whereas the volume under review does not.

The six categories of natural foods that are covered in this companion are fruits; vegetables; grains; legumes; nuts, seeds, and oils; and herbs, spices, and other foods. For each food item, of which there are about 400, Onstad includes general information; buying tips; culinary uses; health benefits; and a sidebar of information on the nutritional value per portion, such as number of calories, protein, minerals, vitamins, and the like. Of added interest is the lore and legend section associated with some of the foods. For instance, spinach has been regarded in folklore as a wonder plant that can restore energy, as personified in Popeye, the popular cartoon character.

A number of unusual food items can be found that will appeal to the curious shopper. Readers can learn about bilibi, yautias, or soursops (bilibi and soursops are tropical fruits and a yautia is a potatolike root originating in the American tropics). The work appears to be well researched, based on the extensive annotated bibliography at the end of the text. The companion will appeal to the food enthusiast as well as to the general reader. Public libraries will find it useful on their reference shelves.—**Elaine F. Jurries**

1428. Susser, Allen. **The Great Citrus Book.** Berkeley, Calif., Ten Speed Press, 1997. 158p. illus. $16.95pa. ISBN 0-89815-855-9.

This 4½-by-10¼-inch book starts with an introduction that covers the history of citrus technology; cultivation; pest management; citrus use; world production; citrus growing areas; and characteristics of various types of citrus plants, including hybrids. Next it covers the various types of citrus products, including nutrition; varieties; and excellent photographs of the sweet orange, mandarin, grapefruit, pummelo, lemon, lime, citron, and sour orange. This section is followed by a description of the kumquat in a similar fashion. The next section discusses unusual citrus and root stock fruits and looks at the influence of crossing different species. This segment is followed by recipes using citrus products. Next comes a "Citrus of the World" section that covers variety, origin, harvest dates, and categories in which the various products can be classified. The volume is a glossy, multicolored book with excellent photographs, and it would be useful for anyone interested in the production, purchasing, and use of citrus products. This paperback features above-average paper with excellent printing.—**Herbert W. Ockerman**

Quotation Books

1429. Herbst, Sharon Tyler. **Never Eat More Than You Can Lift, and Other Food Quotes and Quips: 1,500 Notable Quotables About Edibles and Potables.** New York, Broadway Books, 1997. 372p. index. $27.95. ISBN 0-553-06901-2.

Cookbook author and culinary reference expert Herbst has prepared an enticing and amusing quotation book in *Never Eat More Than You Can Lift*. More than 1,500 quotations under 200 subject headings fill this admittedly subjective volume. Contained between these covers are sayings from such people and personalities as Erma Bombeck, Louis Armstrong, Adolf Hitler, and Miss Piggy (who also supplied the title of the book). The A to Z (or nearly so) format stretches from "Abalone" to "Wine," stopping at "Coffee," "Lemons," "Murder and Food," "Salt," and "Toasts; Toasting" in between. Many subject categories are introduced by little snippets from the author; throughout the text, shaded boxes provide yet more interesting tidbits and kitchen tips. More than 50 recipes, some sounding less-than-appetizing ("Peppered Caramel Bacon," "Can't-Be-Beet Fudge Cake," "Tomato (Gin)ger Slush") pepper the text. Cross-references to related topics are found throughout the entries. An author index and a short recipe index provide further access. A reading list is presented at the end of the volume, and unfortunately this is the only reference point to sources—the quotations themselves give only a who, not a where or when. Because of this small caveat, the pure reference value of this sumptuous book is called into question, but for general circulation, Herbst's book is a peach. [R: LJ, 1 May 97, p. 98]—**Melissa Rae Root**

FORESTRY

1430. **European Forests and Timber: Scenarios into the 21st Century.** By the Timber Section, UN/ECE Trade Division. New York, United Nations, 1996. 228p. (Geneva Timber and Forest Discussion Papers; ETTS V Working Papers). $150.00pa. ISBN 92-1-100736-4. S/N GV.E.96.0.38.

This volume consists of a set of detailed charts and tables containing projections, to the year 2020, of European timber production and consumption. It is a working paper exhibiting material too voluminous to be included in the set of papers published by the Food and Agriculture Organization of the United Nations, referred to as ETTS V, or the fifth study of European timber trends. The work under review is in effect a supplement to those. To make full use of this working paper, one must read the ETTS V series of papers to understand the terminology or have a background in economics. Not just timber is covered here; wood products, such as roundwood, sawnwood, panels, pulp, paperboard, and waste paper, are also featured.

Introductory material includes a discussion of the "consistency analysis" model, which calculates demand for roundwood. This model is the basis for the tables projecting consumption and production of wood and wood products by country, called "base scenarios." The scenarios are based on assumptions about rates of growth in wood demand. There are regional tables, again with consumption and production forecasts for wood products. These tables are based on "alternate scenarios," which involve various permutations of high- and low-cost factors and different product price levels.

This is a valuable compilation of projection figures. The volume should be purchased by any library holding the complete set of ETTS V papers.—**John Laurence Kelland**

1431. **Forest and Forest Industries Country Fact Sheets. Fiches Récapitulatives par Pays des Forêts et des Industries Forestières.** By the Timber Section, UN-ECE/FAO Secretariat. New York, United Nations, 1997. 91p. (Geneva Timber and Forest Study Papers, no.12). $28.00pa. ISBN 92-1-016322-2. S/N E/F.97.II.E.7.

This compendium contains accessible data on forests and forestry arranged by country for 47 nations in North America, the former USSR, and the United Nations/Economic Commission for Europe (UN/ECE) region of Europe. The document is printed in both English and French. Each country is represented by tabular data on area of forest and other wooded land (FOWL), exploitable forest, and net change in FOWL from 1990 to 1995; the percentage of FOWL that is publicly or privately owned; the amount of FOWL per inhabitant; the total growing stock in coniferous and nonconiferous forest; the amount (volume or weight) of production, import, export, and consumption of wood in the rough, fuelwood, sawnwood, panels, woodpulp, paper and paperboard, and waste paper; and the net trade and net trade as percentage of consumption of sawnwood, panels, woodpulp, and paper and paperboard. A pie chart is included for each country, showing the percentage distribution of land area among forests, other wooded land, and other land. Data on the net annual increment of forest volume and the annual fellings are contained in a bar chart that allows a quick assessment of the balance between growth and removal. A useful self-sufficiency ratio is calculated for each country with a comparison for Europe as a whole. Finally, the consumption per capita of sawnwood, panels, and paper and paperboard is shown in bar charts, again with values for Europe included for comparison. Readers should note when comparing countries that scales of the bar chart axes vary substantially among countries. A glossary of terms, symbols, and abbreviations is included. Further information may be obtained from individuals identified for each country.

This compilation is recommended for readers desiring at-a-glance data for comparing the covered countries. It is unfortunate that a similar document does not exist for all nations, but World Wide Web addresses are supplied for other Food and Agriculture Organization sources. An address is provided to which readers can direct comments, because this is the first publication of country fact sheets, and its authors welcome feedback.—**Michael G. Messina**

HORTICULTURE

Dictionaries and Encyclopedias

1432. **The American Horticultural Society A-Z Encyclopedia of Garden Plants.** Christopher Brickell and Judith D. Zuk, eds. New York, DK Publishing, 1997. 1092p. illus. $79.95. ISBN 0-7894-1943-2.

This heavy volume is a mammoth endeavor by the joint forces of the Royal Horticultural Society and the American Horticultural Society, which resulted in a reference book that should be useful to gardening novices and professionals alike. On its 1,000-plus pages are descriptions of more than 15,000 plants and trees, each one illustrated with stunning full-color photographs. The book is devised for the American gardener, and it includes the customary regional maps with regional plant-growing information. The front of the book contains basics, such as getting acquainted with plant terminology and parts of trees, flowers, roots, and rhizomes and methods of pruning, propagation, and the like, whereas in the back is a thorough cross-referencing index. Professionals, of course, will know where to look for such a common thing as a "fir," but casual gardeners will be sent to the appropriate place in the book, which is "Abies"; searching for "privet" will send one to "Ligustrum," "rhubarb" to "Rheum," "rubber plant" to "Ficus elastica," and so forth. Each entry includes detailed information on the plant's geographic origins as well as concise but extremely clear instructions on cultivation, propagation, possible problems, and general care.

An impressive list of contributors took part in this endeavor: gardening experts, nomenclature professionals, regional advisers, editors, proofreaders, and professional plant photographers. An enormous amount of time was spent on producing this encyclopedia, but it has resulted in a flawless, well-produced, extremely attractive and useful reference resource for anyone even vaguely interested in gardening. As for professionals, they will find it an invaluable tool that will find daily use in nurseries, labs, and gardening stores.—**Koraljka Lockhart**

1433. Jantra, Ingrid, and Ursula Krüger. **House Plant Encyclopedia.** Willowdale, Ont., Firefly Books, 1997. 384p. illus. index. $40.00. ISBN 1-55209-027-2.

A better title for this excellent volume might have been *The Container Plant Encyclopedia*, as not all of the plants featured can be grown indoors (the definition of a houseplant). A number of them are for patios and balconies and some are best off in flower beds. This caveat aside, it is doubtful any gardening enthusiast will be able to put the book down before looking at every page. The lush photographs and concise descriptions of plants will make even "brown-thumbed" readers want to try their hand at tending to green plants.

The first 100 pages are divided into 4 sections that give a wonderful overview of house plants in general. The sections—"Placement and Purchase"; "What You Should Know About Plants"; "Successful Care and Propagation"; and "Living Greener, Living Better"—discuss their respective subjects in detail and offer wonderful advice intended to get the user off to a good start. Nearly 1,000 common plants are then arranged alphabetically by botanical name, with information on family, native habitat, flowering time, location, care, propagation, pests and diseases, and uses given for each. Symbols are provided for each plant that quickly explain the light, watering, and feeding needs. Boxes and sidebars appear routinely, giving further information, anecdotal notes, or special tips. Finally, there is an index that is a boon to the neophyte as well as to the gardener who does not bother with botanical names, as it lists the plants by both Latin and common names.

Almost every book on plants has its attractions, but this one is particularly well thought out, taking into account the wide range of readers who might pick it up. This work is highly recommended for the gardener who likes the challenge of container plants, indoors or out. [R: LJ, 15 Mar 97, p. 56]

—Jo Anne H. Ricca

Handbooks and Yearbooks

1434. Clebsch, Betsy. **A Book of Salvias: Sages for Every Garden.** Portland, Oreg., Timber Press, 1997. 221p. illus. index. $29.95. ISBN 0-88192-369-9.

Salvia is an enormously varied genus in the mint family. Its members include annuals, perennials, and shrubby species; its colors range from blue and purple to red, pink, and white. Most of the plants have highly aromatic foliage. Amateur botanist and horticulturist Clebsch has selected more than 100 species for inclusion in this book. The species are arranged alphabetically by the plants' botanical names. Each entry is approximately 500 words in length and includes information on the plant's geographic origin, its physical description, and growing and propagation instructions. In addition, 87 color photographs and 9 illustrations are included and cross-referenced to the text. The book also contains sections on where to see and buy salvias. Of particular use are lists of salvias arranged by various factors, such as cold and heat tolerance, color, and flowering season. The book concludes with a bibliography of 39 works on the subject.

The reference has a significant omission in that the author has not included the popular names of the plants. For example, someone who is looking for information on scarlet sage, gentian sage, clary, or ramona will have to obtain the botanical name from another source first. This limits the work's usefulness, especially to the novice gardener. It is also interesting to note that although salvias are known for their aromatic leaves, Clebsch does not give much attention to this attribute. Most of the entries do not mention scent. Yet gardeners often plant salvias by walkways where the bruising of their foliage by passersby exudes a pleasant fragrance.

Overall, however, *A Book of Salvias* is an attractive work on a subject that rarely has an entire book devoted to it. As such, it fills a void in gardening literature. Libraries frequented by gardeners will certainly want to include a copy in their collections.—**January Adams**

1435. Elliott, Jack. **The Smaller Perennials.** Portland, Oreg., Timber Press, 1997. 176p. illus. $29.95. ISBN 0-88192-383-4.

This small book of smaller perennials offers readers a dictionary of perennial plants, including descriptions and photographs, that grow no higher than 30 inches. This useful subset of the perennial world has value for gardeners who wish to select plants for small garden spaces, those who wish to design rock gardens, or those who wish to focus on the front of the perennial border. The book does not include bulbs or shrubs.

The more than 400 genera listed, with numerous individual species included, are handsomely displayed, with many photographs in bright color, although there is not a picture for each genera. Each plant is listed under its genus, followed by species. The descriptions are thorough, with special emphasis on size at maturity. The plants are physically well described with sound botanical nomenclature. The entries also illustrate the usefulness of each plant in a garden setting. Plants that have received awards of merit or are personal favorites of the author are noted with symbols. A brief introduction with tips on growing and planting is included. Two brief appendixes are provided—one listing shade-loving plants, the other, various plant societies and their addresses.

This book should be included in libraries along with other gardening titles. Its special focus on smaller plants will fill a niche not generally covered in this detail. As a reference title, however, the book has one major drawback, and that is no index of common names. Library patrons often wish to see the scientific description, but do not know the scientific name with which to begin. It is true that common names are as changeable as the region in which they are developed, but an attempt could have been made—peony, poppy, and baby's breath are fairly universal. Although the book is arranged in dictionary format, a central index with some cross-references would have been a useful addition. Also, a library cannot rely on this title as its main source of reference information for perennial gardening: The book is not designed as such. Three classic perennial books are available and can serve this purpose—*Perennials for American Gardens* (Random House, 1989); *Encyclopedia of Perennials* (see ARBA 93, entry 1508); and *Rodale's Illustrated Encyclopedia of Perennials* (see ARBA 94, entry 1620).

Smaller Perennials is beautifully designed and bound; save the dust jacket for exhibit use. Although the author is British, he is aware of the North American garden and includes plants that are adaptable to a variety of climates. Certainly a lovely book, this title is recommended for public and academic libraries that have fairly large gardening collections, which, given the popularity of this hobby, will be many.
—**Paul A. Mogren**

1436. **Eyewitness Garden Handbooks: Annuals & Biennials.** New York, DK Publishing, 1997. 192p. illus. maps. index. $17.95 flexbinding. ISBN 0-7894-1983-1.

Like all DK Publishing books, including those for children, this handbook of annuals and biennials is clear, focused, and well written; and most of all, the pictures are crisp, true to color, and beautiful. The word *handbook* in the title is accurate, because this book is of the size to carry to the garden or to the garden store as one plans for one's own garden design or selects plants. It is especially helpful for choosing a proper site for a particular plant, determining whether it is suitable for containers, and predicting what it will look like at maturity.

The unique feature of this book is that the flowers are arranged by color, according to a provided color wheel, and by size, with the capacity to join these criteria together for a perfect garden match. The book uses scientific nomenclature, grouping flowering plants by family name, genus, and species and variety. Common names are also provided. Other useful information provided includes the origin of the plant—whether of garden origin or an original native of a particular locale. Also furnished is information about propagation, cultivation, site, and variant common names. For plants that have many species or varieties, an introduction is provided for the entire genus (*Viola*, *Petunia*, and *Begonia*, for example).

Following the dictionary listings, supplemental material is given to help gardeners—sections on how to buy annuals or biennials, how to actually plant them, and tips on garden design. The index and glossary of terms are thorough and helpful to readers. The only objection is one not unique to this title: that of an unclear map of hardiness zones. The shading that distinguishes one zone from another is blurred.

For libraries, this is a fine reference book and unique with its color/size arrangement. For a reference collection, this volume would certainly answer patrons' questions about plant names, cultivation, and variety. One would hope that patrons could check this book out to carry in the garden, as that is its best use. It is well bound and best of all carries a low price that is just right for even small libraries.
—**Paul A. Mogren**

1437. **Knott's Handbook for Vegetable Growers.** 4th ed. By Donald N. Maynard and George J. Hochmuth. New York, John Wiley, 1997. 582p. illus. index. $75.00pa. ISBN 0-471-13151-2.

First published in 1956, this handbook is an indispensable, up-to-date companion both in the field and in the marketplace. Topics include the vegetable industry, greenhouse vegetable production, soils and fertilizers, water, pests, weed control, harvesting, storage, and seed production. Packed with quick-access graphs, tables, charts, and line drawings, the 4th edition offers new information on drip irrigation, seed germination, plant tissue and sap testing, windbreaks, and weed management. It also gives advice on allowable pesticide and herbicide use and on the latest worker protection standards.

The appendix contains sources of vegetable information, providers of vegetable seeds, periodicals for vegetable growers, and U.S. units of measurement and the metric conversion factors. A change from the spiralbound 3d edition (see ARBA 89, entry 1392) is a sturdy, flexible cover to help hold pages flat. Libraries with patrons interested in vegetable gardening should find this a helpful reference tool.

—**Rachael Green**

1438. Vogelsong, Diana. **Landscape Architecture Sourcebook: A Guide to Resources on the History and Practice of Landscape Architecture in the United States.** Detroit, Omnigraphics, 1997. 382p. index. (Design Reference Series, v.1). $45.00. ISBN 0-7808-0196-2.

The first volume in Omnigraphics's Design Reference Series, this guide describes English-language publications and other resources containing information on landscape architectural history and practice in the United States. A small number of important works that survey international activities are also included. It is a selective rather than comprehensive list concentrating on titles published since the mid-1970s.

The entries are alphabetically arranged under 10 major chapters covering the following topics: reference works, general texts and histories, landscape architects and architectural firms, practical handbooks, plant materials, core works on places and projects, environmental concerns, periodicals, institutional resources, and computer and media resources. The subjects treated are somewhat similar to *Bibliography of Landscape Architecture, Environmental Design, and Planning* (see ARBA 88, entry 1032).

Entries typically give full bibliographic data for books and periodicals. Paragraph-length annotations describe the work's contents. For institutional resources, current addresses and telephone numbers are given, along with fax numbers and World Wide Web sites when available. Core titles deemed essential for a well-rounded basic collection are identified with an asterisk. The appendix contains a glossary of key terms for understanding the literature of landscape architecture. Author/title and subject indexes are provided. Despite minor similarities to the bibliography mentioned earlier, the annotated entries, title recommendations, and timeliness of the information included in this volume should well serve the needs of landscape architect students, instructors, information specialists, and practicing professionals.

—**Rachael Green**

31 Biological Sciences

GENERAL WORKS

1439. Juo, Pei-Show. **Concise Dictionary of Biomedicine and Molecular Biology.** Boca Raton, Fla., CRC Press, 1996. 983p. $69.95. ISBN 0-8493-2460-2.

There are numerous dictionaries available in the bookstores on microbiology or biochemistry combined with the subject of molecular biology, but this concise dictionary on biomedicine and molecular biology is one of the first with such a combination. The author claims to have collected "23,000 entries, including 4,000 chemical structures and their functions, 1,100 equations of enzymatic reactions, 600 restriction endonucleases and their modes of action, a large number of commonly used drugs and antibiotics and their mechanisms of action and medical applications" in this source. This dictionary is a quick reference guide to terms and chemical structure, molecular weight, and brand names and generic names of common drugs or antibiotics. It is strong in molecular basis of terms, but not on the biomedicine side. Many terms relating to telemedicine or molecular medicine are not included. However, Pei consulted a large number of reference tools, such as dictionaries, reference books, research journals, and textbooks before the production of this concise dictionary.

The consolidation of information, designed for scientists, general public, or anyone interested in knowing more about specific chemical structures, is well researched. Some of the information might be considered too condensed, but the cost of this book is reasonable considering this is a publication by the CRC Press. This concise dictionary does offer phenomenal data and is a good purchase for the price. [R: Choice, June 97, p. 1641]—**Polin P. Lei**

1440. **McGraw-Hill Dictionary of Bioscience.** Sybil P. Parker, ed. New York, McGraw-Hill, 1997. 511p. $17.95pa. ISBN 0-07-052430-0.

McGraw-Hill Dictionary of Bioscience is a spin-off from the *McGraw-Hill Dictionary of Scientific and Technical Terms* (5th ed.; see ARBA 95, entry 1493). Definitions for the 16,000 terms in bioscience and related fields included in the former work are taken from the latter. Appendixes supply metric conversion tables and information on selected environmental causes of human cancer, cranial nerves of vertebrates, slow virus infections, and so on.

Libraries owning the latest edition of the *McGraw-Hill Dictionary of Scientific and Technical Terms* do not need the present volume, nor will libraries owning a relatively up-to-date biological dictionary, such as *Henderson's Dictionary of Biological Terms* (10th ed.; see ARBA 90, entry 1479) or *The Facts on File Dictionary of Biology* (rev. ed.; see ARBA 89, entry 1417). However, given its reasonable price, the dictionary under review would be useful for offices, laboratories, or classrooms. The source of the definitions is a guarantee of quality.—**Jonathan F. Husband**

BIOLOGY

1441. Burns, John T. **Cosmic Influences on Humans, Animals, and Plants: An Annotated Bibliography.** Pasadena, Calif., Salem Press and Lanham, Md., Scarecrow, 1997. 205p. index. (Magill Bibliographies). $34.50. ISBN 0-8108-3313-1.

The title of this work may imply to many readers an astrological roundup of annotated listings. Nothing could be further from the truth. In fact, the 400-plus citations to the literature contained within this volume are based on scientific studies. According to the author, in order for a citation to be included it must be a study that involves the collection of data or be a commentary on studies based on data.

The work is divided into 4 sections that consider the influence of sunspots, solar wind, and auroras on humans, animals, plants, and bacteria; the influence of the moon and tide on humans, animals, and plants; the influence of planets on humans; and the possible mechanisms for cosmic influences. The cosmic influences treated deal with gravitation, magnetism, radiation, earthquakes, volcanoes, and the like. Each of the sections begins with an introduction that introduces the reader to the particular field of study.

The majority of the citations are from the journal literature; a number of monographs are also included. The citations, for the most part, reflect material published in the 1970s, 1980s, and 1990s. The annotations, which are lengthy, consider the scientific aspects of the paper. The number of humans or animals in the study, the way the study was structured, and so forth, are included within the description. In essence, the annotations themselves make for some interesting reading, and those not wishing to track down the original paper can gain insight into many aspects of the topic. A separate author index and a brief subject index are provided at the end of the bibliography.

Finally, it should be noted that a topic such as this one is not easy to research, even with networked CD-ROMs, Websites, and the like. It would take some time and effort to search through the many bibliographic databases that may contain information on the subject. Therefore, for those readers wishing to pursue study of cosmic influences, this volume will prove a head start. It is recommended for large public libraries as well as college and university libraries.—**George H. Bell**

1442. **Encyclopedia of Virology PLUS.** [CD-ROM]. Robert G. Webster and Allan Granoff, eds. San Diego, Calif., Academic Press, 1996. Minimum system requirements: can be used on Windows, Macintosh, and UNIX machines. $475.00/single user; $800.00/network. ISBN 0-12-000103-9.

Owners of Academic Press's 1994 print work *Encyclopedia of Virology* (see ARBA 95, entry 1680) should be advised that the articles on the CD-ROM version are unchanged. Thus, for example, the article on bovine spongiform encephalopathy (mad cow disease) does not reflect the scare that struck Great Britain in March 1996. What is on the CD-ROM version that is not in the print version? One feature is color photographs (the print version is illustrated in black-and-white). More spectacular is a special section on virus visualization, including animated videos of virus particles, that has been added. (QuickTime software must be loaded on the computer in order to view the videos, and they will run only on a Windows or a Macintosh platform.) As fine as the videos are, however, the clear prose of section author Jean-Yves Sgro is even more enjoyable. What an achievement this special section is.

Being a CD-ROM, the electronic version of this work naturally offers more capabilities than the print version. For instance, one can annotate the text, or record a pathway through the work to be saved and replayed later, perhaps as part of a class lecture. Users can teach themselves to create a pathway following both the on-screen instructions and those provided by DynaText, the software used by the CD-ROM to move through the text. Unlike the print work, the CD-ROM contains no index, but this does not matter, as it is full-text searchable.—**Penny Papangelis**

1443. Glick, David M. **Glossary of Biochemistry and Molecular Biology.** rev. ed. London, Portland Press; distr., Brookfield, Vt., Ashgate Publishing, 1997. 214p. $28.00pa. ISBN 1-85578-088-7.

This work includes more than 3,000 molecular biology and biological terms. Lengthy definitions of certain terms, such as *genetic footprinting* and *protein splicing*, suggest that the intended audience has a basic knowledge of the field. Short bibliographic citations following some of the entries are helpful. There are cross-references to such acronyms as ENDOR and NOESY. Closely related terms such as *gel, paper,*

isotachophoresis, and *capillary electrophoresis* are defined under the single entry *electrophoresis*. Frequent *see also* references allow the reader to note appropriate connections between terms. For example, it is clear that *free radical* and *antioxidant* are related terms. Despite the omission of pronunciations, this inexpensive dictionary is recommended for research and academic libraries. [R: Choice, June 97, p. 1639]
—**Marilynn Green**

1444. **Oxford Dictionary of Biochemistry and Molecular Biology.** A. D. Smith and others, eds. New York, Oxford University Press, 1997. 738p. $49.95. ISBN 0-19-854768-4.

This work includes more than 17,000 molecular biology and biochemistry terms. Short definitions of certain terms are intended to serve as a reference for those with a basic knowledge of the field. Acronyms such as ENDOR and NOESY are spelt out. There are cross-references to such terms as *electrophoresis*. Frequent *see also* references allow the reader to note appropriate connections between terms. For example, it is clear that *free radical* and *antioxidant* are related terms.

The *Oxford Dictionary of Biochemistry and Molecular Biology* contains 2,000-plus protein and enzyme entries, which describe the functions they perform and the reactions they catalyze. Entries also include encoding information to aid locating their entries in genetic sequence databases. One significant omission is the lack of pronunciations, particularly for unusual or esoteric terms. Despite this shortcoming, this dictionary is recommended for academic libraries.—**Marilynn Green**

1445. Rudin, Norah. **Dictionary of Modern Biology.** Hauppauge, N.Y., Barron's Educational Series, 1997. 504p. illus. $15.95pa. ISBN 0-8120-9516-2.

Covering all major areas of the biological sciences, this dictionary exemplifies the best of its genre. The definitions are well written and explain the terms in an understandable manner. The length of the definitions varies based upon the biological nomenclature being defined. Many of the terms are explained in a mini-encyclopedic format. In addition to the explanations, and what sets this dictionary so much apart from others of its kind, are the excellent diagrams. Many of these illustrations are the kind one would normally find in a biology textbook. A number of the diagrams are so explanatory in nature as to be appropriate in a high school or lower undergraduate classroom setting. The "Electron Transport and Photophosphorylation in Chloroplasts," "Glycolysis," "Molecular Basis of Muscle Contraction" are just some examples. This work also has an excellent cross-referencing system. Common names, such as "birds," "elephants," and so forth, are referenced to their scientific ones.

In addition to the definitions, there are numerous appendixes; 16 in all. These appendixes represent a mini-reference themselves. Such topics as "Geologic Time Scales," "Phanerozoic Time Scales," "Phylogenetic Classification of Organisms," "Nobel Prize Winners," and a "List of Endangered Species" are some examples.

It is a formidable task to include and define the major terminology from all the vast areas of the biological sciences. This work has achieved that goal. *Dictionary of Modern Biology* is strongly recommended for all high school, junior college, college, university, and public libraries. For the market price of $15.95, no library can go wrong with this purchase.—**George H. Bell**

BOTANY

General Works

1446. Chase, A. R. **Foliage Plant Diseases: Diagnosis and Control.** St. Paul, Minn., APS Press, 1997. 169p. illus. index. $69.00. ISBN 0-89054-179-5.

Chase has summarized current information about foliage plant diseases. The brief introduction includes 4 tables listing scientific and common names of 28 frequently grown foliage plant families, active ingredients and trade names for 29 pesticides used to kill bacteria and fungi, levels of phytotoxicity for 19 bactericides and fungicides on 36 genera (including many squares lacking safety information), and symptoms and possible causes of indoor foliage plant problems. The introduction closes with 17 recent references to ornamental plant diseases.

Next come descriptions of 46 ornamental plants arranged alphabetically from *Aeschynanthus* (Lipstick vine) to *Yucca*. Each plant is given a brief summary of its native habitat, interior uses and growing conditions, blooming (if pertinent), and diseases and pests. Each disease condition is named and given a figure number corresponding to the color photograph illustrating that condition. Also detailed are the cause, signs and symptoms, disease control, and often one or more selected references for controlling that condition or disease. A six-page glossary elucidates pathogenic aspects of such common terms as *additive* or *streak*. Most useful are 69 pages containing 403 crisp, detailed color photographs illustrating the earlier prose descriptions. Finally, the index includes disease conditions, such as *Botrytis* blight, on 14 different plants with both text page references and figure numbers for each. A beautiful photograph of Nashville's Opryland Hotel, Cascades Interiorscape, forms a suitable cover for this American Phytopathological Society pictorial guide that will be helpful to commercial growers and amateur gardeners wisely seeking to use not only chemical but all available control methods to maximize their harvest and enjoyment.—**Helen M. Barber**

1447. **Flora of North America North of Mexico. Volume 3: Magnoliophyta: Magnoliidae and Hamamelidae.** Edited by the Flora of North America Editorial Committee. New York, Oxford University Press, 1997. 590p. illus. maps. index. $85.00. ISBN 0-19-511246-6.

This new volume continues the standard of clarity and coverage set by the first 2 volumes (see ARBA 94, entry 1643). The series is intended to be the definitive professional reference on the flora of North America, covering terrestrial plants from mosses to the angiosperms. It will extend to 30 volumes when completed. The 3d volume of *Flora of North America* provides coverage of the native and naturalized species of the magnolia and witch hazel subclasses of flowering plants of the United States and Canada. Although more detailed information may be sought in the primary literature for many of the plants described here, no other source reviews the entire North American flora in such detail and to a standard format.

Following a list of contributors and an introduction, the volume treats the plants, arranged in phylogenetic sequence by order and then family. Summaries of characters and pertinent literature are provided for each family, followed by a key to the genera occurring in North America. Within each genus, a key is provided to the species. Each generic treatment is presented by a specialist; the generic and specific descriptions are detailed and include comments and references concerning taxonomic history, site ecology, phenology, distribution, and medical and economic uses of the taxon in question. Each species description is accompanied by an (all too small) distribution map, and many are illustrated by excellent line drawings of the foliage, flowers, and other critical characteristics. This series should be a standard reference in any collection with a commitment to the natural history of North America.—**Bruce H. Tiffney**

Flowering Plants

1448. Case, Frederick W., Jr., and Roberta B. Case. **Trilliums.** Portland, Oreg., Timber Press, 1997. 285p. illus. maps. index. $29.95. ISBN 0-88192-374-5.

Every spring a beautiful woodland flower blooms in the Smokey Mountains and northeastern regions of the United States. Known by many names, this plant is actually trillium—a genus of perennials with petals, sepals, and leaves appearing in threes. Although these plants are native only to North America and Asia, there is interest in them around the world, especially among naturalists, botanists, and horticulturists. Therefore, it is surprising that no recent work in English—technical or popular—covers all its species. Indeed, most gardening books contain only brief entries on trilliums, if they mention them at all. Written for amateur field botanists and horticulturists, this book is intended to fill that gap.

After an introduction that includes the history of the plant, the authors discuss structure, biology, cultivation, propagation, conservation, and taxonomy. The rest of the work is devoted to information on 43 species. Each of these subdivisions includes a list of the plant's common names; a large color photograph; a map showing its distribution; and text on its habit, growing season, and any other information the authors deem important. Line drawings appear throughout the text. The result is a book that is as beautiful as it is useful. The drawings and photographs combine to give readers extraordinarily clear pictures of this genus. These are complemented by a well-written and thorough text. The authors have an obvious love and knowledge of their subject. This book belongs in all but the smallest gardening collections.
—**January Adams**

1449. Grey-Wilson, Christopher. **Cyclamen: A Guide for Gardeners, Horticulturists, and Botanists.** Portland, Oreg., Timber Press, 1997. 192p. illus. maps. index. $39.95. ISBN 0-88192-386-9.

When approached to write an updated edition of *The Genus Cyclamen* (1988), Christopher Grey-Wilson consented. As is frequently the case with new editions, additional studies and observations were so prolific that an entirely new work transpired. The author examined recognized habitats, reproduction techniques, and fungi eradication methods, then incorporated vigorous inquiry and current findings, resulting in an abundance of cyclamen science.

Grey-Wilson explains that cyclamen is an accessory plant easily overwhelmed in nature. It hides under shrubs and trees or flourishes in remote limestone outcroppings. It prefers to bloom in fall, winter, and spring rather than summer. Yet cyclamen is copious in floral shops throughout the world due to ease of commercial level propagation, resplendent blooms, and the ability to live for over a hundred years.

Written with artful precision and sharp enthusiasm, *Cyclamen* satisfies the fussiest botanist and the armchair reader. There is plenty of cyclamen history, including such gems as Theophrastus referring to the plant in the second century B.C.E. And, as recently as 1986, a new species, *C. somalense*, was discovered in a remote region of northern Somalia. The exact location remains a secret to protect this particular variety.

A minor drawback of this work is the obvious European bias, which excludes U.S. interest in cyclamen while giving only mere mention to the huge cyclamen industry in Japan. This book also contains some dreadfully barren maps that cannot be understood without an atlas or globe. However, these annoyances can be brushed aside in reference to the ardor and complexity of the author's scrutiny.—**Mary Pat Boian**

1450. **New England's Mountain Flowers: A High Country Heritage.** By Jeff Wallner and Mario J. DiGregorio, with the New England Wild Flower Society. Missoula, Mont., Mountain Press Publishing, 1997. 221p. illus. index. $17.00pa. ISBN 0-87842-337-0.

This book is more like a course on alpine wildflower appreciation than a field guide. Although there are hundreds of different species of wildflowers present in the 5 mountainous New England states (New Hampshire, Connecticut, Massachusetts, Vermont, and Maine), only 85 of the showiest, most interesting, or most rare are included here. There is no key to the species, and they are not presented in either the taxonomic order or the arrangement by color most common in field guides.

That said, this is a delightful book. The entries are arranged in chapters, by habitat starting at the lower elevation "Forest Slopes" and moving up the mountains through "Streambanks and Pond Shores," "Cliffs, Ledges, and Talus Slopes," to the "Alpine Zone." This is a great learning tool, because as any hiker knows, mountain wildflowers, more than most, stick to particular elevations, exposures, and soil types. For each species, there are one or two outstanding color photographs and a full-page entry that includes description, flowering times, habitat, and interesting facts about traditional uses of the plant and derivations of the common and scientific names. The prose is readable and fascinating throughout. The authors emphasize evolution of the plants and their present status as either common, threatened, or endangered. Appendixes include a bibliography, a glossary, and state lists of rare and endangered wildflowers.—**Carol L. Noll**

Fungi

1451. Crane, J. L., and Almut G. Jones. **An Annotated Catalogue of Types of the University of Illinois Mycological Collections (ILL).** Champaign, Ill., University of Illinois Press, 1997. 365p. (Illinois Biological Monographs, no.58). $35.00. ISBN 0-252-02319-6.

This is a book for the serious mycologist. Fungi are listed alphabetically by scientific name within chapters. Information about each specimen is organized consistently by fungus name, reference, type category, substrate or host, locality data, date of collection, name of collector, collector number, and University of Illinois accession number. A list of other institutions (where known) that duplicate specimens is also included. The book contains information about the name on which the species name is based for each type specimen. Synonyms are listed, as are the name and citation for author of the description. Orthographic errors in names are corrected according to the *International Code of Botanical Nomenclature* and other reference tools for naming species. The University of Illinois is the main depository of types for names published by T. J. Burrill, the founder of the University of Illinois Department of Plant Biology. This book accomplishes the goal of providing an annotated list of mycological types in that collection.—**Constance Rinaldo**

1452. Menser, Gary P. **Hallucinogenic and Poisonous Mushroom Field Guide.** Berkeley, Calif., Ronin Publishing, 1997. 124p. illus. index. $14.95pa. ISBN 0-914171-89-5.

This slim volume is a reprint of a 1977 publication of very limited subject matter. Of the 5,000 species of mushrooms occurring in the United States, this book illustrates and describes only 32—24 hallucinogenic ones and the 8 poisonous species with which they can be most easily confused. Furthermore, the species and habitat descriptions are only applicable to the western United States, particularly the Pacific Coast. For each mushroom, there is one page of description and a full-page black-and-white line drawing. There are also color plates of some of the species. A simple, three-page botanical key helps in identification. Use of technical language is kept to a minimum throughout.

Although the author includes a few warnings and disclaimers about the difficulty of identifying many of these species, this volume is clearly meant for those interested in the consumption of hallucinogenic mushrooms. There is information on potency (mostly reputed, as there has not been adequate scientific analysis of many of these species, and mushrooms vary from place to place and season to season anyway) and on how to dry mushrooms to best preserve chemical activity. There are valuable introductory material on methods of collecting and identifying mushrooms and an extensive bibliography and glossary.

Most of these mushrooms are included in more general field guides, although with less discussion of the types of active chemicals and potency. A good general mushroom guide, such as *Mushrooms in Color* by Orson K. Miller Jr. and Hope M. Miller (see ARBA 82, entry 1465) should always be consulted first when identifying an unknown specimen. A specialized guide such as the one under review should be used as a supplement only. Even then, consumption of most of these species, given the variety of potency levels and the vagaries of individual body chemistry, is risky at best. When it comes to these mushrooms, a little knowledge can truly be a dangerous thing.—**Carol L. Noll**

Grasses and Weeds

1453. Uva, Richard H., Joseph C. Neal, and Joseph M. DiTomaso. **Weeds of the Northeast.** Ithaca, N.Y., Comstock Publishing/Cornell University Press, 1997. 397p. illus. index. $60.00; $29.95pa. ISBN 0-8014-3391-6; 0-8014-8334-4pa.

When an out-of-place plant interrupts aesthetics, crop production, or the health of humans and other animals, it is called a weed. Identification is necessary in order to eradicate the weed, and to this end the authors of *Weeds of the Northeast* have accomplished their task. Does the plant have thorns? A square stem? Milky sap oozing from the flower? Simple questions guide the user to the proper identification table. Once the weed of interest is located, users are given its botanical name, common name, description, how it propagates, whether it flowers, what it looks like in the winter, where it occurs (both geographically and in what type soil), and names of other plants similar enough to fool people.

Weeds of the Northeast emphasizes but is not limited to weeds from southern Canada, west to Wisconsin, and south to Virginia. In addition to categorizing more than 200 weeds, the book includes a pull-out chart for 38 grasses and detailed information on numerous shrubs, saplings, and thistles. The authors provide color photographs of the weeds in four stages of growth (seed, seedling, immature, and flowering); a photograph of the weed in its habit; a user-friendly table of contents; a glossary; and an extensive bibliography citing references back to 1913. Author Neal supplied his address for correspondence.

The appeal of *Weeds of the Northeast* is broad, ranging from home gardeners to professional golf course managers to farmers. The book deserves a slot in the reference library.—**Mary Pat Boian**

Herbaceous Plants

1454. Stebbings, Geoff. **The Gardener's Guide to Growing Irises.** Portland, Oreg., Timber Press, 1997. 160p. illus. index. $29.95. ISBN 0-88192-388-5.

Easy to grow and immensely satisfying as an addition to a perennial or annually planted landscape, irises produce some of the most spectacular flowers in the bounty of the garden. An authoritative overview discusses the varied forms and colors that irises produce and explores some of the new hybrids being introduced. Cultivated irises date from 7000 B.C.E., and other facts of their early history and development are provided in engaging prose. The rich, bright white paper is well suited for presenting the lush photographs and informative line drawings that add immeasurably to the appeal of this tastefully produced volume.

Distinctly British in presentation and focus, this guide includes a classification and botany section that emphasizes flower structure, bracts and pods that are helpful in distinguishing different varieties of irises, body and leaf variations, a discussion of genus, and an account of how the bearded iris has become a staple in many gardens because they are so resistant to drying out and amenable to being moved frequently. Practical advice is given on cultivation, propagation, and pest and disease control. Although not definitive, the list of cultivars is a useful reference for locating the names of the individuals who raise prize plants and the dates registered. A list of National Collections in the United Kingdom where one can see irises has descriptive annotations that include viewing times, type of garden structure, and specialized collections. Nurseries in Australia, Canada, France, Holland, New Zealand, the United States, and the United Kingdom are listed, and in some cases telephone numbers appear with a four- or five-word description of irises available for purchase. No e-mail or fax numbers are given. As a nod toward global readers, a growing season translation chart from the United Kingdom informs users of the best times to plant worldwide. Award-winning irises and guidelines for where to place them in a garden setting appear in the appendix. A glossary, a bibliography, and an index complete the book.

A one-volume reference for North American gardeners is *Taylor's Master Guide to Gardening* (see ARBA 96, entry 1550), which features pronunciation guides, botanical names, photographs, and flower descriptions with an emphasis on environmentally sound gardening practices using only safe, organic compounds for growing a variety of irises. Designed to inspire and intrigue iris lovers, *The Gardener's Guide to Growing Irises* will arouse interest in a new generation of plant growers, and it is recommended for circulating collections.—**Judy Gay Matthews**

Ivy

1455. Rose, Peter Q. **The Gardener's Guide to Growing Ivies.** Portland, Oreg., Timber Press, 1996. 160p. illus. index. $29.95. ISBN 0-88192-364-8.

This new work is an expansion of and update to the work *Ivies* (Poole, England, Blandford Press, 1980) by the same author. Some of the same text is used for the plant descriptions, cultivation, the use of ivies in the landscape, and the glossary. However, this new work has expanded the number of plants described (more than 270); has updated the information in some instances; and includes more background information, such as the history of ivy and its use in medicine. It is also in a more attractive format, with many quality, full-color photographs of ivy varieties.

The book is easy reading, yet comprehensive in its coverage of information. Chapters on the history of ivy and ivy botany and nomenclature are presented before botanical descriptions of plants, from *Hedera azorica* to *Hedera rhombea* "Variegata." Each plant is described with information on its form, color, history, habit, stems, petioles, and leaves. The many uses of ivies in gardens, landscapes, walls, terraria, and topiaries are also discussed, as well as ivy cultivation, planting, grafting, budding, and pests and diseases. A glossary, an index of ivies, and a list of places to see and buy ivies in the United Kingdom and the United States are provided before a brief bibliography and a two-page index. Photographs are liberally sprinkled throughout the book, with several two-page plates illustrating the ivies described in the book. The photographs make identification of ivies an easy task.

This book should appeal to the amateur as well as the horticulturist, with a balance of easy reading and fine illustrations and detailed information on the many varieties of the genus *Hedera*. It succeeds in enticing the reader to the amazing variety, beauty, and uses of ivies in indoor and outdoor gardens. This is the most recent work on ivies, and there does not appear to be another work of its type. The guide is recommended for all public, agricultural, and academic libraries.—**Diane B. Rhodes**

Trees and Shrubs

1456. Dirr, Michael A. **Dirr's Hardy Trees and Shrubs: An Illustrated Encyclopedia.** Portland, Oreg., Timber Press, 1997. 493p. illus. index. $69.95. ISBN 0-88192-404-0.

Sit down with *Dirr's Hardy Trees and Shrubs* and be gratified by nearly 500 pages of sensational photographs accompanied by clear, smooth, and visceral text. This book was compiled by a tree expert with a camera who spent a lifetime documenting the colors, shapes, preferences, and idiosyncrasies of trees and shrubs acclimated to the cooler growth zones of the United States. It is a beautiful work replete with photographs ranging from spring full-bloom *Malus floribunda* (Japanese flowering crabapple) to giant naked sycamores bared to the winter onslaught of wind and ice. The text and photographs have been meticulously merged into a pure volume that delights the eyes and mind. Dirr's treatise on trees describes similarities of species and differences in character (what differentiates a weeping willow from a pussy willow) and describes what type of tree is best suited for what circumstances (which type to plant on campus or the golf course).

This book is a labor of love, obvious by its collection of seasonal and intricate pictures, which took author and photographer Dirr 25 years to accumulate. There are charts to assist in choosing salt-resistant trees, there are asides complaining about poplars, ("dirty trees susceptible to fungal leaf spot and canker that drop leaves and twigs without any provocation . . ."), and there is supervision for planting groundcover, shade-tolerant evergreens, and fragrant vines. Honest, parochial, personal, and glib, *Dirr's Hardy Trees and Shrubs* is a trove of beauty and substance.—**Mary Pat Boian**

1457. Galle, Fred C. **Hollies: The Genus *Ilex*.** Portland, Oreg., with the Holly Society of America, Timber Press, 1997. 573p. illus. maps. index. $59.95. ISBN 0-88192-380-X.

This book is an exceptionally thorough and clear exposé of a popular plant species. A brief history of the holly is provided, and an orderly progression follows, leading the reader ever so gently into the identification of the many species. A subtle discussion of taxonomy is furnished to nudge the holly enthusiast toward the use of scientific names as an adjunct to the more popular use of common names. A Herculean job was performed with considerable success in identifying, describing, and cataloging the exceptionally large population of holly varieties, cultivars, clones, and forms. After important discussions of growth, care, propagation, and disease, the volume ends with a review of paleobotany and information on the location of some of the more important fossil finds. To the serious student of hollies, whether in academia or in the home garden, this resource is a useful and valuable assembly of pertinent data on the subject.

—**James H. Flynn Jr.**

NATURAL HISTORY

1458. **Pockets: Nature Facts.** By Scarlett O'Hara. New York, DK Publishing, 1997. 128p. illus. maps. index. (DK Pockets). $6.95pa. ISBN 0-7894-1494-5.

DK Publishing has enlarged its original selection of 4-by-5-inch, full-color pocket book titles with a guide to nature facts. The choices of topics, pleasing layout, crisp-clear photographs, and labeled drawings and schematics are well worth the dollar increase in price over the original set, which sold for $5.95. Each book follows a pattern: color-coded sections, illustrated text, running heads, and annotations. The reference section at the end stresses peripheral information on species classification. The writers anticipate the kinds of questions children will ask about different types of mammals. The glossary and index introduce children to the types of data that quality reference works should include.

DK continues to respect the intelligence and to anticipate the needs of children by challenging and enticing the reader to turn another page, read another fact, and add to a growing base knowledge of the subject, for instance, the types of reproduction in fruit. The entries are brief enough to cover central facts and to raise a few points that readers may not have encountered in science class or personal encounters with nature.

Since the publication of the first set of pocketbooks, DK's editors have made no attempts to address weaknesses, particularly the lack of phonetic spellings of such daunting terms as *rhizoid*. Also puzzling is the deletion of color in the reference section. Still muddling the quality of DK reference works in the heyday of inclusion is the absence or de-emphasis of important women scientists and researchers.

—Mary Ellen Snodgrass

ZOOLOGY

Birds

1459. **American Bird Conservancy's Field Guide to All the Birds of North America.** By Jack L. Griggs. New York, HarperPerennial/HarperCollins, 1997. 172p. illus. maps. index. $19.95pa. ISBN 0-06-273028-2.

The task of designing a new approach to a field guide for birds was no doubt formidable, particularly with so many esteemed competitors. Griggs and the American Bird Conservancy have done a marvelous job in producing an accurate and impressive field guide. Birds are grouped not by taxonomy but by feeding strategies and adaptations. The book is designed to allow rapid access by birds' identifying field characteristics. It has achieved this goal quite well.

The book is divided into four major groupings with several subgroupings: Pelagic Waterbirds (aerialists, swimmer); Waterbirds (aerialists, swimmers, wading birds, shore birds, upland waterbirds); Landbirds (nocturnal, aerialists, ground-walkers, tree-climbers); and Perching Landbirds (divided by type of bill: flycatching bills, curved bills, straight bills, and conical bills). The inside front and back covers act as the table of contents, with the various sections color-coded to match the page color bars.

The book has 172 keys, double-page spreads showing the smallest groupings (e.g., Crows/Ravens, E. Warblers Yellow/Wing Bars). Each key has a short description of identifying characteristics; individual listings have a range map, along with common name, Latin binomial, size, habits, and habitats as well as identifying marks and songs. The collection of keys is punctuated with one- to five-page descriptions discussing the distinctive features of types of birds (e.g., aerialists: raptors, warbler-size straight bills). Conservation notes on habitat destruction and the health of various species are included in many of these descriptions. These descriptive pages are not numbered, so the actual size of the book is close to 400 pages. The index doubles as a checklist and has entries by both common name and Latin name.

Most of the groupings make sense, for instance, the dipper is shown along with kingfishers. At times, though, different birds are found together in a way that might make some other order more sensible. But this is a minor issue. Users need to learn to use each field guide on its own terms.

The illustrations are beautiful, showing birds in their natural habitats. Most show birds in flight and any distinctive features needed for identification, such as tail or wing details. The writing is terse but not dry. The presentation on the whole is quite impressive and functional. It is not without personality and some humor. True to the American Bird Conservancy's mission, concern for bird habitats and the environmental pressures on birds is evident throughout the book.

This work is both an excellent field guide and a beautiful book. Highly recommended for all libraries.—**Stephen Haenel**

1460. Kaufman, Kenn. **Lives of North American Birds.** New York, Houghton Mifflin, 1996. 675p. illus. maps. index. (Peterson Natural History Companions). $35.00. ISBN 0-395-77017-3.

This reference, which gives detailed life histories of North American birds, is intended for the amateur bird enthusiast. Complete species accounts are provided for 680 commonly occurring birds. Briefer detail is given for 230 species that occur occasionally. An introduction to the biology and social history of birds is given in the initial 25 pages.

The species accounts are arranged in taxonomic order and average a page in length. The author provides a brief introduction to each family. Under this heading feeding, nesting, and display behavior are covered. Within each species account the natural history of the bird is described in clear, concise, nontechnical language. Particularly useful is that each account includes a color photograph (usually the male of the species in summer plumage) and a range map. The author has made a real effort to include photographs that are of high quality. Although the range maps are small, and therefore lack detail for birds in a restricted range, it is handy to have them with the account.

Not all birds are depicted in this way. Occasionally occurring birds merit only a short description and have no photographs or range maps. Unfortunately, there is no definition of what is an occasionally occurring or a commonly occurring bird, which would have been useful. Because the author is writing for nonscientists, he does not include references with each account. Instead, these are found in the back pages with the index and photograph credits. The index is arranged by both scientific and common name. Although not intended to be taken into the field, this volume is highly recommended as a companion to any field guide to the birds of North America. [R: RBB, 15 April 97, p. 1451]—**Katherine Margaret Thomas**

1461. Withers, Martin B., and David Hosking. **Common Birds of East Africa.** New York, HarperCollins, 1996. 160p. illus. index. (Collins Safari Guides). $16.00pa. ISBN 0-00-220034-1.

This physically small guidebook (a mere 4½ by 7 inches) contains within its pages full-color illustrations of 360 common bird species of East Africa. The book is geographically limited to the sites of most tourist safaris—Kenya, Tanzania, and Uganda. Descriptive text for each bird faces its color photograph (five or six species photographs per plate) and gives brief comments on the species' seasonal distribution, size, identifying features, and habitats. The authors have been leading wildlife tours and photographing the birdlife of East Africa for 20 years, which is reflected in the book's excellent illustrations and the details of the text.

Restrictions of the pocket-size guide are the exclusion of uncommon and rare species and the general limit of one illustration per species (usually male). Sexual and seasonal changes of plumage are briefly indicated in the text. An introductory section also provides the traveler with many helpful suggestions for safari photography of birds and mammals. For most nature tourists, this book is ideal as a lightweight bird guide.—**Charles Leck**

Domestic Animals

1462. **The Complete Book of Pet Names: An ASPCA Book.** George Greenfield, comp. and ed. Kansas City, Mo., Andrews and McMeel, 1997. 238p. illus. $12.95pa. ISBN 0-8362-2162-1.

Those looking for pet names that go beyond Spot or Tiger will find a giant selection in this book and be entertained at the same time. Attila the Bun (rabbit), Pounce de Leon (cat), and Jack the Gripper (python) are just a few of the thousands of pet names that will spice up the naming game.

Compiled and edited by Greenfield from the National Veterinarian Pet Names Survey, this directory lists more than 6,000 names. The names are grouped under dogs, cats, birds, rabbits and guinea pigs, reptiles and amphibians, and horses. A chapter on pet names from literature treats names from Shakespeare (Lady Macbeth), mythology (Thor), and others, even angels (Furlac, the Angel of the Earth). Anecdotes on "how I named my cat/dog/horse, etc." are included, along with information on how to name dogs according to the American Kennel Club rules. Chapters on pet care basics, dog and cat grooming, and lists of plants poisonous to pets and horses round out the book.

Fun lists feature the top 500 pet names (Max is first, Barkley is 500) and an alphabetic list of the most popular pet names, from Aaron to Zydeco. Another good pet naming book is Wayne Bryant Eldrige's *Best Pet Name Book Ever* (Barron's Educational Series, 1996), now in its 2d edition. However, it provides a different approach than Greenfield's book, and a percentage of the proceeds from Greenfield's book goes to the American Society for the Prevention of Cruelty to Animals (ASPCA). The book under review is recommended for all public libraries.—**Diane B. Rhodes**

1463. Fogle, Bruce. **The Encyclopedia of the Cat.** New York, DK Publishing, 1997. 240p. illus. index. $34.95. ISBN 0-7894-1970-X.

It has taken 60 million years of evolution to produce the domestic cat, now the most popular animal companion in many regions of the world. Entertaining text and more than 1,300 full-color illustrations shed insight into cats and all their splendor. From the cat's age-old relationship with humans through cat worship in ancient cultures to cats in folklore, art, and the media, this complete cat manual provides information on 23 longhair and 36 shorthair varieties.

This book is concerned only with recognized cat breeds. (Household pets are covered in 5 poses on 2 pages with a paragraph of approximately 150 words.) A history of selective breeding, coat colors and patterns, face shapes and body forms, eye shapes and colors, and breed profiles precede the lush color photographs. The cats are not presented in alphabetic order by name, so the useful index is essential. Key facts are presented about each breed in a sidebar, which includes date and place of origin, ancestry, weight range, temperament, and a color guide for coat variations. The illustrations are beautifully presented, and many body attitudes and poses are represented. The section on caring for cats offers routine information on choosing an appropriate breed, equipment for safety and comfort, feeding and nutrition, grooming, training and travel, behavioral problems and possible solutions, signs of illness, and emergency first aid.

The Encyclopedia of the Cat is lavish and informative and joins a number of other ready-reference sources such as *Legacy of the Cat* (see ARBA 91, entry 1578) and *The Ultimate Cat Book* (see ARBA 91, entry 1579) that all cat lovers will delight in using over and over again.—**Judy Gay Matthews**

1464. Foster, Race, and Marty Smith. **The Complete Cat Health Manual.** New York, Howell Book House/Simon & Schuster Macmillan, 1997. 266p. illus. index. $19.95. ISBN 0-87605-675-3.

Divided into 16 chapters, this work walks one through the biological systems of the cat and the major diseases affiliated with each of the systems. In addition, chapters devoted to parasites and infections are included. For each system considered, a general introduction to the system, along with labeled diagrams of the system, are provided. Major diseases of each biological system are then presented and explained. For each disease mentioned, general information on the disease is given along with the answers to the following questions: "What are the symptoms?", "What are the risks?", and "What is the Treatment?" The sections on parasites and infections follow the same basic format as stated above. A total of 191 diseases are covered along 14 biological systems.

The appendixes, found at the end of the work, cover normal physiological data for the feline; the role of ash in the diet; and feline medications, uses, and common dosages. A brief glossary and index complete the work. This manual is a wonderful book with excellent labeled diagrams and text in easy-to-understand language. It belongs on the shelf of every public library. Colleges and universities may wish to consider this work. All cat lovers would do well to purchase a copy.—**George H. Bell**

1465. Morris, Desmond. **Cat World: A Feline Encyclopedia.** New York, Penguin Books, 1997. 496p. illus. index. $29.95. ISBN 0-670-10006-4.

Morris has created a cat fancier's dream in this feline encyclopedia. Both informative and entertaining, *Cat World* is the guide to the kitty kingdom that cat enthusiasts will want in their collection. One can learn the difference between "autogrooming" and "allogrooming" or the real name for the mountain lion. Approximately 1,000 feline figures are listed in this volume, which contains 80 domestic and 36 wild breeds. Behavioral habits to biology are included as well. Bibliographies are noted where they are appropriate for reference to topics not found in this book. The work is alphabetically organized and has an index so that the reader may locate information in an expedient fashion, but also contains many photographs for those who like to browse. Also within its pages is a listing of the 100 best cat books, according to the author. The book's focus is on domestic cats; however, there is a wide range of material that encompasses fictional cats, famous cat owners, and legendary cats. One thing the book does not cover is veterinary care, which was intentionally omitted by the author, who preferred that this information come from qualified veterinary professionals.

Morris is an expert on all types of cats—he was responsible for the largest collection of felines at the London Zoo. He studied zoology at Birmingham and Oxford Universities from 1959 to 1971. Cat lovers or anyone in need of general information will want to read this book. Public libraries should certainly have a copy on hand.—**Christopher Byrne**

1466. Pavia, Audrey. **The Guinea Pig.** New York, Howell Book House/Simon & Schuster Macmillan, 1997. 126p. illus. (An Owner's Guide to a Happy, Healthy Pet). $12.95. ISBN 0-87605-527-7.

The Guinea Pig is well-written, has wonderful color photographs, is thorough, and is a delight to read. The book has four parts: "About Guinea Pigs," "Caring for Your Guinea Pig," "Enjoying Your Guinea Pig," and "Beyond the Basics." The work looks into the background of guinea pigs; describes their physical characteristics; and has an extensive section on how and where to adopt a guinea pig, how to care for them, the various breeds, and how to name them. There are comprehensive sections on equipment needed, toys, how to handle a guinea pig, and how to accustom the guinea pig to other pets.

The book also devotes considerable space to whether to keep a pet guinea pig indoors or outdoors, and addresses their needs based on those environments. Nutrition and grooming are also covered in detail, as are how to understand the guinea pig, having fun with them, and even how to travel with them. The back of the book includes recommended reading, guinea pig publications, and a handy resource section. *The Guinea Pig* is highly recommended.—**Pamela J. Getchell**

1467. **Pockets: Dogs.** By David Taylor. New York, DK Publishing, 1997. 128p. illus. maps. index. (DK Pockets). $6.95pa. ISBN 0-7894-1493-7.

DK Publishing has enlarged its original selection of 4-by-5-inch, full-color pocketbook titles with a guide to dogs. The choice of topics, pleasing layout, crisp-clear photographs, and labeled drawings and schematics are well worth the dollar increase in price over the original set, which sold for $5.95. Each book follows a pattern: color-coded sections, illustrated text, running heads, and annotations. The writers anticipate the kinds of questions children will ask about famous dogs from history and their deeds. The reference section at the end stresses peripheral information with an overview of first aid for dogs plus a glossary and index, which introduce readers to the types of data that quality reference works should include.

DK continues to respect the intelligence and to anticipate the needs of children by challenging and enticing the reader to turn another page, read another fact, and add to a growing base knowledge of the subject, for instance, different tasks performed by working animals. The entries are brief enough to cover central facts and to raise a few points that readers may not have encountered, as demonstrated by the section on traditional dog behaviors and the reasons for each, such as the sniffing of sebaceous glands as a means of identifying other dogs.

Since the publication of the first set of pocketbooks, DK's editors have made no attempts to address weaknesses, particularly the lack of phonetic spellings of such daunting terms as *Aichi*. Also puzzling is the deletion of color in the reference section. Still muddling the quality of DK reference works in the heyday of inclusion is the absence of women as dog handlers and veterinarians.—**Mary Ellen Snodgrass**

Fishes

1468. Grove, Jack Stein, and Robert J. Lavenberg. **The Fishes of the Galapagos Islands.** Stanford, Calif., Stanford University Press, 1997. 863p. illus. index. $125.00. ISBN 0-8047-2289-7.

The Galápagos Islands are justly famed among evolutionary biologists. To such biologists and indeed most people these islands conjure up exotic finches, huge turtles, strange lizards, and the name of Charles Darwin, who is almost synonymous with the word Galápagos. The isolation of these islands from each other and from mainland South America created a natural laboratory where animal and plant groups have changed in a microcosm less biologically complex than continents. Yet, whereas most of the ever-increasing number of visitors to the islands see only the fauna above the waterline, a large number of fishes (more than 440 species) are to be found below this line. This large book is the first comprehensive study of the fish groups. Both authors have spent many years working on the island fishes.

The book is arranged in the usual fashion for faunal studies: an introduction that includes discussion of methodologies, collections examined, a history of the islands culturally as well as geologically and physiographically, their climate, oceanography evolution, and endemism of the fishes. The majority of the book comprises species accounts of cartilaginous and bony fishes. There are six appendixes, including lists of regional distribution and habitats of the fishes, the endemics (almost 10 percent of the fauna), common and scientific names, snorkeling and diving sites, plus a report on efforts to protect the marine fauna. The book concludes with a glossary, a nearly 100-page bibliography, and indexes to common and scientific names. More than 350 illustrations of fishes (black-and-white line drawings or photographs) are augmented with approximately 140 color photographs—mostly of fishes, and many of these in natural settings. A dozen photographs show significant coastal views of well-known sites on several of the islands.

The ordinal/familial/species accounts provide useful information on both taxonomic and broader physiological and ecological characteristics of each group; important references; and, if available, habitat and distribution in the Galápagos Islands. The book is a welcome addition to the literature on the Galápagos fauna.—**David Bardack**

Mammals

1469. **Encyclopedia of Mammals.** Tarrytown, N.Y., Marshall Cavendish, 1997. 17v. illus. maps. index. $459.95/set. ISBN 0-7614-0575-5.

The 17-volume *Encyclopedia of Mammals* is a treat to browse, with its high-quality photographs, drawings and graphics, and its lively informational style. It also provides copious information about mammals from aardvarks to zebras. The set will meet the needs of students from elementary through high school levels as well as the casual reader. Each volume is manageable, with fewer than 200 pages. The A to Z organization is easy to navigate. More than 1,700 photographs add both interest and information to the set. Introductory material explains the characteristics of mammals, where mammals fit on the geologic timeline, how mammals are categorized into orders, and where mammals live in the six zoogeographic regions.

Each entry has 3 sections: profile, behavior, and survival. The profile provides a physical description of the animal and describes different varieties of the mammal. The behavior section investigates all aspects of the animal's life from reproduction and raising its young to its habitat and life cycle. The survival section looks at both endangered animals as well as species that are flourishing. Each volume is indexed, and the final volume contains a comprehensive index and six specialized indexes covering classes of mammals, endangered species, geographic locations, scientific organizations, scientific names for species, and wildlife preserves and parks. The format, quality and depth of information and the fact that mammals are a fascinating and frequently requested topic will make this set popular and useful in any school or public library.—**Lynda Welborn**

1470. Hosking, David, and Martin B. Withers. **Larger Animals of East Africa.** New York, HarperCollins, 1996. 158p. illus. index. (Collins Safari Guides). $16.00pa. ISBN 0-00-220036-8.

The purpose of this guide is to help visitors identify larger animals found in East Africa's game reserves. No pretensions to scholarship are here, but there is a small bibliography for those needing more information after returning home from their safari. To help the more curious reader, the authors have supplied scientific names for each species pictured. The written descriptions comment on feeding habits, size, breeding, life span, lifestyle, and (of interest to many users today) conservation concerns. Animals are shown in their natural habitats, most looking straight into the camera. Users will need to thumb through the book to get an idea of the arrangement; large cats are grouped together, for example. Another large grouping is deer-like animals, such as the common waterbuck, the mountain reedbuck, and the like. Smaller animals, such as mongooses and genets, form another animal grouping.

The photographs aid identification, and descriptions are helpful to laypersons on their first safari. There is advice to those wishing to take their own pictures of wildlife. In essence, this is a field guide for rank beginners who want to survey the passing scene from an air-conditioned van, and therefore not a required purchase for libraries.—**Milton H. Crouch**

Primates

1471. **International Directory of Primatology.** 3d ed. Lawrence Jacobsen and Raymond Hamel, eds. Madison, Wis., Wisconsin Regional Primate Research Center, 1996. 1v. (various paging). maps. index. $25.00 spiralbound. ISBN 0-299-15284-7. ISSN 1064-3826.

This volume is the 3d edition of a directory that serves as a sourcebook on primate research, education, and conservation. The directory is a product of the cooperative efforts of the editors, the Wisconsin Regional Primate Research Center, the International Primatological Society, and primate organizations and primatologists around the world.

Prefaced comments, acknowledgments, a list of corporate supporters, and information on use of the directory precede the 5 major information sections of the directory. Section 1 is a geographic, alphabetically arranged list of organizations, including those pertaining to animal welfare and conservation, government agencies, foundations, museums, primate centers and laboratories, educational programs, sanctuaries, and zoological gardens. Listed data typically provide mission statements, training opportunities, research specialties, field sites, publications, primate species supported, staff, addresses, telephone and fax numbers, and World Wide Web and Gopher sites.

Section 2 is the Primate Society of Great Britain's worldwide guide to primate field studies. Project locations, species, goals, and contact data are described, as are comparisons of primate species studied with the International Union for Conservation of Nature and Natural Resources Red List of Threatened Animals. Section 3 consists of a regional list of names, addresses, and telephone and fax numbers of population management groups. The International Species Inventory System Abstract Report on primate holdings in zoological gardens is furnished as well. Section 4 lists the International Primatological Society membership list. Addresses (postal and e-mail) and telephone numbers are given. Section 5 discusses country-specific resources for information and referral, including libraries. Detailed descriptions and addresses are supplied. Four indexes (organizational, species, subject, name) and two appendixes (scope notes and order forms) complete the directory.

This directory is a superbly organized, comprehensive, and information-packed volume that will be indispensable to anyone with active interests in primates. It is highly recommended for general purchase by colleges, universities, and municipal libraries serving large population centers.—**Edmund D. Keiser Jr.**

1472. Rowe, Noel. **The Pictorial Guide to the Living Primates.** East Hampton, N.Y., Pogonias Press, 1996. 263p. illus. maps. index. $79.95; $59.95pa. ISBN 0-9648825-0-7; 0-9648825-1-5pa.

This book provides information and illustrations for each of the 234 species of living primates. The species are described uniformly, so that the most obscure lemur is treated in equal detail to the chimpanzee. Most of the species are illustrated by one or more color photographs, many of which were taken by the author. Aside from a photograph showing general appearance, there are often additional photographs highlighting characteristic structures and behaviors. A few species for which photographs are not available are illustrated with drawings. The photographs of several new primate species discovered in Madagascar and Brazil during the past few years are a particular treat.

The biological information is arranged in nine standard categories—taxonomy, distinguishing characteristics, physical characteristics, habitat, diet, life history, locomotion, social structure, and behavior. Unavailable information is indicated. It is extraordinary how many species are not well known, lacking even the most basic data. The categories and associated terminology are explained in an introductory overview and a glossary. Each piece of information is linked by a superscript number to the 1,020-item bibliography. A range map accompanies each species account. Primate conservation is an important theme throughout. The conservation status of each species is indicated. The book presents a foreword by Jane Goodall and an introduction by Russell Mittermeier, president of Conservation International.

This book is the first attempt to bring together in a compact and convenient form biological data and illustrations for all primates. It is a splendid achievement. Many of the photographs are stunning, the text is clearly written and informative, and the detailed referencing of the data is of great value. This book belongs in any reference collection with even a modest zoological section. [R: RBB, 1 April 97, pp. 1357-58]

—**Frederic F. Burchsted**

Reptiles and Amphibians

1473. Davies, Robert, and Valerie Davies. **The Reptile & Amphibian Problem Solver: Practical & Expert Advice on Keeping Reptiles & Amphibians.** Blacksburg, Va., Tetra Press, 1997. 208p. illus. index. $29.95. ISBN 1-56465-194-0.

This book is for people who are serious about maintaining amphibians and reptiles as healthy captives for use as pets or for husbandry. It was written to address numerous questions likely to be asked by these individuals. Five major topic units provide focus and organization for the narrative. The first, "Starting Out," succinctly overviews general information necessary for a novice. Coverage includes legal aspects, nomenclature, species and stock selection, captive-bred versus wild-caught individuals, animal health, and handling tips.

"Reptile Care" is next, with definitions and characteristics of lizards, snakes, and turtles followed by comments on housing, cage habitats, heating, lighting, humidity, foods, feeding, breeding, health, and disease. The "Reptile Species" unit discusses specific species or groups of species that are likely to be maintained in captivity. The species or group is typified, and habits appropriate for maintenance of captive specimens are emphasized. Specific questions are addressed for each group or species and each has a table titled "Vivarium Conditions." The table includes information on vivarium size, substrate, habitats, cooling, feeding, and incubation.

Subsequent units called "Amphibian Care" and "Amphibian Species" deal with frogs and salamanders and are organized similarly to those on reptiles. A section entitled "Herptiles and the Law," a glossary, suggested readings and addresses, and an index complete the book. The book is lavishly illustrated with superb color photographs and artwork, and the illustrations complement and add immeasurably to the narrative. Technical terminology is kept to a minimum, and the narrative requires little literary sophistication for easy comprehension. There are some erroneous statements (e.g., lizards and geckos have no eyelids) and oversimplifications, but for the most part, the contents are authoritative and represent considerable practical experience on the part of the writers. This volume is a bargain purchase, and it is recommended enthusiastically for acquisition by municipal, high school, and college libraries.—**Edmund D. Keiser Jr.**

1474. Murphy, John C. **Amphibians and Reptiles of Trinidad and Tobago.** Malabar, Fla., Krieger Publishing, 1997. 245p. illus. maps. index. $72.50. ISBN 0-89464-971-X.

Amphibians and Reptiles of Trinidad and Tobago is surely a labor of love. The author is well qualified to present his subject in a scholarly way but also provides lucid explanations for a layperson. He points out that this is not a comprehensive treatise. General information about the physical and biological environment sets the stage for clearly written species accounts, which have distribution maps and descriptions, species descriptions, natural history, voice for anuran amphibians, and common name etiology, where appropriate. Keys are easy to follow and should be helpful in field settings, although the book is a bit large to carry on a field trip. Identifying characteristics of genera and species are illustrated by clear drawings. The photographs are beautiful and distinct. The glossary is helpful. The literature cited section seems complete and should guide any interested reader to more in-depth information. The book is a bit pricey for individuals, but this title certainly should be on the shelves of libraries with natural history collections or an interest in the fauna of islands or of South and Central America.

—**Constance Rinaldo**

1475. Roze, Janis A. **Coral Snakes of the Americas: Biology, Identification, and Venoms.** Malabar, Fla., Krieger Publishing, 1996. 328p. illus. maps. index. $95.00. ISBN 0-89464-847-0.

The dust cover of this book is engaging and the contents enticing. Chapter 1, an overview, with its colorful, descriptive language, makes the subject understandable even to a nonherpetologist. The author's first-person comments, explanations, insights, and personal scientific background add credence to the subject matter. Roze's interest in coral snakes spans 30 years. The book covers all aspects of coral snakes: anatomy, ecology, feeding and food, reproduction, enemies, mimicry, biogeography, evolution, venoms, and consequences to humans of a coral snake bite. These topics take up the first 123 pages. Next comes a key to the species and subspecies. Then, for each taxon, he gives taxonomic history, range, description, remarks, food, references, and etymology of the name. References to a color plate and range map, along with page number, are given for many of the snakes. There is a section of color drawings that show scale patterns and is useful for identifying a snake at hand. The bibliography is extensive but not comprehensive—there are few entries for the years between 1992 and 1996. Roze concludes with four indexes: name, subject, scientific name, and venom and snakebite. Anyone interested in herpetology will find this a useful reference book.—**Nathan M. Smith**

32 Engineering

GENERAL WORKS

1476. **McGraw-Hill Dictionary of Engineering.** Sybil P. Parker, ed. New York, McGraw-Hill, 1997. 582p. $17.95pa. ISBN 0-07-052435-1.

This paperback dictionary provides the user with 16,700 terms covering the realm of engineering. Based on the 5th edition of the *McGraw-Hill Dictionary of Scientific and Technical Terms* (see ARBA 95, entry 1493), this resource has terms that are fundamental to understanding engineering. Terms are listed alphabetically on a letter-by-letter basis, and each definition provides the field of engineering it is used in. The definitions are brief and understandable even to the layperson. Cross-referencing and a synopsis of each field in engineering are provided. The appendix gives the user conversion factors for the U.S. Customary System, the metric system, and the International System, as well as special mathematical constants and variables, indefinite integrals, and trigonometric identities used in engineering.

For more in-depth definitions, researchers and others may wish to use specific reference works in the fields of civil engineering, electrical engineering, and the like. The *McGraw-Hill Dictionary of Engineering* is reasonably priced and recommended for engineering students and public and academic libraries.
—**Diane J. Turner**

AUTOMOTIVE ENGINEERING

1477. **Delmar's Automotive Dictionary.** By David W. South and Boyce H. Dwiggins. Albany, N.Y., Delmar, 1997. 281p. $22.95pa. ISBN 0-8273-7405-4.

Although there are any number of automotive dictionaries to choose from, many public libraries may find that this resource is an inexpensive alternative to other more costly or specialized texts that are available on the market, simply because it is brief, easy-to-read, and meant for a wide audience. Intended for everyone from the automotive professional to the enthusiast and the general public, this dictionary provides information on automobile parts and repair terminology, terms used in repair shops, language used in trucking and medium- to heavy-duty truck repair, and words and slang commonly used in automotive racing and hot-rodding.

Terminology is arranged alphabetically. All of the defined terms are highlighted in bold typeface. Brief and concise definitions of words, abbreviations, and automotive phrases are included. After consultation with linguistic experts, the publisher decided not to include parts of speech and pronunciation guides, because most of the terms are taken from commonly used words. Among the user-friendly features of this dictionary is the insertion of a shadow alphabet, running A to Z from the top to bottom on the outside of each page, which includes a boldfaced letter indicating the alphabetic location to the user or reader. In a practice commonly found with dictionaries, the top of each page also indicates the first and last words defined on that page.

The text is followed by two brief appendixes. The first provides a breakdown of decimal and metric equivalents, and the second includes some of the more common abbreviations used today in the automotive industry.—**James M. Murray**

CHEMICAL ENGINEERING

1478. Crowley, William R. **Chemicals on the Internet: A Directory of Industry Sites. Volume 1: Organic Chemicals and Petrochemicals.** Houston, Tex., Gulf Publishing, 1997. 244p. index. $69.00pa. ISBN 0-88415-139-5.

As far as a directory of Websites can go, this one does include many places to start, is easy to use, and does include a disk of the URLs for the sites discussed. The first problem is how to keep a directory up-to-date (even the URL for the author's company is out-of-date). Some publishers have addressed this problem by creating a companion Website that fulfills this purpose, but, of course, that is expensive. Crowley does not even touch on the issue of the dynamic content of the World Wide Web; there is no mention of how to find new sites or that URLs included in the book may be defunct. He also does not mention how often the sites covered are updated.

As all experienced researchers know, knowing how to use the Internet does not mean that one has learned research skills. A little more information on this topic would go a long way toward making this a much more useful book. A short paragraph in the introduction entitled "Here's the Procedure" should be expanded to cover development of strategy and problem definition. At the least, a short bibliography should have been included. Any information on the use of virtual libraries and how to find them, as well as special strategies that should be used on search engines for chemical information, would have been useful to all searchers. Often in technical areas, finding a person who knows can be more useful than any other strategy. Creative searching in Usenet and listservs should have been explained in greater detail.
—**Connie Williams**

1479. **Perry's Chemical Engineers' Handbook.** 7th ed. Robert H. Perry, Don W. Green, and James O. Maloney, eds. New York, McGraw-Hill, 1997. 1v. (various paging). illus. index. $125.00. ISBN 0-07-049841-5.

Perry's Chemical Engineers' Handbook, which first appeared in 1934, is virtually the only comprehensive reference book for the chemical processing industry. The editors have assembled a work of some 2,200 pages divided into 30 sections. The individual sections were created by 140 industrial and discipline experts, chiefly drawn from U.S. firms and universities.

An extensive revision and reorganization from the 6th edition of 1984 has been accomplished. New sections include process safety and chemical reactions. Sections extensively revised include physical and chemical data, mathematics, mass transfer, reaction kinetics, and process control. The work is primarily accessed via an excellent, detailed index. The editors note that there are more than 1,700 illustrations, made up of a variety of high-quality diagrams, charts, tables, and photographs. Each section and most subsections are augmented by extensive lists of references with precise information. As has been characteristic of earlier editions, the writing throughout is remarkably uniform and quite clear despite the large number of contributors, a tribute to the editors.

This handbook is an outstanding reference work. The new edition is an essential purchase for appropriate collections serving the profession.—**John M. Robson**

CIVIL ENGINEERING

1480. **Building Construction Cost Data 1997.** 55th ed. Phillip R. Waier and others, eds. Kingston, Mass., R. S. Means, 1996. 663p. illus. index. $79.95pa. ISBN 0-87629-425-5. ISSN 0068-3531.

The 55th annual edition of this reference source is just one of the many valuable products produced by the R. S. Means Company, and it was developed for contractors, architects, engineers, facilities managers, or even homeowners who want to plan and estimate costs of everything from pouring a concrete driveway to building a skyscraper. There are several guides at the beginning explaining how to use either a "quick start" method or the more detailed instructions to get the information and the results needed. All costs depict U.S. national averages, and the book provides brief descriptions on each cost and the factors affecting those costs. The heavily used reference information is easy to spot by the gray bar on the edge of the pages. This includes the extremely valuable "City Cost Indexes," which compare prices from city to city or region to region, and the "Historical Cost Indexes," "Location Factors," and the useful abbreviations section. The alphabetic index aids the user in finding everything from abrasive aggregates to zee bars. This invaluable paperback reference is recommended for large public libraries and academic libraries that serve any clientele interested in building or construction.—**Diane J. Turner**

1481. **Directory of Building and Equipment Grants: A Reference Directory Identifying Building, Renovation, and Equipment Grants Available to Nonprofit Organizations.** 4th ed. Loxahatchee, Fla., Research Grant Guides, 1996. 148p. index. $57.50pa. ISBN 0-945078-14-5. ISSN 1062-6492.

The 4th edition of this special directory now includes 600 qualified sources of grants for building and equipment. Three articles, highly valuable on their own merits, precede the state-by-state bibliographic list of foundations: "Successful Strategies for Winning Building and Equipment Grants," "The Realist's Guide to Foundation and Corporate Grants," and "Computers and the Non-Profit Organization." The computer article suffers the unavoidable fate of being slightly dated, but still provides an adequate overview of generic technological needs. Federal program listings have been removed and wisely left to the realm of more detailed resources. However, the first article suggests sources of federal funding for certain categories of projects related to school programs, transportation, urban development, and scholarly research. Alphabetic and subject indexes and the Foundation Center resource listings continue to make up the appendix. This is a valuable addition to any collection of grant sources, whether academic or public, and it continues to be an important desk reference for nonprofits.—**Barbara Delzell**

1482. **Routledge German Dictionary of Construction. Wörterbuch Bauwesen Deutsch-Englisch/ Englisch-Deutsch.** New York, Routledge, 1997. 345p. $140.00. ISBN 0-415-11242-7.

This is an excellent dictionary for those involved with British or German construction industries. Although each of the countries in the European Union uses its own construction terminology, this dictionary pulls together approximately 25,000 entries for the German and British construction industries. The areas covered include architecture, structural design, building pathology, construction law, project management, specification writing, quality assurance, third-party testing, insurance, liability, and quantity surveying. To a lesser extent, environmental issues are covered, but only where the terms are already in common professional usage.

The introduction clearly notes that coverage of North American terms and spellings were reviewed to ensure coverage. Indeed, North American terms are included here, but the focus is clearly British and German construction vocabulary. The selection of terms for inclusion cast a wide net, and there are both basic and specialized terms in the dictionary; for example, the term *fenestration*. In addition to the inclusion of some very specialized words, coverage in subject areas is proportional. Established areas receive more words than an area that is emerging. This preference has the unfortunate consequence of reinforcing the mainstream practice while downplaying newly important areas, such as environmental issues.

This title is a solid, tight dictionary that will be of immense use to those in the construction professions who must deal with British and German colleagues. As the construction professions become even more global, a work such as this one will become more valuable. As it is, this is a specialized source. It is highly recommended for specialized collections with a heavy British and German focus.—**C. D. Hurt**

1483. **Square Foot Costs 1997.** 18th ed. John H. Ferguson and others, eds. Kingston, Mass., R. S. Means, 1996. 458p. illus. index. $95.95pa. ISBN 0-87629-430-1. ISSN 0732-815X.

R. S. Means publishes a wide variety of building cost annuals. The *Square Foot Costs* volume is the most general in nature and encompasses a wide variety of residential and commercial buildings and individual construction components. It is the one best suited for general reference collections.

The residential section, the first of the three divisions, guides the user with an easy-to-follow method to calculate a general estimate on how much a house will cost to build. A tagged drawing defines 48 elements of a home, then the tables list prices on a per-square foot basis for each style of home (ranch, trilevel, and so forth) in four price levels, from economy to luxury. Estimates for add-ons, such as an extra bathroom or garage, are also noted. The commercial section covers 70 specific buildings, such as apartments, banks, fire stations, and schools, and has the same approach as the residential section. The assemblies section takes buildings down to the various components, such as steel columns, stucco walls, gutters, slabs, and heating/cooling, and provides costs broken down for material and labor per square foot.

There is one more step in the estimation process: The numbers gathered must be modified by the costs in the area of construction. The city multiplier tables adjust figures lower in some cities and much higher in others. Another useful table is the historical index, which compares relative construction costs for each city from 1997 back to 1940. A glossary, a list of abbreviations, and several model work forms are in the back. There is no index, but the intelligent arrangement and tabbing will be all most users will require.

Most public libraries will find this book worthwhile. It is also recommended to academic and special libraries where there is interest.—**Gary R. Cocozzoli**

1484. **The Wiley Dictionary of Civil Engineering and Construction.** L. F. Webster, comp. and ed. New York, John Wiley, 1997. 666p. $49.95pa. ISBN 0-471-18115-3.

This is a straightforward dictionary that is entirely in English (John Wiley has a work with the same title that differs only in that it is an English-Spanish, Spanish-English dictionary [see ARBA 97, entry 1304]). The compiler makes it clear that this is not intended to be a comprehensive source but rather a first stop. The preface is confusing in that apparently the original title for this work was *The Contractor's Dictionary*, and Webster still uses that title. There are more than 30,000 entries here with short definitions ranging from a line to a paragraph in length. Webster hits the mark in offering a no-nonsense work. This is the sort of dictionary that will be used by those in engineering and those who need to interpret construction terminology. The only criticism is including such entries as "inch," which might be best left to more generic dictionaries. This admittedly picky point aside, the work at hand is highly recommended for academic and larger public library collections.—**C. D. Hurt**

ELECTRIC ENGINEERING AND ELECTRONICS

1485. Croft, Terrell, and Wilford I. Summers. **American Electricians' Handbook.** 13th ed. New York, McGraw-Hill, 1996. 1v. (various paging). illus. index. $79.95. ISBN 0-07-013936-9.

American Electricians' Handbook, now in its 13th edition, embodies all the attributes of excellence one typically looks for in a revised edition of any well-established, long-standing work. The revision was professionally implemented and overseen. All entries have been reviewed, revised, and made consistent with most recent requirements of the National Electrical Code 1996 and National Electrical Manufacturers Association and American National Standard Institute s industry standards. The latest state-of-the-art practices have been incorporated. Some specific examples of this include completely revised lamp tables that reflect the 1992 Energy Policy Act mandate to promote energy-efficient lighting. Also, new material on harmonics has been added to the "Fundamentals" section as well as the "Transformers" and "Generators/Motors" divisions.

This handbook goes beyond must-have status for practitioners. It extends nicely into any undergraduate reference collection because of its superb clarity of definitions and the logical, progressive, thoroughly cross-referenced manner in which they are presented. For example, any student in an introductory science class can find a crystal-clear explanation of *emf* (electromotive force), *ohms*, or *volts*, compared to the same definitions in other highly regarded and widely used sources. This handbook is highly recommended for school and academic libraries.—**Barbara Delzell**

1486. **Electrical & Electronics Trades Directory 1996.** [CD-ROM]. Stevenage, England, Peter Peregrinus; distr., Piscataway, N.J., Institution of Electric Engineers, 1996. Minimum system requirements: IBM or compatible 386 (486 recommended). DIN/ISO 9660 CD-ROM drive. MS-DOS 5.0. Windows 3.1. 4MB RAM. 5MB hard disk space. 16-color monitor (256-color recommended). $180.00.

This title is the CD-ROM version of the 114-year-old directory of the same name. The disc is divided into four databases: manufacturer/supplier, representative, wholesaler, and products. Although each database is differentiated by distinct colored lines, all four provide source information on electrical; electronics; allied organizations; and products, materials, and services for any organization having sales outlets to or buying from British industry. The definition of what is included is broad: for example, cable box compounds, water controlled valves, heat shrinkable plastics, wire/cable, and conductive polymers, as well as interconnection components and systems, cable joining accessories, wiring and harness systems, and circuitry. It is also possible to find out who distributes Intel products in Great Britain and which manufacturers are in specific cities or postal codes.

The CD-ROM uses the LASEC Optisearch 2 software system to locate specific information within each database. Once a record has been retrieved, the user can double-click with the right-hand mouse button on any term displayed and start an immediate hypersearch of the entire database. Records supply cross-references that link topics, paragraphs, or words to other documents. Users can annotate individual paragraphs, sections, or words in the document and view this information later. The search engine is efficient, and there are clear, relevant Help screens. Probably the most interesting Help "screen" is found on the main page. From here the user can select the Lotus Screencam, which actively demonstrates the use of every item on the various search screens. It does this surprisingly quickly and in an interesting fashion. All in all, this disc is an interesting and useful product for users who need information on British suppliers and manufacturers.—**Susan B. Ardis**

1487. Horn, Delton T. **The Master Handbook of IC Circuits.** 3d ed. New York, McGraw-Hill, 1997. 440p. illus. index. $49.95; $34.95pa. ISBN 0-07-030562-5; 0-07-0303563-3pa.

Horn, the author of several dozen electronics books published chiefly by TAB Books during the past 17 years, has produced this companion work to his *Master IC Cookbook* (3d ed., 1997). Last revised in 1989, *The Master Handbook of IC Circuits* has as its focus "the most representative, popular, and useful devices." Writing primarily for the hobbyist and technician, Horn does an excellent job of clearly presenting digital, linear, and combination circuits. All are in production as of the creation of the text. Within the three sections, the circuits are presented in numerical order, ignoring manufacturer's alphabetic prefixes. The reader is cautioned to check with the manufacturer or supplier if there is any question about compatibility. Most technicians stockpile the commercial manuals of the circuits they use. The diagrams are large and easy to comprehend; accompanying text is minimal, assuming a knowledgeable user. In addition to a useful subject index, the author has appended a list of symbols and definitions and an index of devices by device number.—**John M. Robson**

1488. **The Illustrated Dictionary of Electronics.** 7th ed. Stan Gibilisco, ed. New York, McGraw-Hill, 1997. 788p. illus. $39.95pa. ISBN 0-07-024186-4.

This title is another edition of a standard electronics dictionary first published in 1980. Originally published by Tab Books as a small handbook, the 7th edition is now a more traditional 23 centimeters. Gibilisco, the current editor, has been involved with this project since 1988 and is a professional technical writer who specializes in books on electronics. He is also the author of the popular *Encyclopedia of Electronics*, which was chosen by *Booklist* as one of the best reference books of the 1980s.

Although some entries, primarily outdated abbreviations and tube-related words, have been eliminated since the 1st edition, the new edition still has many abbreviations, all of which are included in the main dictionary and in a special listing in appendix C. Also included are appendixes that cover electronic and math symbols, Greek letters, and a short and not very useful list of suggested readings. This is a traditional dictionary, and as befits its name, the preponderance of terms are related to electronics and traditional electrical engineering. Computer terms, including network and material science terms, are more selectively included. As with any specialized dictionary, some tangential terms are included and some are not. For example, the Internet is defined but not Ethernet, TCP/IP, Java, and WAIS. However, the book is filled with interesting terms. This inexpensive dictionary should be found in every technical library and any public library that serves people who visit Radio Shack or other electronics stores.—**Susan B. Ardis**

1489. **McGraw-Hill Electronics Dictionary.** 6th ed. By Neil Sclater and John Markus. New York, McGraw-Hill, 1997. 527p. illus. $55.00. ISBN 0-07-057837-0.

This is the 6th edition of a classic dictionary. Previous editions were received favorably, and this edition should be no different. The intent of the dictionary is to be a first stop for information on electronics in general. The dust jacket indicates there are more than 14,000 entries—more than 800 new terms and 220 new illustrations—in this edition. The marketing department and the authors should have communicated better. The preface states that there are "more than 12,000 entries and more than 800 illustrations."

In keeping with previous editions, the entries are alphabetic. The illustrations are all black-and-white and generally informative. Regardless of the number of entries, this is a well-crafted and well-managed dictionary. It is not an in-depth work and was never intended to be used for that purpose. It is a first-stop work that will be used heavily in general reference collections. Some anomalous entries are curious. An example is an entry for "Notices to Mariners." It is true that these can be sent electronically, but the inclusion of this term and not, for instance, "Notices to Airpeople" is curious. Overall, this excellent, general-purpose electronics dictionary will be well used in public and academic reference collections.

—**C. D. Hurt**

GENETIC ENGINEERING

1490. **Biotechnology Abstracts: Agricultural & Environmental. 1983-February 1997.** [CD-ROM]. Baltimore, Md., National Information Services Corporation, 1997. Minimum system requirements: IBM or compatible 386. CD-ROM drive. 3MB RAM. 480K conventional memory. 2.5MB hard disk space. Color or monochrome monitor. $695.00/yr.

The National Information Services Corporation (NISC) purchases the content of numerous abstract and bibliographic tools and combines the text with their own search engine. Their products are available in two formats: CD-ROM and online on their Website (www.nisc.com). Fifty-four CD-ROMs are available, ranging in content from a black studies database to the sciences, including the title under review, *Biotechnology Abstracts*. The software runs under DOS and requires a 386 or greater computer and 180K RAM. (A query to the publisher concerning conversion to Windows was unanswered.) The online products are currently more limited, with a total of 27 databases as of this writing. All one needs to search these sites are a Web browser and a subscription. The search engine used, ROMWright, is the same. Each month, NISC provides a free database for trial.

Even in the novice mode, the search tips on the disc seem a bit advanced. The hints start out with Boolean logic, which is not a concept that most novice library users understand. Perhaps with the advent of sophisticated Web search engines that fact is changing, but it does seem overwhelming for most first-time computer searchers. The search tips are clear if the problem of understanding why Boolean logic is important is overcome, and they should be really useful to those who take the time to learn how to use them. The options available to users, also written in fairly sophisticated language, are extensive.

The novice search mode allows for three search fields; the advanced and expert modes provide much more flexibility, with many more fields added. The Help is written, again, in a technical manner, (e.g., "The NOVICE mode features the most commonly used indexes and fields for searching and emphasizes a Basic Search index for easy retrieval based on the most significant descriptive and textual elements [fields] of the records").

In summary, the search capabilities of this software are sophisticated and well documented for experienced searchers. However, novices will need some training to get started.—**Connie Williams**

MATERIALS SCIENCE

1491. **Jefferson's Welding Encyclopedia.** 18th ed. Robert L. O'Brien, ed. Miami, Fla., American Welding Society, 1997. 758p. illus. $120.00. ISBN 0-87171-506-6.

Long the standard desk reference for the welding profession, *Jefferson's Welding Encyclopedia* in its 18th edition (the 1st edition appeared in 1921) is arranged in dictionary style with a sufficient number of cross-references, illustrations (some colored), tables, and diagrams to guide the experienced practitioner. Common initialisms are inserted parenthetically after the full term. U.S. units of measurement are converted to the international system. Nearly 20 percent of the text is allocated to appendixes, including a history of welding and cutting; diagrams drawn from technical literature; safety, applicable trade, national, and international standards; and a buyer's guide to products, manufacturers, and suppliers. For suppliers, the reader is given (in a separate section) addresses and telephone and fax numbers. Users will find the text clean, the illustrations useful, and the entire work a convenient and efficient reference for those knowledgeable about welding.—**John M. Robson**

1492. **Pearson's Handbook Desk Edition: Crystallographic Data for Intermetallic Phases.** Materials Park, Ohio, ASM International, 1997. 2v. $775.00/set. ISBN 0-87170-603-2.

This two-volume desk set of *Pearson's Handbook* contains 27,686 entries versus the original's 50,000 entries and has a single "best" reference for each phase instead of the multiple references found in the complete work. Entries are updated through 1995 (the 2d edition goes through 1989) and contain complete information. Structure type is given for all entries, 54 percent of the entries have the coordinates of the atoms, and there is a 67-page structure-type index. Many improvements over the original edition have been incorporated into this work, including presenting all crystallographic data in the standard setting used in the *International Tables for Crystallography* and adding such information to the entries as calculated density, color, more detailed diffraction data, standard deviation of unit cell dimension(s), point-set symmetry, and a full reference that includes publication title.—**Jo Anne H. Ricca**

1493. **The Wiley Encyclopedia of Packaging Technology.** 2d ed. Aaron L. Brody and Kenneth S. Marsh, eds. New York, John Wiley, 1997. 1023p. illus. index. $225.00. ISBN 0-471-06397-5.

The goal of the editors is to provide users and students with a comprehensive, single-volume encyclopedia on the diverse subject of packaging technology. This reference is a new edition of the 1986 work (see ARBA 87, entry 1540) and reflects the substantial changes in this industry in the last decade. Forces are driving down costs at the same time that environmental concerns warrant greater safety, simplicity, and recyclability. The encyclopedia was written with the research help of members of the Institute of Packaging Research, and it brings together information that otherwise would have to be found in handbooks dealing with food, plastics, and electronic packaging, among others.

Listed alphabetically and punctuated with numerous cross-references, more than 250 entries cover the fundamental sciences and technologies of packaging. Each entry is signed and contains photographs, helpful tables of physical data and properties, and illustrative diagrams. A short bibliography of cited and general references is also provided for each entry. The references include relevant patents, regulations, and standards. There are two appendixes, the first containing conversion factors, abbreviations, and unit symbols, and the second providing a glossary of packaging terminology and definitions.

—**John M. Robson**

MECHANICAL ENGINEERING

1494. Brown, Harry L., Bernard B. Hamel, and Bruce A. Hedman. **Energy Analysis of 108 Industrial Processes.** 6th ed. Lelburn, Ga., Fairmont Press; distr., New York, Prentice Hall, 1996. 314p. $68.00. ISBN 0-13-576992-2.

The authors have, for 6 editions during a 20-year time period, analyzed the energy consumption of 108 industrial processes as found in the most energy intensive Standard Industrial Classification (SIC) groupings. The goal has been to identify both the quality and the quantity of industrial waste energy that can be recovered in an economically feasible fashion. The authors have used a variety of primary and secondary sources and on-site visits to flowchart the characteristic processes of the various industries that consume 72 percent of the nation's energy output. Each step in a process is described in a tabular form at the inlet and outlet stages of production. Energy and mass balances on a per-unit basis are given. When certain processes within a classification accounted for the vast percentage of the energy usage, the four-digit SIC code was integrated to represent all relevant processes. This reference work is the standard in the area of industrial energy consumption.—**John M. Robson**

SAFETY ENGINEERING

1495. Skelly, Kenneth J., and Elizabeth M. T. Skelly. **Directory of Safety Standards, Literature, and Services.** New York, Van Nostrand Reinhold, 1997. 1964p. $149.95pa. ISBN 0-442-02282-4.

This directory consists of 8 sections, such as federal safety standards; societies, organizations, and associations; safety literature; and state agencies. The largest section, more than half the book, consists of a list of state agencies and safety standards, arranged by state. Interfiled within each state are entries for specific state agencies that deal with safety issues as well as such subject categories as accidents, buildings and facilities, radiation, and waste management. Under each category is a word or phrase with a citation to that state's code. For example, under the listing for Alabama, "sprinkler systems" is the citation to §34-33-1 to 34-33-12 in the Alabama State Code. Because no other information is given, users will need to get a copy of the cited code either from a local university law library, or through interlibrary loan, document delivery, or access to a legal database such as Westlaw or Lexis/Nexis.

The next largest section contains information on industry standards. This same information also can be found in a number of other sources, including KR-Dialog's Standards and Spec file 113; ILI Standards Infodisk (World Wide Web subscription or on CD-ROM); and the paper or CD-ROM index *Industrial Standards* from Information Handling Service (IHS). All of these provide more information, such as citation to specific standards, abstracts, and indexing under keywords. The same can be said for the section on federal safety standards—there are other, much better places to find specific federal safety specifications: KR-Dialog, CFR on the Web, and IHS.

The primary value of this volume is in ascertaining that states have varying standards; for example Maine has a safety standard on training flaggers, whereas Pennsylvania does not. This directory is an esoteric reference book for a specific audience. It would probably be more useful as a personal reference source in a design, law, or engineering firm.—**Susan B. Ardis**

SOILS ENGINEERING

1496. **Compendium of Soil Clean-Up Technologies and Soil Remediation Companies.** By the Economic Commission for Europe. New York, United Nations, 1997. 98p. $60.00pa. ISBN 92-1-116677-2. S/N E.97.II.E. 19.

This compendium results from a United Nations Economic Commission for Europe (ECE) pilot project addressing the "environmental clean-up of selected sites polluted by chemicals in countries in transition of central and eastern Europe and central Asia." It is divided into two sections, a database on 19 soil clean-up technologies and a database on soil remediation companies in 19 ECE countries. The technologies are subdivided into two categories, in situ and ex situ, and each technology is rated on cost, clean-up ability, clean-up time requirements, reliability, and community acceptability. The first three ratings (cost, ability, and time) are quantitative within broad ranges, and the final two (reliability and community acceptance) are qualitative only.

The methodology used to compile the database is not described, so the user is uncertain of the validity of the data. Although not explicit, this work implies that data were collected from questionnaires distributed to and completed by potential technology providers. There is no description of whether raw data were verified, nor any discussion of how subjective rankings were assigned. Each technology is assigned a key number in that technology's description. To connect a technology to a provider of that technology, the user has to manually search over 70 pages of companies for the technology's key number. The company's listing references technologies that are not described in the *Compendium*; furthermore, the *Compendium* describes at least one technology (automated segregation of radioactive soil) that does not link to any listed company.

The preface to the work points out that the database should eventually be published on the Internet, which would greatly improve its ease of use (although electronic publication would not necessarily improve the quality of compiled data). Until that occurs, the *Compendium* does not improve on a telephone call to technology advertisers in soil remediation trade journals, or a quick Internet search.—**Connie Williams**

STATIONARY AND CUSTODIAL ENGINEERING

1497. McKenna, Ted, and Ray Oliverson. **Glossary of Reliability and Maintenance Terms.** Houston, Tex., Gulf Publishing, 1997. 141p. $30.00. ISBN 0-88415-360-6.

The authors, who are reliability consultants, believe that ineffective communication is often an obstacle to achieving a company's goals. This dictionary is their attempt to create a standardized language for important words and phrases used in industry and thereby increase communications. They point out in their introduction that there are many seemingly similar terms used, and they ask the question, what exactly is the difference between repair maintenance, responsive maintenance, routine maintenance, reactive maintenance, and preventive or preventative maintenance? Although several are frankly synonymous, the others refer to different conditions of importance to reliability experts. McKenna and Oliverson's goal is to standardize the meaning of important words while at the same time encouraging the use of certain terms; for example, *preventive maintenance* rather than *preventative maintenance*.

Most of the dictionary is made up of slightly more than 1,000 clearly written definitions for specialized terms, slang, and jargon, such as *DIN*, *insanity*, or *IRAN*. This volume is surprisingly amusing because of a sidebar on each page that consists of pithy and appropriate quotations. For example, on the page with definitions ranging from *Mission time* to *MRD* is a quotation by Samuel Johnson, "Nothing will ever be attempted if all possible objections must first be over come." Definitely reliable words of wisdom.

Aside from the definitions and quotations, there is a 26-item bibliography on the last 2 pages. All in all, this small reference book on a specialized topic is nicely done.—**Susan B. Ardis**

TOOLS

1498. **Home Improvements & Projects Index 1990-1993.** By the Highsmith Press Editorial Staff. Fort Atkinson, Wis., Highsmith Press, 1996. 217p. index. $30.00pa. ISBN 0-917846-30-3.

The 2,900 entries for this index are arranged alphabetically by subject. Each entry contains the title of the article, the author, a concise description of the article, availability of plans, and magazine citation. This index covers nine popular home improvement magazines, including: *Better Homes and Gardens*, *Canadian Workshop*, *Fine Homebuilding*, and *Home Mechanix*. Topics cover 10 articles on installing or repairing doors; 1 article on building a colonial doll house; 2 on making toy trucks; 1 on making a pizza paddle; and 6 on painting, as well as articles on periscopes, hot tubs, biscuit joinery, potting sheds, and removing wallpaper paste. Obviously, a wide range of home improvements is indexed. Coverage is limited to 1990 to 1993. The authors selected the magazines based on library availability and whether the publishers offered reprints or back issues at what the authors consider to be a "reasonable cost."

This index does what it does—no more, no less. Although this volume will fill a need in many public libraries, unfortunately it does not cover a large enough period of time. Most libraries would benefit from a publication of this sort that covered 20 or 30 years of home improvement projects, not to mention projects from the middle and late 1990s.—**Susan B. Ardis**

33 Health Sciences

GENERAL WORKS

Atlases

1499. **Atlas of Anatomy.** English ed. Hauppauge, N.Y., Barron's Educational Series, 1997. 104p. illus. index. $19.95. ISBN 0-7641-5000-6.

Every medical and university library, as well as many public and high school libraries, contains one or more atlases of basic human anatomy. Although the creators of this small, inexpensive volume recognize that there are a number of high-quality, very detailed atlases on this topic currently available, they intend their reference text for an intermediate-level audience, such as high school students or members of the general public who may find advanced atlases too technical.

The body of this volume, which is an English translation of a 1995 Spanish publication, is composed of 84 pages of attractive color plates illustrating normal human anatomy. The plates are organized by body systems (e.g., skeletal, muscular, circulatory, nervous, reproductive). Each plate is clearly labeled, although limited if any explanatory materials are included. There are no illustrations depicting changes caused by pathological conditions.

This volume is well indexed, thus making it easy to use. Public and high school libraries will find this new human anatomy atlas a worthwhile acquisition for their patrons.—**Jonathon Erlen**

1500. **The Ultimate Human Body Version 2.0.** [CD-ROM]. New York, DK Multimedia, 1996. Minimum system requirements: IBM or compatible 486DX/33MHz. Double-speed CD-ROM drive. Windows 3.1x. 8MB RAM (12MB recommended for Windows 95). 22MB hard disk space. 640 x 480 pixels, 256-color monitor (16 bit colors preferred). Mouse. 8 bit sound card. Loudspeakers or headphones. $39.95. ISBN 0-7894-1204-7.

The first version of this CD-ROM, published in 1994, won critical acclaim. This revised version uses a three-dimensional scanner to provide in-depth views of the body and its various systems. Animated sequences show how various organs look from any angle, including a cross-section. "Pop-up" models of each organ can also be dissected. Each view is accompanied by brief descriptions, and sound provides the correct pronunciation. As the user scrolls through the body, the names of various bones and organs are shown on a window in the frame. The program also contains a link to the Body Online Website, the publisher's subscription online "Health Club." The Body Quiz provides an interactive vehicle for exploration of human anatomy.

Aimed at users aged 10 and up, the information is easy to understand, yet comprehensive enough for school reports through high school age. Younger children will also be able to use it if their verbal skills are at 4th-grade level or above, although they will get more out of the disc if it is used with a parent's guidance. The price makes this an appropriate choice for school and public libraries, as well as for home use.

—**Susan B. Hagloch**

Bibliography

1501. Belmonte, Frances R. **Women and Health: An Annotated Bibliography.** Pasadena, Calif., Salem Press and Lanham, Md., Scarecrow, 1997. 203p. index. (Magill Bibliographies). $35.00. ISBN 0-8108-3385-9.

Women's health has finally emerged as a discipline in its own right. This annotated bibliography of approximately 300 books published during the past 30 years demonstrates the evolution of women's health from obstetrics and gynecology to care for the whole woman and the study of her interactions with society. The author, a substance abuse counselor and theologian, takes an interdisciplinary approach.

The chapters cover broad subject areas: descriptions of women, care of women, care by women, self-education and self-help, costs and benefits, and addictions. Each chapter has an introduction that attempts to set the parameters of its contents. Unfortunately, these are so full of jargon that it is hard to decide what the focus is. The actual citations offer only author, title, publisher, and date. The annotations, ranging in length from a one-third to a one-half page, offer brief summaries and some commentary by the author. Author, title, and subject indexes complete the work. The indexes are important because the chapter titles are so vague. The classic title *The New Our Bodies, Ourselves* (Peter Smith, 1996) could appear in several chapters; it is located in the self-education and self-help chapter.

Even though this work may be somewhat valuable for historical purposes in women's studies collections, it is not a necessary purchase for most libraries. The heavy use of jargon and vague organization make it minimally useful at best.—**Barbara M. Bibel**

1502. **Doody's Rating Service 1997: A Buyer's Guide to the 250 Best Health Sciences Books.** Oak Park, Ill., Doody Publishing, 1997. 263p. illus. index. $50.00pa. ISBN 1-885234-07-4. ISSN 1074-9640.

Selecting books in the health sciences can be a formidable task. Many expensive volumes appear each year, and librarians with limited budgets need to spend their money wisely. Doody Publishing is an independent organization that provides reviews of professional and student-level health sciences materials. Doody produces three print and five electronic review products. Reviews are prepared by 140 editorial groups covering the major medical and allied health disciplines. Each group is chaired by an academic health sciences professional who appoints appropriate reviewers and evaluates all titles submitted in the assigned area. The selection of the 250 best books, including the book of the year, is made from a field of 2,900 titles submitted by approximately 200 publishers. A list of review board chairs, submitted titles, and participating publishers appears in the front of this book.

The reviews are divided into broad categories: basic sciences, clinical medicine, nursing, associated health professions, and other disciplines. Within these areas, they are alphabetically arranged by specialties—anatomy, general surgery, case management, veterinary medicine, and so on. Each review contains a full bibliographic citation, a description, a 150-word evaluation, and information about special features and the target audience. In addition to author and title indexes, four appendixes list the titles by specialty, author affiliation, target audience, and book type. Book types are defined on the last page. Videos and CD-ROMs are included.

Health sciences, academic, and special librarians will find this source to be extremely useful for collection development. Public librarians with large collections will also find it helpful because it lists many appropriate titles. The reviews are clear and to the point, and they contain all the relevant acquisition information.—**Barbara M. Bibel**

1503. Haley, Barbara A., and Brian Deevey, comps. **American Health Care in Transition: A Guide to the Literature.** Westport, Conn., Greenwood Press, 1997. 336p. index. (Bibliographies and Indexes in Medical Studies, no.14). $79.50. ISBN 0-313-27323-5.

The compilers call this book a guide rather than an annotated bibliography, although it is a list of sources and the citations are all accompanied by abstracts. According to *Books in Print PLUS* (see ARBA 94, entry 8), it is the only book in print for either compiler, although Haley has published articles in *Humanity and Society*. Neither is a librarian—Haley is an applied sociologist and Deevey is a field data capture specialist for a digital map company. Buyers of this book should know that there are no books represented in this guide, only periodicals and government documents. It would be helpful to have this stated in the introduction. The introduction also fails to state the time span of the entries covered—the earliest one that was noticed had a date of 1979, the latest a date of 1996. Periodicals cited range from health care administration journals such as *Hospitals and Health Networks* to medical and even nursing journals. The government documents included are publications of two agencies, the U.S. General Accounting Office, which audits federal spending in areas like health care, and the Agency for Health Care Policy and Research, part of the U.S. Department of Health and Human Services. At $79.50, this book is a little expensive, but recommended, especially for collections supporting public health departments teaching health care administration.—**Penny Papangelis**

1504. Haynes, Craig. **Ethnic Minority Health: A Selected, Annotated Bibliography.** Lanham, Md., Medical Library Association and Scarecrow, 1997. 503p. index. $65.00. ISBN 0-8108-3225-9.

This work serves to point out the disparities in health between minorities in the United States, who will make up one-third of the population by the year 2000, and nonminorities. The author, head of the Medical Center Library at the University of California, San Diego, Medical Center, concentrates on four minority groups: Native Americans, including Alaska Natives; African Americans; Hispanic Americans; and Asian/Pacific Islander Americans.

The book is organized into chapters devoted to medicine, mental health, medical education, health professions, research, service delivery and access, and prevention and health promotion. Every chapter begins with general information and then treats each group separately, so it is easy to locate relevant sections. What could be either a plus or a minus is that the annotations do not appear with the citations under these topics but are grouped together by main entry in a separate chapter. There are also an author and a subject index. It would have been easier to target specific citations from the subject index if the author had used entry numbers instead of page references, but this is a minor problem.

Sixty percent of the bibliography consists of monographs, although other material, such as government documents, research reports, and conference proceedings, is included. It is important to note that journal citations are not given here. Almost all the citations were published between 1970 and 1995. A list of dissertations and theses, journals, multimedia products, and federal and state publications appear in appendixes. This is a solid bibliography that will be most useful to people without access to OCLC's WorldCat, although the nonmonographs included definitely increase the book's value.—**Hope Yelich**

1505. **Health Statistics: An Annotated Bibliographic Guide to Information Resources.** 2d ed. Frieda O. Weise, Patricia G. Hinegardner, Barbara L. Kuchan, and Phyllis S. Lansing, eds. Chicago, Medical Library Association and Lanham, Md., Scarecrow, 1997. 178p. index. $42.00. ISBN 0-8108-3056-6.

Statistics are an important part of health sciences research. Finding a source with the necessary data for a specific project can be a challenge. This new edition of a basic guide to statistical sources will be helpful. *Health Statistics* was first published in 1980 (see ARBA 81, entry 1554). The 2d edition, by 4 experienced health sciences librarians, updates the material and adds new sources, including electronic databases. Nothing was added after 1994.

The 8 chapters cover broad subject areas, such as general references, vital statistics, demographics, health resources, morbidity, and so forth. Each is subdivided into such topics as specific diseases, age or ethnic groups, and types of health personnel. Within each topic, entries are numbered and arranged alphabetically by title. Entries include title, publisher, and frequency of issue. Entries for electronic sources list dates of coverage. There is no subscription, price, or ISBN/ISSN information. Annotations describe the type and scope of data and their arrangement. Four appendixes contain a brief list of newsletters and journals, a directory of state and federal agencies, a directory of associations and foundations, and a directory of regional federal depository libraries. A short glossary of terms and an index complete the text.

This book is a good starting point for students doing research on health care policy and epidemiology. It would also be helpful for librarians doing reference and collection development work in these areas. *Health Statistics* will be a useful addition to academic health science collections and large public libraries.
—**Barbara M. Bibel**

1506. Nordquist, Joan, comp. **The Health Care Crisis in the United States: A Bibliography.** Santa Cruz, Calif., Reference and Research Services, 1997. 72p. (Contemporary Social Issues: A Bibliographic Series, v.46). $15.00pa. ISBN 0-937855-90-1.

Managed care, managed cost, mangled care, market driven care—these are the words and phrases being used to describe the current evolution of the U.S. medical system. This reference provides a comprehensive list of the most current literature on this state of affairs. More than 850 entries effectively incorporate the spectrum of thinking on health/medical care delivery. Health care delivery "classics" from the 1980s are noted, but the majority of citations are from 1990 to 1996. The entries are organized under broad topical areas, including individual sections on the major populations at risk in the care system: women, children, the elderly, the homeless, minorities, and the poor.

The advantage to this particular reference is that it includes information that would not be found in any one computer database or hardcover medical index. A range of resources are cited—the usual books and journal articles but also dissertations, congressional hearings, and Websites. In addition, the Contemporary Social Issues Series includes literature from the less mainstream publications (e.g., activist organizations and alternative presses). Overall, this book is an excellent, all-inclusive, easy-to-use, quick source for the literature on health care delivery in the 1990s. It is highly recommended, particularly for libraries serving health care students or professionals.—**Mary Ann Thompson**

Biography

1507. **Who's Who in Medicine and Healthcare 1997-1998.** New Providence, N.J., Marquis Who's Who/Reed Reference Publishing, 1996. 1215p. $249.95. ISBN 0-8379-0000-X. ISSN 0000-1708.

This reference provides biographical sketches of 27,800 U.S. and international leaders in health care. The purpose of this publication is to ease networking among medical practitioners and to provide recognition for those making significant contributions to the field. Each entry gives the individual's occupation; personal data such as birthdate, religion, and marital status; education; certifications; and career-related activities, including writings, civic activities, and professional recognitions. Home and office addresses are also noted.

The criteria for inclusion focus on elected members of the Institute of Medicine; deans of U.S. medical, dental, and nursing schools; the board of directors of the American Medical Association and the American Board of Medical Specialties; key positions at U.S. health care agencies; state health and licensing boards; major award recipients such as recent Nobel prize-winners; and senior executives at major health maintenance organizations and pharmaceutical and insurance companies. The introduction states a desire to identify leaders in the delivery of healthcare, as well as providers. In browsing this volume, there is a notable lack of entries for the recognized icons in group practice administration and ambulatory care. Although the individuals listed are no doubt worthy, there is a significant segment of the health care community missing.—**Adrienne Antink Bendel**

Dictionaries and Encyclopedias

1508. Balch, James F., and Phyllis A. Balch. **Prescription for Nutritional Healing.** 2d ed. Garden City Park, N.Y., Avery Publishing, 1997. 600p. index. $19.95p. ISBN 0-89529-727-2.

The 2d edition of *Prescription for Nutritional Healing* is a comprehensive in-home guide of nutritional information for optimum health and fitness. It provides drug-free remedies for more than 300 ailments and disorders, including 50 additional health problems from the last edition. Up-to-date findings in the field of nutrition, the latest research on herbal medicine, and traditional remedies are discussed. The first section of the book, "Understanding the Elements of Health," explains types of nutrients, food supplements, and herbs. Part 2, "The Disorders," describes common health problems from backaches to cancer. Each entry has an excellent description of the problems and often gives information in a table for easy comparison. Helpful nutrients, herbs, and general recommendations for treatment are followed by a section of considerations and further information. Often, sources of further reading and addresses of treatment agencies or associations are given. Part three is a guide to traditional methods of treatment. The book has an index, manufacturer and distributor information, a list of health organizations, and health and medical hot lines.

Written by a medical doctor and a certified nutritionist, this guide provides alternative treatments and information for patients with serious illnesses or for average people who want to design their own nutritional program for better health. This book is designed to help individuals with differing health care needs, and its easy-to-use format makes it an important health resource.—**Natalie Brower-Kirton**

1509. Levinson, David, and Laura Gaccione. **Health and Illness: A Cross-Cultural Encyclopedia.** Santa Barbara, Calif., ABC-CLIO, 1997. 253p. illus. maps. index. (Encyclopedias of the Human Experience). $49.50. ISBN 0-87436-876-6.

Levinson, editor-in-chief of the *Encyclopedia of World Cultures* and senior editor of the *Encyclopedia of Cultural Anthropology*, has written many books on cross-cultural topics since the 1970s. He has edited and produced numerous dictionaries and encyclopedias on human experiences. Gaccione is a professional journalist and Associated Press correspondent. This book is the first of its kind in presenting global information on three different types of medical treatment—biomedicine, alternative and complementary medicine, and traditional medicine. Yet the major emphasis is on the alternative and traditional approaches. The authors reviewed journals, books, encyclopedias, magazines, and materials from organizations and gathered relevant information for this volume. They also collected ethnographic records and medical anthropology from books, articles, doctoral dissertations, reports, and so on.

The A to Z format is easy to use. The book contains unique explanations on wife beating and types of wife beating, supernatural explanations, reflexology, magnet therapy, the Saraguro health system, genital mutilation, culture-bound syndromes, ayurvedic medicine, anthrosophical medicine, and many other topics of interest. However, this book does not attempt to be comprehensive in scope. Only the best-known cultural healing systems and health issues are illustrated. A good bibliography is included.—**Polin P. Lei**

1510. Rognehaugh, Richard. **The Managed Health Care Dictionary.** Gaithersville, Md., Aspen, 1996. 211p. $19.95pa. ISBN 0-8342-0856-3.

Rognehaugh wants his dictionary to "emerge as the Gold Standard in comprehensive managed care terminology." He also wants it to please a widely diverse population—everyone from patients and physicians to government agencies and insurance companies. How well does he succeed? In a word, admirably: He has compiled a unique, comprehensive, up-to-date managed care dictionary with a few correctable elements.

Among the suggested improvements are making the cross-references consistent and always giving terms with the accompanying acronym (e.g., Rognehaugh gives the term *admission per thousand* but not the acronym APT). Another detriment is that medical occupations and specialties are omitted entirely. Patients often do not know an RN from an LPN. Also, some omissions were noted, which can be found in other glossaries.

One of the positive features is the inclusion of 1,100 terms, many cross-referenced; there are 23 entries on Medicare variations alone. In addition, slang and insider terms are included (e.g., *face sheet*, *turfing*, *snif*, and *unbundling*). Nearly 20 percent of the terms are acronyms; some are five unpronounceable letters long (e.g., DXNNH, RBRVS). The definitions are clear and include pros and cons as well as related terms. The terms defined are of all levels of sophistication. Also of benefit are the publisher's solid reputation and its commitment to update and revise (comments and differing perspectives are invited via e-mail, fax, and regular mail).—**Pete Prunkl**

1511. Slee, Vergil N., Debora A. Slee, and H. Joachim Schmidt. **Health Care Terms.** healthy communities ed. St. Paul, Minn., Tringa Press, 1996. 196p. $19.95pa. ISBN 0-9615255-7-6.

The health care reform movement has led to a greater focus on managed health care, prevention, and lifelong health education, rather than simple response to those actively seeking care. The Healthy Communities initiative seeks to incorporate the myriad activities of traditional health care providers with those of educational and public health agencies. Many nonmedical organizations—city councils, legal firms, insurance companies, and support agencies among them—are working with hospitals and nursing services. This volume is designed to help the lay community understand medical terminology as well as to provide medical practitioners with the vocabulary for managed care, law, insurance, payment systems, and other issues.

Arranged alphabetically, with cross-referenced acronyms, the book provides concise definitions of a broad range of terms, from *TQM* to *xenograft*. Obviously, this volume is not as inclusive as specialty dictionaries in any of the subjects covered, but it provides a sufficient cross-section of the vocabulary of each area. The book is small enough to carry in a briefcase and inexpensive enough for copies to be provided to all who want them. Most public and academic libraries probably have this information in other resources, but the work is highly recommended for special libraries serving medical, legal, insurance, and management agencies.—**Susan B. Hagloch**

Directories

1512. **Health Professions Education Directory 1997-1998.** Chicago, American Medical Association, 1997. 459p. $54.95pa. ISBN 0-89970-834-X.

Since its first publication in 1969, this directory has undergone a series of name changes that reflect the changes that have taken place in the medical field. The 1st edition was entitled *Directory of Accredited Allied Medical Educational Programs*. The next year the title was changed to *Directory of Approved Allied Medical Educational Programs*, which succumbed the following year to *Allied Medical Education Directory*. The 7th through 23d editions, published from 1978 through 1996, were succinctly titled *Allied Health Education Directory* (see ARBA 87, entry 1586), *Allied Health and Rehabilitation Professions Education Directory*, and *Health Professions Education Directory 1997-1998*.

Regardless of its name, this American Medical Association (AMA) directory continues to provide comprehensive information on the growing number of health professions, the educational programs that prepare these professionals, and the accrediting agencies that certify such programs. Although the order and number of sections has changed with various editions, the basic content of the directory has remained the same. The new edition is divided into four sections. The first provides detailed information on 13 accrediting agencies, including their structure, purpose, responsibilities, composition, and contact information. The second section, arranged alphabetically by occupation, provides the historic development, an occupation description, a job description, and employment characteristics for each occupation, as well as descriptions of the type of registration or certification required and the educational program necessary to prepare for that occupation. Education requirements range from a high school diploma to baccalaureate and masters level programs. Each occupation entry is followed by a directory, arranged alphabetically by geographic location, to the various educational programs available for that occupation. The third section, also arranged alphabetically by state, provides a directory of institutions that sponsor accredited programs with a list of the programs offered at each institution. The final section summarizes data from the AMA Annual Survey of Accredited Health Education Programs and provides such statistics as the number of programs and enrollments, with attrition and graduation rates, by occupation.

Since the 6th edition, published in 1976, the number of occupations has increased from 26 to 40. Specialties have diversified from medical assistant, occupational therapist, and respiratory therapist, to art therapist, therapeutic recreation therapist, and rehabilitation counselor. Accrediting agencies have expanded and criteria for certification has become more specific. This directory has kept pace with the growth in health professions. It is recommended for vocational guidance, as part of a career development center, and as a reference source for public, high school, and academic libraries.—**Debra S. Van Tassel**

Handbooks and Yearbooks

1513. Field, Shelly. **Career Opportunities in Health Care.** New York, Facts on File, 1997. 228p. index. $29.95; $18.95pa. ISBN 0-8160-3381-1; 0-8160-3382-Xpa.

People seeking information about careers in health care may not realize that so many options are available. In addition to the usual physician, nurse, pharmacist, and dentist, one can consider health services administrator, music therapist, director of hospital funding, biomedical equipment technician, and medical records technician. This book discusses more than 70 different jobs involving direct patient care as well as administration.

The book is divided into 18 sections covering broad areas: medicine, vision care, geriatrics, long-term care, and so on. Within each section, job profiles are listed alphabetically. Each entry is approximately two pages in length. The entries begin with two charts that are next to each other. The "career profile" summarizes the main points of the article, and the "career ladder" shows the path from entry level to the highest position in the field. The narrative portion of the article contains a detailed job description in lay language; salary range; employment prospects; advancement prospects; education and training required; experience, skills, and personality traits useful for the job; best geographic location for employment; unions and professional associations; and job-hunting tips. Appendixes contain a list of education programs for selected occupations by state, a list of trade associations and unions, a brief bibliography, and a glossary of abbreviations and terms.

Career Opportunities in Health Care is a helpful starting point for those exploring options in the job market. It is reasonably priced, so both reference and circulating copies can be purchased. Libraries that own any of the larger career encyclopedias, such as those from J. G. Ferguson or VGM (see entry 215), will not need a reference copy.—**Barbara M. Bibel**

1514. Gastelu, Daniel, and Fred Hatfield. **Dynamic Nutrition for Maximum Performance: A Complete Nutritional Guide for Peak Sports Performance.** Garden City Park, N.Y., Avery Publishing, 1997. 404p. illus. index. $19.95pa. ISBN 0-89529-756-6.

This dietary guide for both professional and amateur athletes or fitness enthusiasts is divided into 4 parts. Part 1 covers nutrients, their roles in fitness and health, and what foods contain them; part 2 discusses anatomy, digestion, and metabolism; part 3 guides users through such activities as building muscle and carbo loading; and part 4 supplies plans specific to individual sports. An introductory section on how to use the book stresses the importance of slowly incorporating new techniques into a fitness regimen and following the advice of a health care provider above all. Helpful tables, charts, and boxes provide information supplementary to the text. Mathematical formulas for determining daily caloric requirements, metabolic rates, and body fat percentages are also useful.

The information combines both time-tested ideas of fitness and nutrition with the latest scientific data and the personal experiences of the two authors (a sports nutritionist/wrestler and a world champion power lifter, respectively). Some of the information may be controversial. The authors appear to espouse carbohydrate consumption over protein, stating that athletes who consume too much meat will suffer from decreased performance and a struggle with body fat. Although many people would agree with this, some nutritionists and weight loss experts would not. Although the book does not seem to overtly promote a vegetarian diet, the preference seems to be there. Proteins are discussed in terms of the amino acids of which they are made; the authors stress that animal protein contains the proper proportions of amino acids, but that vegetarians can have the same quality of protein by combining legumes with grains. Vegetarians will welcome a fitness guide that does not dismiss their dietary choices.

Part 4 will excite the most interest. Featuring 28 sports nutrient plans, each sport is discussed in terms of energy sources, where the energy comes from, dietary guidelines, recommended nutrients, and recommended supplements that may be unique for the activity. For less common sports, a table guides users to comparable sports. For example skateboarding leads to fitness activities (which also incorporates running, aerobics, boating, cheerleading, and many other activities), and water polo directs to swimming. Supplemental materials at the end of the volume include logs for personal use, reference daily intakes for nutrients, illustrations of the muscles of the body, a glossary of unfamiliar or unknown terms, and a bibliography that points the way to further reference sources.

This book would be useful for consultation. The information appears to be accurate and explanatory enough to cover differing sides of issues. However, the true value of this book would come from reading it cover to cover, making it more useful for public and especially individual libraries.—**Melissa Rae Root**

1515. Grohol, John M. **The Insider's Guide to Mental Health Resources Online.** New York, Guilford, 1997. 326p. index. (The Clinician's Toolbox). $21.95pa. ISBN 1-57230-229-1.

Any library with adequate funds should consider buying two copies of this book, one for reference and one for circulation. Although Grohol has geared his book for the mental health practitioner, it is extremely useful for undergraduate or graduate students, researchers, or librarians in any health-related field. What makes it different from so many other Internet search guides is its extensive coverage of search engines plus an entire chapter on how to put together a successful search strategy. Librarians who teach introductory classes on the Internet will find this information useful and may even want to use some of the author's examples in their own teaching. The author uses a rating system of one to four stars for all the Websites and engines he covers and points out the good and bad features of all the addresses. Even experienced searchers will find tips on how to use search engines effectively and will appreciate the author's candid opinions on which sites are a waste of time.

Part 2, called "Getting Answers to Your Professional Questions," is arranged topically. The Websites, listservs, newsgroups, and electronic journals are not limited to psychology but include databases and resources in medicine; alternative medicine; health administration; and some general sites useful for finding professional meetings, looking at publishers' catalogs, and ordering books. A section on patient education resources offers guidelines on helping patients find and evaluate information about their conditions on the Web.

Both the index of Websites and the general index are excellent. Although there are some subjects in the book mostly of interest to the practitioner, such as doing psychotherapy over the Internet and a section on whether "Internet Addiction Disorder" is a real disease, anyone who wants to find useful sites on the Internet could benefit from this book. The author has an excellent Website that provides periodic updates to the book. *The Insider's Guide* is highly recommended for all academic and medical libraries. Public libraries should also purchase the book because of its useful section on patient information.

—**Natalie Kupferberg**

1516. **Health & Medical Year Book 1997.** New York, Collier Newfield, 1997. 336p. illus. index. $33.90. ISBN 1-57161-119-3.

"Feature Articles" at the beginning of this yearbook are mostly by freelance writers in the style of the popular magazines to which they contribute. Subjects vary, but among the outstanding ones are "Learning to Mourn" and the true story "M.D. to Be." These essays reflect current health-related interests and are eminently readable. "Spotlight on Health" contains short discussions on more specific topics, often with practical tips on how to handle these health problems. Examples are "Heartburn and Beyond" and "How to Give Medicine to Children." Liberal use of sidebars and simple illustrations enliven this section.

The section on health and medical news is arranged alphabetically by broad subject and summarizes 1996-1997 news coverage of developments in health and medical care, such as genetic engineering, government policies and programs, and public health concerns. Newly approved drugs and devices and major sources for help and information are listed. Reviews of noteworthy new books of general health interest and brief notes on contributors complete the volume. The index covers 1997, 1996, and 1995 editions of the yearbook, which extends its usefulness as a reference in health science libraries. Its readability, coverage, and general attractiveness make this book a wonderful place for the health care consumer to browse and learn.—**Harriette M. Cluxton**

1517. **Health Care Software Sourcebook 1997.** Lynn Antosz, ed. Gaithersville, Md., Aspen, 1997. 467p. index. $89.00pa. ISBN 0-8342-0904-7.

The *Health Care Software Sourcebook* is intended for the medical information systems manager. Although the book does not claim to be comprehensive, it provides thorough coverage of medical information systems related software. The editor is careful to include information about software that can be integrated with a World Wide Web user access system as well as older access technologies. Such details are included in the descriptions with each entry.

The structure of the book makes it easy to look up subjects by category. The information in each entry describes the purpose, hardware requirements, and other pertinent details about the software. In addition, there are vendor, application, and product name indexes available. Another nice feature is the vendor directory, which lists vendor contact information. This book is strongly recommended for anyone working with medical information systems.—**Diane Kovacs**

1518. **International Handbook of Public Health.** Klaus Hurrelmann and Ulrich Laaser, eds. Westport, Conn., Greenwood Press, 1996. 474p. index. $99.50. ISBN 0-313-29500-X.

Despite its title, this work is not a handbook in the sense of a "concise, ready-reference book." It is not a reference book, but a monograph containing a section on public health theory, training, and research; country reports on Australia, Brazil, Canada, China, France, Germany, Israel, Italy, Japan, Korea,

Malaysia, Mexico, the Philippines, Poland, Russia, South Africa, Tanzania, Thailand, the United Kingdom, and the United States; and a directory of public health organizations around the world. The preface states that the work is arranged to allow easy comparisons between countries, but this is not necessarily the case. When comparing the outlines of the chapters on France and Mexico, for example, the France chapter had sections the Mexico chapter did not and vice versa. In addition, although the individual chapters have statistical tables describing their own countries, the book does not contain any international tables that would allow comparisons of epidemiologic statistics, such as primary cause of death or infant mortality rates across different countries. In fact, much of the factual information is given in the body of the text instead of in tabulated form. This may be the reason for an error found in the country report of the Philippines, which gives the infant mortality rate for the country as 57.0 percent. This would mean that over half of the babies born there die as infants; the World Factbook online (www.odci.gov/cia/publications/nsolo/factbook/rp.htm#People) states the infant mortality rate for the Philippines in 1996 as 35.9 deaths per 1000 live births, or 3.59 percent. Finally, even though the chapters have different authors, this book has a remarkable tendency to contain words and phrases not common in the English language, or at least not in *Webster's Third New International Dictionary* (New York: Merriam-Webster, 1993) or the 2d edition of the *Oxford English Dictionary* (see ARBA 90, entry 1006). Some examples are "autoaggressive," "inhibitional," "bioecopsychosocial," "sociopedagogue," "intersectorality," "aerodigestive," "hospitalocentrism," "sensiblization," "microcensus," "supermortality," "sick funds," "macrospective," "microspective," and "antipromotion," among others.

The work, however, does have its good points, such as the honesty demonstrated by certain chapter authors when admitting that physicians in Poland do not attach importance to educating their patients about the prevention of diseases that are major causes of deaths, or that the resources for mental health care in Mexico serve only patients who have a serious disease, are in acute crisis, or are chronically ill. However, at $99.50, the price is expensive for a monograph.—**Penny Papangelis**

1519. **Major State Health Care Policies: Fifty State Profiles, 1996.** 5th ed. Washington, D.C., Health Policy Tracking Service, 1997. 278p. $147.00 spiralbound. ISBN 1-55516-579-6.

This is without a doubt the most valuable single reference source for current information on state health policy issues. The 1996 edition categorizes state policy activity under 12 headings: health care commissions (formation of study groups/commissions); insurance (various policy reforms, including guaranteed issue, individual and small group reforms, and high-risk pools); medical savings accounts and tax incentives; coverage for targeted populations (indigent care and child health programs, pharmaceutical assistance plans); Medicaid; cost containment (certificate of need, uniform billing forms); data collection and information dissemination; regulation of physician practice; antitrust; managed care (any willing provider legislation, freedom-of-choice clauses, bans on gag clauses); health workforce supply and distribution (scholarships, loan forgiveness programs, telemedicine); and pharmaceuticals.

The policy-level data are gathered from various primary sources (state legislative documents, such as bills and state reports) and selected secondary sources (chiefly publications of the Intergovernmental Health Policy Project at George Washington University). Health Policy Tracking Service also has correspondents in each state capital who collect and verify all information contained in the 50 state profiles that make up the majority of the text. In addition to these four- to six-page profiles, the book contains an excellent narrative overview of relevant federal and state health policies for 1996; tables and maps showing state-by-state activity on selected "hot button" issues (e.g., a map of states suing the tobacco industry); and a concise glossary of terms.

There are various other compilations of state health policies, but most are looseleaf newsletters that are both more difficult to use and far more expensive. The coverage in this volume is current, accurate, and highly accessible. *Major State Health Care Policies* is certain to be a heavily used reference source in any library that purchases it.—**Bruce Stuart**

1520. **Preventive Care Sourcebook 1997-1998.** Betty Ankrapp, ed. Gaithersville, Md., Aspen, 1997. 280p. index. $89.00pa. ISBN 0-8342-0880-6.

Much of the information in this sourcebook is available in other health-related publications, usually directed to health care consumers. However, this large compilation has been selected and arranged as a desk reference for executives and directors charged with planning and implementing programs for health promotion, patient education, prevention and management of diseases and injuries, and so forth. Improving the health of all people in the United States is a national initiative, through prevention, of the U.S. Department of Health and Human Services. Today's managed care and cost containment depend heavily on effective preventive care. This book provides an extensive overview of existing resources.

Each chapter, such as "Substance Abuse," is preceded by a chart listing for-profit and nonprofit organizations, products and services offered, and the page where contact information and a description appear. "Additional Resources" has only contact information. The "Federal Agencies" chapter is fully annotated. Some organizations appear under many different headings with exactly the same wording. This repetition is especially noticeable for publishers of patient educational materials, such as Channing L. Bete Company, Inc., of "scriptography" fame, with 17 listings. State offices and ethnic resources are separately listed. The sourcebook provides subject and organization indexes.

The book is available on disk, and annual updates are planned. Administrators of various health programs should appreciate this excellent sourcebook.—**Harriette M. Cluxton**

1521. Ronzio, Robert A. **The Encyclopedia of Nutrition & Good Health.** New York, Facts on File, 1997. 486p. index. $45.00. ISBN 0-8160-2665-3.

Health care reform has already occurred, regardless of the actions of health care professionals, the health care industry, and politicians. The information explosion has helped more people to take control of their own health. *The Encyclopedia of Nutrition & Good Health* is a reliable source of information about one's body, health, and nutrition.

This source contains current information on foods and food technology; food labels; vitamins; minerals; and major nutrients, such as fats, carbohydrates, and proteins. The encyclopedia includes a discussion of food-related conditions, including eating disorders, dieting and weight loss, food sensitivities, and aging. Special diets, such as Pritikin, are summarized. The volume contains more than 2,500 entries with cross-references and a comprehensive subject index. The encyclopedia is well organized and alphabetically arranged. It evaluates every available nutritional supplement, from vitamin A to zinc, omega-3 fatty acids to ginseng. Bibliographic references are provided after most entries. The evaluations are objective with a few obvious exceptions, such as the link between caffeine and certain symptoms and the ill effects of crash dieting.

This is an unusually well-balanced guide to the facts about nutrition and good health. *The Encyclopedia of Nutrition & Good Health* will find an important place in the resources of physicians, nutritionists, naturopaths, chiropractors, and laypeople with an interest in taking charge of their own nutrition.

—**Marilynn Green**

1522. Sendor, Virginia F., and Patrice M. O'Connor. **Hospice and Palliative Care: Questions and Answers.** Lanham, Md., Scarecrow Press, 1997. 250p. index. $36.00. ISBN 0-8108-3308-5.

According to the authors of this work, hospice is a "coordinated interdisciplinary program of life-affirming compassionate care and supportive services for terminally ill individuals, their families, and significant others." Interestingly, the patient and family are treated as a whole and are to be cared for together. Hospice, when provided by a Medicare-certified program, is paid for entirely by Medicare. Over 340,000 terminally ill persons and their families were served by hospice programs in 1994. The hospice movement is growing, and if a library does not have a reference book on it, this is a good one to select. This work is poised between the academic and the popular to deem appropriate for almost all kinds of libraries. Chapters are devoted to hospice and AIDS, advance directives (orders not to resuscitate, health care proxies, living wills, and durable power of attorney), and answers to questions that deal with the end of life. In addition to being useful, this book is interesting in its treatment of concepts such as total pain (mental, physical, spiritual, social, legal, or financial), migration home syndrome (adult children returning home to be cared for in their last days), and anticipatory grief (grief that begins before the patient has died).

The authors could not be more qualified. Sendor is the founder of the Long Island Foundation for Hospice Care and Research and the former executive director of Life-Care Hospice, and O'Connor, a nurse, is a palliative care consultant and the former director of the hospice at St. Luke's/Roosevelt Hospital Center in New York City. Highly recommended for public, academic, hospital, and personal libraries.

—**Penny Papangelis**

1523. Zand, Janet, Rachel Walton, and Bob Rountree. **A Parent's Guide to Medical Emergencies: First Aid for Your Child.** Garden City Park, N.Y., Avery Publishing, 1997. 186p. illus. index. $11.95pa. ISBN 0-89529-736-1.

No parent likes to think about the possibility of accidents, but the fact is that with children involved, the next medical emergency is just around the corner. This simple paperback is a testament to the Boy Scout's motto—be prepared. The volume has two purposes. First, it shows parents what steps to take before an accident occurs—phone numbers to have ready, supplies to have on hand, measures to take to prevent accidents, even what type of attitude will best reassure a frightened child. There is vital advice on the often overlooked topic of designating legal surrogates to make medical decisions in the parents' absence. Second, the book contains a quick, easy-to-use guide describing what to do in a number of emergencies. Included is advice on treating specific types of poisoning, animal bites, seizures, and just about all the other types of injuries to which children are prone.

In most cases, the information included in this guide is easy to find, easy to read, and the best possible advice in the situation. One idiosyncrasy of this particular volume is that one of the authors is an herbalist and specialist in Oriental medicine, so many of the standard treatments are followed by advice on herbal and homeopathic regimens, which many readers may find puzzling.

Although this guide will have some use as a reference book, it is not designed to sit on a library shelf. Rather, it should be in an accessible place in the home, with all the emergency numbers on the inside cover filled out, the home safety checklist gone over, and the home emergency medical kit already assembled.
—**Carol L. Noll**

MEDICINE

General Works

Dictionaries and Encyclopedias

1524. Cockerham, William C., and Ferris J. Ritchey. **Dictionary of Medical Sociology.** Westport, Conn., Greenwood Press, 1997. 169p. index. $69.50. ISBN 0-313-29269-8.

Since the inception of the discipline of medical sociology over four decades ago a special terminology has evolved in this field. The authors created this small dictionary to define these terms for the broad range of health practitioners, medical economists, health insurance companies, and hospital administrators as well as sociologists working in this area. A brief introductory essay traces the origins and evolution of medical sociology, discussing some of its pioneers such as Talcott Parsons, and the struggle to combine the applied and theoretical aspects of this emerging discipline.

The definitions that comprise the main part of the text vary from one sentence to several pages in length. Cross-references appear in bold typeface. The main problems with this limited dictionary are the inclusion and exclusion of certain terms, and the lack of accuracy and depth of some of the definitions. Although the authors state their rationales for inclusion and exclusion of terms in the preface, one has to question the inclusion of such standard medical concepts as allied health, ambulatory care, chiropractic medicine, and preventive care. Why include AIDS and not tuberculosis and cancer? More troubling are the inaccuracies in some of the definitions. The incorrect date of and information about the significant 1910 Flexner Report, providing only a partial description of the laws governing homeopathy, and the failure to mention the 1957 legal case that created the legal doctrine of informed consent are examples of this. There is a useful unannotated bibliography on medical sociology and an index is provided.

Overall, there is little in this rather expensive volume that cannot be found in other dictionaries. Although academic libraries might find this work of limited use, there is little reason for a health-related library to acquire this reference text.—**Jonathon Erlen**

1525. **CPT '97: Physicians' Current Procedural Terminology.** Chicago, American Medical Association, 1996. 539p. index. $47.95 spiralbound. ISBN 0-89970-793-9. ISSN 0276-8283.

The *CPT* consists of a list of descriptive terms and identifying codes for reporting medical services and procedures performed by physicians. *CPT '97* is the most recent revision of a work that first appeared in 1966 and that has been revised annually since 1977. The terminology is an attempt to provide a uniform language for reliable and effective communication between physicians, patients, and third-party health care providers. This system is the most widely accepted nomenclature for reporting to government and private health insurance programs and is also used for administrative management purposes. The terminology is prepared by an editorial board, physicians from all specialties of medicine, and contributors from the government and third-party sectors.

The main body of the material is listed in six sections: evaluation and management, anesthesiology, surgery, radiology, pathology and laboratory, and medicine. Within each section are subsections with anatomic, procedural, condition, or descriptor subheadings. Users select the name of the procedure or service that most accurately identifies the service performed. Additional terminology is also listed as *see* references. Health sciences libraries supporting hospitals or medical centers may want to include this reference in the collection, but the scope and use of the resource is limited to the actual practitioners or their administrative staff.—**Vicki J. Killion**

1526. Davis, Neil M. **Medical Abbreviations: 12,000 Conveniences at the Expense of Communications and Safety.** 8th ed. Huntington Valley, Pa., Neil M. Davis, 1997. 332p. index. $15.95pa. ISBN 0-931431-08-5.

This text consists of thousands of useful medical abbreviations and symbols. The author has designed this text in an easy-to-use fashion, and individuals involved in health care will probably find this text to be of help when documenting or translating patient reports or medical reports. Basically, if people find a medical symbol or term that does not make sense, they should try looking in this book.

This text has 6 chapters. Chapter 1 is an introduction that offers the reader options on how to use the text and warns the reader that some of the "terms" may need to be confirmed because they may not be universally acceptable. Chapter 2, "A Healthcare Controlled Vocabulary," explains how medical terms are used, and how confusion and possible errors can arise. Individuals who decide to use this text should read chapters 1 and 2 initially to understand how such errors can occur. Chapter 3, "Lettered Abbreviations and Acronyms," comprises the majority of this text and offers thousands of abbreviations and symbols that can be found in the world of medicine. Readers should remember to confirm the proper use of terms and symbols prior to using them in the event that they are not acceptable in their area of specialty. Chapter 4 introduces hundreds of symbols and numbers that the reader will find useful. Chapter 5 is essentially a pharmacology guide to the trade and generic names of select medications. Chapter 6 provides multiple laboratory values, a nice feature to have in such a text. The last few pages of the text are left blank for the user to make notes.

Overall, this work is a user-friendly and practical text from which most individuals involved in health care could probably benefit. Although this text will not help in resuscitating an acutely ill patient, it will be helpful in documenting and charting the patient's medical records and lab reports.—**Paul M. Murphy III**

1527. **Delmar's English/Spanish Pocket Dictionary for Health Professionals.** By Rochelle K. Kelz. Albany, N.Y., Delmar, 1997. 516p. illus. $17.95pa. ISBN 0-8273-6171-8.

With a large Spanish-speaking population seeking health care, providers who have little knowledge of the language need assistance in communicating. This compact dictionary of medical and dental terms will help. The author, a professor who specializes in medical Spanish, has created a work that contains "tens of thousands of words and phrases" (p. vii). The emphasis of the dictionary is pragmatic, everyday usage to promote communication between health care workers and patients. Entries include common slang and vulgarisms as well as medical and scientific cognates from the Latin and Greek. Because most Spanish speakers in the United States come from Mexico, Puerto Rico, Cuba, Central America, and the Dominican Republic, regional words and phrases from these areas are featured.

The text is arranged in two columns with the entry words in bold typeface. Although the book is small, the typeface is clear and easy to read. The translations are brief, and related words or expressions are included in the same entry; for example, *development; arrested —; delayed —; speech—; — of an x-ray film; — of an idea*. A section between the English-Spanish and Spanish-English parts of the dictionary lists anatomic terms and features black-and-white drawings labeled in both languages.

This dictionary will be useful for health care workers who are studying Spanish. Some knowledge of the language is necessary to use it effectively. Those who need to communicate immediately should use a source such as *CommuniMed Multilingual Patient Assessment Manual* (Mosby Lifeline, 1994), which contains a script for obtaining a basic medical history in 20 languages. *Delmar's English/Spanish Pocket Dictionary for Health Professionals* is a welcome addition to both health sciences collections and personal libraries.—**Barbara M. Bibel**

1528. Haubrich, William S. **Medical Meanings: A Glossary of Word Origins.** Philadelphia, American College of Physicians, 1997. 253p. $29.95. ISBN 0-943126-56-8.

Understanding medical terminology can be a challenge. There are several excellent, comprehensive medical dictionaries available, but they provide only brief information about the origins of the words that they define. Serious students of language will want more depth. *Medical Meanings* is a delightful supplement to the traditional dictionary.

The book has approximately 3,000 entries arranged in 2 columns per page. Arrangement is alphabetic with a few exceptions: Broad categories, such as colors, numbers, and phobias, are grouped together under one heading. The entry headings are in bold typeface, and words within the entry in languages other than modern English are in italics. Greek terms are transliterated. The introduction contains instructions for using the book, a Greek transliteration table, and an invitation to send suggestions for improving the work to the author.

What sets *Medical Meanings* apart from the traditional dictionary is the text. Neither syllabication nor pronunciation appear. The entries are short etymological essays tracing the history of the word and offering witty comments. For example, the entry for AIDS states, "Often when a medical condition is poorly understood, it is described rather than specifically named, and it is called a syndrome when its status as an entity is uncertain" (p. 7). The entry on hysterectomy, literally "cutting the uterus," leads to a discussion of Plato's belief that the uterus was an animal roaming freely within the female body and causing moodiness. The author wisely concludes, "A safe assumption is that this notion was proclaimed and promoted, in the main, by men. From this anatomic designation comes the term hysteria, a term doubtless conceived by a confirmed male chauvinist" (p. 107).

Although this is a small volume—the 28th edition of *Dorland's Illustrated Medical Dictionary* (Saunders, 1994) has 115,000 entries—it makes a unique contribution to medical reference by focusing on history and etymology rather than clinical usage. Students of linguistics will find it as useful as students of the health sciences. Those who want more than a definition will find the book enjoyable and entertaining. The work is an excellent companion to traditional dictionaries, and it belongs in health sciences collections. [R: LJ, 15 May 97, p. 72]—**Barbara M. Bibel**

1529. Kurian, George Thomas. **Encyclopedia of Medical Media & Communications.** Gaithersville, Md., Aspen, 1996. 985p. index. $175.00. ISBN 0-8342-0685-4.

The title of this book is misleading in the fact that it is primarily a guide to the print medical literature. As the author states in the preface, "It serves as a roadmap to the universe of print medical literature." With that limitation in mind, the book is useful. There is a substantial section that includes some online and CD-ROM databases. The title leads one to believe that mention is made of electronic medical journals and other multimedia resources distributed through the World Wide Web. Unfortunately, this book does not include WWW-accessible medical publications.—**Diane Kovacs**

1530. **Medical Discoveries: Medical Breakthroughs and the People Who Developed Them.** Bridget Travers and Fran Locher Freiman, eds. Detroit, U*X*L/Gale, 1997. 3v. illus. index. $79.95/set. ISBN 0-7876-0890-4.

Containing 215 entries, this 3-volume set profiles medical and dental inventions, discoveries, and practices that have advanced the health field. The individuals behind these breakthroughs are identified either within the article or in a separate entry devoted to their contributions. The set is alphabetically arranged over the 3 volumes and is written in nontechnical language. Each volume is prefaced with a timeline of medical events, a glossary of 100 terms used within the set, and a bibliography of resources for further investigation. Likewise, each volume contains a master index at the rear.

Entries vary in length from 200 to 2,500 words. Titles are boldfaced, with subheadings also in bold typeface, which assists the user in outlining the topic. Cross-references within and at the end of each entry are in bold typeface to draw the reader's attention to related information. Wide margins allow space for sidebars of related items of interest. Visual appeal is further enhanced by more than 150 black-and-white photographs. Filled boxes provide information that expands a topic. Controversial issues—such as breast implants and abortion—are noted under applicable topics without taking a position. More recent medical procedures, such as radial keratotomy, gamete intrafallopian transfer, and genetic engineering, are discussed.

Although the set covers its intended content, medical breakthroughs and the people behind them, it is not a health encyclopedia or biographical dictionary. Format and reading level are similar to other U*X*L titles. The set is recommended for school libraries in grades 5 through 10 or the children's area of public libraries.—**Elaine Ezell**

1531. **Taber's Cyclopedic Medical Dictionary.** 18th ed. Clayton L. Thomas, ed. Philadelphia, F. A. Davis, 1997. 2439p. illus. $29.95; $32.95 (thumb indexed). ISBN 0-8036-0194-8; 0-8036-0193-X (thumb indexed). ISSN 1065-1357.

Medical dictionaries are useful both for professional health practitioners and for the general public who want more information on a health condition or an unfamiliar term. This well-established dictionary, intended for nursing and allied health students and practitioners, serves both purposes well. With 55,000 entries, *Taber's* defines more terms than, for instance, *The American Heritage Stedman's Medical Dictionary* (see ARBA 96, entry 1697), and its language seems as clear and easy to understand as it can be without losing accuracy and precision. Because of its small but clear typeface and thin paper, the dictionary is a more manageable size than the more comprehensive but monumental *Dorland's Illustrated Medical Dictionary* (27th ed.; see ARBA 89, entry 1538).

Although 2,100 new entries have been added to keep this edition up-to-date, the most striking and useful new feature is the addition of color to the 560 illustrations, including not only medical drawings but photographs and microphotographs, which frequently work better than drawings to illustrate certain conditions. Particularly important "encyclopedic entries" provide more detailed, comprehensive information, such as symptoms, etiology, treatment, and nursing implications. Pronunciation and cross-references for tables and illustrations are given. Forty-seven appendixes cover an amazing variety of subjects: abbreviations, prefixes and suffixes, units of measurement, universal precautions, nursing diagnoses, information on nursing organizations and theory, and medical emergencies, for example.

Unusual features include a manual alphabet and a guide to interviewing patients in Spanish or French for practitioners who do not know the language. An accompanying "Taber's CyberGuide," a Windows 3.1- and Windows 95-compatible introduction on a floppy disk, is amusing but not especially helpful. Because of its comprehensive nature, convenience, and excellent illustrations, this title is highly recommended for both medical libraries and more general collections.—**Marit S. MacArthur**

Directories

1532. **Continuing Medical Education Directory 1996-1997.** Chicago, American Medical Association, 1996. 254p. $49.95pa. ISBN 0-89970-838-2.

The American Medical Association has published a highly informative guide and directory regarding accredited continuing medical education (CME). The reference is comprehensive, seeming to cover everything about CME that would need to be known by a practicing physician or an organization planning to offer such programs. Every format for continuing education is described in detail, from individual journal reading to conferences to the newer technologies of teleconferencing and computer-assisted learning. Accreditation guidelines and application procedures for each type of CME are included. The specific continuing education requirements of specialty medical organizations and individual states are noted. In addition, the index provides a directory of state medical societies and a directory of currently accredited providers. An emphasis on ethics and possible ethical conflicts related to CME is evident throughout the book. Although some sections of the text will be outdated, potential users of this type of reference are encouraged to obtain this edition. The introduction to the text notes that this is the final hard copy; future versions will be available on the Internet. Because of the depth and detail provided, it would seem to be easier to read this information in book form rather than on the computer. The directory is highly recommended for individual physicians, providers of CME, and medical school libraries.—**Mary Ann Thompson**

1533. **Directory of Physicians in the United States.** 35th ed. Chicago, American Medical Association, 1996. 4v. $545.00/set. ISBN 0-89970-827-7.

1534. **Directory of Physicians in the United States.** 35th ed. [CD-ROM]. Chicago, American Medical Association, 1996. Minimum system requirements: IBM or compatible 386DX/33MHz (486DX/66MHz recommended). Double-speed CD-ROM drive. Windows 3.0. 4MB RAM (8MB recommended). 2MB hard disk space. 256-color monitor. $745.00/single user; $1,145.00/networks. ISBN 0-89970-830-7/single user; 0-89970-831-5/networks.

The 35th edition of this standard medical reference tool is produced by the American Medical Association (AMA) in both a 4-volume book and a CD-ROM format. Both formats present difficult-to-find information on more than 723,000 MDs and DOs who are AMA members, living in the United States, the Virgin Islands, Puerto Rico, some Pacific islands, or temporarily out of the United States as of May 1996. This information has been obtained directly from the practitioners and has been verified by material provided by medical schools, the American Board of Medical Specialists, and state licensing boards. The MDs listed include both members and nonmembers of the AMA.

In the traditional book format, volume 1 alphabetically lists all the names found in the other 3 volumes, giving city locations for each name. Volumes 2 through 4 are arranged geographically, by state and then by city. The biographical information for each individual contains, when available, the following items: home/business address, medical school attended and graduation date, board certification, year of licensure, type of specialty practice, and whether the practitioner has received the Physician's Recognition Award for continuing medical education. There are no listings for the doctors' telephone numbers, residency training, academic appointments, or hospital affiliations. This additional information can be found in *The Official ABMS Directory of Board Certified Medical Specialists* (see ARBA 96, entry 1704). However, that reference work only covers 487,306 practitioners, thus making the current work by far the most comprehensive for basic information about U.S. physicians.

The CD-ROM format, although quite expensive and lacking sufficient instructions for the computer challenged, does provide worthwhile additional search capacities. This format allows patrons to formulate a search strategy combining any or all of the following criteria: name, city, state, region, primary specialty, and type of physician. The search feature is the major reason to purchase this expensive software. By double-clicking on the physician's name, the system presents the same information about this individual as appears in the book format.

All academic, large public, and health-related libraries must have this key reference tool. The cost for the CD-ROM format may require many libraries to purchase only the print version.—**Jonathon Erlen**

1535. **Graduate Medical Education Directory 1997-1998.** Chicago, American Medical Association, 1997. 1244p. $62.95pa. ISBN 0-89970-835-8.

The *Graduate Medical Education Directory 1997-1998* is designed to assist individuals who are planning a career in medicine. More specifically, medical students, residents, interns, and physicians will be able to research thousands of medical education programs by consulting this text. The table of contents lists the sections and the appendixes of the text. Specialty topics are also listed under each section. The section topics include graduate medical education information, essentials of accredited residencies in graduate medical education, institutional and program requirements, accredited graduate medical education programs, new and withdrawn programs, and graduate medical education teaching institutions.

The appendixes include combined specialty programs, medical specialty board certification requirements, medical licensure requirements, national medical societies, medical schools in the United States, graduate medical education data tables, and a graduate medical education glossary. This book contains an abundance of useful information. The layout of the book makes it easy to use and read. If preferred, a CD-ROM version is available.—**Paul M. Murphy III**

1536. Randolph, Lillian. **Physician Characteristics and Distribution in the US.** 1997-98 ed. Chicago, American Medical Association, 1997. 356p. index. $125.95pa. ISBN 0-89970-893-5. ISSN 0731-0315.

Since 1906, the Physician Masterfile has been maintained by the American Medical Association as the most comprehensive source of information about doctors of medicine in the United States. Most of this is submitted by the doctors themselves via questionnaires. Analysis of data from this file plus some census and other material became the basis of *Physician Characteristics and Distribution in the US*, published since 1963. The current edition of this extensive statistical compilation, with tables and summaries, is arranged under the following main sections of physician data: trends, characteristics, detailed descriptions, and a new section focusing on primary specialties in which physicians practice. A few new tables have been added in addition to general updating. No personal identification is given.

Medical schools and societies, specialty boards, government agencies, and other groups involved in planning and policy-making concerned with physician supply and demand or doing research on the many healthcare issues (involving doctors) so important today will find this authoritative resource useful. Everything from the counties in Alaska with no doctors, to the age and gender of pediatricians and where they practice, to the percentage of international medical graduates in internal medicine is here somewhere. The resource claims that there are now 737,764 MDs or 278 per 100,000 population, with more than 81 percent in patient care. It is an excellent reference.—**Harriette M. Cluxton**

Handbooks and Yearbooks

1537. **Code of Medical Ethics: Current Opinions with Annotations.** 1996-1997 ed. By the Council on Ethical and Judicial Affairs. Chicago, American Medical Association, 1996. 191p. index. $34.95pa. ISBN 0-89970-807-2.

Medical ethics is an area of fast-paced and complex change. As the book states, "[T]he AMA Principles of Medical Ethics and the Current Opinions of the Council on Ethical and Judicial Affairs have emerged as an important source of guidance for responsible professional medical behavior." The Code of Medical Ethics is only one component of the American Medical Association's Code of Ethics. The others include the Principles of Medical Ethics, Fundamental Elements of the Patient-Physician Relationship, and the Reports of the Council on Ethical and Judicial Affairs. As such, the code alone has limited use.

The code is divided into 9 major sections, including an introduction and opinions in various subissue areas, for example, social policy issues, interprofessional relations, fees and charges, and so forth. Each section in this text provides a position statement with annotated references to journals, court cases, and other appropriate information sources. These are indexed alphabetically, by case and by article title.

For general use, this book is limited because it must be placed in context with the other components of the Code of Ethics. One must also remember that this work is intended to be a statement of the American Medical Association's position, which is certainly important, but does not make for a general reference of broad-based ethical opinion or works. The work's primary value is for practicing physicians and libraries that serve physicians, medical schools, or teaching hospitals.—**Luiz Alberto Cardoso**

1538. **Consumer Health USA, Volume 2.** Alan M. Rees, ed. Phoenix, Ariz., Oryx Press, 1997. 597p. index. $65.00. ISBN 1-57356-068-5.

One of the best sources of medical information is the federal government. Many of the pamphlets and bulletins put out by the National Institutes of Health, the Food and Drug Administration, and the Centers for Disease Control, among other agencies, are authoritative, up-to-date, and comprehensible to the layperson. The numerous publications of health-related nonprofit associations, such as the American Stroke Foundation and the Leukemia Society of America, form another rich source of materials for patient education. Many of these nonbook sources should be the first place to turn for those with a medical question. However, it can be difficult for most libraries to obtain, store, and classify a comprehensive collection of these documents and have them ready for immediate patron access.

This volume, and the 1994 one by the same publisher entitled *Consumer Health USA: Essential Information from the Federal Health Network* (see ARBA 96, entry 1711), are a convenient answer to that problem. They reprint government documents, arranging them in chapters on various diseases and health concerns (such as AIDS, blood diseases and disorders, and genetic disorders) and add a comprehensive subject index. The 1994 book reprinted 151 government publications. This one repeats only 4 of those, and adds 146 new documents from both government and nonprofit association sources. This newer compilation includes more material on stroke, asthma, and connective tissue disorders than did the previous volume. Among the useful appendixes are one that explains the National Cancer Institute's Physician Data Query (PDQ) computer system and an annotated list of toll-free telephone numbers for obtaining health information, arranged by subject.

One notable oversight is that no guidance for the patron is given on obtaining reliable health information off the Internet—many of these government agencies and nonprofit health organizations have Websites, and a list of the best sites, or at least strategies for searching, may be a useful addition to this volume. Nevertheless, this is an information-packed, usable source for patient medical information.

—Carol L. Noll

1539. Inlander, Charles B., and Michael A. Donio. **Medicare Made Easy.** rev. ed. Allentown, Pa., People's Medical Society; distr., Chicago, Independent Publishers Group, 1997. 339p. index. $18.95pa. ISBN 1-882606-67-1.

The title of this book says it all. The guide helps the consumer to understand, access, and work through the conundrum that is Medicare. The authors take the reader step-by-step through Medicare eligibility, coverage (what it pays for and what it does not), the appeals process, rights of the insured, and supplemental insurance policies. Terms and concepts that may be misunderstood are printed in bold typeface and then defined in a glossary in the appendix. A particularly helpful component is the inclusion of samples of all the Medicare forms with accompanying explanations. An extensive appendix includes directories of individual state Medicare intermediaries, insurance offices, and peer review organizations, as well as durable power of attorney and living will forms and the patient's bill of rights.

The book is written in a simple, easy-to-read style and is printed in a large font, sensitive to the vision needs of the majority of the potential readers. Although written for the consumer, the book would be helpful for health care providers who also struggle with Medicare rules and regulations. This book is an absolute must for public libraries and for any library serving a population over the age of 65.

—**Mary Ann Thompson**

1540. **The Merck Manual of Medical Information.** home ed. Robert Berkow, Mark H. Beers, and Andrew J. Fletcher, eds. West Point, Pa., Merck, 1997. 1509p. illus. index. $29.95. ISBN 0-911910-87-5.

The Merck Manual is a standard medical reference source. With its 1st edition appearing in 1899, it is the oldest continuously published medical text in the English language. Although lay readers use it often, it is difficult for them to understand if they are not familiar with medical terminology. This home edition of *The Merck Manual* has been created for the general public. Compiled by an editorial board and contributors with medical school faculty appointments, this new version of the manual contains almost all of the information that is in the professional edition. Such items as descriptions of abnormal heart sounds and the appearance of diseased tissue under the microscope have been omitted, and overviews of anatomy and physiology, charts, and illustrations have been added. The format is larger, with text in two columns, an easy-to-read typeface, and color drawings and sidebars. Instructions for readers and a chart of basic medical prefixes and suffixes provide orientation. Cross-references are marked by symbols.

The book is organized into 24 sections covering broad subject areas, for example, drugs, lung and airway disorders, children's health issues, and so on. Section 1, "Fundamentals," explains basic anatomy and physiology, genetics, aging, and death. The section on drugs emphasizes pharmacology and principles of drug treatment rather than information on specific drugs. Each of the other sections begins with an overview of the organ system and progresses to discussions of various abnormalities and diseases and their diagnosis and treatments. A section on first aid is also provided. Five appendixes cover legal issues, weights and measures, common tests, trade names of generic drugs, and resources for further information. The resources include organizations and government agencies. E-mail and World Wide Web addresses are given.

The home edition of *The Merck Manual* bridges the gap between lay sources and medical textbooks. It provides greater depth than such basic sources as *The Mayo Clinic Family Health Book* (2d ed., William Morrow, 1996), in a format that lay readers can understand. It is an outstanding addition to medical and consumer health collections in all libraries. [R: LJ, 15 June 97, p. 62]—**Barbara M. Bibel**

1541. Morton, Leslie T., and Robert J. Moore. **A Chronology of Medicine and Related Sciences.** Brookfield, Vt., Ashgate Publishing, 1997. 784p. index. $127.95. ISBN 1-85928-215-6.

Many history of medicine-related questions require only a single piece of information; in other words a date, a name, or the location of an event. This new reference tool is probably the best place to begin looking for answers to this type of question. Whereas other medical history reference works provide chronologies, biographies, or bibliographies, no other single volume better combines these aspects of the history of medicine than Morton and Moore's volume.

This reference guide is arranged chronologically, from 3,000 B.C.E. and the Edwin Smith Papyrus through 1996 and the death of Tadeus Reichstein of vitamin C and cortisone fame. Beginning in 1529, there is at least one citation per year through 1996. The following type of entries are provided for each year, when material is available: events (major discoveries; founding of journals, institutions, and societies; Nobel prize-winners); births of significant figures in medical history and a brief mention of their contribution(s); and death dates. These entries range from one to several sentences in length. For items in the first two categories, the authors include citations to journal literature providing further information, as well as citation numbers to the relevant entries in *Morton's Medical Bibliography*, 5th edition (see ARBA 93, entry 1627).

There are a couple of minor weaknesses in this volume. Although the authors wisely state that their timeline is not all-inclusive, there is no explanation for the selection criteria used. Also, there is no clear definition of what the authors mean by medically related sciences: are they including anatomy or biochemistry? Some major aspects of the social history of medicine also lack coverage; for example, Margaret Sanger's work for birth control and the 1957 *Salgo* legal case that established the doctrine of informed consent. Despite these oversights, public, academic, and health-related libraries will find this volume an indispensable reference work.—**Jonathon Erlen**

1542. **Peterson's U.S. & Canadian Medical Schools 1997: 400 Accredited M.D. and Combined Medical Degree Programs.** Princeton, N.J., Peterson's Guides, 1997. 209p. index. $24.95pa. ISBN 1-56079-631-6. ISSN 1089-3342.

Peterson's U.S. & Canadian Medical Schools is a thorough and helpful guide for prospective medical college applicants. Its modest price makes it an affordable addition to most public and academic library collections. However, libraries that have the Association of American Medical Colleges's *Medical School Admission Requirements* (47th ed., 1996) will find that the Peterson's guide is redundant.

The guide under review includes the usual background information in chapters on professional trends, selecting and applying to medical colleges, testing, accreditation, and financing of costly medical educations. One-page profiles of medical colleges in the United States and Canada make up the majority of the publication. Profiles supply information on the institutional setting, student services, campus facilities, medical college personnel and programs, teaching methods, enrollment, expenses and financial aids, and contact information. Listings of information on number of applicants to size of entering class is inconsistent between profiles. Some listings provide percentage of students receiving their top choice for residency.

The information provided in this publication is valuable to prospective medical students. The guide is recommended for libraries without the Association of American Medical Colleges's guide or where demand requires both guides.—**Lynne M. Fox**

1543. **The World Book Health & Medical Annual 1997.** Chicago, World Book, 1997. 352p. illus. index. $29.40. ISBN 0-7166-1197-X.

Because medical information changes rapidly, World Book publishes *The World Book Health & Medical Annual* to update the encyclopedia each year. By providing cross-reference tabs to place in the encyclopedia, users can go from the larger set to the *Health & Medical Annual* for the latest supplemental information.

The 1997 volume has 5 sections. The 1st is a feature called "Spotlight on Stress," containing several articles on all aspects of the topic. The "Healthy Family" section covers such topics as foot care, gum disease, retirement planning, and evaluating health risks. "Medical and Safety Alerts" includes articles on food allergies, glaucoma, and health hazards at the office. "On the Medical Frontier" discusses the latest advances in research on AIDS, laser surgery, artificial joints, and weight control. The weight control article still mentions fen/phen, which has recently been withdrawn by the Food and Drug Administration.

"Health Updates" has alphabetically arranged, brief articles on topics ranging from AIDS to veterinary medicine, including a list of lay health books published in 1995 and 1996. There is also a directory of health resources listing agencies and toll-free numbers.

This volume is an inexpensive, illustrated source that is easy to read. Libraries that own *The World Book Encyclopedia* will want it as a supplement to the set. School libraries and consumer health collections will also find it useful.—**Barbara M. Bibel**

Alternative Medicine

1544. **The Alternative Advisor: The Complete Guide to Natural Therapies & Alternative Treatments.** Alexandria, Va., Time-Life Books, 1997. 400p. $24.95. ISBN 0-7835-4907-5.

Time-Life Books has compiled an easy-to-understand, 400-page volume that should be included in the library of those wanting information concerning the differences between pharmaceutical drugs and natural therapies. The book is divided into two main topics: therapies and conditions. Forty alternative therapies are mentioned, including acupuncture, Ayurvedic medicine, nutrition, massage, hydrotherapy, and yoga. Illustrations are specific and uncluttered. Sidebars include such information as whether or not the therapy is covered by insurance, Medicare, or Medicaid. Also covered are origin of the remedy, what the therapy is good for, where to get it, application techniques, and what critics have to say about it. There are 75 herbs mentioned with their target ailments, preparation methods, and potential side effects listed, which will help relieve any anxiety that comes with exploring the unknown. Thirty of the more common homeopathic remedies, plus descriptions of thirty-two vitamins and minerals, help the neophyte become educated.

The 2d half of *The Alternative Advisor* describes ailments and their symptoms, including when to call a professional health provider. This section discussing conditions has easy-to-read heads at the top edge of each page, making it easy to find the topic of interest. Time-Life Books has published a book that coaches the rookie in entry-level health management, thus making it easier to talk with a doctor about possible health care alternatives. [R: LJ, Aug 97, p. 74]—**Mary Pat Boian**

1545. **The Complete Family Guide to Natural Home Remedies.** Karen Sullivan, ed. Rockport, Mass., Element Books, 1997. 256p. illus. index. $24.95pa. ISBN 1-86204-020-6.

This book is an excellent source of information on five forms of alternative therapy: herbalism, homeopathy, flower remedies, aromatherapy, and diet and nutrition. The book is divided into four parts. "Home Therapies" discusses the five therapies and their application. It explains how the therapies work, their history, and how to prepare various remedies. "The Ailments" lists common problems and injuries grouped under 13 systems of the body (immune, circulatory, respiratory, etc.), plus one group for childhood problems and one group for childhood illnesses. "The Remedy Sources" provides detailed descriptions of 225 well-known and not so well-known substances. "Practical Matters and Useful Information" includes a section on first aid, putting together a home medicine chest, information on vitamins and minerals, a one-page bibliography of related books, a listing of organizations, a glossary, and a subject index.

Parts 2 and 3 make up the bulk of the book. Each ailment listed in part 2 includes a brief description and symptoms, plus a list of possible remedies from one or more of the five therapies; self-care tips are also included. Although some of the body system groups have few entries, the range of illnesses covered is comprehensive. The descriptions are terse, and the list of remedies is often specific. Many of the remedies include cautions such as which substances are to be avoided during pregnancy or with certain medical conditions and symptoms requiring medical attention.

Part 3 is divided into sections on plant and animal remedy sources, elements, compounds and minerals, and food and drink. Each substance includes a few paragraphs on its various uses (homeopathic, herbal, etc.) as well as a "data file" on the properties (herbs and foods), symptom pictures (homeopathic remedies), and extraction method (flower essences), information on dosages, and contradictions when applicable. Like the ailments section, appropriate cautions are included.

The publisher is British and the book does have a British and European slant, which may be confusing to some American readers; for example, suggesting an oil is to be applied "neat." Also, some of the substances are not commonly seen in the United States, such as neroli (bitter orange fruit). Chinese herbs are only mentioned in passing, when there is some overlap with the Western herbs; readers searching for information on Chinese herbs and remedies will have to look elsewhere.

The book can be used as a whole—as an overall guide to incorporating traditional remedies into a healthy lifestyle—or as a reference to individual ailments. The remedies are usually cautious, sensible, and simple enough for most people to adopt. The book is beautifully designed; each page is amply illustrated with color photographs, drawings, and shaded boxed text. Anyone looking for detailed and clear information on traditional Western remedies can find it here.—**Stephen Haenel**

1546. Duke, James A. **The Green Pharmacy: New Discoveries in Herbal Remedies for Common Diseases and Conditions from the World's Foremost Authority on Healing Herbs.** Emmaus, Pa., Rodale Press, 1997. 507p. illus. index. $29.95. ISBN 0-87596-316-1.

The Green Pharmacy is a compendium of herbal treatments for more than 120 common medical conditions. Duke, a world-renowned botanist, has written a book that is highly readable, thorough, and up to date. His approach is a mixture of folklore from around the world combined with clinical research and a large dose of personal anecdotes.

The first part of the book is a guide to using medicinal herbs and includes safety considerations and tips on buying, preparing, and using herbal medicines. The second part is an A to Z listing of diseases and conditions, with descriptions of the conditions and a listing of helpful herbs and foods. The range of maladies covered includes allergies, HIV, insect bites and stings, male and female sexual and genitourinary problems, heart disease, viral infections, Parkinson's disease, asthma, and skin conditions. The list is surprisingly complete, with the exception of children's illnesses, which receive scant attention. The text is sprinkled with recipes and stories of herb lore as well as fine line drawings of many herbs. No bibliography or suggested reading list is included, which would make this an even more useful reference work.

All in all, Duke presents a balanced view of both the advantages and disadvantages of herbs and foods as medicines. He quotes a wide variety of experts—herbalists, naturopaths, physicians, researchers, and the German body Commission E—and provides a full account of the advantages and disadvantages of herbs, especially compared to pharmaceuticals. To his credit, Duke is a bit more guarded than some writers on natural products, often hedging his advice with "herbs that might prove helpful" or "if I had . . . I might try . . . ." Conversely, some of his descriptions of ailments and prescriptions lack the depth of some authorities on natural healing. He often gives details on the chemical constituents of herbs, but this work is not overly technical. His writing is lively and approachable. Using this book is like sitting down with a country herbalist, which lends it a certain charm.—**Stephen Haenel**

1547. Feuerman, Francine, and Marsha J. Handel. **Alternative Medicine Resource Guide.** Chicago, Medical Library Association and Lanham, Md., Scarecrow, 1997. 335p. index. $49.50. ISBN 0-8108-3284-4.

Readers interested in self-regulated health will be pleased with *Alternative Medicine Resources Guide*'s extensive coverage of alternative healing methods. The two librarians responsible for this collection of over 30 noninvasive therapies point out that access to health maintenance information is their objective, and with this goal in mind, they have provided definitions and sources ample enough for novices and explicit enough for professionals.

The book is divided into two sections: resources and bibliography. Resources are extracted from U.S. publications, organizations, universities, treatment resorts, and product suppliers. Systems of alternative medicine mentioned here range from 5,000-year-old methods of healing, such as Ayurveda and herbal therapy, to twentieth-century techniques, such as biofeedback and music therapy. The bibliography section, which is one-third of the book, organizes books, journals, and newsletters including manipulative, sensory, and movement therapies. These entries are based on authors' credentials, understandable ideologies, and universality.

The gratifying element of this work is its success in clearing the misconceptions about the numerous ways to maintain good health. There is no preaching, no judgment, no disdain for conventional medicine. This is a primary guide that will benefit and appease those curious and adventurous enough to take on the responsibility of their own health. As the title says, it is alternative medicine.—**Mary Pat Boian**

1548. Lieberman, Shari, and Nancy Bruning. **The Real Vitamin & Mineral Book.** Garden City Park, N.Y., Avery Publishing, 1997. 342p. index. $12.95pa. ISBN 0-89529-769-8.

This book is an excellent source of information on vitamins and minerals that are necessary for the human body to function properly, and how highly processed food does not supply these nutrients when eating the recommended servings of the basic food groups. The book is divided into 4 parts for easy use. The 1st part is an introduction to these nutrients and explains the basics behind the recommended daily intakes (RDIs) and the optimum daily intakes (ODIs). Part 2, chapters 6-20, gives the details on the fat-soluble vitamins and water-soluble vitamins. Each chapter covers a description of the vitamin, its functions and uses, its relationship to cancer, the organs or parts of the body it affects, symptoms if the body is deficient, how supplements affect the body, ODIs, and the toxicity and adverse affects. Part 3, chapters 21-32, covers the minerals that are necessary building blocks and gives the same information as for vitamins. Part 4, chapters 33-40, discusses other necessary nutrients that are not covered by the previous chapters, with the same information furnished. The last 99 pages consist of in-depth references for the preceding chapters and an extensive index.

This book is well written and easy to understand. It would be useful in any public, academic, or medical library that deals with nutrition. The work is highly recommended for its content and its cost.
—**Betsy J. Kraus**

1549. Lyons, Dianne J. B. **Planning Your Career in Alternative Medicine: A Guide to Degree and Certificate Programs in Alternative Health Care.** Garden City Park, N.Y., Avery Publishing, 1997. 423p. index. $19.95pa. ISBN 0-89529-802-3.

As an introductory guide and selective directory to higher education opportunities in the varied fields of alternative medicine, this work provides the reader with some good basic descriptions of concepts, programs, curricula, sources, and resources. Fields of interest include aromatherapy, Ayurveda, biofeedback, chiropractic, energy healing, environmental medicine, guided imagery, herbal medicine, holistic health care fields, homeopathy, hypnotherapy, integrative medicine, iridology, massage therapy and bodywork, natrapathy, naturopathy, nutrition, polarity therapy, reflexology, traditional Chinese medicine, Vedic psychology, veterinary massage, and yoga. Basic descriptions and overviews are provided for each of these areas, followed by a listing of schools and programs. It is this latter listing that comprises most of the volume. Appendixes include listings and descriptions of accrediting agencies and councils, licensing and certification requirements, professional associations and membership organizations, self-study resources, and conventional medical schools offering courses in alternative medicine.

In an introductory section, the author explains the criteria for inclusion of various schools, but not for all. In some cases, accreditation is a criterion; in others, return of a survey questionnaire. In still other cases, no indication of criteria is given at all. This results in a work of somewhat uneven quality, leaving the reader seeking sound information on shaky ground. A listing of "Top Schools and Programs," based upon a mail questionnaire sent to practitioners, provides no indication of the population sampled or the number of questionnaires returned. Listings of associations are also limited, and can be supplemented by the most current edition of the *Encyclopedia of Associations* (Gale, 1997).

Some public and school libraries might find this volume useful. However, it should be complemented by a variety of other reference tools—dictionaries, encyclopedias, directories—that can provide more substantial information for those contemplating a career in alternative medicine. Although this volume provides some good basic information, it seems too arbitrary and selective in its approach to be able to provide a true picture of the variety of career options.—**Edmund F. SantaVicca**

1550. Null, Gary. **The Woman's Encyclopedia of Natural Healing: The New Healing Techniques of 100 Leading Alternative Practitioners.** New York, Seven Stories Press; distr., Emeryville, Calif., Publishers Group West, 1996. 411p. index. $19.95pa. ISBN 1-888363-35-5.

This paperback volume focuses on how natural (a.k.a., alternative, unconventional, complementary) healing techniques may impact the overall outcome of various ailments that women most often experience. Topics are appropriate for all females regardless of age, race, or cultural heritage; and thus, this work provides a handy reference for all stages of life. Examples include aging, birth control, breast cancer, eating disorders, menopause, osteoporosis, PMS, and varicose veins. In all, 28 topics are explained through causes, symptoms, clinical experience, and therapeutic approaches (e.g., nutrition, exercise, massage, mind/body, and numerous homeopathic supplements).

Most of the information was obtained through interviews with approximately 100 natural healing practitioners. Some chapters include personal testimonies. All chapters include a short bibliography that lists some references in the medical literature. The author is a medical doctor specially trained in gynecologic surgery. This training, when combined with extensive experience in natural healing, provides the expertise necessary to adequately translate complex medical and scientific data into an easy-to-understand format. Any person, whether lay or health care professional, could benefit from the explanations contained within these pages. [R: LJ, Jan 97, p. 90]—**Sue Lyon Mertl**

1551. Schiller, Carol, and David Schiller. **Aromatherapy Oils: A Complete Guide.** New York, Sterling Publishing, 1996. 160p. illus. index. $14.95pa. ISBN 0-8069-6112-0.

An inexpensive alphabetized guide to types and uses of fragrant and stimulating oils, this compendium offers students, librarians, health workers, merchants, and consumers an overview of the role of aromatic oils in health treatments, relaxation, and stress relief. Containing simple explanations and indistinct line drawings of plants from which oils are extracted, the work opens with a thumbnail history of aromatherapy since the time of the Egyptian pharaohs. A three-page chapter on safe selection and handling of oils warns of the danger to eyes and sensitive skin as well as to pregnant and lactating women. Comments on the dangers of mixing aromatherapy with alcohol are also included. A one-sentence warning about the interference of oils with medication leaves much to the imagination. Remaining chapters discuss vegetable oils and butters, essential and infused oils, methods of use, blending oils, and categories of oil properties. The authors conclude with a cross-reference of botanical names, a list of plant families, a glossary, a bibliography, and an index.

The book presents information on individual oils in brief commentaries. Each entry contains botanical and common names, the family name, and the method of extraction. A history of each oil covers its use from numerous ancient cultures. Practical uses are brief to the point of uselessness, as in the comment that oil of fir balsam needles "lessens pain." Documented properties are also listed in terse, one-word commentary. For example, marjoram heads a laundry list of uses: analgesic, aphrodisiac, antibacterial, antifungal, antioxidant, antiseptic, antispasmodic, antistress, antitussive, and antiviral, to name a few. The authors are preoccupied with long lists, which give little useful information to readers. The index lacks significant ties to common ailments such as arthritic joints, sleeplessness, and headaches. Overall, the work provides little more than an alphabetic listing of oils and vague applications to human needs.
—**Mary Ellen Snodgrass**

1552. Woodham, Anne, and David Peters. **Encyclopedia of Healing Therapies.** New York, DK Publishing, 1997. 336p. illus. index. $39.95. ISBN 0-7894-1984-X.

With this publication the authors hope to provide an analysis of the benefits claimed by various healing or complementary therapies (not necessarily alternative therapies to conventional treatments) and to provide readers with a means of identifying therapies that may improve their health.

The book begins with a questionnaire designed to allow readers to assess their general well-being. A second questionnaire is aimed at enabling readers to identify categories of complementary therapies to which they are most suited. These categories—touch and movement, medicinal therapies (including diet or other remedies), and mind and emotion therapies—correspond to headings within the section "Key Healing Therapies." The entry for each therapy includes a definition, brief history, and key principles. But given the many and often gratuitous illustrations, there is only the most basic information conveyed within the several pages devoted to each therapy. Although each complementary therapy is assigned a rating of its effectiveness, the text is clearly biased in its favor. Scant references are made to the primary literature, and no complete bibliographic citations are provided. The section entitled "Treating Ailments" lists over 200 health problems. Entries for each include a brief discussion of conventional treatment along with descriptions of available complimentary treatments. Specific applications of these complimentary treatments for the various ailments are indicated, again without supporting references.

Although this book adequately defines the major complementary therapies currently practiced and provides information for individuals predisposed to their use (including guidance on choosing a practitioner), it does not present information in a substantive or objectively critical manner.—**Michael Weinberg**

Ophthalmology

1553. **Dictionary of Eye Terminology.** 3d ed. By Barbara Cassin and Sheila A. B. Solomon. Melvin L. Rubin, ed. Gainesville, Fla., Triad, 1997. 283p. $24.95 spiralbound. ISBN 0-937404-44-6.

This is the 3d edition of a dictionary of ophthalmic terminology geared toward laypeople, students of optometry and ophthalmology, and medical support staff working in eye-related fields. The 1st edition (see ARBA 85, entry 1592) was published in 1984 and the 2d edition in 1990 (see ARBA 92, entry 1672). Written in plain English, each entry is identified by a category (drug, surgical procedure, symptom, function, and the like) and contains a pronunciation key if needed, synonyms, and a concise definition. Comparison to the 2d edition finds them nearly identical in page length, but because of a slightly larger page size, the more current edition contains approximately 1,000 more entries. Terms new to the 3d edition cover new laser procedures, drugs, surgical techniques, medications, and general medical conditions that affect the eye.

This dictionary occupies a unique niche, because *Stedman's Ophthalmology Words* (Williams & Wilkins, 1992) serves as a source to validate the spelling and accuracy of eye terms (no definitions), and *Dictionary of Visual Science* (4th ed.; see ARBA 90, entry 1691) is intended primarily for professionals. The dictionary under review is a definite acquisition for medical libraries and institutions supporting eye-related health programs.—**Elaine F. Jurries**

Pediatrics

1554. **Columbia University Department of Pediatrics Children's Medical Guide.** By Steve Z. Miller and Bernard Valman. New York, DK Publishing, 1997. 216p. illus. index. $29.95. ISBN 0-7894-1443-0.

It is the sad truth that the growth of managed care, health maintenance organizations, and insurance plans that can force families to switch doctors almost annually has meant that parents must be more knowledgeable than ever about their children's health problems. This quick-reference guide can help parents with that ever-important question, "Should I call the doctor, or can I treat this problem myself?" Along the way, the book also educates readers on normal growth patterns, self-help strategies for numerous conditions, and the meaning of the diagnosis and treatment options they may receive when they do visit a medical clinic.

The book is divided into 4 sections. The 1st describes normal childhood anatomy and development and gives advice on nutrition, home safety, and advice on living with an infant. Here, as elsewhere in the book, much of the information is displayed in easy-to-use charts and illustrations, which emphasize the wide range of growth patterns and behavior that can be considered normal. The 2d section, which comprises the majority of the book, is made up of 41 symptom charts, which are flow charts to help parents assess a child's condition and make an initial diagnosis. As in other guides of this type, such as the *AMA Family Medical Guide* (see ARBA 83, entry 1462), the goal is not to replace the doctor but to help parents decide whether a trip to the doctor is necessary, and if so, how urgent. The flow charts take initial symptoms, such as "painful joints," and by posing a series of questions lead the reader to a possible diagnosis. Most charts also include self-help advice on relieving the problem. A 3d section discusses the diseases and disorders to which children are prone. It is essentially a brief medical encyclopedia, arranged by body systems, such as skeletal, digestive, and so forth, profusely illustrated and written in an easy-to-understand, question-and-answer format. Finally, there is a first aid guide section, which includes illustrated how-tos on choking, rescue-breathing, and cardiopulmonary resuscitation. All place the emphasis on treatment of children, which may be different from similar techniques for adults.

This is an outstanding resource, produced by two doctors from one of the finest pediatric departments in the country. It is authoritative, comprehensive, and easy to use.—**Carol L. Noll**

1555. **The Yale Guide to Children's Nutrition.** William V. Tamborlane and others, eds. New Haven, Conn., Yale University Press, 1997. 415p. illus. index. $18.00pa. ISBN 0-300-07159-8.

In searching the national online catalog, one finds more than 8,000 books published on the subject of nutrition for children and infants. At least 80 books are published with a similar title, including such words as "children's nutrition." However, the guide under review is broad based and has arrived in a timely fashion to enlighten modern parents who have concerns for their children's diet and to provide dietary recommendations.

The Yale Guide is a compilation from more than 50 contributors—physicians, dietitians, nurses, and social workers—writing on a wide spectrum of nutrition-related topics, such as physiology, psychology, health and diseases, social problems, concerns and myths, dietary intake and recommendations, grocery shopping and eating out, and sensible recipes provided by chefs throughout the United States. The editors attempt to be comprehensive in order to address many popular questions adults and children may have about childhood nutrition (e.g., acne and diet). Even though this book is devoted to the nutritional needs of normal children, there are tips on how to deal with special feeding problems, such as cleft palate.

This resource is presented in six parts, from infancy to adolescence: "Developmental Nutrition"; "Common Concerns"; "Beyond the Basics: Special Challenges in Nutrition"; "Building Blocks for Good Nutrition"; "Eating In, Eating Out"; and "Recipes." Appendixes include growth charts, recommended dietary allowances, and a recipe conversion table. The editors' mission in publishing this book was to bring to parents awareness of the importance of good nutrition for the future health of their children. *The Yale Guide* is recommended as a general reference guide for parents who wish to promote healthy eating habits for their children. Also, this is a good reference book for public or health sciences libraries. [R: LJ, 15 Feb 97, p. 129]—**Polin P. Lei**

Psychiatry

1556. Campbell, Robert Jean. **Psychiatric Dictionary.** 7th ed. New York, Oxford University Press, 1996. 799p. $59.95. ISBN 0-19-510259-2.

In preparing the present volume, Campbell has made use of the 4th edition of the American Psychiatric Association's *Diagnostic and Statistical Manual of Mental Disorders* (DSM-IV) (1994), the 10th revision of the *International Statistical Classification of Diseases and Related Health Problems* (ICD-10) (World Health Organization, 1994), and the World Health Organization's lexicons on mental disorders. Some of the 12,311 entries are fascinating; for instance, *insanity* is now obsolete as a medical term (it is still used in its legal sense). Also, a distinction exists between the word *fantasy* (spelled with an "f" and referring to conscious constructions) and the word *phantasy* (spelled with a "ph" and referring to unconscious constructions). Some of the entries go beyond prose definitions to include tables, such as the "Table of Manias and Philias" that is part of the "mania" entry.

It is refreshing to see the author, a Cornell medical school professor as well as director of a New York City hospital, demonstrate open-mindedness toward the supernatural. The word *shaman* is defined as "[a] practitioner whose ability to heal comes from trancelike experiences and inspiration from a supernatural spirit-partner with whom he works in curing sick people" (p. 666). One thing the reader will not find in this work is entries for individual drugs, neither under their brand names (e.g., Prozac) nor under their generic names (e.g., fluoxetine). This is not a failing, because drugs do not really have definitions per se, and anyhow, there would be too many to include even if they did. Campbell does refer to fluoxetine, however (among other drugs listed in the "antidepressant" entry).

One of the stated aims of this work is to provide a dictionary that is comprehensible to the nonspecialist, and Campbell achieves that aim. For this reason, this work is recommended for libraries supporting degree programs in psychology, counseling, and social work. As for selection by medical school libraries, the dictionary is a must; however, it does not replace the DSM-IV or the ICD-10.

—**Penny Papangelis**

Specific Diseases and Conditions

General Works

1557. **Diseases.** Bryan Bunch, ed. Danbury, Conn., Grolier, 1997. 8v. illus. index. $269.00/set. ISBN 0-7172-7617-1.

This excellent encyclopedia is aimed at teens; thus the emphasis is on ailments that particularly affect young people. There is, however, extensive coverage of a wide variety of diseases, both physical and mental; injuries; and body systems. Alphabetically arranged, the 400 main entries include such newly discovered diseases such as the Ebola virus and "mad cow" disease, as well as diseases of historical significance, such as Guam disease and the plague. Sources of infection, symptoms, prognosis, and treatment are fully covered. Each volume contains a full index for the set. Icons provide shortcut information about first aid, prevention, and treatment. Full-color drawings illustrate each volume, although not every entry is illustrated. The set contains extensive cross-referencing.

Diseases is highly recommended for school libraries and for the young adult section of public libraries. The reinforced library binding should hold up well under student use. Although the information may be a little too elementary for adult readers, this set provides a basic introduction to any medical condition.—**Susan B. Hagloch**

1558. Long, James W. **The Essential Guide to Chronic Illness: The Active Patient's Handbook.** New York, HarperPerennial/HarperCollins, 1997. 625p. index. $20.00pa. ISBN 0-06-273137-8.

Studies have shown that patients who understand their illness and take an active part in their treatment do better than those who passively wait for their doctor to tell them what to do. They feel more in control, helping to make crucial care decisions. This book purports to inform patients about 47 common conditions, from acne to Zollinger-Ellis syndrome. The ailments covered were chosen, the author says, based on the relative frequency of occurrence, severity of impact on the patient and the family, and the degree of difficulty of diagnosis and management.

Even using these criteria, the selection seems somewhat arbitrary. AIDS, for example, is covered, although its frequency is considerably less than that of polycystic kidney disease, which is not. Each entry details the principal features of the disease, diagnostic methods and available therapies, and further resources. Additional sections address preventive medicine, terminal illness, special considerations for the elderly patient, and drug-induced disorders. Coverage of the included diseases is thorough, but the restrictions on this coverage make this book of marginal use to public library reference collections. A better choice for reference is *The Mayo Clinic Family Health Book* (2d ed., William Morrow, 1996), but libraries needing more circulating material on diseases should consider the title under review, as it does provide good value for the price.—**Susan B. Hagloch**

AIDS

1559. **AIDS.** 1996 ed. Suzanne B. Squyres, Mark A. Siegel, and Nancy R. Jacobs, eds. Wylie, Tex., Information Plus, 1996. 124p. index. $12.95pa. ISBN 1-57302-025-7.

Information Plus is a for-profit group of former teachers who got together in 1990 to publish current information for middle and high school students doing library research. Students will learn that information if they call the toll-free telephone number on the back cover of *AIDS*. The book itself omits a statement of purpose, the background or credentials of the various in-house writers, a glossary, and a title page. Students writing a term paper or giving an oration on AIDS who find this book in the school library may overlook these points, however, and think only that they have found a gold mine. The 1996 edition of *AIDS* is filled with charts, graphs, quotations, and information in 11 well-organized chapters. Students will write and speak with authority after only a few sessions with *AIDS*. Although the book is scheduled for revision in 1998, one problem may pervade the way Information Plus creates their books. The chapters appear to be written by different people with little coordination between them. Information is both repetitive and inconsistent. With a sparse and incomplete index—one page—students would have a hard time relocating any inconsistencies they discover in their notes. For example, there is no index entry for "women," so it would be difficult to cross-check and question a statement on page 30 ("The actual number of AIDS cases in women is declining . . .") with one on page 101 ("Women now account for roughly 40% . . . of all HIV infections . . ."). Completeness is another issue. The role of the protease inhibitors is slighted in a number of places: how these drugs have increased the cost of care and decreased settlements and how some persons with AIDS cannot tolerate the inhibitors. Reverse transcriptase inhibitors and viral load need to be defined and explained, the role of monkeys and the origin of AIDS clearly resolved, and the opportunistic infections described more fully. Students may find that a trip to their local AIDS service organization will provide current information and firsthand experience to supplement the Information Plus book.—**Pete Prunkl**

1560. Walter, Virginia A., and Melissa Gross. **HIV/AIDS Information for Children: A Guide to Issues and Resources.** Bronx, N.Y., H. W. Wilson, 1996. 261p. index. $35.00. ISBN 0-8242-0902-8.

A remarkable handbook and resource guide aimed at improving information services for children and adolescents, this book is arranged in 5 major sections. The initial 4 provide discussions, overviews, and profiles of issues surrounding children and AIDS. Among the many topics covered are children with AIDS, family issues, concepts of information needs, information-seeking behaviors, information gaps, availability of materials, what libraries can do, readers' advisory and reference services, booktalks, curriculum development, bibliographies, and so on. Each of these 4 sections provides a list of references.

It is the 5th section of this work that provides the reader with an impressive annotated bibliography of resources—both fiction and nonfiction—appropriate for children. Separate sections are provided for annotation of resources pertinent to adoption and foster care, compassion, death and dying, emotions, ethics and values, family, friendship, health and nutrition, homelessness and poverty, homosexuality, illness and disease, medical care, safety and survival, self-esteem, sex education, sexual abuse, social action, and substance abuse. Resources for adults are also included, as well as an appendix that provides evaluation criteria and a checklist for the selection of relevant titles. Four indexes—by grade level, recommendation level, author, and title—conclude the work.

This work should be in every school and public library, as well as in any environment where people address or counsel on issues of AIDS and children. The book is an impressive addition to the literature of AIDS and of children.—**Edmund F. SantaVicca**

Childbirth

1561. **Pregnancy and Birth Sourcebook.** Heather E. Aldred, ed. Detroit, Omnigraphics, 1997. 737p. index. (Health Reference Series, vol.31). $75.00. ISBN 0-7808-0216-0.

This reference book is one of the many sourcebooks from Omnigraphics that health sciences libraries are acquiring for their reference collections. The format is similar to the rest of the Health Reference Series. Some expectant mothers can use this book to identify differences between the normal discomforts of pregnancy and the symptoms that may signal medical problems. The source materials are collected from individual publications and excerpted documents produced by the National Institutes of Health (NIH), its sister agencies and subagencies, and other reliable medical associations. Thus, the contents presented are authoritative and can be used to help women understand, prevent, detect, treat, and cope with the miscellaneous health concerns of pregnancy and childbirth. Most of the basic information is about all aspects of pregnancy and birth. There are 40 chapters in this book, which are arranged in 8 parts: planning for pregnancy, maternal care during pregnancy, fetal development during gestation, labor and delivery, postpartum and prenatal care, pregnancy in mothers with special concerns, disorders of pregnancy, and a glossary. Some chapters discuss common topics that are worth noting, including immunization and pregnancy, genetic counseling, drugs and pregnancy, over-the-counter drugs, amniocentesis, nutrition, weight gain, breast cancer and pregnancy, breast-feeding, mental health, and multiple births. There are historical and statistical data inserted in several chapters. In addition, the detailed index makes it easier to locate information within the book. This resource is recommended for public libraries to have on hand.

—**Polin P. Lei**

Diabetes

1562. **American Diabetes Association Complete Guide to Diabetes.** Alexandria, Va., American Diabetes Association, 1996. 446p. index. $29.95. ISBN 0-945448-64-3.

Diabetes is a disorder that affects more than 16 million Americans—approximately 1 of every 17 people. With a statistic this staggering, the demand for accurate written information about the disease is obviously high. Indeed, there are innumerable texts written on various aspects of diabetes, including a number of popular guides. The highly respected American Diabetes Association has responded with yet another resource book that is a compilation of the best self-care techniques for the diabetic.

Written in a positive, easily understood style, this guide covers all the practical matters that the diabetic must know in order to enjoy a long, healthy life. The different types of diabetes (Type I, Type II, and gestational) are described and a general management plan given for each. A chapter on the health care team that may be especially needed by the person with diabetes (e.g., physician, dietitian, exercise physiologist, podiatrist, eye doctor, mental health counselor) is extensive. Detailed information is given on insulin and how to use it. Techniques for monitoring blood glucose levels are clearly described. A chapter on diabetes tools provides a description of such items as blood glucose meters, test strips, and lancets that are currently available for the diabetic. Other key pieces of the diabetes management plan, proper diet, and exercise are outlined.

Although diabetes can be controlled, there can be complications, such as cardiovascular disease, eye problems, nerve damage, and infections. These complications are discussed and preventive advice given. Because diabetes affects not only the person with the disorder but also family, friends, and coworkers, a chapter is devoted to discussing emotional, psychological, and discrimination issues that may result. A glossary, various appendixes, and a resource list round out this useful guide.

The *Joslin Guide to Diabetes* (Simon & Schuster Trade, 1995), written by doctors at the world-renowned Joslin Diabetes Center (affiliated with Harvard University) is similar in content. The two resource books differ mostly in organization and physical layout. For example, the American Diabetes Association guide contains large margins on each page that may be used by the individual to add personal notes. This is a guide for everyone who is touched by diabetes: the individual with a long history of the disease, the person newly diagnosed with diabetes, and others who desire to be supportive and better informed. The work is highly recommended for personal purchase and for all types of libraries.—**Elaine F. Jurries**

Poisoning

1563. Morelli, Jim. **Poison! How to Handle the Hazardous Substances in Your Home.** Kansas City, Mo., Andrews and McMeel, 1997. 258p. illus. index. $9.95pa. ISBN 0-8362-2721-2.

There is no doubt about it, Morelli has cornered the market on toxicological information for consumers. Although this book is not a replacement for expert assistance, especially during a toxicological emergency, it may decrease the possibility of having such an emergency by providing a necessary element for increased consumer awareness. Readers will learn what to do about the various poisons that lurk in their homes, gardens, and medicine cabinets. According to the author, we live in a toxic dump. However, this book will "add a note of rationality to the mysterious world of poisons . . . by tearing down some enduring myths." Creative and humorous, this conversational volume takes the "science" out of "scientific" jargon. It puts the information at the reader's fingertips in a user-friendly format, and it makes learning fun.

—**Sue Lyon Mertl**

PHARMACY AND PHARMACEUTICAL SCIENCES

1564. Allison, Kathleen Cahill. **EveryWoman's Guide to Prescription and Nonprescription Drugs.** New York, Broadway Books, 1997. 770p. illus. index. $19.95pa. ISBN 0-553-06906-3.

During the past 10 years, efforts have been made to include more women in clinical drug trials. Prior to that time, researchers were reluctant to include women of childbearing age and postmenopausal women because of the differential effects of the menstrual cycle. This exclusion, plus the physiological differences between men and women, resulted in inappropriate dosages and unexpected drug toxicity for many women. In an effort to help women become informed consumers, the editors of this book have created a resource that emphasizes the information women should know about their prescription and nonprescription drugs: Will the medication interact with birth control pills, will hormone replacement therapy affect the medication, can it be taken if pregnant or attempting pregnancy, can it be taken if breast-feeding, will bone density be reduced, and will it affect the menstrual cycle?

The 1st section of the book provides general information on drug testing, types of drugs, interpreting the prescription, routes of administration, and alternative remedies. The chapter on drug safety stresses the communication women must have with the physician and the pharmacist, potential side effects, adverse drug reactions, and drug interactions. In the chapter on choosing drugs for a healthier lifestyle, readers are cautioned about abusing nonprescription products for smoking cessation, weight loss, sun exposure, and constipation. Drug profiles for 200 drugs representing more than 1,000 generic and brand-name drugs, are provided in the 2d section of the book. The profiles are from the database created by the U.S. Pharmacopeial Convention, an independent, not-for-profit organization that sets the official standards of strength, quality, purity, packaging, and labeling of medical products sold in the United States. Each profile includes information on the drug's purpose, information the patient should communicate to the physician or pharmacist, use and administration, precautions, and possible side effects. As the title suggests, the focus is on women's health and well-being. The drug index lists both brand and generic names; the general index provides access to the appropriate drug outline by disease name or symptom.

Although the drug information is written from a woman's point of view, so to speak, it is available in other resources. The value of the book resides in the first few chapters, in which women are encouraged to be informed consumers and learn more about the drugs they use. Women's health issues are extremely important, and this book offers valuable information while fulfilling a current and popular need in many libraries' consumer health collections. [R: RBB, 1 Mar 97, p. 1188]—**Vicki J. Killion**

1565. **Burger's Medicinal Chemistry and Drug Discovery.** 5th ed. Manfred E. Wolff, ed. New York, John Wiley, 1995-1997. 5v. index. $975.00/set. ISBN 0-471-57556-9 (v.1); 0-471-57557-7 (v.2); 0-471-57558-5 (v.3); 0-471-57559-3 (v.4); 0-471-57560-7 (v.5).

This series is divided into 5 hardback volumes. Volume 1 eloquently explains the scientific and legal aspects of drug discovery processes, product development issues, 3-dimensional chemical structure information, and various drug discovery technologies. The remaining volumes are devoted to important individual drug classes. Chapters are structured by disease category (e.g., antihypertensive agents); therapeutic modality (e.g., beta-blockers); or a combination of the two.

Individual chapters contain up-to-date information in each of the basic sciences, including molecular biology, biochemistry, and pharmacology. Every contributor provides a masterful synopsis of the huge quantities of available data. For older drugs, a historical perspective is included that focuses on the product's contribution to improved quality of life and decreased health care costs. Extensive bibliographies conclude each chapter, and indexes appear within each volume (with a cumulative index in volume 5). This reference series is an essential addition to the libraries of medical and allied health professionals, medicinal chemists and biopharmaceutical industry professionals, and certain members of the legal community.—**Sue Lyon Mertl**

1566. **Delmar's A-Z NDR-97: Nurse's Drug Reference.** By George R. Spratto and Adrienne L. Woods. Albany, N.Y., Delmar, 1997. 1415p. illus. index. $29.95pa. ISBN 0-8273-7726-6. ISSN 1089-165X.

NDR-97 provides up-to-date information on the newest and most widely used prescription and over-the-counter drugs and the proper monitoring of drug therapy by the practitioner. Although one of the most important features of the book is the presentation of nursing considerations in a nursing process format, the summary for each drug is presented in clear, concise language that many laypeople will find easy to understand.

The initial chapter gives detailed information on how to use the book. Chapter 2 is an alphabetic list of therapeutic or chemical drug classes with general information for the class and a list of the drugs in the class covered in chapter 3. Each entry in chapter 3 consists of 2 parts: general drug information and nursing considerations. The general drug information includes the Food and Drug Administration pregnancy category, drug schedule, actions, uses, contraindications, side effects, drug interactions, laboratory test interference, and the usual dosage and administration information. The nursing considerations guide the practitioner in applying the nursing process to pharmacotherapeutics to insure safe practice. Suggestions for assessment, intervention, patient education, compliance, and outcomes identification are briefly summarized for each drug. Other useful features of the book include a list of common soundalike drug names, commonly used abbreviations and symbols, commonly used laboratory test values (e.g., normal serum values), and a table of drug compatibility. The index is extensively cross-referenced and simplifies drug location by pairing trade and generic names with the generic name in bold typeface. Purchasers of the book may also register for access to updates online (Delmar@Once). Monthly drug updates, weekly postings of related articles, and a question-and-answer forum are some of the features available electronically.

Because it is the official drug reference of the National Student Nurses' Association, health sciences libraries supporting schools of nursing and hospital nursing staff should have a copy of *NDR-97* on the shelf for the unique combination of comprehensive drug information and nursing interventions. Large public libraries may consider adding this item to the reference collection for the concise, easy-to-read information many laypeople require when searching for information on prescription drugs.—**Vicki J. Killion**

1567. **Delmar's Therapeutic Class Drug Guide for Nurses 1997.** By George R. Spratto and Adrienne L. Woods. Albany, N.Y., Delmar, 1997. 1453p. illus. index. $29.95pa. ISBN 0-8273-7727-4. ISSN 1089-1641.

This is not a pharmacology text, and it does not concern itself with the chemical composition of drugs (like *Physician's Desk Reference*). The guide succeeds admirably in providing a rich source of information about current therapeutic drugs, and it emphasizes the nursing considerations essential to their effective use. The directions to nurses appear at the end of each article and are arranged under assessment, interventions, client/family teaching, and evaluation.

Each section treats a separate classification of therapeutic drugs, with a general discussion of the class and a list of drugs included (e.g., "Cardiovascular Drugs" covers antiarrhythmic agents, antianginal agents, antihypertensive drugs, antihyperlipidemic agents, and drugs for congestive heart failure and peripheral vascular disease). Chapters list appropriate drugs in each category by generic name, with information arranged under general statement, action/kinetics, uses, contraindications, special concerns, side effects, drug interactions, laboratory test interferences, dosage, and nursing considerations. This format allows for quick access to specifics and for extensive subject coverage. Trade names with a tiny maple leaf indicate that the trade name is available only in Canada. Other abbreviations and symbols are commonly used in the text; a reference list and directions on using the guide appear in introductory pages.

There is a brief visual identification guide. Several appendixes give valuable supplemental information, such as common laboratory test values, pregnancy categories, and a "drug preview" of material received from the manufacturers too late for inclusion in this year's guide. Nurses in all specialties should find this book a valuable resource. The address for obtaining Internet updates is provided.—**Harriette M. Cluxton**

1568. Fudyma, Janice. **What Do I Take? A Consumer's Guide to Nonprescription Drugs.** New York, HarperPerennial/HarperCollins, 1997. 177p. $13.00pa. ISBN 0-06-273422-9.

For those people whose bursitis is acting up again, or who need some relief and cannot find the time to schedule a doctor's appointment, this small but informative monograph is the book to consult. By turning to the bursitis/tendinitis page, a number of over-the-counter products are listed and rated by pharmacists. Ratings of each product (based on a 1-to-10 scale) consider the following categories: "Most Effective," "Speed of Relief," "Minimal Side Effects," and "Percentage of Pharmacists Who Most Often Recommend." The participating pharmacists, who are members of the American Pharmaceutical Association, were selected based on three or more years of practice, and were chosen from diversified geographic locations. The results of the ratings represent a 90 percent confidence level, plus or minus 8 points. In the case of bursitis, a total of 11 over-the-counter medications are rated.

For each affliction listed, in addition to the rating scale some general information on the affliction, on the medications themselves, and when it is best to see a doctor are outlined. A total of 57 afflictions are presented with ratings of 400 over-the-counter products. Other afflictions include heartburn, coughs, ringworm, eye redness, fever, and so on. Aside from the alphabetic list of afflictions, a 2d section contains an alphabetic list of the products discussed. For each product listed, dosage form, active ingredients, and warnings are presented. The work concludes with a two-page glossary. This guide is recommended for all public libraries as well as for individual purchase.—**George H. Bell**

1569. Hocking, George Macdonald. **A Dictionary of Natural Products: Terms in the Field of Pharmacognosy....** Medford, N.J., Plexus Publishing, 1997. 994p. $139.50. ISBN 0-937548-31-6.

According to the definition found within this dictionary, *pharmacognosy* is "that branch of pharmacy relating to medicinal substances from the plant, animal, and mineral kingdoms in their natural, crude, or unprepared state, or in the form of such primary derivatives as oils, waxes, gums, and resins." The above statement represents an excellent summary of what this dictionary is about. The majority of the more than 18,000 terms in this work consist of scientific and common names of plants and animals; scientific terms for the families and genera of the plants and animals; drugs acquired from animals and plants; pharmaceutical preparations; animal products, such as antitoxins, sera, and the like; terminology used in pharmacognosy and phytochemistry; and botanical terms associated with the field.

The length of the information given for the types of terms contained within the work varies from several sentences to several pages. For example, in considering the amount of information given when a genera is listed, all appropriate scientific names of the organisms within the genera are considered, along with the type of medicinal product they produce as well as the uses of said product. Many entries of this type can run one or more pages. It should also be noted that a number of abbreviations are used as part of the information given in order to save space. The key to the abbreviations can be found in the beginning of the book; however, most abbreviations can be determined by their context within the definitions. References are identified by means of numbers within the definitions, and a list of these references can be found in appendix A.

This dictionary represents copious, detailed information on medicinal products, their uses, and the biological organisms responsible for the products. The dictionary is extremely well researched, with a total of 2,798 references cited. A bibliography of general reference works on pharmacognosy and economic botany; a list of serials in the field of pharmacognosy; a list of terms describing properties and therapeutic uses of drugs, pesticides, and so forth; diagrams of types of inflorescences and of flowers; a description of a classification scheme; and a list of the scientific names of plants that produce natural rubber can be found at the end of the work. It is highly recommended for college, universities, and large public libraries.—**George H. Bell**

34   High Technology

GENERAL WORKS

1570. **CorpTech CD-ROM Directory of Technology Companies.** [CD-ROM]. Woburn, Mass., Corporate Technology Information Services, 1996. Minimum system requirements: IBM or compatible 386 Intel processor. 2X CD-ROM drive. DOS 3.0. Windows 3.1. 4MB RAM. 2MB hard disk space. Video drive support for 256 colors (optional). Mouse. Laser or dot matrix printer (optional). $5,900.00.

This is the CD-ROM version of the annual four-volume set (see ARBA 96, entry 1749, for a review of the 10th edition). It contains all the information of the print volumes plus some new elements and online links on one CD-ROM. Accompanied by a 126-page manual, installation is quick and easy. It helps to have a World Wide Web browser such as Netscape on the workstation, as parts of the program tie into that.

The search engine is a model of uncluttered design. The search screen layout is in three frames or windows for index searching. The first frame selects the index to search. The box where the term is entered sits atop the alphabetized list of terms to be searched and selected. A third frame tallies the search results and strategy. Searching may be by company; by location; by Internet capability (availability of e-mail or homepage); by ownership; by status (year formed, source of capital, government contract); by size (by sales, employees, and historical and projected growth); by executives; and by products (industry, SIC code, CorpTech group code). In addition to index searching, one may search for text in browse mode. Boolean capabilities using AND and OR are available in text searching.

Company records may be viewed as a list or in full form, or they may be printed or downloaded. The full record includes the company's address; status; government contract standing; size (employees, sales growth); executives; primary industry; SIC code; narrative description; CorpTech product codes; and units (subsidiaries, divisions). Under the item "Internet," there is a link to "Explore: CompanyLink Resources." Clicking here will open the Web browser, link to CompanyLink, and bring up the record for that company. CompanyLink is CorpTech's database on the Web, and it displays an abbreviated version of the record on the CD-ROM product. It does have additional Web links in the record, including a "summary profile" that contains more complete corporate data with an embedded link to the company's homepage and a "CorpTech report (for $2)," consisting of the abbreviated company record with news articles and even more links to stock prices, charts, and SEC filings from EDGAR. The news reports originate from a variety of print and online wire sources. Additional connections to competitors and to *Hoover's Report* (for $2) are provided. These links carry an extra charge ($10/month) or a per-report price of $2. The user may subscribe to these extra features online using a credit card. A free two-week demonstration is also offered online. Free links appear for an Infoseek search on the company, a local street map, and the local weather.

This is a dream database. It is wonderfully simple and intuitive to use. Consulting the manual is a rarity. The search engine is powerful and quick, the displays easy to read. The CompanyLink feature provides an abundance of additional information. A great deal of competitive intelligence may be gathered using this CD-ROM as a gateway. Because the majority of these high tech firms are private, the abundance of information being offered here that would normally encompass several disparate searches is truly significant. This source is highly recommended for any library serving a technology-intensive clientele. For corporate libraries in high technology companies, this disc is a must-have.—**Gerald L. Gill**

1571. **CorpTech Explore Database.** [CD-ROM]. Woburn, Mass., Corporate Technology Information Services, 1997. Minimum system requirements: IBM or compatible 386 with Intel or compatible processor. CD-ROM drive (double-speed or higher recommended). DOS 3.0. Windows 3.1. 2MB hard disk space. 4MB memory. 256-color monitor (optional). Mouse. Laser or dot matrix printer (optional). $5,900.00.

Finding information on private companies, divisions, and subsidiaries is usually difficult and often insufficient. CorpTech has simplified this process for 45,000 high-tech companies. In one location you can find annual sales, number of employees, international business and projected growth, and links to parent company and other operating units. The Explore function quickly links to other relevant records on the CD-ROM or to the company's Website.

Searches can be constructed by choosing terms from the index, by searching the text in either the company or product description fields, or by browsing by company name. The user's manual is clearly written and helpful for more advanced functions.

Although a database with this type of information is not unique to Explore Database, the ease with which you can search and sort on the 30 different indexes is. Another unique feature is the employment trend reports that are categorized by geographic area, by industry, or by product category.

The price is the one negative aspect of this product. Exporting is only available with the Explore Database Gold. For this luxury the cost increases substantially—from $2,450 to $5,900. [R: LJ, 15 April 97, p. 128]—**Deborah S. Hatfield**

1572. Hansen, Brad. **The Dictionary of Multimedia Terms & Acronyms.** Wilsonville, Oreg., Franklin, Beedle & Associates, 1997. 343p. illus. $16.95pa. ISBN 1-887902-14-7.

Given the number of computer and technology dictionaries on the market, is a dictionary for multimedia really necessary? Yes, because multimedia is a cross-disciplinary activity that involves concepts (and words) from many different fields. This dictionary does a worthy job of pulling together the various elements of multimedia; it includes artistic terms and multimedia-specific technical terms, as well as generic computer and technology terms. Acronyms, the phrases represented by acronyms, and variant terms are all provided in the dictionary, with *see* references pointing to a single definition for each term. Definitions are clear and concise, typically running from 10 to 60 words in length. Particularly important concepts such as MIDI and FireWire are explained with extended definitions of a few hundred words. Illustrations help explain some terms.

The definitions are accurate and well written, but there is some inconsistency in what is included. For example, the RS-232 connector is defined, but not the RJ-45. This is a minor criticism, however; most everything that really should be in a multimedia dictionary is featured. In addition to the definitions, a series of appendixes document some topics related to multimedia. An essay on copyright is particularly valuable, providing an explanation of copyright as it relates to multimedia, which may be hard to find elsewhere. A World Wide Web appendix gives an overview of HTML, tables of HTML tags, elements, colors and coded characters, and an explanation of CGI. A list of multimedia standards organizations and a recommended reading bibliography are handy. The appendix on DOS commands is less useful, as this information is of peripheral importance to multimedia and is readily available elsewhere.

The Dictionary of Multimedia Terms & Acronyms brings together a wide spectrum of information on a cross-disciplinary topic. One would have to open many books on an abundance of different subjects to cover all the multimedia topics that are here.—**Ken Feser**

1573. **Jane's Simulation and Training Systems 1996-97.** 9th ed. Ian W. Strachan, ed. Alexandria, Va., Jane's Information Group, 1996. 525p. illus. maps. index. $290.00. ISBN 0-7106-1361-X.

The universe of simulation and training systems is varied and complex, using a broad mix of technology ranging from the extremely sophisticated pilot training device to the simplicity of the dummy land mine. Among these technologies are Image Generation systems that produce visual, often three-dimensional images from photographs or other data; Visual Display Systems, used in simulators and virtual reality technology; and Motion Cuing Systems that provide physical movement to simulators. Most of the products in the publication at hand are used by the military, but many are used for both military and civilian purposes (flight trainers, for instance), and some are purely civilian in nature. Some products assume large, complex tasks, such as ship handling simulators, and some are relatively specialized, such as pistol marksmanship trainers. Of course, the ultimate goal of these systems is not only efficiency but economy; the real equipment is often too precious to risk and too expensive to operate in a training mode.

Readers familiar with Jane's Information Group publications will not be surprised that this title follows the well-known Jane's format: an explanation of the scope of the work and its organization, definitions of terms and a glossary, an overview and recapitulation of developments and trends in the industry, and a product section arranged by function and country of manufacture. This last section is, as usual, notable for its profusion of photographs; for its technical data; and for its narrative descriptions of purpose, employment, and characteristics. A fine work for a limited readership, this title will be of use to libraries serving those with interest in this highly specialized subject. (For an earlier review of this work under the title *Jane's Military Training Systems*, see ARBA 92, entry 656.)—**Eric R. Nitschke**

COMPUTING

1574. Collin, S. M. H. **Dictionary of Personal Computing and the Internet.** Chicago, Fitzroy Dearborn, 1997. 205p. illus. $35.00. ISBN 1-57958-016-5.

The author has designed this dictionary for users wanting to understand the complex terms that are used to describe personal computers (PCs) and the Internet. This can include anything from the components that make up a PC and the way PCs work to the software they run, as well as the communications and technology jargon used for e-mail, transferring files, and the World Wide Web. More than 1,600 terms are covered along with an appendix listing HTML commands.

The terms are arranged in alphabetic order in bold, lowercase letters, with the exception of trademarks, proper names, or acronyms. *See* and *see also* references are included. The definitions given in this work are straightforward with little frills, as Collin does not try to be encyclopedic or verbose. A few illustrations are scattered throughout. Currently used terms can be found here for concepts as well as an array of acronyms such as cookies, cgi script, and RAID. Although the definitions are understandable, this work does not appear to be geared towards a beginner. The more knowledgeable reader may appreciate having access to a dictionary that does not talk down to them.

Although this is a valid reference tool, it may be underused in some libraries due to its audience level. This would be an appropriate reference purchase for larger computer science collections.—**Julia Perez**

1575. **CyberDictionary: Your Guide to the Wired World.** David Morse, ed. Santa Monica, Calif., Knowledge Exchange, 1996. 313p. illus. index. $17.95pa. ISBN 1-888232-04-8.

Wired magazine bothers many people who are unable to get beyond appearance. The colors are bright and sometimes obscure the meaning of the text. Typography can be overwhelmed by exuberance and frankly, one's eyes need a break from all that work. However, beneath the visual farrago is useful and interesting information. Sure, there is the MTV sort of style-mongering that maddens the content crowd, but that is part of the message too. Much of this is also true of *CyberDictionary: Your Guide to the Wired World*. What a reader gets are bright colors, distracting sidebars, cartoons, photographs, and diagrams. The reader also gets well-written definitions without the technical bias that often bewilders the ordinary mortal. In other words, this is a useful and readable dictionary. It will not satisfy an engineer, but for those curious about point-to-point protocol (PPP) or Uniform Resource Locater (URL), this is a reference tool to try.

Strangely, *CyberDictionary* is an interesting place to visit. There are quotations from Mick Jagger and Isaac Asimov and essays on all sorts of topics. The problems are obvious but exist in every dictionary. It is already out-of-date (what about *push and pull?*), and no one can cover everything (where is *ISP—Internet service provider?*). This is a helpful reference book. Patrons who are hooking up to the World Wide Web for the first time or are attempting to decipher an article in the Science section of Sunday's paper will find this a good choice.—**George M. Cumming Jr.**

1576. **Dictionary of Computing.** 4th ed. New York, Oxford University Press, 1996. 550p. $49.95. ISBN 0-19-853855-3.

Revised by a team of computer specialists, the 4th edition of *Dictionary of Computing* contains more than 7,000 terms—1,700 more than the 3d edition (see ARBA 91, entry 1722). Coverage includes computer applications in industry, the office, science, education, and the home; the means of achieving these applications in terms of hardware, software, computer organization, telecommunications, and user interaction; security, safety, and legal aspects of computing; major computer manufacturers and organizations; and underlying concepts and theories of computing and, where appropriate, of electronics, mathematics, and logic. This resource may prove invaluable to a select audience. Readers who already have a good understanding of how computers and computer programs operate will find the dictionary entries more than definitions. Descriptions of terms often put the information in context and point users to related terms. A sample entry illustrates the complexity of terms defined, the cross-references to other dictionary terms (indicated by an asterisk), and the *see also* terms.

> Inquiry station. A terminal from which information can be retrieved from a *database. Generally the terminal has a display and a keyboard, but there may also be ancillary devices such as a *badge reader. The user makes the inquiry via the keyboard either in the form of a question in plain text or by indicating a selection from a menu on the display. The display will show a series of possible selections that successively narrow the field of search. An inquiry station may also update information as the result of an action arising from an inquiry. An airline booking terminal is an example of an inquiry station. *See also* interrogation (p. 244).

Opinions will vary as to how useful this dictionary is, depending largely upon the user's prior knowledge and experience. Some users will appreciate the extensive cross-referencing, but others may find it frustrating to have to look up one or more additional entries to understand what the original entry means. Some individuals will find many definitions easy to understand, whereas others will have difficulty. There is also some variability in the quality and complexity of the definitions; certain definitions may be difficult for nearly everyone. For example, a library user or staff member attempting to understand Boolean operations as an aid to searching (a concept important to accessing online information) will be led through a complicated explanation of the Boolean function in algebra but will probably be unable to apply this explanation to the task of searching for information online.

The book jacket of this attractive dictionary states that it "should prove invaluable to students and teachers of computing as well as computer users in general." The truth is that a significant proportion of the latter group—even those who are skillful users of many computer applications—will find some explanations more complex than they had hoped. As with any reference work, this dictionary should be considered for selection only after careful examination of library patron needs.—**Jan Bakker**

1577. **Oxford Dictionary of Computing for Learners of English.** Sandra Pyne and Allene Tuck, eds. New York, Oxford University Press, 1996. 394p. $13.95. ISBN 0-19-431441-3.

Oxford Dictionary of Computing for Learners of English is the second book in the Oxford University Press series of basic subject dictionaries for learners of English, which is targeted for an intermediate to advanced level. Because of the intended audience, the format is clear and uncluttered, with definitions that pertain to computing only. Because to the majority of computer novices computer-specific vocabulary is a foreign language, this dictionary should prove invaluable to English speakers, too. A notation of the part of speech, a definition with difficult words in the definition glossed, and an example of the word used in the sentence follow each word in the dictionary. In a separate column to the side, the authors give grammatical notes if needed, pronunciation, *see* references, a list of words often used with the word, and synonyms. This column is flexible, showing a different configuration for almost every word. The dictionary notes differences in English and American spelling where it exists. For example, the entry for *logo* (p. 218) reads as follows:

> **LOGO** *noun* (software programming)
> A high-level computer programming language which was
> Designed to be used in education, especially to teach
> Programming to children: *The child typed the simple*
> *LOGO command FORWARD 50.*
> **Note** LOGO is a functional procedural language which was
> Designed in 1968. It is usually translated by an interpreter.
>
> **note** not used with a or an. No plural and used with a singular verb only.
> (also **Logo**)
> ><program in, write **Logo**; a Logo graphic, interpreter, program.
> See turtle

This dictionary is an excellent reference for computer-based English for all library patrons. Its straightforward format makes it easy to use and understand. It should fill an empty niche in any reference collection.—**Nancy P. Reed**

1578. Raymond, Eric S., comp. **The New Hacker's Dictionary.** 3d ed. Cambridge, Mass., MIT Press, 1996. 547p. illus. $32.00; $17.50pa. ISBN 0-262-18178-9; 0-262-68092-0pa.

Raymond refers to this work as a collection of slang terms used by various subcultures of computer hackers. Here, hackers are defined as the opposite of the common public perception of this group—computer criminals. This new edition includes more than 100 new entries and changes that add new meanings, background, and etymological history to the entries found in the 2d edition (see ARBA 93, entry 1680). The compilers has also included terms reflecting the popular interest in the Internet, World Wide Web, and the culture of the hackers who maintain it.

Considering the popularity of anything electronic in today's world, this book should generate interest among an assortment of users. This book is for those who have had to decipher electronic messages like "abend," "angry fruit salad," and "nethack." The main body of the work is arranged in dictionary format and is a combination of humor, anecdotes, and definitions. Several prefaces and appendixes are included. Of interest are the humorous appendixes on hacker folklore and a portrait of a hacker. A bibliography is also available.

More than a typical dictionary, this book goes beyond being a reference tool because much of it makes for entertaining reading by all computer users. Recommended for purchase by public and academic libraries or for personal use.—**Julia Perez**

1579. **Routledge German Dictionary of Information Technology: Deutsch-Englisch/Englisch-Deutsch. Wörterbuch Informationstechnologie.** New York, Routledge, 1996. 436p. $130.00. ISBN 0-415-08646-9.

This work contains 25,000 entries in German and English and covers a wide range of information technology-related fields including computing, data transfer, telecommunications, mathematics, electronics, optics, online services, programming , and client-server systems. It was compiled by terminologists with experience in various subject areas.

The dictionary is divided into two major sections. The A to Z listings (German-English then English-German) are followed by a list of abbreviations. Each entry shows the parts of speech, a subject area label (artificial intelligence, computing, programming, etc.) often with contexts (e.g., the entry *merge sorting* gives the context "of data") and compound forms of terms. Genders are indicated for German noun translations, and British English versus American English spelling (e.g., optical fibre/optical fiber) is noted. Cross-references for all abbreviations are shown in both English and German.

Although one suspects that an entire dictionary could be devoted to each of the subject areas, the coverage here is extensive. Many terms are recent, covering developments in the rapidly changing online world. This work will be of great interest to specialist translators and those libraries, particularly academic, serving bilingual technical specialists. The publisher indicates an electronic version on CD-ROM and diskette is forthcoming.—**Stephen Haenel**

OPTICAL STORAGE DEVICES
Microforms

1580. **Guide to Microforms in Print 1997: Incorporating International Microforms in Print.** New Providence, N.J., K. G. Saur, 1997. 2v. index. $430.00/set. ISBN 3-598-11325-0. ISSN 0164-0747.

This well-known publication was earlier published by Meckler Media and since 1980 has been published by K. G. Saur. *Guide to Microforms in Print* is a title main entry listing, with cross-references from all authors and editors to titles. In addition, cross-references from variant authors and titles are provided where needed. The main entry is as follows: title, author or editor, place of publication, date of publication, collection information, type of microform code, and price. In previous editions, the word "apply" was used to indicate that price information should be obtained directly from the publisher. Although the word "apply" is still found in this edition, it has been removed when possible. The user should contact the publisher when no price is given.—**Bohdan S. Wynar**

ROBOTICS

1581. **World Industrial Robots 1997.** By the Economic Commission for Europe and the International Federation of Robotics. New York, United Nations, 1997. 254p. illus. maps. $120.00pa. ISBN 92-1-100756-9. ISSN 1020-1076. S/N GV.E.97.0.20.

Based on data from national industrial robot associations, this yearbook presents comprehensive global industrial robot statistics for key industrialized nations. Organized in five parts, data collection methods are explained clearly in the introduction along with application classifications, statistical adjustments, and robot types (e.g., assembling and welding). The development of industrial robots is summarized, with time series data (1981 to 1996) analyzed in part 2, and forecasts (1997 to 2000) in part 4. A worldwide economic overview examines important factors, such as GDP, price, technological breakthroughs, and new developments.

Part 3 contains detailed, comparative statistical data for 20 countries, including the United States, Europe, and Asia. These reports, varying in length from short summaries to extensive analyses, identify key techno-economic variables (e.g., industrial branches) through uniform tables, charts, and figures. As each yearbook has a topical section (part 5), there are five articles on industry and country activities and trends in packaging. An appendix with six tables and a figure completes the volume. Although the lack of a separate list of tables or a topical index hinders access, this unique volume is recommended for libraries with engineering and business reference collections.—**Sandra E. Belanger**

TELECOMMUNICATIONS

Directories

1582. **Books and Periodicals Online: A Directory of Online Publications.** 1997 ed. Nuchine Nobari, ed. Washington, D.C., Library Technology Alliance, 1997. 2v. $370.00pa./set. ISBN 0-9630277-3-5. ISSN 0951-838X.

Books and Periodicals Online, now in its 8th edition, has been carefully designed and compiled to determine if a particular publication is online or on CD-ROM in order to ascertain the availability of a publication before actually going online. The advantage, of course, is cost. This directory tells readers where to find it; for what periods; and if it is available in full text, abstract, or indexed format. Included in this edition are more than 180,000 listings, with inclusion from some 85,000 publications, such as journals, newspapers, wire services, newsletters, and other source documents in approximately 2,000 databases around the world.

Among the key features of this edition are (1) databases and the online services that carry them; (2) producers and vendors names, addresses, and telephone numbers; (3) international and foreign-language publications; (4) information on dates and types of coverage (where available); (5) an appendix listing former title names; and (6) extensive coverage of general subject areas, such as engineering, sciences, law, and business. Also included in this directory are listings for titles no longer indexed in a database or published in print or electronic format. This feature, valuable for locating older discontinued publications, will help find journals that remain in a database although the title no longer appears. Only titles removed and purged from databases have been excluded from this directory.

The advantage to using this two-volume directory is that it eliminates the need to maintain separate serial listings for each service. This reference will certainly benefit college and specialized libraries needing access to a wide array of electronic information in an efficient and accurate manner.

—**Barbara B. Goldstein**

1583. **CyberHound's Guide to Companies on the Internet.** Wendy H. Mason and Donna Craft, eds. Detroit, Gale, 1997. 540p. index. $79.00pa. ISBN 0-7876-1023-2. ISSN 1089-2753.

This softbound directory contains basic information and reviews of more than 2,000 World Wide Web and Gopher sites on the Internet. In-house and freelance reviewers surfed the Web, surveying major private and public companies; high-profile entertainment, technology, and consumer product companies; international corporate sites; and unique or otherwise interesting small business sites. In addition to a 2- to 20-line review of a site, an entry includes basic company information; ratings for content, design, technical merit, and entertainment; and a description of the site contents. Two neat tidbits are the "Net Gain" and "Net Loss" categories describing the best and the worst features of a site, respectively. Several indexes provide various points of entry into the information: a directory of business-oriented Websites; a company index; a subject index by product line, industry, and site content; a four-digit Standard Industrial Classification (SIC) index; and a master index of current and former company names, alternate names, and acronyms. Gale could have included an intended audience index, for children, parents, or wholesale distributors, for example. URL and ratings indexes would have been useful, too.

While the information on the 15 or so sites visited was generally still accurate, the tone of the reviews varied widely. Some are all business. Half the review for Peachtree Software (http://www.peach.com) is a laundry list of its products. Others are sarcastic: Prayers Heavenbound (http://www1.primenet.com/~prayers), a site sponsored by a satellite communications company, allows mortals "to broadcast your prayers into space where hopefully God will have a better chance of picking them up" (p. 330). Still others pan a company's products, as on page 436: "Trying to figure out where you want to go today can be difficult here [Microsoft Website]" (http://www.microsoft.com). The site is "as complex, as sophisticated, and as cumbersome as its best-selling word processing software . . . ."

At first glance, this book promises to be useful. Where else can one find reviews of business sites on the Internet? The answer is Gale's searchable Cyberhound database (http://www.cyberhound.com). Instead of dumping out database content to print an obsolete directory, Gale would provide better service by regularly updating its Internet database.—**Susan D. Baird-Joshi**

1584. **CyberHound's Guide to Internet Discussion Groups.** Paul Lewon, ed. Detroit, Gale, 1997. 1058p. index. $79.00pa. ISBN 0-7876-1019-4. ISSN 1089-2931.

The Internet began as a way to sustain communication during a nuclear attack. Nowadays it may seem as if the Internet is doing the attacking. It is ironic that a medium that is supposed to reduce paper usage has spawned so many files and books on how to use it. *CyberHound's Guide to Internet Discussion Groups* is a 1,058-page tome listing 4,400 Internet discussion groups, their purpose, a rating, how to access them, and an overall description.

The areas in the book's focus are relatively small compared to the whole of the Internet—the e-mail discussion groups known as listservs and that independent network, Usenet, which joined the Internet later, consisting of newsgroups. One of this book's flaws is the absence of a clear discussion of the difference between the two as well as the need for potentially different software or at least different applications within the same browser to access each. Because the Internet is rapidly being equated with the World Wide Web, perhaps it is wise to state here that it is not, and that Web browsers (programs used to search the Web) have since added subapplications to allow reading of e-mail and Usenet newsgroups, which were formerly only accessible through separate programs. Also, it is important for the reader to realize that only a percentage of these discussion groups are described—according to the editor's admission, there are 17,000 newsgroups and 55,000 listservs.

The compendium does offer a rating system, although biased, of the groups' content and entertainment value; any warnings of profanity or "adult topics"; as well as the language, geographic coverage, number of subscribers, number of messages daily, whether the group is moderated or archived, and the net gains and losses from the group. The most opinionated feature is a sample quotation of the group's content. How one goes about choosing a single quotation to represent a group that spawns 100 messages a day is beyond comprehension. In comparing the editor's ratings of several of the listservs and newsgroups against this reviewer's own experience, this reviewer disagreed with almost every one, including the choice of *pars pro toto* quotations. More helpful is the book's added Internet glossary and large subject index.

All in all, the book is more of an abridged annotated index than a guide, and although helpful in finding groups on certain subjects, one can try to find the data on the Internet for free before paying the publisher's price of $79. Something like this belongs, after all, in a clearly defined location on the Internet, but it will take a long time to break the habit of going to the bookstore for data about the Internet. Also, of course, one of the big problems of the Internet is the lack of organization, as different search engines and software companies vie for the starting position as people crank up their dialers and open their browsers.
—**Kenneth I. Saichek**

1585. **CyberHound's Guide to People on the Internet.** Deborah Tracy, ed. Detroit, Gale, 1997. 812p. index. $79.00pa. ISBN 0-7876-1026-7. ISSN 1089-2745.

CyberHound's Guide to People on the Internet is one of the newest additions to the CyberHound series of guides to Internet resources. Previous titles gave advice for locating nonprofit organizations, companies, discussion groups, and libraries on the Internet. This guide is divided into three main sections. "Personal Web Sites" lists 1,500 prominent or noteworthy individuals who are the subject of World Wide Web pages. "Who's Who Online" gathers 1,000 sites that qualify primarily as company or institutional directories of personnel or members. The "White Pages" provides access by e-mail to 3,000 professionals and businesspeople who are experts in their fields. A team of Gale in-house and freelance Web surfers was directed to identify "people" sites focusing on newsmakers in the fields of entertainment, sports, business, or politics who would be of interest to a broad audience of Internet users. Value-added features include an annotated bibliography of current instructional Internet books and a glossary of technical terminology used in the first two descriptive sections.

The most compelling reason for purchasing this item is the full description and evaluation of each site in the first two sections. Information includes detailed access and retrieval directions and a presentation of the scope and content of the site. Most noteworthy is the rating system used to evaluate each Website. Evaluation criteria include timeliness, reliability of content, graphic presentation, ease of navigation, and educational or entertainment value. An overall rating measures the comparative worth of the site. However, it would be a mistake to accept this rating as definitive when most sites are "under construction" given the open-ended nature of the WWW. As with most Gale resources, the quality of indexing is outstanding. In particular, the subject index categorizes people listed in the "White Pages" by their area of expertise. This is an improvement upon the arrangement of *The Internet White Pages [1994]* (see ARBA 95, entry 1705), which does not provide any access to its listings except alphabetically or by domain name. This well-organized guide should serve its intended audience well and is recommended for a ready-reference collection in a public library.—**David G. Nowak**

1586. **Internet Tools of the Profession: A Guide for Information Professionals.** 2d ed. Hope N. Tillman, ed. Washington, D.C., Special Libraries Association, 1997. 249p. index. $49.00pa. ISBN 0-87111-467-4.

This 2d edition expands the number of participating Special Libraries Association (SLA) divisions. Of the 14 chapters, the initial 2 provide an introduction to the book and the Internet itself; the 3d, to SLA's online resources. The remaining 11 chapters, alphabetic by topic, cover business and finance; chemistry; education; food, agriculture, and nutrition; information technology; insurance and employee benefits; legal issues; library management; metals/materials; pharmaceuticals; and telecommunications. Within each chapter, resources are listed alphabetically. An index also helps locate sources. Each entry includes the source (i.e., the online address); the cost, if any; the type of resource (e.g., TELNET, World Wide Web); the contact person; the purpose; and the value of the resource when appropriate success stories exist.

The 8½-by-11-inch page layout provides sufficient all-around margins for comments and notes. The apparently camera-ready copy has a crisp, clean look. The entries make it easy to identify data needed at a glance. There is a timely caution about using Gopher and Veronica at this time; because many sites are not being maintained or updated, some links may not be found. To offset this potential problem, the book at hand is to be kept up-to-date via SLA's Website. The authors of each chapter, together with their divisions, will help maintain the site. The SLA Website posts links to the Webpages highlighted in the book, a possible precursor to an electronic version of the book. Secondary school, public, and academic librarians will find many useful sites for report writing and reference.—**Esther R. Sinofsky**

1587. **Mecklermedia's Official Internet World Internet Yellow Pages.** 1996 ed. San Mateo, Calif., IDG Books Worldwide, 1996. 908p. illus. index. $39.99pa. (with disc). ISBN 1-56884-343-7.

With more than 26,000 individual resources listed in the book and an accompanying CD-ROM, *Mecklermedia's Official Internet World Internet Yellow Pages* proclaims itself the "largest and most broadly comprehensive volume in your Internet reference bookshelf." Most of the Internet resources listed, however, are mailing lists and newsgroups. The introduction states that because only a few World Wide Web sites were selected, those in the book represent "the best and most interesting." There are no criteria listed for the best and most interesting, although various resources throughout the book are rated with a world icon to indicate high quality and general usefulness of the Website's content and focus. Interestingly, many Websites do not rate high enough to display a world icon using the book's rating system. There is an adequate table of contents, an index, and multiple appendixes with such listings as Usenet newsgroups, FTP and Gopher addresses of universities, online library catalogs, electronic texts, ARCHIE servers, and MUDDs. A CD-ROM accompanies the books and allows CD-ROM to Internet access only if the Quarterdeck Mosaic browser is also installed (4 MB RAM). There is no CD-ROM to Internet access with other browsers. The search software on the CD-ROM does not allow for Boolean searching. The default between two key words seems to be "or." The help file covers the electronic book commands and options, but does not help with searching.

A check of some of the Internet resources throughout the book produced a high rate of incorrect addresses. Material in this directory is dated and not very useful for reference purposes.—**Elizabeth B. Miller**

1588. **Mecklermedia's Official Internet World World Wide Web Yellow Pages.** 1996 ed. San Mateo, Calif., IDG Books Worldwide, 1996. 862p. illus. index. $39.99pa. (with disc). ISBN 1-56884-344-5.

It is a brave editor who creates a book of URLs. Already some World Wide Web addresses have changed, and nifty new sites have come to the fore. The reader just hopes that Webmasters provide forwarding information. Basically, the editor's colleagues at Vanderbilt University each researched Websites by specific topics. Criteria for inclusion were currency, useful organization, high general interest, and ready access. The umbrella group is Mecklermedia's *Internet World*.

In examining the content itself, one determines that the book opens with essays on Internet use and trends. The body of the work consists of Websites by subject, from aboriginal studies to women; topics are generally broad, such as education, and sometimes have subcategories (e.g., baseball falls under sports). Up to eight entries make up a page. Each entry includes popular title, keywords, description, sponsor or Webmaster, and Webmaster e-mail when available. Coverage is uneven; there is only 1 site under politics and almost 7 pages under religion, 1 site for Russia and 23 pages under television (because it lists individual broadcasting stations). Other topics with multitudinous entries include colleges/universities, the Internet, libraries, and mathematics. The main section also contains FAQ boxes (such as TELNET-accessible browsers), factoids (such as number of people using Yahoo in one week), and smileys on each lower right hand corner (":-F" is a bucktooth vampire with one tooth missing). These added features make for fun browsing.

Appendixes include Internet access providers worldwide; Web resources (e.g., HTML authoring, security); the future of VRML and Java; CGI programming languages; entertainment/lifestyle books and publications (including authors, bookstores, games, actors, MUDs); Windows tools on the Net; a glossary; how to use the CD-ROM included with the book; and some reprints of *Internet World* one-page "Webliographies." One wonders why some of these categories were not included in the main section. An index offers access to the main section entries (not the reprint URLs, however, :-( ). For the casual or recreational Internet user, this book is a fun source of information, although it should not be a first pick as a major reference tool.—**Lesley S. J. Farmer**

1589. **Microsoft Bookshelf Internet Directory.** 1996-97 ed. Redmond, Wash., Microsoft Press, 1996. 699p. $35.00pa. (with disc). ISBN 1-55615-947-1.

Getting a handle on the Internet's varied offerings while avoiding some of its less-desirable aspects can be difficult. There are online search engines and directories, but they can be difficult to use and often do not help narrow down the search. The *Microsoft Bookshelf Internet Directory* is designed to help librarians, teachers, and anyone with an interest in general online information find sites to suit their interests.

This book is a directory of FTP sites, newsgroups, Websites, and other Internet resources. The bulk of this sizable guide is the alphabetic listing of Internet sites grouped under 77 subjects. They cover a wide range of topics concerned with recreation, activism, house and home, work, and hobbies. It is easy to use and safe, ignoring salacious sites while retaining adult material such as sites concerned with abortion, AIDS, gay and lesbian issues, and the like. The sites for teens listed under the section "Youth Resources" are realistic and frank and not patronizing. The introduction (on Internet Service Providers and accounts) and the chapter of frequently asked questions are informative. (To its credit, the presentation is evenhanded when discussing Web browser competitor Netscape.)

Each entry provides the site's title, its type (World Wide Web, newsgroup, etc.), the audience, and access information. The annotations are one paragraph long and are written in a casual, often humorous tone. However, there are some minor problems in the organization and lack of thorough cross-referencing. For instance, both *Interactive Publishing Alert* (dedicated to online publishing) and *Institute for Advanced Metaphysical Studies* are listed under *Shopping*. Also, there is no title index.

The accompanying CD-ROM (Windows only, of course) provides the full contents of the directory in an Explorer-like program. Although there is no print manual to accompany the software, there is online help, and the interface is highly intuitive and simple to navigate. Any computer user with minimal Windows experience and a bit of gumption should be able to jump right on and go.

The contents of the directory appear in the left window, and sites can be accessed with a double-click. The full annotation appears in the right window with the address hotlinked. Once the browser is dialed up and ready to go, the user can go directly to any site listed in the directory. The Find feature allows easy access to the entire contents. To circumvent the usual problem with sites becoming obsolete, the program offers a simple-to-use update feature through the File menu. Updates are available through Microsoft Bookshelf's Website. This reviewer was able to download and insert updates in less than five minutes.

This directory is well thought out and balanced. It is informative and fun to use and will meet the need for a general Internet resource for most libraries. [R: Choice, Jan 97, p. 772]—**Stephen Haenel**

1590. Miller, Elizabeth B. **The Internet Resource Directory for K-12 Teachers and Librarians.** 96/97 ed. Englewood, Colo., Libraries Unlimited, 1997. 220p. index. $25.00pa. ISBN 1-56308-506-2.

The 1997 version of this directory is exactly what it claims to be—a resource presenting a broad sampling of good Internet resources for school library media specialists, educators, and students. The directory will be most welcomed by professionals who are somewhat familiar with navigating the Internet but still feel a little overwhelmed by the unwieldiness of it. Even though the author had to be selective, and therefore may have omitted many high-quality resources, there is no question that this work will be a useful tool in beginning to identify World Wide Web materials that expand the curriculum as well as the professional tools of the librarian and teacher. The author, a librarian, clearly explains her selection criteria in the book's preface. Resources include not only Websites but some Gopher sites (many of which, the author cautions, will soon be no longer available) and listserv discussion groups. More than 900 resources are included—200 more than the previous edition—with 400 retained and updated from last year's edition.

Using the table of contents or the comprehensive index, readers of this directory can find quality resources dealing with the curricular areas of art, music, and drama; foreign languages; language arts; math and computer science; science; and social studies and geography. A nice feature is the inclusion of some reference sites (college guides, entertainment sites, dictionaries, historical documents, and others) and resources for educators (school district sites, lesson plans, discussion groups, and services to which teachers can pose questions). The "School Library Media Applications" section includes Internet material of special interest to school library media specialists, technology coordinators, and teachers of computer science. The author's care in selection of resources is evident from the one- or two-paragraph descriptions of each resource.

School librarians will find that this reference work helps them in their efforts to assist teachers in locating appropriate Internet resources. The author also recommends its use as a supplemental textbook in college courses or professional development workshops focusing on use of the Internet in the classroom. Public libraries may also want to add this title to their collections.—**Jan Bakker**

1591. **Net.Journal Directory: The Catalog of Full Text Periodicals Archived on the World Wide Web. Volume 1, Number 2, Fall 1997.** Lawrence Krumenaker, ed. Hillsdale, N.J., Hermograph, 1997. 364p. $125.00/issue; $220.00/year. ISBN 0-9656775-7-5.

The 2d edition of this reference book, published twice yearly, includes over 25,000 individual listings of nearly 9,500 periodicals offering full-text archives that are accessible online via the World Wide Web for either a fee or at no cost. Periodicals are defined as trade magazines, trade journals, scholarly journals, trade papers, newsletters, business newspapers, and general newspapers. There are three criteria for inclusion in this directory of periodicals on the World Wide Web: sites must be accessible using a Web browser, they must have a searchable or organized archive, and full-text articles must be either readable online or immediately available for downloading to one's computer.

Examples of fee-based sites offering archival Web services to more than one journal or one publisher are *DialogWeb, Dow Jones Publications Library, InfoTrac Search Bank,* and *OCLC's Electronic Collection Online*. Some of the free single-source sites include *Scientific American, USA Today, The New York Times, Fortune, Time Magazine, People,* and *Money*. Not listed from pathfinder.com are *Sports Illustrated, Sports Illustrated for Kids,* and *Time for Kids*.

The appendixes include a subject index of periodicals categorized by subjects such as agriculture, food, forest and paper products, medical, and transportation. There is a brief description with costs of some of the major, individual fee-based services offering Web access. Archives of full-text newspapers are listed by state or by country if outside the United States. Additionally, there is a short listing of periodical Websites with current issues only.

Libraries with Web-based Internet access and subscriptions to multiple fee-based archival Web services will find this resource the most useful. Recommended for corporate, academic, and large public libraries. [R: LJ, July 97, p. 78]—**Elizabeth B. Miller**

Handbooks and Yearbooks

1592. **Finding Images Online:** *Online User's* **Guide to Image Searching in Cyberspace.** By Paula Berinstein. Susan E. Feldman, ed. Wilton, Conn., Pemberton Press, 1996. 357p. illus. index. $29.95pa. ISBN 0-910965-21-8.

How many words does it take to describe a picture? It may require fewer than a thousand but certainly could include enough to make searching for just the right image a bit difficult on an online system. This book's strength is that it tells users what they want, where to find it, how to get it, and what to do with it. The introduction performs an excellent job of explaining what kinds of images are available, how they can be used, who should find the book useful, and how to use the book, including an overview of each chapter.

Knowing where to look for images is only the first step. Knowing how to look is even more important. The section called "A Crash Course in Visual Literacy" defines the various types of visual attributes that a picture researcher needs to know. There is a detailed chapter of systems that contain images, the types of images contained on each system, and how to search the systems. Representative screens and case studies are included for practice. The three case studies provided in the World Wide Web chapter did not produce the same results when this reviewer tried them, but this is certainly due to the volatility of the Web. Search screens change, files go up and down every day, but the basic how-to remains the same.

The book goes on to explain about the different types of software required to view and manipulate the images (viewers), how to find viewers, and how to install them. The book contains a final chapter on copyright and the importance of obtaining permission to use images. Three appendixes, a bibliography, and an index round out the abundant information found in less than four hundred pages. This book is readable and a good bargain. [R: RQ, Spring 97, p. 470]—**Deborah S. Hatfield**

1593. Fist, Stewart. **The Informatics Handbook: A Guide to Multimedia Communications and Broadcasting.** New York, Chapman & Hall, 1996. 746p. (Telecommunications Technology and Applications Series). $64.95pa. ISBN 0-412-72530-4.

Fist states up-front that this entity is not a dictionary and not an encyclopedia. In fact, he seems much concerned in eliminating the possibility of anyone objecting to his definitions. This concern (or lack of) is stated shortly before he calls for corrections and help from the readers. Before that, however, he lets readers know that his background is in film and television, explaining the preponderance of terms dealing with those media. The result is a cross between *Quick Reference to Computer Graphics Terms* (see ARBA 95, entry 1699) and Mitchell Shnier's *Dictionary of PC Hardware and Data Communications Terms* (O'Reilly, 1996); unfortunately, without the accuracy of either.

The author of the work under review states that many terms from the original database are not included in the book, but a number of the definitions are also incomplete. *Address space* refers only to memory, and *applet* makes no mention of Java (and the definition is opposed to the applets that do add bells and whistles to pages and programs). A great deal of content is simply wrong. *Code* is confused with "cipher." The example *IP address* used is invalid (and, in fact, impossible). *Majordomo* is a program, not a function; and so on. Other entries are confusing. A dash must be seen as different from a hyphen by a publishing program, but there is no dash in either ASCII or on a standard keyboard. Fist seems to mix up the Kermit protocol with the Kermit (probably MS-Kermit) program and gets the speed and parameters wrong to boot. Some material, particularly that related to the Internet, is inconsistent. The description of hamming code has some marvelous detail, but part of it makes no sense at all.

The introduction seems to indicate a "joe user" target audience, rather than a specialist group. Still, it is difficult to understand how confusing definitions help the novice.—**Robert M. Slade**

1594. Hahn, Harley. **The Internet Complete Reference.** 2d ed. New York, Osborne/McGraw-Hill, 1996. 802p. index. $32.95pa. ISBN 0-07-882138-X.

The original edition of *The Internet Complete Reference* (1994) was, in its time, the best single guide to the Internet ever seen. Yet time passes quickly on the Internet, and even excellent guides need constant updating to remain current. This 1996 update maintains the quality of the original edition, but it omits discussion of too many of today's components of the Internet to be more than a specialty, niche publication. The niche here is users of UNIX-based systems. Hahn's greatest expertise is in UNIX, and it shows here, for good as well as bad. The book provides rich detail in the use of character-based software running on UNIX servers, programs such as pine (e-mail) and lynx (World Wide Web). Internet beginners who employ UNIX shell accounts will benefit immensely from the detail and quality of the introductions here.

However, these days, most beginners—and even most experienced users of the Internet—rely on software clients that run on Windows 95 or the Macintosh: clients such as Eudora or Pegasus (e-mail), and Netscape or Internet Explorer (World Wide Web). The book does mention these programs, but only briefly and with none of the depth of the UNIX discussions. Similarly, Hahn describes in considerable detail specialized clients for accessing such Internet services as ftp, Usenet news, and Gopher, all but ignoring the fact that most beginners, if they use these services at all, will access them via a Web browser. Treatment of other specialized services—Internet Relay Chat (IRC) and MUDs—is again limited by the emphasis on using UNIX client software.

Even though the technical detail remains good, the occasional omission is troubling. For example, the book includes a long discussion of the uuencode method of encoding program files for transmission via e-mail, but it does not mention the mimencode method that has largely superseded uuencode, even on UNIX systems. Discussions of tar file decoding omit the fact that the better Windows- and Mac-based dearchiving programs now know how to process tar archives.

The book includes a "Catalog of Internet Resources," listing sites with "a variety of interesting and useful resources." Despite the book's now being more than a year old, most of these sites are still in operation; of a dozen site entries checked, fully 75 percent were still in operation. The quality of the listings is mixed, with too many "sites" consisting of category listings at Yahoo. Sometimes established, high-quality sites were absent for no apparent reason; for example, the "Mathematics" section lists four sites but does not include either the Cornell or Swarthmore Web servers, two of the most important math sites on the Web.

In sum, *The Internet Complete Reference* is a book that has not kept up with the times. It remains extremely useful to Internet newcomers who rely on UNIX systems, but it is too narrowly focused to be of much benefit to users of Windows and Macintosh software.—**Ray Olszewski**

1595. Morville, Peter, Louis Rosenfeld, and Joseph Janes. **The Internet Searcher's Handbook: Locating Information, People, & Software.** New York, Neal-Schuman, 1996. 236p. illus. index. (Neal-Schuman NetGuide Series). $35.00pa. ISBN 1-55570-236-8.

This attractive paperback devoted to Internet searching is divided into 2 sections. Each of the initial 4 chapters has a separate author, which means the quality of these chapters varies. Although all provide useful information, chapter 3, "Using the Internet for Research," and chapter 4, "Online Communities as Tools for Research and Reference," are the best organized and provide the most useful information for Internet searching. The 2d section of the book includes chapters 5, 6, and 7 and makes up the heart of the book. Entitled "Virtual Libraries," "Internet Directories," and "Internet Search Tools," respectively, each chapter offers lists and detailed evaluations of the various Internet sources in the category addressed. Each chapter begins with a "developer's perspective" and gives a real-world view of some aspect of developing an Internet tool. For instance, in chapter 5 the perspective is written by Frederick Zimmerman, editor and publisher of the *Internet Book and Information Center*, and he discusses his experience creating and maintaining this virtual library. The perspectives sections are followed by descriptions of a series of Internet resources. These are excellent overviews, and the format that includes meta information, description, evaluation, a sample search, and a sample screen or two for each resource are particularly clear and useful. These 3 chapters alone are well worth the price of the book.

An added attraction is the "Quick Index to Internet Searching Tools and Resources," listed as appendix 1. This index is a list of 44 Internet resources with URLs arranged by category. Appendix 2 is a list of "regular expressions" to aid in searching for those searchers who do not know UNIX. A glossary is a further help to novice users of the Internet. The authors have sought to overcome the current problem that devils all printed material about electronic information sources by including a URL of the Internet Searching Center, where resource updates will be made in a timely manner. This may be the only way authors will be able to handle this ever-present problem. Unfortunately, in this case the URL provided in the book is itself no longer accurate. However, a note is posted at the old address that points to the new location. At this location there are indeed updates that have been made since the book's publication. Several of the sources from the book, the Whole Internet Catalog and Mailbase, for instance, are not listed at the Website, and when checked proved no longer available. Although somewhat inconvenient, this arrangement does seem to work. All in all, this book is well conceived, well researched, well organized, and well worth the price. [R: Choice, June 97, p. 1643]—**Elisabeth Logan**

1596. **Naked in Cyberspace: How to Find Personal Information Online.** By Carole A. Lane. Helen Burwell and Owen B. Davies, eds. Wilton, Conn., Pemberton Press, 1997. 513p. index. $29.95pa. ISBN 0-910965-17-X.

As the amount of information available online continues to grow, more people are using the Internet and other sources of electronic information as research tools. This guide shows users how to find data specifically about people. After a general overview of database searching, the Internet, and privacy issues, the author shows how personal records can be and are being used (e.g., to locate a long-lost friend or relative, to recruit and screen potential employees, to explore genealogical records, and to investigate financial assets). Each type of search is covered in a separate chapter that explains why and how the search is conducted and lists resources that may aid in the endeavor. Lane's step-by-step approach will make online research a satisfying enterprise even for novices.

Types of personal records that are available online (e.g., telephone directories, mailing lists, tax records) and their contents are also reviewed. Lane shares her expertise as an online researcher, thoroughly discussing such issues as accuracy, added content, search capabilities, and use restriction as they relate to the sources. To the inevitable question, "Where do I find out more?" she lists numerous books, periodicals, organizations, databases, and vendors in the appendixes.

The sheer amount of practical information contained in this book will certainly be of value to anyone wishing to search personal records online. The efficiency of research could be aided by more critical and comparative comments and by grouping related resources in their appropriate chapters, but apart from these logistical problems, the book is a useful one, particularly for consumers and novice online searchers. One hopes it will see many editions.—**Barbara Ittner**

35 Physical Sciences and Mathematics

PHYSICAL SCIENCES

General Works

1597. Cardarelli, François, ed. **Scientific Unit Conversion: A Practical Guide to Metrication.** New York, Springer Publishing, 1997. 456p. $39.95pa. ISBN 3-540-76022-9.

On several scores, this work is a unique reference tool. It is international in the extreme—French author, German publisher, printed in Malta, and corrections are solicited via supplied bookmark to an address in Great Britain. It is advertised as a pocketbook despite being 23.5-by-12.5-by-2.5 centimeters, requiring a large pocket, indeed. Depending on how one counts, the International System of Units (SI) is compared to 30 other systems, including the Assyrio-Chaldean-Persian System. Obsolete national and regional systems include those from the "Voyages of Discovery" age. Nearly 260 pages are required to list the units that are subsequently grouped into 26 categories.

To emphasize that this is a scientific tool rather than a technical one, the first 7 engineering handbooks checked averaged 6 pages of conversion tables, whereas the favorite scientific tool, *CRC Handbook of Chemistry and Physics* (5th ed.; see ARBA 95, entry 1711), had 48 pages of such tables in its section 1 alone. This book is essential for scientific libraries, metropolitan public libraries, and academic libraries supporting advanced work in the classics, theology, economic history, or business. [R: Choice, July/Aug 97, p. 1776]—**Eugene B. Jackson**

1598. **Notable Women in the Physical Sciences: A Biographical Dictionary.** Benjamin F. Shearer and Barbara S. Shearer, eds. Westport, Conn., Greenwood Press, 1997. 479p. illus. index. $49.95. ISBN 0-313-29303-1.

Essays in this nicely compiled volume highlight the contributions of women scientists from the United States and a few from Europe, Canada, China, and India. Fields covered include physics, astronomy, physical chemistry, and chemistry, but not applied sciences, such as engineering and materials science. This volume complements other reference works providing biographical information about women scientists—such as Marilyn Bailey Ogilvie's *Women in Science: Antiquity Through the Nineteenth Century* (see ARBA 88, entry 1441) and Martha J. Bailey's *American Women in Science* (see ARBA 96, entry 1486)—by its emphasis on twentieth-century scientists whose work is continuing. Editors Benjamin and Barbara Shearer also produced the earlier work, *Notable Women in the Life Sciences* (see ARBA 97, entry 1231), to which this volume is certainly a welcome companion.

Each entry includes a straightforward biography of 1,000 to 1,500 words, a chronology, and a bibliography comprising both primary works of the scientist and secondary sources. Reviews are signed, and an appendix gives short descriptions of the contributors, who include scientists, librarians, and researchers on women. Essays note if a scientist received a starred entry (denoting outstanding work) in the *American Men of Science* (Jacques Cattell Press, 1906–1he-1968), a detail of help researchers tracing the historical treatment of women scientists. Useful appendixes include a list of scientists by specialty and a compilation of prize-winners. Photographs accompany approximately half of the entries—an excellent addition considering that some of these women scientists are not well known.

Necessary limitations to this volume include the lack of critical analysis in the brief essays and the selective rather than comprehensive approach to inclusion of scientists. Still, this work should be added to collections in high school, public, and academic libraries as a quick reference and first stop for research.
—Jean C. McManus

Chemistry

1599. **Concise Encyclopedia Biochemistry and Molecular Biology.** 3d ed. Revised by Thomas A. Scott and E. Ian Mercer. New York, Walter de Gruyter, 1996. 737p. illus. $99.95. ISBN 3-11-014535-9.

This book, although cataloged as a 3d edition, is more than an update of the earlier *Concise Encyclopedia Biochemistry* (see ARBA 90, entry 1481, and ARBA 85, entry 1678). Although detailed treatment of metabolic pathways and natural products (the focus of the earlier editions) has been maintained, the title of the work has been expanded to reflect a broadening of scope that encompasses recent developments in molecular and cell biology. For example, entirely new entries have been created, such as cell adhesion molecules, DNA binding proteins, DNA fingerprinting, the Human Genome Project, NMR-spectroscopy, and protein folding. Other entries have been updated, rewritten, or reorganized as necessary, including all those pertaining to photosynthesis in higher and lower plants and fungi. As in previous editions, EC numbers (standardized enzyme nomenclature) are provided.

Accompanying the more than 4,500 alphabetically arranged entries, which range in length from a brief paragraph to several pages, are numerous tables, charts, and diagrams. Meticulous indexing maximizes access to the topics covered: common names, synonyms, and chemical names are all cross-referenced. There are also extensive *see* references. Many entries also list citations to the primary literature. This work, intended for advanced students and researchers, is a unique source of biochemical and molecular biological data and is highly recommended for academic biology collections.
—**Michael Weinberg**

1600. **Elements.** By Brian Knapp. Danbury, Conn., Grolier, 1996. 15v. illus. index. $269.00/set. ISBN 0-7172-7572-8.

This highly illustrated set of 15 volumes provides students with in-depth information about individual and groups of elements. The main format of each book is two-page spreads focusing on one aspect of the element in question. In each volume, the reader can find out the definition, natural occurrences, extractions/ preparation, uses, and compounds. Colorful photographs and diagrams make it easy for the reader to get an idea about the relevant information. A key feature of this set is the gradation in typeface size, which corresponds to the level of information. At first glance, one may think that the book is for younger readers because of the introductory large typeface, but the smaller print material can challenge the thinking of most high schoolers. Each volume includes key facts about the specific elements and then provides the same following pages for each: periodical tables (and explanation), how to read equations, and a glossary. In that way, each volume may be used independently without having to refer to a separate key legend volume. The individual volumes also have indexes.

Each volume is slim, with a glossy cover. The binding is stitched. The books do not lie flat easily. Finding good, accessible information on elements can be a daunting task. This set will be most welcome in junior and senior high school library collections. [R: SLJ, May 97, p. 160]—**Lesley S. J. Farmer**

1601. **Macmillan Encyclopedia of Chemistry.** Joseph J. Lagowski, ed. New York, Macmillan Library Reference/Simon & Schuster Macmillan, 1997. 4v. illus. index. $400.00/set. ISBN 0-02-897225-2.

In the increasing gap between the technological haves and have nots, the publication of print encyclopedias still serve a purpose. Although not inexpensive, the *Macmillan Encyclopedia of Chemistry* may be best described as comprising a good general chemical encyclopedia, suitable for high schools or junior colleges. It is nowhere near as comprehensive as large specialized handbooks or the abundance of online information resources associated with the chemical field. A useful entry on literature searching guides users to more comprehensive sources. The limitations of manual access are somewhat alleviated by cross-references and a 149-page index.

The volumes include a broad range of topics reflecting the classical areas of chemistry and biochemistry. Contents are arranged alphabetically, but a synoptic arrangement of articles provides a classified finding tool. Entries are also provided for some industrial applications, medicine, ethics in science, and careers. The nearly 70 signed articles range from concise definitions to extensive overviews and include brief bibliographies. More than 1,500 illustrations of chemical structures, equations, and principles support discussion of important concepts. Biographical sketches are furnished among the articles for chemists who have made a major contribution to the field. Names of Nobel prize-winners in chemistry from 1901 through 1996 are provided. No other information is given about them, although biographical sketches are provided for a few of them.—**Andrew G. Torok**

1602. **McGraw-Hill Dictionary of Chemistry.** Sybil P. Parker, ed. New York, McGraw-Hill, 1997. 454p. $16.95pa. ISBN 0-07-052428-9.

This paperback volume provides up-to-date definitions for approximately 8,500 chemical terms from 6 chemistry disciplines (general, inorganic, organic, physical, analytic, and spectroscopy). Each entry provides the term in bold typeface, identification by field, pronunciations, cross-references, chemical formulas, synonyms, variant spellings, and abbreviations.

Equally impressive is the 21-page appendix, because each topic is presented in a user-friendly, table-style format that easily organizes hundreds of facts and figures. Examples include conversion factors for the U.S. Customary System, metric system, and International System; the periodic table of the elements; natural isotopic compositions of the elements; standard atomic weights; common acid-base indicators; the pH scale; principal organic functional groups; and more.

This book was designed to decipher many chemical complexities into digestible pieces. It will, no doubt, conveniently serve as a single, comprehensive reference for professionals, students, educators, librarians, writers, and general scientific readers.—**Sue Lyon Mertl**

Earth and Planetary Sciences

General Works

1603. **McGraw-Hill Dictionary of Earth Science.** Sybil P. Parker, ed. New York, McGraw-Hill, 1997. 468p. $17.95pa. ISBN 0-07-052427-0.

As the earth sciences have increased in importance in society, there has been a tendency to reduce and simplify them, to make them more understandable for "the general reader with scientific curiosity." One unfortunate effect of this movement is the lumping together of disparate fields, losing much of the essence of each in the resulting amalgam. This consequence is the reason the *McGraw-Hill Dictionary of Earth Science* fails. It claims to "fully define the language of earth science" with 10,400 entries covering geology, geochemistry, geography, geodesy, geophysics, hydrology, oceanography, meteorology, and climatology. To truly and comprehensively cover these fields, however, this dictionary should be three times the length it is. As the volume stands, it simply has too many gaps.

To illustrate the holes: The field of geology is described as the study of "earth, its history, and its life as recorded in the rocks" (p. ix). This statement is fine, but if readers try to find a paleontological term, they will be disappointed. In fact, even the term *paleontology* is missing. Also, how can a dictionary covering geology not define *ophiolite, gabbro, hard ground, Stokes' law, isotope,* or *limestone*? Some geologic definitions are wrong or misleading. *Ripple index,* for example, is defined as "the ratio of crest-to-crest distance to the crest-to-trough distance" (p. 323), rather than wavelength to amplitude, and *Middle Silurian* (p. 224) is listed as a geologic epoch (which it is not). If the other "earth sciences" are treated in the same way as geology, this book is superficial indeed.

Most professional dictionaries have a long list of experts that have been consulted for accuracy and inclusion of definitions. This dictionary lists an editorial staff, but this reviewer did not recognize any name as that of an earth scientist. A dictionary must be authoritative to be useful, but this book has no visible authorities other than for pronunciation. The volume at hand should be avoided in favor of truly professional dictionaries developed for each field of the earth sciences.—**Mark A. Wilson**

Astronomy and Space Sciences

1604. Arnold, H. J. P., P. Doherty, and P. Moore. **The Photographic Atlas of the Stars.** Waukesha, Wis., Kalmbach Publishing, 1997. 220p. illus. maps. index. $59.95. ISBN 0-913135-31-3.

The sky has held a certain fascination for human beings from the earliest times. Efforts to map the objects seen there have been documented from the Stone Age. Accuracy and scale have posed the greatest barriers to people attempting to read and interpret them. Nearly all of the charts and atlases of the sky have been developed for the professional or serious amateur astronomer, and these are not easily interpreted by the casual observer.

The authors of this atlas have taken extraordinary measures to depict the sky as one would see it with the unaided eye. The atlas begins with an introduction to the methodology (the equipment, film, photographic procedures, and climatic conditions) for obtaining the images. The atlas is composed of direct color photographic images (taken by Arnold) of sections of the sky paired with a chart (constructed by Doherty) of the same section, to the same scale. This feature makes the atlas extremely usable to the casual sky observer. By presenting the sky in a way that the inexpert observer can easily identify constellations and stars, the authors have removed a barrier to most people's full appreciation of the universe above them.

Each section is enriched with descriptive text written by the popular writer of astronomy, Moore. The stars and other visible objects are briefly explained, and a little bit of the history of the constellation is provided as well. The authors include tables to assist in locating bright stars and nonstellar objects. They have created a workable and beautiful resource that is highly recommended for public library collections.—**Margaret F. Dominy**

1605. **Cambridge Guide to Stars and Planets.** 2d ed. By Patrick Moore and Wil Tirion. New York, Cambridge University Press, 1997. 256p. illus. maps. index. $14.95pa. ISBN 0-521-58582-1.

Every general library should have a large holding of pocket guides to subjects of natural history, and this book will be an excellent addition to that shelf. Astronomy is a field that is easily accessible to amateurs with inexpensive equipment (or no equipment at all), and yet it holds some of the most profound mysteries of existence. Guidebooks to the stars and planets are checked out by the curious, and they often change lives by showing what complexity and beauty lies waiting for a simple upward glance. This manual for observing the sky is updated to 1996 (even including the speculations about ancient life on Mars) and is well organized. It starts with an introduction to the basics of astronomical observation, with a good review of telescopes and their mounts (although oddly leaving out the popular Dobsonians). The basics of solar observation are included, along with excellent maps of the moon's surface. Each planet is briefly discussed and well illustrated with recent color photographs. Stars and other deep-sky objects are described in lucid terms, aided by a thorough glossary. There is an excellent short introduction to cosmology, complete with a diagram of the hypothesized Big Bang events, which is a topic few books of this type cover. The heart of the manual is a set of star maps arranged in alphabetic order by constellations. The Southern and Northern Hemispheres are covered equally. These maps are produced in color and are easy to interpret. Each map has a page of description discussing the history of the constellation and its major items of interest. The constellations themselves are easily located on the accompanying index maps.

The only reservation about the book as a useful astronomical manual is its minimal number of timetables of future events. Elongation and conjunction dates of Venus are given for the next few years, as are the opposition dates of Mars, Jupiter, and Saturn. The observer who wants to know *now* what that bright planet is in the southern sky will be disappointed with this book alone. Yearly summaries of planet positions or graphical timetables would have solved this problem. Nevertheless, this book can be combined with recent information from astronomy magazines and newspaper almanacs to make any clear night of observation most enjoyable and informative.—**Mark A. Wilson**

1606. **History of Astronomy: An Encyclopedia.** John Lankford, ed. New York, Garland, 1997. 594p. illus. maps. index. $95.00. ISBN 0-8153-0322-X.

Aimed at the educated layperson, this compendium of scholarly articles is one of the best of its kind. Although the work covers the history of astronomy all the way back to ancient times, its focus is on the Scientific Revolution (ca.1543 C.E.) to the present day. The encyclopedia's entries fall into five broad categories: historical overviews, national developments, observatories, social history, and biographies. The latest are only treated briefly so as not to duplicate existing biographical works.

Arranged alphabetically, the articles range from a few paragraphs to more than 5,000 words and include numerous bibliographic references to lead the reader to related materials. These bibliographies are one of the book's strong points. Above all, the quality of the writing is high, and the entries are clearly presented, succinct, and well organized. A word of praise is due to the editor for balancing the coverage of the various aspects of the topic while insuring consistency of style and clarity among the articles themselves. Other features worth mentioning are in-text cross-references in bold typeface, an index to aid location of specific topics, and a number of photographs. The encyclopedia is appropriate for university and large public libraries.—**Robert A. Seal**

1607. Ince, Martin. **Dictionary of Astronomy.** Chicago, Fitzroy Dearborn, 1997. 193p. $35.00. ISBN 1-57958-018-1.

This work is an update of similar resources. The author presents a well-rounded collection of astronomic terms and people. The definitions tend to be brief, but the author occasionally elaborates on a biography or complex concept. When necessary, an illustration is provided. Abbreviations and cross-references are scattered throughout.

Unfortunately, it is unclear what criteria were used for inclusion of terms or biography. For instance, Henrietta Leavitt is listed but her colleague and contemporary, Annie "Jump" Canon, is omitted. Of concern is the fact that only 10 of the 27 sources listed in the bibliography are published in the 1990s. The target audience is strictly popular, making this resource appropriate for public or school library collections.
—**Margaret F. Dominy**

1608. **McGraw-Hill Dictionary of Astronomy.** Sybil P. Parker, ed. New York, McGraw-Hill, 1997. 246p. $12.95pa. ISBN 0-07-052434-3.

The terms in this dictionary appeared originally in the *McGraw-Hill Dictionary of Scientific and Technical Terms* (5th ed.; see ARBA 95, entry 1493). Although one would not guess the fact from the title, a large percentage of the 3,400 terms come from astrophysics and aerospace engineering, not astronomy. The definitions are terse and technical in nature. Each definition includes a pronunciation. There are no illustrations. The editor appears to have made no attempt to update the definitions from their original 1994 content. There are numerous, generally useful, cross-references. However, there are some omissions. Although both *neutron star* and *pulsar* have definitions, neither definition indicates that a pulsar is a rapidly spinning, magnetized neutron star. Most definitions one might look for can be found, although terms that have emerged since 1994 are missing, including *extrasolar planets*, *MACHOs* (massive compact halo objects), *WIMPs* (weakly interacting massive particles), and *microlensing*. The entry for Halley's Comet is certainly justified. However, why is there an entry for Kohoutek's Comet, a major cometary disappointment in 1973, but no entries for such spectacular comets as West (1976), Bennett (1970), or Ikeya-Seki (1965)? The work's content is apparently too old to include Comet Shoemaker-Levy 9, which crashed into Jupiter in July 1994, and the work naturally omits 1996's Comet Hyukutake and 1997's Comet Hale-Bopp.

The work includes many useful appendixes, including eclipses, meteor showers, constellations, nearby and bright stars, and so forth. One curious omission from a list of large radio telescopes is the National Radio Observatory Very Large Array near Socorro, New Mexico, which plays a prominent role in such movies as *Contact* and *2010* and which has been fully operational since 1982. In summary, this inexpensive dictionary contains thousands of brief, generally reliable definitions written at a college textbook reading level, but it could have been improved with some effort at updating its content and with a title indicating the true breadth of the terms included. Libraries already owning the *McGraw-Hill Dictionary of Scientific and Technical Terms* may want to think twice before purchasing the smaller title.
—**Richard S. Watts**

1609. **The NASA Atlas of the Solar System.** By Ronald Greeley and Raymond Batson. New York, Cambridge University Press, 1997. 369p. illus. maps. index. $150.00. ISBN 0-521-56127-2.

This volume is an atlas of craters in a coffee-table-sized format. It contains maps of the surfaces of the members of the solar system that the National Aeronautics and Space Administration has probed (every planet except Pluto), and most satellites are included. Only the objects enshrouded with thick atmospheres or volcanically active (the four gas giants: Jupiter, Saturn, Uranus, and Neptune, along with Venus and the Earth) appear uncratered, because they are large enough to have processes that remove them. All the others are cratered as a result of the bombardment by the residue of the early solar system. What a variety of worlds they are—from Io, the volcano-drenched inner satellite of Jupiter, to the tiny airless potato-shaped moons of Mars.

This atlas is a work likely to have a devoted but limited readership. It will gain adherents, particularly among young readers, who retain or may develop interest in space and the neighboring worlds of all kinds. The maps include the names of the features on each planet or satellite. The names were chosen by the International Astronomical Union, the organization responsible for this task. Institutions with libraries devoted to science, discovery, and education would find this a unique and stimulating addition. [R: LJ, 15 May 97, p. 72]—**Arthur R. Upgren**

1610. **Nine Worlds Hosted by Patrick Stewart.** [CD-ROM]. Larkspur, Calif., Palladium Interactive, 1996. Minimum system requirements (Windows version): IBM or compatible 486/33MHz (486/66MHz recommended). Double-speed CD-ROM drive. Windows 3.1. 8MB RAM. 4MB hard disk space (10MB recommended). SVGA, 640 x 480, 256-color monitor. 8-bit sound card. 9600 bps modem (optional). Minimum system requirements (Macintosh version): 68040/25MHz. Double-speed CD-ROM drive. System 7.0.1. 8MB RAM. 4MB hard disk space (10MB recommended). 9600 bps modem (optional). $39.99.

Patrick Stewart, known from his role in the *Star Trek: The Next Generation* series, narrates this interactive tour of the planets. Screens are highly graphic, and sound is a must for using the program because much information is given orally, including instructions on manipulating the program. The main screen offers the user three methods of exploration: by planets, humankind's view, and resource explorer. The planets section provides verbal and text information as well as photographs, images, and video on each planet. Information includes how humans learned about the planet, exploratory voyages, its moons, and physical characteristics. "Interplanetary Tourist" guides one through a lighthearted vacation on the planet, giving a fun postcard and such necessary information as one's weight on the planet and the temperature so a person will know what clothing to carry. The humankind's view is a chronological look at astronomy, people, and discoveries through nine periods from the ancients to the future. The program allows scrolling through the time frame and clicking on a specific topic or period for further exploration. The resource explorer provides eight options for related information, which include shareware, publications, points of interest, a quiz, and an online launcher.

The program also has a glossary of more than 180 terms and individuals, audio controls, and an index of topics that are linked within the program. The print function opens a list of topics that can be printed. The program also links to Palladium's proprietary Nine Worlds Website, with links to space-related Webpages, such as newsletters, chat rooms, the National Aeronautics and Space Administration, and labs. The extensive graphics, sounds from classical to modern music, and Stewart's commanding voice make this a captivating program. Although much of the information is not of great depth, it will be useful and hold the interest of and fascinate users. [R: LJ, 15 May 97, p. 112]—**Elaine Ezell**

Climatology and Meteorology

1611. Engelbert, Phillis. **The Complete Weather Resource.** Detroit, U*X*L/Gale, 1997. 3v. illus. maps. index. $49.95/set. ISBN 0-8103-9787-0.

This three-volume set offers excellent value for its modest price. Aimed at students in grades 5 and up, the set approaches the comprehensiveness of a college-level meteorology text in terms of content but not difficulty. By breaking the topics up into 3 volumes, the author has made these complex weather topics simple and easy to understand. Volume 1 covers weather basics: clouds, fog, winds, and other primary meteorology topics. Volume 2 introduces the reader to such topics as precipitation, thunderstorms, tornadoes, hurricanes, temperature extremes, floods, droughts, and optical weather phenomena. The final volume treats weather forecasting, climate, and environmental problems like ozone depletion. Each volume contains a separate glossary, bibliography, and index. These tools provide ready access to information covered and are well laid out and pleasing to use. The set is extensively illustrated with many photographs and line drawings of weather events. The author also describes several easy-to-do weather projects throughout the volumes.

Overall, the set is attractive in design and layout and will please and entice the reader to further explore the science of meteorology. The binding is excellent and sturdy. Bibliographic references are easy to locate and provide good jumping-off points for further student exploration. One minor quibble is that the picture credits do not always reflect the source of the information. For example, on page 251 of volume 2 there is a map depicting "Months of Peak Tornado Occurrence (1950-1990)." This map is not listed in the picture credits for the volume and is unlikely to have been compiled from data collected by the author. Nonetheless, the set is highly recommended for all collections through the university reference level.—**Ralph Lee Scott**

1612. **Glossary of Weather and Climate with Related Oceanic and Hydrologic Terms.** Ira W. Geer, ed. Boston, American Meteorological Society, 1996. 272p. $29.95; $21.95pa. ISBN 1-878220-19-5; 1-878220-21-7pa.

This book is a glossary produced by scientists and teachers of grades K-12. Students will need help to understand the book's contents. An update of *Glossary of Meteorology*, also by the American Meteorological Society (1959), this volume has fewer entries than the older one. Geer not only covers meteorology but oceanography and hydrology as well. All entries are nicely cross-referenced. There are few errors or debatable points. One such error occurs in the "Acclimatization" entry, which says "see 'Climatization,'" but "Climatization" merely says "same as acclimatization." Also, "Fog" is defined as water droplets, yet "Ice Fog" says it is a type of fog composed of ice particles. In addition, "Heavy Snow" is defined as 4 inches (150 mm), but these measurements are not equal. The relationship between the Kelvin, Absolute, and Celsius temperature scales is nicely defined under "Absolute Zero" but left undefined in the three temperature scale entries.

A list of references is provided. *Glossary of Weather and Climate* is suitable for teachers and scientists, but it is not as extensive as the earlier *Glossary of Meteorology* mentioned above. [R: Choice, May 97, p. 1475]—**Allen E. Staver**

1613. Lyons, Walter A. **The Handy Weather Answer Book.** Detroit, Visible Ink Press/Gale, 1997. 397p. illus. maps. index. $16.95pa. ISBN 0-7876-1034-8.

This entertaining work is a collection of 1,055 questions and answers on weather written in nontechnical language for the general reader. The author's stated purpose is to interest the reader in weather and related phenomena. His definition of *related phenomena* includes aspects of oceanography, seismology, volcanology, and environmental science. This broad definition is evident in the titles of the 17 sections: "Weather Fundamentals"; "Instruments and Observations"; "The Upper Atmosphere and Beyond"; "Clouds"; "Hurricanes and Tropical Storms"; "Thunderstorms, Floods, and Hail"; "Lightning and Thunder"; "Optical Phenomena"; "Tornadoes"; "Cold and Winter Storms"; "Heat and Humidity"; "Earthquakes and Volcanoes"; "Air Pollution and the Environment"; "Weather and the Human Body"; "Weather Forecasting"; "Climate Change"; and "Careers in Meteorology." The questions and answers are not arranged in an organized manner within each section, but an excellent index makes it easy to locate the desired pieces of information.

The questions included in the book vary in relevance to the topic. Although the appropriateness of most of the questions is obvious, there are some that are truly trivial and irrelevant (e.g., "Is there malaria in Switzerland?"). Unfortunately, the answers do not include bibliographic source information, even though there is an 8-page bibliography. The author also notes in the introduction that he was unable to verify some of the weather phenomena that are included in this book. These shortcomings limit the book's usefulness as a reference tool, but school and public libraries should consider purchasing a copy for their circulating collection.—**John R. Burch Jr.**

Geology

1614. **McGraw-Hill Dictionary of Geology and Mineralogy.** Sybil P. Parker, ed. New York, McGraw-Hill, 1997. 346p. $16.95pa. ISBN 0-07-052432-7.

The editor has taken the approximately 8,700 definitions of terms in the areas of geology, petrology, and mineralogy from the *McGraw-Hill Dictionary of Scientific and Technical Terms* (5th ed.; see ARBA 95, entry 1493) and has published them in this separate dictionary. She indicates that all terms, definitions, and pronunciations are taken from the parent work.

Acronyms, synonyms, and abbreviations are included, and cross-references are made to related terms. There is also a pronunciation guide for each term, regardless of how common the term may be (e.g., *age, foam, gallery, event*). Definitions of minerals include formula, hardness, and one or more other identifiers, such as color. Each term is defined briefly, often with only a phrase or brief sentence. Some are defined so briefly as to be nearly useless, or the definition requires that one go to a second definition to understand the first definition. The brief definitions make use somewhat awkward, even for someone with a background in geology, because it is often necessary to go from definition to definition to obtain a useful definition of a term.

Included in the appendix are such diverse pieces of information as conversion factors for U.S., metric, and international systems of measurement; a list of some volcanic eruptions since the eleventh century; a list of minerals found in meteorites; and indicator plants useful in mineral prospecting. Of the numerous dictionaries in the field of geology and mineralogy, this may be among the more comprehensive in number of terms. Additional information per term so that the user need not follow terms from definition to definition would enhance its usefulness.—**Ann E. Prentice**

Mineralogy

1615. Schumann, Walter. **Gemstones of the World.** rev. ed. New York, Sterling Publishing, 1997. 271p. illus. index. $24.95. ISBN 0-8069-9461-4.

Gemstones of the World is filled with endsheet diagrams and maps of gemstone types and locations; glossy color photographs; charts ranking gemstones by properties, such as hardness; and substantial background text on many aspects of gemstones. This guide is visually appealing, with excellent photographs and accompanying text. Interesting features of this volume include a list of false names of gems and their corresponding correct names, diagrams of crystal systems, descriptions of optical properties, a section on mining methods and cutting, and descriptions of new varieties of gemstones on the market.

The organization of this book follows that of a field guide, grouping gemstones by their chemical composition. Each group entry includes a list of properties (color, Moh's hardness, crystal system, transparency, refractive index, and absorption spectra), a brief history of deposits and use, gemstones that might be confused with the featured gem, and a full-page photograph of rough and polished varieties. The inclusion of technical properties that can only be measured with sophisticated equipment causes one to wonder what use a gemstone collector or student would have for this work. Also, a geologist or chemist seeking this information might not think to look in a work devoted to gemstones. Even with more information than might be needed, this work is best suited to the interested amateur.—**Jean C. McManus**

Oceanography

1616. **Oceanographic & Marine Resources: 1960-January 1997.** [CD-ROM]. Baltimore, Md., National Information Services Corporation, 1997. Minimum system requirements: IBM or compatible 386. CD-ROM drive. 3MB RAM. 480K conventional memory. 2.5MB hard disk space. Color or monochrome monitor. $1,445.00/yr.

This CD-ROM product is a comprehensive database of more than 550,000 bibliographic records covering multidisciplines related to oceanography and marine life, with a strong emphasis on physical oceanography. Additional topics include but are not limited to law and policy, climatology, mining and engineering, pollution, and energy. The database is a compilation of 11 databases; the 5 most significant ones are the Institute of Oceanographic Sciences Deacon Laboratory/Proudman Oceanographic Laboratory, Plymouth Marine Laboratory/Marine Biological Association Library, GeoArchive subset, SeaGrant Abstracts, and NOAA Library and Information Network. Coverage of North American coasts, sounds, bays, wetlands, and estuaries is thorough, although overall coverage is worldwide. Documented sources include not only books, journals, and periodicals but also monographs, proceedings, government reports, and theses and dissertations. The National Information Services Corporation uses composite records to handle any duplications.

There are three modes for searching: Novice, advanced, and expert accommodate the inexperienced as well as the advanced user. Each search mode displays in a different color combination, and the user can easily toggle between the three levels. The user can also switch between two user-interface languages: English and Spanish. Bibliographic citations provide basic information on each document, including library location, database, and language and translation. There are few abstracts. Entries are well indexed, including keyword. The Autodex (automatic index) assists the user in all three search modes by displaying words close to the term entered; however, the user has the option to turn off this feature. Updates are semiannual and install automatically. A User's Guide and Quick Guide are included. This CD-ROM is a good resource for specialized and large academic libraries and is available for a free, 30-day trial period.—**Elaine Ezell**

Paleontology

1617. **The Complete Dinosaur.** James O. Farlow and M. K. Brett-Surman, eds. Bloomington, Ind., Indiana University Press, 1997. 752p. illus. maps. index. $59.95. ISBN 0-253-33349-0.

The worldwide renaissance in dinosaur studies is approximately 30 years old and is marked by increased efforts to collect, describe, and reconstruct the life histories of dinosaurs. During that time only a few, often idiosyncratic, books with substantial information on these extinct animals were published. Yet since 1990, publications suitable for interested laypeople as well as paleontologists have burgeoned, beginning with *The Dinosauria*, a multiauthored systematic and paleobiological study. A few texts designed for class use have appeared, as have at least three heavy weight tomes, two of which are termed encyclopedias—D. F. Glut's *Dinosaurs: The Encyclopedia* (see entry 1618) and *The Encyclopedia of Dinosaurs* (Academic Press) by P. Currie and K. Padian. Both of these are treasure chests of information with a multiplicity of illustrations. *The Complete Dinosaur* is the third of this trio, all of which bear 1997 publication dates.

Among the nearly 50 authors of articles in this book are some by the editors and authors of the encyclopedias listed above. Together, these contributors are the principal researchers on dinosaurs, and the information found in each of the 43 chapters of *The Complete Dinosaur* is state-of-the-art. The book is divided into six sections: "The Discovery of Dinosaurs," "The Study of Dinosaurs," "The Groups of Dinosaurs," "Biology of the Dinosaurs," "Dinosaur Evolution in the Changing World of the Mesozoic Era," and "Dinosaurs and the Media." The first section examines the earliest discoveries, then moves on to review the occurrences of dinosaurs by continent. The second section answers the classic question of "how do you know where to look?" but goes on to systematic methodologies; dinosaurs in geologic time; and, most significantly, a chapter on molecular paleontology. The third section provides short but readable introductions to each dinosaur group, the basic characters, and some noteworthy biological features. The fourth section strives to look at dinosaurs as though they were living animals. There are chapters on foods eaten, combat, courtship, eggs, growth, physiology, pathology, and trackways. The fifth section looks at the changing configuration of continents during the age of dinosaurs and their contemporaries in several different faunas. A single chapter briefly reviews contrasting theories of dinosaurian extinction. The last section traces the use of dinosaurs in everything from movies to stamps. Here one can find lists of movies, novels, stamp issues country by country, and dinosaur Websites.

Most chapters contain illustrations or photographs, some have tables and cladograms, and all include numerous references. Because references are useful for more than one chapter, the result is some duplication in different chapters. Illustrations are clear but not numerous. A section of 22 color plates shows some old but predominantly avant-garde restorations of dinosaurs in their Mesozoic world, dinosaurs on stamps, dinosaurs in comics, and so forth. There are a chronology of dinosaur discoveries, a glossary, a brief biography of the authors, and an index.

The amount of information in just 750 pages is amazing. This book should be on the shelves of dinosaur freaks as well as those who need to know more about the paleobiology of extinct animals. It will be an invaluable library reference.—**David Bardack**

1618. Glut, Donald F. **Dinosaurs: The Encyclopedia.** Jefferson, N.C., McFarland, 1997. 1076p. illus. index. $145.00. ISBN 0-89950-917-7.

Although there are enough dinosaur names here to send a six-year-old into ecstasy, this 1,000-plus page encyclopedia is much more than a listing of published names: It is the first extensive compilation of data on dinosaur genera. The book begins with a background section on the Mesozoic Era, dinosaurian relationships, the warm-blooded/cold-blooded debate, the relationships of dinosaurs and birds, and the types of evidence that must be considered to develop a biologically meaningful explanation of dinosaurian extinction. The next section is devoted to dinosaurian systematics, especially at the suprageneric level. For most of these groups, Glut provides a diagnosis, a brief description, the geologic age range, the geographic distribution, and included taxa.

However, the majority of the text, in excess of 900 pages, covers genera of dinosaurs, including publications into the mid-1990s. For each genus the basic systematic data are provided, as is a listing of known material, catalog numbers, type species, and name derivation. For most genera, Glut includes a section of comments that form an essential element of the encyclopedia. Here Glut reviews the principal published studies on the genus, the taxonomic and biological questions raised by the material, and the changing interpretations of the fossils. Where necessary, he provides diagnoses of species referred to the genus. There are 35 pages of references and a short glossary.

As useful as the text and references will be, an essential part of this book is the hundreds of illustrations of mounted specimens, isolated bones, restorations, and the like. Readers will gain a sense of the material on which dinosaur groups are based. All illustrations are black-and-white; some, however, are rather dark, but most are good and complement the text. This book presents in one place descriptions, analyses, pictures, and references to the growing group of dinosaurs. This will be a base from which later dinosaur encyclopedias can be developed.

Twenty-five years ago Glut produced *The Dinosaur Dictionary* (see ARBA 73, entry 1460) just as the renaissance in dinosaurian studies was emerging. This is a much more comprehensive work with an altogether different audience in mind. Producing such an immense tome is the product of long-term commitment and vast effort. Literature on dinosaurs is voluminous, and the animals under discussion are geographically widely distributed in many institutions. Two pages of brief acknowledgments show how much help was received from specialists at museums and academic institutions. This book is a welcome resource for all libraries and individuals who seek information on dinosaurs.—**David Bardack**

Physics

1619. **Encyclopedia of Acoustics.** Malcolm J. Crocker, ed. New York, John Wiley, 1997. 4v. illus. index. $475.00/set. ISBN 0-471-80465-7.

This four-volume epic work devoted to the total aspects of the subject of acoustics deserves the highest of recommendations on authorship, clarity, discipline, and interconnectedness. First of all, the hand of James Lighthill, University College, London, is clearly evident here. The editor in chief is Crocker, professor at Auburn University, who instigated the project in the 1980s. Assurances have been received from a member of the editorial team that no subsequent international meeting in the subject was held without Crocker having an updating session with working authors/willing reviewers to attain the goal of a treatment of acoustics that was accessible to the layperson yet technically correct.

Some figures of interest include 180 authors of the 166 chapters and 500 reviewers (of which 150 preferred to remain anonymous). The 4 volumes are made up of different parts. Volume 1 consists of 4 parts: general linear acoustics, nonlinear acoustics and cavitation, aeroacoustics and atmospheric sound, and underwater sound. Volume 2 also has 4 parts: ultrasonics, quantum acoustics, and physical effects of sound; mechanical vibrations and shock; statistical methods in acoustics; and the effects and control of noise. Volume 3's 4 parts are architectural acoustics, acoustical signal processing, physiological acoustics; and psychological acoustics. Finally, volume 4 contains parts on speech communication, music and musical acoustics, bioacoustics, animal bioacoustics, acoustical instruments and instrumentation, and transducers. The list of parts is repeated on the covers of the 4 bound volumes. Each part is a "mini-monograph" that includes an introduction intended to be accessible to a layperson.

The *Encyclopedia of Acoustics* is essential for all science/technology libraries serving lower-division level students and for metropolitan libraries.—**Eugene B. Jackson**

1620. **Handbook of Physical Quantities.** Igor S. Grigoriev, Evgenii Z. Meilikhov, and A. A. Radzig, eds. Boca Raton, Fla., CRC Press, 1997. 1548p. illus. maps. index. $99.00. ISBN 0-8493-2861-6.

What is the coefficient of thermal radiation for moon grounds from the Mare Foecunditatis region at various temperatures? Where to find a complete table of baryons? What is the chemical composition of some irons and steels? The resource for questions such as these is the *Handbook of Physical Quantities*. This immense volume contains numerical information, in tabular and graphical form, on the vast array of the physical universe.

The editors divided the book into topic chapters, each written by an authority on that subject. Chapters on acoustics, thermometry, and pressure of saturated vapors are examples. Each chapter begins with an introductory essay on the topic and ends with extensive references. Tables and graphs are presented with descriptions, explanations of units, and any other parameters pertinent to the data. The index provides access to tables and figures in addition to page references to text material. However, attempting to locate a figure or a table without its corresponding page number is inconvenient.

The book is printed on high-quality paper. The typeface is clear even for small sub- and superscript notations. This is a formidable resource of numerical information. It is well organized, well indexed, and uncrowded. The handbook is highly recommended for any science collection.—**Margaret F. Dominy**

1621. **McGraw-Hill Dictionary of Physics.** 2d ed. Sybil P. Parker, ed. New York, McGraw-Hill, 1997. 498p. $16.95pa. ISBN 0-07-052429-7.

There is nothing unusual in this second, spin-off physics edition from the *McGraw-Hill Dictionary of Scientific and Technical Terms* (5th ed.; see ARBA 95, entry 1493). The 1st edition of this dictionary was cited as a supplementary and updated physics dictionary in ARBA 87 (see entry 1723). Similarly, this volume "concentrates on the vocabulary of those disciplines that constitute physics and related fields," with a special nod to the fact that "the language of physics embraces many unique disciplines which are usually represented in specialized dictionaries and glossaries" (p. v). Parker is well recognized for her fine reference sources crossing many scientific disciplines.

Users of McGraw-Hill titles will find few surprises in this latest contribution, either in coverage or format. The 15 fields that commonly define the breadth of physics are covered: acoustics, atomic physics, fluid mechanics, mechanics, nuclear physics, optics, particle physics, physics, plasma physics, quantum mechanics, relativity, solid-state physics, spectroscopy, statistical mechanics, and thermodynamics. As in other titles, the first part of each definition gives the particular field with which it is associated (e.g., *Euler angles* [mechanics] or *OW unit* [acoustics]). If used in more than one branch of physics, then the general term [physics] is applied. Definitions also include pronunciations, synonyms, acronyms, and abbreviations with alphabetically organized cross-references from the last three items. The definitions are succinct, averaging 25 to 30 words in length with an occasional exception where appropriate to the term's complexity.

The editor claims that the 9,200 entries (down from 11,200 covered in the 1st edition) are up-to-date and "fully define the language of physics" (cover blurb). Fourteen table appendixes include a variety of data both common (e.g., conversion factors, fundamental particles) and not so common (e.g., "Defining fixed points of the International Temperature Scale of 1990 [ITS-90]"; "The 14 Bravais lattices, derived by centering of the seven crystal classes [P and R] defined by symmetry operators"). Unfortunately, the tables as well as the text itself are printed in such a reduced font size that even well-sighted users may find it difficult to read. There are no illustrations or diagrams, and biographies are not included. The volume has a "how to use" introduction, basic definitions of the 15 fields covered, and a pronunciation key. Available only in paperback and reasonably priced, the work is of enough authority to ensure that it should be added to any collection serving students of this rapidly changing discipline.—**Laurel Grotzinger**

1622. Yaws, Carl L. **Handbook of Thermal Conductivity, Volume 4: Inorganic Compounds and Elements.** Houston, Tex., Gulf Publishing, 1997. 372p. index. (Library of Physico-Chemical Property Data). $85.00. ISBN 0-88415-395-9.

This handbook presents thermal conductivity gas phase and solid/liquid phase data for 343 inorganic compounds. The format, functional fits of temperature in graph form, arranged by chemical formula, follows the previous three volumes by this author devoted to organic compounds (see ARBA 96, entries

1821, 1822, and 1823). The preface, in this case, is not an optional read. Because the majority of data are actually estimates, the preface describes the basis for these estimates. Specifically, 66 percent of the solid/liquid phase data are estimated, and 86 percent of the solid phase data are estimated.

In order to determine which graphs are experimental results, estimates, or a combination of both, one needs to check appendix C, "Data Code for Compounds." A more user-friendly approach would be to include code notation on the graphs themselves. Appendixes F and G point the reader to available computer programs for calculating gas and solid/liquid thermal conductivity. There is a useful bibliography. This is a practitioner's volume whose value is probably best determined on a situational basis.

—Barbara Delzell

1623. Yaws, Carl L. **Handbook of Viscosity, Volume 4: Inorganic Compounds and Elements.** Houston, Tex., Gulf Publishing, 1997. 372p. index. (Library of Physico-Chemical Property Data). $75.00. ISBN 0-88415-370-3.

This handbook provides graphs of absolute viscosity of inorganic compounds and elements in liquid and gas phases as a function of temperature. The graphs are arranged by chemical formula; an appendix indexes the compounds by name. Appendixes give coefficients for the equations used in the graphs. Viscosities are given in units of micropoise for gases and centipoise for liquids; conversion factors to English units are given on each graph.

The virtues and faults of this work both stem from the fact that experimental data on gas and liquid viscosities of inorganic compounds are scarce. Thus, one will find here data that are hard to come by elsewhere; however, many of the graphs are based on estimates. The alert reader will notice the remark in the preface that the estimates for inorganics should be considered as rough approximations. However, the graphs themselves give no indication of their source—one must turn to appendix C to find out whether any given graph derives from experimental data or from an estimate, and even here there is no indication of which of the 138 references is the source of the experimental data or estimate for the graph.

An older standard source, *Data Book on the Viscosity of Liquids* (see ARBA 90, entry 1774), gives explicit references to sources of the viscosities it presents, along with evaluations of accuracy. Yaws's book will be useful as an additional source for inorganic compounds, with the caution that the data presented may be approximate.—**Robert Michaelson**

MATHEMATICS

1624. **Assistantships and Graduate Fellowships in the Mathematical Sciences, 1996-1997.** Compiled by the AMS-IMS-MAA Data Committee. Providence, R.I., American Mathematical Society, 1996. 126p. $20.00pa.; $12.00pa. (members). ISBN 0-8218-0189-9. ISSN 1040-7650.

Published by the American Mathematical Society (AMS), this is the 9th issue of *Assistantships and Graduate Fellowships in the Mathematical Sciences* (A&GF), the successor to the former special December issue of *Notices of the AMS*. The publication is primarily intended as a source of information on graduate programs in the mathematical sciences for prospective graduate students and their advisers. Its content will also be useful to others in the mathematical community who are interested in support patterns for graduate education. A&GF is a complement to the annual AMS publications, *Combined Membership List* (see ARBA 97, entry 1412) and *Mathematical Sciences Professional Directory* (see entry 1625).

The book under review begins with an overview of mathematical employment in the 1990s. United States institutions are listed alphabetically by state, followed by Canadian institutions. There is also a section on stipends for study and travel. The data describe assistantship and fellowship support for the academic year 1996-1997. The publication and distribution schedule is designed to provide timely information to applicants for graduate programs and for support for 1997-1998.

Free copies of A&GF are sent to institutional members of the AMS and to other departments of mathematical sciences at four-year institutions listed in the *Professional Directory*. Individual AMS members may request a free copy by returning the form included with their first membership dues notice mailed in June. Also recommended is the publication *Graduate School and You: A Guide for Prospective Graduate Students* (Council of Graduate Schools, 1989) for general information on the graduate school application process. Comments and suggestions to the AMS are welcome.—**Janet Mongan**

1625. **Mathematical Sciences Professional Directory 1997.** Providence, R.I., American Mathematical Society, 1997. 216p. index. $50.00pa.; $40.00pa. (members). ISBN 0-8218-0192-9. ISSN 0737-4356.

The 1997 edition of the American Mathematical Society's (AMS) *Mathematical Sciences Professional Directory* contains 8 major sections. The 1st section, the most detailed, is really a 13-page subdirectory with a separate index. This section not only offers a staff resource page and a list of non-user-specific electronic addresses but a list of officials, committees, and trustees as well. When appropriate, individual terms of service are given.

Sections 2 through 8, the remainder of the directory, consist of 5 alphabetic lists and 2 more indexes. The 2d section is a list of 40 other professional societies in the discipline. As in the 1st section, officers, committees, staff, and trustees are listed with terms of service. Section 3 is a list of government agencies. This list is composed of the Departments of Commerce, Defense, Education, Energy, and Health and Human Services. The National Aeronautics and Space Administration and the National Science Foundation are also listed. Only discipline-related offices are listed under each agency. The 4th section is a list of worldwide reciprocity societies. The order here is alphabetic by continent. The next section is an alphabetic list of all individuals listed in the first 4 sections. Telephone numbers and electronic addresses are included when provided to the AMS. Section 6 is an alphabetic list of academic institutions by state. Degrees in the discipline offered at each institution are given, as well as department chairs. Lists of academic institutions in Canada, Central America, and the Caribbean follow the list of states. The directory closes with an alphabetic list of nonacademic organizations and an alphabetic index of colleges and universities. This feature is most useful if the state or country of the institution is not known.

What is most impressive about this directory is its scope. It includes worldwide organizations of every type in the mathematical sciences. The major indexes, two for individuals and one for college and universities, make this title especially useful to academic libraries that support a major in mathematics.
—**C. Michael Phillips**

1626. **McGraw-Hill Dictionary of Mathematics.** Sybil P. Parker, ed. New York, McGraw-Hill, 1997. 306p. $12.95pa. ISBN 0-07-052433-5.

The *McGraw-Hill Dictionary of Mathematics* contains 4,000 entries that define the language of mathematics. All definitions are drawn from the *McGraw-Hill Dictionary of Scientific and Technical Terms* (5th ed.; see ARBA 95, entry 1493). This dictionary concentrates on terms that are fundamental to the understanding of mathematics and its related fields. It serves as a major compendium of the specialized language that is essential to understanding mathematics and its many distinct branches. The dictionary covers all the branches of mathematics, including those taught in high school and college, such as algebra, geometry, analytic geometry, trigonometry, calculus, and vector analysis, as well as more advanced areas of mathematics, such as group theory and topology. It provides a single comprehensive reference for students, teachers, librarians, writers, scientists, engineers, researchers, and the general public.

Along with definitions and pronunciations, defined terms include synonyms, acronyms, and abbreviations. Such synonyms, acronyms, and abbreviations also appear in the alphabetic sequence as cross-references to the terms. A definition may conclude with a mention of a variant spelling or other such information. Included are a pronunciation key and appendixes on the equivalents of commonly used units for the U.S. Customary System and the metric system; conversion factors for the U.S. Customary System, metric system, and International System; mathematical notations with definitions; symbols commonly used in geometry; a common logarithm table, giving log $(a + b)$; values of trigonometric functions; compound amount: $(1 + r)^n$; and regular polytopes in n dimensions.—**Janet Mongan**

36 Resource Sciences

ENERGY RESOURCES

1627. **Energy Balances for Countries in Transition 1993, 1994-2010, and Energy Prospects in CIS Countries.** By the Economic Commission for Europe. New York, United Nations, 1997. 149p. $42.00pa. ISBN 92-1-100743-7. S/N GV.E.97.0.8.

This publication is a valuable statistical contribution in world energy production and consumption. It presents for the first time relatively compatible information about energy balances for the Commonwealth of Independent States since 1993 and energy prospects up to the year 2010. The book contains an introduction, explanatory notes, country and regional tables, summary tables, and an annex. The introduction says that the Energy Data Bank contains energy balances from 1965 to 1990 for the transition economies. Projections for the years 1990, 1995, 2000, and 2010 are received through the end of July. They are incomplete and do not cover all countries. "Explanatory Notes" contains five issues: structure of the energy balance sheet, description of commodities, description of transactions, unit conversion factors and symbols, and a country case example.

The major part of the book has the following structure. The balance of the rows is subdivided into 3 broad parts. The 1st part (rows 1-3) is devoted to primary and equivalent energy sources. The 2d part (rows 4-6) is a condensed version of the energy conversion sector where primary fuels are converted into secondary or derived forms of energy, such as electricity (row 4). The 3d part covers final consumption of derived forms of energy or final energy (row 7). The link between the 1st part and the 3d part is the energy conversion sector (rows 4-6), and care should be taken when entering the relevant primary fuels that undergo conversion before final use. The balance of the columns is divided into 9 different forms of energy and a total column.

Designers used the new standard: the equivalent of assumed conversion efficiencies of 100 percent, 33 percent, and 10 percent for electricity produced by hydroelectric plants (and other nonthermal sources); nuclear power plants; and geothermal heat, respectively. Prior to 1989, efficiencies of 38.4 percent had been used for nuclear, hydroelectric, and geothermal energy. There are 22 countries included in the major part of this book. Regrettably, regions of the former Yugoslavia (one-third of the Balkans) are excluded, as well as Slovenia, which is going to be a member of the North Atlantic Treaty Organization.
—**Ludmila N. Ilyina**

1628. Palmer, Clare. **Environmental Ethics.** Santa Barbara, Calif., ABC-CLIO, 1997. 192p. index. (Contemporary Ethical Issues). $39.50. ISBN 0-87436-840-5.

Since Rachel Carson's *Silent Spring* was published in 1962, environmental issues have moved to the forefront of popular concern. Environmental ethics is one study that "examines how human beings should interact with the nonhuman world around them." This book seeks to provide a reference and review source of information on all aspects of environmental ethics.

This work is divided into 10 chapters and includes a chronology of events that led to the development of environmental ethics, biographical sketches of key individuals, the major issues in environmental ethics (atmospheric pollution, biodiversity, climate change, deforestation, ecosystems, energy resources, and others), environmental law, and codes of practice in environmental ethics. A helpful annotated directory of organizations involved in research and teaching, pressure groups, federal and state agencies, and international organizations is provided. Finally, a listing of reference books, key periodicals, videos, CD-ROMs, software and Websites, a brief glossary, and an index complete the volume.

This book is part of the publisher's Contemporary Ethical Issues series, which features books on journalism, law enforcement, and business as well. It provides a good sampling of facts, biographies, issues, directories, bibliographies, and other basic reference material, which will make it a good addition to libraries, especially because environmental ethics is a relatively new discipline. There is no comparable book, but *Environmental Ethics*, 2d ed. by Joseph R. DesJardins (Wadsworth, 1997) is a good textbook treatment of the subject. Recommended for all public and academic libraries.—**Diane B. Rhodes**

ENVIRONMENTAL SCIENCE

Bibliography

1629. **Bibliographic Guide to the Environment 1996.** New York, G. K. Hall/Simon & Schuster Macmillan, 1997. 770p. $195.00. ISBN 0-7838-1757-6. ISSN 1063-6153.

G. K. Hall's environmental annual, last reviewed in ARBA 94 (see entry 1988), is compiled from the cataloging records of materials acquired and processed in the previous calendar year by the Library of Congress and the New York Public Library. Full bibliographic data are given, items are listed in an integrated main entry format, and New York Public Library holdings are identified. Works in all languages are included, and serials are listed along with book and nonbook materials. The scope is interdisciplinary, with the following topics among those emphasized: conservation, endangered species, energy, environmental laws and legislation, and pollution. Interest in these disciplines varies from students writing reports to lawyers interpreting public policy. This authoritative resource's wide-ranging usefulness and appeal will dictate purchase by many libraries. (See entry 109 for a thorough review of the series.)—**Ed Volz**

1630. **Free Market Environmental Bibliography 1995-1996.** 4th ed. Washington, D.C., Competitive Enterprise Institute, [1996]. 116p. $10.00pa. ISBN 1-889865-00-1.

This bibliography lists books and articles dealing with environmental issues, and in particular the potential for free market environmentalism (FME) to deal with current environmental problems. The FME movement believes that government involvement in environmental issues through regulation ultimately results in even more environmental woes, whereas free market enterprise is the best avenue for ensuring environmental quality. The bibliography was compiled by the Environmental Studies Program at the Competitive Enterprise Institute to provide a reading list for those interested in FME. The compilers admit in their foreword that this should be considered a work in progress, which is likely missing some pertinent articles that they hope to include in future editions. They invite the reader to suggest additions and provide complete contact information.

The bibliography is divided into 12 broad sections containing citations identified as either books, articles, or studies. Each section is preceded by a short essay on the section topic that identifies the major points of key readings. Excerpts of selected works are highlighted in colored boxes to tempt the reader to read further. The 12 sections include free market environmental theory; property rights; land management; forests; fisheries; wildlife management; water policy; pollution; solid waste, hazardous waste, and recycling; environmental risks; environmental education; and environmentalism, economics, and other topics.

The works included in the bibliography range from essays to college textbooks. There is no attempt at balance by including works from the opposing view, but the editors make no pretense at being balanced. The literature included has been selected simply to further the FME movement, but this bibliography should complement nicely other works that promulgate saving the environment through strict governmental involvement. [R: Choice, July/Aug 97, pp. 1779-80]—**Michael G. Messina**

Biography

1631. **World Who Is Who and Does What in Environment & Conservation.** Lynn M. Curme, comp. Nicholas Polunin, ed. New York, St. Martin's Press, 1997. 592p. $75.00. ISBN 0-312-17448-9.

This valuable reference book profiles 1,300 major figures from around the world in environment and conservation. Persons included were selected by recommendations of the World Conservation Union, World Wildlife Fund International, United Nations Environment Programme, and other organizations. Biographies were prepared from detailed questionnaires sent to each person profiled. Each includes career and achievement information, relevant publications, language capabilities, willingness to consult, address, and telephone and fax numbers. There is a detailed appendix by specialty: Examples are advocacy, environmental; fish, early life history; fisheries; flows, hydraulic research of; forestry; nature conservation; nutrient cycling; rehabilitation, environmental; sustainable agricultural development; taxonomic botany; whale conservation; wilderness; wildlife (plant and animal); wind energy; and women. Even some unusual specialties are noted (e.g., "Zen teaching" for Peter Matthiessen). There is also an appendix by country, which is broken down by state for the United States.

Although this reviewer found herself wondering why some individuals considered notable were not included, there is no way the book could be complete, especially in its premier edition. This is a useful book for libraries and for the many organizations and agencies that need to know who's who in environment and conservation.—**Marquita Hill**

Dictionaries and Encyclopedias

1632. Dunster, Julian, and Katherine Dunster. **Dictionary of Natural Resource Management.** Vancouver, B.C., University of British Columbia Press, 1996. 363p. illus. maps. $74.95. ISBN 0-7748-0503-X.

The field of natural resource management is growing and encompassing more and more disciplines. *Dictionary of Natural Resource Management* provides the exact meaning attached to natural resource management terms in a single source. More than 6,000 entries are included. This dictionary is thoroughly cross-referenced and illustrated. Formulas are included for certain technical terms (e.g., *Sorenson Quantitative Index*). The dictionary encompasses terminology from the following disciplines: forestry, landscape ecology, wildlife management, mycology, forest fire control, pedology, conservation biology, silviculture, pest management, botany, geology, geomorphology, and engineering and harvesting.

A detailed set of appendixes covers the classification of organisms, geologic time scales, and conversion factors. A synopsis of classification divides living organisms into five kingdoms as well as breaking down the classification of plants. The animal kingdom is subdivided into phylum, subphylum, class, subclass, and order. Appendix 2 outlines the geologic time scales, including the Mesozoic Era and its various periods (Jurassic, Triassic, and so on). Appendix 3 includes valuable tools for interpreting data, such as conversion tables and measurements. *Dictionary of Natural Resource Management* will be an essential reference work for resource managers, planners, resource lawyers, students, decision-makers, and anyone involved in any aspect of managing the planet's natural resources.—**Marilynn Green**

1633. Gilpin, Alan. **Dictionary of Environment and Sustainable Development.** New York, John Wiley, 1996. 247p. illus. maps. $65.95. ISBN 0-471-96219-8.

Dictionary of Environment and Sustainable Development is well organized and easy to understand. This dictionary covers information pertaining to environmental issues and protection. "Key Terms and Concepts: A User's Guide" introduces the reader to major environmental topics. Gilpin follows with a list of abbreviations that are frequently used throughout the work. This list identifies related organizations and terms. In the main dictionary section, the definitions are clear yet concise. Gilpin includes cross-references when applicable. Of course, the dictionary terms are in alphabetic order. Throughout the main dictionary section, Gilpin has interspersed charts, diagrams, and illustrations. All are precise and easy to read and are placed near their identified dictionary terms. Various countries' environmental policies are arranged chronologically in charts. These charts are informative and reflect a positive trend toward international environmental concern and regulation. This work will be useful for anyone researching an environmental topic. Students in introductory environmental studies courses will find this dictionary to be a convenient and efficient reference tool.—**Marjorie H. Jones**

1634. **Glossary of Environment Statistics.** By the Department for Economic and Social Information and Policy Analysis, Statistics Division. New York, United Nations, 1996. 83p. (Studies in Methods, Series F, no.67). $25.00pa. ISBN 92-1-161386-8. S/N 96.XVII.12.

The *Glossary of Environment Statistics* is a United Nations' publication created so that statisticians could have a quick reference tool for terms pertaining to environmental data production and use. The glossary defines nearly 1,200 terms and includes a list of references that were employed for those definitions not commonly known, which are cited from specific publications. The definitions are brief—usually one or two sentences—and a number of them can be found in such standard works as *The Encyclopedia of the Environment* (see ARBA 95, entry 1765) and the *McGraw-Hill Encyclopedia of Environmental Science & Engineering* (3d ed.; see ARBA 94, entry 1999). However, the volume under review also includes some economic and statistical terms (e.g., *capital accumulation*, *market valuation*, *line transect sampling*) that do not appear in environmental encyclopedias.

At $25, this 83-page thriftily printed paperback is no bargain. It will be useful in the personal libraries of statisticians who do environmental work, and libraries that support such statisticians could consider purchasing it. Most libraries will be able to provide the same information from more general environmental reference sources already on hand.—**Donald A. Barclay**

1635. Lewis, Richard J. **Hazardous Chemicals Desk Reference.** 4th ed. New York, Van Nostrand Reinhold, 1997. 1644p. index. $119.95. ISBN 0-442-02322-7.

The need for knowledge about hazardous properties of common chemicals is driven by a combination of increased public awareness and stricter legislation. Despite the increased interest, even a well-informed person may have difficulty finding this type of information. Many of the available reference sources either give so much data that they require significant training before being used or only offer data on a limited number of compounds. This work is an excellent balance between these two extremes and should be very useful to readers from a broad range of backgrounds.

This is the 4th edition of a reference source that has been popular in the past (see ARBA 95, entry 1781, ARBA 92, entry 1727, and ARBA 88, entry 1748). The new edition maintains the same format, which has worked well previously, but the data has been significantly updated. The author has added 400 more compounds, bringing the total number of chemicals covered to over 5,000, and has also revised the information for many of the other entries. One particularly helpful change is the addition of many new synonyms, making it easier to locate compounds.

At a time when the public is increasingly concerned about toxicity, flammability, explosion, and reactivity hazards of chemicals, this book should be a useful resource for readers who have some background in chemistry and biology. It is an appropriate purchase, even for libraries that aim to maintain only a basic reference collection in this area.—**Harry E. Pence**

1636. Porteous, Andrew. **Dictionary of Environmental Science and Technology.** 2d ed. New York, John Wiley, 1996. 635p. illus. $22.95pa. ISBN 0-471-96075-6.

This dictionary focuses on terms in science and technology that are relevant to environmental protection and resource management. The author's hope is that the book's definitions will contribute to environmental literacy. At the same time, he points out that the reader needs some acquaintance with ecology, economics, sociology, technology, physics, and chemistry. A useful aspect of the dictionary is that the definitions often go beyond simple definitions to brief descriptions. For example, *acid mine drainage* is not just defined but described, and a page-and-a-half are used to describe *acid rain*. Numerous figures and tables make the book more interesting while also providing more information. As the title implies, not just environmental but technological terms are discussed. For example, there are good descriptions of *wind energy* and *solar energy*. The term *sewage treatment* includes a brief description (with figures) of the technology used in treatment. One caveat is that the author is British, examples given are often relevant to Great Britain, and when laws are described, they are British laws.—**Marquita Hill**

1637. **Routledge French Dictionary of Environmental Technology: French-English/English-French. Dictionnaire Anglais du Génie de l'Environnement.** New York, Routledge, 1997. 260p. $140.00. ISBN 0-415-13918-X.

Compiled by an authoritative team of professional terminologists, this dictionary covers more than 25,000 terms and references in one volume. The contexts include 70-plus subject areas, such as analysis and sampling, waste management, policy and legal instruments, safety engineering, general environmental management, marine pollution, noise pollution, air quality control, recycling, and alternative energy sources.

This dictionary is arranged alphabetically. Both abbreviations and their full forms are linked together with cross-references. Abbreviations and acronyms are written in uppercase letters. They appear after entry terms of the same form written in lowercase letters. For example, "cap" comes before "CAP," which stands for controlled-atmosphere packaging. Parts of speech are indicated. If there is more than one technical definition for the same term, multiple labels are given as appropriate. Gender indications are provided for every French noun. One significant omission is the lack of pronunciation. A unique feature is the comprehensive labeling of subject areas. Labels are indicated in uppercase. The layout is clear, and the typography is also clear and concise. Entries appear in bold typeface.

The *Routledge French Dictionary of Environmental Technology* is an authoritative reference source of the highest quality. It is more comprehensive in its coverage than the *Vocabulary of Enzyme Engineering* (see ARBA 95, entry 1618). This reference tool should be useful to a wide group of environmental professionals. The dictionary will certainly enhance communication among those committed to finding realistic solutions to global environmental problems.—**Marilynn Green**

1638. Wells, Edward R., and Alan M. Schwartz. **Historical Dictionary of North American Environmentalism.** Lanham, Md., Scarecrow, 1997. 226p. illus. (Historical Dictionaries of Religions, Philosophies, and Movements, no.14). $47.00. ISBN 0-8108-3331.

According to the preface, "this volume follows in a series of new historical dictionaries of religions, philosophies, and movements. It is neither a dictionary of environment science nor environmental issues, but rather an attempt to capture the people, places and events that have contributed to the development of environmentalism around the world." Both authors mention more complete dictionaries of environmental science—for example *Encyclopedia of Environmental Studies* (see ARBA 92, entry 1773) or the *Green Encyclopedia* (see ARBA 94, entry 1996)—but nothing more recently published, such as *The Grolier Library of Environmental Concepts and Issues* (see ARBA 97, entry 1427) or *Conservation and Environmentalism: An Encyclopedia* (see ARBA 97, entry 1426). In examining the article on Chernobyl, the worst nuclear power plant disaster in history, one finds that its length is identical to the article on China's one-child program. There is no need to discuss this skimpy article on Chernobyl; it is sufficient to say that this nuclear disaster not only "rocked the Soviet Ukraine," but also Russia and Belarus: Thousands of people were forced to leave both republics. Statistics provided in this article are not accurate. This volume adds very little to the voluminous scholarly and reference literature on the environment.—**Bohdan S. Wynar**

Directories

1639. Shipp, Steve. **Rainforest Organizations: A Worldwide Directory of Private and Governmental Entities.** Jefferson, N.C., McFarland, 1997. 184p. index. $38.50pa. ISBN 0-7864-0381-0.

This volume is a directory of more than 120 organizations worldwide that deal with rainforests. The organizations range from federal agencies, such as the U.S. Department of Agriculture, to private groups that charge memberships dues, such as the Sierra Club, to professional organizations requiring certain educational criteria for membership, such as the Society of American Foresters. Geographically, groups dealing with all types of rainforests from lowland to montane, temperate to tropical, and both wet and dry, are included. Information for each organization includes names of principal contacts, their address, telephone and fax numbers, and e-mail and Internet addresses where available. For the larger groups, their mission statement, their publications, and their history and current projects are included. Entries are arranged in alphabetic order only, so readers looking for organizations concerned with specific forest types or geographic areas will have to depend upon the index for help. Organizations listed in the main body of the book are cross-referenced in the index as well.

Four appendixes are included that deal with assessment of U.S. tropical forests, the International Tropical Timber Agreement, the history of the Caribbean/Luquillo Forest in Puerto Rico, and the Hawaii Tropical Forest Recovery Act. A useful introduction acquaints the reader with the types of rainforests and the current major issues and lists the countries containing extensive rainforest acreage. An extensive bibliography rounds out the book.

Organizations included are the more responsible groups, whereas the radical extremist environmental groups are omitted. This lends the directory an air of professionalism and respectability for readers interested in serious rainforest issues. This book is recommended for anyone wanting to learn more about rainforests as a good first-source reference.—**Michael G. Messina**

Handbooks and Yearbooks

1640. **Greening the College Curriculum: A Guide to Environmental Teaching in the Liberal Arts.** Jonathan Collett and Stephen Karakashian, eds. Washington, D.C., Island Press, 1996. 328p. $40.00; $22.00pa. ISBN 1-55963-421-9; 1-55963-422-7pa.

In a unique attempt to foster environmental literacy across the curriculum, this resource is jam-packed with good ideas and useful resources. Arranged in 12 chapters, the first and last are about reinventing education and the classroom. Each of the other 10 chapters covers a discipline: anthropology, biology, economics, geography, history, literature, media and journalism, philosophy, political science, and religion. Each chapter gives a brief introductory essay about integration of environmental issues into an area of expertise, then gives detailed course plans for at least one lower- and one upper-division course. At the end of each chapter, an annotated resources section lists many readings and a few even provide Internet sites, films, computer programs, and pertinent organizations. The bibliographies do not have any references more recent than 1995. The book is not indexed. Because this book is specifically geared toward teaching in the liberal arts, it is recommended for faculty development and circulating academic collections. [R: Choice, Jan 97, p. 740]—**Christine Drew**

1641. **The Guide to Graduate Environmental Programs.** By the Student Conservation Association. Washington, D.C., Island Press, 1997. 447p. index. $29.95; $16.95pa. ISBN 1-55963-339-5; 1-55963-340-9pa.

This book is written for the undergraduate interested in applying to graduate environmental programs. Part 1 has 3 concise and useful chapters providing the undergraduate student with information on how to research graduate schools, the application process, and an overview of different program areas. Most of the volume is the "program profiles" in part 2. The profiles, arranged alphabetically by university, were gathered by the Student Conservation Association (SCA) from a questionnaire sent to participating schools. More than 150 American graduate schools with over 400 programs are listed. Each profile contains a brief general overview of the university, detailed information about programs offered, faculty and admissions contacts, World Wide Web addresses and e-mail addresses, background facts about the program, areas of specialization available, features of the program, admission and degree requirements, information about the students and faculty affiliated with the program, tuition and financial aid, facilities, and career counseling and job placement information.

An appendix listing "additional programs not profiled in this volume" provides names and contact information only. Part 4 has indexes by state and area of specialization. The information provided in this resource is more detailed than that found in other graduate school guides such as the popular annual *Peterson's Guide to Graduate and Professional Programs* (see ARBA 96, entry 349), but the coverage of schools in SCA's guide is not as complete. For instance, only 15 graduate biology programs are profiled in SCA's guide. Because of its ease of use and reasonable price, this guide is highly recommended for undergraduate libraries and career resource centers.—**Christine Drew**

1642. **Hazardous Substances Resource Guide.** 2d ed. Richard P. Pohanish and Stanley A. Greene, eds. Detroit, Gale, 1997. 800p. index. $198.00. ISBN 0-8103-9062-0.

The lack of a comprehensive work understandable to the public, when coupled with the public's increasing concern over the environment and the effects of chemical materials on humans and their world, resulted in this publication, which is now in its 2d edition. The relatively high cost of this well-conceived and -executed resource may, however, limit its acquisition to specialized libraries, academic libraries, or larger public libraries. Nearly 1,200 hazardous substances are outlined and profiled, indicating the potential dangers and storage of these materials. Entries are arranged in alphabetic order with a minimum of technical and medical jargon. However, the editors have taken care not to oversimplify the vital information presented.

As is true with many Gale publications, the main text or body of the work is preceded by contents listings, an introduction, a statement of the scope of the work, and a list of selected but common abbreviations. Following the introductory information, this expansive document is broken down into 5 major sections covering the following: explanation and understanding of hazardous substances, such as pesticides, solvents, and asbestos; detailed definitions and profiles of chemicals; a list of resources from print and nonprint media; 4 indexes, including by chemical name, resource, and chemical abstract service number; and a glossary and appendix. Twenty-three tables are interspersed throughout the text to highlight and expand upon the information.—**James M. Murray**

1643. **Information Sources in Environmental Protection.** Selwyn Eagle and Judith Deschamps, eds. New Providence, N.J., Bowker-Saur/Reed Reference Publishing, 1997. 280p. index. (Guides to Information Sources). $75.00. ISBN 1-85739-062-8.

This guide to information sources in the evolving and interdisciplinary area of environmental protection effectively covers a broad range of topics from a decidedly European/British perspective. Each chapter describes a coherent subject, resulting in separate discussions of the effects of pollutants and chemicals on humans, animals, water, and atmosphere, respectively. The editors' inclusive approach to the subject of environmental protection results in chapters on such topics as noise as a pollutant, environmental information and decision-making, environmental law and land use, and education and training.

The considerable strength in coverage is somewhat offset by the lack of consistency in style and format throughout the volume. The individually authored chapters differ in style, citation format, and historical depth and give variant weight to the description of broad issues versus the description and annotation of sources. Although this approach means that the individual contributors can highlight what they think most important, it makes the book less likely to be used for ready-reference. The best apparent use for this volume would be to read individual chapters as necessary. Readers will probably find the concise index most useful for finding specific reference book titles, acronyms, and organizations. Although subject headings are included in the index, the chapter arrangement provides better access to topics.

This book will prove useful to collections needing a guide to British sources on environmental protection. It will help students and researchers to get acquainted with specialized areas quickly.

—**Jean C. McManus**

37 Transportation

GENERAL WORKS

1644. **Annual Bulletin of Transport Statistics for Europe and North America 1996, Volume XLVI.** By the Economic Commission for Europe. New York, United Nations, 1996. 235p. $60.00pa. ISBN 92-1-016319-2. ISSN 0250-9911. S/N E/F/R.96.II.E.26.

Last reviewed in ARBA 96 (see entry 1877), this is the 46th edition of transportation statistics for Europe and North America. The coverage includes those countries once comprising the Soviet Union: Georgia, Kazakhstan, the Russian Federation, Tajikistan, and others. It also contains the countries emerging from the breakup of Yugoslavia. General statistics grouped by commodity or means of transport are covered. Some examples are railways, air travel, roads, inland waterways, transportation, pipelines, seaports, and so on. Individual countries also have specific statistics. The volume uses three languages—English, French, and Russian—for ease of use for the researcher. The most recent statistics are dated 1994, with comparative statistics from 1993 and 1990. An appendix with definitions of many terms encountered in the volume rounds out the work. These definitions are especially useful for researchers that may need comparative statistics for transportation methods with which they may not be familiar. There are numerous instances, as noted in the previous review, of statistics being unrecorded. This is not the fault of the United Nations, the publishers of this work, but the unavailability of the statistics themselves.

This work continues to provide useful comparative statistics for transportation-related issues, along with the interesting statistics recorded for each country. This work is recommended for any library with a need for comparative statistics or transportation-related information.—**Gregory Curtis**

AIR

1645. **Pockets: Aircraft.** By David Jefferis. New York, DK Publishing, 1997. 128p. illus. maps. index. (DK Pockets). $6.95pa. ISBN 0-7894-1496-1.

DK Publishing has enlarged its original selection of 4-by-5-inch, full-color pocket book titles with a guide to aircraft. The choices of topics, pleasing layout, crisp-clear photographs, and labeled drawings and schematics are well worth the dollar increase in price over the original set, which sold for $5.95. Each book follows a pattern: color-coded sections, illustrated text, running heads, and annotations. The reference section at the end stresses peripheral information with a timeline of aircraft development. The publisher continues to respect the intelligence and to anticipate the needs of children by challenging and enticing the reader to turn another page, read another fact, and add to a growing base knowledge of the subject. In this guide, the author stresses the growing sophistication and purpose of the lighter-than-air devices that preceded airplanes. He anticipates the kinds of questions children will ask about flying aces and their deeds. In each book, a glossary and an index introduce children to the types of data that quality reference works should include. The main entries are brief enough to cover central facts, such as the uses of aircraft for peacetime tasks as well as for war.

Since the publication of the first set of pocketbooks, DK's editors have made no attempts to address weaknesses, particularly the lack of phonetic spellings of unfamiliar names of airplane types and parts. Also puzzling is the deletion of color in the reference section, particularly troubling on pages 104-05, a dull pair of pages in contrast to the main text. Still muddling the quality of DK reference works in the heyday of inclusion is the absence of women in its illustration of the operation and maintenance of aircraft.—**Mary Ellen Snodgrass**

1646. Sterling, Christopher H. **Commercial Air Transport Books: An Annotated Bibliography of Airlines, Airliners, and the Air Transport Industry.** McLean, Va., Paladwr Press, 1996. 303p. index. $65.00. ISBN 0-9626483-9-6.

In 1986 and 1988, Myron J. Smith produced the first two volumes of *The Airline Bibliography* (see ARBA 89, entry 1684, and ARBA 87, entry 1732). This title is and will remain one of the most extensive bibliographies on commercial air transportation. One of its strengths is the extensive coverage of the periodical literature. As time has gone on, there has been a need for an update of this fine work.

Sterling's book, although excellent, does only a partial job because it is limited to English-language books, monographs, reports, and serials. Works of fiction, children's literature, and engineering and highly technical works are excluded. Its 2,707 annotated citations are listed in 9 groupings: history, airliners, airlines, airline operations, regulation, air mail, airports, periodicals, and bibliographies. The bibliography covers a century's publication output, from 1894 through 1995. An outstanding feature is its "star rating" system indicating relative levels of importance of each book. This is supplemented by an appendix in which 16 authorities in the field list their dozen favorite airline and airliner books. The volume will find heavy use from book collectors, book dealers, and librarians who wish to build their collection in this field. [R: Choice, April 97, p. 1316]—**Robert J. Havlik**

GROUND

1647. McShane, Clay. **The Automobile: A Chronology of Its Antecedents, Development, and Impact.** Westport, Conn., Greenwood Press, 1997. 222p. illus. index. $69.50. ISBN 0-313-30308-8.

McShane has compiled a straightforward, year-by-year (more specific dates are not given) chronology of the automobile and the earlier forms of transportation from which it derived, starting with the domestication of draft animals ca.8000 B.C.E. and extending through 1994. Pertinent ancillary industries (especially petroleum and road-building) and businesses created by the automobile (e.g., motels and all the various drive-ins) are also included. The work treats both the technological and the socioeconomic aspects of the motor car evenhandedly.

The entries are terse (sometimes leaving the reader wishing for more detail) and clear. A thorough index to topics, persons, firms, and places provides reference access to the contents. A selection of statistical tables and a directory of United States and Canadian automobile museums are useful appendixes.

The book's most serious drawback is its complete lack of documentation; not even a basic bibliography is provided. Research libraries may find this to be a significant liability. Public libraries should find the book useful; it is enjoyable for browsing as well as for a reference tool, and it can provide much amusement for trivia fans. Where else can one easily find the answer to the question "Who was the first American pedestrian killed by a car?" Answer: one H. H. Bliss in 1899 (in New York City, and the vehicle was a taxi—is anyone surprised?).—**Paul B. Cors**

1648. **Standard Catalog of American Cars, 1946-1975.** 4th ed. Ron Kowalke, ed. Iola, Wis., Krause Publications, 1997. 976p. illus. $34.95pa. ISBN 0-87341-521-3.

The *Standard Catalog of American Cars* series has become a basic tool in identification and specifications of makes and models of cars and as a basis for at least preliminary research on them. This 4th edition continues the original policy of building and adding to the database with the help of many specialist members of the Society of Automotive Historians, museum curators, restorers, club technical specialists, and individual owners. Both format and data vary from edition to edition; the basic information stays the same except for needed corrections, additions, and so forth. This edition includes many additional illustrations (black-and-white and color), a few new dream cars, Indianapolis 500 winners, Indy pace cars, and factory lightweights (cars modified for drag racing). Deleted are lists of car clubs and museums, no real loss because these are readily available elsewhere and change too often to be reliable in a volume designed to last for five or more years. Pages of price estimates, listed by condition categories, are grouped together rather than placed with each make, model, and year, and are heavily and realistically revised, mostly upward. In sum, this is an excellent revision of a basic tool in the field, at a most reasonable price.—**Walter C. Allen**

1649. **32nd Annual Steam Passenger Service Directory: A Guide to Tourist Railroads and Railroad Museums.** Waukesha, Wis., Kalmbach Publishing, 1997. 404p. illus. index. (Railroad Reference Series, no.19). $14.95pa. ISBN 0-89024-309-3.

Kalmbach Publishing's *Steam Passenger Service Directory* is as important to travelers seeking railroad-theme attractions as the Fodor's or Michelin guides are to travelers in general. Despite the limited scope implied by "steam passenger service," the directory actually tries to cover all the important tourist railroads, historic trolley lines, railroad museums, and public model train exhibits in the United States and Canada. The 1997 edition includes approximately 400 of these attractions, ranging from small depot museums to preserved railroads offering steam, diesel, and trolley excursions. The directory is arranged alphabetically by state or province and then by town, making it particularly useful to people planning trips.

Each entry occupies a single page and provides a surprising amount of detailed information, including photographs, brief descriptions, hours, train schedules, admission costs, lists of equipment on display, specific instructions on how to reach the attractions, names of people to contact, mailing addresses, telephone numbers, Internet addresses, fax numbers, and e-mail addresses—not to mention locomotive radio frequencies for tourists who want to eavesdrop on the engineers. Through a series of 20-some standard icons, entries also indicate whether attractions offer handicapped accessibility, car and bus parking, gift shops, refreshments, restaurants, dining cars, guided tours, picnic areas, excursions, and brochures by mail, as well as which credit cards they accept and whether they are listed on the National Register of Historic Places. The directory is indexed by the name of the attraction.

Steam Passenger Service Directory provides an excellent and unbiased balance of coverage and a vast amount of useful information, all at a modest price. It is the best book of its type and a standard work in the field.—**Frederick A. Schlipf**

1650. Willson, Quentin. **Classic American Cars.** New York, DK Publishing, 1997. 192p. illus. index. $29.95. ISBN 0-7894-2083-X.

Classic American Cars is primarily a coffee-table book for the mildly interested layperson, not really of much use to the researcher of automotive history or development. Content is limited to 60 cars, from the 1943 wartime Jeep through the 1978 Cadillac Seville. There is a chapter of commentary on "The Most Influential Cars in the World" (nearly all American) and two pages on "Future Classics" (seven American candidates). This is followed by two- or four-page spreads on the individual classics, from such obvious examples as the 1957 Chevrolet Bel-Air and 1965 Chrysler 300L to the less obvious 1958 Rambler Ambassador and the 1971 Chevrolet Nova SS. Each entry offers at least one large profile photograph; front and rear views; and details of engine, interior, and so on. The captions and comments are well written and to the point. There are brief specifications also. The captions point out unique or unusual features. What makes the volume of at least some reference use for the nonspecialist using a general collection is the high quality of the illustrations. They are some of the best available short of usually more expensive single-marque works.—**Walter C. Allen**

WATER

1651. Paine, Lincoln P. **Ships of the World: An Historical Encyclopedia.** New York, Houghton Mifflin, 1997. 680p. illus. index. $50.00. ISBN 0-395-71556-3.

In many respects the story of shipping is the story of mankind. Who would dispute, for instance, the role of the *Santa María* in the discovery of North America; and of the *Victoria*, Magellan's ship, in revolutionizing global relationships? The *Thermopylae* brought tea from China, lessening the distance from Britain to Australia to a mere 69 days. The *Titanic* lives on in our imagination, providing enduring insights into social stratification, emigration, and human behavior in response to disaster and tragedy.

Ships of the World provides an excellent tool of first recourse for all users seeking information on more than 1,000 individual vessels throughout history, including those in literature (listed separately). Paine credits numerous named advisors as well as unnamed librarians from the public libraries of New York, Brooklyn, and Portland, Maine. Transportation as diverse as the *Bounty* and Darwin's *Beagle*, the Skuledev ships from the Viking era, the *Gjøa* (in which Roald Amudsen first traversed the Northwest Passage), the *Bathysphere*, and the *Queen Mary* (now a floating hotel and museum to a recently bygone era), all are to be found within its pages. Numerous entries are illustrated, and 16 pages of color plates are in the centerfold. Maps, chronologies, and a glossary are provided, as well as an index. For each vessel, basic specifications are given, followed by a commendably readable article and a source reference or two (full citations are provided in the bibliography). This approach is excellent because it allows the casual reader to glean a general understanding in a minute or so, while at the same time directing the more serious student to fuller material. Literary ships include several in novels by children's author Arthur Ransome, Hillaire Belloc's yacht *Nona* (which actually existed), the legendary Flying Dutchman, and the Yellow Submarine of Beatles fame.

The index is easy to use, listing the names of ships, persons, places, wars, and other topics. It omits, however, the Seven Stones and the Isles of Scilly (notorious for numerous shipwrecks) off Britain's Land's End, although these places are mentioned in the entry for the *Torrey Canyon* (the world's first supertanker disaster). Users should not give up if the ship they seek is not found under the entry heading they expect, but should consult the index. For example, the *Merrimac* is entered under its later name *Virginia*; the *Stefan Batory* is briefly mentioned in the article on the *Batory*, which it succeeded. Although abbreviations for specifications are given, a fuller list is needed, because terms such as RMS and CSS are not universally understood, particularly in a work intended for so general a readership. No explanation is provided why one of the two ships named *Queen Elizabeth*, but not the other, is labeled HMS. It is also distracting, at the head of individual entries, for these abbreviations to precede the names. Names of persons used as names of ships are entered directly rather than inverted. In the list of literary ships, one regrettable omission is *Noah's Ark*, which deserves mention for several reasons, not least its technical specifications (which disaccord with the traditional picture) and of the efforts over time to locate it. Users seeking "world's first" records can peruse the chronology of "Maritime and Related Technology," which ominously lists, in 1958, the first commercial transatlantic jet plane service. A separate listing of records for size, speed, and so forth would be a useful addition.

This work is most suitable for academic, public, and school libraries. Indeed, all libraries serving a general readership will welcome it. Users should be advised, as the preface states, that it is selective rather than exhaustive.—**Ian Fairclough**

Author/Title Index
Reference is to entry number.

A&E entertainment almanac, 1997, 1264
A-Z of contract clauses, 531
A-Z of horror films, 1297
Aaker, Everett, 1276
Abate, Frank R., 993
Abate, Randall S., 558
Abbey, Cherie D., 21
ABC-CLIO companion to the disability rights movement, 775
ABC-CLIO companion to the 1960s counterculture in America, 437
Abortion, 1996 ed, 753
Abortion & reproductive rights [CD-ROM], 754
Abridged Dewey decimal classification & relative index, 13th ed, 579
Aby, Stephen H., 782
Academic American ency, 36
Achar, Rajani, 178
ACS style gd, 2d ed, 872
Action! the action movie A-Z, 1293
Acton, Edward, 481
Acts of the Apostles, 1370
Adamec, Ludwig W., 110
Adams, Bruce, 731
Adams, McCrea, 1059
Aday, Kathryn L., 757
Aday, Ronald H., 757
Addison-Wesley sci hndbk, 1412
Address bk for German genealogy, 6th ed, 363
Adelman, Irving, 1108
Adolescence: the survival gd for parents & teenagers, 802
Africa, 103
Africa in figures 1996, 102
Africa S of the Sahara 1997, 26th ed, 108
African acronyms & abbrevs, 104
African American almanac, 346
African American almanac, 7th ed, 335
African American ency suppl, 336
African-American orators, 337
African American theatre dir, 1816-1960, 1328
African art, 956
African intl relations, 2d ed, 699
African studies companion, 2d ed, 105
African traditional religion in S Africa, 1344
African writers, 1167
Aghion, Irene, 1257
AIDS, 1996 ed, 1559
Aldred, Heather E., 1561
All music gd, 3d ed, 1228
All music gd to country, 1230
All music gd to rock, 2d ed, 1238
Allen, Chris, 106
Allison, Jonathan, 1174
Allison, Kathleen Cahill, 1564
Allison, Stephen, 1401

Almanac of ...
   business & industrial financial ratios 1996, 27th ed, 177
   the executive branch 1997/98, 642
   the unelected, 649
Alternative advisor: the complete gd to natural therapies & alternative treatments, 1544
Alternative medicine resource gd, 1547
Altman, Susan, 338
AMA style gd for business writing, 873
America in histl fiction, 1114
America in so many words, 1000
American assn: yr-by-yr stats for the baseball minor league, 1902-52, 738
American Bird Conservancy's field gd to all the birds of N America, 1459
American bk trade dir 1997-98, 596
American casino gd, 1997 ed, 411
American Diabetes Assn complete gd to diabetes, 1562
American electricians' hndbk, 13th ed, 1485
American elves, 1255
American eras: Civil War & Reconstruction, 1850-77, 444
American eras: dvlpmt of the industrial US, 1878-99, 445
American evangelicalism 2: 1st bibliographical suppl, 1990-96, 1383
American expatriate writers, 1127
American Film Inst catalog, within our gates: ethnicity in American feature films, 1911-60, 1288
American govt & pols, 646
American health care in transition, 1502
American Heritage children's thesaurus, 1016
American Heritage dict of idioms, 1006
American Heritage talking dict [CD-ROM], 997
American Horticultural Society A-Z ency of garden plants, 1432
American Indian: a multimedia ency [CD-ROM], 352
American legislative leaders in the West, 1911-94, 650
American lib dir 1996-97, 49th ed, 572
American marketplace, 3d ed, 246
American novelists since WWII, 5th series, 1128
American poets since WW II, 4th series, 1140
American poets since WW II, 5th series, 1141
American presidency [CD-ROM], 668
American salaries & wages survey, 4th ed, 229
American women, 247
American women's almanac, 826
Americans at play, 726
America's best bed & breakfasts, 2d ed, 408
America's best hotels & restaurants, 409
America's religions, 1364
America's top internships, 1998 ed, 221
America's top jobs for people without college degrees, 3d ed, 227
America's top office, mgmt, sales, & professional jobs, 3d ed, 228

America's top-rated cities 1997, 5th ed, 820
America's top-rated smaller cities 1996-97, 2d ed, 821
Ammer, Christine, 1006
Ammon, Bette D., 1090
Amphibians & reptiles of Trinidad & Tobago, 1474
Ancestors: a beginner's gd to family hist & genealogy, 372
Ancient Egypt, 486
Ancient Greeks, 472
Andacht, Sandra, 890
Anderson, James D., 1142, 1185
Andrews, Joyce, 1038
Andrews, Robert, 80
Andrews, Shelly, 1061, 1062, 1063
Andrews, William L., 1129
Anglim, Christopher Thomas, 515
Ankrapp, Betty, 1519
Ann Sheridan: a bio-bibliog, 1274
Annotated catalogue of types of the Univ of Ill. mycological collections (ILL), 1451
Annual bibliog of modern art, 1995, 939
Annual bulletin of housing & bldg stats for Europe & N America 1996, 822
Annual bulletin of transport stats for Europe & N America 1996, v.46, 1644
Answer atlas, 380
Anthony, Michael, 484
Anthropological lit on disc [CD-ROM], 317
Anthropology of religion, 1359
Anti-abortion movement, 755
Antiquarian, specialty, & used bk sellers 1997-98, 2d ed, 597
Antique & collectible buttons, 902
Antique trader's gd to games & puzzles, 891
Antokoletz, Elliott, 1210
Antosz, Lynn, 1516
Applied sci & tech index 1996, 1418
Arakin, V. D., 1045
Arany-Makkai, Agnes, 1043
ARBA gd to subject encys & dicts, 2d ed, 5
Archibald, Chestina Mitchell, 1369
Architecture, 976
Architecture sourcebk, 977
ArchivesUSA [CD-ROM], 430
Area bibliog of China, 112
Argentine novel, 1168
Arkin, William M., 617
Armstrong, C. J., 849
Armstrong, Neil, 45
Arnold, Claude Graveley, 1225
Arnold, Guy, 120
Arnold, H. J. P., 1604
Aromatherapy oils, 1551
Art & architecture in the poetry of Robert Browning, appendix A, 1154
Art & artists of 20th-century China, 967
Art bks, 2d ed, 940
Art diary 97/98, 953
Art index, Nov 1995 to Oct 1996, 968
Art of the ancient Mediterranean world, 957
Arthur Bliss: a source bk, 1211

Articles describing archives & ms collections in the US, 577
Artists communities, 954
Artist's resource hndbk, rev ed, 964
Artwords: a glossary of contemporary art theory, 951
Artz, Joan W., 76
Arweck, Elisabeth, 1343
A's & B's of academic scholarships 1997/98, 19th ed, 285
Asante, Clement E., 850
Asia-Pacific in figures, 10th ed, 811
Asian higher educ, 295
Aspen, Kristan, 1218
Assistantships & graduate fellowships in the math scis, 1996-97, 1624
Associate Pr stylebk & libel manual, 6th ed, 874
Association of American Univ Prs dir 1996-97, 598
Atkins, Beryl T., 1024
Atkins, G. Pope, 695
Atlas of anatomy, English ed, 1523
Atlas of threatened cultures, 318
Atwater, Kevin G., 650
Augsburger, Jeff, 921
Australasia & S Pacific Islands bibliog, 144
Authors & artists for YAs, v.20, 1100
Authors & artists for YAs, v.21, 1101
Autobiographies by Americans of color 1980-94, 347
Automobile, 1647
AV market place 1997, 884
Avery, Christine, 241
Avery index to architectural pers at Columbia Univ [CD-ROM], 970
Avery's choice: 5 centuries of great architectural bks, 971
Avisson bk of contests & prize competitions for poets, 864
Awards, honors, & prizes 1997, 13th ed, 49
Awe, Susan C., 5
Axelrod, Alan, 763
Aycock, Wendell M., 1118

Babiel, Nikolai, 1044
Bacon's mag dir 1998, 46th ed, 876
Bacon's newspaper dir 1998, 46th ed, 877
Bacon's radio dir 1998, 12th ed, 885
Bacon's TV/cable dir 1998, 12th ed, 886
Bahm, Archie J., 1340
Baker, Charles F., III, 472
Baker, Rosalie F., 472
Baker's biogl dict of 20th-century classical musicians, 1197
Balch, James F., 1507
Balch, Phyllis A., 1507
Baldwin, Carl R., 702
Ball, J., 1015
Ball, Robert W. D., 630
Ballard, Ednalou C., 791
Baltics info sources dir 1996, 124
Banham, Joanna, 935
Banks, Robert, 1385
Barbier, Karen, 185
Barbillon, Claire, 1257
Barish, Eileen, 402

Barlowe, Wayne Douglas, 979
Barlowe's gd to fantasy, 979
Barnes, Rik, 410
Barnhart dict companion, v.10, no.1, summer 1997, 1010
Barnhart, Clarence L., 1009
Barnhart, David K., 1000, 1010
Barnhart, Phillip A., 313
Barnhart, Robert K., 996
Barrera, Rosalinda B., 1087
Barrett, David V., 1360
Barron's Russian dict, 1044
Barstow, Jane Missner, 1124
Barthelmas, Della Gray, 434
Baseball pioneers: ratings of 19th century players, 730
Baseball records registry, 728
Basic music lib, 3d ed, 1186
Basic word list, 3d ed, 992
Bassett, Jane, 983
Batalden, Sandra L., 125
Batalden, Stephen K., 125
Batson, Raymond, 1609
Batten, Donna, 49
Battleships of the world, 626
Bauml, Betty J., 711
Bauml, Franz H., 711
Baumohl, Jim, 765
Baxter, Craig, 460
Baxter, Joan, 1301
Baxter, Mark, 562
Beall, Julianne, 579
Beasley, Heather, 272
Beatles memorabilia price gd, 3d ed, 921
Beaton, K. B., 1029
Bed & breakfast ency, 427
Beene, LynnDianne, 1143
Beers, Mark H., 1540
Beider, Alexander, 375
Bela Bartok: a gd to research, 2d ed, 1210
Belmonte, Frances R., 1500
Bendall, Sarah, 394
Benet's reader's ency, 4th ed, 843
Benin, 106
Bennett, Bev, 1420
Bennett, Fordyce R., 1135
Bennett, Ruth M., 191
Bennett, Suzanne, 1106
Bentley, Chantelle, 868
Benyukh, Oleg P., 1047
Benz, Wolfgang, 470
Bercovitch, Jacob, 696
Berent, Irwin M., 362
Berinstein, Paula, 1592
Berkman, Bob I., 575
Berko, Robert L., 703
Berkow, Robert, 1540
Berman, Allen G., 915
Berman, Daniel K., 1249
Berman, Louis A., 1249
Berman, Matt, 1076
Bernhard, Elizabeth A., 274, 764, 792
Bernikow, Louise, 826

Bernson, Carol, 1241
Berry, Barbara, 279
Berry, Dawn Bradley, 513
Berthold-Bond, Annie, 1425
Best bks for YA readers, 1094
Best of the Latino heritage, 358
Betrus, Michael, 218
Bevans, Stephen B., 1350
Bever, Edward, 103
Bewes, Diccon, 500
Biblical quotation & allusion in the canata libretti of
    J. S. Bach, 1245
Bibliographic gd to ...
    anthropology & archaeology 1995, 319
    art & architecture 1996, 941
    black studies 1995, 339
    business & economics 1995, 147
    dance 1995, 1267
    E Asian studies 1995, 109
    educ 1996, 265
    Latin American studies 1996, 139
    law 1996, 509
    maps & atlases 1996, 391
    Middle Eastern studies 1996, 143
    music 1996, 1187
    psychology 1996, 707
    Slavic, Baltic, & Eurasian studies 1996, 126
    tech 1996, 1398
    the environment 1996, 1629
    theatre arts 1996, 1322
Bibliographic index 1996, 6
Bibliography for hist, hist curatorship, & museums, 495
Bibliography of British hist 1914-89, 464
Bibliography of Jane Austen, [new ed], 1153
Bibliography on writing & written lang, 984
Bibo (Pui Bo), Bai, 1034
Bidding dict, 744
Bieber's dict of legal citations, Prince's 5th ed, 516
Bierley, Paul E., 1229
Big bk of opportunities for women, 269
Big broadcast, 1920-50, 2d ed, 887
Billboard 1996 music yrbk, 1205
Billboard's American rock 'n' roll in review, 1239
Billman, Larry, 1268, 1272
Billy Murray: the phonograph industry's 1st great
    recording artist, 1198
Biographical companion to lit in English, rev ed, 1066
Biographical dict of ...
    modern American educators, 266
    professional wrestling, 752
    psychology, 710
Biographical dir of the American Congress, 1774-
    1996, 651
Biographical hndbk of Hispanics & US film, 1277
Biography index, Sept 1995-Aug 1996, 20
Biography today, 1996 annual cum, 21
Biotechnology abstracts: agricultural & environmental,
    1983-Feb 1997 [CD-ROM], 1490
Biskupic, Joan, 526, 529
Bjorklund, Dennis A., 1302
Black Americana price gd, 892

Black bk, 4th ed, 796
Black demographic data, 1790-1860, 342
Black, John, 151
Blackwell gd to recorded contemporary music, 1221
Blair, Karen J., 828
Blanchard, Dallas A., 755
Bliese, Richard H., 1350
Bloedow, Steve, 906
Bloomfield, B. C., 588
BNA's directory of state & fed courts, judges, & clerks, 1997 ed, 521
Bock, Hanne, 517
Bock, Ian, 517
Bodart, Joni Richards, 1081, 1082, 1083
Bogart, Dave, 576
Bogdanov, Vladimir, 1228, 1230
Boice, Daniel, 592
Boire, Richard Glen, 527
Bolles, Richard Nelson, 222
Bonavita, Mark, 742
Book of Amos, 1372
Book of salvias, 1434
Book review digest, Mar 1996 to Feb 1997 inclusive, 65
Booking Hawaii Five-O: an episode gd & critical hist of the 1968-80 TV detective show, 1313
Books & pers online, 1997 ed, 1582
Books for you, 1095
Books from Chapel Hill 1922-97, 595
Books in print 1997-98, 15
Booktalking the award winners: children's retrospective volume, 1081
Booktalking the award winners 3, 1082
Borck, Jim Springer, 7
Botterweck, G. Johannes, 1375
Bourie, Steve, 411
Bowbeer, Anne Aull, 1275
Bowker annual lib & bk trade almanac 1997, 576
Bowker, John, 1357, 1361
Boxing register, 743
Boyd, Alex, 327
Boyd, Margaret A., 931
Bracken, James K., 594
Brand, Juliane, 1059
Brazil, rev ed, 140
Brecka, Shawn, 893
Breining, Greg, 412
Bremer, Ronald A., 364
Bremer-David, Charissa, 946
Brent, Bill, 796
Bressett, Kenneth, 910
Brett-Surman, M. K., 1617
Breuilly, Elizabeth, 1348
Brickell, Christopher, 1432
British Army campaign medals, 630
British cinema sheet music, 1195
British co-operative movement film catalogue, 1289
British dirs, 2d ed, 132
British literary bk trade, 1475-1700, 594
British novel 1680-1832, 1146
British secret servs, 686
British women writers, 1700-1850, 1144

British writers, suppl 4, 1149
Britton, John A., 697
Brockman, Norbert C., 1349
Brod, Joanna, 1080
Brody, Aaron L., 1493
Brook, Barry S., 1188
Brookman US, UN, & Canada stamps & postal collectibles, 928
Brooks, Joan, 878
Broussard, Mark, 741, 742
Brown, Harry L., 1494
Brown, Neil L., 273
Brown, Risa W., 1099
Brown, Thomas J., 444
Brownmiller, Sara, 841
Brownstein, Samuel C., 992
Brownstone, David, 803
Bruccoli, Matthew J., 1127
Bruning, Nancy, 1548
Brunk, Gregory G., 635
Bruno, Leonard C., 1402
Bruntjen, Scott, 17
Bryan, George B., 1157, 1254
Bud Collins' tennis ency, [3d ed], 750
Budapest, 133
Budlong, Tom, 878
Buening, Alice P., 936
Building construction cost data 1997, 55th ed, 1480
Bunch, Bryan, 1557
Burger's medicinal chemistry & drug discovery, 5th ed, 1565
Burgess, William E., 280
Burns, John T., 1441
Burt, Bernard, 405
Burton, Alan, 1289
Burton, T. L., 1156
Burwell, Helen, 1596
Bush, Betsy Hills, 539
Business: name & business type index [CD-ROM], 158
Business & industry [CD-ROM], 189
Business & legal forms for authors & self-publishers, 605
Business multimedia explained, 242
Business pers index, v.38: Aug 1995-July 1996, 167
Business sales leads, 1997 ed [CD-ROM], 248
Butler, J. Douglas, 754
Butler, Marian, 18
Butt, John, 1050
Buttress's world gd to abbrevs of orgs, 11th ed, 1
Buxton, Frank, 887
Bynagle, Hans E., 1330

Calhoun, Milburn, 100
California, 413
Calvert, Stephen J., 1094
Cambridge companion to the Bible, 1377
Cambridge dict of scientists, 1399
Cambridge ency, 3d ed, 37
Cambridge ency of lang, 2d ed, 989
Cambridge factfinder, 2d ed, 38
Cambridge gd to stars & planets, 2d ed, 1605

Campaign & election reform, 679
Campbell, Donal, 134
Campbell, Peter, 1214
Campbell, Robert Jean, 1556
Canadian bks in print 1997, 18
Canadian co hists, v.1, 208
Canadian film & video, 1271
Canadian music & music educ, 1194
Canadian newsmakers 1997, 33
Canadian parliamentary, 683
Cane, Paul W., Jr., 530
Cantarella, Gina Marie, 787
Cardarelli, Francois, 1597
Career discovery ency, 213
Career opportunities in health care, 1512
Career perspectives software series [CD-ROM], 223
Careers in intl affairs, 6th ed, 698
Carl H. Pforzheimer Lib, English lit, 1475-1700, 1997 ed, 1148
Carland, Maria Pinto, 698
Carlson, Barbara, 414
Carlton, R. Scott, 909
Carpenter, Allan, 823
Carpenter, Charles A., 1105
Carroll, Bob, 747
Carroll, Frances Laverne, 574
Carter, Craig, 741
Carty, Dick, 1198
Carvajal, Carol Styles, 1051
Casati, Roberto, 1331
Case, Christopher, 1303
Case, Frederick W., Jr., 1448
Case, Roberta B., 1448
Casino gaming in the US, 724
Cassell dict of cliches, 1018
Cassell dict of Norse myth & legend, 1259
Cassin, Barbara, 1553
Castagno, John, 980
Castronova, Frank V., 25
Cat world, 1465
Catala, Rafael, 1142, 1185
Catalog of catalogs 5, 183
Cate, Thomas, 152
Cates, Jo A., 851
Catholic Internet, USA ed, 1390
Catholicism on the Web, 1391
Cavazos-Gaither, Alma E., 82
CD-ROM for librarians & educators, 2d ed, 282
Celtic baby names, 378
Certification & accreditation programs dir, 270
Chaliand, Gerard, 807
Chalip, Laurence, 725
Chambers, Steven D., 606
Chapman, Antony J., 710
Chapman, Jeff, 1068
Characters in YA lit, 1103
Charles, Jill, 1325
Charlton standard catalogue of chintz, 2d ed, 924
Charlton standard catalogue of Royal Doulton beswick figurines, 5th ed, 925

Charlton standard catalogue of Royal Doulton beswick jugs, 4th ed, 926
Charmed circle: 20-game-winning pitchers in baseball's 20th century, 732
Chase, A. R., 1446
Chaucer's Miller's, Reeve's, & Cook's Tales, 1156
Checklist of American imprints for 1845, 17
Chemical & biological warfare, 607
Chemicals on the Internet, v.1, 1478
Cherniaev, Vladimir Iu., 481
Cherry, R. L., 784
Chesler, Andrew, 79
Chestochowski, Ben, 745
Chevalier, Tracy, 1107
Chidester, David, 1344, 1345, 1382
Child abuse, 1997 ed, 568
Children's catalog, 17th ed, 586
Children's ency [CD-ROM], 39
Children's fiction series, 1088
Children's illus atlas, 1997 ed, 381
Chilton, John, 1235
China, new ed, 111
Chinese filmography, 1296
Chinese 1000, 1022
Chinese synonyms usage dict, 1023
Cho, Elisa, 783
Choices for young readers [CD-ROM], 1086
Christensen, Karen, 721
Christian music dirs: printed music 1997-98, 1244
Christianity in S Africa, 1382
Christophory, Jul, 135
Chronicle of America, rev ed, 435
Chronicle of the cinema, rev ed, 1282
Chronology of European hist, 462
Chronology of medicine & related scis, 1541
Ciment, James, 355
Cities of the biblical world, 1378
City crime rankings, 3d ed, 552
Civil trial practice deskbk, 528
Civil War bks: a critical bibliog, 432
Civil War in bks, 433
Civil War sites, memorials, museums, & lib collections, 448
Clark, David Lindsey, 1220
Clark, Edward, 340
Clark, M., 1030
Clark, Sandra, 1161
Clarke, Peter B., 1343
Classic American cars, 1650
Classic FM gd to classical music, 1222
Claudio, Virginia S., 1422
Clebsch, Betsy, 1434
Clemens, Joe, 906
Clements, Frank A., 689
Cliches, 1019
ClinPSYC: 1980-Dec 1996 [CD-ROM], 712
Clive Barker's A-Z of horror, 1306
Clough, David G., 791
Clough, Leonard G., 791
Clucas, Richard A., 657
Clute, John, 1116

Cockerham, William C., 1524
Code of medical ethics: current opinons with annots, 1996-97 ed, 1537
Cogan, Neil H., 669
Cohen, Richard M., 746
Colander, David C., 152
Cold War ref gd, 508
Coleman, Gordon J., 1412
Collaborative bibliog of women in philosophy, 1332
Collected eds histl series & sets & monuments of music, 1190
Collecting dolls ref & price gd, 917
Collecting in cyberspace, 893
Collector's gd to TV memorabilia, 1960s & 1970s, 922
Collectors value gd to Oriental decorative arts, 890
College hndbk for transfer students 1997, 296
College majors & careers, 3d ed, 316
College.educ: on-line resources for the cyber-savvy, 301
CollegeSource [CD-ROM], 297
Collett, Jonathan, 1640
Collier's ency, 40
Collier's ency 1998 [CD-ROM], 41
Collin, S. M. H., 1574
Collinge, William J., 1384
Collins concise atlas of the world, rev ed, 382
Collins, Bud, 750
Collins, James T., 264
Collins-Robert French-English, English-French dict, 3d ed, 1024
Color of words: an encyclopaedic dict of ethnic bias in the US, 328
Columbia companion to British hist, 465
Columbia ency [CD-ROM], 42
Columbia Univ Dept of Pediatrics children's medical gd, 1554
Comics buyer's gd 1998, 908
Comics values annual, 1998 ed, 907
Commercial air transport bks, 1646
Common birds of E Africa, 1461
Companion ency of geography, 397
Comparative gd to American suburbs, 824
Compendium of histl sources, rev ed, 364
Compendium of soil clean-up technologies & soil remediation cos, 1496
Compilation of state & fed privacy laws, 1997 ed, 543
Complete anime gd, 1307
Complete atlas of world hist, 491
Complete bill of rights, 669
Complete bk of Catholic colleges, 1998 ed, 288
Complete bk of colleges, 1998 ed, 286
Complete bk of everyday Christianity, 1385
Complete bk of personal legal forms, 2d ed, 541
Complete bk of pet names, 1462
Complete bk of small business legal forms, 2d ed, 542
Complete cat health manual, 1464
Complete dinosaur, 1617
Complete dir for people with disabilities, 1997-98, 770
Complete family gd to natural home remedies, 1545
Complete film dict, 1285
Complete gd to American bed & breakfast, 410
Complete gd to whiskey, 1426

Complete hist of our presidents, 658
Complete Marquis Who's Who on CD-ROM [CD-ROM], 28
Complete scholarship bk, 287
Complete weather resource, 1611
Comprehensive annot bk of Mormon bibliog, 1397
Comprehensive dissertation index, 1996 suppl, 844
Comprehensive name index for The American Slave, 341
Concise atlas of the world, 3d ed, 383
Concise conservative ency, 691
Concise dict of ...
    American biog, 5th ed, 29
    biomedicine & molecular biology, 1439
    Indian philosophy, rev ed, 1336
Concise ency biochemistry & molecular biology, 3d ed, 1599
Concise world atlas, 384
Congressional Quarterly almanac, v.52, 670
Congressional Quarterly's gd to the US Supreme Court, 3d ed, 529
Congressional roll call 1996, 671
Congressional staff dir fall 1997, 652
Congressional yrbk 1996, 104th Congress, 2nd session, 672
Connecting cultures, 1093
Conroy, Wendy A., 710
Consolidated bibliog of urban hist, 825
Constitutional law & YAs, 2d ed, 540
Consumer health USA, v.2, 1538
Consumer Latin America 1997, 4th ed, 209
Consumer sales leads, 1997 ed [CD-ROM], 249
Conte, Joseph, 1140, 1141
Contemporary authors autobiog series, v.25, 1061
Contemporary authors autobiog series, v.26, 1062
Contemporary authors autobiog series, v.27, 1063
Contemporary authors on CD [CD-ROM], 1064
Contemporary Canadian authors, v.1, 1169
Contemporary democracy, 638
Contemporary Jewish-American novelists, 1125
Contemporary Latin American artists, 955
Contemporary literary criticism, v.90, 1068
Contemporary novel, 2d ed, 1108
Contemporary popular writers, 1058
Contemporary quotations in black, 78
Contemporary women's issues 1992-July 1997 [CD-ROM], 838
Continuing medical educ dir 1996-97, 1532
Conway, George L., 933
Cook, Chris, 500
Cook, Mary F., 224
Cook, Rhodes, 673
Cooley, Laurel, 6
Cooper, Gail, 281
Cooper, Garry, 281
Copyright laws & treaties of the world 1991-95 suppl, 566
Coral snakes of the Americas, 1475
Cordry, Harold V., 1250
Core collection for small libs, 1077
Corke, Bettina, 35
Cormier, Ramona, 1342
Cornell, Charles R., 20

Corporate & fndn fundraising manual for Native Americans, 3d ed, 793
Corporate fndn profiles, 785
CorpTech CD-ROM dir of tech cos [CD-ROM], 1570
CorpTech explore database [CD-ROM], 1571
Correard, Marie-Helene, 1026, 1027
Corsica, 131
Cosgrove, Holli, 213
Cosmic influences on humans, animals, & plants, 1441
Coulmas, Florian, 984
Counties USA 1997, 662
Country Americana price gd, 894
Country music, 1234
Cowgill, Allison A., 724
Cowlard, Keith A., 467
Cowley, Robert, 616
Cox, C. Brian, 1167
Cox, Elizabeth M., 829
Coykendall, Ralf, Jr., 895
Coykendall's complete gd to sporting collectibles, 895
CPI.Q: Canadian per index [CD-ROM], 75
CPT '97: physicians' current procedural terminology, 1525
CQ's state fact finder 1997, 817
Craft, Donna, 1583
Crafts supply source bk, 4th ed, 931
Craggs, Stewart R., 1211
Crainer, Stuart, 148
Cramer, Clayton E., 342
Cran, Angela, 136
Crane, J. L., 1451
Crane, Nancy B., 875
Crawford, Tad, 605
Crime & the justice system in America, 550
Criminal quotes, 79
Critical companion to the Russian revolution 1914-21, 481
Critical hist & filmography of Toho's Godzilla series, 1294
Crocker, Malcolm J., 1619
Croddy, Eric, 607
Croft, Terrell, 1485
Cross, F. L., 1389
Crossy, Tiffany, 427
Crowley, William R., 1478
Crystal, David, 37, 38, 989
Cullen-DuPont, Kathryn, 563
Cultural atlas of India, 113
Cultural ency of baseball, 733
Culturally diverse lib collections for youth, 1099
Cumulative bk index 1995, 11
Cupboard love: a dict of culinary curiosities, 1423
Curme, Lynn M., 1631
Current biog yrbk 1996, 22
Custard, Ed, 288
Custer & the battle of Little Bighorn, 441
Custy, Mary C., 638
Cutten, Mervyn, 982
Cutting for all! the satorial arts, related crafts, & the commercial paper pattern, 934
CyberDictionary, 1575
CyberHound's gd to ...
  cos on the Internet, 1583
  Internet discussion groups, 1584
  people on the Internet, 1585
CyberTools for business, 163
Cybriwsky, Roman, 461
Cyclamen: a gd for gardeners, horticulturists, & botanists, 1449
Cyclopedia Anatomicae, 978
Cyclopedia of world authors, 3d ed, 1059

D'Agostino, Annette M., 1316
Daily planetary gd 1997, 713
Dakin, Shaun, 204
Dale, Jean, 925, 926
Dance on disc [CD-ROM], 1269
Daniels, David, 1226
Danopoulos, Constantine P., 621
Dardanelles campaign, 1915, 494
Davidson, Pamela, 1181
Davies, Owen B., 1596
Davies, Philip H. J., 686
Davies, Robert, 1473
Davies, Valerie, 1473
Davies, Vitoria, 1041
Davis, Greg, 922
Davis, Neil M., 1526
Dawson, Jeff, 780
Day, Alan, 146
Day, David Howard, 1290
De Angelis, Carl, 988
Deans, Candace, 204
Decalo, Samuel, 453, 454
DeCoste, F. C., 510
Deever, Beverly Ann Deepe, 852
Deevey, Brian, 1502
DeFranco, Laurence J., 329
DeHart, Jean, 1131
Deivert, Bert, 1287
DeLancey, Mark W., 699
Delmar's A-Z NDR-97: nurse's drug ref, 1566
Delmar's automotive dict, 1477
Delmar's English/Spanish pocket dict for health professionals, 1527
Delmar's therapeutic class drug gd for nurses 1997, 1567
DeLong, Janice A., 1077
Demastes, William W., 1175
Demographic yrbk, 1995, 47th ed, 804
Depression in the elderly, 760
DeRyan, Tim, 1390
Deschamps, Judith, 1643
Desert Mag subject index, 878
DesJardins, Dawn Conzett, 50
Devereux, Daniel T., 1334
DeVries, LaMoine F., 1378
Dewar, David, 1412
DeWitt, Donald L., 577
Diana, Joan P., 756
Dickenson, John, 140
Dickey, Alison Adams, 968
Dickey, Jerry, 1132
Dickstein, Ruth, 841

Dictionary catalog of the collection of African American lit in the Mildred F. Sawyer Lib of Suffolk Univ, 340
Dictionary of ...
  Afro-American slavery, updated ed, 438
  American & English law, 520
  art, 947
  astronomy, 1607
  British & Irish travellers in Italy, 1701-1800, 476
  communication & media studies, 4th ed, 857
  computing, 4th ed, 1576
  dicts & encys, 2d ed, 45
  economics, 151
  environment & sustainable dvlpmt, 1633
  environmental sci & tech, 2d ed, 1636
  eye terminology, 3d ed, 1553
  healthful food terms, 1420
  Irish family names, 376
  Japanese loanwords, 1003
  Jewish surnames from the Kingdom of Poland, 375
  land surveyors & local map-makers of Grt Brit & Ireland, 1530-1850, 394
  literary biog documentary series, v.14, 1089
  media literacy, 856
  medical sociology, 1524
  Mexican rulers, 1325-1997, 485
  mission, 1350
  modern biology, 1445
  multicultural educ, 267
  multimedia terms & acronyms, 1572
  natural products, 1569
  natural resource mgmt, 1632
  19th century British bk illustrators & caricaturists, rev ed, 944
  1000 Jewish proverbs, 1251
  1000 Polish proverbs, 1252
  personal computing & the Internet, 1574
  philosophy & religion, new ed, 1337
  portrait painters in Britain up to 1920, 982
  real estate, 263
  Scottish quotations, 136
  social & market research, 253
  the English lang [CD-ROM], 1020
  20th-century world hist, 504
  Ukrainian composers, 1217
  who, what, & where in Shakespeare, 1161
  women artists, 948
  worldwide gestures, 711
Die cast price gd, 930
Diefenderfer, William M., III, 329
DiGregorio, Mario J., 1450
Dillard, Philip H., 1212
Diller, Daniel C., 653
Dimond, Peter, 1213
Dinosaurs, 1618
Directories in print, 15th ed, 50
Directory of ...
  agencies & orgs serving individuals who are deaf-blind, rev ed, 771
  American philosophers 1996-97, 18th ed, 1340
  bldg & equipment grants, 4th ed, 1481
  business info resources, 1997, 5th ed, 250
  business to business catalogs, 1997, 190
  college facilities & services for people with disabilities, 4th ed, 772
  Congressional voting scores & interest group ratings, 2d ed, 678
  educ grants, 271
  environmental law educ opportunities at American law schools, 558
  fed libs, 3d ed, 573
  grants for orgs serving people with disabilities, 10th ed, 773
  intl economic org, 161
  lib technical servs home pages, 591
  listed derivative contracts 1996/97, 171
  operating grants, 3d ed, 786
  physicians in the US, 35th ed, 1533
  physicians in the US, 35th ed [CD-ROM], 1534
  poetry publishers, 599
  publishing 1997, 22d ed, 600
  rare bk & special collections in the UK & the Republic of Ireland, 2d ed, 588
  safety standards, lit, & servs, 1495
  small pr/mag editors & publishers 1997-98, 28th ed, 601
  special libs & info centers, v.1, 21st ed, 589
  special libs & info centers, v.2, 21st ed, 590
  theatre training programs 1997-99, 6th ed, 1325
  US labor orgs, 1997 ed, 219
Dirr, Michael A., 1456
Dirr's hardy trees & shrubs, 1456
Discography of 78 rpm era recordings of the horn, 1203
DISCovering authors, Canadian ed [CD-ROM], 1065
DISCovering biog [CD-ROM], 23
DISCovering sci [CD-ROM], 1413
DISCovering US hist [CD-ROM], 446
DISCovering world hist [CD-ROM], 505
Diseases, 1557
DiTomaso, Joseph M., 1453
Dittmar, Joseph J., 728
Divine inspirations: pearls of Bible wisdom from the O. & N.T.s, 1369
Dodd, David G., 1240
Dodd, Janet S., 872
Dodds de Wolf, Gaelan, 1012
Doerper, John, 415
Doherty, Charles, 960
Doherty, P., 1604
Doll values antique to modern, 918
Dominic, Catherine C., 1163, 1164
Donahue, Mildred A., 279
Donio, Michael A., 1539
Doody's rating serv 1997, 1501
Douchant, Mike, 739
Douglas, Ian, 397
Douglas, J. D., 1373
Dressman, Mark, 1087
Drew, Bernard A., 1102
DuBoff, Leonard D., 1265
Duckle, Vincent H., 1189
Duke, James A., 1546

Duke of Newcastle, 1693-1768, & Henry Pelham, 1694-1754, 687
Dunn, Jerry, 1014
Dunster, Julian, 1632
Dunster, Katherine, 1632
DuPree, Mary, 1200
Durant, David N, 1011
Duskis, Neil, 979
Dutch art, 949
Duval, Alain, 1024
DuVall, Audre, 898
Dwiggins, Boyce H., 1477
Dworkin, Rita, 1108
Dynamic nutrition for maximum performance, 1513

Eades, J. S., 106
Eagle, Selwyn, 1643
Early TV, 889
Eastern Europe & the Commonwealth of Independent States 1997, 3d ed, 127
Eberle, Linda, 924
Ecclesia: a theological ency of the Church, 1387
Eck, Marty, 921
Economic Commission for Europe, 1496, 1581
Economic survey of Latin America & the Caribbean 1995-96, 210
Eddy Arnold discography, 1944-96, 1231
Edinburgh ency, 137
Education index, July 1995 to June 1996, 279
Edwardian fiction, 1152
Edwards, Alan F., Jr., 289
Edwards, Paul M., 1291
Eggers, Ellen K., 455
Ehlich, Konrad, 984
Ehrens, Cheryl, 93
Ehrlich, Eugene, 1017, 1025
Eicher, David J., 433
Eighteenth-century Anglo-American women novelists, 1111
Eighteenth century, n.s.15 for 1989, 7
Einstein, Daniel, 1304
Elder, George R., 1352
Election results dir 1997, 663
Electrical & electronics trades dir 1996 [CD-ROM], 1486
Electronic & computer music, 1196
Electronic styles: a hndbk for citing electronic info, 2d ed, 875
Elements, 1600
El-Hi textbooks & serials in print 1997, 283
Elias, Stephen, 534
Eliceiri, Ellen M. Enright, 856
Elliott, Jack, 1435
Elmer Rice: a research & production sourcebk, 1326
Elsevier's dict of European Community co/business/financial law in English, Danish, & German, 517
Elsevier's dict of info tech in English, German, & French, 581
Emblidge, David, 871
Embree, Lester, 1335

Emerson, William K., 624
Employment discrimination law, 3d ed, 530
Encyclopaedia Judaica [CD-ROM], 1393
Encyclopedia of ...
   acoustics, 1619
   African-American heritage, 338
   American farm implements & antiques, 1419
   American Indian civil rights, 562
   American pol reform, 657
   ancient civilizations of the Near East & Mediterranean, 487
   angels, 1355
   archetypal symbolism, v.1, 1351
   archetypal symbolism, v.2: the body, 1352
   bioethics, rev ed [CD-ROM], 1333
   careers & vocational guidance, 2d ed [CD-ROM], 214
   careers & vocational guidance, 10th ed, 215
   classical philosophy, 1334
   cryptology, 855
   early Christianity, 2d ed, 1386
   famous suicides, 767
   fantasy, 1116
   frontier lit, 1130
   geographical features in world hist, 399
   German resistance to the Nazi movement, 470
   healing therapies, 1552
   interior design, 935
   Keynesian economics, 152
   Latin American lit, 1178
   lib & info sci, v.57, 569
   lib & info sci, v.59, 570
   mammals, 1469
   medical media & communications, 1529
   Mexico, 141
   Minor League Baseball, 2d ed, 729
   Native American biog, 350
   N American Indians, 353, 354
   nutrition & good health, 1520
   phenomenology, 1335
   religion [CD-ROM], 1353
   religious controversies in the US, 1354
   rural America, 98
   sacred places, 1349
   sports sci, 720
   statl scis: update v.1, 809
   the American Constitution [CD-ROM], 518
   the cat, 1463
   the essay, 1107
   the inter-American system, 695
   the Republican Party & the ency of the Democratic Party, 659
   the war of 1812, 612
   TV, 888
   TV sci fiction, 1283
   20th century conflict, 613
   US Army insignia & uniforms, 624
   US foreign relations, 660
   virology plus [CD-ROM], 1442
   world sport, 721
   world terrorism, 551

Encyclopedia plus of world problems & human
    potential, 4th ed [CD-ROM], 86
Encyclopedia USA, suppl v.1, 439
Encyclopedia USA, v.24, 440
Energy analysis of 108 industrial processes, 6th ed, 1494
Energy & environmental industry survey 1997, 191
Energy balances for countries in transition 1993, 1994-
    2010, & energy prospects in CIS countries, 1627
Engel, Margaret, 731
Engelbert, Phillis, 1611
English lang & orientation programs in the US, 11th
    ed, 988
English novel, 1660-1700, 1145
English-Ukrainian dict of business, 155
English-Yiddish, Yiddish-English dict, [rev ed], 1054
Enhanced occupational outlook hndbk, 226
Environmental ethics, 1628
Environmental law hndbk, 14th ed, 559
Epics for students, 1069
Erlewine, Michael, 1228, 1230, 1238
Erlewine, Stephen Thomas, 1228, 1230
Ernst, Carl R., 63, 524, 525, 665, 666, 706
Essential business buyer's gd, 179
Essential gd to chronic illness, 1558
Estes, Ellen G., 791
Ethnic cultures of the world, 331
Ethnic minority health, 1503
Ethridge, James M., 597
Ethridge, Karen, 597
Europe on file, 121
European art since 1850, 958
European art to 1850, 959
European forests & timber, 1430
European hist on file, 463
Evans, Linda, 1236
Evans, Philip R., 1236
Evans, Robert C., 1119
Evans, Toshie M., 1003
Everthing Civil War, 447
EveryWoman's gd to prescription & nonprescription
    drugs, 1564
Evinger, William R., 573
Experimental TV, test films, pilots, & trial series,
    1925-95, 1314
Exploring poetry [CD-ROM], 1184
Exploring Shakespeare [CD-ROM], 1162
Exter, Thomas G., 225
External degrees in the info age, 308
Extractives, manufacturing, & servs, 162
Extraordinary women in support of music, 1199
Eyewitness ency of sci [CD-ROM], 1403
Eyewitness garden hndbk: annuals & biennials, 1436

Faber, Charles F., 730
Fabry, Heinz-Josef, 1375
Facts about the cities, 2d ed, 823
Facts about the Supreme Court of the US, 538
Facts on File ency of black women in America, 343
Facts on File ency of word & phrase origins, rev ed, 1001
Facts on File world news CD-ROM 1997 [CD-ROM], 506

Faerber, Marc, 589, 590
Fagan, Brian M., 428
Fales, Alexcia, 770
Falk, Byron A., Jr., 67, 68
Falk, Valerie R., 67, 68
Falkenstein, Jeffrey A., 790
Famous lines: a Columbia dict of familiar quotations, 80
Far Eastern art, 960
Farlow, James O., 1617
Farndon, John, 48
Farr, J. Michael, 226, 227, 228
Feather, John, 571
Feder, Jody, 274, 792
Federal regulatory dir, 8th ed, 664
Feher, Gyorgy, 978
Feldman, Susan E., 1592
Felts, Eva M., 166
Female offenders, 549
Feminism worldwide, 831
Feminist ency of Italian lit, 1177
Fenton, R. R., 849
Fenwick, Elizabeth, 802
Ferguson, Everett, 1386
Ferguson, John H., 1483
Feuerman, Francine, 1547
Feuerstein, Georg, 1338
Field, Shelly, 1512
Fiesta, 1262
50 most influential women in American law, 513
50 yrs of events, 1331
Film & video finder, 5th ed, 310
Film & video on the Internet, 1287
Film choreographers & dance directors, 1268
Film researcher's hndbk, 1309
Filmmakers in The Moving Picture World, 1316
Financial aid bk, 2d ed, 298
Financial aid financer, 306
Finch, Jim, 1112
Find it fast, 4th ed, 575
Find public records fast, 665
Finding images online, 1592
Finding your Hispanic roots, 368
Finland, rev ed, 123
Fisher, Helen S., 229
Fishes of the Galapagos Islands, 1468
Fist, Stewart, 1593
Fitton, Robert A., 81
Fitzsimmons, Richard, 756
Flea market trader, 11th ed, 896
Fletcher, Andrew J., 1540
Fletcher, Beverly R., 549
Flexner, Stuart Berg, 1002
Flora of N America n of Mexico, v.3, 1447
Florida, 416
Florida: atlas of histl county boundaries, 431
Florida almanac 1997-98, 11th ed, 99
Fodor's ballpark vacations, 731
Fodor's exploring Canada, 421
Fodor's exploring the Greek Islands, 424
Fodor's healthy escapes, 5th ed, 405
Foerstel, Herbert N., 584

Fogelman, Peggy, 983
Fogle, Bruce, 1463
Foliage plant diseases, 1446
Folklore, culture, & aging, 761
Folsom, W. Davis, 153
Foner, Eric, 344
Food festivals, 414
Forest & forest industries country fact sheets, 1431
Forty, George, 613
Fosbrook, Deborah, 531
Foster, Frances Smith, 1129
Foster, Race, 1464
Fostoria, v.2: identification & value gd to etched, carved & cut designs, 899
Foundation dir 1997, 19th ed, 787
Foundation dir suppl, 788
Foundation giving, 1997 ed, 794
Fox, Ken, 1311
Fox, Thomas C., 1391
Frame by frame 2: a filmography of the African American image, 1978-94, 1295
Franck, Irene, 803
Francoeur, Robert T., 797
Frank, Frederick S., 1137
Frank, Sam, 1273
Frankenhoff, Brent, 908
Franklin, Laurel F., 700
Fred Astaire: a bio-bibliog, 1272
Freda, Michael D., 1231
Fredriksen, John C., 608
Free expression & censorship in America, 584
Free market environmental bibliog 1995-96, 4th ed, 1630
Freedom's lawmakers: a dir of black officeholders during Reconstruction, rev ed, 344
Freelance Editorial Assn yellow pages & code of fair practice, 1997-98, 863
Freese, Mel R., 732
Freiman, Fran Locher, 1530
Freitag, Wolfgang M., 940
French feminist theory 3, 832
French tapestries & textiles in the J. Paul Getty Museum, 946
Frey, Gisela, 517
Friedman, Norman, 629, 634
Frois, Jeanne, 100
From headline hunter to Superman: a journalism filmography, 1298
From talking drums to the Internet, 854
Fromm, Joy, 821
Frost-Knappman, Elizabeth, 563
Fudyma, Janice, 1568
Fulltext sources online, July 1997, 51
Fulton, Len, 599, 601
Fulton, Roger, 1283
Funding in aging, 758
Fund-Raising regulation, 539

G. A. Henty 1832-1902: a bibliographical study of his British eds...., 1159
Gaccione, Laura, 1508

Gage Canadian dict, rev ed, 1012
Gagne, Louise, 603, 880
Gaither, Carl C., 82
Galazka, Jacek, 1253
Gall, Susan, 834
Gall, Susan Bevan, 119
Gall, Tim, 834
Gall, Timothy L., 119
Galle, Fred C., 1457
Gallery of her own: an annot bibliog of women in Victorian painting, 981
Gallup, George, Jr., 87
Gallup Poll, 87
Gander, Terry J., 633
Garage sale & flea market annual, 5th ed, 897
Garcia, Frank, 1286
Garcia, Richard A., 349
Gardener's gd to growing irises, 1454
Gardener's gd to growing ivies, 1455
Gardiner, Juliet, 465
Gardner, Robert, 854
Garland, Henry, 1173
Garland, Mary, 1173
Garment & textile dict, 933
Garner, Carolyn, 1099
Garner, Roberta, 690
Garnier, Camille, 1151
Garoogian, Andrew, 820, 821
Garoogian, Rhoda, 820, 821
Gaschnitz, K. Michael, 722
Gastelu, Daniel, 1513
Gay & lesbian biog, 781
Gay & lesbian online, rev ed, 780
Gaze, Delia, 948
Geer, Ira W., 1612
Gelbart, Marsh, 631
Gelbert, Doug, 448
Gemstones of the world, rev ed, 1615
Genealogical & local hist bks in print: gen ref & world resources, 5th ed, 359
Genealogical & local hist bks in print: US sources & resources, 5th ed, 360
Genealogy annual, 1995, 361
Generation X: the young adult market, 256
Geographic database for US economy, tech, & growth [CD-ROM], 818
George F. Kennan: an annot bibliog, 700
George Gordon, Lord Byron, 1155
German Baroque writers, 1661-1730, 1172
German theatre, 1323
Gershman, Michael, 737
Gevinson, Alan, 1288
Gibilisco, Stan, 1488
Gibson, Gloria J., 1295
Gifford, C. D., 219
Giles, James R., 1128
Giles, Wanda H., 1128
Gillaspie, Jon A., 1220
Gillespie, John T., 1091, 1103
Gilpin, Alan, 1633
Gilson, David, 1153

Giroux, Christopher, 1068
Glazier, Stephen D., 1359
Glick, David M., 1443
Global data locator, 812
Glossary of ...
    biochemistry & molecular biology, rev ed, 1443
    environment stats, 1634
    reliability & maintenance terms, 1497
    weather & climate with related oceanic & hydrologic terms, 1612
Glut, Donald F., 1618
God on the Internet, 1365
Goddard, Ives, 356
Gods & heroes of classical antiquity, 1257
Goehlert, Robert U., 646
Goerss, John Mark, 1369
Going out in style: the architecture of eternity, 973
Golden age of Walt Disney records 1933-88, 1209
Goldstein, Joshua, 675
Goldstein, Norm, 874
Gonzalez, Alexander G., 1176
Good old index: the Sherlock Holmes hndbk, 1158
Goodall, Francis, 149
Goode, Clement Tyson, Jr., 1155
Googins, Bradley K., 777
Gorbachev bibliog, 1985-91, 482
Goreham, Gary A., 98
Gorman, Robert F., 564
Gottlieb, Nicholas, 770
Gould, Dennis E., 483
Goulding, Phil G., 1223
Gourvish, Terry, 149
Government financial aid bk, 2d ed, 299
Government job finder, 234
Government phone bk USA 1997, 5th ed, 52
Gozdecka-Sanford, Adriana, 479
Graber, Steven, 220
Graduate medical educ dir 1997-98, 1535
Graduate programs in journalism & mass communications, 309
Graefen, Gabriele, 984
Graff, Gary, 1233
Graham, Ian, 1404
Graham, Judith, 22
Grammatically correct, 1005
Grammatically correct hndbk, 1004
Grandparents, 779
Granoff, Allan, 1442
Grant, Carl A., 267
Grant, Daniel, 865, 964
Grant, Edmond, 1311
Grant, John, 1116
Grant, Tina, 208
Grants register 1998, 16th ed, 300
Grateful Dead & the deadheads, 1240
Graves, Genevieve, 174
Graying of America: an ency of aging, health, mind, & behavior, 759
Great citrus bk, 1428
Great escapes: the spring breaker's gd to beaches & beyond, 417

Great events from hist: N American series, rev ed, 497
Great world trials, 532
Greece: Athens & the mainland, 425
Greek Islands, 426
Greeley, Ronald, 1609
Green kitchen hndbk, 1425
Green pharmacy, 1546
Green, Don W., 1479
Green, Joseph, 1112
Green, Sharon Weiner, 992
Greene, Stanley A., 1642
Greenfield, George, 1462
Greenfieldt, John, 1122
Greening the college curriculum: a gd to environmental teaching in the liberal arts, 1640
Greenspon, Joanna, 846
Greentree, Rosemary, 1156
Greger, Rene, 626
Gregg, Robert J., 1012
Grehan, Ida, 376
Grey-Wilson, Christopher, 1449
Gridiron greats: a century of Polish Americans in college football, 745
Griggs, Jack L., 1459
Grigoriev, Igor S., 1620
Grimes, John, 1336
Grinde, Donald A., Jr., 350
Groenier, Paul D., 72
Grohol, John M., 1514
Grolier lib of sci biogs, 1400
Grolier lib of WW I, 614
Grolier multimedia ency, 1998, deluxe ed [CD-ROM], 43
Gross, David C., 1251
Gross, Melissa, 1560
Grossman, Ellie, 1004
Grossman, Paul, 530
Group work with the elderly, 757
Grove, Jack Stein, 1468
Grubel, Monika, 1394
Guernsey, Lisa, 301
Guerrilla warfare, 620
Guide to ...
    background investigations, 7th ed, 640
    British prose fiction explication: 19th & 20th centuries, 1143
    college programs in hospitality & tourism, 5th ed, 314
    executive recruiters, new ed, 218
    fed funding for anti-crime programs, 2d ed, 553
    fed funding for educ, 1997, 23d ed, 274
    fed funding for govts & nonprofits, 19th ed, 792
    fed funding for housing & homeless programs, 3d ed, 764
    films on the Korean War, 1291
    graduate environmental programs, 1641
    literary agents, 1997, 866
    microforms in print 1997, 1580
    multicultural resources 1997/98, 327
    natl professional certification programs, 313
    naturalization records of the US, 332
    ref works for the study of the Spanish lang & lit & Spanish American lit, 1183

S African ref bks, 6th ed, 19
the evaluation of educl experiences in the armed servs, 1996, v.1: Army, 275
the evaluation of educl experiences in the armed servs, 1996, v.2: Navy, 276
the evaluation of educl experiences in the armed servs, 1996, v.3: Air Force, Coast Guard, Dept of Defense, Marine Corps, 277
the presidency, 2d ed, 674
the US supreme court, 526
US fndns, their trustees, officers, & donors, 1997 ed, 789
Guidebook for publishing philosophy, 1997 ed, 867
Guiley, Rosemary Ellen, 1355
Guinea pig, 1466
Guitar music by women composers, 1218
Gun digest, 920
Gustav Mahler's symphonies, 1248

Hadro, Jane E., 528
Hager, Alan, 1060
Hahn, Harley, 1594
Haines, David W., 801
Hajnal, Peter I., 693
Haley, Barbara A., 1502
Halfdanarson, Guomundur, 474
Hall, David E., 104
Hall, Hal W., 1117
Halliwell, Leslie, 1305
Halliwell's filmgoer's companion, 12th ed, 1305
Hallucinogenic & poisonous mushroom field gd, 1452
Hamadeh, Samer, 221
Hamel, Bernard B., 1494
Hamel, Raymond, 1471
Hamer, Frank, 932
Hamer, Janet, 932
Hamilton, Neil A., 437
Hammer, Patricia Cahape, 272
Hammond explorer atlas of the world, 385
Handbook of ...
    intl financial terms, 184
    N American Indians, v.17: langs, 356
    physical quantities, 1620
    population & housing censuses, pt.4, 805
    the American frontier, v.4: the far West, 357
    thermal conductivity, v.4: inorganic compounds & elements, 1622
    US coins, 1998, 55th ed, 910
    US labor stats, 230
    viscosity, v.4: inorganic compounds & elements, 1623
    world mineral trade stats 1990-95, 251
Handbook to Bach's sacred cantata texts, 1247
Handel, Marsha J., 1547
Handy sci answer bk, 2d ed, 1414
Handy weather answer bk, 1613
Hani-English/English-Hani dict, 1034
Hannah Arendt 2: a bibliog, 636
Hans Holbein the younger: a gd to research, 943
Hansen, Brad, 1572
Harcourt, Geoff, 152

Hardin, James, 1172
Harduf, David Mendel, 1054, 1055
Harduf's transliterated English-Hebrew dict, 4th v., L-M, 1035
Harduf's transliterated English-Yiddish, Yiddish-English dict, [rev ed], 1055
Hardy, Gayle J., 60
Harland, Mike, 1041
Harmony theory, 1193
Harms, Jeanne McLain, 284
Harner, James L., 1165
HarperCollins Portuguese dict, college ed, 1041
Harries, Dan, 1287
Harris, Barbara P., 1012
Harris, Elree I., 981
Harris, John M., 1227
Harris, Laurie Lanzen, 21
Harris, Nigel G. E., 1341
Harris, Trudier, 1129
Harris, Wayne, 163
Harrison, Ben, 546
Hartman, Stephen W., 263
Harvey, Robert, 1171
Hatch, Thom, 441
Hatfield, Fred, 1513
Hatfield, John T., 1364
Haubrich, William S., 1528
Haught, James A, 1347
Hauser, Barbara R., 544
Hayford, Charles W., 111
Haynes, Craig, 1503
Hayward, Susan, 1284
Haywood, John, 487
Hazardous chemicals desk ref, 4th ed, 1635
Hazardous substances resource gd, 2d ed, 1642
Hazen-Hammond, Susan, 351
Healey, Jon, 672
Health & illness, 1508
Health & medical yrbk 1997, 1515
Health care crisis in the US, 1505
Health care software sourcebk 1997, 1516
Health care terms, healthy communities ed, 1510
Health professions educ dir 1997-98, 1511
Health stats, 2d ed, 1504
Heard, J. Norman, 357
Hearn, Daniel Allen, 554
Heaton, Donald D., 1421
Hedman, Bruce A., 1494
Heidler, David S., 612
Heidler, Jeanne T., 612
Helbig, Alethea K., 1084, 1092
Hellweg, Paul, 1016
Henderson, Helene, 1263
Hendrickson, Robert, 1001, 1007
Henriques, Gary, 898
Herald, Diana Tixier, 1096
Herbert, Stephen, 1280
Herbst, Philip H., 328
Herbst, Sharon Tyler, 1429
Heritage ency of band music, suppl v.3, 1229
Herlocher, Dawn, 916

Herrmann, Joachim, 507
Heslop, Janet, 246
Hester, M. L., 864
Hester, Stanley, 1236
Hester, Stephen, 1236
Heuvel, Michael Vanden, 1326
Hewett, Janet B., 451, 452
Heyman, Charles, 555
High school senior's gd to merit & other no-need funding 1996-98, 307
Highly selective dict for the extraordinarily literate, 1017
Hill, Anne, 857
Hill, Brad, 1206
Hill, George R., 1190
Hine, Darlene Clark, 343
Hinegardner, Patricia G., 1504
Hipple, Ted, 1104
Hischak, Thomas S., 1327
Hispanic firsts, 348
Historic docs index, 1972-95, 682
Historical atlas of the Holocaust, 492
Historical atlas of the Holocaust [CD-ROM], 493
Historical dict of ...
    Afghanistan, 2d ed, 110
    Bangladesh, 2d ed, 460
    Burundi, 455
    Catholicism, 1384
    Chad, 3d ed, 453
    Germany's Weimar Republic, 1918-33, 471
    Hinduism, 1392
    human rights & humanitarian orgs, 564
    Hungary, 473
    Iceland, 474
    Ireland, 475
    Latvia, 477
    Lithuania, 478
    Morocco, new ed, 458
    Niger, 3d ed, 454
    N American environmentalism, 1638
    Palestine, 488
    Stockholm, 483
    Tanzania, 2d ed, 457
    the British Empire, 466
    the civil rights movement, 565
    the Gulf Arab States, 489
    the Republic of Guinea-Bissau, 3d ed, 456
    the UK, v.1: England & the UK, 467
    the UNESCO, 694
    the World Bank, 186
    Tokyo, 461
    Trinidad & Tobago, 484
    Tunisia, 2d ed, 459
    Venezuela, 2d ed, 142
    war journalism, 881
    Warsaw, 479
Historical stats of the US, bicentennial ed [CD-ROM], 819
History of ...
    art for young people, 5th ed, 965
    astronomy, 1606
    humanity, v.3, 507
    music for harpsichord or piano & orchestra, 1227

    photography, v.3, 938
    physical anthropology, 320
    the ancient & medieval world, 501
HIV/AIDS info for children, 1560
Hochmuth, George J., 1437
Hocking, George Macdonald, 1569
Hoepelman, J. P., 581
Hoffman, Eric, 867
Hoffman, Marian, 359, 360
Hoffman, Miles, 1202
Hoffmann, Frank, 1198
Hofling, Charles Andrew, 1040
Hogg, Ian V., 633
Holidays, festivals, & celebrations dict, 2d ed, 1263
Hollander, Zander, 749, 750
Hollies, 1457
Hollings, Robert L., 644, 704
Holm, Kirsten C., 870
Holmes, Kim R., 169
Holmes, Robyn, 1214
Holocaust, 502
Holston, Kim R., 1292
Holtin, Alice Y., 1232
Hombs, Mary Ellen, 799
Home improvements & projects index 1990-93, 1498
Homelessness in America, 765
Hone, E. Wade, 365
Hoover's billion dollar dir, 159
Hoover's co capsules on CD-ROM [CD-ROM], 192
Hoover's co profiles on CD-ROM [CD-ROM], 193
Hoover's global 250, 202
Hoover's gd to media cos, 859
Hoover's hndbk of emerging cos 1997, 173
Hoover's hndbk of private cos 1997, 164
Hoover's hndbks index 1997, 168
Hoover's masterlist of major Latin American cos 1996-97, 211
Hopkinson, Barbara, 12, 13
Horn Bk gd to children's & YA bks, v.7, no.2, 1078
Horn, Delton T., 1487
Horowitz, Amy, 788
Horror & sci fiction films 4, 1300
Horton, Tara A., 868
Horwitz, Barbara J., 1144
Horwood, Jane, 1051
Hosking, David, 1461, 1470
Hospice & palliative care, 1521
Hostelling N America, 1997, 403
Houck, Susan, 574
Houfe, Simon, 944
Houghton Mifflin dict of geography, 395
House plant ency, 1433
Household hints & tips, 180
Hovey, Harold A., 817
Hovey, Kendra A., 817
How much can I make?, 174
How to be a perfect stranger, 1362
How to be a perfect stranger, v.2, 1363
Howard, Carol, 1149
Howard, Joyce M., 1418
Hoxie, Frederick E., 353

Hubbard, Benjamin J., 1364
Hudson, Grace L., 131
Hudson's subscription newsletter dir, 13th ed, 76
Huggett, Richard, 397
Hughes, H. G. A., 145
Human resources yrbk 1996/97, 224
Humanities abstracts full text [CD-ROM], 845
Humanities index, April 1995 to Mar 1996, 846
Humor in British lit, from the Middle Ages to the Restoration, 1150
Hunt, Caroline C., 1089
Hurrelmann, Klaus, 1517
Husfloen, Kyle, 892, 894, 927
Husni, Samir A., 882
Hutchings, Noel, 1332
Huxford, Bob, 896, 905
Huxford, Sharon, 896, 905
Hymnology, 1246

IDEA: intl dir of educl audiovisuals [CD-ROM], 311
Identities & issues in lit, 1070
Idiom savant: slang as it is slung, 1014
Idrogo, Curt, 327
Illustrated bk of world rankings, rev ed, 813
Illustrated dict of electronics, 7th ed, 1488
Illustrated ency of ...
    divination, 714
    world hist, 503
    world religions, 1356
Illustrated sci ency, 1405
Immigration questions & answers, rev ed, 702
Impact of Napoleon, 1800-15, 469
Ince, Martin, 1607
Index of ...
    American per verse: 1994, 1185
    American per verse: 1995, 1142
    economic freedom, 1997, 169
Index to ...
    AV producers & distrs 1997, 10th ed, 312
    black pers 1995, 345
    dance pers: 1995, 1270
    the Wilson authors series, 1075
    the Wilson booktalking series, 1083
    translated short fiction by Latin American women in English lang anthologies, 1179
    women's studies anthologies, 841
Indiana: atlas of histl county boundaries, 379
Informatics hndbk, 1593
Information sources in ...
    environmental protection, 1643
    law, 2d ed, 533
    official pubns, 61
Ingamells, John, 476
Ingraham, Holly, 377
Inlander, Charles B., 1539
Inside Sports Mag college basketball, 2d ed, 739
Inside Sports Mag golf, 748
Inside Sports Mag hockey, 1997 ed, 749
Insider's gd to mental health resources online, 1514
Instant natl locator gd, 3d ed, 53

Interdisciplinary undergraduate programs, 2d ed, 289
International bibliog of business hist, 149
International biog dir of natl archivists, documentalists, & librarians, 574
International bk trade dir 1997, 602
International bks in print 1997, 12, 13
International children's Bible dict, 1376
International conflict, 696
International dir of ...
    consumer brands & their owners, 200
    philosophy & philosophers 1997-98, 10th ed, 1342
    primatology, 3d ed, 1471
International encyclopaedic dict of numismatics, 909
International ency of ...
    info & lib sci, 571
    secret societies & fraternal orders, 763
    sexuality, 797
    the sociology of educ, 268
International Federation of Robotics, 1581
International gd to securities market indices, 175
International hndbk of public health, 1517
International index to music pers 1997:2 [CD-ROM], 1208
International info documents, 693
International standards desk ref, 206
International trade sources, 199
International trade stats yrbk, 1995, 252
International treaties on intellectual property, 2d ed, 567
International yrbk 1997, 44
International yrbk of industrial stats 1997, 194
Internet & lib & info servs, 582
Internet complete ref, 2d ed, 1594
Internet gd for the legal researcher, 2d ed, 535
Internet resource dir for K-12 teachers & librarians, 96/97 ed, 1590
Internet searcher's hndbk, 1595
Internet tools of the profession, 2d ed, 1586
Irish almanac & yrbk of facts 1997, 134
Irish playwrights, 1880-1995, 1175
Islam, Hinduism, & Judaism in S Africa, 1345
Israel, Fred L., 661
Israeli secret servs, 689
ITP Nelson Canadian dict of the English lang, 1013
It's only rock 'n' roll: the ultimate gd to the Rolling Stones, 1241
Itzaj Maya-Spanish-English dict, 1040
IVP Bible background commentary: Genesis-Deuteronomy, 1379
Izod, Irene, 12, 13

Jackson, Richard, 696
Jacobs, Eva E., 230
Jacobs, Nancy R., 753, 1559
Jacobsen, Lawrence, 1471
Jaegly, Peggy J., 1115
James A. Garfield, 645
Jandora, John Walter, 609
Jane's air-launched weapons image lib [CD-ROM], 632
Jane's ammunition hndbk 1996-97, 5th ed, 633
Jane's electro-optic systems 1996-97, 2d ed, 619
Janes, Joseph, 1595

Jane's military aircraft image lib [CD-ROM], 623
Jane's military communications, 1997-98, 618
Jane's police & security equipment 1996-97, 9th ed, 555
Jane's simulation & training systems 1996-97, 9th ed, 1573
Jane's warships image lib [CD-ROM], 627
Janson, Anthony F., 965
Janson, H. W., 965
Jantra, Ingrid, 1433
Japanese studies in Canada: the 1990s, 115
Jay, Antony, 641
Jefferis, David, 1645
Jefferson's welding ency, 18th ed, 1491
Jentleson, Bruce W., 660
Jewish sports legends, 2d ed, 719
Jewish writers of Latin America, 1180
Jewish yrbk 1997, 1395
JIST's electronic enhanced dict of occupational titles, 2d ed [CD-ROM], 216
JIST's electronic occupational outlook hndbk, 2d ed [CD-ROM], 231
JIST's multimedia occupational outlook hndbk, 2d ed [CD-ROM], 232
Job hunter's sourcebk, 3d ed, 233
Job-Hunting on the Internet, 222
JobBank gd to employment servs 1998-99, 220
Joes, Anthony James, 620
Johansen, Bruce E., 350
Johnson, Arthur, 725
Johnson, Bryan T., 169
Johnson, Dana, 929
Johnson, Donald Leslie, 972
Johnson, Gordon, 113
Johnson, Hans, 654
Johnson, Jean E., 783
Johnson, Lloyd, 729
Johnson, Samuel, 1020
Johnston, Deborah, 107
Johnston, William M., 1346
Jones, Almut G., 1451
Jones, Constance, 766
Jones, Francine, 785
Jones, Stephen, 1306
Joseph, Andrew, 1311
Journalism, 2d ed, 851
Judaism, 1394
Judicial staff dir, 1997, 522
Julius, Marshall, 1293
Junior chronicle of the 20th century, 498
Junior timelines on file, 499
Junior Worldmark ency of the Canadian provinces, 119
Juo, Pei-Show, 1439

K & W gd to colleges for the learning disabled, 1998 ed, 290
Kabdebo, Thomas, 45
Kalat, David, 1294
Kaleidoscope: a multicultural Booklist for grades K-8, 1087
Kamm, Antony, 1066
Kanellos, Nicolas, 348
Kaplan, Steven M., 157, 519
Kaptur, Marcy, 833
Karakashian, Stephen, 1640
Karasik, Theodore W., 128
Karcher, Stephen, 714
Karnbach, James, 1241
Karney, Robyn, 1282
Kaufman, Kenn, 1460
Kausler, Barry C., 759
Kausler, Donald H., 759
Kavanagh, Gaynor, 495
Kear, Lynn, 715
Kee, Howard Clark, 1377
Keeler, Todd E., 649
Keeling, Richard, 1191
Keen, Peter G. W., 242
Keenan, Sheila, 836
Keister, Douglas, 973
Keller, Estela, 1277
Keller, Gary D., 1277
Kellner, Mark A., 1365
Kelly, Douglas R., 930
Kelz, Rochelle K., 1527
Kemp, Sandra, 1152
Kemp, Thomas J., 361
Kemp, Thomas Jay, 366
Kemper, Robert E., 243
Kent, Allen, 569, 570
Kent, Cassandra, 180
Kepars, I., 118
Kerr, Ann, 899
Keuper, Jerome P., 1022
Key concepts in cinema studies, 1284
Key gd to electronic resources: art & art hist, 942
Key gd to electronic resources: lang & lit, 985
Key indicators of county growth 1970-2025, 1996 ed, 806
Killpatrick, Frances, 723
Killpatrick, James, 723
Kimball, Michelle R., 830
King, Anita, 78
King, Constance, 917
Kinnear, Karen L., 839
Kipps, Harriet Clyde, 795
Kirkpatrick, Betty, 1019
Kirkpatrick, Melanie, 169
Klotman, Phyllis R., 1295
Knapp, Brian, 1600
Knappman, Edward W., 532
Knight, Denise D., 1126
Kniskern, Nancy V., 418
Knott's hndbk for vegetable growers, 4th ed, 1437
Knowledge Exchange business ency, 154
Konigsberg, Ira, 1285
Kope, Spencer, 447
Korch, Rick, 746
Koschnick, Wolfgang J., 253
Kostenko, Dmytro, 155
Kotz, Samuel, 809
Kovacs, Diane K., 985
Kowalke, Ron, 1648

Kozub, Robert M., 264
Kratz, E. Ulrich, 986
Krause, Chester L., 911, 912
Kravets, Marybeth, 290
Krebs, Gary M., 1242
Krell, Robert, 708
Krouglov, Alexander, 155
Kruegler, Christopher, 692
Kruger, Ursula, 1433
Krumenaker, Lawrence, 1591
Kuchan, Barbara L., 1504
Kuhn, Laura, 1197
Kulisheck, P. J., 687
Kurds & Kurdistan, 116
Kurian, George Thomas, 659, 812, 813, 1529
Kuroff, Barbara, 936
Kurylko, Katya, 155

Laaser, Ulrich, 1517
Labor, employment, & the law, 515
Ladson-Billings, Gloria, 267
LaFrance, Ronald, 355
Lagowski, Joseph J., 1601
Lagua, Rosalinda T., 1422
Laing, Adrian C., 531
Land & property research in the US, 365
Landes, Alison, 568, 753
Landon, Grelun, 1234
Lands & peoples, 95
Lands & peoples special ed: the changing face of Europe, 96
Landscape architecture sourcebk, 1438
Landskroner, Ronald A., 244
Lane, Carole A., 1596
Lane, Jan-Erik, 684
Lang, Robert, 1169
Langley, Myrtle, 1381
Langmead, Donald, 972, 974
Lankford, John, 1606
Lansing, Phyllis S., 1504
Larger animals of E Africa, 1470
Larousse dict of women, 24
Larry Sitsky: a bio-bibliog, 1214
Latin American films, 1932-94, 1299
Latin for the illiterati, 1039
Lauber, Daniel, 234, 235
Laufenburg, Cindy, 1207
Laura Ingalls Wilder: an annot bibliog of critical, biogl, & teaching studies, 1139
Lauria, Angela E., 643
Lavenberg, Robert J., 1468
Law & legal info dir, 9th ed, 523
Law for the layperson, 2d ed, 511
Law, religion, theology, 510
Law, values, & the environment, 560
Lawrence, Robert L., 520
Lawyers' law bks, 3d ed, 512
Lazzari, Marie, 1069
Lea, Christine, 1050

Leadership: quotations from the world's greatest motivators, 81
Leaffer, Marshall A., 567
Ledoux, Trish, 1307
Lee, Loyd E., 622
Leeman, Richard W., 337
Leeming, David Adams, 1256
Leeson, Richard M., 1136
Legal executions in N.Y. State, 554
Legal research, 5th ed, 534
Leiter, Samuel L., 1324
Lemke, Bob, 906
Lentz, Harris M., III, 752, 1308
Leonard, Bill J., 1354
Leonard, Kathy S., 1179
Lerner, Loren, 1271
Les bon mots: how to amaze tout le monde with everyday French, 1025
Lesotho, rev ed, 107
Lester, David, 767
Letellier, Robert Ignatius, 1145
Lettow, Lucille J., 284
Levinkind, Susan, 534
Levinson, David, 721, 1508
Levy, Barbara R., 784
Lewis, Helene M. A., 1024
Lewis, Katie, 785
Lewis, Paul W., 1034
Lewis, Richard J., 1635
Lewon, Paul, 1584
Li, Xia, 875
Librarian's gd to public records, rev ed, 666
Lichtblau, Myron I., 1168
Lieberman, Shari, 1548
Life & death in the US, 769
Light, Jonathan Fraser, 733
Light 'n lively reads, 1057
Lighter, J. E., 1015
Lignor, Amy, 250
Lilley, William, III, 329
Lillian Russell: a bio-bibliog, 1275
Lilly, Teri Ann, 777
Lin, Alvin C., 274, 553, 792
Lin, Lin, 694
Lindemann, Barbara, 530
Lineback, Richard H., 1340, 1342
Linguistic cultures of the world, 990
Lipinski, Miroslaw, 1252
Lipset, Seymour Martin, 639
Lissarrague, Francois, 1257
Literary almanac, 1071
Literature & its times, 1072
Literature of the nonprofit sector, v.8, 783
Little, Anne C., 1119
Liu, Lewis-Guodo, 582
Lives & works in the arts from the renaissance to the 20th century, 847
Lives of N American birds, 1460
Lives of the great composers, 3d ed, 1216
Livingstone, E. A., 1389
Llompart, Ana Cristina, 1051

Lobban, Richard Andrew, Jr., 456
Lockhart, Darrell B., 1180
Logue, Calvin McLeod, 1131
Lomer, Cecile, 105
London Philharmonic discography, 1204
Long, James W., 1558
Long, John H., 379, 431
Longman companion to America in the era of the 2 world wars, 1910-45, 449
Looking at European sculpture, 983
Loos, John L., 497
Lorraine Hansberry: a research & production sourcebk, 1136
Louisiana almanac, 1997-98 ed, 100
Lowenstein, Barbara, 703
Lubin, Bernard, 709
Lucas, Phillip Charles, 1366
Lucchesi, Tony, 959
Luck, Steve, 47
Ludden, LaVerne L., 226
Luebking, Sandra Hargreaves, 370
Luker, Ralph E, 565
Lumpkin, Betty S., 282
Lunt, Susie, 122
Luxembourg, rev ed, 135
Lynching & vigilantism in the US, 547
Lyons, Dianne J. B., 1549
Lyons, Walter A., 1613

Mabunda, L. Mpho, 335
MacAuslan, Janna, 1218
Mack, Kibibi Voloria, 336
Mackenzie, Leslie, 250, 770
MacLeod, Don, 535
Macmillan centennial atlas of the world, 386
Macmillan ency of chemistry, 1601
Macmillan ency of sci, rev ed, 1406
MacPherson, Lillian, 510
Madden, W. C., 734
Madrid, 138
Magazines for kids & teens, rev ed, 879
Magida, Arthur J., 1362, 1363
Magill, Frank N., 497, 1059, 1085, 1123
Magistrale, Anthony, 1137
Magnuson, Norris A., 1383
Major state health care policies, 5th ed, 1518
Major Tudor authors, 1060
Mak, Grace C. L., 295
Makers of 20th century modern architecture, 972
Maki, Kathleen E., 233
Makinson, Larry, 675
Malbin, Michael J., 676
Maleson, Sandra, 305
Malloy, Alex G., 907, 915
Malloy, Nancy, 958
Malone, John, 88
Maloney, James O., 1479
Managed health care dict, 1509
Management consulting [CD-ROM], 245

Mandated benefits, 236
Mandler, Crystal, 794
Mangin, Paul, 226
Manley, Bill, 490
Mann, David D., 1151
Mann, Susan Garland, 1151
Mann, Thomas E., 676
Man's gd to coping with disability, 774
Mansfield, Brian, 1233
Manufactures phone bk USA 1997, 195
Maps & mapping of Africa, 392
Maps of the world, 387
Margiotta, Jennifer, 642
Marguerite Duras: a bio-bibliog, 1171
Marijuana law, 2d ed, 527
Marion, Donald J., 1296
Market share & business rankings worldwide [CD-ROM], 254
Markus, John, 1489
Maroney, James F., 1219
Marra, Jean M., 70
Marsh, Kenneth S., 1493
Marth, Del, 99
Marth, Martha J., 99
Martin, Fenton S., 646
Martindale, Carolyn, 852
Mason, Paul, 318
Mason, Wendy H., 1583
Massil, Stephen W., 1395
Master hndbk of IC circuits, 3d ed, 1487
Masterplots 2: juvenile & YA lit series suppl, 1085
Matchbox toys 1947-96, 2d ed, 929
Mathematical scis professional dir 1997, 1625
Matlins, Stuart M., 1363
Matter of fact: statements containing stats on current social, economics, & pol issues, v.24, 814
Matthews, Winton E., Jr., 579
Matthews, Alison, 913
Matthews, Victor H., 1379
Matulka, Denise I., 1097
Matuz, Roger, 748
Maxford, Howard, 1297
Maximov, Andrei, 688
Maximov's companion to who governs Moscow, 688
Mayer, R., 581
Maynard, Donald N., 1437
Mazza, Debora, 1036, 1037
Mazzeno, Laurence W., 1146
McArt, Pat, 134
McBeth, Amy, 1203
McCall, Mary Reilly, 827
McCarthy, Ronald M., 496, 692
McCready, Sam, 1166
McDermott, Anne, 1020
McDonald, Steve, 729
McDonald's collectibles, 898
McElroy, Lorie Jenkins, 840
McFadden, Margaret, 837
McGillivray, Alice V., 673
McGovern, Bernie, 99

McGraw-Hill dict of ...
 astronomy, 1608
 biosci, 1440
 chemistry, 1602
 earth sci, 1603
 engineering, 1476
 geology & mineralogy, 1614
 mathematics, 1626
 physics, 2d ed, 1621
McGraw-Hill electronics dict, 6th ed, 1489
McGraw-Hill ency of sci & tech, 8th ed, 1407
McGuckin, Frank, 557
McHugh, Michael P., 1386
McIlwaine, John, 392
McIntire, Dennis, 1197
McKay, David, 684
McKay, Ian, 903
McKenna, Ted, 1497
McKernan, Luke, 1280
McKim, Donald K., 1358
McKnight, Jean Sinclair, 511
McLerran, Jennifer, 951
McMahon, Thomas, 1100, 1101
McShane, Clay, 1647
Mecklermedia's official Internet World Internet yellow pages, 1996 ed, 1587
Mecklermedia's official Internet World WWW yellow pages, 1996 ed, 1588
Media courses UK 1997, 4th ed, 860
Media in Africa & Africa in the media, 853
Medical abbrevs, 8th ed, 1526
Medical & psychological effects of concentration camps on Holocaust survivors, v.4: genocide, 708
Medical discoveries, 1530
Medical meanings: a glossary of word origins, 1528
Medicare made easy, rev ed, 1539
Medieval & early modern data bank [CD-ROM], 165
Meho, Lokman I., 116
Meier, Matt S., 349
Meilikhov, Evgenii Z., 1620
Meiners, Phyllis A., 793
Melton, J. Gordon, 1321, 1366
Mender, Mona, 1199
Mendy, Peter Karibe, 456
Menser, Gary P., 1452
Mercer, E. Ian, 1599
Merck manual of medical info, home ed, 1540
Merriam-Webster's collegiate dict, deluxe audio ed [CD-ROM], 998
Merriam-Webster's geographical dict, 3d ed, 396
Meserole, Mike, 727
Metcalf, Allan A., 1000
Metz, Allan, 255, 800
Mexican, Central, & S American art, 961
Meyer, Ulrich, 1245
Meyers, Eric M., 429, 1377
Michael, Erika, 943
Michael Singer's film directors, 1997, 12th ed, 1317
Mickolus, Edward F., 556
Microsoft Bkshelf Internet dir, 1996-97 ed, 1589
Mid-Youth market, 261

Mieder, Wolfgang, 1157, 1254
Mihalkanin, Edward S., 564
Milepost: trip planner for Ala. & Western Canada, 49th ed, 406
Miletich, John J., 760
Militarism in Arab society, 609
Millar, David, 1399
Miller, Elizabeth B., 1590
Miller, Jeanette W., 1397
Miller, Joseph, 580
Miller, Judith, 903
Miller, Judith A., 521
Miller, Randall M., 438
Miller, Sally E., 72
Miller, Steve Z., 1554
Miller's intl antiques price gd 1997, 18th ed, 903
Mills, Watson E., 1370, 1371
Milne, Rosemary C., 1024
Mimms, Kenneth A., 346
Mina, Robin, 185
Miner, Brad, 691
Minnesota, 412
Minor ballet composers, 1215
Minority orgs, 5th ed, 330
Mirkovich, Thomas R., 724
Mishler, Clifford, 911, 912
Mitchell, Charlotte, 1152
Mitchell, Joan S., 579
Mitchell Kennerly imprint: a descriptive bibliog, 592
Mitchell, Robert, 302
Mitchell, Susan, 256
Mitsis, Phillip T., 1334
Mix, Ann Bennett, 367
Modern campaigns, 615
Modern collectible dolls identification & value gd, 919
Modern drama scholarship & criticism 1981-90, 1105
Modern ency of E Slavic, Baltic, & Eurasian lits, v.10, 1170
Modern Irish writers, 1176
Mogelonsky, Marcia, 257
Moles, Peter, 184
Monaghan, Patricia, 1258
Money for graduate students in the humanities 1996-98, 848
Money for graduate students in the scis 1996-98, 1411
Money for graduate students in the social scis 1996-98, 91
Monroe, Jacqueline Wasserman, 523
Montalvo, Rene J., 20
Moon, Beverly, 1351
Moon, Spencer, 1278
Mooney, Martha T., 65
Moore, P., 1604
Moore, Patrick, 1605
Moore, Robert J., 1541
Moran, Edward, 26
More opening nights on Broadway: a critical quotebk of the musical theatre 1965-81, 1329
Morelli, Jim, 1563
Morey, Carl, 1192
Morgan, Bill, 922

Morgan, Jenny, 1309
Morgan, Kathleen O'Leary, 552
Morgan, Scott, 552
Morris, Bruce B, 1310
Morris, Desmond, 1465
Morris, Neil, 1033
Morris, Roswitha, 1033
Morse, David, 1575
Morton, Brian, 1221
Morton, Leslie T., 1541
Morton, Mark, 1423
Morville, Peter, 1595
Moses, Norton H., 547
Moses, Robert, 1264
Moss, Joyce, 1072
Mote, Dave, 1058
Motion picture gd, 1311
Mountain range: a dict of expressions from Appalachia to the Ozarks, 1007
Moyer, Patsy, 918, 919
Moys, Elizabeth M., 533
Mozart diary, 1213
Mulder, John M., 647
Mullay, Sandy, 137
Muller, Karl, 1350
Muller, Sheila D., 949
Multicultural dict of proverbs, 1250
Multicultural educ dir, 273
Multicultural student's gd to colleges [rev ed], 302
Murphy, Bruce, 843
Murphy, John C., 1474
Murray, Jim, 1426
Murray, Linda, 950
Murray, Peter, 950
Murray, R. Michael, 1209
Museum premieres, exhibitions, & special events, 72
Museums of the world, 73
Music, David W., 1246
Music for voice & classical guitar, 1945-96, 1219
Music in Canada, 1192
Music ref & research materials, 5th ed, 1189
Musical Americans: a biogl dict 1918-26, 1200
MusicHound country, 1233
Musiker, Naomi, 19
Musiker, Reuben, 19
Muslim women throughout the world, 830
MVR bk motor servs gd, 1997 ed, 536
MVR decoder digest, 1997 ed, 537
Myths & hero tales, 1084

Naden, Corinne J., 1091, 1103
NAFTA & GATT: environmental & economic issues, 705
NAFTA bibliog, 255
Naked in cyberspace: how to find personal info online, 1596
Nantz, Jim, 739
Narins, Brigham, 1068
NASA atlas of the solar system, 1609
Nash, Jay Robert, 701
Nash, Rose, 1048

National accounts stats, 203
National cultures of the world, 90
National dir of ...
    bereavement support grps & servs, 1996, 768
    catalogs 1997, 181
    corporate giving, 790
National gd to ...
    educl credit for training programs, 1997 ed, 315
    funding for higher educ, 4th ed, 291
    funding for info tech, 583
National Hispanic media dir, 1997, 861
National jobbank 1998, 237
National museum of American art [CD-ROM], 966
National road race ency, 751
National serv & AmeriCorps, 800
National sports politicies, 725
Nations of Africa, 321
Native educ dir 1997, 272
Naval Institute gd to the ships & aircraft of the US Fleet, 16th ed, 628
Naval Institute gd to world naval weapons systems 1997-98, 634
Nazzal, Laila A., 488
Nazzal, Nafez Y., 488
NCAA basketball: the official 1997 women's college basketball records bk, 740
Neal, Joseph C., 1453
Neft, David S, 746
Nelson, Michael, 674
Ness, Richard R., 1298
Net.journal dir, vol. 1, no. 2, 1591
Never eat more than you can lift, & other food quotes & quips, 1429
Nevins, Allan, 432
New Bible dict, 3d ed, 1373
New bk of goddesses & heroines, 3d ed, 1258
New bk of knowledge, 46
New comparative world atlas, 388
New England's mountain flowers, 1450
New, Gregory R., 579
New hacker's dict, 3d ed, 1578
New intl dict of O.T. theology & exegesis, 1374
New Kabuki ency, 1324
New members of Congress almanac: 105th US Congress, 654
New religious movements in Western Europe, 1343
New shorter Oxford English dict [CD-ROM], 999
New Sotheby's wine ency, 1424
New York, the city in more than 500 memorable quotations, 101
New York Times almanac 1998, 2
Newbery companion, 1091
Newbolt, Peter, 1159
Newcomb, Horace, 888
Newly independent states of Eurasia, 2d ed, 125
Newman, John, 1056
Newsletters in print 1998, 10th ed, 880
Newsmakers 1997, 25
Newsome, Chevelle, 862
Newton, David E., 855
Newton, Kenneth, 684

Nicholas, Jeremy, 1222
Nilsen, Don L. F., 1150
Nimmo, Dan, 862
Nine worlds hosted by Patrick Stewart [CD-ROM], 1610
Nineteenth-century American women writers, 1126
NIV complete Bible lib [CD-ROM], 1380
Nobari, Nuchine, 1582
Nobel prize winners 1992-96 suppl, 26
Noffsinger, James Philip, 610
Nolan, Cathal J., 655
Nonprofit manager's resource dir, 244
Non-profits & educ job finder 1997-2000, 235
Nonviolent action, 496
Nordquist, Joan, 548, 636, 637, 705, 831, 832, 1505
Norfolk, Elizabeth, 903
Norris, Frederick W., 1386
North American art since 1900, 962
North American art to 1900, 963
North American Indian music, 1191
Northwest women: an annot bibliog of sources on the hist of Oreg. & Wash. women, 1787-1970, 828
Notable Latino Americans, 349
Notable US Ambassadors since 1775, 655
Notable women in the physical scis, 1598
Novels for students, v.1, 1109
Novels for students, v.2, 1110
NPR classical music companion, 1202
NSFRE fund-raising dict, 784
NTC's compact Swedish & English dict, 1053
NTC's dict of Latin American Spanish, 1049
NTC's dict of Spanish cognates thematically organized, 1048
NTC's new college Russian & English dict, 1045
NTIS ordernow [CD-ROM], 62
Nuiry, Octavio, 861
Null, Gary, 1550
Numbers: how many, how far, how long, how much, 810
Nurcombe, Valerie J., 61
Nutrition & diet therapy ref dict, 4th ed, 1422

Oakes, Elizabeth H., 330
O'Brien, Geoffrey, 8
O'Brien, Joanne, 1348
O'Brien, Robert L., 1491
Occupational outlook hndbk, 1996-97 ed, 238
Oceanographic & marine resources: 1960-Jan 1997 [CD-ROM], 1616
O Ceirin, Cyril, 34
O Ceirin, Kit, 34
O'Connor, J., 1015
O'Connor, Patrice M., 1521
O'Donnell, Christopher, 1387
Ofcansky, Thomas P., 457
Official baseball rules 1997, 735
Official gd to American incomes, 2d ed, 225
Official Major League Baseball fact bk 1997, 736
Ogden, Tom, 716
O'Handley, Kathryn, 683
O'Hara, Scarlett, 1458
O'Leary, A. P., 619

Ohles, Frederik, 266
Ohles, Shirley M., 266
Okonski, Walter, 480
Old masters, 980
Oldman, Mark, 221
Oliveres, Raphael A., 1049
Oliverson, Ray, 1497
Olsen, Margaret, 913
Olson, Elizabeth A., 269
Olson, James S., 466, 562
Omlid, Steve, 796
On common ground: world religions in America [CD-ROM], 1367
150 yrs of America's Smithsonian [CD-ROM], 74
100 greatest, 27
100 most popular YA authors, rev ed, 1102
One hundred yrs of American women writing, 1848-1948, 1124
O'Neill, James, 1318
O'Neill, Mary, 1027
Onstad, Dianne, 1427
Open secrets: the ency of congressional money & pols, 4th ed, 675
Operas in 1 act, 1224
Orchard, Andy, 1259
Orchestra on record, 1896-1926, 1225
Orchestral music, 3d ed, 1226
Orenstein, Ruth M., 51
Orion blue bk, 182
Ornstein, Norman J., 676
Orodenker, Richard, 883
Orton, Lavinia, 860
Oryx gd to distance learning, 280
Oscar stars from A-Z, 1279
O'Shea, Kathleen A., 549
Osifchin, Gary P., 642, 654
Our Sunday Visitors ency of Catholic doctrine, 1388
Outline maps on file, 398
Owen, Bill, 887
Oxford color Italian dict, 1036
Oxford companion to ...
    African American lit, 1129
    archaeology, 428
    Christian art & architecture, 950
    German lit, 3d ed, 1173
    20th-century lit in English, 1073
Oxford desk dict & thesaurus, American ed, 993
Oxford desk ref atlas, 389
Oxford dict & thesaurus, American ed, 994
Oxford dict of ...
    biochemistry & molecular biology, 1444
    computing for learners of English, 1577
    pol quotations, 641
    quotations, 4th ed, 83
    the Christian Church, 3d ed, 1389
    the Jewish religion, 1396
    world religions, 1357
Oxford-Duden German desk dict, new ed, 1030
Oxford-Duden German dict [CD-ROM], 1032
Oxford-Duden German dict, rev ed, 1031
Oxford ency of archaeology in the Near East, 429

Oxford family ency, 47
Oxford-Hachette French desk dict, 1026
Oxford Italian desk dict, 1037
Oxford Italian minidict, 2d ed, 1038
Oxford pa Portuguese dict, 1042
Oxford pa Spanish dict & grammar, 1050
Oxford starter French dict, 1027
Oxford starter German dict, 1033
Oxford starter Russian dict, 1046
Oxford starter Spanish dict, 1051
Oxford 3-in-1 bilingual dict [CD-ROM], 1021

Pacific NW, 415
Paddock, Lisa, 538
Paine, Lincoln P., 1651
PAIS select [CD-ROM], 89
Palder, Edward L., 183
Palidvor-Sonevyts'ka, Nataliia, 1217
Palmer, Clare, 1628
Palmer, Martin, 1348
Palmer, Pete, 737
Palmowski, Jan, 504
Palombo, Fulvio, 959
Pancza-Graham, Arleen, 963
Panton, Kenneth J., 467
Pare, Michael A., 270, 718
Parenting A to Z, 2d ed, 803
Parent's gd to medical emergencies, 1522
Parish, Peter J., 442
Park, Amy Lynn, 166
Park, Thomas K., 458
Parker, Geoffrey, 616
Parker, Philip M., 90, 331, 990, 1368
Parker, Sybil P., 1407, 1440, 1476, 1602, 1603, 1608, 1614, 1621, 1626
Parry, Donald W., 1397
Parry, Melanie, 24
Partington, Angela, 83
Patent law index, 1997, 545
Paterson, Thomas G., 660
Patin, Thomas, 951
Patrick Kavanagh: a ref gd, 1174
Patten, Fred, 1307
Patterson, Lotsee, 327
Patterson, Michael, 1323
Pavia, Audrey, 1466
Pavlov, A. S., 629
PCI: pers contents index [CD-ROM], 66
Pearson's hndbk desk ed, 1492
Peck, David, 1070
Peck, Malcolm C., 489
Pehle, Walter H., 470
Pelka, Fred, 775
Pellam, John L., 150
Penguin atlas of diasporas, 807
Penguin histl atlas of ancient Egypt, 490
Penn, James R., 399
People's names, 377

Peoples of ...
  Central Africa, 322
  E Africa, 323
  N Africa, 324
  Southern Africa, 325
  W Africa, 326
Performing arts business ency, 1265
Perilli, Barry, 751
Periodical source index CD-ROM [CD-ROM], 373
Perkins, Agnes, 1092
Perkins, Agnes Regan, 1084
Perkins, Kenneth J., 459
Perlman, Seth, 539
Perone, James E., 1193
Perry, Robert H., 1479
Perry's chemical engineers' hndbk, 7th ed, 1479
Personal name index to The New York Times Index, v.5, 67
Personal name index to The New York Times Index, v.6, 68
Peters, David, 1552
Peters, Diane E., 1194
Peterson, Bernard L., Jr., 1328
Peterson, Jane T., 1106
Peterson's college money hndbk 1998, 15th ed, 303
Peterson's competitive colleges 1997-98, 16th ed, 292
Peterson's gd to MBA programs 1998, 160
Peterson's gd to 2-yr colleges 1998, 28th ed, 293
Peterson's scholarship almanac, 304
Peterson's scholarships for study in the USA & Canada 1998, 294
Peterson's US & Canadian medical schools 1997, 1542
Petonito, Gina, 650
Petretti, Allan, 923
Petretti's Coca-Cola collectibles price gd, 10th ed, 923
Pfaff, Bonnie Shaw, 523
Phifer, Paul, 316
Phillips, Mark, 1286
Philosophy: a gd to the ref lit, 2d ed, 1330
Phoenix award of the children's lit assn 1990-94, 1092
PhoneDisc powerfinder [CD-ROM], 54
Photographer's market, 1998, 936
Photographers on disc [CD-ROM], 937
Photographic atlas of the stars, 1604
Physician characteristics & distribution in the US, 1536
Piacente, Steve, 649
Pickard, Roy, 1279
Pickett, Christopher M., 545
Pictorial gd to the living primates, 1472
Picture bks to enhance the curriculum, 284
Picture this: picture bks for young adults, 1097
Pierce, Anne, 1369
Pierce, James R., 1369
Pierson, Darren, 562
Pietrusza, David, 737
Pike-Nase, Christal, 704
Pingatore, Diana R., 1138
Pitman, L. M., 1
Pitt-Catsouphes, Marcie, 777

Pitts, Michael R., 1312
Placenames of the world, 401
Placzek, Adolf K., 971
Plakans, Andrejs, 477
Planet Earth: Macmillan world atlas, 390
Planning your career in alternative medicine, 1549
Platinum & palladium buyer's gd, 913
Plunkett, Jack W., 185, 259
Plunkett's financial servs industry almanac, 185
Plunkett's retail industry almanac, 259
Pockets: aircraft, 1645
Pockets: Bible companion, 1381
Pockets: dogs, 1467
Pockets: ency, 48
Pockets: English dict A to Z, 995
Pockets: French dict, 1028
Pockets: nature facts, 1458
Pockets: Spanish dict, 1052
Poe ency, 1137
Poet's market, 1998, 868
Pohanish, Richard P., 1642
Poison! how to handle the hazardous substances in your home, 1563
Political commentators in the US in the 20th century, 862
Political data hndbk: OECD countries, 2d ed, 684
Political geography, 393
Political leaders & military figures in the 2d World War, 606
Political role of the military, 621
Pollock, Bruce, 1243
Pollock, Sean R., 25
Polmar, Norman, 628
Polunin, Nicholas, 1631
POPLINE: through Dec 1996 [CD-ROM], 778
Porteous, Andrew, 1636
Portman, Janet, 534
Portugal with Madeira & the Azores, 422
Postiglione, Gerard A., 295
Potter, Alicia, 1264
Potter's dict of materials & techniques, 4th ed, 932
Pottery & porcelain ceramics price gd, 927
Potts, Howard E., 341
Potts, Karen, 588
Poverty Row studios, 1929-40: an illus hist of 53 independent film cos...., 1312
Powell, John, 462
Powers, Roger S., 692
Practical dict of German usage, 1029
Practical gd to planned giving 1998, 791
Prague, 122
Predicting the future, 88
Pregnancy & birth sourcebk, 1561
Prescription for nutritional healing, 1507
Preservation yellow pages, rev ed, 975
Presidential Medal of Freedom, 30
Presidents, 661
Presidents, first ladies, & vice presidents, 653
Presidents of the US—their written measure, 648
Press freedom & dvlpmt, 850
Preventive care sourcebk 1997-98, 1519
Price, Anne, 586

Prime time network serials, 1310
Prime-time religion, 1366
Prince, Mary Miles, 516
Princeton Review student advantage gd to visiting college campuses, 1997 ed, 305
Pro-choice/pro-life issues in the 1990s, 756
Produce ref gd to fruits & vegetables from around the world, 1421
Professional & occupational licensure in the US, 704
Professional codes of conduct in the UK, 2d ed, 1341
Professional sports stats, 722
Protest, power, & change, 692
Protocol: a hndbk for legislative staff, 677
Proverb wit & wisdom, 1249
Proverbial Charles Dickens, 1157
Proverbs in world lit, 1254
Provorse, Carl, 823
Prues, Don, 870
Prues, Donald M., 866
Psychiatric dict, 7th ed, 1556
Public records online, 1997 ed, 706
Publishers dir, 1998, 18th ed, 603
Publishers' intl ISBN dir 1997/98, 604
Pyne, Sandra, 1577

Qiu, Minjia, 174
Quality mgmt sourcebk, 241
Quality, TQC, TQM: a meta lit study, 243
Questions & answers bk of sci facts, 1404
Quiram, Jacquelyn, 568
Quitno, Neal, 552

Race, crime, & the criminal justice system, 548
Radzig, A. A., 1620
Rageau, Jean-Pierre, 807
Rahman, Syedur, 460
Rainforest orgs, 1639
Raish, Martin, 942
Raistrick, Donald, 512
Raitt, Lia Correia, 1042
Ramsay, John G., 266
Randolph, Lillian, 1536
Random House histl dict of American slang, v.2: H-O, 1015
Rann, Rick, 921
Ranney, Doug, 1307
Rap whoz who, 1237
Rapalje, Stewart, 520
Rasor, Eugene L., 611
Raycraft, Carol, 904
Raycraft, Don, 904
Rayhawk, Peggie, 642, 654
Raymond, Eric S., 1578
Re, Joseph M., 306
Rea, William R., 956
Reader's catalog, 2d ed, 8
Reader's companion to military hist, 616
Readers' gd abstracts full text mega ed [CD-ROM], 69
Readers' gd for young people [CD-ROM], 77

Readers' gd to ...
  american hist, 442
  per lit 1995, 70
  the short stories of Eudora Welty, 1138
  the short stories of Stephen Crane, 1133
Real vitamin & mineral bk, 1548
Recent ref bks in religion, 1346
Recommended bks in Spanish for children & YAs, 1991-95, 1079
Recommended ref bks for small & medium-sized libs & media centers 1997, 9
Red Nichols story, 1236
Reed, Ida, 1189
Reed, William Cyrus, 699
Reel black talk: a sourcebk of 50 American filmmakers, 1278
Rees, Alan M., 1538
Rees, Nigel, 1018
Reese, William L., 1337
Reference gd to the Bible in Emily Dickinson's poetry, 1135
Refugees in America in the 1990s, 801
Rehill, Anne Collier, 1281
Rehrig, William H., 1229
Reif, Joe, 262
Reincarnation: a selected annot bibliog, 715
Reinventing govt, 644
Religions of the world, 1348
Religious cultures of the world, 1368
Renshaw, Patrick, 449
Renstrom, Peter G., 540
Renz, Loren, 794
Representative American speeches 1995-96, 1131
Reptile & amphibian problem solver, 1473
Research on professional consultation & consultation for organizational change, 709
Resource gd to travel in sub-Saharan Africa v.2, 420
Resources of the Third World, 120
Review of maritime transport 1997, 260
Rhodes, Karen, 1313
Rich, Elizabeth H., 291, 583, 758, 789
Richards, Chris, 1356
Richardson, David A., 1147
Riggs, Quentin, 1198
Riggs, Thomas, 945
Rinderknecht, Carol, 17
Ringgren, Helmer, 1375
Rinker, Harry L., 891
R.I.P.: the complete bk of death & dying, 766
Ritchey, Ferris J., 1524
Robb, H. Amanda, 79
Robbins, Keith, 464
Robbins, Robert A., 528
Roberto, Deborah, 703
Roberts, James B., 743
Robert's rules in plain English, 681
Robertson, Jack S., 969
Robertson, James, 136
Robertson, James I., Jr., 432
Robertson, Lawrence R., 129

Robertson, Malcolm J., 171
Robertson, Stephen L., 653
Robinson, Jo Ann, 315
Robinson, Judith Schiek, 60
Robinson, Mike, 397
Rock & roll reader's gd, 1242
Rock song index, 1243
Rodger, Richard, 825
Rogal, Samuel J., 1160
Roger Ebert's video companion, 1319
Rogers, Joan C., 528
Rogerson, John, 1377
Rognehaugh, Richard, 1509
Rollberg, Peter, 1170
Romans, 1371
Romantic hearts: a personal ref for romance readers, 3d ed, 1115
Ronald Colman: a bio-bibliog, 1273
Rony, A. Kohar, 114
Ronzio, Robert A., 1520
Room, Adrian, 401, 1260
Roosens, Laurent, 938
Rosa Luxemburg & Emma Goldman: a bibliog, 637
Rose, Peter Q., 1455
Rosenberg, William G., 481
Rosenfeld, Louis, 1595
Rosenthal Collection of printed bks with ms annots, 578
Rosenthal, Bernard M., 578
Rosow, La Vergne, 1057
Ross, Leon T., 346
Ross, Thomas W., 1158
Roster of Confederate soldiers 1861-65, 451
Roster of Union soldiers 1861-65: US colored troops, 452
Roth, John E., 1255
Roth, Mitchel P., 881
Rountree, Bob, 1522
Routldege French dict of environmental technology, 1637
Routledge German dict of business commerce & finance, 156
Routledge German dict of construction, 1482
Routledge German dict of info tech, 1579
Routledge Spanish technical dict, 1408
Rowe, Noel, 1472
Rowe, Sara, 589, 590
Rowen, Beth, 1264
Roy, Michelle, 237
Roze, Janis A., 1475
Rubel, David, 436, 443
Rubin, Melvin L., 1553
Rudin, Norah, 1445
Rudolph, Donna Keyse, 142
Rudolph, G. A., 142
Rulau, Russell, 914
Rumsey, William D., 1332
Rupp, Robert O., 645
Russell, Cheryl, 261
Russell, Rinaldina, 1177
Russell, Timothy O., 419
Russia & Eurasia facts & figures annual, v.21, 128
Russia & Eurasia facts & figures annual, v.22, 129

Russian-English comprehensive dict, 1047
Russian idioms, 1043
Ryskamp, George R., 368

Saar, Doreen Alvarez, 1111
Saari, Peggy, 834, 1401
Sabin Collection catalog [CD-ROM], 10
Safety & health on the Internet, 239
Saha, Lawrence J., 268
St. Helena, Ascension, & Tristan da Cunha, 146
St. James gd to black artists, 945
Sakach, Deborah Edwards, 427
Salda, Anne C. M., 186
Saldarini, Anthony J., 1377
Salu, Luc, 938
Samir Husni's gd to new consumer mags, 1997 ed, 882
Samoa (American Samoa, Western Samoa, Samoans abroad), 145
Sanjurjo, Annick, 955
Sankey, Michael, 63, 419, 536, 537, 665, 706
Sankey, Michael L., 524, 525, 666
Santucci, James A., 1364
Saraceno, Dan, 288
Sarkozi, Matyas, 133
Sayler, James, 648
Scargill, Matthew H., 1012
Schaefer, Christina K., 332
Schaefer, Michael W., 1133
Schenkenberg, Amy, 676
Schiller, Carol, 1551
Schiller, David, 1551
Schimke, Ann, 285, 417
Schlachter, Gail Ann, 91, 307, 848, 1411
Schleifer, Jay, 369
Schlueter, June, 1067
Schlueter, Paul, 1067
Schmalleger, Frank, 550
Schmidt, H. Joachim, 1510
Schmittroth, Linda, 827
Schofield, Mary Anne, 1111
Scholastic children's dict, rev ed, 1008
Scholastic ency of ...
    the N American Indian, 355
    the presidents & their times, updated ed, 443
    women in the US, 836
Scholze-Stubenrecht, Werner, 1031
Schon, Isabel, 358, 1079
Schonberg, Harold C., 1216
School violence, 278
Schraepler, Hans-Albrecht, 161
Schrank, Bernice, 1175
Schreiber, Mae N., 199
Schroeder's antiques price gd, 15th ed, 905
Schuenenman, Bruce R., 1215
Schultz, Jeffrey D., 659
Schultz, Margie, 1274
Schumann, Walter, 1615
Schwartz, Alan M., 1638
Schwartz, Donald Ray, 1275
Schwartz, Richard Alan, 508

Schwedt, Rachel E., 1077
Science & tech firsts, 1402
Science fiction & fantasy reference index 1992-95, 1117
Science fiction, fantasy, & horror film sequels, series, & remakes, 1292
Science fiction TV series, 1286
Science on file [CD-ROM], 1415
Science yr 1997, 1416
Science yr 1998, 1417
Scientific unit conversion, 1597
Scientists, 1401
Sci-Fi on tape, 1318
Sclater, Neil, 1489
Scott, David L., 170
Scott, John F., 961
Scott, Shirley R., 981
Scott, Susan, 924
Scott, Thomas A., 1599
Screen, J. E. O., 123
Scroggins, Daniel C., 1182
Seabourne, Joan, 789
Sears list of subject headings, 16th ed, 580
Sects, 'cults,' & alternative religions, 1360
Seligman, Kevin L., 934
Sendor, Virginia F., 1521
Senick, Gerard J., 1080
Senior high school lib catalog, 15th ed, 587
Serri, Conchita Franco, 349
Services—the export of the 21st century: a gdbk of US serv exporters, 262
Sexuality & the elderly, 798
Shadle, Robert, 466
Shakespeare for students, bk 2, 1163
Shakespeare's characters for students, 1164
Shambhala ency of yoga, 1338
Sharp, Gene, 496
Sharp, J. Michael, 678
Sharp, James Roger, 650
Sharp, Nancy Weatherly, 650
Shatzky, Joel, 1125
Shaw, Gareth, 132
Shaw, Patricia, 1214
Shaw, Russell, 1388
Shearer, Barbara S., 1598
Shearer, Benjamin F., 1598
Sheehy, Noel, 710
Sherman, Gale W., 1090
Sherman, Marc I., 708
Shields, Graham, 138
Shiers, George, 889
Shiers, May, 889
Shilling, Henry, 175
Shim, Jae K., 263
Shipp, Steve, 1639
Ships of the world, 1651
Shopping with a conscience, 178
Short fiction: a criticial companion, 1119
Short stories for students, v.1, 1120
Short stories for students, v.2, 1121
Short story index 1995, 1122
Short story writers, 1123

Shortelle, Dennis, 854
Shou-hsin, Teng, 1023
Shriver, George H., 1354
Shuldiner, David P., 761
Siegel, Joel G., 263
Siegel, Mark A., 753, 1559
Siegman, Joseph, 719
Sienkewicz, Thomas J., 1261
Sierra, Judy, 378
Signers of the Declaration of Independence, 434
Signs of the zodiac, 717
Silver, Joel, 594
Silverblatt, Art, 856
Silverman, David P., 486
Simmons, Susan L., 556
Simpson, James B., 84
Simpson's contemporary quotations, rev ed, 84
Singer, Michael, 1317
Singers of the century, 1201
Singleton, Carl, 117
Sinko, Peggy Tuck, 379, 431
Siochain, Etain O, 45
Sir Arthur Sullivan: a resource bk, 1212
Sitarz, Daniel, 541, 542
Sixteenth-century British nondramatic writers, 4th series, 1147
Sixties [CD-ROM], 450
Skelly, Elizabeth M. T., 1495
Skelly, Kenneth J., 1495
Skutt, Alexander G., 743
Slee, Debora A., 1510
Slee, Vergil N., 1510
Sleuths, sidekicks, & stooges, 1112
Slonimsky, Nicolas, 1197
Small business sourcebk, 10th ed, 166
Smaller perennials, 1435
Smith, A. D., 1444
Smith, Darren L., 418
Smith, John David, 438
Smith, Marty, 1464
Smith, Robert Ellis, 543
Smith, Ron, 736
Smith, Tony, 802
Smith, Verity, 1178
Smoley, Lewis M., 1248
Snodgrass, Mary Ellen, 717, 1130
Social movement theory & research, 690
Social scis abstracts full text [CD-ROM], 92
Social scis index, April 1995 to Mar 1996, 93
Sociofile: 1974-Dec 1996 [CD-ROM], 94
Sociology: a gd to ref & info sources, 782
Sofer, Morry, 991
Sollberger, Martha Park, 1185
Solomon Islands campaign, Guadalcanal to Rabaul, 611
Solomon, Sheila A. B., 1553
Something about the author autobiog series, v.24, 1080
Sonevyts'kyi, Ihor, 1217
Song Writers Market, 1998, 1207
Sophie Treadwell: a research & production sourcebk, 1132
Sorrow, Barbara Head, 282
Soukhanov, Anne H., 1002

Source: a gdbk of American genealogy, 370
Sourcebook for Jewish genealogies & family hists, 362
Sourcebook of county court records, 3d ed, 524
Sourcebook of local court & county record retrievers, 3d ed, 525
South, David W., 1477
Southeast Asian langs & lits, 986
Spanish artists from the 4th to the 20th century, 952
Spaulding, Seth, 694
Speaking freely, 1002
Special edition: a gd to network TV documentary series & special news reports, 1980-89, 1304
Spencer, Frank, 320
Spencer, Janet, 305
Spencer, Pam, 1098
Spies, 701
Spille, Henry A., 308
Sporting News official NBA gd, 1997-98 ed, 741
Sporting News official NBA register, 742
Sports ency: pro football, 746
Sports stars, series 3, 718
Spratto, George R., 1566, 1567
Spurge, Lorraine, 154
Spyke, Rebecca, 699
Square foot costs 1997, 18th ed, 1483
Squyres, Suzanne B., 568, 1559
Stachura, Lisa, 725
Stade, George, 1149
Stambler, Irwin, 1234
Stancell, Steven, 1237
Standard catalog of
    American cars, 1946-75, 1648
    baseball cards, 1998, 906
    football cards, 900
    US tokens 1700-1900, 914
    world coins, 18th century 1701-1800, 911
    world coins, 1998, 912
Star gd, 1997-98, 1266
Stars in blue: movie actors in America's sea servs, 1281
State & local taxation answer bk, 264
State atlas of pol & cultural diversity, 329
State staff dir, summer 1997, 667
Statistical yrbk for Asia & the Pacific 1996, 815
Statistical yrbk 1994, 41st ed, 816
Statistically speaking: a dict of quotations, 82
Statler Brothers discography, 1232
Steane, J. B., 1201
Stebbings, Geoff, 1454
Steen, Peter, 699
Steen, Sara J., 988
Stein, Barry Jason, 625
Stephen Crane ency, 1134
Stephens, Norris L., 1190
Sterling, Christopher H., 1646
Sterry, Paul, 1404
Stevens, R. Paul, 1385
Stevenson, Neil, 976
Stevenson, Tom, 1424
Stewart, Barbara, 591
Stewart, Brian, 982
Stewart, David W., 308

Stewart, Sean, 742
Stilman, Anne, 1005
Stilwell, Steven A., 1113
Stoll, Donald R., 879
Stone, Jon R., 1039, 1366
Stoneham, Marshall, 1220
Storytelling ency, 1256
Stover, Lois T., 1095
Strachan, Ian W., 1573
Strauss, Carol Ann, 779
Strickland, Ruth Ann, 679
Stringer, Jenny, 1073
Stuart, Philip, 1204
Stuart, Ralph B., III, 239
Stubblebine, Donald J., 1195
Student's dict of lang & linguistics, 987
Student's gd to Jewish American genealogy, 369
Studwell, William E., 1215
Stuhr-Rommereim, Rebecca, 347
Sturges, Paul, 571
Subject gd to bks in print 1997-98, 16
Subject gd to US govt ref sources, 2d ed, 60
Subramanian, Jane M., 1139
Sukhwal, B. L., 393
Sukhwal, Lilawati, 393
Sullivan, Bruce M., 1392
Sullivan, Eugene, 308
Sullivan, Karen, 1545
Sullivan, Michael, 967
Sullivan, Thomas F. P., 559
Summers, W. Franklin, 1224
Summers, Wilford I., 1485
Sumner, David E., 309
Sundermeier, Theo, 1350
Suskin, Steven, 1329
Susser, Allen, 1428
Sutcliffe, Andrea, 810
Sutherland, Caroline, 683
Suziedelis, Saulius, 478
Swinerton, E. Nelson, 315
Switzer, Teri R., 212
Sykes, J. B., 1031
Szucs, Loretto Dennis, 370

Taber's cyclopedic medical dict, 18th ed, 1531
Tamborlane, William V., 1555
Tanks, 631
Tasmania, 118
Taub, Michael, 1125
Taussig, Louis, 420
Taylor, David, 1467
Teen genreflecting, 1096
Telecommuters, the workforce of the 21st century, 212
Television musicals, 1301
Television western players of the 50s, 1276
Television westerns episode gd, 1308
Telgen, Diane, 1109, 1110
Tenuto, John, 690
Terrace, Vincent, 1314
Terrorism in the US, 557

Terrorism, 1992-95, 556
Terry, Nicholas, 184
Tesucun, Felix Fernando, 1040
Tetzloff, Jason M., 562
Thawley, John, 144
Theatregoer's almanac, 1327
Thematic catalogues in music, 2d ed, 1188
Theological dict of the O.T., v.8, 1375
Theories of myth, 1261
Theories of pol processes, 635
Thinking from A to Z, 1339
32nd annual steam passenger serv dir, 1649
Thode, Ernest, 363
Thoma, Emile, 135
Thomas, Avril, 475
Thomas, Charles Flint, 1154
Thomas, Clayton L., 1531
Thomas, Colin, 475
Thomas Cook intl air travel hndbk 1997, 407
Thomas, Rebecca L., 1093
Thomas register of American manufacturers, 1997, 87th ed, 196
Thomas register on CD-ROM, 1997 [CD-ROM], 197
Thompson, Clifford, 26
Thompson, Della, 1046
Thompson, Henry O., 1372
Thompson, Kathleen, 343
Thompson, Maggie, 908
Thompson, Sue Ellen, 1263
Thompson, Verlinda D., 1087
Thomsett, Jean Freestone, 85
Thomsett, Michael C., 85
Thorn, John, 737
Thorndike, E. L., 1009
Thorndike-Barnhart jr dict, 1009
Thorne, Kathryn Ford, 431
Thorne, Sandra A., 1397
Thunderbird gd to intl business resources on the WWW, 204
Thyen, O., 1030
Ticket to the opera, 1223
Tigges, Julie A., 544
Tillman, Hope N., 1586
Timelines of Native American hist, 351
Tipper, Allison, 132
Tirion, Wil, 1605
Toasting Cheers: an episode gd to the 1982-93 comedy series...., 1302
Tobler, Judy, 1345, 1382
Toll-Free phone bk USA 1997, 55
Tolliday, Steven, 149
Tomaselli-Moschovitis, Valerie, 499
Tompkins, Vincent, 445
Topline ency of histl charts, Mar 1997 ed, 176
Total baseball, 737
Total football, 747
Toth, Georgetta, 785
Totten, Herman L., 1099
Touchstones: a gd to records, rights, & resources for families of American WW II casualties, 367
Tracy, Deborah, 1585

Trammell, Jeffrey B., 654
Tran, Trinh C., 794
Translator's hndbk 1997, 991
Trask, R. L., 987
Travel & vacation phone bk USA, 404
Traveler's sourcebk 1997, 418
Travers, Bridget, 1530
Travis, William G., 1383
Treasure hard to attain: images of archaeology in popular film, 1290
Treasury of Polish aphorisms, 1253
Trilliums, 1448
Trogdon, Robert W., 1127
Trotter, David, 1152
Troy, Leo, 177
Trucano, Michael, 698
True crime narratives, 546
Trumbull, Priscilla, 198
Truscott, Alan, 744
TSCA hndbk, 3d ed, 561
Tuck, Allene, 1577
Tuller, Michael N., 787, 788
Tun-Atz, Hilary Henri, 793
Turner, C. M. E. P., 962
Turner, Jane, 947
Turner, John R., 593
Twayne's masterwork studies on CD-ROM [CD-ROM], 1074
Twentieth-century American sportswriters, 883
Twentieth-century artists on art, 2d ed, 969
Twentieth-century hist of US population, 808
Twentieth-century short story explication: new series, v.3: 1993-94, 1118
20,000 Spanish American pseudonyms, 1182
200 yrs of dolls, 916
2000 yrs of disbelief: famous people with the courage to doubt, 1347
Tyrkus, Michael J., 781
Tyson, Jacqueline, 783

Ultimate bk of sports lists 1998, 727
Ultimate business lib, 148
Ultimate family tree deluxe [CD-ROM], 371
Ultimate human body version 2.0 [CD-ROM], 1499
Ultimate movie thesaurus, 1303
Ultimate pocket: flags of the world, 374
Understanding American business jargon, 153
Unger, Melvin P., 1247
United States & Latin America, 697
U.S. Army patches, 625
U.S. employment opportunities, 240
U.S. homes [CD-ROM], 56
U.S. homes & business [CD-ROM], 57
United States in the 19th century, 436
U.S.-Mexican treaties, 680
U.S. military online, 617
U.S. news coverage of racial minorities, 852
U.S. primary elections 1995-96, 673
Unveiling Indonesia, 114
Using public records to find & investigate anyone, 703

USSR population census, 1989 [CD-ROM], 130
Utter, Glenn H., 679
Uva, Richard H., 1453
U*X*L multicultural CD [CD-ROM], 333

Vardy, Steven Bela, 473
Vacationing with your pet, 402
Valman, Bernard, 1554
van Hartesveldt, Fred R., 494
van Heel, K. Donker, 503
Van Vynckt, Virginia, 1420
van Wyk, J. J., 638
VanGemeren, Willem A., 1374
VanMeter, Vandelia L., 1114
Variety & Daily Variety TV reviews, v.18: 1993-94, 1315
Varzi, Achille C., 1331
Vazquez-Gomez, Juana, 485
Verify those credentials: do you know who you're dealing with?, 63
VGM's careers ency, 4th ed, 217
Viacheslav Ivanov: a ref gd, 1181
Viano, Richard, 1188
Victorian database on CD-ROM, 1970-95 [CD-ROM], 468
VideoHound's sci-fi experience, 1320
VideoHound's vampires on video, 1321
Vietnam studies, 117
Vietnam War lit, 3d ed, 1056
Vincent, C. Paul, 471
Virtual field trips, 281
Virtual musician, 1206
Virtual roots: a gd to genealogy & local hist on the WWW, 366
Vital stats on Congress 1995-96, 676
Vogele, William B., 692
Vogelsong, Diana, 1438
Volat, Helene, 1171
Volunteer America, 4th ed, 795
von Schlegell, Barbara R., 830

Wagman, Robert J., 643
Wagner, J., 581
Waier, Phillip R., 1480
Walker, Bonnie L., 798
Walker, John, 1305
Walker's manual of community bank stocks, 187
Walker's manual of unlisted stocks, 172
Wall Street words, 170
Wallace-Homestead price gd to American country antiques, 904
Waller, Lynn, 1376
Wallner, Jeff, 1450
Walsh, Gretchen, 853
Walter Scott Publishing Co., 593
Walter, Virginia A., 1560
Walton, John H., 1379
Walton, Rachel, 1522
Wang, Richard T., 112
Wanted to buy, 6th ed, 901
War & conflict quotations, 85

War of 1812 eyewitness accounts, 608
Warburton, Nigel, 1339
Warman's coins & currency, 2d ed, 915
Warner, Jay, 1239
Warner, Ken, 920
Warsaw, 423
Warships of the USSR & Russia, 1945-95, 629
Wartime Poland, 1939-45, 480
Washburn, David E., 273
Washington '97, 14th ed, 58
Wasserman, Steven, 523
Watson, Cynthia, 621
Watson, James, 857
Wax, Imy, 290
Wayne, Kathryn M., 977
Weber, R. David, 91, 307, 848, 1411
Webster, L. F., 1484
Webster, Robert G., 1442
Webster's new world dict of media & communications, rev ed, 858
Weddington, Michael, 751
Weeds of the NE, 1453
WEFA industrial monitor 1997, 198
Weiner, Mitchel, 992
Weiner, Richard, 858
Weiner, Robert G., 1240
Weingart, Patrice Walsh, 820
Weise, Frieda O., 1504
Welfare reform, 799
Wellner, Alison S., 726
Wellner, Alison Stein, 258
Wells, Edward R., 1638
Wells, Stuart, III, 907
Wells, Robert N., Jr., 560
Wenborn, Neil, 465
Wendel, C. H., 1419
Werblowsky, R. J. Zwi, 1396
Werner, Michael S., 141
Wertheim, Stanley, 1134
Wertsman, Vladimir F., 101
Westin, Richard A., 680
Westminster dict of theological terms, 1358
Weston, Mary Ann, 852
Wetterau, Bruce, 30
Wetzel, Bethann, 1317
Whaley, Leigh Ann, 469
What do I take? a consumer's gd to nonprescription drugs, 1568
What do YAs read next? v.2, 1098
What else should I read? guiding kids to good bks, v.2, 1076
What happened where, 500
What mystery do I read next? a reader's gd to recent mystery fiction, 1113
Wheeler, Helen Rippier, 762
Where Queen Elizabeth slept & what the butler saw, 1011
Where to play in the USA: the gaming gd, 419
Whisenhunt, Donald W., 439, 440
Whisler, Kirk, 861
Whitaker's bks in print 1997, 14
Whitburn, Joel, 1205

White, Ernest M., 647
White, Ethel S., 647
Whitlam, John, 1041, 1042
Whitten, Bessie E., 162
Whitten, David O., 162
Whole foods companion, 1427
Who's buying food & drink, 257
Who's buying for the home, 258
Who's who in ...
   American law 1996-97, 514
   Asian banking & finance, 150
   classical mythology, 1260
   Congress 1997, 656
   democracy, 639
   European pols, 3d ed, 685
   Latin America, 4th ed, 35
   medicine & healthcare 1997-98, 1506
   the East 1997-98, 26th ed, 31
   the West 1998-99, 26th ed, 32
Who's who of British jazz, 1235
Who's who of Victorian cinema, 1280
Wick, Robert L., 1196
Wieczynski, Joseph L., 482
Wiedemann, Barbara, 1119
Wigoder, Geoffrey, 502, 1396
Wiley, Bell I., 432
Wiley dict of civil engineering & construction, 1484
Wiley ency of packaging tech, 2d ed, 1493
Wiley's English-Spanish, Spanish-English business dict, 157
Wiley's English-Spanish, Spanish-English legal dict, 2d ed, 519
Willard, Jim, 372
Willard, Terry, 372
Willem Marinus Dudok, a Dutch modernist, 974
William Butler Yeats ency, 1166
William Somerset Maugham ency, 1160
Williamson, John, 618
Willins, Michael, 936
Willis, Donald C., 1300
Willson, Quentin, 1650
Wilson, Bernice, 957
Wilson, C. Dwayne, 709
Wilson, George, 1072
Wilson, Jane, 372
Wilson, Katharina M., 1067
Wilson, Kathleen, 1120, 1121
Winchester, Tom, 1292
Wind ensemble sourcebk & biogl gd, 1220
Winning edge: the student-athlete's gd to college sports, 5th ed, 723
Winterton, Jules, 533
Wise, James E., 1281
Wisniewski, Debra J., 902
Withers, Martin B., 1461, 1470
Witt, Elder, 526, 529
Wizards & sorcerers, 716
WLN interlibrary loan policies dir, 5th ed, 585
Wolff, Manfred E., 1565
Wolff, Miles, 729
Woman's ency of natural healing, 1550

Woman's gd to coping with disability, 2d ed, 776
Women & aging, 762
Women & health, 1500
Women in modern American pols, 829
Women in the Third World, 839
Women of Congress, 833
Women of Ireland, 34
Women of the All-American Girls Professional Baseball League, 734
Women playwrights in England, Ireland, & Scotland 1660-1823, 1151
Women playwrights of diversity, 1106
Women writers of Grt Brit & Europe, 1067
Women's almanac, 827
Women's chronology, 834
Women's firsts, 835
Women's issues, 837
Women's legal gd, 544
Women's rights on trial, 563
Women's studies index 1995, 842
Women's voices, 840
Wong, Mary M., 768
Wong, Nancy C., 11
Wood, D. R. W., 1373
Woodbridge, Hensley C., 1183
Woodham, Anne, 1552
Woodrow Wilson, 647
Woods, Adrienne L., 1566, 1567
Woodstra, Chris, 1228, 1230
Work-Family research, 777
World almanac & bk of facts 1997, 3
World almanac for kids 1998, 4
World almanac of US pols, 1997-99 ed, 643
World Bk dict, 996
World Bk ency of sci, 1409
World Bk health & medical annual 1997, 1543
World Bk yr bk, 1997, 64
World Bks young scientist, 1410
World country analyst [CD-ROM], 205
World databases in humanities, 849
World dir of minorities, 334
World economic outlook, May 1997, 188
World facts & maps, 400
World gd 1997/98, 10th ed, 97
World industrial robots 1997, 1581
World investment dir 1996, v.5: Africa, 201
World investment dir 1996, v.6: w Asia, 207
World religions, 1361
World Shakespeare bibliog on CD-ROM 1990-93 [CD-ROM], 1165
World War I aviation, rev ed, 610
World War II in Europe, Africa, & the Americas, with general sources, 622
World who is who & does what in environment & conservation, 1631
Worth a 1,000 words: an annot gd to picture bks for older readers, 1090
Wratten, Darrel, 1345, 1382
Wright, John W., 2
Wright, Marshall D., 738
Wright, Russell O., 769, 808
Writers for YAs, 1104
Writer's market, 1998, 870
Writer's market, 1998, electronic ed [CD-ROM], 869
Writer's resource, 871
Writer's resource hndbk, 865
Wynar, Bohdan S., 9

Yaakov, Juliette, 586, 587
Yale gd to children's nutrition, 1555
Yamashita, Kenneth, 327
Yampolsky, Selma, 26
Yang, Hiyol, 167
Yaws, Carl L., 1622, 1623
Yeager, Rodger, 457
Yearbook of intl orgs 1997/98, 71
Yeoman, R. S., 910
Young, Philip H., 1088

Zabel, Diane, 241
Zagars, Julie, 975
Zand, Janet, 1522
Zell, Hans M., 105
Zenker, Stephanie F., 1095
Zeyl, Donald J., 1334
Zheutlin, Barbara, 871
Zilboorg, Caroline, 835
Zimmerman, Doris P., 681
Zip code finder, 59
Zubatsky, David S., 362
Zuckerman, Amy, 206
Zuk, Judith D., 1432
Zumerchik, John, 720
Zurcher, Erik, 507

Subject Index
Reference is to entry number.

ABBREVIATIONS
Buttress's world gd to abbrevs of orgs, 11th ed, 1

ABORTION
Abortion, 1996 ed, 753
Abortion & reproductive rights [CD-ROM], 754
Anti-abortion movement, 755
Pro-choice/pro-life issues in the 1990s, 756

ACCREDITATION (EDUCATION)
Certification & accreditation programs dir, 270

ACOUSTICS. *See* **SOUND**

ACRONYMS
Buttress's world gd to abbrevs of orgs, 11th ed, 1

ACTORS. *See also* **MOTION PICTURE ACTORS & ACTRESSES**
Ann Sheridan: a bio-bibliog, 1274
Lillian Russell: a bio-bibliog, 1275

ADJUSTMENT (PSYCHOLOGY)
Woman's gd to coping with disability, 2d ed, 776

ADMINISTRATIVE AGENCIES
Federal regulatory dir, 8th ed, 664
Government phone bk USA 1997, 5th ed, 52
State staff dir, summer 1997, 667

ADOLESCENCE
Adolescence: the survival gd for parents & teenagers, 802

AERONAUTICS
Commercial air transport bks, 1646
Pockets: aircraft, 1645

AFGHANISTAN
Historical dict of Afghanistan, 2d ed, 110

AFRICA
Africa in figures 1996, 102
African intl relations, 2d ed, 699
Nations of Africa, 321

AFRICA—ACRONYMS
African acronyms & abbrevs, 104

AFRICA, CENTRAL
Peoples of Central Africa, 322

AFRICA, EAST
Common birds of E Africa, 1461
Larger animals of E Africa, 1470
Peoples of E Africa, 323

AFRICA IN MASS MEDIA
Media in Africa & Africa in the media, 853

AFRICA—MAPS
Maps & mapping of Africa, 392

AFRICA, NORTH
Peoples of N Africa, 324

AFRICA, NORTH—ANTIQUITIES
Oxford ency of archaeology in the Near East, 429

AFRICA—POLITICS & GOVERNMENT
Africa, 103

AFRICA, SOUTHERN
Peoples of Southern Africa, 325

AFRICA—STUDY & TEACHING
African studies companion, 2d ed, 105

AFRICA, SUB-SAHARAN
Africa S of the Sahara 1997, 26th ed, 108
Resource gd to travel in sub-Saharan Africa v.2, 420

AFRICA, WEST
Benin, 106
Historical dict of the Republic of Guinea-Bissau, 3d ed, 456
Peoples of W Africa, 326

AFRICAN LITERATURE
African writers, 1167

AFRO-AMERICANS
African American almanac, 346
African American almanac, 7th ed, 335
African American ency suppl, 336
African-American orators, 337
Autobiographies by Americans of color 1980-94, 347
Bibliographic gd to black studies 1995, 339
Black demographic data, 1790-1860, 342
Comprehensive name index for The American Slave, 341
Dictionary of Afro-American slavery, updated ed, 438
Encyclopedia of African-American heritage, 338
Frame by frame 2: a filmography of the African American image, 1978-94, 1295
Freedom's lawmakers: a dir of black officeholders during Reconstruction, rev ed, 344
Historical dict of the civil rights movement, 565
Reel black talk: a sourcebk of 50 American filmmakers, 1278
U*X*L multicultural CD [CD-ROM], 333

AFRO-AMERICANS—COLLECTIBLES
Black Americana price gd, 892

AFRO-AMERICANS—QUOTATIONS
Contemporary quotations in black, 70

AFRO-AMERICANS IN LITERATURE
Lorraine Hansberry: a research & production sourcebk, 1136
Oxford companion to African American lit, 1129

AFRO-AMERICAN THEATER
African American theatre dir, 1816-1960, 1328

AFRO-AMERICAN WOMEN
Facts on File ency of black women in America, 343

AGED. *See also* **GERONTOLOGY**
Depression in the elderly, 760
Folklore, culture, & aging, 761
Graying of America: an ency of aging, health, mind, & behavior, 759
Group work with the elderly, 757
Sexuality & the elderly, 798
Women & aging, 762

AGNOSTICS
2000 yrs of disbelief: famous people with the courage to doubt, 1347

AGRICULTURAL IMPLEMENTS
Encyclopedia of American farm implements & antiques, 1419

AIDS (DISEASE)
AIDS, 1996 ed, 1559
HIV/AIDS info for children, 1560

AIRLINES
Commercial air transport bks, 1646

AIRPLANES
Pockets: aircraft, 1645

AIRPLANES, MILITARY
Jane's military aircraft image lib [CD-ROM], 623
Naval Institute gd to the ships & aircraft of the US Fleet, 16th ed, 628

AIRPORTS
Thomas Cook intl air travel hndbk 1997, 407

AIR TRAVEL
Thomas Cook intl air travel hndbk 1997, 407

ALASKA
Milepost: trip planner for Ala. & Western Canada, 49th ed, 406

ALL AMERICAN GIRLS PROFESSIONAL BASEBALL LEAGUE
Women of the All-American Girls Professional Baseball League, 734

ALMANACS
A&E entertainment almanac, 1997, 1264
African American almanac, 346
Irish almanac & yrbk of facts 1997, 134
Literary almanac, 1071
New York Times almanac 1998, 2
Women's almanac, 827
World almanac & bk of facts 1997, 3
World almanac for kids 1998, 4
World gd 1997/98, 10th ed, 97

ALTERNATIVE MEDICINE. *See also* **MEDICINE, POPULAR**
Alternative advisor: the complete gd to natural therapies & alternative treatments, 1544
Alternative medicine resource gd, 1547
Aromatherapy oils, 1551
Complete family gd to natural home remedies, 1545
Encyclopedia of healing therapies, 1552
Green pharmacy, 1546
Health & illness, 1508
Woman's ency of natural healing, 1550

ALTERNATIVE MEDICINE—VOCATIONAL GUIDANCE
Planning your career in alternative medicine, 1549

AMBASSADORS—UNITED STATES
Notable US Ambassadors since 1775, 655

AMERICA—FOREIGN RELATIONS
Encyclopedia of the inter-American system, 695

AMERICANA
Black Americana price gd, 892
Country Americana price gd, 894

AMERICAN ASSOCIATION (BASEBALL LEAGUE)
American assn: yr-by-yr stats for the baseball minor league, 1902-52, 738

AMERICAN DRAMA
Women playwrights of diversity, 1106

AMERICAN FICTION
American novelists since WWII, 5th series, 1128
Contemporary Jewish-American novelists, 1125
Contemporary novel, 2d ed, 1108
Eighteenth-Century Anglo-American women novelists, 1111

AMERICANISMS
America in so many words, 1000
American Heritage dict of idioms, 1006
Idiom savant: slang as it is slung, 1014
Oxford dict & thesaurus, American ed, 994
Speaking freely, 1002

AMERICAN LITERATURE
American expatriate writers, 1127
Contemporary popular writers, 1058
Encyclopedia of frontier lit, 1130
Identities & issues in lit, 1070

Nineteenth-century American women writers, 1126
One hundred yrs of American women writing, 1848-1948, 1124

AMERICAN LITERATURE—AFRO-AMERICAN AUTHORS
Dictionary catalog of the collection of African American lit in the Mildred F. Sawyer Lib of Suffolk Univ, 340
Oxford companion to African American lit, 1129

AMERICAN POETRY
American poets since WW II, 5th series, 1140
American poets since WW II, 4th series, 1141

AMERICORPS
National serv & AmeriCorps, 800

AMMUNITION
Jane's ammunition hndbk 1996-97, 5th ed, 633

AMPHIBIANS
Amphibians & reptiles of Trinidad & Tobago, 1474
Reptile & amphibian problem solver, 1473

ANARCHISTS
Rosa Luxemburg & Emma Goldman: a bibliog, 637

ANATOMY, HUMAN
Atlas of anatomy, English ed, 1523
Science on file [CD-ROM], 1415

ANGELS
Encyclopedia of angels, 1355

ANIMATED FILMS
Complete anime gd, 1307

ANNUALS (PLANTS)
Eyewitness garden hndbk: annuals & biennials, 1436

ANONYMS & PSEUDONYMS
20,000 Spanish American pseudonyms, 1182

ANTHROPOLOGY
Anthropological lit on disc [CD-ROM], 317
Anthropology of religion, 1359
Bibliographic gd to anthropology & archaeology 1995, 319
History of physical anthropology, 320

ANTHROPOLOGY—JUVENILE LITERATURE
Atlas of threatened cultures, 318

ANTI-NAZI MOVEMENT—GERMANY
Encyclopedia of German resistance to the Nazi movement, 470

ANTIQUARIAN BOOKSELLERS
Antiquarian, specialty, & used bk sellers 1997-98, 2d ed, 597

ANTIQUES
Collectors value gd to Oriental decorative arts, 890
Miller's intl antiques price gd 1997, 18th ed, 903
Schroeder's antiques price gd, 15th ed, 905
Wallace-Homestead price gd to American country antiques, 904

APHORISMS
Treasury of Polish aphorisms, 1253

ARAB COUNTRIES
Militarism in Arab society, 609

ARCHAEOLOGY
Bibliographic gd to anthropology & archaeology 1995, 319
Oxford companion to archaeology, 428
Treasure hard to attain: images of archaeology in popular film, 1290

ARCHETYPE (PSYCHOLOGY)
Encyclopedia of archetypal symbolism, v.1, 1351
Encyclopedia of archetypal symbolism, v.2: the body, 1352

ARCHITECTS
Makers of 20th century modern architecture, 972
Twentieth-century artists on art, 2d ed, 969
Willem Marinus Dudok, a Dutch modernist, 974

ARCHITECTURE
Architecture, 976
Architecture sourcebk, 977
Avery index to architectural pers at Columbia Univ [CD-ROM], 970
Avery's choice: 5 centuries of great architectural bks, 971
Bibliographic gd to art & architecture 1996, 941
Oxford companion to Christian art & architecture, 950

ARCHITECTURE IN LITERATURE
Art & architecture in the poetry of Robert Browning, appendix A, 1154

ARCHIVES
ArchivesUSA [CD-ROM], 430
Articles describing archives & ms collections in the US, 577

ARCHIVISTS
International biogl dir of natl archivists, documentalists, & librarians, 574

ARENDT, HANNAH
Hannah Arendt 2: a bibliog, 636

ARGENTINE FICTION
Argentine novel, 1168

ARNOLD, EDDY
Eddy Arnold discography, 1944-96, 1231

AROMATHERAPY
Aromatherapy oils, 1551

ART
African art, 956
Art of the ancient Mediterranean world, 957
European art since 1850, 958
European art to 1850, 959
Far Eastern art, 960
Mexican, Central, & S American art, 961
North American art since 1900, 962
North American art to 1900, 963
Art index, Nov 1995 to Oct 1996, 968
Bibliographic gd to art & architecture 1996, 941
Dictionary of art, 947
Dictionary of women artists, 948
History of art for young people, 5th ed, 965
National museum of American art [CD-ROM], 966

ART—BIBLIOGRAPHY
Art bks, 2d ed, 940

ART, CHINESE
Art & artists of 20th-century China, 967

ART, DUTCH
Dutch art, 949

ART IN LITERATURE
Art & architecture in the poetry of Robert Browning, appendix A, 1154

ARTIST COLONIES
Artists communities, 954

ARTISTS
Art bks, 2d ed, 940
Artist's resource hndbk, rev ed, 964
Dictionary of 19th century British bk illustrators & caricaturists, rev ed, 944
Twentieth-century artists on art, 2d ed, 969

ARTISTS, BLACK
St. James gd to black artists, 945

ARTISTS' MARKS
Old masters, 980

ARTISTS, SPANISH
Spanish artists from the 4th to the 20th century, 952

ART, LATIN AMERICAN
Contemporary Latin American artists, 955

ART, MODERN
Annual bibliog of modern art, 1995, 939
Art & artists of 20th-century China, 967
Contemporary Latin American artists, 955

ART & RELIGION
Encyclopedia of archetypal symbolism, v.1, 1351
Encyclopedia of archetypal symbolism, v.2: the body, 1352

ARTS
Art diary 97/98, 953
Crafts supply source bk, 4th ed, 931
Lives & works in the arts from the renaissance to the 20th century, 847

ARTS—INFORMATION SERVICES
Key gd to electronic resources: art & art hist, 942

ART—TERMINOLOGY
Artwords: a glossary of contemporary art theory, 951

ASCENSION ISLAND
St. Helena, Ascension, & Tristan da Cunha, 146

ASIA
Asia-Pacific in figures, 10th ed, 811
Asian higher educ, 295
Cultural atlas of India, 113
Statistical yrbk for Asia & the Pacific 1996, 815
World investment dir 1996, v.6: West Asia, 207

ASIANS
Who's who in Asian banking & finance, 150

ASTAIRE, FRED
Fred Astaire: a bio-bibliog, 1272

ASTROLOGY
Cosmic influences on humans, animals, & plants, 1441
Daily planetary gd 1997, 713
Signs of the zodiac, 717

ASTRONOMY
Dictionary of astronomy, 1607
History of astronomy, 1606
McGraw-Hill dict of astronomy, 1608
Nine worlds hosted by Patrick Stewart [CD-ROM], 1610
Photographic atlas of the stars, 1604

ATHEISTS
2000 yrs of disbelief: famous people with the courage to doubt, 1347

ATHLETES
Jewish sports legends, 2d ed, 719
Sports stars, series 3, 718

ATHLETES—NUTRITION
Dynamic nutrition for maximum performance, 1513

ATLASES
Answer atlas, 380
Collins concise atlas of the world, rev ed, 382
Complete atlas of world hist, 491
Concise world atlas, 384
Florida: atlas of histl county boundaries, 431
Hammond explorer atlas of the world, 385
Macmillan centennial atlas of the world, 386
Maps of the world, 387
NASA atlas of the solar system, 1609

New comparative world atlas, 388
Outline maps on file, 398
Oxford desk ref atlas, 389
Penguin atlas of diasporas, 807
Photographic atlas of the stars, 1604
Planet Earth: Macmillan world atlas, 390

ATLASES—HISTORY
Bibliographic gd to maps & atlases 1996, 391

AUDIO-VISUAL MATERIALS
AV market place 1997, 884
IDEA: intl dir of educl audiovisuals [CD-ROM], 311
Index to AV producers & distrs 1997, 10th ed, 312

AUSTEN, JANE
Bibliography of Jane Austen, [new ed], 1153

AUSTRALASIA
Australasia & S Pacific Islands bibliog, 144

AUTHORS
Authors & artists for YAs, v.20, 1100
Authors & artists for YAs, v.21, 1101
Benét's reader's ency, 4th ed, 843
Biographical companion to lit in English, rev ed, 1066
Contemporary authors autobiog series, v.25, 1061
Contemporary authors autobiog series, v.26, 1062
Contemporary authors autobiog series, v.27, 1063
Contemporary authors on CD [CD-ROM], 1064
Contemporary Canadian authors, v.1, 1169
Contemporary popular writers, 1058
Cyclopedia of world authors, 3d ed, 1059
DISCovering authors, Canadian ed [CD-ROM], 1065
Major Tudor authors, 1060
Novels for students, v.1, 1109
Novels for students, v.2, 1110
100 most popular YA authors, rev ed, 1102
Oxford companion to 20th-century lit in English, 1073
Short stories for students, v.1, 1120
Short stories for students, v.2, 1121
Short story writers, 1123
Something about the author autobiog series, v.24, 1080
Writers for YAs, 1104

AUTHORS, AFRICAN
African writers, 1167

AUTHORS, AMERICAN
American expatriate writers, 1127
Poe ency, 1137

AUTHORS—BIOGRAPHY
Index to the Wilson authors series, 1075

AUTHORS, ENGLISH
British writers, suppl 4, 1149
G. A. Henty 1832-1902: a bibliographical study of his British eds...., 1159
Guide to British prose fiction explication: 19th & 20th centuries, 1143
Sixteenth-century British nondramatic writers, 4th series, 1147

William Somerset Maugham ency, 1160
Women writers of Gt Brit & Europe, 1067

AUTHORS, EUROPEAN
Women writers of Gt Brit & Europe, 1067

AUTHORS, FRENCH
Marguerite Duras: a bio-bibliog, 1171

AUTHORS, GERMAN
German Baroque writers, 1661-1730, 1172

AUTHORSHIP. *See also* **PUBLISHERS & PUBLISHING**
AMA style gd for business writing, 873
Freelance Editorial Assn yellow pages & code of fair practice, 1997-98, 863
Guidebook for publishing philosophy, 1997 ed, 867
Writer's resource, 871
Writer's resource hndbk, 865

AUTHORSHIP—STYLE MANUALS
Associate Pr stylebook & libel manual, 6th ed, 874

AUTHORS, IRISH
Modern Irish writers, 1176

AUTHORS & PUBLISHERS
Business and legal forms for authors and self-publishers, 605
Guide to literary agents, 1997, 866
Poet's market, 1998, 868
Writer's market, 1998, 870
Writer's market, 1998, electronic ed [CD-ROM], 869

AUTOBIOGRAPHIES
Autobiographies by Americans of color 1980-94, 347

AUTOMOBILE DRIVERS' RECORDS
MVR bk motor servs gd, 1997 ed, 536
MVR decoder digest, 1997 ed, 537

AUTOMOBILES
Automobile, 1647
Classic American cars, 1650
Delmar's automotive dict, 1477
Standard catalog of American cars, 1946-75, 1648

AVERY LIBRARY
Avery's choice: 5 centuries of great architectural bks, 971

AVIATION
World War I aviation, rev ed, 610

AWARDS
Awards, honors, & prizes 1997, 13th ed, 49
Literary almanac, 1071

BACH, JOHANN SEBASTIAN
Biblical quotation & allusion in the cantana libretti of J. S. Bach, 1245
Handbook to Bach's sacred cantata texts, 1247

BALLET
Minor ballet composers, 1215

BALTIC STATES
Baltics info sources dir 1996, 124
Bibliographic gd to Slavic, Baltic, & Eurasian studies 1996, 126

BAND MUSIC
Heritage ency of band music, suppl v.3, 1229

BANGLADESH
Historical dict of Bangladesh, 2d ed, 460

BANKS & BANKING. *See also* **ECONOMICS; FINANCE**
Plunkett's financial servs industry almanac, 185
Who's who in Asian banking & finance, 150

BANK STOCKS
Walker's manual of community bank stocks, 187

BAROQUE LITERATURE
German Baroque writers, 1661-1730, 1172

BARTOK, BELA
Bela Bartok: a gd to research, 2d ed, 1210

BASEBALL
American assn: yr-by-yr stats for the baseball minor league, 1902-52, 738
Baseball records registry, 728
Charmed circle: 20-game-winning pitchers in baseball's 20th century, 732
Cultural ency of baseball, 733
Encyclopedia of Minor League Baseball, 2d ed, 729
Fodor's ballpark vacations, 731
Official baseball rules 1997, 735
Official Major League Baseball fact bk 1997, 736
Total baseball, 737
Women of the All-American Girls Professional Baseball League, 734

BASEBALL CARDS
Standard catalog of baseball cards, 1998, 906

BASEBALL PLAYERS
Baseball pioneers: ratings of 19th century players, 730

BASKETBALL
Inside Sports Mag college basketball, 2d ed, 739
NCAA basketball: the official 1997 women's college basketball records bk, 740
Sporting News official NBA gd, 1997-98 ed, 741
Sporting News official NBA register, 742

BATTLES
Modern campaigns, 615

BEATLES, THE
Beatles memorabilia price gd, 3d ed, 921

BED & BREAKFAST ACCOMMODATIONS
America's best bed & breakfasts, 2d ed, 408
Bed & breakfast ency, 427
Complete gd to American bed & breakfast, 410

BENIN
Benin, 106

BEST BOOKS
Best bks for YA readers, 1094
Books for you, 1095
Booktalking the award winners 3, 1081
Booktalking the award winners: children's retrospective volume, 1082
Choices for young readers [CD-ROM], 1086
Civil War bks: a critical bibliog, 432
Core collection for small libs, 1077
Doody's rating serv 1997, 1501
Kaleidoscope: a multicultural booklist for grades K-8, 1087
Newbery companion, 1091
Reader's catalog, 2d ed, 8
Recommended bks in Spanish for children & YAs, 1991-95, 1079
Senior high school lib catalog, 15th ed, 587
Ultimate business lib, 148

BEVERAGES
Who's buying food & drink, 257

BEVERAGES—QUOTATIONS
Never eat more than you can lift, & other food quotes & quips, 1429

BIBLE
Cambridge companion to the Bible, 1377
NIV complete Bible lib [CD-ROM], 1380
Pockets: Bible companion, 1381

BIBLE—CONCORDANCES
Biblical quotation & allusion in the cantana libretti of J. S. Bach, 1245

BIBLE—DICTIONARIES
International children's Bible dict, 1376
New Bible dict, 3d ed, 1373

BIBLE—GEOGRAPHY
Cities of the biblical world, 1378

BIBLE—IN LITERATURE
Reference gd to the Bible in Emily Dickinson's poetry, 1135

BIBLE. N.T.
Acts of the Apostles, 1370
Romans, 1371

BIBLE. O.T.
Book of Amos, 1372
IVP Bible background commentary: Genesis-Deuteronomy, 1379

New intl dict of O.T. theology & exegesis, 1374
Theological dict of the O.T., v.8, 1375

BIBLE—QUOTATIONS
Divine inspirations: pearls of Bible wisdom from the O. & N.T.s, 1369

BIBLIOGRAPHY
Bibliographic index 1996, 6
Books in print 1997-98, 15
Subject gd to bks in print 1997-98, 16
Canadian bks in print 1997, 18
Checklist of American imprints for 1845, 17
Cumulative bk index 1995, 11
Directory of business info resources, 1997, 5th ed, 250
Eighteenth century, n.s.15 for 1989, 7
El-Hi textbooks and serials in print 1997, 283
International bks in print 1997, 12
International bks in print 1997, 13

BIBLIOGRAPHY—EARLY PRINTED BOOKS
Sabin Collection catalog [CD-ROM], 10

BIBLIOGRAPHY—EUROPE
Rosenthal Collection of printed bks with ms annots, 578

BIENNIALS (PLANTS)
Eyewitness garden hndbk: annuals & biennials, 1436

BIOCHEMISTRY
Concise ency biochemistry & molecular biology, 3d ed, 1599
Oxford dict of biochemistry & molecular biology, 1444

BIOETHICS
Encyclopedia of bioethics, rev ed [CD-ROM], 1333

BIOGRAPHY
Biographical companion to lit in English, rev ed, 1066
Biography index, Sept 1995-Aug 1996, 20
Biography today, 1996 annual cum, 21
British literary bk trade, 1475-1700, 594
Canadian newsmakers 1997, 33
Complete Marquis Who's Who on CD-ROM [CD-ROM], 28
Concise dict of American biog, 5th ed, 29
Contemporary authors autobiog series, v.25, 1061
Contemporary authors autobiog series, v.26, 1062
Contemporary authors autobiog series, v.27, 1063
Contemporary Canadian authors, v.1, 1169
Current biog yrbk 1996, 22
Cyclopedia of world authors, 3d ed, 1059
DISCovering authors, Canadian ed [CD-ROM], 1065
DISCovering biog [CD-ROM], 23
Encyclopedia of Native American biog, 350
50 most influential women in American law, 513
Gay & lesbian biog, 781
Grolier lib of sci biogs, 1400
Larousse dict of women, 24
Newsmakers 1997, 25
Nobel prize winners 1992-96 suppl, 26
Notable Latino Americans, 349

Notable women in the physical scis, 1598
100 greatest, 27
100 most popular YA authors, rev ed, 1102
Scholastic ency of women in the US, 836
Scientists, 1401
Singers of the century, 1201
Stars in blue: movie actors in America's sea servs, 1281
Twentieth-century American sportswriters, 883
Who's who in Asian banking & finance, 150
Who's who in Latin America, 4th ed, 35
Who's who in medicine & healthcare 1997-98, 1506
Who's who in the East 1997-98, 26th ed, 31
Who's who in the West 1998-99, 26th ed, 32
Women of Ireland, 34

BIOLOGICAL WARFARE
Chemical & biological warfare, 607

BIOLOGY
Concise dict of biomedicine & molecular biology, 1439
Concise ency biochemistry & molecular biology, 3d ed, 1599
Dictionary of modern biology, 1445
Glossary of biochemistry & molecular biology, rev ed, 1443
McGraw-Hill dict of biosci, 1440

BIOTECHNOLOGY
Biotechnology abstracts: agricultural & environmental, 1983-Feb 1997 [CD-ROM], 1490

BIRDS
American Bird Conservancy's field gd to all the birds of N America, 1459
Common birds of E Africa, 1461
Lives of N American birds, 1460

BIRTH CONTROL
POPLINE: through Dec 1996 [CD-ROM], 778

BLACKS—QUOTATIONS
Contemporary quotations in black, 78

BLACKS—SOUTH AFRICA—RELIGION
African traditional religion in South Africa, 1344

BLIND—DEAF
Directory of agencies & orgs serving individuals who are deaf-blind, rev ed, 771

BLISS, ARTHUR
Arthur Bliss: a source bk, 1211

BOARD GAMES
Antique trader's gd to games & puzzles, 891

BOOKSELLERS & BOOKSELLING. *See also* **PUBLISHERS & PUBLISHING**
American bk trade dir 1997-98, 596
Bowker annual lib and bk trade almanac 1997, 576
British literary bk trade, 1475-1700, 594
International bk trade dir 1997, 602

BOOKS—REVIEWS
Book review digest, Mar 1996 to Feb 1997 inclusive, 65

BOOKSTORES
Antiquarian, specialty, & used bk sellers 1997-98, 2d ed, 597

BOOK TALKS
Booktalking the award winners 3, 1081
Booktalking the award winners: children's retrospective volume, 1082
Index to the Wilson booktalking series, 1083

BOTANY
Flora of N America of Mexico, v.3, 1447

BOXING
Boxing register, 743

BRAND NAME PRODUCTS
International dir of consumer brands & their owners, 200

BRAZIL
Brazil, rev ed, 140

BROADCASTING
Encyclopedia of TV, 888
Informatics hndbk, 1593

BROWNING, ROBERT
Art & architecture in the poetry of Robert Browning, appendix A, 1154

BUDAPEST
Budapest, 133

BUILDING
Annual bulletin of housing & bldg stats for Europe & N America 1996, 822
Building construction cost data 1997, 55th ed, 1480
Directory of bldg & equipment grants, 4th ed, 1481
Square foot costs 1997, 18th ed, 1483
Wiley dict of civil engineering & construction, 1484

BURLESQUE (THEATER)
Bibliographic gd to dance 1995, 1267

BURUNDI
Historical dict of Burundi, 455

BUSINESS. *See also* **BANKS & BANKING; CORPORATIONS; ECONOMICS; FINANCE; MANAGEMENT; MARKETING**
Bibliographic gd to business & economics 1995, 147
Business & industry [CD-ROM], 189
Business pers index, v.38: Aug 1995-July 1996, 167
Economic survey of Latin America & the Caribbean 1995-96, 210
Elsevier's dict of European Community co/business/financial law in English, Danish, & German, 517
Knowledge Exchange business ency, 154
Market share & business rankings worldwide [CD-ROM], 254

NAFTA & GATT: environmental & economic issues, 705
National accounts stats, 203
Routledge German dict of business commerce and finance, 156
Ultimate business lib, 148
Understanding American business jargon, 153
Wiley's English-Spanish, Spanish-English business dict, 157

BUSINESS—DICTIONARIES
English-Ukrainian dict of business, 155

BUSINESS—DIRECTORIES
Directory of business info resources, 1997, 5th ed, 250

BUSINESS ENTERPRISES
Canadian co hists, v.1, 208
Hoover's billion dollar dir, 159
Hoover's co capsules on CD-ROM, 192
Hoover's co profiles on CD-ROM [CD-ROM], 193
Hoover's global 250, 202
Hoover's gd to media cos, 859
Hoover's hndbk of emerging cos 1997, 173
Hoover's hndbk of private cos 1997, 164
Hoover's hndbks index 1997, 168
Hoover's masterlist of major Latin American cos 1996-97, 211
National jobbank 1998, 237

BUSINESS—HISTORY
International bibliog of business hist, 149

BUSINESS NAMES
International dir of consumer brands & their owners, 200

BUSINESS WRITING
AMA style gd for business writing, 873

BUTTONS
Antique & collectible buttons, 902

BYRON, GEORGE GORDON
George Gordon, Lord Byron, 1155

CALIFORNIA
California, 413

CAMPAIGN FUNDS
Campaign and election reform, 679
Open secrets: the ency of congressional money & pols, 4th ed, 675

CANADA
Canadian bks in print 1997, 18
Canadian film & video, 1271
Fodor's exploring Canada, 421
Milepost: trip planner for Ala. & Western Canada, 49th ed, 406

CANADA—BIOGRAPHY
Canadian newsmakers 1997, 33
Contemporary Canadian authors, v.1, 1169

CANADA—ENCYCLOPEDIAS
Junior Worldmark ency of the Canadian provinces, 119

CANADA—POLITICS & GOVERNMENT
Canadian parliamentary, 683

CANADIANISMS
Gage Canadian dict, rev ed, 1012

CANADIAN LITERATURE
Identities & issues in lit, 1070

CANADIAN PERIODICALS
CPI.Q: Canadian per index [CD-ROM], 75

CANTATAS
Handbook to Bach's sacred cantata texts, 1247

CAPITAL PUNISHMENT
Legal executions in N.Y. State, 554

CARD GAMES
Bidding dict, 744

CAREERS
Career discovery ency, 213
College majors & careers, 3d ed, 316
Encyclopedia of careers & vocational guidance, 2d ed [CD-ROM], 214

CARIBBEAN AREA
Bibliographic gd to Latin American studies 1996, 139

CARL H. PFORZHEIMER LIBRARY
Carl H. Pforzheimer Lib, English lit, 1475-1700, 1997 ed, 1148

CARTOGRAPHERS
Dictionary of land surveyors and local map-makers of Gt Brit and Ireland, 1530-1850, 394

CARTOGRAPHY
Bibliographic gd to maps & atlases 1996, 391
Maps & mapping of Africa, 392

CASINOS
American casino gd, 1997 ed, 411
Casino gaming in the US, 724
Where to play in the USA: the gaming gd, 419

CATALOGS, COLLEGE
CollegeSource [CD-ROM], 297

CATALOGS, COMMERCIAL
National dir of catalogs 1997, 181

CATHOLIC CHURCH
Catholicism on the Web, 1391
Ecclesia: a theological ency of the Church, 1387
Historical dict of Catholicism, 1384
Our Sunday Visitors ency of Catholic doctrine, 1388

CATHOLICISM
Catholic Internet, USA ed, 1390

CATHOLIC UNIVERSITIES & COLLEGES
Complete bk of Catholic colleges, 1998 ed, 288

CATS
Cat world, 1465
Complete cat health manual, 1464
Encyclopedia of the cat, 1463

CD-ROM
CD-ROM for librarians & educators, 2d ed, 282
Key gd to electronic resources: art & art hist, 942
Key gd to electronic resources: lang & lit, 985

CD-ROMS
Abortion & reproductive rights [CD-ROM], 754
American Heritage talking dict [CD-ROM], 997
American Indian: a multimedia ency [CD-ROM], 352
American presidency [CD-ROM], 668
Anthropological lit on disc [CD-ROM], 317
ArchivesUSA [CD-ROM], 430
Avery index to architectural pers at Columbia Univ [CD-ROM], 970
Biotechnology abstracts: agricultural & environmental, 1983-Feb 1997 [CD-ROM], 1490
Business & industry [CD-ROM], 189
Business: name & business type index [CD-ROM], 158
Business sales leads, 1997 ed [CD-ROM], 248
Career perspectives software series [CD-ROM], 223
Children's ency [CD-ROM], 39
Choices for young readers [CD-ROM], 1086
ClinPSYC: 1980-Dec 1996 [CD-ROM], 712
CollegeSource [CD-ROM], 297
Collier's ency 1998 [CD-ROM], 41
Columbia ency [CD-ROM], 42
Complete Marquis Who's Who on CD-ROM [CD-ROM], 28
Consumer sales leads, 1997 ed [CD-ROM], 249
Contemporary authors on CD [CD-ROM], 1064
Contemporary women's issues 1992-July 1997 [CD-ROM], 838
CorpTech CD-ROM dir of tech cos [CD-ROM], 1570
CorpTech explore database [CD-ROM], 1571
CPI.Q: Canadian per index [CD-ROM], 75
Dance on disc [CD-ROM], 1269
Dictionary of the English lang [CD-ROM], 1020
Directory of physicians in the US, 35th ed [CD-ROM], 1534
DISCovering authors, Canadian ed [CD-ROM], 1065
DISCovering biog [CD-ROM], 23
DISCovering sci [CD-ROM], 1413
DISCovering US hist [CD-ROM], 446
DISCovering world hist [CD-ROM], 505
Electrical & electronics trades dir 1996 [CD-ROM], 1486
Encyclopaedia Judaica [CD-ROM], 1393
Encyclopedia of bioethics, rev ed [CD-ROM], 1333
Encyclopedia of careers & vocational guidance, 2d ed [CD-ROM], 214

Encyclopedia of religion [CD-ROM], 1353
Encyclopedia of the American Constitution [CD-ROM], 518
Encyclopedia of virology plus [CD-ROM], 1442
Encyclopedia plus of world problems & human potential, 4th ed [CD-ROM], 86
Exploring poetry [CD-ROM], 1184
Exploring Shakespeare [CD-ROM], 1162
Eyewitness ency of sci [CD-ROM], 1403
Facts on File world news CD-ROM 1997 [CD-ROM], 506
Geographic database for US economy, tech, & growth [CD-ROM], 818
Grolier multimedia ency, 1998, deluxe ed [CD-ROM], 43
Historical atlas of the Holocaust [CD-ROM], 493
Hoover's co capsules on CD-ROM, 192
Hoover's co profiles on CD-ROM [CD-ROM], 193
Humanities abstracts full text [CD-ROM], 845
IDEA: intl dir of educl audiovisuals [CD-ROM], 311
International index to music pers 1997:2 [CD-ROM], 1208
Jane's air-launched weapons image lib [CD-ROM], 632
Jane's military aircraft image lib [CD-ROM], 623
Jane's warships image lib [CD-ROM], 627
JIST's electronic enhanced dict of occupational titles, 2d ed [CD-ROM], 216
JIST's electronic occupational outlook hndbk, 2d ed [CD-ROM], 231
JIST's multimedia occupational outlook hndbk, 2d ed [CD-ROM], 232
Management consulting [CD-ROM], 245
Market share & business rankings worldwide [CD-ROM], 254
Medieval & early modern data bank [CD-ROM], 165
Merriam-Webster's collegiate dict, deluxe audio ed [CD-ROM], 998
National museum of American art [CD-ROM], 966
New shorter Oxford English dict [CD-ROM], 999
Nine worlds hosted by Patrick Stewart [CD-ROM], 1610
NIV complete Bible lib [CD-ROM], 1380
NTIS ordernow [CD-ROM], 62
Oceanographic & marine resources: 1960-Jan 1997 [CD-ROM], 1616
On common ground: world religions in America [CD-ROM], 1367
150 yrs of America's Smithsonian [CD-ROM], 74
Oxford-Duden German dict [CD-ROM], 1032
Oxford 3-in-1 bilingual dict [CD-ROM], 1021
PAIS select [CD-ROM], 89
PCI: pers contents index [CD-ROM], 66
Periodical source index CD-ROM [CD-ROM], 373
PhoneDisc powerfinder [CD-ROM], 54
Photographers on disc [CD-ROM], 937
POPLINE: through Dec 1996 [CD-ROM], 778
Readers' gd abstracts full text mega ed [CD-ROM], 69
Readers' gd for young people [CD-ROM], 77
Sabin Collection catalog [CD-ROM], 10
Sixties [CD-ROM], 450
Social scis abstracts full text [CD-ROM], 92
Sociofile: 1974-Dec 1996 [CD-ROM], 94
Thomas register on CD-ROM, 1997 [CD-ROM], 197
Twayne's masterwork studies on CD-ROM [CD-ROM], 1074

Ultimate family tree deluxe [CD-ROM], 371
Ultimate human body version 2.0 [CD-ROM], 1499
U.S. homes [CD-ROM], 56
U.S. homes & business [CD-ROM], 57
USSR population census, 1989 [CD-ROM], 130
U*X*L multicultural CD [CD-ROM], 333
Victorian database on CD-ROM, 1970-95 [CD-ROM], 468
World country analyst [CD-ROM], 205
World Shakespeare bibliog on CD-ROM 1990-93 [CD-ROM], 1165
Writer's market, 1998, electronic ed [CD-ROM], 869

CELEBRITIES
Biography today, 1996 annual cum, 21
Newsmakers 1997, 25
Star gd, 1997-98, 1266

CELTS
Celtic baby names, 378

CENSORSHIP
Free expression & censorship in America, 584

CERAMIC MATERIALS
Potter's dict of materials & techniques, 4th ed, 932

CHAD
Historical dict of Chad, 3d ed, 453

CHAMBER MUSIC
Discography of 78 rpm era recordings of the horn, 1203

CHARACTERS & CHARACTERISTICS IN LITERATURE
Characters in YA lit, 1103
Dictionary of who, what, & where in Shakespeare, 1161
Shakespeare's characters for students, 1164

CHARITABLE USES, TRUSTS, & FOUNDATIONS. *See also* **ENDOWMENTS; FUND RAISING; GRANTS-IN-AID**
Fndn dir 1997, 19th ed, 787
Fndn dir supplement, 788
Fndn giving, 1997 ed, 794
Funding in aging, 758
Guide to US fndns, their trustees, officers, & donors, 1997 ed, 789

CHAUCER, GEOFFREY
Chaucer's Miller's, Reeve's, & Cook's Tales, 1156

CHEERS (TELEVISION PROGRAM)
Toasting Cheers: an episode gd to the 1982-93 comedy series...., 1302

CHEMICAL ENGINEERING
Chemicals on the Internet, v.1, 1478
Perry's chemical engineers' hndbk, 7th ed, 1479

CHEMICAL LITERATURE—AUTHORSHIP
ACS style gd, 2d ed, 872

CHEMICALS
Hazardous chemicals desk ref, 4th ed, 1635

CHEMICAL WARFARE
Chemical & biological warfare, 607

CHEMISTRY
Burger's medicinal chemistry & drug discovery, 5th ed, 1565
Concise ency biochemistry & molecular biology, 3d ed, 1599
Elements, 1600
Glossary of biochemistry & molecular biology, rev ed, 1443
Macmillan ency of chemistry, 1601
McGraw-Hill dict of chemistry, 1602

CHILD ABUSE
Child abuse, 1997 ed, 568

CHILDBIRTH
Pregnancy and birth sourcebk, 1561

CHILD REARING
Parenting A to Z, 2d ed, 803

CHILDREN—NUTRITION
Yale gd to children's nutrition, 1555

CHILDREN'S ATLASES
Atlas of threatened cultures, 318
Children's illus atlas, 1997 ed, 381
Concise atlas of the world, 3d ed, 383

CHILDREN'S ENCYCLOPEDIAS & DICTIONARIES
Atlas of threatened cultures, 318
Career discovery ency, 213
Children's ency [CD-ROM], 39
Diseases, 1557
Elements, 1600
Encyclopedia of mammals, 1469
Encyclopedia of N American Indians, 354
Fiesta, 1262
Grolier lib of sci biogs, 1400
Grolier lib of WW I, 614
Holocaust, 502
Illustrated ency of world hist, 503
Illustrated sci ency, 1405
International children's Bible dict, 1376
Junior chronicle of the 20th century, 498
Junior Worldmark ency of the Canadian provinces, 119
Lands & peoples, 95
Macmillan ency of sci, rev ed, 1406
Maps of the world, 387
Medical discoveries, 1530
Modern campaigns, 615
Nations of Africa, 321
Peoples of Central Africa, 322
Peoples of E Africa, 323
Peoples of N Africa, 324
Peoples of Southern Africa, 325
Peoples of W Africa, 326
New bk of knowledge, 46
100 greatest, 27
Presidents, 661
Questions & answers bk of sci facts, 1404
Religions of the world, 1348
Scholastic children's dict, rev ed, 1008
Scholastic ency of the N American Indian, 355
Scholastic ency of the presidents & their times, updated ed, 443
Scholastic ency of women in the US, 836
Thorndike-Barnhart jr dict, 1009
Unites States in the 19th century, 436
Women's voices, 840
World Bk ency of sci, 1409
World Bk yr bk, 1997, 64
World Bk's young scientist, 1410

CHILDREN'S LITERATURE
Booktalking the award winners 3, 1081
Booktalking the award winners: children's retrospective volume, 1082
Index to the Wilson booktalking series, 1083
Children's catalog, 17th ed, 586
Children's fiction series, 1088
Connecting cultures, 1093
Core collection for small libs, 1077
Kaleidoscope: a multicultural booklist for grades K-8, 1087
Masterplots 2: juvenile & YA lit series suppl, 1085
Newbery companion, 1091
Phoenix award of the children's lit assn 1990-94, 1092
What else should I read? guiding kids to good bks, v.2, 1076

CHILDREN'S LITERATURE—BIBLIOGRAPHY
Choices for young readers [CD-ROM], 1086
Horn Bk gd to children's & YA bks, v.7, no.2, 1078

CHILDREN'S LITERATURE—BIOGRAPHY
Dictionary of literary biog documentary series, v.14, 1089
Laura Ingalls Wilder: an annot bibliog of critical, biogl, & teaching studies, 1139
Something about the author autobiog series, v.24, 1080

CHILDREN'S LITERATURE, SPANISH
Recommended bks in Spanish for children & YAs, 1991-95, 1079

CHILDREN'S PERIODICALS
Magazines for kids & teens, rev ed, 879
Readers' gd for young people [CD-ROM], 77

CHINA
Area bibliog of China, 112
Bibliographic gd to E Asian studies 1995, 109
China, new ed, 111
Chinese filmography, 1296

CHINESE LANGUAGE—DICTIONARIES—ENGLISH
Chinese 1000, 1022
Chinese synonyms usage dict, 1023

CHINTZ WARE
Charlton standard catalogue of chintz, 2d ed, 924

CHOREOGRAPHERS
Film choreographers & dance directors, 1268

CHRISTIAN ART
Oxford companion to Christian art & architecture, 950

CHRISTIANITY—DICTIONARIES
Compete bk of everyday Christianity, 1385
Oxford dict of the Christian Church, 3d ed, 1389

CHRISTIANITY—SOUTH AFRICA
Christianity in S Africa, 1382

CHRONIC DISEASES
Essential gd to chronic illness, 1558

CHRONOLOGY, HISTORICAL
Junior chronicle of the 20th century, 498
Junior timelines on file, 499
Women's chronology, 834

CHURCH CONTROVERSIES
Encyclopedia of religious controversies in the US, 1354

CHURCH HISTORY
Encyclopedia of early Christianity, 2d ed, 1386
Historical dict of Catholicism, 1384

CHURCH MUSIC
Hymnology, 1246

CITATION OF ELECTRONIC INFORMATION SOURCES
Electronic styles: a hndbk for citing electronic info, 2d ed, 875

CITIES & TOWNS
America's top-rated smaller cities 1996-97, 2d ed, 821
Comparative gd to American suburbs, 824
Consolidated bibliog of urban hist, 825
Facts about the cities, 2d ed, 823

CITIES & TOWNS, ANCIENT
Cities of the biblical world, 1378

CITRUS FRUITS
Great citrus bk, 1428

CIVIL ENGINEERING
Wiley dict of civil engineering & construction, 1484

CIVILIZATION, ANCIENT
Encyclopedia of ancient civilizations of the Near East & Mediterranean, 487

CIVIL PROCEDURE
Civil trial practice deskbk, 528

CIVIL RIGHTS
ABC-CLIO companion to the disability rights movement, 775
Encyclopedia of American Indian civil rights, 562
Historical dict of the civil rights movement, 565

CIVIL SERVICE POSITIONS
Government job finder, 234

CIXOUS, HELENE
French feminist theory 3, 832

CLASSIFICATION, DEWEY DECIMAL
Abridged Dewey decimal classification & relative index, 13th ed, 579

CLIMATE
Handy weather answer bk, 1613

CLIMATOLOGY
Complete weather resource, 1611
Glossary of weather & climate with related oceanic & hydrologic terms, 1612

CLOTHING TRADE
Garment & textile dict, 933

COCA-COLA
Petretti's Coca-Cola collectibles price gd, 10th ed, 923

COINS
Handbook of US coins, 1998, 55th ed, 910
International encyclopaedic dict of numismatics, 909
Platinum & palladium buyer's gd, 913
Standard catalog of world coins, 18th century 1701-1800, 911
Standard catalog of world coins, 1998, 912
Warman's coins & currency, 2d ed, 915

COLD WAR
Cold War ref gd, 508
George F. Kennan: an annot bibliog, 700

COLLECTIBLES
Beatles memorabilia price gd, 3d ed, 921
Black Americana price gd, 892
Collecting in cyberspace, 893
Collector's gd to TV memorabilia, 1960s & 1970s, 922
Country Americana price gd, 894
Coykendall's complete gd to sporting collectibles, 895
Everything Civil War, 447
Flea market trader, 11th ed, 896
Garage sale & flea market annual, 5th ed, 897
Golden age of Walt Disney records 1933-88, 1209
McDonald's collectibles, 898
Petretti's Coca-Cola collectibles price gd, 10th ed, 923
Schroeder's antiques price gd, 15th ed, 905
Wanted to buy, 6th ed, 901

COLLEGE CHOICE
College hndbk for transfer students 1997, 296
Peterson's competitive colleges 1997-98, 16th ed, 292
Peterson's gd to 2-yr colleges 1998, 28th ed, 293
Peterson's US & Canadian medical schools 1997, 1542
Princeton Review student advantage gd to visiting college campuses, 1997 ed, 305

COLLEGE COSTS
Financial aid financer, 306
Peterson's college money hndbk 1998, 15th ed, 303

COLLEGE MAJORS
College majors & careers, 3d ed, 316

COLLEGE SPORTS
Gridiron greats: a century of Polish Americans in college football, 745
NCAA basketball: the official 1997 women's college basketball records bk, 740
Winning edge: the student-athlete's gd to college sports, 5th ed, 723

COLMAN, RONALD
Ronald Colman: a bio-bibliog, 1273

COMIC BOOKS, STRIPS, ETC.
Comics buyer's gd 1998, 908
Comics values annual, 1998 ed, 907

COMMERCIAL CATALOGS
Catalog of catalogs 5, 183
Directory of business to business catalogs, 1997, 190

COMMERCIAL LAW
A-Z of contract clauses, 531

COMMONWEALTH OF INDEPENDENT STATES
Energy balances for countries in transition 1993, 1994-2010, & energy prospects in CIS countries, 1627

COMMUNICATION
Dictionary of communication & media studies, 4th ed, 857
Media courses UK 1997, 4th ed, 860
Webster's new world dict of media & communications, rev ed, 858

COMMUNICATION IN MEDICINE
Encyclopedia of medical media & communications, 1529

COMMUNICATION & TECHNOLOGY
From talking drums to the Internet, 854

COMMUNITY BANKS
Walker's manual of community bank stocks, 187

COMMUNITY COLLEGES
Peterson's gd to 2-yr colleges 1998, 28th ed, 293

COMPOSERS
Arthur Bliss: a source bk, 1211
Baker's biogl dict of 20th-century classical musicians, 1197
Bela Bartok: a gd to research, 2d ed, 1210
Classic FM gd to classical music, 1222
Larry Sitsky: a bio-bibliog, 1214
Lives of the great composers, 3d ed, 1216
Minor ballet composers, 1215
Mozart diary, 1213
Sir Arthur Sullivan: a resource bk, 1212

COMPUTER-ASSISTED INSTRUCTION
CD-ROM for librarians & educators, 2d ed, 282

COMPUTER MUSIC
Electronic & computer music, 1196

COMPUTER NETWORK RESOURCES
Internet searcher's hndbk, 1595

COMPUTERS. *See also* MICROCOMPUTERS
Dictionary of multimedia terms & acronyms, 1572
Orion blue bk, 182

COMPUTER SIMULATION
Jane's simulation & training systems 1996-97, 9th ed, 1573

COMPUTERS—SLANG
New hacker's dict, 3d ed, 1578

COMPUTING
Dictionary of computing, 4th ed, 1576
Dictionary of personal computing and the Internet, 1574
Oxford dict of computing for learners of English, 1577

CONFEDERATE STATES OF AMERICA. ARMY
Roster of Confederate soldiers 1861-65, 451

CONSERVATIONISTS
World who is who & does what in environment & conservation, 1631

CONSERVATISM
Concise conservative ency, 691

CONSTRUCTION EQUIPMENT
Wiley dict of civil engineering & construction, 1484

CONSTRUCTION INDUSTRY
Building construction cost data 1997, 55th ed, 1480
Routledge German dict of construction, 1482
Square foot costs 1997, 18th ed, 1483

CONSUMER BEHAVIOR
American marketplace, 3d ed, 246
Consumer Latin America 1997, 4th ed, 209
Generation X: the young adult market, 256
Mid-Youth market, 261
Who's buying food & drink, 257
Who's buying for the home, 258

CONSUMER COOPERATIVES
British co-operative movement film catalogue, 1289

CONSUMER EDUCATION
Orion blue bk, 182
Shopping with a conscience, 178

CONTRACT BRIDGE
Bidding dict, 744

CONTRACTS
A-Z of contract clauses, 531

COOKERY
Cupboard love: a dict of culinary curiosities, 1423
Food festivals, 414
Whole foods companion, 1427

COPYRIGHT
Copyright laws & treaties of the world 1991-95 suppl, 566

CORAL SNAKES
Coral snakes of the Americas, 1475

CORPORATIONS. *See also* **BUSINESS ENTERPRISES**
Business: name & business type index [CD-ROM], 158
Business sales leads, 1997 ed [CD-ROM], 248
Canadian co hists, v.1, 208
CorpTech CD-ROM dir of tech cos [CD-ROM], 1570
CorpTech explore database [CD-ROM], 1571
CyberHound's gd to cos on the Internet, 1583
Hoover's billion dollar dir, 159
Hoover's co capsules on CD-ROM, 192
Hoover's co profiles on CD-ROM [CD-ROM], 193
Hoover's global 250, 202
Hoover's gd to media cos, 859
Hoover's hndbk of emerging cos 1997, 173
Hoover's hndbk of private cos 1997, 164
Hoover's hndbks index 1997, 168
Hoover's masterlist of major Latin American cos 1996-97, 211
National jobbank 1998, 237
PhoneDisc powerfinder [CD-ROM], 54
Thomas register of American manufacturers, 1997, 87th ed, 196
Thomas register on CD-ROM, 1997 [CD-ROM], 197
U.S. homes & business [CD-ROM], 57

CORRECTIONS
Guide to fed funding for anti-crime programs, 2d ed, 553

CORSICA (FRANCE)
Corsica, 131

COSTUME
Cutting for all! the satorial arts, related crafts, & the commercial paper pattern, 934

COUNTERCULTURE. *See* **SUBCULTURE**

COUNTRY MUSIC
All music gd to country, 1230
Country music, 1234
MusicHound country, 1233
Statler Brothers discography, 1232

COUNTY COURTS
Sourcebook of county court records, 3d ed, 524

COUNTY GOVERNMENT
Counties USA 1997, 662

COURT RECORDS
Sourcebook of county court records, 3d ed, 524
Sourcebook of local court & county record retrievers, 3d ed, 525

COURTS
BNA's directory of state & fed courts, judges, & clerks, 1997 ed, 521
Congressional Quarterly's gd to the US Supreme Court, 3d ed, 529
Great world trials, 532
Guide to fed funding for anti-crime programs, 2d ed, 553
Judicial staff dir, 1997, 522

CRANE, STEPHEN
Reader's gd to the short stories of Stephen Crane, 1133
Stephen Crane ency, 1134

CRIME
City crime rankings, 3d ed, 552
Crime & the justice system in America, 550
Criminal quotes, 79
School violence, 278
True crime narratives, 546

CRIMINAL JUSTICE, ADMINISTRATION OF
Race, crime, & the criminal justice system, 548

CRITICAL THINKING
Thinking from A to Z, 1339

CRYPTOGRAPHY
Encyclopedia of cryptology, 855

CRYSTALLOGRAPHY
Pearson's hndbk desk ed, 1492

CULTS
New religious movements in Western Europe, 1343
Sects, 'cults,' & alternative religions, 1360

CULTURE
Atlas of threatened cultures, 318
Lands & peoples, 95
World facts & maps, 400

CURRICULA
Greening the college curriculum: a gd to environmental teaching in the liberal arts, 1640

CUSTER, GEORGE ARMSTRONG
Custer & the battle of Little Bighorn, 441

CYCLAMEN
Cyclamen: a gd for gardeners, horticulturists, & botanists, 1449

CZECH REPUBLIC
Prague, 122

DANCE
Bibliographic gd to dance 1995, 1267
Dance on disc [CD-ROM], 1269
Index to dance pers: 1995, 1270

DANCE IN MOTION PICTURES
Film choreographers & dance directors, 1268

DANCERS
Fred Astaire: a bio-bibliog, 1272

DANISH LANGUAGE—DICTIONARIES—GERMAN
Elsevier's dict of European Community co/business/financial law in English, Danish, & German, 517

DATABASES
Fulltext sources online, July 1997, 51
Global data locator, 812
World databases in humanities, 849

DEADHEADS
Grateful Dead & the deadheads, 1240

DEAF—BLIND. See BLIND—DEAF

DEATH
Life & death in the US, 769
National dir of bereavement support grps & servs, 1996, 768
R.I.P.: the complete bk of death & dying, 766

DECORATIVE ARTS
Collectors value gd to Oriental decorative arts, 890

DEMOCRACY
Contemporary democracy, 638
Who's who in democracy, 639

DEMOCRATIC PARTY
Encyclopedia of the Republican Party & the ency of the Democratic Party, 659

DEMOGRAPHICS
American marketplace, 3d ed, 246
American women, 247
Consumer sales leads, 1997 ed [CD-ROM], 249
Generation X: the young adult market, 256
Mid-Youth market, 261
Official gd to American incomes, 2d ed, 225
PhoneDisc powerfinder [CD-ROM], 54

DEMOGRAPHY
Americans at play, 726
Demographic yrbk, 1995, 47th ed, 804
Geographic database for US economy, tech, & growth [CD-ROM], 818
Key indicators of county growth 1970-2025, 1996 ed, 806

DEPRESSION IN OLD AGE
Depression in the elderly, 760

DERIVATIVE SECURITIES
Directory of listed derivative contracts 1996/97, 171

DESERT MAGAZINE
Desert Mag subject index, 878

DESIGNERS
Twentieth-century artists on art, 2d ed, 969

DETECTIVE & MYSTERY STORIES
Good old index: the Sherlock Holmes hndbk, 1158
Sleuths, sidekicks, & stooges, 1112
What mystery do I read next? a reader's gd to recent mystery fiction, 1113

DEVELOPING COUNTRIES
Resources of the Third World, 120

DIABETES
American Diabetes Assn complete gd to diabetes, 1562

DICKENS, CHARLES
Proverbial Charles Dickens, 1157

DICKINSON, EMILY
Reference gd to the Bible in Emily Dickinson's poetry, 1135

DICTIONARIES, MEDICAL
Medical meanings: a glossary of word origins, 1528

DICTIONARIES, POLYGLOT
Elsevier's dict of European Community co/business/financial law in English, Danish, & German, 517
Elsevier's dict of info tech in Enigsh, German, & French, 581
Itzaj Maya-Spanish-English dict, 1040
Oxford 3-in-1 bilingual dict [CD-ROM], 1021

DIE-CAST TOYS
Die cast price gd, 930

DIET
Dictionary of healthful food terms, 1420
Nutrition & diet therapy ref dict, 4th ed, 1422
Prescription for nutritional healing, 1507
Yale gd to children's nutrition, 1555

DINOSAURS
Complete dinosaur, 1617
Dinosaurs, 1618

DIRECTORIES
British dirs, 2d ed, 132
Directories in print, 15th ed, 50

DISABLED. See HANDICAPPED

DISCRIMINATION IN EMPLOYMENT
Employment discrimination law, 3d ed, 530

DISEASES
Diseases, 1557
Preventive care sourcebk 1997-98, 1519

DISSERTATIONS, ACADEMIC
Canadian music & music educ, 1194
Comprehensive dissertation index, 1996 suppl, 844

DISTANCE EDUCATION
External degrees in the info age, 308
Oryx guide to distance learning, 280

DIVINATION
Illustrated ency of divination, 714

DOCUMENTARY TELEVISION PROGRAMS
Special edition: a gd to network TV documentary series & special news reports, 1980-89, 1304

DOGS
Pockets: dogs, 1467

DOLLS
Collecting dolls ref & price gd, 917
Doll values antique to modern, 918
Modern collectible dolls identification & value gd, 919
200 yrs of dolls, 916

DOYLE, ARTHUR CONAN, SIR
Good old index: the Sherlock Holmes hndbk, 1158

DRAMA
Directory of theatre training programs 1997-99, 6th ed, 1325
German theatre, 1323
Modern drama scholarship & criticism 1981-90, 1105
Theatregoer's almanac, 1327

DRAMATISTS
Elmer Rice: a research & production sourcebk, 1326
Irish playwrights, 1880-1995, 1175
Sophie Treadwell: a research & production sourcebk, 1132

DRESS MAKING
Cutting for all! the satorial arts, related crafts, & the commercial paper pattern, 934

DRUGS. See PHARMACOLOGY
Delmar's A-Z NDR-97: nurse's drug ref, 1566
Delmar's therapeutic class drug gd for nurses 1997, 1567
Dictionary of natural products, 1569
EveryWoman's gd to prescription & nonprescription drugs, 1564
What do I take? a consumer's gd to nonprescription drugs, 1568

DURAS, MARGUERITE
Marguerite Duras: a bio-bibliog, 1171

DWELLINGS
Consumer sales leads, 1997 ed [CD-ROM], 249
PhoneDisc powerfinder [CD-ROM], 54
U.S. homes [CD-ROM], 56
U.S. homes & business [CD-ROM], 57

DWELLINGS—REMODELING
Home improvements & projects index 1990-93, 1498

EARTH SCIENCES. See also GEOLOGY
McGraw-Hill dict of earth sci, 1603
Science on file [CD-ROM], 1415

EAST ASIA
Bibliographic gd to E Asian studies 1995, 109

ECOLOGY
Bibliographic gd to the environment 1996, 1629

ECONOMIC DEVELOPMENT—SOCIETIES
Directory of intl economic org, 161

ECONOMIC INDICATORS
Illustrated bk of world rankings, rev ed, 813

ECONOMICS. See also BANKS & BANKING; BUSINESS; FINANCE
Bibliographic gd to business & economics 1995, 147
Business pers index, v.38: Aug 1995-July 1996, 167
Dictionary of economics, 151
Encyclopedia of Keynesian economics, 152
Index of economic freedom, 1997, 169
Knowledge Exchange business ency, 154
NAFTA & GATT: environmental & economic issues, 705
National accounts stats, 203
World economic outlook, May 1997, 188

EDINBURGH (SCOTLAND)
Edinburgh ency, 137

EDITING
Freelance Editorial Assn yellow pages & code of fair practice, 1997-98, 863

EDUCATION
Bibliographic gd to educ 1996, 265
Education index, July 1995 to June 1996, 279
El-Hi textbooks and serials in print 1997, 283
Guide to fed funding for educ, 1997, 23d ed, 274
International ency of the sociology of educ, 268
Multicultural educ dir, 273
Native educ dir 1997, 272

EDUCATION, ELEMENTARY
Internet resource dir for K-12 teachers & librarians, 96/97 ed, 1590
Picture bks to enhance the curriculum, 284

EDUCATION, HIGHER
Asian higher educ, 295
College.educ: on-line resources for the cyber-savvy, 301
CollegeSource [CD-ROM], 297
Directory of college facilities & services for people with disabilities, 4th ed, 772

English lang & orientation programs in the US, 11th ed, 988
External degrees in the info age, 308
Greening the college curriculum: a gd to environmental teaching in the liberal arts, 1640
Guide to the evaluation of educl experiences in the armed servs, 1996, v.1: Army, 275
Guide to the evaluation of educl experiences in the armed servs, 1996, v.2: Navy, 276
Guide to the evaluation of educl experiences in the armed servs, 1996, v.3: Air Force, Coast Guard, Dept of Defense, Marine Corps, 277
Interdisciplinary undergraduate programs, 2d ed, 289
Media courses UK 1997, 4th ed, 860
Money for graduate students in the humanities 1996-98, 848
National gd to funding for higher educ, 4th ed, 291

EDUCATION, SECONDARY
Internet resource dir for K-12 teachers & librarians, 96/97 ed, 1590

EDUCATION, VOCATIONAL
Guide to the evaluation of educl experiences in the armed servs, 1996, v.1: Army, 275
Guide to the evaluation of educl experiences in the armed servs, 1996, v.2: Navy, 276
Guide to the evaluation of educl experiences in the armed servs, 1996, v.3: Air Force, Coast Guard, Dept of Defense, Marine Corps, 277

EDUCATORS
Biographical dict of modern American educators, 266

EGYPT
Ancient Egypt, 486
Penguin histl atlas of ancient Egypt, 490

ELECTIONS
Campaign and election reform, 679

ELECTIONS—UNITED STATES
US primary elections 1995-96, 673

ELECTRIC ENGINEERING
American electricians' hndbk, 13th ed, 1485
Electrical & electronics trades dir 1996 [CD-ROM], 1486

ELECTRONIC JOURNALS
Books & pers online, 1997 ed, 1582
Net journal dir, vol. 1, no. 2, 1591

ELECTRONIC MUSIC
Electronic & computer music, 1196

ELECTRONIC PUBLISHING
Books & pers online, 1997 ed, 1582

ELECTRONICS
Electrical & electronics trades dir 1996 [CD-ROM], 1486
Illustrated dict of electronics, 7th ed, 1488

Jane's electro-optic systems 1996-97, 2d ed, 619
Jane's military communications, 1997-98, 618
McGraw-Hill electronics dict, 6th ed, 1489

ELEMENTS
Elements, 1600

ELVES
American elves, 1255

EMIGRATION & IMMIGRATION
Immigration questions & answers, rev ed, 702

EMPLOYEE FRINGE BENEFITS
Mandated benefits, 236

EMPLOYEE SCREENING
Guide to background investigations, 7th ed, 640

EMPLOYEES—RECRUITING
Guide to executive recruiters, new ed, 218

EMPLOYMENT AGENCIES
JobBank gd to employment servs 1998-99, 220

ENCYCLOPEDIAS & DICTIONARIES. *See also* **CHILDREN'S ENCYCLOPEDIAS & DICTIONARIES**
Academic American ency, 36
Cambridge ency, 3d ed, 37
Cambridge factfinder, 2d ed, 38
Collier's ency, 40
Collier's ency 1998 [CD-ROM], 41
Columbia ency [CD-ROM], 42
Dictionary of dicts & encys, 2d ed, 45
Grolier multimedia ency, 1998, deluxe ed [CD-ROM], 43
Merriam-Webster's collegiate dict, deluxe audio ed, 998
Oxford family ency, 47
Pockets: ency, 48

ENCYCLOPEDIAS & DICTIONARIES—BIBLIOGRAPHY
ARBA gd to subject encys & dicts, 2d ed, 5

ENDOWMENTS. *See also* **CHARITABLE USES, TRUSTS, & FOUNDATIONS; GRANTS-IN-AID**
National gd to funding for higher educ, 4th ed, 291

ENERGY CONSUMPTION
Energy analysis of 108 industrial processes, 6th ed, 1494

ENERGY INDUSTRIES
Bibliographic gd to the environment 1996, 1629
Energy & environmental industry survey 1997, 191
Energy balances for countries in transition 1993, 1994-2010, & energy prospects in CIS countries, 1627

ENGINEERING
Bibliographic gd to tech 1996, 1398
McGraw-Hill dict of engineering, 1476

ENGLISH DRAMA
Dictionary of who, what, & where in Shakespeare, 1161
Irish playwrights, 1880-1995, 1175
Women playwrights in England, Ireland, & Scotland 1660-1823, 1151

ENGLISH FICTION
British novel 1680-1832, 1146
Contemporary novel, 2d ed, 1108
Edwardian fiction, 1152
Eighteenth-century Anglo-American women novelists, 1111
English novel, 1660-1700, 1145
Guide to British prose fiction explication: 19th & 20th centuries, 1143

ENGLISH LANGUAGE—CANADA—DICTIONARIES
Gage Canadian dict, rev ed, 1012
ITP Nelson Canadian dict of the English lang, 1013

ENGLISH LANGUAGE—COGNATE WORDS—SPANISH
NTC's dict of Spanish cognates thematically organized, 1048

ENGLISH LANGUAGE—DICTIONARIES
American Heritage talking dict [CD-ROM], 997
Barnhart dict companion, v.10, no.1, summer 1997, 1010
Dictionary of the English lang [CD-ROM], 1020
ITP Nelson Canadian dict of the English lang, 1013
Merriam-Webster's collegiate dict, deluxe audio ed, 998
New shorter Oxford English dict [CD-ROM], 999
Oxford desk dict & thesaurus, American ed, 993
Pockets: English dict A to Z, 995
World Bk dict, 996

ENGLISH LANGUAGE—DICTIONARIES—DANISH
Elsevier's dict of European Community co/business/financial law in English, Danish, & German, 517

ENGLISH LANGUAGE—DICTIONARIES—FRENCH
Collins-Robert French-English, English-French dict, 3d ed, 1024
Oxford-Hachette French desk dict, 1026
Oxford starter French dict, 1027
Pockets: French dict, 1028
Routldege French dict of environmental technology, 1637

ENGLISH LANGUAGE—DICTIONARIES—GERMAN
Elsevier's dict of European Community co/business/financial law in English, Danish, & German, 517
Oxford-Duden German desk dict, new ed, 1030
Oxford-Duden German dict [CD-ROM], 1032
Oxford-Duden German dict, rev ed, 1031
Oxford starter German dict, 1033
Practical dict of German usage, 1029
Routledge German dict of business commerce and finance, 156

Routledge German dict of construction, 1482
Routledge German dict of info tech, 1579

ENGLISH LANGUAGE—DICTIONARIES—HANI
Hani-English/English-Hani dict, 1034

ENGLISH LANGUAGE—DICTIONARIES—HEBREW
Harduf's transliterated English-Hebrew dict, 4th v., L-M, 1035

ENGLISH LANGUAGE—DICTIONARIES—ITALIAN
Oxford color Italian dict, 1036
Oxford Italian desk dict, 1037
Oxford Italian minidict, 2d ed, 1038

ENGLISH LANGUAGE—DICTIONARIES, JUVENILE
Scholastic children's dict, rev ed, 1008

ENGLISH LANGUAGE—DICTIONARIES—LATIN
Latin for the illiterati, 1039

ENGLISH LANGUAGE—DICTIONARIES—PORTUGUESE
HarperCollins Portuguese dict, college ed, 1041
Oxford pa Portuguese dict, 1042

ENGLISH LANGUAGE—DICTIONARIES—RUSSIAN
NTC's new college Russian & English dict, 1045
Oxford starter Russian dict, 1046

ENGLISH LANGUAGE—DICTIONARIES—SPANISH
Delmar's English/Spanish pocket dict for health professionals, 1527
NTC's dict of Latin American Spanish, 1049
Oxford pa Spanish dict & grammar, 1050
Oxford starter Spanish dict, 1051
Pockets: spanish dict, 1052
Routledge Spanish technical dict, 1408
Wiley's English-Spanish, Spanish-English business dict, 157
Wiley's English-Spanish, Spanish-English legal dict, 2d ed, 519

ENGLISH LANGUAGE—DICTIONARIES—SWEDISH
NTC's compact Swedish & English dict, 1053

ENGLISH LANGUAGE—DICTIONARIES—UKRAINIAN
English-Ukrainian dict of business, 155

ENGLISH LANGUAGE—DICTIONARIES—YIDDISH
English-Yiddish, Yiddish-English dict, [rev ed], 1054
Harduf's transliterated English-Yiddish, Yiddish-English dict, [rev ed], 1055

ENGLISH LANGUAGE—ERRORS OF USAGE—DICTIONARIES
Highly selective dict for the extraordinarily literate, 1017

ENGLISH LANGUAGE—ETYMOLOGY
America in so many words, 1000
Facts on File ency of word & phrase origins, rev ed, 1001
Medical meanings: a glossary of word origins, 1528
Speaking freely, 1002

ENGLISH LANGUAGE—FOREIGN WORDS & PHRASES—JAPANESE
Dictionary of Japanese loanwords, 1003

ENGLISH LANGUAGE—GRAMMAR
Grammatically correct, 1005
Grammatically correct hndbk, 1004

ENGLISH LANGUAGE—IDIOMS
American Heritage dict of idioms, 1006

ENGLISH LANGUAGE—OBSOLETE WORDS
Random House histl dict of American slang, v.2: H-O, 1015
Where Queen Elizabeth slept & what the butler saw, 1011

ENGLISH LANGUAGE—RHETORIC
Grammatically correct, 1005

ENGLISH LANGUAGE—SLANG
Idiom savant: slang as it is slung, 1014
Random House histl dict of American slang, v.2: H-O, 1015
Speaking freely, 1002

ENGLISH LANGUAGE—STUDY & TRAINING
English lang & orientation programs in the US, 11th ed, 988

ENGLISH LANGUAGE—STYLE
ACS style gd, 2d ed, 872

ENGLISH LANGUAGE—SYNONYMS & ANTONYMS
Highly selective dict for the extraordinarily literate, 1017
Oxford desk dict & thesaurus, American ed, 993

ENGLISH LANGUAGE—SYNONYMS & ANTONYMS—JUVENILE LITERATURE
American Heritage children's thesaurus, 1016

ENGLISH LANGUAGE—TERMS & PHRASES
Cassell dict of cliches, 1018
Cliches, 1019
Facts on File ency of word & phrase origins, rev ed, 1001

ENGLISH LANGUAGE—UNITED STATES—DICTIONARIES
Oxford dict & thesaurus, American ed, 994

ENGLISH LITERATURE
Biographical companion to lit in English, rev ed, 1066
British women writers, 1700-1850, 1144
British writers, suppl 4, 1149
Carl H. Pforzheimer Lib, English lit, 1475-1700, 1997 ed, 1148
Contemporary popular writers, 1058
Humor in British lit, from the Middle Ages to the Restoration, 1150
Major Tudor authors, 1060
Shakespeare for students, bk 2, 1163
Sixteenth-century British nondramatic writers, 4th series, 1147

ENGLISH LITERATURE—19TH CENTURY
George Gordon, Lord Byron, 1155

ENGLISH LITERATURE—IRISH AUTHORS
Modern Irish writers, 1176

ENGLISH—STUDY AND TEACHING
Light 'n lively reads, 1057
Oxford dict of computing for learners of English, 1577

ENGLISH WIT & HUMOR
Humor in British lit, from the Middle Ages to the Restoration, 1150

ENTERTAINERS
A&E entertainment almanac, 1997, 1264

ENTREPRENEURSHIP
Small business sourcebk, 10th ed, 166

ENVIRONMENTAL ECONOMICS
Dictionary of environment & sustainable dvlpmt, 1633

ENVIRONMENTAL EDUCATION
Greening the college curriculum: a gd to environmental teaching in the liberal arts, 1640

ENVIRONMENTALISM
Historical dict of N American environmentalism, 1638

ENVIRONMENTALISTS
World who is who & does what in environment & conservation, 1631

ENVIRONMENTAL LAW
Environmental ethics, 1628
Environmental law hndbk, 14th ed, 559
Law, values, and the environment, 560

ENVIRONMENTAL POLICY
Dictionary of environment and sustainable dvlpmt, 1633
Free market environmental bibliog 1995-96, 4th ed, 1630
NAFTA & GATT: environmental & economic issues, 705

ENVIRONMENTAL PROTECTION
Dictionary of natural resource mgmt, 1632
Information sources in environmental protection, 1643
Rainforest orgs, 1639

ENVIRONMENTAL SCIENCES
Companion ency of geography, 397
Dictionary of environmental sci & tech, 2d ed, 1636

Glossary of environment stats, 1634
Guide to graduate environmental programs, 1641

EPIC LITERATURE
Epics for students, 1069

ESPIONAGE
Spies, 701

ESSAYS
Encyclopedia of the essay, 1107

ETHNIC FOLKLORE
American elves, 1255

ETHNIC GROUPS. *See also* **MINORITIES**
Ethnic cultures of the world, 331
Ethnic minority health, 1503

ETHNIC GROUPS IN LITERATURE
Identities & issues in lit, 1070

ETHNOLOGY
Nations of Africa, 321
Peoples of Central Africa, 322
Peoples of E Africa, 323
Peoples of N Africa, 324
Peoples of Southern Africa, 325
Peoples of W Africa, 326

ETIQUETTE
Protocol: a hndbk for legislative staff, 677

EURASIA
Bibliographic gd to Slavic, Baltic, & Eurasian studies 1996, 126
Russia & Eurasia facts & figures annual, v.21, 128
Russia & Eurasia facts & figures annual, v.22, 129

EUROPE
Europe on file, 121
European forests & timber, 1430
Lands & peoples special ed: the changing face of Europe, 96
New religious movements in Western Europe, 1343
Who's who in European pols, 3d ed, 685

EUROPEAN COMMUNITIES
Elsevier's dict of European Community co/business/ financial law in English, Danish, & German, 517
Political data hndbk: OECD countries, 2d ed, 684

EUROPEAN LITERATURE
Major Tudor authors, 1060

EUROPE, EASTERN
Eastern Europe & the Commonwealth of Independent States 1997, 3d ed, 127

EUROPE—HISTORY
Chronology of European hist, 462
European hist on file, 463
Medieval & early modern data bank [CD-ROM], 165

EVANGELICALISM
American evangelicalism 2: 1st bibliogl suppl, 1990-96, 1383

EVENTS (PHILOSOPHY)
50 yrs of events, 1331

EXECUTIONS AND EXECUTIONERS
Legal executions in N.Y. State, 554

EXECUTIVE DEPARTMENTS. UNITED STATES
Almanac of the executive branch 1997/98, 642

EXHIBITIONS
Museum premieres, exhibitions, & special events, 72

EXOBIOLOGY
Cosmic influences on humans, animals, & plants, 1441

EXPATRIATE ARTISTS
American expatriate writers, 1127

EXPORT MARKETING
International standards desk ref, 206
Services—the export of the 21st century: a gdbk of US serv exporters, 262

EYE
Dictionary of eye terminology, 3d ed, 1553

FAMILY
Work-Family research, 777

FANTASTIC FICTION
Encyclopedia of fantasy, 1116
Science fiction & fantasy ref index 1992-95, 1117

FANTASTIC FILMS
Sci-Fi on tape, 1318

FANTASY IN ART
Barlowe's gd to fantasy, 979

FARM EQUIPMENT
Encyclopedia of American farm implements & antiques, 1419

FEDERAL GOVERNMENT
American govt & pols, 646
Federal regulatory dir, 8th ed, 664

FEMALE OFFENDERS
Female offenders, 549

FEMINISM
Feminism worldwide, 831
French feminist theory 3, 832
Women's issues, 837

FESTIVALS
Fiesta, 1262
Food festivals, 414
Holidays, festivals, & celebrations dict, 2d ed, 1263

FICTION
Argentine novel, 1168
Children's fiction series, 1088
English novel, 1660-1700, 1145
Novels for students, v.1, 1109
Novels for students, v.2, 1110

FICTION GENRES
Teen genreflecting, 1096

FINANCE
Almanac of business & industrial financial ratios 1996, 27th ed, 177
Bibliographic gd to business & economics 1995, 147
Elsevier's dict of European Community co/business/ financial law in English, Danish, & German, 517
Handbook of intl financial terms, 184
Knowledge Exchange business ency, 154
Plunkett's financial servs industry almanac, 185
Routledge German dict of business commerce and finance, 156
Who's who in Asian banking & finance, 150

FINANCE, PERSONAL
Numbers: how many, how far, how long, how much, 810

FINLAND
Finland, rev ed, 123

FIREARMS
Gun digest, 920

FIRST AID IN ILLNESS & INJURY
Parent's gd to medical emergencies, 1522

FISHES
Fishes of the Galapagos Islands, 1468

FISHING
Coykendall's complete gd to sporting collectibles, 895

FLAGS
Ultimate pocket: flags of the world, 374

FLEA MARKETS
Flea market trader, 11th ed, 896
Garage sale & flea market annual, 5th ed, 897

FLORIDA
Florida, 416
Florida almanac 1997-98, 11th ed, 99
Florida: atlas of histl county boundaries, 431

FLOWERS
Cyclamen: a gd for gardeners, horticulturists, & botanists, 1449

FOLIAGE PLANTS
Foliage plant diseases, 1446

FOOD
Dictionary of healthful food terms, 1420
Green kitchen hndbk, 1425
Who's buying food & drink, 257

FOOD—QUOTATIONS
Never eat more than you can lift, & other food quotes & quips, 1429

FOOTBALL
Gridiron greats: a century of Polish Americans in college football, 745
Sports ency: pro football, 746
Total football, 747

FORECASTING
Predicting the future, 88

FORESTRY
European forests & timber, 1430

FORESTS & FORESTRY
Forest & forest industries country fact sheets, 1431

FORMER SOVIET REPUBLICS. *See also* RUSSIA; SOVIET UNION
Eastern Europe & the Commonwealth of Independent States 1997, 3d ed, 127
Newly independent states of Eurasia, 2d ed, 125
Russia & Eurasia facts & figures annual, v.21, 128
Russia & Eurasia facts & figures annual, v.22, 129

FORMS (LAW)
Complete bk of personal legal forms, 2d ed, 541
Complete bk of small business legal forms, 2d ed, 542

FRANCE—HISTORY
Impact of Napoleon, 1800-15, 469

FRANCHISES (RETAIL TRADE)
How much can I make?, 174

FRATERNAL ORDERS. *See* SECRET SOCIETIES

FREEDOM OF SPEECH
Free expression & censorship in America, 584

FREEDOM OF THE PRESS
Press freedom & dvlpmt, 850

FREE ENTERPRISE
Free market environmental bibliog 1995-96, 4th ed, 1630

FREE TRADE
NAFTA bibliog, 255

FRENCH LANGUAGE—DICTIONARIES— ENGLISH
Collins-Robert French-English, English-French dict, 3d ed, 1024
Les bon mots: how to amaze tout le monde with everyday French, 1025
Oxford-Hachette French desk dict, 1026
Oxford starter French dict, 1027
Pockets: french dict, 1028
Routldege French dict of environmental technology, 1637

FRIENDLY SOCIETIES
International ency of secret societies & fraternal orders, 763

FRONTIER & PIONEER LIFE
Encyclopedia of frontier lit, 1130
Handbook of the American frontier, v.4: the far West, 357

FRUIT
Produce ref gd to fruits & vegetables from around the world, 1421

FUNDAMENTALISM
American evangelicalism 2: 1st bibliogl suppl, 1990-96, 1383

FUND RAISING
Corporate & fndn fundraising manual for Native Americans, 3d ed, 793
Fund-Raising regulation, 539
NSFRE fund-raising dict, 784

FUNERAL RITES & CEREMONIES
R.I.P.: the complete bk of death & dying, 766

FUNGI
Annotated catalogue of types of the Univ of Ill. mycological collections (ILL), 1451
Hallucinogenic & poisonous mushroom field gd, 1452

GAMBLING
American casino gd, 1997 ed, 411
Casino gaming in the US, 724
Where to play in the USA: the gaming gd, 419

GARAGE SALES
Garage sale & flea market annual, 5th ed, 897

GARDENING
Eyewitness garden hndbk: annuals & biennials, 1436
Gardener's gd to growing irises, 1454
Gardener's gd to growing ivies, 1455
Smaller perennials, 1435

GARFIELD, JAMES A.
James A. Garfield, 645

GATT (GENERAL AGREEMENT ON TARIFFS & TRADE)
NAFTA & GATT: environmental & economic issues, 705

GAYS
Gay & lesbian biog, 781
Gay & lesbian online, rev ed, 780

GAZETTEERS
Merriam-Webster's geographical dict, 3d ed, 396

GENEALOGY
Address bk for German genealogy, 6th ed, 363
Ancestors: a beginner's gd to family hist & genealogy, 372
Compendium of histl sources, rev ed, 364
Finding your Hispanic roots, 368
Genealogical & local hist bks in print: gen ref & world resources v., 5th ed, 359
Genealogical & local hist bks in print: US sources & resources v., 5th ed, 360
Genealogy annual, 1995, 361
Periodical source index CD-ROM [CD-ROM], 373
Source: a gdbk of American genealogy, 370
Student's gd to Jewish American genealogy, 369
Touchstones: a gd to records, rights, & resources for families of American WW II casualties, 367
Ultimate family tree deluxe [CD-ROM], 371
Virtual roots: a gd to genealogy & local hist on the WWW, 366

GENETIC ENGINEERING
Biotechnology abstracts: agricultural & environmental, 1983-Feb 1997 [CD-ROM], 1490

GEOGRAPHY
Answer atlas, 380
Children's illus atlas, 1997 ed, 381
Companion ency of geography, 397
Encyclopedia of geographical features in world hist, 399
Houghton Mifflin dict of geography, 395
Lands & peoples, 95
Maps of the world, 387
McGraw-Hill dict of earth sci, 1603
Merriam-Webster's geographical dict, 3d ed, 396
Political geography, 393
World facts & maps, 400

GEOLOGY. *See also* **EARTH SCIENCES**
McGraw-Hill dict of earth sci, 1603
McGraw-Hill dict of geology & mineralogy, 1614

GERMAN AMERICANS
Address bk for German genealogy, 6th ed, 363

GERMAN LANGUAGE—DICTIONARIES—ENGLISH
Elsevier's dict of European Community co/business/financial law in English, Danish, & German, 517
Oxford-Duden German desk dict, new ed, 1030
Oxford-Duden German dict [CD-ROM], 1032
Oxford-Duden German dict, rev ed, 1031
Oxford starter German dict, 1033
Practical dict of German usage, 1029
Routledge German dict of business commerce and finance, 156
Routledge German dict of construction, 1482
Routledge German dict of info tech, 1579

GERMAN LITERATURE
German Baroque writers, 1661-1730, 1172
Oxford companion to German lit, 3d ed, 1173

GERMANY—HISTORY
Encyclopedia of German resistance to the Nazi movement, 470
Historical dict of Germany's Weimar Republic, 1918-33, 471

GERONTOLOGY. *See also* **AGED**
Graying of America, 760

Group work with the elderly, 757
Women & aging, 762

GESTURES
Dictionary of worldwide gestures, 711

GLASSWARE
Fostoria, v.2: identification & value gd to etched, carved & cut designs, 899

GODDESSES
New bk of goddesses & heroines, 3d ed, 1258

GODZILLA FILMS
Critical hist & filmography of Toho's Godzilla series, 1294

GOLDMAN, EMMA
Rosa Luxemburg & Emma Goldman: a bibliog, 637

GOLF
Inside Sports Mag golf, 748

GOVERNMENT EXECUTIVES
Almanac of the unelected, 649
Maximov's companion to who governs Moscow, 688

GOVERNMENT LIBRARIES
Directory of fed libs, 3d ed, 573

GOVERNMENT PUBLICATIONS
Information sources in official pubns, 61
NTIS ordernow [CD-ROM], 62
Subject gd to US govt ref sources, 2d ed, 60

GRANDPARENTS
Grandparents, 779

GRANTS-IN-AID. *See also* **CHARITABLE USES, TRUSTS, & FOUNDATIONS; ENDOWMENTS; FUND RAISING**
Corporate fndn profiles, 785
Directory of bldg & equipment grants, 4th ed, 1481
Directory of educ grants, 271
Directory of grants for orgs serving people with disabilities, 10th ed, 773
Directory of operating grants, 3d ed, 786
Funding in aging, 758
Grants register 1998, 16th ed, 300
Guide to fed funding for anti-crime programs, 2d ed, 553
Guide to fed funding for govts & nonprofits, 19th ed, 792
National dir of corporate giving, 790
National gd to funding for higher educ, 4th ed, 291
National gd to funding for info tech, 583

GRATEFUL DEAD
Grateful Dead & the deadheads, 1240

GREAT BRITAIN
Directory of rare bk & special collections in the UK & the Republic of Ireland, 2d ed, 588
Media courses UK 1997, 4th ed, 860

GREAT BRITAIN—DIRECTORIES
British dirs, 2d ed, 132

GREAT BRITAIN—HISTORY
Bibliography of British hist 1914-89, 464
Columbia companion to British hist, 465
Historical dict of the British Empire, 466
Historical dict of the UK, v.1: England and the UK, 467
Victorian database on CD-ROM, 1970-95 [CD-ROM], 468

GREAT BRITAIN—POLITICS & GOVERNMENT
British secret servs, 686
Duke of Newcastle, 1693-1768, & Henry Pelham, 1694-1754, 687

GREAT BRITAIN—SOCIAL LIFE & CUSTOMS
Where Queen Elizabeth slept & what the butler saw, 1011

GREECE
Fodor's exploring the Greek Islands, 424
Greece: Athens & the mainland, 425
Greek Islands, 426

GREECE—CIVILIZATION—JUVENILE LITERATURE
Ancient Greeks, 472

GREEN TECHNOLOGY
Routldege French dict of environmental technology, 1637

GRIEF
National dir of bereavement support grps & servs, 1996, 768

GUERRILLA WARFARE
Guerrilla warfare, 620

GUINEA-BISSAU
Historical dict of the Republic of Guinea-Bissau, 3d ed, 456

GUINEA PIGS
Guinea pig, 1466

GUITAR MUSIC
Guitar music by women composers, 1218
Music for voice & classical guitar, 1945-96, 1219

HANDBOOKS, VADE MECUMS, ETC.
Numbers: how many, how far, how long, how much, 810

HANDICAPPED
ABC-CLIO companion to the disability rights movement, 775
Complete dir for people with disabilities, 1997-98, 770
Directory of agencies & orgs serving individuals who are deaf-blind, rev ed, 771
Directory of college facilities & services for people with disabilities, 4th ed, 772
Directory of grants for orgs serving people with disabilities, 10th ed, 773
Man's gd to coping with disability, 774

HANDICRAFT
Crafts supply source bk, 4th ed, 931

HANI LANGUAGE—DICTIONARIES—ENGLISH
Hani-English/English-Hani dict, 1034

HANSBERRY, LORRAINE
Lorraine Hansberry: a research & production sourcebk, 1136

HARMONY
Harmony theory, 1193

HARPSICHORD
History of music for harpsichord or piano & orchestra, 1227

HAWAII FIVE-O (TELEVISION PROGRAM)
Booking Hawaii Five-O: an episode gd & critical hist of the 1968-80 TV detective show, 1313

HAZARDOUS SUBSTANCES
Hazardous chemicals desk ref, 4th ed, 1635
Hazardous substances resource gd, 2d ed, 1642
TSCA hndbk, 3d ed, 561

HEADS OF STATE
Political leaders & military figures in the 2d World War, 606

HEALTH
Encyclopedia of medical media & communications, 1529
Ethnic minority health, 1503
Fodor's healthy escapes, 5th ed, 405
Health & medical yrbk 1997, 1515
Major state health care policies, 5th ed, 1518
Managed health care dict, 1509
Preventive care sourcebk 1997-98, 1519
Who's who in medicine & healthcare 1997-98, 1506

HEALTH CARE REFORM
Health care crisis in the US, 1505

HEAT
Handbook of thermal conductivity, v.4: inorganic compounds & elements, 1622

HEBREW LANGUAGE—DICTIONARIES—ENGLISH
Harduf's transliterated English-Hebrew dict, 4th v., L-M, 1035
Theological dict of the O.T., v.8, 1375

HENTY, GEORGE ALFRED
G. A. Henty 1832-1902: a bibliographical study of his British eds...., 1159

HERBS
Complete family gd to natural home remedies, 1545
Green pharmacy, 1546

HERO (GREEK MYTHOLOGY) IN LITERATURE
Myths & hero tales, 1084

HIGH INTEREST-LOW VOCABULARY BOOKS
Light 'n lively reads, 1057

HIGH TECHNOLOGY
CorpTech explore database [CD-ROM], 1571
CyberDictionary, 1575

HINDUISM
Historical dict of Hinduism, 1392
Islam, Hinduism, & Judaism in S Africa, 1345

HISPANIC AMERICANS
Biographical hndbk of Hispanics & US film, 1277
Finding your Hispanic roots, 368
Hispanic firsts, 348
National Hispanic media dir, 1997, 861
Notable Latino Americans, 349
U*X*L multicultural CD [CD-ROM], 333

HISTORICAL FICTION
America in histl fiction, 1114

HISTORICAL GEOGRAPHY
Historical atlas of the Holocaust, 492
Historical atlas of the Holocaust [CD-ROM], 493
Indiana: atlas of histl county boundaries, 379

HISTORIC PRESERVATION
Preservation yellow pages, rev ed, 975

HISTORIC SITES
What happened where, 500

HISTORY, ANCIENT—JUVENILE LITERATURE
History of the ancient & medieval world, 501

HISTORY—BIBLIOGRAPHY
Bibliography for hist, hist curatorship, & museums, 495

HISTORY IN LITERATURE
Literature & its times, 1072

HISTORY, MODERN
Dictionary of 20th-century world hist, 504
Facts on File world news CD-ROM 1997 [CD-ROM], 506
Junior chronicle of the 20th century, 498
Matter of fact: statements containing stats on current social, economics, & pol issues, v.24, 814
Sixties [CD-ROM], 450
What happened where, 500
World War II in Europe, Africa, & the Americas, with general sources, 622

HOCKEY
Inside Sports Mag hockey, 1997 ed, 749

HOLBEIN, HANS
Hans Holbein the younger: a gd to research, 943

HOLIDAYS
Holidays, festivals, & celebrations dict, 2d ed, 1263

HOLLY
Hollies, 1457

HOLMES, SHERLOCK
Good old index: the Sherlock Holmes hndbk, 1158

HOLOCAUST, JEWISH
Historical atlas of the Holocaust, 492
Historical atlas of the Holocaust [CD-ROM], 493
Holocaust, 502

HOLOCAUST SURVIVORS
Medical & psychological effects of concentration camps on Holocaust survivors, v.4: genocide, 708

HOME ECONOMICS
Green kitchen hndbk, 1425
Household hints & tips, 180

HOME LABOR
Telecommuters, the workforce of the 21st century, 212

HOMELESSNESS
Guide to fed funding for housing & homeless programs, 3d ed, 764
Homelessness in America, 765

HOMEOPATHY
Complete family gd to natural home remedies, 1545

HORN MUSIC
Discography of 78 rpm era recordings of the horn, 1203

HORROR FILMS
A-Z of horror films, 1297
Clive Barker's A-Z of horror, 1306
Science fiction, fantasy, & horror film sequels, series, & remakes, 1292

HORROR IN LITERATURE
Clive Barker's A-Z of horror, 1306

HOSPICE CARE
Hospice & palliative care, 1521

HOSPITALITY INDUSTRY
Guide to college programs in hospitality & tourism, 5th ed, 314

HOSTELS
Hostelling N America, 1997, 403

HOTELS
America's best hotels & restaurants, 409

HOUSEHOLD SUPPLIES
Poison! how to handle the hazardous substances in your home, 1563
Who's buying for the home, 258

HOUSE PLANTS
House plant ency, 1433

HOUSING
Annual bulletin of housing & bldg stats for Europe & N America 1996, 822
Guide to fed funding for housing & homeless programs, 3d ed, 764

HUMAN ANATOMY
Ultimate human body version 2.0 [CD-ROM], 1499

HUMAN CAPITAL
Human resources yrbk 1996/97, 224

HUMANITIES
Benét's reader's ency, 4th ed, 843
Comprehensive dissertation index, 1996 supplement, 844
Humanities abstracts full text [CD-ROM], 845
Humanities index, April 1995 to Mar 1996, 846
World databases in humanities, 849

HUMAN RIGHTS
Historical dict of human rights & humanitarian orgs, 564

HUNGARY
Budapest, 133
Historical dict of Hungary, 473

HUNTING
Coykendall's complete gd to sporting collectibles, 895

HYMNS
Christian music dirs: printed music 1997-98, 1244
Hymnology, 1246

ICELAND
Historical dict of Iceland, 474

IDEOLOGY
Social movement theory & research, 690

IDIOMS
Mountain range: a dict of expressions from Appalachia to the Ozarks, 1007
Russian idioms, 1043

ILLUSTRATED BOOKS, CHILDREN'S
Worth a 1,000 words: an annot gd to picture bks for older readers, 1090

ILLUSTRATORS
Authors & artists for YAs, v.20, 1100
Authors & artists for YAs, v.21, 1101
Dictionary of 19th century British bk illustrators & caricaturists, rev ed, 944

IMAGE TRANSMISSION
Finding images online, 1592

IMMIGRATION
Guide to naturalization records of the US, 332
NAFTA & GATT: environmental & economic issues, 705

IMPERIALISM
Historical dict of the British Empire, 466

INCOME
American salaries & wages survey, 4th ed, 229
Official gd to American incomes, 2d ed, 225

INCUNABULA
Rosenthal Collection of printed bks with ms annots, 578

INDEXES
PCI: pers contents index [CD-ROM], 66

INDIA
Cultural atlas of India, 113

INDIANA
Indiana: atlas of histl county boundaries, 379

INDIANS OF NORTH AMERICA
American Indian: a multimedia ency [CD-ROM], 352
Encyclopedia of American Indian civil rights, 562
Encyclopedia of Native American biog, 350
Encyclopedia of N American Indians, 353, 354
Handbook of N American Indians, v.17: langs, 356
Handbook of the American frontier, v.4: the far West, 357
Native educ dir 1997, 272
North American Indian music, 1191
Scholastic ency of the N American Indian, 355
Timelines of Native American hist, 351
U*X*L multicultural CD [CD-ROM], 333

INDONESIA—BIBLIOGRAPHY
Unveiling Indonesia, 114

INDUSTRIAL MANAGEMENT
Almanac of business & industrial financial ratios 1996, 27th ed, 177

INDUSTRIAL REVOLUTION
American eras: dvlpmt of the industrial US, 1878-99, 445

INDUSTRIAL SAFETY
Directory of safety standards, lit, & servs, 1495
Safety & health on the Internet, 239

INDUSTRY. *See also* **MANUFACTURES**
Business & industry [CD-ROM], 189
Energy analysis of 108 industrial processes, 6th ed, 1494
Extractives, manufacturing, & servs, 162
International yrbk of industrial stats 1997, 194
Thomas register of American manufacturers, 1997, 87th ed, 196
Thomas register on CD-ROM, 1997 [CD-ROM], 197
WEFA industrial monitor 1997, 198
World industrial robots 1997, 1581

INFORMATION RETRIEVAL
Find it fast, 4th ed, 575
Verify those credentials: do you know who you're dealing with?, 63

INFORMATION SCIENCE
Dictionary of computing, 4th ed, 1576
Encyclopedia of lib & info sci, v.57, 569
Encyclopedia of lib & info sci, v.59, 570

INFORMATION STORAGE & RETRIEVAL SYSTEMS
Key gd to electronic resources: lang & lit, 985

INFORMATION TECHNOLOGY
Elsevier's dict of info tech in Engish, German, & French, 581
Routledge German dict of info tech, 1579

INORGANIC COMPOUNDS
Handbook of viscosity, v.4: inorganic compounds & elements, 1623

INSIGNIA
Encyclopedia of US Army insignia & uniforms, 624

INSTRUCTIONAL MATERIALS CENTERS. *See also* **SCHOOL LIBRARIES**
Recommended ref bks for small & medium-sized libs & media centers 1997, 9

INTEGRATED CIRCUITS
Master hndbk of IC circuits, 3d ed, 1487

INTELLECTUAL PROPERTY
Copyright laws & treaties of the world 1991-95 suppl, 566
International treaties on intellectual property, 2d ed, 567

INTERDISCIPLINARY APPROACH TO EDUCATION
Interdisciplinary undergraduate programs, 2d ed, 289

INTERIOR DECORATION
Ency of interior design, 935

INTERLIBRARY LOAN
WLN interlibrary loan policies dir, 5th ed, 585

INTERNATIONAL AGENCIES
Historical dict of human rights & humanitarian orgs, 564
International info documents, 693
Yearbook of intl orgs 1997/98, 71

INTERNATIONAL BUSINESS ENTERPRISES
International bibliog of business hist, 149
International trade sources, 199
International trade stats yrbk, 1995, 252
World investment dir 1996, v.6: West Asia, 207

INTERNATIONAL ECONOMIC RELATIONS
Directory of intl economic org, 161
World economic outlook, May 1997, 188

INTERNATIONAL FINANCE
Handbook of intl financial terms, 184

INTERNATIONAL RELATIONS
African intl relations, 2d ed, 699

Careers in intl affairs, 6th ed, 698
International conflict, 696

INTERNATIONAL TRADE
Handbook of world mineral trade stats 1990-95, 251
International trade sources, 199
National accounts stats, 203
Thunderbird gd to intl business resources on the WWW, 204
World country analyst [CD-ROM], 205

INTERNET (COMPUTER NETWORK)
Business multimedia explained, 242
Catholic Internet, USA ed, 1390
Catholicism on the Web, 1391
Chemicals on the Internet, v.1, 1478
CyberDictionary, 1575
CyberHound's gd to cos on the Internet, 1583
CyberHound's gd to Internet discussion groups, 1584
CyberHound's gd to people on the Internet, 1585
CyberTools for business, 163
Dictionary of personal computing and the Internet, 1574
Film & video on the Internet, 1287
Finding images online, 1592
Gay & lesbian online, rev ed, 780
God on the Internet, 1365
Insider's gd to mental health resources online, 1514
Internet & lib & info servs, 582
Internet complete ref, 2d ed, 1594
Internet gd for the legal researcher, 2d ed, 535
Internet resource dir for K-12 teachers & librarians, 96/97 ed, 1590
Internet searcher's hndbk, 1595
Internet tools of the profession, 2d ed, 1586
Key gd to electronic resources: lang & lit, 985
Mecklermedia's official Internet World Internet yellow pages, 1996 ed, 1587
Mecklermedia's official Internet World WWW yellow pages, 1996 ed, 1588
Microsoft Bkshelf Internet dir, 1996-97 ed, 1589
Naked in cyberspace: how to find personal info online, 1596
Safety & health on the Internet, 239
U.S. military online, 617
Virtual field trips, 281
Virtual musician, 1206
Virtual roots: a gd to genealogy & local hist on the WWW, 366

INTERNSHIP PROGRAMS
America's top internships, 1998 ed, 221

INVESTMENTS
International gd to securities market indices, 175
Plunkett's financial servs industry almanac, 185
Topline ency of histl charts, Mar 1997 ed, 176
Walker's manual of unlisted stocks, 172
Wall Street words, 170
World investment dir 1996, v.5: Africa, 201

IRELAND
Directory of rare bk & special collections in the UK & the Republic of Ireland, 2d ed, 588
Irish almanac & yrbk of facts 1997, 134
Women of Ireland, 34

IRELAND—BIOGRAPHY
Modern Irish writers, 1176

IRELAND—HISTORY
Historical dict of Ireland, 475

IRELAND IN LITERATURE
Patrick Kavanagh: a ref gd, 1174

IRIGARAY, LUCE
French feminist theory 3, 832

IRISH AMERICANS
Dictionary of Irish family names, 376

IRIS (PLANT)
Gardener's gd to growing irises, 1454

ISLAM
Islam, Hinduism, & Judaism in S Africa, 1345

ISRAEL
Israeli secret servs, 689

ITALIAN LANGUAGE—DICTIONARIES—ENGLISH
Oxford color Italian dict, 1036
Oxford Italian desk dict, 1037
Oxford Italian minidict, 2d ed, 1038

ITALIAN LITERATURE
Feminist ency of Italian lit, 1177

ITALY
Dictionary of British & Irish travellers in Italy, 1701-1800, 476

ITZA DIALECT
Itzaj Maya-Spanish-English dict, 1040

IVANOV, VIACHESLAV
Viacheslav Ivanov: a ref gd, 1181

IVY
Gardener's gd to growing ivies, 1455

JAPAN
Bibliographic gd to E Asian studies 1995, 109

JAPAN—STUDY & TEACHING
Japanese studies in Canada: the 1990s, 115

JAZZ MUSIC
All music gd, 3d ed, 1228
Who's who of British jazz, 1235

JAZZ MUSICIANS
Red Nichols story, 1236

JEWISH AMERICANS
Student's gd to Jewish American genealogy, 369

JEWISH-ARAB RELATIONS
Historical dict of Palestine, 488

JEWISH ATHLETES
Jewish sports legends, 2d ed, 719

JEWISH AUTHORS
Jewish writers of Latin America, 1180

JEWS
Dictionary of Jewish surnames from the Kingdom of Poland, 375
Encyclopaedia Judaica, 1393
Jewish yr bk 1997, 1395

JEWS—GENEALOGY
Sourcebook for Jewish genealogies & family hists, 362

JEWS IN LITERATURE
Contemporary Jewish-American novelists, 1125

JOB DESCRIPTIONS
Enhanced occupational outlook hndbk, 226

JOB HUNTING
America's top jobs for people without college degrees, 3d ed, 227
America's top office, mgmt, sales, & professional jobs, 3d ed, 228
Government job finder, 234
Guide to executive recruiters, new ed, 218
JIST's multimedia occupational outlook hndbk, 2d ed [CD-ROM], 232
Job hunter's sourcebk, 3d ed, 233
Job-Hunting on the Internet, 222
Management consulting [CD-ROM], 245
National jobbank 1998, 237
Non-profits and educ job finder 1997-2000, 235
U.S. employment opportunities, 240

JOURNALISM
From headline hunter to Superman: a journalism filmography, 1298
Graduate programs in journalism & mass communications, 309
Journalism, 2d ed, 851
U.S. news coverage of racial minorities, 852

JOURNALISTS
Political commentators in the US in the 20th century, 862

JUDAISM
Dictionary of 1000 Jewish proverbs, 1251
Encyclopaedia Judaica, 1393
Islam, Hinduism, & Judaism in South Africa, 1345
Jewish yr bk 1997, 1395

Judaism, 1394
Oxford dict of the Jewish religion, 1396

JUDGES
BNA's directory of state & fed courts, judges, & clerks, 1997 ed, 521

JUDICIARY. *See* **COURTS**

JUVENILE & YOUNG ADULT FICTION SERIES
Masterplots 2: juvenile & YA lit series suppl, 1085

KABUKI
New Kabuki ency, 1324

KAVANAGH, PATRICK
Patrick Kavanagh: a ref gd, 1174

KENNAN, GEORGE FROST
George F. Kennan: an annot bibliog, 700

KENNERLEY, MITCHELL
Mitchell Kennerly imprint: a descriptive bibliog, 592

KEYNESIAN ECONOMICS
Encyclopedia of Keynesian economics, 152

KOREAN WAR, 1950-53
Guide to films on the Korean War, 1291

KURDISTAN
Kurds & Kurdistan, 116

LABOR
Handbook of US labor stats, 230

LABOR LAWS & LEGISLATION
Employment discrimination law, 3d ed, 530
Labor, employment, & the law, 515

LANDMARK YELLOW PAGES
Preservation yellow pages, rev ed, 975

LANDSCAPE ARCHITECTURE
Landscape architecture sourcebk, 1438

LANGUAGE & CULTURE
Linguistic cultures of the world, 990

LANGUAGE & LANGUAGES
Bibliography on writing & written lang, 984
Cambridge ency of lang, 2d ed, 989
Handbook of N American Indians, v.17: langs, 356
Southeast Asian langs & lits, 986
Student's dict of lang & linguistics, 987

LATIN AMERICA
Bibliographic gd to Latin American studies 1996, 139
Economic survey of Latin America & the Caribbean 1995-96, 210
Encyclopedia of the inter-American system, 695
Hoover's masterlist of major Latin American cos 1996-97, 211
Who's who in Latin America, 4th ed, 35

LATIN AMERICA—JUVENILE LITERATURE
Best of the Latino heritage, 358

LATIN AMERICAN FICTION
Index to translated short fiction by Latin American women in English lang anthologies, 1179

LATIN AMERICAN LITERATURE
Encyclopedia of Latin American lit, 1178
Jewish writers of Latin America, 1180

LATIN AMERICA—RELATIONS—UNITED STATES
United States & Latin America, 697

LATIN LANGUAGE—DICTIONARIES—ENGLISH
Latin for the illiterati, 1039

LATVIA
Historical dict of Latvia, 477

LAW
Bibliographic gd to law 1996, 509
Bieber's dict of legal citations, Prince's 5th ed, 516
Compilation of state & fed privacy laws, 1997 ed, 543
Dictionary of American and English law, 520
Elsevier's dict of European Community co/business/ financial law in English, Danish, & German, 517
50 most influential women in American law, 513
Fund-Raising regulation, 539
Information sources in law, 2d ed, 533
Law & legal info dir, 9th ed, 523
Law for the layperson, 2d ed, 511
Wiley's English-Spanish, Spanish-English legal dict, 2d ed, 519

LAW—BIBLIOGRAPHY
Lawyers' law bks, 3d ed, 512

LAW ENFORCEMENT
Guide to fed funding for anti-crime programs, 2d ed, 553

LAW—POPULAR WORKS
Complete bk of personal legal forms, 2d ed, 541
Complete bk of small business legal forms, 2d ed, 542
Law for the layperson, 511

LAW—STUDY AND TEACHING
Directory of environmental law educ opportunities at American law schools, 558

LAWYERS
Who's who in American law 1996-97, 514

LEADERSHIP
Leadership: quotations from the world's greatest motivators, 81

LEARNING DISABLED
K & W gd to colleges for the learning disabled, 1998 ed, 290

LEGAL RESEARCH
Information sources in law, 2d ed, 533
Internet gd for the legal researcher, 2d ed, 535
Law & legal info dir, 9th ed, 523
Legal research, 5th ed, 534
Sourcebook of local court & county record retrievers, 3d ed, 525

LEGENDS
Cassell dict of Norse myth & legend, 1259

LEGISLATION
Congressional roll call 1996, 671

LEGISLATORS
American legislative leaders in the West, 1911-94, 650
Election results dir 1997, 663
Protocol: a hndbk for legislative staff, 677
Vital stats on Congress 1995-96, 676

LESBIANS
Gay & lesbian biog, 781
Gay & lesbian online, rev ed, 780

LESBIANS IN LITERATURE
Women playwrights of diversity, 1106

LESOTHO
Lesotho, rev ed, 107

LIBEL & SLANDER
Associate Pr stylebook & libel manual, 6th ed, 874

LIBRARIANS
American lib dir 1996-97, 49th ed, 572
International biogl dir of natl archivists, documentalists, & librarians, 574

LIBRARIES
American lib dir 1996-97, 49th ed, 572
Articles describing archives & ms collections in the US, 577

LIBRARIES—SPECIAL COLLECTIONS
Directory of rare bk & special collections in the UK & the Republic of Ireland, 2d ed, 588

LIBRARY OF CONGRESS—CATALOGS
Unveiling Indonesia, 114

LIBRARY SCIENCE
Bowker annual lib and bk trade almanac 1997, 576
Encyclopedia of lib & info sci, v.57, 569
Encyclopedia of lib & info sci, v.59, 570
Internet & lib & info servs, 582

LIFE SCIENCES
McGraw-Hill dict of biosci, 1440

LILLIES
Trilliums, 1448

LINGUISTICS
Student's dict of lang & linguistics, 987

LISTSERVS (INTERNET)
CyberHound's gd to Internet discussion groups, 1584
Mecklermedia's official Internet World Internet yellow pages, 1996 ed, 1587

LITERARY AGENTS
Guide to literary agents, 1997, 866

LITERARY PRIZES
Avisson bk of contests and prize competitions for poets, 864
Booktalking the award winners 3, 1081
Booktalking the award winners: children's retrospective volume, 1082
Phoenix award of the children's lit assn 1990-94, 1092

LITERATURE
Benét's reader's ency, 4th ed, 843
Cyclopedia of world authors, 3d ed, 1059
Lives & works in the arts from the renaissance to the 20th century, 847
Proverbs in world lit, 1254
Reader's catalog, 2d ed, 8
Southeast Asian langs & lits, 986
Twayne's masterwork studies on CD-ROM [CD-ROM], 1074

LITERATURE & HISTORY
Literature & its times, 1072

LITERATURE, MODERN
Contemporary literary criticism, v.90, 1068
Literary almanac, 1071
Modern ency of E Slavic, Baltic, & Eurasian lits, v.10, 1170
Oxford companion to 20th-century lit in English, 1073

LITHUANIA
Historical dict of Lithuania, 478

LITTLE BIGHORN, BATTLE OF THE
Custer & the battle of Little Bighorn, 441

LOCAL HISTORY
Genealogical & local hist bks in print: gen ref & world resources v., 5th ed, 359

LONDON PHILHARMONIC ORCHESTRA
London Philharmonic discography, 1204

LOUISIANA
Louisiana almanac, 1997-98 ed, 100

LOVE STORIES
Romantic hearts: a personal ref for romance readers, 3d ed, 1115

LUXEMBOURG
Luxembourg, rev ed, 135

LUXEMBURG, ROSA
Rosa Luxemburg & Emma Goldman: a bibliog, 637

LYNCHING
Lynching & vigilantism in the US, 547

MADRID (SPAIN)
Madrid, 138

MAGIC
Wizards & sorcerers, 716

MAHLER, GUSTAV
Gustav Mahler's symphonies, 1248

MAIL ORDER BUSINESS
Catalog of catalogs 5, 183

MAINTENANCE
Glossary of reliability & maintenance terms, 1497

MAMMALS
Encyclopedia of mammals, 1469
Larger animals of E Africa, 1470

MAN
Encyclopedia plus of world problems & human potential, 4th ed [CD-ROM], 86
History of humanity, v.3, 507
Lands & peoples, 95

MANAGED CARE
Managed health care dict, 1509

MANAGEMENT. See also BUSINESS
Business pers index, v.38: Aug 1995-July 1996, 167
Management consulting [CD-ROM], 245
Nonprofit manager's resource dir, 244
Ultimate business lib, 148

MANAGEMENT INFORMATION SYSTEMS
Business multimedia explained, 242

MAN—MIGRATIONS
Penguin atlas of diasporas, 807

MANUFACTURES. See also INDUSTRY
Extractives, manufacturing, & servs, 162
International yrbk of industrial stats 1997, 194
Manufactures phone bk USA 1997, 195
Thomas register of American manufacturers, 1997, 87th ed, 196
Thomas register on CD-ROM, 1997 [CD-ROM], 197

MANUSCRIPTS
Articles describing archives & ms collections in the US, 577

MAPS—BIBLIOGRAPHY
Bibliographic gd to maps & atlases 1996, 391

MARIJUANA
Marijuana law, 2d ed, 527

MARINE BIOLOGY
Oceanographic & marine resources: 1960-Jan 1997 [CD-ROM], 1616

MARKETING
American marketplace, 3d ed, 246
American women, 247
Business sales leads, 1997 ed [CD-ROM], 248
Consumer Latin America 1997, 4th ed, 209
Consumer sales leads, 1997 ed [CD-ROM], 249
Generation X: the young adult market, 256
Market share & business rankings worldwide [CD-ROM], 254
Mid-Youth market, 261
World country analyst [CD-ROM], 205

MARKETING RESEARCH
Dictionary of social & market research, 253

MASS MEDIA
Dictionary of communication & media studies, 4th ed, 857
Graduate programs in journalism & mass communications, 309
Media in Africa & Africa in the media, 853
National Hispanic media dir, 1997, 861
Political commentators in the US in the 20th century, 862
Press freedom & dvlpmt, 850
Webster's new world dict of media & communications, rev ed, 858

MASS MEDIA—STUDY & TEACHING
Dictionary of media literacy, 856

MASTER OF BUSINESS ADMINISTRATION DEGREE
Peterson's gd to MBA programs 1998, 160

MATERIALS
Pearson's hndbk desk ed, 1492

MATHEMATICAL STATISTICS
Encyclopedia of statl scis: update v.1, 809

MATHEMATICIANS
Mathematical scis professional dir 1997, 1625

MATHEMATICS
Assistantships & graduate fellowships in the math scis, 1996-97, 1624
McGraw-Hill dict of mathematics, 1626
Statistically speaking: a dict of quotations, 82

MAUGHAM, W. SOMERSET
William Somerset Maugham ency, 1160

MAUSOLEUMS
Going out in style: the architecture of eternity, 973

MAYA LANGUAGE
Itzaj Maya-Spanish-English dict, 1040

MCDONALD'S (RESTAURANT)
McDonald's collectibles, 898

MEDICAL CARE
American health care in transition, 1502
Health care terms, healthy communities ed, 1510
Health stats, 2d ed, 1504

MEDICAL EDUCATION
Graduate medical educ dir 1997-98, 1535

MEDICAL ETHICS
Code of medical ethics: current opinons with annots, 1996-97 ed, 1537

MEDICAL POLICY
Dictionary of medical sociology, 1524
Health care crisis in the US, 1505

MEDICAL SCIENCES
Chronology of medicine & related scis, 1541
Concise dict of biomedicine & molecular biology, 1439
Doody's rating serv 1997, 1501

MEDICAL SCIENTISTS
Medical discoveries, 1530

MEDICARE
Medicare made easy, rev ed, 1539

MEDICINE
Burger's medicinal chemistry & drug discovery, 5th ed, 1565
Continuing medical educ dir 1996-97, 1532
CPT '97: physicians' current procedural terminology, 1525
Dictionary of natural products, 1569
Encyclopedia of medical media & communications, 1529
Health & illness, 1508
Health & medical yrbk 1997, 1515
Health professions educ dir 1997-98, 1511
Medical discoveries, 1530
Medical meanings: a glossary of word origins, 1528
Taber's cyclopedic medical dict, 18th ed, 1531
Who's who in medicine & healthcare 1997-98, 1506
World Bk health & medical annual 1997, 1543

MEDICINE—ABBREVIATIONS
Medical abbrevs, 8th ed, 1526

MEDICINE—DICTIONARIES
Delmar's English/Spanish pocket dict for health professionals, 1527

MEDICINE, POPULAR. See also ALTERNATIVE MEDICINE
Complete family gd to natural home remedies, 1545
Consumer health USA, v.2, 1538
Encyclopedia of healing therapies, 1552
Essential gd to chronic illness, 1558
Merck manual of medical info, home ed, 1540

MEDICINE—VOCATIONAL GUIDANCE
Career opportunities in health care, 1512

MEDITERRANEAN REGION—CIVILIZATION
Encyclopedia of ancient civilizations of the Near East & Mediterranean, 487

MEETINGS
Robert's rules in plain English, 681

MENTAL HEALTH
Insider's gd to mental health resources online, 1514

METEOROLOGY
Complete weather resource, 1611
Glossary of weather & climate with related oceanic & hydrologic terms, 1612

METRIC SYSTEM—CONVERSION TABLES
Scientific unit conversion, 1597

METROPOLITAN AREAS
Comparative gd to American suburbs, 824

MEXICO
Bibliographic gd to Latin American studies 1996, 139
Encyclopedia of Mexico, 141

MEXICO—FOREIGN RELATIONS
U.S.-Mexican treaties, 680

MEXICO—POLITICS & GOVERNMENT
Dictionary of Mexican rulers, 1325-1997, 485

MICROBIOLOGY
Encyclopedia of virology plus [CD-ROM], 1442

MICROCOMPUTERS. *See also* **COMPUTERS**
CyberDictionary, 1575

MICROFORMS
Guide to microforms in print 1997, 1580

MICROSOFT NETWORK
Microsoft Bkshelf Internet dir, 1996-97 ed, 1589

MIDDLE AGES—HISTORY
Medieval & early modern data bank [CD-ROM], 165

MIDDLE AGES—HISTORY—JUVENILE LITERATURE
History of the ancient & medieval world, 501

MIDDLE EAST
Bibliographic gd to Middle Eastern studies 1996, 143

MIDDLE EAST—ANTIQUITIES
Encyclopedia of ancient civilizations of the Near East & Mediterranean, 487
Oxford ency of archaeology in the Near East, 429

MILITARISM
Militarism in Arab society, 609

MILITARY BIOGRAPHY
Political leaders & military figures in the 2d World War, 606

MILITARY DECORATIONS
British Army campaign medals, 630

MILITARY HISTORY
Encyclopedia of 20th century conflict, 613
Modern campaigns, 615
Reader's companion to military hist, 616

MILITARY SUPPLIES
Jane's electro-optic systems 1996-97, 2d ed, 619
Jane's military communications, 1997-98, 618

MILITARY UNIFORMS
Encyclopedia of US Army insignia & uniforms, 624

MILITARY WEAPONS
Jane's air-launched weapons image lib [CD-ROM], 632

MINERALOGY
McGraw-Hill dict of geology & mineralogy, 1614

MINERALS
Handbook of world mineral trade stats 1990-95, 251

MINERALS IN HUMAN NUTRITION
Real vitamin & mineral bk, 1548

MINNESOTA
Minnesota, 412

MINORITIES. *See also* **ETHNIC STUDIES**
Guide to multicultural resources 1997/98, 327
Minority orgs, 5th ed, 330
Race, crime, & the criminal justice system, 548
World dir of minorities, 334

MINORITIES—EDUCATION
Multicultural student's gd to colleges, rev, 302

MINORITIES IN MOTION PICTURES
American Film Inst catalog, within our gates: ethnicity in American feature films, 1911-60, 1288

MINORITIES—PRESS COVERAGE
U.S. news coverage of racial minorites, 852

MINORITY WOMEN IN LITERATURE
Women playwrights of diversity, 1106

MISSING PERSONS
Using public records to find and investigate anyone, 703

MISSIONS
Dictionary of mission, 1350

MOLECULAR BIOLOGY
Oxford dict of biochemistry & molecular biology, 1444

MONEY
International encyclopaedic dict of numismatics, 909
Warman's coins & currency, 2d ed, 915

MONOGRAMS
Old masters, 980

MORMON CHURCH
Comprehensive annot bk of Mormon bibliog, 1397

MOROCCO
Historical dict of Morocco, new ed, 458

MORTALITY—STATISTICS
Life & death in the US, 769

MOSCOW (RUSSIA)
Maximov's companion to who governs Moscow, 688

MOTION PICTURE ACTORS & ACTRESSES.
See also **ACTORS**
Fred Astaire: a bio-bibliog, 1272
Halliwell's filmgoer's companion, 12th ed, 1305
Oscar stars from A-Z, 1279
Ronald Colman: a bio-bibliog, 1273
Stars in blue: movie actors in America's sea servs, 1281
Who's who of Victorian cinema, 1280

MOTION PICTURE—DICTIONARIES
Complete film dict, 1285

MOTION PICTURE INDUSTRY
Biographical hndbk of Hispanics & US film, 1277
Chronicle of the cinema, rev ed, 1282
Key concepts in cinema studies, 1284

MOTION PICTURE MUSIC
British cinema sheet music, 1195

MOTION PICTURE PRODUCERS & DIRECTORS
Marguerite Duras: a bio-bibliog, 1171
Michael Singer's film directors, 1997, 12th ed, 1317
Reel black talk: a sourcebk of 50 American filmmakers, 1278
Who's who of Victorian cinema, 1280

MOTION PICTURE—REVIEWS
Motion picture gd, 1311
Roger Ebert's video companion, 1319

MOTION PICTURES
A&E entertainment almanac, 1997, 1264
A-Z of horror films, 1297
Action! the action movie A-Z, 1293
American Film Inst catalog, within our gates: ethnicity in American feature films, 1911-60, 1288
British co-operative movement film catalogue, 1289
Canadian film & video, 1271
Chronicle of the cinema, rev ed, 1282
Critical hist & filmography of Toho's Godzilla series, 1294
Encyclopedia of fantasy, 1116
Film & video on the Internet, 1287
Filmmakers in The Moving Picture World, 1316
Frame by frame 2: a filmography of the African American image, 1978-94, 1295
From headline hunter to Superman: a journalism filmography, 1298
Key concepts in cinema studies, 1284
Michael Singer's film directors, 1997, 12th ed, 1317
Science fiction, fantasy, & horror film sequels, series, & remakes, 1292
Ultimate movie thesaurus, 1303

MOTION PICTURES—ARCHIVAL RESOURCES
Film researcher's hndbk, 1309

MOTION PICTURES—CHINA
Chinese filmography, 1296

MOTION PICTURES—LATIN AMERICA
Latin American films, 1932-94, 1299

MOTION PICTURES—REVIEWS
Guide to films on the Korean War, 1291
Horror & sci fiction films 4, 1300
VideoHound's sci-fi experience, 1320
VideoHound's vampires on video, 1321

MOTION PICTURE STUDIOS
Poverty Row studios, 1929-40: an illus hist of 53 independent film cos...., 1312

MOUNTAIN PLANTS
New England's mountain flowers, 1450

MOVING PICTURE WORLD
Filmmakers in The Moving Picture World, 1316

MOZART, WOLFGANG AMADEUS
Mozart diary, 1213

MULTICULTURAL EDUCATION
Dictionary of multicultural educ, 267

MULTICULTURALISM
Connecting cultures, 1093
Culturally diverse lib collections for youth, 1099
Ethnic cultures of the world, 331
Guide to multicultural resources 1997/98, 327
Kaleidoscope: a multicultural booklist for grades K-8, 1087
Linguistic cultures of the world, 990
Multicultural dict of proverbs, 1250
Multicultural educ dir, 273
National cultures of the world, 90
Religious cultures of the world, 1368

MULTIMEDIA SYSTEMS
Business multimedia explained, 242
Dictionary of multimedia terms & acronyms, 1572

MURRAY, BILLY
Billy Murray: the phonograph industry's 1st great recording artist, 1198

MUSEUMS
Art diary 97/98, 953
Museum premieres, exhibitions, & special events, 72
Museums of the world, 73

MUSEUM TECHNIQUES
Bibliography for hist, hist curatorship, & museums, 495

MUSHROOMS
Hallucinogenic & poisonous mushroom field gd, 1452

MUSIC
Baker's biogl dict of 20th-century classical musicians, 1197
Bibliographic gd to music 1996, 1187
Billboard 1996 music yrbk, 1205
Classic FM gd to classical music, 1222
Gustav Mahler's symphonies, 1248
Harmony theory, 1193
International index to music pers 1997:2 [CD-ROM], 1208
Lives & works in the arts from the renaissance to the 20th century, 847
North American Indian music, 1191
Virtual musician, 1206

MUSIC—20TH CENTURY
Blackwell gd to recorded contemporary music, 1221

MUSICALS
More opening nights on Broadway: a critical quotebk of the musical theatre 1965-81, 1329

MUSIC—BIBLIOGRAPHY
Basic music lib, 3d ed, 1186
Collected eds histl series & sets & monuments of music, 1190
Music ref & research materials, 5th ed, 1189

MUSIC—CANADA
Canadian music & music educ, 1194
Music in Canada, 1192

MUSIC—CATALOGS
Thematic catalogues in music, 2d ed, 1188

MUSIC—DICTIONARIES
NPR classical music companion, 1202

MUSICIANS
Baker's biogl dict of 20th-century classical musicians, 1197
Musical Americans: a biographical dict 1918-26, 1200
Star gd, 1997-98, 1266

MUSIC LIBRARIES
Basic music lib, 3d ed, 1186

MUSIC—TERMINOLOGY
NPR classical music companion, 1202

MUSLIM WOMEN
Muslim women throughout the world, 830

MYSTERY & DETECTIVE STORIES. *See* DETECTIVE & MYSTERY STORIES

MYTHOLOGY
Gods & heroes of classical antiquity, 1257
New bk of goddesses & heroines, 3d ed, 1258
Theories of myth, 1261
Who's who in classical mythology, 1260

MYTHOLOGY—JUVENILE LITERATURE
Myths & hero tales, 1084

MYTHOLOGY, NORSE
Cassell dict of Norse myth & legend, 1259

NAFTA (NORTH AMERICAN FREE TRADE AGREEMENT)
NAFTA & GATT: environmental & economic issues, 705
NAFTA bibliog, 255

NAMES, GEOGRAPHICAL
Houghton Mifflin dict of geography, 395
Placenames of the world, 401

NAMES, PERSONAL
Celtic baby names, 378
Dictionary of Irish family names, 376
Dictionary of Jewish surnames from the Kingdom of Poland, 375
People's names, 377

NAPOLEON I
Impact of Napoleon, 1800-15, 469

NATIONAL SERVICE
National serv & AmeriCorps, 800

NATIONAL SOCIALISM
Encyclopedia of German resistance to the Nazi movement, 470

NATURAL FOODS
Whole foods companion, 1427

NATURALIZATION RECORDS
Guide to naturalization records of the US, 332

NATURAL RESOURCES
Dictionary of natural resource mgmt, 1632
Resources of the Third World, 120

NATURE
Pockets: nature facts, 1458

NEWBERY MEDAL
Newbery companion, 1091

NEWCASTLE, THOMAS PELHAM-HOLLES, DUKE OF
Duke of Newcastle, 1693-1768, & Henry Pelham, 1694-1754, 687

NEWSGROUPS (INTERNET)
CyberHound's gd to Internet discussion groups, 1584
Mecklermedia's official Internet World Internet yellow pages, 1996 ed, 1587

NEWSLETTERS
Hudson's subscription newsletter dir, 13th ed, 76
Newsletters in print 1998, 10th ed, 880

NEWSPAPERS
Bacon's newspaper dir 1998, 46th ed, 877

NEWSPAPERS—DATABASES
Fulltext sources online, July 1997, 51

NEW YORK (N.Y.)
New York, the city in more than 500 memorable quotations, 101

NEW YORK TIMES
Personal name index to The New York Times Index, v.5, 67
Personal name index to The New York Times Index, v.6, 68

NICHOLS, RED
Red Nichols story, 1236

NIGER
Historical dict of Niger, 3d ed, 454

NOBEL PRIZES
Nobel prize winners 1992-96 suppl, 26

NONPROFIT ORGANIZATIONS
Directory of grants for orgs serving people with disabilities, 10th ed, 773
Directory of operating grants, 3d ed, 786
Guide to fed funding for govts & nonprofits, 19th ed, 792
Literature of the nonprofit sector, v.8, 783
Nonprofit manager's resource dir, 244
Non-profits and educ job finder 1997-2000, 235
NSFRE fund-raising dict, 784

NONVERBAL COMMUNICATION
Dictionary of worldwide gestures, 711

NONVIOLENCE
Nonviolent action, 496
Protest, power, & change, 692

NORTH AMERICA—HISTORY
Great events from hist: N American series, rev ed, 497

NOVELISTS, AMERICAN
American novelists since WWII, 5th series, 1128

NUMISMATICS
International encyclopaedic dict of numismatics, 909
Standard catalog of US tokens 1700-1900, 914

NURSING
Delmar's A-Z NDR-97: nurse's drug ref, 1566
Delmar's therapeutic class drug gd for nurses 1997, 1567

NUTRITION
Dictionary of healthful food terms, 1420
Encyclopedia of nutrition & good health, 1520
Green kitchen hndbk, 1425
Nutrition & diet therapy ref dict, 4th ed, 1422
Prescription for nutritional healing, 1507
Yale gd to children's nutrition, 1555

OCCULTISM. *See also* PARAPSYCHOLOGY
Illustrated ency of divination, 714
Wizards & sorcerers, 716

OCCUPATIONAL TRAINING
National gd to educl credit for training programs, 1997 ed, 315

OCCUPATIONS
America's top jobs for people without college degrees, 3d ed, 227
America's top office, mgmt, sales, & professional jobs, 3d ed, 228
Career perspectives software series [CD-ROM], 223
Encyclopedia of careers & vocational guidance, 10th ed, 215
Enhanced occupational outlook hndbk, 226
Health professions educ dir 1997-98, 1511
JIST's electronic enhanced dict of occupational titles, 2d ed [CD-ROM], 216
JIST's electronic occupational outlook hndbk, 2d ed [CD-ROM], 231
JIST's multimedia occupational outlook hndbk, 2d ed [CD-ROM], 232
Occupational outlook hndbk, 1996-97 ed, 238
VGM's careers ency, 4th ed, 217

OCCUPATIONS—LICENSES
Professional & occupational licensure in the US, 704

OCEANIA
Australasia & S Pacific Islands bibliog, 144

OCEANOGRAPHY
Oceanographic & marine resources: 1960-Jan 1997 [CD-ROM], 1616

OFFICE EQUIPMENT & SUPPLIES
Essential business buyer's gd, 179

ONLINE DATABASES
Fulltext sources online, July 1997, 51
Public records online, 1997 ed, 706

OPERA
Operas in 1 act, 1224
Ticket to the opera, 1223

OPHTHALMOLOGY
Dictionary of eye terminology, 3d ed, 1553

ORAL TRADITION
Storytelling ency, 1256

ORCHESTRA
London Philharmonic discography, 1204

ORCHESTRAL MUSIC
Heritage ency of band music, 1229
History of music for harpsichord or piano & orchestra, 1227
Orchestra on record, 1896-1926, 1225
Orchestral music, 3d ed, 1226

ORDNANCE
Jane's ammunition hndbk 1996-97, 5th ed, 633
Naval Institute gd to world naval weapons systems 1997-98, 634

ORGANIZATIONAL CHANGE
Research on professional consultation & consultation for organizational change, 709

ORGANIZATIONS
Buttress's world gd to abbrevs of orgs, 11th ed, 1

ORNAMENTAL TREES
Dirr's hardy trees & shrubs, 1456

OUTDOOR RECREATION
Americans at play, 726

OUTLINE MAPS
Outline maps on file, 398

PACIFIC AREA
Asia-Pacific in figures, 10th ed, 811
Statistical yrbk for Asia & the Pacific 1996, 815

PACIFIC NORTHWEST
Pacific NW, 415

PACKAGING
Wiley ency of packaging tech, 2d ed, 1493

PAINTERS
Dictionary of portrait painters in Britain up to 1920, 982
Hans Holbein the younger: a gd to research, 943

PAINTING
Gallery of her own: an annot bibliog of women in Victorian painting, 981

PALESTINE
Historical dict of Palestine, 488

PALLADIUM
Platinum & palladium buyer's gd, 913

PAN-AMERICANISM
Encyclopedia of the inter-American system, 695

PARAPSYCHOLOGY. See also OCCULTISM
Bibliographic gd to psychology 1996, 707

PARENTING
Grandparents, 779
Parenting A to Z, 2d ed, 803

PARLIAMENTARY PRACTICES
Robert's rules in plain English, 681

PATENT LAWS & LEGISLATION
Patent law index, 1997, 545

PEDIATRICS
Columbia Univ Dept of Pediatrics children's medical gd, 1554
Parent's gd to medical emergencies, 1522

PELHAM, HENRY
Duke of Newcastle, 1693-1768, & Henry Pelham, 1694-1754, 687

PERENNIALS
Smaller perennials, 1435

PERESTROIKA
Gorbachev bibliog, 1985-91, 482

PERFORMING ARTS
Bibliographic gd to theatre arts 1996, 1322
Performing arts business ency, 1265

PERIODICALS
Bacon's mag dir 1998, 46th ed, 876
Desert Mag subject index, 878
Fulltext sources online, July 1997, 51
Hudson's subscription newsletter dir, 13th ed, 76
Index to black pers 1995, 345
Index to dance pers: 1995, 1270
International index to music pers 1997:2 [CD-ROM], 1208
National Hispanic media dir, 1997, 861
PCI: pers contents index [CD-ROM], 66
Readers' gd abstracts full text mega ed [CD-ROM], 69
Readers' gd for young people [CD-ROM], 77
Readers' gd to per lit 1995, 70
Samir Husni's gd to new consumer mags, 1997 ed, 882

PERSIAN GULF STATES
Historical dict of the Gulf Arab States, 489

PERSONNEL MANAGEMENT
Human resources yrbk 1996/97, 224
Mandated benefits, 236

PERSONNEL RECORDS
Verify those credentials: do you know who you're dealing with?, 63

PETS—NAMES
Complete bk of pet names, 1462

PETS & TRAVEL
Vacationing with your pet, 402

PHARMACOGNOSY
Dictionary of natural products, 1569

PHARMACOLOGY
Burger's medicinal chemistry & drug discovery, 5th ed, 1565

PHENOMENOLOGY
Encyclopedia of phenomenology, 1335

PHILANTHROPY
Fndn dir 1997, 19th ed, 787
Fndn dir suppl, 788
Fndn giving, 1997 ed, 794
Guide to US fndns, their trustees, officers, & donors, 1997 ed, 789
National gd to funding for info tech, 583
Practical gd to planned giving 1998, 791

PHILOLOGY
Key gd to electronic resources: lang & lit, 985

PHILOSOPHERS
Collaborative bibliog of women in philosophy, 1332
Directory of American philosophers 1996-97, 18th ed, 1340
Encyclopedia of classical philosophy, 1334
Encyclopedia of phenomenology, 1335
Hannah Arendt 2: a bibliog, 636
International dir of philosophy & philosophers 1997-98, 10th ed, 1342

PHILOSOPHY
Concise dict of Indian philosophy, rev ed, 1336
Dictionary of philosophy & religion, new ed, 1337
Encyclopedia of classical philosophy, 1334
Guidebook for publishing philosophy, 1997 ed, 867
International dir of philosophy & philosophers 1997-98, 10th ed, 1342
Philosophy: a gd to the ref lit, 2d ed, 1330

PHOENIX AWARD
Phoenix award of the children's lit assn 1990-94, 1092

PHOTOGRAPHERS
Photographers on disc [CD-ROM], 937

PHOTOGRAPHY
History of photography, v.3, 938
Photographer's market, 1998, 936

PHYSICAL ANTHROPOLOGY
History of physical anthropology, 320

PHYSICAL FITNESS
Fodor's healthy escapes, 5th ed, 405

PHYSICALLY HANDICAPPED
Man's gd to coping with disability, 774
Woman's gd to coping with disability, 2d ed, 776

PHYSICIANS
Directory of physicians in the US, 35th ed, 1533
Directory of physicians in the US, 35th ed [CD-ROM], 1534
Physician characteristics and distribution in the US, 1536

PHYSICS
Handbook of physical quantities, 1620
McGraw-Hill dict of physics, 2d ed, 1621

PICTURE BOOKS
Picture this: picture bks for young adults, 1097

PICTURE BOOKS FOR CHILDREN
Picture bks to enhance the curriculum, 284
Worth a 1,000 words: an annot gd to picture bks for older readers, 1090

PITCHERS (BASEBALL)
Charmed circle: 20-game-winning pitchers in baseball's 20th century, 732

PLANETS
Cambridge gd to stars & planets, 2d ed, 1605
NASA atlas of the solar system, 1609

PLANTS, ORNAMENTAL
American Horticultural Society A-Z ency of garden plants, 1432

PLATINUM
Platinum & palladium buyer's gd, 913

POE, EDGAR ALLAN
Poe ency, 1137

POETRY
Avisson bk of contests and prize competitions for poets, 864
Directory of poetry publishers, 599
Exploring poetry [CD-ROM], 1184
Index of American per verse: 1994, 1185
Index of American per verse 1995, 1142

POETS
George Gordon, Lord Byron, 1155
Index of American per verse: 1994, 1185
Poet's market, 1998, 868
Viacheslav Ivanov: a ref gd, 1181
William Butler Yeats ency, 1166

POETS, AMERICAN
American poets since WW II, 5th series, 1140
American poets since WW II, 4th series, 1141

POISONS
Poison! how to handle the hazardous substances in your home, 1563
TSCA hndbk, 3d ed, 561

POLAND
Dictionary of Jewish surnames from the Kingdom of Poland, 375
Wartime Poland, 1939-45, 480

POLICE
Jane's police & security equipment 1996-97, 9th ed, 555

POLISH AMERICANS
Gridiron greats: a century of Polish Americans in college football, 745

POLITICAL GEOGRAPHY
Political geography, 393

POLITICAL ORATORY
African-American orators, 337

POLITICAL SCIENCE
Bibliographic gd to law 1996, 509
Contemporary democracy, 638
Hannah Arendt 2: a bibliog, 636
Political data hndbk: OECD countries, 2d ed, 684
Reinventing govt, 644
Theories of pol processes, 635

POLITICAL SCIENCE—QUOTATIONS
Oxford dict of pol quotations, 641

POLITICIANS
Maximov's companion to who governs Moscow, 688
New members of Congress almanac: 105th US Congress, 654
State staff dir, summer 1997, 667
Who's who in Congress 1997, 656
Who's who in European pols, 3d ed, 685
Who's who in Latin America, 4th ed, 35
World almanac of US pols, 1997-99 ed, 643

POLITICIANS—QUOTATIONS
Oxford dict of pol quotations, 641

POPULAR MUSIC
A&E entertainment almanac, 1997, 1264
All music gd, 3d ed, 1228

POPULAR MUSIC—WRITING AND PUBLISHING
Song Writers Market, 1998, 1207

POPULATION
Handbook of population & housing censuses, pt.4, 805
POPLINE: through Dec 1996 [CD-ROM], 778
Twentieth-century hist of US population, 808

PORCELAIN
Pottery and porcelain ceramics price gd, 927

PORTUGAL
Portugal with Madeira & the Azores, 422

PORTUGUESE LANGUAGE—DICTIONARIES—ENGLISH
HarperCollins Portuguese dict, college ed, 1041
Oxford pa Portuguese dict, 1042

POSTAGE STAMPS
Brookman US, UN, & Canada stamps & postal collectibles, 928

POSTAL SERVICE
Zip code finder, 59

POTTERY
Charlton standard catalogue of chintz, 2d ed, 924
Charlton standard catalogue of Royal Doulton beswick figurines, 5th ed, 925
Charlton standard catalogue of Royal Doulton beswick jugs, 4th ed, 926
Pottery and porcelain ceramics price gd, 927

POTTERY CRAFT
Potter's dict of materials & techniques, 4th ed, 932

POWER RESOURCES
Energy balances for countries in transition 1993, 1994-2010, & energy prospects in CIS countries, 1627

PRAGUE (CZECH REPUBLIC)
Prague, 122

PRECIOUS STONES
Gemstones of the world, rev ed, 1615

PREDICTIONS
Predicting the future, 88

PREGNANCY
Pregnancy and birth sourcebk, 1561

PREJUDICES
Color of words: an encyclopaedic dict of ethnic bias in the US, 328

PRESIDENTIAL MEDAL OF FREEDOM
Presidential Medal of Freedom, 30

PRESIDENTS—MEXICO
Dictionary of Mexican rulers, 1325-1997, 485

PRESIDENTS' SPOUSES—UNITED STATES
Presidents, first ladies, & vice presidents, 653

PRESIDENTS—UNITED STATES
American presidency [CD-ROM], 668
Guide to the presidency, 2d ed, 674
Presidents, 661
Presidents, first ladies, & vice presidents, 653
Presidents of the US—their written measure, 648
Scholastic ency of the presidents & their times, updated ed, 443

PRESIDENTS—UNITED STATES—JUVENILE LITERATURE
Complete hist of our presidents, 658

PRESSURE GROUPS
Directory of Congressional voting scores & interest group ratings, 2d ed, 678

PRIMARIES—UNITED STATES
US primary elections 1995-96, 673

PRIMATES
International dir of primatology, 3d ed, 1471
Pictorial gd to the living primates, 1472

PRINTERS
British literary bk trade, 1475-1700, 594

PRIVACY, RIGHT OF
Compilation of state & fed privacy laws, 1997 ed, 543

PROCESSING (LIBRARIES)
Directory of lib technical servs home pages, 591

PRO-CHOICE MOVEMENT
Pro-choice/pro-life issues in the 1990s, 756

PROFESSIONAL EMPLOYEES—CERTIFICATION
Guide to natl professional certification programs, 313

PROFESSIONAL ETHICS
Professional codes of conduct in the UK, 2d ed, 1341

PROFESSIONAL SPORTS
Professional sports stats, 722

PROFESSIONS—CERTIFICATION
Certification & accreditation programs dir, 270

PROFESSIONS—LICENSES
Professional & occupational licensure in the US, 704

PRO-LIFE MOVEMENT
Anti-abortion movement, 755
Pro-choice/pro-life issues in the 1990s, 756

PROVERBS
Dictionary of 1000 Jewish proverbs, 1251
Dictionary of 1000 Polish proverbs, 1252
Multicultural dict of proverbs, 1250
Proverb wit & wisdom, 1249
Proverbial Charles Dickens, 1157
Proverbs in world lit, 1254

PSYCHIATRY
Insider's gd to mental health resources online, 1514
Psychiatric dict, 7th ed, 1556

PSYCHOLOGISTS
Biographical dict of psychology, 710

PSYCHOLOGY
Bibliographic gd to psychology 1996, 707
ClinPSYC: 1980-Dec 1996 [CD-ROM], 712

PUBLIC HEALTH
International hndbk of public health, 1517

PUBLIC HEALTH—DIRECTORIES
Health stats, 2d ed, 1504

PUBLIC LAND RECORDS
Land & property research in the US, 365

PUBLIC OPINION
Gallup Poll, 87

PUBLIC RECORDS
Find public records fast, 665
Guide to background investigations, 7th ed, 640
Librarian's gd to public records, rev ed, 666
MVR bk motor servs gd, 1997 ed, 536
MVR decoder digest, 1997 ed, 537
Public records online, 1997 ed, 706
Sourcebook of county court records, 3d ed, 524
Sourcebook of local court & county record retrievers, 3d ed, 525
Using public records to find and investigate anyone, 703
Verify those credentials: do you know who you're dealing with?, 63

PUBLIC WELFARE
Welfare reform, 799

PUBLISHERS & PUBLISHING. *See also* **BOOKSELLERS & BOOKSELLING**
Association of American Univ Prs dir 1996-97, 598
Books from Chapel Hill 1922-97, 595
British literary bk trade, 1475-1700, 594
Directory of poetry publishers, 599
Directory of publishing 1997, 22d ed, 600
Directory of small pr/mag editors & publishers 1997-98, 28th ed, 601
Mitchell Kennerly imprint: a descriptive bibliog, 592
Publishers dir, 1998, 18th ed, 603
Publishers' intl ISBN dir 1997/98, 604
Walter Scott Publishing Co., 593

PURCHASING
Essential business buyer's gd, 179

PUZZLES
Antique trader's gd to games & puzzles, 891

QUALITY CONTROL
International standards desk ref, 206
Quality, TQC, TQM: a meta lit study, 243

QUOTATIONS
Contemporary quotations in black, 78
Criminal quotes, 79
Dictionary of Scottish quotations, 136
Famous lines: a Columbia dict of familiar quotations, 80
Leadership: quotations from the world's greatest motivators, 81
New York, the city in more than 500 memorable quotations, 101
Oxford dict of quotations, 4th ed, 83
Simpson's contemporary quotations, rev ed, 84
Statistically speaking: a dict of quotations, 82
War & conflict quotations, 85

RACE RELATIONS
Race, crime, & the criminal justice system, 548

RACISM
Color of words: an encyclopaedic dict of ethnic bias in the US, 328

RADIO BROADCASTING
Bacon's radio dir 1998, 12th ed, 885
Big broadcast, 1920-50, 2d ed, 887
National Hispanic media dir, 1997, 861

RAILROADS
32nd annual steam passenger serv dir, 1649

RAIN FORESTS
Rainforest orgs, 1639

RAP MUSICIANS
Rap whoz who, 1237

RARE BOOKS
Directory of rare bk & special collections in the UK & the Republic of Ireland, 2d ed, 588

RATIO ANALYSIS
Almanac of business & industrial financial ratios 1996, 27th ed, 177

READING INTERESTS
Teen genreflecting, 1096
What else should I read? guiding kids to good bks, v.2, 1076

REAL ESTATE BUSINESS
Dictionary of real estate, 263

REAL PROPERTY
Dictionary of real estate, 263

REASONING
Thinking from A to Z, 1339

RECONSTRUCTION
Freedom's lawmakers: a dir of black officeholders during Reconstruction, rev ed, 344

REFERENCE BOOKS
ARBA gd to subject encys & dicts, 2d ed, 5
Dictionary of dicts & encys, 2d ed, 45
Global data locator, 812
Guide to S African ref bks, 6th ed, 19
Journalism, 2d ed, 851
Music ref & research materials, 5th ed, 1189
Recent ref bks in religion, 1346
Recommended ref bks for small & medium-sized libs & media centers 1997, 9
Sociology: a gd to ref and info sources, 782
Subject gd to US govt ref sources, 2d ed, 60

REFERENCE WORKS
Guide to ref works for the study of the Spanish lang and lit and Spanish American lit, 1183

REFUGEES
Refugees in America in the 1990s, 801

REINCARNATION
Reincarnation: a selected annot bibliog, 715

RELIABILITY (ENGINEERING)
Glossary of reliability & maintenance terms, 1497

RELIGION
Anthropology of religion, 1359
Dictionary of philosophy & religion, new ed, 1337
Encyclopedia of religion [CD-ROM], 1353
God on the Internet, 1365
Oxford dict of the Christian Church, 3d ed, 1389
Oxford dict of the Jewish religion, 1396
Oxford dict of world religions, 1357

RELIGION—BIBLIOGRAPHY
Recent ref bks in religion, 1346

RELIGION & LAW
Law, religion, theology, 510

RELIGIONS
America's religions, 1364
Illustrated ency of world religions, 1356
On common ground: world religions in America [CD-ROM], 1367
Religions of the world, 1348
Religious cultures of the world, 1368
Sects, 'cults,' & alternative religions, 1360
World religions, 1361

RELIGIOUS BROADCASTING
Prime-time religion, 1366

RELIGIOUS ETIQUETTE
How to be a perfect stranger, 1362
How to be a perfect stranger, v.2, 1363

REPTILES
Amphibians & reptiles of Trinidad & Tobago, 1474
Reptile & amphibian problem solver, 1473

REPUBLICAN PARTY
Encyclopedia of the Republican Party & the ency of the Democratic Party, 659

RESEARCH
Find it fast, 4th ed, 575

RESTAURANTS
America's best hotels & restaurants, 409

REVOLUTIONARIES
Who's who in democracy, 639

RICE, ELMER
Elmer Rice: a research & production sourcebk, 1326

RIGHT OF PROPERTY
Free market environmental bibliog 1995-96, 4th ed, 1630

ROBOTICS
World industrial robots 1997, 1581

ROCK MUSIC
All music gd, 3d ed, 1228

All music gd to rock, 2d ed, 1238
Billboard's American rock 'n' roll in review, 1239
It's only rock 'n' roll: the ultimate gd to the Rolling Stones, 1241
Rock & roll reader's gd, 1242
Rock song index, 1243

ROLLING STONES
It's only rock 'n' roll: the ultimate gd to the Rolling Stones, 1241

ROYAL DOULTON CHARACTER JUGS
Charlton standard catalogue of Royal Doulton beswick jugs, 4th ed, 926

ROYAL DOULTON FIGURINES
Charlton standard catalogue of Royal Doulton beswick figurines, 5th ed, 925

RUNNING
National road race ency, 751

RURAL CONDITIONS
Encyclopedia of rural America, 98

RUSSELL, LILLIAN
Lillian Russell: a bio-bibliog, 1275

RUSSIA. *See also* **FORMER SOVIET REPUBLICS; SOVIET UNION**
Russia & Eurasia facts & figures annual, v.21, 128
Russia & Eurasia facts & figures annual, v.22, 129
Warships of the USSR & Russia, 1945-95, 629

RUSSIAN LANGUAGE—DICTIONARIES—ENGLISH
Barron's Russian dict, 1044
NTC's new college Russian & English dict, 1045
Oxford starter Russian dict, 1046
Russian-English comprehensive dict, 1047
Russian idioms, 1043

SACRED SPACE
Encyclopedia of sacred places, 1349

SACRED VOCAL MUSIC
Handbook to Bach's sacred cantata texts, 1247

SAFETY EDUCATION
Preventive care sourcebk 1997-98, 1519

SAFETY REGULATIONS
Directory of safety standards, lit, & servs, 1495

SAGE
Book of salvias, 1434

SAILORS
Stars in blue: movie actors in America's sea servs, 1281

SAINT HELENA
St. Helena, Ascension, & Tristan da Cunha, 146

SALARY SURVEYS. *See* **WAGE SURVEYS**

SALVIA
Book of salvias, 1434

SAMOAN ISLANDS
Samoa (American Samoa, Western Samoa, Samoans abroad), 145

SANITARY ENGINEERING
Dictionary of environmental sci & tech, 2d ed, 1636

SANSKRIT LANGUAGE
Concise dict of Indian philosophy, rev ed, 1336

SCHOLARSHIPS
A's & B's of academic scholarships 1997/98, 19th ed, 285
Assistantships & graduate fellowships in the math scis, 1996-97, 1624
Complete scholarship bk, 287
Financial aid bk, 2d ed, 298
Government financial aid bk, 2d ed, 299
Grants register 1998, 16th ed, 300
High school senior's gd to merit & other no-need funding 1996-98, 307
Money for graduate students in the scis 1996-98, 1411
Money for graduate students in the social scis 1996-98, 91
Peterson's scholarship almanac, 304
Peterson's scholarships for study in the USA & Canada 1998, 294

SCHOOL FIELD TRIPS
Virtual field trips, 281

SCHOOL LIBRARIES. *See also* **INSTRUCTIONAL MATERIALS CENTERS**
Children's catalog, 17th ed, 586
Senior high school lib catalog, 15th ed, 587

SCHOOL VIOLENCE
School violence, 278

SCIENCE
Applied sci & tech index 1996, 1418
Bibliographic gd to tech 1996, 1398
DISCovering sci [CD-ROM], 1413
Eyewitness ency of sci [CD-ROM], 1403
Handy sci answer bk, 2d ed, 1414
Illustrated sci ency, 1405
Macmillan ency of sci, rev ed, 1406
McGraw-Hill ency of sci & tech, 8th ed, 1407
Questions & answers bk of sci facts, 1404
Science & tech firsts, 1402
Science on file [CD-ROM], 1415
Science yr 1997, 1416
Science yr 1998, 1417
World Bk ency of sci, 1409
World Bk's young scientist, 1410

SCIENCE FICTION
Encyclopedia of TV sci fiction, 1283

Science fiction & fantasy reference index 1992-95, 1117
VideoHound's sci-fi experience, 1320

SCIENCE FICTION FILMS
Critical hist & filmography of Toho's Godzilla series, 1294
Horror & sci fiction films 4, 1300
Science fiction, fantasy, & horror film sequels, series, & remakes, 1292
Sci-Fi on tape, 1318

SCIENCE FICTION—ILLUSTRATIONS
Barlowe's gd to fantasy, 979

SCIENCE FICTION TELEVISION PROGRAMS
Science fiction TV series, 1286

SCIENCE—HANDBOOKS
Addison-Wesley sci hndbk, 1412

SCIENTISTS
Cambridge dict of scientists, 1399
Grolier lib of sci biogs, 1400
Mathematical scis professional dir 1997, 1625
Notable women in the physical scis, 1598
Scientists, 1401

SCOTLAND
Dictionary of Scottish quotations, 136

SCULPTURE
Looking at European sculpture, 983

SECRET SERVICE—GREAT BRITAIN
British secret servs, 686

SECRET SERVICE—ISRAEL
Israeli secret servs, 689

SECRET SOCIETIES
International ency of secret societies & fraternal orders, 763

SECTS
New religious movements in Western Europe, 1343
Sects, 'cults,' & alternative religions, 1360

SECURITIES
Directory of listed derivative contracts 1996/97, 171
International gd to securities market indices, 175
Topline ency of histl charts, Mar 1997 ed, 176
Wall Street words, 170

SELF-HELP GROUPS
National dir of bereavement support grps & servs, 1996, 768

SELF-PUBLISHING
Business and legal forms for authors and self-publishers, 605

SERVICE INDUSTRIES
Services—the export of the 21st century: a gdbk of US serv exporters, 262

SEX
Black bk, 4th ed, 796
International ency of sexuality, 797
Sexuality & the elderly, 798

SHAKESPEARE, WILLIAM
Dictionary of who, what, & where in Shakespeare, 1161
Exploring Shakespeare [CD-ROM], 1162
Shakespeare for students, bk 2, 1163
Shakespeare's characters for students, 1164
World Shakespeare bibliog on CD-ROM 1990-93 [CD-ROM], 1165

SHERIDAN, ANN
Ann Sheridan: a bio-bibliog, 1274

SHIPPING
Review of maritime transport 1997, 260

SHIPS
Naval Institute gd to the ships & aircraft of the US Fleet, 16th ed, 628
Ships of the world, 1651

SHORT STORIES
Index to translated short fiction by Latin American women in English lang anthologies, 1179
Reader's gd to the short stories of Eudora Welty, 1138
Reader's gd to the short stories of Stephen Crane, 1133
Short fiction: a criticial companion, 1119
Short stories for students, v.1, 1120
Short stories for students, v.2, 1121
Short story index 1995, 1122
Short story writers, 1123
Twentieth-century short story explication: new series, v.3: 1993-94, 1118

SHRUBS
Dirr's hardy trees & shrubs, 1456

SINGERS
Billy Murray: the phonograph industry's 1st great recording artist, 1198
Lillian Russell: a bio-bibliog, 1275
Singers of the century, 1201

SITSKY, LARRY
Larry Sitsky: a bio-bibliog, 1214

SLAVERY
Comprehensive name index for The American Slave, 341
Dictionary of Afro-American slavery, updated ed, 438

SLAVIC COUNTRIES
Bibliographic gd to Slavic, Baltic, & Eurasian studies 1996, 126

SMALL BUSINESS
Small business sourcebk, 10th ed, 166

SMITHSONIAN INSTITUTION
150 yrs of America's Smithsonian [CD-ROM], 74

SNAKES
Coral snakes of the Americas, 1475

SOAP OPERAS
Prime time network serials, 1310

SOCIAL INDICATORS
Illustrated bk of world rankings, rev ed, 813

SOCIALISM
Rosa Luxemburg & Emma Goldman: a bibliog, 637

SOCIAL MEDICINE
Dictionary of medical sociology, 1524

SOCIAL MOVEMENTS
Social movement theory & research, 690

SOCIAL PROBLEMS
Encyclopedia plus of world problems & human potential, 4th ed [CD-ROM], 86

SOCIAL RESPONSIBILITY OF BUSINESS
Shopping with a conscience, 178

SOCIAL SCIENCES
Comprehensive dissertation index, 1996 supplement, 844
Education index, July 1995 to June 1996, 279
PAIS select [CD-ROM], 89
Social scis abstracts full text [CD-ROM], 92
Social scis index, April 1995 to Mar 1996, 93
Sociofile: 1974-Dec 1996 [CD-ROM], 94
Sociology: a gd to ref and info sources, 782

SOCIAL SCIENCES—RESEARCH
Dictionary of social & market research, 253

SOCIAL SCIENCES—STATISTICS
National cultures of the world, 90

SOCIETIES
Women & aging, 763

SOCIOLOGY
Sociology: a gd to ref and info sources, 782

SOCIOLOGY, RURAL
Encyclopedia of rural America, 98

SOIL MECHANICS
Compendium of soil clean-up technologies and soil remediation companies, 1496

SOLAR SYSTEM
NASA atlas of the solar system, 1609

SOLDIERS
Roster of Union soldiers 1861-65: US colored troops, 452

SONGS WITH GUITAR
Music for voice & classical guitar, 1945-96, 1219

SOUND
Encyclopedia of acoustics, 1619

SOUND RECORDINGS
Blackwell gd to recorded contemporary music, 1221
Golden age of Walt Disney records 1933-88, 1209

SOUTH AFRICA
Lesotho, rev ed, 107

SOUTH AFRICA—BIBLIOGRAPHY
Guide to S African ref bks, 6th ed, 19

SOUTH AFRICA—RELIGION
African traditional religion in S Africa, 1344
Christianity in S Africa, 1382
Islam, Hinduism, & Judaism in S Africa, 1345

SOUTHEAST ASIAN LANGUAGES
Southeast Asian langs & lits, 986

SOUTHEAST ASIAN LITERATURES
Southeast Asian langs & lits, 986

SOVIET UNION. *See also* **FORMER SOVIET REPUBLICS; RUSSIA**
Critical companion to the Russian revolution 1914-21, 481
Gorbachev bibliog, 1985-91, 482
USSR population census, 1989 [CD-ROM], 130
Warships of the USSR & Russia, 1945-95, 629

SPAIN—JUVENILE LITERATURE
Best of the Latino heritage, 358

SPANISH AMERICAN LITERATURE
Guide to ref works for the study of the Spanish lang and lit and Spanish American lit, 1183

SPANISH LANGUAGE—DICTIONARIES—ENGLISH
Delmar's English/Spanish pocket dict for health professionals, 1527
NTC's dict of Latin American Spanish, 1049
NTC's dict of Spanish cognates thematically organized, 1048
Oxford pa Spanish dict & grammar, 1050
Oxford starter Spanish dict, 1051
Pockets: Spanish dict, 1052
Routledge Spanish technical dict, 1408
Wiley's English-Spanish, Spanish-English business dict, 157
Wiley's English-Spanish, Spanish-English legal dict, 2d ed, 519

SPECIAL LIBRARIES
Directory of special libs & info centers, v.1, 21st ed, 589
Directory of special libs & info centers, v.2, 21st ed, 590

SPEECHES
Representative American speeches 1995-96, 1131

SPIES
Spies, 701

SPORTS
Encyclopedia of sports sci, 720
Encyclopedia of world sport, 721
Ultimate bk of sports lists 1998, 727

SPORTS CARDS
Standard catalog of football cards, 900

SPORTS & STATE
National sports policies, 725

SPORTSWRITERS
Twentieth-century American sportswriters, 883

STARS
Cambridge gd to stars & planets, 2d ed, 1605
Photographic atlas of the stars, 1604

STATESMEN
Who's who in democracy, 639

STATISTICS
City crime rankings, 3d ed, 552
Encyclopedia of statl scis: update v.1, 809
Geographic database for US economy, tech, & growth [CD-ROM], 818
Global data locator, 812
Handbook of US labor stats, 230
Illustrated bk of world rankings, rev ed, 813
Key indicators of county growth 1970-2025, 1996 ed, 806
Matter of fact: statements containing stats on current social, economics, & pol issues, v.24, 814
Statistical yrbk for Asia & the Pacific 1996, 815
Statistical yrbk 1994, 41st ed, 816
Statistically speaking: a dict of quotations, 82

STATLER BROTHERS
Statler Brothers discography, 1232

STOCKHOLM (SWEDEN)
Historical dict of Stockholm, 483

STOCKS
Topline ency of histl charts, Mar 1997 ed, 176
Walker's manual of unlisted stocks, 172

STORES, RETAIL
Plunkett's retail industry almanac, 259

STORYTELLING
Storytelling ency, 1256

STUDENT AID
Big bk of opportunities for women, 269
Complete scholarship bk, 287
Financial aid financer, 306
High school senior's gd to merit & other no-need funding 1996-98, 307
Money for graduate students in the scis 1996-98, 1411
Money for graduate students in the social scis 1996-98, 91
Peterson's college money hndbk 1998, 303

SUBCULTURE
ABC-CLIO companion to the 1960s counterculture in America, 437

SUBJECT HEADINGS
Sears list of subject headings, 16th ed, 580

SUBURBS
Comparative gd to American suburbs, 824

SUICIDE
Encyclopedia of famous suicides, 767

SULLIVAN, ARTHUR, SIR
Sir Arthur Sullivan: a resource bk, 1212

SURVEYORS
Dictionary of land surveyors and local map-makers of Gt Brit and Ireland, 1530-1850, 394

SUSTAINABLE DEVELOPMENT
Dictionary of environment & sustainable dvlpmt, 1633

SWEDISH LANGUAGE—DICTIONARIES—ENGLISH
NTC's compact Swedish & English dict, 1053

SYMBOLISM
Encyclopedia of archetypal symbolism, v.1, 1351
Encyclopedia of archetypal symbolism, v.2: the body, 1352

SYMPHONIES
Gustav Mahler's symphonies, 1248

SYMPTOMATOLOGY
Columbia Univ Dept of Pediatrics children's medical gd, 1554

SYNTHETIC TRAINING DEVICES
Jane's simulation & training systems 1996-97, 9th ed, 1573

TAILORING
Cutting for all! the satorial arts, related crafts, & the commercial paper pattern, 934

TANKS (MILITARY)
Tanks, 631

TANZANIA
Historical dict of Tanzania, 2d ed, 457

TAPESTRY
French tapestries & textiles in the J. Paul Getty Museum, 946

TARIFF
NAFTA bibliog, 255

TASMANIA
Tasmania, 118

TAXATION
State & local taxation answer bk, 264

TEACHING—AIDS & DEVICES
Film & video finder, 5th ed, 310

TECHNOLOGY
Applied sci & tech index 1996, 1418
Bibliographic gd to tech 1996, 1398
Dictionary of multimedia terms & acronyms, 1572
Handy sci answer bk, 2d ed, 1414
Macmillan ency of sci, rev ed, 1406
McGraw-Hill ency of sci & tech, 8th ed, 1407
Questions & answers bk of sci facts, 1404
Routledge Spanish technical dict, 1408
Science & tech firsts, 1402
Science yr 1997, 1416
Science yr 1998, 1417
World Bk's young scientist, 1410

TEENAGERS
Adolescence: the survival gd for parents & teenagers, 802

TELECOMMUNICATIONS
Informatics hndbk, 1593

TELECOMMUTING
Telecommuters, the workforce of the 21st century, 212

TELEPHONE DIRECTORIES
Business: name & business type index [CD-ROM], 158
Business sales leads, 1997 ed [CD-ROM], 248
Consumer sales leads, 1997 ed [CD-ROM], 249
Government phone bk USA 1997, 5th ed, 52
Instant natl locator gd, 3d ed, 53
PhoneDisc powerfinder [CD-ROM], 54
Toll-Free phone bk USA 1997, 55
U.S. homes [CD-ROM], 56
U.S. homes & business [CD-ROM], 57

TELEVISION
Bacon's TV/cable dir 1998, 12th ed, 886
Collector's gd to TV memorabilia, 1960s & 1970s, 922
Early TV, 889
Encyclopedia of TV, 888
National Hispanic media dir, 1997, 861

TELEVISION ACTORS & ACTRESSES
Television western players of the 50s, 1276

TELEVISION MUSICALS
Television musicals, 1301

TELEVISION PERSONALITIES
Star gd, 1997-98, 1266

TELEVISION PROGRAMS
Booking Hawaii Five-O: an episode gd & critical hist of the 1968-80 TV detective show, 1313
Encyclopedia of TV sci fiction, 1283
Experimental TV, test films, pilots, & trial series, 1925-95, 1314
Prime time network serials, 1310
Science fiction TV series, 1286
Television westerns episode gd, 1308
Toasting Cheers: an episode gd to the 1982-93 comedy series...., 1302
Variety & Daily Variety TV reviews, v.18: 1993-94, 1315

TELEVISION PROGRAMS—JAPAN
Complete anime gd, 1307

TELEVISION SPECIALS
Special edition: a gd to network TV documentary series & special news reports, 1980-89, 1304

TENNIS
Bud Collins' tennis ency [3d ed], 750

TERRORISM
Encyclopedia of world terrorism, 551
Terrorism, 1992-95, 556
Terrorism in the US, 557

TEXTBOOKS
El-Hi textbooks and serials in print 1997, 283

TEXTILES
French tapestries & textiles in the J. Paul Getty Museum, 946
Garment & textile dict, 933

THEATER
Bibliographic gd to theatre arts 1996, 1322
Directory of theatre training programs 1997-99, 6th ed, 1325
German theatre, 1323
More opening nights on Broadway: a critical quotebk of the musical theatre 1965-81, 1329
Theatregoer's almanac, 1327

THEATER—JAPAN
New Kabuki ency, 1324

THEOLOGY
Dictionary of mission, 1350
New intl dict of O.T. theology & exegesis, 1374
Oxford dict of world religions, 1357
Westminster dict of theological terms, 1358

THESAURI
American Heritage children's thesaurus, 1016
Merriam-Webster's collegiate dict, deluxe audio ed, 998
Oxford desk dict & thesaurus, American ed, 993

TOKENS
Standard catalog of US tokens 1700-1900, 914

TOKYO (JAPAN)
Historical dict of Tokyo, 461

TOLL-FREE TELEPHONE CALLS
Toll-Free phone bk USA 1997, 55

TOTAL QUALITY MANAGEMENT
Quality mgmt sourcebook, 241
Quality, TQC, TQM: a meta lit study, 243

TOURIST TRADE
Guide to college programs in hospitality & tourism, 5th ed, 314

TOXIC TORTS
TSCA hndbk, 3d ed, 561

TOYS
Matchbox toys 1947-96, 2d ed, 929

TRADE. See also **BUSINESS; MARKETING**
Economic survey of Latin America & the Caribbean 1995-96, 210

TRADE & PROFESSIONAL ASSOCIATIONS
Professional codes of conduct in the UK, 2d ed, 1341

TRADE—UNIONS
Directory of US labor orgs, 1997 ed, 219

TRADING CARDS
Standard catalog of football cards, 900

TRANSLATING & INTERPRETING
Translator's hndbk 1997, 991

TRANSPORTATION
Annual bulletin of transport stats for Europe & N America 1996, v.46, 1644

TRAVEL
Americans at play, 726
America's best bed & breakfasts, 2d ed, 408
California, 413
Everything Civil War, 447
Fodor's ballpark vacations, 731
Fodor's exploring Canada, 421
Fodor's exploring the Greek Islands, 424
Fodor's healthy escapes, 5th ed, 405
Great escapes: the spring breaker's gd to beaches & beyond, 417
Greece: Athens & the mainland, 425
Greek Islands, 426
Milepost: trip planner for Ala. & Western Canada, 49th ed, 406
Travel & vacation phone bk USA, 404
Traveler's sourcebk 1997, 418
Vacationing with your pet, 402

TRAVELERS
Dictionary of British & Irish travellers in Italy, 1701-1800, 476

TREADWELL, SOPHIE
Sophie Treadwell: a research & production sourcebk, 1132

TREATIES
Copyright laws & treaties of the world 1991-95 suppl, 566
International treaties on intellectual property, 2d ed, 567

TRIAL PRACTICE
Civil trial practice deskbk, 528

TRIALS
Great world trials, 532
Women's rights on trial, 563

TRILLIUMS
Trilliums, 1448

TRINIDAD & TOBAGO
Historical dict of Trinidad & Tobago, 484

TRISTAN DA CUNHA ISLANDS
St. Helena, Ascension, & Tristan da Cunha, 146

TUNISIA
Historical dict of Tunisia, 2d ed, 459

UNESCO
Historical dict of the UNESCO, 694

UNIONS. See **TRADE—UNIONS**

UNITED NATIONS
Historical dict of the UNESCO, 694

UNITED STATES—ARMED FORCES
Guide to the evaluation of educl experiences in the armed servs, 1996, v.1: Army, 275
Guide to the evaluation of educl experiences in the armed servs, 1996, v.2: Navy, 276
Guide to the evaluation of educl experiences in the armed servs, 1996, v.3: Air Force, Coast Guard, Dept of Defense, Marine Corps, 277

UNITED STATES. ARMY
U.S. Army patches, 625

UNITED STATES—ARMY-AFRO-AMERICAN TROUPS
Roster of Union soldiers 1861-65: US colored troops, 452

UNITED STATES—BIOGRAPHY
Presidential Medal of Freedom, 30

UNITED STATES—CENSUS
Historical stats of the US, bicentennial ed [CD-ROM], 819
State atlas of pol & cultural diversity, 329

UNITED STATES—CIVILIZATION—1865-1918
American eras: Civil War & Reconstruction, 1850-77, 444
American eras: dvlpmt of the industrial US, 1878-99, 445

UNITED STATES. CONGRESS
Almanac of the unelected, 649
Biographical dir of the American Congress, 1774-1996, 651
Congressional Quarterly almanac, v.52, 670

Congressional roll call 1996, 671
Congressional staff dir fall 1997, 652
Congressional yrbk 1996, 104th Congress, 2nd session, 672
Directory of Congressional voting scores & interest group ratings, 2d ed, 678
New members of Congress almanac: 105th US Congress, 654
Open secrets: the ency of congressional money & pols, 4th ed, 675
Vital stats on Congress 1995-96, 676
Who's who in Congress 1997, 656
Women of Congress, 833

UNITED STATES—CONSTITUTION
Complete bill of rights, 669
Encyclopedia of the American Constitution [CD-ROM], 518

UNITED STATES—CONSTITUTIONAL LAW
Constitutional law & YAs, 2d ed, 540

UNITED STATES. DECLARATION OF INDEPENDENCE
Signers of the Declaration of Independence, 434

UNITED STATES—DEPARTMENT OF COMMERCE
NTIS ordernow [CD-ROM], 62

UNITED STATES—DEPARTMENT OF DEFENSE
U.S. military online, 617

UNITED STATES—FOREIGN RELATIONS
Encyclopedia of US foreign relations, 660
George F. Kennan: an annot bibliog, 700
Notable US Ambassadors since 1775, 655
U.S.-Mexican treaties, 680
U.S. and Latin America, 697

UNITED STATES—GENEALOGY
Land & property research in the US, 365
Source: a gdbk of American genealogy, 370

UNITED STATES—HISTORY
DISCovering US hist [CD-ROM], 446
Encyclopedia USA, suppl v.1, 439
Encyclopedia USA, v.24, 440
Great events from hist: N American series, rev ed, 497
Historic documents index, 682
Historical stats of the US, bicentennial ed [CD-ROM], 819
Readers' gd to American hist, 442
Scholastic ency of the presidents & their times, updated ed, 443
Sixties [CD-ROM], 450

UNITED STATES—HISTORY—20TH CENTURY
Longman companion to America in the era of the 2 world wars, 1910-45, 449

UNITED STATES—HISTORY—CHRONOLOGY
Chronicle of America, rev ed, 435
Unites States in the 19th century, 436

UNITED STATES—HISTORY—CIVIL WAR, 1861-1865
Civil War bks: a critical bibliog, 432
Civil War in bks, 433
Civil War sites, memorials, museums, & lib collections, 448
Everything Civil War, 447
Roster of Confederate soldiers 1861-65, 451
Roster of Union soldiers 1861-65, 452

UNITED STATES—HISTORY—WAR OF 1812
Encyclopedia of the war of 1812, 612
War of 1812 eyewitness accounts, 608

UNITED STATES—IMPRINTS—CATALOGS
Books from Chapel Hill 1922-97, 595

UNITED STATES—IN LITERATURE
America in histl fiction, 1114

UNITED STATES—OFFICIALS & EMPLOYEES
Freedom's lawmakers: a dir of black officeholders during Reconstruction, rev ed, 344

UNITED STATES—POLITICS & GOVERNMENT
American govt & pols, 646
Congressional Quarterly almanac, v.52, 670
Election results dir 1997, 663
Encyclopedia of American pol reform, 657
Historic docs index, 1972-95, 682
Protocol: a hndbk for legislative staff, 677
World almanac of US pols, 1997-99 ed, 643

UNITED STATES—POPULATION
State atlas of pol & cultural diversity, 329
Twentieth-century hist of US population, 808

UNITED STATES—RELIGION
America's religions, 1364
Encyclopedia of religious controversies in the US, 1354

UNITED STATES—SOCIAL LIFE & CUSTOMS
ABC-CLIO companion to the 1960s counterculture in America, 437

UNITED STATES—STATISTICS
CQ's state fact finder 1997, 817
Historical stats of the US, bicentennial ed [CD-ROM], 819

UNITED STATES. SUPREME COURT
Congressional Quarterly's gd to the US Supreme Court, 3d ed, 529
Facts about the Supreme Court of the US, 538
Guide to the US Supreme Court, 526

UNITS—CONVERSION TABLES
Scientific unit conversion, 1597

UNIVERSITIES & COLLEGES
College hndbk for transfer students 1997, 296
Complete bk of colleges, 1998 ed, 286
Guide to graduate environmental programs, 1641

K & W gd to colleges for the learning disabled, 1998 ed, 290
Multicultural student's gd to colleges, rev, 302
Peterson's competitive colleges 1997-98, 16th ed, 292
Peterson's gd to 2-yr colleges 1998, 28th ed, 293
Peterson's US & Canadian medical schools 1997, 1542
Princeton Review student advantage gd to visiting college campuses, 1997 ed, 305

VACATIONS
Great escapes: the spring breaker's gd to beaches & beyond, 417

VAMPIRE FILMS
VideoHound's vampires on video, 1321

VEGETABLE GARDENING
Knott's hndbk for vegetable growers, 4th ed, 1437

VEGETABLES
Produce ref gd to fruits & vegetables from around the world, 1421

VENEZUELA
Historical dict of Venezuela, 2d ed, 142

VICE-PRESIDENTS—UNITED STATES
Presidents, first ladies, & vice presidents, 653

VIDEO RECORDINGS
Billboard 1996 music yrbk, 1205
Canadian film & video, 1271
Film & video finder, 5th ed, 310
Film & video on the Internet, 1287
Roger Ebert's video companion, 1319
Sci-Fi on tape, 1318
VideoHound's sci-fi experience, 1320
VideoHound's vampires on video, 1321

VIETNAM
Vietnam studies, 117

VIETNAMESE CONFLICT, 1961-1975
Vietnam War lit, 3d ed, 1056

VIGILANTES
Lynching & vigilantism in the US, 547

VIROLOGY
Encyclopedia of virology plus [CD-ROM], 1442

VISCOSITY
Handbook of viscosity, v.4: inorganic compounds & elements, 1623

VITAMINS
Real vitamin & mineral bk, 1548

VOCABULARY
Basic word list, 3d ed, 992

VOCATIONAL EDUCATION
Continuing medical educ dir 1996-97, 1532
National gd to educl credit for training programs, 1997 ed, 315

VOCATIONAL GUIDANCE
America's top jobs for people without college degrees, 3d ed, 227
America's top office, mgmt, sales, & professional jobs, 3d ed, 228
Career discovery ency, 213
Career perspectives software series [CD-ROM], 223
Careers in intl affairs, 6th ed, 698
College majors & careers, 3d ed, 316
Encyclopedia of careers & vocational guidance, 2d ed [CD-ROM], 214
Encyclopedia of careers & vocational guidance, 10th ed, 215
Enhanced occupational outlook hndbk, 226
Health professions educ dir 1997-98, 1511
JIST's electronic enhanced dict of occupational titles, 2d ed [CD-ROM], 216
JIST's electronic occupational outlook hndbk, 2d ed [CD-ROM], 231
JIST's multimedia occupational outlook hndbk, 2d ed [CD-ROM], 232
Job hunter's sourcebk, 3d ed, 233
Occupational outlook hndbk, 1996-97 ed, 238
U.S. employment opportunities, 240
VGM's careers ency, 4th ed, 217

VOLUNTARISM
Volunteer America, 4th ed, 795

WAGE SURVEYS
American salaries & wages survey, 4th ed, 229

WAR
International conflict, 696
War & conflict quotations, 85

WAR CORRESPONDENTS
Historical dict of war journalism, 881

WAR IN LITERATURE
Vietnam War lit, 3d ed, 1056

WARSAW (POLAND)
Historical dict of Warsaw, 479
Warsaw, 423

WARSHIPS
Battleships of the world, 626
Jane's warships image lib [CD-ROM], 627
Naval Institute gd to the ships & aircraft of the US Fleet, 16th ed, 628
Warships of the USSR & Russia, 1945-95, 629

WASHINGTON, D.C.
Washington '97, 14th ed, 58

WEAPONS
Jane's police & security equipment 1996-97, 9th ed, 555

WEAPONS SYSTEMS
Jane's simulation & training systems 1996-97, 9th ed, 1573
Naval Institute gd to world naval weapons systems 1997-98, 634

WEATHER
Complete weather resource, 1611
Glossary of weather & climate with related oceanic & hydrologic terms, 1612
Handy weather answer bk, 1613

WEB SITES
Chemicals on the Internet, v.1, 1478
Directory of lib technical servs home pages, 591
Job-Hunting on the Internet, 222

WEEDS
Weeds of the NE, 1453

WEIGHTS & MEASURES
Numbers: how many, how far, how long, how much, 810

WELDING
Jefferson's welding ency, 18th ed, 1491

WELTY, EUDORA
Reader's gd to the short stories of Eudora Welty, 1138

WESTERNS (TELEVISION PROGRAMS)
Television western players of the 50s, 1276
Television westerns episode gd, 1308

WEST (UNITED STATES)
Who's who in the West 1998-99, 26th ed, 32

WHISKEY
Complete gd to whiskey, 1426

WILDER, LAURA INGALLS
Laura Ingalls Wilder: an annot bibliog of critical, biogl, & teaching studies, 1139

WILD FLOWERS
New England's mountain flowers, 1450

WILSON, WOODROW
Woodrow Wilson, 647

WIND ENSEMBLES
Wind ensemble sourcebk & biogl gd, 1220

WINE & WINE MAKING
New Sotheby's wine ency, 1424

WOMEN
American women, 247
Big bk of opportunities for women, 269
Collaborative bibliog of women in philosophy, 1332
Contemporary women's issues 1992-July 1997 [CD-ROM], 838
Facts on File ency of black women in America, 343
50 most influential women in American law, 513
Larousse dict of women, 24
Muslim women throughout the world, 830
Northwest women: an annot bibliog of sources on the hist of Oreg. & Wash. women, 1787-1970, 828
Women of Ireland, 34
Women's almanac, 827
Women's issues, 837
Women's rights on trial, 563
Women's voices, 840

WOMEN ARTISTS
Dictionary of women artists, 948

WOMEN AUTHORS
Nineteenth-century American women writers, 1126
One hundred yrs of American women writing, 1848-1948, 1124
Women writers of Gt Brit & Europe, 1067

WOMEN BASEBALL PLAYERS
Women of the All-American Girls Professional Baseball League, 734

WOMEN BASKETBALL PLAYERS
NCAA basketball: the official 1997 women's college basketball records bk, 740

WOMEN COMPOSERS
Baker's biogl dict of 20th-century classical musicians, 1197
Guitar music by women composers, 1218

WOMEN—DEVELOPING COUNTRIES
Women in the Third World, 839

WOMEN—DISEASES
Woman's ency of natural healing, 1550

WOMEN DRAMATISTS
Women playwrights of diversity, 1106

WOMEN—HEALTH & HYGIENE
EveryWoman's gd to prescription & nonprescription drugs, 1564
Woman's ency of natural healing, 1550
Women & health, 1500

WOMEN—HISTORY
Scholastic ency of women in the US, 836
Women's chronology, 834
Women's firsts, 835

WOMEN IN LITERATURE
Feminist ency of Italian lit, 1177

WOMEN IN POLITICS
Women in modern American pols, 829

WOMEN IN THE PERFORMING ARTS
Extraordinary women in support of music, 1199

WOMEN—LEGAL STATUS
Women's legal gd, 544

WOMEN LEGISLATORS
Women of Congress, 833

WOMEN & LITERATURE
British women writers, 1700-1850, 1144
Eighteenth-century Anglo-American women novelists, 1111
Laura Ingalls Wilder: an annot bibliog of critical, biogl, & teaching studies, 1139
Lorraine Hansberry: a research & production sourcebk, 1136
Women playwrights in England, Ireland, & Scotland 1660-1823, 1151

WOMEN MUSICIANS
Baker's biogl dict of 20th-century classical musicians, 1197
Extraordinary women in support of music, 1199

WOMEN PAINTERS
Gallery of her own: an annot bibliog of women in Victorian painting, 981

WOMEN PHYSICAL SCIENTISTS
Notable women in the physical scis, 1598

WOMEN PRISONERS
Female offenders, 549

WOMEN'S RIGHTS
Women in the Third World, 839
Women's voices, 840

WOMEN'S STUDIES
Index to women's studies anthologies, 841
Women's studies index 1995, 842

WOMEN—UNITED STATES
American women's almanac, 826

WORDS, NEW
Barnhart dict companion, v.10, no.1, summer 1997, 1010

WORK & FAMILY
Work-Family research, 777

WORLD BANK
Historical dict of the World Bank, 186

WORLD HEALTH
International hndbk of public health, 1517

WORLD HISTORY
Complete atlas of world hist, 491
Dictionary of 20th-century world hist, 504
DISCovering world hist [CD-ROM], 505
Encyclopedia of geographical features in world hist, 399
History of humanity, v.3, 507
Illustrated ency of world hist, 503

WORLD POLITICS
Cold War ref gd, 508
World facts & maps, 400
World gd 1997/98, 10th ed, 97

WORLD RECORDS
Women's firsts, 835

WORLD WAR, 1914-1918
Dardanelles campaign, 1915, 494
Grolier lib of WW I, 614
World War I aviation, rev ed, 610

WORLD WAR, 1939-1945
Medical & psychological effects of concentration camps on Holocaust survivors, v.4: genocide, 708
Political leaders & military figures in the 2d World War, 606
Solomon Islands campaign, Guadalcanal to Rabaul, 611
Touchstones: a gd to records, rights, & resources for families of American WW II casualties, 367
Wartime Poland, 1939-45, 480
World War II in Europe, Africa, & the Americas, with general sources, 622

WORLD WIDE WEB
Catholic Internet, USA ed, 1390
Collecting in cyberspace, 893
College.educ: on-line resources for the cyber-savvy, 301
CyberTools for business, 163
Finding images online, 1592
God on the Internet, 1365
Internet complete ref, 2d ed, 1594
Internet gd for the legal researcher, 2d ed, 535
Key gd to electronic resources: art & art hist, 942
Mecklermedia's official Internet World WWW yellow pages, 1996 ed, 1588
Naked in cyberspace: how to find personal info online, 1596
Net journal dir, vol. 1, no. 2, 1591
Thunderbird gd to intl business resources on the WWW, 204
Virtual field trips, 281
Virtual musician, 1206
Virtual roots: a gd to genealogy & local hist on the WWW, 366

WRESTLERS
Biographical dict of professional wrestling, 752

WRITING
Bibliography on writing & written lang, 984

YEARBOOKS
A&E entertainment almanac, 1997, 1264
Congressional yrbk 1996, 104th Congress, 2nd session, 672
Health & medical yrbk 1997, 1515
International yr bk 1997, 44
Science yr 1997, 1416
Science yr 1998, 1417

World Bk health & medical annual 1997, 1543
World Bk yr bk, 1997, 64

YEATS, W. B. (WILLIAM BUTLER)
William Butler Yeats ency, 1166

YIDDISH LANGUAGE—DICTIONARIES—ENGLISH
English-Yiddish, Yiddish-English dict, [rev ed], 1054
Harduf's transliterated English-Yiddish, Yiddish-English dict, [rev ed], 1055

YOGA
Shambhala ency of yoga, 1338

YOUNG ADULT LITERATURE
Authors & artists for YAs, v.20, 1100
Authors & artists for YAs, v.21, 1101
Best bks for YA readers, 1094
Books for you, 1095
Booktalking the award winners 3, 1081
Booktalking the award winners: children's retrospective volume, 1082
Characters in YA lit, 1103
Culturally diverse lib collections for youth, 1099
Horn Bk gd to children's & YA bks, v.7, no.2, 1078
100 most popular YA authors, rev ed, 1102
Picture this: picture bks for young adults, 1097
Teen genreflecting, 1096
What do YAs read next? v.2, 1098
What else should I read? guiding kids to good bks, v.2, 1076
Writers for YAs, 1104

YOUNG ADULT LITERATURE—BIOGRAPHY
Something about the author autobiog series, v.24, 1080

YOUNG ADULT LITERATURE, SPANISH
Recommended bks in Spanish for children & YAs, 1991-95, 1079

YOUTH HOSTELS
Hostelling N America, 1997, 403

ZIP CODES—DIRECTORIES
Instant natl locator gd, 3d ed, 53
Zip code finder, 59

ZODIAC
Signs of the zodiac, 717